The Rungs of Ladders

The Rungs of Ladders

A WYATT HISTORY IN ENGLAND & THE UNITED STATES, FROM 1066 TO MODERN TIMES

♀ | | ♂

Hélène Andorre Hinson Staley

Dedicated to

James Noah Hinson, M.D.

Written & compiled by

Hélène Andorre Hinson Staley

Illustrated by

Kaspars Gailītis

The Rungs of Ladders
A Wyatt History in England & the United States, from 1066 to Modern Times

Dedicated to
James Noah Hinson, M.D.

Written & compiled by
Hélène Andorre Hinson Staley

Illustrated by
Kaspars Gailītis

This book is intended to inspire readers to conduct their own genealogical research and to inform readers of materials, thus gathered and / or quoted by the author via contacts and documents.

This book is in part the creative expression of the author's memories and those of interviewees. No part of *The Rungs of Ladders, A Wyatt History in England & the United States, from 1066 to Modern Times* is intended to offend any person, profession, culture, religion or country.

The front cover of this book and interior artwork are by illustrator Kaspars Gailītis. At the time of this publication, the dates of birth, marriage, death and other events are recorded according to public documents or records and include those from tombstones and family sources. Some information is gathered from historical articles, interviews or conversations, studies, letters and encyclopedia reports.

If you find a misprint, or error or something you disagree with, note it in the pages labeled: *"Notes,"* located in the back matter. Then, contact the researcher or Metallo House Publishers [MHP].

Many people with the surname of Wyatt have the same first names. Consequently, lifespans whenever available are provided repeatedly to distinguish people having the same or similar names with similar lifespans. All quotations are properly attributed and fall within fair use, or they are used by permission either from family members and via personal interviews.

There are no final drafts while compiling such history. There is always room for refinement, clarifications, additions. In other words, not one edition is the final word. Additionally, not all known Wyatt descendants are included in this book.

Some Eagle descendants are also Wyatt descendants and can be found listed in *The Eagle Family of America: Egley, Egle, Egli, Eagle, 1690-1998* by Rachel Hinson Hill.

This book was printed in the United States of America.

To order additional copies of *The Rungs of Ladders, A Wyatt History in England & the United States, from 1066 to Modern Times* contact Amazon.com, barnesandnoble.com, or order it from your favorite bookstore or book distributor.

ISBN: 1508528284
ISBN 13: 9781508528289

* If you want to help support this research and writing efforts, please feel encouraged to seek Metallo House books on Amazon.com, as well as other online booksellers, or from your favorite bookstores.

♀ | | ♂

"Duriora virtus -- Virtue tries harder things."

-- WYATT MOTTO FOR ITS COAT OF ARMS

"Let us read, and let us dance -- two amusements that
will never do any harm to the world."

-- VOLTAIRE

Voltaire, known as François-Marie Arouet [November 21, 1694-May 30, 1778]
French Enlightenment playwright, writer historian, philosopher; Paris, France.

Note from the Author

♀ | | ♂

*V*OLTAIRE'S QUOTE ON DANCING AND reading entertains and inspires curiosity. The experience is much like dancing. For three years after my second son was born, I studied ballet. As a child, I took a couple years of ballet and tap classes. In college I studied an elective course of aerobic dance. I am by no means an expert in dance. Many dreams have me jumping 15 and 20 feet into the air. The physical reality is another calculation altogether.

As you turn the pages of this book, or any of my books, remember this quote from Voltaire. *"Let us read, and let us dance – two amusements that will never do any harm to the world."* As you advance through the pages of *The Rungs of Ladders, A Wyatt History in England & the United States, from 1066 to Modern Times* take notice of quotations from various sources. Each is not made lightly but with a quest to apply the wisdom of others to my personal voice.

Despite Voltaire's belief that witty sayings prove nothing – they are entertaining and often cause us to take a deeper, or second look at a point, opinion, conclusion or hope.

François-Marie Arouet, born November 21, 1694 [Voltaire claimed his birthday as February 20, 1694] in Paris, France, wrote under the pen name *"Voltaire."* He was the partner of Émilie du Châtelet and son of Marie Marguerite d'Aumart and François Arouet. His quotations, inserted periodically in this book, break some of the monotony of genealogical presentation. The quotations are placed appropriately to draw an emphasis to various points.

Voltaire, who passed away May 30, 1778, was an historian, writer and philosopher who became famous for his wit. His writings were brave in attacks on the Roman Catholic Church. He advocated freedom of religion, expression and separation of church and state.

Voltaire wrote in nearly every literary form – stage plays, poems, novels, essays, historical and scientific documentations, letters, books, pamphlets. He lived during a time when it was not generally physically *or emotionally* safe to express opinions in the written and published word.

Some of his works incorporated his criticism of intolerance from the French institutions of his time. He was the youngest of five children born to his parents and one of three whom survived longer than infancy. His father was a lawyer, and his mother was from the Province of Poitou.

WAS HE RELATED to the Guyots? [Guyott, Wiotus, Wiot, Wyot, Wyotte, Wyat, Wyatt, Wiat, Wiatt, Wiett]

If readers of *The Rungs of Ladders, A Wyatt History in England & the United States, from 1066 to Modern Times* find out, send the information to Metallo House Publishers [MHP] and the author of this book.

The name Voltaire was used by François-Marie Arouet in the year 1718. His pen name is viewed by some historians to symbolically mark his separation from his family and past. The pen name *"Voltaire"* was adopted after he was incarcerated at the Bastille, which was a fortress in Paris used as a prison via the kings of France. The pen name can be interpreted as declaring his uniqueness in a sea of human souls. More specifically, he was declaring his place in history and those ways in which he could mirror or reflect his interests.

The name Voltaire is an anagram or word play, much like some writers do with character names in books that secretly hide the names of real people. The word play of **AROVET LI** is the Latin spelling of *"Arouet."*

In addition to Voltaire's quotes, others are included from:

* Mahatma Gandhi [Mohandas Karamchand Gandhi, born October 2, 1869, Porbandar, Kathiawar Agency, British India; died January 30, 1948, New Delhi, Delhi, India], led India to independence and inspired civil rights and freedom movements worldwide.
* Mother Teresa [Anjezë Gonxhe Bojaxhiu] born August 26, 1910, Skopje, now capital of the Republic of Macedonia- died September 5, 1997, Roman Catholic nun who lived most of her life in India.
* Buddha [Gautama Shakyamuni, born 563 BCE, Lumbini, Sakya Republic; died 483 BCE, Kushinagar, Malla Republic.] A sage who lived and taught in Eastern India.

♀ | | ♂

The Rungs of Ladders

A WYATT HISTORY IN ENGLAND
& THE UNITED STATES, FROM
1066 TO MODERN TIMES

Contents

♀ | | ♂

*Additional pictures are found within the body of the book, which may not appear in the content pages. These are identified with cutlines. The back cover of the book contains a photo of the author with her father James Noah Hinson, M.D. in 1964 during a trip to Rowan County, N.C. from New Orleans, La.

Explanation

♀ | | ♂

THE RUNGS OF LADDERS

"He who knows nothing of the past can't be trusted with the future,"

UNKNOWN SOURCE QUOTED OFTEN BY VIRGIE IRENE EAGLE HINSON TO
HER CHILDREN AS RECALLED BY MARGARET ANN HINSON GORDON.

"The beginning is the most important part of the work."

– PLATO [BORN 428/427 BCE, ATHENS; DIED 348/347 BCE, ATHENS,
GREECE] PHILOSOPHER AND MATHEMATICIAN IN CLASSICAL GREECE.

*W*HEN YOU FIRST SELECTED THIS book *The Rungs of Ladders, A Wyatt History in England & the United States, from 1066 to Modern Times* or examined its cover, you might have asked what *rungs of ladders* have to do with genealogical history?

Several years ago, I drew circles and boxes while deducing connections of various people – some passed long ago while others are still living.

I thought about the process of entering information into the *Family Tree Maker*™ program. The program is designed to archive names, dates, etc. The program has an option for the user to plug in any given name and then see a list of that person's cousins to every degree, aunts and uncles to every degree. In other words, a list is only limited by the researcher's time to add individuals into it.

How in the world is the computer able to do this?

I worked for IBM a short while as a technical writer in 1990 and 1991 in the Information Development Department, which was located in the Cary Regency Park in Cary, N.C. in the late 1980s and early 1990s. Still, such an experience left me clueless.

I imagined blinking lights covered by the exterior of the computer playing a mathematical tune. I am not mathematically inclined, or even that computer savvy.

My first exposure to computers was at *The Salisbury Post* in Salisbury, N.C. There, I wrote occasional features and cutlines. I have been using computers regularly since college years and daily in newsrooms I worked in during the late 1980s.

Nevertheless, there is this void called:

"You are not a computer programmer."

Computers continuously evolve. They evolved while I worked as a reporter and writer for newspapers – interning at *The Durham Morning Herald* and *The Durham Sun,* now defunct, while a student in the School of Journalism – renamed *The School of Media and Journalism* at the University of North Carolina at Chapel Hill. We adjust to the improvements – but using one does not necessarily mean we understand the programming.

Many young adults today begin using computers as early as preschool! I did not resolve the question, but some other quest.

Subsequently, with a pen and paper I sketched ladders. At the top I plugged in on each vertical parallel line | | two siblings and to the sides of each, I added a plus mark + to the symbols for female ♀ and male ♂ accordingly to represent the spouses.

On the first rung == at the top of the ladder I wrote *"siblings."* Then, on the second rung ==, I wrote: *"first cousins."* On the third rung ==: *"second cousins,"* the fourth rung ==, *"third cousins"* and continued doing this down the ladder to sixth or seventh cousins – whatever I needed to see at the time.

The vertical line to the first rung perpendicular to it represented the offspring from each sibling who married into another family obviously – *not one another.* (This is the South [eastern U.S.], yes, and the joke of cousins marrying cousins, etc. from the North is abused *to what seems an infinite yawn.*)

The children, nevertheless, then were first cousins to one another, and the offspring of these children are second cousins to one another. The offspring of the second cousins are third cousins to one another and so forth.

From looking at the ladder either written down, or imagining it in one's mind, one can count readily and see that say your grandmother's first cousin's grandchildren are your third cousins, or that your offspring's child is a 5th cousin to the 2nd great grandchild of your grandmother's first cousin, and the offspring of your child is then a first cousin four generations removed to your grandmother's first cousin.

Do not count the rung that joins your grandchild to his 5th cousin, but the rungs above it that lead on the diagonal from him to his second great grandmother's first cousin.

Simply reading these words or hearing them in conversation can confuse and bore the daylights out of people -- even people who love genealogical research. This is with one exception: The ladder, visualizing it, or drawing it and plugging in the information in which you wish to discern.

The rungs of the ladder help one to remember to count the generations removed starting with the person one is looking at and counting the rungs towards the two who are first cousins with one another. The image of the ladder, whether one starts at the bottom of the ladder, or the top to insert the names of the first cousins and so forth is helpful.

```
X -----Siblings----------X
X-----1st Cousins-------X
X-----2nd Cousins------X
X-----3rd Cousins-------X
X-----4th Cousins-------X
X-----5th Cousins-------X
X -----6th Cousins------X
X-----7th Cousins-------X
X-----8th Cousins-------X
```

Later, I looked at DNA ladders out of curiosity and without being a scientist, I said to myself –

"Oh, how funny."

Deoxyribonucleic acid [DNA] is the hereditary material in humans and most all organisms. Nearly each cell in a person's body has the same DNA. Most of it is found in the cell nucleus, where it is called nuclear DNA. The structure of it forms a ladder that twists a bit like a stretched coil or curl. The concept of counting generations on a physical ladde is, *as well in the scientific way of visualization*, a DNA ladder.

While the standard ladder is different than the DNA ladder, both are ladders and each contains information that shows relationships. It was one of those funny moments one gets after spending 12 hours in one spot too long – but the visualization of a ladder is the point.

Say someone introduces to you your second cousin and says nothing else. You can sit there and just pretend to know what this actually means, or you can draw this ladder diagram, then deduce with enthusiasm and a friendly handshake:

"How do you do!

"Your father and my mother were first cousins.

"Your father is my first cousin one generation removed.

"That indeed makes us second cousins!"

If you say this, you are terribly good – but *what if* someone introduces you as an eighth cousin?

Can you do it?

Yes!

Take a blank paper and draw the ladder I have described – it looks like the rusty ladder in the shed behind your house, or the shamefully in-need of paint ladder stored in your basement, or the stick figure you sketch is perfectly fine.

Visualize, and draw the ladder with its rungs and each rung after the siblings represents first, second, third, fourth, fifth, sixth, seventh, eighth cousin relationships. Next, begin counting from the rung just above the generations removed and counting to the first cousin and higher if needed to find other relationships.

[6th great grandparent]	X ---Siblings----X	[8th C's 6th G grandparent]
[5th great grandparent]	X---1st Cousins--X	[8th C's 5th G grandparent]
[4th great grandparent]	X------2nd C-----X	[8th C's 4th G grandparent]
[3rd great grandparent]	X-----3rd C-----X	[8th C's 3rd G grandparent]
[2nd great grandparent]	X-----4th C-------X	[8th C's 2nd G grandparent]
[Great-grandparent]	X-----5th C-------X	[8th C's great grandparent]
[Grandparent]	X -----6th C------X	[8th C's grandparent]
[Parent]	X-----7th C------X	[Your 8th cousin's parent]
[You]	X---8th Cousin'sX	[Your 8th cousin]

- C's = Cousin
- G=Great

So you can then say:

"Yes, I am happy to make your acquaintance!

"I know exactly how we are related.

"Your sixth great grandfather, who fought in the Revolutionary War by the way, was a brother to my sixth great grandmother!

"Oh wow – double wow, what a terribly small world!"

Wait.

You cannot say *"what a terribly small world"* unless you really understand that as truth – even though it really is!

Say:

"Your fifth great grandmother was a first cousin to my fifth great grandmother."

Certainly, you can look at the ladder and determine other relationships. Your 8th cousin's fifth great grandmother, for instance, is your first cousin seven generations [counting the rungs] removed.

If by chance you don't like this visual, look at the first tree outside your window – preferably one without leaves with the season being the dead of winter. Now, you can use that as your visual and connect your relatives to you.

Oh, you say you prefer the ladder?

I thought you might.

It gets more complicated when you discover your fourth cousin is also your sixth cousin once removed.

Tangles!

Oh what tangled rungs are woven when we practice what we've chosen!

In case you don't understand that joke it is a play or spoof on Sir Walter Scott's:

"Oh, what a tangled web we weave when first we practice to deceive."

This is word play. Hopefully, it removes any bricks resting on your shoulders regarding the comprehension of genealogy being for a select few.

It's for us all.

♀ | | ♂

$$♀ \mid \mid ♂$$

Author's Note:

One hurdle pertains to double first cousins. When for instance two siblings of one family marry persons in another family, such offspring are regarded as double first cousins to one another instead of only first cousins. For instance, if two brothers named Smith each marry women from say the Jones family – the women, being sisters to one another. The Smith offspring of such unions are deemed double first cousins to one another.

In regard to uncles and aunts: The siblings of your father and mother are your aunts and uncles. The siblings of your grandmother or grandfather are your grandaunts and granduncles. The siblings of your great grandmother or great grandfather are your great-grandaunts and great-granduncles. The siblings of say your third great-grandfather are your third great-granduncles and third great-grandaunts. The expression *"great aunt"* is slang for grand-aunt or grandaunt. It is proper to refer to the brother of your grandfather as your *"grand-uncle"* or *"granduncle."* *"Great-grand"* is preferred over the slang expression: *"great-great."*

The proper progression: mother, grandmother, great grandmother, second great grandmother, third great grandmother, fourth great grandmother and so forth. The same is for the male: father, grandfather, great grandfather, second great grandfather, etc. For uncles: uncle, granduncle, great-granduncle, second great-granduncle and so forth. For aunts: aunt, grandaunt, great-grandaunt, second great-grandaunt, etc.

4th great grandparents have siblings who are your 4th great granduncles, et. al.
3rd great grandparents have siblings who are your 3rd great granduncles, et. al.
2nd great grandparents have siblings who are your 2nd great granduncles, et. al.
Great grandparents have siblings who are your great granduncles, et. al.
Grandparents have siblings who are your granduncles & grandaunts.
Parents have siblings who are your uncles & aunts.

In regard to *"half"* cousins, some genealogists use this precision, while some legal authorities call them simply *"cousin."* Some say: *"No such thing."* Half siblings exist, and when they become part of family tree, half cousins are deduced while determining relationships. This book uses the words *"half cousin"* and *"step"* even though it is considered slang or not proper by some genealogists – it is well understood. The word *"removed"* indicates two people are from different generations. Once removed, for instance, means there is the difference of one generation. Your father's first cousin is your first cousin once removed. Your grandmother's first cousin is your first cousin twice removed – two generations removed.

In regard to the title: *"step daughter,"* some genealogists say: *"daughter of the husband"* or *"daughter of the wife."* Of course, *"step"* relations are extended family references.

In-laws are additionally extended family ties: The parents of your sister-in-law are simply called *"the parents of your sister-in-law."* The same applies to your brother-in-law. Your father-in-law and mother-in-law are the parents of your husband or wife. The brother of your husband or wife is called your brother-in-law. The sister of your husband or wife is called your sister-in-law.

In this book, first cousins are referred to as such; however, some genealogists refer to them as full-cousins or cousins-german or cousin-german.

For a more extensive list of explanations and terms [heraldry terms, mottos, symbols, Old French and Latin terms, last will and testament terms, calendars, abbreviations, etc.], refer to chapters 2 and 5.

The Rungs of Ladders
A Wyatt History in England &
the United States, from 1066 to Modern Times
is dedicated to my beloved father

James Noah Hinson, M.D.

♀ | | ♂

Dedication

♀ | | ♂

"Life is full of coincidences."

– JAMES NOAH HINSON, M.D.

A s you read on the cover and previous page – *The Rungs of Ladders, A Wyatt History in England & the United States, from 1066 to Modern Times* is dedicated to James Noah Hinson, M.D. Genealogical history fascinated him since childhood. It took most of my life thus far to develop a similar interest. He planted, nevertheless, this possibility in my mind:

Remember your ancestors.

Certainly, his fascination with Wyatt history – as well as those wrapped tightly in the history of Rowan County, and immigrants to the United States -- Müllers [Millers] Parks, Eagles [Egles], Morgans, Ellers – to name a few, influenced how we put this book together. He was the first to ask what new things I learned about the Wyatts. My father, a keystone contributor and an encouragement for this book, never tired to hear genealogical stories.

When I was a child, he occasionally asked:

"Do you know who Mary Jane Morgan was?"

I suppose most often I nodded,

"No."

What child knows the name of his or her second great grandmother? Gradually, nods to affirmation evolved by age 15:

"She was connected to us…."

"She was the mother of Grandpa Eagle."

(Noah Jenkins Eagle – a great grandfather to me [Egle]).

"And who was Mary Jane's mother?" he asked.

"Mary Jane was the daughter of Rachel Evelyn Wyatt and John Morgan …

"…Don't you want to know where my sister Rachel got her name?"

He smiles as he speaks of the Wyatts, and all those associated by blood or marriage and even those adopted. People are significant. Each person is important and comes with history from which we might learn.

One goal with this book is to capture the essence of our conversations. His mind was much like a modern-day computer. When I was a child, he recited stories and connections Sunday afternoons when I returned from church. I would find after a while I was the only one sitting in the breakfast room with him.

Maybe my siblings knew his stories? I needed to be reminded. I thank God for those minds, which have kept these things safe before the invention and wide-use of computers.

Part of my father's childhood was spent living on a River Road farm, formerly owned by his great grandfather Solomon Eagle, Jr. Solomon's first wife was Mary Jane Morgan, daughter Rachel Evelyn Wyatt and John Calvin Morgan. Mary Jane Morgan inherited this farm from her parents.

When she married Solomon and later died, it was passed into the Eagle family. Mary Jane died in 1928 before James Noah Hinson, M.D. was born. His fate was to absorb the stories. The River Road farm once owned by the Morgan-Wyatt-Eagle family is today owned by the Gribble family. Directly across the road from it is another farm known as The Briggs Place. It was during my father's childhood owned by Lottie Morgan [1879-1956] and her husband Phillip Ranson Briggs [1881-1966].

*Lottie Morgan, daughter of Jacob and Ann James *"Jim"* Kirk Morgan, was a niece to her father's siblings: Rhoda, Nathaniel, John, Mack Camey, Mary, Noah, Moses, James, Elizabeth, David and Silas. Lottie was a first cousin and third cousin to Mary Jane Morgan Eagle – wife of Solomon Eagle, Jr.

The house that once stood on *The Briggs Place* was burned in 1972 by a lunatic. It was never re-built. The only thing left of it afterward was the well and a bathtub amongst the charred rubble.

Another barn, though, was added later. What can never be destroyed are those memories of my father and his brother Chub working together late nights and weekends to renovate and restore the house so the Wilson family could occupy it. Their own home had fallen victim to fire in prior months.

Part of my father's growing years were spent on another family farm located on Hinson Road in a house that Loveless Morgan and his brother Mack Camey Morgan had once resided in.

When Mack Camey Morgan [1836-1913] returned from the American Civil War [ACW] – referred to as the War Between the States, or specifically as the War by Southerners, his wife Mary Elizabeth *"Betty"* Arey [1842-1904] did not wish to live there and wanted to return to Riles Creek, where she grew up. Mack Camey's father Moses Green Morgan [1810-1879] deeded the house to Mack. Mack Camey's daughter Lavina Morgan Russell [1858-1880] is said to have been born in the house on Hinson Road, which still stands today.

My father remarked that emphasis be on the Wyatts. At such times, I would remind him I give emphasis to the Wyatt family no doubt, but the dedication I wrote to honor him. I believe intuitively that his soul understood. Every good thing a human does comes from Our Heavenly Father. The Book of John tells us so in chapter 15, verses four through seven.

"Abide in me and I in you as the branch cannot bear fruit itself, unless it abides in the vine, neither can you unless you abide in me. I am the vine; you are the branches. Those who abide in me and I in them will bear much fruit; because without me you can do nothing."

Everything good is wrapped in truth. It comes to us through God. We hope everything in this book reflects truth. We hope all motives flow from good intentions.

Part of his journey…

My father practiced medicine in Rowan County, N.C. for nearly 45 years. He retired from it in 2011, selling his portion of a building to Rowan Memorial Hospital – currently known as [N: Novant] Rowan Regional Hospital. His office was located on Mocksville Avenue next door to the Salisbury Pharmacy. Recently, the pharmacy and medical offices connected to it were torn down so that as of June 2016, all that remains of it is an empty lot.

He was born in Mabery Place, Porter Station, Stanly County, N.C. to a former Ponds School teacher Virgie Irene Eagle Hinson on January 12, 1929. He was affectionately called *"Jim"* and *"Jimmy"* and was amongst five siblings. His elder brothers June and Chub attended Palmerville Elementary School.

My father attended first grade until Christmastime at Baden School in Baden, N.C. He attended this school while living at what he called the Coggins House [that did not have electricity at the time], in Palmerville, N.C.

Later, he moved with his family to Millingport, located between one or two miles north of the town of Finger, N.C. This house had electricity. He attended Millingport School for the remainder of first grade and half of the second grade school year. After this, he moved with his family to his great grandfather's farm on River Road – directly across from what we still to this day call The Briggs Place.

"Moving to Solomon Eagle's house was the luckiest day of my life," he said.

"Solomon became my mentor.

"While there, I went to Shaver School for the second half of second grade through the seventh grade, graduating from grammar school in nineteen-forty-two.

"Before nineteen thirty-five, there were one room school houses.

"Shaver School was a four-room school house on Reeves Island Road."

From 8th grade to 12th grade, he attended *Richfield School*, graduating in 1947. His brothers attended and graduated from this school when it did not yet have 12th grade incorporated.

His siblings: William *"Bill"* Crowell Hinson, Jr. – nicknamed *"June,"* [b. 1926-2014]; Richard Clyde *"known as Chub or Chubby,"* [1927-2006]; Betty Lou Hinson Heath [b. 1930]; Rachel Evelyn Hinson Hill [1932-1994]; Margaret Ann Hinson Gordon [b. 1934].

Shaver School, Reeves Island Road, Gold Hill, Rowan County, N.C.

Bottom photo: James *"Jim"* Noah Hinson, M.D. [1929-2015] far right & his siblings: Margaret Ann Hinson Gordon, b. 1934; Rachel Evelyn Hinson Hill [1932-1994]; Betty Lou Hinson Heath, b. 1930; William *"June"* Crowell Hinson [1926-2014], Richard Clyde *"Chub"* Hinson [1927-2006].Top photo: Jim. Chub, June, Rachel, Margaret & Betty.

James N. Hinson, M.D.

My father's maternal grandmother Laura Lou Eller Eagle [1883-1959] used a code phrase whenever a child entered a room in which adults were conversing. If the content of the conversation was not appropriate for children, she said:

"Pictures have ears."

It is remarkably similar to what some nobility in England said during the Medieval Period when one felt a spy might be near. Only then, such people said:

"Pictures have eyes."

One day my father recalled:

"She was laughing and said: 'I never believed that I would have to read in The Stanly News and Press that my grandson was going to the medical school at Wake Forest."

Evidently, no one had told her before. *The Stanly News & Press* came out twice a week. A month later the announcement was in *The Salisbury Post.* His mother Virgie discovered the news through her mother Laura.

His Education:

* 1947: Graduated from Richfield High School, Richfield, Rowan County, N.C.
* 1947-1948: Attends Mars Hill College, Mars Hill, N.C., known currently as Mars Hill University.
* 1948-1950: Works in Baden, N.C. at ALCOA Aluminum Company of America: aluminum factory.
* 1950-1952: Serves in the United States Army during the Korean War – spending the initial part as a rifleman in Camp Atterbery, located 40 miles south of Indianapolis, Ind. He served as military policeman [MP]. While in the army, he attends Candidates for Officers Training School. He served in Company E, 2nd or 3rd Battalion, 112 Regiment, Army 28th Division. Company E was made up of five brigades including three brigades of infantry.

"A colonel was inspecting my performance of stabbing with a bayonet.

"He told me to point to the hollow of the neck and lunge at him.

"…I lunged at him again, and I saw his eyes get bigger.

"He thought I was going to hit him."

- 1952-1953: Works in Baden at ALCOA.
- 1953-1956: Graduates from *Catawba College* in Salisbury, N.C. with a double major in chemistry and biology.

*Catawba College – established in 1851, is one of the oldest colleges in North Carolina. Originally, this college was created to educate students seeking to be ministers in the German Reformed Church.

- 1956-1960: Graduates from *Bowman Gray School of Medicine, Wake Forest University,* Winston-Salem. N.C. [In 1997, the school was renamed Wake Forest University School of Medicine.]
- 1960-1961: Completes Internship at North Carolina Baptist Hospital, Winston-Salem, N.C.
- 1961-1962: Completes a 1-year residency in Internal Medicine at Charleston Memorial Hospital in Charleston, W.Va.
- 1962-1964: Completes a 2-year residency in New Orleans, La. in General Medicine via Tulane University School of Medicine.
- 1964-1965: Completes a 2-year residency in the Chest & Cardiology, New Orleans, La. via Tulane University School of Medicine.
- 1965-1966: Completes a 1-year residency in Cardiology, New Orleans, La. via Tulane University School of Medicine.
- March 1967: Sets up a private practice in Salisbury, N.C.

After retiring from medicine, he continued running farms* in Rowan County. His love of the outdoors – seeing the progress of corn, soybeans, wheat, hay and other growing adventures, was at the core of everything he did there. In recent years, he added the watchful guards of donkeys to protect cattle from coyotes.

*The Briggs Place, The Hoffner Place, The Hill-Arey Farm, The Morgan Place, The Basinger Farm, The Shaver Place, Hinson Road Farm.

He said in recent years:

"I got to do everything I ever wanted to do in my life.

"I wanted to be a soldier, and I did that.

"I wanted to become a doctor, and I did that.

"I wanted to become a farmer, and I still do that."

Possibly he should add:

"I wanted to do family research,

"...and I do that

"...and motivated my daughter Hélène to piece this book together!"

> *"Feeling gratitude and not expressing it is like*
> *wrapping a present and not giving it."*

–William Arthur Ward [1921, Louisiana – March
30, 1994] – author of *Fountains of Faith*.

One day in recent years, my father recalled medical meetings in Salisbury. A friend Dr. Frank B. Marsh -- a general practice physician, who later specialized in cardiology and internal medicine, led the prayer.

"Oh Lord give us the insight or patience to understand and forever be mindful of the needs of others."

Dr. Marsh, who later retired at age 92, no doubt emphasized this prayer for the doctors in attendance. It is a consistent prayer my father recalled. Perhaps, it is one we might remember as we continue to build upon this history called: *Genealogy.*

James Noah Hinson, M.D.

♀ | | ♂

James Noah Hinson, M.D. & his wife Patricia Ann Leighton Hinson

♀ | | ♂

Appreciation

♀ | | ♂

*"Appreciation in others is a wonderful thing: It makes
what is excellent in others belong to us as well."*

-- VOLTAIRE

-- Voltaire – known as François-Marie Arouet
[November 21, 1694-May 30, 1778]
French Enlightenment, playwright,
writer, historian, philosopher; Paris, France

♀ | | ♂

FIRST AND FOREMOST, WE ARE thankful to God – Our Heavenly Father and Creator. Without Him, we can do nothing. In every endeavor, we must remember to lean on Him and not forget He is the reason we breathe, think, stand, walk.

Anything good a human soul hopes to do is channeled from Heaven. Any success gained belongs to God. This project is tremendous responsibility. Through the years many people trust us to protect and preserve genealogical history. With this book, we are able to breathe some relief that it is complete enough to publish.

Thankfulness. We possess much. It is the emotion, demeanor and feeling that rules. It should be expressed in a list as long as the pages of this book. There are going to be people left out due to an inability to recall every name of those encountered in libraries and every unrelated and related soul who points in various directions.

Not one researcher of genealogy does it alone. Each person we come in contact with -- *no matter how brief,* influences everything we do.

Collectively, we influence one another – good *or bad* – no one more important than the other.

A seemingly tiny tip from a librarian, or a relative can lead to something great in terms of information, or understanding how people and history fit together – a lineage, or a particular person in history relevant to the genealogical pursuits.

Thankfulness… we are grateful to my father James *"Jim" "Jimmy"* Noah Hinson, M.D. for introducing genealogy to me as a child -- emphasizing its importance. He emphasized this with just about everyone he knew.

It was introduced at an age I did not always follow what he conveyed. It was, however, the seeds he planted that are growing today. Even the smallest bits of what we recall from conversations become the footholds of those things we learn later.

Genealogical research is done in layers. This includes digging through those efforts and accomplishments of other researchers when the paper and stone trails grow cold.

"To the living we owe respect, but to the dead, we owe only the truth,"

– Voltaire

♀ | | ♂

So, here we are -- *a kiss* for James Noah Hinson, M.D.

To Patricia Ann Leighton Hinson, I am grateful for instilling the importance of accuracy at the age 7. It was then my first attempts at writing.

This took form in letters to her mother Mary Ruth McTall [Metallo] Leighton [1920-2003] and grandmother Susan *"Susie"* Frances Biller McTall [1896-1984].

For every card, letter or present, I was instructed to write appreciation. I was to detail things received for birthdays, or things I learned in school, on the swim team and in ballet.

Writing letters instills persistence and accuracy. My mother Patricia was adamant. I recall writing with the fat pencil used by grammar-school students that my father accompanied me to buy a pair of boots. I wrote the word *"shoes"* and later, was required to rewrite and edit out *"shoes"* replacing it with *"boots."*

Via my mother, I learned every person has talents that can be expanded upon with diligence and persistence. We are each a link to a greater picture.

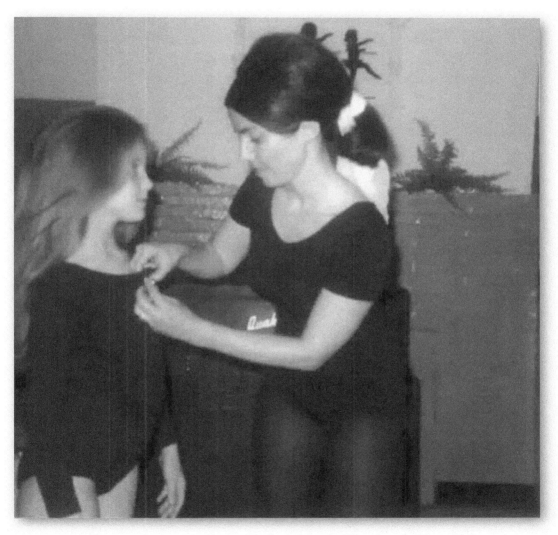

Hélène, age 8 & Mrs. Tadlock of Tadlock School of Dancing, Salisbury, N.C.

To most of the rest, I give hand-shakes and hugs.

Thank you to my cousin and author in his own right William *"Billy"* Ashley Hinson, who has as much interest in genealogy as I do.

He has on many occasions discussed genealogy on the telephone from sunrise of one day to sunrise of the next day. He is a seeker of truth.

Refer to *Suggested Reading & References*. Billy's first genealogical book is titled: *Hinson & Related Families*, a compilation of records, his transcriptions of records, family photographs, newspaper articles, etc.

He told me:

"No matter what lineages I research and compile, Uncle Jim always takes an interest. He always buys my books."

His Uncle Jim is my father – the youngest of three brothers and the third child of six.

Billy's courage to move forward with his Hinson project set the precedence. His actions to get it done despite the goal of perfection or lacking perfection – is perfection itself. It is saying by showing:

"I am going to step on these wobbly stones in a river bed of rushing water. I will make it to the other side even if I fall a hundred times. I am going to get this done!"

Appreciation is extended to beloved Aunt Rachel Evelyn Hinson Hill [1932-1994] and Uncle Richard *"Chub"* Clyde Hinson [1927-2006]. Rachel's book was used often as a reference regarding Eagles – here in particular to the Eagles who connect into the Wyatt lineage. Chub's assistance came towards the end of his life when I interviewed him.

We are obliged to Rachel's children: Norman, Glenda and Paula [1962-1981] and Rachel's husband ♫ ♫ ♫ Paul Junior *"Bud"* Hill [1930-2013] ♫ ♫ ♫ -- each provided influence.

We are thankful to my paternal aunts Betty Lou Hinson Heath and Margaret Ann Hinson Gordon for sharing memories and answering genealogical questions. Margaret assisted with proofreading the earliest drafts.

For years, Betty and her daughter Frances LuAnne Heath Tywater have organized Eagle reunions, which have facilitated and encouraged genealogical discussions and education. Hugs to you both too.

Thank you Uncle June [William C. Hinson, Jr. [1926-2014] and Aunt Dee [Delah Mae Brady Hinson] and cousins Melanie Joan Hinson Saramaha, Rebecca *"Becky"* Ann Hinson Wikle and Mary Lynn Hinson Mangieri.

Appreciation is extended to my great aunt Zylpha Almetta Wright Eagle and granduncle Robert *"Bob"* Noah Eagle and first cousin once removed Norman Paige Barringer [1928-2013] and his wife Mary Ruth Pinion Barringer. They collectively shared stories. These were seeds that grew and led to more answers.

For all relatives not mentioned in the front matter pages, readers can refer to the back matter. Know we are obliged.

Heartfelt gratitude is extended to illustrator Kaspars Gailītis for artwork and photos as prescribed for *The Rungs of Ladders*. Kaspars helped *not only* with this project, but he assisted with three others prior:

- *The Fairyselves* [fantasy fiction, 2012] with cover designs and interior illustrations;
- *The Dish Keepers of Honest House* [fiction 2010] cover design and interior artwork;
- *Paper & Stone, A Leighton History in England & the United States* [genealogical history, 2011]. [With co-researcher by Robert Allen DeVries, Ph.D., a fourth cousin via Leighton lineage.]

We can never express enough appreciation. Kaspars is an inspiration, an intuitive muse and creative thinker. During discussions regarding possible cover designs for any project I present, he offers possibilities.

We build together with imagination. From that, whatever we come up with seems to be an evolution of thought – steps in the journey. Creative thinkers and artists have a role to play in a giant journey we all take together.

Most of the photos published in *The Rungs of Ladders, A Wyatt History in England & the United States, from 1066 to Modern Times* were stained, faded and damaged by time. Kaspars meticulously cleaned these images making them appear as new. His work goes beyond this. He designed the front cover, resized photos so they would fit the perimeters.

It was his suggestion as well we include little journal entries to break up the monotony genealogical presentations oftentimes display.

We appreciate as well my former classmate William *"Bill"* B. Styple. In 2010, we ran into one another on the Internet's Facebook. Soon after we spoke again on the telephone after not having spoken in decades. It is utterly amazing how Heaven places on Earth human angels who dot in and out of lives supplying clues and hints as to what is needed to move forward.

These human-angels transform our ignorant moments into higher learning. They forgive what we don't know. We work with what we have. Before such angels walk away – a part of them becomes us.

We may not initially recognize why these people are meeting with us at all. We are certainly blessed by the souls we have known.

One day I glanced out the office window over the garage. A mail carrier arrived with a large box. It was a package from Bill. It was like Christmas – only it was not a holiday. In the box was Bill's first book titled: *The Little Bugler, The True Story of A Twelve-Year-Old Boy in the Civil War*. He signed it for my sons Zachary, Nicholas and Benjamin.

What a treasure this book is too. It is a true story about Gustav Albert Schurmann who served as a musician ♫♪♪♪♫ in *Company I, 40th, New York Infantry* from 1861 to 1864. Certainly, it is a keepsake to be kept for an eternity.

In this package from Kearny, N.J. was a hardback copy of *Writing & Fighting the Confederate War, The Letters of Peter Wellington Alexander Confederate War Correspondent* and another book titled: *Our Noble Blood, The Civil War Letters of Major-general Régis de Trobriand*, translated by Nathalie Chartrain. There were other books and a disc on ACW veterans.

Refer to a list of his publications in the back matter. [These plugs are my hugs.] When I met Bill at *Catawba College* in Salisbury, N.C. he was knowledgeable about history and particularly enthusiastic about history on the War Between the States. At 18, I never imagined I might find him years later and consult his expertise.

Thank you Bill for reading my initial drafts. *Most of all*, thank you for editing, compiling and researching those books in your own repertoire. We cannot conduct genealogical research without having reliable sources of history within reach.

> *"Stand upright, speak thy thoughts, declare the truth thou hast, that all*
> *may share; Be bold, proclaim it everywhere: They only live who dare."*

> – VOLTAIRE

♀ | | ♂

Appreciation is extended to deceased genealogical British researcher Martyn Freeth who shared in years before his passing June 24, 2012 some of his Wyatt research. Martyn supplied prior direction while researching Leightons in England and the United States in *Paper & Stone, A Leighton History in England & the United States.*

It's ironic that someone who was asked to answer questions about Leightons should be related to the Wyatts. He told me this as we went about assisting me whenever he could. We are appreciative of Sir Michael Leighton for passing my initial letter to Martyn. It led to many insightful correspondences'.

We are grateful to Julian and Alice Wyatt who posted at the familytreemaker.genealogy.com a compilation quite similar to my own and to others I have come across. That research effort was made by John Hampton Wyatt and adapted by his grandchildren for that site.

Gretchen Beilfuss Witt – I bow to her! Gretchen is the Edith M. Clark History Room Librarian at Rowan County Library, #201 West Fisher Street in Salisbury, N.C.

Gretchen has the patience of a saint. It is a delight to pull from my mailbox large envelopes she has stuffed with documents – marriage records, last will and testaments, land grants, census records, tax documents, etc.

To Dewey Snider, Genealogy History Room at Lexington Public Library, Lexington, N.C. thank you for answering questions. Dewey is blessed with the *know-how* of library science – *skilled to the max* for assisting researchers.

Dewey told a story of finding a footstone that sank and settled. Had he not looked a little closer, it would have possibly been lost forever.

Stones too will eventually turn to dust. Caretakers need to preserve the reminders that once on Earth this person laughed, sang, played. One day we will join them.

We are thankful to all librarians in Special Collections at Wilson Library and Davis Library at the University of North Carolina at Chapel Hill. Specifically, we thank *"Harry"* now retired.

A few years ago, while gathering records and researching Dandridges, I mentioned to Harry *Dishonest Housekeepers*, an avant-guard fiction. A year or so later, while perusing the UNC-CH's online site, I saw this book had been made available for *in library use only* at Wilson. It was the most wonderful feeling to learn this. Thank you, Harry!

Thanks to Eli with the Lexington Public Library, #140 E. Main Street Lexington, Ky. Eli sent promptly census records regarding the whereabouts of three sons of John Wiatt [1743-1815] [Sylvester, James and Eli Wiatt] when they left Rowan County, N.C. and traveled to Kentucky.

Gratitude is extended to the University of North Carolina at Chapel Hill. I graduated from UNC-CH in 1987 with a bachelor's degree in Journalism with an emphasis in the news editorial sequence.

I return often to UNC-Chapel Hill using its treasures and beautiful libraries particularly the archives in Special Collections of Wilson Library. My sons visit this campus and as I like to say, *"have since they were eggs."*

The eldest son Zachary graduated Mother's Day, Sunday, May 11th, 2014 with a bachelor of science degree in Chemistry and Physics from this university. I am thankful to my sons Nicholas and Benjamin for their patience – and *lack of patience* that prompted occasional breaks.

We thank Howard. In the mid-to-late 1990s, he helped find a genealogical computer program, which allows archiving – *The Family Tree Maker* ®. His beloved parents Marie Cecelia Euker [1919-1998] and Milton Carlton Staley [1920-1998] provided inspiration and information specifically on the Lucas lineage. This information prompted me to think more deeply about the Wyatts who were involved in the American Civil War.

We extend our warm hugs to my 4th cousin Robert *"Bob"* Allen DeVries, Ph.D. whose work on the Leighton book extended beyond its pages and found expression in this Wyatt book as well.

My sister Nicky – Nicole Suzanne Hinson, M.D., we thank for supportive conversations and proof-reading.

Hans Leighton Hinson, M.D.;
Nicole *"Nicky"* Suzanne Hinson, M.D.

Patricia Ann Leighton Hinson, Hélène Andorre Hinson (Staley) & James Noah
Hinson, M.D.; Hans Leighton Hinson & Hélène Andorrre Hinson (Staley).

My brother Hans Leighton Hinson, M.D. is to be recognized for his curiosity, questions and direction.

On Friday, October 10th, 2014, Maryann Price Zane called regarding Lucas lineage. Ironically, she wanted to share a photo of former ACW Union soldier [ranked sergeant and corporal at varying times] Irish immigrant Timothy Lucas [1831-1910], a man mentioned while discussing William Wesley Wyatt's history [1831-1863] and connections.

Maryann is a third cousin once removed to my sons. Although she is not related to the Wyatt family that I know of, she is a second great granddaughter of Timothy Lucas. Timothy Lucas is a third great grandfather to my sons via their father's father's mother's Lucas lineage.

The blue-clad Union soldier Timothy Lucas fought in the *Battle of Gettysburg*. He fought in this same battle where Confederate soldier William Wesley Wyatt battled. This William Wesley Wyatt [1831-1863] was a brother of my third great grandmother Rachel Evelyn Wyatt Morgan [1835-1915]. William fought beside his brother Silas Wyatt [1838-1864] and second cousin Nathaniel Morgan [1832-1904], husband of Delilah Wyatt Morgan [b. 1834].

William Wesley Wyatt, Silas Wyatt, Nathan Morgan and Timothy Lucas [1831-1910] were part of more than 165,000 soldiers who fought at Gettysburg. Around 51,000 men from both the Union and Confederacy were killed, wounded, captured or missing. So, to Maryann, we say thank you for sending Lucas family photos, from which I obtained one of Timothy.

Gratitude is extended to Pastor Tommy Beaver of Luther's Lutheran Church in Richfield, N.C. for his beautiful sermon, which is included in the back matter.

Dr. Brian Futrell -- I am thankful to him. Brian told a patient in June 2015:

"Hélène says we all have at least one book in ourselves."

Brian's innocent reiteration drove a point home.

We are each a spirit inside a body. Our experiences tell the stories of how we live.

In another transition and a discovery that steps on this genealogical path, I read Emanuel Swedenborg's theologies. Such emphasizes our lives are summations of every action, thought, deed, intent. Intent is what we are shaped by. Even intent evolves as we mature and grow.

Swedenborg wrote on many subjects – not just those pertaining to theologies. One that caught my interest is:

"Heaven and Hell," [originally in Latin and titled: *"Heaven and Its Wonders and Hell from Things Heard and Seen -- De Caelo et Eius Mirabilibus et de inferno, ex Auditis et Visis.*]

We are thankful to Swedenborg – a Swedish scientist, anatomist, botanist, physicist, chemist, philosopher, theologian, mathematician, known as the *"Father of Swedish Mechanics,"* who lived from 1688 to 1772. None of us does anything alone – We have as angels those seen and unseen souls influencing our insights – openly and spiritually. He is such an angel.

Swedenborg emphasizes it is the intent of a person, which comes to define a human soul. Who we are and what we become is defined by what we love most. It is additionally defined by how we regard and treat our fellow humankind. We are essentially souls traveling the earthly realm in bodies we will leave behind – taking within the soul unique, treasured and not-so-treasured experiences.

Mega rays of sunlight to my friend Patrick de Broux. He is one of our earthly angels. On November 13, 2014, he sent his honest, wise and much needed awakenings regarding the appropriate uses of boldface font and symbols.

From there, he wrote and sent several pages of suggestions. Patrick's input is a Godsend. He is a source of continued support and guidance.

Thank you to the New Hanover County Public Library's genealogical section on Chestnut Street in Wilmington, N.C. It supplied eight news clippings on various Wyatts in North Carolina from:

- *The Charlotte Chronicle* [1905]
- *The Messenger* [1900]
- *The Greenville Weekly* [1900]
- *The Greenville Daily Reflector* [1897].

We are immensely grateful to all public record keepers – tombstone engravers, clerks, etc. and those editors and writers listed in the suggested reading back matter section.

Thankfulness is extended to all of the souls of this planet who influence, teach, inspire and lead us through this *Rungs of Ladders'* journey. The other souls referred to are divided only by the physical and spiritual realms of Heaven.

Appreciation travels from this Earth to those ancestors and relatives [and all adopted members too] we would not know in this earthly realm without the assistance of researchers, writers and archivists.

Nevertheless, there are whispers we receive in dreams. Such experiences are *magical*. Suddenly, we find a tidbit we did not know before, or someone we do not expect steps out of the woodwork to lend a hand.

From age four, I grew up in Salisbury, where I went to school with students who may or may not have known they were my blood relatives. At Knox Junior High School, the then main principal Frank B. Shaver was my third cousin once removed, and the principal of Salisbury High School was Ninion Windsor Eagle, my third cousin once removed. Even my dentist James Eagle is my cousin.

Many of my father's patients were cousins. The entire town and its county is riddled with Shavers, Eagles, Caspers, Stoners, Wyatts, Ellers, Morgans, Millers [Mullers], Park, [Parks, Parke], Pooles, Reeds, Reids, Hodges, and others – and from these family names I am a descendant – along with Norbitts, Hendleys and others.

From each of these I have additionally cousins who are Basingers, Barringers, Briggs, Carters, Hills, Kirks, Earnhardts, Trexlers, Misenheimers, Peelers, Files, Whitakers, Hoffners and many more.

These lineages are the strands that are braided through Rowan County and the North Carolina's other 99 counties. They travel into Virginia and Maryland and throughout the U.S. and the globe.

In regard to the Wyatts, a man recently told me:

"It sounds like a French braid."

Indeed, it is if one considers the origins of the Wyatt family having been people using the Guyot name in France. Through the corridors of time we have lineages from Germany, Switzerland, England, Ireland and other areas of the world. They are woven together in each of us. Its evolutions took a little rest in Rowan County, N.C. along the way. For that, we are thankful too.

I cannot ever thank enough the people who names and stories alone caught my interest and that of my father as those he loved and respected all of his life.

♀ | | ♂

Genealogical Games

♀ | | ♂

- Not all those who wander are lost...

♀ | | ♂

"*NOT ALL THOSE WHO WANDER are lost,*" is a quotation from John Ronald Reuel Tolkein's [1892-1973] book: *The Lord of the Rings*. When applied to the Wyatt lineage, it rings true as well.

The Wyatts of Virginia are indicated in historical accounts to come from an ancient English family. They are believed to be of Norman-French origin.

People who can trace their lineages past their backyards find ancestors who wandered this planet to such a degree genealogists today are much like the children in a game of *Hide & Seek*.

Children must pay attention to clues and likely places their friends might hide. If they are afraid of heights, they are not likely to hide in a tree or a barn's loft. If they fear the neighbor's dog, they will not venture into the dog's area.

The Wyatts have wandered we can say with confidence since the *Norman Invasion of 1066*. They continue to do this probably in less time since the invention of ships, trains and jets. From an historical perspective, many brave souls are Wyatts.

As you read, take into account the writer speaks from the present. There is an underlying quest to make sense of English language through the centuries.

One must discern, or at least try to discern discrepancies in public records and discrepancies from family stories or beliefs passed from one generation to the next.

This can be much like the *game of whispering* a message into your friend's ear. The friend whispers the message into the next person's ear. That person does the same over the course of a large circle of people. When what is whispered gets to the end of the circle, it is likely not to resemble what the first person uttered. This is true of public records.

Public records can be from the military, births recorded in Bibles, or on a public register, or in a church, or on a tombstone. The same is true of death records. All begin with what is uttered.

This account will take you from 1066 and through the Medieval Period or the Middle Ages to the Colonial Period up to our Modern Era.

This book makes no pretenses to become a carbon copy in style or presentation of others before. I am using a computer and have advantages that others before this invention did not have. There are others doing Wyatt research, and perhaps this presentation, assessment and compilations herein will be helpful in the scope of everything done and being done.

Included occasionally are journal entries. I hope you find them entertaining and lighten any weight when wondering how will you get your mind around this information. We are with you every step of the way.

The task here is to communicate the genealogical past and how it fits into the history of its time. Since the establishment of the United States – U.S. Americans have solved disagreements by fighting. This has not changed much today; however, the attitudes of rebelling have. Today, Americans are more likely to request our government seek and discern alternatives to war.

In some sections of this book the reader will encounter humor to offset dates. The repetition, although used sparingly, is necessary to discern identities and clarify points.

The process is to follow, decipher and discern discrepancies of record and in conversation, in stories handed down and to apply such an analysis to additional discrepancies that are inadvertently added during the drafting phase.

While sorting past errors, or worse believing something to be an error and *not discovering at all it is not* is one paranoia in organizing the research into this presentation. We don't need to entertain the possibility of nightmares. Our human experiences and imaginations often supply that on their own.

For the genealogical researcher....

There will be discrepancies.

There will be debates.

There will be frustration and headaches, or temporary roadblocks cluttering up the pathways with multiple persons and cousins, parents and offspring with the exact same names.

There will be satisfaction in knowing we are souls on a mission to gain a better understanding of what it is like to travel in the human body and venture about the globe.

What is it like to untangle Wyatts?

Hopefully, when this book is laid to rest, additional tangles will be fewer.

There are tangles – possibly unyielding knots as well, we have not sorted. Those are left for readers and future researchers. Possibly, a lightbulb may go off and lead to more answers. If so, send your *eureka* moments to Metallo House Publishers [MHP].

Whether proof of a connection, or a discrepancy, feel at ease to send comments. The goal is preservation and presentation. It is not to seek skeletons.

It is simply to keep ancestral heritage intact. When the next few hundred years have passed, researchers with the task of archiving and recording will have in place information that will assist.

Pictures, Photographs & Illustrations

♀ | | ♂

"It is our spirit that sees, not our eye; our spirit sees through our eyes."

— Emanuel Swedenborg

⁕   Illustrations, photograph & art image restorations by Kaspars Gailītis.

About the Cover Design

*T*REES ARE SYMBOLIC OF FAMILIES because they have branches. Each branch of a tree holds itself outward like an opened hand or arm to the sky as if embracing our Creator. In other words, the branches are like the arms of a child reaching for parents.

This cover shows the leaves of a tree suggested to be nearby but not seen completely. Often those still living are invisible to other members. The ladder, although symbolic as well, leans on a white background. The rungs lead us from one generation to the next.

The Photographs

James Noah Hinson, M.D. & daughter Hélène at age 1 appears on the back cover.

Rachel Evelyn Wyatt Morgan [born 1835, Rowan County, N.C.; died 1915, Rowan County, N.C.]

Eli Wyatt [born: 1841, North Carolina; died: 1912, Rowan County, N.C.], husband of Malinda Wise [1833-1902]; son of Mary Hendly and Noah Calvin Wyatt [1805-1871] – who is a son to Thomas Wiatt [1774-1845] → son of: John Wiatt [1743-1815]; enlisted in the Confederate Army in Rowan County, N.C. February 22, 1862 and served in the 10th Regiment Company D, 1st Regiment North Carolina Artillery; NCST ACW. Buried: Saint Matthews Lutheran Church Cemetery, Salisbury, N.C. Row #22.

Noah *"Noe"* Calvin Wyatt [born: 1843, North Carolina], husband of Nancy Daniels Reid; son of Mary Polly Hendly and Noah Calvin Wyatt, enlisted for the Confederacy in Iredell

County, N.C. August 8th, 1862; 5th Regiment -- Company H, North Carolina State Troops, ACW.

James *"Jim"* Noah Wyatt [1861-1957], husband of Barbara Ann E. Basinger [1862-1957] This James *"Jim"* Noah Wyatt is the son of Mary Buchanan and William Wesley Wyatt [1831-1863] who enlisted for the Confederacy September 4th, 1862 and served in the 23rd Regiment -- Company H, North Carolina State Troops ACW and was wounded in the Battle of Gettysburg, Pa. dying of his injuries on July 20th, 1863. James' wife Barbara Basinger is the daughter of Rhoda Isabelle Morgan and D. *"Whit"* Whitson Basinger.

Mary Jane Morgan Eagle [born 1856, Rowan County, N.C.; died 1928, Rowan County, N.C.], wife of Solomon Eagle, Jr. [1857-1939]. She is the daughter of Rachel E. Wyatt and John Morgan.

Collage of five of the Morgan siblings– sons of: Barbara Shaver [1813-1896] Moses Greene or Green Morgan [1810-1879] of Rowan County, N.C.

1) Nathaniel *"Nathan"* Morgan – husband of Lila Delilah *"Delila"* Wyatt [born 1834, Rowan County, N.C.] & later husband to Linda *"Linna"* Surratt [1842-1921]; Nathan's lifespan: 1832-1904 – born and died in Poole Town District, Morgan Township, N.C., Confederate soldier who enlisted August 8th, 1862 in Iredell County and served in 5th Regiment -- Company H, North Carolina State Troops, ACW, farmer.
2) John Calvin Morgan - husband of Rachel Evelyn Wyatt Morgan [1835-1915] [John Morgan was born: 1834, Poole Town District, Morgan Township, N.C.; died 1864, Spotsylvania, Va.], farmer, who with his wife owned a farm on River Road in Rowan County with nine slaves. Enlisted August 8th, 1862 for the Confederacy; served in the 5th Regiment -- Company H of the North Carolina Troops, ACW; mortally wounded in the Battle of Spotsylvania Court House, Va. May 12th, 1864.
3) Mack Camey Morgan [born 1836; died 1913, Rowan County, N.C. – husband of 1) Mary Elizabeth *"Betty"* Arey [1842-1904] 2) Martha Jane Stoner [b. 1844] former wife of Reuben Monroe Eller [b. 1858, Liberty, N.C.], enlisted August 8th, 1862 in Iredell County for the Confederacy and served in the 5th Regiment -- Company H of the North Carolina Troops, ACW, farmer.
4) Jacob Morgan [1847-1919] married: 1) Sinie Surratt; 2) Ann Jim Kirk [1854-1924].
5) James Loveless *"Love"* Morgan [1849-1915] married Louisa *"Louise"* Clementine Kirk [1849-1923].

John Thomas Wyatt [1851-1933] *"Venus of Faith"* – two photos; son of Wilson Riley *"Wiley"* Wyatt and Mary Ann Park [1831-Aft. 1870]; served the Confederacy in an unofficial capacity [ACW], stone cutter, newspaper columnist, inventor of a unique salve formula for eczema, millstone carver. He married December 16, 1880 Charlotte Elizabeth Phillips Dyer [born abt. 1836].

THE ILLUSTRATIONS

Illustration of Confederate soldier telling his wife goodbye during the American Civil War [ACW] [1861-1865].

Illustration of the Wyatt Coat of Arms

Paintings by Hans Holbein, the Younger

Sir Henry Wyatt [1460-1536], born in Southange, [South Haigh or Upper Haigh] West Riding, Yorkshire, England; died in Allington Castle, Kent County, England; in 1502 married 1) Anne Skinner, born 1485 in Reigate Surry County or Arleigh, Essex, England and had issue: Margaret *"Lady Lee,"* around 1506; Henry about 1500 and Thomas [the Elder] in 1503. Some sources report Sir Henry Wyatt [1460-1536] married 2) a Margaret Bailiff. Sir Henry Wyatt was a son of Margaret Jane Clarke or Bailiffe and Richard Wiat [1435-1475], born in Southange and Tickhill, West Riding, Yorkshire, England; died in Barking, Essex, England. His image in this book is from a painting by one of the greatest portrait painters of the 16th century: Hans Holbein, the Younger [1497-1543].

Sir Thomas Wyatt – the Elder [1503-1542]; born in Allington Castle, Kent County, England; died Sherbourne or Sherborne, Dorset, England; married 1) Elizabeth Brooke [1503-1560] 2) Elizabeth Darrell or Darell. Sir Thomas Wyatt, the Elder, served in the court of King Henry VII, was a poet, was High Sheriff of Kent County in 1537, among other occupations. The sketch herein was made by Hans Holbein [1497-1543], portrait artist of the 16th century.

Margaret *"Lady Lee"* Wyatt or Wiatt [Abt. 1506-Abt. 1535], born Allington Castle, Kent County, England, wife of Sir Anthony Lee who was born in Quarendon or Quarrendon, Buckinghamshire, England and died in 1549. Issue or children of Margaret and Sir Anthony Lee: Henry, [b. Abt. 1532], Robert, Cromwell, Thomas, Anne, Lettice, Katherine, Joyce, Jane. Some sources claim she married secondly a John Thomas Rogers. This portrait of Margaret herein was painted by 16th century portrait artist Hans Holbein [1497-1543].

* Reminder: Margaret Wyatt [Abt. 1506-Abt. 1535] is a daughter of Sir Henry Wyatt [1460-1536]. Margaret is a sister to the elder / poet Wyatt.

Sir Thomas Wyatt – the Younger [1521-1554]; born Allington Castle, Kent County, England; died Tower Hill, London, England; married Lady Jane Haute *"Hawte"* [Abt. 1522-1600]. He led Wyatt's Rebellion against Queen Mary I. This image herein was produced by 16th century portrait artist Hans Holbein, the Younger [1497-1543].

The Image of Allington Castle

Allington Castle, the ancestral Wyatt home, was erected by Stephen de Penctester [Penshurst] sometime between 1279 and 1299 passing to his son-in-law Sir Henry de Cobham in the early 14th century. Located five miles from Maidstone in Kent County, the castle was bought by Sir Henry Wiatt or Wyatt [1460-1535 or 36]. Sir Henry altered Allington Castle after the year 1492.

It was in 1554 forfeited to the British Crown when Sir Thomas Wyatt – the Younger, was charged with treason after leading a rebellion against Queen Mary I – daughter of Henry VIII – Mary I – being the half-sister of then Princess Elizabeth I.

The castle, where the Younger and Elder were born, is said to have been turned into two farm houses that later fell into ruin. The castle is reportedly to have been restored by Lord Martin Conway and his architect W.D. Caroe between the years 1905 and 1929.

When Sir Henry Wyatt [1503-1542] resided in this castle, he added timber-framed buildings in the south-east corner. These became offices and a kitchen.

Reports indicate Sir Henry Wyatt altered most of the windows while there. A wing of the building that divides the courtyard in half was built by Sir Henry Wyatt. It contained a long gallery, which was destroyed later and restored by Lord Conway.

Visitors to Allington Castle include: Tudor Kings Henry VII and Henry VIII, Queen Consorts Anne Boleyn and Catherine Parr, Cardinal Wolsey and Thomas Cromwell.

Additional photos herein have not been cleaned of spots, stains, blurriness or Father Time. They are presented as the following in varying places throughout *The Rungs of Ladders*.

Additional images:

* Portrait photo of James Noah Hinson, M.D. & his wife Patricia Ann Leighton Hinson.
* Portrait photograph of James Noah Hinson, abt. 1956.
* Candid photograph of James Noah Hinson, M.D. & his sister Margaret feeding a calf with a bottle.
* James Noah Hinson, M.D. visiting the Park-Wyatt-Bean Graveyard, Rowan County, N.C.
* Shaver School, Rowan County, N.C.
* Group photos of James Noah Hinson, M.D. as a child growing up with his siblings June, Chub, Rachel, Betty and Margaret.
* Dance illustration
* Photo of Lick Creek Baptist Church Cemetery
* Land map of 300 acres for John Wyatt [Wiatt] 1743-1815.
* Photo of Luther's Lutheran Church, Richfield, N.C.

♀ | | ♂

Sir Henry Wyatt – Father of Sir Thomas Wyatt, the Elder.

Allington Castle at Boxley Parish, Kent County, England.

How to begin

♀ | | ♂

"It is dangerous to be right in matters on which the
established authorities are wrong."

-- VOLTAIRE

PAIN IS NOT AN ILLUSION…

"Pain is not an illusion in this physical world, but it is an illusion to truth."

THESE WORDS FILLED MY THOUGHTS the morning of Tuesday, October 29th, 2013.

Pain is what enemies wish to inflict on the living. Some seek to destroy, wipe out, cause to disappear and to kill. The truth is -- as far as Heaven is concerned – the killing of a living body gets rid of no one. Physical death does not dissolve them into nothingness, nor does it wipe from the minds of souls a person's existence. The body is merely the soul's vehicle – not the religion, not the race, not the nationality. It's a lesson humans seem to forget on earth: We all belong to and begin with God.

Pain is the realization of harm we each cause and mend in others just by living here.

Just prior to this contemplation, I pondered at great length Europe and the United Kingdom [U.K.] -- its kings and queens through history and time.

All these things come with discrepancies we either suspect or *never learn.* We swallow each spoonful often without questioning things, which may have been exaggerations, or propaganda, or gossip, or things that were completely covered up.

What encompassed exactly my thoughts on October 29th, 2013 is pretty much the stories and histories passed from one time to the next – things recorded on paper, in monuments, on grave stones and church walls, floors and tombs. At some point, humans naturally need or want to express opinions and conclusions about what goes on and about what they experience living here.

Trying to figure out how the earliest Wyatts fit into the history and genealogies that surrounded them prompts the seeker to better understand the times in which they lived. This insight and understanding is necessary.

One cannot simply say:

"I am related to nobility or royalty"

[or anyone who is otherwise a stranger to us]

without this deeper want of understanding not only *how* we all fit into this puzzle of genealogy, but *into the ebb and flow of living here.*

Even bonafide genealogical proof does NOT raise our status in God's Eyes. The quest is never to turn up a nose, or to act or behave as if anyone has rights over another person's privacy, or power to live in this world.

A human who wears a robe of velvet and silk is not somehow better than a human who wears a cotton tunic or a burlap cover. A human who fights in a battle for any number of perceived or brainwashed assaults, is no better than a human who lives say remotely in a mountain cave minding his own business and killing no one.

On Saturday, February 21, 2015, I ventured with two of my three children and husband to visit the North Carolina Museum of Natural Sciences at #11 West Jones Street in Raleigh, N.C. The temperature was in the 20s Fahrenheit.

On the Thursday prior the weather report stated a high would be 17 degrees Fahrenheit [-8.3 degrees Celsius] and a low would reach 2 degrees Fahrenheit [-16.6 degrees Celsius]. This high was in error and climbed to around 25 degrees F – and with the snow and ice was good reason to stay indoors. The venure to Raleigh beckoned all the stronger.

So, after driving nearly an hour to the museum and walking over the iced and snowy sections of parking lots, walkways and sidewalks, we entered. It is a place endeavored many times. February 21st, 2015 would be different.

There for the first time I see John Muir's words:

"When we try to pick out anything by itself, we find it hitched to everything else in the Universe."

It was one of those moments we feel the angels of Heaven speaking to us. Certainly, one might say the ghosts of the earth speak in such moments. It was a sparkle nevertheless that what remains in this physical plane of John Muir – imprints of his ghost, spirit, words of paper or plaque. His words fashioned a deep impression.

I doubt he was speaking of genealogy – The museum's plaque was simply quoting John Muir's book: *My First Summer in the Sierra* [published in 1911].

Here is it again:

"When we try to pick out anything by itself, we find it hitched to everything else in the Universe."

Later, I came across this other version of his honest and profound quote:

"When we try to pick out anything by itself, we find that it is bound fast by a thousand invisible cords that cannot be broken, to everything in the Universe."

Reading his words for the first time and being in the midst of piecing this Wyatt book together had a profound eureka consequence.

My mind raced. Everything is connected. You know math and science are connected, and the history of it is connected. We know the evolution of the English language is connected to English literature, and its history is its timeline. We know the evolution of language of any sort – French, Italian, German, etc., is connected to everything we learn or never learn. History records our lives – even if not in any official capacity – every human has a history, and every step we take is connected to one another.

The reference to a thousand invisible cords is profound. It is reminiscent or suggestive of a quote from the Book of Ecclesiastes in the Bible. First, it is important to point out John Muir [April 21, 1838-December 24, 1914] was a Scottish-American naturalist, engineer, writer, botanist and geologist. He was an advocate of preserving the wilderness in the United States.

His quote in the second version stated earlier rings so closely with the *Book of Ecclesiastes 12:6-7*:

"Remember Him before the silver cord is severed, or the golden bowl is broken; before the pitcher is shattered at the spring, or the wheel broken at the well, and the dust returns to the ground it came from, and the spirit returns to God who gave it."

Some might interpret the severing of a silver cord or breaking of the bowl as a symbol of death and the cord as our body's connection to the soul or to God. God is the life Source outside the realms of the Earth and yet it influences and gives life on this Earth.

This silver cord we all possess represents our connection to one another – We are all connected, and whether one uses the argument of the descendants of Noah who survived the Great Flood, or any other way of thinking about the significance of each soul on this Earth, we are all connected to something far greater than our human brains have processed so far.

Genealogy helps us discover it from a point of view that further supports the idea in Muir's quote regarding nature and the universe. We are all connected to one another. We are all here to help one another – not to fight, kill and hinder.

We are not here to invent and discover ways to harm our brothers and sisters. We are here to use our differences to the collective advantage of mankind. The differences are to help one another discover tolerance through love, peace and a safe path in the midst of a difficult physical existence.

A soul or spirit in this world cannot do it without a body, and it must have other souls inside more vehicles or bodies to ensure a safe journey.

So many meet with destructive forces that hinder experiences and rob one another of vehicles that would otherwise render protection and growth.

I am but one soul. There is the advantage of being in a world full of souls here for the same reasons. This means we each benefit from one another simply by being here, living, questioning those things that interest us.

What are those reasons we are here?

The reasons are to journey into the physical confines of this existence, to gain knowledge and understanding before our physical brains malfunction or slow considerably with our bodies. Personally, I do not believe we are here to destroy one another, or to worship one another. Even with mistakes humans make collectively or individually – there is something to be gained. We are here to love.

We learn eventually destructive forces are outside the nature of our natural souls. Simply being in this physical world is a fight to survive. We are spiritual creatures inside a physical body. The only reprieve for our souls while in these human bodies seems to be when we experience love on one level, or another with other humans, or earthly creatures, or those visiting from the Spiritual Realm – angels, or in prayer to God, or when the body is at rest and the mind is dreaming.

Granted, we wish that *sticks and stones* for such battles never became part of the decisions people make, or that their perception ever be that the material world is the ultimate prize. Certainly, it is not. It is what we learn. The prize is in the understanding and wisdom. This is not held between our hands, or felt beneath our feet. The prize is held between our ears …. and inside hearts.

So on Tuesday, October 29th 2013 as I first mentioned in the beginning of this introduction ….

I thought of King Henry Tudor VIII [1491-1547] -- his arrogance and misdirection. England's King Henry Tudor no doubt knew his accusations were lies. His thinking led to Consort Queen Anne Boleyn's [1501- May 19, 1536] execution by sword at the Tower of London [north bank of the River Thames].

King Henry VIII's misguided thinking and evolution of thought led to the execution of Catherine Howard [1523- February 13, 1541/42] whose youth made her death at Tower Hill more inhumane.

Historical accounts record a rumor that Sir Thomas Wyatt – the Elder [Abt. 1503-1542], had a love interest in Anne Boleyn. Some of his poems suggest it. Sir Thomas Wyatt's – the Elder's marriage to Elizabeth Brooke [1503-1560; daughter of Dorothy Heydon and Thomas Brooke, 8th Baron of Cobham] is said to have been an unhappy union.

I thought about Henry VIII's second daughter Queen Elizabeth I [1533-1603]. Reports from her advisors and information conveyed by spy Francis Walsingham and gossip made her suspicious of her first cousin once removed Mary Queen of Scots [1542-1587] possessing motives to be Queen of England. So, on February 1, 1587, Elizabeth I signed her cousin's death warrant.

Mary Queen of Scots is said to have been the unluckiest queen in British history and the saddest of all political figures in the British Isles.

Mary Queen of Scots [1542-1587] was the great granddaughter of King Henry Tudor VII [1456/57-April 21, 1509]. Elizabeth I was a granddaughter of this same King Henry Tudor VII – the father of King Henry VIII. Mary Queen of Scot's [1542-1587] was a legitimate descendant of King Henry VII; whereas Elizabeth the First had been claimed by her father Henry VIII to be a bastard or illegitimate child, along with Elizabeth I's half sister Mary I *"Bloody Mary."*

King Henry VII → Margaret *"Mary Queen of Scots"* Tudor → King James Stuart V of Scotland → Mary *"Mary Queen of the Scots"* Stuart → James Stuart VI & I *"King of Scotland"* and *"King of England"* [1603].

King Henry VII → King Henry VIII Tudor → Elizabeth I Tudor.

```
        King H VII-----------[same]--------------King H VII
              ^                                        ^
   ♀ + King H VIII---------[siblings]-------------Margaret Tudor + ♂
              ^                                        ^
        Queen Eliz. I--------[1ˢᵗ cousins]----------James Stuart V [King of Scotland]
              ^                                        ^
```

No descendants----[2ⁿᵈ cousins]----------Mary Stuart [Queen of Scots]

   ∧   ∧

No descendants----[3ʳᵈ cousins]----------James VI & I

As pages of history traveled through my thoughts, so did the timeline of King George V [1865-1936]. He refused his first cousin Nicholas II [1868-1918] asylum in England. He looked so much like him he could have been his twin. George V's actions to refuse Nicholas II's entry unknowingly strengthened forces against Nicholas II. This led to Nicholas II and his family being rounded up and slaughtered. *

    * In the back matter, see *Footnote to Introduction*.

As if positioned in the middle of the story the universe is writing about the human-kind of our earth, the doors of my mind opened to the life of Edward VIII. His reign lasted not more than a year before he abdicated. His father George V and mother, and others in his family disapproved of his choice of wife: Wallace Warfield Simpson [1896-1986].

Edward VIII [1894-1972] was an uncle to Elizabeth II and a brother to George VI [1895-1952]. This George VI was the father of Elizabeth II, who is Queen of 16 of the 53 member states of the Commonwealth of Nations and Head of the Commonwealth and Supreme Governor of the Church of England.

On that October day of 2013...I thought longer.

Is the idea of royalty an illusion?

Are royal families throughout mankind's history supposed to be for the public the example of a model family -- the supreme way to behave?

The year 1788 opens like a playwright turning the pages of a script. The British had lost its hold on the American colonies. I remember a humorous, but seemingly historically accurate film made in 1994 titled: *The Madness of King George* [directed by Nicholas Hytner; based on a play written by Alan Bennett]. It's one of my favorite films of all time.

One of the king's lines -- George III of Great Britain and Ireland played by Nigel Hawthorne [1929-2001] is an emphasis that George, his wife and children should give the people what they want and *"be the model family."* *

    * In the back matter, see *2ⁿᵈ Footnote to Introduction*.

As King George III, Hawthorne in the film, says:

"We must try to be more of a family…There are model farms now…model villages…We must be a model family for the Nation to look to…Smile to the people…Let them see we are happy…That is why we are here."

EXAMINATION OF HUMANKIND….

Cousin killed cousin. Sister threatened death to another. Queen Bloody Mary, Henry VIII's eldest daughter Mary I – threatened her half-sister Elizabeth I. One must certainly conclude mankind in its physical mind has entertained fantasy and illusion throughout real life dramas. We seemingly do it without objection like sheep to slaughter or open field.

What strikes or hints at being such an illusion is if royalty is ordained by God -- if Henry VIII, for instance, had his power from God Almighty, then it does not seem at all God would cause Henry to have affairs with women through the country sides of England.

If we judge, we are taught we can expect some similar judgment of ourselves. If we do not make some sort of discernment about what we should be doing and what hinders mankind, we get stuck in arrogance, fear, greed – a rut. The whispers of evil lie to us – and cause us to make poor judgments on behalf of ourselves and others.

If kings are ordained by God, and royalty by definition would not tolerate adultery no matter how it is defined and bent to a will, then King Henry VIII was not royal by definition or action.

Undoubtedly, he was regarded as royal by his adoring and not-so-adoring public. Maybe not. If royalty meant kings and queens were authoritative figure heads – then they were unquestionably royal. They fought diligently to gain control and harder than that to keep it.

In those ways, they are quite extraordinary. Nevertheless, when arrogance and greed for power enters motive or intent –battle is then an illusion. The illusion will pass as we leave our mark here and figure out this was temporary and not real in the long-run.

My thoughts wrapped King Henry Tudor VIII and other associated royalty.

The history of Henry VIII's own genealogy traces to Edward IV [April 28, 1442 – conceived in the summer of 1441 when Edward IV's mother's husband Richard 3rd Duke of York was in Pontoise, which was several days of marching from Rouen, France.

Edward IV's mother Cecily Neville, Duchess of York, stayed behind and was in Rouen. Edward IV's biological father is said to have been an archer -- and he the result of an affair his mother had while his mother Cecily Neville's spouse [Richard – 3rd Duke of York,

Richard Platagenet] was away at war. Math and historical documents brought this under scrutiny. These speculations were there during their lifetimes and remain to this day.

Such an emphasis is recorded in an historical play titled: *King Richard The Third,* written around 1592, act 3, scene 5: *The Tower of Walls* by William Shakespeare. It depicts the Machiavellian rise to power and the short time in power of King Richard III.

Tell them, how Edward put to death, a citizen,

Only for saying he would make his son

Heir to the crown; meaning, indeed, his house,

Which, by the sign thereof, was termed so.

Moreover, urge his hateful luxury,

And bestial appetite in charge of lust;

Which stretch'd unto their servants, daughters, wives,

Even where his lustful eye, or savage heart,

without control, listed [lusted] to make a prey.

Nay, for a need, thus far come near my person:--

Tell them, when that my mother went with child

Of that unsatiate Edward, noble York

My princely father then had wars in France;

And by true computation of the time

Found that the issue was not his begot;

Which well appeared in his lineaments,

Being nothing like the noble duke my father:

But touch this sparingly, as 't were far off:

Because you know, my Lord, my mother lives.

*Footnote: King of England Edward IV [1442-1483] and Richard III [1452-1485] were brothers – more precisely half-brothers if the historical assertions are correct. The earliest known copy of this play was published in 1597 and titled: *The Tragedy of King Richard the Third.* A copy of this play can be found in THE GLOBE ILLUSTRATED SHAKESPEARE, THE COMPLETE WORKS ANNOTATED, DELUXE EDITION, EDITED BY HOWARD STAUNTON © Copyright 1983 Edition, The Globe Illustrated Shakespeare, Greenwich House Crown Publishers, Inc. New York.

In those days, a writer of plays both factual and fiction was what the Internet news and television are today. There is more to this than Shakespeare, so dig it up. Read until you can't stand it another second.

Edward IV [1442-1483], who had dislodged the House of Lancaster from the throne and became king in 1461, died in 1483, and his half-brother Richard III [1452-1485] regarded as his full brother, became king – the last of the House of York. Interesting, Richard III had prior to this been put in charge of Edward IV's young sons.

Hmm, and what happened to those innocent boys sleeping in the tower?

Aspects of royal protocol occupied my thoughts in 2013. Such things dictated a future Queen of England must be a virgin. The public knows definitely of Lady Diana Spencer [1961-1997] in 1981 and the *"check-list"* she passed before marrying Prince Charles.

By requirements of Royalty, was Wallace Simpson unfit to be included in the royal family? Edward VIII's love prevailed. Love forever and a day does.

Wallace Simpson became Prince Edward's wife even though she could not be Queen Consort. Wallace Simpson [1896-1986] became the wife of Edward VIII who was also called *"David."* Edward VIII's wife then became an aunt by marriage to Queen Elizabeth II [born: Elizabeth Alexandra Mary on April 21, 1926 – still living as of July 2016].

When Wallace Simpson suffered especially the last 10 years of her life, she reportedly and allegedly fell victim to her attorney Suzanne Blum who gained power of attorney over the Duchess.

What is really a model family?

What are human beings if not a family?

Family stretches the world through nationalities and centuries. Perhaps, royalty in any century is a model family. Maybe there is truly no such thing when one considers the vast ways in which people define what family means.

It is an illusion of an illusion -- this definition of what constitutes or creates royalty. Possibly what is considered a model family -- be it royal or not -- is also an illusion.

What does this mean *"an illusion of an illusion"*?

When a human kills another via war, or in anger, or with a crazy maladjusted brain – that person is killing a body. Whether they are deemed royalty, nobility, servant, slave or *"regular folk,"* it is an illusion.

Why is it an illusion?

It is an illusion because the essence of a person is the spirit! It is impossible to truly get rid of anyone's essence.

Chopping off heads under the order of a king, for instance, disrupts the soul's journey on this planet. In other words, it gets rid of the spirit's vehicle on the physical or earthly plane. Just like a car's commander is the driver, if one removes the vehicle --- the soul returns to the realm of its creation or Creator – God. The soul or essence of a person, is a passenger in the human body.

The truth is we cannot kill one another and believe it is a done deal. The soul belongs to God. It cannot die. The body does and will die. That is not an illusion -- but the essence inside the body is our truest identity. It does not die with the body.

It survives. Possibly, the soul can come back into a new earthly body? Maybe it is enough that its truest existence no longer requires the physical body. Certainly, though, the soul or spirit enters a physical body and exits it. Upon exiting, it takes with it all experiences it had while here.

* So, an illusion of an illusion simply means in this instance that earthly titles are an illusion to those things deemed heavenly. Titles on earth do not define intent, what we love the most and how we treat others. Our bodies are not part of the heavenly realm either. Two illusions.

Now, what does this have to do with the Wyatts?

EARLY WYATT EMPLOYMENT…

> *"There is only one Christ, Jesus, on faith. All else is a dispute over trifles."*

> – QUEEN ELIZABETH I.

In early Wyatt history, Sir Henry Wyatt [1460-1537], father of Sir Thomas Wyatt, the Elder and poet and grandfather of Sir Thomas Wyatt, the Younger, each served in the courts of the English Monarchy at varying times.

Sixteenth century English ambassador and lyrical poet Sir Thomas Wyatt [1503-1542], the Elder, was married to Elizabeth Brooke [1503-1560], the mother of the Younger Wyatt beheaded for treason in 1554. Brooke's lineage ties into the Boleyn family -- making Queen Elizabeth I a half third cousin to Sir Thomas Wyatt, the Younger – via her maternal lineage.

A 1537 letter in which the elder Sir Thomas Wyatt wrote in Paris, France to his son, Wyatt gave advice on love and marriage. The spellings reflect the English language before it was standardized.

> *"Loue well and agree with your wife, for where there is noyse and debate in the howse, there is vnquiett dwellinge, and much the more where it is in one bed. Frame well yourself to loue and reuerence you as her head. Such as you are to her, such shall she be to you. Obey and reuerence your father in lawe as you would me, and remember that long lief followeth them that reuerence **theire parents and elders, and the blessings of God for** good agreement betwene the wief and the husbande —as fruite of manye children, which I for the like thinge doe lacke, and the faulte is both in your mother and me, but cheifliein her."*

In *Modern Language Notes*, Vol. 49., No. 7 on page 447, the elder Wyatt is quoted to have written in 1537 to his son:

> *"I remitt you wholie to youre father in lawe. Recommend me to my daughter Iane and my daughter Besse, and write vnto me, at the least to exercise your hand. And farewell, with God's blessinge…"*

Sir George *"Georgius"* Thomas Wiatt, Knt. [Abt. 1554-1624] and his wife Lady Jane Finch [1555-1644] were the parents of Reverend Haute *"Haut" "Hawte"* Wiatt [1594-1638] and Royal Governor Sir Francis Wiatt [1588-1644]. It is through Rev. Haute Wiatt that many Wyatts in the United States are descended.

George Thomas Wiatt's father was Sir Thomas Wiatt or Wyatt – the Younger. This connection helps in understanding one of the ways in which the original Wyatts of Virginia and many of those Wyatts connected to the descendants of Rev. Hawte Wiatt are connected as well to the Hawte, Brooke, Heydon or Hayden and Boleyn families.

So, yes, these Wyatts are related to Queen Consort Anne Boleyn. She was a noble who married into a then so-proclaimed by tooth, blood, nail and battle -- a royal family. She was the mother of Queen Elizabeth I – so if you are a fan of Elizabeth I – rejoice.

A SMALL WORLD…

The more we gather and trace, the more we realize how small this world really is. Even those considered to be the most mundane and lowly of creatures are collecting experiences in this world attaching such to his or her soul's memory and taking them to Heaven like a letter from Earth.

The Earth cannot dwell in Heaven. Experiences are recorded by each and every living soul that arrives here no matter how long or short its stay might be, and no matter if its body's brain understands this or not. What the human brain does not understand, the soul certainly does, or comes to at the very least when it passes from this place called Earth into Heaven.

So with this introduction, you have gained my perspective. You have gained observations that have come about from a great deal of thought due to souls who came here before we ever did. They left their words and observations – and those parts of their journeys teach us in this quest.

They left records of having been here. They are our teachers and voices. They left their stories of trial and error, trust and gains, illusions and truth. We all will join them one day and leave such things for others to find as well.

When you read about the Wyatt people, know they are connected to you either by blood or marriage or simply by soul.

CHAPTER 1

The Original Name Was *"Guyot."*

♀ | | ♂

"Virtue tries harder things"

-- WYATT MOTTO FOR ITS COAT OF ARMS.

PART 1. BEFORE 1066 & AFTER

THE NAME *"GUYOT"* EVOLVED OR transformed as many names do. *"Guyot"* is *Old French.* It was introduced into England after the *Battle of Hastings* in 1066 [Norman Conquest] via a man some call *"Admiral* or *Captain Adam Guyott* or *Guyot* or *Wyot."*

The surname *"Guyot"* may be derived from a diminutive of the first or personal name *"Guy."* This is the French form of the Germanic first name *"Wido."* It is possible by some reports this name *"Wido"* is from the *Old High German* word: *"witu."* In *Old English* before the 7th century, the words: *"widu"* and *"wudu"* meant *"wood."* It meant *"wide"* from the German *"wit"* and Olde English *"wid."*

This name was used much amongst the Normans in the forms of *"Wi"* and *"Why."* In France, it was used as *"Guy."* Some followed an occupation. It may have been used by a person who was a *guide.* In Old French *"gui"* means in modern French *"guide"* or *"guider,"* which means *to lead, steer, guide, direct.*

Some variant spellings of *"Guyot"* include:

* Guitt
* Guiet
* Guite
* Guyet
* Guyott

The next known transformations are *"Wyot"* and *"Wyotte."* From there, other spellings evolved such as: *"Wiat"* and *"Wiatt."* The spelling of *"Wyatt"* is most commonly used. It is used when referring to ancestors who have been found in records of both paper and stone as *"Wiat"* and as *"Wiatt."* The spellings of *"Wyot"* and *"Wyotte"* are incorporated.

These spellings are found:

* *Wiatt*
* *Wiat*
* *Wyat*
* *Wyatt*
* *Wyet*
* *Wiett*

Variations seemingly have been used for the exact same people in the course of their lifetimes -- depending upon the preference of the person recording information in marriage bonds, tax records and land deeds.

The name *"Guyot,"* as it is stipulated and mentioned earlier, came to England during the Norman Conquest. It was led by Normandy's Duke William II, who later became known as *William the Conqueror* [known as *"William the Bastard"* son of Robert I, Duke of Normandy [1008-1035] and Herleva Falasia]. William I, father of Henry I, was the first Norman King of England or King of the English from 1066-1087. He lived roughly from 1027-September 9, 1087.

Some forms of the *"Guyot"* name are:

* Wyatt
* Wyon
* Guyon
* Guise
* Guy

The name Guyot was *anglicized* from the Normandy spelling to:

* Wiot
* Wyot
* Wyotte
* Wiatt
* Wiat
* Wyatt

The name *"Wyatt"* is traced as far back as the year 912 in Wales. During that time there were two clans with one being known as *"Black Wyatts"* and the other as *"Red Wyatts."*

In England's history, the name first appears in the year 1273. The *Red Wyatts* with a **fealty grant** from the English Crown built *"Wyatt Hall"* in Devonshire.

[Fealty means allegiance that a tenant owes to his feudal lord. The word *"feoffee"* is a person in whom is vested or granted a fief or lands under certain conditions. In the Feudal system of Europe in the ninth and fifteenth centuries nobility regarded those persons who held a fief [fee, feoff, fiefdom], which were inheritable lands, properties. To hold land in fief or office meant the holder had a right to revenues the land produced – hunting, fishing, etc. The term *"fief"* is used by historians to simply mean *"property;"* however, its exact meaning was not more precise until the middle of the 12th century.]

There is a Malcolm Wyatt recorded in Scotland's history at Anegos. Malcolm Wyatt rendered homage to the king in 1296. There is another named James Wyatt who was a burgess of Arbroath in the year 1464. Arbroath is a former royal burgh [town], which was founded by or granted a royal charter.

[A royal charter is a formal document issued by the Crown or Monarchy as letters of patent. It grants power to a person or group. Arbroath is located in the council area of Angus, Scotland.]

An early record of this name is cited by some as being *Wiotus de Colnbrook* who held land at Langley Marish – east of Windsor and Eton and was living in the year 1315.

An Adelle Bartlett-Harper studied the origins of the Wyatt family. Adelle points out that ancient English manuscripts state the first Wyatt to come to England was an Admiral Guyot – known as Admiral Adam Wyatt. Others such as Alexander Lloyd Wiatt in *The Wiatt Family of Virginia* refer to him as having been a captain in one of William the Conqueror's ships and so called Captain Adam Guyott.

One familytreemaker source from Steven E. Wyatt states:

> *"Guyot had charge of the Norman fleet when William the Conqueror landed in 1066. He married one of the Conqueror's daughters and along with others was awarded large estates, which were located in Yorkshire, near the ancient town of Southange. In the time the name Guyot was anglicized to Wiot, then Wiat and finally to Wyatt, by Sir Francis Wyatt, while Governor of Virginia; this being one of the five spellings he used during his term of office 1621-29, when signing official documents...There is definite evidence that the Wyatts owned land at Southange...in the township of Kexburgh, near Darton"*

> — NORTHEAST OF BARNSLEY, YORKSHIRE.

Wiats in the U.S. and in England are said to be descendants of, or associated in some genealogical capacity with the Wiat families who occupied *Allington Castle* in Kent County, England.

Sir George Thomas Wiatt [1554-1624]: Earliest Known to Record Wyatt History:

Sir George Thomas Wiatt [born at *Allington Castle* in Kent County, England in 1554 and died September 16, 1624] wrote in his lifetime a Wyatt family history. He supposedly died in Ireland, but his remains were buried Nov. 10, 1624 in Boxley, Kent County, England. There is some controversy whether or not this man George Wiatt had three names with *"Thomas"* being the middle name, or just two names.

George's father was Sir Thomas Wiatt, the Younger, who led *Wyatt's Rebellion* against Queen Mary the First. The Younger Wyatt was executed for treason April 11, 1554 at Tower Hill, London, England.

The Wyatt estate of Boxley Kent County was restored to George after his father's execution by Queen Mary I [1515/16-1558], and Wavering Estate was restored to him by Queen Elizabeth I [1533-1602/03] in 1570.

George Wiatt's genealogical claims supposedly go back to the 1300s. He claims the line of descent as:

* Adam Wyote or Wiat [1320-1385] father of: → William Wyot [1350-1388] father of: → Robert Wyot [1383-1440] father of: →Geoffrey Wiat [1404 or 1410-1460] father of: → Richard Wiat [1420 or 1435-1475] father of: → Sir Henry Wiatt [1460-1536 or 1537] father of: → Sir Thomas Wyatt, the Elder [1503-1542] father of: → Sir Thomas Wyatt, the Younger [1521-1554] father of: → Sir George *"Georgius"* Thomas Wiatt, Knt. [1554-1624] father of: Reverend Haute *"Haut" "Hawte"* Wiatt [1594-1638].

Allington Castle in Boxley Parish of Kent County, England is known historically for an ancient abbey …

"…where the 'Rod of Grace' wrough miracles, in the popular fancy only second to those of St. Thomas of Canterbury: second, Peneden Heath, where Norman Bishops met to try Odo, the half brother of William the Conqueror, and Wiat Tyler rallied his Kentish malcontents; third the Wiatt family, who had their seal there for centuries; they became possessors of the Abbey, after it was confiscated by the Crown."

♀ | | ♂

♀ | | ♂

PART 2.
SUNDAY EVENING
APRIL 27, 2014
JOURNAL ENTRY

It occurs to me as I am working on this book in a season that jumped from the freezer to sweat box, with all such distractions, I cannot fail to point out Odo [Abt. 1030-1097] was Earl of Kent and Bishop of Bayeux and was second in power after the King of England.

The first and only time I ever saw in person the Bayeux tapestry I had read about in high school French class was as a teen on a trip to Europe. I recall standing in front of it in the Louvre Museum, where it was exhibited at the time. It depicts the Battle of Hastings, Sussex, England, where Harold II [some refer to as Harold Godwineson or Godwinson], 1020-Oct. 14, 1066 was defeated by William I of Normandy. Harold II of Wessex, a loyal supporter of Edward the Confessor [1003-1053], felt he should be king of the English after Edward's passing, as Edward, a proclaimed celibate during his marriage to Eadgyth or *"Edith,"* had no children.

In it, William the Conqueror's half-brother Odo is depicted with a wooden stick in hand. He appears to be encouraging then [Duke of Normandy's] William's troops in that battle of 1066. He looks to be riding side saddle. Odo is riding a horse and carrying a weapon – a club, possibly. Odo, as depicted, organizes William's troops. He is said to have been the most trusted of William's supporters.

*William I's half-brother Odo was the son of William's mother Herleva and Herluin de Conteville. William I was the son of Robert I Duke of Normandy [1008-1035].

I note today a free e-book: *Abbeys, Castles and Ancient Balls of England and Wales, their Legendary Lore* by John Timbs.

Transcription with limited punctuation from page 313 on Henry Wyatt [1460-1536 or 37] & Sir Thomas Wyatt – the Elder [1503-1542]:

Allington Castle and the Wyatts This ivy mantled pile is all that remains of Allington Castle on the left bank of the Medway just below Maidstone but with the fatality which often attends places of historical renown this Castle is now occupied as two tenements It was built by William de Columbariis in the reign of King Stephen Here lived Sir Henry Wyatt the father of the Poet a man of high principles and strict conduct of whom his son states that he was deeply impressed

with reverence for religion that there was no man more pitiful no man more true of his word no man faster to his friend no man diligenter nor more circumspect which thing both the Kings his masters noted in him greatly His attachment to the House of Lancaster brought him under the displeasure of Richard III who sent him into prison in Scotland where he was kept in irons and stocks for upwards of two years and put to the rack under the eyes of the tyrant As soon however as Henry VII succeeded to the throne Sir Henry was restored to liberty appointed to high offices and at the coronation of Henry VIII he was created a Knight of the Bath Having distinguished himself at the battle of the Spurs he was made a Knight Banneret on the field He held the office of Keeper of the King's Jewels and King's Ewerer and in 1527 entertained the King at Allington Castle which he had purchased in 1493 Here Thomas Wyatt the poet was born in 1503 As an elegant courtier and a statesman of great sagacity and integrity he takes a prominent position in the history of the reign of Henry VIII who in 1542 created him steward of the King's manor of Maidstone The brief remainder of his life he passed in retirement at Allington hunting and hawking and shooting with the bow and in bad weather devoting himself to the study and composition of verses but he died October 11 1542 of fever brought on by his zeal in attending an unexpected summons from his sovereign Wyatt has left us writings both in prose and verse but taking into account the time at which he wrote his prose is the more remarkable.

Abbeys, Castles and Ancient Balls of England and Wales, their Legendary Lore by John Timbs.

How meanly Wyatt estimated the courtier in life he thus sings:

> *"In court to serve decked with fresh array*
> *Of sugar d meats feeling the sweet repast*
> *The life in banquets and sundry kinds of play*
> *Amid the press the worldly looks to waste*
> *Hath with it join d oft times such bitter taste*
> *That whoso joys such kind of life to hold*
> *In prison joys fefter d with chains of gold."*

   ✧   King Stephen who ruled with Matilda from 1135-1154, was a grandson of William the Conqueror via William's daughter Adela.

On page 84 of *Genealogical Gleanings in England*, the following quote regarding Sir Henry Wiatt's – father of the poet, severe imprisonment:

"…. *once in a cold and narrow Tower, where he had neither bed to lie on, nor clothes sufficient to warm him, nor meat for his mouth; he had starved there had not God… sent a cat both to feed and warm him.*"

The account continues stating that the cat came to him daily and delivered pigeons, which the guard or jailor, dressed and prepared for Sir Henry.

♀ | | ♂

PART 3. THE EARLIEST WYATTS OF ENGLAND

The earliest Wyatts kept company with those in the British Monarchy and to the ultimate dread of one such was Sir Thomas Wyatt – the Younger. He was the son of the Elder who was a poet. The Younger having been accused of treason, was executed after leading a rebellion against Queen Mary I – the half-sister of Queen Elizabeth I – both daughters of King Henry VIII.

Wyatts are said or thought to be descendants from the Wyatts or Wiatt families who occupied Allington Castle, Boxley Parish, Kent County, England. What American Wyatts might find intriguing is at Boxley Church in Kent County there is an inscription dedicated to the Wiatt family.

It states:

"Rev. Haute Wyatt died Vicar of Boxley Parish, and he had issue living in Virginia."

♀ | | ♂

CHAPTER 2

The Wyatt Coat of Arms

♀ | | ♂

"What most persons consider as virtue, after the
age of 40, is simply a loss of energy,"

-- Voltaire

❖ Voltaire, known as François-Marie Arouet [November 21, 1694-May 30, 1778]
French Enlightenment, playwright, writer, historian, philosopher; Paris, France.

Part 1. Heraldry Terms

THE WYATT COAT OF ARMS in heraldic language [heraldry is pictorial representation or armorial insignias of family names through a *Coat of Arms* or crests, the emblem used to decorate the helmet.] is first described as *"Arms Quarterly of Six."*

❖ The word *"quarterly"* refers to when the shield is divided into four sections or parts.

In heraldry, quartering is the method of bringing several different Coats of Arms together. This is done by dividing the shield into equal parts and placing different Coats of Arms in each division.

❖ *"1 and 6 Per fesse azure and gules, a pair of barnacles argent, enclosed by a ring or. (Wiat)"*
❖ The *"fesse"* refers to a single broad line, bar or band across the shield.

The word *"or"* refers to the color *"gold"* or *"yellow."* The word *"gules"* means *"red"* in heraldic terms for colors and has since the year 1165. It comes from the French word: *"gueules."*

There are nine tinctures or colors in heraldry language. Two are metals. There are additionally some that are incidental such as: ash colour, bay color, chief brown color, etc.

❖ *"Or"* refers to *"gold"*
❖ *"Argent"* to *"silver"*
❖ *"Gules"* to *"red"*

- *"Azure"* to *"blue"*
- *"Sable"* to *"black"*
- *"Vert"* to *"green"*
- *"Purpure"* to *"purple"*
- *"Tenné"* to *"tenny"* [tawny – an orange-tawny color]
- *"Sanguine"* to *"blood color."*
- Furs are considered as tinctures too – *ermine* is considered as *"argent,"* and ermines is *"sable."*
- *"Barnacle"* refers to a Barnacle goose – known as the *"Cleg or Clark goose."*
- *"Martlet"* refers to a *"black bird or a bird that resembles a swallow"* that reveals the thighs of the bird, but not lower legs or feet -- anything below that point.
- *"Cinquefoils"* refers to some form *"having five leaves."*
- *"Bordure"* refers to a *"border."*
- *"Bezantee"* is *"bezant or besant or besaunte:"* a roundlet or. It is gold coinage symbolic of, or representing the money used in Constantinople drawn flat. Known as *"Besant d'or,"* *"Besant d'argent,"* *"Besant de gueules."*
- *Engrailed* is *"ingrailed"* or *"engélé "* which is a word used to describe the cutting edge of a border, bend or fesse into small semi-circular indentations.
- The *"fesse,"* again, is the broad horizontal stripe across the center field of the shield.
- *"2 On a fesse or, between three boars' heads coupled argent as many lioncels rampant sable. (Wyat).* Symbols such as boars represent *"bravery."*
- *"3 Argent on a bend gules a martlet between two cinquefoils or, a bordure azure bezantee.* (Bailife alias Clarke)
- *Or, a cross engrailed gules.* (Hawte)
- *5 Per pale --- and --- Lion rampant ermine.* (Sheluring)

The crest is located above the shield and helmet. The crest is described as:

"An ostrich proper, in the beak of horseshoe argent. A demi-lion rampant sable, holding in the dexter paw, an arrow in bend or flighted and headed argent."

- The heraldic terms *"sable"* means *"black."*
- The term *"argent"* means *"the tincture of silver."*
- The term *"dexter"* refers to the right-hand side of the shield, thus being left of the onlooker or spectator.
- The phrase *"lioncels"* refers to lions, rampant refers to animals rearing – going up on hindquarters -- especially lions.

♀ | | ♂

♀ | | ♂

PART 2. MOTTOS

"Virtue tries harder things"

-- WYATT MOTTO FOR ITS COAT OF ARMS.

Family mottos are thought to have originated from battle cries during the Medieval Period – spanning from the 5th to 15th century. The Wyatt family motto for the Wyatt Coat of Arms is *"Duriora virtus,"* which means *"Virtue tries harder things."*

Coats of Arms were originally designed to identify knights in battle. Knights needed the exteriors of the armor they wore to identify or distinguish them as one particular group.

For aristocratic families or nobility, *Coats of Arms* include a shield, a crest at the top of the shield, and in some cases at the top of a helmet and a motto. The motto [which is Italian for *"word"*] can reference the bearer's name or accomplishments. Mottos later came to represent the skills and accomplishments of families.

Mottos were army or war cries – phrases used to lead, rally and inspire troops into battle. Consequently, slogans or sayings developed. The word *"slogan"* is derived from a Gaelic word: *"slogorn,"* which means *"army cry."*

Sometimes mottos were just family names shouted over and over again, or the word: *"Forward!"* Some mottos encompassed religious invocations, assembly or rally cries, some were to encourage troops, while others were intended to instill fear or insult in the opponent.

Symbols such as bears [strength and cunning] boars [bravery] eagles [nobility, protection] lions [unending courage], etc. are found on such shields in general.

In Medieval England, heralds were responsible for organizing tournaments, so naturally they were familiar with the contestants – the knights, their crests and arms. The number and variety of coats of arms grew to the point the College of Arms in England was established in 1484 to keep track of them.

Coats of Arms are the property of the person who was issued the insignia [badge, emblem, crest, sign, symbol, logo, motif], and are regarded often as belonging to the

direct male descendant of the person to whom it was originally issued to. Others – even with the same surname, cannot rightfully claim ownership, or use their particular motif.

Nobility used *Coats of Arms* as a way to officially set them apart.

♀ | | ♂

♀ | | ♂

PART 3. SYMBOLS

There is a Roman mythological character, or deity, named *"Virtus."* He/she is symbolic or represents bravery and military strength. After the Virginia Colony declared its independence from Great Britain in 1776 – Virtus, the mythological character, was made into a central figure for the *Seal of Virginia*. A Committee was appointed to come up with a design for the seal for the Commonwealth of Virginia.

One of these committee men was Richard Henry Lee – a descendant from the original immigrant Colonel Richard Henry Lee and his wife Anne Constable Lee – both are said to have known personally Rev. Haute Wyatt and his brother Royal Governor Francis Wyatt in Jamestown, Va. when it was still a British colony.

Richard Lee [1733-1794] – a former President Pro-Tempore of the U.S. Senate for several months in 1792 was the son of: → Colonel Thomas Lee [1690-1750] son of: → Colonel Richard Lee II [1647-1715] son of: → Colonel Richard Henry Lee [The British immigrant [1618-1664].

The original committee included: George Mason IV [1725-1792] – called *"the Father of the Bill of Rights;"* George Wythe [1726-1806] – signer of the *U.S. Declaration of Independence*; Robert Carter Nicholas [1728-1780] – Justice of the Supreme Court of Virginia.

The *Flag of Virginia* has Virtus holding what appears to be a sword upward in the left arm and a spear in the right pointing to the sky. Virtus stands over a fallen soldier. Virtus has one foot on the soldier's chest near the neck. There is a fallen gold crown on the ground next to the fallen soldier. The fallen or defeated soldier holds a chain and whip. One can't get more symbolic than this!

The fallen soldier represents *Tyranny* or England at the time. The seal of Virginia was, as stated earlier, adopted in 1776 and modified in 1930.

The motto for Virginia:

"Sic Semper Tyrannis" appears on it and means:

"Thus Always to Tyrants."

Above Virtus is the word: *"Virginia."*

♀ | | ♂

Artistic depiction of the Wyatt or Wiat Coat of Arms.

CHAPTER 3

Some Celebrated Wyatts

♀ | | ♂

"C'est un poids bien pesant qu'on nom trop tôt fameux."

= *"Quote a heavy weight, a name too quickly famous."*

-- Voltaire

*W*YATTS LEFT GREAT INFLUENCE AND courage. Their lives remain even in this modern day, figures of fascination. The Wyatts, though, are links to others who forge ahead in the journeys we each partake of, support or encourage. This chapter points out some Wyatts you might have heard of in England and the United States.

Sir Henry Wiatt, Knt. (father of the poet) [born: 1460 in Southange, West Riding, Yorkshire; died: 1536 in Allington Castle, Boxley, Kent County, England] – was an advisor to England's King Henry VIII in 1509 when he came to the throne. Henry Wiatt, husband of Margaret Bailiff & Anne Skinner, is said by historians to have been the *"most beloved"* man in England during his day. His parents: Margaret Jane Clarke or Bailiffe & Richard Wiat [b. 1420], of Southange -- known as South Haigh and Upper Haigh, Yorkshire, England.

Not much is known of his life before he took up the cause of supporting Henry Tudor VII, who later became known as King Henry VII of England. Sir Henry Wyatt purchased Allington Castle, close to Maidstone in Kent County in 1492. King Henry VIII visited Sir Henry Wyatt in 1527.

Sir Thomas Wiatt *"The Elder"* [1503-1542] – who was employed by King Henry VIII at times, is remembered as a lyrical poet who was accused by King Henry VIII of having a love interest in the later Consort Queen Anne Boleyn, who became the second wife of King Henry VIII.

Sir Thomas Wiatt the Elder is the son of: → Anne Skinner [b. 1485 in Reigate, Surry County, or Ardleigh, Essex, England] & Sir Henry Wiatt [born: 1460 in Southange, West

Riding, Yorkshire; died: 1536, Allington Castle, Boxley, Kent County, England]. This elder Wiatt was referred to as *"The Father of the Drab Age"* by C.S. Lewis.

This Thomas Wyatt has been reported to have been over six feet tall, exceptionally strong in body and very handsome. He was an ambassador serving King Henry VIII. He first entered the service of King Henry VIII in the year 1515.

Sir Thomas Wiatt *"The Younger"* [1521-1554] served as a squire in King Henry VIII's Court and later led a rebellion against Queen Mary I – the half-sister of then Princess Elizabeth I [Elizabeth Tudor]. Sir Thomas Wiatt the Younger is the son of Elizabeth Brooke [1503-1560] & Sir Thomas Wiatt the Elder [1503-1542]. Elizabeth Brooke Wiatt, mother of the younger Thomas Wiatt, is the daughter of: → Dorothy Heydon & Thomas Brooke [d. 1529]. Dorothy is the daughter of Elizabeth or Anne Boleyn & Sir Henry Heydon *"Haydon"* *"Hayden"* – This Elizabeth or Anne Boleyn is not to be confused with Queen Anne Boleyn.

This E. or A. Boleyn is the daughter of an unknown wife of Sir Geoffrey Boleyn [1406-1471] son of: → Anne *"Jane"* Bracton & Sir Thomas Boleyn. Sir Geoffrey Boleyn [1406-1471] married an Anne Mary Hoo [1424-1484] and had a son named Sir William Boleyn [1451-1505] father of: → Thomas Boleyn --1st Earl of Wiltshire & Ormonde [1477-1538/39] – father of: → Consort Queen Anne Boleyn [1501-1536] – mother of: → Queen Elizabeth I [1533-1602/03].

Sir Thomas Wiatt the Younger is thus a half third cousin to Elizabeth I.

Sir George *"Georgius"* **Thomas Wiatt, Knt**. [1554-1624] wrote a history on the *Life of Queen Anne Boleigne* or Boleyn – also spelled *"Bullen,"* a manuscript that is in the British Museum. He also recorded a Wyatt history during his lifetime.

Sir George Wiatt was a son of: → Lady Jane Haute or Hawte [Abt. 1522-1600], as it is sometimes spelled & of Sir Thomas Wiatt the Younger [1521-1554]. George's paternal grandfather is the Elder Thomas, the poet.

Sir Francis Wyatt [1588-1644] a son of Lady Jane Finch [1555-1644] & Sir George *"Georgius"* Thomas Wiatt, Knt. [1554-1624] of Allington Castle or Boxley Hall, Kent County, England, was the English Royal Governor of Virginia from 1621-1626 and again in 1639-1642. Sir Francis Wyatt [1588-1644], husband of Lady Margaret Sandys, rallied in 1622 the defense of Jamestown, which was attacked by Native Americans. Four hundred settlers died as a result of the attack. Gov. Wyatt's remains are buried at Boxley Abbey Church, Kent County, England.

Royal Governor Sir Francis Wyatt was a brother to Rev. Haute Wyatt and is believed to have brought his nephews to Jamestown, Va. during his second term as governor. Gov. Wyatt is said to have brought with him to Virginia the first written constitution for the English colony. Sir Francis Wyatt is credited with organizing the General Assembly, which was called in 1619. This was the first legislative body in America. Sir Francis, according to historical articles, *"caused its privileges to be embodied in a written constitution, the first of its kind in the new world."*

Reverend Haute *"Hawte"* Wiatt [1594-1638] was minister of Jamestown, Va. from 1621-1625. He was Vicar of Boxley Parish, Kent County, England from 1625-1638. He was the son of Lady Jane Finch [1555-1644] & Sir George *"Georgius"* Thomas Wiatt, Knt. [1554-1624] of Allington Castle or Boxley Hall, Kent County, England.

According to historians Rev. Haute Wyatt is the common ancestor *"to those who claim kinship to the pre-1700 Wyatt family in the Americas."*

Henry Wiatt [1685-1743] married Elizabeth Dandridge [1703-1750] – a sister to Colonel John Dandridge II, who was with his wife Frances Orlando Jones, a parent to Martha Dandridge Custis Washington [1731-1832] – known as *"Lady Washington."*

Henry Wiatt, known as Henry Wyatt [Abt. 1685-1743], was of Gloucester County, Va. & Saint Peter's Parish, New Kent County, Va. He was a son of: → Richard Wiatt [1650-Abt.1704] son of: → George Wiatt [1622 to Abt. 1670/71] son of: → Reverend Haute *"Haut"* *"Hawte"* Wiatt [1594-1638] son of: → Sir George *"Georgius"* Thomas Wiatt, Knt. [1554-1624] son of: → Sir Thomas Wiatt the Younger [1521-1554] son of: → Sir Thomas Wiatt the Elder [Abt. 1503-1542] son of: → Sir Henry Wiatt, Knt. [father of the poet] [Abt. 1460-1535] son of: → Sir Richard Wiatt, Knt. [1435-1475] son of → Geoffrey *"Jeoffrey"* Wiat [1404-1460] son of: → Robert or Richard Wiot [1383- 1440] son of: → William Wiot [1350-1388] son of: → Adam Wiot 1320-1385] great grandson of: → Admiral or Captain Adam Guyott [b. Bef. 1066-d. Aft. 1066].

[See the Wyatt Section.]

Henry Wyatt [born September 17, 1794; died February 27, 1840 in Prestwich, close to Manchester, England] – the portrait painter should not be confused with other Henry Wyatt's mentioned in this compilation. This Henry Wyatt, born in 1794 in Thickbroom, close to Lichfield, Staffordshire moved to Birmingham, accompanied by a guardian named Francis Eginton when Henry was three years old. Shortly before this, Henry's father had died. Eginton was a glass-painter, sent his ward to London in 1811 and in 1812 Henry was admitted into a school of the Royal Academy.

He studied art under Sir Thomas Lawrence. This Henry Wyatt's artistic works include: *"Fair Forester," "Juliet," "Chapeau Noir," "Gentle Reader," "Mars and Venus,"* and *"The Romance."* Among portraits he painted include one of Thomas Harrison [1744-1829], an English architect and bridge engineer.

Henry Lawson Wyatt [born in Richmond, Va. Feb. 12, 1842 to Isham Belcher & Lucinda N.L. Wyatt] is purported to have been the first Confederate soldier to have been killed in action. There is a statue dedicated to him in Wake County, N.C. on the State Capitol grounds. This was done June 10, 1912.

• See *War Records & Discrepancies.*

Harriet *"Hattie"* Ophelia Wyatt [born in Bakersville, Humphreys County, Tennessee in 1878 and lived until 1950] was the first elected woman to the U.S. Senate. She was known as *"Silent Hattie."* She opposed the repeal of Prohibition, supported *Equal Rights Amendment* to the U.S. Constitution, served on the U.S. Employees Compensation Appeals Board from 1946 until 1950.

Harriet Wyatt's husband was Thaddeus Horatius Caraway, who served in the U.S. House of Representatives [1913-1921] and the U.S. Senate [1921-1931]. Hattie Wyatt is the daughter of: Louisa Lucy Mildred Burch & William Carroll Wyatt [Abt. 1815-1901] son of: → Robert Henry Wyatt [1782-1850, of North Carolina] son of: → James Wyatt [born 1751] son of: → Colonel Joseph Wyatt [1728-1767] son of: → **Elizabeth Dandridge & Henry Wyatt** [Abt. 1685-Abt. 1743] – Henry & Elizabeth – being paternal aunt and uncle to Martha Custis Washington [1731-1802].

See *Suggested Reading & References.* See the Wyatt Section.

John T. Wyatt [1851-1933] – founder of the town of Faith in Rowan County, N.C. is known to the world as *"Venus of Faith."* He settled on the rocky land five miles east of Salisbury, N.C. Faith, the town in which he named, is located in the eastern part of Rowan.

"Two other fellows and I wrote Washington, and they suggested a short name," John T. Wyatt once said.

"...we settled on Faith because it was short and sort of fitted."

Writer and country correspondent, whose articles ran in *The Salisbury Post* and were picked up by other newspapers throughout the country.

John Thomas Wyatt [1851-1933] son of: → Mary Ann Park Wyatt Phillips [1831-Abt. 1870] & Wilson Riley Wyatt [1830-1862] son of: → Jesse *"Jessey"* Wyatt [1800-1860] son of: → John *"Johney"* Wyatt, Jr. [d. 1819] son of: → John *"Johney"* Wyatt, Sr. [1743-1815].

Edgar Marshall Wyatt [1917-1999] – seed seller and Raleigh historian. He was the co-founder of *Wyatt-Quarles Seed Company*, which in 1955 assumed the space of another business owned by his family called: Job P. Wyatt & Sons. Edgar Wyatt retired from the seed business in 1986.

During his retirement, Edgar Wyatt began publishing stories of life in Raleigh when it was *"a sleepy little village."* These stories are in two books: *Growing Up in Raleigh and Memories of Old Raleigh.* Edgar Wyatt husband of: → Katherine *"Bebe"* Dickerson Wyatt; father of: → Emily, Chuck & Marshall.

Author's Note: We have not discerned how Edgar fits into the Wyatt family as a whole; however, he carried the name during his lifetime. This fact justifies mentioning.

* If you discover or find additional famous Wyatts [Wiatts, Wiats, et. al.], please jot notations in the blank back matter note pages of this book. Send comments and observations.

CHAPTER 4

Understanding Titles

♀ | | ♂

"Les mortel sont égaux, ce n'est pas la naissance,
c'est la seule vertu qui fait la différence."

Translation:

"All men are equal; it is not their birth, but virtue that makes the difference."

-- VOLTAIRE

OR A MODERN U.S. CITIZEN, British titles can be somewhat confusing when one is not accustomed to hearing, using or studying them on a regular basis. For purposes herein, the simplest of explanations is provided.

These titles are for a body of peers, or titled nobility in England. The word *"nobility'* is derived from the Latin word: *"nobilis,"* which means well-known or famous. The term was reserved and applied prior to the Industrial Revolution [Abt. 1760 to Abt. 1840 – middle of the 18th century to the middle of the 19th century] to those in the highest social class.

In the Feudal system of Europe in the ninth and fifteenth centuries nobility regarded those persons who held a fief [fee, feoff, fiefdom], which were inheritable lands, properties. To hold land in fief or office meant the holder had a right to revenues the land produced – hunting, fishing, etc.

The term *"fief"* is used by historians to simply mean *"property;"* however, its exact meaning was not more precise until the middle of the 12th century. Land lawyers fine-tuned its meaning. Being wealthy does not make one noble, and not all true nobles are wealthy.

There are five ranks:

* Duke
* Marquess

- Earl or Count
- Viscount
- Baron.

Up until the year 1999, peers were entitled to sit in the *House of Lords.* Peers were exempted from jury duty. Historically, some titles are hereditary, and some are granted for life.

- A DUKE [Latin: Dux, means *"leader"*] is a nobleman of the highest hereditary rank in Great Britain below the monarch. It was created in 1337. Historically, a duke or duchess controlled or ruled the duchy or dukedom, which was his or her territory or domain.
- A MARQUIS [Marquess, Marchioness] is a French word, which is derived from *"marche"* or *"march."* The marches refer to the borders of England, Scotland and Wales. This title was created in 1385. It is a nobleman who ranks below a duke and above a count or earl.
- An EARL in the Scandinavian form meant *"Chieftain,"* but in Medieval England it became equal to a count. From the Anglo Saxon or Old English *"eorl"* meant a *"military leader."* The rank was created sometime between circa. 800 and 1000. Countess is the feminine title for Earl.
- A VISCOUNT is nobleman that ranked below an earl or count -- but above a baron. The word *"viscount"* comes from the Latin word: *"vicecomes"* or vice-count. It was created in the year 1440. Viscountess is the feminine title for Viscount.
- A BARON is a British nobleman of the lowest rank. The word *"baron"* comes from the Old Germanic word, *"baro,"* which means *"freeman."* The late Latin form of *"baro"* means man, servant, soldier. It was created in 1066. Baroness is the feminine title for Baron.
- FITZROY means son of the king. It was incorporated into the names of illegitimate offspring of kings and used for those offspring acknowledged by the king. In ancient documents *"Fitz"* is spelled: *"Fiz, filz."* In modern French: *"fils de"* – son of.

Historically, peerages were hereditary -- meaning they passed from a father to a son, or from one person to another heir. In our modern age, no hereditary peerages are created.

There are, however, life peerages and such grants all the privileges of a hereditary one -- including a seat in the *House of Lords* -- but it cannot be passed to a son or heir. The *House of Lords, House of Commons and Sovereign or Monarchy* are the United Kingdom's Parliament.

The House of Lords is the Upper House of Parliament in the United Kingdom, and its purpose is to scrutinize legislation proposed by the Lower House by debating about it. The House of Lords proposes amendments of legislation. It is officially referred to as *"The Lords Spiritual and Temporal."* It is commonly known as *"the Lords,"* and during ceremonial purposes, it is called: *"House of Peers."*

A seat or membership in the *House of Lords* was once a right of heredity or birth. Today it consists almost entirely of *appointed* members. Membership in the House of Lords is by inheritance, appointment, or by virtue of an ecclesiastical role with the Lords Spiritual – which consists of 26 senior bishops in the Church of England.

The Sovereign is a ceremonial Head of State. *Oaths of Allegiance* are made to the Queen.

In a nutshell – in our most modern times today, there are various avenues in which members of the House of Lords [about 750] are appointed. There are three main categories of member:

1) There are life peers, appointed for their lifetimes
2) Archbishops and bishops serve in the House of Lords
3) Elected hereditary members.

The *House of Lords* and the *House of Commons* meet in the Palace of Westminster, located on the northern bank of the River Thames. The House of Commons is a democratically elected body of 650 members since the 2010 general election. These members are known as MPs, or the *Members of Parliament*. The *House of Commons*, referred to as the *Commons*, is the lower house of Parliament. MPs in the House of Commons consider and propose new laws, scrutinize government policies, etc.

Nobility titles do not exist in the U.S. Class distinctions and mean something different -- even though such things are forever in evolution, how it is filtered is not the same; otherwise we would not be the United States.

Names are really the focus – but titles in British culture and life -- both currently and historically are sometimes required for identity purposes. This requirement in such research is the same no matter where one grows up and no matter in what country a person is a citizen of.

In a court of law in the United States, judges are addressed as *"Your Honor."* If anyone dared address a judge in the U.S. as *"Your Majesty,"* one would not wish to think too long on what might happen.

As far as class distinctions in this modern age of the U.S., to describe someone in some circles as being of low class can have connotations of being *"dirty"* or *"uneducated"* when the truth reveals the opposite. Low class is described as *"low income."* Upper class in the U.S. is described as *"high income."* So, in the U.S., there are great achievers who might be thought of as the nobility of the United States with official titles – but those achievers bridge some regard as the upper, middle and lower classes.

There are exceptions, however, regarding titles for achievements in sports, for example: *"the greatest ball player of all time."*

Doctors are addressed as *"Dr. Jones, Dr. Smith, Dr. Wyatt, Dr. Parke,"* etc. This is true no matter if the doctorate is a D.C., D.D.S., D.O., D.P.M., D.V.M., O.D. or M.D.or D.M. With Ph.Ds., the title is used but not required. Outside the academic setting, people possessing a J.S.D. or a S.J.D. [Doctor of Juridical Science] or a J.D. [Doctor of Law or Juris Doctor] or LL.D [Legum Doctor] are simply addressed by their names or as *Mister Wyatt,* for instance.

♀ | | ♂

"Tous les genres sont bons, hors le genre ennuyeux,"

Translation: *"All styles are good except the boring kind."*

"Le superflu, chose très nécessaire."

Translation: *"The superfluous, a very necessary thing."*

Or:

"The superfluous is very necessary."

CHAPTER 5

Terms

♀ | | ♂

PART 1. MEDIEVAL ENGLISH, OLD FRENCH & LATIN

*T*HIS SECTION MAY HELP READERS understand words genealogists sometimes encounter in old records and within writings and compilations of other times.

- *"Relict"* and *"relicta"* and *"renupta."* The word *"relict"* refers to *"widow."* The word *"relicta"* comes from the Latin: *"relictus,"* which means forgotten, lost or abandoned, left behind. *"Relict"* or *"relicta"* refers to the survivor of a person who has passed on. *"Renupta"* refers to being remarried. In Latin *"nupta"* means bride or married.

For the modern-day researcher these words can be confusing. For example, sometimes a researcher will see the words:

- *"Filius et hæres,"* [Latin] or *"son and heyre"* or *"sonne and heyre"* [Medieval or Middle English] or *"son and heir or eir or heire"* [Old French] and all these mean: *"son and heir"* – the person who inherits, or who is legally entitled to inherit.

Classical Latin & Old English:

- *"æ"* [aesc pronounced, *"ash"*] is the diphthong for *"aj."* In Old English, *"æ"* is the sound between an *"a"* and an *"e,"* like the short *"a"* in the word *"cat."*
- The word *"filia,"* is Latin for *"daughter."*
- The word: *"militis,"* is Latin for *"soldier, knight or warrior."*
- The word *"uxor"* is Latin for wife or spouse.
- The word for *"son"* in French is *"fils"* and for *"daughter,"* it is: *"fille."* Seeing the words: *"filius"* and *"filia"* is then readily discernible.
- The words *"without issue"* occasionally appear in this book and simply mean: *"without descendants"* or *"childless."*

Additional Latin terms for genealogical researchers:

- <u>Decessit sine prole</u>: Died without issue.
- <u>Decessit sine prole legitima</u>: Died without legitimate issue.

- Decessit sine prole superstite: Died without surviving issue.
- Decessit sine prole mascula superstite: Died without surviving male issue.
- Decessit vita matris: Died in the lifetime of the mother.
- Decessit vita patris: Died in the lifetime of the father.
- Sine: Means *"without."*
- Obdormio: Means to fall asleep.
- Decessit: Died.
- Prole: Issue or offspring.
- Consort: Comes from the Latin *"consortium,"* which means *"partnership."* Consider this fictitional statement: *"Mrs. Jacqueline Brown, consort of Mr. John Brown."* This indicates that the husband survived his wife – that the death ended the partnership of marriage.

In this book – *The Rungs of Ladders, A Wyatt History in England & the United States, from 1066 to Modern Times,* the words *"Unknown," "Unknown Wife"* or *"Unknown Husband"* are used because this data is not yet determined.

♀ | | ♂

Part 2. Terms Used in Last Wills & Testaments & Land Deeds & Land Grants

- **Moyety** means [moiety means a portion of]. As a legal term, this word describes a portion other than complete ownership of property. The Old French word is *"moitié,"* which meant *"half."* It is defined the same way in modern day French. The Latin, it is *"medietas,"* meaning *"middle."*

In English law, this term is utilized in parsing – breaking down or defining aspects of ownership and liability in all forms of property. In the Middle Ages, however, this word *"moiety"* – is spelled seeming as *"moyety"* in one 18th century wills transcribed in April 2014. It is discussed later.

In the 18th century [1701-1800] for the purpose of such last will & testaments the term refers to a *"portion"* of the original whole. A moiety in centuries prior to this refers to two groups, or dividing into two parts, and this would be influenced by negotiation of two heirs.

- **Bequeathed** or to bequeath means to pass on or will property to another after a person's leaves the physical body. In the legal sense it is the verb meaning: *"to make a bequest."* In Old English, this word is known as *"Becwethan,"* and it meant to declare or express into words to *"quoth,"* which means *"said."*
- **Double** *"s"* old wills appear as what modern-day readers might mistake "∫" as an *"F."* I noticed in one will, for instance, the word: *"Consisted."* While the two *"s's"* are not double *"ss,"* it appears to modern readers as: *"Consifted"* and *"Confisting"* or "Con∫isting"– which should be discerned not as an *"F,"* but as an *"S"* – *"Consisted"* and *"Consisting."* Witne∫s or Witne∫s is *"witness,"* and is another example. The word *"Session"* can appear as *"Sefsion"* or *"Sepsion"* or worse as *"Sepion"* to the undiscerning eye. The name *"Jesse"* can appear in handwritten presentation as *"Isep"* or as *"Ie∫se"* or *"IeFse."*
- The long ∫ can be confused with the lowercase or miniscule "f" in printed materials, but in handwritten materials the confusion, as stated earlier, can slow a transcriber and researcher considerably. The long ∫ is a form of the miniscule *"s."* If the writer adds a little nub to the long s's left [but not cross threw it completely as a regular *"F"* or *"f"* or ∫ it might still further appear as a lowercase *"F"* when in fact it is an *"s."* The French phonetic symbol, which sounds like: *"chou"* comes close in how it appears; however, the line one third through the middle of the long ∫ appears as a little clef to the left and does not cross all the way through it.

Papers from periods prior to the American Civil War [1861-1865], can introduce confusion for modern readers. One must decipher faded and often illegible or unreadable penmanship of the time's communicator. For the literate, I find they either did not have rules, or did not impose grammatical rules, or they wrote in the way they pronounced words – like one might find in Geoffrey Chaucer's lifetime [Abt. 1343-October 25, 1400.] Chaucer – his name comes from the French *"Chausseur,"* meaning *"shoemaker,"* was born in London and known as the Father of English literature. The grammar of his day reflects inconsistencies in spellings, which may have come from later editors. Chaucer authored works such as *The Canterbury Tales*.

* Grammatical rules and spelling:

A Dictionary of the English Language was published April 15, 1755. It was compiled and written by Samuel Johnson. This dictionary is sometimes referred to as *Johnson's Dictionary*. It was written in response of dissatisfaction with the dictionaries of the time period. A group of London booksellers contracted the task with Johnson in 1746. It took him nearly nine years to complete it. He claimed originally he could finish it in three years.

The Oxford English Dictionary was not completed until 173 years later.

The first English language dictionary was published in 1604 by a Robert Cawdrey.

A man named Thomas Blount published an English dictionary in 1656. There were many inconsistencies in spellings in everyday documents and papers during these time periods.

In the United States, Noah Webster [1758-1843] compiled and wrote an English dictionary that became a best seller. His first dictionary was titled: *A Compendious Dictionary of the English Language* was published in 1806.

It is too bold to suggest not a single grammatical rule was followed because that simply is not true. In typesetting the general rule for a font containing the long *"s,"* or ſ, the German typographic guidelines or rules required the common *"s"* when it is used by itself at the end of a syllable. The long *"s"* was to be used at the beginning of a syllable.

Author of *Jane Eyre*, Charlotte Brontë [1816-1855] in her time used a long *"s"* as the first letter in words with double *"s."* If one looks at early modern English in say the *U.S. Bill of Rights* – the first ten amendments to the U.S. Constitution [passed by Congress September 25, 1789], one will see *"Congress"* in combination of the long *"s"* and the short *"s"* as *"Congreſs."*

* **Royal Charter** is a formal document issued by the Crown or monarch as letters of patent, which grant power to a person or group.
* The word *"presents"* is sometimes written in wills to mean *"in the presence of"*
* The words *"Just Debts"* refers to lawful debts – debts that are already due to be paid out of a person's estate.

- The letters *"N"* and *"S"* are sometimes used to relay direction as in north and south or as in name of state *"N. Carolina"* for *"North Carolina."*
- **An executor** is a person, or *executors* are people one names in a will who will be responsible for handling an estate and ensuring wishes are carried out after one passes away.
- **Heretofore** means in the legal sense *"until now"* or *"before this time."* It means *"up to the present time"* or *"before this previously."*
- **Headright** is a legal grant of land to settlers. The Virginia Company of London held titles to a lot of land and had very few workers. The headright system was introduced in the year 1618. Its focus was to remedy the labor shortage for tobacco. Virginia colonists were granted two headrights – this meant they were granted two tracts of land 50 acres each or 100 acres. New settlers who paid their passage to the Colony of Virginia were granted one headright. Some individuals accumulated headrights by paying for the passage of others. Some settlers came under this agreement as indentured servants and promising to work five-to-seven years for the landowner.
- **Cousin** – When this word was used in the 1600s – it often meant *"niece"* or *"nephew."*
- **Son-in-law, daughter-in-law** - During the 17th century these terms often meant stepson, step-daughter, etc.
- **Esquire** – a title in the 17th century used for the son of a knight or a member of the Council or to a Naval Collector.
- **Guardians** – The courts in the 17th century appointed guardians for minors. Children over age 14 were allowed by approval of the courts to choose their own guardians.
- **Servant** – In the 17th century, usage of this term was done in the sense of *"employee."* Younger sons of gentry in England were listed as *"indentured servant."*
- **Dower** – according to the Caswell County Historical Association online.
  North Carolina dower rights:
  - Years 1663-1783: During a marital union – the wife had a right to one-third of the real estate owned by her husband. She was not allowed to sell it; however, the husband was not allowed to sell the property without her permission. In this sense, it was referred to as a dower as a matter of common law.
  - Years 1784-1868: A woman's right to one-third of her spouse's land became effective when he died. During their marriage, the husband had absolute control. This meant he could sell some of the property or all of it. His control of the property was known as *"curtesy."*
  - In 1869, a dower via common law was reinstated.

  By year 1960, the dower was abolished with the husband's *"curtesy."* Some interesting points made on dowers include:
  - A widow's dower was protected from the husband's creditors.
  - A widow was entitled to the house they shared and its property buildings – barns, tool sheds, etc. If the widow remarried, she was still entitled to the dower.

❧ Upon the demise of the widow, the land transfers to the heirs of her first marriage.

Taxes:

❧ *"WP"* on tax list records for Rowan County, N.C. means *"white pole."* This means a tax was levied on a white male over 16 years of age. Males over the age of 16 years were taxable and eligible for the militia.

❧ *"A"* refers to *"acres."*

❧ A poll tax – a capital tax levied on every adult in a community.

♀ | | ♂

Part 3. Measurements

- **Chain:** Unit of length, measuring 66 feet, or 22 yards, or 100 links, or 4 rods, which is 20.1168 meters.
- **Furlong:** A measurement of distance in imperial units, which is equal to 10 chains, or 1/8ᵗʰ of a mile, or 220 yards, or 660 feet, or 40 rods.
- **Rod:** This measurement is used by surveyors. It is a perch or pole and a unit measuring 5.5 yards or 16.5 feet or 1/320ᵗʰ of a statute mile. A rod is ¼ of a surveyor's chain. Imperial units – *British Imperial Units*, is a system of units defined in the year 1824 by the *British Weights and Measures Act*.
- **Statute mile** is equal to 80 chains. An acre is the area of 10 square chains – the area of one chain by one furlong.
- **Hogshead** [hogz'hed] is a large cask or barrel designed to hold 63 wine gallons, or 52.5 imperial gallons, or 54 gallons of beer, 46 gallons of claret, or in the U.S. containing tobacco varying 750 to 1200 pounds. Quote using word hogshead:
  - *"In 1827, a ship carrying some 300 giant hogsheads – a hogshead is a cask containing 56 imperial gallons or 63 US gallons – was wrecked in the Irish Sea, bound for India."*

♀ | | ♂

PART 4. PLACES & CALENDARS

⬧ Southange -- known as *South Haigh* and *Upper Haigh*, Yorkshire, England.

CALENDARS
When eleven days of 1752 vanished into thin air....

In 1752 on September 2nd the sleepy-eyed pulled their covers to their chins and snored the night hours away. When they woke to the chirping sounds of dawn, it was 11 days later decreed by an act of Parliament.

Their calendar read: Sept. 14th, 1752. It was due to the Calendar [New Style] Act of 1750 as a measure to bring Great Britain in alignment with much of the world. For the year 1752 in Great Britain, Sept. 3rd –13th vanished. From then on, no one needed to double date their letters in the confusion the previous calendar no doubt caused for 170 years.

In the compilations for Wyatt, Dandridge, Boleyn and Tudor, the reader will note some years for marriage or death or birth appear, for example as 1618/1619. The archiving in the Family Tree Maker® program adjusts the year due the lack of using the Gregorian Calendar prior to 1752 by the British and its colonies.

⬧ **Anno Domini** [A.D. or AD] means specifically: *"Anno Domini Nostri Lesu (Jesu) Christi."* This means: *"In the Year of the Lord"* or Medieval Latin: *"In the Year of Our Lord."* 1 A.D. is said to be the estimated birth year of Jesus Christ or the *Year of the Nativity*. His birth is speculated as well to have occurred between 5 B.C. and 1 B.C. based on King Herod's death being 4 B.C.
⬧ **Lunisolar Calendar** had 13 months every second or third year.
⬧ **Gregorian Calendar** [Western Calendar or Christian Calendar] is the most widely used calendar in the world. It is modeled after the **Julian Calendar**. The Gregorian Calendar, introduced in February1582] was decreed by Pope Gregory XIII [1502-1585] and is named for him. It was designed in order to bring about the date of Easter to the time of year as it had been agreed upon in the year 325 by the *First Council of Nicaea*. The years in this calendar are numbered from the traditional birth year of Jesus. This is called the Anno Domini [A.D.] Era, or Common Era, or Common Christian Era. It is solar based on 365 days a common year, which is divided in 12 months. Each month consists of 30 and 31 days except February during the common year. It contains a **Leap Year** every four years, which adds a day to February. The Gregorian Calendar's year is 365.2425 days. There is a difference of 0.002 percent between it and the Julian Calendar.

According to ***Introduction to Calendars United States Naval Observatory***:

"Every year that is exactly divisible by four is a leap year, except for years that are exactly divisible by 100, but these centurial years are leap years if they are exactly divisible by 400."

The years 1700, 1800 and 1900 are not Leap Years; however, the year 2000 is designated as such.

The Calendar Act of 1750 in Great Britain's Parliament reformed the calendar of England and British Dominions so the New Legal Year began on January 1ˢᵗ instead of March 25ᵗʰ. It then adopted the Gregorian Calendar used by most of western Europe.

This took effect – as stated earlier, in 1752. It was to align with the calendar used in much of the world. Scotland's year began January 1, 1600 and had partly changed; however, it adopted the Gregorian Calendar in 1752. This new reformed calendar took effect in Russia in 1918; Greece held out for the change until 1923.

- **Julian Calendar** was introduced in 46 BC by Julius Caesar. It was the reform calendar for the Roman Calendar. It has 365 days divided into 12 months with a leap day added every four years to February. The Julian year is 365.25 days long. The tropical or solar year [length of time it takes the ☼ Sun to return to the same position in the cycle of seasons. The tropical year is about 20 minutes shorter than the time it takes the Earth to complete one full orbit around the ☼ Sun, as measured with respect to the fixed stars.] The tropical year is a few minutes shorter than 365.25 days. The Julian calendar did not compensate the difference in time and gained three days every four centuries. This discrepancy was corrected by the Gregorian calendar in 1582.

♀ | | ♂

PART 5. ABBREVIATIONS

- ACW: American Civil War
- CSA: Confederate States of America
- MP: Members of Parliament
- Maj. Gen.: Major General – two-star rank
- Brig. Gen.: Brigadier General – one-star rank
- Col.: Colonel
- Capt.: Captain
- Lieut. Col.: Lieutenant Colonel
- Lieut. Gen. Lieutenant General
- Sgt.: Sergeant
- Sgt. Maj. : Sergeant Major
- Pvt.: Private
- Gov.: Governor
- Sen.: Senator
- Rep.: Representative

United States State Abbreviations:

1) Alabama: AL & Ala.
2) Alaska: AK & Alas.
3) Arizona: AZ & Ariz.
4) Arkansas: AR & Ark.
5) California: CA, Ca. Calif & Cal.
6) Colorado: CO, Col. Colo. & Col.
7) Connecticut: CT, Ct. & Conn.
8) Delaware: DE, Del. & De.
9) Florida: FL, Fla., Fl. & Flor.
10) Georgia: GA & Ga.
11) Hawaii: HI
12) Idaho: ID, Ida & Id.
13) Illinois: IL, Ill. & Ills.
14) Indiana: IN, Ind. & In.
15) Iowa: IA, Ia. & Ioa.
16) Kansas: KS, Ks., Ka. & Kans.
17) Kentucky: KY, Ky., Ken. & Kent.
18) Louisiana: LA & La.
19) Maine: ME & Me.
20) Maryland: MD & Md.

21) Massachusetts: MA & Mass.
22) Michigan: MI & Mich.
23) Minnesota: MN, Minn. & Mn.
24) Missouri: MO & Mo.
25) Mississippi: MS & Miss.
26) Montana: MT & Mont.
27) Nebraska: NE, Neb., & Nebr.
28) Nevada: NV & Nev.
29) New Hampshire: NH & N.H.
30) New Jersey: NJ & N.J.
31) New Mexico: NM & N.M.
32) New York: NY & N.Y.
33) North Carolina: NC & N.C.
34) North Dakota: ND, N.D. & N.Dak.
35) Ohio: OH, Oh. & O.
36) Oklahoma: OK & Okla.
37) Oregon: OR, Ore & Or.
38) Pennsylvania: PA, Pa. & Penn.
39) Rhoda Island: RI
40) South Carolina: SC & S.C.
41) South Dakota: SD & S.D.
42) Tennessee: TN & Tenn.
43) Texas: TX, Tx. & Tex.
44) Utah: UT & Ut.
45) Vermont: VT & Vt.
46) Virginia: VA & Virg.
47) Washington: WA, Wash. & Wa.
48) West Virginia: WV, W.Va. & W. Virg.
49) Wisconsin: WI, Wisc. & Wis.
50) Wyoming: WY, Wy. or Wyo.

Commonwealth & Territories

1) District of Columbia: D.C.
2) American Samoa: AS
3) Federated States of Micronesia: FM
4) Guam: GU
5) Marshall Islands: MH
6) Northern Mariana Islands: MP & M.P.
7) Palau: PW
8) Puerto Rico: PR & P.R.
9) Virgin Islands: VI & U.S.V.I.

♀ | | ♂

English
by T.S. Watt

I take it you already know
of tough and bough and cough and dough?
Others may stumble, but not you
on hiccough, thorough, slough and through.
Well done! And now you wish, perhaps,
To learn of less familiar traps?

Beware of heard, a dreadful word
That looks like beard and sounds like bird.
And dead; it's said like bed, not bead.
For goodness sake, don't call it deed!
Watch out for meat and great and threat,
(They rhyme with suite and straight and debt)

A moth is not a moth in mother,
Nor both in bother, broth in brother.
And here is not a match for there,
Nor dear and fear for bear and pear,
And then there's dose and rose and lose --
Just look them up -- and goose and choose,

And cork and work and card and ward
And font and front and word and sword.
And do and go and thwart and cart --
Come, come, I've hardly made a start.
A dreadful language? Man alive,
I mastered it when I was five.

♀ | | ♂

* In *The Rungs of Ladders, A Wyatt History in England & the United States, from 1066 to Modern Times* the upper case *"X"* is used in some legal documents, such as wills as a signature. It is quoted with the understanding of *"making one's mark."* In cases found in this book, *"X"* refers to Unknown Wife, Unknown Surname, Unknown Husband, Unknown Child. Such refers to the name being at this time unknown to the researcher.

♀ | | ♂

CHAPTER 6

A Necessary Note On Location

♀ | | ♂

"Many noble persons .... Resolved to send an expedition to Virginia....
This notice is published to announce the expedition of all workmen of
whatever occupation – blacksmiths, carpenters, barrel-makers, architects,
bakers, weavers, shoemakers, sawers of lumber, spinners of wool ... both
men and woman, of any occupation—who wish to join this voyage to
Virginia, where they will have houses to live in, vegetable gardens and
orchards, and food and clothing provided by the Company...they will
receive share in all products and profits...they will also receive a share of
the land that is to be divided, for themselves and their heirs forever..."

-- QUOTE FROM VIRGINIA COMPANY BROADSIDE, IN
THE GENESIS OF THE UNITED STATES, ED. ALEXANDER
BROWN [BOSTON, 1890], VOL. 1, PPS. 248-249.

*W*ITHIN THIS BOOK, YOU WILL find Wyatt history in England and the United States –
specifically the original Wyatts in historic Jamestown, Va. [on the Chesapeake Bay,
settled in 1607] and those in Rowan County, N.C.

This book presents Wyatt genealogical history and contains information you may agree
or disagree with – and hopefully recognize as a contribution within the scope of genealogical
research.

* The purpose is not to argue genealogical history.
* The purpose is to record Wyatt and associated histories as accurately as possible
  given the vast and conflicting information available.
* If you find something you don't agree with – make a note in the back of this book.
  Send proof of what you claim. When and if another edition of this book is printed,
  the changes or additions will be included.

Location of the Wyatts for the purposes of this book include:

1. Kent County & Yorkshire, England.
2. The British Colony of Virginia, which comprised 8 counties or shires originally created in 1634.
3. Rowan County, N.C., U.S.A.

PART 1. WYATT ORIGINS IN ENGLAND: KENT COUNTY & YORKSHIRE

Yorkshire or York's shire is a county in Northern England. It is the county or shire of the City of York, which derives its name for the city Jorvik – which is Viking term. The word *"shire"* is derived from Old English: *"scir,"* and means to shear in regard *"to divide land."*

Yorkshire is the largest county in the United Kingdom. Current-day areas of the county include North Yorkshire, South Yorkshire, West Yorkshire and East Riding of Yorkshire. Yorkshire is nicknamed *"God's Own County."* It is regarded as being amongst the greenest counties in England.

The white rose of the English royal House of York is the emblem for Yorkshire. The flag of Yorkshire has a dark blue background with the white rose emblem at its center.

Some readers may recognize Yorkshire in its association with the Brontë sisters – Emily [author of *Wuthering Heights*], Anne [author of *The Tenant of Wildfell Hall*] and Charlotte [author of *Jane Eyre*] of Haworth, a small historic town. Haworth is located in the City of Bradford metropolitan borough of West Yorkshire, England. Historically, a section of West Riding of Yorkshire is located in Pennines, three miles or 4.8 kilometers southwest of Keighley and 10 miles or 16 kilometers west of Bradford. Yorkshire is beautiful beyond words.

♀ | | ♂

PART 2. THE BRITISH COLONY OF VIRGINIA

"We came with our ships to Cape Comfort, where we saw five [Virginia Indians] running on the shore. . ... [After] rowing ashore, the captain called to them a sign of friendship, but they were at first very [fearful] until they saw the captain lay his hand on his heart. Upon that they laid down their bows and arrows and come very boldly to us, making signs to come ashore to their town, which [they call] Kecoughtan."

--- GEORGE PERCY, *"OBSERVATIONS GATHERED OUT OF A DISCOURSE OF THE PLANTATION OF THE SOUTHERN COLONY OF VIRGINIA BY THE ENGLISH, 1606,"* AS QUOTED IN HAILE, P. 91.

Jamestown [Jamestowne & James Towne], founded by the Virginia Company of London, England and named for James I of England, was a settlement in the Colony of Virginia. On May 24, 1607, it was established as *"James Fort"* by the Virginia Company of London. By 1619, it was regarded as *"Jamestown."* It was considered permanent after it was briefly abandoned in 1610. It served as the capital of the Virginia colony from 1616 until 1699.

The Jamestown settlement was located within territory known as: Tsenacommacah -- pronounced *"Sen-ah-com-ma-cah,"* also known as:

* Attankkoughkomouck
* Attanakamik
* Tenakomakah
* Tscenocomoco
* Tsenacomoco.

This territory was named by the Powhatan also known as Powatan and Powhaten native Americans, claiming this area as their native homeland. The area encompassed Tidewater Virginia and the Eastern shore.

The boundaries reached 100 miles or 160 kilometers by 100 miles or 160 kilometers from close to the south end of the mouth of the James River all the way north to the south end of the Potomac River.

It spanned from the Eastern Shore west to about the fall zone or line of the two rivers. The Powhatan Native Americans were part of a Chiefdom of Virginia Native American tribes. They were regarded as the Powhatan Confederacy. These native people spoke Algonquian.

[Chief Powhatan said] . . . 'Therefore lay me down all your commodities together. What I like I will take, and in [return] give you what I think fitting their value.' . . . He fixed his humor upon a few blue beads. A long time he . . . desired them, [and] Smith . . . [described the beads] as being composed of the most rare substance of the color of the skies, and not to be worn but by the greatest kings in the world. . . . [Before] we departed, for a pound or two of blue beads [John Smith] bought . . . 2[00] or 300 bushels of corn, yet parted good friends.

---- JOHN SMITH, *THE GENERAL HISTORY OF VIRGINIA, NEW-ENGLAND, AND THE SUMMER ISLES*, AS QUOTED IN HAILE, P. 246.

According to records in *Adventurers of Purse and Person 1607-1625 and Their Families* the following counties or divisions were formed in the Colony of Virginia:

1. James City County – James City & Surry [formed by April 1652]
2. Henrico County – Henrico, Goochland, 1728; Chesterfield, 1749
3. Charles City County – Charles City, Prince George, 1703
4. Elizabeth City County – Elizabeth City, New Norfolk [formed, 1636 from a portion of Elizabeth City on the south side of Hampton Roads]; From this, Lower County of New Norfolk, 1637; [Lower Norfolk] and Upper County of New Norfolk [Upper Norfolk] 1637 – by 1642, Nansemond.
5. Warwick River County [Denbigh County taken from the name of the Parish, abt. 1635; It became known as Warwick in March 1642/43.
6. Warrosquyoake County – By 1637, it became known as the Isle of Wight, and from Warrosquyoake, Southampton was formed in 1749.
7. Charles River County – In March 1642/43, it was changed to York County and from upper York, New Kent was formed in 1654; Gloucester was formed in 1651. King and Queen was formed in 1691 and King William in 1702. From Gloucester – Lancaster [formed from York and Northumberland, mentioned January 1, 1651/52 – Old Rappahannock, 1656 and Lancaster.
8. Northumberland County – was formed from Indian district Chickacoan, first mentioned January 31, 1644/45, mentioned in Maryland records. From it, Northumberland, Westmoreland in 1653 and Stafford in 1664.
9. Accawmack County – This county was known as Northampton by March 1642-/43 and from it formed Accomack, 1663 and Northampton.

On April 10, 1606, James the first granted a charter to a group of London citizens: Sir Thomas Gates, Sir George Somers, Richard Hakluyt and Edward-Maria Wingfield, Thomas Hanham, Raleigh Gilbert, William Parker and George Popham to form the first colony to be called Virginia. This first charter was revised. A second charter was issued May 23, 1609.

"This charter is notable for the inclusion of the names of all the adventurers (i.e. stockholders) 659 in number and a list of 56 trade guides of London as subscribers."

The corporate title became known as *"The Treasurer and Company of Adventurers and Planters of the City of London for the First Colony in Virginia."*

On March 12, 1612, a third charter extended the boundaries of the colony and increased the privileges of the company, and the names of the stockholders added since the second charter were included. The company operated for 18 years. Through its ups and downs, it was blamed in 1622 for the Indian Massacre. This company never withdrew its support in efforts to establish and support the colony.

On June 26, 1624, the British Crown took over controlling the colony. Some historians believe that the Colony would not have survived more than two or three years had it been from its beginning under the control and direction of the Monarchy.

♀ | | ♂

PART 3. ROWAN COUNTY, N.C.

Wyatts and Wyatt descendants live in Rowan County today. Many there and in others parts of the United States can trace their Wyatt lineages to Jamestown, Va.

Rowan County was created from a part of Anson County in 1753. Around 350 Anson County citizens petitioned at that time the North Carolina State Legislature to create a separate county. When Rowan was incorporated, it was named in honor of Irish immigrant Matthew Rowan, then acting North Carolina Governor [1753-1754].

Gov. Matthew Rowan was additionally a councilor, assemblyman and Surveyor-General. His parents were Reverend John and Margaret Rowan of Antrim County, Ireland. Gov. Rowan immigrated in 1724 with the goal of constructing two vessels for a Dublin merchant.

In 1755, the Town of Salisbury became the county seat for Rowan. The town of Salisbury was named in honor of Salisbury, England – which is a Cathedral City in Wiltshire, England less than 10 miles from Stonehenge.

Rowan County, N.C. is divided into the following townships:

* Atwell
* China Grove
* Cleveland
* Franklin
* Gold Hill
* Litaker
* Locke
* Morgan
* Mount Ulla
* Providence
* Salisbury
* Scotch Irish
* Steele
* Unity.

Morgan Township -- one of 14 townships in Rowan, is comprised of 61.13 square miles or 158.3 kilometers squared in the southeastern part of the county. It is the largest township by land area. There are no incorporated municipalities in Morgan Township. The eastern border of Morgan Township is the Yadkin River, and the township contains a portion of High Rock Lake. In the 2010 federal census, a population of 3,424 is recorded for Morgan Township.

Rowan County communities in addition to Salisbury include: Bear Poplar, Chine Grove, Craven, Spencer and Faith. North Carolina is divided into 100 counties. Rowan County is flanked by Davie County to the north, Davidson County to its east and northeast, Mecklenburg, Cabarrus, Stanly and Mongomery counties to its south and Iredell to its west. Mecklenburg County is where Charlotte is located.

The total population for Rowan County in 2010 was reported as 138,428: Salisbury: 28,205; Atwell: 12,428; China Grove: 24,501; Cleveland: 2,817; Franklin: 12,322; Gold Hill: 11,278; Litaker: 11,867; Locke: 14, 149; Mount Ulla: 1,694; Providence: 9,985; Scotch Irish: 1, 820; Steele: 1,725; Unity: 2,215.

♀ | | ♂

PART 4.
SUNDAY AFTERNOON
APRIL 27, 2013
JOURNAL ENTRY

A year ago maybe it was – my father recalled as a little boy asking his mother Virgie Irene Eagle [Egle] Hinson [1902-1984], a great granddaughter to Rachel Evelyn Wyatt Morgan [1835-1915] who was related to him in the Morgan Township?

Virgie replied:

"It would be easier to tell you who you are not related to" (in the Morgan Township).

♀ | | ♂

As one travels down West Innes Street, where it meets North Church Street in Salisbury, Rowan County, N.C., the presence of a winged muse named *"Fame"* holding a fallen Confederate soldier echo voices of another time.

On its base are the words:

"In memory of Rowan's Confederate soldiers that their heroic deeds sublime self-sacrifice and undying devotion to duty and country may never be forgotten. 1861-1865"

This statue, created by a Frederic Wellington Ruckstuhl, was purchased from a company in Brussels, Belgium in 1908 at a cost of $10,000. The Hoke Chapter of the United Daughters of the Confederacy dedicated it on May 10th of that same year.

The monument was financed via funds raised from the production of a play titled: *Under the Southern Cross* by Christian Reid – known as Frances Tieran Fisher.

When I was a child growing up in Salisbury after my family had moved there from New Orleans, La., I viewed this statue as an angel -- not a muse.

…but who is to say muses cannot have wings?

♀ | | ♂

CHAPTER 7

Challenges…Rowan County, North Carolina

♀ | | ♂

*T*HE WYATTS PRESENT UNIQUE GENEALOGICAL hurdles. There are Wyatts who carry the Wyatt surname in various spellings. There are many who descend from Wyatts who understandably do not carry the surname.

There is a fear of recording inaccurate dates or spellings. One can easily discern in Rowan County this fear of the researcher need be forgiven. Many of the marriage bonds, land records, tax records, census records, last wills and testaments contain discrepancies in spellings.

The name Wyatt, which is thought originally to have been Guyot, Wyot and Wyotte in England and France, has evolved into expected spelling variations of Wiat, Wiatt, Wyat, Wyatt.

In Rowan County, N.C. some recorded *"Wyatt"* as *"Wyett"* and as *"Wiett."* Also, as *"Wyotte."* In paper and stone trails – names, whether misspellings or variations such as Park, Parks and Parke are often in Rowan County the exact same group.

Weeding through the McCubbins file in the Rowan County Public Library's history room in Salisbury, N.C., among other files, revealed such discrepancies and slowed the process a bit. The greatest hurdles, however, are not so much name variations and misspellings.

One figure in this genealogical endeavor John Wyatt [1743-1815] has his name as *"Wiat"* and as *"Wyat"* in his last will and testament. It is shown as *"Wiatt"* *with* two T's on his tombstone. One of his sons Thomas Wyatt has in the marriage bond record notes [in the McCubbins file at Rowan Public Library] spelled as *"Wiett."*

A great hurdle in sorting these Wyatts is not as much the careful manner in which information is woven around the process -- but in conveying how it fits together. The goal is accuracy.

♀ | | ♂

CHAPTER 8

England's Earliest Wyatts

♀ | | ♂

THE GREAT GRANDFATHER OF ADAM WIOT OR WIOTUS [1320-ABT. 1385] & HOW HE TIES IN....

*T*HE INTERNET OFFERS NUMEROUS ARCHIVAL and genealogical discussions on Captain Adam Guyott. This man is sometimes known as Wiot or Wyot. His great grandson is seemingly his namesake. Additionally known as *"Adam Wyotte,"* Captain Guyot is purported as the earliest known Wyatt ancestor. Both Adam Wiots or Guyotts are at the forefront of Wyatts. They are said to be ancestors of Rev. Hawte [Haute] Wyatt. Rev. Hawte Wyatt resided from 1621 until 1625 in what is today historic Jamestown, Va. None of us really knew either Adam, or Rev. Hawte Wyatt. We get to know them through records they left behind.

The second Adam Wiot, Abt. 1320- Abt. 1385, and his wife Lady Agnes Wigton [also known as Wiggen or Wiggon de Norwoods, or Agnes Wigton or Wiggen de Norwoods] married around 1340. Some researchers report the marriage ceremony as 1349.

Not all such sources are in agreement. Many in general contain errors in script or typing. Several sources seem to be in agreement, however, this great grandson of Captain Adam Guyott -- Adam Wyot was a descendant of a family called *"Guyot."* They agree apparently the Guyots came from a French/Norman origin. Admiral or Captain Adam Guyott or Guyot or Wyot – lived during and prior to the Battle of Hastings in 1066.

ADAM WYOT OR GUYOT [ABT.1320- ABT.1385]

The great grandson of the immigrant Adam Wyot or Guyot, born around 1320, had two sons: William and John Wiot. This John is claimed. William, born around 1350, had a son named either Robert or Richard born around 1383.

This Robert or Richard had a son named Geoffrey born around 1404. He had a son named Richard born around 1420, and from this Richard was born Sir Henry Wiatt, the father of the poet – Sir Thomas Wiatt – the Elder.

Adam is reported to have been born in Yorkshire, England. He lived early on in the ancient town of Southange [also known as South Haigh and Upper Haigh], Yorkshire, England.

A bibliography from myheritage.com and a few others also promote this information. Adam Wiot is first mentioned in the Roger Twyden Roll.

It states this is:

"…borne out by reference in the pipe rolls, the Assize Rolls and other ancient records of the 14th and 15th centuries."

The claim he is first mentioned is in the Roger Twyden Roll, which came out of a reference in the pipe rolls and other records of the 1300 and 1400s. Historical articles state Henry Wiatt [1460-Abt. 1536] – husband of Anne Skinner and Margaret Bailiff, is said to have applied for a new Grant of Arms in January 1507 or 08.

The Grant of Arms was granted because he is said to have descended from the House of Blood and the name of Wiat. It is said as well that because Henry Wiatt [father of Sir Thomas Wyatt – the Elder [poet], Margaret *"Lady Lee,"* and few others, was by then a privy councilor, he may not have been asked to produce further proof such as a pedigree.

In Henry Wiatt's career, he was rewarded for his bravery as a soldier and appointed *"Keeper"* and later *"Constable"* of Norwich Castle. Norwich Castle today is known as Norwich Castle Museum & Art Gallery, located on Castle Meadow, Norwich, East Anglia – an area East of England; one of nine official regions of England. Norwich Castle is a Medieval fortification founded by William the Conqueror [1027-1087] in the aftermath of the Norman Conquest.

Later, another honor was added in 1490 as Henry Wiatt [Wyatt] was made *"Master of the King's Jewels"* for 34 years. In the year 1488, he became the *"Controller of the Mint."* This job required he assist with reorganizing mint and coinage.

Around the year 1492 he bought Allington Castle in Kent County, England from the trustees of Robert Gainsford. The castle then was in strong need of repair. Henry and his son Thomas the Elder made extensive renovations. Large Tudor windows were added. A porch was also added. Other additions include: a fire place, long gallery, a newer kitchen and staircase.

He used funds from the selling of a Hall in the village of [Southange] South Haigh or Upper Haigh in Yorkshire, to purchase Allington Castle.

This Henry Wyatt or Wiatt was visited in the castle by Henry VII in the year 1527 and was visited by Cardinal Thomas Wolsey *"Woolsley"* [March 1474 to November 29, 1530] of the Roman Catholic Church. Cardinal Wolsey was the king's almoner – a chaplain or church officer in charge of distributing funds to poor.

♀ | | ♂

Sir Thomas Wyatt – the Elder [1503-1542], the poet & his sister
Margaret *"Lady Lee"* Wyatt, [Abt.1506-Abt. 1535].

♀ | | ♂

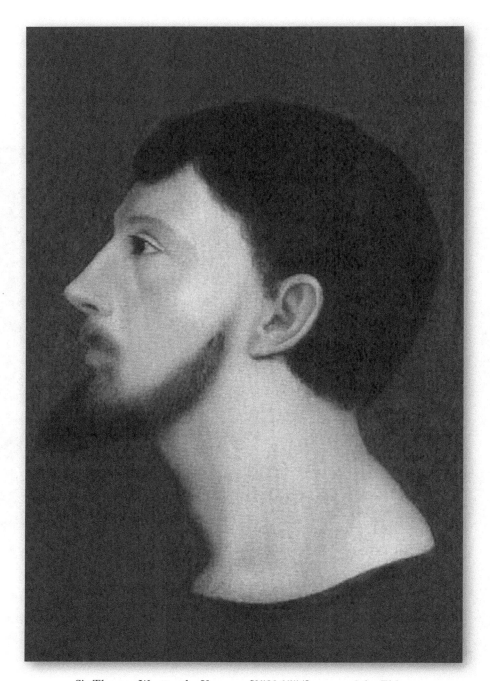

Sir Thomas Wyatt – the Younger [1521-1554], a son of the Elder.

♀ | | ♂

CHAPTER 9

The Twysden Roll

♀ | | ♂

*T*HE TWYSDEN ROLL CONTAINS PEDIGREES and the arms of Twysden and other families including Wyatt and Scott. The Twysden Roll contains pedigrees and arms of the family of Elizabeth Woodville, the Queen of Edward IV.

Edward IV's aunt is said to have married around the year 1430 a William Haute. William Haute is said to have been an ancestor of Jane Haute or Hawte – the wife of Sir Thomas Wiatt – the Younger, who was born at Allington Castle in Kent County, England in 1521 and executed at Tower Hill, London, England April 11th, 1554. The Younger Wyatt was executed for leading a rebellion against Queen Mary I – Henry VIII's eldest living child at the time.

The Hautes or Hawtes of Bishopsbourne and Wavering Manor in Kent County, England are said to have been neighbors to the Wiatt family of Allington Castle. The Haute lineage left no more heirs after the year 1530. Lady Jane Haute or Hawte, [1522-Abt. 1600] wife of Sir Thomas Wyatt – the Younger, was born in Bishopsborne, Kent County, England.

One interesting side note is Sir Thomas Wyatt the Younger had a daughter Anne Wyatt [1542-1592] who was married to Sir Roger Twisden de Peckham or Twysden. Some accounts refer to this Anne as having been his sister.

This man – Sir Roger Twisden in the year 1578, compiled a genealogical tree of 11 generations of Wiats, thus producing in the year 1619 a pedigree for the Wyatt family -- originally of Yorkshire and Allington Castle, Kent County, England.

♀ | | ♂

CHAPTER 10

Queen Elizabeth I [1533-1603] & Sir Thomas Wyatt – the Younger [1521-1554]

♀ | | ♂

*H*OW ARE THEY RELATED?

The answer is of great interest. Elizabeth I – the second daughter of King Henry VIII to survive past infancy has a family connection via the Bolyen lineage. Elizabeth I and Sir Thomas Wyatt – the Younger, are related. Sir Thomas Wiatt's mother Elizabeth Brooke is a half second cousin once removed to Queen Elizabeth I. This means that to Sir Thomas Wiatt – the Younger, Elizabeth the First was a half third cousin.

This relationship is traced to the Younger Wyatt's mother Elizabeth Brooke [1503-1560], who was married to Sir Thomas Wiatt – the Elder [Abt. 1503-1542]. Elizabeth Brooke was a daughter to Dorothy Heydon and Thomas Brooke, 8th Baron and Lord of Cobham [d. 1529]. Dorothy Heydon's parents were Sir Henry Heydon and Anne or Elizabeth Boleyn.

This Anne or Elizabeth Boleyn was the daughter of an unknown woman and Geoffrey Boleyn. Geoffrey Boleyn's son William via his wife Anne Mary Hoo was William Boleyn [1451-October 10, 1505] This William Boleyn of Norfolk, England married Lady Margaret Ormond Butler [1454-1539] and had amongst their 10 children: Thomas Boleyn – the 1st Earl of Wilshire. One of the children born to this Thomas Boleyn 1st Earl of Wiltshire and his wife Lady Elizabeth Howard was Anne Boleyn – the second wife of King Henry VIII. [1491-1547].

❧ The name *"Boleyn"* is sometimes referred to as *"Bullen."*

Elizabeth Brooke Wyatt – wife of Sir Thomas Wyatt – the Elder, had a brother named George who married a woman named Anne. Together, they had a daughter they may have named in honor of George's sister. The child was called Elisabeth Brooke [1526-1565]. This niece Elisabeth Brooke of Elizabeth Brooke Wyatt married William Parr, 1st Marquess of Northampton. This William Parr was the brother of Katharine [Katherine, Katheryn] Parr [1512-Sept. 5th, 1548] – this Katharine being the sixth wife of Henry VIII [1491-1546/47]. What is even more interesting is this Katharine Parr later married

[Thomas Seymour – the one executed for treason while King Edward VI was on the throne.] – this Thomas being the brother of Jane Seymour – Jane being King Henry VIII's third wife.

In compilations, the reader will note some years for marriage or death or birth appear, for example as 1618/1619. The archiving in the Family Tree Maker® program adjusts the year due the lack of using the Gregorian Calendar prior to 1752 by the British and its colonies.

Henry VIII's wives:

* Katherine of Aragon, former princess of Spain [1485-1535/36]; m. 1509
* Anne Boleyn [1501-1536]; m. 1532/33
* Jane Seymour [d. 1537] m. 1536
* Anne of Cleves [1515-1557] m. 1538/39
* Katherine Howard [abt. 1525-1541/42] m. 1540
* Katharine Parr [abt. 1512-1548] m. 1543

His mistresses were:

* Elizabeth Stafford [1491-1546/47]
* Elizabeth Blount by whom he had a son that was recognized as illegitimate:

Henry Fitzroy Tudor, 1519-1536, married Mary Howard.

* *The passing of Queen Elizabeth the First marked the end of the Tudor line. Her end in 1603 brought about the Union of Crowns with Scotland.

Ladder #1:

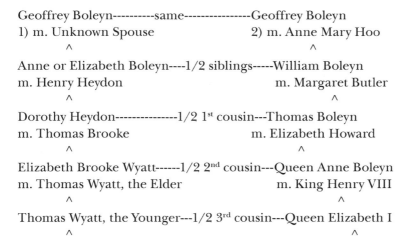

Geoffrey Boleyn----------same----------------Geoffrey Boleyn
1) m. Unknown Spouse   2) m. Anne Mary Hoo
         ∧   ∧
Anne or Elizabeth Boleyn----1/2 siblings-----William Boleyn
m. Henry Heydon   m. Margaret Butler
         ∧   ∧
Dorothy Heydon--------------1/2 1st cousin---Thomas Boleyn
m. Thomas Brooke   m. Elizabeth Howard
         ∧   ∧
Elizabeth Brooke Wyatt------1/2 2nd cousin---Queen Anne Boleyn
m. Thomas Wyatt, the Elder   m. King Henry VIII
         ∧   ∧
Thomas Wyatt, the Younger---1/2 3rd cousin---Queen Elizabeth I
         ∧   ∧

George Thomas Wiatt, Knt.----1/2 4th cousin ---No descendants of QEI

* QEI is a half 2nd cousin one generation removed to Elizabeth Brooke Wyatt. ½ equals one-half.

Ladder #2:

Elizabeth Brooke Wyatt-----siblings------------George Brooke
m. Thomas Wyatt, the Elder---in-laws----------m. Anne
    ∧   ∧
Thomas Wyatt, the Younger-----1st cousins----Elisabeth Brooke
m. Jane Hawte---------------------in laws-------William Parr
    ∧   ∧
George Thomas Wiatt, Knt.-----2nd cousins----Offspring?

Ladder #3:

William Parr -----------siblings -----------------Queen Katharine Parr
m. Elisabeth Brooke   6th wife of King Henry VIII

* Katharine Parr married as well Thomas Seymour, a brother of Queen Jane Seymour, the 3rd wife of King Henry VIII.
* Note: Do not confuse the two Eliz. Brookes – one is Elizabeth Brooke, wife of the Elder Wyatt and one is Elisabeth Brook, wife of William Parr.

Ladder #4:

Queen Anne Boleyn--siblings--Rochford Boleyn--siblings--Mary
m. King Henry VIII   m. William Carey
    ∧   ∧
Queen Elizabeth I --------------1st cousins--------------- Catherine Carey
                                            m. Francis Knollys
                                                  ∧
No descendants of QE----------2nd cousins-------------Anne Knollys
                                            m. Thomas West
                                                  ∧
                                            Gov. John West
                                            m. Ann
                                                  ∧
                                            Cap. John West
                                            m. Unity Croshaw
                                                  ∧
                                            Nathaniel West
                                            m. Martha Woodward
                                                  ∧

Unity West m.
William Dandridge

- Sibling of William Dandridge: John Dandridge II m. Frances Orlando Jones and has daughter Martha Dandridge Custis Washington – wife of U.S. President George Washington. Martha's great granddaughter Mary Anne Randolph Custis married General Robert E. Lee. Robert E. Lee and 12th U.S. President Zachary Taylor both descend from Anne Constable and Colonel Richard Henry Lee I, *"The Immigrant."*
- Sibling of William Dandridge: Elizabeth Dandridge [1703-Abt. 1750] m. Henry Wiatt or Wyatt [Abt. 1685-Abt. 1743] – possible parents of John Wiatt [1743-1815] – the John Wiatt of the Lick Creek Baptist Church, Davidson County, N.C.
- This Anne Knollys who married Thomas West de la Warr had a sister named Elizabeth named Thomas Leighton [Abt. 1530-1610]. This union is discussed more in *Paper & Stone, A Leighton History in England & the United States.*

CHAPTER 11

Anne Boleyn [Bullen], [1501-1536]
2nd wife of King Henry VIII [1491-1547]

♀ | | ♂

"Aisi sera groigne qui groigne," Latin for *"Let them grumble; that is how it is going to be."*

– CONSORT QUEEN ANNE BOLEYN.

*W*HY DEVOTE A CHAPTER TO Queen Consort Anne Boleyn in this Wyatt book?

Queen Anne Boleyn's genealogy partly reflects she was a half second cousin once removed to Sir Thomas Wyatt, the Younger. Consort Queen Anne Boleyn was the second wife of King Henry VIII. With him, she was a parent of Elizabeth I Tudor, born September 7, 1533.

Two other babies – sons born after Elizabeth I, then did not survive. They were Henry Tudor, born 1534 and titled: *"Duke of Cornwall;"* and another son who died as an infant – born January 29, 1535/36.

There is a painting titled: *"Anne Boleyn Say a Final Farewell to Her Daughter, Princess Elizabeth"* by artist Gustaf Wapper, 1838. In this painting, Queen Boleyn is looking away as her daughter Elizabeth, less than three months from turning 3 years old, rests her angelic face against her mother's chest. The image stirs the heart. It reveals the innocence of their union.

Anne Boleyn – Queen Consort of King Henry VIII, had a brother named Viscount Rochford Boleyn. He was executed May 19, 1536 having been accused of adultery and incest by Henry VIII. Henry VIII got rid of people who stood in his way for what he wanted.

King Henry VIII had attempted to accuse his first wife Katharine of Aragon of adultery simply because she had been married to Henry's brother: Arthur Tudor who died less than five months into his marriage.

King Henry VIII grabbed at straws – but each straw was cemented to the belief that he acted in a way as to seek God's will. There were other factors to consider with his first wife, her being royal by birth and being held in high regard by Spain. He could not have her killed simply because he said she was guilty of adultery. The Roman Catholic Church said no – so he sent her away and founded a church that would grant him a divorce.

Something That Makes the World Smaller...

Consort Queen Anne Boleyn – a queen not by blood, but by marriage, had a sister named Mary. Mary had as historians speculate two illegitimate children with Henry VIII. One child was Catherine Carey or Cary, who married Sir Francis Knollys, a member of Parliament [MP] and of Oxfordshire, England.

Together one of their children was Lady Anne Knollys. She has been referred to as Elizabeth Knollys – and this is not to be confused with Anne's sister Elizabeth Knollys who married a Sir Thomas Leighton, mentioned in a previous book titled: *Paper & Stone, A Leighton History in England & the United States.*

This Lady Anne Knollys married Sir Thomas West and amongst their children record-ed is (New World) Royal Governor John West [1590-1659], born in Hampshire, England and died at West Point Plantation, Va. This John West and his wife Ann had a son Colonel John West around the year 1632. This John West [1632-1691] married Unity Croshaw and had amongst their children a Nathaniel West, who died after October 1723.

Before then, however, Nathaniel West married Martha Woodward and had daughter Unity West who grew up and married Captain Colonel William Dandridge [1689-1743].

This William Dandridge was a brother to Colonel John Dandridge II [1700-1756].

John Dandridge II was the father of Martha Washington Dandridge Custis Washington [1731-1802] Colonel John Dandridge II was a brother to Martha Washington's aunt Elizabeth Dandridge Wyatt [1703-1750]. Elizabeth Dandridge Wyatt's husband was Henry Wyatt [1685-1743] a great grandson to Reverend Haute *"Hawte"* Wiatt [1594-1638]. This Martha Washington is the wife of U.S. First President George Washington.

Henry Carey, [abt. 1525/26-1596] – son of Mary Boleyn and William Carey and brother of Catharine Carey Knollys, was on April 15, 1535 living at Syon, Isleworth, Middlesex when referred to as King Henry VIII's son. By 1545, Henry Carey was at age 19 living in King Henry VIII's household. His mother Mary and aunt Queen Anne Boleyn are half-second cousins once removed to Sir Thomas Wyatt the Younger. Henry is believed to have been an illegitimate child of King Henry VIII.

Initially, British genealogist Martyn Freeth, who passed away June 24, 2012, mentioned this connection in a letter and later sent an historical article with more information. The letter is as follows:

6:58 a.m., April 21, 2011

Hélène…. Turning now to the question of ancestors shared by QE I and Sirs Thomas Wyatt, I see two.

Sir Henry Heydon married a daughter of the first Sir Geoffrey Bullen. Their daughter Dorothy married Thomas Brooke, 8th Baron Cobham (died 19.7.1529). Their daughter Elizabeth married Sir TW senior (died 1541). Sir Gewoffrey B was great-grandfather of Anne, the Queen.

The other is a bit more remote. Richard Woodville / Wydeville, of Grafton, Northants (died Dec 1441) was grandfather of Elizabeth, wife of King E IV; while RW's daughter Joan or Matilda married in 1429 William Haut, of Ightham / Bishopsbourne. The line from there you will know.

I need to break off now; but hope to come back with other titbits.

Pip, pip,

Martyn.

❧ *The Rungs of Ladders* footnote:

Boleyn is sometimes known as *"Bullen."* Genealogist Martyn Freeth uses short-hand in his letter *"QE I,"* meaning *"Queen Elizabeth I." "RW"* is *"Richard Woodville." "Sir TW senior"* refers to Sir Thomas Wiatt – the Elder. Freeth's reference to *"King E IV"* is, of course, Edward IV, [1442-1483] King of England and of the House of York. A daughter of Elizabeth Woodville [Wydville or Wydeville] [1437-1492] was Elizabeth of York [Plantagenet] [1465-1503] was the wife of King Henry VII [Tudor] – the father of King Henry VIII. Freeth points as follows: An unknown woman marries Geoffrey Boleyn *"Bullen"* father of: → Elizabeth or Anne Boleyn or Bullen mother of: → Dorothy Heydon – Dorothy who married Thomas Brooke, 8th Baron of Cobham; Dorothy Heydon Brooke mother of: → Elizabeth Brooke [b. 1503] who marries Sir Thomas *"The Elder"* Wiatt. Geoffrey Boleyn [1406-1471] married an Anne Mary Hoo [1424—1484] parents of: → Sir William Boleyn [1451-1505] → father of: Thomas Boleyn *"Bullen"* 1st Earl of Wiltshire b. 1477 → father of: *Queen Consort* Anne Boleyn, 2nd wife of King Henry VIII. So, Geofrey Boleyn is indeed the great grandfather of Queen Anne and of Elizabeth Brooke Wiatt – mother of: → Sir Thomas Wiatt, the Younger: father of: → Sir George Thomas Wiatt [1554-1624] father of: → the two Wiatt brothers who traveled to Jamestown, Va. one being Royal Governor Sir Francis Wiatt [Wyatt] and the other Rev. Haute Wyatt.

The following brief sketch clarifies this tangled genealogical web.

Sir Thomas Wiatt – the Younger son of: → Elizabeth Brooke Wiatt [wife of Sir Thomas Wiatt, the poet] daughter of: → Dorothy Heydon Brooke [wife of Thomas Brooke] daughter of: → Elizabeth or Anne Boleyn [wife of Sir Henry Heydon "Haydon" "Hayden"] daughter of: → Unknown Wife & Sir Geoffrey Boleyn son of: → Sir Thomas Boleyn & Anne Jane Bracton

Queen Elizabeth I daughter of → Consort Queen Anne Boleyn [2nd wife of King Henry VIII] daughter of: → Lady Elizabeth Howard, Countess of Wilshire & Thomas Boleyn [1477-1538/39] --1st Earl of Wiltshire & Ormonde son of: → Lady Margaret Ormond Butler & Sir William Boleyn [1451-1505] son of: → Sir Geoffrey Boleyn [1406-1471] [& 1st wife: Anne Mary Hoo [1424-1484]

Sir Geoffrey Boleyn's 2nd unknown wife had a daughter named: Elizabeth or Anne Boleyn who married Sir Henry Heydon "Haydon" "Hayden" & had a daughter named:

Dorothy Heydon, wife of Thomas Brooke & had a daughter named Elizabeth Brooke, who became the wife of: Sir Thomas Wiatt, the Elder and mother of the Younger.

Incidentally, Dorothy Heydon Brooke's son George Brooke [brother of Elizabeth Brooke Wiatt] had a daughter named Elisbeth Brooke, who married William Parr, 1st Marquess of Northampton – making Dorothy Heydon Brooke's grand-daughter Elisabeth Brooke Parr a sister-in-law of Catharine Parr, King Henry VIII's 6th wife/queen.

Sir Thomas Parr father of: → William Parr, 1st Marquess of Northampton, husband of Elisabeth Brooke [1526-1565]

Sir Thomas Parr is the father of: → Katherine Parr, the 6th wife of King Henry VIII. Katherine was a widow twice before she married King Henry Tudor VIII [1491-1546/47]. Death dates found in historical articles for Katherine Parr are September 5, 1548 at Whitehall Palace, London, England & January 28, 1547.

Refer to the Bolyen Section for more details.

♀ | | ♂

♀ | | ♂

Queen Consort Anne Bolyen Tudor [1501-1536] & her daughter
Queen Elizabeth I [Tudor] [1533-1603]

CHAPTER 12

Wyatts & the British Colony of Virginia

♀ | | ♂

PART 1. NOVA BRITANNIA

*I*N THE UNITED STATES THE identity of John Wiatt [1743-1815] has been a focus for years. Some claim him as the son of Elizabeth Dandridge and Henry Wyatt. This Henry Wyatt was a great grandson of Rev. Haute [Hawte] Wyatt who lived and worked briefly in Jamestown, Va.

Rev. Haute Wyatt's descendants are found in Virginia and North Carolina and other states of the U.S. Some researchers may find information debatable in how some relatives are connected. For instance, one researcher who descends from Rev. Hawte Wyatt's son Edward, claims his ancestor Edward was the second son of Hawte Wyatt instead of the first as is claimed by others. In opposition to this assertion, I read on page 374 of *Adventurers of Purse and Person 1607-1625 and Their Families*:

* ***"EDWARD WYATT (Hautel) appears to have been the elder son, born about 1620 despite what was probably an error in listing the children of Haute Wyatt in an administration account, which named Edward as the second son."*** *

* *See footnote in back matter.

One controversy is such that George -- son of Rev. Hawte Wyatt is dismissed as having descendants -- but not by other groups who readily embrace George as their ancestor.

There is another group -- one from Kentucky that suggests possibly my ancestor John Wiatt [1743-1815] as theirs -- but as tying in with their clan, which most likely ties in with those first Wyatt brothers Rev. Haute Wyatt and Royal Governor Sir Francis Wyatt -- sons of Sir George Wyatt [Wiat, Wiatt] of Allington Castle and Boxley Manor in Kent County, England.

In regard to assertions that George was the eldest, the inclination is disbelief -- *but it makes not one bit of difference as to what I believe* -- but what I read, and in this book the intent is to shape the information into some sort of understandable form that might inspire readers and researchers to continue to dig. The quest is to at least inform you as to the information we have in which to work.

In a letter dated July 25, 1621, word of Hawte's appointment as minister was sent to the Colony of Virginia.

One very important book mentioned earlier titled: *Adventurers of Purse and Person 1607-1625 and Their Families* has a section on the earliest Wyatts of Virginia. It quotes various documents, and from this the following: A letter dated July 25, 1621:

> **"We have sent you Sir Francis Wyatt to be the future Governor...and likewise sent you two sufficient preachers, Mr. Haute Wyatt who is to be the Preacher of the Governor's tenents & Mr. Bolton whom we have consigned to Elizabeth City."**

It is recorded in *Adventurers of Purse and Person 1605-1625 and Their Families* that less than six months after Rev. Haute Wyatt [Wiat] took over his position in Virginia -- *"the massacre occurred, but Jamestown having been warned in time, the Governor, his entourage and settlers there escaped the holocaust."* pg. 372-373.

A census [referred to as a muster] recording the inhabitants of Virginia [minus the Native Americans] began on January 20 and continued until February 7, 1624/1625. This was done while Gov. Francis Wyatt served. This archive is in England in the *State Papers of the British Public Record Office.*

This assessment of population and goods and properties was put together when Charles I was reigning, and Royal British government had decided to abrogate or abolish the Charter of the Virginia Company and bring the affairs of the Virginia Colony under control of the British Crown.

The U.S. Government Printing Office has published four volumes of *The Records of the Virginia Company of London.* The University of North Carolina at Chapel Hill keeps in its Davis Library copies of these – volumes 1, 2 and 4 in the stacks and volume 3 via special request. Volume I [1619-1622] titled: *THE COURT BOOK, "AT A COURTE HELD YE 16: OF July 1621* on page 516 of volume 1, it is mentioned the brother of Sir Francis Wyatt, which is, of course Rev. Haute Wyatt.

Rev. Haute Wyatt appears in these records as a person then being considered for the job of minister of Jamestown or James City, as it was also known. The record is, as stated earlier via the record title, from July 16, 1621, and Rev. Haute Wyatt began officially as minister there on November 18, 1621 as the date he arrived on the vessel called: *The George.*

Here is a quote minus the sub and superscripts from volume 1 page 516. Take into consideration there are no consistent spellings it seems in the English language of the time. In one quote Francis is referred to as *"Wyat"* and here as *"Wyatte."* – *"courte"* with and without an *"e,"* *"very"* as *"verie,"* *"entertained"* as *"entertayned,"* *"entertain"* as *"enterteine,"* *"surgeons,"* as *"chirurgeions"* or *"surgery"* as *"chirurgery"* or *"chest"* as *"chyest"* or *"we have"* as *"wee haue,"* *"whole"* as *"wholl," "April"* as *"Aprile,"* etc. Sir Francis Wyatt is referred to in such records as *"Sr ffraun-cis Wyat."*

- *A Dictionary of the English Language* was published April 15, 1755 and compiled and written by Samuel Johnson. It is sometimes referred to as *Johnson's Dictionary*. It was written in response of dissatisfaction with the dictionaries of the time period. A group of London booksellers contracted the task with Johnson in 1746, and it took him nearly nine years to complete it. He claimed originally he could finish it in three years. *The Oxford English Dictionary* was not completed until 173 years later.
- The first English language dictionary was published in 1604 by a Robert Cawdrey. A man named Thomas Blount published an English dictionary in 1656, but one can discern there were many inconsistencies in spellings in everyday documents and papers during these time periods. In the United States, Noah Webster [1758-1843] compiled and wrote an English dictionary that became a best seller. His first dictionary was titled: *A Compendious Dictionary of the English Language w*as published in 1806.

Sr Fraunces Wyatte entertained for Mynister

Itt was signified that Sir Frauncis Wyatte brother beinge a Mr of Arte and a good Divine and very willinge to goe wth him this present Voy-adge, might be entertayned and placed as Mynister ouer his people and have ye same allowance towards the furnishinge of himselfe wth necessaries as others have hadd, and that his wife might have her transporte freed, wch mocon was thought verie reasonable and ordered by ereccon of hande that hee should be entertayned and haue the place hee desyred and the same ‖ like‖ allowance of monny graunted vnto mr Bolton lately entertayned.

Volume II [1622-1624] is what is titled: *The Court Book*. In this volume 2, *"A COURT HELD FOR VIRGINIA ON WEDNESDAY IN YE AFTERNOONE THE 21ST OF APRILL—1624"* a list of those present is given on page 518 of the bound records. The record on page 519 records that a letter from the Royal Governor Francis Wyatt or Wiatt was read. The reference to the George it is assumed is the vessel or ship by this name.

As recorded on page 519 of volume 2, a section of such a note is indicated below transcribed in the English of that time minus the sub and super type. Its purpose in *The Rungs of Ladders* is to mention that his name [Sir Francis Wyatt] appears in this reference volume of the Virginia Company of London's records. If you care to see this in its entirely, you have the source name.

As recorded on page 519 of volume 2:

Mr. Deputy acquainted the Court hee had received by the George lately Returned from Virginia a Packett of lers: enclosed in a Box, Wch beinge dyrected to the

Earle of Southampton Treasuror hee sent to his LoP: wch his LoP: haveinge pvsed had returned back vnto him: Since wch time noe Courts had been kept in regaurd of this buissie time of Parlyament, and for that little or noe occasion till now, was offered of ballinge a Court. Whervppo ye generally letter from the Gouernor and Counsell of Virginia vnto the Company here was read: bearinge date At Iames Citty the 29: of Ianuary—1623.

Next was read a letter from Sr ffrauncis Wyat the present Gouernor Of Virginia dated att Iames Citty the Second of ffebruary 1623 breiflie Relatinge the manner of proceedinge against the Saluages in divers Places and by what Commanders the service was pformed; And hopeth in the general Assembly now called in Virginia some good order wilbe taken to maynteyne an Army for securinge of the wholl Collony.

Volume III of *The Records of The Virginia Company of London,* as edited by Susan Myra Kingsbury, A.M., Ph.D. of Bryn Mawr College in 1933 has transcribed in the English of the time period. The letter is signed from Sir Edwin Sandis, Gibbs, Wrote, Worth, et. al. beginning on page 485 of the bound records of this volume.

It is dated July 25th, 1621. As mentioned earlier, the purpose here is to quote the source, and for further reading you may run to a library that holds in its treasures these volumes. This quote is minus the sub and super scripts.

...We haue sent youe (Sir Francis Wyatt) to be the future Governor, to whom we require all respect and obedience be given. Mr. Sandys we haue elected or Treasuror, and Stated his place, and given him authority to see and cause all or orders concerninge staple commodities to be putt in executon.... Wee haue likewise sent youe two sufficient preachers: mr. Haut Wyatt; who is to be Preacher to the Governors Tennts: and mr Bolton, whom we have consigned to Elizabeth Citty, to inhabit wth Capt Tho: Nuce to whom we recommend him, vndrstandinge that mr Stockton is otherwise seated. And for supply of the Phisitions place wee haue sent youe Doctor Pott, wth two Chirurgeions and a Chyest of Phisicke and Chirurgery; not doubtinge but youe will enterteine and supplie him well att his landinge, wth all necessaries and accordinge vnto the Companies promise, giue him helpe for the speedy buildinge of a house imediaely vppon his arivall...

According to an account recorded in *Adventurers of Purse and Person 1607-1625 and Their Families* [Adventurers refers to stockholders, and later planters who settled the colony of Virginia] – a vessel called the Southampton arrived in Virginia March 4, 1623/24. It brought with it a

"commission authorizing Captain John Harvey, John Pory, Abraham Peirsey and Samuel Matthews" to gather information on the exact and then current *"state of the Plantation in diver points."*

[page 3, *Adventurers of Purse and Person 1607-1625 and Their Families*].

While Captain Harvey visited the Colony of Virginia gathering answers to such questions as:

- ❧ *"How many several plantations there be public and private?*
- ❧ *What people, men, women and children be in each plantation?*
- ❧ *What houses?*
- ❧ *What cattle?*
- ❧ *What corn?*
- ❧ *What fortications?*
- ❧ *What arms, etc.*
- ❧ *What boats?"*

he was met with embittered or resentful colonists regarding this Royal decision. Surrendering their constitutional rights afforded to them through the generous guidelines of the Virginia Company most likely seemed outrageous and an arrogant stomping upon their good works.

Ultimately, the Virginia Assembly, before it was disbanded, May 1624 was required to enable commissioners to take this assessment of the then current state of the Virginia colony and transport them from one plantation to the next in order to perform this work.

When the January 1625 census [muster] was done 1,232 inhabitants were recorded. Precision is lacking for those people who traveled to the Virginia Colony from the years 1607 to 1624. Records are reported to be incomplete. A fair estimate would, according to *Adventurers of Purse and Person 1607-1625 and Their Families*, place the number of inhabitants since 1607 between 7,100 and 7,200.

It is believed and reported that roughly one-seventh of an estimated 7,200 colonists from 1607 to 1624 survived. Certainly, they endured the harsh travel of the time crossing the ocean in vessels that were unsanitary and overcrowded. Without doubt, the weather conditions during summer months were humid and hot as compared to what they might have been accustomed to in England.

The stockholders invested in the settlement of the colony mentioned in the first, second and third charters from 1607 to 1625 is reported at less than 1,000 -- nine hundred is the approximate number supplied in *Adventurers of Purse and Person 1607-1625 and Their Families* [1964 edition].

The Royal government succeeded or followed this Virginia Company on June 26, 1624. The census of 1625 of the colony enabled the British Crown to gain information on all settlements there. The census in 1625 supplies the name of each colonist. It gives the location of home, number of family members, properties regarding livestock, ammunition, houses, etc.

Adventurers of Purse and Person 1607-1625 and Their Families identifies 109 individuals who either 1) Came to the Virginia colony from 1607 to 1625 and had descendants; or 2) who did not come to the colony between 1607 to 1625 – but *"whose grandchildren were residents there as immigrants to Virginia"* [xv]

"The descendants of each of the 109 individuals are presented through three generations, bringing the history of the family of that individual through the 17ᵗʰ century." [xv, front matter pages of *Adventurers of Purse and Person 1607-1625 and Their Families.*]

What is pointed out directly by the editors of *Adventurers of Purse and Person 1607-1625 and Their Families* is President Thomas Jefferson's genealogical connections – Christopher Branch, recorded as living in Henrico County in 1625, had a granddaughter Martha Branch who married the great grandfather of President Thomas Jefferson and carried his same name –Thomas Jefferson. This is all well and good, but what about Jamestown connections to the Wyatts – even those by marriage?

John West is recorded in this census – his lifespan being 1590-1659. He was the 12ᵗʰ child of Sir Thomas West, who in title was the second Lord De La Warr and his wife Lady Anne Knollys, daughter of Sir Francis Knollys and his wife Catherine Cary. This Catherine or Katherine Cary or Carey Knollys [Abt. 1524-Abt. 1568] was one of the children of or daughters of William Carey and Mary Boleyn [1499-1543] – Mary being a sister of Queen Consort Anne Boleyn [1501-1536] – second wife of King Henry Tudor VIII.

Refer to The Boleyn and Tudor sections for more details.

2) On the British 1623 census, Rev. Haute [Hawte] Wyatt is listed, but his wife and children are not, so it is speculative they did not accompany him to Virginia. Haute and his brother Francis returned to England from Virginia in 1626 after they had been called to do so and after the demise of their father George in 1624. Haute settled back in at Boxley. There his wife gave birth to a third son in October 1626. This infant died soon after. Haute married again in 1629 Ann Cox who gave birth to two children before she died in February 1631. In 1632, Haute lived at Boxley, where he was Vicar. He lived there with his mother Lady Jane Finch and his children until he died in July 1638. He left no will.

3) Haute's mother appeared in the Archdeaconry Court of Canterbury on October 26, 1638. There, she petitioned for the administration of the estate of her son Haute Wyatt.

Quote page 373 of *Adventurers of Purse and Person 1607-1625 and Their Families:*

"In the administration accounts filed by Lady Jane, rent due to Sir Francis Wyatt of Boxley was listed and also money paid out in behalf of Haute Wyatt's children namely: George, age 19; Edward, age 17; John, age 10; Ann, aged 7."

A very important notation appears as a footnote in *Adventurers of Purse and Person 1607-1525 and Their Families*: It is quoted from the Parish Register mentioned in *The History of Boxley Parish*.

It states as follows:

"The names and ages of the two elder sons appear to have been reversed, as information hereafter indicates Edward (b. 1620) was the elder."

Furthermore, the book titled: *Adventurers of Purse and Person 1607-1625 and Their Families* emphasizes on page 374 that Edward Wyatt, son of Haute Wyatt

"...appears to have been the elder son, born about 1620 despite what probably was an error in listing the children of Haute Wyatt in an administration account, which named Edward as the second son. This is borne out by a claim of his descendants in Virginia to 'Boxley' in England when the Wyatt line through Sir Francis became extinct."

Adventurers of Purse and Person 1607-1625 and Their Families furthermore states Edward Wyatt is first mentioned in Virginia records as *"Edwin Wyatt"* is declared headright in a land patent issued September 29, 1643 to his uncle Sir Francis. Edward had apparently come to the Virginia Colony when Gov. Francis Wyatt was sent a second time as Governor of Virginia in 1639. George Wyatt probably came as well with his uncle on the second trip to Virginia

"for he purchased along with George Lake, 12 April 1642, 400 acres in James City County and the land was divided 4 October 1645. He was living in York County in 1661 at which time mention was made of his land, and he died prior to 15 January 1671/72 at which time 'Henry Wyatt, son and heir of George Wyatt of Middle Plantation, deceased, sold to Colonel John Page 50 acres...George married probably Susanna _____." page 375.

The term *"headright"* simply refers to evidence as to right to land. People who came to the Virginia colony after the year 1616 -- arrived after either crossing the sea or from another settlement, and they were entitled to 50 acres of land. Those arrivals that came by or before the year 1616, were entitled to 100 acres of land in their own names or in the names of those whom paid for them to travel. Such was made possible by the Virginia Company because it was trying to inspire people to relocate to the colony.

Interestingly enough, headrights were issued or granted in the names of nobility, gentry, indentured servants and Negroes. Also, headrights in a land patent did not consistently arrive in the colony the same year the patent was issued. The dates of such patents are clues to first appearances in Virginia, though. Claimants to land were asked to show a receipt that passage was paid by them regardless if the payer arrived later.

A mural monument at Boxley is placed in memory of the members of the Wyatt family. It names Rev. Haute Wyatt and states he had *"issue now living in Virginia."*

According to a book titled: *The History of Boxley* by J. Cave-Brown, Maidstone, 1892, pps. 117 & 171, the Rev. Hawte Wyatt accompanied his brother Sir Francis Wyatt to Virginia on a vessel called the Georgia on Nov. 18, 1621. The ages of his children given in the Archdeaconry Court of Canterbury, Accounts, Box 3 were used in this compilation to calculate approximately birth years. *The History of Boxley* states referring to two of Hawte's children -- George and Edward:

"From these two brothers descend the numerous Wyatts of Virginia."

An inscription is located at Boxley Church, Kent County, England, to the Wiatt family.

It states:

"Rev. Haute Wyatt died Vicar of Boxley Parish, and that he had issue living in Virginia."

On pages 228 to 229 of Volume IV of *The Records of the Virginia Company of London* are notes made from letters, which arrived in England from Virginia in a vessel called the *"Abigail."* They are labeled: *"The Manchester Papers"* numbers 338, 339, Document in Public Records Office, London, England List of Records no. 523. *"lre"* refers to *"letter."*

June. 19. 1623....

1. **The Lady Wyatts lre to her Mother] that she is recouered of her sicknes&c That they prouisions there at unreasonable rates and not good. This yeare we liue hard by reason of the Indians and gett little or no meate for we canot send out vnder 4 or 5 and they we out 2 or 3 dayes and gett so little it is not worth their labour. We lack about ...and most of these are dead this Winter. Here hath ben a generall death of men and Cattle but now I thank [God]... it is ceased. We want all almost three partes of or men: And if we receaue not or due of them how can they looke for anything from him: or kine are we haue to liue on and or garden wch we haue none but I am about one: All the last Sumer Mr Wyatt lay sick &c**
2. **Sr Francis Wyatts lre to his father George Wyatt Esqre dat 4 Ap. 1623 Jams City sayes, Mrs Boyse reporteth of a great deal of miserie that or people endure and not least Hunger in whch th' Indians also suffer extreame....**

♀ | | ♂

♀ | | ♂

PART 2.
SATURDAY
MAY 17, 2014
JOURNAL ENTRY

My eldest son who graduated May 11th of 2014 with a double major – Bachelor' of Science degree in Physics and Chemistry, respectfully, skillfully and carefully lugged across campus these four volumes from the Davis Library at UNC-Chapel Hill in April 2014.

- *The Records of The Virginia Company of London, THE COURT BOOK, FROM THE MANUSCRIPT IN THE LIBRARY OF CONGRESS*, volumes 1-2;
- *The Records of The Virginia Company of London, Volume 3, Documents I.*
- *The Records of The Virginia Company of London*, Volume 4.

His legwork is a Godsend. My back is forever indebted. The pages are brittle. They do, however, contain necessary examples that reflect as well the language of the time.

Although the father of English literature Geoffrey Chaucer lived from about 1343 until October 25, 1400, some 200 plus years prior to those adventurers to Jamestown, Va. in the 1620s – even the smallest familiarity of the English spoken then will help readers discern these English records of the 1600s.

♀ | | ♂

CHAPTER 13

The Park-Wyatt-Bean Graveyard

♀ | | ♂

THE REMAINS OF RACHEL EVELYN Wyatt Morgan [wife of John Morgan] are buried at Luther's Lutheran Church formerly called Piney Woods -- Lutherans used it, and the primitive Baptists used it -- alternated Sundays.

The remains of Rachel Evelyn Wyatt's parents, however, are buried in a graveyard called the Park-Wyatt-Bean Graveyard. Rachel's father was Noah Calvin Wiatt [1805-1871].

Several years ago, having attempted to cross on foot a field my father planted in soybeans and getting stuck in muddy areas, I decided to make the trip again. This time, the same field was planted in corn. The ground was dry.

Corn leaves and husks touched the bordering rows and bowed only momentarily by an intermittent wind. Rare breezes offered little mercy to the thirsty, overheated, itchy or phobic. I carried a pad of paper, camera, pencils, pens.

My feet marked the way as if on a balance beam – which was the narrow path between the rows. Leaves from the corn husks and stalks were rough like sandpaper. My father – clad in long sleeves and sunhat, pushed them gently like little swinging doors.

"When will we reach the graveyard, Daddy?"

A few moments passed, and there we stood where the end of the corn rows reached the edge of the forest.

"So, where is this Park-Wyatt-Bean Graveyard?"

"It's in there," he pointed.

We stood motionless. Resting, *yes.* I was eyeing the white snares woven by critters no one really cares to meet. This covered the spaces between branches like closed doors -- some like hammocks and trapezes.

My father smiled and said:

"We spray, but it does nothing to arachnids."

The scratchy-itchy husks were like poison ivy and sumac in disguise. What difference would it make? A few eight-legged critters? As long as I did not see a fat, juicy one with hundreds of eyes or *fangs* – I would concentrate.

Just inside the *Park-Wyatt-Bean Graveyard* were grave stones riddled between trees, roots and leaves.

"Mind you don't fall in there," my father said, pointing to a six-foot pit, adding he once fell into it as a little boy. He climbed out rather quickly, running home as it was getting dark. Through the canopy of treetops only the smallest bits of blue and fuzzy light shown.

Walking about, he showed me the stone of Noah Calvin Wiatt. Noah's stone is the 4th stone from the right on the first row.

Words on stone:

"--- OF WIATT of Feb. 3 1805 DIED -- of March 1871 -- Aged 66 yrs. I mos. -- 26 days."

Rachel's mother's [Mary Polly Hendly [Henly] [1806-Abt. 1861] remains are also in this historical cemetery.

It is located at the third stone from the right. The stone is engraved with the following words:

"SACRED POLLY WIATT Was born Jan. 5th, 1806 AND Died About 1861."

The stone is located around 100 feet from a field my father plants alternatively in corn and soybeans.

Also buried in this family cemetery are the remains of Rachel Wyatt Morgan's paternal grandfather Thomas Wiatt [Wyatt] [1774-1845]. In some records, such as his marriage bond recording his union with Rachel Park there are discrepancies in spelling, such as:

"Thomas Wiett" marrying *"Rachel Parks"* on January 12, 1793 and the document being witnessed by a Jordan Wiett.

This Thomas Wiatt or Wyatt is referred to as *"Tommey Wyatt"* by John Thomas Wyatt [1851-1933], known as a columnist /newspaper writer whose personal notes are stored in a collection in the History Room at Rowan Public Library in Salisbury, N.C.

In these papers *Venus of Faith* – John Thomas Wyatt, claims in his own handwriting to descend from Thomas' father John Wiatt [1743-1815] whose remains are buried at the Lick Creek Baptist Church Cemetery in Davidson County, N.C.

Venus of Faith, who is discussed in other areas of this Wyatt history, claims his Wyatt ancestry as beginning with himself: John Thomas Wyatt [1851-1933] son of: → Wilson Riley Wyatt [b. 1830-1862] who is the son of: → Jesse *"Jessey"* Wyatt [1800-1860] son of: → John Wyatt, Jr. [d. 1819] son of: → John Wiatt, Sr. [1743-1815]. Venus of Faith in his hand written notes refers to John Wiatt, Sr. as *"Old Johny Wyatt"* as being the father of his great grandfather John Wyatt, Jr.

The point is that John Wiatt, Jr.'s brother Thomas Wiatt [Wyatt], the father of Noah Calvin Wyatt [1805-1871] is buried in the Park-Wyatt-Bean Graveyard. Thomas Wiatt [1774-1845] was married to Rachel Park [referred to in public records as Rachel Parks, Rachel Parke] [1774-1850]. She is a daughter to Joanna *"Ann"* *"Anna"* *"Anny"* Reed [1746-1833] and Noah Park, Sr. [1742-1815].

Part of the original 690 acres owned by Noah Park, Sr. [1742-1815] [father-in-law to Thomas Wiatt] was used to start the Park-Wyatt-Bean Graveyard. It is located off of the Bringle Ferry Road in the eastern section of Rowan County, N.C. on Cedar Creek.

One hundred and four point five acres of the original tract from a land grant is the portion owned by my family today. It was part of the stomping grounds my father explored with his siblings, cousins and uncle while growing. Noah Park, Sr. [1743-1815] by the way, fought in the American Revolutionary War -- also called: The American War of Independence, [1775-1783]. During this time, Noah served as a guard at Salisbury District Gaol, 1778. [Listed on the tax list for Berger District in 1778.]

The word, *"Gaol"* refers to *"jail."*

There are several means of service in the Revolutionary War. One way was to serve in the Continental Army for the duration of the war. Another way was to serve in the militia for three month terms. Another way was to donate goods [1 horse and 3 bales of hay, etc.].

Noah was supposedly born in King George County, Va.; however, New Jersey is claimed as being an area in which he was either born or lived. While in New Jersey, he obtained a land grant for the 690 acres.

Noah Park, Sr. is the original owner of the land on which the Park-Wyatt-Bean Graveyard is located. Noah Park, Sr. is reportedly to have served in the Rowan County, North Carolina Militia in the French and Indian War in 1760 and in 1763.

The Park family ties in with the Wyatts and the Morgans. The visual of rungs and ladders begin resembling the weaves of a homemade pot-holder. The father of Noah Park, Sr.

[1742-1815 or 1820] was John Parke II [1703 or 1707-1758], born in Hopewell, Huntingdon, N.J., died in Hampshire County, Va. The validity of this story is not known for sure.

One day while sitting in my office over the garage and talking to my father on the telephone a bit of Park history was communicated.

"No one makes or gets you angry or upset, but yourself. You get yourself upset."

-- James Noah Hinson, M.D.

My father recollected:

"The father of Noah Park is said to have taken up residence on properties in New Jersey, where he was born.

"He lived there for years with his family without paying taxes or obtaining proper papers to show ownership of the land.

"He was approached by a man claiming to have purchased the land from its rightful owner.

"The father of Noah Park was annoyed by this man's persistence in trying to claim ownership to the land he believed was his property.

"Consequently, Noah Park's father is said to have 'tarred and feathered' the newcomer.

"Legal authorities in New Jersey placed a bounty of three hundred on Noah Park's father.

"This Park family moved to Virginia, where Noah Park's father is believed to have been bushwhacked around 1758 by Indians. Approximately eight years later, Noah Park's mother remarried in 1766."

To write and piece together a book on the Park [Parks, Parke] family is not part of the quest…*at the moment.* It makes, however, perfect sense to mention the Park family. As you will find in the back matter – many Park descendants not only tie in with Wyatts at this juncture, but in more ways than one might predict.

♀ | | ♂

James Noah Hinson, M.D. at the Park-Wyatt-Bean Graveyard, Rowan County, N.C.

CHAPTER 14

Genealogical Webs
John Wiatt [1743-1815]

♀ | | ♂

*Researchers cannot cram the feet of all John Wiatts of the same century into
the same boot. One is going to pinch and another will completely flop off. The
genealogist must search for the perfect fit given the discrepancies of the day.*

PART 1. HURDLES

*T*HE PREFERENCE IS TO BEGIN without discrepancies. It would be unfair, though,
not to address the differences. The intent is to inform. There are genealogical
researchers and family researchers who claim this John Wiatt [1743-1815] as being from
Tryon, Buncombe County, N.C. The John Wiatt under examination is the one whose son
Thomas has remains at the Park-Wyatt-Bean Graveyard.

There are researchers whose work hints they do not have enough information on John
Wiatt, Sr. or his sons to completely validate or confirm this connection. Such researchers
state there was a John Wyatt, born March 29 1772 in Tryon, North Carolina who died Feb.
24, 1869 in Cumberland County, Tenn.

Clarification is required....

Now, the John *"Johney"* Wiatt, *JR.* – a son of John Wiatt, Sr., -- Sr. being the one whose
remains are said to be buried at Lick Creek, was born in Davidson County, N.C. and died in
1819, or in 1813, according to Park research. He was married to Hannah Park [1770-1855],
who died in Rowan County, N.C. A child of this *John Jr.* Wiatt was Jessy Wyatt, a paternal
grandfather of John Thomas Wyatt – *"Venus of Faith"* columnist. What others doing this research may not be aware of is that Hannah Park, daughter of Noah Park, Sr. [1742-1815 or
1820] and Joanna *"Ann" "Anna" "Anny"* Reed [1746-May 22, 1833] was a sister to Rachel Park
[1774-1850] who married Thomas Wyatt [1774-1845] – the latter being the parents of Noah
Calvin Wyatt [1805-1871], among others.

These details distinguish this John Wiatt, Jr. from the other claimed from Tryon, N.C. How is John Wiatt [1743-1815] – whose remains are buried at the Lick Creek Baptist Church, connected? There are no doubts as to how he is connected to his descendants – *how they are linked together.*

The task is to properly identify him in records and to show him being someone's son! Certainly, many of the people he is connected to by blood and marriage have remained in Rowan County records. This difference is in being able to distinguish which Revolutionary War records in North Carolina simply belong to another John Wyatt with one remaining in Maryland that might be a match.

John Wiatt's tombstone at Lick Creek Baptist Church Cemetery, Davidson County, N.C.

♀ | | ♂

♀ | | ♂

PART 2. AUTHOR'S NOTES

"… there is the very strong suggestion this John Wiatt was the youngest son of Henry Wyatt and Elizabeth Dandridge."

On February 18th, 2007, I find at ancestry.com a military record listing a John Wyatt, born in Maryland, then a resident of Alby, who worked as a carpenter and had *"accidental marks scar cut in the right knee."* This listing for a John Wyatt is found in **Muster and Pay Rolls of the Revolutionary War, 1775-1783.**

"New York Line -- 1st Regiment

Captain John H. Wendell's Company. We the Subscribers have Severally inlisted ourselves as Soldiers in the Continental Army for the Defence of the United States of America in Captain John H. Wendall's Company of Colo Goose Van Schaick's Regiment Raised for that purpose to serve in said Army during the present War, and we do Respectively Bind ourselves to conform in every Instance to such Rules, Laws & Regulations as are or shall be made for the ordering and Government of said Army."

This above tidbit is possible. I have yet to prove it. There is a handwritten statement by a John Thomas Wyatt known as *Venus of Faith* in his lifetime – that this John Wyatt [1743-1815] he descended from – the one whose remains are buried at Lick Creek, came from either Virginia or Maryland. Venus emphasized, though, his belief Maryland was more probable.

The John Wyatt listed in the *ROSTER OF SOLDIERS FROM NORTH CAROLINA IN THE AMERICAN REVOLUTION WITH AN APPENDIX CONTAINING A COLLECTION OF MISCELLANEOUS RECORDS,* ROWAN PUBLIC LIBRARY, Jo White Linn Collection, GENEALOGICAL PUBLISHING CO., INC. BALTIMORE 1972, however, <u>died in the year 1777 -- and is not one in the same as the John Wyatt</u> found in New York Line 1st Regiment and being born in Maryland.

Wyatt research on the Internet trees and compilations can appear authentic when one glances at the source list. The trouble with some sources cited is that often I can at this point in time October 15, 2014 weed out other John Wyatts who are connected, or are named in records – who are in fact <u>not one in the same</u> as this one at Lick Creek.

I can find citations on the Internet that are at face value *"proof"* but when examined *are in conflict* with other sources. This means they do not each time period back the other up. The search should recover at least three records or sources – the more, the better. If the record is too scant, then one must search for another record.

Many researchers are excited about this John Wiatt [1743-1815]. Their assertion does not dispute his connection. The bottom line is researchers cannot cram the feet of all John Wiatts of the same century into the same boot. One is going to pinch and another will completely flop off. The genealogist must search for the perfect fit given the discrepancies of the day.

Author's Notes:

February 18, 2007

On this same day, I find a *1790 U.S. Federal Census for Rowan County* listing in the second column of one page marked #310 in the first column and #311 in the second column -- a John Wyatt, Jr. Census records of this time period in Rowan County, N.C. do not seem to acknowledge females of households or children except in number. There are two small narrow columns in the second column of residents; however, the top portion of the census does not indicate what these numbers stand for. In the first column next to John Wyatt, Jr.'s name is the number one. The next column after this is blank, and the next column after this contains the number one.

The 1790 census is scant. It contains the heads of households – one being this John Wyatt Jun [Jun referring to *"Junior"* or *"Jr."*] referenced in my notes from 2007. His household is reported to have one free white male in the column labeled *"10 years and over."* Zero is listed in the column for *"Free White Males 10 and under"* and one is indicated in the column for *"Free White Females."* This Wyatt comes between the household of Thomas Williams and John Yont. There are no persons indicated for the columns *"All Other Free Persons"* and the column indicated for *"Slaves."* The John Wyatt Jr. who supposedly died in 1819 – had a son named William in the year 1790. This may be the same John Wyatt Jr. who is on the 1794 Rowan County Tax List of Capt. Davis along with a Nathan Wiatt as *"Wiatt, Nathan: 200 A, 1 WP."* Directly under him is Wiatt, Jordan: 1 WP; Wiatt, John Junr: 1 WP; Wiatt, John Senr: 300 A, 1 WP -- seemingly a match to our John Wiatt ancestor buried at Lick Creek. Wiatt, Thomas: 1 WP.

This information will be repeated again in this book. Also supporting the claim of John having a brother named Nathan in addition to the tax record is the 1790 Census record showing John Wyatt directly next to [just over him] Nathan who is indicated in his household to have two free white males 10 years and over; three free white males 10 years and younger and three free white females. They are not indicated as owning any slaves.

The 1790 U.S. Census for Rowan County [the first census by the *Department of Commerce & Labor*] contains two other heads of households of interest. One is a John Wyatt – spelled not as *"Wiatt,"* but as *"Wyatt."* This one has two white free males at least 10 years or over, three free white males 10 and under and five free white females. The remaining sections for other free person and slave columns are blank. John Wiatt [1743-1815] has four possible daughters and seven possible sons. We have approximate and more firm dates of birth for

Sylvester, Cecilia, Thomas, Elizabeth and Eli; however, birthdays for the others are not yet firmed up. So counting his wife and daughters there would be as indicated on the census five white females by the year 1790. Eli Wyatt was born around 1789, so one of these might be him. One of these males over age 10 might be his son Thomas Wiatt, born in 1774. Sylvester would be around 28 years old in the year 1790 and likely to be living on his own.

Several researchers claim John Wiatt [1743-1815] as coming directly from Virginia and being the youngest son of Henry [abt. 1685- abt. 1743] and Elizabeth Dandridge Wyatt [1703-1750] – Henry being a son of Sarah *"Sallie"* Peyton [b. 1665] & Richard Wiatt [1650 to about 1704] & Elizabeth being a daughter of Ann Dugale [1670-1731] & John Dandridge I [1655-1731].

The first time I saw this assertion or claim regarding John Wiatt, Sr. [1743-1815] being the son of Henry Wyatt and Elizabeth Dandridge was at *"Death Records Online"* myheritage. com.

More specifically:

http://dgmweb.net/FGS/W/WyattJohn-RachelHannah.html.

While there within my gut is the inclination to believe it – there is not enough evidence in my opinion to say if it is true or not. Deductive reasoning with the records we do have can be used, however. *With that, there is the very strong suggestion this John Wiatt was the youngest son of Henry Wyatt and Elizabeth Dandridge.*

♀ | | ♂

PART 3. DISCERNING HISTORICAL TRUTHS
How can this conclusion then be drawn?

One of the persons purported to have been a daughter to Elizabeth Dandridge and Henry Wyatt was a *"Mary,"* and a record from *Saint Peter's Parish*, New Kent County, Va. as a Mary being born Sept. 20, 1726. Many claim this Mary is one in the same as a Mary whose remains are buried in Warren or Bute, County, N.C. and having married in the year 1743 – the year John was born. [Warren County was formed from the northern half of Bute County in 1779. Warren County is between Vance and Halifax counties and borders Virginia to the north.]

A child named William Wiatt [1738-1802] is said to be buried at Lick Creek Baptist Church Cemetery in Davidson County, N.C. This William is said to have at least two sons Henry and Aaron – one of whom is buried in Wilkes County, N.C.

Another claim is that Henry and Elizabeth Dandridge Wyatt had a daughter named Abbey in 1732 and has her remains in Morgan District, Wilkes County, N.C. Wilkes County borders Iredell County to the north of the state.

The most profound assertion is a Nathan Wiatt, born in 1740 Churchill, Gloucester County, Va. and is said to be buried at *Lick Creek Baptist Church Cemetery* in Davidson County, N.C. While his actual grave has not been identified in that cemetery by this researcher [Hélène Hinson Staley] there are tax records showing a Nathan recorded specifically in the *"1794 Rowan County Tax List of Capt. Davis."* This is Nathan Wiatt as "Wiatt, Nathan: 200 A, 1 WP." Directly under him is

Wiatt, Jordan: 1 WP
Wiatt, John Junr: 1 WP
Wiatt, John Senr: 300 A, 1 WP -- a match to our John Wiatt ancestor buried at Lick Creek.
Wiatt, Thomas: 1 WP

Recorded in the *"1796 Rowan County Tax List"* on page 346 is the following:

Wyatt, Nathan: 200 A, 1WP
Wyatt, Thomas: 1 WP
Wyatt, John Junr. 1 WP

"WP" on tax list records for Rowan County means *"white pole."* This means that a tax was levied on a white male over 16 years of age. Males over the age of 16 years were taxable and eligible for the militia.

What can be asserted profoundly is that people including Wyatts 150 years ago in Rowan County, N.C. and those known to be connected to these Wyatts of Rowan County in question claimed publicly genealogical roots to Rev. Hawte Wyatt. Granted some pointed to his brother Royal Governor Sir Francis Wyatt, but Francis descendants died off in England. [I don't believe Francis has any living descendants today.]

Henry Wyatt and Elizabeth Dandridge are mentioned in family trees associated with Wyatt and Dandridge lineages and this Henry Wyatt [Abt. 1685-1743], son of Richard Wiatt [Abt. 1650-1704] son of: → George Wiatt son of: → Rev. Hawte Wyatt [Wiat] [1594-1638] son of: → Sir George *"Georgius"* Thomas Wiatt, Knt. [Abt. 1554-1624] son of: → Sir Thomas *"The Younger"* Wiatt [1521-1554] and so forth is in all probability connected to Henry Wyatt – the Henry [1685-1743] who married Elizabeth Dandridge, aunt of Martha Custis Washington, spouse of the United States First President George Washington.

On the internet site ancestry.com some claim our John Wiatt [1743-1815] as having been born in Staunton, Augusta, Va. Staunton is nicknamed the *"Queen City of the Shenandoah Valley,"* and was incorporated in 1871. Staunton is the county seat of Augusta County. It is known as the birthplace of the 28th President of the United States Woodrow Wilson. To date, the researcher and writer of this book has not found this claim valid.

Most of the children of Henry Wiatt [Aft. 1685-1743] and Elizabeth Dandridge [1703-Abt.1750] are thought to have lived in Gloucester County and in New Kent County, Va. Gloucester County, Va. was founded in 1651, named for Henry Stuart, Duke of Gloucester –third son of King Charles I of England. New Kent County was founded in 1654 and named for Kent, England.

Hélène,

There is listed four accounts of slaves belonging to Henry Wyatt/Wiatt in the 1684-1786 ***Vestry Book & Register for St. Peter's Parish*** in New Kent County, Virginia. They are as follows:

Page 405
Phillis a negro girle belonging to Mr. Henry Wyatt borne the 6 June 1700

Page 406
Name: negro belonging to Mr. Henry Wyatt borne ye 23 July 1702

Page 406
Peter negro son of Doxy, belonging to Mrs. Wyatt borne ye 7 November 1704

Page 448
Bess a negro woman of Henry Wyatts Dyed 11 of November 1724

Cousin
Billy Hinson

♀ | | ♂

There are genealogical posts via *WikiTree* that this John Wiatt. Sr. was the stepson of this aforesaid Henry Wyatt's supposed second wife Mary Wynne, born in 1708 Brunswick, Va., daughter of Peter Wynne and Frances Anderson; died Sept. 17, 1767, in Butte, N.C.

It is probable these are associated somehow; however, there is some uncertainty how. The first discrepancy in this *WikiTree* claim is this Henry Wyatt somehow was married to Mary Wynne, while if one considers she was having children for many years with the site's claimed Thomas Twitty – *it would be physically impossible.* The possibility that she was a second wife would be wrong according to Henry's supposed demise date of 1743, and Elizabeth's demise of 1750.

So, for the researcher speaking to you right now, one should not place much faith in the WikiTree claim as it stands in July and August 2014.

DNA testing would help resolve this matter, but it is already suspected with much certainty all these Wyatts and those who have Wyatt ancestors fit together somehow – just discovering exactly how is a bit tricky. One gets to a point where one can say:

*"Looks possible...**but maybe not exactly** as you want to believe."*

DNA testing calls into play laws that may prevent without direct consent publishing medical facts about those living without consent.

Most readers of this book have access to the Internet. Readers may wish to peruse countless computer screen pages of Wyatt research from researchers in the U.K. and the U.S. and possibly those bearing the surname *"Guyot"* from France.

The main point is that each of these internet reports are speaking of the same group of Wyatts connected with Rev. Hawte Wyatt whose sons Edward and George traveled with their paternal uncle Sir Francis Wyatt [1588-1644] in November 1639 to Virginia after their father Hawte's death [June 4, 1594-August 1638]. Their mother Barbara Elizabeth *"Eliza"* Mitford Wiatt [Wyatt] lived from 1598 until October 31, 1626. It is believed Edward and George came with their uncle when Francis was *to begin and serve* a second term as Royal Governor of the Virginia Colony.

Rev. Hawte Wiatt [Wyatt] [1595-1638] married twice and with his second wife had a son named John Wiatt [1630-1666]. This Captain John Wiatt traveled from England to Virginia in 1652 and claimed headright by Col. Thomas Pettus for land. The land was patented in Westmoreland County, Va. From Rev. Wiatt's son John there are descendants who traveled to the Albemarle Precinct, Perquimans area of North Carolina.

There will inevitably be discrepancies even though the quest is to discern such. Information published in *The Rungs of Ladders* on John Wiatt [1743-1815] in Rowan and Davidson counties is confirmed by matters of record.

Information quoted in this book regarding the earliest Wyatts of England and in the Virginia Colony is according to records and historical articles. Keep in mind records have discrepancies, and whenever noted or recognized they are pointed out.

A genealogical battle is not the quest. There are many on the Internet who are routinely curious about John Wiatt [1743-1815] – the John Wiatt, whose remains are buried at Lick Creek Baptist Church Cemetery in Denton, Davidson County, N.C. – the John Wiatt, who left in his *Last Will and Testament* two acres for the church to be built on. Without understanding the connections of Park, Morgan, Millers, Eagles – we would be completely lost. Perhaps, this book will assist these endeavors.

♀ | | ♂

Part 4. Proof of Records
John Wiatt
1743-1815
What we have is…

* September 25, 1778 land grant.
* Land Entry #1573 on 25 Sept 1778 is for 300 acres bordering James Story on both sides of Lick Creek and includes two improvements, one where John now lives, the other where George Story formerly lived. John obtained Land Grant #1786, dated 18 May 1789, for 300 acres on Lick Creek adjoining Moses Park and William Cole.
* *"1778 Rowan County Tax Lists,"* where he is listed as *"John Wiett"* under the heading: *"Capt. Cox's District"* with the number: *"110"* next to his name.
* His *"1784 Taxable Return of Cap: Runnions Co. A Lis. of the Taxable Property of the Inhabitants of Capt Runyons District, Rowan* County, North Carolina, Taken by William Cole for the year 1784.
* *"1794 Rowan County Tax List of Capt. Davis"* is a Nathan Wiatt as *"Wiatt, Nathan: 200 A, 1 WP."* Directly under him is *"Wiatt, Jordan: 1 WP, then Wiatt, John Junr: 1 WP; then: Wiatt, John Senr: 300 A, 1 WP and then Wiatt, Thomas: 1 WP."*
* *"1796 Rowan County Tax List"* on page 346 is the following -- Wyatt, Nathan: 200 A, 1WP; Wyatt, Thomas: 1 WP; Wyatt, John Junr. 1 WP
* 1790 Rowan County census - John Wyatt (entry #749)
* The *Last Will & Testament* of John Wiatt [1743-1815].
* His tombstone at the Lick Creek Baptist Church, Denton, Davidson County, N.C.
* Handwritten claims of *Venus of Faith* newspaper columnist and unique salve formula inventor John Thomas Wyatt [1851-1933].
* Several land surveys of John Wiatt's property.

On February 18th, 2007, I find at ancestry.com a military record listing a John Wyatt, born in Maryland, then a resident of Alby, who worked as a carpenter and had *"accidental marks scar cut in the right knee."* This listing for a John Wyatt is found in **Muster and Pay Rolls of the Revolutionary War, 1775-1783.**

The American Revolutionary Era began in 1763.

"New York Line -- 1st Regiment

Captain John H. Wendell's Company. We the Subscribers have Severally inlisted ourselves as Soldiers in the Continental Army for the Defence of the United States of America in Captain John H. Wendall's Company of Colo Goose Van Schaick's Regiment Raised for that purpose to serve in said Army during the present War, and we do Respectively Bind ourselves to conform in every Instance to such Rules, Laws & Regulations as are or shall be made for the ordering and Government of said Army."

* Clarification: This finding is included not to support that the John Wiatt buried at Lick Creek fought in the Revolutionary War – but that a document that might be his, or may not be his, was found. The point it is in contrast to the Revolutionary War record recorded for another John Wiatt in North Carolina – that man dying in 1777.

♀ | | ♂

Outside this list of paper and stone trails are those of his son Thomas Wiatt [1774-1845] and daughter-in-law Rachel *"Parks" "Park" "Parke."* Thomas Wiatt is mentioned in the Last Will & Testament of Noah Park, Sr., his father-in-law. Other records as well solidify John Wiatt – the one whose remains are at Lick Creek, is without doubt connected to Wyatts of Rowan County, N.C.

There are no doubts as to John Wiatt's presence in North Carolina and those of his son Thomas. Thomas's remains are buried in the Park-Wyatt-Bean Graveyard. Perhaps, such facts and matters of record will help other researchers say with more certainty how he may connect with Henry Wyatt, husband of Elizabeth Dandridge, the aunt of Martha Custis Dandridge Washington. This Elizabeth Dandridge should NOT be confused with Martha's sister Elizabeth Dandridge [1749-1800] who married twice – an Aylet and a Henley or Henly.

John Wiatt, born in 1743 -- died November 11, 1815, buried at the Lick Creek Baptist Church near what is today known as Denton, Davidson County, N.C., married a woman named Rachel. It is speculated that either her surname or middle name was *"Hannah."* There is as well some speculation that she had a daughter named *"Rachel."*

The land grant map done by Bert Lanier many years ago of the southern part of Davidson County reveals 300 acres to John Wiatt. It is dated 1778, numbered as 1786 and located on Lick Creek. It spans the creek. It includes the area where Lick Creek Baptist Church is located.

Lick Creek Baptist Church was organized in 1787. The church received land from John Wiatt on which to build the original church.

The remains of John Wiatt [1743-1815] are buried in the church cemetery.

His stone is inscribed:

JOHN WIATT, DEC'D NOV THE 11TH 1815. AGD 72.

Additionally, *Cemetery Records of Davidson County, N.C., vol. 2, Southern Section*, compiled by The Genealogical Society of Davidson County list as #9 of Row #14 of Lick Creek Baptist Church Cemetery this same information.

♀ | | ♂

PART 5.
SATURDAY
MARCH 31, 2012
SALISBURY, N.C.
JOURNAL ENTRY

To walk into the History Room at Rowan Public Library from the parking lot flanking Fisher Street the goal is:

1. Find more information on John Wiatt.
2. Find more information on John Wiatt
3. Find more information on John Wiatt and ….

The goal prompts each step. The warm Spring day continues while I sit with documentations – many handwritten by those who are certainly sipping tea with angels. Possibly, they wonder what is taking so long! I wish for a ghost visitation. It will not be easy. The man who willed land on which to build a church may certainly not visit me as a ghost and allow me to know it!

The land grant map mentioned earlier is supported by the *"1784 Taxable Return of Cap: Runnions Co. A List of the Taxable Property of the Inhabitants of Capt Runyons District, Rowan County, North Carolina,"* taken by William Cole for the year 1784. 85.706.1, North Carolina State Archives, Southern Davidson County area. This John Wiatt [Wyatt] is listed third from the top in the left-hand column as:

John Wiatt: 300 A, 1 WP.

On page 140 of the *"1778 Rowan County Tax Lists,"* there is a *"John Wiett."* listed under the heading: *"Capt. Cox's District" with the number:* "110" next to his name.

Recorded in the *"1794 Rowan County Tax List of Capt. Davis"* is a Nathan Wiatt as:

Wiatt, Nathan: 200 A, 1 WP.

Directly under this listing:

Wiatt, Jordan: 1 WP
Wiatt, John Junr: 1 WP
Wiatt, John Senr: 300 A, 1 WP -- a match to John Wiatt ancestor buried at Lick Creek.
Wiatt, Thomas: 1 WP

Recorded in the *"1796 Rowan County Tax List"* on page 346 is the following --

Wyatt, Nathan: 200 A, 1WP
Wyatt, Thomas: 1 WP
Wyatt, John Junr. 1 WP

On the Account of Delinquent Land & Poles for 1798 – also known as the Treasurer's and Comptroller's Papers, Box 78, County Settlements, North Carolina State Archives is listed a John Weyett: 1 poll.

♀ | | ♂

PART 6.
FEBRUARY 18ᵀᴴ, 2007
JOURNAL ENTRY

My fingers are tapping keys through Internet search engines. I arrive at ancestry.com. Before me, I see a military record listing a John Wyatt, born in Maryland, then a resident of Alby, who worked as a carpenter and had *"accidental marks scar cut in the right knee."* This listing for a John Wyatt is found in Muster and Pay Rolls of the Revolutionary War, 1775-1783.

"New York Line -- 1st Regiment

Captain John H. Wendell's Company. We the Subscribers have Severally inlisted ourselves as Soldiers in the Continental Army for the Defence of the United States of America in Captain John H. Wendall's Company of Colo Goose Van Schaick's Regiment Raised for that purpose to serve in said Army during the present War, and we do Respectively Bind ourselves to conform in every Instance to such Rules, Laws & Regulations as are or shall be made for the ordering and Government of said Army."

Is this the John Wiatt of Lick Creek?

I do <u>not</u> believe this one is one in the same – but I note him nevertheless and *just in case*. He might be. There are many John Wyatts using all of the variations of this name. Perhaps, this information may serve in this journey, and if not my own, some other researcher down the road. I keep waving and waiting for that researcher. Presently, though, he or she is on a separate journey and appears as a tiny dot even with binoculars.

Another soldier with the same name appears in....

ROSTER OF SOLDIERS FROM NORTH CAROLINA IN THE AMERICAN REVOLUTION WITH AN APPENDIX CONTAINING A COLLECTION OF MISCELLANEOUS RECORDS, ROWAN PUBLIC LIBRARY, Jo White Linn Collection, GENEALOGICAL PUBLISHING CO., INC. BALTIMORE 1972.

A John Wyatt is listed as #2323 having been received by Griffin Dauge. This John Wyatt listed in the roster died in the year 1777, so perhaps he is cousin to the John Wiatt buried at Lick Creek.

On this same day February 18, 2007 ....

I come across a 1790 U.S. Federal Census for Rowan County listing in the second column of one page marked #310 in the first column and #311 in the second column -- a

John Wyatt, Jr. Census records of this time period in Rowan County, N.C. do not seem to acknowledge females of households or children except in number. There are two small narrow columns in the second column of residents; however, the top portion of the census does not indicate what these numbers stand for. In the first column next to John Wyatt, Jr.'s name is the number one. The next column after this is blank, and the next column after this contains the number one. Maybe, this one is the son of our John Wiatt [1743-1815]. I believe it is.

♀ | | ♂

PART 7.
APRIL 2012
JOURNAL ENTRY

Gretchen Witt of the Rowan Public Library sends an envelope with several documents.

Abstract of Deed Books 11-14 of Rowan County North Carolina 1786-1797 [Jo White Linn Collection of the Rowan Public Library]. Highlighted is: *"1277."*

It states:

"p. 206 18 May 1789. State Grant #1786 @ 50 sh per 100 A to John Wiatt, 300 A on Lick Crk and Yadkin R adj Moses Park and William Cole."

Attached to it is faded chicken scratch of the day. It does not verify with documentation that he came from Virginia! If Virginia is mentioned, it is buried in this scratch, I cannot discern completely. Gretchen sends an attempted translation in anticipation. It is compared during the research of *The Rungs of Ladders* to the original document.

♀ | | ♂

Note from Gretchen Witt:

"This is my transcription of the beginning of the grant 1786. Much is formulaic. To my mind it does not name where John is from...Sorry."

Gretchen Witt's brief transcription of this Land Grant for Sept. 25, 1778:

State of North Carolina ' No. 1786. To all to whom those presents shall [ ]

Know ye that we in consideration of fifty shillings for ever hundred acres hereby paid into our Treasury by John Wyatt have given and granted and by this Do give and grant unto said John Wyatt a tract of Land containing three hundred acres lying and being in the county of Rowan on Lick creek the waters of the Yadkin River beginning at [???] sapling in Moses Parks line and with William Cole's line North sixty four [?] west forty five chains to...

© 2014, 2015, 2016 Translation of Land Grant by Gretchen Witt to John Wiatt prior to 2014 in the Rowan County Library's History & Genealogy Department, Salisbury, N.C. 28144

Below is my transcription of the original. It is transcribed beginning to end with the assistance of my father.

State of North Carolina No. 1786 to all to whom those presents shall come Greeting

Know ye that we fore and in consideration of the sum of Fifty Shillings for every hundred acres hereby Grant paid Into our Treasury by John Wyatt have given and granted and by this do give and grant unto this day John Wyatt a tract of Land containing Three hundred acres Lying and being in the County of Rowan on Lick creek the waters of the Yadkin River beginning at an oak sapling in Moses Parks line and with William Cole's line North Sixty four ....west forty five chains to [looks like apir or apen – possibly it is: *"to a pin"*] *thence North forty five* [indiscernible word looks like: *"inches"*] *to a post gate* [looks like *"the a foot"* or *"then a sot seven"*?] *by Eight Chains to a stake on said Coles line thence along his line south five chains and six tenth is a black oak Sapling his corner there east with said ...20... 80... a miory... ... South 5 ... N 50 links from there with _80 links to the beginning North of this...reserved....together with all woods, waters mines ...consisting....*

John Wyatt has here and also in forever....having... May from time to time...that the Said John Wyat Shall... this Grant to be...in the Reg is ...of our said county of Rowan... ... from the Date...of otherwise the farm [sum?] shall be Void and of ...Effect In Testimony Whereof within Cause ...our sellers take made ... and our ... Seal to the... ...this 18th day of May with XIIIIth year ...By His ....land S. [seal] John ....1786 ...John Wyatt 300 acres...Rowan County...Recorded in the Secretary Office....

© Copyright April 2014 as Land Grant for John Wiatt [Wyatt] transcribed and interpreted by Hélène Andorre Hinson Staley & James Noah Hinson, M.D., Metallo House Publishers, Moncure, N.C. 27559. All Rights Reserved. This transcription is according to the researcher; however, another partial transcription of this land grant maybe found via other sources.

* A chain is a unit of length. A chain measures 66 feet or 22 yards or 100 links or 4 rods, which is 20.1168 meters. A furlong, a measurement of distance in imperial units, is equal to 10 chains or 1/8th of a mile or 220 yards or 660 feet or 40 rods. Rods used by surveyors is a perch or pole and a unit measuring 5.5 yards or 16.5 feet or 1/320th of a statute mile. A rod is ¼ of a surveyor's chain. Imperial units – British Imperial units, is a system of units defined in the year 1824 by the British Weights and Measures Act. A statute mile is equal to 80 chains. An acre is the area of 10 square chains – the area of one chain by one furlong.

This September 25, 1778 land grant is mentioned in *Abstract of Deed Books 11-14 of Rowan County North Carolina 1786-1797 [Jo White Linn Collection of the Rowan Public Library]*. It is mentioned on page 206 for the date 18 May 1789. State Grant #1786 @ 50 sh per 100 A to John Wiatt, 300 A on Lick Crk and Yadkin R adj Moses Park and William Cole.

Land Entry #1573 on 25 Sept 1778 is for 300 acres bordering James Story on both sides of Lick Creek and includes two improvements, one where John now lives, the other where

George Story formerly lived. John obtained Land Grant #1786, dated 18 May 1789, for 300 acres on Lick Creek adjoining Moses Park and William Cole.

♀ | | ♂

State of North Carolina   No. 1573

James Brandon Entry Office of Chains
for Lands in the County of Rowan
To the Surveryor ...fair County Greeting

You are required as from as may be to lay off and Survey for John Wyatt a tract or parcel of Land containing Three Hundred Acres lying in the County aforesaid [one indiscernible words] James Storys Line on Lick Creek on both Sides of Said Creek including Two Improvements one of which he now lives on [in?] and the other that George Story formerly lived on.

Observing the Distinctions of the Act of Assembly in with [indiscernible] made and provided for farming Out Lands [indiscerible words] fair plans of each survey with a proper certificate [indiscernible word] to each you are to [indiscernible words -- transport?] this warrant to the Secretary's office without Delay.

Given under my Hand at Salisbury the Twenty Fifth Day of September Anno Dom 1778.

[indiscernible name]

© Copyright April 2014 as Land Grant #1573 dated September 25, 1778 for John Wiatt [Wyatt] transcribed and interpreted by Hélène Andorre Hinson Staley & James Noah Hinson, M.D., Metallo House Publishers, Moncure, N.C. 27559. All Rights Reserved. This transcription is according to the researcher.

Readers and researchers compare the Gretchen's translation and the Hinson/Staley transcription of it to the original handwritten document in further attempts to discern the writing. There is a difference between a translation and a transcription. A translation is an attempt to gain some meaning of what is said. A transcription is in this case the attempt of discerning it word for word. While reading these records, keep in mind North Carolina officially became a state of the United States on Nov. 21, 1789. By 1712, the Carolina Colony became separate colonies North Carolina and South Carolina. These colonies became royal colonies in 1729.

♀ | | ♂

PART 8.
6:41 P.M., SUNDAY
APRIL 13, 2014
JOURNAL ENTRY

I am sitting in my office over the garage with one hurt knee, one hurt third absent toe-nail and ankles that feel like those of an elephant. I hold pages from Will Book G, Rowan County, pages 453-454. Here too is the original – a photocopy of the original. God hears my prayers. I shrink at the thought of transcribing another will today [previously this morning Noah Park, Sr.'s will – this Noah being the father-in-law of Thomas Wiatt [1774-1845] – this Thomas Wiatt being a son of the John Wiatt. I suddenly recall I had transcribed his will a few years ago. Possibly, his ghost got my attention.

♀ | | ♂

The *Last Will & Testament* of John Wiatt [1743-1815] – the one buried at Lick Creek Baptist Church, is as follows:

Will Book, Rowan County, North Carolina, Mrs. Stahle Linn, Jr., regent; Elizabeth Maxwell Steele Chapter, Salisbury, North Carolina; Mrs. Noble Shumate, state chairman; page 269: Will of John Wiatt, Rowan County, North Carolina; Will Book G, pp. 453, 454; will probated in 1816; Testator: John Wiatt; Place: County of Rowan and State of North Carolina; Date: Fifth day of Nov. in the yr. of our Lord 1815; Beneficiaries: Wife, son, Eli; son, John; grandson, John Wiatt; son, James Wiatt; William Bean; Allen Wiatt; Silvester Wiatt; Granddaughter, Betsey Eston; Thomas Wiatt; Aszor Parks; Executors: Son, Wm Bean; son, Thomas Wiatt; Witnesses: Obed Parrish, David Cox.

The Last Will and Testament of
John Wiatt [1743-1815]
November 1815

In the name of [God,]... Amen. I John Wiatt of the County of Rowan and the State of N. Carolina, being very sick & weak in body but of Perfect mind and memory thanks be to ...[God]... for the same Calling to mind the mortality of my body and knowing that it is appointed for all men once to die do make and ordain this my last will and testament in the name and form following, that is to say, First of all, I will let my Just Debts and funeral layperson be paid out of my personal estate, further it is my will that my house hold furniture plantation tools with all Stock of Horses, Cattle, hogs sheep to my wife & son Eli Wiatt also Two Acres of land where the Lick Creek Meeting house now stands to the use of the Methodist & Baptist Church also all the Lands on the South side of the dry branch to my son John during his life and thence to my grand son John Wiatt after my son John dies -- also to my son James Wiatt one hundred acres on the North side

of S. dry Branch also all the rest of my lands I leave to my son Eli with my P. sons John Wiatt, James Wiatt & Eli Wiatt paying each the Sum of Forty Dollars to be equally Divided between William Bean, Allen Wiatt, Silvester Wiatt, Betsy Eston my grand daughter, Thomas Wiatt & Aazor Parks the P. money to be paid within Three years. I likewise Institute My faithful and well beloved Sons Wm Bean andThomas Wiatt my sole Executors of this my last will + testament revoking all other wills or Legacies register + Executors by me heretofore made ratifying & confirming this to be my last will & testament in Witness whereof I have my hand and seal this fifth day of Nov. in the yr. of our Lord 1815 Signed sealed & acknowledged in the presence of us –

Obed Parrish	X	His				
& David Cox		John	X	Wiatt	(Seal)	Seal
		Mark				

Children of John Wiatt & Rachel *"Hannah"*

* Allen Wiatt?
* Sarah *"Sally"* Wiatt
* Dempsey Wyatt
* Eli [Ely] Wyatt
* James Wyatt
* John Wyatt, Jr., born in Davidson County, N.C.; died 1819
* Rachel Wyatt
* Sylvester *"Silvester"* Wiatt
* Cecelia Wyatt
* Thomas Wiatt [Wyatt, Wiett] born 1774 in Rowan County, N.C.; died 1845; remains buried in the Park-Wyatt-Bean Graveyard, Rowan County, N.C.
* Elizabeth Wiatt, born in 1778; married a *"Park."*

In John Wiatt's will, he refers to *"…beloved sons William Bean and Thomas Wiatt my sole Executors…"* This is part of the language of the day. Just as in *Adventurers of Purse & Person 1607-1625 and Their Families* records of the Virginia Colony in the 1600s a nephew or niece may be referred to as *"cousins"* when in fact they are not.

The 1700s are not much changed in this respect. John Wiatt's will in 1815 refers to William Bean as a *"son"* when in fact he is a son-in-law. It is likely this William Bean is the William Bean [1754-1829; b. Londondairy, Northern Ireland; died in the Piney Woods District, Morgan Township, Rowan County, N.C.] is the husband of John's daughter Cecelia Wyatt – [est. birth 1761].

♀ | | ♂

In the name of God Amen I John Wiatt of the County
of Rowan and State of N: Caroline being very sick &
weak in body but of Perfect mind and memory thanks
be to God for the same calling to mind the mortality of
my body and knowing that it is appointed for all men
once to die do make and ordain this my last will and
testament in the name and form following that is to say,
     First of all I will let my Just Debts be paid out of
my personal estate, further it is my will that my house
hold furniture plantation tools with all Stock of Horses

also all the rest of my lands I leave to my Son Eli with my d. Sons John Hiatt, James Hiatt & Eli Hiatt paying each the Sum of Forty Dollars to be equally Divided be- tween William Bean, Allen Hiatt, Silvester Hiatt, Betsey Eston my grand daughter, Thomas Hiatt & Mazor Parks the d. money to be paid within three years, I likewise Institute My faithful & well beloved Sons Wm Bean and Thomas Hiatt my sole Executors of this my last will & testament revoking all other wills or Legacies registers & Executors by me heretofore made ratifying & conforming this to be my last will & Testament in Witness whereof I have my hind and seal this fifth day of Nov. in the Yr. of our Lord 1815. Signed sealed & Acknowledged in the presence of us –

Obed Parrish
David Bo

X

John ┼ Hiatt
mark

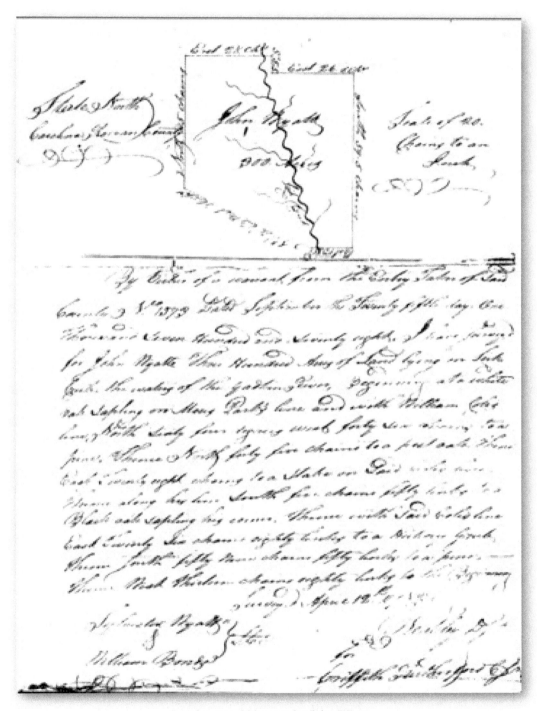

Land survey 300 acres for John Wiatt

♀ | | ♂

PART 9. DISCERNING IDENTITIES

A List of Taxable Property in the County of Rowan, North Carolina Anno 1778 from the August term of 1778 include *"John Wiett"* [Wiatt, Wyatt] in the Capt. Cox District being taxed 110 pounds. Included is a William Wiatt in the same district with a tax of 140 pounds and Ebenezer Park of the same district with a tax of 349 pounds. John Wiatt's son Thomas Wiatt was four years old in 1778, and 19 years after this tax recorded John's debt. *Rowan County, North Carolina Tax Lists, 1757-1800, Annotated Transcriptions,* Jo White Linn Collection, Davidson County Public Library also record this same information.

Likeforex.com on the Internet advertises a currency converter, which is updated every 15 minutes. According to its calculations, and as of August 11th, 2014, 110 pounds by today's U.S. dollar equivalent is $184.69; 140 British pounds sterling is as of today: $235.06 USD, and 349 pounds is equal to $585.96 USD. As of August 11th, 2014, one British Pound Sterling equals $1.6790 USD, so five British Pounds is equal to $8.3949 USD. Conversely, as of August 11th, 2014, one U.S. dollar is equal to 0.5956 British Pound Sterling. You are most likely reading this book in 2015 or after this time. Converters for British and U.S. currencies can be found online using a google search; however, the one used for this book is at www.likeforex.com/currency-converter/british-pound-sterling-gbp-usd-us-dollar.htm/349.

Thomas Wiatt [1774-1845] married into the Park family as did his brother John Wiatt, Jr. [d. 1819] in 1789 – John Wiatt, Jr. marrying Hannah Park [1770-1855] and Thomas marrying Rachel Park [1774-1815] – two daughters of Noah Park, Sr. [1742-1815] Rachel and Hannah Park's brother Noah Park, Jr. married a Joanna Peeler and had George Anthony Park [1808-1882] who married Hannah Hodge [Abt. 1813-1885] and had several children including William Alexander Park [Abt. 1831-1865] – the latter of whom is discussed in other parts of this book. William Alexander Park died as a POW June 7, 1865 during the War at Point Lookout, Md. William's mother Hannah Hodge [1813-1885] was a daughter of Ruhamah Palmer [1792-1840] and Jesse Hodge [1792-1864], brother of Joseph Hodge [b.1786] – the father of Agnes Nancy Hodge [1817-1880], wife of Solomon Eagle, Sr. [1811-1877]– whose son by the same name is mentioned in other parts of this book.

One can see from this example the families of Rowan, Davidson, Stanly and Cabarrus counties are strongly tied. Solomon Eagle, Sr.'s sister Sophia Eagle [1818-1888] married Jesse Hodge [1820-1890], brother of Agnes Nancy Hodge [1817-1980]. The offspring of Solomon Eagle, Sr. and his wife Agnes N. Hodge are double first cousins to the offspring of Sophia Eagle and Jesse Hodge.

In regard to this 1778 tax record, it could very well be that the William Wiatt [1738-Abt. 1802] listed at being taxed 140 pounds [when Davidson County was still in part Rowan

County before 1822] is the brother of John Wiatt, Sr. who is buried at Lick Creek Baptist Church Cemetery.

The *1791 Tax List of Capt. Enochs* [CRX 244, 1791], North Carolina State Archives for the Davie County area, which is just above [north] Rowan County and between Davidson and Iredell counties, has listed a John Wiyatt: 1WP and a William Wiyatt: 200 A, 2 WP and an Aaron Wiyatt: 70 A, 1 WP on page 309. There is a claim that John Wiatt [1743-1812] had a brother William Wiatt [1738-1802] who married Margaret Bostick, born about 1740 in Rowan County, N.C. and had two sons: Henry in 1763 and Aaron Wiatt around 1765. This Aaron is said to have been born at Lick Creek, Rowan County, N.C. and his remains are in Wilkes County, N.C. Wilkes County is northwest of Iredell, Davie, Davidson and Rowan counties.

In the *1800 Rowan County Rowan County List of the Persons who Failed to give their Taxables Property & the Sums Collected from Each for the year 1800* [Treasurer's and Comptroller's Papers, Box 78, County Settlements, North Carolina State Archives] from the country-wide list not divided into tax districts, is a John Wyatt: 1 poll found under heading: *"Additional List of Taxes."*

"WP" on tax list records for Rowan County means *"white pole."* This means that a tax was levied on a white male over 16 years of age. Males over the age of 16 years were taxable and eligible for the militia. *"A"* refers to *"acres."*

An *"Ebenezer Park"* of the Capt. Cox District is taxed in the year 1778. Although John Wiatt's sons Thomas and John Jr. marry daughters of Noah Park, Sr. long after this tax record, one can then look at the Park lineage to try to discern which *"Ebenezer"* this might have been. Noah Park, Sr.'s son Ebenezer, born in 1768? No, it could not be him. [This Ebenezer Park born in 1768, by the way married an *"Elizabeth Wiatt."* He also married a Sarah *"Sally"* Poole in 1820.]

What about Ebenezer Park's first cousin Ebenezer Park, Jr., born in 1775? No, it could not be him either; however, it might have been Eb's father Ebenezer Park [1747-1839] – This *"Ebenezer Park"* was a brother to Noah Park, Sr. Prior to 1797 when this Ebenezer moved to Madison County, Ky. This Ebenezer *"Eb"* Park [1747-1839] lived at least 24 years in Salisbury, Rowan County, N.C., where he in 1772 married his wife Tabitha Mills. This Eb Park was from Frederick County, Va., and he died in Drowning Creek, Madison County, Ky.

This Ebenezer Park is an uncle to Rachel and Hannah Park – the two sisters who married two of John Wiatt's [1743-1815] sons – Thomas and John Wiatt, Jr. – making the offspring of these unions double first cousins to one another, thus Ebenezer Park, born in 1747 – brother of Noah Park, Sr., is a granduncle to the grandchildren John Wiatt [1743-1815] and Noah Park, Sr.

Three sons of John Wiatt, Sr. [1743-1815] moved to Kentucky as stipulated by Venus of Faith in his notes and as further supported by the 1840 and 1850 U.S. Federal Census Records.

Sylvester [Silvester] [1761-1850] appears with his brother James Wiatt on the 1840 federal census in Calloway County, Ky. Sylvester Wiatt appears on the 1850 census along with his brother Eli Wiatt then being in McCracken County, Ky. and Sylvester in Marshall County. James Wiatt does not appear on the 1850 census. Sylvester is said by family to have died in Marshall County, Ky. Sylvester Wiett [Wiatt] is listed as being a farmer at age 88 on the August 24, 1850 census for Marshall County, Ky.

U.S. Federal Census for August 24th, 1850 Marshall County, Kentucky
Sylvester Wiett, 88 years old, farmer from North Carolina
Thomas T. Wiett, 23, male, farmer from North Carolina
Sally Wiett, 23, female checked as being able to read and write, born in Ky.
Mary, 3 months old, born in Ky.

❋   Wiett is a typo of Wiatt.

**State of North
Carolina, Rowan County
John Wyatte 300 acres
Scale of 20 chains to an inch**

By virtue of a warrant from the Entry Taken of Said County No. 1573 dated September the Twenty Fifth day, One Thousand Seven Hundred and Seventy Eight I have Surveyed for John Wyatte 300 Acres of Land lying on Cedar [or Said or Sedar] Creek, the Waters of the Yadkin River, Beginning at a white Oak Sapling on Moses Park's line and with William Coles line North Sixty Four degrees West forty six chains to a pine, Thence North forty five chains to a post ["sale" or "pale"?] then East twenty eight chains fifty links to a Black Oak Sapling [indiscernible word] corners, Thence with Said Cole's line East twenty six chains eighty links to a [two indiscernible words] Thence South fifty nine chains eighty links to the Beginning

Surveyed April 12th [year indiscernible][is though the year 1783]

Sylvester Wyatt

      &   **[indiscernible names]**
William Bonds   **Griffith Rutherford CS**

Eli *"Ely"* Wiatt [Born abt. 1789] married a *"Sarah"* and had a William P. Wyatt in 1829.

♀ | | ♂

♀ | | ♂

PART 10.
FEBRUARY 18, 2007
JOURNAL ENTRY

On ancestry.com, there is the 1830 Federal Census for Davidson County, N.C. an Eli Wyatt is listed as a male between the ages of 30 and 40 -- specifically:

"Of thirty and under forty." There are no other criteria to indicate whether this is Eli Wyatt -- brother to Thomas Wyatt, Sr.

On the same day for District #2 in McCracken County, Ky. a census record for September 12th, 1850 reveals: Eli, Dempsey and John Wyatt. On this record, they are grown men and listed in separate households.

Eli Wyatt, 61, male, farmer from North Carolina; Sarah Wyatt, 53, female of ----- a word that is indiscernible; William P. Wyatt, 21; farmer of North Carolina;

Dempsey Wyatt, 35; male, a blacksmith from North Carolina; Martha Wyatt, 18, female; of ---- a word that is indiscernible; William S.D. Wyatt, six months; male of Kentucky; William Wyatt, 27; male, blacksmith from North Carolina;

Three households after this is listed:

John Wyatt, 41, male, farmer from North Carolina; Delaney Wyatt, 31, female of ---- a word that is indiscernible; Margaret Wyatt, 10, female of Kentucky; William Wyatt, 8; male, of Kentucky; James, B. Wyatt, 6; male, of Kentucky; looks like "Nancy" Wyatt, 4, female, of Kentucky; looks like Eda, 2; female; of Kentucky. There appears to be two boarders in this household; however, the word boarder is not used to distinguish them as such. Their names are Jacob Browning, 25; male, farmer of the same indiscernible place as all those mentioned above; Sidney Hickman, 20; female of the same indiscernible place. The indiscernible place in all instances here and above for the Kentucky census looks like: *"Benn"* or *"Bern."* It could be an abbreviation for *"Penn;"* HOWEVER, the first letter resembles more of a *"B"* than a *"P."*

The following record is for Eli Wyatt [1841-1912], husband of Melinda. This Eli Wyatt is the son of Noah Calvin Wyatt [1805-1871] – who is a son to Thomas Wiatt [1774-1845] → son of: John Wiatt [1743-1815]:

McCubbins File at Rowan Public Library contains the Book 41 page 616, March 16, 1870: Eli Wyatt & wife Melinda make a deed of trust to Lawrence A. Bringle -- all of Rowan County, N.C. for 256 acres at the mouth of Dutch Second Creek next [to] Alexander Frick, Moses Lemly & up said creek for $1.00 as they owe him $390.00.

Additional records reveal this Eli Wyatt [1841-1912] served in Company D, 10th Regiment N.C.S.T. (1st Regiment N.C. Light Artillery Battery).

Wyatt, Eli, Private
resided in Rowan County, where he enlisted
at age 21, February 22, 1862 for the war.
Wounded at Battle of Second Manassas, Va.,
August 29, 1862. Present and accounted for
through February 1865. Captured at Amelia
Court House, Va., April 5, 1865 and confined
at Point Lookout, Md. until released after
taking Oath of Allegiance June 21, 1865.

❦   From the McCubbins file at the Rowan Public Library in Salisbury, N.C.:

May 20, 1819: Esq. William Bean, Jacob Goss, John Houser & Christopher Stokes are to act as commissioners to lay off one year's provision for the widow & family of deceased John Wyatt [Wiatt]. Administration on the estate of John Wyatt is granted to Hannah Wyatt & James Carrick *"who gave bend of 250 pounds with Jesse Parks & William Burridge."*

CHAPTER 15

† Lick Creek Baptist Church †

♀ | | ♂

"What is faith? Is it to believe that which is evident? No. It is perfectly evident to my mind that there exists a necessary, eternal, supreme, and intelligent being. This is no matter of faith, but of reason."

-- VOLTAIRE

PART 1. LOCATION & HISTORY

ON A HILL BETWEEN CABIN Creek and Lick Creek the cemetery whispers its memories into our modern day. According to a brief history supplied by the History & Genealogy Department of the Rowan Public Library in Salisbury, N.C., Lick Creek Baptist Church is an historic landmark of the county.

There is a paved road between North Carolina Highway #8 and High Rock passing the church. The original church is no longer standing. It may have been some sort of log or brush arbor construction; however, a wood-framed church was built later to replace it.

According to Dewey Snider, a genealogical researcher with the Davidson County Public Library, #602 South Main Street, Lexington, N.C., the second building known burned down in 1931. Today's Lick Creek Baptist Church was built to replace the previous one. It is on the property in which the cemetery marks its history.

The current Lick Creek Baptist Church was dedicated in August 1936, according to Dewey Snider, who retired from the Lexington Public Library Genealogy Department in late 2014. The Lick Creek Baptist Church is located on Lick Creek Church Road – State Road # 2501 in the Healing Springs Township .3 of a mile east of Cole Road, which is SR #2502.

Records of the church's founding have not been located and seemingly do not exist. It is assumed such documentation is lost or destroyed. It is deduced by modern-day historians the church held meetings before the year 1787. Abbotts Creek Church – as it is reported, received a letter asking for a church *"in order to be constituted."* This brief history of the Lick

Creek Baptist Church [1784-1907] states the Jersey Baptist Church was in receipt of an August 3, 1805 letter in which assistance is requested *"to constitute the Lick Creek congregation."* It is speculated this request was most likely granted in August 1807.

Building records for the Lick Creek Baptist Church do not seemingly exist. A brush arbor is suggested as having been where church services were held in the church's earliest beginnings. Brush arbors were crude constructions that could give some relief from weather.

The brief written history obtained from the Rowan Public Library's History & Genealogy Department points out that the Pee Dee Association meeting was held at the Lick Creek Baptist Church in October, 1819.

† From this aforementioned department the following quote is rendered:

"In August, 1808, Lick Creek Church joined the Sandy Creek Association and remained a member until 1815. Later, the Pee Dee Association was formed in October, 1816 ....in Montgomery County. Lick Creek remained a member of this association until 1825. Then Lick Creek joined other churches and formed Abbotts Creek Union Association at Liberty Meeting House in Davidson County in November, 1825.

In 1832, the split in the Baptist churches occurred in the Abbotts Creek Association. The churches in favor of missions formed the Liberty Baptist Association and Lick Creek...a charter member. Lick Creek Church led the missionary movement after the split and became the strongest church in the association. The Primitive Baptist believers of Lick Creek moved across the Yadkin River and formed the Flat Creek Baptist Church."

†Recorded ministers of the Lick Creek Baptist Church [1784-1907]†

The dates are approximated by years supplied in the aforementioned history.

* † **1825-1839: Elder Eli Carroll**
* † **1839-1862: Elder Alfred Kinney**
* † **1861-1865: Elder W.H. Hammer**
* † **1865-1868: A. Cornish**
* † **1868-1880: H. Morton**
* † **1880-1881: S.A. Roper**
* † **1881-1889: U.F. Haithcock**
* † **1889-1890: J.H. Booth**
* † **1890-1893: William Turner**
* † **1893-1895: J.M. Bennett**
* † **1895-1903?: H. Morris**
* † **1904-1905: J.A. Summey**

♀ | | ♂

Part 2. Cemetery Records

Cemetery Records of Davidson County, N.C. Volume 2 Southern Section, compiled by The Genealogical Society of Davidson County in Lexington, N.C. show several graves in Row #14. where the remains of John Wiatt [1743-1815] are buried in plot: #9. There are marble and slate markers and fieldstones. In Row #14 alone there are nine noted to have the surname of *"Cole,"* two with the surname of *"Stafford,"* one *"Thompson."* The others are indiscernible. There are 19 marked plots indicated in Row #14. It is discerned from the list of records on page 125 that there are 27 plots in Row #14.

Row #15, indicated on the same page 125 of this record book lists 20 plots – two by the surname of *"Jarvis,"* one by the surname of *"Taylor,"* four by the surname of *"Cole,"* including a *"Cole"* who married a *"Beckom,"* two by the surname of *"Beckom,"* including the one whose maiden name was *"Cole,"* one with the surname of *"Williams."* Two slates with only initials – one with *"O.P."* and the other with *"E.W."* are in this 15th row. There are slate and fieldstone markers that contain no information. For detailed information on the individuals with the other surnames mentioned, refer to page 125 of *Cemetery Records of Davidson County, N.C. Volume 2 Southern Section*.

There are 24 rows, including a few subsection rows indicated as 8X, 11X and 13X. They are recorded with names and without – some with markers or stone and some without not much more than a fieldstone or slate, broken marble markers or footstones. To date – as of August 29th, 2014, graves of a Nathan Wiatt, born in about 1740 and as being indicated by some family members as having been a brother to John Wiatt [1743-1815], is not readily discerned in this cemetery.

A William Wiatt, who has been claimed as being a brother to John Wiatt [1743-1815] by sources outside of records discerned by the researcher of this book, is not found in the Lick Creek Baptist Church Cemetery; *however, this research does not claim his remains are not in the cemetery* – only that they are not readily discerned due to nameless markers.

This William Wiatt [April 9, 1738- Abt. 1802] is said to have married a Margaret Bostick [born about 1740 in Rowan County]. Both have been claimed to been buried at Lick Creek Baptist Church Cemetery in Denton, Davidson County, N.C. in the section prior to the years 1822 known to be part of Rowan County. †

Lick Creek Baptist Church Cemetery, Davidson County, N.C.

♀ | | ♂

♀ | | ♂

PART 3.
SATURDAY
MAY 24, 2014
JOURNAL ENTRY

One hundred and fifteen years ago, Venus of Faith – John Thomas Wyatt, the newspaper correspondent or columnist, as he might be known as in our modern times – a collector of historical memorabilia, sketched his thoughts in note form. They are riddled with a few indiscernible words, nicknames and misspellings. As most people know – especially writers, misspelled words in notes do not bother us too much. It is when they are published we are unsettled by seeing them or others pointing them out.

I am not insensitive or cold regarding this – however, because I must be terribly careful – I have transcribed today word-for-word as he noted. I have <u>not</u> corrected his spelling, grammar, punctuation or nicknames used and short-hand. In the following information – his notes are transcribed and discerned. Corrections appear in brackets as discernments of what Venus of Faith meant. This is done for clarification; however, if by some chance someone disagrees – the original here is still intact.

Gretchen Witt of the Rowan Public Library's History Room in Salisbury, N.C. was especially good to send photocopies of the originals.

From the handwritten notes, supplied from the Rowan Public Library via Gretchen Witt, John Thomas Wyatt -- known as *"Venus of Faith"* wrote:

"John Wyatt and wife Rachael Hannah was the first Wyatts known to come to Davidson County, N.C. + is supposed to come from Va or Maryland but think they came from Maryland + they lived here in time of the Revolutionary War. They married and had the following children: Sylvester Wyatt ... John Wyatt who was my great grandfather + who went blind before he died, one child died ... his name was Dempsy Wyatt... James Wyatt ... Ely Wyatt, Selery Wyatt ... Elizabeth Wyatt ... Tomy Wyat. ..."

John Thomas Wyatt -- Venus of Faith -- wrote in his handwritten script:

"Old Johney Wyatt was the father of my Greatee grandfather John Wyatt, and he was he father of my grandfather Jessey Wyatt, and he was the father of my father Wilson Riley Wyatt + he was the father of John Thomas Wyatt who is myself the writer + of Columbus Ceciro Wyatt, my Brother and Columbus Ceciro Wyatt was the father of harvey A. Wyatt + Minney [Looks like Minney] Wyatt + Johnie M. Wyatt + Sidney Wyatt."

In another personal note entry, Venus of Faith writes:

"William Hunter Cole the father of Thomas Cole was Raised in 1/2 mile apart in davidson Co., N.C. of the old Wyatt family and is not more than half a mile from where the olde original John Wyatt Settled from where Thomas Cole now lives and about 2 miles from Bringles ferry in davidson Co., about East course, on the Yadkin River + on a creek called Lick Creek. The name Lick Creek got its name from having so many [word left out -- is blank] *+ other wild cattle...*

"Salty Places where deer could lick salt + other wild cattle hence it was called lick creek...

"Miss Rushes Living on her own the land now that Jimmy Rusher (Has old House Place) + Lee Rusher = was owned by the Wyatt Family...

"Thomas Cole...and [means "an old"] *old man now living in davidson Co. N.C. this July 8th 1899 and was then in about 150 yards from where he now lives + was Born Mar 20th 1815 + is 84 years old + is living with his son James Milton Cole who married a Miss Smith, daughter of Davie Smith...*

"Samuel Clark Bailey Miller at W.P. Staffords Mill in davidson Co. mar [married] *Bringles ferry one of daughters married William Clark who works at carpenter work at Spencer Nancy Jane Bailey he married...*

"Lawrence Talbert married Minnie Bailey...Trading ford P.O. is doing farm work...Son Book ago [Some book ago] *1+ 2 daughters at home...*

"Jimmey Bailey wants to learn to drill + cut granite...had Brother named Guss Bailey + knows me + Bro Ceciro + Run the Butcher Stand for Jim Love near where John Henderson now lives in time of the war...

"... water is running in his house from a mountain spring

(old mill House Shingles get eaten)...

"old man John Wyatt & Sons as follows:

"Silvester Wyatt + Jimey Wyatt + Ely Wyatt all went together to Kentucky and Settled 7 miles from Paddukill [Paducah, which is the county seat of McCracken County, Kentucky.] *Ky., and was mighty* [indiscernible word]*, Jimey Wyatt had lots of money, sold 4 or 5 hundred acres when he left here...Macracken Co. Ky* [McCracken County, Ky.] *is where they moved to."*

CHAPTER 16

Public Records Unveil Truths

♀ | | ♂

*"If people we love are stolen from us, the way to have them live on is to never
stop loving them. Buildings burn, people die, but real love is forever."*

-- VOLTAIRE

PART 1. THOMAS WIATT [1774-1845]

*T*RY TO IMAGINE WHAT THOMAS Wiatt saw around him. In his adult years, Rowan
County certainly would be a colonial theme of knicker-breeches, long wool, cotton, linen and silk waistcosts. Town streets and shops were dotted by elderly conservatives in fully skirted red-scarlet cloaks, white cravats or neck cloths, sailors and slaves in monmouth caps, farmers and European wagoners in cornflower blue hunting shirts made up the evolving terrain of people he saw and knew.

In the farming communities of Rowan – there were probably few three-piece suits. If Thomas walked on the floor boards of churches or other buildings – he no doubt heard the clacking of low-heeled shoes and boots of every man – whether or not he was a sportsman, farmer or doctor. Bonneted heads of females in stay makers of varying ages and classes – Thomas certainly saw them in his routines and traveling about. Hats under the sun with hands grasping the brims through fingerless gloves north of the shuffling of petticoats camouflaged by the gowns of work and play.

He saw these things – just as we see the fashion of our modern times. Thomas Wiatt would have known of Saint Luke's Episcopal Church – its parish established in 1753 and its present building as it was erected in 1828 in Salisbury, even if he never ventured into it.

Thomas Wiatt lived through ten U.S. Presidents – George Washington, John Adams, Thomas Jefferson, James Madison, James Monroe, John Quincy Adams, Andrew Jackson, Martin Van Buren, William Henry Harrison and John Tyler.

The bodily remains of Thomas Wiatt rest in the Park-Wyatt-Bean Graveyard – along with those remains of his wife. The remains of Thomas Wiatt are not all we can imagine from that time period. He was more than the dust an earthly body leaves behind. John Wiatt, Sr.'s son Thomas Wiatt -- recorded as Thomas Wiett, Wyat, and Wyatt [1774-1845], married a Rachel Parke, whose name sometimes appears as *"Parks."*

Rachel Parke Wiatt [1774-May 1850] of Rowan County, had several children, including another possible Rachel Wyatt born in 1802, who married a John Jacob Bean [1802-1876], born in the Piney Woods District of Morgan Township, Rowan County, N.C. and is buried in Murray County, Calloway, Ky. This Rachel was supposedly born in or near the Lick Creek area of Rowan County, a section of which became in 1822 Davidson County.

Thomas Wiatt's wife Rachel Parke Wiatt was a daughter of Joanna *"Ann" "Anna" "Anny"* Reed [1746-1833] and Noah Park, Sr. [1743-1815 or was his DOD 1820?] There are two mentions of a Thomas Wiatt in Noah Park. Sr.'s will – the first as a Thomas Wiatt Kaylor Line [which possibly means this Thomas Wiatt's property next to a Kaylor property owned by Leonard Kalor or Kaylor – Noah's son-in-law via Noah's daughter Mary Park Kaylor. The other mention of Thomas Wiatt in Noah Park, Sr.'s will is a *"Thomas F or J Wiatt"* as a witness to Noah Park, Sr.'s *Last Will and Testament.*

The footsteps of Noah Park, Sr. and his son-in-law Thomas Wiatt speak to us in this modern day. We turn the pages of public records and find their names inscribed with those who married, owned land, inherited and paid taxes. Such records confirm they existed beyond a tombstone or grave plot.

The following excerpts from the *Abstracts of Deed Books 20-24 of Rowan County, North Carolina 1807-1818,* donated by James W. Kluttz mention this same Thomas Wiatt – but spell his name as *"Wyatt."* Given the other people mentioned and his connection to them by blood and marriage, it is clear this *"Thomas Wiatt"* is one in the same with *"Thomas Wyatt."*

493. p. 489. 9 Apr 1808. Noah Parks Sr. to his son Noah Parks Jr. for $60, 207 A on S side of Yadkin R on Cedar Crk adj Anthony Peeler, Lewis Kaylor, and Noah Parks. Wit. Nathan Morgan, David Woodson, Prvd by Woodson At Nov Ct. 1815.

Signature of Noah Park
Noah Park's name on 20:489

494. p. 490. 4 May 1812. Noah Parks Sr. to his son John Parks for 5 shillings, 169 A on both sides of Cedar Crk adj Ebenezer Parks, Thomas Wiatt, Evan Alexander, Noah Parks, Jr. and Lewis Kaylor. Wit: Nathan Morgan, David Woodson, Prvd by Woodson at Nov. Ct. 1815.

This is made more clear if you understand that the children of Noah Park, Sr. are brother-in-laws and sister-in-laws to Thomas Wiatt via his wife Rachel Park – Noah Park, Sr.'s daughter. Children of Noah Parks: Ebenezer, Hannah, Rachel, Mary, Jesse, Noah, Jr., Amos, John Davis, Elizabeth Betty and Sarah.

Thomas's sister-in-law Sarah Park married James Morgan [1780-1847], son of Naomie Poole [Pool] & Nathan Morgan, Sr. [1756-1842]. Thomas Wiatt's sister-in-law Elizabeth Betty Park married Nathan Morgan, Jr. – a brother to the aforesaid James Morgan. Understanding that Hannah Park – Thomas Wiatt's sister-in-law married John Wyatt, Jr. – Thomas' brother who supposedly died in 1819 – brings things into better focus for the researcher. Thomas's brother-in-law Ebenezer Park [1768-1854] was married twice: 1) Elizabeth Wiatt in 1791 and 2) Sarah *"Sally"* Poole in 1820. Thomas's sister-in-law married Leonard Kaylor [Kaler]. The mention of Lewis Kaylor – Leonard's father's property makes sense.

Thomas' brother-in-law Jesse Park, husband of Sarah Todd is mentioned in these records and in handwritten documents. It is important to remember the rule about the double S's. A handwritten *"J"* often in such documents resembles on *"T"* uppercase, and the first *"s"* appears as a *"P"* when it is the upper *"S"* and then next to it is the lowercase *"s."* What looks like *"Iepe"* or *"Isep"* is *"Jesse."* The mention of Thomas' brother-in-law Amos Park, husband of Margaret *"Molly"* *"Milly"* Mildred Briggs, prevents misunderstanding.

It is indeed nearly impossible to speak of the Wyatts of Rowan County [in light of the spelling versions of this name] without speaking of the Morgan and Park [Parks, Parke] families. The visualization is much like if one holds his or her hands with the fingers joining between its opposite – like a child playing:

"This is the Church, this is the steeple, open the doors and here are the people"

494. p. 490 4 May 1812. Noah Parks Sr. to his son John Parks for 5 shillings, 169 A on both sides of Cedar Crk adj Ebenezer Parks, **Thomas Wyatt**, Evan Alexander, Noah Parks, Jr. and Lewis Kaylor. Wit: Nathan Morgan, David Woodson. Prvd by Woodson at Nov Ct 1815.

Of same on page 28:

491. p. 487. 4 May 1812, Noah Parks Sr. to his son Jesse Parks for 5 shillings, 169 A on S side of Yadkin R at Cedar Crk adj Leonard Kayor [sic: Kaylor] and Noah Parks, Jr. Wit.: Nathan Morgan, David Woodson, Prvd by Woodson at Nov Ct. 1815.

492. p. 488. 15 Nov 1811, Noah Parks, Sr. to Ebenezer Parks for 5 shillings, 151 A on Cedar Crk adj this Grantee,

Thomas Wyatt, John Parks, and Lewis Kaylor. Wit: David
Barclay, David Woodson. Prvd by Woodson at Nov Ct 1815.

493. p. 489. 9 Apr 1808 Noah Parks Sr. to his son Noah
Parks Jr. for $60, 207 A on S side of Yadkin R on Cedar
Crk adj Anthony Peeler, Lewis Kaylor, and Noah Parks.
Wit: Nathan Morgan, David Woodson. Prvd by Woodson
at Nov Ct 1815.

Rowan County North Carolina Will Abstracts, volume II, 1805-1850.

2402. p. 307. 29 Feb 1851. Alexander Parks and Ebenezer Parks Sr. to Noah Wiatt
[?] for $104.22 ½, 49 acres and 18 poles on Cedar Crk adj David Park, Jonathan
Bean, Brantly Wiatt, Noah Wiatt and Dempsey Park. Wit: Willie Bean, George A.
Park. Prvd by Bean at Aug Ct 1851. Reg 30 Oct 1851.

♀ | | ♂

PART 2.
7:41 P.M., SUNDAY
APRIL 13, 2014
JOURNAL ENTRY

I transcribed Noah Park, Sr.'s will today as Mother Nature in all of her flowering shower of pollen scratched my throat and danced on my nose to stay alert.

It appears below and is included in this Wyatt history because Noah Park, Sr. was the father-in-law of Thomas Wiatt. It supports original assertions stated in the front matter.

Transcription from the original will of Noah Park, Sr. – father-in-law of Thomas Wyatt [Wiett, Wyat, Wiatt] and father of Rachel Park Wyatt – parents of Noah Calvin Wyatt, father of Rachel Wyatt Morgan – the wife of John Morgan is as follows:

Last Will & Testament of Noah Park, Sr.

In the Name of [...God,] **Amen. I, Noah Park, of the County of Rowan, Being sick and weak of Body, but of Sound Mind Memory and Understanding _____ be ...[God] for It; and considering the certainty of Death and the uncertainty of time that is left and to the End, I may be the Better _____ and to leave this World, whenever it may be Please ...[God] to call me Thence; Do Therefore I Make and Declare this my Last Will and Testament in Manner Following, that is to Say, First and Principally I Command my soul into the hands Of Almighty God. My benefactor hoping for His Pardon and Remission of all my sins and to enjoy Everlasting Happiness In His Heavenly Kingdom through the Soul Merrits of Jesus Christ, My Savior. My Body commit to the Earth at the Discretion of my Executors. Here after mentioned and also my Worldly Goods and Property, which it hath been pleasing God To benefit me with; I dispose of the same as [follow with?] _____ First, I Give and Bequeath unto my beloved Wife Anny Park One Feather bed and Furniture there unto Belongings _____ all of our House hold Furniture. Excepting What I may herein afterward mention to some of my beloved. Daughter, Sara, Also, I Further Give and bequeath unto her One Blazed Face Mare and Colt of Two years Old, and also Two Milk Cows and Their Calves, which she Shall have Out of My Stock of Meat Cattle also all My Stock of Sheep and Hogs. Then, I also Give and Bequeath unto my First Born and beloved Son Ebenezer Parks One Moyelty Or Fifth Part of all my Land consisting of Six Hundred And Ninety acres in the whole of which my Desire is that He Shall Take his Part, which will Consist of One Hundred And thirty Eight Acres, To be Said of in the South west Corner of My Land, so as to include a field which he now Has in [Dendany] on Said Land, but not to include _____ at the East of the [Yrafoy] Ridge known by the name of [Ropy] mend and Spring; Then, I also Give and Bequeath unto second and beloved Son, Jesse Park, One Fifth Part or Moyety of My Land Consisting of One Hundred and Thirty-Eight Acres, to be Land of giving the, Yadkin River From the mouth of Cedar Creek up the River to Kaylors Line Thence a Long his Line including the Land on the North Side Of Said Cedar creek for Quantity; Also, I Give and bequeath to My Said Son Jesse Parks My Sorrell mare and one Cow and calf.**

_____ I also Give and Bequeath unto my Third and Beloved Son Noah Park One Moyety or Fifth Part of My Land Consisting of One Hundred and Thirty Eight Acres to be Said of forming the Yadkin River Beginning at the mouth Of Cedar Creek and Running Down the River to Peelers Line Thence along his Line _____ I include for Quantity the Land On the South Side of Cedar Creek from Peelers Line. I also Give and Bequeath to My said third son Noah Park, One Year Old Heifer of my Stock of Meat Cattle _____ I also Give and Bequeath unto my Fourth and Dear beloved son Amos Parks One moiety of Fifth Part of my Land to consist of One Hundred and Thirty Eight acres to Be said of giving to the Land which shall be said of to his Brother Noah and Peelors Line and the Line of Alexanders Land for Compliment. Also, I Give and Bequeath to my Said Fourth Son Amos Park my yellow Bay mare and One Cow and Calf of my Stock of Meat

Cattle – ___ I also Give and Bequeath to Fifth and Most Beloved Son John Davis Park One Moyety or Fifth Part of My Land consisting of One Hundred and Thirty Eight Acres To be Said of forming the Lines of the Land It Shall be Said of for his Brothers Ebenezer and Amos and the Lines of Thomas Wyat Kaylor ___ I also Give and bequeath to My aforesaid Fifth son John Davis Park one yearlin Heifer Of my Stock of Meat Cattle and One milek [milk] cow and calf ____ I also Give and Bequeath unto my ____Most Dutifull and beloved Daughter Hannah Wiatt one Ewe of my flock of sheep _____I also Give and Bequeath unto my Dutifull and beloved Daughter Rachel Wiatt one Calf of My Stock of Meat Cattle

_____ I also give and Bequeath unto Dutifull and beloved Daughter Mary Kaylor one Calf of My Stock of Meat Cattle – _____I also Give and Bequeath unto my Dutifull and beloved Daughter Sarah Parks one Cow and Calf of my Stock of Meat Cattle and one Feather Bed and furniture for the same.

_____ I also Give and Bequeath unto Dutifull and beloved Daughter Elizabeth Park one Cow and Calf of my Stock Of Meat Cattle and one Feather bed and Furniture for the Beloved Wife Anny Park Shall remain in Full possession Of any Dwelling House and One Third Part of the cleared Lands If she Shall require the same During the Time of her Life

Or widowhood and I do further will and Bequeath unto her all The Flax Cotton and all the House Hold and Kitchen furniture Also my Loom and gear _____ and I also further will andBequeath unto my two Sons Jesse Park and Amos Park All my Plantation tools and Farming Utensils the wagon And gear Excepted and I also Give and Bequeath unto my son Jesse Park all my Black Smith Tools and I do give By Constitute Nominate and Appoint my Trusty and Beloved Sons Ebenezer Park and Amos Park go into And Soul Executor, to this My Last will and Testament In witness thereof I, said Noah Park hath to this My Last will consisting of One that of Paper here unto It my Hand and Seal this Fifth Day of April in the year Of Our Lord Christ 1801

Noah Park [signature]

Seal

Signed Sealed _____ and Declared
By Noah Park, as his Last will and
Testaments in Presents of us –
David Woodson & Thomas __[F?] Wiatt
Mark
[signature is indiscernible but looks like:
Nichols or Lionel Lösloe]

* First born son of Noah Park [Parke, Parks] is indicated as Ebenezer Parke. The other sons are indicated as Jesse, Noah, Amos and John Davis Parke. The daughters: Hannah, Rachel, Mary Kailor, Sarah and Elizabeth. Executors: Ebenezer and Amos Parke; Witnesses: David Woodson and Thomas Wyatt.

⁕ *Footnote for John Davis Park, son of Noah Park, Sr. State of North Carolina Rowan County.

KNOW all Men by these presents, That we John Park
+ Thomas Todd
in the state aforesaid, are held and firmly
bound unto the Governor of the State of North Carolina for the
time being, in the just and full sum of Five Hundred Pounds,
current money of this state, to be paid to the said Governor, or his
successors or assigns: To the which payment well and truly to be
made and done, we bind ourselves, our Heirs, Executors and
Administrators. Sealed with our seals and dated this 20th
day of October Anno Domini 1812.

The Condition of the above obligation is such, That whereas the
above bounden John Park hath made
application for a License for a marriage to be celebrated between
him and Polly Bean of the county aforesaid:
Now in safe it shall not appear hereafter, that there is any lawful
cause to obstruct the said marriage, then the above obligation to be
void, otherwise to remain in full force and virtue.
Sealed and delivered
in the presence of us
John Park [Seal]
mark
John Park
Geo Dunn

♀ | | ♂

PART 3.
7:56 P.M., SUNDAY
APRIL 13, 2014
JOURNAL ENTRY

The sun is setting. The sky turns to blues, pinks and lavenders. The pigments are those of a beautiful painting – compliments of Mother Nature. I am stretching. I guard my painful right knee and third nail-less toe on the right foot as well. Today is the birthday of a great grandfather on another lineage not related to the Wiatts or Wyatts – Oliver Richard Leighton [April 13, 1873-March 27, 1927] Oliver was the father of my mother's father Clarence H. Leighton. Dates – birthdays as in this instance have a way of ♪ ♫ ♪ singing cheers and good blessings ♪ ♫ ♪ when we least expect.

Earlier today I woke at the crack of dawn. I thought of my 4th cousin Robert Allen DeVries. He is the co-researcher for *Paper & Stone, A Leighton History in England & the United States*. It was a workout prerequisite to buckling down, committing to writing to the best of my ability *The Rungs of Ladders, A Wyatt History in England & the United States, from 1066 to Modern Times*.

In the southwest, the clouds grow thick. My stomach desires dinner. Before you eat and sleep this evening please take into consideration the points about Noah Park, Sr.'s will as they appear below.

The word, *"moyety,"* which is used in Noah Park's last will and testament may not be readily understood by modern-day researchers. It is referring to *"moiety,"* meaning *"a portion of."* As a legal term, this word describes a portion other than complete ownership of property. The Old French word is *"moitié,"* which meant *"half."* It is defined the same way in modern day French. The Latin is *"medietas"* meaning *"middle."*

In English law, this term is utilized in parsing – breaking down or defining aspects of ownership and liability in all forms of property. In the Middle Ages, however, this word *"moiety"* – spelled seeming as *"moyety"* in Noah Park, Sr.'s will means something else in a feudal system, which incorporated a set of legal and military customs in the 9th and 15th centuries in Europe.

Noah Park, Sr. was born in 1742 – in the 18th century [1701-1800]. His will refers to *"a portion"* of the original whole. A moiety in centuries prior to this it seems to refer to two groups, or dividing into two parts and this would be influenced by negotiation of two heirs.

"*Bequeathed*" means to pass on, or will property to another after a person's leaves the physical body. In the legal sense this word is used in Noah Park Sr.'s will, for instance; and in that sense it is a verb meaning "*to make a bequest.*" In Old English, this word is known as "*Becwethan,*" and it meant to declare or express into words to "*quoth,*" which means "*said.*"

Double "*s*" in old wills appear as what modern-day readers might mistake as an "*F*". Often in Noah's will is the word: Consisted. While the two "*s's*" are not double "*s's*" it is written as "*Consifted*" and "*Confisting*" – which should be discerned not as an "*F*" but as an "*S*" – "*Consisted*" and "*Consisting.*"

The point concerns people carrying the exact same names in order. One of Thomas Wiatt's ' eight known children to date of this writing was a Noah Calvin Wyatt [1805-1871] married a Mary Polly Hendly -- also known as "*Henly,*" [1806-abt. 1871]. One of the children was known as Rachel Evelyn Wyatt [1835-1915] married John Noah Calvin Morgan, born 1834 – referred to as John Calvin Morgan in the Poole Town District of Morgan Township. John Morgan died at the Battle of Spotsylvania [sometimes spelled with two "*Ts*" – "*Spottsylvania.*"] Court House in Spotsylvania, Va. while serving in the 5th Regiment -- Company H of North Carolina Troops [ACW].

♀ | | ♂

Part 4. Public Records

Book 36, page 402: November 24, 1842:

The State Grants [warrant 529 entered December 10, 1840 & surveyed August 19, 1841 to Brantly Wyatt 27 acres on Sedar [sic: Cedar] Creek next Wila Bean, **Thomas Wyatt**, Abraham Miller & Lawrence Bringle.

* *Brantley Wyatt is the son of Rachel Park and Thomas Wyatt or Wiatt – a son of John Wiatt [1743-1815].

Scale 64 poles to the [indiscernible word]

State of North Carolina
Rowan County
This plot represents a tract
of land surveyed for
Brantly Wyatt by virtue of
his warrant dated the 2nd
of April 1841 and No. 529
on the waters of the Cedar Creek
Beginning at a heap of
Stones Wily Beans corner on a
runs with his West 20
poles to a Post Oak Thos Wyatt
corner thence with his line [looks like 118]
205 poles to a stake his corner
in a wod thence East 22 poles to a stake
Abraham Millers corner on Lawrence A. Bringles
line thence North 205 poles to the Beginning
containing twenty Seven Acres
Surveyed the 19th of Augs 1841

George Parks
Daniel Miller   } CB James Crosby [indiscernible word]

© Copyright Wednesday, October 15, 2014 survey 1841 27acres for Brantly Wyatt as transcribed from the original by Hélène Andorre Hinson Staley, Metallo House Publishers, Moncure, N.C. 27559. All Rights Reserved. This transcription is according to the researcher;

however, another transcription of this may be found by other researchers who may agree or disagree.

♀ | | ♂

State of North Carolina No. 529
Rowan County

I JS Beard Entry officer of claims for land in
the county of Rowan to the Surveyor of Said County
Greetings

You are hereby required to lay off and survey
for Brantley Wyatt a tract of land or parcel of land
lying in Rowan County Containing 50 acres
more or leSs on the waters of Cedar Creek
forming Wiley Bean Thomas Wyatt + others entered
the 10th day of December 1840. Observing
the directions of the act of aSsurably in that case
made and Provided for surveying out Lands two
Just + fair Plans of such survey, with a surveyor
certificate [indiscernible word allotted?] to each together with this
warrant you are to transport to the Secretarys
Office without delay.

Given under my hand at office in
Salisbury the 2 day of Aprile 1841

     JS Beard ETRC

© Copyright Wednesday, October 15, 2014 survey year 1841 for 50 acres for Brantly Wyatt as transcribed from the original by Hélène Andorre Hinson Staley, Metallo House Publishers, Moncure, N.C. 27559. All Rights Reserved. This transcription is according to the research-er; however, another transcription of this may be found by other researchers who may agree or disagree.

Also summarized from McCubbins file:

Book 86, page 136: April 13, 1899: D.C. Reid -- no wife signs -- lets R.J. Reid (both of Rowan County, N.C.) have the undivided half interest in 215 acres (which T.C.

Wyatt inherited from his deceased father, Brantly Wyatt) also in the land bought of Abraham Miller -- see mortgage from T.C. Wyatt to said Reid on October 9, 1892 in Book 10, page 82 to secure $407.58 & sold now for $609.00., witnessed by W.W. Reid & acknowledged on the same day.

♀ | | ♂

Others in the Park-Wyatt- Bean Graveyard as indicated in the McCubbins file are some children I am not sure how they connect; unless, they are descendants of Thomas Wyatt or one of his brothers.

They are: James P. Wyatt died Sept. 3, 1870, age 3 years, 8 months & 14 days old
Anna Wyatt died Dec. 12, 1888
Elizabeth Wyatt died Aug. 19, 1857 age 1 year & 6 days
Polly Wiatt born Jan. 5, 1806; died about 1861

♀ | | ♂

The following is a brief summary of McCubbins file notes [History Room, Genealogical section, Rowan Public Library, Salisbury, N.C.]

Book 37, page 379, May 10, 1845: Thomas Wyatt -- no wife signs -- out of leve [sic love] for Brantly Wyatt (both of Rowan County, N.C.) gives him 188 acres next Ebenezer Parks, heirs of --- Shephard, Widow Miller, --- Burrage, near a branch, Brantly Wyatt & Wiley Bean, witness and proved by Wiley Bean in Aug. 1845.

On better typed pages, McCubbins has this same note as the following:

Book 37, page 379, May 10, 1845: Thomas Wyatt -- no wife signs -- lets Brantly Wyatt (both of Rowan County, N.C.) have 188 acres on Cedar Creek next Ebenezer Parks, heirs of --- Shephard, Widow Miller, --- Burrage, near a branch, Brantly Wyatt & Wiley Bean, out of love, witness and proved by Wiley Bean in Aug. 1845.

* The original documents have Thomas Wyatt or Wiatt or *"Thomas Wiott."*

Book 37, page 354, May 10, 1845: Thomas Wyatt -- no wife signs -- lets Noah Wyatt (both of Rowan County, N.C.) have 133 acres on Cedar Creek next Ebenezer Parks, out of love, witnessed by Buckner Crowell & Wiley Bean Jr. & proved by the latter on Sept. 10 1845.

Excerpt of page 354:

This indenture made this the tenth day of May in the year of our Lord. One thousand Eight Hundred and forty five Between Thomas Wiot of the County of Rowan and the State of No. Carolina of the one part + Noah Wiot of the county and state aforesaid of the other part witness that the said Thomas Wiot for and in consideration of the Natural Love + affection, which he has unto the Noah Wiot has Given Granted [indiscernible word] realized and confirmed and by these presents [indiscernible words] onto the said Noah Wiot [indiscernible words] and assigns all that [indiscernible words] ….

Summarized:

The will of Brantley: [sic Brantly] Wyatt (Book K, page 315) made January 18, 1863 & probated in May 1863. Wife Juleyan (187 1/2 acres), where I live & 27 1/2 acres next above & the plantation of Camey Morgan)...Sons P.L. James J.? & T.C. Daughter: Josey Ann (unmarried); Exrs: friends James J? Wyatt & David C. Reid: Witnesses: Willie Bean & George P. Burrage.

The McCubbins file contains a marriage document summary -- which already matches with the one collected. McCubbins file contains spelling variations of the name Julian and Julie as *"Juleyan"* and *"Juley."* Her notes on birth and death either came from cemetery stones or census records and match those I have collected as well.

Children of Rachel *"Parks"* *"Park"* Parke & Thomas *"Tommy"* Wiatt, Sr. (Wyatt, Wiett):

* Allen Wiatt ?
* Sarah *"Sally"*
* Dempsy
* James
* John
* Rachel
* Sylvester
* Cecila or Cecilia
* Thomas
* Elizabeth
* Ely

♀ | | ♂

♀ | | ♂

Part 5. A Small World

The following property paper mentions Thomas Wiatt's land as part of the perimeters of other property owners -- Michael Miller, John Shaver, Joseph and Jesse Hodges and Willie Morgan in regard to a tract of land roughly 300 acres formerly owned by R.A. Alexander. A few commas and boldface font are the only changes made in order to bring some clarity for the modern reader.

Deed Book 35, p.336.

This Indenture made this 14th day of
September 1841 Between Nathaniel W. Alexander by his
attorney in trust Wm. I. Alexander of the County of
Mecklenburg + State of North Carolina of the one part
and **Abraham Miller** of the County of Rowan and
State of North Carolina of the other part witness on that the
[indiscernible word] + party of the first part for and in consideration
of the sum of one hundred and fifty Dollars the receipt
of which is hereby acknowledged hath sold and conveyed
and doth hereby sell and convey to the said party of the
second part + his heirs all that tract or parcel of Land
lying in the county of Rowan State of N Carolina
as follows lying on the waters of Little Creek adjoining
the Lands of **Micheal Miller's heirs**, the lands of **John
Shaver, Joseph** and **Jesse Hodges, Willie Morgan** +
of **Thomas Wiatt** containing about 300 acres
it being a tract of Land formerly owned by
the late R.A. Alexander and now held by the said --
NW Alexander as Devisee of said R.A. Alexander
To have and to hold the same with the [appus]
[indiscernible word[thenceunto belonging to the said party
of the second part of the first part for [indiscernible word] the
consideration aforesaid doth hereby [indiscernible word]
[indiscernible word] to warrant and defend the premises
aforesaid to the said party of the second part +
his heirs [indiscernible looks like: Exss] admin. and assigns against the
claim + entry of all persons whatsoever in witness
thereof the (s) party of the first part hath [indiscernible word]
[indiscernible word] his and and seal on the day and year above
written Signed Sealed and Delivered in
presence of   Nathaniel W. Alexander [Seal]
W.C. Owens   Wm I. Alexander. his atty.

© Copyright September 7, 2014 Deed Book 35, page 336 as transcribed from the original by Hélène Andorre Hinson Staley, Metallo House Publishers, Moncure, N.C. 27559. All Rights Reserved. This transcription is according to the researcher; however, another transcription of this may be found by other researchers who may agree or disagree.

Identities of Abraham Miller, Michael Miller, John Shaver, Joseph and Jesse Hodges, Willie Morgan and Thomas Wiatt: This document in and of itself to the modern-day reader may at face value just appear to be a land document declaring ownership.

The date of 1841 and community suggest this is Thomas Wiatt – referred to by other sources as *"Tommy" Wiatt, Wiett, Wyatt and Thomas Wiatt, Sr."* [1774-1845] – husband of Rachel Park [Parks, Parke] 1774-May 1850.

Jesse Hodge [1792-1864] is the spouse of Ruhamah or Ruhamar Palmer [1792-1840]. This Jesse Hodge is a brother to Joseph Hodge [born 1786], spouse of Mary Polly Norbitt. These two brothers Jesse and Joseph Hodge are likely the *"Hodges"* referred to in this document. The names *"Hodge"* and *"Hodges"* [with and without an *"s"*] appear in handwritten documents as both.

The August 1st, 1850 U.S. Federal Census for Rowan County, North Carolina has listed #227:

Jesse Hodges [Hodge], 57; male
Sally M. Hodges, 20, female
Abram A., 17, male, laborer
John F., 15, male, laborer

Jesse's brother Joseph Hodges is living one household down next to the Wilson Airy household in 1850.

Joseph Hodges, 63;
Mary, 67;
William, 42; Elizabeth, 39;

Joseph Hodges' household is directly next door to the Richard Hodges household in 1850.

The father of Jesse and Joseph Hodge was Joseph Hodge [1765-Abt. 1808] who is said to have come from England. Noted on August 18, 1778 this Joseph Hodge, father of Jesse and Joseph, served as a guard in Salisbury, N.C. during the Revolutionary War. Jesse Hodge [1792-1864] and Ruhamah Palmer [1792-1840] are the parents of Hannah Hodge, born about 1813, who married George Anthony Park [1808-1882] and had several children, including William Alexander Park [Abt. 1831-June 7, 1865] – the Confederate soldier mentioned in a previous chapter, who died at Union Prison, Point Lookout, Saint Mary's County,

Md. William married his first cousin once removed [via Park lineage] Nancy Carolina Park [1829-1901], daughter of Mary Polly Bean and John Davis Park – the youngest son of Noah Park, Sr. [1742-1815].

There are two John Shavers who lived during the time frame in which the above document is dated in September 1841. One is John S. Shaver [1755-1844] who married Anna Maria *"Mary"* Müller [Miller] [1770-1839], whose remains are buried at Reid Graveyard, on the Tuckertown Lake off the Yadkin River, Rowan County, N.C. This John Shaver came to Rowan County, N.C. sometime in the 1780s from Germany.

The other John Shaver is named for this one and is the son of the first one mentioned here. John S. Shaver, Jr. [1801-1853], spouse of Rebecca Reed [Reid] [1806-1882]. The John S. Shaver, Jr.'s son was John I. Shaver [1848-1910] who married Rhoda E. Wyatt [1844-1920] – this Rhoda Wyatt, being a daughter of Mary Polly Hendly [Henly] [1806-1861] and Noah Calvin Wyatt [1805-1871] – the parents of Henry Thomas, Malinda [Delinda], William Wesley, Emanuel James M., Lila Delilah *"Delila,"* Rachel Evelyn and Silas Wyatt – each discussed in this book.

Now, who are Abraham Miller and Michael Miller – the Miller men referred to in the property document mentioned earlier along with Thomas Wiatt? Michael Miller [1818-1911], spouse of Amanda Jane Owen was the son of Sophia, died abt. 1850 and Abraham Miller, b. 1793. Michael Miller [1818-1911] father of: → Abraham Philip Miller [b. 1861, Morgan Township] father of: Amanda Mayetta Miller [1894-1971] wife of Pleasant Loveless Wyatt [1895-1986] parents of: → Zula, Baxter, Polly, Margaret, Raymond and Ruby. Of these children: Margaret Evelyeen Wyatt [b.1922, Rowan County, N.C.], married Wilson Smith [1917-2011] and had two sons: Ronald Lee and Timothy Ray. Wilson Smith was the former business partner of Ralph Ketner, the Food Lion Store founders in Salisbury, N.C.

Rowan County North Carolina Deed Book #35, p. 21:

241. p. 336. 14 Sep 1843. Wm J. Alexander of Mecklenberg County, NC, as attorney in fact of Nathan/Nathaniel W. Alexander, to Abraham Miller for $150, 300 A on Little Crk adj Michael Miller's heirs, John Shaver, Joseph Hodges, Jesse Hodges, Willie Morgan, and **Thomas Wiatt**. It had been owned by R.H. Alexander who devised it to this Grantor. Wit: H.C. Owens. Prvd by Owens before Judge J.L. Bailey on 14 Sep 1841. Reg 14 Sep 1841.

♀ | | ♂

Part 6. Author's Note

The significance of a document can change the more we know about those people mentioned in it – witnesses, fellow landowners, attorneys, etc. How they lead up to the current day is amazing. I was a little girl in the 1970s in Salisbury, N.C. My mother shopped weekly at Food Town, which became later known as Food Lion®. Wilson Smith's wife is my third and fifth cousin – give or take a *"removed"* here and there. I don't doubt many of the store's patrons through the years in Salisbury, N.C. are cousins of

Margaret Evelyeen Wyatt Smith [b. 1922] daughter of: → Amanda Mayetta Miller [1894-1971] and Pleasant Loveless Wyatt [1895-1986] son of: → Ciscero L. Wyatt [1861-1945] and Polly Louise *"Louisa"* Park [Abt. 1861]. This Ciscero Wyatt is the son of: → Lazarus Pleasant Wyatt and Delilia *"Delilah"* Park [Abt. 1837] daughter of: → Hannah Hodge and George Anthony Park [1808-1882]. This Delilah Park Wyatt is a sister to William Alexander Park who died at Point Lookout, Md. during the ACW – as mentioned earlier. Lazarus Pleasant Wyatt is one of the children of Rachel Park and Thomas Wiatt [1774-1845] – the remains of which are buried in the Park-Wyatt-Bean Graveyard.

Is this world smaller? Yes, it is!

♀ | | ♂

CHAPTER 17

Brave Farewells

♀ | | ♂

Rachel Evelyn Wyatt Morgan [1835-1915]
John Calvin Morgan [1834-1864]
Mary Jane Morgan Eagle [1856-1928]
Solomon Eagle, Jr. [1857-1939]

"…For all sad words of tongue or pen,
The saddest are these: 'It might have been!'
Ah, well! For us all some sweet hope lies
Deeply buried from human eyes;
And, in the hereafter, angels may
Roll the stone from its grave away!"

❋   JOHN GREENLEAF WHITTIER [1807-1892] – SOME
LINES FROM HIS POEM TITLED: *"MAUD MULLER."*

PART 1. 1862

*"*D*ID YOU BY CHANCE LOSE a small silver spoon?"*

The conductor addressed Rachel Wyatt Morgan as she made her way into the train that would transport her to Salisbury, N.C. from Richmond, Va. Apparently, Rachel had left the spoon behind during her travel North.

Weeks or perhaps months prior to that earlier journey, Rachel Wyatt received news [possibly from the War Department in Richmond or regimental officer] that her husband John Morgan was ill. She was requested to go to a hospital in Richmond, Va., where John was recovering. *

When John enlisted for the Confederate Army in 1862, his eldest child and only daughter Mary Jane Morgan [Eagle] was nearly five years old.

Mary Jane Morgan's last visual memory of seeing her father was him disappearing behind a tree from where she stood near their home on River Road in Rowan County. After telling his expectant wife Rachel goodbye, he rode away on horseback to Statesville, Iredell County August 8th of that fateful year 1862.

Three months later, Rachel and John's second child John Noah Calvin Morgan was born on November 6, 1862. John's hospitalization had been a blessing in disguise: had Rachel not been summoned by the military to travel to Richmond, John might never have seen his baby son.

The day the train conductor placed baby John's spoon back into his mother's hand turned out to be the last day Rachel saw her husband alive.

* Chimborazo Hospital was erected in Richmond, Va. to serve the needs of the Confederate Army between 1862 and 1865. Over 76,000 injured gray-clad soldiers were treated in Chimborazo Hospital.

♀ | | ♂

Part 2. 1864

"When a company of soldiers were in formation, a line of soldiers in a single line, the command would be: 'Count off by twos!' The soldiers would count off: 'One, two... One, two...' et cetera. Then, the officer would command: 'Twos one pace to the rear!' The number twos would step back. Then, the officer calls out: 'Dress on the right guide, dress!' The single line of soldiers would now be two lines of soldiers – ready for battle or parade...."

-- William B. Styple, author and historian

John's brother Mack Camey Morgan [lifespan: 1836-1913] returned at the end of the War recounting that John's regiment during the Battle of Spotsylvania on May 12, 1864 had been ordered to charge.

The 5th Regiment of the North Carolina Infantry -- Company H - which was in Brig. Gen. Robert D. Johnston's Brigade, part of Major General Jubal A. Early's Division, under Lt. Gen. Richard Ewell's Second Corps of the Army of Northern Virginia at Spottsylvania – was readied for battle into six lines. The first three lines were armed. The rows of soldiers who followed gathered arms from the dead and wounded in order to fight.

The butt of John's rifle was reportedly shot off within moments of the order to charge. He did not hear the second order to fall back and continued forward holding only the rifle barrel. Consequently, he was, as his record indicates: *"mortally wounded."*

John's brother Nathan did not escape the watchful eyes of their brother Mack. He returned describing Nathan's red beard as appearing white from the foam of saliva during this same battle at the *Spotsylvania Court House* in Virginia.

Rachel's nine slaves had fled by the end of the War. She was left to raise Mary Jane and John alone on the River Road farm. Rachel never remarried.

♀ | | ♂

Part 3. 1939

Her daughter Mary Jane Morgan married Solomon Eagle, Jr. [1857-1939]. When Solomon passed away December 27th, 1939 his great-grandson James Noah Hinson, M.D. was two weeks from his 11th birthday.

"Two days after Christmas Grandpa Solomon died. Chub had not gotten up yet. June was telling this tale.

"I asked,

"Who was there with you?"

"He answered that Chub was there.

"I did not say anything because I knew Chub was still sleeping that day.

"June and I were there sawing long hickory logs. We lived in the house that Solomon had built as a wedding present for his daughter Lillie [Mary Lillie Eagle Troutman] *and her husband Love Troutman.*

[Love Troutman, July 14, 1897- August 11, 1980; son of Amanda C. Frick and Daniel A. Troutman; Mary Lillie Eagle, May 18, 1898- July 12, 1979, daughter of Mary Jane Morgan and Solomon Eagle, Jr.]

"Solomon later got the house back after Love and Lillie moved to town in Salisbury, where they both went to work in a cotton mill. The house Solomon built for his daughter as a wedding present had a porch on both sides.

"On the day Solomon died, Hattie, his second wife and her sister Kate came out of Solomon's house hollering:

'Pet is dying.'

"Hattie and Katie referred to Solomon as 'Pet' -- he was their human pet. Rowser and Bullie were their actual pets -- bulldogs.

"Solomon was in the bed on his back and somewhere within the next five minutes he took a deep breath and slowly exhaled. It was an agonal breath. That is the last breath that most people usually take when they die.

"They breathe one time, and it occurs one-to-fifteen minutes after they stop breathing. Usually it occurs within three-to-five minutes after they stop breathing. In medical school, we were taught not to be quick to pronounce death before the last breath.

"I saw Grandpa Solomon take his last breath.

"After that, we went down to the Briggs house and asked Burley "Bertie" Morgan who was there visiting his sister Lottie Morgan Briggs – Phillip Ranson Briggs' wife, if he could come over and attend Grandpa Solomon [Eagle] *who had just died.*

[Lottie was a daughter to Jacob Morgan – who was a brother to Mack Camey, Nathan, John, Moses, Noah, James, Silas, David, Elizabeth, Rhoda and Mary.]

"When we returned, Bertie asked for two quarters.

"He placed the quarters over Solomon's eyes to keep them closed."

Luther's Lutheran Church, Richfield, N.C.

SOLOMON EAGLE
BORN JAN 18, 1857 - DIED DEC 27, 1939
MARY JANE MORGAN
WIFE OF SOLOMON EAGLE
BORN NOV 20, 1856 - DIED OCT 15, 1928

♀ | | ♂

PART 4. 2002

James Noah Hinson, M.D. recalls conversations with his great grandfather, Solomon Eagle, Jr. He asked him what he remembered of Federal Officer Major General George Stoneman's raid into Salisbury.

Solomon remembered hearing the firing of cannons, which he thought at the time was in celebration of the War ending. More than likely, what he had heard were the explosions going off at Grant's Creek.

It is possible he heard the firing of cannons from York Heights across from the Yadkin River at Spencer, N.C. This is where the Federal Maj. Gen. Stoneman was coming to liberate prisoners from the Confederate prison for Union soldiers.

In *To Escape Into Dreams*, volume 1, this account is recorded from Christmas Day 2002. The following excerpt is from pages 329-330 of that book.

Fighting was still going on even though the war had been over for two weeks. What Solomon likely heard as a boy was the explosion of a bridge at Grant's Creek. Yankee soldiers were on it coming in from Mocksville. Part of Salisbury's Garrison [unit of the military] was at Grant's Creek Bridge at Catawba College.

They met the Yankees marching down from Mocksville at Grant's Creek Bridge. They [Confederate soldiers] mined the bridge with explosives, and when they could no longer resist advancing federal troops, they pulled back.

They ... blew up the bridge. There may or may not have been cannons fired at this location. As well as there may or may not have been cannons fired from York Heights on the east bank of the Yadkin River. Toward Spencer to the west. Solomon lived around two miles below Liberty.

Wiley Morgan....was a guard then at the Confederate Prison in Salisbury. His fellow guard asked him what he thought the commotion coming from the direction of the train station was about.

Wiley replied:

"I think the Yankees have arrived, and I am going to get the Hell out of here! What are you going to do?"

The fellow guard replied he would keep walking his post and stay to guard the prison. So Wiley jumped off the prison wall with his rifle, got on his horse and rode sixteen miles non-stop back home, took off his uniform and hid it.

A day or so later, Wiley returned to the prison grounds and found his fellow guard had been shot and buried. The gun was broken in half. The barrel of the gun was used as a marker for one end of the grave, and the stock [or butt] of the gun was used for the opposite end.

♀ | | ♂

Major Wiley Sean Morgan [1814-1901] served during the Mexican War [1845-46].

Appears on the School District #41 of North Carolina U.S. Census July 31st, 1850:

Willa Morgan, 37, male; farmer
Catharine Morgan, 39; female
Sephona J. Morgan, 12; female
Elizabeth C., 10; female
Polly L. Morgan, 7; female
Jesse Austin, 5; male

Around 5,000 Union soldiers raided western North Carolina in late March 1865 under the command of the blue-clad Federal Officer Maj. Gen. George Stoneman. His focus was to destroy Confederate supply lines, and Salisbury was part of this goal. Union Maj. Gen. Stoneman met significant resistance from Confederate forces.

This accelerated at Grant's Creek. Five hundred Confederates with two artillery batteries and 200 former prisoners from the Confederate Prison removed the bridge flooring and defended the bridge crossing as the trains loaded with supplies continued transport. Union forces were divided and crossed the river at varying points instead of assaulting from the front. They eventually flanked the Confederates and captured the City of Salisbury.

Incidentally, Confederate Prison for Union soldiers in Salisbury was the only such prison in North Carolina during the War. It was essentially a former textile mill. In May 1862, it held nearly 1,400 Union prisoners. According to the North Carolina History Project, by October 1864, the inmate population increased to around 10,000. Overcrowding and unsanitary conditions precipitated a death rate of over 25 percent with 4,000 of the Union prisoners dying during the prison's operation. It has been reported that an estimated 100 Union prisoners tunneled out of the prison and escaped in January 1865.

Recapping:

    Rachel E. Wyatt Morgan, whose nine slaves abandoned her at the end of the War and whose husband was killed in the *Battle of Spottsylvania,* was left a widow with two children to raise:

1) <u>Mary Jane Morgan</u> [1856-1928] who married Solomon Eagle, Jr. [1857-1939] and had one son Noah Jenkins Eagle [1878-1976] and two daughters: Rachel Minnie Dora Eagle [b. 1885; m. Cain Morgan] and Mary Lillie Eagle [lifespan: 1898-1975; m. Love Troutman].
2) <u>John Noah Calvin Morgan</u> [lifespan: 1862-1927; m. Eugenia A. *"Jennie"* Culp.

♀ | | ♂

PART 5.
MAY 28, 2008
JOURNAL ENTRY

I called my father today, a Wednesday, to ask him to relay a question about Ada Leighton to my mother. Somehow, the conversation evolved into recollections as to word expressions commonly used by Solomon Eagle, Jr.

"I was sitting on the front porch of Solomon's home when he said:

'By gum, someone's killed a beef.'

"He used the expression 'by gum' in order to avoid saying, 'By God.'

"No one had butchered a cow that day, so most people might deduce what Solomon was saying without any further explanation."

Rachel Wyatt Morgan's son-in-law Solomon Eagle, Jr. helped saw the timber used for building the new Saint Matthew's Lutheran Church in Salisbury, N.C. and then he helped build this church when his son Noah was four or five years old.

"Rev. John Hodge was Baptist minister who delivered sermons at East Corinth.

This Baptist minister was asked to preach the homecoming service because a Lutheran minister could not be found at the time. He arrived at the old church, where Saint Matthew's Lutheran Church is currently located.

During the sermon the minister stomped his feet repeatedly as he stood on top of the hogshead. He shouted:

"If you don't change your ways, you will go straight to hell!"

After repeated stomping, he plummeted through the hogshead.* Startled and shaken by the unexpected, the minister said:

"Service dismissed."

* A hogshead [hogz'hed] is a large cask or barrel designed to hold 63 wine gallons, or 52.5 imperial gallons, or 54 gallons of beer, 46 gallons of claret, or in the U.S. containing tobacco varying 750 to 1200 pounds.

Robert Noah Eagle, a grandson of Solomon and maternal uncle to James said in May 2016: *"Grandpa always called me Robert – not Bob. One day he said: 'I hear you* [and Chub] *took the buggy out for a ride. I don't mind, but if you want to do it again. I would appreciate if you let me know.' Another time, I recall asking Grandpa how he was doing. He said: 'I'm doing all right, but this gout is about to kill me.' "*

The following Rowan County petition records information on the property formerly owned by John Morgan [1834-1864], husband of Rachel E. Wyatt Morgan. Eli Wyatt [1841-1912], who is present when the document is drawn up, is a brother to Rachel Wyatt Morgan. Eli Wyatt is a son of Mary Polly Hendly (Henly or Hendley) and Noah Calvin Wyatt, son of Rachel Park and Thomas Wiatt.

Do not confuse this Eli with another Eli Wiatt [b. Abt. 1789] who is one of the three sons of John Wiatt [1743-1815] who moved to Kentucky. John Wiatt's son Eli is on the Kentucky census for 1840 and 1850 -- the years he was living in McCracken County, Ky.

McCracken County is very close to Calloway and Marshall counties - Calloway borders Marshall to the south, and McCracken borders Marshall to the northeast.

John Buchanan [1828-1889] is a brother-in-law to Rachel E. Wyatt Morgan, as he is then married to Malinda [Delinda] Wyatt [1829-1903].

The Rowan County, N.C. document is dated April 8, 1866.

State of North Carolina Rowan County,
Whereas John Buchanan Administrator of John Morgan,
deceased, did file his petition to the May Session A.D.
1866 of Rowan County Court against the heirs at law
of the Said John Morgan, deceased, praying for the date
of the Real Estate of the said John Morgan, deceased,
descended to his heirs, and whereas at the said May
Session A.D. 1866 of said Court a decree was made
ordering him, the said John Buchanan, Admin to sell
the said land of the said John Morgan deceased
subject to the widow's right of dower, and to make
title to the purchaser upon the payment of the purchase
money, and whereas, the said sum was exposed to
public sale subject to the widow's rights of dower
upon the premises upon the 30th day of June
1866, when and where Rachel E. Morgan was the
last and highest bidder of the sum of three hundred
Dollars to him, now the said John Buchanan Admin. for and
in consideration of the said sum of three hundred

Dollars to him in hand paid by the said Rachel E.

Morgan the receipt whereof he doth hereby acknowledge, hath bargained, and sold by these presents, and

doth bargain and sell to the said Rachel E. Morgan

her heirs and [indiscernible word], That tract on parcel of land

subject to the widows right of dower, situated and

lying in the said County of Rowan and State of North

Carolina bounded as follows to wit: situation on the

water of little creek, Beginning at a white oak a little

North of Nathan Morgan's dwelling House by a Black Oak

+ 2 white oaks and a Hickory, and runs North 14 [degrees] East

5 chains and 25 links to a Persimon in the field. Thence

North 14 [degrees] West 20 chains and 25 links to a Rock in the old

field. Thence South 82 [indiscernible words] West [indiscernible]

Chains and 21 links to a Rock, South East corner of Chapel Church lot. Thence [indiscernible word] 8 chains and 16 links to a Small Pine another the said Church lot, Thence North 5 [degrees] East and a 11 links to a Stone. Thence North 85 [degrees] West one chain and 55 links to a double persimon. Thence North 25 [degrees] 111 chains

and 40 links to a Post -Oak on Richard Hodge's line.

Thence South 74 [degrees] West 14 chains to a Pine-Not and

Cedar-Birch. Thence South 41 chains +35 links to a

Pine-not. Thence North 74 [degrees] East 39 Chains and

40 links to the place of beginning containing in all

one hundred and twenty-one and a half Acres of

Land be the same more or less

To have and to hold to her the said Rachel E. Morgan

his heirs forever and the said John Buchanan Admin.

doth covenant to warrant and defend the title to the

premises only so far as empowered to do by said decree

and no further. In witness whereof I have hereunto

set my hand and fixed my seal this the 8th day

of April A.D. 1866. Signed, Sealed and delivered

in the presence of

Eli Wyatt   John Buchanan (Seal)

Author's note: A *"dower"* is a spouse's legal entitlement to share of the deceased spouse's real estate or other property during his or her lifetime. It is the provision the law makes for the widow out of the lands or tenement of her husband for her support and nurture of her children. Dower rights applied to widow's giving them one-third of the total land owned by her husband. She could choose in substitution for the dower to accept other property left to her in her husband's will.

Notation:

According to James N. Hinson, M.D., the land formerly owned by John Morgan [1834-1864] – husband of Rachel Wyatt Morgan, eventually became the property of Solomon Eagle Jr. [1857-1939] and was around 122.5 acres – Solomon being the son-in-law of Rachel Wyatt Morgan and the husband of Mary Jane Morgan Eagle [1856-1928]. Around two acres of this land was willed to Noah Jenkins Eagle [1878-1976], a son of Solomon and Mary Jane Morgan Eagle.

Rachel Evelyn Wyatt Morgan [1835-1915]

John Calvin Morgan [1834-1864]

CHAPTER 18

Echoes of Love

♀ | | ♂

*"Everyone should do all in his power to collect and disseminate the truth,
in hope that it may find a place in history and descend posterity."*

❦   CONFEDERATE GEN. ROBERT E. LEE [1807-1870]

*"...When Sherman's army marched through Georgia and the Carolinas,
the soldiers who went into the countryside to rob or pillage, were called
Sherman's Bummers...Sometimes, Yankees were called Lincolnites."*

❦   WILLIAM B. STYPLE, CIVIL WAR HISTORIAN AND RESEARCHER.

PART 1. 1865

RACHEL EVELYN WYATT MORGAN'S MEMORIES unfolded like a neatly preserved letter. She was 30 years old. Her world had been torn into bloody pieces. She clung to those fragments as if to reinforce the strength and will to survive. The words were passed to her daughter and son and so forth.

Tears welled in the would-be thief's eyes. He was more than just a thief. He was a Yankee soldier. The federal was exhausted *no doubt* – dirty, tired and eager to find his way back to the North. If he fought against John Morgan in the Battle of Spottsylvania – then who was to say *or not* whether one of his bullets entered the body of Rachel's husband?

John's widow saw through a glass pane the Union man – his blue uniform tattered and covered in the dust of carnage and of those filthy layers of sleeping in the realm of the paranoid mindset of all soldiers during wartime. The hem of Rachel's dark clothes of mourning moved like a curtain in an opened window as she walked to the door of her River Road home in Rowan County, N.C.

Opening the entrance, pushing herself to the porch, she bravely took note of what he was doing.

"My slaves have run off," she yelled out to gain his attention. *"…and that horse is the only thing I have left to raise my two children with."*

The Union soldier's motive to steal the dregs of what Rachel had left at the end of the War was no doubt thwarted by her tone and brought to the forefront any goodness or dignity the man possessed.

The soldier stood holding the halter to steady the plow horse. Through his tears, he saw this honestly and innocently vulnerable, but focused woman, dressed in her homemade farm dress. The Union soldier placed the horse back into the barn. He left on foot to seek some other form of transportation.

♀ | | ♂

PART 2.

Described as *"a woman of resolve in making her plans with determination"* by her great-great grandson James Noah Hinson, M.D. -- Rachel would have been the first to relay this story, which was passed to her grandson Noah Jenkins Eagle and others through the generations.

From that one story – Rachel's perspective is preserved.

Rachel Evelyn Wyatt Morgan [1835-1915] had 12 siblings. Rachel, as mentioned earlier, married John Morgan and her sister Lila Delilah *"Delila"* Wyatt, born in 1834, married Nathaniel *"Nathan"* Morgan [1832-1904], who was born and died in the Poole Town District of Morgan Township, N.C.

The name *"Rachel,"* which means *"lamb"* did not stop with Mary Jane Morgan Eagle's daughter Rachel Minnie Dora Eagle. Mary Jane Morgan Eagle's son Noah Eagle [1878-1976] had a daughter, amongst six other children. That daughter was Virgie Irene Eagle [1902-1984] who married a Hinson. Virgie's remains are buried with those of her parents in the Wyatt Grove Missionary Baptist Church Cemetery on the corner of Bringle Ferry and Wyatt Grove Church roads in Richfield, Rowan County, N.C.

Virgie had six children, including my father James Noah Hinson, M.D. Virgie's second daughter was Rachel Evelyn Hinson [1932-1994]. This Rachel was named for her second great grandmother Rachel Evelyn Wyatt Morgan. The name *"Evelyn"* is sometimes spelled *"Eveline."*

Rachel Evelyn Wyatt Morgan [1835-1915] whose remains are buried at Luther's Lutheran Church in an area formerly called Piney Woods District of Morgan Township of Rowan County is the point in which this research began.

Wyatt history travels to Rachel Evelyn Wyatt [who married John Morgan – [1834-1864,] the one who was *"mortally wounded"* in the Battle of Spottsylvania [Spotsylvania] Court House in Virginia during the American Civil War.

Rachel Evelyn Wyatt Morgan daughter of: → Noah Calvin Wyatt [1805-1871] son of: → Thomas Wiatt [1774-1845] son of: → John Wiatt [1743-1815].

John Morgan [1834-1864] son of: → Moses Green Morgan [1810-1879] & Barbara Shaver [1813-1896] – this Moses Green Morgan being a brother to Maj. Wiley Sean Morgan [1814-1901] – who served in the Mexican War from 1845-46; was a prison guard at the Salisbury Prison that housed Union soldiers. Maj. Wiley Sean Morgan was a private at age 47 who trained troops at Morgan Muster ground during the War Between the States.

* Dr. John Morgan [minister], son of Julia E. [1858-1935] & Moses L. Morgan [1860-1893] restored the Morgan Cemetery around November 1965. Barbara Shaver and her husband Moses G. Morgan [1810-1879] – not to be confused with Moses L. Morgan, have their remains buried in the Morgan Cemetery, located on Stokes Ferry Road, Rowan County, N.C. Many relatives of John Morgan [1834-1864] are buried in the Morgan Cemetery, and those closest to him whose remains are there include his father Moses Green Morgan [1810-1879], his mother Barbara Shaver Morgan [1813-1896], his paternal grandparents Nathan Morgan, Jr. [1785-1844] and Elizabeth *"Betty"* Park Morgan [b. 1781], brother Mack Camey Morgan [1837-1915], brother Silas Green Morgan [1857-1921]; sister Mary Morgan Arey [1836-1913] and brother Noah Morgan, who was born about 1845 and killed during the American Civil War.

Note:

The July 31st, 1850 United States Federal Census of North Carolina for School District #41 list the following:

*Moses G. Morgan, 39, male, farmer; Barbara, 35; Nathan, 17; ***John, 15**; McKay* [Mack Camey], *13; Mary, 11; Rhoda, 9, Moses G. 7; Noah, 5; Jacob, 3; Loveles, 1; Rachel, 37.*

Continuation:

Found at the top of the page for School District #41 -- 1st day of _____ 1850:

Mary Morgan, 11; female
Rhoda Morgan 9; female
Moses G. Morgan, 7; male
Noah Morgan, 5; male
Jacob Morgan, 3; male
Loveles, 1; male*
Rachel Shaver, 39; female

*Loveles meaning "Loveless."

♀ | | ♂

PART 3.
FRIDAY EVENING
JUNE 13, 2014
JOURNAL ENTRY

The telephone rings. I am talking with my father about the Wyatts. Naturally, a conversation about the Morgans ties in. The Eagle and the Briggs families tie in soon after. It is quite easy to have a conversation about the Müllers [Millers], Shavers and Park families because at some juncture they have married into these lineages. Some became my direct lineages. Other branches grew making some double cousins to me and one another.

There are several Nathan Morgans. Specifically, Nathan Morgan [1832-1904] who married Lila Delilah *"Delila"* Wyatt, born in 1834 is a focus this evening. This Nathan, as mentioned earlier is a son to Barbara Shaver and Moses Greene Morgan.

Glancing a photo of Nathan's tombstone, one sees the inscription includes the name of a Linda *"Linna"* Surratt and a daughter: Mammie Esther Morgan [1880-1948].

My father confirms my eyes do not deceive – Nathan married twice. This leads into a conversation about Nathan's niece – Lottie Barbara E. Morgan Briggs [1879-1956] who was born in Rowan County and died in Davidson County, N.C. Lottie is a daughter to Ann James *"Jim"* Kirk [1854-1924] and Jacob Morgan [1847-1919]. Lottie's husband referred to by my father simply as *"Ranson Briggs"* [Phillip Ranson Briggs, 1881-1966] used to live in a house referred to as the *"Briggs Place."*

The Briggs Place was a house and still is a farm on River Road in Rowan County. The Briggs Place is located across the now paved road of the farm, formerly owned by John Morgan and his wife Rachel Wyatt, and later by Mary Jane Morgan and Solomon Eagle, Jr. [That place was essentially the Morgan-Wyatt-Eagle Place] and is no longer owned by our family members. I refer to the Briggs Place as the main farm, or the hub of my father's other farms.

The calendar page flips to the year 1972. Night hours became a temporary routine for renovations on The Briggs Place. My father with the assistance of his brother Chub pounds nails, rips out rotten floor boards and replaces with new.

At age nine, I watch as the flooring on the porch is removed and replaced with lumber he cut. Soon after, the house is rented to the Wilson family. The Wilson's home was clean, warm and welcoming. Their presence made the Briggs Place feel alive. For years prior, I would go there and gather pecans from the yard. My father said then if I did not stop fussing with Hans we would wake up Mister Briggs. Of course, Mr. Briggs was not in there – but I was convinced some old man in the then vacant house, was sleeping much.

The barn and house of the Wilson family had burned, so they needed a place to live. The former Briggs Place was later burned as well by a person who supposedly burned other structures and fields in Rowan County. I've never forgotten the sadness in my father's demeanor and face when that historical family landmark was lost to flames.

As if a gust of wind blowing over and along the roads of Rowan turns the calendar page to the year 1902, my father's focus addresses another time. In 1902 – the year Virgie Irene Eagle [Hinson] was born, a visitor appears at the door of Noah Jenkins Eagle on Orchard Road.

The visitor is a former slave of the Benson family. She walked 17 miles stopping at *"Pop Eagle's"* [Noah Jenkins Eagle, 1878-1976] house. Noah's daughter Virgie Irene [my father's mother] was a baby then. The slave woman asks Noah Eagle where she might find *"Master Nathan."*

This makes better sense if one understands that Noah's mother is Mary Jane Morgan [1856-1928] who married Solomon Eagle, Jr. [1857-1939]. This Mary Jane is the daughter as mentioned earlier in this book of John Morgan [1834-1864] and Rachel E. Wyatt Morgan. This John Morgan is a son of Moses Greene Morgan [1810-1879] and Barbara Shaver Morgan [1813-1896]. Moses's son and John's brother Nathan [1832-1904] is the person the slave woman was inquiring of.

This Nathan – there are several, is the one who married Lila Delilah *"Delila"* Wyatt in 1855 and later Linda *"Linna"* Surratt, 1842-1921 and had a daughter Mammie Esther Morgan, whose remains are with her parents at East Corinth Baptist Church Cemetery, Gold Hill, Rowan County, N.C.

Jacob Morgan – a brother of Nathan, has a daughter Lottie who married Ranson Briggs as I mentioned earlier. *"Master Nathan,"* as the slave woman referred to him, was an uncle to Mary Jane Morgan Eagle, a great uncle to Noah Jenkins Eagle to whom she directed the conversation. Nathan was a brother to John – the husband of Rachel Evelyn Wyatt who died at Spottsylvania; and brother to McCamey [Mack Camey], Mary, Rhoda, Moses, Jacob, James Loveless, Elizabeth, David and Silas. Nathan lived next door to the slave woman's former owners – the Benson family. The Benson family lived close to the Briggs home as well.

My father says:

"One day the former slave woman came walking down that dirt road that ran by Pop Eagle's. She – the slave woman, was old then – and walked seventeen miles from Salisbury. I believe she lived in Salisbury after she gained her freedom. I used to go down there [to the Benson's

house] *and find broken dishes. They had slave quarters there. She had lived down there where the spring was."*

I asked:

"What did the slave woman want of Nathan?"

He replied:

"She wanted to talk with Nathan about those things old people want to talk about."

Nathan died two years later at the age of 72.

The term *"master"* might have appeared as part of the former slave's training during years prior to the ACW. All free white men were addressed as *"master"* by their slaves; however, given that the year was 1902, it might have been used by the former slave simply as affection as she had called him in her youth. The term *"master"* was reserved for boys in forms of address; whereas *"mister"* is used for grown men. Knowing that Nathan was by then elderly, it follows the address was affection. Not all former slaves disliked their former white neighbors or owners. Some slave owners of Rowan loved their slaves so much they buried the remains of slaves in family cemeteries. [Example: The Reed Graveyard near Tuckertown Lake.]

♀ | | ♂

*"Nothing fills me with deeper sadness than to see a Southerner
apologize for the defense we made for our heritage."*

⚜ LIEUTENANT & CONFEDERATE PRESIDENT JEFFERSON FINIS DAVIS [1808-1889].

Mary Jane Morgan Eagle [1856-1928] – mother of Noah Jenkins Eagle, Rachel
Minnie Dora Eagle Morgan & Mary Lillie Eagle Troutman.

CHAPTER 19

Surviving Point Lookout
The Morgan Brothers

♀ | | ♂

*"Mack Camey and his brother Nathan were in infantry. The amazing
thing was that they were in the infantry and came home at all."*

☀ JAMES N. HINSON, M.D. THURSDAY, DECEMBER 11TH,
2008 DURING A TELEPHONE CONVERSATION.

PART 1. NATHANIEL *"NATHAN"* MORGAN [1832-1904]

THE RED BEARDED CONFEDERATE SOLDIER Nathan returned to Rowan County with his brother Mack. The scars of battle – the loss of brothers and cousins followed them as ghosts no doubt. Through the dirt and gravel roads of Morgan Township few now paved, they found the courage to speak of their experiences.

Of those conversations that were lost – public records fill in the gaps. Of those horrors never spoken, the bones of Union Prison at Point Lookout will forever speak.

Nathan Morgan [1832-1904], being the third Nathan Morgan, not from his father Moses Green Morgan [1810-1879], but from his grandfather and great grandfather to carry the name, served during the American Civil War in the 5th Regiment -- Company H of the North Carolina Infantry. Nathaniel Morgan, resided in Rowan County and enlisted in Iredell County at the age of 30 August 8, 1862.

Nathan was captured at Gettysburg, Pa. after being wounded in the right thigh sometime between July 1st and 4th, 1863. He was confined at Fort McHenry, Md. and at Fort Delaware, Del. until he was transferred to Point Lookout, Md. between October 15th and 18th, 1863.

Fourteen-foot wooden walls encased the 40 acres that comprised the camp of Point Lookout Prison. From the vantage point of the Heavens, it certainly was a festering wound in Saint Mary's County, Md. During the course of its operation Point Lookout Prison Camp contained 50,000 enlisted confederate men. Disease from contaminated and polluted water, inadequate food, icy temperatures, the absence of barracks, daily abuse by guards shook newcomers into Hell on earth.

Confederates were given tents, but as conditions worsened and the population of the camp grew, the deficit opened the doors of death and carnage. It is suggested that the capacity of Point Lookout Prison was 10,000, but at any given time the prison population was between 12,000 and 20,000.

Today, Point Lookout is known as Point Lookout State Park. It is located in the southernmost spot on Maryland's western shore and coastal regions of the western side of the Chesapeake Bay. Specifically, it is on the southern tip of Saint Mary's County on a peninsula formed by the confluence of the lower Potomac River, Point Lookout Creek and Chesapeake Bay. Over 14,000 prisoners died at Point Lookout. One source states that 3,384 bodies are buried there in a mass grave without records to back this number. Estimates from Point Lookout State Park report that out of the over 50,000 prisoners held there – only 4,000 died.

Discrepancies, yes.

Nathan Morgan was paroled at Point Lookout March 23, 1864 and transferred to City Point, Va. for an exchange. This means the Union traded him for a Union soldier who had been captured by the Confederacy. He rejoined his company prior to November 1, 1864. Nathan Morgan was paroled at Appomattox Court House, Va. April 9, 1865 after the War ended, according to troop records. Some historical accounts report this occurred three days after that.

Appomattox Court House is now part of a National Historical Park. On April 9, 1865 Confederate General Robert E. Lee, surrendered the Army of Northern Virginia to Lieutenant-General Ulysses Grant. Several other confederate armies under different commanders were still in the field when Lee's surrender took place. Lee's actions signaled the four-year-long war was officially over. The futile attempt of the Southern states to create a separate nation had ended.

Three days after April 9, 1865, the men of the Army of Northern Virginia -- Lee's men, were marched before the Union Army. They stacked their muskets and furled their banners. The soldiers had placed the furled flag on top of the muskets with the bayonets attached. This ending of the War was a new beginning. Nathan – who may be related to you in any number of ways, was my third great-granduncle. This fact is to supply focus as to how he connects with the writer of this book and to others.

Nathan *"Nath"* Morgan, certainly stood exhausted amongst his comrades at Appomattox. The flashing of the horrors he had witnessed in battle playing through his mind like a nightmare in which one does not wake.

My father remembered what had been told to him about Nathan Morgan, husband of Lila Wyatt. While in battle, Nathan, fighting along side his Wyatt cousins, took on the appearance of intolerable fear, mouth breathing and dehydration.

"Nathan had a red beard, and he foamed at the mouth so much it looked like he had a white beard."

In summation so far, we have Rachel Wyatt and her sister Lila marrying two Morgan brothers -- John, who died at Spotsylvania and Nathan who surrendered at Appomattox.

The point about complicated lineages is not yet complete. Brothers John and Nathan had another sibling named Noah Green Morgan, born around 1845, who -- although he did not marry a Wyatt, served in Company G, 6th North Carolina Infantry, was killed in the War.

Mack Camey *"McCamy"* Morgan [1836-1913], a brother to John, Nathan and Noah, did not marry a Wyatt, but was yoked twice -- first to Mary Elizabeth *"Betty"* Arey [1842-1904] in September 1857; and secondly, he married Martha Jane Stoner, born October 1844.

Martha Jane Stoner was the wife of Reuben Monroe Eller -- both the parents of three children, including my great grandmother Laura Lou Eller Eagle. The only child Mack Camey had with Martha was Greenleaf Whittier Morgan. McCamey or Mack Camey or Camy, being my third great granduncle on the Morgan lineage, had 15 children with his first wife. His second marriage created a new title. With that, he became [after I was born] my *step* second great grandfather.

Martha is quoted as saying prior to her engagement:

"I don't want anything to do with that tobacco-chewing man."

Tangles!

The layers of families in Rowan must be explained in order to grasp the intricate patterns of its genealogy. These examples are few as compared to the bulk and the ones that accurately define *complicated*. The quest is to explain it as simply as the English language will allow.

Note: The July 31st, 1850 United States Federal Census of North Carolina for School District #41 list the following:

Moses G. Morgan, 39, male, farmer; Barbara, 35; Nathan, 17; John, 15; McCamy, 13; Mary, 11; Rhoda, 9, Moses G. 7; Noah, 5; Jacob, 3; Loveles, 1; Rachel, 37.

Continuation:

Found at the top of the page for School District #41 -- 1st day of _____ 1850:

Mary Morgan, 11; female
Rhoda Morgan 9; female
Moses G. Morgan, 7; male
Noah Morgan, 5; male
Jacob Morgan, 3; male
Loveles, 1; male
Rachel Shaver, 39; female

> *"General Lee surrendered about 26,000 men, of whom only 7,892 were armed...I assert without fear of contradiction that there were more fighting men at the close of the war in Point Lookout Prison alone, not to mention Fort Delaware, Hart's Island, Johnson's Island, Newport News and other questionable places.... than there were in Lee's whole army at the surrender..."*

- CONFEDERATE SERGEANT CHARLES T. LOEHR [B. AUGUST 8, 1842, ALTENA, GERMANY; D. MARCH 5, 1915, RICHMOND, VA.] IN AN ADDRESS BEFORE PICKETT CV CAMP, OCTOBER 10, 1890.

♀ | | ♂

Part 2. Mack Camey Morgan [1836-1913]

The October winds of 1863 lifted in flight the great blue heron that nested near the Federals' insanity of Point Lookout. It seemed possibly a place in waiting – a place that stretched its dirty skeleton arms like a demon from the bowels of War to those whose luck it would be to enter it.

Pvt. Mack Camey Morgan fell out from the march from Front Royal, Va. July 24, 1863. After having been captured at Manassas Gap, Va., July 24, 1863, he was still full of the stamina that comes with youth. One week later after being confined at Washington, D.C., he was transferred to Point Lookout. His imprisonment and health would not dictate an early death, as he stayed there for eight months until March 3, 1864. Mack's brother Nathan's arrival in October 1863 was one of the bearded faces that peered out in the shuffle and fast stepping of those tortured by starvation and disease.

Mack and Nathan's 26-year-old cousin Silas Wyatt traveled there across the bumpy mountainous terrain as well. Maryland and its early icy temperatures coupled with the filthiness of tents and lack of tents and blankets dictated resistance in body, mind and spirit.

Silas, a young school teacher, was confined nearly three and a half months at Fort Delaware since his capture at the Battle of Gettysburg in July 1863. He grew weaker each day. Silas passed through the same gates of Point Lookout as his cousins in the same days, and within 11 days of this, fell deathly ill. Silas was hospitalized at Point Lookout dying two and a half months later [January 19, 1864] of chronic diarrhea due to the poor quality of water given to prisoners.

For Mack, though later exchanged to rejoin Company H, Point Lookout was a hungrier state of affairs six months later. Mack was captured again September 19, 1864 at Winchester, Va., in the state where he had with his brother Nathan been paroled March 3, 1864 at Point Lookout and then exchanged. He was confined at Harper's Ferry, W.Va. and then at Point Lookout., Md. for six months collectively until paroled and transferred to Aiken's Landing, James River, Va., March 15, 1865, for exchange.

Mack took the Oath of Allegiance at Salisbury on June 9, 1865 – just two days after his cousin William A. Park, who served in Company D -- 10th Regiment – the 1st Regiment N.C. Light Artillery, died of typhoid fever in the cruel, cold clutches of Point Lookout. Nathan and Mack's cousin William Alexander Park had been wounded at Sharpsburg, Md. September16, 1862. He was present and accounted for through February 1865. Luck ran out when he was captured at Amelia Court House, April 5, 1865 and confined at Point Lookout, Md.

At Saint Peter's Lutheran Church Cemetery in Rockwell, Rowan County, N.C., there is a stone for William Alexander Park. It is inscribed: *"Co D 1 NC Artillery 1830 1865."* It is located in the 4th row.

Mack Camey Morgan [1836-1913], repeating he is a brother to John and Nathan who married two Wyatt sisters, resided as his brothers did in Rowan County when he enlisted in Iredell County for the Confederacy. He joined the army at age 27 on August 8th, 1862 with his brothers Nathaniel and John along with their cousin Noah Wyatt, a brother to Silas Wyatt.

No recollections of Fort Delaware are found from Wyatts and Morgans who experienced Fort Delaware. On pages 158-161 of *Writing & Fighting from the Army of Northern Virginia, A Collection of Confederate Soldier Correspondence,* edited by William B. Styple, is a personal account of Fort Delaware from an R.A. Gains writing to his brother on October 11, 1862 from Richmond, Va.

The following excerpt is from such letter written after R.A. Gaines was paroled and sent under the flag of truce to Aiken's [Aken's] Landing on the James River. When he arrived in Richmond, Va., he was very ill with a bowel disease. He was rescued from a side walk by a Louisiana Lieutenant and taken to a hospital. His account from Styple's collections:

"At Baltimore we took the boats for Fort Delaware. This fort is situated on a small island in the Delaware Bay.

"Here we were placed in charge of a set of the most brutal, inhuman demons that ever blacked the pages of history. They did not give us as much to eat in two days' time, as we could eat at one meal, and gave us scarcely any water to drink, except salt water out of the bay, when instead of quenching our thirst, made it worse and fevered our brain almost to a frenzy...."

Gains describes the inhuman actions of those Union soldiers who wanted Confederates to take an oath of allegiance to the Federal Government and abandon their cause of defending the South to the point they inflicted tyrannical brutality. Even Rains in vain attempt to trade his knife for a piece of bread to eat was met with the threat of death.

Gains wrote:

"I owe no allegiance to any infernal government that would deny a prisoner food and water... I will perish before I forsake our glorious little Confederacy, the land of my father and my mother...."

"...It was not uncommon for a Yankee Sergeant to come into the yard, single out a man, follow him all around the yard kicking him at every step...

"One of the prisoners lost a small sum of money and told one of the Yankee Corporals he believed 'that man stole it,' pointing to another prisoner who occupied the bunk next to him, upon which his corporal-ship stepped up to the accused and ordered him to draw his shirt, when he received on his bare back twenty-five or thirty strokes with the flat side of the Corporal's sabre, which drew the blood at almost every stroke..."

Within R.A. Gain's account includes him talking in the prison yard with *"a gentleman from South Carolina by the name of Parker,"* who was then 56 years old. The same Corporal who beat the younger prisoner walked up and began beating Parker with his sabre and at the same time asking him why he did not get out of his way.

Top, left to right: Morgan brothers: Nathaniel & John; 2nd row,
left to right: Mack Camey, Jacob, James Loveless.

CHAPTER 20

Wyatts & Related Soldiers

♀ | | ♂

"It is forbidden to kill; therefore, all murderers are punished unless
they kill in large numbers and to the sound of trumpets."

– VOLTAIRE

Known as François-Marie Arouet
[November 21, 1694-May 30, 1778]
French Enlightenment, playwright
writer, historian, philosopher
Paris, France.

"The duty of its citizens, then appears to me too plain to admit of doubt.
All should unite in honest efforts to obliterate the effects of the war and to
restore the blessing of peace.... promote harmony and good feelings..."

❧   ON GETTYSBURG, CONFEDERATE GEN. ROBERT E. LEE, IN A
LETTER TO VIRGINIA GOVERNOR JOHN LETCHER [1813-1844].

WILLIAM WESLEY WYATT [1831-1863]
PART 1. 1861-1865

*R*OY ELI WYATT [1929-2005] WAS a great grandson of William Wesley Wyatt. Of Roy's grandmother Barbara Ann E. Basinger Wyatt [1862-1957] James Noah Hinson, M.D. said:

"She came outside and said, ' I want to show you something. I have my second eye sight...'.
She goes into the house...She kept the fences clear of briars. She did not like the kitchen...I was
doubly kin to some of these people."

A stillness hung in the air of Rowan County's near ending summer on September 4, 1862. As the clouds moved across the blue yonder, and all of Mother Nature seemed well with the world, the souls of mankind were torn both in body and in spirit. Soon more would be joining them on the battlefields as carnage and heroes – victors and victims.

The young faces of children and of pretty Southern wives of Confederate soldiers no doubt stayed in the minds of those men who left to enlist. William Wesley Wyatt shared those things in common with all soldiers who fought in the War.

His final goodbyes to his wife Mary Buchanan Wyatt and young sons John C. and James *"Jim"* Noah were those pictures his eyes and emotions drew close to his heart. They were like hands and arms grasping and holding on to those things one fears never touching again.

His second cousins Mack Camey, Nathan and John Morgan had already enlisted in Iredell County on August 8, 1862.

A little over a year later William Wesley Wyatt, who fought with his North Carolina comrades in Company H of the 23rd Regiment was present and accounted for until he was wounded in the back and arm. He was captured sometime between July 1-3, 1863 during the Battle of Gettysburg. He succumbed to his wounds July 20 of the same year.

William's second cousin Nathaniel *"Nathan"* Morgan fought at Gettysburg. Sometime between July 1- 4, 1863 he was injured in the right thigh. Of course, Nathan survived the War as you read in a previous chapter.

William's brother Silas Wyatt fought at Gettysburg and later on in the war died of *"chronic diarrhoea"* while a prisoner at Point Lookout, Md. Later, the U.S. Government erected a tribute to those men who died at Point Lookout in Saint Mary's County, Md. The Federal Confederate cemetery memorial plaque is inscribed:

ERECTED BY THE UNITED STATES TO MARK THE BURIAL PLACE OF CONFEDERATE SOLDIERS AND SAILORS – WHO DIED AT POINT LOOKOUT, MD. WHILE PRISONERS OF WAR AND WERE THERE BURIED TO THE NUMBER OF 3,384 BUT WHOSE REMAINS WERE SUBSEQUENTLY REMOVED, EITHER TO THEIR RESPECTIVE HOMES OR TO THIS CEMETERY WHERE THE INDIVIDUAL GRAVES CANNOT BE IDENTIFIED.

Military records are found for all – but one of William Wesley Wyatt's brothers: Emanuel James M. Wyatt, born in 1832. The other brothers of that household who served in the Confederacy: John P. Wyatt in the 2nd Regiment Company B North Carolina Junior Reserves; Henry Thomas Wyatt in the 7th Regiment Company F N.C.S.T.; Eli Wyatt in Company D, 10th Regiment N.C.S.T. (1st Regiment N.C. Light Artillery Battery); Noah Wyatt in the 5th Regiment -- Company H N.C.S.T.

William Wesley Wyatt, born in 1831, succumbing to his wounds on July 20, 1863 at Gettysburg, Pa. [having served in the 23rd Regiment -- Company H] was a brother to Rachel Evelyn Wyatt Morgan, and both of whom were second cousins to the Morgan men who fought for the Confederacy.

Explaining genealogical webs is similar to re-braiding those ties, which got scattered like bones mixed with the related and unrelated.

Martyn Freeth, the British genealogist who passed away in 2012, emphasized that many in England, the United States and other parts of the world commonly married their second, third, fourth cousins and so forth. Genealogists may find people in the modern day who marry their cousins without realizing it.

Timothy Lucas appears in the middle. On the far left, which is right of Timothy, is Timothy Lucas' eldest son Peter. The child is Clinton Howard Lucas, Peter's eldest child. The woman is Ann Fitzpatrick Lucas, wife of Timothy.

♀ | | ♂

PART 2.
SUMMER, 2014
LUCAS & WYATT IN 1863
JOURNAL ENTRY

Beneath our feet on former battle grounds, each blade of grass was once drenched in the blood of hellish screams. The American Civil War [ACW] or the War Between the States that lasted four years, three weeks and six days with the last shot fired June 22, 1865 [April 12, 1861- May 10, 1865] is said to have been a war of brother against brother, cousin against cousin. When we peek through the remnants of time, it is difficult to imagine the battles fought on ground we now stroll upon.

William Wesley Wyatt, a brother to my third great grandmother Rachel E. Wyatt Morgan was at Gettysburg, Pa. fighting on the same day as an ancestor from my son's paternal lineage – an Irish immigrant from Belfast. He was a weaver named Timothy Lucas [1831-1910].

He was a Union soldier and third great grandfather of my children and their first cousins on their paternal side. Timothy Lucas needed work. He enlisted for the Union on August 12, 1861 at Philadelphia, Pa. He joined Captain William Raughman's Company E Third Regiment, Penn Cavalry --- Army of the United States, was honorably discharged from the service on the Twenty fourth day of August 1864.

[It has been speculated he had a brother named Benjamin who had immigrated to the U.S. and moved South. It is known Timothy Lucas had a son named George Benjamin Lucas [born 1862] whose name appears as Benjamin on Timothy's death certificate.

Possibly had Timothy moved South he might have fought for the Confederacy. Sergeant Timothy Lucas of the Regiment 3rd Penn Cavalry was recovering in the General Hospital of Baltimore, Md. on July 25, 1863 after his horse fell on him during the Battle of Gettysburg [July 1-3, 1863, Gettysburg, Adams County, Pa.]

Parvis General Hosp'l
Baltimore, Md.
Aug: 29, 1863

Sergt. Tim Lucas
    3rd Pa: Cav'y
    Asks transfer
to Philadelphia
M.D.O.8 "At Balto. Md.

Sept. 1st 1863 Respectfully
referred to Asst. Surg. D.C.
Peters U.S.A. Transfer
authorized "if necessary to
recovery."
[signed]   Geo. Luther
           Surgeon M.S. Vols
           Act. Med. Director

August 29, 1863
Parivs. U.S.A.
General Hospital   Baltimore, M.D.
Sir,
     I have been now in this Hospital
since the 25th Day of July 1863, and I
am not improving. But am somewhat
weaker than when I came hear [sic--here.
     Therefore I desire to be transfered
to some Philadelphia Hospital for the
Following Reasons: In consequence
of injuries received at the Battle
of Gettysburg by my horse falling.
I am partly ruptured and ..
inwardly so that I am in continual
pain, and as Philadelphia is my
Home, and my family resides there,
I consider it would forward my
convalescence by having my friends
near me. I have been in active
service since August 1861 and have
never been away from the Regiments.
Sir, if you consider my request
reasonable, order my transfer
through
     S.E. Witt. B. Peters
Surgeon in Charge
Parvis U.S.S. General Hospital
        Baltimore M.D.
And by doing so, you will
confer a great favor on
        your obedient servant
Sargt Timothy Lucas
     ..Co. 3rd Penn Cavalry

Timothy's hospitalization in Baltimore began five days after William Wesley Wyatt [1831-1863] died from his injuries in the same battle. Union soldier Timothy Lucas was on August 29th of that same year still at the Baltimore Hospital and obvious by the letter requesting he be moved to Philadelphia Hospital to recover from being ruptured.

No one knows – except God and the souls of Heaven if these men crossed paths at Gettysburg. We know only that they were there and fought on opposing sides. The Battle of Gettysburg had the largest number of casualties during the entire war.

On my maternal side a third great grandfather -- a William Sines [July 20, 1820-March 1921] who served for the blue-clad Union, may have walked the same paths as Timothy Lucas [a third great grandfather to my sons on their paternal side]. Possibly, Sines and Lucas caught the same sights as those of Wyatts and Morgans who fought for the Confederacy.

William Sines, originally of Cranesville, Preston County, Va., served for the Union with his sons John and Henry Sines, the youngest. They served in Company D, 3rd Regiment Maryland Infantry. Henry Sines, son of William, enlisted April 10, 1863 at age 16 and served under Capt. Garyhan. This Henry is said to have seen battles at Frederick's Junction and Harper's Ferry. He was under the command of General Wallace. He was discharged from the Union Army on May 29, 1865 at Baltimore, Md. at age 17.

"In 1862 William Sines volunteered for service
in the Union Army and served faithfully with his
sons, John and Henry, all in Co. "D," 3rd Md. Regi-
sment, until the close of the Civil War. John
enlisted first, followed by his father; then Henry
a boy of sixteen, much needed at home, insisted
that he also be taken to the war, threatening to
run away if refused. Finally, his parents consented,
leaving at home only the mother and many small
children."

[*The Hoye's Pioneer Families of Garrett County*, Garrett County Historical Society, 1988.]

Our ancestors were really trying to kill one another before we became even a hope. Had they succeeded – our souls might have elected to stay in Heaven.

Harper's Ferry – known as Harpers Ferry by some –without an apostrophe, was a town in Virginia where white abolitionist John Brown attempted to start an armed slave revolt in 1859. His plan was to seize a U.S. arsenal there. Accompanying him were 20 men. He was defeated by a detachment of U.S. Marines led by Confederate Gen. Robert E. Lee.

William Wesley Wyatt, brother to Rachel Wyatt Morgan and Lila Wyatt Morgan -- two sisters who married two Morgan brothers, married Mary Buchanan, daughter of Phelpena

Shaver and James Buchanan -- Phelpena Shaver Buchanan being a sister to my 4th great grandmother Barbara Shaver Morgan -- wife of Moses Green Morgan – the parents of John, Nathan and Mack who fought for the Confederacy.

Amongst the siblings of William Wesley Wyatt and his sister Rachel E. Wyatt Morgan -- wife of John Morgan, who died May 12, 1864 at Spotsylvania Court House, is Malinda or Delinda Wyatt who married John Buchanan -- the brother of Mary Buchanan, being the wife of William Wesley Wyatt.

♀ | | ♂

According to the National Park Service, the 5th Regiment of North Carolina Infantry State Troops was organized in Halifax, N.C. in July 1861. One hundred men made up a company and 10 companies that came together in a central location could then form a regiment. The 5th Regiment's companies were recruited from the following counties: Cumberland, Gates, Johnston, Graven, Rowan, Bertie, Wilson and Caswell. The 5th Regiment was ordered to Virginia and reached Manassas on July 19, 1861. This Confederate regiment fought under General James Longstreet. By April 1862, it had 460 effectives [members of the armed service fit for active duty]. During the war, it was brigaded under Generals Early, Garland, Iverson, R.D. Johnston. It participated in military campaigns of the Army of Northern Virginia from Williamsburg, Va. to Cold Harbor. It was involved in General Early's operations in the Shenandoah Valley and Appomattox Campaign. It had 180 men in action at Seven Pines, 10 killed, 22 wounded, 4 missing during the Seven Days Battles, 4 killed and 37 wounded at Chancellorsville. The unit took 473 men to Gettysburg and lost more than half. There it reported 16 disabled at Bristoe and three at Mine Run. It surrendered with 7 officers and 76 men of which 48 were armed. The field officers were Colonels Thomas M. Garrett and Duncan K. McRae and Lieutenant Colonels John C. Badham, William J. Hill, Joseph P. Jones, John W. Lea and Peter J. Sinclair.

♀ | | ♂

Part 3.
Summer, 2014
Journal Entry
1862-1865

On August 8, 1862 three brothers traveled from Rowan County together to Iredell County, N.C. They were accompanied by their 19-year-old second cousin Noah Wyatt [b.1843] who served with them in the 5th Regiment -- Company H, N.C. State Troops. The brothers Nathaniel Morgan, age 30; John Morgan, age 29; Mack Camey Morgan, age 27; signed up to fight for the Confederacy. Of these men, one John Morgan – husband of Rachel E. Wyatt, died at Spotsylvania Court House in Virginia May 12, 1864.

John's brother Nathaniel Morgan [1832-1904], who was wounded in the right thigh between July 1- 4, 1863 and captured at Gettysburg, seemingly fought alongside his second cousin William Wesley Wyatt [1831-1863] [Rachel's brother] at the Battle of Gettysburg, as they were both there. With them was William's brother Silas, who was captured at Gettysburg between July 4-5, 1863. Silas was in the 5th Regiment, Company G and eventually died of *"chronic diarrhoea"* at Point Lookout, Md., where he was a POW.

The Battle of Gettysburg ended with Union proclaiming a victory in this fight. This is how history is recorded – victory or defeat. Around 3,155 Union were reported dead and 4,708 of the Confederates dead. Yes, a victory of killing one another.

One wonders if any crossed paths with Timothy Lucas who avoided his own name being added to the list of Union dead. There are probably many in the U.S. who might learn or already know the identities of ancestors who fought on opposing sides during this battle. Nathaniel Morgan, whose wife was Lila Delilah *"Delila"* Wyatt, born 1834, a sister of Rachel E. Wyatt Morgan, was amongst those soldiers paroled at the end of the War at Appomattox Court House, Va. in April 1865.

♀ | | ♂

PART 4. APPOMATTOX, 1865

On the morning of April 9th, 1865, Gen. Robert E. Lee and his Army of Northern Virginia had one last battle before it surrendered to the Union Army of Ulysses S. Grant. It was one of the last battles of the War. Gray-clad Gen. Lee is said to have abandoned the Confederate capital of Richmond, Va.

Following a 10-month siege of Petersburg, he retreated west in hope of uniting his army with the Confederate forces of North Carolina. Such a confederate retreat was cut off by the Union soldiers at Appomattox Court House. Rebel Gen. Lee soon realized he could not continue trying to break a Union force to his front when the Union forces of cavalry were supported by two corps of Union infantry.

The only choice left was to surrender. The surrender documents were signed in the parlor of a house owned by a Wilmer McLean during the afternoon of April 9. The 12th of April marked disbandment of the Army of Northern Virginia, paroling its officers, soldiers and ended the war in Virginia. This set off the wave of surrenders throughout the South that the war was over.

♀ | | ♂

PART 5.
JOURNAL ENTRY
SUMMER 2014
BATTLE OF SPOTTSYLVANIA, 1864

The Battle of Spottsylvania (19th Century spelling) Court House, Va. was one of the bloodiest battles of the American Civil War. Desperate fighting continued for nearly two weeks from May 8 until May 21, 1864, as the Federal Army of the Potomac led by General Ulysses S. Grant tried to outflank and destroy Confederate General Robert E. Lee's Army of Northern Virginia. Although the end results of this battle were inconclusive, with Grant failing to destroy Lee's army, both armies suffered nearly 32,000 casualties -- soldiers killed, wounded or captured.

Amongst those Confederate dead in this battle, was my third great grandfather –- a farmer-turned-soldier -- John Calvin Morgan of the Poole Town District of Rowan County, N.C.

Private John Morgan of the 5th Regiment of the North Carolina Infantry -- Company H, was mortally wounded four days into this battle on May 12, 1864. As mentioned in the *Brave Farewells* chapter of this book, the butt of John's rifle was shot off within moments of an order to charge. So deafening were the sounds of battle, John did not hear the second order to fall back and continued forward holding only the rifle barrel.

Historians consider May 12th to be the most intense day of the Battle of Spottsylvania. Union casualties were reported as 9,000 that day, compared to 8,000 Confederate casualties, which included 3,000 soldiers taken prisoner.

The fighting on May 12th began at 4:30 in the morning, in a fog so dense that no one could hardly see a hand before him. The Federal battle-plan was a direct assault of 15,000 men charging against a strongly entrenched Confederate line. Due to the damp foggy conditions, many of the Confederate defenders were unable to fire their weapons and desperate hand-to-hand fighting ensued with bayonet and clubbed musket.

This area of fighting later became known as the Bloody Angle, where thousands perished. After several hours of hard fighting in the drizzly rain, a Confederate counter attack drove the Union troops back. In some places not entirely, each army was separated by only a six-foot-high earthen wall.

Several hours later the Confederates attempted to complete a fallback position -- a final line nearly a mile to their rear. More Union attacks followed with darkness ending the fighting for that day.

The Battle of Spottsylvania continued for nine more days, through May 21, 1864, with almost continuous flank attacks and maneuvering.

The eye-witnesses to Pvt. John Morgan's fatal injury are said to have been his brothers Nathan and Mack Camey Morgan who had prior to May 12, 1864 been paroled March 3, 1864 from Point Lookout POW camp and exchanged to rejoin their company. So two months and nine days passed before that fatal day.

The stoicism and courage was rallied by the commanders. For certainly, as the fog was lifting and dust from booted traffic and cannon wheels settled – the field cradled the dead – some in uniforms – some in whatever clothing was found on them. Eyes, mouths and buttons opened to the sky. Some bodies were flanked by the guns they used or the drum they had pounded.

John's remains have not been located. Possibly buried in Spotsylvania Confederate Cemetery in Spotsylvania County, Va. or in the Fredericksburg Confederate Cemetery. The remains of his wife Rachel Evelyn Wyatt Morgan are buried in the Luther's Lutheran Church Cemetery in Richfield, N.C. It is located at the intersection of Richfield Road [SR 1005] and Stokes Ferry Road [SR 1004]. It is three miles west of the Yadkin River. The remains of John's son John Noah Calvin Morgan [1862-1927] and son's wife: Eugenia A. *"Jennie"* Culp [1856-1954] are there as well. The remains of John's daughter Mary Jane Morgan Eagle are at Luther's Lutheran with those of Solomon Eagle and many other relatives.

Today, there are monuments and stones to remind us what all has happened on the battlefield of Spottsylvania Court House – that where the birds can be heard chirping their daily songs – once young men were told to fight to the death. Fight to defend the cause.

♀ | | ♂

One of Ulysses S. Grant's aides Horace Porter in Campaigning with Grant:

> **The appalling sight presented was harrowing in the extreme. Our own killed were scattered over a large space near the *"angle,"* while in front of the captured breastworks the enemy's dead, vastly more numerous than our own, were piled upon each other in some places four layers deep, exhibiting every ghastly phase of mutilation. Below the mass of fast-decaying corpses, the convulsive twitching of limbs and the writhing of bodies showed that there were wounded men still alive and struggling to extricate themselves from the horrid entombment. Every relief possible was afforded, but in too many cases it came too late. The place was well named the *"Bloody Angle."***

Horace Porter's account, although accurate about the realities of war, are deplorable. Some depict war as a glorious way to die. There is nothing glorious about it. Certainly, when soldiers fight they are not filled with anger, but fear. The fear frees itself from their clutches as the Light of our Lord rescues souls from further injury.

John Morgan is said to have owned nine slaves who lived on his farm on River Road in Rowan County. When he rode off to defend the South his wife had under her wings first child: Mary Jane Morgan [m. Solomon Eagle, Jr.] [Lifespan: 1856-1928] and was expecting John Noah Calvin Morgan [m. Eugenia A. *"Jennie"* Culp] [Lifespan: 1862-1927]. John Morgan served in the 5th Regiment -- Company H of the North Carolina Troops.

All that is known of the nine slaves to date is that they ran away. Many former slaves perished, starved to death on their way to the freedom that was then proclaimed. Some of the speculative ruminants of those slaves owned by various lineages on my paternal side include a stone wall that is surrounded by trees of a forest that has since grown around the Park-Wyatt-Bean Graveyard in Rowan County, N.C. It remains to this day on that property. Few people know of this wall today or the cemetery.

Confederate troop records reveal William S. Eagle of Rowan County. At age 16 in Rowan County William – who in family files is listed as William Sidney Eagle [1846-1926] enlisted March 3, 1862 with Company 2nd B Infantry Regiment and was promoted to full corporal on May 30, 1864. This William Sidney Eagle was a son of Nancy Shandy and George Adam Eagle.

William's father George Adam Eagle [Egle] was a brother to Solomon Eagle, Sr., making William a first cousin to Solomon Eagle, Jr. who married Mary Jane Morgan – a daughter of Rachel Evelyn Wyatt Morgan. Tangled genealogies of Rowan County are simply because so many of its residents were [and are] related to one another by blood or marriage. It is remarkable when we consider today how protective parents are of their children. A 16-year-old boy was then an acceptable choice for military duty. William Sidney Eagle [Egle] survived the War and at age 21 married on March 12, 1867 Mary Elizabeth Barnsley and had five children.

♀ | | ♂

Part 6. Wyatt & Park

Pathways of the men who became Confederate soldiers from Rowan County, joined brothers and cousins to defend the South. Southerners viewed the War as a way to keep its property and to divide itself from the rest the U.S. It evolved for the Federals as a means at keeping the U.S. together, and political maneuvers regarding slavery became the focal point.

A second cousin to William Wesley Wyatt [1831-1863] who died July 20th from wounds sustained at Gettysburg, Pa. was William Alexander Parke, Parke [Park] died in the Union Prison at Point Look Out, Saint Mary's County. Md. William Alexander Parke was mustered out on June 7, 1865 having died a prisoner of war. He had enlisted March 13, 1862 into Company D -- 1st NC Artillery. He is sometimes referred to in records as *"William A. Parks."*

1850 U.S. Federal Census School District #41, Rowan County, N.C. U.S. Federal Census the Park family for number 219:

George A. Park, 43, male; farmer
Hannah Park, 40; female
* William A. Park, 19; male
Ruhama Jane Park, 14; female
Delila A. Park, 13; female
Jesse A. Park, 11; male
Mary Park, 8; female
John F. Park, 6; female

* Parks, William A., Private
Enlisted at Rowan County at age 31, March 13,
1862 for the war. Wounded at Sharpsburg, Md.,
September 16, 1862. Present and accounted for
through February 1865. Captured at Amelia
Court House, April 5, 1865 and confined
at Point Lookout, Md. where he died June 7,
1865 of typhoid fever.

* William Park -- known as *"Parks,"* served in Company D, 10th Regiment N.C.S.T. (1st Regiment N.C. Artillery).

At Saint Peter's Lutheran Church Cemetery in Rockwell, Rowan County, N.C. is stone for William Alexander Park. It is inscribed: *"Co D 1 NC Artilliary 1830 1865."* It is located in the 4th row.

The two Williams – one being a Parke or Park or Parks and the other a Wyatt were connected. William Alexander Parke was the son of Hannah Hodge [1813-1885] and George Anthony Park [1808-1882]. George's parents were: Joanna Peeler [1779-1839] and Noah Parke, Jr. [1779-1829]. Noah Parke, Jr.'s parents were Joanna *"Ann"* Reed and Noah Parke, Sr. [1742-1815] Noah Parke and Joanna Reed's daughter Rachel Parke [1774-1850] married Thomas Wyatt [Wiatt] [1774-1845] and had a son named Noah Calvin Wyatt [1805-1871]. He married Mary Henley or Henly – and this name has been recorded by some as *"Henry."* One of their sons was William Wesley Wyatt. Because Rachel Parke Wyatt and Noah Parke, Jr. were siblings, George Anthony Parke and Noah Calvin Wyatt are first cousins and William Alexander Parke and William Wesley Wyatt so then are second cousins.

Serving in the same Company D, 10th Regiment was Eli Wyatt – a brother to William Wesley Wyatt and a second cousin to William Alexander Park [Parks, Parke].

Wyatt, Eli, Private
resided in Rowan County, where he enlisted
at age 21, February 22, 1862 for the war.
Wounded at Battle of Second Manassas, Va.,
August 29, 1862. Present and accounted for
through February 1865. Captured at Amelia
Court House, Va., April 5, 1865 and confined
at Point Lookout, Md. until released after
taking Oath of Allegiance June 21, 1865.

Company E, 10th Regiment N.C.S.T. (1st Regiment N.C. Artillery), page 89 North Carolina Troops 1861-1865 A Roster Volume 1 Artillery, compiled by Louis H. Manarin.

Eli Wyatt served in Company D, 10th Regiment N.C.S.T. (1st Regiment N.C. Artillery). Eli's brother Silas Wyatt died in this same prison as his second cousin William Alexander Park [Parks, Parke].

During the same period when Eli Wyatt was captured at Amelia Court House, Va. April 5, 1865 and confined at Point Lookout, Md. until released June 29th of the same year of 1865 was Private Daniel P. Morgan, born 1841 and a son of Susan Isenhour, b. Abt. 1818; and Wiley Morgan, b. Abt. 1818 – this Wiley being a son of Sarah Hill, b. 1800 and John Morgan, b. 1794. Daniel P. Morgan is a great grandson of Nathan Morgan, Sr. [1756-1842] and Naomi Poole [1760-1851]. John Morgan [1834-1864] – the Confederate soldier who married and had two children with Rachel Wyatt – daughter of Mary Polly Hendly and Noah Calvin Wyatt, is also a great grandson of Nathan Morgan, Sr. and Naomi Poole. Eli Wyatt, as stated earlier, was one of the brothers of John's wife Rachel.

Daniel P. Morgan, b. 1841 son of: → Wiley Morgan, b. 1818 son of: → John Morgan, b. 1794 son of: → Nathan Morgan, Sr., 1756-1842

John Morgan [1834-1864] son of: → Moses Greene Morgan, b. 1810 son of: → Nathan Morgan, Jr. [1785-1844] son of → Nathan Morgan, Sr. 1756-1842

Rachel and Eli are siblings. John and Rachel are spouses to one another. Daniel P. Morgan and John Morgan [1834-1864] are second cousins to one another.

Rachel E. Wyatt Morgan [1835-1915] daughter of: → Noah Calvin Wyatt [1805-1871] son of: → Thomas Wiatt [1774-1845] son of: → John Wiatt [1743-1815]

Eli Wyatt [1841-1912] son of: → Noah Calvin Wyatt [1805-1871] son of: → Thomas Wiatt [1774-1845] son of: → John Wiatt [1743-1815]

North Carolina Troop Records, Volume I, Artillery, first row, page 85:

MORGAN, DANIEL P., Private
Resided in Rowan County where he enlisted at age 21, March 19, 1862 for the war as a substitute for Leonard Hofferer. Present or accounted for through February 1865. Captured at Amelia Court House, Va., April 5, 1865 and confined at Point Lookout, Md., until released after taking an Oath of Allegiance June 29, 1865.

Point Lookout Prison designed for Confederate soldiers was the saddest of family reunions ever held. From the perspective of the soldiers who suffered starvation, dehydration, freezing temperatures, indiscriminate beatings, disease and lack of medical care, seeing a familiar face may have brought some comfort.

James *"Jim"* Noah Wyatt

⚜ This photograph is of James *"Jim"* Noah Wyatt [1861-1957], a son of Mary Buchannan and William Wesley Wyatt. In this book there are many instances one cannot hardly speak of the Wyatts at large without speaking of the Park family, or the Morgan family, or the Miller family, which is really the Müller family. James Wyatt, although he carries the Wyatt name and his wife that of *"Basinger,"* are cousins, and by that day's standards not too close to marry. They are both second and third cousins to one another. People did not travel as much as they do in more recent decades and tended to stay most all of their lives in the communities where they grew up. In North Carolina it is legal to marry a first cousin, although the majority of people [including those mentioned herein] shy away from this. <u>It is illegal</u> to marry your first cousin in the following states:

⚜ Arkansas
⚜ Delaware
⚜ Idaho
⚜ Iowa
⚜ Kansas
⚜ Kentucky
⚜ Louisiana
⚜ Michigan
⚜ Minnesota
⚜ Mississippi
⚜ Missouri
⚜ Montana
⚜ Nebraska
⚜ Nevada
⚜ New Hampshire
⚜ North Dakota
⚜ Ohio
⚜ Oklahoma
⚜ Oregon
⚜ Pennsylvania
⚜ South Dakota
⚜ Texas
⚜ Washington
⚜ West Virginia
⚜ Wyoming

According to the National Conference of State Legislatures (NCSL):

"Twenty-five states prohibit marriages between first cousins. Six states allow first cousin marriage under certain circumstances, and North Carolina allows first cousin marriage but prohibits double-cousin marriage. States generally recognize marriages of first cousins married in a state where such marriages are legal."

Of those states that allow first cousin marriages <u>Arizona</u> allows it ONLY IF both are 65 or older, or one is unable to reproduce; <u>Illinois</u> allows ONLY IF both are 50 or older, or one is unable to reproduce; <u>Indiana</u>: ONLY IF both are at least 65; <u>Maine</u>: if couple obtains a physician's certificate of genetic counseling; <u>Utah</u>: ONLY IF both are 65 or older, or if both are 55 or older and one is unable to reproduce; <u>Wisconsin</u>: ONLY IF the woman is 55 or older, or one is unable to reproduce. These laws are according to a May 2010 report from the NCSL, and are, of course, subject to change. Additionally, first cousins once removed [offspring of your first cousin] are prohibited to marry in Indiana, Kentucky, Nevada, Ohio, Washington and Wisconsin. Second cousins evidently can marry legally in all states of the U.S.

An article titled, *"The Surprising Truth About Cousins and Marriage,"* in an internet site called *"Today I Found Out,"* [www.todayifoundout.com] stated in February 2014 that the state of Kansas banned in 1858 cousin marriage. New Hampshire, Nevada, North Dakota, South Dakota, Washington and Wyoming banned it in the 1860s and by the 1920s other states followed. Texas banned cousin marriage in 2005. The 2014 article states that first cousins MAY NOT marry in Arkansas, Delaware, Iowa, Idaho, Kansas, Kentucky, Louisiana, Michigan, Minnesota, Mississippi, Montana, Missouri, Nebraska, Nevada, New Hampshire, North Dakota, Ohio, Oklahoma, Oregon, Pennsylvania, South Dakota, Texas, Washington and West Virginia. First cousin marriage is allowed with restrictions in Arizona, Illiniois, Indiana, Maine, Utah, Wisconsin and North Carolina. As stated earlier, the union or marriage of double first cousins is banned in North Carolina. This leaves 19 states of the U.S. that allow it without restriction.

* How are second and third cousins discerned in this instance? Barbara Ann E. Basinger and her husband James Noah Wyatt are third cousins via the Park and Morgan lineages. Barbara's mother was Rhoda Isabelle Morgan who married D. Whit *"Whitson"* Whit Basinger. James Wyatt's father was William Wesley Wyatt, the Confederate soldier who fought at Gettysburg, Pa. and later died of his injuries. Rhoda Isabelle Morgan [1839-1922] and William Wesley Wyatt are second cousins. Draw the rungs of a ladder and mark them as such. Now, the third rung up from them write Moses Greene Morgan on one side and Noah Calvin Wyatt on the other side of the rung. [You may write them going up the ladder or down the ladder – the result is nevertheless the same.] They are first cousins. Moses Greene Morgan is the father of Rhoda Isabelle Morgan. Noah Calvin Wyatt is the father of William Wesley Wyatt. The mother of Moses Greene Morgan is Elizabeth *"Betty"* Park who married Nathan Morgan, Jr. A sister to Elizabeth *"Betty"* Park Morgan is Rachel Park, the wife of Thomas Wiatt [1774-1845].

* Both sisters are daughters of Joanna *"Anne"* *"Anna"* Reed [1746-1833] and Noah Park, Sr. [1742-1815 or 1820]. Draw this on the ladder, according to the rungs rule – then it is clear they are third cousins. What about the other connection? Barbara Basinger and James Wyatt are second cousins via their mothers? James Wyatt's mother is Mary Buchanan, a daughter of Phelpena Shaver and James *"Jim"*

Buchannan. Barbara Basinger's mother again is Rhoda Isabelle Morgan Basinger. Mary and Rhoda are first cousins.

* Note them on the ladder you are sketching on paper, or in your mind. Mary Buchanan's mother is Phelpena Shaver Buchanan and Phelpena is a sister to Barbara Shaver Morgan. Thus, the rung under Mary and Rhoda joins James to Barbara as 2nd cousins. Barbara Shaver Morgan – wife of Moses Greene Morgan, is a daughter of Anna Maria Müller [1770-1839] and John S. Shaver [1755-1844] – of Germany. Anna Maria Müller Shaver is the daughter of Elizabeth Blackhawk *"Na Me Qua" "Red Fawn"* [Abt. 1736-1780] of Tultehocken Township, Berks County, Va.; buried Rockwell, Rowan County, N.C. Elizabeth's husband was Johann Wendal Müller [1733-1805] and was born in Manheim or Helmstat in the Dutchy of Brunswick, Germany or Southwestern Germany. Wendal Müller, a Lutheran, arrived here at the age of 25 years on a vessel called *the Brothers*. He helped build a road from Salisbury, N.C. to meet Buffalo Creek Road. Wendal was Lieutenant and later Captain during the Revolutionary War. He tttowned 2, 400 acres and many slaves. Wendal's wife – a Cherokee Indian Princess, was the daughter of Chief Blackhawk *"Na Na Ma Kee"* – Thunder Blackhawk, born around 1711 in what is today known as Tultehocken Township, Berks County, W.Va. and whose remains maybe in Blackhawk Hollow, W.Va. – near Charleston. Wendal is well-known among genealogical researchers of Rowan County – and his connection to Morgan family is a solid connection to the Morgans, Shavers, Buchanans and Wyatts. The Park family connecting into the Wiatt and Morgan families is another indisputable connection.

* Footnote: Noah Park, Sr. [1742-1815] and his wife Joanna *"Anna"* Reed [1746-1833] had the following children: Ebenezer Park [1768-1854] married Elizabeth Wyatt & Sally Poole; Hannah Park [1770-1855] married John Wyatt. Jr., d. 1819; Rachel Park [1774-1850] married Thomas Wiatt [1774-1845]; Mary Park [1775-1845] married Leonard Kaylor [1774-1854]; Jesse Park [Bef. 1777-1837] married Sarah Todd [1781-Bef. 1860]; Noah Park, Jr. [1779-1829] married Joanna Peeler [1779-1829]; Amos Park [Abt. 1780-1856] married Margaret Mildred Briggs [b. 1780]; John Davis Park [Abt. 1780-1856] married Mary Polly Bean [1780-1845]; Elizabeth *"Betty"* Park [b. Abt. 1781] married Nathan Morgan [1785-1844]; Sarah Park [1785-1844] married James Morgan [1780-1847].

* Noah Park, Sr.   [same]   Noah Park, Sr.
[1742-1815 or 1820] m. Joanna Reed [1746-1833]
         ^   ^

Elizabeth   [sisters]   Rachel [m. Thomas Wiatt]
[m. Nathan Morgan, Jr.]
         ^   ^

Moses Green Morgan   [Double 1st C]   Noah C. Wyatt
[m. Barbara Shaver]   [m. Mary Hendly]
         ^   ^

John C. Morgan   [2nd C]   Rachel E. Wyatt

^   ^

Mary J. Morgan   [same]   Mary J. Morgan
[m. Solomon Eagle, Jr.]   [m. Solomon Eagle, Jr.]
^   ^

Noah J. Eagle   [same]   Noah J. Eagle
[m. Laura L. Eller]   [m. Laura L. Eller]
^   ^

Virgie I. Eagle   [same]   Virgie I. Eagle

Reminder: Two of Noah Park, Sr.'s daughters married Morgan brothers – sons of Naomi Poole & Nathan Morgan, Sr. [1756-1842]. Two of Noah Park, Sr.'s daughters married Wiatt brothers – sons of Rachel Hannah & John Wiatt, Sr. [1743-1815].

John Wiatt [1743-1815]
^

Thomas Wiatt [1774-1845]   In-laws   Nathan Morgan, Jr.
m. Rachel Park-----------------------Sisters------------m. Elizabeth *"Betty"* Park
^   ^

Noah Calvin Wyatt [1805-1871]   Double 1st Cousins   Moses Green Morgan
^   ^

William Wesley Wyatt [1831-1863]----2nd Cousins---- Rhoda Isabelle Morgan
                                                    wife of: D.W. Basinger
^   ^

James Noah Wyatt [1861-1957]   married   Barbara Basinger
^   ^

David Eli Wyatt [1887-1966]   [same]   David Eli Wyatt [1887-1966]
m. Amanda Fannie Ester Frick   m. Amanda Fannie Ester Frick
                                                          ^

Roy Eli Wyatt [1929-2005]   [same]   Roy Eli Wyatt [1929-2005]

*Roy Eli Wyatt lived on Orchard Road in Rowan County, N.C.; never married. Childhood friend of James Noah Hinson, M.D., and of his siblings and maternal uncle Robert Noah Eagle. Children of David and Amanda Wyatt: Lula, Paul, Mary & Roy Eli.

Eli Wyatt [1841-1912], son of Mary Polly Hendly & Noah Calvin Wyatt

".... Gen. Robert E. Lee concentrated his full strength against Maj. Gen. George G. Meade's Army of the Potomac at the crossroads county seat of Gettysburg. On July 1, Confederate forces converged on the town from the west and north, driving Union defenders back through the streets to Cemetery Hill. During the night, reinforcements arrived for both sides. On July 2, Lee attempted to envelop the Federals, first striking the Union left flank at the Peach Orchard, Wheatfield, Devil's Den, and the Round Tops with Longstreet's and Hill's divisions, and then attacking the Union right at Culp's and East Cemetery Hills with Ewell's divisions. By evening, the Federals retained Little Round Top and had repulsed most of Ewell's men. During the morning of July 3, the Confederate infantry were driven from their last toe-hold on Culp's Hill. In the afternoon, after a preliminary artillery bombardment, Lee attacked the Union center on Cemetery Ridge. The Pickett-Pettigrew assault (more popularly Pickett's Charge) momentarily pierced the Union line but was driven back with severe casualties. Stuart's Cavalry attempted to gain the Union rear but was repulsed. On July 4, Lee began withdrawing his army towards Williamsport on the Potomac River. His train of wounded stretched more than fourteen miles...."

--- Quoted from: iml.jou.ufl.edu/projects/Fall03/Peters/ Gettysburg/htm ©2015 on Gettysburg, Pa., July 1-3, 1863. The result of this Gettysburg Campaign June –August 1863, was a victory for the Union in Adams County, between July 1-3, 1863 with principal commanders Maj. General George G. Meade [Federal government] and General Robert E. Lee [Confederate States of America]. Estimated casualties 51,000 – 23,000 for the Union and 28,000 for the CSA.

♀ | | ♂

PART 7. WYATT BROTHERS

❀ SONS OF MARY POLLY HENDLY & NOAH CALVIN WYATT

Henry Thomas Wyatt [Born: 1828]

Silas *"Siles"* Wyatt [1838-1864]

Noah Wyatt [b. 1843]

John P. Wyatt [1846-1924]

Emanuel James M. Wyatt [b. 1832]

Ghosts or spiritual imprints of those souls that lived in Rowan County and who fought on behalf of their communities and state drift in on summer clouds and the air of cool autumn nights. Their history perseveres. They are remembered. Their blood and sweat rests in Rowan's soil. Such is now in the fabric of Mother Nature.

Henry Thomas Wyatt [b. 1828] was a brother to Malinda Delinda Wyatt Buchanan [1829-1903], William Wesley Wyatt [1831-1863], Rachel E. Wyatt Morgan [1835-1915], and this Henry served in the 7th Regiment -- Company F, North Carolina. Another one of these Wyatt siblings -- a Silas *"Siles"* Wyatt [1838- January 19,1864] served in the Confederate Army as a private in the 5th Regiment, Company G of N.C. Troops. Silas died around six months after his brother William Wesley Wyatt in the ACW. Silas Wyatt [1838-1864] is one of the POWs who died at Point Lookout, Md.

Henry and Silas' brother Eli Wyatt [1841-1912] served having lived and then enlisted in Rowan County on Feb. 22, 1862 at age 21. He served in Company D, NC Company A 1st Light Artillery Battery, according to North Carolina Troop Records 1861-1865. His remains are in the Saint Matthew's Lutheran Church Cemetery in Salisbury, N.C. in row #22 having died at age 71.

Wyatt, Silas, Private
Enlisted in Northampton County at age 25, August 13, 1862 for the war. Captured at Gettysburg, Pennsylvania, July 4-5, 1863. Confined at Fort Delaware, Delaware, until transferred to Point Lookout, Maryland, October 15-18, 1863. Hospitalized at Point Lookout October 29, 1863, with *"chronic diarrhoea"* and died on January 19, 1864.

Silas Wyatt served in Company G, 5th Regiment
N.C. State Troops. The August 8, 1860 U.S. Federal Census for South of Salisbury, Rowan
County, N.C. shows a Silas Wyatt, age 23, working as a school teacher in the same household
as Lewiston? Wyatt, then age 25. His wife was Lucetta *"Settie"* Rufty, b. 1835, and his daughters: Laura and Lucinda.

Noah *"Noe"* Calvin Wyatt, born in 1843, son of Mary Polly Hendly & Noah Calvin Wyatt.

Noah Wyatt [b. 1843]

Brother to William Wesley, Henry, Siles or Silas, and Eli was Noah [b. 1843] who served as a private in the 5th Infantry Regiment -- Company H, N.C. According to North Carolina troop records, he enlisted for the confederacy in Iredell County at age 19 on August 8th, 1862 as stated earlier in this book.

Notes for Noah *"Noe"* Calvin Wyatt:

Book #57, page 194: Feb. 25, 1880: Noah C. Wyatt and his wife Nancy E. let John A. Snider -- all of Rowan County, N.C., have 8 3/4 acres on the dividing line between the said Wyatt and W.R. Barker on the Old Mocksville Road next to Charles Stanard and Obadiah Belt for $550.00; witnessed by Andrew Murphy and acknowledged on the same day. (Craig and Caldwell as administrators of deceased C.F. Fisher let him 4 acres of the above on Jan. 29, 1873 -- See Book #48, page 42 -- the other from C.E. Miller and wife on Feb. 18, 1874. See Book # 48, page 43 -- who got it from Craige and Caldwell as administrators of C.F. Fisher on Dec. 19, 1873; See Book #47, page 525.

Book #46, page 152: Feb. 26, 1872: Harriet C. Bringle and husband David L. Bringle let Noah C. Wyatt, all of Rowan County, N.C., have 4 acres on the Mocksville Road next to C.F. Fisher, John I. Shaver and others for $900.00, acknowledged on the same day.

Book #52, page 382: June 3, 1876 Noah C. Wyatt and wife Nancy E. of Rowan County, N.C., let Lucinda J. Daniel of Davidson County, N.C., have 8 acres next to W.M. Barker, W.P. Terrell and others fronting the Homestead of the late Obadiah Woodson on the Old Mocksville Road for $200.00; marked paid in full.

Book #5, page 322, March 27, 1880: James A. Craige, no wife signs, lets Nancy E. Wyatt -- both of Rowan County, N.C., have _____in the northwest square of Salisbury beginning on the corner of Liberty and Ellis streets, &c for $275.00, witnessed and proved by James R. Crawford on March 27, 1880. This is what Edwin Shaver said Craige have April 22, 1875; See Book #50, page 14.

Noah *"Noe"* Calvin Wyatt, b. 1843, son of Mary Polly Hendly & Noah Calvin Wyatt.

Rowan County Marriage Bonds lists Noah C. Wyatt as groom, and Nancy E. Reid as bride, with the date of the marriage bond being March 15, 1866. T The bondsman and witnesses: Levi Trexler J.P., officiating.

Children of Noah Wyatt and Nancy Reid are: 1) Zeb, 2) Walter, 3) M.D. 4) Taves.

JOHN P. WYATT [1846-1924] & EMANUEL JAMES M. WYATT [B. 1832]

Honorably -- these men certainly lived their duties and obligations to defend the Southern states. From this same group of brothers -- sons of Mary Polly Hendly [Henly] and Noah Calvin Wyatt – are more heroes of Rowan County.

John P. Wyatt [1846-1924] served in the 2nd Regiment Company B (N.C. Junior Res.). This group had another brother -- Emanuel James M. Wyatt, born 1832. Emanuel is listed on the *1860 U.S. Federal Census* as a farmer as Manuel Wyatt, then 27, living with his wife Mary and child.

J.P. Wyatt's record is found as Private J.P. Wyatt and states he was born in Rowan County on or about November 5, 1846 – while the birth date in archives shows October 23rd of the same year. The record indicates he was a farmer prior to enlisting at Camp Holmes, near Raleigh, N.C. at age 17, May 23, 1864. He was present and accounted for on August 31, 1864.

".... Reported on detached duty at Neuse River Bridge from September 21 through October 31, 1864. No further records."

John P. Wyatt served in the 2nd Regiment Company B of the Junior Reserves. He is said to have been a grammar school teacher at the Yadkin Valley School. Specifically, one of his pupils was Noah Jenkins Eagle [1878-1976] son of → Solomon Eagle, Jr. [1857-1939] and Mary Jane Morgan [1856-1928], daughter of → John Morgan [1834-1864] who was *"mortally wounded"* at Spottsylvania Court House, Va. & Rachel Evelyn Wyatt [1835-1915] daughter of → Noah Calvin Wyatt [1805-1871] son of → Thomas Wiatt [1774-1845] son of → John Wiatt, Sr. [1743-1815], the one whose remains are buried at Lick Creek Baptist Church in Davidson County, N.C.

Notes for John P. Wyatt:

On the June 2, 1900 United States Federal Census for Morgan Township, Rowan County, North Carolina there is on the same page as Solomon Eagle, Jr. and his family a listing for the family of a John P. Wyatt. This John P. Wyatt, then age 58, a farmer, was born October, 1846 and married a woman whose name is indiscernible on this census. The name resembles *"Meryl."* The wife is listed as age 49, born January 1857. The children listed are: Sarah, A, then age 24, born April 1876; Henry N., then age 18, born October 1881. All on this page have birthplace: North Carolina. Directly above this John P. Wyatt is a Sallie Hodge, listed as a mother-in-law, age 70, born July 1820.

McCubbins file at Rowan Public Library indicates the following notation:

John P. Wyatt:
Book #60 Page 255: Dec. 14, 1881 Paul B. Taylor &wife Sarah R. let John P. Wyatt --
all of Rowan Co., N.C. -- have 53 acres (being lot#3 in the estate of deceased Caleb
Shaver] next Jane Shaver, ot #2 & Jesse A. Parks also his third of the threshing machine &c, (unless he repays with interest,) for $200.00, witnessed by Caswell Taylor
& acknowledged before William Bean (J.P.) on the same day.

Book #71 page 353: Aug. 15 1896, John P. Wyatt (as the trustee of Paul B. Taylor &
wife Sarah R. who made the trust on Dec. 14 1881 for $200.00 -- see Book 60 page
255) let John F. Hodge, both of Rowan County, N.C. have 53 acres next [to] Jane
Shaver, lot #2 & Jesse A. Park for $150.00, acknowledged on Aug. 15 1896. (This is
lot #3 in the estate of deceased Caleb Shaver.)

Military & Census Records

2nd Regiment Company B (North Carolina Junior Reserves); ACW.

More About John P. Wyatt:

* August 02, 1850, U.S. Federal Census in School District #41 Rowan Co.,
  N.C. birth: Abt. 1847
* 1860, U.S. Federal Census in Salisbury, Rowan Co., N.C. birth: Abt. 1847
* 1880, U.S. Federal Census in Morgan Township, Rowan Co., N.C. birth:
  Abt. 1847
* 1900, U.S. Federal Census in Rowan Co., N.C. birth: October 1846.
* 1910, U.S. Federal Census in Morgan Township, Rowan Co., N.C. birth:
  Abt. 1847
* 1920, U.S. Federal Census in Morgan Township, Rowan Co., N.C. birth:
  Abt. 1847
* 2nd Regiment Company B (North Carolina Junior Reserves); ACW.

According to James Noah Hinson, M.D., as mentioned earlier, John P. Wyatt
was a teacher for his maternal grandfather Noah Jenkins Eagle. John P. Wyatt
taught grammar school Rowan County, N.C. for grades first through seventh at the
Yadkin Valley School.

The remains of John P. Wyatt [1846-1924], son of Mary Polly Hendly and Noah
Calvin Wyatt, are buried at Wyatt's Grove Baptist Church Cemetery, Rowan County,
N.C.

His wife Mary Frances Hodge Wyatt:

Buried at Wyatt's Grove Baptist Church Cemetery, Rowan County, N.C.

Rowan County Marriage Bonds lists John P. Wyatt as groom, and Mary F. Hodge as bride, with the date of the marriage bond being March 6, 1871 and the wedding date as: March 9, 1871. The groom is listed as being the son of Noah & Mary Wyatt. The bride is listed as the daughter of Richard & Sallie Hodge. The bondsman and witnesses: Obadiah Woodson, R.D., H. Morton, officiating.

Children of John Wyatt and Mary Hodge are: 1) Martha *"Lou"* Louise[19] Wyatt, born October 24, 1873; died May 01, 1951; 2) Ann Wyatt? 3) Henry Walter Wyatt, born October 14, 1881; died February 01, 1928. He married Cole?

Emanuel James M. Wyatt [b. 1832] son of Mary Polly Hendly & Noah Calvin Wyatt.

Notes for Emanuel James M. Wyatt:

Via ancestry.com an 1860 United States Federal Census for South of Salisbury, Rowan County, August 16th, 1860, Bringles Post Office, a Manuel Wyatt -- probably *"Emanuel"* Wyatt is listed as age 27, male, farmer of North Carolina; Mary A. Wyatt, 22, female of North Carolina; the child's name is indiscernible, but it begins with a *"C"* and ends in a *"y."* This child is two years old and from North Carolina.

Directly under Emanuel's listing is a John Bean, 35, male farm of North Carolina with an Elizabeth Bean, 35, female "home keeper" of North Carolina and children: Edmond, 9; and Daniel, 5.

Children of Emanuel Wyatt and Mary Bean are: 1) Calvin Wyatt, 2) Casandra Wyatt, 3) James Wyatt, 4) Moses Wyatt.

♀ | | ♂

PART 8. MORE WYATTS

Truths can get buried with the dead. We cannot solely rely on what is taught in textbooks. We must strive to discern truth, uncover it and remember it as a means of promoting good. To advance the good of mankind – is to block evil. Either is discerned by the intent of the heart. Whatever side an ancestor fought on – there was both suffering and compassion. Love and disdain. Good and evil.

The victory of the North was resolution – the putting down of weapons and collecting the bones of the dead and the flesh of the wounded. Getting to that point, though, was walking through Hades on earth. Whenever the doors of Hades open and find expression through a human body – there is going to be destruction. Point Lookout in Saint Mary's County, Md. must have felt like hell on earth.

According to some accounts Confederate soldiers were tortured as entertainment for the Negro guards and Union.

There is one *"Guyot,"* a Thomas without any other information on a list of POWs who are buried in the point Lookout Cemetery in Saint Mary's County, Md. Perhaps, his Guyots tie into our earliest Wyatts – known then as Guyots.

An article titled: *"Descendants of Point Lookout POW Organization," located* at a website on Confederate POWs. It asserts that Point Lookout Prison's list of 3,384 names inscribed on monument plaques is not accurate. It is said that dairies from prisoners and other reports suggest that over 14,000 men died while incarcerated at Point Lookout.

Accounts have included a description that prisoners were forced to discard anything containing the initials: *"U.S."* The men were confined to tents. They were given one blanket regardless of season. There was a lack of firewood and other supplies for living.

From North Carolina Troop records, it is discerned several Wyatts were held at Point Lookout Prison for Confederate soldiers and several of their cousins by the surnames of Park and Morgan passed through and some died there as well.

From Companies G & H, 45th Regiment N.C. Troops, a Corporal William Wyatt, is recorded to have been from *"Pittsylvania County,"* Va. – but who had resided in Rowan or Rockingham County, N. C., where he worked as a farmer prior to enlisting at Rockingham County at age 20, March 11, 1862, was captured at Spottsylvania Court House, Va. May 10, 1864 and confined at Point Lookout, Md. May 18, 1864. Apparently, he was transferred to Elmira, New York August 3, 1864. He was released there after taking an Oath of Allegiance May 13, 1865.

Another Wyatt from the Infantry – a Private Roland H. Wyatt, [Company B 46th Regiment of N.C. Troops] who had resided in Rowan County, where he enlisted for the Confederacy at age 38 April 15, 1863 was wounded in the leg at Wilderness, Va. around May 6, 1864. He was captured at Amelia Court House, Va. April 5 1865 and confined at Point Lookout Prison April 13, 1865 and released from Point Lookout June 21, 1865 after taking an Oath of Allegiance.

Another is recorded:

Wyatt Private Victory Wyatt – born in Wilkes County, where he resided and worked as a farmer prior to enlisting April 22, 1862 in Wilkes County at age 22. This Victory Wyatt was captured at Rappahannock Station, Va. on November 7, 1863 and confined at Point Lookout Prison November 11, 1863. He was released from Point Lookout January 29, 1864 after taking an Oath of Allegiance and joining the U.S. Army and assigned to Company F, 1st Regiment of U.S. Volunteer Infantry.

What a twist or turn-around this seems to be! Apparently he lived up to his name and joined the side that was ultimately victorious. Who is to say, though, there is any glory when human beings fight about those things they might have otherwise resolved without the loss of human lives – without the loss of interrupting the soul's journey?

There is another Wyatt who spent time at Point Lookout Prison. This is a J.E. Wyatt who resided in Rowan County and enlisted in Iredell County on or about September 2, 1862 for the war. He deserted on October 17, 1862 and was captured at Gettysburg, Pa. July 1, 1863; confined at Fort Delaware, Del. until he was transferred to Point Lookout sometime between the 15 and 18 of October 1863. He was paroled from Point Lookout February 18, 1865 and transferred to Boulware's and Cox's Wharves, James River, Va. He was received sometimes between the 20th and 21st of February 1865 for exchange. He took an Oath of Allegiance at Salisbury, N.C. on June 13, 1865.

There is a J.E. Wyatt who supposedly had a son named Noah Calvin Wyatt, who married a Ruth J. Hodge and had a daughter named Mary Beulah Daisy Wyatt, born 1900. She was the wife of Jesse Calvin Kluttz [1892-1969]. This J.E. Wyatt's granddaughter Mary Beulah Daisy Wyatt's husband Jesse Calvin Kluttz. His mother was Mary Jane Ribelin Kluttz [1856-1941]. Her paternal grandfather was Isaac Ribelin [1800-1863] who married Mary Polly Eagle [1807-1878] –a daughter to George Egle, Jr. [1781-1864] and Mary Madeline Haldeman [1784-1868].

The Egles or Eagles are traced into Cocalico, Lancaster County, Pa. and from there into Zurich, Switzerland. For more information of the Eagle [Egle] genealogical history, refer to *To Escape Into Dreams,* volume 1; *Appendices of: To Escape Into Dreams,* volume 3 and to *The Eagle Family of America, Egley, Egle, Egli, Eagle. 1690-1998* by Rachel Hinson Hill.

The common point here is J.E. Wyatt is another Confederate soldier who spent time at Point Lookout Prison.

In the N.C. Troop Records 1861-1865, there is Infantry Regiments 22nd-26th, a record for a Private John F. Wyatt who resided in Wilkes County and enlisted at Camp Holmes at age 24 September 22, 1862, He was wounded in the head and captured at Gettysburg, Pa. July 3, 1863. He was confined at Baltimore, Md. and transferred to Point Lookout Prison on or about October 30, 1864.

Naturally, I check our indexes and just because I do not find him, or connect him readily and properly at this point, is not reason to leave him out of this Wyatt book. Those soldiers with the Wyatt surname found listed in the *N.C. Troop Records* are noted. A listing of those can be found in the back of this book. Readers may note assertions in the back matter pages and contact Metallo House Publishers. Clarifications can be made in future editions.

The article on the internet titled: *"Descendants of Point Lookout POW Organization,"* includes an account from a Confederate Sergeant Charles T. Loehr, captured April 1, 1865 at the Battle of Five Forks. The article stipulates he was one of 40 men placed into a tent designed for sixteen. It reports that six or seven prison soldiers died by dawn – and two of these were on both sides of Loehr.

It asserts prisoners died for lack of food, medical care and unsanitary conditions. One of the most profound quotes from Loehr relays a sense of the stress Point Lookout no doubt inevitably evolved*:*

> *"Negroes of the worst sort and very brutal; when the prisoners were driven out of their tents at night by diarrhea, the guards would make them carry them on their back* [sic: backs]*; they were quick-stepped about the grounds, forced to kneel and pray for Abe Lincoln..."*

The article describes what is referred to as *"Dead Line Ditch,"* which was located approximately 15 feet from the fence. Any prisoners approaching it was fired upon.

The article furthermore quotes a Confederate Sergeant Major of the Camp, P. Thoroughgood that

> *"...conduct and conversation of the colored men evidence that thre is a sort of rivalry among them to distinguish themselves by shooting some of us....one who does so gains an eclat which the others envy; and animated frequently by vindictive feelings, they make pretexts to vent them."*

The article further states:

> *"The man responsible for these atrocities was Provost Marshall (Major) A.G. Brady, who, as it turned out, personally made in excess of $1,000,000 during his time as camp commander. The mortality rate at Point Lookout was greater than that of the Confederate prison at Andersonville, Georgia. Even more damning is that the fatalities at Point Lookout were due to unnecessary neglect, while those at Andersonville were due to a real want in the Confederacy*

as a whole. The official number of Confederate dead at Point Lookout was 3,384, but other accounts suggest that many more perished. Sergeant Loehr wrote that it was "not unusual to hear of 60-65 deaths per day and `it is said that 8,600 Confederate dead were buried near [the] prison pen.'" .Prof. Bart Talbert, University of Salisbury, MD."

♀ | | ♂

♀ | | ♂

PART 9.
SATURDAY
JUNE 27, 2015
JOURNAL ENTRY

I mull through notes. A letter from fourth cousin on my maternal lineages Robert Allen DeVries, Ph.D. touches my fingertips.

I call him *"Cousin Bob."* He co-researched with me *Paper & Stone, A Leighton History in England & the United States.* His correspondence is dated October 23, 2014. He writes of a mutual Leighton relative who fought for the blue-clad Union – this Richard Watt Leighton [1839-1918], being a grandnephew to a second great grandfather of mine Isaac Leighton [1828-1911].

DeVries, a great grandnephew of Edward Isaac Leighton [1850-1916], refers to Ed. Most profoundly he refers to Richard Watts Leighton, born in Old Swinford, Worcester or Stourbridge, England; died at Cleveland, Cuyahoga County, Ohio.

He writes:

"I wasn't really searching much on this family, but found two interesting things while in the library:

Uncle Ed was also an inventor!
Edward I Leighton, US Patent #526,576 on Sept 25, 1894
"Machine for Shearing Wooden Railroad Ties"

His oldest brother Richard Leighton - which I was told was a drummer boy in the civil war, does actually have a "draft record" in ward 4 of Cleveland in ancestry.com. I have NOT, however found any other records or his unit. I will try to find local experts in civil war from the area to help me."

DeVries 'mention of this Richard Watts Leighton, a first cousin three generations removed to me, prompts one to wonder of what all he saw in terms of faces of his enemy.

Did he cross paths with Wyatt Confederates?

Did he cross paths with Irish immigrant Union soldier Timothy Lucas?

Did he glance in passing the surviving or dying eyes of Morgan, Park, Eagle or Hodge men who fought for the South, or those Sines who fought for the North?

The answers to these questions we may never know. Once while sitting in mounds of records, notes and papers scattered about a desk and floor, I began to feel sorry for myself. I told my father how frustrated I felt when I became stumped and doubly so to be sitting in a mess of papers that just seemed to grow more with every new question that presented.

He said:

"Be grateful you have such things to research."

He meant most likely that the mess is just part of the quest.

On December 10, 2015, this cousin Bob sends a record on a John Leighton. His Graves Registration Card in Cuyahoga County, Ohio [Birth: 1816; Burial: May 6, 1872] contains a service record for the ACW. We speculate this John is possibly the same as our John Leighton [1817-1872] – son of Diana Maybury and Richard Leighton. John Leighton enlisted in Ohio August 10, 1861, was discharged Oct. 20, 1864 and served in the Cavalry as a Sergeant for Company H, 4th O.V.C. Seeing such records of relatives on my maternal side and then considering those of the Wyatts who fought as well in the ACW on my paternal side further supports this notion: Our ancestors were trying to kill one another long before they became friends, lovers and married. Otherwise, well, none of us would be here today!

CHAPTER 21

John T. Wyatt [1851-1933]
Venus of Faith

♀ | | ♂

PART 1. TROT IT OUT

"If you can beat that, then trot it out."

– JOHN THOMAS WYATT

*"...in about one hundred years from now, it would be very
interesting for the people to read and see what date their grandfather
or great grandfather was born or married or died..."*

– JTW daybook.

JOHN THOMAS WYATT WROTE SOME of his observations and thoughts in his 59 day-books – which were essentially notes or notations, names and dates, etc. he made in preparation for the *"Items of Faith"* newspaper columns.

This John Thomas Wyatt was known to the world as *"Venus of Faith."* He was a writer and country correspondent, whose articles ran in *The Salisbury Post* of Salisbury, N.C. and were picked up by other newspapers throughout the country.

He was known additionally as the inventor of an eczema salve and as a millstone carver. John Thomas Wyatt pitched his product in his articles via a column he wrote for local newspapers. His *"advertising"* was overlooked by editors due to the popularity of his articles.

Newspapers statewide picked up his articles and ran them. Venus of Faith found material for his columns by attending reunions, picnics, social gatherings. He is said to have focused on strange-shaped vegetables, unusually large farm animals, etc. He once claimed to own the largest boulder in the county.

John Thomas Wyatt collected antiques, arrowheads, and was most interested in collecting items 100 years old or older. He wanted to open a museum with all he collected. When John T. Wyatt was 12 years old, he ran errands for the Confederate Army's Company B, Freeman's Battalion stationed at Murphy's Grove in Salisbury, N.C. Company B provided guards for Salisbury's Confederate Prison for Union soldiers.

John Thomas Wyatt was charged with guarding the Union prisoners held in Salisbury. He attended all the Confederate soldier reunions well into the last years of his life. He considered himself a veteran of the ACW and a former soldier of the Confederate States of America [CSA].

The Bicentennial Edition of *The Salisbury Post* ran a story that was originally published in June 1969 and written by the now deceased Heath Thomas. The article states that the Payne Building of the Nazareth Children's Home was in 1969 *"recently"* torn down. Within a cornerstone of this building, a copper box was discovered. Inside the box were notes from John Thomas Wyatt stating his identity and those of his parents.

He died of cancer in 1933 and left his collections and notes to Catawba College. Many of the items from his collection were put up for sale by his family in order to pay estate expenses. He was known for his claim of shipping the first carload of granite out of Rowan County. Enoch E. Phillips, the father of his wife operated a granite business in Davidson County.

A newspaper obituary recorded that John T. Wyatt was once asked why his newspaper columns never addressed politics or religion. He is quoted to have said:

"I'm just not interested...

"But there is one thing I claim to hold the palm for, and if any of you newspaper folks can beat it, just trot out your man.

"I'm 78 years old and never used a profane word in my life."

♀ | | ♂

John Thomas Wyatt, also known as *"Venus of Faith,"* which
was his pen name for a newspaper column.

1860 U.S. Federal Census, P.O. Bringles -- home in 1860 to this family: Salisbury, N.C. Wilson R. Wyatt, 30; Mary Ann Wyatt, 25; **John T. Wyatt**, 9; Columbus C. Wyatt, 7;

The father of **John Thomas Wyatt** is Wilson R. Wyatt -- more specifically as Wilson Riley Wyatt. For *Company K, 8th Regiment North Carolina Infantry State Troops* he appears on the ***"Company Muster-in and Descriptive Roll"*** as joining at Camp Macon in Warren County on September 14, 1861 and mustered into service on that same day. This record states he was born in Davidson County and was then age 32 and worked as a farmer. It states he enrolled July 6, 186_ for active service in Salisbury and was enrolled by Capt. P.A. Kennerly. The record states he took an Oath of Allegiance to the State of North Carolina and was then *"on furlough."* It states after *"a remark made by verifying officer."*

On another page of the same record for Company K, 8th Regiment North Carolina Troops it reiterates he entered into service on July 6, 1861 at age 32. Under *"Remarks,"* is *"Died March 1862 of disease."* The Copyist signing the document is W.M. Potter.

Furthermore, on page 624 of NC Troop records for Company K, a Wilson R. Wyatt, a private born in Davidson County and resided in Rowan County *"where he was by occupation a farmer. Enlisting in Rowan County at age 32, July 1861, for the war. Died at Salisbury on March 1862 of disease."*

Family of John Thomas Wyatt's [Venus of Faith's] wife:

On the U.S. Federal Census for Rowan County, N.C. November 1, 1850 in School District #24 -- Enoch E. Phillips is listed in dwelling #1512 at age 42, then being a stone cutter with $400.00 worth of real estate. Also listed are his children: Charlotte E. Phillips, 14; John L. Phillips, 13; Calvin, 12; Adam B., 10; Joseph, 9; Ellen, 7; Jane, 4; Solomon, 3.

On the census for June 15th & 16th 1880 for the Litaker Township in Rowan County, N.C., Enoch Phillips is listed at age 71 and being a stone cutter. His daughter Ellen is listed as keeping house at age 37; Charlotte Dyer, daughter, keeping house at age 44 is listed as well. Someone else with the surname and age being indiscernible with the first name of *"Lewis"* follows. Each are recorded as having been born in North Carolina.

*Charlotte's first husband was Frank Dyer.

Book 65, page 90: Aug. 29, 1885, Henry Peeler (as administrator of deceased E.E. Phillips) let Charlotte E. Wyatt -- all of Rowan Co., N.C. -- have 34 1/2 acres *"Known as the Rock Quarry owned by E.E. Phillips"* next Daniel Stirewalt -- Newsom W. Williams, Greem Heilig & others, for $172.50. (This was sold Aug. 30, 1884 to make assets for the said estate but doesn't include the 1 1/2 acre, which he let Jacob Holshouser & others have for a church on July 19 1870).

♀ | | ♂

Part 2. Quotes from John Thomas Wyatt
known as Venus of Faith
[1851-1933]

In the Bicentennial Edition of *The Salisbury Post* titled: *"Venus of Faith, Country Correspondent's Motto Was 'If You Can Beat That, Trot It Out'"* by the late Heath Thomas, John Thomas Wyatt is quoted:

> *"...I, John Thomas Wyatt, was born in Davidson County, N.C. on October 31, 1851. My parents moved to Salisbury when I was just a little boy and I was raised in or near Salisbury. I am a son of Mr. and Mrs. Wilson Wiley* [Sic: Riley] *Wyatt and grandson of Jessie Wyatt Jr. and his wife and great-grandson of Jessie Wyatt Sir.,* [sic: John *"Johney"* Wyatt, Jr.], *all of Davidson and Rowan counties on the Yadkin River. I am a member of the Reformed Church at Faith...and a newspaper correspondent and have been writing for several papers for over 40 years. I shipped the first carload of granite that went from this section and started up the great granite industry...That has given employment to hundreds of people...."*

Reiterated from John Thomas Wyatt's handwritten notes:

> *"John Wyatt and wife Rachael Hannah was the first Wyatts known to come to Davidson County, N.C. + is supposed to come from Va or Maryland but think they came from Maryland + they lived here in time of the Revolutionary War. They married and had the following children: Sylvester Wyatt .. John Wyatt who was my great grandfather + who went blind before he died, one child died .. his name was Dempsy Wyatt. .. James Wyatt .. Ely Wyatt, Selery Wyatt .. Elizabeth Wyatt .. Tomy Wyat. .. "*

John Thomas Wyatt a.k.a. *Venus of Faith* -- wrote in his handwritten script:

> *"Old Johney Wyatt was the father of my Greatee grandfather John Wyatt, and he was he father of my grandfather Jessey Wyatt, and he was the father of my father Wilson Riley Wyatt + he was the father of John Thomas Wyatt who is myself the writer + of Columbus Ceciro Wyatt, my Brother and Columbus Ceciro Wyatt was the father of harvey A. Wyatt..."*

John Thomas Wyatt or Venus of Faith is discussed in more detail in Chapter 13: Park-Wyatt-Bean Graveyard and in Chapter 14: Genealogical Webs John Wiatt [1743-1815].

♀ | | ♂

CHAPTER 22

War Records & Discrepancies

♀ | | ♂

Part 1. Records

$\mathcal{R}$ecords are only as accurate as the person in charge of logging the information noted. A researcher can wave records in the air as bonafide proof of *this or that* – but if another researcher steps forward and says the record is wrong then certainly the assertion must be considered.

In researching, the genealogist must look for discrepancies and then from those find other records or information to either *prove or disprove* the information. Some discrepancies are variances in spelling or interpretation of spelling via pronunciation. Some may be due to oversights.

In particular, Company A's Private Henry Lawson Wyatt of North Carolina's Volunteers is recorded as being *the first Confederate killed during combat.* * He is referred to by historians as being the first of 40,000 North Carolinians to lose his life in the *American Civil War.*

A monument erected on Capital grounds in Raleigh, N.C. honors Private Henry L. Wyatt killed during the Battle of Big Bethel in Virginia on June 10, 1861.

The wording is of the utmost importance if we are to truly understand record keeping and its influence on what is regarded later as facts. A Confederate Captain John Q. Marr of the 17th Virginia Infantry was killed at the *Battle of Fairfax Courthouse* June 1, 1861. His demise was not circulated adequately by the media of the time.

Some genealogists use quite readily newspaper articles, which can and often report misunderstandings of facts. *The Battle of Big Bethel* was hooted by the media or press of the day as being the first battle of the American Civil War. Some then etched the fate of Pvt. Henry Lawson Wyatt's memory as *"the first Confederate martyr"* and the *"first to fall at the Altar."*

The *North Carolina Civil War Death Study* backs these things. It is argued as Virginians additionally pointed out that Wyatt was by birth in 1842 from Richmond, Va. – and a resident since age 12 of North Carolina. The challenge from Virginia's assertions that Captain John Q. Marr was the first to die in battle and not Wyatt was then refined by one veteran. This was reported in the *North Carolina Civil War Death Study*. The report makes the distinction between a *"skirmish"* and a *"battle."* A North Carolina veteran of the time is quoted:

"Wyatt was the first to fall in open flight when troops met for the first time in battle array."

The argument thus evolved into a matter of the meaning of language or semantics and not one of order in military confrontations.

Some historians point to Confederate soldier William P. Clark of Baltimore, Md. Clark was awaiting transport to the South when a riot erupted. He was killed in Baltimore April 19, 1861. The Civil War death study points out *"the first North Carolina soldier to lose his life in the war"* was of Company B -- 1st North Carolina Volunteers' Private James Hudson. He died of pneumonia in Raleigh May 11, 1861.

The death study challenges the claim that North Carolina contributed more men and lost more men serving the Confederacy than any other Southern state. Some assert the reported 40,000 dead Confederates from North Carolina may have been between 33,000 and 35,000. It is claimed North Carolina's traditional assertion 40,000 disregards black- African Americans and white North Carolinians who died while serving the Union.

Company commanders during the War were responsible for recording the deaths of fallen soldiers. This was done via the muster roll. This muster roll or register was compiled monthly. Such documents state rather or not a soldier is *present and accounted for*, if absent, then why and those soldiers who had died. After each battle engagement, armies were required to compile casualty lists.

Medical records from army hospitals recorded who died, what they died of – disease or wounds. Military prisons records for POWs were to record deaths as well. If a soldier was executed due to desertion or war crimes this would be recorded in Courts Martial records. Muster-out records were kept by Union regiments to account for soldiers who were wounded or died during the unit's service. These things do not account for:

* Soldiers missing in combat. They were presumed dead or captured.
* Those captured by the enemy may have died as POWs and then been listed as POWs by their army.
* Titles of soldiers having the same names or similar names can cause discrepancies that are not readily discerned without extensive searching.
* If the soldier used a different name when entering a POW camp, this would add to more inaccuracies in record keeping. The *North Carolina Civil War Death Study* states that prison clerks wanting to return home at the end of the war listed men who died the previous month *"as having taken the Oath of Allegiance."*

* HENRY LAWSON WYATT: Amongst those articles housed in the files of the genea-logical Wyatt collection at the New Hanover Public Library is an account dated January 25, 1895 regarding Henry Lawson Wyatt [Feb. 12, 1842-1861]

The following contains some excerpts:

The papers in and out of North Carolina as to the first man killed in the great War of Second Independence. Henry Lawson Wyatt, of Tarboro, was the first man to be killed, but he was a native of Richmond, Va., born in [sic: on] February 12th, 1842. He was a worthy carpenter and joined the Edgecombe Guards, under Capt. John L. Bridgers. He was a very gallant soldier and was but nineteen when he was killed in the battle of Bethel, Va. We write this now because we have before us a sketch of him in a paper from another State in which it was stated he was born in North Carolina. Virginia is entitled to the honor of producing such a yalliant [sic galliant or valiant] and true hero. North Carolina has enough of heroes without pre-tending to take those of other States. Many soldiers like D.H. Hill, Charles C. Lee, James H. Lane, Cooke and others were born in other States, but closely identified with North Carolina in commanding her troops.

An account of Wyatt's death (in "Brief Sketches of North Carolina Troops") says:

"Young Wyatt lost his life under circumstances of great gallantry and heroism. In the begin-ning of the battle in which he fell the sharpshooters of the enemy occupied a house between the two opposing lines, blue and gray. A call was made for volunteers to advance across the intervening distance, through an open field 200 yards wide, and fire the building. Corporal George W. Williams, Private Henry Lawson Wyatt, Johyn H. Thorpe, Thomas Fallod and Robert H. Bradley responded to the call and attempted to perform the duty. They had pro-ceeded but a short distance into the field when Henry Wyatt fell with a bullet in his brain in a volley fired from the building. The other four soldiers dropped to the earth and remained until they could with safety rejoin their command, went through the entire war and are yet living." ....

Two and a half years later the following transcription of an article published on June 22, 1897 in *The Greenville Daily Reflector*:

The Greenville Daily Reflector settles the question as to Henry Wyatt's nativity....

"Henry Wyatt was not a native of North Carolina, but was born in the city of Richmond, Va. His father, John Wyatt, came to Greenville from Richmond some years before the war, and engaged in work at the coach shops of James Nelson, then located on the corned [sic: corner] of Pitt and Third streets. Finding that he could get permanent work he sent back to Richmond after his son Henry, then a boy about 4 years old. The two went to live with a woman known as Miss Cloudy who had a house on Pitt street about 100 yards south of Fifth street, the place now owned by Daniel Foreman's children.

"Henry Wyatt grew up in Greenville, and was nearly grown when the war came on. When companies were being organized here, he wanted to join one of them but his father objected because of his age. Young Wyatt then ran away and went to Tarboro where he joined a company."

"We said yesterday that we believed he was born in Richmond. It had been so stated since the day he was killed at the skirmish at Bethel, Va."

Approximately three years later, John Wilder Atkinson wrote to *The Messenger* his thoughts on Henry Lawson Wyatt. The following he penned in 1900.

...In regard to the question as to the state in which Wyatt was born, I may, I think, with propriety pronounce. Wyatt was a Richmond boy, well known to me. He lived in Richmond, all his life until shortly before the war, when he removed to Edgecombe county, North Carolina. He was a member of a volunteer company in Richmond, of which I was captain, and was by me transferred to the company, of which he was subsequently a member on his removal to this state.

I saw him at Bethel, when he was fatally shot, having, with two others, volunteered to advance in front of our line for the purpose of burning a barn which obstructed the fire of the Richmond Howitzers, then commanded by Major George W. Randolph – afterwards secretary of war in President Davis' cabinet.

It is true he was the only man killed at Bethel and the first killed in any regular battle, but unless my memory deceives me, he was not the first man killed after the war was declared. According to my recollection, about one week before the battle of Bethel, a Cavalry scouting party was sent down the Peninsula by General John B. Magruder, who was in command of that army in 1861, and these scouts meeting an advance party of videttes, sent out from Fortress Monroe, one of them was shot and killed.

This young man was, I think, from Williamsburg, or that vicinity.

The Virginia Infantry present at Bethel, under Liet.-Col. Stuart, was a portion of the Fifteenth Virginia regiment, of which Colonel Thomas August was commander, and not the Third Virginia, as stated by Mr. Hale. Of this detachment from the regiment I was captain of Company A.

On Feb. 8th, 1900, *The Greenville Weekly* professed that this Henry Wyatt lived in Greensville for several years.

An excerpt from that account:

"On June 1st, 1861, at Hallifax Court House, Va., a company of federal Cavalry and a body of confederates had a fight, in which Captain Marr of the Warrenton Virginia Rifles was killed. He was the first confederate soldier killed in battle...."

Another five years passed when the following article published by *The Charlotte Chronicle* on Feb. 2, 1905 stated:

The proposition before the Legislature to erect a monument on the Bethel battlefield, to Henry A. Wyatt of North Carolina, the first Confederate soldier killed in the Civil war, should enlist the favorable attention of the members of that body. Wyatt was but a boy. There are men living in Charlotte today who saw him shot down as he advanced across an open to set fire to a house behind which a body of Federals were massed, and from which position, they were able to command the Confederate position. The story of Wyatt's bravery and of his death is familiar to all North Carolinians, but not to the outside world. By all means, Wyatt should have a monument.

♀ | | ♂

PART 2. MISSING WYATTS [WIATTS, WIATS]

Note pages in the back matter will assist the reader as a means of adding people who may be missing from this account.

The following list of Wyatts was gathered from *North Carolina Troop Records* and other sources. If you know how, or discover how they fit into this Wyatt history, record your assertions in the note pages found in the back of the book. Send findings to *Metallo House Publishers*. The Wyatts in this section are not listed in the back matter because the author/researcher could not readily discern how they connect.

North Carolina Troops 1861-1865 – A Roster Volume 1 Artillery, compiled by Louis H. Manarin, First Printing 1968, 1989, 2004:

Company E, 10th Regiment N.C.S.T. 91st Regiment N.C. Artillery), page 246

Wyatt, J.F., Private
Captured at Gettysburg, Pa., July 5, 1863 and
Confined at Fort Delaware, Del., July 7-12, 1863.

Company B, page 558

Wyatt, James A., Private
Transferred from Company B, 12th Battalion
Va. Light Artillery November 4, 1863. Present
Or accounted for through February 1865.

North Carolina Troops 1861-1865 – A Roster Volume 2 Cavalry, compiled by Louis H. Manarin, First Printing 1968, 1989, 2004:

4th Battalion N.C. Cavalry, page: 264

Wyatt, Horace D., Corporal
Enlisted in Martin County at age 34, October
27 1861 for twelve months' service. Mustered in
as Corporal on November 6, 1861 and reported
on muster-in roll date Washington, N.C., February 19, 1862. No further records.

4th Battalion N.C. Cavalry, page: 366

Wyatt, Colton, Private Born in Ashe County, where he resided as a farmer and enlisted at age 20, July 8, 1862 for the war. Present or accounted for until transferred to Company B, 65th, Regiment N.C. Troops (6th Regiment N.C. Cavalry) August 3, 1863.

Company I, 63rd Regiment North Carolina Troops [5th Regiment N.C. Cavalry]

4th Battalion N.C. Cavalry, page: 437

Wyatt, W.H., Private
Enlisted in Davie County at age 29, July 12,
1862 for the war. Present and accounted for
through October 1862.

Company C, 65th Regiment North Carolina Troops [6th Regiment N.C. Cavalry]

4th Battalion N.C. Cavalry, page: 469

Wyatt, Alfred, Private
Enlisted in Lenoir County October 2, 1864 for
the war. Present and accounted for through
November 1864.

*Wyatt, Colton, Private
Transferred from Company D, 5th Battalion N.C.
Cavalry August 3, 1863. Present and accounted for
Through November 1864.

4th Battalion N.C. Cavalry, page 683

Wyatt, Robert L., Private
Transferred from Company H -- 7th Regiment
Confederate Cavalry July 11, 1864. Present or
accounted for through October 1, 1864.

The following is a list of Confederate soldiers by the surname of *"Wyatt"* and one spelled as *"Wiatt"* who were paroled at the *Appomattox Court House,* Va. The place of *Appomattox Court House* is significant in that actions signal General Lee's surrender and that the American Civil War was officially over. This list of Wyatts or Wiatts is from the third edition of *The Appomattox Paroles, April 9-15, 1865.*

Wiatt, William Edward: Chaplain, Wise's Brigade 26th Virginia Regiment, Infantry. [1st column, page 224];

Wyatt, Benjamin Franklin, 6th Virginia Regiment, Company A

Wyatt, George Washington, 34th Virginia Regiment, Company C

Wyatt, Joseph M., Ord. Sergeant 30th Virginia Regiment

Wyatt, Lewis L., Corp., 44th Alabama Regiment, Company F

Wyatt, Richard S., 57th Virginia Regiment, Company F

Wyatt, W.W., Palmetto Sharpshooters Company K

[*The Appomattox Paroles, April 9-15, 1865*; 1st column, page 231]

Civil War Courts-Martial of North Carolina Troops by Aldo S. Perry reported in his that Confederate military courts *"sentenced to death more soldiers from North Carolina than from any other state."*

He mentions an Andrew Wyatt of the 26th North Carolina Infantry. He reports that prior to January 26, 1863, Sergeant Andrew Wyatt was one of a few Confederate soldiers spared moments before execution.

Perry states in book:

"The events that led Sergeant Wyatt to his harrowing experience at Magnolia, Duplin County, began with his conscription from his home in Ashe County in September 1862. Three others with the same surname went into service that day. Eleven weeks later, Sergeant Wyatt deserted from Garysburg, NC, where a camp of instruction was located. He was arrested ten days after departing Garysburg..." [page 70].

According to this account, Andrew Wyatt was attempting to cross the Roanoke River. He was hospitalized after the arrest. A court-marital followed. One ghastly account reported that he was blindfolded and ordered to kneel down by a freshly dug grave. The firing squad readied itself. The officer was reading the sentence just as an orderly arrived with an order from General French granting a pardon. Perry reports that Wyatt's life was extended by five months returning to duty and *"death at Gettysburg, PA."*

Perry mentions another Wyatt – a William W. Wyatt of Wilkes County, N.C. in the 4th Regiment Company E of the NC Troops who was executed with two other men for desertion. Private William W. Wyatt it is speculated by Perry was the only of the three who could read and write. He wrote a letter to then North Carolina Governor Z.B. Vance on April 21st, 1864 asking for clemency or to at least give them more time to present their side of what happened.

"This note will inform you that we have been so unfortunate to have the sentence of death passed on us we started home and was arrested near warren ferry on James River the 25th of

March 1864 and brought back and court marchaled there was noting but desertion charged against us we did not take any arm nor nothing of that sort and we was influenced [ink blot] as we would not have started but we did not make this appear at the tryal as we did not know it was necessary and our sentence was to be shot to death with muskerty within seven days from the publication of the sentence which was read to us yesterday we understand that we are to be shot for an example to skair others and not principally for crime & we privates J.F. Owens, Wm. W. Wyatt and R. Sparks of Wilkes County...." [page 129].

Perry points out in his book that Governor Vance received the letter and did not note any action he wanted to take concerning the men. These three men were caught as far as the James River with five others. It was a second attempt at desertion for the three executed. What is particularly sinister is the decision to shoot the three men was made three weeks before the three learned the outcome of their trial. One of the eight men caught and accused of deserting was Private Philo Benefield. He was sentenced to serve a prison term in Salisbury, N.C., where he was held until December 1864.

Perry further quotes a letter of another from the 30th Regiment:

"I must say something a bout what I saw the other day I saw men Co. E 4th NC regment marched out into a cold field an tyed to stakes and 36 men shot them I wish I could tel you how I felt I never felt so bad in all my life the guns fiered that trimbliled and the blud run down their sids tha were berried their in the cold field...." [page 131].

Outside of the ACW records are mentions of Wyatts. For instance, *The North Carolina Higher-Court Records, 1670-1696,* edited by Mattie Erma Edwards Parker, published by the State Department of Archives and History, Raleigh, N.C. in 1968 contains a record from the County Court of Albemarle that mentions a William Wyatt – along with a few others, to take inventory of a deceased person.

The record simply states:

"Ordered that William Wyatt, John Barrow, Caleb Calloway and Stephen Hancock take an Inventory of the estate of Walter Greene, deceased and Appraise the same."

In a fiction book titled: *To Lay One's Life Down For You, Brother,* a novel by Dr. Sean M.J. McCarthy, there is a list of Vietnam veterans [1954-1975] that includes 14 soldiers by this surname:

* Alvie Clinton Wyatt
* Billy Herdon Wyatt
* Billy Joe Wyatt
* Charles Rembert Wyatt
* Edward W. Wyatt
* Everett Albert Wyatt, Jr.

- James Edward Wyatt
- John Wesley Wyatt, Jr.
- Marvin Leon Wyatt
- Phillip Edgar Wyatt
- Richard Coleman Wyatt
- Robert Paul Wyatt
- Ronald Wyatt
- Tommy Lloyd Wyatt

* While none from this list are noted in the back matter – these men are nevertheless people who served in the U.S. Military whose surname was *"Wyatt."*

♀ | | ♂

This is an illustration of a Confederate soldier telling his wife
goodbye during the American Civil War [1861-1865].

"This is a different kind of army...No man has to bow, no man born to royalty. Here we judge you by what you do, not by who your father was. Here you can be something.... It's the idea that we all have value, you and me. What we're fighting for, in the end...we're fighting for each other."

* COLONEL JOSHUA LAWRENCE CHAMBERLAIN [SEPTEMBER 8, 1828 – FEBRUARY 24, 1914], AMERICAN COLLEGE PROFESSOR FROM MAINE ON GETTYSBURG.

Footnotes

♀ | | ♂

* Footnote to Introduction

$\mathcal{E}$NGLAND'S KING GEORGE V WAS formerly known as George V of Saxe-Coburg-Gotha, which was changed to the House of Windsor after he declared on July 17th, 1917:

"Now, therefore, We, out of Our Royal Will and Authority, do hereby declare and announce that as from the date of this Our Royal Proclamation Our House and Family shall be styled and known as the House and Family of Windsor, and that all the descendants in the male line of Our said Grandmother Queen Victoria who are subjects of these Realms, other than female descendants who may marry or may have married, shall bear the said Name of Windsor."

Nicholas II Tsar of Russia [born May 18, 1868 in the Alexander Palace, Tsarskoye Selo, Saint Petersburg, Russian Empire; died July 17, 1918 in Yekaterinberg, Russian Soviet Union] and his wife Alexandra Hesse or Alix of Hesse, [born June 6, 1872 in Darmstadt, German Empire; died July 17, 1918] with their children: Olga, born 1895; Tatiana, born 1897; Maria, born 1899; Anastasia, born 1901 and Alexei, born 1904, who suffered with hemophilia.

On March 2, 1917, Nicholas II gave up the throne. The throne could not be passed to his son whose illness rendered him not appropriate. Nicholas II's brother Mikhail *"Michael"* did not want the position, so the Romanov Dynasty ended. Nicholas II, the last Emperor of Russia, was known as *"Nikolai Alexandrovich Romanov."*

Certainly, it would be unfair to paint King George V as completely heartless in the aftermath of the Boleshvik Revolution [known as the October Uprising, also: Red October, The Great October Socialist Revolution of 1917*].

The British government feared a trendy reaction if it decided to allow Nicholas II and his family asylum in England. Nicholas II was arrested by the New Provisional Government at Tsarskoe Selo. In August 1917, he was moved with his family to the town of Tobolsk in the region of Urals [a mountain range running from north to south through western Russia and from the Arctic Ocean coast to the Ural River and northwestern Kazakhstan. The eastern side of the Urals is a natural boundary between Europe and Asia.] This was located 1,200 miles east of Moscow.

There existed fears that opponents of the Bolshevik Government might try to rescue Nicholas II. Consequently, in the later part of April 1918, Nicholas II and his family were moved once more – then to Yekartenberg. This was the center of Bolsehvik power in the Ural region. An order in the middle of July 1918 came from Moscow that Nicholas II and his family would be killed. This family was awakened from their beds in the early morning of July 17, 1918, and shot to death. Their bodies were thrown into an old mineshaft until the collapse of the Soviet Union in 1991.

Their remains were gathered in 1998 and taken to Saint Petersburg and interred in the Peter-Paul Fortress. Nicholas II is a first cousin to George V of Saxe-Colburg-Gotha [Windsor] because George and Nicholas' mothers are sisters to one another. Nicholas II's mother Maria Feodorovna Frederikke Dagmar [1847-1928], of Denmark and the wife of Alexander III Tsar of All the Russias; is a sister to Alexandra [1844-1925] of Denmark, wife of Albert Edward VII of Saxe-Coburg-Gotha who are the parents of George V of Saxe-Coburg-Gotha [1865-1936].

Alexandria and Maria's brother George I [known as William, 1845-1913] is the mother of Andrew de Laszlo [1882-1944] who is the father of Prince Philip Mountbatten, born 1921 – who is the husband of our modern day's Queen Elizabeth II [born 1926]. So, Prince Philip's father Prince Andrew of Greece and Denmark is a first cousin to George V and to Nicholas II.

What do their genealogical relationships have to do with my point here? Nothing really. I spent hours drawing it out with pencil and paper so I could understand it, so it is part of your genealogical lesson – possibly it is torture – but not likely as the assumption is you are at least curious about genealogy.

* The Bolshevik Revolution was the seizure of state power, which was essential in the larger Russian Revolution of 1917. It capitalized on the February Revolution of 1917 that overthrew the Tsar Nicholas II of Russia and established The Russian Provisional Government, consisting of former nobles and aristocrats. Urban workers organized into councils. Revolutionaries criticized the provisional government. The October Revolution in Petrograd overthrew this government and gave the power to local soviets. The Bolshevik Part was supported by the soviets. The Russian Civil War followed from 1917 to 1922, the latter being the year the Soviet Union was created.

* 2nd Footnote to Introduction

This footnote refers to section of Introduction discussing King George III and the film titled: *The Madness of King George* [directed by Nicholas Hytner; based on a play written by Alan Bennett].

George III seeming was losing his grip on reality due to a rare illness that turned his urine blue [Porphyria]. By the end of the film, he regains his sanity, wit and charm. In the midst of all he had been through and his family as well, there is this inner strength or push to *"appear"* that all is well.

George III, was on the British throne from 1760 until 1820. George III [June 4, 1738-January 29, 1820], was married to Queen Consort Charlotte of the House of Mecklenburg-Streilitz [a North German dynasty of West Slavic origin that ruled until 1918] [died 1818] and had several children, including: Prince Edward Augustus, George IV, Frederick, William IV, Charlotte, Augusta Sophia, Octavia, Alfred, Amelia. Prince Edward Augustus [1767-1820] married Victoria of Saxe-Coburg-Gotha [1786-1861].

Edward and Victoria's daughter Alexandrina Victoria [1819-1901] married Francis Albert Augustus of Saxe-Colburg-Gotha [1819-1861] and had several children – one being Albert Edward VII [1841-1910] – the father of George V.

*Footnote: Chapter 12, Wyatts & the British Colony of Virginia; Part 1. Nova Britannia

The *Adventurers of Purse and Person 1607-1625 and Their Families:*

"EDWARD WYATT (Haute1) appears to have been the elder son, born about 1620 despite what was probably an error in listing the children of Haute 1 Wyatt in an administration account, which named Edward2 as the second son. This is borne out by a claim of the descendants in Virginia to 'Boxley' in England, when the Wyatt line through Sir Francis became extinct. Edward Wyatt, first mentioned in Virginia records as Edwin Wyatt a headright in a land patent issued 29 September 1643, to his uncle, Sir Francis, apparently, had come to the colony when Sir Francis was sent a second time as Governor of Virginia, 1639. He is mentioned 23 April 1646, as the administrator of the estate of John Clarke of York County and represented his widow Hannah Clarke in 1652. He acquired by 3 September 1663, 850 acres of Middle Plantation (Williamsburg) York County formerly belonging to John Clarke, deceased, and which had been found to escheat. Subsequently, with his wife Jane, Edward Wyatt sold the Clarke tract. 1667 to George Poindexter and Otho Thorpe of Middle Plantation. In the meantime, 20 July 1662, 'Edward Wyatt, Gent' obtained a patent for 1,230 acres in Gloucester County 'upon the Pianketank River' for transportation of 25 persons. This probably confirmed a gift of land in the Pianketank area made to Edward Wyatt, 29 October 1655 by 'Pindavako,' protector of the young King of Chiskoyack by signed agreement, the original now in the possession of the Huntington Library at San Marino, California.

"The Wyatt Plantation "Boxley" upon the Pianketank River, was eventually divided and 'Old Upton' and 'New Upton' cut from it."

Some accounts have Rev. Hawte leaving his sons Edward and George in Virginia and others point that it was more likely Francis -- the uncle brought them with him during his second trip to Virginia and second term as governor there.

Luther's Lutheran Church, Richfield, N.C.

In Honor of James Noah Hinson, M.D. [1929-2015]

♀ | | ♂

".... death is a continuation of life, but a continuation in another world. That world is invisible to the eyes of the physical body.... but can be seen there in light that outshines the noonday of this world a thousand times."

—Emanuel Swedenborg

Part 1. Saying Good-bye

*A*T 4:25 P.M., Monday, March 30th, 2015, my father's heart stopped. My mother held him in her arms whispering into his ear the *"I love yous"* one says when we know the journey for a soul has ended here and is about to begin a new life in Heaven. He wanted I finish this book before he passed away – and in not doing so, I failed. He became frustrated occasionally because I did not work quickly enough. He felt we would run out of time before he said his farewells to this earth. Three weeks before he passed, I gave him the manuscript *in better progress* – with some of the photos, pictures and artwork that would be published.

That version of the manuscript did not contain this back matter. It contained enough that he understood we were close to finishing. I wanted so much to put the published project into his hands. Something inside of me – my soul, I believe this is what it was, knew I would not obtain that goal. His view now is from Heaven's gates, windows, doors, and tunnels and those unique dreams that sometimes grace one's sleep. He is reading it as each of you read it, nevertheless.

His wake was held between 5:30 p.m. and 6 p.m. for immediate family members and from 6 p.m. to 8 p.m. Friday, April 3rd, 2015 for extended family and friends at the Summersett Funeral Home just off of Innes Street in Salisbury, N.C. So many of his closest friends, neighbors and relatives gathered there. They said the nicest things one could possibly express.

Mary Ann Wyatt Eagle [1839-1902], daughter of Mary Polly
Hendly & Noah Calvin Wyatt & wife of Joseph Eagle

Dr. Myron Goodman said:

"Jim was the best doctor to treat diabetes that I have ever known. He just had a knack for it."

*Myron Goodman, M.D. is related to my father via the Eagles, Wyatts, Hodge, Heilig, Haldeman [Halderman], Norbitts, Henly [Hendley, Henley] and Park families – and according to calculations is his 3rd cousin once removed, also a 4th cousin and a 6th cousin. Myron is the son of Myron A.O. Goodman who is the son of Enoch Arthur Goodman, the son of Nancy Jane Eagle [Goodman], daughter of Mary Ann Wyatt and Joseph Travis Eagle – Joseph Travis Eagle being a brother to Solomon Eagle, Jr. – the Solomon whose remains are buried at Luther's Lutheran Church in Richfield. The Eagle lineage is traced to Solomon Eagle, Sr., son of George Egle, Jr., son of George Egle, Sr., son of Adam Egle of the Canton of Zurich, Switzerland – Adam being the son of Marcus Egle of the same. Eleven generations of Egles can be traced prior to Marcus Egle to Ulrich *"Ulric"* Egli or Eglé to the Swiss Confederation around the year 1350. Joseph Travis Eagle's [1839-1911] wife Mary Ann Wyatt [1839-1902] has ancestors that are traced to the Virginia Colony at Jamestown to Reverend Haute *"Haut" "Hawte"* Wiatt and on into England back to Admiral or Captain Adam Guyot [Wyot, Wyatt]. This Mary Ann Wyatt was a sister of William Wesley Wyatt, Rachel E. Wyatt Morgan, Silas, Lila, Emanuel, Henry, among others. In half of a nutshell, Myron's second great grandmother Mary Ann Wyatt [Eagle] was a sister to Rachel E. Wyatt [Morgan]. Myron's second great grandfather Joseph T. Eagle was a brother to Solomon Eagle, Jr. – making him a 3rd cousin once removed via the Eagles and a 4th cousin via the Wyatts to James Noah Hinson, M.D.

One face I had not seen since I was a teenager appeared through the long line of attendees.

"Len [Hélène], I bet you can't tell me who he is?" Hans said reaching to the man's shoulder.

Light eyes through a tanned face and sandy hair smiled through a veil of sadness.

"She does not know who you are!" Hans joked.

"He's Mike Morgan," I said.

Mike worked on the farms for my father for many years. Mike is the son of Arlene Hoffner and J.T. Morgan.

*J.T. Morgan is the son of Freda Maybelle Kirk and Jacob *"J."* Thomas *"Tom"* Morgan, son of Ann James *"Jim"* Kirk and Jacob Morgan, son of Barbara Shaver and Moses Green Morgan [1810-1879].

One by one – those people who knew and loved my father – made their way through the line of my uncles, aunts, siblings, sons, nephews, sister-in-law, husband and cousins.

Extended cousins shook hands and hugged. They greeted my mother at the end of the reception line before reaching the dark gray suited remains that lay in coffin.

The remains that lay in the coffin are not all that is left of my father, or any soul that gathers the courage to come to this earth. For the most part, I avoided talking about death to my father. Occasionally, he mentioned it and managed to get a response.

"Daddy, when you pass from this earth, your soul is going to say:

'Oh, what was I doing before I ventured there?'

"When you leave your body, it will be as if you discarded a coat you no longer require."

The obituary herein is an adaptation of what appeared in *The Salisbury Post* the day before his funeral, which was held at 2 p.m., Saturday at Luther's Lutheran Church in Richfield, N.C. His remains were buried in the cemetery there – the same cemetery in which the remains of one of his great grandfathers are located since 1939.

Solomon Eagle, Jr., my father remarked within two weeks of his passing, was the reason he decided to go to medical school. In the previous year, my father referred to Solomon Eagle, Jr. as his mentor and as having tremendous influence on him during his earliest years. Solomon understood how to work, survive and succeed in a world full of uncertainty.

Although my father as a little boy was surrounded in many male figures – Solomon was the person whose words and actions spoke to him the deepest. Solomon made him feel safe and in control of his future. They both shared the same month of being born – my father on the 12th of January, and Solomon on January 18th.

My father lived 86 years, two months, two weeks and four days. Solomon – his mentor, lived 82 years, 11 months, one week and two days. His first name was given in honor of his great grandfather James Henry Hinson [born in April 1867, Stanly County, N.C.; died in 1904, Woods, Tx.] His middle name *"Noah"* was given to honor his grandfather Noah Jenkins Eagle [born January 28th, 1878, Morgan Township, Rowan County, N.C.; died August 18th, 1976, Richfield, Rowan County, N.C.]. The name *"Noah"* seemingly has been passed down from Noah Parks, Sr. [1743-1815] as it is popular in the Park, Wyatt, Morgan and Eagle families.

At 2 p.m., Saturday, April 4th friends and family gathered at the vibrant red doors of Luther's Lutheran Church in Richfield. The coolness of winter was still suspended in the air, as the sun was not hidden by clouds.

What does one do to make a difference after a person has passed away?

There is nothing left to do, I suppose except to give the best funeral one is able to, or to express openly condolences, or to listen to those condolences.

Prayers.

Flowers.

Poems.

Music.

Honorary salutes and the firing of guns into the sky.

We do this for the souls who leave. Then, we go home. We see their faces in our minds. We hear their words and voices as if they are still here with us.

Some of us cry outwardly, while others are in agony deep inside hearts behind locked doors. Having one's parents in this world gives most people a sense of strength, so when one passes – we are left with a feeling that part of ourselves departed this planet too.

White lilies, carnations and other white flowers gathered in two silver-toned vases were placed left and right of the altar. The closed casket was positioned in the front of the church as the minister lay his hand over the lid and gave his blessing asking God to give His blessings.

During my father's funeral, he was given military honors having served during the Korean War. An American flag draped his casket as the coming Easter winds kissed the cheeks of every attendee and flapped the cloth of the tent that sheltered those seated under it. The guns fired into the sunny skies. The bugle played away those last moments of the ceremony.

Tree at Luther's Lutheran Church, Richfield, Rowan County, N.C.

♀ | | ♂

PART 2. THE OBITUARY

"Our soul or spirit is our inner part, and our body is our outer part … when we
rise after death, we shed our body, because we then inhabit our inner part…"

-- EMANUEL SWEDENBORG

JAMES NOAH HINSON, M.D. [1929-2015]

James Noah Hinson, M.D, 86, of Salisbury, N.C. passed away at 4:25 p.m., Monday, March 30, 2015. He had been in declining health for the past few years. He was the husband of Patricia Ann Leighton Hinson.

Dr. Hinson was born January 12, 1929 at Mabery Place, Porter Station, Stanly County. He was the third son of Virgie Irene Eagle, a former Ponds School teacher, and William Crowell Hinson, a farmer. Dr. Hinson and his wife Patricia had three children: Hélène Andorre Hinson Staley of Moncure; Häns Leighton Hinson, M.D. of Mount Pleasant, S.C. and Nicole Suzanne Hinson, M.D. of Huntersville. Mrs. Hinson is the daughter of the late Clarence Harland and Ruth McTall [Metallo] Leighton.

A resident of Salisbury since 1967, Dr. Hinson is survived by seven grandsons: Zachary Christopher Staley, Nicholas Staley, Benjamin *"Ben"* Noah Patrick Staley – each of Moncure; Jonah Karsch Hinson, Noah Karsch Hinson, Elijah Karsch Hinson and Micah Karsch Hinson – each of Mount Pleasant, S.C.

He is survived by his sisters Betty Lou Hinson Heath of High Point and Margaret Ann Hinson Gordon of Rowan County; 12 nieces, 8 nephews; 14 grandnephews, 12 grandnieces, 3 great grandnephews, 7 great grandnieces. He is survived by one uncle: Robert Noah Eagle, age 92, son of Noah and Laura Lou Eller Eagle and brother of Virgie Irene Eagle Hinson, mother of Dr. Hinson. Dr. Hinson is also survived by many cousins.

Dr. Hinson was the brother of the late Rachel Evelyn Hinson Hill, brother-in-law of the late Paul Junior *"Bud"* Hill; brother of the late Richard Clyde *"Chub or Chubby,"* Hinson; and the late William *"Bill"* Crowell Hinson, Jr. – nicknamed *"June;"* brother-in-law of the late John Arthur Gordon; brother-in-law of the late James Edwin *"Ed"* Heath; brother-in-law of the late Merrell Lenora Goodman Hinson; brother-in-law of the late Pansy Ruth Hampton Hinson.

He leaves behind his daughter-in-law Vanessa Karsch Hinson, M.D., wife of Hans; son-in-law Howard Anthony Staley, D.P.M., husband of Hélène.

Dr. Hinson, who specialized in internal medicine with an emphasis on cardiology, pulmonary and hematologic diseases, practiced medicine in Rowan County over 40 years. He retired in 2008. His office was located on Mocksville Avenue.

In addition to his medical practice, Dr. Hinson owned and operated farms in Rowan County, N.C. since the late 1960s.

During grammar school years, Dr. Hinson attended Baden School in Baden; Millingport School in Millingport; Shaver School, a four-room school house on Reaves Island Road in Rowan County. From 8th grade to 12th grade, he attended Richfield School, graduating from there in 1947. From 1947 to 1948, he attended Mars Hill College. From 1948-1950, Dr. Hinson worked in Baden, at ALCOA Aluminum Company of America, an aluminum factory.

From 1950 to 1952, Dr. Hinson served in the United States Army during the Korean War – spending the initial part as a rifleman in Camp Atterbury [or Atterbery] near Edinburgh, Ind. and later as military policeman [MP]. While in the army, he attended Candidates for Officers Training School. He served in Company E, 112 Regiment, Army 28th Division.

From 1953 to 1956, he was a student at Catawba College in Salisbury, graduating with bachelor's degree and a double major in chemistry and biology. From 1956 to1960, he attended Bowman Gray School of Medicine at Wake Forest University, Winston-Salem. In 1997, Bowman Gray was renamed Wake Forest School of Medicine.

From 1960 to 1961, Dr. Hinson completed an internship at North Carolina Baptist Hospital, Winston-Salem. From 1961 to 1962, he completed a chest medicine residency at Charleston Memorial Hospital in Charleston, W.Va. From 1962 to 1966, he completed a residency in New Orleans, La. focused on cardiology, pulmonology, hematology and neurology under the auspices of Tulane University School of Medicine.

Dr. Hinson enjoyed genealogical research and history, gardening, poetry, cooking, spending time with his children and grandchildren.

The family will receive family and friends at Summersett Funeral Home in Salisbury. The funeral will be held at Luther's Lutheran Church with the Rev. Tommy Beaver officiating. Pallbearers: Phillip Van Gordon, Ph.D., M.D.; Hans Leighton Hinson, M.D.; William Eugene Heath, Zachary Christopher Staley, Nicholas Staley and Jonah Karsch Hinson. Lawrence *"Larry"* Walker Tywater to serve as an alternate pallbearer.

Memorial donations can be given to the American Cancer Society. Online condolences and memorial tributes may be made at:

www.summersetfuneralhome.com.

Interment will be at Luther's Lutheran Church Cemetery – known as Piney Woods Church Cemetery, located at the intersection of Richfield Road (State Road 1005) and Stokesferry Road (SR 1004), #4955 Richfield Road, Morgan Township, southeastern Rowan County.

♀ | | ♂

PART 3. I HAVE A RENDEZVOUS WITH DEATH

Before the Rev. Tommy Beaver delivered the eulogy, Vanessa Karsch Hinson, Ph.D., M.D. read the poem by Alan Seeger [1888-1916] titled: *"I Have A Rendez Vous With Death."*

I HAVE A rendezvous with Death
At some disputed barricade,
When Spring comes back with rustling shade
And apple blossoms fill the air –
I have a rendezvous with Death
When Spring brings back blue days and fair.

IT MAY BE he shall take my hand,
And lead me into his dark land
And close my eyes and quench my breath –
It may be I shall pass him still.
I have a rendezvous with Death
On some scarred slope of battered hill,
When Spring comes round again this year
And the first meadow flowers appear

GOD KNOWS 'TWERE better to be deep
Pillowed in silk and scented down,
Where love throbs out in blissful sleep,
Pulse nigh to pulse, and breath to breath,
Where hushed awakenings are dear...
But I've a rendezvous with Death
At midnight in some flaming town,
When Spring trips north again this year,
And I to my pledged word am true,
I shall not fail that rendezvous.

♀ | | ♂

Part 4. Eulogy by Rev. Tommy Beaver

What can we say about James Hinson?

He was beloved by his patients. He was a person who loved his interactions with people….

Dr. Hinson cared about people – his wife, children, family members, friends, patients and colleagues.

Dr. Hinson had an uncanny sense of fairness and honesty. He expected the same treatment from others.

James was committed to trying to be a better person – he wanted to learn from his mistakes.

…No one was above the other – all human beings.

….

Care is something other than cure.

Cure means *"change."*

A doctor, a lawyer, a minister, a social worker, they all want to use their professional skills to bring about changes in people's lives. They get paid for whatever kind of cure they can bring about. But cure, desirable as it may be, can easily become violent, manipulative and even destructive, if it does not grow out of care.

Care is being with, crying with, suffering with, feeling with. Care is compassion; it is claiming the truth that the other person is my brother or sister, human, mortal, vulnerable, like I am.

When care is our first concern, cure can be received as a gift. Often we are not able to cure, but we are always able to care. To care is to be human.

To me that certainly describes Dr. Hinson. He cared for his wife, children, family, friends and patients, and they cared for him.

Dr. Hinson grew up several miles from here. He attended the elite local schools – Baden, Millingport, Shaver, a four-room school house up the Stokes Ferry Road from here. He graduated from the prominent Richfield High School.

I am exaggerating about the schools as Doc learned in spite of the fact that these schools had limited libraries and resources. They did the best they could do in that time period. Maybe the fact that his mother was a former school teacher helped.

It is obvious that Doc had the ability to absorb knowledge. He would slowly read something, and when he finished he could recite it from memory. He graduated from Catawba College with a double major in chemistry and biology. Can't get much tougher than that. In a medical school residency, he pursued specialized areas of medicine – lung diseases, cardiology, pulmonology, hematology and neurology.

When James was in the Army, his superiors selected him to attend Officer's Training School, and he was told that he would be on the fast track to becoming a general. After a while, he asked if he could get out of OTS – it wasn't for him.

Dr. Hinson was human, yes, he made mistakes, and he learned from them. He was committed to trying to become a better person. He had an uncanny sense of fairness and honesty. He expected that the same treatment from others. Sometimes, he had to be creative.

A patient came to see Dr. Hinson for treatment. When he got ready to leave, Doc noticed he was behind in paying his bill for previous treatments. The doctor said to him,

"When are you going to pay your bill?"

The man said, *"I don't have enough money."*

Doc said, *"Well, how much do you have?"*

He pulled out his wallet and counted out $18. Doc took it and proceeded to divvy it out. He said to the man,

"Well, you are going to need this amount to pay for your pills downstairs."

He put that amount in a stack.

"You have to have money for gas to get home."

He made another stack.

"You have to eat."

He laid out a few dollars for that.

Finally, after everything was divided out, there was one dollar left.

Doc said: *"That is mine. Bill paid in full."*

He would have given the shirt off his back if someone really needed it. He checked into their situation rather than just hand them money without questioning.

A woman came to him with an ugly cut on her face from a bar fight. Dr. Hinson looked at the gaping wound and said:

"I am not a surgeon, but I think I can sew up your wound so there won't be an ugly scar on your face."

He went to work making very fine stitches – he took his time being very careful to sew up the wound. [He said while working, *"I understand why women sew; it's so relaxing."*] He was quite content and enjoyed neat work. A week or so later she came back to have the stitches out – before he got started she asked how much removing the stitches was going to cost.

He said, *"Well, removing the stitches is included in the suturing."*

He told her how much it was going to be, and she replied that she only had half of the money now and would pay the rest later. Doc thought that once she left he would not see her again. So, he proceeded to take out every other stitch.

She asked, *"Why did you not take out all of the stitches?"*

He said: *"When you pay the rest of your bill, I will take out the rest."*

Needless to say, she didn't return – She must have removed the rest of the stitches herself.

James and Patricia raised three intelligent and talented children. They wanted their children to be all they could be. Doc practiced the Socratic method of teaching, that originated with the philosophy of Socrates, in which one asks a series of easily answered questions that inevitably lead to a logical conclusion foreseen by the questioner.

He wanted them to develop a method of resolving questions and problems that they could use all through life. Of course, it is much easier to answer a child's questions and be done with it, but that's teaching them to rely on others instead of working through questions themselves.

Obviously, the children thrived from the guidance their parents gave them in their early formative years. They have been very successful in their work.

In describing his father, Hans said, that his Dad was more spiritual than religious. By that meaning he was a person of integrity, not a shyster, out to gain at someone else's expense. James' mother kept all the letters that her children wrote to her while they were away from home, in school, or in the military.

One day when Hans was with his grandmother Hinson, she took him up in the attic and pulled out one of the letters that James had written her while he was in Medical School.

He wrote:

"I know there must be a God – He is the only one who could have put all of this together for me."

Dr. Hinson did his first year of residency at Charleston Memorial Hospital in Charleston, West Virginia. One day a young lady came into the clinic [where he was on call]. She presented a rash that was giving her problems.... since she was in nursing school, she thought she could tell the doctor what she needed. ...

Dr. Hinson shook his head. He wasn't sure she needed to be taking that dosage of medication [even though it was the dosage recommended for adults.] Well, she was young and pretty, so I guess he didn't want to disappoint the young lady so he wrote a prescription. She took the pills right away and went to her class.

Before long after she got into class she slid out of her desk. The medicine put her away. That was how James and Patricia met. One thing led to another, and they eventually married and raised three children, welcomed son- and daughter-in-laws into the family and had seven grandsons.

He loved history and genealogy. He was especially interested in protecting and extending the history of this part of Eastern Rowan County. He was especially fond of Luther's Lutheran Church and its history since his great grandfather Eagle is buried in this cemetery as well as a number of relatives. I am hoping that someone has recorded the history that Doc loved to recite.

Once an East Rowan student athlete came to his office for a physical. Doc was to do physicals for the school. The nurse had him to dress in a paper gown for his physical. The story goes that it was very cold in the exam room and the young man only had this paper gown on – and he was shivering.

Finally, Doc arrived. I understand that he never hurried – he was extremely patient with everyone. The first words out of Doc's mouth:

"Do you know who you are?"

The young man said he thought he did but after an hour lecture of all the ancestors of this student, he did not believe he knew anything. To top it all, Doc left and went to the next patient without giving him his physical. He had to be called back in later to do that.

Doc loved this part of the county. He spent a lot of time, money and sweat on his farm, raising grain and hay for his beef cattle herds. Since the 60s, he has been involved in farming, especially in cattle ranching. If you ever brought into the conversation with Doc either farming, history or cows, you were in for a rather long discussion. For a number of years now coyotes have been invading our area. They caused thousands of dollars of damage to Dr. Hinson's calves.

Someone told Doc to get a donkey to chase the coyotes away from the calves. He did and that stopped most of the poaching by the coyotes. The cows bonded with the donkey and wherever the donkey would go, the cows would follow. In these last few years he and his care taker would go to the farm and drive out into the pasture and find the donkey.

Doc brought carrots to feed the donkey. He got a great deal of pleasure from feeding the donkey as it stuck its head through the window of the truck and let Doc rub its ears and head. That is what you can call Donkey therapy.

Dr. Hinson was quite a man. He loved God, Patricia, his children, in-laws, grandsons, family and many friends. He made the most of the gifts and talents God had given him.

He lived life to the fullest, being well suited to being a medical doctor helping people find healing and hope in their lives. He loved his connection to this part of Rowan County, all that God had made, but especially God's crowning creation of mankind.

James Noah Hinson, M.D. and his sister Margaret Hinson Gordon; Abt. 2013.

♀ | | ♂

PART 5. SOME MEMORIES....

The following is a draft copy of a letter written by my father James Noah Hinson, M.D. to his mother Virgie Irene Eagle Hinson five days after the birth of my brother Häns. It is written from the standpoint of baby Häns -- writing as if Häns is relaying his perceptions of the world. This fact becomes readily apparent halfway through the letter. Upon reading it a second time, however, it became obvious this is the perspective from beginning-to-end.

In 1964, we live in New Orleans, La. There is a reference to cock roaches. If one does not live in, or visit New Orleans, it is impossible to know the cock roaches in New Orleans seem as common as birds in plain sight -- even in the cleanest of homes. In fact, the cock roaches because of their immense size, might view themselves as birds. The word, *"Varicella"* is used casually, and for non-medically inclined persons. This simply means, *"Chickenpox."*

My mother gave me the original letter on Saturday late afternoon, April 11th, 2009 during a visit to Salisbury, N.C. It is, to date, being preserved in one of our family scrapbooks with acid-free materials.

The original cursive scripted letter is written in blue ink on ringed notebook paper. There are two places in this letter where the script is not legible. These are noted within inserted brackets with *"sic"* and the words: *"not discernible."*

The paper is only slightly faded on its edges. It is in good condition. My father is 35 years old in June 1964 having had a recent birthday the preceding January 12th.

After I was born, my father wrote a series of letters to his mother from my perspective -- as if I am speaking to her. This letter, however, is from the perspective of baby Hans speaking. It is quite good -- the style and tone; highly creative.

> June 7, 1964
> Dear Grandma,
>   Since Hélène has been so busy
> scratching her varicella that she has had
> little time left except to eat and sleep.
> I am going to write you a letter
> all by myself. Of course, most of this will
> be about her since
> she is attracting a lot of attention
> with all her sore spots and new bangs.

In fact, her first bangs. [Sometimes she
gets all excited and will say, *"See! See! See!*
See! See?," or *"Butchie, go Bye Bye."*
At first, I was told she said, "Butchie
Butchie Bee --" and this is what I think she
calls herself. Sometimes, I wonder if
she knows what she is saying; for she will point
at a picture and say, *"Ba-by! Ba-by!*
Ba-by!" and again she will just point at
anything and say, *"Ba-by."* Maybe that's pretty good
after all for 16 months old. [But, Grandma
what is confusing is that she will give
all her toys away including the donkey, the monkey
and the kitty, the baby doll, and play with mush melon rind,
water melon rind, peach seeds, corn cobs and cock-
roaches when she can find one. And just
to tell you something else, she is afraid of
an electric fan and refuses to get within
6 feet of one. I guess it must be the noise it makes.

Since she can make so much noise on her own
this does not sound right; but, on my
honor that is the way she is, Grandma.
[Well, before I sound gobby like
Hélène, or some other rattle trap
female, I had better tell you
these are things I heard and observed
before I got stuck in this dad-blasted
Hospital on Napoleon Avenue. Well,
Grandma, this all took place
in the middle of the night, to be exact -
5:05 a.m., June 2nd. I got tired of
staying in the same place all the time,
or just tagging around everywhere with
a bunch of girls -- I felt so out of place!
After all, I weighed 5 whole pounds and
another half-pound. [Well, all the
people made a big fuss
over my [sic: ----- word not discernible here] and put me in
a little old box with glass sides
to it - well, at least I could see out
without too much difficulty, and it
was nice to breathe good fresh air
right through my Royal nose.

This sure beats that long line of communication
with free air that I have been putting up
with for the past 8 1/2 months. Well, anyways, I had
[sic: words not discernible here ----] to beg to wonder if it
was really free.
[I think my Mama was a little sore with
me for being what she calls, *"small."* Well, you know how people are, just because
I am *"small,"* whatever that means. Yesterday, she put on her high heel shoes and
Sunday dress and went walking off [sic: to] home without me.

Here I am, Grandma, all alone in the world, weighing in at 5 lbs. today with some fuzzy-faced, big, fat man telling me I can't get out of this damn little old box except to eat until I weigh 5 lbs. 8 oz. again. By that time, maybe Mama will be tired of being angry with me and will come and take me home. When that day comes Hélène had better not point her index finger at me and say, *"Ba-by."* For anybody without taking a second look can tell I am *"boy"* -- Häns Leighton Hinson.

♀ | | ♂

PART 6. JOURNAL ENTRY 2007
Childhood Recollections from late 1970s:

...I wake one morning to find a mouse pinched -- caught, but unharmed. I wake my father ....

He walks to the kitchen.

He says:

"I will let it go .... but it had better not come back."

.... I walk through the woods and notice two black birds. One is dead, and the other is alive. The bird that is alive is missing a leg and has one leg dangling by a thread of skin ... my brother has been setting old metal traps .... The traps belonged to the former owner of our house – Dr. Robert Lowery [died 1972].

In the kitchen I request my father doctor the bird. He splints its good leg and tapes the other one on. Afterwards, we place the bird into a box on top of an upright freezer in the garage. Every time, I open the box, the bird pecks -- outraged and angry.

♀ | | ♂

The cat is eyeing the bird as an owl might a rabbit. The cat is ultimately obedient. The bird later passes away.

Through prior years, we held funerals for dead birds [and pieces of birds] .... Daddy makes crosses .... cuts roses for bird graves. He conducts bird funerals -- encouraging us to say: *"The Lord's Prayer."* This time my father is not at home. I hold the funeral for the bird ....

♀ | | ♂

In case you missed the purpose of this entry, the emphasis is that love is the foundation of everything that really matters in this world. The Wyatts are not mice or birds – but are like those creatures in my child's mind that required love and respect even in death.

The concept carries into my adult years. Not only do I frequently visit cemeteries as part of genealogical research on humans, I keep in my backyard two animal cemeteries. They include remains from former pets and forest animals.

♀ | | ♂

PART 7. CLIPPINGS

On Sunday, August 19th, 2007, my parents present two notebooks of articles. Amongst them is the following with a photo of my father appearing right of the article just under the headline.

The article ran in January 1967 in *The Salisbury Post.*

Dr. J.N. Hinson announces
Opening Of Office Here
Dr. James N. Hinson, an-
nounces the opening of an office
at 102 Mocksville Avenue Tuesday for the practice of internal
medicine.

Dr. Hinson did his undergraduate studies at Mars Hill College, Mars Hill, and Catawba
College. He received his M.D.
degree from the Bowman Gray
School of Medicine, Wake Forest College.

For the past three years he
has been an instructor in medicine in the Department of Medicine of the Tulane University
School of Medicine.

Prior to that, Dr. Hinson had
served his internship at Baptist
Hospital in Winston-Salem. The
following year, he spent a year
of residency training in internal
medicine at Memorial Hospital,
Charleston, West Virginia.

Dr. Hinson did four years of
additional residency training in
internal medicine in New Orleans, La. in association with
the Tulane University School of
Medicine in Charity Hospital of
New Orleans and the Veterans

Administration of New Orleans.

Dr. Hinson's final two years of residency were primarily devoted to the study of disorders of the heart and lungs.

During the Korean Conflict, Dr. Hinson served two years with the U.S. Army. He is a native of Rowan County, son of William C. Hinson Sr. and Virgie Eagle Hinson of Morgan Township. He is married to the former Patricia Ann Leighton. They are parents to two children.

Dr. Hinson is a member of the staff of Rowan Memorial Hospital. He will hold regular office hours and prefers to see patients by appointment, but will see them on a drop-in basis as time permits.

Announcement cards:

JAMES N. HINSON, M.D.

ANNOUNCES THE OPENING OF HIS OFFICE
FOR THE PRACTICE OF
INTERNAL MEDICINE
AT
SUITE 204
102 MOCKSVILLE AVENUE
SALISBURY, NORTH CAROLINA

OFFICE HOURS:
MON., TUES., WED., THURS. AND FRI.
9:00 UNTIL 5:00
TELEPHONE: 633-3136
SAT. 9:00 UNTIL 1:00

♀ | | ♂

The following articles and other documents pertain to both my father and mother.

It is assumed both of the following clippings ran in *The Republican*, Oakland, Md. and in *The Salisbury Post*, Salisbury, N.C. in 1962. The engagement ran with a photograph of the bride.

Announce Engagement

Mr. and Mrs. Clarence H. Leighton, 7th and Alder streets, Oakland, announce the engagement of
their daughter, Patricia Ann, to
Dr. James Noah Hinson, son of Mr. and
Mrs. William C. Hinson of Fair-
field, [sic: Richfield], North Carolina.

The wedding will be an event of
early spring.

Miss Leighton is a student at
Alderson-Broaddus college at Philippi, W. Va., where she is studying
for a B.S. degree in nursing. She
attended Southern High school
and was graduated from St. Mary's
Seminary in 1959. At present she
is taking courses at Memorial hospital in Charleston and Morris
Harvey college.

Dr. Hinson is taking special work
at Memorial hospital in Charleston.

The following news clipping was published on March 15, 1962 and ran with a photo of the bride and groom in front of their wedding cake.

Hinson-Leighton Nuptials Held

Miss Patricia Ann Leighton,
daughter of Mr. and Mrs. Clarence
H. Leighton, Oakland, became the
bride of Dr. James Noah Hinson,
son of Mr. and Mrs. William C. Hinson, Richfield, N.C., March 3, in
Oakland.

The double-ring ceremony was performed in St. Mark's Lutheran church with the Rev. Wm. Ernest Fox officating. Mrs. Donald Sincell was organist, accompanying Mrs. Jay Bell, vocalist, who sang "O Lord Most Holy," "Wedding Prayer," "The Lord's Prayer," "O Perfect Love."

The altar was decorated with palms and lilies.

The bride, given in marriage by her father, was attired in a pure silk Peau-De-Sole sheath grown with a sweep traciss. She wore an all-jewel Queen's Crown of crystals and pearls. She carried a crescent bouquet of lilies and white roses.

Miss Becky Michael, the flower girl, scattered rose petals, while Bill Leighton, brother of the bride, was the ring bearer.

Miss Carol Browning was maid of honor. Miss Nancy Plusquellie and Miss Carolyn Leighton were bridesmaids. The three attendants wore white silk-organza sheath dresses with matching peplums fastened with bouffant bows. The head-dresses were of matching bouffant bows.

Dr. Raphael Gomez served as best man. Thomas Nally and Jack Gnegy were ushers. Acolyte was Robert Leighton, brother of the bride.

A reception was held at Cornish Manor. The table was centered with a four-tiered cake topped with a miniature bride and groom. Mrs. John Swain, aunt of the bride, served the cake. Mrs. Eugene Helbig and Mr. and Mrs. Floyd Leigh-

ton, uncle and aunt of the bride,
served at the punch bowls.

The couple left for a trip to
Bradenton, Florida.

Dr. Hinson was graduated from
Catawba College in Salisbury, Bowman Gray School of Medicine and
Wake Forest College at Winston-
Salem. He interned at North Carolina Baptist hospital. At present he
is a resident of internal medicine
at Memorial hospital in Charleston,
W.Va.

Mrs. Hinson attended Southern
High School and was graduated
from St. Mary's Seminary in 1959.
At the time of her marriage she
was a student at Alderson-Broaddus
college at Philippi, W.Va. and taking courses at Memorial hospital
and Morris Harvey college in
Charleston, W.Va. She will resume
her studies in the summer.

In the year 2013, Herbert Vernon Leighton, a son of Dr. Herbert Houck Leighton
of Oakland, Md., sent via surface mail the following note attached to a wedding
invitation.

He wrote:

"I found this in some memorabilia at my father's house. Thought you would enjoy it."

The envelop is addressed to Mr. and Mrs. H.C. Leighton, Oakland, Maryland and post-
marked: OAKLAND, MD. FEB. 2, 1962. It contains in the upper right hand corner a
Lincoln 4 cent stamp in purple.

The invitation:

Mr. and Mrs. Clarence H. Leighton
request the honour of your presence
at the marriage of their daughter
Patricia Ann
to

> Doctor James Noah Hinson
> on Saturday, the third of March
> Nineteen hundred and sixty-two
> at three o'clock
> St. Marks's Lutheran Church
> Oakland, Maryland

On September 15th, 1958, my mother was 17 years old. For an English III paper, she wrote by hand the following essay. It was found among the paper properties of her mother Ruth. It reflects the time period in which both of my parents lived as children.

"My Autobiography"

> In 1941 Adolf Hitler, believing to give
> Germany world domination, invaded Russia.
> On December 7 of the same year, Japan
> made an unexpected attack upon
> Pearl Harbor, Hawaii. The year 1941
> was a year of memorable happenings.
> In July of the same year another
> event commenced. This occurrence
> did not make the headlines, but
> it will be remembered by the
> persons involved. Mr. and Mrs. Clarence
> Leighton became the proud parents of
> a baby girl. Many things happen in
> a year; Many people are born while
> others begin their life after death.
> Death remains miraculous mystery
> even to the very wise. Death comes
> as a surprise even to those who
> are expecting to die. It comes
> quickly and quietly as a thief
> in the night.
> At the moment I am concerned
> with the living or this wouldn't be
> an autobiography. [underlines "auto."]
> I reside in a small town called
> Oakland in the state of Maryland.
> I have attended Oakland Elementary
> School, Oakland Annex; and Southern
> Garrett County Junior Senior High School.
> I am beginning my second year at

St. Mary's Seminary Junior College.

My interests are many and varied.
As a child of seven I began my
study of the piano. At the age of
thirteen I served as organist at
St. Mark's Lutheran Church. I also have
a great appreciation for voice. Since
grade school I've sung in choruses,
girl's sextets, church choirs, and other
organizations. Last year at St. Mary's
I got the leading role in the
operetta *"Girls Will Be Girls."*

I am a devout Christian, and a
member of St. Mark's Lutheran in Oakland.
In St. Mark's I've served as organist,
assistant pianist, sang in the
choir, member and served as
treasurer of the Luther League. For
six years I've attended Camp Luther
in Cowen, West Virginia. In my
last year I received an award
for the most outstanding senior
girl camper.

In the time I have spent at
St. Mary's, I have strengthened my
intellectual faculties. Not only in the
sense of scholastic ability and mental
cultivation, but in widening my
reasoning powers, judgment, and understanding of people.

One of the greatest values that
man can ascertain is that of
understanding his fellowman. When
he attains this ability many problems of our society will be solved.

Practically all of my life I have
longed for an older sister. At St.
Mary's I found her. She is Spanish
and I American, but because of
God's kindness I have finally found
her. Though she is married now and
I may never see her again I shall
always remember and be thankful.

My aim in life is to become

a medical doctor. I believe that
it is the will of God that I
should do so. Sometimes I find
it hard to distinguish between
my own selfish desires and the
will of my Father. He suffered
and died for me so that I
might live. I can never repay that
debt, but in thankfulness I can
serve him the best I know how.
If I am destined to become a
doctor or to become a washwoman,
I must give my life of service,
whatever it may be, because without
Him I am nothing.

*"For I am not ashamed of
the gospel: it is the power of God
for salvation to everyone who has
faith."* Romans 1:16.

On Sunday, August 19th, 2007, my parents presented me with a collection of newspaper articles during a visit to Moncure, N.C. Within the collection is the following news article that ran in *The Salisbury Post*, March 4th, 1968. The article ran and was published left of a photograph of my mother.

Mrs. Hinson
Is Named
To RMH Staff

Mrs. Patricia Leighton Hinson, wife of Dr. James Noah Hinson, has recently accepted a position as clinical instructor in medical and surgical nursing on the staff of the Rowan Memorial Hospital School of Nursing.

Mrs. Hinson attended Alderson-Broaddus College School of Nursing in Philippi, West Virginia and completed her course of study at Louisiana State University Department of Nursing in New Orleans, receiving a bachelor of science degree in

nursing education. She is a
member of the America
Nurses' Association and the National League for Nursing.

Under the auspices of Louisiana State University, Department of Nursing, Mrs. Hinson
had experience in psychiatric
nursing at Charity Hospital, Administration of the Nursing
Team at Oschner Foundation
Hospital in New Orleans and
Public Health Nursing in Jefferson Parish.

For two years following graduation in 1965, Mrs. Hinson
functioned as charge nurse on a
medical-surgical unit at Southern Hospital in New Orleans.

Mrs. Hinson is the former
Patricia Ann Leighton, daughter of Mr. and Mrs. Clarence H.
Leighton Oakland, Md. Dr. and
Mrs. Hinson are the parents of
three children, Helene, Hans
and Nicole.

My mother met my father during the early 1960s when my father was a resident at Charleston Memorial Hospital in West Virginia [1961-1962] and my mother was a student nurse doing OB-pediatric rotations.

* Casted in Piedmont Players Theatre On Stage: *"Lil' Abner,"* a musical comedy, March 5-7, 10-14, 1987, Hedrick Little Theatre, celebrating Piedmont Players 26th year. Patricia Ann Leighton Hinson played 'Stupefyin' Jones.'

*Note: Patricia was born on a Friday, July 11, 1941.

The following article ran in *The Salisbury Post* with a photograph around 1972.

Mrs. Hinson To Be
Instructor Of
Nursing At DCCC

Mrs. Patricia Leighton Hinson, wife of Dr. James Noah

Hinson, has recently been appointed to the position of instructor of medical-surgical nursing at Davidson County Community College.

Mrs. Hinson attended Alderson-Broaddus College, School of Nursing, Philippi, W.V. and completed her course of study at Louisiana State University, Department of Nursing, in New Orleans, La., graduating with a bachelor of science in nursing degree.

Under the auspices of Lousiana State University, Department of Nursing, Mrs. Hinson studied psychiatric nursing at Charity Hospital administration of the nursing team at Osscner Foundation Hospital in New Orleans, and public health nursing in Jefferson Parish.

Following graduation in 1965, Mrs. Hinson functioned as charge nurse on a medical-surgical unit at Southern Baptist Hospital in New Orleans for two years. In 1968, Mrs. Hinson joined the teaching staff at Rowan Memorial Hospital School of Nursing and was responsible for instruction of students in medical-surgical nursing, including coronary care, intensive care and the administration of the nursing team.

In January of this year, Mrs. Hinson was accepted as a student in the Graduate School of the University of North Carolina in Charlotte, College of Human Development and Learning. She is a member of the American Nurse Association, National

league for Nursing, National
Council on Cardiovascular Nursing and is an officer in the
Rowan-Davie Medical Aux-
illary.

Dr. and Mrs. Hinson are the
parents of three children. Mrs.
Hinson is the former Patricia
Ann Leighton, daughter of Mr.
and Mrs. Clarence H. Leighton,
Oakland, Md.

$$♀ \mid \mid ♂$$

PART 8. MEMORIES

James Noah Hinson, M.D., son of Virgie Irene Eagle Hinson, was born Jan. 12th, 1929 in Mabery Place, Porter Station, Stanly County, N.C.

The following are excerpts from notes.

My father used to sing to us. He sang a German poem he learned in college. My brother and I listened to him … on the way to Jack and Jill Nursery …I suspect he sang the poem to remember it. Nevertheless, he sang the poem titled: *'Heidenroslein.'* When I was in college, he gave me a copy of the poem. The poem is printed below for those who read German. I have included it because it is the only song my father taught me … he concentrated on a few lines:

'Röslein, Röslein, Röslein rot, Röslein auf der heide' and *part of one of the lines from the first stanza: '… lief er schnell, es nah' zu seh'n.'* I note only now he changed these words when he sang it to us to: *'lief er schnell, es nah' morgen schön'* instead of: *' Lief er schnell, es nah zu seh'n….'*

I stood behind the front seat … as we rode to nursery. Occasionally, we got too loud singing any hodgepodge of our kindered repertoire. Sometimes, we fought. Then, he resorted to telling us to be quiet. Our direct response was to listen for about 30 seconds, and then start singing: *'Röslein, Röslein.'*

Heidenröslein
By Johann Wolfgang von Goethe
[1749-1832]

[Pronounced: yo han volfgang fn go t;
also pronounced: yo hän vôlf gang fen gö te]

Sah ein Knab' ein Röslein steh'n,
Röslein auf der Heide,
War so jung und morgen schön,
lief er schnell, es nah' zu seh'n,
Sah's mit vielen Freuden,
Röslein, Röslein, Röslein rot,
Röslein auf der heide.
Knabe sprach: Ich breche dich
Röslein auf der Heide,
Röslein sprach: Ich steche dich,
daß du ewig denkst an mich,

und ich will's nicht leiden
Röslein, Röslein, Röslein rot,
Röslein auf der heide.
Und der wilde Knabe brach 's
Röslein auf der Heide,
Röslein wehrte sich und stach,
half ihm doch kein Weh und Ach,
mußt es eben leiden.
Röslein, Röslein, Röslein rot,
Röslein auf der heide.

[Note: Goethe, who was born in Frankfurt, Germany, was a German poet, dramatist, novelist, scientist and master of world literature. He was also a researcher in biological morphology.]

A translation of the poem in German into English by Walter Meyer appears below:

Passing lad a rose blossom spied,
Blossom on the earth growing,
'Twas so fair and of youthful pride,
Raced he fast to be near its side,
Saw it with joy o'erflowing.
Blossom, blossom, blossom red,
Blossom on the heath growing.

Said the lad: I shall pick thee,
Blossom on the heath growing,
Blossom spoke: Then I'll prick thee,
That thou shalt ever think of me,
And I'll not be allowing
Blossom, blossom, blossom red,
Blossom on the heath growing.

And the lusty lad did pick
The blossom, in defense, did prick,
'Twas, alas, but a harmless nick,
Had to be allowing.
Blossom, blossom, blossom red,
Blossom on the heath growing.

[Translation of the poem *"Heidenröslein"* from German into English is by Walter Meyer. This translation is quoted with written permission from Walter Meyer, © Copyright 1996, All Rights Reserved.]

Some of my father's favorite sayings or quotes include:

* *"Fool me once, shame on you; fool me twice, shame on me."*
* *"If a man feels the need to drink -- even once a month, he is an alcoholic."*
* *"Just because everyone is doing something, does not mean you should be doing it."*
* *"No one makes or gets you angry or upset, but yourself. You get yourself upset."'*
* *"If you can't respect a person for anything other than his age, respect him for that."*
* *"Life is full of coincidences."*
* *"If one does not have any brain himself, he should keep company with those who do. He will get more out of life."*

A quote he said later is one doctors of his time memorized: *"Ontogeny recapitulates phylogeny,"* a biogenic law [theory] developed in 1866 by Ernst Haeckel (1834-1919).

Ontogeny is the development of an individual beginning with a fertilized ovum to maturity and in this theory it is, contrasted with the development of a group or species (phylogeny).

In this theory, disproven many years ago and is nevertheless still taught as fact -- uses the word *"recapitulates"* to explain the repeating of stages from the evolution of a species during the embryonic period of an animal's life.

Phylogeny is a noun that refers to the development of a species over a period of time as contrasted with the development of an individual.

Here's a better way to explain it:

It means that as an embryo of an advanced organism grows or advances, it will travel or pass through stages that look much like the adult phase of less-advanced organisms...at one point each human embryo has gills, resembles a tadpole.

Although further research demonstrated that early stage embryos are not representative of mankind's evolutionary ancestors, Haeckel's general concept that the developmental process reveals clues about evolutionary history is correct.

Animals with recent common ancestors tend to share more similarity during development than those that do not. A dog embryo and a pig embryo resemble the other through most stages of development than a dog embryo and a salamander embryo, for instance.

When he was an undergraduate at Catawba College, two of his teachers impressed upon him during their class talks two bits of advice that influenced him to the point he made a point to quote them.

"You are here to learn how to think," he says in reference to students attending college.

"Entertain yourself with your own thoughts," in regard to a teacher advising students after chapel on how to behave when they are not interested in listening to the morning service.

Two of his favorite quotations from English literature are from William Shakespeare. He read the play *"Macbeth"* when he was in high school. He felt moved by the cadence, the flow of its words.

During dinner July 4th, 2007, my father asks my eldest if he has read this play from Shakespeare's *MacBeth*. Then, he proceeds to quote this passage:

"To-morrow, and to-morrow, and to-morrow,
Creeps in this petty pace from day to day,
To the last syllable of recorded time;
And all our yesterdays have lighted fools
The way to dusty death. Out, out brief candle!
Life's but a walking shadow, a poor player,
That struts and frets his hour upon the stage,
And then is heard no more; it is a tale
Told by an idiot, full of sound and fury,
Signifying nothing."

In years prior he often would ask,

"Do you know what 'to thine own self be true' means."

This quote comes from Shakespeare's play called *"Hamlet."* In Act I, scene III, the character Polonius prepares his son Laertes for traveling abroad with advice. In this advice, he directs Laertes to memorize that *"neither a borrower not a lender be."*

"This above all: to thine own self be true, and it must follow, as the night the day, thou cans't not be false to any man."

My father's childhood memories:

It is 2002.

My father says his mother used to have a bantam (banty) hen sit on fertile guinea eggs to hatch and raise the guineas. He explains her reasoning was because guinea mothers often lead their offspring into wet grass after a rain; whereas hens prefer not getting their feet and legs wet and were more likely to stay on their nests after a rain.

Young guineas, like chickens, follow the mother bird that hatches them. They go wherever the mother bird takes them. Placing the fertile guinea eggs under the hen offers some assurance young birds will not get sick or die.

"One day I notice a black snake coiled up in a bantam hen's nest," he says.

'The snake moved to a lumber pile. I got the snake out. It had lumps in its body, so I took an axe and chopped it in two. I squeezed the eggs out. All, but two were crushed. I put the un-damaged eggs back in the nest. They hatched into feathered-legged bantams like their mother. A rooster hatched from one of the eggs; it was named Thomas. A hen hatched from the other egg; it was named Jefferson. Later Jefferson sat on guinea eggs. When they hatched, she raised and loved them like her own.'

Guineas are not loner birds, he explains. They like to stick together in a group of guineas and usually have little-to-nothing to do with chickens. They fly in groups out into fields and back to their houses before nightfall. Virgie liked to keep guineas around because guinea birds as a group kill snakes without fear.

The guineas hatched by Jefferson loved her so much, one could tell it worried her.

He said:

"They recognized her more than the hen recognized them. This was unusual. They loved her so much they nearly loved her to death. They were always so happy to see her."

When they would fly back from a field, they ran up to that hen loving on her like they had just found their long lost mother. The hen put up with them for a long time. All of their attentions just about wore her out. The hen would have to find solace up under the roof of the hen house to get away from them for a while.

It is Thanksgiving Day, 2001. My father speaks about swimming in the Yadkin River with his brothers when he was growing up. He says he was out on the bank of the Yadkin.

He says:

"We [Chub, June and I] were running up the river bank. We had been running up the bank, jumping into the river, floating down, climbing out and doing this over and over again ...I pulled some branches back that were dangling over the water. Just as I was about to jump into the water, a cottonmouth reared its head from the water, opened its mouth and hissed ...'Had I jumped in just a second earlier, I would have jumped in with that snake," he explained.

On March 4th, 2001, I videotaped him telling his grandson Nicholas Staley the following account of his childhood years growing up with two older brothers June and Chub as his primary playmates.

1939

"In the winter of nineteen thirty-nine or forty or it could have been the next year ... Anyway, it had been the coldest year in many moons ...it just stayed that way. It was maybe four degrees below zero ... The creek was frozen over.

"Grandpa," he said referring to his father William Crowell Hinson, *"on a Saturday had gone to market."*

"Grandma," [he said referring to his mother Virgie Eagle Hinson,] *"gave us specific instructions. She said we were not to go to the creek ... and we were not to get wet ...we wondered how we would get out of this.*

"We made our way to the barn ... June was the scout leader. So we got to the barn with our little wagon ...We went down the cow trail or the lane, came to a right angle, turned and went through what was really a mud hole with rock in it ... it was frozen over. We went right across it and went down to the creek. The creek was all frozen over, which we knew from our previous observations. We wanted to be careful that we did not get wet to get away with this thing ... we went down to the creek.

"The creek was running where we used to cross it, but it was frozen every place else in between. We went down to the place where Grandpa Hinson's frog pond ran into the creek ...The water was unusually deep there ...We dug a hole in the ice. It was very deep, and as I remember, we dug down a foot ...We never got through the ice, so we figured the ice was safe to be on not realizing that the ice was deeper in this hole in the shade than in other places...We ventured out on down the creek and passed by the catfish hole, which was frozen over

"...Finally we got down to the fishing hole ...It was the largest hole of all, but the water was not so deep. We played with a little wagon. A lot of the times June was pulling, and Chub was pushing .... We went down to the lower end of this hole. We looked, and there was a stump under the ground ...The ice was thin. We realized that the stump was decaying and putting off heat ...it made the ice thin, so we pointed out,

'We want to stay off of that part. It's okay to play on the rest.'

"Well, actually, the weather had warmed up [by then] ... It wasn't a terribly cold day because the sun came out. The ice had melted up top and gave us better traction. It wasn't so slick. Chub was pushing me, and June was pulling. We took a little curve, and as Chub liked to do was ...he swung the tail end of the wagon around. He was scooting on the ice. He landed up

258

over the stump, and within seconds he was up to his waist in ice; cold ice water … The ice was breaking, but he finally got some solid ice and got [himself] up …

"We said,

'What do we do? If we went home, we had been promised a whipping if we got wet.' … So June was the engineer and decided,

'Let's go up to Grandma Eagle's. Grandma Eagle…maybe she would help us get through this thing because we knew Chub would get sick…This was the main reason we were not supposed to get wet.'

" So, we hurried across the pasture and left the wagon at the creek…We got up behind the barn… June stationed Chub behind the barn … for him to wait there until the signal was right for him to come to the house…So, he proceeds to go up to see Grandma, and I tagged along with him to hear all of these negotiations. He got Grandma [Laura] Eagle to promise she would not tell Grandma [Virgie] Hinson we had been wet in the creek …if she would let us come in the house to dry off. Our idea of drying off was standing before the fireplace. Grandma [Laura] promised at least three or four times to never tell Grandma Hinson that we fell into the creek, and Chub got wet …Grandma got us before the fireplace and took off all of Chub's clothes … and hung them up to dry. She gave him some dry clothes to put on. After she got Chub's clothes dry, she gave them back to him to put on.

"After he got his clothes on, we went home. Grandma Hinson never said a word then except [to ask] where we had been. We told her over at Grandma's … June was holding a straight face all the time this talking was going on …Grandma [Virgie] never suspected Chub had gotten wet …June may remember this differently than I do …Our choices that day were to have a pity party. We did not want to stay home and pity ourselves. So, we listened to June …He was the good scout master who carried us on our excursion for that day, and it was so exciting that I have not forgotten it to this day…"

♀ | | ♂

PART 9. 2015

To gaze across a field or pasture at one of his farms in Rowan County today, I am reminded of a quote. I never starved growing up, and neither do many who understand the Earth's purpose is to serve the physical bodies while our souls venture to the earth – even if not more than 120 years or less than an hour. The earthly realm is the place that allows a soul to love his neighbor and therefore shape his soul.

My mother's mother Mary Ruth McTall [Metallo] Leighton [1920-2003] said in mid-October 1999:

"Your father said…

"'As long as you own a piece of land, you will never starve.'"

On Sunday, October 4th, 2015, I drove to Richfield, N.C. and attended a service at Luther's Lutheran Church. It was a sunny day with a cool breeze. I sat in the same general area I had the Sunday following his funeral.

Rev. Beaver was making a point about souls not being able to take any of the physical possessions of the earth into Heaven. I was listening and feeling my father's spirit within.

After the service – I was greeted by Lee Roy Kirk [son of Lee Roy Kirk, Sr., 1914-1994 and Stella Basinger 1917-2007, buried: Luther's Lutheran Church]. He said my father walked one day around the Hill-Arey Place in the rain examining the property.

"Hans was just a little boy then. Jim kept walking around, but when it began to rain, Hans and I found a hollowed tree and stood inside of it to keep dry. Jim was the only of the three of us who got a cold later."

Others approached with the warmest smiles a human might ever make. He left them with wonderful memories.

Albert and Shirley *"Sherley"* Arey Shepherd expressed they had known him – my heart swelled in smiles. Shirley is a third cousin to my father via the Eagles and additionally related to us via the Wyatt, Hodge and Morgan lineages.

Shirley Arey → daughter of: Anna *"Anner"* Lillian Pauline Eagle Arey → daughter of William Lawson Eagle → son of Daniel Calvin Eagle → son of Solomon Eagle, Sr.

Shirley Arey → daughter of: Anna *"Anner"* Lillian Pauline Eagle → daughter of: William Lawson Eagle → son of: Amanda Jane Wyatt Eagle [wife of Daniel Calvin Eagle] Amanda Wyatt is the daughter of Noah Calvin Wyatt → son of Rachel Park and Thomas Wyatt – this Thomas being the son of John Wiatt, [1743-1815].

Shirley Arey is the daughter of James Ross Arey → son of James G. Arey → son of Eliza Hodge → daughter of Jesse Hodge → son of Joseph Hodge.

Sylvia Morgan Casper – a fourth cousin twice removed to me and her husband Irving approached and pointed out the stones in the cemetery that flanks the church. [Sylvia is a third cousin once removed to Shirley Arey Shepherd.]

Sylvia is the → daughter of: Gilmer Austin Morgan → son of Charlie Calvin Morgan → son of Noah Wesley Morgan → son of Charlie Morgan → son of Nathan Morgan, Jr. → son of Nathan Morgan, Sr. and so forth.

*Noah Wesley Morgan was married to Polly Belinda Hodge → daughter of Nancy Morgan and Abram A. Hodge → son of Jesse Hodge → son of Joseph Hodge – the immigrant from England.

Before leaving Luther's Lutheran Church to head towards Salisbury to have lunch with my mother, I ran up the hill of the cemetery. I stood in front of the marker of my father's remains. The silk flowers were still on the grave from a previous visit.

Every time before his passing I told him good-bye with hugs and kisses. This time I could not say good-bye – I could not kiss his cheek or hug him. I can no longer tell him good-bye when a part of him lives in the hearts of every person he ever loved and who ever loved him. There are no good-byes – those are simply an illusion. It is now just *"Hello, I am thinking of you."*

What a nice view it is to stand there at Luther's Lutheran. To look north, south, east or west – all views are pleasant. Daddy wanted his remains be placed in the land, where people he knew have left echoes – their memories that will for eternity be cherished.

His spirit and soul – the essence of who he was and who he became, never died. It transformed and was reborn into God's Kingdom. Whatever love we feel for another and whatever good deed we do in life has its origins with God – as it is first created in Heaven. It flows through the human channels that choose to keep those doors opened like a tree's branches reaching into the sky.

With these words, I say from this earthly realm into the spiritual – *"I love you Daddy. I always love you."*

Post Scripts

♀ | | ♂

"Life is full of coincidences,"

JAMES NOAH HINSON, M.D.

Some interesting tidbits ...

*I*N 2007, WHILE READING HISTORICAL articles online, I ventured to the genforum. A post included descendants of John Wyatt [1743-1815] and his wife Rachel Hannah Wyatt -- specifically pointing out Thomas Wyatt and his wife Rachel Park and the Park-Wyatt-Bean Graveyard -- two things already familiar.

At the same forum, are the names Henry Wyatt and Elizabeth Dandridge. They are indicated as being the parents of John Wyatt -- Thomas' father. From here, another site at rootsweb.com includes Elizabeth Dandridge and Henry Wyatt and claims a link to Adam Wyatt, in the 1300s.

Certainly, one's research must question fully those making claims -- and include looking at the paper and stone trails they follow.

Also, I find in this research many who are claimed to descend from one of Adam's historically known descendants Rev. Haute Wyatt's and his children.

Based on these assertions, I deduce my supposed or speculative 10th great grandfather via Wyatt lineage accompanied Anne Constable Lee prior to her meeting and marrying Colonel Richard Lee [1618-1664] in America, according to historical articles. This Ann or Anne Constable Lee [born 1622] is the 7th great grandmother of Hélène Claire Hero Rufty. Hélène is a family friend I am named for.

Hélène Claire Hero Rufty → daughter of: & Alvin Anthony Hero [1908-1977] & Marie Hélène Alice Stauffer Hero [1913-1965] → daughter of Hélène Maury [1887-1957] & Isaac

Hull Stauffer III [1885-1967] → son of Isaac Hull Stauffer, Jr. & Myrthé Bianca Taylor Stauffer [1864-1897] → daughter of Louise Marie Myrthé Bringier & Lieutenant General Richard *"Dick"* Taylor [1826-1879] → son of Margaret *"Peggy"* Mackall Smith [1788-1852] & U.S. President Zachary Taylor [1784-1850] → son of Sarah Dabney *"Sally"* Strother [b. Abt. 1760] & Richard Taylor [1744-1826] → son of Zachary Taylor [1707-Abt. 1768] & Elizabeth Lee [1703-1750] daughter of → Sarah Elizabeth Allerton [1671-1731] & Captain Hancock Lee I, Hon.[1653-1709] → son of Colonel Richard Henry Lee I, *"The Immigrant"* [1618-1664] & Ann Constable Lee [Abt. 1620-1666].

Col. Richard Lee's Lee lineage is actually traced 14 generations from him to Hugo *"Hugh"* de Lega who traveled with William the Conqueror from Normandy [France] to England in 1066. Hugh de Lega's son Reginald de la Lega was high Sheriff of Shropshire, England and known as *"Reinder de Lega."*

It was upon reading Robert E. Lee [1807-1870] was a fourth cousin once removed to 12th U.S. President Zachary Taylor [1784-1850], a third great grandfather to Hélène Rufty, I searched for confirmation and checking collections to see if I had put this in and forgotten about it. I did not find Robert E. Lee in my notes or trees at the time, but I thought I should check historical articles for information on Col. Richard Lee.

When I did, I found initially, the name Sir Francis Wyatt, Royal Colonial Governor of Virginia. One historical source article states Anne Constable lived in the household of Gov. Francis Wyatt of Jamestown, Va. and while still living in the Wyatt household, Anne met Col. Richard Lee [1617 or 1618-1664] and later married him.

Anne Constable [Abt. 1620-1666] was the ward of: Sir John Thoroughgood, a personal attendant of Charles I, King of England. King Charles I then served as king from 1600 to 1649.

Col. Richard Lee I is often referred to as *"the immigrant"* Lee to the first British Virginia colony, having arrived in the year 1639 at the age of 22, according to some accounts. He arrived with little in his pockets and was given a step in the right direction from the first governor of the Virginia colony -- Sir Francis Wyatt.

Col. Lee worked in the fur trading industry with Native Americans. He has been called the first white man to settle the northern neck of Virginia.

Col. Lee became Attorney General of the Colony of Virginia, Colonial Secretary of State and member of the King's Council. He became known as the Clerk of the Quarter Court at Jamestown. He served as High Sheriff and was Colonel of the Militia. Lee traded slaves and fur, planted tobacco.

He employed and imported indentured British servants. Those servants paid for their passage with seven years of labor. When he passed away, he owned 13,000 acres of land and was the largest landowner in Virginia. He was a second great grandfather to U.S. President Zachary Taylor and a 3rd great grandfather of ACW CSA Gen. Robert E. Lee.

General Robert Edward Lee [1807-1870] → son of Anne Hill Carter [1773-1829] & Major Henry *"Light-Horse"* Harry Lee [1756-1818] son of → Lucy Grymes [1734-1792] & Henry Lee [1729-1787] → son of Mary Bland [1704-1764] & Captain Henry Lee I [1691-1747] → son of Laetitia Corbin [1657-1706] & Colonel Richard Lee II, Esq. [1647-1715] → son of Anne Constable [Abt. 1620-1666] & Colonel Richard Henry Lee I, *"The Immigrant"* [1618-1664] and so forth.

Jamestown [Jamestowne & James Towne], founded by the Virginia Company of London, England and named for James I of England, was a settlement in the Colony of Virginia. On May 24, 1607, it was established as James Fort by the Virginia Company of London. By 1619, it was regarded as Jamestown. It was considered permanent after it was briefly abandoned in 1610. It served as the capital of the Virginia colony from 1616 until 1699.

The Jamestown settlement was located within territory known as: Tsenacommacah -- pronounced *"Sen-ah-com-ma-cah,"* known as:

- Attanoughkomouck
- Attanakamik
- Tenakomakah
- Tscenocomoco
- Tsenacomoco.

This territory was named by the Powhatan also known as Powatan and Powhaten native Americans, claiming this area as their native homeland. The area encompassed Tidewater Virginia and the Eastern shore.

The boundaries reached 100 miles or 160 kilometers by 100 miles or 160 kilometers from close to the south end of the mouth of the James River all the way north to the south end of the Potomac River. It spanned from the Eastern Shore west to about the fall zone or line of the two rivers. The Powhatan Native Americans were part of a Chiefdom of Virginia Native American tribes. They were regarded as the Powhatan Confederacy. They spoke Algonquian.

While researching Wyatts, I was additionally writing a short rather avant-guard novella titled: *Dishonest Housekeepers*. During this time, I had a very curious dream. It is curious because the dream itself seemed to direct me in genealogical pursuits the following morning.

Later, I wrote a screenplay version of it and incorporated the dream as fiction. This was my first attempt at writing a screenplay incorporating the rules and requirements of the *Screenwriter's Bible* by David Trottier.] With the exception of one attempt, I have not tried to sell the screenplay or to publish it.

It sits patiently awaiting I promote it to an interested reader. One cannot gain readers unless one advertises -- but despite a lack of advertisements readers occasionally trickle in for other writings I have published.

Much of the story *Dishonest Housekeepers* is based on dreams. The dreams are woven around a fictional story about a woman named Ella. She is tricked and hurt often by dishonest housekeepers. It is to the point her Soul and Spirit get involved.

You might be wondering why I decided to include this mention in a genealogical history. Well, if this has not been done before – then mark me the first to do it. If you do not care for this section – then concentrate on those sections of the book you do appreciate.

The following is an excerpt from two scenes deep into the screenplay. The excerpt is included because it demonstrates a dream that readers of the screenplay do not know the writer of the screenplay actually had.

In the dream the woman I am named for was serving a platter of prunes and plums to guests, including an American Indian chief. Of course, it is easy now to discern the dream transported me into Jamestown, Va. from Chatham County, N.C. -- but the fictional character Ella from England into Jamestown, Va.

INT. ELLA'S BEDROOM - DAY - (SUMMER)

ELLA (VO)

It is yesterday afternoon.

Ella begins writing in her journal. Ella sits in her bed propped by pillows with a pen in one hand and her journal opened flat against her abdomen. She writes.

INSERT: Journal page.

ELLA (VO)

Writes.

> This is a reflection.
> I nap after a morning swim
> and soaking in a warm tub and
> showering. I nurse my baby.
> I drift into a dream.

BACK TO SCENE

INT. COLONY OF VIRGINIA – JAMESTOWN - NIGHT- DREAM

The dream escorts Ella to a door. Walls are white-cream colored. The rooms are large with white brick-like tile on the floors. The furnishings are white.

Ella finds herself with her parents, children, a few relatives and a friend of her mother. This friend makes haste in a kitchen. This friend prepares platters of fruit. Ella is offered fruit; it includes dried plums or prunes. Ella picks one up. She places it into her mouth.

To her right is a fireplace with a white-cream wall above it and a raised lettering for the word: *"Jamestown."*

Ella has a difficult time discerning the word. She decides it says: *"Jamesplace."* The letters are no more than three-inches high. They are raised and recessed at the same time in a rectangular-shaped indenture of the wall above a fireplace.

The entire time she is here, she is distracted by the urge to go to the restroom. She worries about privacy. She avoids the restroom.

ELLA

She crosses, uncrosses and re-crosses her legs.

ELLA'S FRIEND

You have a one-way ticket. But you
can return home on another
ticket anytime you wish.

Ella chews a bite of fruit as she listens.

Ella's friend places a fruit platter on a coffee table directly front of Ella.

ELLA'S FRIEND (referring to ticket)

It might cost you.

An AMERICAN INDIAN CHIEF sits next to Ella. He is tall and between ages fifty and seventy. He cries quietly. No one speaks. Ella wakes.

BACK TO PRESENT DAY

INT. ELLA'S BEDROOM - DAY - (SUMMER)

Ella finishes her journal entry. She closes the cover. She re-opens the journal and adds two sentences.

ELLA (VO)

This dream is about purification.
The Indian chief is symbolic
of a spiritual protector.

She stands and answers the door. On the front step is another PROSPECT looking for work.

DISSOLVE....

The point is ...

- I had this dream, recorded long before I wanted to analyze Lee ancestry for the sake of understanding if it was a fact Robert E. Lee was blood kinship to Zachary Taylor. Of course, this information was always there -- I just did not know it at that point in time and perhaps some subconscious part of me was attempting to get my attention.
- Searching to understand the South's Gen. Robert E. Lee's connection to 12th U.S. President Zachary Taylor introduced an avenue that led a unique journey to the Wyatt lineage.
- The dream precipitated the search, and the symbols in the dream such as the Indian Chief and the words: *"Jamestown"* and *"Jamesplace"* now in hindsight feel as if some higher good was cutting a path to further inspire interest.
- The genealogical finds in other words leads to Jamestown, Va., where Ann Constable lived with the Wyatt family. Coincidences are one thing -- but to have one like this! Royal Gov. Sir Francis Wyatt, who became Royal Colonial Virginia Governor in 1621, rallied a defense of Jamestown when this town was attacked by Native Americans.

Four hundred settlers died during this attack. In the screenplay I allude to the American Indian as a symbol in another dream the character Ella has. Here is a section of that which is recorded in the screenplay.

INT. WOODS - NIGHT - (SUMMER) DREAM

Ella walks in the woods in a white cotton gown and bared feet.

Birds sleep in treetop nests, deer walk about.

DREAM:

It is gentle peace. This is what she sees: A miasma of mist and vapor. It imbues air like cottony clouds. It is continuous by miles wide and miles tall. Unmistakable luminance. Young birds prod and nestle mothers' feathery wings like puppies scratching noses against weedy turf.

SNUGGLE sounds secure these hours like cradles of angels' arms for all newborns of humankind and all life forms in between.

Ella's FEET find passage around cracked acorn shells and minuscule pieces of quartz and granite. She walks with a sixth sense around such things.

She is like a NATIVE AMERICAN INDIAN over 200 years ago. She STEPS WITH PURPOSE and care. She steps in the sense of a ghost who does not know of its own passing until the sun rising with angels lined along its corridors beckons it home.

Tree frogs swim in nearby ponds. There are shadowy branches and vines. DEER graze in paths of camouflage of PEARLY LUMINOSITY. Thick clouds glide across the moon. SHADOWS STRETCH against the lofty-bend of broom straw. Clustered rabbit's tobacco disappears into fog.

POSSEUMS and WEASELS run toward the local chicken plant that turn portions of a nearby town into Stinkville.

Ella's FEET brush the dewy ground through a steady and slow gait towards the deer. Ella raises a flashlight. Corn and rabbit FOOD ROLL LIKE MINIATURE BEADS OF GRAY IRON THROUGH YELLOW OIL FROM PALM AND FINGERS TO THE GROUND. Gentle chewing ceases and seeks to discern what she is. What does she want? Why is she here? What will she do?

ELLA (VO)

Retrace your steps. (whispers) Retrace
your steps! (louder whisper)

SUPER: *"Forty winks from a rooster's call."*
A FOGGY STEAM DISSIPATES, as the sun rises.
BACK TO PRESENT DAY

INT. ELLA'S BEDROOM – DAY

Soft, warm covers garland Ella.

Loose and hard corn is scattered about the floor.

Spirit and Soul sit on either side of Ella's bed. Soul is dressed as if he's been on a hiking and fishing trip. He wears a hat with an abundance of fishing lures. Spirit is dressed in a long nightshirt and nightcap. He holds a candle.

SPIRIT

Here we are! In this glorious
universe of stars and planets,
the greens and blues of Mother
Nature, her children of every life
form and the misfits of maladjusted
housekeepers who run between beauty
and Hades making us miserable.
Ella ignores them to survive.

SOUL

Well, thank you for that little
speech. She's awake now. Did
you notice?

SPIRIT

Yes. I did. Now, why don't you
shower and spray before she
notices you.

Soul looks down and breathes in as if to check for offensive odor.

DISSOLVE

♀ | | ♂

The Wyatt Section

♀ | | ♂

*T*HE WYATT SECTION follows. The name Wyatt, Wyat, Wiot, Guyot or Guyott, Wyot is discussed at great length in Chapter 1: *The Original Name was "Guyot."* It is purported to mean *"little warrior."* It is derived from the Old English name *"Wigheard"* – comprised of elements: *wig war plus heard, hardy, brave* and *strong.*

Refer to Chapter 1 for a more detailed account of its meaning. This account is by far from complete. There is no such thing as a final draft in this history to date. If you discern any point as a discrepancy, please send Metallo House Publishers your assessment. We will be happy to consider it.

In researching historical articles, no concrete proof is cited that Admiral or Captain Adam Guyot or Guyott in fact married one of the daughters of William the Conqueror. Nevertheless, the possibility is not disputed. William the Conqueror with his wife Maude or Matilda of Flanders [d. 1083] had many children – one named Agatha, whose absolute existence may be disputed. Another was Adeliza. More children included: Matilda, Robert, Richard, William II *"Rufus"* King of England, Cecilia, Constance, Adela, Henry I King of England. William I's daughter Adela, married Stephen II and had a son who later became King of England.

We include this connection until proof is found to dispute it. If true, then the Wyatts can claim this ancestral or relative connection to William the Conqueror.

The Wyatts are connected to Dandridge lineage via Henry Wyatt [Lifespan: Abt. 1685 to Abt. 1743] who married Elizabeth Dandridge [Abt. 1703-Abt.1750] – daughter of John Dandridge I and sister to John Dandridge II – the father of Martha Dandridge Custis Washington [1731-1802]. Martha's great granddaughter Mary Anne or Anna Randolph Custis became the wife of Confederate General Robert E. Lee [1807-1873].

The Lee family is additionally traced to Jamestown, Va., where its immigrant Colonel Richard Henry Lee I, [1618-1664] met his bride Anne Constable, who ironically lived temporarily in the household of Sir Francis Wyatt, then the Royal Governor of the Virginia Colony. At the time, Anne Constable was a ward of Sir John Thoroughgood, personal attendant: Charles I, King of England. This Gov. Wyatt, commissioned by King Charles I, brought with him a written constitution – the first of its kind in the New World. It became the model for subsequent Anglo-American governments.

Anne Constable and Col. Richard Henry Lee are ancestors of not only Robert E. Lee – but also of the 12th U.S. President Zachary Taylor [1784-1850]. Robert E. Lee and Zachary Taylor were third cousins once removed to one another. Rev. Hawte Wyatt, brother to Sir Francis Wyatt, would have certainly known Anne Constable and Col. Richard Lee.

The social and employment circles of early Jamestown, Va. created the foundation in which many Wyatts are genealogically connected today.

DESCENDANTS OF CAPTAIN OR ADMIRAL ADAM GUYOTT OR WIOT

Generation No. 1

1. Captain or Admiral Adam Guyott or[1] Wiot died Aft. 1066. He married Daughter of William the Conqueror, daughter of William and Maude Flanders.

More About Captain or Admiral Adam Guyott or Wiot:
Fact 1: Was Captain of one of the ships of William I coming into England from Normandy.

Child of Captain Wiot and Daughter Conqueror is:
+ 2   i.   Guyott[2], born in England.

Generation No. 2

2. Guyott[2] (Captain or Admiral Adam Guyott or[1] Wiot) was born in England. He married Unknown.

Child of Guyott and Unknown is:
+ 3   i.   Guyott3.

Generation No. 3

3. Guyott[3] (Guyott[2], Captain or Admiral Adam Guyott or[1] Wiot) was born in Normandy. He married Unknown.

Child of Guyott and Unknown is:

+ 4   i.   Adam Wiot or Wyote or[4] Wyot, born Abt. 1320 in moved Southange known as South Haigh or Upper Haigh, Yorkshire, England; died Abt. 1385 in Kexburgh, near Darton, northeast of Barnsley in Yorkshire, England.

Generation No. 4

4. Adam Wiot or Wyote or[4] Wyot (Guyott[3], Guyott[2], Captain or Admiral Adam Guyott or[1] Wiot) was born Abt. 1320 in moved Southange also known as South Haigh or Upper Haigh, Yorkshire, England, and died Abt. 1385 in Kexburgh, near Darton, northeast of Barnsley in Yorkshire, England. He married Lady Agnes Wigton Wiggen or Wiggon de Norwoods Abt. 1340. Some sources say married 1349, England, daughter of Lord Cobham and X.

More About Adam Wiot or Wyote or Wyot:
Fact 1: Was Norman/French.
Fact 2: Wyote -- another spelling of this name.

Children of Adam Wyot and Lady de Norwoods are:

+ 5   i.   William Wiot or[5] Wyot, born 1350 in Southange -- also known as South Haigh or Upper Haigh, Yorkshire, England; died 1388.
+ 6   ii.   John Wiot, born 1340 in Langley Marish Church, near Slough, England; died 1410 in buried at Langley Marish Church, near Slough, England.

Generation No. 5

5. William Wiot or[5] Wyot (Adam Wiot or Wyote or[4], Guyott[3], Guyott[2], Captain or Admiral Adam Guyott or[1] Wiot) was born 1350 in Southange -- known as South Haigh or Upper Haigh, Yorkshire, England, and died 1388. He married Jane Bailiffe or Bayliffe de Barnsley 1372, daughter of Roger de Barnsley and X.

More About Jane Bailiffe or Bayliffe de Barnsley:
Fact 1: Abt. 1373, date provided by Church of the Latter Day Saints genealogical records.

Children of William Wyot and Jane de Barnsley are:

+ 7   i.   Robert or Richard[6] Wiot, born 1383 in Southange -- known as South Haigh or Upper Haigh, Yorkshire, England; died 1440.
  8   ii.   John Wiot.

More About John Wiot:
Fact 1: 2010, supposedly died childless, according to Alexander Lloyd Wiatt's research.

6.   John[5] Wiot (Adam Wiot or Wyote or[4] Wyot, Guyott[3], Guyott[2], Captain or Admiral Adam Guyott or[1] Wiot) was born 1340 in Langley Marish Church, near Slough, England, and died 1410 in buried at Langley Marish Church, near Slough, England. He married Philippa Rouet 1366, daughter of Rouet and X.

More About John Wiot:
Fact 1: 1377, was a friend of Geoffrey Chaucer, [Abt. 1343-October 25, 1400.] father of English poetry.
Fact 2: 1383-1388, was the tax commissioner for Buckingham.
Fact 3: He spent the last years of his life as secular cleric of Horton rectory [Bucks]
Fact 4: One source claimed him childless, while others claim the opposite.
Buried at Langley Marish in 1410.

More About Philippa Rouet:
Fact 1: Sister of Catherine Rouet Swinford

        Child of John Wiot and Philippa Rouet is:
        9   i.   William6 Wiot, born 1360; died 1427 in buried at Langley Marish.

Generation No. 6

7.   Robert or Richard[6] Wiot (William Wiot or[5] Wyot, Adam Wiot or Wyote or[4], Guyott[3], Guyott[2], Captain or Admiral Adam Guyott or[1] Wiot) was born 1383 in Southange -- also known as South Haigh or Upper Haigh, Yorkshire, England, and died 1440. He married Jane Skipwith (Skipworth) 1408, daughter of Richard de Southange and Unknown Wife.

        Children of Robert Wiot and Jane (Skipworth) are:
        +   10   i.   Geoffrey "Jeoffrey" Wiot or[7] Wiat, born 1404 in Southange --
                               also known as South Haigh and Upper Haigh, Yorkshire,
                               England; died 1460.
            11   ii.   John Wiatt [Wyatt].

Generation No. 7

10. Geoffrey "Jeoffrey" Wiot or[7] Wiat (Robert or Richard[6] Wiot, William Wiot or[5] Wyot, Adam Wiot or Wyote or[4], Guyott[3], Guyott[2], Captain or Admiral Adam Guyott or[1] Wiot) was born 1404 in Southange -- also known as South Haigh and Upper Haigh, Yorkshire, England, and died 1460. He married Anna "Anne" Skipworth (Skipwith) or Anne Wiot

in Southgate, Kent County, England, daughter of Richard Skipworth and Unknown Wife.

More About Geoffrey "Jeoffrey" Wiot or Wiat:
Fact 1: 1410, sited by some as the birth year.

More About Anna "Anne" Skipworth (Skipwith) or Anne Wiot:
Fact 1: Welch cousin of husband.

    Children of Geoffrey Wiat and Anna Wiot are:

+	12	i.	Richard Wiat or[8] Wyatt, born 1435 in Southange and Tickhill, West Riding, Yorkshire, England; died 1475 in Barking, Essex, England.
	13	ii.	John Wiat.

    More About John Wiat:
    Fact 1: No children.

Generation No. 8

12.   Richard Wiat or[8] Wyatt (Geoffrey "Jeoffrey" Wiot or[7] Wiat, Robert or Richard[6] Wiot, William Wiot or[5] Wyot, Adam Wiot or Wyote or[4], Guyott[3], Guyott[2], Captain or Admiral Adam Guyott or[1] Wiot) was born 1435 in Southange and Tickhill, West Riding, Yorkshire, England, and died 1475 in Barking, Essex, England. He married (1) Margaret Jane Clarke or Bailiffe in England, daughter of William Southange and Unknown wife. He married (2) Harde or Herne or Herme.

More About Richard Wiat or Wyatt:
Fact 1: 1435, Date of birth from another source.
Fact 2: Southange -- known as South Haigh and Upper Haigh, Yorkshire, England
Fact 3: 1428-1478, lifespan cited by some historians.

More About Margaret Jane Clarke or Bailiffe:
Fact 1: Referred to as *"Anne Wiot"* in some genealogies.

    Children of Richard Wyatt and Margaret Bailiffe are:

	14	i.	Joan[9] Wiatt.
+	15	ii.	John Wiat, born 1458 in Allington Castle, Kent County, England; died 1525.
+	16	iii.	Sir Henry Wiatt, Knt. [father of the poet], born 1460 in Southange, West Riding, Yorkshire, England; died November 10, 1536 in Allington Castle, Kent County, England.
+	17	iv.	William Wiatt, born 1463 in Barking, Essex, England; died 1532.
+	18	v.	Thomas Wiatt of Kent, born Abt. 1467 in of Kent County, England.

Child of Richard Wyatt and Harde Herme is:

19   i.   John[9] Wyatt.

More About John Wyatt:
Died with his mother at birth. The existence of this child and his mother is cited on page 6 of The Wiatt Family of Virginia compiled by A.L. Wiatt.

Generation No. 9

15. John[9] Wiat (Richard Wiat or[8] Wyatt, Geoffrey "Jeoffrey" Wiot or[7] Wiat, Robert or Richard[6] Wiot, William Wiot or[5] Wyot, Adam Wiot or Wyote or[4], Guyott[3], Guyott[2], Captain or Admiral Adam Guyott or[1] Wiot) was born 1458 in Allington Castle, Kent County, England, and died 1525. He married Unknown Wife Bef. 1526.

More About John Wiat:
Fact 1: Died with his mother at birth.

Child of John Wiat and Unknown Wife is:

+ 20   i.   Phillip10 Wiat, born 1500 in Braunton, Devon, England; died 1591 in Braunton, Devon, England.

16. Sir Henry[9] Wiatt, Knt. [father of the poet] (Richard Wiat or[8] Wyatt, Geoffrey "Jeoffrey" Wiot or[7] Wiat, Robert or Richard[6] Wiot, William Wiot or[5] Wyot, Adam Wiot or Wyote or[4], Guyott[3], Guyott[2], Captain or Admiral Adam Guyott or[1] Wiot) was born 1460 in Southange, West Riding, Yorkshire, England, and died November 10, 1536 in Allington Castle, Kent County, England. He married (1) Margaret Bailiff, daughter of Richard Bailiff and Unknown Wife. He married (2) Anne Skinner 1502 in Kent County, England, daughter of John Skinner and Unknown Wife.

More About Sir Henry Wiatt, Knt. [father of the poet]:
Fact 1: March 10, 1536/37, Date of demise given by another source.
Fact 2: 1460, Another date given as birth in Allington Caste, Kent County, England.
Fact 3: 1509, Was an advisor to King Henry VIII when King Henry came to the throne.
Fact 4: Historians say to have been the most beloved man in England during his day.
Fact 5: Had been one of Henry VII's Privey Councilors.
Fact 6: Knight Banneret.
Fact 7: Was Privy Council to King Henry VII & King Henry VIII.
Fact 8: English courtier.
Fact 9: Attended Eton College with Henry Tudor -- later King Henry VII.
Fact 10: Was Treasurer of the King's Chamber until 1528.
Fact 11: Was Master of the King's Jewels for 34 years until 1524.
Buried in Milton, near Gravesend, Kent County, England. Aged 76 or 77 years old at time of demise. Died about 1536 or 37.

Children of Sir Wiatt and Anne Skinner are:

+	21	i.	Henry[10] Wiatt, born 1500 in Allington Castle, Kent County, England; died 1544.
+	22	ii.	Sir Thomas "The Elder" Wiatt, born Abt. 1503 in Allington Castle, Kent County, England; died October 11, 1542 in Sherbourne or Sherborne, Dorset, England.
+	23	iii.	Margaret "Lady Lee" Wiatt, born Abt. 1506 in Allington Castle, Kent County, England; died March 10, 1535/36.
	24	iv.	Thomas Wiatt?.
	25	v.	Richard Wiatt?
	26	vi.	Joan Wiatt?

17. William[9] Wiatt (Richard Wiat or[8] Wyatt, Geoffrey "Jeoffrey" Wiot or[7] Wiat, Robert or Richard[6] Wiot, William Wiot or[5] Wyot, Adam Wiot or Wyote or[4], Guyott[3], Guyott[2], Captain or Admiral Adam Guyott or[1] Wiot) was born 1463 in Barking, Essex, England, and died 1532. He married Jane Harde.

More About William Wiatt:
Fact 1: Was a tax collector for king's war with France.

Children of William Wiatt and Jane Harde are:

+	27	i.	Thomas[10] Wiatt, born Abt. 1494 in Lupset, Yorkshire, England.
	28	ii.	John Wiatt.
	29	iii.	William Wiatt.
+	30	iv.	Anne Wiatt, born Abt. 1493 in Lupset, Yorkshire, England.

18. Thomas Wiatt of[9] Kent (Richard Wiat or[8] Wyatt, Geoffrey "Jeoffrey" Wiot or[7] Wiat, Robert or Richard[6] Wiot, William Wiot or[5] Wyot, Adam Wiot or Wyote or[4], Guyott[3], Guyott[2], Captain or Admiral Adam Guyott or[1] Wiot) was born Abt. 1467 in of Kent County, England. He married Unknown Wife.

More About Thomas Wiatt of Kent:
Fact 1: Wyatts of Crosbury descend from him.

Children of Thomas Kent and Unknown Wife are:

	31	i.	Richard Wiatt of[10] Slindon.

More About Richard Wiatt of Slindon:
Fact 1: Rector of Slindon.

+	32	ii.	Robert Wiatt of Slindon, born in of Slindon, England.
+	33	iii.	John Wiatt of Flansham, born in of Flansham, England.

Generation No. 10

20. Phillip[10] Wiat (John[9], Richard Wiat or[8] Wyatt, Geoffrey "Jeoffrey" Wiot or[7] Wiat, Robert or Richard[6] Wiot, William Wiot or[5] Wyot, Adam Wiot or Wyote or[4], Guyott[3], Guyott[2], Captain or Admiral Adam Guyott or[1] Wiot) was born 1500 in Braunton, Devon, England, and died 1591 in Braunton, Devon, England. He married Jane Patty Bef. 1526 in Devon, England.

> Children of Phillip Wiat and Jane Patty are:
>
> | | | |
> |---|---|---|
> | 34 | i. | Sedwell[11] Wiat. |
> | 35 | ii. | Agnes Wiat, born Abt. 1526 in Braunton, Devon, England. She married John Sheppard January 26, 1554/55. |
> | 36 | iii. | Margaret Wiat, born Abt. 1530 in Braunton, Devon, England. She married John Poyntz. |
> | 37 | iv. | George Wiat, born Abt. 1532 in Braunton, Devon, England; died September 15, 1594. |
> | 38 | v. | Hugh Wiat, born Abt. 1534 in Shillinsford, Berkshire, England. He married (1) Mary Hill. He married (2) Mary Maria Bourchier November 28, 1566. |
> | 39 | vi. | William Wiat, born December 14, 1539 in Braunton, Devon, England. He married Elizabeth Sheppard October 19, 1560 in Braunton, Devon, England. |
> | 40 | vii. | Nicholas Wiat, born 1540 in Braunton, Devon, England; died 1596. |
> | 41 | viii. | Thomas Wiat, born February 27, 1543/44 in 1544, Braunton, Devon, England. He married Margaret Risdon October 03, 1569. |
> | 42 | ix. | Adam Wiat, born Abt. 1548 in Barnstaple, Devon, England; died October 10, 1611. He married Elizabeth Harris September 23, 1576. |
> | 43 | x. | Phillip Wiat, born August 03, 1550 in Braunton, Devon, England; died August 22, 1608. He married Alice Brooke October 25, 1579. |
> | + 44 | xi. | John Wiat, born November 27, 1558 in Braunton, Devon, England; died December 22, 1598. |

21. Henry[10] Wiatt (Sir Henry[9], Richard Wiat or[8] Wyatt, Geoffrey "Jeoffrey" Wiot or[7] Wiat, Robert or Richard[6] Wiot, William Wiot or[5] Wyot, Adam Wiot or Wyote or[4], Guyott[3], Guyott[2], Captain or Admiral Adam Guyott or[1] Wiot) was born 1500 in Allington Castle, Kent County, England, and died 1544. He married Unknown Wife.

> Child of Henry Wiatt and Unknown Wife is:
>
> | | | |
> |---|---|---|
> | 45 | i. | Edward[11] Wiatt, born in lived in Essex; died 1544 in buried at Tillingham, England, where a brass monument in his honor is located. He married Miss Brown. |

22. Sir Thomas "The Elder"[10] Wiatt (Sir Henry[9], Richard Wiat or[8] Wyatt, Geoffrey "Jeoffrey" Wiot or[7] Wiat, Robert or Richard[6] Wiot, William Wiot or[5] Wyot, Adam Wiot or Wyote or[4], Guyott[3], Guyott[2], Captain or Admiral Adam Guyott or[1] Wiot) was born Abt. 1503 in Allington Castle, Kent County, England, and died October 11, 1542 in Sherbourne or Sherborne, Dorset, England. He met (1) Elizabeth Darrell or Darell, daughter of Sir Edward Darell. He married (2) Elizabeth Brooke 1520 in 1521 another possible year of marriage., daughter of Thomas Brooke and Dorothy Heydon.

More About Sir Thomas "The Elder" Wiatt:
Fact 1: C.S. Lewis called him the *"Father of the Drab Age."*
Fact 2: 1541, date of death cited by Martyn Freeth.
Buried at the great church of Sherbourne, Dorset, England.

More About Elizabeth Darrell or Darell:
Fact 1: Was long time mistress and muse of Sir Thomas Wyatt -- the Elder.

More About Elizabeth Brooke:
Fact 1: Considered for a possible wife for Henry VIII while his 5th wife awaited execution.
Fact 2: Separated from her husband and lived openly in adultery.

Children of Sir Wiatt and Elizabeth Darell are:
46   i.   Francis Darell[11] Wyatt, born 1540.

        More About Francis Darell Wyatt:
        Fact 1: Took the surname Darrell instead of using the Wyatt name in any of its spellings.

47   ii.   Henry Wyatt Darrell.

        More About Henry Wyatt Darrell:
        Fact 1: Died in infancy.

48   iii.   Edward "Edwardus Wyat" Darell Wyatt, died 1554.

        More About Edward "Edwardus Wyat" Darell Wyatt:
        Fact 1: Was executed for his part in Wyatt's Rebellion against Queen Mary.
        Fact 2: January 21, 1553/54, was present among family and friends at Allington Castle, Kent County, England.
        Fact 3: January 24, 1553/54, is named as one of the participants meeting to discuss the upcoming rebellion.
        Fact 4: January 25, 1553/54, 1554, marched with Sir Thomas Wyatt to London.

Fact 5: Surrendered at Ludgate Hill with about 60 other rebels and taken to the tower.

Fact 6: Possibly a son instead of a half-brother of Sir Thomas Wyatt the Younger.

Children of Sir Wiatt and Elizabeth Brooke are:

+ 49   i.   Sir Thomas "The Younger"[11] Wiatt, born 1521 in Allington Castle, Kent County, England; died April 11, 1554 in Tower Hill, London, England.

  50   ii.   Frances Wiatt? born Abt. 1522; died July 16, 1578. She married (1) Thomas Lighe. She married (2) William Patrickson.

23. Margaret "Lady Lee"[10] Wiatt (Sir Henry[9], Richard Wiat or[8] Wyatt, Geoffrey "Jeoffrey" Wiot or[7] Wiat, Robert or Richard[6] Wiot, William Wiot or[5] Wyot, Adam Wiot or Wyote or[4], Guyott[3], Guyott[2], Captain or Admiral Adam Guyott or[1] Wiot) was born Abt. 1506 in Allington Castle, Kent County, England, and died March 10, 1535/36. She married (1) John Thomas Rogers? in Deritend, Warwickshire, England. She married (2) Sir Anthony Lee, son of Sir Lee and Jane Cope.

More About Margaret "Lady Lee" Wiatt:
Fact 1: Some accounts have her only marrying once; others report twice.

More About Sir Anthony Lee:
Fact 1: Knight of Quorndon.
Fact 2: Was a Member of Parliament.

Children of Margaret Wiatt and John Rogers? are:
  51   i.   Rev. John[11] Rogers.
  52   ii.   William Rogers.
  53   iii. Edward Rogers.
  54   iv.   Eleanor Rogers.
  55   v.   Joan Rogers.

Children of Margaret Wiatt and Sir Lee are:
+ 56   i.   Sir Henry11 Lee, born March 1532/33 in Kent County, lived in Ditchley, England; died February 12, 1610/11.
  57   ii.   Robert Lee, died Abt. 1598.
  58   iii. Cromwell Lee, died Abt. 1601 in Oxford, England. He married Mary Harcourt.

        More About Cromwell Lee:
        Fact 1: Compiled an Italian-English dictionary,

  59   iv.   Thomas Lee.
  60   v.   Anne Lee.

61	vi.	Lettice Lee.
62	vii.	Katherine Lee.
63	viii.	Joyce Lee.
64	ix.	Jane Lee.

27. Thomas[10] Wiatt (William[9], Richard Wiat or[8] Wyatt, Geoffrey "Jeoffrey" Wiot or[7] Wiat, Robert or Richard[6] Wiot, William Wiot or[5] Wyot, Adam Wiot or Wyote or[4], Guyott[3], Guyott[2], Captain or Admiral Adam Guyott or[1] Wiot) was born Abt. 1494 in Lupset, Yorkshire, England. He married Margaret Scott.

Children of Thomas Wiatt and Margaret Scott are:

65	i.	Thomas11 Wiatt.
66	ii.	Francis Wiatt.
67	iii.	Edmund Wiatt.

30. Anne[10] Wiatt (William[9], Richard Wiat or[8] Wyatt, Geoffrey "Jeoffrey" Wiot or[7] Wiat, Robert or Richard[6] Wiot, William Wiot or[5] Wyot, Adam Wiot or Wyote or[4], Guyott[3], Guyott[2], Captain or Admiral Adam Guyott or[1] Wiot) was born Abt. 1493 in Lupset, Yorkshire, England. She married (1) John Spilman. She married (2) Leonard Bates. She married (3) John Saville or Savile, son of Thomas Seville and Margaret Basforth.

Child of Anne Wiatt and John Savile is:

68	i.	Henry11 Saville, born 1518; died January 05, 1567/68. He married Joan Vernon.

More About Henry Saville:
Fact 1: Sheriff of Yorkshire

32. Robert Wiatt of[10] Slindon (Thomas Wiatt of[9] Kent, Richard Wiat or[8] Wyatt, Geoffrey "Jeoffrey" Wiot or[7] Wiat, Robert or Richard[6] Wiot, William Wiot or[5] Wyot, Adam Wiot or Wyote or[4], Guyott[3], Guyott[2], Captain or Admiral Adam Guyott or[1] Wiot) was born in of Slindon, England. He married Unknown Wife.

Child of Robert Slindon and Unknown Wife is:

69	i.	Richard11 Wiat, born 1554; died 1619 in buried at Isleworth Church. He married Margaret Shears.

33. John Wiatt of[10] Flansham (Thomas Wiatt of[9] Kent, Richard Wiat or[8] Wyatt, Geoffrey "Jeoffrey" Wiot or[7] Wiat, Robert or Richard[6] Wiot, William Wiot or[5] Wyot, Adam Wiot or Wyote or[4], Guyott[3], Guyott[2], Captain or Admiral Adam Guyott or[1] Wiot) was born in of Flansham, England.

Child of John Wiatt of Flansham is:

+	70	i.	William[11] Wiatt.

Generation No. 11

44. John[11] Wiat (Phillip[10], John[9], Richard Wiat or[8] Wyatt, Geoffrey "Jeoffrey" Wiot or[7] Wiat, Robert or Richard[6] Wiot, William Wiot or[5] Wyot, Adam Wiot or Wyote or[4], Guyott[3], Guyott[2], Captain or Admiral Adam Guyott or[1] Wiot) was born November 27, 1558 in Braunton, Devon, England, and died December 22, 1598. He married Frances Chichester in Braunton, Devon, England.

More About John Wiat:
Fact 1: Christened November 27, 1558, Braunton, Devon, England.

Children of John Wiat and Frances Chichester are:

71	i.	Anne[12] Wiat.
72	ii.	Agnes Wiat.
73	iii.	Joan Wiat.
74	iv.	Phillip Wiat.
75	v.	Hugh Wiat.
76	vi.	Margaret Wiat.

49. Sir Thomas "The Younger"[11] Wiatt (Sir Thomas "The Elder"[10], Sir Henry[9], Richard Wiat or[8] Wyatt, Geoffrey "Jeoffrey" Wiot or[7] Wiat, Robert or Richard[6] Wiot, William Wiot or[5] Wyot, Adam Wiot or Wyote or[4], Guyott[3], Guyott[2], Captain or Admiral Adam Guyott or[1] Wiot) was born 1521 in Allington Castle, Kent County, England, and died April 11, 1554 in Tower Hill, London, England. He married Lady Jane Haute "Hawte" "Haut" "Hawt" 1536 in or 1537 Kent County, England, daughter of Sir Haute and Maria Guldeford.

More About Sir Thomas "The Younger" Wiatt:
Fact 1: Was brought up a Roman Catholic.
Fact 2: Changed to Protestant after witnessing Spanish Inquisition in Spain on trip.
Fact 3: Was imprisoned at Tower of London for breaking windows while drunk.
Fact 4: After release, fought for Hapsburg emperor -- then also King of Spain.
Fact 5: Fragment of Allington Castle still inhabited near Maidstone on bank of Medway.
Fact 6: Served King Henry VIII as a squire and soldier.
Fact 7: Was an only son of his parents.
Fact 8: Executed near Hyde Park, London, England.
Fact 9: 1522, cites his birth year as -- Alexander Lloyd Wiatt.
Fact 10: 1542, he inherited Allington Castle and Boxley Abbey.
Fact 11: 1543, took part in siege of Landrecies and in 1544 the siege of Boulogne.
Fact 12: 1547, was knighted.
Fact 13: Resting place provided: St. Mary the Virgin and All Saints Churchyard, Boxley, Kent, England.
Executed. Churchyard, Boxley, Kent County, England.

More About Lady Jane Haute "Hawte" "Haut" "Hawt":

Fact 1: 1537, Manor of Boxley passed to him via his wife Jane Haute.

Fact 2: 1554, Property was confiscated after husband's rebellion by Queen Mary I

Fact 3: 1571, Boxley Manor property was restored to her by Elizabeth I.

Fact 4: Abbey property, Abbey House and Upper Grange.

Children of Sir Wiatt and Lady "Hawt" are:

77	i.	Arthur[12] Wiatt.
78	ii.	Charles "Carolus" Wiatt.
79	iii.	Henry "Henricus" Wiatt.

More About Henry "Henricus" Wiatt:
died Abt. 1624?

80	iv.	Jocosa "Joyce" Wiatt.
81	v.	Richardus "Richard" Wiatt.
82	vi.	Ursula Wiatt.
83	vii.	Frances Wiatt? He married Sir Thomas Leigh?
+ 84	viii.	Anne or Ann Anna Wiatt, born September 19, 1542 in Kent, England; died June 04, 1592 in East Peckham, Kent County, England.
+ 85	ix.	Jane or Joan Wiatt, born 1553 in England; died 1617.
+ 86	x.	Sir George "Georgius" Thomas Wiatt, Knt., born Abt. 1554 in Allington Castle or Boxley Hall, Kent County, England; died September 16, 1624 in Ireland, buried Nov. 10, 1624 in Boxley, Kent, England.

56. Sir Henry[11] Lee (Margaret "Lady Lee"[10] Wiatt, Sir Henry[9], Richard Wiat or[8] Wyatt, Geoffrey "Jeoffrey" Wiot or[7] Wiat, Robert or Richard[6] Wiot, William Wiot or[5] Wyot, Adam Wiot or Wyote or[4], Guyott[3], Guyott[2], Captain or Admiral Adam Guyott or[1] Wiot) was born March 1532/33 in Kent County, of Ditchley, England, and died February 12, 1610/11. He married Anne Paget.

More About Sir Henry Lee:

Fact 1: Master of the Armory under Queen Elizabeth I of England.

Children of Sir Lee and Anne Paget are:

87	i.	John[12] Lee.
88	ii.	Henry Lee.
89	iii.	Mary Lee.

70. William[11] Wiatt (John Wiatt of[10] Flansham, Thomas Wiatt of[9] Kent, Richard Wiat or[8] Wyatt, Geoffrey "Jeoffrey" Wiot or[7] Wiat, Robert or Richard[6] Wiot, William Wiot or[5] Wyot,

Adam Wiot or Wyote or[4], Guyott[3], Guyott[2], Captain or Admiral Adam Guyott or[1] Wiot). He married Unknown Wife.

Child of William Wiatt and Unknown Wife is:
+ 90   i.   Richard[12] Wiatt, born 1726.

Generation No. 12

84. Anne or Ann Anna[12] Wiatt (Sir Thomas "The Younger"[11], Sir Thomas "The Elder"[10], Sir Henry[9], Richard Wiat or[8] Wyatt, Geoffrey "Jeoffrey" Wiot or[7] Wiat, Robert or Richard[6] Wiot, William Wiot or[5] Wyot, Adam Wiot or Wyote or[4], Guyott[3], Guyott[2], Captain or Admiral Adam Guyott or[1] Wiot) was born September 19, 1542 in Kent, England, and died June 04, 1592 in East Peckham, Kent County, England. She married Sir Roger Twisden de Peckham or Twysden.

More About Anne or Ann Anna Wiatt:
Remains buried at Saint Michael's Churchyard. east Peckham, Tonbrdige and Malling Borough, Kent, England.

More About Sir Roger Twisden de Peckham or Twysden:
Fact 1: Of Royal Hall, England.

Child of Anne Wiatt and Sir Twysden is:
+ 91   i.   William[13] Twysden, born in of Roydon Hall, England; died January 08, 1627/28.

85. Jane or Joan[12] Wiatt (Sir Thomas "The Younger"[11], Sir Thomas "The Elder"[10], Sir Henry[9], Richard Wiat or[8] Wyatt, Geoffrey "Jeoffrey" Wiot or[7] Wiat, Robert or Richard[6] Wiot, William Wiot or[5] Wyot, Adam Wiot or Wyote or[4], Guyott[3], Guyott[2], Captain or Admiral Adam Guyott or[1] Wiot) was born 1553 in England, and died 1617. She married Sir Charles Scott or Scot, son of Sir Scott and Mary Tuke.

More About Sir Charles Scott or Scot:
Fact 1: A younger son of Sir Reynold Scott.
Fact 2: Was Captain of the Castles of Calais and Langette, France.
Fact 3: 1541-1542, Was Sheriff of Kent

Children of Jane Wiatt and Sir Scot are:
+ 92   i.   Dorothea "Deborah"[13] Scott.
  93   ii.   Thomas Scott.

86. Sir George "Georgius" Thomas[12] Wiatt, Knt. (Sir Thomas "The Younger"[11], Sir Thomas "The Elder"[10], Sir Henry[9], Richard Wiat or[8] Wyatt, Geoffrey "Jeoffrey" Wiot or[7] Wiat, Robert or Richard[6] Wiot, William Wiot or[5] Wyot, Adam Wiot or Wyote or[4], Guyott[3], Guyott[2], Captain or Admiral Adam Guyott or[1] Wiot) was born Abt. 1554 in Allington Castle or Boxley Hall,

Kent County, England, and died September 16, 1624 in Ireland, buried Nov. 10, 1624 in Boxley, Kent, England. He married Lady Jane Finch October 08, 1582 in Caswell, Kent County, England, daughter of Sir Finch and Lady Moyle.

More About Sir George "Georgius" Thomas Wiatt, Knt.:

Fact 1: 1550, possible birth year.

Fact 2: Admitted to Grays' Inn at age 17

Fact 3: Married at age 18.

Fact 4: Wrote *The Life of Anne Boleyn.*

Fact 5: Wrote a history of the Wyatt family.

Fact 6: Both manuscripts mentioned above are in the British Museum.

Fact 7: Was a soldier.

Fact 8: Wrote Extracts from *The Life of Queen Anne Boleigne.*

Fact 9: September 01, 1624, a date cited as a possible as by date of death.

Died at age 73 years.

Buried at Boxley Manor (Abbey), Kent County, England. Possible death years 1624 and 1625. Saint Mary the Virgin and All Saints Churchyard, Boxley, Maidstone Borough, Kent, England.

More About Lady Jane Finch:

Fact 1: April 29, 1639, takes administration of her son Hawte's estate upon his demise.

Fact 2: With Jane's efforts, she identifies Hawte's children in documents.

Outlived her husband by 20 years. Died at age 84.

Children of Sir Wiatt and Lady Finch are:

	94	i.	George Thomas[13] Wiatt?
+	95	ii.	Thomas Wiatt.
+	96	iii.	Sir Francis Wyatt, born 1588 in Boxley Abbey, Kent County, England; died August 1644 in Jamestown, Va. buried in Boxely, Kent County, England.
	97	iv.	Eleanora "Eleanor" Wiatt, born 1591 in Allington Castle, Boxley, Kent County, England. She married Lord John Finch February 06, 1617/18 in Boxley, Kent, County, England.

More About Lord John Finch:

Fact 1: 1627, Was Speaker of the House of Commons.

Fact 2: Baron of Fordetch

+	98	v.	Rev. Haute "Haut" "Hawte" Wiatt, born June 04, 1594 in Allington Castle, Maidstone, Kent County, England; died July 31, 1638 in Allington Castle, Kent County, England.
+	99	vi.	Isabel Wiatt, born Abt. 1595 in Allington Castle, Kent, England; died Abt. 1655.

+ 100 vii. Henry Wiatt, born November 07, 1596 in Kerstening, Berks, Kent County, England; died November 10, 1624 in buried January 1, 1624 Boxley, Kent County, England.

90. Richard[12] Wiatt (William[11], John Wiatt of[10] Flansham, Thomas Wiatt of[9] Kent, Richard Wiat or[8] Wyatt, Geoffrey "Jeoffrey" Wiot or[7] Wiat, Robert or Richard[6] Wiot, William Wiot or[5] Wyot, Adam Wiot or Wyote or[4], Guyott[3], Guyott[2], Captain or Admiral Adam Guyott or[1] Wiot) was born 1726. He married Mary Greenfield.

Children of Richard Wiatt and Mary Greenfield are:
101 i. Richard[13] Wiatt, born 1810.

More About Richard Wiatt:
Fact 1: Was High Sheriff of Sussex
Fact 2: From Richard are descended the Wyatts of Cissbury

+ 102 ii. Miriam Wiatt.

Generation No. 13

91. William[13] Twysden (Anne or Ann Anna[12] Wiatt, Sir Thomas "The Younger"[11], Sir Thomas "The Elder"[10], Sir Henry[9], Richard Wiat or[8] Wyatt, Geoffrey "Jeoffrey" Wiot or[7] Wiat, Robert or Richard[6] Wiot, William Wiot or[5] Wyot, Adam Wiot or Wyote or[4], Guyott[3], Guyott[2], Captain or Admiral Adam Guyott or[1] Wiot) was born in of Roydon Hall, England, and died January 08, 1627/28. He married Anne Finch.

Child of William Twysden and Anne Finch is:
103 i. Sir Roger[14] Twysden.

More About Sir Roger Twysden:
Fact 1: Inherited George Wyatt's manuscript on Anne Boleyn *Extracts from The Life of Queen Anne Boleigne* by Geo Wyat, written at the end of the 16th century

92. Dorothea "Deborah"[13] Scott (Jane or Joan[12] Wiatt, Sir Thomas "The Younger"[11], Sir Thomas "The Elder"[10], Sir Henry[9], Richard Wiat or[8] Wyatt, Geoffrey "Jeoffrey" Wiot or[7] Wiat, Robert or Richard[6] Wiot, William Wiot or[5] Wyot, Adam Wiot or Wyote or[4], Guyott[3], Guyott[2], Captain or Admiral Adam Guyott or[1] Wiot). She married William Fleet.

More About William Fleet:
Fact 1: Was a member of the Virginia Company of London under the 3rd charter.

Children of Dorothea Scott and William Fleet are:
104 i. Henry[14] Fleet.

More About Henry Fleet:
Fact 1: Was among early immigrants to Virginia and Maryland.
Fact 2: 1638, Was a member of the Maryland Legislature.

105   ii.   Reginald Fleet.

More About Reginald Fleet:
Fact 1: Was among early immigrants to Virginia and Maryland.
Fact 2: 1638, Was a member of the Maryland Legislature.

106   iii.   John Fleet.

More About John Fleet:
Fact 1: Was among early immigrants to Virginia and Maryland.
Fact 2: 1638, Was a member of the Maryland Legislature.

107   iv.   Edward Fleet.

More About Edward Fleet:
Fact 1: Was among early immigrants to Virginia and Maryland.
Fact 2: 1638, Was a member of the Maryland Legislature.

108   v.   Son Fleet.
109   vi.   Son Fleet.
110   vii.   Son Fleet.
111   viii.   Daughter Fleet.
112   ix.   Daughter Fleet.
113   x.   Daughter Fleet.
114   xi.   Daughter Fleet.

95. Thomas[13] Wiatt (Sir George "Georgius" Thomas[12], Sir Thomas "The Younger"[11], Sir Thomas "The Elder"[10], Sir Henry[9], Richard Wiat or[8] Wyatt, Geoffrey "Jeoffrey" Wiot or[7] Wiat, Robert or Richard[6] Wiot, William Wiot or[5] Wyot, Adam Wiot or Wyote or[4], Guyott[3], Guyott[2], Captain or Admiral Adam Guyott or[1] Wiot).

More About Thomas Wiatt:
Fact 1: There is a Virginia record stating on September 24, 1643, a Thomas Wyat, patented 2,000 acres on South side of the Rappahannock River. "

Child of Thomas Wiatt is:
+   115   i.   William[14] Wyatt?

96. Sir Francis[13] Wyatt (Sir George "Georgius" Thomas[12] Wiatt, Knt., Sir Thomas "The Younger"[11], Sir Thomas "The Elder"[10], Sir Henry[9], Richard Wiat or[8] Wyatt, Geoffrey "Jeoffrey" Wiot or[7] Wiat, Robert or Richard[6] Wiot, William Wiot or[5] Wyot, Adam Wiot or

Wyote or[4], Guyott[3], Guyott[2], Captain or Admiral Adam Guyott or[1] Wiot) was born 1588 in Boxley Abbey, Kent County, England, and died August 1644 in Jamestown, Va. buried in Boxely, Kent County, England. He married Lady Margaret Sandys 1618, daughter of Sir Samuel Sandys and Culpeper?

More About Sir Francis Wyatt:
Fact 1: 1621-1626, served as English Royal Colonial Governor of Virginia in November.
Fact 2: 1639-1642, English Royal Colonial Governor of Virginia.
Fact 3: 1618, was knighted.
Fact 4: 1623, inherited *"Boxley Abbey,"* the Wyatt family seat.
Fact 5: March 1621/22, Indians went to war with white settlers.
Fact 6: 1624, Colony at Jamestown, Va. came under Royal control.
Fact 7: Was Crown-appointed Royal Governor of Virginia.
Fact 8: 1626, temporarily leaves Va. to attend to his family's estate matters in England.
Fact 9: 1639, returns in November to resume his position as governor of Virginia.
Fact 10: August 24, 1644, buried at Boxley Abbey Church, Kent County, England.
Fact 11: 1621, was the first English Royal Governor of Virginia.
Fact 12: 1624, Virginia became a royal colony in this year.
Fact 13: 1621-1639, listed Nov. 18, 1621 and Nov. 1639 in Virginia register as Governor of Virginia.
Wyatt monument erected in the Boxley Church in 1702 by Francis' son Edwin Wiat states: *"George Wiat left also Hawte Wiat who died vicar of this parish, and hath issue living in Virginia."*

More About Lady Margaret Sandys:
Fact 1: Also known as *"Lady Wyatt."*
Fact 2: 1621, Settled in Virginia for a while after her husband became Royal governor there.

    Children of Sir Wyatt and Lady Sandys are:
+   116   i.   Edwin Wyatt[14] (Wiatt).
    117   ii.   Francis Wyatt (Wiatt).
    118   iii.   Henry Wyatt (Wiatt).

        More About Henry Wyatt (Wiatt):

    119   iv.   Richard Wyatt (Wiatt)?
+   120   v.   Maj. William (Wiatt?), born July 22, 1621 in Boxley, Maidenstone, England; died in St. Peter's Parish, New Kent County, Va.

98. Rev. Haute "Haut" "Hawte"[13] Wiatt (Sir George "Georgius" Thomas[12], Sir Thomas "The Younger"[11], Sir Thomas "The Elder"[10], Sir Henry[9], Richard Wiat or[8] Wyatt, Geoffrey "Jeoffrey" Wiot or[7] Wiat, Robert or Richard[6] Wiot, William Wiot or[5] Wyot, Adam Wiot or Wyote or[4], Guyott[3], Guyott[2], Captain or Admiral Adam Guyott or[1] Wiot) was born June "Jeoffrey" Wiot or[7] Wiat, Robert or Richard[6] Wiot, William Wiot or[5] Wyot, Adam Wiot or Wyote or[4], Guyott[3], Guyott[2], Captain or Admiral Adam Guyott or[1] Wiot) was born June 04, 1594 in Allington Castle, Maidstone, Kent County, England, and died July 31, 1638 in Allington Castle, Kent County, England. He married (1) Barbara Elizabeth "Eliza" Mitford February 06, 1618/19 in London, England, daughter of Philip Mitford and Unknown Wife. He married (2) Anna "Ann" Lee Cox (Cocke) 1629 in England, daughter of John Cox and Ann Lee.

More About Rev. Haute "Haut" "Hawte" Wiatt:

Fact 1: November 18, 1621, Travels from England to Jamestown on the Georgia or George vessel.

Fact 2: 1621-1625, serves as minister at Jamestown, Va.

Fact 3: 1625-1638, Minister or Vicar of Boxley Parish, Kent County, England.

Fact 4: July 31, 1638, possible date of demise at Boxley Abbey, Kent County, England.

Fact 5: Was the second son of Sir George Wiat of Allington Castle and Boxley Manor, Kent County, England.

Fact 6: October 1621, arrived on vessel called the George at Jamestown.

Fact 7: July 16, 1621, London court Rev. Wiat was *"entertayned as minister"* to accompany his brother.

Fact 8: 1632, was vicar in charge of Boxley Parish, Kent County, England.

Fact 9: Attended Queen's College at Oxford and was a student at Gray's Inn.

Cause of Death: Tuberculosis

Buried Aug. 1st, 1638, Boxley Parish, Kent County, England. Interred in center aisle at Boxley Church.

More About Barbara Elizabeth "Eliza" Mitford:

Fact 1: Barbara Elizabeth Mitford is also name combination listed.

Cause of Death: Had given birth to a third son on Oct. 16, 1626.

In the book titled: *The History of Boxley Parish* on page 168 of the parish register Barbara is recorded as *"Elizabeth"* with the burial recorded as October 31, 1626.

More About Anna "Ann" Lee Cox (Cocke):

Fact 1: 1607, another possible birth year.

Cause of Death: Died in February 1631

Gave birth to two children before her passing.

Children of Rev. Wiatt and Barbara Mitford are:

+ 121   i.   Edward[14] Wiatt, born Abt. 1619 in Kent County, England; died Abt. 1670 in Gloucester County, Va.

+ 122 ii. George Wiatt, born 1622 in "Boxley," Gloucester County, of Middle Plantation [Williamsburg] Va.; died January 15, 1670/71 in Gloucester County, Va.

+ 123 iii. Richard Wiatt? born 1623 in Boxley Manor, Maidenstone, Kent County, England; died in Mobjack, Gloucester County, Va.

+ 124 iv. Maj. Anthony Wiatt? born 1624 in Boxley Manor, Maidenstone, Kent County, England; died 1698 in Middle Plantation, Williamsburg, James City, Va.

125 v. Thomas Wiatt, born October 16, 1626 in October 15, 1626, baptized Boxley Manor, Boxley Parish, Kent County, England; died April 10, 1627 in buried on this day in Kent County, England.

More About Thomas Wiatt:
Fact 1: Was Rev. Haute Wiat's third son -- died in infancy. Remains are buried at Boxley Abbey, Kent County, England on April 10th, 1627.

126 vi. Nicholas Wiatt, born 1620-1673.

More About Nicholas Wiatt:
Fact 1: This person is cited in CLP research.

Children of Rev. Wiatt and Anna (Cocke) are:

+ 127 i. Captain John[14] Wiatt, born 1630 in Boxley Manor, Boxley, Kent County, England; died 1666 in Virginia.

128 ii. Ann or Anne "Anna" Katherine Wiatt, born February 06, 1630/31 in baptized Feb. 19, 1631 at Boxley Manor, Boxley, Kent County, England; died January 01, 1648/49 in Charleston, S.C. She married Charles Nicholas Everleigh or Eveliegh in Virginia.
More About Ann or Anne "Anna" Katherine Wiatt:
Fact 1: Married; moved to Charleston, S.C.
Fact 2: Ann is mentioned with her brother John in in the will of cousin Eleanor Wyatt.
Fact 3: Eleanor lived 1624-1649, only child of Henry Wyatt, brother to Haute.

More About Charles Nicholas Everleigh or Eveliegh:
Fact 1: Everleigh is also known as *"Everly"* and as *"Heverley."*

99. Isabel[13] Wiatt (Sir George "Georgius" Thomas[12], Sir Thomas "The Younger"[11], Sir Thomas "The Elder"[10], Sir Henry[9], Richard Wiat or[8] Wyatt, Geoffrey "Jeoffrey" Wiot

or[7] Wiat, Robert or Richard[6] Wiot, William Wiot or[5] Wyot, Adam Wiot or Wyote or[4], Guyott[3], Guyott[2], Captain or Admiral Adam Guyott or[1] Wiot) was born Abt. 1595 in Allington Castle, Kent, England, and died Abt. 1655. She married Francis Page Abt. 1622 in Virginia.

More About Isabel Wiatt:
Fact 1: Lived at Middle Plantation fortified in 1634; Williamsburg by 1700.
Fact 2: Lived also Bedfont in Harrow
Died at age 73.

More About Francis Page:
Remains buried in Bedford, England.

Children of Isabel Wiatt and Francis Page are:

129	i.	Francis[14] Page, born Abt. 1622.
130	ii.	Matthew Page, born Abt. 1624.
131	iii.	Elizabeth Page, born Abt. 1625 in England.
132	iv.	John Page, born Abt. 1628.
133	v.	Robert Page, born Abt. 1635.
134	vi.	Gibbs Page, born Abt. 1637.
135	vii.	Ince Page, born Abt. 1639.

100. Henry[13] Wiatt (Sir George "Georgius" Thomas[12], Sir Thomas "The Younger"[11], Sir Thomas "The Elder"[10], Sir Henry[9], Richard Wiat or[8] Wyatt, Geoffrey "Jeoffrey" Wiot or[7] Wiat, Robert or Richard[6] Wiot, William Wiot or[5] Wyot, Adam Wiot or Wyote or[4], Guyott[3], Guyott[2], Captain or Admiral Adam Guyott or[1] Wiot) was born November 07, 1596 in Kerstening, Berks, Kent County, England, and died November 10, 1624 in buried January 1, 1624 Boxley, Kent County, England. He married Catherine Finch December 08, 1618 in Saint Andrews Church,

More About Henry Wiatt:
Fact 1: Christened November 7, 1596, Otham, Kent County, England

Child of Henry Wiatt and Catherine Finch is:

136	i.	Eleanor[14] Wiatt, born 1624; died 1649.

More About Eleanor Wiatt:
Fact 1: Only child.

102. Miriam[13] Wiatt (Richard[12], William[11], John Wiatt of[10] Flansham, Thomas Wiatt of[9] Kent, Richard Wiat or[8] Wyatt, Geoffrey "Jeoffrey" Wiot or[7] Wiat, Robert or Richard[6] Wiot, William Wiot or[5] Wyot, Adam Wiot or Wyote or[4], Guyott[3], Guyott[2], Captain or Admiral Adam Guyott or[1] Wiot). She married Hugh Penfold.

Child of Miriam Wiatt and Hugh Penfold is:
137   i.   Hugh[14] Penfold.

More About Hugh Penfold:
Fact 1: November 14, 1839, assumed the Wyatt name and arms by Royal license.

Generation No. 14

115.   William[14] Wyatt? (Thomas[13] Wiatt, Sir George "Georgius" Thomas[12], Sir Thomas "The Younger"[11], Sir Thomas "The Elder"[10], Sir Henry[9], Richard Wiat or[8] Wyatt, Geoffrey "Jeoffrey" Wiot or[7] Wiat, Robert or Richard[6] Wiot, William Wiot or[5] Wyot, Adam Wiot or Wyote or[4], Guyott[3], Guyott[2], Captain or Admiral Adam Guyott or[1] Wiot).

Child of William Wyatt? is:
+ 138   i.   Thomas[15] Wyatt?

116.   Edwin Wyatt[14] (Wiatt) (Sir Francis[13] Wyatt, Sir George "Georgius" Thomas[12] Wiatt, Knt., Sir Thomas "The Younger"[11], Sir Thomas "The Elder"[10], Sir Henry[9], Richard Wiat or[8] Wyatt, Geoffrey "Jeoffrey" Wiot or[7] Wiat, Robert or Richard[6] Wiot, William Wiot or[5] Wyot, Adam Wiot or Wyote or[4], Guyott[3], Guyott[2], Captain or Admiral Adam Guyott or[1] Wiot). He married Frances Crispe of Quex, daughter of Thomas Crispe of Quex.

Children of Edwin (Wiatt) and Frances Quex are:
139   i.   Thomas[15] (Wiatt).
140   ii.   Edwin (Wiatt).
141   iii. Margareta (Wiatt).
142   iv.   Frances (Wiatt).
143   v.   Richard (Wiatt).

120.   Maj. William[14] (Wiatt?) (Sir Francis[13] Wyatt, Sir George "Georgius" Thomas[12] Wiatt, Knt., Sir Thomas "The Younger"[11], Sir Thomas "The Elder"[10], Sir Henry[9], Richard Wiat or[8] Wyatt, Geoffrey "Jeoffrey" Wiot or[7] Wiat, Robert or Richard[6] Wiot, William Wiot or[5] Wyot, Adam Wiot or Wyote or[4], Guyott[3], Guyott[2], Captain or Admiral Adam Guyott or[1] Wiot) was born July 22, 1621 in Boxley, Maidenstone, England, and died in St. Peter's Parish, New Kent County, Va. He married Anna.

More About Maj. William (Wiatt?):
Fact 1: April 27, 1653, William Wyatt, patented 400 acres in Gloucester County, Va.
Fact 2: 1655, William Wyatt witness to a deed to Mr. Wyat from the "Chiscoyake indians"
May 20, 1664, Maj. William Wyatt patented 1,900 acres in New Kent County, Va.
Fact 3: May 20, 1664, William Wyatt patented 300 acres in New Kent County, Va.
Fact 4: June 06, 1665, William Wyatt patented 300 acres in New Kent County, Va.
Fact 6: 1671, New Kent County, Va. Maj. and High sheriff [York records].

Children of Maj. (Wiatt?) and Anna are:

144   i.   Anna[15] (Wiatt?), born in Saint Peter's Parish, New Kent County, Va.

145   ii.   William (Wiatt, Jr.?), born in New Kent County, Va.

More About William (Wiatt, Jr.?):
Fact 1: June 20, 1670, William Wyatt, Jr. patented 500 acres of land in New Kent County, Va.

121. Edward[14] Wiatt (Rev. Haute "Haut" "Hawte"[13], Sir George "Georgius" Thomas[12], Sir Thomas "The Younger"[11], Sir Thomas "The Elder"[10], Sir Henry[9], Richard Wiat or[8] Wyatt, Geoffrey "Jeoffrey" Wiot or[7] Wiat, Robert or Richard[6] Wiot, William Wiot or[5] Wyot, Adam Wiot or Wyote or[4], Guyott[3], Guyott[2], Captain or Admiral Adam Guyott or[1] Wiot) was born Abt. 1619 in Kent County, England, and died Abt. 1670 in Gloucester County, Va. He married Jane Conquest 1644, daughter of Lewis Conquest and Dorothy Hewett.

More About Edward Wiatt:
Fact 1: April 19, 1662, had patents for land 370 acres in Boxley, Kingston, Gloucester County, Va.
Fact 2: 1655, witnessed to a deed to *"Mr. Edward Wyat from the "Chiscoyake indians."*
Fact 3: Was a cousin to Edwin Wiat who set up the monument at Boxley Abbey Church.
Fact 4: 1619, possible birth year.
Fact 5: 1690, possible date of demise.

Children of Edward Wiatt and Jane Conquest are:

+   146   i.   Conquest[15] Wiatt, born 1645 in Boxley Plantation, Gloucester County, Va.; died 1720 in Upton Plantation, Va.

147   ii.   Francis Wyatt: Remains are buried at Ware Episcopal Church, Gloucester County, Va.

More About Francis Wyatt:
Died at age 2. Remains are buried at Ware Episcopal Church, Gloucester County, Va.

148   iii.   Haute Wyatt, died in Remains are buried at Ware Episcopal Church, Gloucester County, Va.

More About Haute Wyatt:
Died at age 5. Remains are buried at Ware Episcopal Church, Gloucester County, Va.

149   iv.   Edward Wyatt, died in Remains are buried at Ware Episcopal Church, Gloucester County, Va.

More About Edward Wyatt:
Died at age 12. Remains are buried at Ware Episcopal Church, Gloucester County, Va.

122. George[14] Wiatt (Rev. Haute "Haut" "Hawte"[13], Sir George "Georgius" Thomas[12], Sir Thomas "The Younger"[11], Sir Thomas "The Elder"[10], Sir Henry[9], Richard Wiat or[8] Wyatt, Geoffrey "Jeoffrey" Wiot or[7] Wiat, Robert or Richard[6] Wiot, William Wiot or[5] Wyot, Adam Wiot or Wyote or[4], Guyott[3], Guyott[2], Captain or Admiral Adam Guyott or[1] Wiot) was born 1622 in "Boxley," Gloucester County, of Middle Plantation [Williamsburg] Va., and died January 15, 1670/71 in Gloucester County, Va. He married Susannah "Susanna" R. Baynham.

More About George Wiatt:
Fact 1: 1642, patented lands at Williamsburg, Va.
Fact 2: 1677, possible demise year.
Fact 3: December 12, 1619, baptized-- birthday not known, but some claim it as named for Haute's father.
Fact 4: 1645, lived at Middle Plantation.
More About Susannah *"Susanna" R. Baynham."*

Children of George Wiatt and Susannah Baynham are:

	150	i.	Alice[15] Wiatt.
	151	ii.	Susannah Wiatt.
+	152	iii.	Henry Wiatt, born July 11, 1647 in Middle Plantation, [Fort] -- Williamsburg, 1698 James City, Va.; died 1705 in Churchill, Gloucester County, Va.
+	153	iv.	Richard Wiatt, born 1650 in Middle Plantation, [Fort] -- Williamsburg, 1698 James City, Va.; died Abt. 1704 in Gloucester County, Va.
	154	v.	Peyton Wiatt, born 1652 in Middle Plantation, [Fort] -- Williamsburg, 1698 James City, Va.

123. Richard[14] Wiatt? (Rev. Haute "Haut" "Hawte"[13] Wiatt, Sir George "Georgius" Thomas[12], Sir Thomas "The Younger"[11], Sir Thomas "The Elder"[10], Sir Henry[9], Richard Wiat or[8] Wyatt, Geoffrey "Jeoffrey" Wiot or[7] Wiat, Robert or Richard[6] Wiot, William Wiot or[5] Wyot, Adam Wiot or Wyote or[4], Guyott[3], Guyott[2], Captain or Admiral Adam Guyott or[1] Wiot) was born 1623 in Boxley Manor, Maidenstone, Kent County, England, and died in Mobjack, Gloucester County, Va.

More About Richard Wiatt?
Fact 1: August 20, 1645, Richard Wyatt patented 500 acres of land in Mobjack Bay, Gloucester County, Va.
Fact 2: Richard Wyatt orders by York Court to pay a hogshead of tobacco to Dr. Thomas Eton of London, *"surgeon."*

Child of Richard Wiatt? is:

155   i.   Thomas[15] Wyatt? born in Boxley, Gloucester County, Va.; died in Mobjack, Gloucester County, Va.

More About Thomas Wyatt?
Fact 1: May 09, 1666, Thomas Wyatt patented 500 acres of land in Mobjack Bay, Gloucester County, Va.

124. Maj. Anthony[14] Wiatt? (Rev. Haute "Haut" "Hawte"[13] Wiatt, Sir George "Georgius" Thomas[12], Sir Thomas "The Younger"[11], Sir Thomas "The Elder"[10], Sir Henry[9], Richard Wiat or[8] Wyatt, Geoffrey "Jeoffrey" Wiot or[7] Wiat, Robert or Richard[6] Wiot, William Wiot or[5] Wyot, Adam Wiot or Wyote or[4], Guyott[3], Guyott[2], Captain or Admiral Adam Guyott or[1] Wiot) was born 1624 in Boxley Manor, Maidenstone, Kent County, England, and died 1698 in Middle Plantation, Williamsburg, James City, Va.

More About Maj. Anthony Wiatt?
Fact 1: Anthony Wyatt, a burgess from Charles City in 1645, 1655 and 1656
Fact 2: June 28, 1664, Anthony Wyatt patented 282 acres of land in New Kent County, Va.
Fact 3: July 24, 1669, Anthony Wyatt patented 398 acres of land in Middleton Plantation [1698 Williamsburg, Charles City, Va.]

Children of Maj. Anthony Wiatt? are:
156   i.   Nicholas[15] Wyatt? born in Middle Plantation, Williamsburg, Va.

More About Nicholas Wyatt?
Fact 1: Fought in Bacon's Rebellion.
Fact 2: 1686, Nicholas Wyatt patented land "Chaplin's Choice" Plantation.

157   ii.   Christopher Wyatt? born 1643.

127. Captain John[14] Wiatt (Rev. Haute "Haut" "Hawte"[13], Sir George "Georgius" Thomas[12], Sir Thomas "The Younger"[11], Sir Thomas "The Elder"[10], Sir Henry[9], Richard Wiat or[8] Wyatt, Geoffrey "Jeoffrey" Wiot or[7] Wiat, Robert or Richard[6] Wiot, William Wiot or[5] Wyot, Adam Wiot or Wyote or[4], Guyott[3], Guyott[2], Captain or Admiral Adam Guyott or[1] Wiot) was born 1630 in Boxley Manor, Boxley, Kent County, England, and died 1666 in Virginia. He married (1) Mary [Katharine?] Cocke. He married (2) Jane Osborne 1662 in Carlina, Va., daughter of Thomas Osborne and Anne Bert.

More About Captain John Wiatt:
Fact 1: 1670, possible year of demise.
Fact 2: 1652, came to Virginia by this year.

Fact 3: 1652, went to Virginia as he was claimed as headright by Col. Thomas Pettus for land.

Fact 4: The land was patented in Westmoreland County, Va.

Child of Captain Wiatt and Mary Cocke is:

+ 158   i.   William[15] Wiatt, born April 26, 1656 in Perquimans, N.C.; died January 14, 1686/87 in Perquimans County, N.C.

Child of Captain Wiatt and Jane Osborne is:

+ 159   i.   John[15] Wiatt, born 1663 in Gloucester County, Va.; died 1684.

Generation No. 15

138. Thomas[15] Wyatt? (William[14], Thomas[13] Wiatt, Sir George "Georgius" Thomas[12], Sir Thomas "The Younger"[11], Sir Thomas "The Elder"[10], Sir Henry[9], Richard Wiat or[8] Wyatt, Geoffrey "Jeoffrey" Wiot or[7] Wiat, Robert or Richard[6] Wiot, William Wiot or[5] Wyot, Adam Wiot or Wyote or[4], Guyott[3], Guyott[2], Captain or Admiral Adam Guyott or[1] Wiot).

Child of Thomas Wyatt? is:

+ 160   i.   Thomas[16] Wyatt?

146. Conquest[15] Wiatt (Edward[14], Rev. Haute "Haut" "Hawte"[13], Sir George "Georgius" Thomas[12], Sir Thomas "The Younger"[11], Sir Thomas "The Elder"[10], Sir Henry[9], Richard Wiat or[8] Wyatt, Geoffrey "Jeoffrey" Wiot or[7] Wiat, Robert or Richard[6] Wiot, William Wiot or[5] Wyot, Adam Wiot or Wyote or[4], Guyott[3], Guyott[2], Captain or Admiral Adam Guyott or[1] Wiot) was born 1645 in Boxley Plantation, Gloucester County, Va., and died 1720 in Upton Plantation, Va. He married Sallie Pate, daughter of Col. Pate and X.

More About Conquest Wiatt:

Fact 1: Lived at Upton, Gloucester County, Va.

Remains are buried at Petsworth Church, Gloucester County, Va.

Children of Conquest Wiatt and Sallie Pate are:

+ 161   i.   Francis[16] Wiatt, born 1670 in Gloucester, Va.? died 1730 in Gloucester County, Va.

+ 162   ii.   Conquest Wiatt, born 1672; died Aft. February 1744/45.

+ 163   iii.   James Wiatt, born 1674; died January 27, 1744/45.

+ 164   iv.   Captain Edward Wiatt, born 1677 in Prince William County, Va. or Boxley, Gloucester County, Va.; died January 23, 1744/45.

+ 165   v.   Sarah Wiatt, born 1679 in Virginia; died in Virginia.

+ 166   vi.   Captain John W. Wiatt, born 1683 in Boxley, Gloucester County, Va.; died December 10, 1765 in Boxley, Gloucester County, Va.

+ 167   vii.   Mary Wiatt, born Abt. 1680.

152. Henry[15] Wiatt (George[14], Rev. Haute "Haut" "Hawte"[13], Sir George "Georgius" Thomas[12], Sir Thomas "The Younger"[11], Sir Thomas "The Elder"[10], Sir Henry[9], Richard Wiat or[8] Wyatt, Geoffrey "Jeoffrey" Wiot or[7] Wiat, Robert or Richard[6] Wiot, William Wiot or[5] Wyot, Adam Wiot or Wyote or[4], Guyott[3], Guyott[2], Captain or Admiral Adam Guyott or[1] Wiot) was born July 11, 1647 in Middle Plantation, [Fort] -- Williamsburg, 1698 James City, Va., and died 1705 in Churchill, Gloucester County, Va. He married Alice Bradbridge.

More About Henry Wiatt:
Fact 1: 1671, Henry Wyatt of Gloucester, sold land at Middle Plantation [1698 – Williamsburg]
Fact 2: James City, Va. to John Page [York Records]
Fact 3: 1686, Vestryman of Saint Peter's Parish Church, Saint Peter's Parish, New Kent County.
Fact 4: 1686, He sold land mentioned in the deed as having belonged to his father: *"George Wyatt of Middleton Plantation."*
Fact 5: Served as a church warden, processional, and vestryman of Saint Peter's Parish, New Kent County, Va.
Fact 6: He lived with his wife in New Kent County, Va.

Children of Henry Wiatt and Alice Bradbridge are:
168   i.   Henry[16] Wyatt, born in Saint Peter's Parish, New Kent County, Va.; died in Prince George County, Va.

More About Henry Wyatt:
Fact 1: 1728, Henry Wyatt of Prince George County, Va. released a mill in New Kent County, Va.

169   ii.   Richard Wyatt, born in Saint Peter's Parish, New Kent County, Va.

More About Richard Wyatt:
Fact 1: 1705, Saint Peter's Parish, New Kent County, Va.
Fact 2: Was legatee of his father Henry Wiatt, deceased.

153. Richard[15] Wiatt (George[14], Rev. Haute "Haut" "Hawte"[13], Sir George "Georgius" Thomas[12], Sir Thomas "The Younger"[11], Sir Thomas "The Elder"[10], Sir Henry[9], Richard Wiat or[8] Wyatt, Geoffrey "Jeoffrey" Wiot or[7] Wiat, Robert or Richard[6] Wiot, William Wiot or[5] Wyot, Adam Wiot or Wyote or[4], Guyott[3], Guyott[2], Captain or Admiral Adam Guyott or[1] Wiot) was born 1650 in Middle Plantation, [Fort] -- Williamsburg, 1698 James City, Va., and died Abt. 1704 in Gloucester County, Va. He married (1) Catherine Long. He married (2) Sarah "Sallie" Peyton 1685 in Saint Peter's Church, Gloucester County, Va.

Children of Richard Wiatt and Sarah Peyton are:

+ 170   i.   Frances[16] Wiatt, born 1680 in Gloucester County, Va.

+ 171   ii.   Henry Wiatt, born Abt. 1685 in Gloucester County, Va. Saint Peter's Parish, New Kent County, Va.; died 1743 in Prince George, Va.

+ 172   iii.   Richard Wiatt, born Abt. 1686.

   173   iv.   Peyton Wiatt, born 1688 in Saint Peter's Parish, New Kent County, Va.

   174   v.   Thomas Wiatt, born 1700.

   175   vi.   Richard Wiatt, born 1702.

   176   vii.   Suzannah Wiatt, born 1704.

158. William[15] Wiatt (Captain John[14], Rev. Haute "Haut" "Hawte"[13], Sir George "Georgius" Thomas[12], Sir Thomas "The Younger"[11], Sir Thomas "The Elder"[10], Sir Henry[9], Richard Wiat or[8] Wyatt, Geoffrey "Jeoffrey" Wiot or[7] Wiat, Robert or Richard[6] Wiot, William Wiot or[5] Wyot, Adam Wiot or Wyote or[4], Guyott[3], Guyott[2], Captain or Admiral Adam Guyott or[1] Wiot) was born April 26, 1656 in Perquimans, N.C., and died January 14, 1686/87 in Perquimans County, N.C. He married Rebecca Kent [Evans] 1675 in Perquimans County, N.C., daughter of Richard Evans and Elizabeth Perry.

Children of William Wiatt and Rebecca [Evans] are:

+ 177   i.   John[16] Wyatt, born April 26, 1679 in Perquimans County, N.C.; died December 26, 1739 in Perquimans County, N.C.

   178   ii.   Vinson Wyatt.

   179   iii.   Elizabeth Wyatt.

   180   iv.   Sarah Wyatt.

   181   v.   Thomas Wyatt.

   182   vi.   Samuel Wyatt.

159. John[15] Wiatt (Captain John[14], Rev. Haute "Haut" "Hawte"[13], Sir George "Georgius" Thomas[12], Sir Thomas "The Younger"[11], Sir Thomas "The Elder"[10], Sir Henry[9], Richard Wiat or[8] Wyatt, Geoffrey "Jeoffrey" Wiot or[7] Wiat, Robert or Richard[6] Wiot, William Wiot or[5] Wyot, Adam Wiot or Wyote or[4], Guyott[3], Guyott[2], Captain or Admiral Adam Guyott or[1] Wiot) was born 1663 in Gloucester County, Va., and died 1684. He married Anne Jones 1682 in Rappahannock, Va., daughter of Rice Jones.

Child of John Wiatt and Anne Jones is:

+ 183   i.   John[16] Wyatt, born 1684; died 1750.

Generation No. 16

160. Thomas[16] Wyatt? (Thomas[15], William[14], Thomas[13] Wiatt, Sir George "Georgius" Thomas[12], Sir Thomas "The Younger"[11], Sir Thomas "The Elder"[10], Sir Henry[9], Richard Wiat or[8] Wyatt, Geoffrey "Jeoffrey" Wiot or[7] Wiat, Robert or Richard[6] Wiot, William Wiot

or[5] Wyot, Adam Wiot or Wyote or[4], Guyott[3], Guyott[2], Captain or Admiral Adam Guyott or[1] Wiot).

   Child of Thomas Wyatt? is:
+ 184   i.   William[17] Wyatt?

161. Francis[16] Wiatt (Conquest[15], Edward[14], Rev. Haute "Haut" "Hawte"[13], Sir George "Georgius" Thomas[12], Sir Thomas "The Younger"[11], Sir Thomas "The Elder"[10], Sir Henry[9], Richard Wiat or[8] Wyatt, Geoffrey "Jeoffrey" Wiot or[7] Wiat, Robert or Richard[6] Wiot, William Wiot or[5] Wyot, Adam Wiot or Wyote or[4], Guyott[3], Guyott[2], Captain or Admiral Adam Guyott or[1] Wiot) was born 1670 in Gloucester, Va.? and died 1730 in Gloucester County, Va. He married Ann or Elizabeth Kennon.

More About Francis Wiatt:
Fact 1: Purchased 3,000 acres of land in Spotsylvania County, Va.
Fact 2: 1714-1730, was a vestryman at Petsworth Parish.
Fact 3: May 19, 1732, died before this day.

   Children of Francis Wiatt and Ann Kennon are:
185   i.   Edward[17] Wyatt.
186   ii.   John Wyatt, died Abt. 1739.

    More About John Wyatt:
    Drowns at sea.

187   iii.   Francis Wyatt, born January 1716/17; died 1761. He married Lucy Rowe 1742.

    More About Francis Wyatt:
    Fact 1: 1751, possible date of demise.

188   iv.   Thomas Wyatt, born Abt. 1720; died 1781. He married Sukey Edmondson 1747.

    More About Thomas Wyatt:
    Fact 1: Justice of the Peace.
    Fact 2: Planter.
    Fact 3: Resided in Essex and Spotsylvania counties, Va.

189   v.   William Wyatt, born 1720.

    More About William Wyatt:
    Fact 1: 1739, Became a merchant and sea Captain -- moved to Liverpool, England.

Fact 2: 1734, Worked also as "writer and clerk" for lawyer: Benjamin Needler, Williamsburg, Va.

Fact 3: *"William the Mariner."*

190   vi.   Ann Wyatt, born 1725. She married John Thurston.

More About Ann Wyatt:
Fact 1: Claimed 667 acres of land left to her by Francis Wiatt in 1745.

191   vii.   Elizabeth Wyatt, born 1731.

192   viii.   Peter Wyatt, born 1722. He married X Bef. 1756.

162. Conquest[16] Wiatt (Conquest[15], Edward[14], Rev. Haute "Haut" "Hawte"[13], Sir George "Georgius" Thomas[12], Sir Thomas "The Younger"[11], Sir Thomas "The Elder"[10], Sir Henry[9], Richard Wiat or[8] Wyatt, Geoffrey "Jeoffrey" Wiot or[7] Wiat, Robert or Richard[6] Wiot, William Wiot or[5] Wyot, Adam Wiot or Wyote or[4], Guyott[3], Guyott[2], Captain or Admiral Adam Guyott or[1] Wiot) was born 1672, and died Aft. February 1744/45. He married (1) Nancy Sayre or Sawyer or Sawer. He married (2) Martha "Millie" Gaines or Gains.

Children of Conquest Wiatt and Nancy Sawer are:
193   i.   John[17] Wyatt, born 1704.
194   ii.   Elizabeth Wyatt, born 1711. She married Thomas T. Royston.
195   iii.   Conquest Wyatt, born 1735-1815.

Children of Conquest Wiatt and Martha Gains are:
+   196   i.   John Edward17 Wiatt, Jr., born May 15, 1732 in Gloucester County, Va.; died January 05, 1805 in Virginia.
197   ii.   Conquest Wiatt, born 1735.
198   iii.   Unknown Daughter Wiatt. She married X 1756.

163. James[16] Wiatt (Conquest[15], Edward[14], Rev. Haute "Haut" "Hawte"[13], Sir George "Georgius" Thomas[12], Sir Thomas "The Younger"[11], Sir Thomas "The Elder"[10], Sir Henry[9], Richard Wiat or[8] Wyatt, Geoffrey "Jeoffrey" Wiot or[7] Wiat, Robert or Richard[6] Wiot, William Wiot or[5] Wyot, Adam Wiot or Wyote or[4], Guyott[3], Guyott[2], Captain or Admiral Adam Guyott or[1] Wiot) was born 1674, and died January 27, 1744/45. He married (1) Grace Newton, daughter of John Newton and Mary Allerton. He married (2) Margaret.

More About James Wiatt:
Fact 1: 1728, moved to Prince William County, Va.
Fact 2: Was sub-sheriff in the county.

Children of James Wiatt and Grace Newton are:

199	i.	Daniel[17] Wyatt, born 1703.
200	ii.	William Wyatt, born 1705.
201	iii.	James Wyatt, born 1707 in Gloucester County, Va.
202	iv.	Sallie Wyatt, born 1710.
203	v.	John Wyatt, born 1712.
204	vi.	Frances Wyatt, born 1715.
205	vii.	Elizabeth Wyatt, born 1718.
206	viii.	Conquest Wyatt, born 1720.

Children of James Wiatt and Margaret are:

| 207 | i. | William[17] Wiatt, born Bef. 1735. |
| 208 | ii. | Ann Wiatt. |

164. Captain Edward[16] Wiatt (Conquest[15], Edward[14], Rev. Haute "Haut" "Hawte"[13], Sir George "Georgius" Thomas[12], Sir Thomas "The Younger"[11], Sir Thomas "The Elder"[10], Sir Henry[9], Richard Wiat or[8] Wyatt, Geoffrey "Jeoffrey" Wiot or[7] Wiat, Robert or Richard[6] Wiot, William Wiot or[5] Wyot, Adam Wiot or Wyote or[4], Guyott[3], Guyott[2], Captain or Admiral Adam Guyott or[1] Wiot) was born 1677 in Prince William County, Va. or Boxley, Gloucester County, Va., and died January 23, 1744/45. He married (1) Margaret Cook Buchannan? He married (2) Frances Newton Abt. 1705, daughter of John Newton and Mary Allerton.

More About Captain Edward Wiatt:

Fact 1: Lived at Boxley, Gloucester County, Va.

Fact 2: Purchased lands in Dettingen Parish, Prince William County, Va.

Fact 3: 1750, possible date of demise.

Fact 4: Owned land in Prince William County, Va.

Fact 5: Captain in the Colonial Militia.

Fact 6: 1739-1744, Vestryman at Petsworth Parish

Children of Captain Wiatt and Frances Newton are:

| + | 209 | i. | William Edward17 Wiatt, Sr., born 1707 in Gloucester County, Va.; died 1774 in Prince William County, Va. |
| | 210 | ii. | John Wiatt, born 1709; died 1768 in Gloucester County, Va. |

More About John Wiatt:

Fact 1: Remained in Gloucester County, Va.

211	iii.	Elizabeth Wiatt, born 1712. She married John Cocke or Coke.
212	iv.	Anne Wiatt, born May 05, 1719. She married Thomas Shirley.
213	v.	Conquest Wiatt, born 1717. He married Agnes Grigsby.

More About Conquest Wiatt:
Fact 1: Moved to Stafford County, Va.

214	vi.	Edward Wiatt, Jr.
215	vii.	Sarah Wiatt. She married Richard Cate.

165.   Sarah[16] Wiatt (Conquest[15], Edward[14], Rev. Haute "Haut" "Hawte"[13], Sir George "Georgius" Thomas[12], Sir Thomas "The Younger"[11], Sir Thomas "The Elder"[10], Sir Henry[9], Richard Wiat or[8] Wyatt, Geoffrey "Jeoffrey" Wiot or[7] Wiat, Robert or Richard[6] Wiot, William Wiot or[5] Wyot, Adam Wiot or Wyote or[4], Guyott[3], Guyott[2], Captain or Admiral Adam Guyott or[1] Wiot) was born 1679 in Virginia, and died in Virginia. She married Richard Cate.

Child of Sarah Wiatt and Richard Cate is:
216	i.	Ann[17] Cate, died 1822.

166.   Captain John W.[16] Wiatt (Conquest[15], Edward[14], Rev. Haute "Haut" "Hawte"[13], Sir George "Georgius" Thomas[12], Sir Thomas "The Younger"[11], Sir Thomas "The Elder"[10], Sir Henry[9], Richard Wiat or[8] Wyatt, Geoffrey "Jeoffrey" Wiot or[7] Wiat, Robert or Richard[6] Wiot, William Wiot or[5] Wyot, Adam Wiot or Wyote or[4], Guyott[3], Guyott[2], Captain or Admiral Adam Guyott or[1] Wiot) was born 1683 in Boxley, Gloucester County, Va., and died December 10, 1765 in Boxley, Gloucester County, Va. He married Elizabeth Buckner Abt. 1720.

More About Captain John W. Wiatt:
Fact 1: Vestryman at Petsworth Parish, Va.
Fact 2: Captain of Militia.

Children of Captain Wiatt and Elizabeth Buckner are:
	217	i.	John[17] Wiatt, died 1775 in Liverpool, England. He married Martha.
+	218	ii.	James Wyatt.
	219	iii.	Conquest Wiatt, born 1724.
	220	iv.	Francis Wiatt, born 1727.
	221	v.	Elizabeth Wiatt, born September 15, 1730; died February 23, 1803. She married Cornelius Collier 1753.

More About Cornelius Collier:
Fact 1: He owned large estates in Virginia, South Carolina, Georgia and Alabama.

222	vi.	Sally Wyatt, born 1732. She married Samuel Blackwell.

167. Mary[16] Wiatt (Conquest[15], Edward[14], Rev. Haute "Haut" "Hawte"[13], Sir George "Georgius" Thomas[12], Sir Thomas "The Younger"[11], Sir Thomas "The Elder"[10], Sir Henry[9], Richard Wiat or[8] Wyatt, Geoffrey "Jeoffrey" Wiot or[7] Wiat, Robert or Richard[6] Wiot, William Wiot

or[5] Wyot, Adam Wiot or Wyote or[4], Guyott[3], Guyott[2], Captain or Admiral Adam Guyott or[1] Wiot) was born Abt. 1680. She married John Royston.

       Children of Mary Wiatt and John Royston are:

223	i.	John[17] Royston, born 1702-1748.	
224	ii.	Thomas T. Royston, born 1705 in Gloucester County, Va.; died Bef. September 12, 1783 in Caroline County, Va. He married (1) Ann Garrett. He married (2) Elizabeth Wiatt.	
225	iii.	Conquest Royston, born Abt. 1720; died Aft. 1793.	

              More About Conquest Royston:
              Fact 1: Lived in Gloucester County, Va.

226	iv.	Richard Wiatt Royston, born Abt. 1720 in Gloucester County, Va.; died Bef. November 20, 1790 in Caroline County, Va. He married Anne Kemp Abt. 1750.

170. Frances[16] Wiatt (Richard[15], George[14], Rev. Haute "Haut" "Hawte"[13], Sir George "Georgius" Thomas[12], Sir Thomas "The Younger"[11], Sir Thomas "The Elder"[10], Sir Henry[9], Richard Wiat or[8] Wyatt, Geoffrey "Jeoffrey" Wiot or[7] Wiat, Robert or Richard[6] Wiot, William Wiot or[5] Wyot, Adam Wiot or Wyote or[4], Guyott[3], Guyott[2], Captain or Admiral Adam Guyott or[1] Wiot) was born 1680 in Gloucester County, Va. She married Benard Sykes.

       Child of Frances Wiatt and Benard Sykes is:

+	227	i.	rebecca[17] Sykes, born 1715.

171. Henry[16] Wiatt (Richard[15], George[14], Rev. Haute "Haut" "Hawte"[13], Sir George "Georgius" Thomas[12], Sir Thomas "The Younger"[11], Sir Thomas "The Elder"[10], Sir Henry[9], Richard Wiat or[8] Wyatt, Geoffrey "Jeoffrey" Wiot or[7] Wiat, Robert or Richard[6] Wiot, William Wiot or[5] Wyot, Adam Wiot or Wyote or[4], Guyott[3], Guyott[2], Captain or Admiral Adam Guyott or[1] Wiot) was born Abt. 1685 in Gloucester County, Va. Saint Peter's Parish, New Kent County, Va., and died 1743 in Prince George, Va. He married Elizabeth Dandridge 1725 in Prince George County, Va., daughter of John Dandridge and Ann Dugale.

More About Henry Wiatt:
Fact 1: 1690, another possible birth date.
Fact 2: 1762, date of demise cited by CLP Research on Dandridges of Virginia.

More About Elizabeth Dandridge:
Fact 1: 1703, possible birth year.

       Children of Henry Wiatt and Elizabeth Dandridge are:

228	i.	Mary17 Wiatt? born September 20, 1726 in Saint Peter's Parish, New Kent County, Virginia; died May 10, 1784 in Warren

			County or Beute County, North Carolina. She married John Daniel Hawkins 1743 in Grandville, N.C.
+	229	ii.	Colonel Joseph Wyatt, born Abt. 1728 in associated with Saint Peter's Parish, New Kent County, Virginia; died Abt. 1767 in New Kent County, Va.
	230	iii.	Elizabeth Wiatt, born September 15, 1730 in Churchill, Gloucester County, Va.; died February 23, 1803.
	231	iv.	Francis Wiatt, born March 29, 1731 in Churchill, Gloucester County, N.C.; died 1804 in Gloucester County, Va. Saint Peter's Parish, New Kent County, Va.

> More About Francis Wiatt:
> Fact 1: Place of birth said to have been Prince George, Virginia.

	232	v.	Abby Wiatt*? born 1732; died in Morgan District, Wilkes County, N.C.
	233	vi.	Sarah "Sally" Wiatt, born 1735 in Churchill, Gloucester County, Va.
+	234	vii.	William Wiatt, born April 09, 1738 in Churchill, Gloucester County,Va; died Abt. 1802 in Lick Creek, Rowan County [1822-Davidson County], N.C.
	235	viii.	Nathan Wiatt, born 1740 in Churchill, Gloucester County, Va.; died in Lick Creek, Rowan County [1822-Davidson County], N.C.
+	236	ix.	John Wiatt, born May 06, 1743 in Virginia or Maryland? died November 11, 1815 in Lick Creek Baptist Church, Denton, Davidson County, N.C.

172. Richard[16] Wiatt (Richard[15], George[14], Rev. Haute "Haut" "Hawte"[13], Sir George "Georgius" Thomas[12], Sir Thomas "The Younger"[11], Sir Thomas "The Elder"[10], Sir Henry[9], Richard Wiat or[8] Wyatt, Geoffrey "Jeoffrey" Wiot or[7] Wiat, Robert or Richard[6] Wiot, William Wiot or[5] Wyot, Adam Wiot or Wyote or[4], Guyott[3], Guyott[2], Captain or Admiral Adam Guyott or[1] Wiot) was born Abt. 1686. He married Sarah Overstreet.

Child of Richard Wiatt and Sarah Overstreet is:
+ 237   i.   Richard[17] Wyatt, born 1725 in King and Queen County, Va.

177. John[16] Wyatt (William[15] Wiatt, Captain John[14], Rev. Haute "Haut" "Hawte"[13], Sir George "Georgius" Thomas[12], Sir Thomas "The Younger"[11], Sir Thomas "The Elder"[10], Sir Henry[9], Richard Wiat or[8] Wyatt, Geoffrey "Jeoffrey" Wiot or[7] Wiat, Robert or Richard[6] Wiot, William Wiot or[5] Wyot, Adam Wiot or Wyote or[4], Guyott[3], Guyott[2], Captain or Admiral Adam Guyott or[1] Wiot) was born April 26, 1679 in Perquimans County, N.C., and died December 26, 1739 in Perquimans County, N.C. He married Rachel Callaway November 17, 1696 in Albemarle Precinct, Perquimans, N.C.

Children of John Wyatt and Rachel Callaway are:

238	i.	John[17] Wyatt.
239	ii.	Sarah Wyatt.
240	iii.	Elizabeth Wyatt.

183. John[16] Wyatt (John[15] Wiatt, Captain John[14], Rev. Haute "Haut" "Hawte"[13], Sir George "Georgius" Thomas[12], Sir Thomas "The Younger"[11], Sir Thomas "The Elder"[10], Sir Henry[9], Richard Wiat or[8] Wyatt, Geoffrey "Jeoffrey" Wiot or[7] Wiat, Robert or Richard[6] Wiot, William Wiot or[5] Wyot, Adam Wiot or Wyote or[4], Guyott[3], Guyott[2], Captain or Admiral Adam Guyott or[1] Wiot) was born 1684, and died 1750. He married Jennie Pamplin 1711 in England.

Children of John Wyatt and Jennie Pamplin are:

+	241	i.	Anne[17] Wyatt, born 1717.
	242	ii.	John Wyatt.
	243	iii.	William Wyatt.
	244	iv.	Richard Wyatt.
	245	v.	Mary Wyatt.
	246	vi.	Thomas Wyatt.
	247	vii.	Henry Wyatt.
	248	viii.	Lucy Wyatt.

Generation No. 17

184. William[17] Wyatt? (Thomas[16], Thomas[15], William[14], Thomas[13] Wiatt, Sir George "Georgius" Thomas[12], Sir Thomas "The Younger"[11], Sir Thomas "The Elder"[10], Sir Henry[9], Richard Wiat or[8] Wyatt, Geoffrey "Jeoffrey" Wiot or[7] Wiat, Robert or Richard[6] Wiot, William Wiot or[5] Wyot, Adam Wiot or Wyote or[4], Guyott[3], Guyott[2], Captain or Admiral Adam Guyott or[1] Wiot). He married Mary Unknown Wife.

Child of William Wyatt? and Mary Wife is:

+	249	i.	Aaron[18] Wyatt.

196. John Edward[17] Wiatt, Jr. (Conquest[16], Conquest[15], Edward[14], Rev. Haute "Haut" "Hawte"[13], Sir George "Georgius" Thomas[12], Sir Thomas "The Younger"[11], Sir Thomas "The Elder"[10], Sir Henry[9], Richard Wiat or[8] Wyatt, Geoffrey "Jeoffrey" Wiot or[7] Wiat, Robert or Richard[6] Wiot, William Wiot or[5] Wyot, Adam Wiot or Wyote or[4], Guyott[3], Guyott[2], Captain or Admiral Adam Guyott or[1] Wiot) was born May 15, 1732 in Gloucester County, Va., and died January 05, 1805 in Virginia. He married Mary Elizabeth Todd November 13, 1856 in Virginia, daughter of Christopher Todd and Elizabeth Mason.

More About John Edward Wiatt, Jr.:
Fact 1: 1900, listed in the Daughters of the American Revolution [DAR] Patriot Index Centennial Edition Part III, Washington.

Remains are with his wife at Ware Episcopal Church, Gloucester County, Va. -- originally buried at Toddsbury and moved later.

More About Mary Elizabeth Todd:
Remains are with her husband at Ware Episcopal Church, Gloucester County, Va. -- originally buried at Toddsbury and moved later.

Children of John Wiatt and Mary Todd are:

| | 250 | i. | Mary[18] Wiatt, born 1759. |
| + | 251 | ii. | Dr. William Edward Wiatt, born October 17, 1762; died December 26, 1802 in buried at Boxley, Gloucester County, Va. |

209.   William Edward[17] Wiatt, Sr. (Captain Edward[16], Conquest[15], Edward[14], Rev. Haute "Haut" "Hawte"[13], Sir George "Georgius" Thomas[12], Sir Thomas "The Younger"[11], Sir Thomas "The Elder"[10], Sir Henry[9], Richard Wiat or[8] Wyatt, Geoffrey "Jeoffrey" Wiot or[7] Wiat, Robert or Richard[6] Wiot, William Wiot or[5] Wyot, Adam Wiot or Wyote or[4], Guyott[3], Guyott[2], Captain or Admiral Adam Guyott or[1] Wiot) was born 1707 in Gloucester County, Va., and died 1774 in Prince William County, Va. He married (1) Martha Gaines? He married (2) Lettice Nicoll or Nichols Abt. 1730.

More About William Edward Wiatt, Sr.:
Fact 1: 1786, Cited as having died after this year by A.L. Wiatt.

Child of William Wiatt and Martha Gaines? is:

| 252 | i. | Two Children[18] Wyatt. |

More About Two Children Wyatt:
Fact 1: Died young.

Children of William Wiatt and Lettice Nichols are:

	253	i.	Micajah[18] Wyatt.
	254	ii.	Edward Wyatt. He married Unknown Wife.
	255	iii.	Frances Wyatt. She married Thomas Scott.
+	256	iv.	William Wyatt, Jr.
	257	v.	Elizabeth Wyatt.

More About Elizabeth Wyatt:
Fact 1: never married

| 258 | vi. | Conquest Wyatt. He married Jane Redmond? |
| 259 | vii. | Elijah Wyatt. He married (1) Margaret Chilton. He married (2) Wife #2. He married (3) Wife #3. He married (4) Wife #4. |

218. James[17] Wyatt (Captain John W.[16] Wiatt, Conquest[15], Edward[14], Rev. Haute "Haut" "Hawte"[13], Sir George "Georgius" Thomas[12], Sir Thomas "The Younger"[11], Sir Thomas "The Elder"[10], Sir Henry[9], Richard Wiat or[8] Wyatt, Geoffrey "Jeoffrey" Wiot or[7] Wiat, Robert or Richard[6] Wiot, William Wiot or[5] Wyot, Adam Wiot or Wyote or[4], Guyott[3], Guyott[2], Captain or Admiral Adam Guyott or[1] Wiot).

> Child of James Wyatt is:
> 260   i.   Edward[18] Wyatt.

227. Rebecca[17] Sykes (Frances[16] Wiatt, Richard[15], George[14], Rev. Haute "Haut" "Hawte"[13], Sir George "Georgius" Thomas[12], Sir Thomas "The Younger"[11], Sir Thomas "The Elder"[10], Sir Henry[9], Richard Wiat or[8] Wyatt, Geoffrey "Jeoffrey" Wiot or[7] Wiat, Robert or Richard[6] Wiot, William Wiot or[5] Wyot, Adam Wiot or Wyote or[4], Guyott[3], Guyott[2], Captain or Admiral Adam Guyott or[1] Wiot) was born 1715. She married Thomas Cates 1702 in Prince George County, Va.

> Children of Rebecca Sykes and Thomas Cates are:
> 261   i.   Frances[18] Cates.
> +   262   ii.   Thomas Cates, Jr, born 1733 in Orange County, N.C.; died 1816 in Orange County, N.C.

229. Colonel Joseph[17] Wyatt (Henry[16] Wiatt, Richard[15], George[14], Rev. Haute "Haut" "Hawte"[13], Sir George "Georgius" Thomas[12], Sir Thomas "The Younger"[11], Sir Thomas "The Elder"[10], Sir Henry[9], Richard Wiat or[8] Wyatt, Geoffrey "Jeoffrey" Wiot or[7] Wiat, Robert or Richard[6] Wiot, William Wiot or[5] Wyot, Adam Wiot or Wyote or[4], Guyott[3], Guyott[2], Captain or Admiral Adam Guyott or[1] Wiot) was born Abt. 1728 in associated with Saint Peter's Parish, New Kent County, Virginia, and died Abt. 1767 in New Kent County, Va. He married Dorothy "Virginia" Peyton Smith.

More About Colonel Joseph Wyatt:
Fact 1: Married and then moved to New Kent County, Va.
Fact 2: 1767, possible demise year.
Fact 3: Virginia State Senator for New Kent County, Va.
Fact 4: Abt. 1728, possibly born in Gloucester County, Va.

> Children of Colonel Wyatt and Dorothy Smith are:
> +   263   i.   William Hodges?[18] Wyatt.
>   264   ii.   Dorothy Wyatt? born in Colonial Georgia; died in Harmons Creek, Benton, Tenn.
> +   265   iii.   James Wyatt, born 1751.
>   266   iv.   Peyton Wyatt, born 1755 in Saint Peter's Parish, New Kent County, Va.; died 1805 in Lincoln, Ga. He married Hannah Bibb.

More About Peyton Wyatt:
Fact 1: November 15, 1763, possible date of birth.

+ 267 v. Sarah Sallie "Sally" Smith Wyatt, born 1759 in New Kent County, Va.; died August 15, 1826 in Robinson Springs, Elmore County, Ala.

268 vi. Ann Wyatt, born Abt. 1760 in New Kent County, Va.; died Abt. 1836 in Lawrence, Ala.

269 vii. Nancy Ann "Nannie" Wyatt, born November 17, 1760 in New Kent County, Va.; died 1836 in Lawrence, Ala. She married Capt. Francis Scott.

More About Nancy Ann "Nannie" Wyatt:
Fact 1: Moved to Alabama.

+ 270 viii. Ballard S. Wyatt, born 1765 in Va.

271 ix. Zachariah Sacker Wyatt, born 1765 in Durants Neck, Perquimans, North Carolina; died 1807 in Henry, Tennessee.

+ 272 x. Colonel Joseph Hawte Wyatt, born August 24, 1767 in New Kent County, Virginia; died April 28, 1843 in Charlotte House, Charlotte, Virginia.

234. William[17] Wiatt (Henry[16], Richard[15], George[14], Rev. Haute "Haut" "Hawte"[13], Sir George "Georgius" Thomas[12], Sir Thomas "The Younger"[11], Sir Thomas "The Elder"[10], Sir Henry[9], Richard Wiat or[8] Wyatt, Geoffrey "Jeoffrey" Wiot or[7] Wiat, Robert or Richard[6] Wiot, William Wiot or[5] Wyot, Adam Wiot or Wyote or[4], Guyott[3], Guyott[2], Captain or Admiral Adam Guyott or[1] Wiot) was born April 09, 1738 in Churchill, Gloucester County, Va., and died Abt. 1802 in Lick Creek, Rowan County [1822-Davidson County], N.C. He married Margaret Bostick 1822 in Davidson County, N.C.

Children of William Wiatt and Margaret Bostick are:
273 i. Henry[18] Wyatt, born 1763 in Lick Creek, Rowan County [1822-Davidson County], N.C.

274 ii. Aaron Wyatt, born Abt. 1765 in Lick Creek, Rowan County [1822-Davidson County], N.C.; died 1831 in Wilkes County, N.C.

236. John[17] Wiatt (Henry[16], Richard[15], George[14], Rev. Haute "Haut" "Hawte"[13], Sir George "Georgius" Thomas[12], Sir Thomas "The Younger"[11], Sir Thomas "The Elder"[10], Sir Henry[9], Richard Wiat or[8] Wyatt, Geoffrey "Jeoffrey" Wiot or[7] Wiat, Robert or Richard[6] Wiot, William Wiot or[5] Wyot, Adam Wiot or Wyote or[4], Guyott[3], Guyott[2], Captain or Admiral Adam Guyott or[1] Wiot) was born May 06, 1743 in Virginia or Maryland?, and died November 11, 1815 in Lick Creek Baptist Church, Denton, Davidson County, N.C. He married Rachel "Hannah".

More About John Wiatt:
Fact 1: May 06, 1743, possible birthday
Fact 4: 1760, possible marriage date
Fact 5: November 11, 1815, buried near High Rock Lake.
Fact 6: According to John Thomas Wyatt Venus of Faith, this John Wiatt was the first Wyatt to come to Davidson County, N.C. from Virginia or Maryland.
Died at age 72 years. Grave is marked with a stone in Davidson County, a part that used to be Rowan County. Remains are at the Lick Creek Baptist Church Cemetery in Row #14 -- #9 as *John Wiatt.*

More About Rachel "Hannah":
Fact 1: Possible birth abt. 1745.
Fact 2: Death date. possible 1820.

Children of John Wiatt and Rachel "Hannah" are:

	275	i.	Allen[18] Wiatt?
	276	ii.	Sarah "Sally" Wiatt.
	277	iii.	Dempsey "Dempsy" Wiatt.

More About Dempsey "Dempsy" Wyatt:
Died young, according to John Thomas Wyatt "Venus of Faith" handwritten notes.

+	278	iv.	James Wyatt, born Abt. 1805.
+	279	v.	John "Johney" Wyatt, Jr., born in Davidson County, N.C.; died 1819.
	280	vi.	Rachel Wyatt?
	281	vii.	Sylvester "Silvester" Wiatt, born 1762 in Church Hill, Va.; died Aft. August 1850 in Marshall County, Ky.

More About Sylvester "Silvester" Wiatt:
Fact 1: Moved to Kentucky.

+	282	viii.	Cecelia "Celia" Wyatt, born 1761 in Churchill, Gloucester, Va.
+	283	ix.	Thomas "Tommy" Wiatt, Sr. (Wyatt, Wiett), born 1774 in Rowan County, N.C.; died 1845 in buried in Wyatt, Park Bean Graveyard, Rowan County, N.C.
	284	x.	Elizabeth Wiatt, born 1778; died Bef. 1820. She married Park.
+	285	xi.	Eli "Ely" Wyatt, born Abt. 1789.

237. Richard[17] Wyatt (Richard[16] Wiatt, Richard[15], George[14], Rev. Haute "Haut" "Hawte"[13], Sir George "Georgius" Thomas[12], Sir Thomas "The Younger"[11], Sir Thomas "The Elder"[10], Sir Henry[9], Richard Wiat or[8] Wyatt, Geoffrey "Jeoffrey" Wiot or[7] Wiat, Robert or Richard[6]

Wiot, William Wiot or[5] Wyot, Adam Wiot or Wyote or[4], Guyott[3], Guyott[2], Captain or Admiral Adam Guyott or[1] Wiot) was born 1725 in King and Queen County, Va. He married Anne Garrett, daughter of Humphrey Garrett.

Children of Richard Wyatt and Anne Garrett are:

+   286   i.   Overstreet[18] Wyatt, born 1753 in Lunenburg County, Va.

+   287   ii.   Col. John Wyatt, born 1755.

241.   Anne[17] Wyatt (John[16], John[15] Wiatt, Captain John[14], Rev. Haute "Haut" "Hawte"[13], Sir George "Georgius" Thomas[12], Sir Thomas "The Younger"[11], Sir Thomas "The Elder"[10], Sir Henry[9], Richard Wiat or[8] Wyatt, Geoffrey "Jeoffrey" Wiot or[7] Wiat, Robert or Richard[6] Wiot, William Wiot or[5] Wyot, Adam Wiot or Wyote or[4], Guyott[3], Guyott[2], Captain or Admiral Adam Guyott or[1] Wiot) was born 1717. She married John Stark May 25, 1735.

Child of Anne Wyatt and John Stark is:

+   288   i.   Col.[18] Stark, born 1740 in Hanover County, Va.; died in Wilkes County, Ga.

Generation No. 18

249.   Aaron[18] Wyatt (William[17] Wyatt? Thomas[16], Thomas[15], William[14], Thomas[13] Wiatt, Sir George "Georgius" Thomas[12], Sir Thomas "The Younger"[11], Sir Thomas "The Elder"[10], Sir Henry[9], Richard Wiat or[8] Wyatt, Geoffrey "Jeoffrey" Wiot or[7] Wiat, Robert or Richard[6] Wiot, William Wiot or[5] Wyot, Adam Wiot or Wyote or[4], Guyott[3], Guyott[2], Captain or Admiral Adam Guyott or[1] Wiot). He married Ansley.

Child of Aaron Wyatt and Ansley is:

+   289   i.   Aaron[19] Wyatt, born 1790 in Rowan County or Wilkes County, N.C.

251.   Dr. William Edward[18] Wiatt (John Edward[17], Conquest[16], Conquest[15], Edward[14], Rev. Haute "Haut" "Hawte"[13], Sir George "Georgius" Thomas[12], Sir Thomas "The Younger"[11], Sir Thomas "The Elder"[10], Sir Henry[9], Richard Wiat or[8] Wyatt, Geoffrey "Jeoffrey" Wiot or[7] Wiat, Robert or Richard[6] Wiot, William Wiot or[5] Wyot, Adam Wiot or Wyote or[4], Guyott[3], Guyott[2], Captain or Admiral Adam Guyott or[1] Wiot) was born October 17, 1762, and died December 26, 1802 in buried at Boxley, Gloucester County, Va. He married Mary Graham February 18, 1781, daughter of Dr. Graham and Elizabeth Cocke.

More About Dr. William Edward Wiatt:

Fact 1: 1790, Physician and Justice of the Peace in Prince William County, Va.

Fact 2: 1802, Sheriff of Gloucester County, Va.

Fact 3: Was Master of Botetourt Lodge #7 of Ancient and Free Accepted Masons.

Children of Dr. Wiatt and Mary Graham are:

290	i.	John Todd Cocke[19] Wiatt, born 1781-1850. He married Cecilia Dabney.
291	ii.	Dr. William Graham Wiatt, born 1784-1854. He married Louisa Campbell Stubbs.
292	iii.	Eliza Maria Wiatt, born 1789-1844. She married Walker Jones.
293	iv.	Eleanor Wiatt. She married Col. Thomas Scott.
294	v.	Col. Thomas Todd Wiatt, died 1865.

More About Col. Thomas Todd Wiatt:
Fact 1: Did not marry.

295	vi.	Maj. Haute C. Wiatt, died 1861.

More About Maj. Haute C. Wiatt:
Fact 1: Did not marry.

256.   William[18] Wyatt, Jr. (William Edward[17] Wiatt, Sr., Captain Edward[16], Conquest[15], Edward[14], Rev. Haute "Haut" "Hawte"[13], Sir George "Georgius" Thomas[12], Sir Thomas "The Younger"[11], Sir Thomas "The Elder"[10], Sir Henry[9], Richard Wiat or[8] Wyatt, Geoffrey "Jeoffrey" Wiot or[7] Wiat, Robert or Richard[6] Wiot, William Wiot or[5] Wyot, Adam Wiot or Wyote or[4], Guyott[3], Guyott[2], Captain or Admiral Adam Guyott or[1] Wiot). He married (1) Frances Newton, daughter of William Newton and Mary Holloway. He married (2) Elizabeth Snoe [Snow].

More About William Wyatt, Jr.:
Fact 1: Served as a soldier during the American Revolution in Virginia.
Fact 2: Lived in Maca, Prince William County, Va.
Fact 3: 1788-1792, lived in South Carolina near Greenville Church.
Fact 4: Private in the 5th Virginia Regiment during Revolutionary War.

Children of William Wyatt and Frances Newton are:

296	i.	Frances[19] Wyatt. She married James Mattison.

More About Frances Wyatt:
Fact 1: Remained in South Carolina
Remains are buried at Broadmouth Baptist Church, Abbeville County, S.C.

More About James Mattison:
Remains are buried at Broadmouth Baptist Church, Abbeville County, S.C.

+   297   ii.   Micajah Wyatt.

    298   iii.   Lettice Nicoll Wyatt. She married Nimrod Smith in South Carolina.

More About Lettice Nicoll Wyatt:
Fact 1: Remained in South Carolina.

+   299   iv.   Elijah Wyatt, born 1774 in Abbeville County, S. C.; died 1858.
+   300   v.   William Wyatt.

    301   vi.   Zadock Wyatt. He married Mary Cammack.

More About Zadock Wyatt:
Fact 1: Moved to Christian County, Ky.

    302   vii.   Elizabeth Wyatt. She married Noah English.

More About Elizabeth Wyatt:
Fact 1: Lived in South Carolina for a few years. Fact 2: Returned to Prince William County, Va.

Children of William Wyatt and Elizabeth [Snow] are:

    303   i.   Talitha Cumi[19] Wyatt. She married Henry Rosseau Payne.

More About Talitha Cumi Wyatt:
Fact 1: Settled in Daviess County, Mo.

    304   ii.   Malina Wyatt. She married William Dunnington.

More About Malina Wyatt:
Fact 1: Remained in Virginia.

    305   iii.   Mary Frances "Fanny" Wyatt. She married John Wyatt.

More About Mary Frances "Fanny" Wyatt:
Fact 1: Married and moved to Kentucky.

    306   iv.   Mahala Wyatt. She married James Rosser.
    307   v.   Melissa Wyatt. She married John Rosser.

More About Melissa Wyatt:
Fact 1: Moved to Missouri.

262. Thomas[18] Cates, Jr. (Rebecca[17] Sykes, Frances[16] Wiatt, Richard[15], George[14], Rev. Haute "Haut" "Hawte"[13], Sir George "Georgius" Thomas[12], Sir Thomas "The Younger"[11], Sir Thomas "The Elder"[10], Sir Henry[9], Richard Wiat or[8] Wyatt, Geoffrey "Jeoffrey" Wiot or[7]

Wiat, Robert or Richard[6] Wiot, William Wiot or[5] Wyot, Adam Wiot or Wyote or[4], Guyott[3], Guyott[2], Captain or Admiral Adam Guyott or[1] Wiot) was born 1733 in Orange County, N.C., and died 1816 in Orange County, N.C. He married Sara Esteridge.

Child of Thomas Cates and Sara Esteridge is:

+ 308   i.   Frances[19] Cates, born 1772; died Aft. 1805 in Orange County, N.C.

263.   William Hodges?[18] Wyatt (Colonel Joseph[17], Henry[16] Wiatt, Richard[15], George[14], Rev. Haute "Haut" "Hawte"[13], Sir George "Georgius" Thomas[12], Sir Thomas "The Younger"[11], Sir Thomas "The Elder"[10], Sir Henry[9], Richard Wiat or[8] Wyatt, Geoffrey "Jeoffrey" Wiot or[7] Wiat, Robert or Richard[6] Wiot, William Wiot or[5] Wyot, Adam Wiot or Wyote or[4], Guyott[3], Guyott[2], Captain or Admiral Adam Guyott or[1] Wiot). He married Susannah E. Jones?

Children of William Wyatt and Susannah Jones? are:

+ 309   i.   James[19] Wyatt, Sr., born in Georgia; died June 14, 1847.
    310   ii.   Peyton Wyatt.
    311   iii.   Eliza Wyatt.
    312   iv.   Joseph Wyatt.
    313   v.   William Wyatt.

265.   James[18] Wyatt (Colonel Joseph[17], Henry[16] Wiatt, Richard[15], George[14], Rev. Haute "Haut" "Hawte"[13], Sir George "Georgius" Thomas[12], Sir Thomas "The Younger"[11], Sir Thomas "The Elder"[10], Sir Henry[9], Richard Wiat or[8] Wyatt, Geoffrey "Jeoffrey" Wiot or[7] Wiat, Robert or Richard[6] Wiot, William Wiot or[5] Wyot, Adam Wiot or Wyote or[4], Guyott[3], Guyott[2], Captain or Admiral Adam Guyott or[1] Wiot) was born 1751. He married Lethia Brown.

Child of James Wyatt and Lethia Brown is:

+ 314   i.   Robert Henry[19] Wyatt, born 1782 in North Carolina; died 1850.

267.   Sarah Sallie "Sally" Smith[18] Wyatt (Colonel Joseph[17], Henry[16] Wiatt, Richard[15], George[14], Rev. Haute "Haut" "Hawte"[13], Sir George "Georgius" Thomas[12], Sir Thomas "The Younger"[11], Sir Thomas "The Elder"[10], Sir Henry[9], Richard Wiat or[8] Wyatt, Geoffrey "Jeoffrey" Wiot or[7] Wiat, Robert or Richard[6] Wiot, William Wiot or[5] Wyot, Adam Wiot or Wyote or[4], Guyott[3], Guyott[2], Captain or Admiral Adam Guyott or[1] Wiot) was born 1759 in New Kent County, Va., and died August 15, 1826 in Robinson Springs, Elmore County, Ala. She married (1) Capt. William Crawford Bibb. She married (2) William Barrett March 21, 1807 in Elbert County, Ga.

More About Sarah Sallie "Sally" Smith Wyatt:
Fact 1: August 05, 1826, possible date of demise.
Fact 2: Died possibly in Elbert, Ga.

More About Capt. William Crawford Bibb:
Fact 1: Capt. of the Calvary during the Revolution.

Fact 2: Moved to Alabama.

More About William Barrett:
Fact 1: Congressman of Georgia.

    Children of Sarah Wyatt and Capt. Bibb are:

315   i.   Gov. William Wyatt[19] Bibb, M.D., born 1780; died 1820.

    More About Gov. William Wyatt Bibb, M.D.:
    Fact 1: Studied at William and Mary University.
    Fact 2: Studied medicine at Pennsylvania University
    Fact 3: 1801, received M.D.

316   ii.   Gov. Thomas Bibb, born 1784; died 1840.

    More About Gov. Thomas Bibb:
    Fact 1: President of the first State Senate of Alabama.
    Fact 2: Became Governor of Alabama after his brother's demise.

317   iii.   Delia Bibb. She married Pope.
318   iv.   John Dandridge Bibb.
319   v.   Joseph Wyatt Bibb, M.D.
320   vi.   Martha Bibb. She married Freeman.
321   vii.   Judge B. Smith Bibb.

270. Ballard S.[18] Wyatt (Colonel Joseph[17], Henry[16] Wiatt, Richard[15], George[14], Rev. Haute "Haut" "Hawte"[13], Sir George "Georgius" Thomas[12], Sir Thomas "The Younger"[11], Sir Thomas "The Elder"[10], Sir Henry[9], Richard Wiat or[8] Wyatt, Geoffrey "Jeoffrey" Wiot or[7] Wiat, Robert or Richard[6] Wiot, William Wiot or[5] Wyot, Adam Wiot or Wyote or[4], Guyott[3], Guyott[2], Captain or Admiral Adam Guyott or[1] Wiot) was born 1765 in Va.

    Child of Ballard S. Wyatt is:
+ 322   i.   Charles[19] Wyatt, born 1812.

272. Colonel Joseph Hawte[18] Wyatt (Colonel Joseph[17], Henry[16] Wiatt, Richard[15], George[14], Rev. Haute "Haut" "Hawte"[13], Sir George "Georgius" Thomas[12], Sir Thomas "The Younger"[11], Sir Thomas "The Elder"[10], Sir Henry[9], Richard Wiat or[8] Wyatt, Geoffrey "Jeoffrey" Wiot or[7] Wiat, Robert or Richard[6] Wiot, William Wiot or[5] Wyot, Adam Wiot or Wyote or[4], Guyott[3], Guyott[2], Captain or Admiral Adam Guyott or[1] Wiot) was born August 24, 1767 in New Kent County, Virginia, and died April 28, 1843 in Charlotte House, Charlotte, Virginia. He married Dorothy.

More About Colonel Joseph Hawte Wyatt:
Fact 1: Married; moved to Georgia [as in the state of the U.S.]

Child of Colonel Wyatt and Dorothy is:

323   i.   Joseph[19] Wyatt.

278. James[18] Wyatt (John[17] Wiatt, Henry[16], Richard[15], George[14], Rev. Haute "Haut" "Hawte"[13], Sir George "Georgius" Thomas[12], Sir Thomas "The Younger"[11], Sir Thomas "The Elder"[10], Sir Henry[9], Richard Wiat or[8] Wyatt, Geoffrey "Jeoffrey" Wiot or[7] Wiat, Robert or Richard[6] Wiot, William Wiot or[5] Wyot, Adam Wiot or Wyote or[4], Guyott[3], Guyott[2], Captain or Admiral Adam Guyott or[1] Wiot) was born Abt. 1805. He married Unknown.

More About James Wyatt:

Fact 1: According to Venus of Faith, moved to Kentucky.

Fact 2: Census records in Kentucky back this.

Fact 3: 1840, Federal Census Calloway, Ky.

Fact 4: Two white males under age 5 and one male between 40 and 50.

Fact 5: Wife is not indicated on the 1840 Kentucky Census.

Children of James Wyatt and Unknown are:

324   i.   Child[19] Wyatt, born Abt. 1835.

325   ii.   Child Wyatt, born Abt. 1838.

279. John "Johney"[18] Wyatt, Jr. (John[17] Wiatt, Henry[16], Richard[15], George[14], Rev. Haute "Haut" "Hawte"[13], Sir George "Georgius" Thomas[12], Sir Thomas "The Younger"[11], Sir Thomas "The Elder"[10], Sir Henry[9], Richard Wiat or[8] Wyatt, Geoffrey "Jeoffrey" Wiot or[7] Wiat, Robert or Richard[6] Wiot, William Wiot or[5] Wyot, Adam Wiot or Wyote or[4], Guyott[3], Guyott[2], Captain or Admiral Adam Guyott or[1] Wiot) was born in Davidson County, N.C., and died 1819. He married Hannah Park 1789 in Lick Creek, Davidson County, N.C., daughter of Noah Park and Joanna Reed.

More About John "Johney" Wyatt, Jr.:

Fact 1: 1813, *Descendants of Roger Park, Immigrant 1648-1739* states he died in this year. According to John Thomas Wyatt *"Venus of Faith"* personal handwritten notes -- this John Wyatt, Jr. was his great grandfather and went blind before he passed away.

More About Hannah Park:

Fact 1: 1772, possible birth year.

Children of John Wyatt and Hannah Park are:

326   i.   William[19] Wyatt, born 1790 in Rowan County (1822 Davidson County), N.C.

327   ii.   Cornelius Wyatt, born 1795 in Rowan County (1822 Davidson County), N.C.

+   328   iii.   Jesse "Jessey" Wyatt, born 1800 in Rowan County (1822 Davidson County, N.C.), N.C.; died 1860 in Bringles P.O.,

Westside of River Road, Pooletown District, Morgan Township, N.C.

+ 329   iv.   John Wyatt III, born 1802 in North Carolina; died 1894 in Brinkley, Calloway County, Ky.

330   v.   Noah Wyatt, born 1807 in Rowan County (1822 Davidson County), N.C.; died in Murray County, Calloway, Ky.

282. Cecelia "Celia"[18] Wyatt (John[17] Wiatt, Henry[16], Richard[15], George[14], Rev. Haute "Haut" "Hawte"[13], Sir George "Georgius" Thomas[12], Sir Thomas "The Younger"[11], Sir Thomas "The Elder"[10], Sir Henry[9], Richard Wiat or[8] Wyatt, Geoffrey "Jeoffrey" Wiot or[7] Wiat, Robert or Richard[6] Wiot, William Wiot or[5] Wyot, Adam Wiot or Wyote or[4], Guyott[3], Guyott[2], Captain or Admiral Adam Guyott or[1] Wiot) was born 1761 in Churchill, Gloucester, Va. She married William Bean 1778 in Lick Creek Baptist Church, Davidson County, N.C., son of William McBean and Naomi Bates.

More About William Bean:
Fact 1: Is said by family to have immigrated at age 13 with his father.

Children of Cecelia Wyatt and William Bean are:

+ 331   i.   John Jacob[19] Bean, born February 28, 1802 in Piney Woods District, Morgan Township, Rowan County, N.C.; died January 01, 1876 in Murray County, Calloway, Ky.

332   ii.   10 other children Bean.

283. Thomas "Tommy"[18] Wiatt, Sr. (Wyatt, Wiett) (John[17], Henry[16], Richard[15], George[14], Rev. Haute "Haut" "Hawte"[13], Sir George "Georgius" Thomas[12], Sir Thomas "The Younger"[11], Sir Thomas "The Elder"[10], Sir Henry[9], Richard Wiat or[8] Wyatt, Geoffrey "Jeoffrey" Wiot or[7] Wiat, Robert or Richard[6] Wiot, William Wiot or[5] Wyot, Adam Wiot or Wyote or[4], Guyott[3], Guyott[2], Captain or Admiral Adam Guyott or[1] Wiot) was born 1774 in Rowan County N.C., and died 1845 in buried in Wyatt, Park Bean Graveyard, Rowan County, N.C. He married Rachel "Parks" "Park" Parke January 12, 1793 in Piney Woods District, Rowan County, N.C., daughter of Noah Park and Joanna Reed.

More About Thomas "Tommy" Wiatt, Sr. (Wyatt, Wiett):
Fact 1: Is recorded in his father-in-law's will as a witness along with David Woodson. Buried in Park-Wyatt- Bean Graveyard, Richfield, N.C.

Children of Thomas Wiatt and Rachel Parke are:

+ 333   i.   Lazarus Pleasant[19] Wyatt.

334   ii.   Rebecca Wyatt.

335   iii.   James Noah Wyatt?

More About James Noah Wyatt?

	336	iv.	Rachel Wyatt, born 1802 in Lick Creek, Rowan County, (1822 Davidson County, N.C.); died March 08, 1877 in Murray County, Calloway, Ky.
+	337	v.	Richmond Wyatt? born 1804 in Lick Creek, Davidson County, N.C.; died in Providence Township, N.C.
+	338	vi.	Noah Calvin Wyatt, born February 03, 1805 in Rowan County, N.C.; died March 30, 1871 in Rowan County, N.C.
+	339	vii.	Brantley or Brantly Wyatt, born December 20, 1813 in Rowan County, N.C.; died February 03, 1863 in Rowan County, N.C.
+	340	viii.	Thomas Wyatt, Jr., born Abt. 1820.

285. Eli "Ely"[18] Wyatt (John[17] Wiatt, Henry[16], Richard[15], George[14], Rev. Haute "Haut" "Hawte"[13], Sir George "Georgius" Thomas[12], Sir Thomas "The Younger"[11], Sir Thomas "The Elder"[10], Sir Henry[9], Richard Wiat or[8] Wyatt, Geoffrey "Jeoffrey" Wiot or[7] Wiat, Robert or Richard[6] Wiot, William Wiot or[5] Wyot, Adam Wiot or Wyote or[4], Guyott[3], Guyott[2], Captain or Admiral Adam Guyott or[1] Wiot) was born Abt. 1789. He married Sarah.

   More About Eli "Ely" Wyatt:
   Fact 1: According to Venus of Faith, moved to Kentucky.
   Fact 2: 1840, McCracken County Ky. census with two females and one other male
   Fact 3: 1850, McCracken County Ky. census with wife Sarah and son William Wyatt.

   Child of Eli Wyatt and Sarah is:
   341   i.   William P.[19] Wyatt, born Abt. 1829.

286. Overstreet[18] Wyatt (Richard[17], Richard[16] Wiatt, Richard[15], George[14], Rev. Haute "Haut" "Hawte"[13], Sir George "Georgius" Thomas[12], Sir Thomas "The Younger"[11], Sir Thomas "The Elder"[10], Sir Henry[9], Richard Wiat or[8] Wyatt, Geoffrey "Jeoffrey" Wiot or[7] Wiat, Robert or Richard[6] Wiot, William Wiot or[5] Wyot, Adam Wiot or Wyote or[4], Guyott[3], Guyott[2], Captain or Admiral Adam Guyott or[1] Wiot) was born 1753 in Lunenburg County, Va. He married Sarah Tomlinson, daughter of Col. Benjamin Tomblinson.

   Children of Overstreet Wyatt and Sarah Tomlinson are:
+	342	i.	Martha[19] Wyatt, born 1792; died 1857.
	343	ii.	Ermine Wyatt.
	344	iii.	Mary Wyatt.
	345	iv.	Lucy Wyatt.
	346	v.	Sally Wyatt.
	347	vi.	Harriet Wyatt.
	348	vii.	John Wyatt. He married Sallie Williams.
	349	viii.	Benjamin Wyatt.
	350	ix.	Thomas Wyatt.
	351	x.	Henry Wyatt.
	352	xi.	Harris Wyatt. He married Elizabeth Webb.

287. Col. John[18] Wyatt (Richard[17], Richard[16] Wiatt, Richard[15], George[14], Rev. Haute "Haut" "Hawte"[13], Sir George "Georgius" Thomas[12], Sir Thomas "The Younger"[11], Sir Thomas "The Elder"[10], Sir Henry[9], Richard Wiat or[8] Wyatt, Geoffrey "Jeoffrey" Wiot or[7] Wiat, Robert or Richard[6] Wiot, William Wiot or[5] Wyot, Adam Wiot or Wyote or[4], Guyott[3], Guyott[2], Captain or Admiral Adam Guyott or[1] Wiot) was born 1755. He married Mary Tomlinson, daughter of Benjamin Tomlinson.

   Children of Col. Wyatt and Mary Tomlinson are:

	353	i.	Col. Richard[19] Wyatt.
	354	ii.	Martha Wyatt. She married Charles Gilliam.
	355	iii.	Benjamin Wyatt.
	356	iv.	Sarah Wyatt.
	357	v.	John Wyatt.
+	358	vi.	Thomas Wyatt, born 1809.

288. Col.[18] Stark (Anne[17] Wyatt, John[16], John[15] Wiatt, Captain John[14], Rev. Haute "Haut" "Hawte"[13], Sir George "Georgius" Thomas[12], Sir Thomas "The Younger"[11], Sir Thomas "The Elder"[10], Sir Henry[9], Richard Wiat or[8] Wyatt, Geoffrey "Jeoffrey" Wiot or[7] Wiat, Robert or Richard[6] Wiot, William Wiot or[5] Wyot, Adam Wiot or Wyote or[4], Guyott[3], Guyott[2], Captain or Admiral Adam Guyott or[1] Wiot) was born 1740 in Hanover County, Va., and died in Wilkes County, Ga. He married Elizabeth.

   Child of Col. Stark and Elizabeth is:

+	359	i.	Mary[19] Stark.

Generation No. 19

289. Aaron[19] Wyatt (Aaron[18], William[17] Wyatt? Thomas[16], Thomas[15], William[14], Thomas[13] Wiatt, Sir George "Georgius" Thomas[12], Sir Thomas "The Younger"[11], Sir Thomas "The Elder"[10], Sir Henry[9], Richard Wiat or[8] Wyatt, Geoffrey "Jeoffrey" Wiot or[7] Wiat, Robert or Richard[6] Wiot, William Wiot or[5] Wyot, Adam Wiot or Wyote or[4], Guyott[3], Guyott[2], Captain or Admiral Adam Guyott or[1] Wiot) was born 1790 in Rowan County or Wilkes County, N.C. He married Susie Sheets, daughter of Sheets and Unknown Wife.

More About Aaron Wyatt:
Fact 1: 1860, Aaron was living in Ashe County, N.C.

   Children of Aaron Wyatt and Susie Sheets are:

360	i.	Aaron[20] Wyatt.
361	ii.	Alex Wyatt.
362	iii.	Daughter Wyatt.
363	iv.	Hannah Wyatt? She married John Garvey October 14, 1851.
364	v.	Joseph Wyatt?

365	vi.	Louisa Wyatt?
366	vii.	Polly Wyatt?
367	viii.	Sally Wyatt?
368	ix.	Susie Wyatt?
369	x.	William Wyatt?
370	xi.	Wilson Wyatt? She married Olive Faller October 18, 1855.
371	xii.	Malvinia Wyatt? born May 29, 1840.
372	xiii.	John Andrew Wyatt? born August 17, 1852.
373	xiv.	Solomon Wyatt? born 1855.
374	xv.	Jane Wyatt? born 1857.
375	xvi.	Ellen Wyatt? born May 15, 1859.

297. Micajah[19] Wyatt (William[18], William Edward[17] Wiatt, Sr., Captain Edward[16], Conquest[15], Edward[14], Rev. Haute "Haut" "Hawte"[13], Sir George "Georgius" Thomas[12], Sir Thomas "The Younger"[11], Sir Thomas "The Elder"[10], Sir Henry[9], Richard Wiat or[8] Wyatt, Geoffrey "Jeoffrey" Wiot or[7] Wiat, Robert or Richard[6] Wiot, William Wiot or[5] Wyot, Adam Wiot or Wyote or[4], Guyott[3], Guyott[2], Captain or Admiral Adam Guyott or[1] Wiot). She married Unknown.

More About Micajah Wyatt:
Fact 1: Remained in Halifax County, Va.

Child of Micajah Wyatt and Unknown is:
376   i.   Four children[20] Unknown.

299. Elijah[19] Wyatt (William[18], William Edward[17] Wiatt, Sr., Captain Edward[16], Conquest[15], Edward[14], Rev. Haute "Haut" "Hawte"[13], Sir George "Georgius" Thomas[12], Sir Thomas "The Younger"[11], Sir Thomas "The Elder"[10], Sir Henry[9], Richard Wiat or[8] Wyatt, Geoffrey "Jeoffrey" Wiot or[7] Wiat, Robert or Richard[6] Wiot, William Wiot or[5] Wyot, Adam Wiot or Wyote or[4], Guyott[3], Guyott[2], Captain or Admiral Adam Guyott or[1] Wiot) was born 1774 in Abbeville County, S. C., and died 1858. He married Mary Grigsby Foster September 15, 1793 in Fairfax County, Va., daughter of Colonel Foster and Elizabeth Grigsby.

More About Elijah Wyatt:
Fact 1: 1799, Moved to South Carolina.
Remains are buried at Broadmouth Baptist Church, Abbeville County, S.C. with his wife and next to his sister Frances N. Wyatt and her husband James Mattison.

More About Mary Grigsby Foster:
Fact 1: Moved to South Carolina.
Remains are buried at Broadmouth Baptist Church, Abbeville County, S.C. with her husband and next to her sister-in-law Frances N. Wyatt and brother-in-law James Mattison.

Children of Elijah Wyatt and Mary Foster are:

	377	i.	Eliza[20] Wyatt. She married William Mattison.
	378	ii.	Edna Esther Wyatt. She married Ephraim Mitchell.
+	379	iii.	Colonel James Foster Wyatt, born 1801; died 1868.
	380	iv.	William Newton Wyatt. He married Eliza Miller.

More About William Newton Wyatt:
Fact 1: Moved to Marion, Alabama.

+	381	v.	Redmond Grigsby Wyatt, born 1806; died 1857.
	382	vi.	Mildred Luani Wyatt. She married Abner Cox.
	383	vii.	Susan Cecile Wyatt. She married Elias Kay.
	384	viii.	Harriet Wyatt. She married John Mauldin.

More About Harriet Wyatt:
Fact 1: Moved to Franklin County, Ga.

385   ix.   Malina Wyatt. She married Hugh C. Alexander.

More About Malina Wyatt:
Fact 1: Moved to Arkansas.

300. William[19] Wyatt (William[18], William Edward[17] Wiatt, Sr., Captain Edward[16], Conquest[15], Edward[14], Rev. Haute "Haut" "Hawte"[13], Sir George "Georgius" Thomas[12], Sir Thomas "The Younger"[11], Sir Thomas "The Elder"[10], Sir Henry[9], Richard Wiat or[8] Wyatt, Geoffrey "Jeoffrey" Wiot or[7] Wiat, Robert or Richard[6] Wiot, William Wiot or[5] Wyot, Adam Wiot or Wyote or[4], Guyott[3], Guyott[2], Captain or Admiral Adam Guyott or[1] Wiot). He married Mary Martha Gaines.

Child of William Wyatt and Mary Gaines is:
386   i.   Child[20] Wyatt.

More About Child Wyatt:
Fact 1: Moved to Illinois as an adult -- only child of parents.

308. Frances[19] Cates (Thomas[18], Rebecca[17] Sykes, Frances[16] Wiatt, Richard[15], George[14], Rev. Haute "Haut" "Hawte"[13], Sir George "Georgius" Thomas[12], Sir Thomas "The Younger"[11], Sir Thomas "The Elder"[10], Sir Henry[9], Richard Wiat or[8] Wyatt, Geoffrey "Jeoffrey" Wiot or[7] Wiat, Robert or Richard[6] Wiot, William Wiot or[5] Wyot, Adam Wiot or Wyote or[4], Guyott[3], Guyott[2], Captain or Admiral Adam Guyott or[1] Wiot) was born 1772, and died Aft. 1805 in Orange County, N.C. She married John Thomas Sykes.

Child of Frances Cates and John Sykes is:
+   387   i.   James B.[20] Sykes, born 1804 in Orange County, N.C.; died 1880 in Orange County, N.C.

309. James[19] Wyatt, Sr. (William Hodges?[18], Colonel Joseph[17], Henry[16] Wiatt, Richard[15], George[14], Rev. Haute "Haut" "Hawte"[13], Sir George "Georgius" Thomas[12], Sir Thomas "The Younger"[11], Sir Thomas "The Elder"[10], Sir Henry[9], Richard Wiat or[8] Wyatt, Geoffrey "Jeoffrey" Wiot or[7] Wiat, Robert or Richard[6] Wiot, William Wiot or[5] Wyot, Adam Wiot or Wyote or[4], Guyott[3], Guyott[2], Captain or Admiral Adam Guyott or[1] Wiot) was born in Georgia, and died June 14, 1847. He married Nancy Hodges.

> Children of James Wyatt and Nancy Hodges are:
> 388   i.   Permelia[20] Wyatt, born September 18, 1804.
> 389   ii.   Jessie Wyatt, born September 02, 1805.
> 390   iii. William Hodges Wyatt, born January 09, 1808 in Henry County, Ga.; died June 07, 1888 in Marysville, Cooke County, Texas. He married Anna Ray October 18, 1827 in Caldago, Talladega, County, Alabama.
> 391   iv.   Wiley Wyatt, born December 03, 1809. He married Jamima Johnson.

314. Robert Henry[19] Wyatt (James[18], Colonel Joseph[17], Henry[16] Wiatt, Richard[15], George[14], Rev. Haute "Haut" "Hawte"[13], Sir George "Georgius" Thomas[12], Sir Thomas "The Younger"[11], Sir Thomas "The Elder"[10], Sir Henry[9], Richard Wiat or[8] Wyatt, Geoffrey "Jeoffrey" Wiot or[7] Wiat, Robert or Richard[6] Wiot, William Wiot or[5] Wyot, Adam Wiot or Wyote or[4], Guyott[3], Guyott[2], Captain or Admiral Adam Guyott or[1] Wiot) was born 1782 in North Carolina, and died 1850. He married Mary Jane Jones.

More About Robert Henry Wyatt:
Fact 1: Moved to Tennessee.

> Child of Robert Wyatt and Mary Jones is:
> + 392   i.   William Carroll[20] Wyatt, born Abt. 1815; died 1901.

322. Charles[19] Wyatt (Ballard S.[18], Colonel Joseph[17], Henry[16] Wiatt, Richard[15], George[14], Rev. Haute "Haut" "Hawte"[13], Sir George "Georgius" Thomas[12], Sir Thomas "The Younger"[11], Sir Thomas "The Elder"[10], Sir Henry[9], Richard Wiat or[8] Wyatt, Geoffrey "Jeoffrey" Wiot or[7] Wiat, Robert or Richard[6] Wiot, William Wiot or[5] Wyot, Adam Wiot or Wyote or[4], Guyott[3], Guyott[2], Captain or Admiral Adam Guyott or[1] Wiot) was born 1812. He married Delilah Butcher.

> Child of Charles Wyatt and Delilah Butcher is:
> + 393   i.   Gilbert Newton[20] Wyatt, born 1839 in Greenbriar, W.Va.

328. Jesse "Jessey"[19] Wyatt (John "Johney"[18], John[17] Wiatt, Henry[16], Richard[15], George[14], Rev. Haute "Haut" "Hawte"[13], Sir George "Georgius" Thomas[12], Sir Thomas "The Younger"[11], Sir Thomas "The Elder"[10], Sir Henry[9], Richard Wiat or[8] Wyatt, Geoffrey "Jeoffrey" Wiot or[7] Wiat, Robert or Richard[6] Wiot, William Wiot or[5] Wyot, Adam Wiot or Wyote or[4], Guyott[3],

Guyott[2], Captain or Admiral Adam Guyott or[1] Wiot) was born 1800 in Rowan County (1822 Davidson County, N.C.), N.C., and died 1860 in Bringles P.O., Westside of River Road, Pooletown District, Morgan Township, N.C. He married Sarah Briggs June 16, 1826 in Lick Creek Baptist Church, Davidson County, N.C.

Children of Jesse Wyatt and Sarah Briggs are:

394   i.   Barbara[20] Wyatt.

More About Barbara Wyatt:
Fact 1: The eldest, according to Venus of Faith John Thomas Wyatt 1851-1933.

395   ii.   James "Jimmy" Wyatt.

More About James "Jimmy" Wyatt:
Fact 1: Went West with one of the brothers of Sarah Briggs Wyatt and then to Illinois.
Fact 2: Settled in Brown County, Ill.

396   iii. James "Jimmy" Wyatt.

More About James "Jimmy" Wyatt:
Fact 1: Traveled West with one of his mother's brothers' -- a Briggs.
Fact 2: Settled in Brown County, Ill.

397   iv.   Noah Wyatt.

More About Noah Wyatt:
Fact 1: The youngest, according to Venus of Faith: John Thomas Wyatt 1851-1933.

398   v.   Thomas "Tommey" Wyatt.
399   vi.   William Wyatt.

More About William Wyatt:
Fact 1: Died young.

+ 400   vii. Gilbert Ivey Wyatt, born March 29, 1830 in Davidson County, N.C.; died August 28, 1863 in Battery Wagoner, Morris Island, S.C.

+ 401   viii. Wilson Riley Wyatt, born March 29, 1830 in Davidson and Rowan counties on Yadkin River, N.C.; died March 1862 in Salisbury, Rowan County, N.C.

402   ix.   Ann "Anney" Wyatt, born Abt. 1831. She married Milas J.S. Parks.

403   x.   Noah Wyatt, born Aft. 1831.

More About Noah Wyatt:
Fact 1: Was the youngest and last child of his parents.

329. John[19] Wyatt III (John "Johney"[18], John[17] Wiatt, Henry[16], Richard[15], George[14], Rev. Haute "Haut" "Hawte"[13], Sir George "Georgius" Thomas[12], Sir Thomas "The Younger"[11], Sir Thomas "The Elder"[10], Sir Henry[9], Richard Wiat or[8] Wyatt, Geoffrey "Jeoffrey" Wiot or[7] Wiat, Robert or Richard[6] Wiot, William Wiot or[5] Wyot, Adam Wiot or Wyote or[4], Guyott[3], Guyott[2], Captain or Admiral Adam Guyott or[1] Wiot) was born 1802 in North Carolina, and died 1894 in Brinkley, Calloway County, Ky. He married (1) Elizabeth Houser 1824. He married (2) Deannah Day 1838 in Kentucky. He married (3) Sarah "Sally" Gillimore or Gallemore 1842 in Kentucky.

More About John Wyatt III:
Fact 1: 1790, is indicated in Index of North Carolina Ancestors Vol 2. as being birth year.
Fact 2: Note: It is not certain our John III married these three women two being from Kentucky.

Children of John Wyatt and Elizabeth Houser are:
404   i.   William[20] Wyatt, born 1828 in Calloway, Murray County, Ky.
405   ii.   John A. Wyatt, born 1829 in Calloway, Murray County, Ky.
406   iii.   Elizabeth Wyatt, born 1836 in Calloway, Murray County, Ky.

Child of John Wyatt and Deannah Day is:
407   i.   Elendor[20] Wyatt, born 1840 in Calloway, Murray County, Ky.

Children of John Wyatt and Sarah Gallemore are:
408   i.   Clarandes[20] Wyatt, born 1842 in Murray County, Calloway, Ky.
409   ii.   Newton Wyatt, born 1849 in Murray County, Calloway, Ky.
410   iii.   Adaline Wyatt, born 1857 in Murray County, Calloway, Ky.
411   iv.   Amanda P. Wyatt, born 1858 in Murray County, Calloway, Ky.

331. John Jacob[19] Bean (Cecelia "Celia"[18] Wyatt, John[17] Wiatt, Henry[16], Richard[15], George[14], Rev. Haute "Haut" "Hawte"[13], Sir George "Georgius" Thomas[12], Sir Thomas "The Younger"[11], Sir Thomas "The Elder"[10], Sir Henry[9], Richard Wiat or[8] Wyatt, Geoffrey "Jeoffrey" Wiot or[7] Wiat, Robert or Richard[6] Wiot, William Wiot or[5] Wyot, Adam Wiot or Wyote or[4], Guyott[3], Guyott[2], Captain or Admiral Adam Guyott or[1] Wiot) was born February 28, 1802 in Piney Woods District, Morgan Township, Rowan County, N.C., and died January 01, 1876 in Murray County, Calloway, Ky. He married Rachel Wyatt in Lick Creek Baptist Church, Davidson County, N.C., daughter of Thomas Wiatt and Rachel Parke.

Children of John Bean and Rachel Wyatt are:

412	i.	Five Children[20] Bean.
413	ii.	Elvira Bean, born October 15, 1824 in Piney Woods District, Morgan Township, Rowan County, N.C.; died May 06, 1894 in Murray County, Calloway, Ky.
414	iii.	Eveline Bean, born 1832 in Piney Woods District, Morgan Township, Rowan County, N.C.
415	iv.	John C. Bean, born 1836 in Piney Woods District, Morgan Township, Rowan County, N.C.
416	v.	Jesse L. Bean, born 1839 in Piney Woods District, Morgan Township, Rowan County, N.C.
417	vi.	Miles M. Bean, born 1841 in Piney Woods District, Morgan Township, Rowan County, N.C.

333. Lazarus Pleasant[19] Wyatt (Thomas "Tommy"[18] Wiatt, Sr. (Wyatt, Wiett), John[17], Henry[16], Richard[15], George[14], Rev. Haute "Haut" "Hawte"[13], Sir George "Georgius" Thomas[12], Sir Thomas "The Younger"[11], Sir Thomas "The Elder"[10], Sir Henry[9], Richard Wiat or[8] Wyatt, Geoffrey "Jeoffrey" Wiot or[7] Wiat, Robert or Richard[6] Wiot, William Wiot or[5] Wyot, Adam Wiot or Wyote or[4], Guyott[3], Guyott[2], Captain or Admiral Adam Guyott or[1] Wiot). He married Delilia "Delilah" Park, daughter of George Park and Hannah Hodge.

Children of Lazarus Wyatt and Delilia Park are:

	418	i.	Adam[20] Wyatt?
+	419	ii.	John Wyatt?
+	420	iii.	Ciscero "Cicero" L. Wyatt, born February 02, 1861; died January 21, 1945.
	421	iv.	James L. Wyatt, born Abt. 1866. He married Linda Bringle March 06, 1887 in Rowan County N.C.

336. Rachel[19] Wyatt (Thomas "Tommy"[18] Wiatt, Sr. (Wyatt, Wiett), John[17], Henry[16], Richard[15], George[14], Rev. Haute "Haut" "Hawte"[13], Sir George "Georgius" Thomas[12], Sir Thomas "The Younger"[11], Sir Thomas "The Elder"[10], Sir Henry[9], Richard Wiat or[8] Wyatt, Geoffrey "Jeoffrey" Wiot or[7] Wiat, Robert or Richard[6] Wiot, William Wiot or[5] Wyot, Adam Wiot or Wyote or[4], Guyott[3], Guyott[2], Captain or Admiral Adam Guyott or[1] Wiot) was born 1802 in Lick creek, Rowan County, (1822 Davidson County, N.C.), and died March 08, 1877 in Murray County, Calloway, Ky. She married John Jacob Bean in Lick Creek Baptist Church, Davidson County, N.C., son of William Bean and Cecelia Wyatt.

Children of Rachel Wyatt and John Bean are:

422	i.	Five Children[20] Bean.
423	ii.	Elvira Bean, born October 15, 1824 in Piney Woods District, Morgan Township, Rowan County, N.C.; died May 06, 1894 in Murray County, Calloway, Ky.

424	iii.	Eveline Bean, born 1832 in Piney Woods District, Morgan Township, Rowan County, N.C.
425	iv.	John C. Bean, born 1836 in Piney Woods District, Morgan Township, Rowan County, N.C.
426	v.	Jesse L. Bean, born 1839 in Piney Woods District, Morgan Township, Rowan County, N.C.
427	vi.	Miles M. Bean, born 1841 in Piney Woods District, Morgan Township, Rowan County, N.C.

337. Richmond[19] Wyatt? (Thomas "Tommy"[18] Wiatt, Sr. (Wyatt, Wiett), John[17], Henry[16], Richard[15], George[14], Rev. Haute "Haut" "Hawte"[13], Sir George "Georgius" Thomas[12], Sir Thomas "The Younger"[11], Sir Thomas "The Elder"[10], Sir Henry[9], Richard Wiat or[8] Wyatt, Geoffrey "Jeoffrey" Wiot or[7] Wiat, Robert or Richard[6] Wiot, William Wiot or[5] Wyot, Adam Wiot or Wyote or[4], Guyott[3], Guyott[2], Captain or Admiral Adam Guyott or[1] Wiot) was born 1804 in Lick creek, Davidson County, N.C., and died in Providence Township, N.C. He married Lucy Foster February 23, 1822 in Union Lutheran Church, Providence Township, N.C.

Child of Richmond Wyatt? and Lucy Foster is:
428   i.   Seven children[20] Wyatt?.

338. Noah Calvin[19] Wyatt (Thomas "Tommy"[18] Wiatt, Sr. (Wyatt, Wiett), John[17], Henry[16], Richard[15], George[14], Rev. Haute "Haut" "Hawte"[13], Sir George "Georgius" Thomas[12], Sir Thomas "The Younger"[11], Sir Thomas "The Elder"[10], Sir Henry[9], Richard Wiat or[8] Wyatt, Geoffrey "Jeoffrey" Wiot or[7] Wiat, Robert or Richard[6] Wiot, William Wiot or[5] Wyot, Adam Wiot or Wyote or[4], Guyott[3], Guyott[2], Captain or Admiral Adam Guyott or[1] Wiot) was born February 03, 1805 in Rowan County, N.C., and died March 30, 1871 in Rowan County, N.C. He married Mary Polly Hendly (Henly or Hendley) December 27, 1824, daughter of Hendly and Unknown Wife.

More About Noah Calvin Wyatt:
Fact 1: Resided in the Morgan Township, Rowan County, N.C.
Fact 2: Rachel Wyatt Morgan 's father.
Fact 3: Lived up the creek from Virgie Eagle Hinson's former house on Hinson Road.
Fact 4: August 02, 1850, according to McCubbins file had real estate value $600.00.
Fact 5: August 02, 1850, is a farmer age 45 years; wife Polly then, 44 years.
Fact 6: March 29, 1871, died according to Park Family.
Fact 7: Tombstone is in the Park-Wyatt-Bean Graveyard in Rowan County, N.C.
Fact 8: The name *"Noah"* is missing from the stone.
Fact 9: Transcribed: *"OF WIATT of Feb. 3, 1805 DIED of March 1871; Aged 66 yrs. I mos. 26 days."*
Buried in the Park-Wyatt-Bean Graveyard, Richfield, N.C. 4th stone from right. --1st row. Words on stone: *"--- OF WIATT of Feb. 3 1805 DIED -- of March 1871 -- Aged 66 yrs. I mos. -- 26 days."*

More About Mary Polly Hendly (Henly or Hendley):

Fact 1: Mother of Rachel E. Wyatt -- the mother of Mary Jane Morgan Eagle.

Fact 3: Named *"Henry"* in Park research.

Buried at Bean-Park-Wyatt Graveyard, Richfield, N.C.

Is located at the third stone from the right. Stone reads: *"SACRED POLLY WIATT Was born Jan. 5th, 1806 AND Died About 1861."* Stone located about 100 feet from the corn-soy field, Richfield, N.C.

Children of Noah Wyatt and Mary Hendley) are:

+ 429   i.   Henry Thomas[20] Wyatt, born 1828 in North Carolina.

+ 430   ii.   Malinda [Delinda] Wyatt, born February 05, 1829; died January 23, 1903.

+ 431   iii.   William Wesley "Brantly" Wyatt, born 1831 in North Carolina; died July 20, 1863 in Gettysburg, Pa.

+ 432   iv.   Emanuel James M. Wyatt, born 1832.

+ 433   v.   Lila Delilah "Delila" Wyatt, born 1834 in North Carolina.

+ 434   vi.   Rachel Evelyn "Eveline" Wyatt, born October 02, 1835 in North Carolina; died April 24, 1915 in North Carolina.

+ 435   vii.   Silas "Siles" Wyatt, born 1838 in North Carolina; died January 19, 1864 in Point Lookout, Md.

+ 436   viii.   Mary Ann Wyatt, born March 20, 1839 in North Carolina; died October 12, 1902 in Rowan County N.C.

+ 437   ix.   Eli Wyatt, born January 30, 1841 in North Carolina; died June 01, 1912 in Rowan County N.C.

+ 438   x.   Noah "Noe" Calvin Wyatt, born 1843 in North Carolina.

+ 439   xi.   Rhoda E. Wyatt, born October 10, 1844 in North Carolina; died April 22, 1920 in Rowan County N.C.

+ 440   xii.   John P. Wyatt, born October 23, 1846 in Rowan County, N.C.; died April 07, 1924 in Rowan County N.C.

+ 441   xiii.   Amanda Jane Wyatt, born January 28, 1848 in Rowan County, N.C.; died April 23, 1907 in Rowan County N.C.

339.   Brantley or Brantly[19] Wyatt (Thomas "Tommy"[18] Wiatt, Sr. (Wyatt, Wiett), John[17], Henry[16], Richard[15], George[14], Rev. Haute "Haut" "Hawte"[13], Sir George "Georgius" Thomas[12], Sir Thomas "The Younger"[11], Sir Thomas "The Elder"[10], Sir Henry[9], Richard Wiat or[8] Wyatt, Geoffrey "Jeoffrey" Wiot or[7] Wiat, Robert or Richard[6] Wiot, William Wiot or[5] Wyot, Adam Wiot or Wyote or[4], Guyott[3], Guyott[2], Captain or Admiral Adam Guyott or[1] Wiot) was born December 20, 1813 in Rowan County, N.C., and died February 03, 1863 in Rowan County, N.C. He married Julia "Juley" "Julyan" "Julianna" Ann Daniel April 05, 1836 in Lick Creek Baptist Church, Rowan County, N.C., daughter of Daniel and Nancy.

More About Brantley or Brantly Wyatt:

Fact 1: This son named Brantley existed, according to James N. Hinson, M.D.

Fact 2: 1840, confirmed on U.S. N.C. Federal Census -- listed with Thomas Wyatt.

Fact 3: Sometimes his name is misspelled as *"Brantley."*

Fact 4: Also misspelled as *"Brently."*

Died at age 50; Buried in the Park-Wyatt-Bean Graveyard off of Brinkle Ferry Road, which is off of River Road in Richfield, Rowan County, N.C.

More About Julia "Juley" "Julyan" "Julianna" Ann Daniel:

Fact 1: Also known as "Julianna Daniels."

Children of Brantley Wyatt and Julia Daniel are:

442	i.	Delilah Ann[20] Wyatt.
+ 443	ii.	Pleasant L. Wyatt, born March 1837; died July 09, 1916 in Gold Hill, Morgan Township, Rowan County, N.C.
444	iii.	James J. Wyatt, born 1840.

More About James J. Wyatt:

Fact 1: fought along side Gilbert Ivey Wyatt -- cousins.

445	iv.	Travis Calvin Wyatt, born October 1845; died March 28, 1921 in Gold Hill, Morgan Township, Rowan County, N.C. He married Anne Hooks March 10, 1878 in Gold Hill Township, Rowan County N.C.
446	v.	Joice A. Wyatt, born October 13, 1850; died March 14, 1880. She married David Bean March 13, 1879.

340. Thomas[19] Wyatt, Jr. (Thomas "Tommy"[18] Wiatt, Sr. (Wyatt, Wiett), John[17], Henry[16], Richard[15], George[14], Rev. Haute "Haut" "Hawte"[13], Sir George "Georgius" Thomas[12], Sir Thomas "The Younger"[11], Sir Thomas "The Elder"[10], Sir Henry[9], Richard Wiat or[8] Wyatt, Geoffrey "Jeoffrey" Wiot or[7] Wiat, Robert or Richard[6] Wiot, William Wiot or[5] Wyot, Adam Wiot or Wyote or[4], Guyott[3], Guyott[2], Captain or Admiral Adam Guyott or[1] Wiot) was born Abt. 1820. He married Nancy L.

More About Thomas Wyatt, Jr.:

Fact 1: 1840, appears on the U.S. N.C. Federal Census next to *"Amos Parks."*

Fact 2: July 25, 1870, appears on census for Gold Hill, Rowan County, N.C.

Child of Thomas Wyatt and Nancy L. is:

447	i.	Jesse Franklin[20] Wyatt, born Abt. 1861 in Morgan Township, Rowan County, N.C. He married Amanda Nash October 23, 1879.

342. Martha[19] Wyatt (Overstreet[18], Richard[17], Richard[16] Wiatt, Richard[15], George[14], Rev. Haute "Haut" "Hawte"[13], Sir George "Georgius" Thomas[12], Sir Thomas "The Younger"[11],

Sir Thomas "The Elder"[10], Sir Henry[9], Richard Wiat or[8] Wyatt, Geoffrey "Jeoffrey" Wiot or[7] Wiat, Robert or Richard[6] Wiot, William Wiot or[5] Wyot, Adam Wiot or Wyote or[4], Guyott[3], Guyott[2], Captain or Admiral Adam Guyott or[1] Wiot) was born 1792, and died 1857. She married John Smith.

Children of Martha Wyatt and John Smith are:

448	i.	Mary[20] Smith.
449	ii.	Thomas Smith.
450	iii.	Sarah Smith.
451	iv.	Benjamin Smith.
452	v.	Martha Smith.
453	vi.	John Smith.
454	vii.	William Smith.
455	viii.	Emily Smith.
456	ix.	Andrew Smith.

358.   Thomas[19] Wyatt (Col. John[18], Richard[17], Richard[16] Wiatt, Richard[15], George[14], Rev. Haute "Haut" "Hawte"[13], Sir George "Georgius" Thomas[12], Sir Thomas "The Younger"[11], Sir Thomas "The Elder"[10], Sir Henry[9], Richard Wiat or[8] Wyatt, Geoffrey "Jeoffrey" Wiot or[7] Wiat, Robert or Richard[6] Wiot, William Wiot or[5] Wyot, Adam Wiot or Wyote or[4], Guyott[3], Guyott[2], Captain or Admiral Adam Guyott or[1] Wiot) was born 1809. He married Frances Allen, daughter of Judge Nathaniel? Allen.

Child of Thomas Wyatt and Frances Allen is:

457	i.	Eva[20] Wyatt, born 1844.

359.   Mary[19] Stark (Col.[18], Anne[17] Wyatt, John[16], John[15] Wiatt, Captain John[14], Rev. Haute "Haut" "Hawte"[13], Sir George "Georgius" Thomas[12], Sir Thomas "The Younger"[11], Sir Thomas "The Elder"[10], Sir Henry[9], Richard Wiat or[8] Wyatt, Geoffrey "Jeoffrey" Wiot or[7] Wiat, Robert or Richard[6] Wiot, William Wiot or[5] Wyot, Adam Wiot or Wyote or[4], Guyott[3], Guyott[2], Captain or Admiral Adam Guyott or[1] Wiot). She married Stephen Staples.

Children of Mary Stark and Stephen Staples are:

458	i.	Daughter #1[20] Staples.
459	ii.	Daughter #2 Staples.
460	iii.	Daughter #3 Staples.
461	iv.	Daughter #4 Staples.
462	v.	Daughter #5 Staples.
463	vi.	Daughter #6 Staples.
464	vii.	Daughter #7 Staples.
465	viii.	Daughter #8 Staples.
466	ix.	Daughter #9 Staples.
467	x.	Daughter #10 Staples.

468	xi.	Daughter #11 Staples.
469	xii.	Daughter #12 Staples.
470	xiii.	Daughter #13 Staples.
471	xiv.	Son #1 Staples.
472	xv.	Son #2 Staples.

Generation No. 20

379. Colonel James Foster[20] Wyatt (Elijah[19], William[18], William Edward[17] Wiatt, Sr., Captain Edward[16], Conquest[15], Edward[14], Rev. Haute "Haut" "Hawte"[13], Sir George "Georgius" Thomas[12], Sir Thomas "The Younger"[11], Sir Thomas "The Elder"[10], Sir Henry[9], Richard Wiat or[8] Wyatt, Geoffrey "Jeoffrey" Wiot or[7] Wiat, Robert or Richard[6] Wiot, William Wiot or[5] Wyot, Adam Wiot or Wyote or[4], Guyott[3], Guyott[2], Captain or Admiral Adam Guyott or[1] Wiot) was born 1801, and died 1868. He married Nancy Rosamond Pyles, daughter of William Pyles and Mary Rosamond.

More About Colonel James Foster Wyatt:
Remains are buried at Pisgah Baptist Church, Anderson County, S.C.

More About Nancy Rosamond Pyles:
Remains are buried at Pisgah Baptist Church, Anderson County, S.C.

Children of Colonel Wyatt and Nancy Pyles are:

473	i.	Ludy Asbury21 Wyatt. He married Mary Woodfin.

More About Ludy Asbury Wyatt:
Fact 1: Moved to Marion, Ala.

474	ii.	Redmond Foster Wyatt. He married Nancy Ophelia Rasor.
475	iii.	Isaac Allerton Newton Wyatt.

More About Isaac Allerton Newton Wyatt:
Died at age 18, single.

476	iv.	William Rosamond Wyatt, died in Marion, Ala.

More About William Rosamond Wyatt:
Never married.

477	v.	Essie Elizabeth Wyatt. She married Thomas William Martin.
478	vi.	Cornelia Virginia Wyatt. She married James Hamilton Burdine.
479	vii.	James Jasper Wyatt.

More About James Jasper Wyatt:
Died at age 24. Never married.

381. Redmond Grigsby[20] Wyatt (Elijah[19], William[18], William Edward[17] Wiatt, Sr., Captain Edward[16], Conquest[15], Edward[14], Rev. Haute "Haut" "Hawte"[13], Sir George "Georgius" Thomas[12], Sir Thomas "The Younger"[11], Sir Thomas "The Elder"[10], Sir Henry[9], Richard Wiat or[8] Wyatt, Geoffrey "Jeoffrey" Wiot or[7] Wiat, Robert or Richard[6] Wiot, William Wiot or[5] Wyot, Adam Wiot or Wyote or[4], Guyott[3], Guyott[2], Captain or Admiral Adam Guyott or[1] Wiot) was born 1806, and died 1857. He married (1) Eleanor Ann "Nelly" Seawright, daughter of Andrew Seawright and Margaret Richey. He married (2) Elizabeth Dunn Richey Abt. 1829, daughter of James Richey and Elizabeth Dunn.

More About Redmond Grigsby Wyatt:
Fact 1: 1867, possible date of death.
Fact 2: Planter in Anderson County, S.C.

Children of Redmond Wyatt and Eleanor Seawright are:

480	i.	Margaret Luani[21] Wyatt. She married John Robert Henderson.
481	ii.	Eugenia Ann Wyatt. She married Enoch Smith Pepper.
482	iii.	Andrew Grigsby Wyatt. He married Eveline Garrison Lenhardt.
483	iv.	Redmond Caldwell Wyatt. He married Frances Jospehine Sitton.
484	v.	Rebecca Josephine Wyatt. She married Lemuel G. Hendricks.

Children of Redmond Wyatt and Elizabeth Richey are:

485	i.	James Elijah[21] Wyatt. He married Mary Wilson.
486	ii.	William Franklin Wyatt. He married Dorcas Sara Ann LaBoon.
487	iii.	Mary Jane Wyatt. She married Auguste Andrea.

More About Auguste Andrea:
Fact 1: A planter in Italia Plantation, Greenville County, S.C.

| 488 | iv. | Harriet Elizabeth Wyatt. She married Enoch Wigington. |

More About Harriet Elizabeth Wyatt:
Fact 1: Moved to Alabama.

489	v.	John Newton Wyatt. He married Elizabeth Caroline Smith.
490	vi.	Samuel Thompson Wyatt. He married Sara Richley.
491	vii.	Elizabeth D. Richey Wyatt.

More About Elizabeth D. Richey Wyatt:
Remains are buried at Greenville Church, Anderson County, S.C.

387.   James B.[20] sykes (frances[19] cates, thomas[18], Rebecca[17] Sykes, Frances[16] Wiatt, Richard[15], George[14], Rev. Haute "Haut" "Hawte"[13], Sir George "Georgius" Thomas[12], Sir Thomas "The Younger"[11], Sir Thomas "The Elder"[10], Sir Henry[9], Richard Wiat or[8] Wyatt, Geoffrey "Jeoffrey" Wiot or[7] Wiat, Robert or Richard[6] Wiot, William Wiot or[5] Wyot, Adam Wiot or Wyote or[4], Guyott[3], Guyott[2], Captain or Admiral Adam Guyott or[1] Wiot) was born 1804 in Orange County, N.C., and died 1880 in Orange County, N.C. He married cynthia cheek.

Child of james Sykes and cynthia cheek is:

+   492   i.   Martha C.[21] Sykes, born July 14, 1847 in Orange County, N.C.; died August 31, 1914 in melville, alamance, n.c.

392.   William Carroll[20] Wyatt (Robert Henry[19], James[18], Colonel Joseph[17], Henry[16] Wiatt, Richard[15], George[14], Rev. Haute "Haut" "Hawte"[13], Sir George "Georgius" Thomas[12], Sir Thomas "The Younger"[11], Sir Thomas "The Elder"[10], Sir Henry[9], Richard Wiat or[8] Wyatt, Geoffrey "Jeoffrey" Wiot or[7] Wiat, Robert or Richard[6] Wiot, William Wiot or[5] Wyot, Adam Wiot or Wyote or[4], Guyott[3], Guyott[2], Captain or Admiral Adam Guyott or[1] Wiot) was born Abt. 1815, and died 1901. He married (1) Louisa Lucy Mildred Burch. He married (2) Harriet O'Guin.

More About William Carroll Wyatt:
Fact 1: Farmer and general store owner.
Fact 2: 1818-1901, lifespan given in the CLP research for Arkansas.

Children of William Wyatt and Louisa Burch are:
493   i.   Harriett "Hattie" Ophelia[21] Wyatt, born 1878 in Bakersville, Humphreys County, Tn.; died 1950. She married Thaddeus Horatius Caraway.

More About Harriett "Hattie" Ophelia Wyatt:
Fact 1: Was the first elected woman to U.S. Senate.
Fact 2: Democrat and school teacher.
Fact 3: Nicknamed: *"Silent Hattie."*
Fact 4: Supported the Equal Rights Amendment to the U.S. Constitution.
Fact 5: 1931-1945, served in the United States Senate.
Fact 6: Opposed repeal of Prohibition.
Fact 7: Supported Equal Rights Amendment to U.S. Constitution.

More About Thaddeus Horatius Caraway:
Fact 1: Worked as a cotton picker, teacher and lawyer.
Fact 2: 1908-1912, Judicial District Prosecutor in Arkansas.
Fact 3: 1913-1921, served in the U.S. House of Representatives.

Fact 4: 1921-1931, served in the United States Senate.

Fact 5: 1883, moved with his mother to Arkansas.

Fact 6: Was a Democrat.

494	ii.	Child #2 Wyatt.
495	iii.	Child #3 Wyatt.
496	iv.	Child #4 Wyatt.

Children of William Wyatt and Harriet O'Guin are:

497	i.	Child #1[21] Wyatt.
498	ii.	Child #2 Wyatt.
499	iii.	Child #3 Wyatt.
500	iv.	Child #4 Wyatt.
501	v.	Child #5 Wyatt.

393.   Gilbert Newton[20] Wyatt (Charles[19], Ballard S.[18], Colonel Joseph[17], Henry[16] Wiatt, Richard[15], George[14], Rev. Haute "Haut" "Hawte"[13], Sir George "Georgius" Thomas[12], Sir Thomas "The Younger"[11], Sir Thomas "The Elder"[10], Sir Henry[9], Richard Wiat or[8] Wyatt, Geoffrey "Jeoffrey" Wiot or[7] Wiat, Robert or Richard[6] Wiot, William Wiot or[5] Wyot, Adam Wiot or Wyote or[4], Guyott[3], Guyott[2], Captain or Admiral Adam Guyott or[1] Wiot) was born 1839 in Greenbriar, W.Va. He married Mary E. Pritchlett.

Child of Gilbert Wyatt and Mary Pritchlett is:

502	i.	Valentine B.[21] Wyatt, born in Mt. Erie, Wayne, Il.; died in Amarillo, Potter, Tx. He married Mary Joanna Gallagher 1892.

400.   Gilbert Ivey[20] Wyatt (Jesse "Jessey"[19], John "Johney"[18], John[17] Wiatt, Henry[16], Richard[15], George[14], Rev. Haute "Haut" "Hawte"[13], Sir George "Georgius" Thomas[12], Sir Thomas "The Younger"[11], Sir Thomas "The Elder"[10], Sir Henry[9], Richard Wiat or[8] Wyatt, Geoffrey "Jeoffrey" Wiot or[7] Wiat, Robert or Richard[6] Wiot, William Wiot or[5] Wyot, Adam Wiot or Wyote or[4], Guyott[3], Guyott[2], Captain or Admiral Adam Guyott or[1] Wiot) was born March 29, 1830 in Davidson County, N.C., and died August 28, 1863 in Battery Wagoner, Morris Island, S.C. He married Eve Ann Ludwig.

More About Gilbert Ivey Wyatt:

Fact 1: Company K, Infantry, captured early in war.

Fact 2: Killed at Battery Wagoner, shot through the eye.

Children of Gilbert Wyatt and Eve Ludwig are:

503	i.	William H.[21] Wyatt, born 1852 in Bringles P.O., Westside of River Road, Pooletown District, Morgan Township, N.C.
504	ii.	Margaret Jane Wyatt, born 1857 in Bringles P.O., Westside of River Road, Pooletown District, Morgan Township, N.C.

401. Wilson Riley[20] Wyatt (Jesse "Jessey"[19], John "Johney"[18], John[17] Wiatt, Henry[16], Richard[15], George[14], Rev. Haute "Haut" "Hawte"[13], Sir George "Georgius" Thomas[12], Sir Thomas "The Younger"[11], Sir Thomas "The Elder"[10], Sir Henry[9], Richard Wiat or[8] Wyatt, Geoffrey "Jeoffrey" Wiot or[7] Wiat, Robert or Richard[6] Wiot, William Wiot or[5] Wyot, Adam Wiot or Wyote or[4], Guyott[3], Guyott[2], Captain or Admiral Adam Guyott or[1] Wiot) was born March 29, 1830 in Davidson and Rowan counties on Yadkin River, N.C., and died March 1862 in Salisbury, Rowan County, N.C. He married Mary Ann Park September 29, 1850 in Lick Creek, Davidson County, N.C., daughter of John Park and Mary Bean.

More About Wilson Riley Wyatt:
Fact 1: 1860, U.S. Federal Census with wife and two sons.

Children of Wilson Wyatt and Mary Park are:

505   i.   John Thomas[21] Wyatt, born October 31, 1851 in Davidson and Rowan counties, N.C.; died November 03, 1933 in Rockwell, Litaker, Rowan County N.C. He married Charlotte Elizabeth Phillips December 16, 1880 in Rowan County N.C.

More About John Thomas Wyatt:
Fact 1: *"Venus of Faith"* pen name used for John Thomas Wyatt as a newspaper columnist.
Fact 2: 1860, appears on the U.S. Federal Census Salisbury Rowan County, N.C. birth: Abt. 1851
Fact 3: 1900, appears on the U.S. Federal Census in Litaker, Rowan County, N.C.; Born: Oct. 18
Fact 4: 1930, appears on the U.S. Federal Census in Faith, Rowan County, N.C. birth: Abt. 1852
Fact 5: November 03, 1933, listed in North Carolina Death Indexes, 1908-2004; Rowan County, N.C.
Fact 6: November 03, 1933, listed in North Carolina Death Certificates, 1909-1975; Rowan County, N.C.
Fact 7: 1851-1933, listed in the North Carolina Find A Grave Index, 1716-2012.
Died at 2 a.m. November 3, 1933.
Passed in the home of his nephew Henry Wyatt in Rockwell, N.C., according to a newspaper article; however, this may have been *"Harvey Wyatt."*

+ 506   ii.   Columbus Ciscero Wyatt, born September 23, 1853 in Davidson County, N.C.; died January 18, 1920 in Baden, Stanly County, N.C.

419. John[20] Wyatt? (Lazerus Pleasant[19] Wyatt, Thomas "Tommy"[18] Wiatt, Sr. (Wyatt, Wiett), John[17], Henry[16], Richard[15], George[14], Rev. Haute "Haut" "Hawte"[13], Sir George "Georgius"

Thomas[12], Sir Thomas "The Younger"[11], Sir Thomas "The Elder"[10], Sir Henry[9], Richard Wiat or[8] Wyatt, Geoffrey "Jeoffrey" Wiot or[7] Wiat, Robert or Richard[6] Wiot, William Wiot or[5] Wyot, Adam Wiot or Wyote or[4], Guyott[3], Guyott[2], Captain or Admiral Adam Guyott or[1] Wiot). He married Wife.

More About John Wyatt?:
Died in PEST House.

    Children of John Wyatt? and Wife are:

	507	i.	Gracie[21] Wyatt?. She married Hagler.
+	508	ii.	Beulah Wyatt?.

420. Ciscero "Cicero" L.[20] Wyatt (Lazerus Pleasant[19], Thomas "Tommy"[18] Wiatt, Sr. (Wyatt, Wiett), John[17], Henry[16], Richard[15], George[14], Rev. Haute "Haut" "Hawte"[13], Sir George "Georgius" Thomas[12], Sir Thomas "The Younger"[11], Sir Thomas "The Elder"[10], Sir Henry[9], Richard Wiat or[8] Wyatt, Geoffrey "Jeoffrey" Wiot or[7] Wiat, Robert or Richard[6] Wiot, William Wiot or[5] Wyot, Adam Wiot or Wyote or[4], Guyott[3], Guyott[2], Captain or Admiral Adam Guyott or[1] Wiot) was born February 02, 1861, and died January 21, 1945. He married Polly Louise "Louisa" Park November 19, 1882 in Rowan County N.C., daughter of Milas Parks and Anna Wyatt.

More About Polly Louise "Louisa" Park:
Fact 1: Referred to as "Parks" in Rowan County, N.C. marriage bonds.

    Children of Ciscero Wyatt and Polly Park are:

+	509	i.	Pleasant Loveless[21] Wyatt, born 1895 in Rowan County, N.C.; died 1986 in Rowan County, N.C.
	510	ii.	Infant Daughter? Wyatt?, born 1891.
	511	iii.	Columbus L. Wyatt?, born 1895.

429. Henry Thomas[20] Wyatt (Noah Calvin[19], Thomas "Tommy"[18] Wiatt, Sr. (Wyatt, Wiett), John[17], Henry[16], Richard[15], George[14], Rev. Haute "Haut" "Hawte"[13], Sir George "Georgius" Thomas[12], Sir Thomas "The Younger"[11], Sir Thomas "The Elder"[10], Sir Henry[9], Richard Wiat or[8] Wyatt, Geoffrey "Jeoffrey" Wiot or[7] Wiat, Robert or Richard[6] Wiot, William Wiot or[5] Wyot, Adam Wiot or Wyote or[4], Guyott[3], Guyott[2], Captain or Admiral Adam Guyott or[1] Wiot) was born 1828 in North Carolina. He married Mary Kisler or Kesler.

More About Henry Thomas Wyatt:
Fact 1: 7th Regiment Company F, North Carolina Troops ACW.
Was his name Henry R. Wyatt?

    Children of Henry Wyatt and Mary Kesler are:

512	i.	Nancy "Nan" Jane[21] Wyatt, born Abt. 1857.
513	ii.	Barbara Lou Wyatt, born Abt. 1861.

+   514   iii.   Elizabeth Augusta Wyatt, born May 24, 1867; died November 05, 1933.

      515   iv.   Mary Annie Wyatt, born December 07, 1871.

430. Malinda [Delinda][20] Wyatt (Noah Calvin[19], Thomas "Tommy"[18] Wiatt, Sr. (Wyatt, Wiett), John[17], Henry[16], Richard[15], George[14], Rev. Haute "Haut" "Hawte"[13], Sir George "Georgius" Thomas[12], Sir Thomas "The Younger"[11], Sir Thomas "The Elder"[10], Sir Henry[9], Richard Wiat or[8] Wyatt, Geoffrey "Jeoffrey" Wiot or[7] Wiat, Robert or Richard[6] Wiot, William Wiot or[5] Wyot, Adam Wiot or Wyote or[4], Guyott[3], Guyott[2], Captain or Admiral Adam Guyott or[1] Wiot) was born February 05, 1829, and died January 23, 1903. She married John Buchanan August 26, 1848 in Rowan County, N.C., son of James Buchanan and Phelpena Shaver.

More About Malinda [Delinda] Wyatt:
Fact 1: Nicknamed: *"Linda."*
Remains are buried at East Corinth Baptist Church Cemetery, Rowan County, NC

More About John Buchanan:
Fact 1: 1850, appears on N.C. Census with father James and other family members.
East Corinth Baptist Church Cemetery, Rowan County, NC

      Children of Malinda Wyatt and John Buchanan are:
      516   i.   Eli[21] Buchanan.
      517   ii.   Grant Buchanan.
      518   iii.   Lou Buchanan.
      519   iv.   Mack Buchanan.
      520   v.   Mary Jane Buchanan.
      521   vi.   Moses L. Buchanan.

431. William Wesley "Brantly"[20] Wyatt (Noah Calvin[19], Thomas "Tommy"[18] Wiatt, Sr. (Wyatt, Wiett), John[17], Henry[16], Richard[15], George[14], Rev. Haute "Haut" "Hawte"[13], Sir George "Georgius" Thomas[12], Sir Thomas "The Younger"[11], Sir Thomas "The Elder"[10], Sir Henry[9], Richard Wiat or[8] Wyatt, Geoffrey "Jeoffrey" Wiot or[7] Wiat, Robert or Richard[6] Wiot, William Wiot or[5] Wyot, Adam Wiot or Wyote or[4], Guyott[3], Guyott[2], Captain or Admiral Adam Guyott or[1] Wiot) was born 1831 in North Carolina, and died July 20, 1863 in Gettysburg, Pa. He married Mary Buchanan Abt. 1859 in Rowan County N.C., daughter of James Buchanan and Phelpena Shaver.

More About William Wesley "Brantly" Wyatt:
Fact 1: 23rd Regiment Company H, North Carolina State Troops ACW.
Fact 2: August 02, 1850, is a laborer.

      Children of William Wyatt and Mary Buchanan are:
+   522   i.   John C.[21] Wyatt, born Abt. 1860 in Rowan County, N.C.
+   523   ii.   James "Jim" Noah Wyatt, born April 04, 1861 in North Carolina; died February 02, 1957.

432. Emanuel James M.[20] Wyatt (Noah Calvin[19], Thomas "Tommy"[18] Wiatt, Sr. (Wyatt, Wiett), John[17], Henry[16], Richard[15], George[14], Rev. Haute "Haut" "Hawte"[13], Sir George "Georgius" Thomas[12], Sir Thomas "The Younger"[11], Sir Thomas "The Elder"[10], Sir Henry[9], Richard Wiat or[8] Wyatt, Geoffrey "Jeoffrey" Wiot or[7] Wiat, Robert or Richard[6] Wiot, William Wiot or[5] Wyot, Adam Wiot or Wyote or[4], Guyott[3], Guyott[2], Captain or Admiral Adam Guyott or[1] Wiot) was born 1832. He married Mary Bean.

        Children of Emanuel Wyatt and Mary Bean are:
       524   i.   Calvin[21] Wyatt.
       525   ii.   Casandra Wyatt.
       526   iii.   James Wyatt.
       527   iv.   Moses Wyatt.

433. Lila Delilah "Delila"[20] Wyatt (Noah Calvin[19], Thomas "Tommy"[18] Wiatt, Sr. (Wyatt, Wiett), John[17], Henry[16], Richard[15], George[14], Rev. Haute "Haut" "Hawte"[13], Sir George "Georgius" Thomas[12], Sir Thomas "The Younger"[11], Sir Thomas "The Elder"[10], Sir Henry[9], Richard Wiat or[8] Wyatt, Geoffrey "Jeoffrey" Wiot or[7] Wiat, Robert or Richard[6] Wiot, William Wiot or[5] Wyot, Adam Wiot or Wyote or[4], Guyott[3], Guyott[2], Captain or Admiral Adam Guyott or[1] Wiot) was born 1834 in North Carolina. She married Nathaniel "Nathan" Morgan October 18, 1855 in Rowan County, N.C., son of Moses Morgan and Barbara Shaver.

More About Nathaniel "Nathan" Morgan:
Fact 1: Served in 5th Regiment Co. H, N.C. Troops.
Fact 2: Was the third Nathan.
Remains are buried at East Corinth Baptist Church Cemetery, Gold Hill, Rowan County, N.C.

        Children of Lila Wyatt and Nathaniel Morgan are:
       528   i.   Jane Alice[21] Morgan. She married Dow Surratt.
       529   ii.   John Wesley Morgan. He married Mandy File.

                   More About John Wesley Morgan:
                   Fact 1: Aunt Betty was born in John Wesley Morgan's house -- Betty being Daddy's sister.

       530   iii.   Lee Morgan. He married (1) Essie Bringle. He married (2) Lynda Loftin.
       531   iv.   Mamie Morgan. She married Mock Loftin.
       532   v.   Mock Morgan. He married Eva A. Morris.
+   533   vi.   Rhoda Isabelle Morgan, born February 07, 1862 in North Carolina; died January 04, 1909 in North Carolina.
       534   vii.   William Collie Morgan, born April 04, 1873; died September 24, 1935. He married Emma L. Basinger.

434. Rachel Evelyn "Eveline"[20] Wyatt (Noah Calvin[19], Thomas "Tommy"[18] Wiatt, Sr. (Wyatt, Wiett), John[17], Henry[16], Richard[15], George[14], Rev. Haute "Haut" "Hawte"[13], Sir George "Georgius" Thomas[12], Sir Thomas "The Younger"[11], Sir Thomas "The Elder"[10], Sir Henry[9], Richard Wiat or[8] Wyatt, Geoffrey "Jeoffrey" Wiot or[7] Wiat, Robert or Richard[6] Wiot, William Wiot or[5] Wyot, Adam Wiot or Wyote or[4], Guyott[3], Guyott[2], Captain or Admiral Adam Guyott or[1] Wiot) was born October 02, 1835 in North Carolina, and died April 24, 1915 in North Carolina. She married John Calvin Morgan June 28, 1855 in Rowan County, N.C., son of Moses Morgan and Barbara Shaver.

> More About Rachel Evelyn "Eveline" Wyatt:
> Fact 1: *"Evelyn"* also spelled: *"Eveline."*
> Fact 2: October 02, 1913, Celebrates 78th birthday with family dinner: Shavers, Morgans, Wyatts attended.
> Fact 3: August 02, 1850, In McCubbins file listed as *"Rachel C."* age 14.
> Buried on Row #14; aged 79 years, 6 months, 23 days
> Buried Luther's Lutheran Church formerly called Piney Wood's -- Lutherans used it and the primative baptists used it -- alternated Sundays.

> More About John Calvin Morgan:
> Fact 1: 1/8 Cherokee Indian from Shavers, according: W.A. Hinson (1987).
> Fact 2: 5th Regiment Company H North Carolina Troops ACW.
> Fact 3: Died at the Battle of Spotsylvania Court House, Va.
> Fact 4: Had nine slaves.
> Died at the Battle of Spotsylvania Court House, Va. Possibly buried in Spotsylvania Confederate Cemetery in Spotsylvania County, Va. or in the Fredericksburg Confederate Cemetery.

> Children of Rachel Wyatt and John Morgan are:
> + 535   i.   Mary Jane[21] Morgan, born November 20, 1856 in Rowan County, N.C.; died October 15, 1928 in died at a state hospital, N.C.
>
> 536   ii.   John Noah Calvin Morgan, born November 06, 1862; died October 25, 1927 in died in Morganton in state hospital, Richfield, Rowan County, N.C. He married Eugenia A. *"Jennie"* Culp.
>
> > More About John Noah Calvin Morgan:
> > Buried at Luther's Lutheran Church, Richfield, N.C.
> >
> > More About Eugenia A. "Jennie" Culp:
> > Buried in the Luther's Lutheran Church Cemetery, Richfield, N.C.

435. Silas "Siles"[20] Wyatt (Noah Calvin[19], Thomas "Tommy"[18] Wiatt, Sr. (Wyatt, Wiett), John[17], Henry[16], Richard[15], George[14], Rev. Haute "Haut" "Hawte"[13], Sir George "Georgius"

Thomas[12], Sir Thomas "The Younger"[11], Sir Thomas "The Elder"[10], Sir Henry[9], Richard Wiat or[8] Wyatt, Geoffrey "Jeoffrey" Wiot or[7] Wiat, Robert or Richard[6] Wiot, William Wiot or[5] Wyot, Adam Wiot or Wyote or[4], Guyott[3], Guyott[2], Captain or Admiral Adam Guyott or[1] Wiot) was born 1838 in North Carolina, and died January 19, 1864 in Point Lookout, Md. He married Lucetta "Settie" Rufty.

More About Silas "Siles" Wyatt:
Fact 1: 5th Regiment Company G, North Carolina Troops ACW.
Fact 2: August 02, 1850, age 12.
Fact 3: August 08, 1860, listed on U.S. Federal Census living in Salisbury N.C. with his wife.

> Children of Silas Wyatt and Lucetta Rufty are:
> 537   i.   Laura[21] Wyatt.
> 538   ii. Lucinda Wyatt.

436. Mary Ann[20] Wyatt (Noah Calvin[19], Thomas "Tommy"[18] Wiatt, Sr. (Wyatt, Wiett), John[17], Henry[16], Richard[15], George[14], Rev. Haute "Haut" "Hawte"[13], Sir George "Georgius" Thomas[12], Sir Thomas "The Younger"[11], Sir Thomas "The Elder"[10], Sir Henry[9], Richard Wiat or[8] Wyatt, Geoffrey "Jeoffrey" Wiot or[7] Wiat, Robert or Richard[6] Wiot, William Wiot or[5] Wyot, Adam Wiot or Wyote or[4], Guyott[3], Guyott[2], Captain or Admiral Adam Guyott or[1] Wiot) was born March 20, 1839 in North Carolina, and died October 12, 1902 in Rowan County N.C. She married Joseph Travis Eagle December 01, 1859, son of Solomon Eagle and Agnes Hodge.

More About Mary Ann Wyatt:
Fact 1: August 02, 1850, was age 11
Fact 2: October 02, 1902, possible date of demise Remains are buried in the Liberty United Methodist Church Cemetery, Gold Hill, Rowan County, N.C. Inscription: *"Aged 63 y's 6 m's 12 dy's"*

More About Joseph Travis Eagle:
Fact 1: Lived in the Liberty community of Rowan County, N.C.
Fact 2: December 01, 1859, marriage cited: Rachel Hinson Hill's book: p. 134 *Egley, Egle, Egli, Eagle, 1690-1998.*
Remains are buried at the Liberty United Methodist Church Cemetery, Gold Hill, Rowan County, N.C. Inscription: "Aged 71 yrs 7 ms 3 ds"

> Children of Mary Wyatt and Joseph Eagle are:
> + 539   i.   Noah Calvin[21] Eagle, born April 30, 1861 in Rowan County N.C.; died August 14, 1951.
> + 540   ii. Eli Esau Eagle, born October 14, 1861 in Rowan County N.C.; died March 07, 1935.
> + 541   iii. Nancy Jane Eagle, born October 07, 1862 in Rowan County N.C.; died April 26, 1943 in Gold Hill, Morgan Township, Rowan County, N.C.

+ 542   iv.   Mary Malinda Eagle, born August 22, 1866 in Rowan County N.C.; died January 09, 1945.

   543   v.   Frances Lou "Lieu" Eagle, born September 10, 1868 in Rowan County N.C.; died January 27, 1953 in Rowan County N.C. She married (1) James Hugh "Huey" Morgan. She married (2) William Alexander Agner April 07, 1887 in Rowan County N.C.

More About Frances Lou "Lieu" Eagle:
East Corinth Baptist Church cemtery, Gold Hill, Rowan County, N.C.Inscription: *"GONE BUT NOT FORGOTTEN."*

More About James Hugh "Huey" Morgan:
East Corinth Baptist Church cemtery, Gold Hill, Rowan County, N.C. Inscription: *"GONE BUT NOT FORGOTTEN."*

More About William Alexander Agner:
Providence United Methodist Church Cemetery, Salisbury, Rowan County, N.C. Row #2; Inscription: *"27yrs, 7 mos, and 20 dys."*

   544   vi.   Amanda Caroline "Carolina" Eagle, born 1870 in Rowan County N.C.; died 1958. She married Pheonix N. Trexler.

+ 545   vii.   William Grant Eagle, born July 28, 1872 in Rowan County N.C.; died April 11, 1943 in Rowan County N.C.

+ 546   viii.   Josephine Eagle, born March 10, 1875 in Rowan County N.C.; died February 07, 1968 in Rowan County N.C.

   547   ix.   John Solomon Eagle, born 1877 in Rowan County N.C.; died 1910 in Rowan County N.C. He married Lillie Rufty.

   548   x.   Joseph Travis Eagle, born 1878 in Rowan County N.C.; died 1914 in Rowan County N.C. He married Ollie Earnhardt.

   549   xi.   Walter C. Eagle, born 1881 in Rowan County N.C.; died 1881 in Rowan County N.C.

437. Eli[20] Wyatt (Noah Calvin[19], Thomas "Tommy"[18] Wiatt, Sr. (Wyatt, Wiett), John[17], Henry[16], Richard[15], George[14], Rev. Haute "Haut" "Hawte"[13], Sir George "Georgius" Thomas[12], Sir Thomas "The Younger"[11], Sir Thomas "The Elder"[10], Sir Henry[9], Richard Wiat or[8] Wyatt, Geoffrey "Jeoffrey" Wiot or[7] Wiat, Robert or Richard[6] Wiot, William Wiot or[5] Wyot, Adam Wiot or Wyote or[4], Guyott[3], Guyott[2], Captain or Admiral Adam Guyott or[1] Wiot) was born January 30, 1841 in North Carolina, and died June 01, 1912 in Rowan County N.C. He married Malinda Wise July 30, 1868 in Rowan County North Carolina, daughter of Charles Wise and Sophie May.

More About Eli Wyatt:
Fact 1: 10th Regiment Company D, 1st Regiment North Carolina Artillery; NCST ACW.

Fact 2: August 02, 1850, listed as age 9 in McCubbins file.
Remains are buried at Saint Matthews Lutheran Church Cemetery, Salisbury, N.C. Row #22; Plot #293.

More About Malinda Wise:
Remains are buried at Saint Matthew's Lutheran Church Cemetery, Salisbury, Rowan County, N.C. Row #22; Plot # 294.

Children of Eli Wyatt and Malinda Wise are:

+ 550   i.   Laura Jane[21] Wyatt, born May 20, 1869; died February 20, 1940.
+ 551   ii.   Mary Sophia Wyatt, born November 26, 1870 in Rowan County N.C.; died June 30, 1933 in Rowan County N.C.
+ 552   iii.   William Mock Wyatt, born August 05, 1872 in Rowan County N.C.; died October 27, 1939 in Rowan County N.C.
   553   iv.   Melinda Lou Wyatt, born May 05, 1876; died November 29, 1933.

438. Noah "Noe" Calvin[20] Wyatt (Noah Calvin[19], Thomas "Tommy"[18] Wiatt, Sr. (Wyatt, Wiett), John[17], Henry[16], Richard[15], George[14], Rev. Haute "Haut" "Hawte"[13], Sir George "Georgius" Thomas[12], Sir Thomas "The Younger"[11], Sir Thomas "The Elder"[10], Sir Henry[9], Richard Wiat or[8] Wyatt, Geoffrey "Jeoffrey" Wiot or[7] Wiat, Robert or Richard[6] Wiot, William Wiot or[5] Wyot, Adam Wiot or Wyote or[4], Guyott[3], Guyott[2], Captain or Admiral Adam Guyott or[1] Wiot) was born 1843 in North Carolina. He married Nancy Daniels Reid March 15, 1866 in Not sure of wedding date or place Rowan County N.C.?.

More About Noah "Noe" Calvin Wyatt:
Fact 1: 5th Regiment Company H, North Carolina State Troops, ACW.
Fact 2: August 02, 1850, listed as age 7.
Fact 3: August 08, 1862, enlisted in Iredell County for Confederacy.

Children of Noah Wyatt and Nancy Reid are:

   554   i.   Zeb[21] Wyatt.
   555   ii.   Walter Wyatt.
   556   iii.   M. D. Wyatt.
   557   iv.   Traves Wyatt.

439. Rhoda E.[20] Wyatt (Noah Calvin[19], Thomas "Tommy"[18] Wiatt, Sr. (Wyatt, Wiett), John[17], Henry[16], Richard[15], George[14], Rev. Haute "Haut" "Hawte"[13], Sir George "Georgius" Thomas[12], Sir Thomas "The Younger"[11], Sir Thomas "The Elder"[10], Sir Henry[9], Richard Wiat or[8] Wyatt, Geoffrey "Jeoffrey" Wiot or[7] Wiat, Robert or Richard[6] Wiot, William Wiot or[5] Wyot, Adam Wiot or Wyote or[4], Guyott[3], Guyott[2], Captain or Admiral Adam Guyott or[1] Wiot) was born October 10, 1844 in North Carolina, and died April 22, 1920 in Rowan County N.C. She married John I. Shaver December 03, 1868 in Rowan County N.C., son of John Shaver and Rebecca [Reid].

More About Rhoda E. Wyatt:
Fact 1: August 02, 1850, listed age 5 in McCubbins file at Rowan Public Library. Remains are buried at Zion United Methodist Church Cemetery, Rowan County, N.C.; Row #2.

More About John I. Shaver:
Buried at Zion United Methodist Church Cemetery, Rowan County, N.C.; Row #2.; Aged 67 Yrs 2 Mos 3 Days.

Children of Rhoda Wyatt and John Shaver are:

	558	i.	Billie[21] Shaver.
	559	ii.	Mary Shaver.
+	560	iii.	Ollie Lou Ada Shaver, born March 10, 1870; died July 03, 1955.
	561	iv.	Amanda Barbara Shaver, born 1873-1937. She married Noah Calvin File 1895.

More About Amanda Barbara Shaver:
Chestnut Hill Cemetery, Salisbury, N.C.

More About Noah Calvin File:
Chestnut Hill Cemetery, Salisbury, N.C.

+	562	v.	Emanuel Calvin Shaver, born 1875-1930 in Rowan County N.C.; died in Rowan County N.C.
	563	vi.	Jane Alice Shaver, born 1877-1950. She married Hoffman.

440. John P.[20] Wyatt (Noah Calvin[19], Thomas "Tommy"[18] Wiatt, Sr. (Wyatt, Wiett), John[17], Henry[16], Richard[15], George[14], Rev. Haute "Haut" "Hawte"[13], Sir George "Georgius" Thomas[12], Sir Thomas "The Younger"[11], Sir Thomas "The Elder"[10], Sir Henry[9], Richard Wiat or[8] Wyatt, Geoffrey "Jeoffrey" Wiot or[7] Wiat, Robert or Richard[6] Wiot, William Wiot or[5] Wyot, Adam Wiot or Wyote or[4], Guyott[3], Guyott[2], Captain or Admiral Adam Guyott or[1] Wiot) was born October 23, 1846 in Rowan County, N.C., and died April 07, 1924 in Rowan County N.C. He married Mary Frances Hodge March 09, 1871 in Rowan County N.C., daughter of Richard Hodge and Sallie.

More About John P. Wyatt:
Fact 1: August 02, 1850, U.S. Federal Census in School District #41 Rowan Co., N.C. birth: Abt. 1847
Fact 2: 1860, U.S. Federal Census in Salisbury, Rowan Co., N.C. birth: Abt. 1847
Fact 3: 1880, U.S. Federal Census in Morgan Township, Rowan Co., N.C. birth: Abt. 1847
Fact 4: 1900, U.S. Federal Census in Rowan Co., N.C. birth: October 1846.
Fact 5: 1910, U.S. Federal Census in Morgan Township, Rowan Co., N.C. birth: Abt. 1847

Fact 6: 1920, U.S. Federal Census in Morgan Township, Rowan Co., N.C. birth: Abt. 1847

Fact 7: 2nd Regiment Company B (North Carolina Junior Reserves); ACW.

Fact 8: 1850, Was a teacher for Noah Jenkins Eagle -- grammar school Rowan County, N.C.

Fact 9: Yadkin Valley School 1-7 grades.

Remains are buried at Wyatt Grove Missionary Baptist Church Cemetery, Richfield, Rowan County, N.C.

More About Mary Frances Hodge:

Remains are buried at Wyatt Grove Missionary Baptist Church Cemetery, Richfield, Rowan County, N.C.

Children of John Wyatt and Mary Hodge are:

564   i.   Martha "Lou" Louise[21] Wyatt, born October 24, 1873; died May 01, 1951.

565   ii.   Ann Wyatt?

566   iii.   Henry Walter Wyatt, born October 14, 1881; died February 01, 1928. He married Cole?.

441. **Amanda Jane[20] Wyatt** (Noah Calvin[19], Thomas "Tommy"[18] Wiatt, Sr. (Wyatt, Wiett), John[17], Henry[16], Richard[15], George[14], Rev. Haute "Haut" "Hawte"[13], Sir George "Georgius" Thomas[12], Sir Thomas "The Younger"[11], Sir Thomas "The Elder"[10], Sir Henry[9], Richard Wiat or[8] Wyatt, Geoffrey "Jeoffrey" Wiot or[7] Wiat, Robert or Richard[6] Wiot, William Wiot or[5] Wyot, Adam Wiot or Wyote or[4], Guyott[3], Guyott[2], Captain or Admiral Adam Guyott or[1] Wiot) was born January 28, 1848 in Rowan County, N.C., and died April 23, 1907 in Rowan County N.C. She married Daniel Calvin Eagle September 17, 1868 in Rowan County, N.C., son of Solomon Eagle and Agnes Hodge.

More About Amanda Jane Wyatt:

Fact 1: August 02, 1850, listed age 2, according to McCubbins file: Rowan Pub. Lib., Salisbury, N.C.

Remains are buried at Saint Matthew's Lutheran Church Cemetery, Salisbury, N.C.; Row #3; plot #17.

More About Daniel Calvin Eagle:

Remains are buried in the Saint Matthew's Lutheran Church Cemetery, Salisbury, Rowan County, N.C.

Children of Amanda Wyatt and Daniel Eagle are:

    567   i.   Delinda Isabelle[21] Eagle.

+ 568   ii.   William Lawson Eagle, born January 31, 1870 in Rowan County, N.C.; died November 27, 1928.

+ 569   iii.   Adolphus Grant Eagle, born August 30, 1873 in North Carolina; died June 06, 1941 in North Carolina.

+ 570   iv.   John Murphy Eagle, born August 28, 1874 in Rowan County N.C.; died August 29, 1945.

571   v.   Solomon Luther Eagle, born April 14, 1876 in Salisbury, N.C.; died January 28, 1950 in Rowan County N.C. He married Margaret Anna Peeler November 25, 1909 in Rowan County, N.C.

More About Solomon Luther Eagle:
Remains are buried at the Saint Matthews Lutheran Church Cemetery, Rowan County, N.C.

More About Margaret Anna Peeler:
Remains are buried at the Saint Matthews Lutheran Church Cemetery, Rowan County, N.C.

+ 572   vi.   Mary Lillie Eagle, born June 14, 1878 in Rowan County N.C.; died March 02, 1938.

+ 573   vii.   David Leo Eagle, born December 11, 1880; died February 03, 1963.

+ 574   viii.   Noah Walter Eagle, born November 27, 1884; died August 14, 1937.

+ 575   ix.   Albert Lee Eagle, born June 09, 1887; died May 04, 1922.

+ 576   x.   Amanda Dora Eagle, born October 03, 1888; died October 03, 1966.

443. Pleasant L.[20] Wyatt (Brantley or Brantly[19], Thomas "Tommy"[18] Wiatt, Sr. (Wyatt, Wiett), John[17], Henry[16], Richard[15], George[14], Rev. Haute "Haut" "Hawte"[13], Sir George "Georgius" Thomas[12], Sir Thomas "The Younger"[11], Sir Thomas "The Elder"[10], Sir Henry[9], Richard Wiat or[8] Wyatt, Geoffrey "Jeoffrey" Wiot or[7] Wiat, Robert or Richard[6] Wiot, William Wiot or[5] Wyot, Adam Wiot or Wyote or[4], Guyott[3], Guyott[2], Captain or Admiral Adam Guyott or[1] Wiot) was born March 1837, and died July 09, 1916 in Gold Hill, Morgan Township, Rowan County, N.C. He married Delilah A. Park.

Child of Pleasant Wyatt and Delilah Park is:
+ 577   i.   Pleasant LaFayette[21] Wyatt?, born July 11, 1864 in Rowan County, N.C.; died November 28, 1942 in Charlotte, Mecklenburg County, N.C.

Generation No. 21

492. Martha C.[21] Sykes (James B.[20], frances[19] cates, thomas[18], Rebecca[17] Sykes, Frances[16] Wiatt, Richard[15], George[14], Rev. Haute "Haut" "Hawte"[13], Sir George "Georgius" Thomas[12], Sir Thomas "The Younger"[11], Sir Thomas "The Elder"[10], Sir Henry[9], Richard Wiat or[8] Wyatt, Geoffrey "Jeoffrey" Wiot or[7] Wiat, Robert or Richard[6] Wiot, William Wiot or[5] Wyot, Adam Wiot or Wyote or[4], Guyott[3], Guyott[2], Captain or Admiral Adam Guyott or[1] Wiot) was born

July 14, 1847 in Orange County, N.C., and died August 31, 1914 in Melville, Alamance, N.C. She married John C Qualls.

More About John C. Qualls:
Fact 1: Confedrate army -- enlisted private.
Fact 2: Enlisted either Alamance or Orange County, N.C.
Fact 3: Army of Northern Virginia under Genral Robert E. Lee.

Child of Martha Sykes and John C. is:

+ 578   i.   James Franklin[22] Qualls, born 1879 in Hillsbourough, Orange County, N.C.; died June 19, 1951 in Thomason Township, Alamance County, N.C.

506. Columbus Ciscero[21] Wyatt (Wilson Riley[20], Jesse "Jessey"[19], John "Johney"[18], John[17] Wiatt, Henry[16], Richard[15], George[14], Rev. Haute "Haut" "Hawte"[13], Sir George "Georgius" Thomas[12], Sir Thomas "The Younger"[11], Sir Thomas "The Elder"[10], Sir Henry[9], Richard Wiat or[8] Wyatt, Geoffrey "Jeoffrey" Wiot or[7] Wiat, Robert or Richard[6] Wiot, William Wiot or[5] Wyot, Adam Wiot or Wyote or[4], Guyott[3], Guyott[2], Captain or Admiral Adam Guyott or[1] Wiot) was born September 23, 1853 in Davidson County, N.C., and died January 18, 1920 in Baden, Stanly County, N.C. He met (1) Sarah Ann Rainey 1874 in year of Bond is 1874 Rowan County N.C., daughter of Milas Rainey and Caroline. He married (2) Amanda Rebecca McCombs November 28, 1875 in Gold Hill Township, Rowan County N.C., daughter of James McCombs and Mary Wife. He married (3) Mary V. Cauble 1895 in Year of Bond 1895 Rowan County N.C., daughter of Adam Cauble and Lunda.

More About Columbus Ciscero Wyatt:
Fact 1: Married at age 20 years.

Children of Columbus Wyatt and Amanda McCombs are:

+ 579   i.   Harvey Addison[22] Wyatt, born February 16, 1877; died January 05, 1956 in Rockwell, Rowan County, N.C.
   580   ii.   John T. or M. Wyatt.
   581   iii.   Minney Wyatt?.
   582   iv.   Sidney Wyatt?.

508. Beulah[21] Wyatt? (John[20], Lazerus Pleasant[19] Wyatt, Thomas "Tommy"[18] Wiatt, Sr. (Wyatt, Wiett), John[17], Henry[16], Richard[15], George[14], Rev. Haute "Haut" "Hawte"[13], Sir George "Georgius" Thomas[12], Sir Thomas "The Younger"[11], Sir Thomas "The Elder"[10], Sir Henry[9], Richard Wiat or[8] Wyatt, Geoffrey "Jeoffrey" Wiot or[7] Wiat, Robert or Richard[6] Wiot, William Wiot or[5] Wyot, Adam Wiot or Wyote or[4], Guyott[3], Guyott[2], Captain or Admiral Adam Guyott or[1] Wiot). She married Unknown.

More About Beulah Wyatt?:
Fact 1: Never married.

Child of Beulah Wyatt? and Unknown is:
583   i.   Noah[22] Wyatt.

More About Noah Wyatt:
Fact 1: moved to Arkansas, then to Charlotte or Kannapolis, N.C.

509. Pleasant Loveless[21] Wyatt (Ciscero "Cicero" L.[20], Lazerus Pleasant[19], Thomas "Tommy"[18] Wiatt, Sr. (Wyatt, Wiett), John[17], Henry[16], Richard[15], George[14], Rev. Haute "Haut" "Hawte"[13], Sir George "Georgius" Thomas[12], Sir Thomas "The Younger"[11], Sir Thomas "The Elder"[10], Sir Henry[9], Richard Wiat or[8] Wyatt, Geoffrey "Jeoffrey" Wiot or[7] Wiat, Robert or Richard[6] Wiot, William Wiot or[5] Wyot, Adam Wiot or Wyote or[4], Guyott[3], Guyott[2], Captain or Admiral Adam Guyott or[1] Wiot) was born 1895 in Rowan County, N.C., and died 1986 in Rowan County, N.C. He married Amanda Mayetta Miller, daughter of Abraham Miller and Laura Morgan.

More About Pleasant Loveless Wyatt:
Buried in Oakdale Cemetery, Spencer, N.C.

Children of Pleasant Wyatt and Amanda Miller are:
584   i.   Zula Irene[22] Wyatt, born March 03, 1915 in Rowan County, N.C.
585   ii.   Baxter Loveless Wyatt, born December 03, 1916 in Rowan County, N.C.
586   iii.   Polly Louise Wyatt, born August 29, 1918 in Rowan County, N.C.
+ 587   iv.   Margaret Evelyeen Wyatt, born May 13, 1922 in Rowan County, N.C.
588   v.   Raymond Lewis Wyatt, born November 23, 1926 in Rowan County, N.C.
589   vi.   Ruby Valeria Wyatt, born July 16, 1930 in Rowan County, N.C. She married Walton.

514. Elizabeth Augusta[21] Wyatt (Henry Thomas[20], Noah Calvin[19], Thomas "Tommy"[18] Wiatt, Sr. (Wyatt, Wiett), John[17], Henry[16], Richard[15], George[14], Rev. Haute "Haut" "Hawte"[13], Sir George "Georgius" Thomas[12], Sir Thomas "The Younger"[11], Sir Thomas "The Elder"[10], Sir Henry[9], Richard Wiat or[8] Wyatt, Geoffrey "Jeoffrey" Wiot or[7] Wiat, Robert or Richard[6] Wiot, William Wiot or[5] Wyot, Adam Wiot or Wyote or[4], Guyott[3], Guyott[2], Captain or Admiral Adam Guyott or[1] Wiot) was born May 24, 1867, and died November 05, 1933. She married John A. Lylery.

More About Elizabeth Augusta Wyatt:
Remains are buried at Saint Peter's Lutheran Church Cemetery, Rockwell, Rowan County, N.C.; Row #17.

More About John A. Lylery:
Remains are buried at Saint Peter's Lutheran Church Cemetery, Rockwell, Rowan County, N.C.; Row #17.

Child of Elizabeth Wyatt and John Lylery is:
590   i.   Minnie Esther[22] Lylery, born July 16, 1907 in Rowan County N.C.; died May 01, 1960 in Greensboro, Guilford County, N.C. She married Hollie Alexander Ritchie.

More About Minnie Esther Lylery:
Remains are buried at Saint Peter's Lutheran Church Cemetery, Rockwell, Rowan County, N.C.; Row #17.

More About Hollie Alexander Ritchie:
Remains are buried at Saint Peter's Lutheran Church Cemetery, Rockwell, Rowan County, N.C.; Row #17.

522. John C.[21] Wyatt (William Wesley "Brantly"[20], Noah Calvin[19], Thomas "Tommy"[18] Wiatt, Sr. (Wyatt, Wiett), John[17], Henry[16], Richard[15], George[14], Rev. Haute "Haut" "Hawte"[13], Sir George "Georgius" Thomas[12], Sir Thomas "The Younger"[11], Sir Thomas "The Elder"[10], Sir Henry[9], Richard Wiat or[8] Wyatt, Geoffrey "Jeoffrey" Wiot or[7] Wiat, Robert or Richard[6] Wiot, William Wiot or[5] Wyot, Adam Wiot or Wyote or[4], Guyott[3], Guyott[2], Captain or Admiral Adam Guyott or[1] Wiot) was born Abt. 1860 in Rowan County, N.C. He married Ally Jane Hodge February 19, 1882 in Rowan County N.C., daughter of Abram Hodge and Nancy Morgan.

More About John C. Wyatt:
Remains are buried in the Saint Matthew's Lutheran Church Cemetery, Salisbury, Rowan County, N.C. Plot #644.

Child of John Wyatt and Ally Hodge is:
591   i.   Harvey[22] Wyatt. He married Wife.

523. James "Jim" Noah[21] Wyatt (William Wesley "Brantly"[20], Noah Calvin[19], Thomas "Tommy"[18] Wiatt, Sr. (Wyatt, Wiett), John[17], Henry[16], Richard[15], George[14], Rev. Haute "Haut" "Hawte"[13], Sir George "Georgius" Thomas[12], Sir Thomas "The Younger"[11], Sir Thomas "The Elder"[10], Sir Henry[9], Richard Wiat or[8] Wyatt, Geoffrey "Jeoffrey" Wiot or[7] Wiat, Robert or Richard[6] Wiot, William Wiot or[5] Wyot, Adam Wiot or Wyote or[4], Guyott[3], Guyott[2], Captain or Admiral Adam Guyott or[1] Wiot) was born April 04, 1861 in North Carolina, and died February 02, 1957. He married Barbara Ann E. Basinger March 06, 1884 in Rowan County N.C., daughter of D. Basinger and Rhoda Morgan.

More About James "Jim" Noah Wyatt:
Fact 1: Nicknamed: *"Jim."*

> Child of James Wyatt and Barbara Basinger is:

+ 592   i.   David Eli[22] Wyatt, born November 21, 1887 in Rowan County N.C.; died March 01, 1966 in Rowan County N.C.

533. Rhoda Isabelle[21] Morgan (Lila Delilah "Delila"[20] Wyatt, Noah Calvin[19], Thomas "Tommy"[18] Wiatt, Sr. (Wyatt, Wiett), John[17], Henry[16], Richard[15], George[14], Rev. Haute "Haut" "Hawte"[13], Sir George "Georgius" Thomas[12], Sir Thomas "The Younger"[11], Sir Thomas "The Elder"[10], Sir Henry[9], Richard Wiat or[8] Wyatt, Geoffrey "Jeoffrey" Wiot or[7] Wiat, Robert or Richard[6] Wiot, William Wiot or[5] Wyot, Adam Wiot or Wyote or[4], Guyott[3], Guyott[2], Captain or Admiral Adam Guyott or[1] Wiot) was born February 07, 1862 in North Carolina, and died January 04, 1909 in North Carolina. She married William Alexander Kirk.

More About Rhoda Isabelle Morgan:
Luther's Lutheran Church Cemetery, Rowan County, N.C. Remains are next to her husband.

More About William Alexander Kirk:
Luther's Lutheran Church Cemetery, Rowan County, N.C. next to the remains of his wife.

> Children of Rhoda Morgan and William Kirk are:

    593   i.   J. Eugene[22] Kirk.

    594   ii.   Mack Lee Kirk.

+ 595   iii.   Freda Maybelle Kirk, born December 12, 1886 in Stanly County, N.C.; died January 24, 1955 in Rowan County N.C.

535. Mary Jane[21] Morgan (Rachel Evelyn "Eveline"[20] Wyatt, Noah Calvin[19], Thomas "Tommy"[18] Wiatt, Sr. (Wyatt, Wiett), John[17], Henry[16], Richard[15], George[14], Rev. Haute "Haut" "Hawte"[13], Sir George "Georgius" Thomas[12], Sir Thomas "The Younger"[11], Sir Thomas "The Elder"[10], Sir Henry[9], Richard Wiat or[8] Wyatt, Geoffrey "Jeoffrey" Wiot or[7] Wiat, Robert or Richard[6] Wiot, William Wiot or[5] Wyot, Adam Wiot or Wyote or[4], Guyott[3], Guyott[2], Captain or Admiral Adam Guyott or[1] Wiot) was born November 20, 1856 in Rowan County, N.C., and died October 15, 1928 in died at a state hospital, N.C. She married Solomon Eagle, Jr. November 02, 1876, son of Solomon Eagle and Agnes Hodge.

More About Mary Jane Morgan:
Died in Morganton, N.C. Buried at Luther's Lutheran Church Cemetery in Rowan County, N.C.

More About Solomon Eagle, Jr.:
Fact 1: Resided in Morgan Township, Rowan County, N.C.

Fact 2: 1870, appears on N.C. Federal Census with parents and siblings.

Fact 3: June 22, 1880, appears on N.C. Federal Census with his mother, Joel and Mary.

Fact 4: June 02, 1900, appears on N.C. Federal Census with wife, children and mother.

Fact 5: 1920, appears on N.C. Federal Census with his wife and family.

Fact 6: 1930, appears on N.C. Federal Census with his wife Hattie, then age 46.

Buried at Luther's Lutheran Church Cemetery – Piney Woods formerly known as this. Changed to Luther's Lutheran Church.

Children of Mary Morgan and Solomon Eagle are:

+ 596   i.   Noah Jenkins[22] Eagle, born January 28, 1878 in Morgan Township, Rowan County, N.C.; died August 18, 1976 in Richfield, Rowan County, N.C.

+ 597   ii.   Rachel Minnie Dora Eagle, born February 1885 in Rowan County, N.C.

+ 598   iii.   Mary Lillie Eagle, born May 18, 1898 in Providence Township, Rowan County, N.C.; died July 12, 1979 in North Carolina.

539. Noah Calvin[21] Eagle (Mary Ann[20] Wyatt, Noah Calvin[19], Thomas "Tommy"[18] Wiatt, Sr. (Wyatt, Wiett), John[17], Henry[16], Richard[15], George[14], Rev. Haute "Haut" "Hawte"[13], Sir George "Georgius" Thomas[12], Sir Thomas "The Younger"[11], Sir Thomas "The Elder"[10], Sir Henry[9], Richard Wiat or[8] Wyatt, Geoffrey "Jeoffrey" Wiot or[7] Wiat, Robert or Richard[6] Wiot, William Wiot or[5] Wyot, Adam Wiot or Wyote or[4], Guyott[3], Guyott[2], Captain or Admiral Adam Guyott or[1] Wiot) was born April 30, 1861 in Rowan County N.C., and died August 14, 1951. He married (1) Elizabeth Christenburgh Kirk February 10, 1884, daughter of Daniel Kirk and Mary Shaver. He married (2) M. Florence Shaver August 29, 1889, daughter of Alexander Shaver and Nancy Bost.

More About Noah Calvin Eagle:

Fact 1: 1884, lived near Reeves Island, River Rd., Stanly County line.

Fact 2: Was a farmer.

Fact 3: Later in his life moved to Rine St., Salisbury, N.C. and worked: Salisbury Mill.

Fact 4: Retired from Salisbury Mill, Salisbury, N.C.

Fact 5: Known for growing a beautiful vegetable garden each year.

Buried at Liberty Methodist Church Cemetery, Liberty, N.C.; was of small stature.

More About Elizabeth Christenburgh Kirk:

Buried at Liberty Methodist Church Cemetery, Liberty, N.C.

More About M. Florence Shaver:

Buried at Liberty Methodist Church Cemetery.

Children of Noah Eagle and Elizabeth Kirk are:

+ 599   i.   Mary Frances[22] Eagle, born November 25, 1884 in Jan. 30, 1979; died January 30, 1979.

+ 600   ii.   Albert Thadeus Eagle, born December 24, 1885; died May 19, 1986.

+ 601   iii.   Roxie Dora Eagle, born August 14, 1887; died September 24, 1955.

Children of Noah Eagle and M. Shaver are:

+ 602   i.   Annie Luada[22] Eagle, born November 03, 1890; died August 21, 1929.

+ 603   ii.   Nannie Manola Eagle, born January 03, 1894; died June 03, 1965.

604   iii.   Enos Calvin Eagle, born October 01, 1895 in Rowan County N.C.; died July 29, 1905 in Rowan County N.C.

More About Enos Calvin Eagle:
Buried at Liberty Methodist Church Cemetery, Liberty, N.C.

+ 605   iv.   Martin Junius Eagle, born June 08, 1897 in Morgan Township, Rowan County, N.C.; died September 21, 1970.

606   v.   Thomas C. Eagle, born January 30, 1900 in Rowan County N.C.; died January 30, 1901 in Rowan County N.C.

More About Thomas C. Eagle:
Buried at Liberty Methodist Church Cemetery, Liberty, N.C.

+ 607   vi.   Mattie E. Eagle, born July 22, 1902.

+ 608   vii.   Carpenter L. Eagle, born March 29, 1904.

609   viii.   John Ervin Eagle, born September 08, 1906; died June 22, 1908.

More About John Ervin Eagle:
Buried at Liberty Methodist Church Cemetery, Liberty, N.C.

540. Eli Esau[21] Eagle (Mary Ann[20] Wyatt, Noah Calvin[19], Thomas "Tommy"[18] Wiatt, Sr. (Wyatt, Wiett), John[17], Henry[16], Richard[15], George[14], Rev. Haute "Haut" "Hawte"[13], Sir George "Georgius" Thomas[12], Sir Thomas "The Younger"[11], Sir Thomas "The Elder"[10], Sir Henry[9], Richard Wiat or[8] Wyatt, Geoffrey "Jeoffrey" Wiot or[7] Wiat, Robert or Richard[6] Wiot, William Wiot or[5] Wyot, Adam Wiot or Wyote or[4], Guyott[3], Guyott[2], Captain or Admiral Adam Guyott or[1] Wiot) was born October 14, 1861 in Rowan County N.C., and died March 07, 1935. He married Nancy Ann Kirk June 10, 1883 in N.C., daughter of David Kirk and Mary Shaver.

More About Eli Esau Eagle:
Remains buried at Liberty United Methodist Church Cemetery, Gold Hill, N.C.

More About Nancy Ann Kirk:
Remains buried at Liberty United Methodist Church Cemetery, Gold Hill, N.C.

Children of Eli Eagle and Nancy Kirk are:

	610	i.	Elbert Lee[22] Eagle, born June 15, 1898; died December 31, 1945. He married Elouise Smith.
+	611	ii.	William Armstrong Eagle, born April 08, 1900; died February 25, 1978.
+	612	iii.	Carrie Etta Eagle, born March 30, 1884; died February 19, 1974.
+	613	iv.	Emma Dora Eagle, born April 24, 1885; died March 06, 1967.
+	614	v.	Mary Christine Eagle, born August 07, 1886.
	615	vi.	Fannie Isabell Eagle, born January 26, 1888; died March 27, 1899.
+	616	vii.	Grover Victor Eagle, born February 22, 1891; died May 28, 1966.
+	617	viii.	Joseph Calvin Eagle, born November 14, 1892; died November 18, 1973.
+	618	ix.	Walter Eli Eagle, born September 11, 1894.
+	619	x.	Annie Zenobia Eagle, born September 20, 1896; died May 12, 1962.
+	620	xi.	Ida Lou Eagle, born July 10, 1899; died April 27, 1952.
+	621	xii.	Elizabeth "Elisbeth" Nora Eagle, born January 14, 1902 in Gold Hill, N.C; died January 30, 1983.
+	622	xiii.	James Harvey Eagle, born April 30, 1905 in Gold Hill, N.C.
	623	xiv.	John Kirk Eagle, born May 12, 1909 in Morgan Township, Rowan County, N.C.; died March 31, 1974. He married Kathleen Loop January 29, 1928.

More About John Kirk Eagle:
Remains are buried in the Rowan Memorial Park Cemetery, Salisbury, N.C.

More About Kathleen Loop:
Fact 1: Born Feb. 12

541. Nancy Jane[21] Eagle (Mary Ann[20] Wyatt, Noah Calvin[19], Thomas "Tommy"[18] Wiatt, Sr. (Wyatt, Wiett), John[17], Henry[16], Richard[15], George[14], Rev. Haute "Haut" "Hawte"[13], Sir George "Georgius" Thomas[12], Sir Thomas "The Younger"[11], Sir Thomas "The Elder"[10], Sir Henry[9], Richard Wiat or[8] Wyatt, Geoffrey "Jeoffrey" Wiot or[7] Wiat, Robert or Richard[6] Wiot, William Wiot or[5] Wyot, Adam Wiot or Wyote or[4], Guyott[3], Guyott[2], Captain or

Admiral Adam Guyott or[1] Wiot) was born October 07, 1862 in Rowan County N.C., and died April 26, 1943 in Gold Hill, Morgan Township, Rowan County, N.C. She married Moses Goodman February 29, 1880 in Rowan County N.C., son of Christopher Goodman and Amelia Canup.

More About Nancy Jane Eagle:
Fact 1: 1943, Buried Liberty Methodist Cemetery, Salisbury, N.C.
Buried at Liberty Methodist Cemetery, N.C.

More About Moses Goodman:
Fact 1: 1939, Buried Liberty Methodist Cemetery, Salisbury, N.C.
Buried at Liberty Methodist Cemetery, N.C.

Children of Nancy Eagle and Moses Goodman are:
+ 624   i.   Enoch Arthur[22] Goodman, born February 07, 1881; died April 17, 1974.
+ 625   ii.   Linus Giles Goodman, born September 05, 1884; died October 03, 1971.
+ 626   iii. Amanda Louise Goodman, born September 12, 1886; died September 29, 1905.
+ 627   iv.   Paul Talmadge Goodman, born April 26, 1889; died July 23, 1965.
  628   v.   Mary Josephine Goodman, born May 17, 1891; died January 18, 1977.
+ 629   vi.   Leland Quincy Goodman, born March 20, 1893; died July 21, 1982.
+ 630   vii. Nannie Jane Goodman, born December 26, 1894.
+ 631   viii. Bennett Francis Goodman, born July 12, 1883 in Rowan County, N.C.; died December 09, 1964.

542. Mary Malinda[21] Eagle (Mary Ann[20] Wyatt, Noah Calvin[19], Thomas "Tommy"[18] Wiatt, Sr. (Wyatt, Wiett), John[17], Henry[16], Richard[15], George[14], Rev. Haute "Haut" "Hawte"[13], Sir George "Georgius" Thomas[12], Sir Thomas "The Younger"[11], Sir Thomas "The Elder"[10], Sir Henry[9], Richard Wiat or[8] Wyatt, Geoffrey "Jeoffrey" Wiot or[7] Wiat, Robert or Richard[6] Wiot, William Wiot or[5] Wyot, Adam Wiot or Wyote or[4], Guyott[3], Guyott[2], Captain or Admiral Adam Guyott or[1] Wiot) was born August 22, 1866 in Rowan County N.C., and died January 09, 1945. She married Abraham Daniel Shaver in married September 6, 188_, son of Alexander Shaver and Nancy Bost.

More About Mary Malinda Eagle:
Remains are buried at Liberty Methodist Church Cemetery, Rowan County, N.C.

More About Abraham Daniel Shaver:
Remains are buried at Liberty Methodist Church Cemetery, Rowan County, N.C.

Children of Mary Eagle and Abraham Shaver are:

+ 632   i.   Josephine Erma[22] Shaver, born August 12, 1890.

   633   ii.   John Burlie Shaver.

   634   iii.   Joseph Shaver, born January 10, 1896 in Rowan County N.C.; died March 03, 1896 in Rowan County N.C.

     More About Joseph Shaver:
     Remains are buried at Liberty Methodist Church Cemetery, Rowan County, N.C.

   635   iv.   Edith Ann Shaver, born February 01, 1898 in Rowan County N.C.; died September 03, 1898 in Rowan County N.C.

     More About Edith Ann Shaver:
     Remains are buried at Liberty Methodist Church Cemetery, Rowan County, N.C.

   636   v.   Daniel Mackey Shaver, born July 21, 1901 in Rowan County N.C.; died December 23, 1901 in Rowan County N.C.

     More About Daniel Mackey Shaver:
     Remains are buried at Liberty Methodist Church Cemetery, Rowan County, N.C.

+ 637   vi.   Curtis Bewey Shaver.

545. William Grant[21] Eagle (Mary Ann[20] Wyatt, Noah Calvin[19], Thomas "Tommy"[18] Wiatt, Sr. (Wyatt, Wiett), John[17], Henry[16], Richard[15], George[14], Rev. Haute "Haut" "Hawte"[13], Sir George "Georgius" Thomas[12], Sir Thomas "The Younger"[11], Sir Thomas "The Elder"[10], Sir Henry[9], Richard Wiat or[8] Wyatt, Geoffrey "Jeoffrey" Wiot or[7] Wiat, Robert or Richard[6] Wiot, William Wiot or[5] Wyot, Adam Wiot or Wyote or[4], Guyott[3], Guyott[2], Captain or Admiral Adam Guyott or[1] Wiot) was born July 28, 1872 in Rowan County N.C., and died April 11, 1943 in Rowan County N.C. He married Dovie Laura Cranford March 19, 1893, daughter of Henry Cranford and Lundy Porter.

More About William Grant Eagle:
Remains buried at Liberty United Methodist Church Cemetery, Gold Hill, N.C.

More About Dovie Laura Cranford:
Remains buried at Liberty United Methodist Church Cemetery, Gold Hill, N.C.

Children of William Eagle and Dovie Cranford are:

+ 638   i.   William Grant[22] Eagle, Jr., born 1894 in Rowan County, N.C.; died 1918.

+ 639   ii.   Beulah Ann Eagle, born 1895 in Rowan County, N.C.; died 1947.

+ 640   iii.   Addie Louise Eagle, born 1897 in Rowan County, N.C.; died 1977.

+ 641   iv.   Esther Ethel Eagle, born 1898 in Rowan County, N.C.

+ 642   v.   Octa Mae Eagle, born July 26, 1903 in Rowan County, N.C.; died 1995.

   643   vi.   Agnes Dovie Eagle, born June 26, 1905 in Rowan County, N.C.; died January 21, 1925. She married John Earnhardt December 22, 1923.

More About Agnes Dovie Eagle:
Buried at Liberty Methodist Church Cemetery, Rowan County, N.C.

More About John Earnhardt:
Buried at Liberty Methodist Church Cemetery, Rowan County, N.C.

+ 644   vii.   Norvie Lundy Eagle, born March 02, 1907 in Rowan County, N.C.

+ 645   viii.   Paul Thomas Eagle, born March 13, 1908 in of Misenheimer, Rowan County, N.C.

+ 646   ix.   Mary (Phene) Josephine Eagle, born February 10, 1910 in Rowan County, N.C.; died March 13, 1994.

+ 647   x.   Kate Eursel "Ercle" Eagle, born November 09, 1912 in Morgan Township, Rowan County, N.C.

+ 648   xi.   Doy Hollis Eagle, born January 10, 1915 in of Gold Hill, Rowan County, N.C.; died 2007 in Rowan County, N.C.

+ 649   xii.   Jessie Bernice Eagle, born September 10, 1916 in Rowan County, N.C.

   650   xiii.   William Banks Eagle, born 1919 in Rowan County, N.C.; died 1947.

+ 651   xiv.   Emma Dora Eagle, born June 26, 1901 in Morgan Township, Rowan County, N.C.; died September 21, 1993.

546. Josephine[21] Eagle (Mary Ann[20] Wyatt, Noah Calvin[19], Thomas "Tommy"[18] Wiatt, Sr. (Wyatt, Wiett), John[17], Henry[16], Richard[15], George[14], Rev. Haute "Haut" "Hawte"[13], Sir George "Georgius" Thomas[12], Sir Thomas "The Younger"[11], Sir Thomas "The Elder"[10], Sir Henry[9], Richard Wiat or[8] Wyatt, Geoffrey "Jeoffrey" Wiot or[7] Wiat, Robert or Richard[6] Wiot, William Wiot or[5] Wyot, Adam Wiot or Wyote or[4], Guyott[3], Guyott[2], Captain or Admiral Adam Guyott or[1] Wiot) was born March 10, 1875 in Rowan County N.C., and died February 07, 1968 in Rowan County N.C. She married James Calvin Cranford December 20, 1898.

More About Josephine Eagle:
Buried at Liberty Methodist Church Cemetery, Rowan County, N.C.

More About James Calvin Cranford:
Buried at Liberty Methodist Church Cemetery, Rowan County, N.C.

Children of Josephine Eagle and James Cranford are:

+ 652   i.   McCoy Lee[22] Cranford, born September 30, 1899 in Rowan County, N.C; died June 18, 1984.

653   ii.   Murray Cranford, born in Rowan County, N.C.

654   iii.   Lundy Cranford, born in Rowan County, N.C.

655   iv.   Lucy Minerva Cranford, born in Rowan County, N.C.

656   v.   Gaither Cranford, born in Rowan County, N.C.

550. Laura Jane[21] Wyatt (Eli[20], Noah Calvin[19], Thomas "Tommy"[18] Wiatt, Sr. (Wyatt, Wiett), John[17], Henry[16], Richard[15], George[14], Rev. Haute "Haut" "Hawte"[13], Sir George "Georgius" Thomas[12], Sir Thomas "The Younger"[11], Sir Thomas "The Elder"[10], Sir Henry[9], Richard Wiat or[8] Wyatt, Geoffrey "Jeoffrey" Wiot or[7] Wiat, Robert or Richard[6] Wiot, William Wiot or[5] Wyot, Adam Wiot or Wyote or[4], Guyott[3], Guyott[2], Captain or Admiral Adam Guyott or[1] Wiot) was born May 20, 1869, and died February 20, 1940. She married Leroy Davis Linn November 29, 1888 in Rowan County N.C., son of Moses Linn and Elizabeth Wormington.

Child of Laura Wyatt and Leroy Linn is:

657   i.   Ida Luciel[22] Linn, born 1906; died 1908.

551. Mary Sophia[21] Wyatt (Eli[20], Noah Calvin[19], Thomas "Tommy"[18] Wiatt, Sr. (Wyatt, Wiett), John[17], Henry[16], Richard[15], George[14], Rev. Haute "Haut" "Hawte"[13], Sir George "Georgius" Thomas[12], Sir Thomas "The Younger"[11], Sir Thomas "The Elder"[10], Sir Henry[9], Richard Wiat or[8] Wyatt, Geoffrey "Jeoffrey" Wiot or[7] Wiat, Robert or Richard[6] Wiot, William Wiot or[5] Wyot, Adam Wiot or Wyote or[4], Guyott[3], Guyott[2], Captain or Admiral Adam Guyott or[1] Wiot) was born November 26, 1870 in Rowan County N.C., and died June 30, 1933 in Rowan County N.C. She married Henry Lee Owens August 08, 1907 in Rowan County N.C., son of Drew Owens and Effie.

More About Mary Sophia Wyatt:
Saint Matthew's Lutheran Church Cemtery, Salisbury, Rowan County, N.C. Row #31.

More About Henry Lee Owens:
Saint Matthew's Lutheran Church Cemtery, Salisbury, Rowan County, N.C. Row #31.

Child of Mary Wyatt and Henry Owens is:

658   i.   Daisy Lula owens[22] Owens, born February 15, 1911 in Rowan County N.C.; died June 17, 1964 in Rowan County N.C.

More About Daisy Lula owens Owens:
Saint Matthew's Lutheran Church Cemtery, Salisbury, Rowan County, N.C. Row #31. Inscription: "Dau of H L and Mary Owens.".

552. William Mock[21] Wyatt (Eli[20], Noah Calvin[19], Thomas "Tommy"[18] Wiatt, Sr. (Wyatt, Wiett), John[17], Henry[16], Richard[15], George[14], Rev. Haute "Haut" "Hawte"[13], Sir George "Georgius" Thomas[12], Sir Thomas "The Younger"[11], Sir Thomas "The Elder"[10], Sir Henry[9], Richard Wiat or[8] Wyatt, Geoffrey "Jeoffrey" Wiot or[7] Wiat, Robert or Richard[6] Wiot, William Wiot or[5] Wyot, Adam Wiot or Wyote or[4], Guyott[3], Guyott[2], Captain or Admiral Adam Guyott or[1] Wiot) was born August 05, 1872 in Rowan County N.C., and died October 27, 1939 in Rowan County N.C. He married (2) Delphra Newsom March 25, 1894 in Rowan County N.C., daughter of Abram Newsom and Anna.

More About William Mock Wyatt:
Remains are buried in the Saint Matthew's Lutheran Church Cemetery, Salisbury, Rowan County, N.C. Plot #292.

More About Delphra Newsom:
Remains are buried at Saint Matthew's Lutheran Church Cemtery, Salisbury, Rowan County, N.C. Row #22; Plot # 292.

Child of William Mock Wyatt is:
+ 659   i.   MacDonald[22] Wyatt.

Child of William Wyatt and Delphra Newsom is:
660   i.   Pearl Lee[22] Wyatt, born September 05, 1908 in Rowan County N.C.; died December 02, 1989 in Rowan County N.C. She married Theodore Franklin Surratt December 23, 1923 in Rowan County N.C.

More About Pearl Lee Wyatt:
Saint Matthew's Lutheran Church Cemtery, Salisbury, Rowan County, N.C. Row #23.

More About Theodore Franklin Surratt:
Saint Matthew's Lutheran Church Cemtery, Salisbury, Rowan County, N.C. Row #23.

560. Ollie Lou Ada[21] Shaver (Rhoda E.[20] Wyatt, Noah Calvin[19], Thomas "Tommy"[18] Wiatt, Sr. (Wyatt, Wiett), John[17], Henry[16], Richard[15], George[14], Rev. Haute "Haut" "Hawte"[13], Sir George "Georgius" Thomas[12], Sir Thomas "The Younger"[11], Sir Thomas "The Elder"[10], Sir Henry[9], Richard Wiat or[8] Wyatt, Geoffrey "Jeoffrey" Wiot or[7] Wiat, Robert or Richard[6] Wiot, William Wiot or[5] Wyot, Adam Wiot or Wyote or[4], Guyott[3], Guyott[2], Captain or Admiral

Adam Guyott or[1] Wiot) was born March 10, 1870, and died July 03, 1955. She married (1) Howell Parker. She married (2) Howell Parker.

More About Ollie Lou Ada Shaver:
Fact 1: Sister to Emanuel Shaver.
Luther's Lutheran Church, Rowan County, N.C.

More About Howell Parker:
Luther's Lutheran Church, Rowan County, N.C.

Child of Ollie Shaver and Howell Parker is:

+ 661   i.   J. Columbus[22] Parker, born March 17, 1849; died June 18, 1926.

Children of Ollie Shaver and Howell Parker are:

   662   i.   Nettie M.B.[22] Parker.
   663   ii.   William Narvie Parker, died 1982.
+ 664   iii.   Bertha Lillie Ann Parker, born 1894-1981.
   665   iv.   James Burley Parker, born 1895.
   666   v.   Eva Mae Parker, born 1903.
   667   vi.   Vargie McNealey Parker, born 1905.
   668   vii.   Verna Viola Parker, born 1908.
   669   viii.   Jennie Parker, born 1909.
   670   ix.   George Hubert Parker, born 1914.

562. **Emanuel Calvin[21] Shaver** (Rhoda E.[20] Wyatt, Noah Calvin[19], Thomas "Tommy"[18] Wiatt, Sr. (Wyatt, Wiett), John[17], Henry[16], Richard[15], George[14], Rev. Haute "Haut" "Hawte"[13], Sir George "Georgius" Thomas[12], Sir Thomas "The Younger"[11], Sir Thomas "The Elder"[10], Sir Henry[9], Richard Wiat or[8] Wyatt, Geoffrey "Jeoffrey" Wiot or[7] Wiat, Robert or Richard[6] Wiot, William Wiot or[5] Wyot, Adam Wiot or Wyote or[4], Guyott[3], Guyott[2], Captain or Admiral Adam Guyott or[1] Wiot) was born 1875-1930 in Rowan County N.C., and died in Rowan County N.C. He married Mary Refina Hope Miller, daughter of J. Miller and Joicy.

Children of Emanuel Shaver and Mary Miller are:

+ 671   i.   Jacob Frank[22] Shaver, born 1900.
   672   ii.   Ill Blauch Shaver, born 1904.
   673   iii.   Ralph Kiser haver, born 1906.
   674   iv.   Lottie Shaver, born 1909.
   675   v.   Maggie Ellen Shaver, born July 04, 1909 in North Carolina; died March 18, 1955 in North Carolina. She married C. Roscoe Morgan.

     More About Maggie Ellen Shaver:
     Remains are buried in Luther's Lutheran Church in Richfield, N.C. next to her husband.

More About C. Roscoe Morgan:
Remains are buried in the Luther's Lutheran Church in
Richfield, N.C. next to his wife.

676 vi. Ruby Alice Shaver, born 1912.

More About Ruby Alice Shaver:
Fact 1: Taught James Noah Hinson, M.D. during grammar
school years.
Fact 2: Shaver Elementary, Rowan County, N.C.

568. William Lawson[21] Eagle (Amanda Jane[20] Wyatt, Noah Calvin[19], Thomas "Tommy"[18] Wiatt,
Sr. (Wyatt, Wiett), John[17], Henry[16], Richard[15], George[14], Rev. Haute "Haut" "Hawte"[13], Sir George
"Georgius" Thomas[12], Sir Thomas "The Younger"[11], Sir Thomas "The Elder"[10], Sir Henry[9],
Richard Wiat or[8] Wyatt, Geoffrey "Jeoffrey" Wiot or[7] Wiat, Robert or Richard[6] Wiot, William
Wiot or[5] Wyot, Adam Wiot or Wyote or[4], Guyott[3], Guyott[2], Captain or Admiral Adam Guyott or[1]
Wiot) was born January 31, 1870 in Rowan County, N.C., and died November 27, 1928. He mar-
ried Fannie Alice Dell or Dale Shaver, daughter of Daniel Shaver and Sara Miller.

More About William Lawson Eagle:
Buried at Luther's Lutheran Church Cemetery, Richfield, N.C. Row #13.

More About Fannie Alice Dell or Dale Shaver:
Remains are buried at Luther's Lutheran Church Cemetery, Richfield, N.C.

Children of William Eagle and Fannie Shaver are:
 677 i. Infant Son[22] Eagle, born 1897.
+ 678 ii. Calvin DeBerry Eagle, born March 09, 1898 in Rowan County N.C.; died June 18, 1973 in Salisbury, Rowan County, N.C.
+ 679 iii. Anna "Anner" Lillian Pauline Eagle, born June 21, 1911 in Rowan County N.C.; died August 14, 1993 in Salisbury, Rowan County, N.C.
+ 680 iv. Virgie Lou Vera Eagle, born September 25, 1900; died 1980.
+ 681 v. Sarah Jane Eagle, born July 11, 1904.
+ 682 vi. Esther Mae Eagle, born November 20, 1906.

569. Adolphus Grant[21] Eagle (Amanda Jane[20] Wyatt, Noah Calvin[19], Thomas "Tommy"[18]
Wiatt, Sr. (Wyatt, Wiett), John[17], Henry[16], Richard[15], George[14], Rev. Haute "Haut" "Hawte"[13],
Sir George "Georgius" Thomas[12], Sir Thomas "The Younger"[11], Sir Thomas "The Elder"[10],
Sir Henry[9], Richard Wiat or[8] Wyatt, Geoffrey "Jeoffrey" Wiot or[7] Wiat, Robert or Richard[6]
Wiot, William Wiot or[5] Wyot, Adam Wiot or Wyote or[4], Guyott[3], Guyott[2], Captain or Admiral
Adam Guyott or[1] Wiot) was born August 30, 1873 in North Carolina, and died June 06, 1941
in North Carolina. He married Nancy "Elisabeth" Elizabeth Morgan December 22, 1898 in
Rowan County, N.C., daughter of Mack Morgan and Mary Arey.

More About Adolphus Grant Eagle:
Fact 1: Worked on the South Bound Rail Road with Noah Eagle.
Fact 2: Sometimes listed as Adolphus G. Eagle on public records.
Fact 3: May 14, 1941, date cited as well as day of demise.

Children of Adolphus Eagle and Nancy Morgan are:

+ 683   i.   Bertha Louise[22] Eagle, born February 1900 in North Carolina; died December 24, 1932.

+ 684   ii.   Beulah Jane Eagle, born March 06, 1900 in Morgan Township, Rowan County, N.C.

   685   iii.   Daisy Mae Eagle, born March 25, 1902 in Rowan County, N.C.

More About Daisy Mae Eagle:
Fact 1: Never married.
Fact 2: Worked 50 years in nursing service.
Fact 3: 1977, received Rowan County Nurse of the Year Award.

   686   iv.   Leroy "Leron" "Lee Roy" Eagle, born January 30, 1904 in North Carolina; died December 30, 1931 in North Carolina.

More About Leroy "Leron" "Lee Roy" Eagle:
Remains are buried in the Greenlawn Memorial Gardens Cemetery, Spartanburg, S.C.

+ 687   v.   Jennie Elizabeth Eagle, born September 01, 1906 in Rowan County, N.C.

   688   vi.   Linda "Delinda T." Belle Eagle, born January 06, 1908 in North Carolina; died December 26, 1923.

More About Linda "Delinda T." Belle Eagle:
Remains are buried at Flat Creek Primitive Church Cemetery, River Road, Rowan County, N.C.

+ 689   vii.   Viola Martha Eagle, born November 10, 1910 in North Carolina.

+ 690   viii.   Bessie Carolina "Caroline" Eagle, born June 20, 1913 in Rowan County, N.C.

   691   ix.   Martha Ethel Eagle, born October 15, 1913 in North Carolina; died 1914.

More About Martha Ethel Eagle:
Remains are buried at Flat Creek Primitive Baptist Church Cemetery, Rowan County, N.C.

+ 692   x.   Marnie Della "Delle" Eagle, born May 10, 1916 in Rowan County, N.C.

570. John Murphy[21] Eagle (Amanda Jane[20] Wyatt, Noah Calvin[19], Thomas "Tommy"[18] Wiatt, Sr. (Wyatt, Wiett), John[17], Henry[16], Richard[15], George[14], Rev. Haute "Haut" "Hawte"[13], Sir George "Georgius" Thomas[12], Sir Thomas "The Younger"[11], Sir Thomas "The Elder"[10], Sir Henry[9], Richard Wiat or[8] Wyatt, Geoffrey "Jeoffrey" Wiot or[7] Wiat, Robert or Richard[6] Wiot, William Wiot or[5] Wyot, Adam Wiot or Wyote or[4], Guyott[3], Guyott[2], Captain or Admiral Adam Guyott or[1] Wiot) was born August 28, 1874 in Rowan County N.C., and died August 29, 1945. He married Amanda K. Kesler August 13, 1899, daughter of Joseph Kesler and Elisabeth Wyatt.

> More About John Murphy Eagle:
> Remains buried at Salisbury Memorial Park, Salisbury, N.C.

> Children of John Eagle and Amanda Kesler are:

+ 693   i.   Weathler Lee[22] Eagle, born October 06, 1900 in Rowan County N.C.; died February 11, 1947.
+ 694   ii.   Mary Kate Eagle, born January 30, 1903; died November 08, 1968.
+ 695   iii.   Ethel Viola Eagle, born November 05, 1908; died March 13, 1977.
+ 696   iv.   Lizzie Remelle Eagle, born September 23, 1912.
+ 697   v.   Margaret Marie Eagle, born July 22, 1916; died July 03, 1971.

572. Mary Lillie[21] Eagle (Amanda Jane[20] Wyatt, Noah Calvin[19], Thomas "Tommy"[18] Wiatt, Sr. (Wyatt, Wiett), John[17], Henry[16], Richard[15], George[14], Rev. Haute "Haut" "Hawte"[13], Sir George "Georgius" Thomas[12], Sir Thomas "The Younger"[11], Sir Thomas "The Elder"[10], Sir Henry[9], Richard Wiat or[8] Wyatt, Geoffrey "Jeoffrey" Wiot or[7] Wiat, Robert or Richard[6] Wiot, William Wiot or[5] Wyot, Adam Wiot or Wyote or[4], Guyott[3], Guyott[2], Captain or Admiral Adam Guyott or[1] Wiot) was born June 14, 1878 in Rowan County N.C., and died March 02, 1938. She married John Harkey.

> Children of Mary Eagle and John Harkey are:

+ 698   i.   Martin L.22 Harkey.
+ 699   ii.   Annie Harkey.
+ 700   iii.   Onnie Harkey.

573. David Leo[21] Eagle (Amanda Jane[20] Wyatt, Noah Calvin[19], Thomas "Tommy"[18] Wiatt, Sr. (Wyatt, Wiett), John[17], Henry[16], Richard[15], George[14], Rev. Haute "Haut" "Hawte"[13], Sir George "Georgius" Thomas[12], Sir Thomas "The Younger"[11], Sir Thomas "The Elder"[10], Sir Henry[9], Richard Wiat or[8] Wyatt, Geoffrey "Jeoffrey" Wiot or[7] Wiat, Robert or Richard[6] Wiot, William Wiot or[5] Wyot, Adam Wiot or Wyote or[4], Guyott[3], Guyott[2], Captain or Admiral

Adam Guyott or[1] Wiot) was born December 11, 1880, and died February 03, 1963. He married (1) Sophia Ollie Poole. He married (2) Ammie Ethel Starnes December 12, 1930 in Rowan County, N.C., daughter of Henry Starnes and Mary Frick.

More About Sophia Ollie Poole:
Fact 1: November 03, 1884, date of birth given in Rachel Hinson Hill's Eagle book. Remains arre buried at the Saint Matthews Church Cemetery, Rowan County, N.C.

Children of David Eagle and Sophia Poole are:

701	i.	Daughter[22] Eagle, born December 12, 1907; died December 12, 1907.
702	ii.	Son Eagle, born July 12, 1918; died July 20, 1918.

Children of David Eagle and Ammie Starnes are:

+	703	i.	Mary Frances[22] Eagle, born January 25, 1932 in Rowan County N.C.
	704	ii.	Annie Mae Eagle, born August 01, 1933 in Rowan County N.C. She married Gilbert Lee Winders May 04, 1952.

More About Gilbert Lee Winders:
Remains are buried at Saint Matthews Lutheran Church Cemetery, Rowan County, N.C.

+	705	iii.	Janie Catherine Eagle, born August 01, 1935 in Rowan County N.C.
+	706	iv.	Barbara Jean Eagle, born April 17, 1942 in Rowan County N.C.
+	707	v.	Martin Luther Eagle, born October 04, 1944 in Rowan County N.C.
	708	vi.	David Leo Eagle, born November 03, 1937 in Rowan County N.C.; died June 11, 1959.

More About David Leo Eagle:
Remains at buried at the Saint Matthews Lutheran Church Cemetery, Rowan County, N.C.

	709	vii.	Henry Irvin Eagle, born March 16, 1940 in Rowan County N.C.; died October 09, 1954.

574. Noah Walter[21] Eagle (Amanda Jane[20] Wyatt, Noah Calvin[19], Thomas "Tommy"[18] Wiatt, Sr. (Wyatt, Wiett), John[17], Henry[16], Richard[15], George[14], Rev. Haute "Haut" "Hawte"[13], Sir George "Georgius" Thomas[12], Sir Thomas "The Younger"[11], Sir Thomas "The Elder"[10], Sir Henry[9], Richard Wiat or[8] Wyatt, Geoffrey "Jeoffrey" Wiot or[7] Wiat, Robert or Richard[6] Wiot, William Wiot or[5] Wyot, Adam Wiot or Wyote or[4], Guyott[3], Guyott[2], Captain or Admiral Adam Guyott or[1] Wiot) was born November 27, 1884, and died August 14, 1937.

He married Delindia Belle Morgan December 23, 1911, daughter of Jacob Morgan and Mary Casper.

More About Noah Walter Eagle:
Committed suicide -- shot himself at Cedar Creek, Rowan County, N.C. Remains are buried at Saint Matthews Lutheran Church Cemetery, Rowan County, N.C.

Child of Noah Eagle and Delindia Morgan is:

+   710   i.   Helen Lois[22] Eagle, born December 16, 1912 in Wilmington, Del.

575. Albert Lee[21] Eagle (Amanda Jane[20] Wyatt, Noah Calvin[19], Thomas "Tommy"[18] Wiatt, Sr. (Wyatt, Wiett), John[17], Henry[16], Richard[15], George[14], Rev. Haute "Haut" "Hawte"[13], Sir George "Georgius" Thomas[12], Sir Thomas "The Younger"[11], Sir Thomas "The Elder"[10], Sir Henry[9], Richard Wiat or[8] Wyatt, Geoffrey "Jeoffrey" Wiot or[7] Wiat, Robert or Richard[6] Wiot, William Wiot or[5] Wyot, Adam Wiot or Wyote or[4], Guyott[3], Guyott[2], Captain or Admiral Adam Guyott or[1] Wiot) was born June 09, 1887, and died May 04, 1922. He married Cora Lee Trexler July 28, 1908, daughter of Adison Trexler and Sarah File.

More About Albert Lee Eagle:
Buried at St, Matthews Church Cemetery, Rowan County, N.C.

More About Cora Lee Trexler:
Buried at St. Matthews Church Cemetery, Rowan County, N.C.

Children of Albert Eagle and Cora Trexler are:

+   711   i.   Ruth Anne[22] Eagle, born May 18, 1901 in Rowan County, N.C.
+   712   ii.   Carrie Etta Eagle, born December 13, 1917 in Rowan County, N.C.

576. Amanda Dora[21] Eagle (Amanda Jane[20] Wyatt, Noah Calvin[19], Thomas "Tommy"[18] Wiatt, Sr. (Wyatt, Wiett), John[17], Henry[16], Richard[15], George[14], Rev. Haute "Haut" "Hawte"[13], Sir George "Georgius" Thomas[12], Sir Thomas "The Younger"[11], Sir Thomas "The Elder"[10], Sir Henry[9], Richard Wiat or[8] Wyatt, Geoffrey "Jeoffrey" Wiot or[7] Wiat, Robert or Richard[6] Wiot, William Wiot or[5] Wyot, Adam Wiot or Wyote or[4], Guyott[3], Guyott[2], Captain or Admiral Adam Guyott or[1] Wiot) was born October 03, 1888, and died October 03, 1966. She married John Calvin Morgan April 12, 1908, son of David Morgan and Barbara.

Children of Amanda Eagle and John Morgan are:

+   713   i.   Rosa Belle[22] Morgan, born February 07, 1909.
     714   ii.   Otta Byron Morgan, born October 17, 1911.
     715   iii.   Doris Morgan, born August 03, 1913.
     716   iv.   Myrtle Lee Morgan, born September 25, 1915; died May 12, 1976.

717	v.	Ira Mae Morgan, born August 04, 1918.
+ 718	vi.	Amanda Catherine Morgan, born March 08, 1921.
+ 719	vii.	John Calvin Morgan, Jr., born August 20, 1923; died 1995.
+ 720	viii.	William Howard Morgan, born September 24, 1925.
+ 721	ix.	Mildred Bernice Morgan, born August 16, 1927.

577. Pleasant LaFayette[21] Wyatt? (Pleasant L.[20] Wyatt, Brantley or Brantly[19], Thomas "Tommy"[18] Wiatt, Sr. (Wyatt, Wiett), John[17], Henry[16], Richard[15], George[14], Rev. Haute "Haut" "Hawte"[13], Sir George "Georgius" Thomas[12], Sir Thomas "The Younger"[11], Sir Thomas "The Elder"[10], Sir Henry[9], Richard Wiat or[8] Wyatt, Geoffrey "Jeoffrey" Wiot or[7] Wiat, Robert or Richard[6] Wiot, William Wiot or[5] Wyot, Adam Wiot or Wyote or[4], Guyott[3], Guyott[2], Captain or Admiral Adam Guyott or[1] Wiot) was born July 11, 1864 in Rowan County, N.C., and died November 28, 1942 in Charlotte, Mecklenburg County, N.C. He married Mary Elizabeth Gilbert.

> Children of Pleasant Wyatt? and Mary Gilbert are:
>
> | | | |
> |---|---|---|
> | 722 | i. | Belle[22] Wyatt?, born 1882; died 1972. She married Smith. |
> | 723 | ii. | James Henry Wyatt?, born 1885-1955. |
> | 724 | iii. | Charles Lorenzen Wyatt?, born 1889-1971. |
> | 725 | iv. | Emma Mary Wyatt?, born 1891-1976. She married Tate. |
> | 726 | v. | William David Wyatt?, born 1898-1964. |
> | 727 | vi. | Jack Wyatt?, born 1904-1905. |

Generation No. 22

578. james frankin[22] qualls (Martha C.[21] Sykes, James B.[20], frances[19] cates, thomas[18], Rebecca[17] Sykes, Frances[16] Wiatt, Richard[15], George[14], Rev. Haute "Haut" "Hawte"[13], Sir George "Georgius" Thomas[12], Sir Thomas "The Younger"[11], Sir Thomas "The Elder"[10], Sir Henry[9], Richard Wiat or[8] Wyatt, Geoffrey "Jeoffrey" Wiot or[7] Wiat, Robert or Richard[6] Wiot, William Wiot or[5] Wyot, Adam Wiot or Wyote or[4], Guyott[3], Guyott[2], Captain or Admiral Adam Guyott or[1] Wiot) was born 1879 in hillsbourough, orange co, nc, and died June 19, 1951 in thomason yownship, alamance co, n.c. He married Lucy Jane Riley.

More About James Frankin Qualls:
Fact 1: Was a street car conductor.

More About Lucy Jane Riley:
Fact 1: Had 13 children.

> Children of James Qualls and Lucy Riley are:
>
> | | | |
> |---|---|---|
> | 728 | i. | 13 children[23] qualls. |
> | + 729 | ii. | Joseph Marshall Qualls, born March 10, 1900 in mebane, alabance co, n.c.; died August 26, 1980 in graham, Alamance County, N.C. |

579. Harvey Addison[22] Wyatt (Columbus Cicero[21], Wilson Riley[20], Jesse "Jessey"[19], John "Johney"[18], John[17] Wiatt, Henry[16], Richard[15], George[14], Rev. Haute "Haut" "Hawte"[13], Sir George "Georgius" Thomas[12], Sir Thomas "The Younger"[11], Sir Thomas "The Elder"[10], Sir Henry[9], Richard Wiat or[8] Wyatt, Geoffrey "Jeoffrey" Wiot or[7] Wiat, Robert or Richard[6] Wiot, William Wiot or[5] Wyot, Adam Wiot or Wyote or[4], Guyott[3], Guyott[2], Captain or Admiral Adam Guyott or[1] Wiot) was born February 16, 1877, and died January 05, 1956 in Rockwell, Rowan County, N.C. He married (1) Lilly Roxcine "Roxie" "Rozanna" Lyerly. He met (2) Charity Luiada "Ada" Eagle, daughter of Moses Eagle and Caroline Frick.

More About Harvey Addison Wyatt:
Remains are buried in the Rockwell Cemetery, Rockwell, Rowan County, N.C.

More About Lilly Roxcine "Roxie" "Rozanna" Lyerly:
Remains are buried in the Rockwell Cemetery, Rockwell, Rowan County, N.C.

More About Charity Luiada "Ada" Eagle:
Fact 1: 1886, year of birth given by James Noah Hinson, M.D. in notes.
Buried at Faith Lutheran Cemetery, Rowan County, N.C.

Children of Harvey Wyatt and Lilly Lyerly are:

730	i.	Nora Lee[23] Wyatt, born October 07, 1903.
731	ii.	Pearl Wyatt, born October 09, 1905; died December 17, 1990 in buried in Rockwell, Rowan County, N.C. She married Thomas Huneycutt.
732	iii.	Stella Wynita Wyatt, born June 13, 1909; died August 06, 1998. She married Bond Overcash.
733	iv.	Hazel Jamia Wyatt, born May 11, 1911.
734	v.	Nema Pauline Wyatt, born December 31, 1913; died February 23, 1995 in Rockwell, N.C. She married a Vanderburg.
735	vi.	Roy Wyatt, born Aft. 1914.

More About Roy Wyatt:
Remains are buried in the National Cemetery in Salisbury, N.C.

| 736 | vii | Elma E. Wyatt, born April 04, 1920; died November 30, 1922 in Rockwell, Rowan County, N.C. |

More About Elma E. Wyatt:
Remains are buried in the Rockwell Cemetery, Rockwell, Rowan County, N.C.

| 737 | viii | Genieve or Genevieve Wyatt, born May 29, 1922; died in buried in Rockwell, Rowan County, N.C. |

More About Genieve or Genevieve Wyatt:
Remains are buried in Rockwell. N.C.

Child of Harvey Wyatt and Charity Eagle is:

+ 738   i.   Effie Jeanette "Genetta" Eagle[23] Wyatt, born March 21, 1900; died July 08, 1986.

587. Margaret Evelyeen[22] Wyatt (Pleasant Loveless[21], Ciscero "Cicero" L.[20], Lazerus Pleasant[19], Thomas "Tommy"[18] Wiatt, Sr. (Wyatt, Wiett), John[17], Henry[16], Richard[15], George[14], Rev. Haute "Haut" "Hawte"[13], Sir George "Georgius" Thomas[12], Sir Thomas "The Younger"[11], Sir Thomas "The Elder"[10], Sir Henry[9], Richard Wiat or[8] Wyatt, Geoffrey "Jeoffrey" Wiot or[7] Wiat, Robert or Richard[6] Wiot, William Wiot or[5] Wyot, Adam Wiot or Wyote or[4], Guyott[3], Guyott[2], Captain or Admiral Adam Guyott or[1] Wiot) was born May 13, 1922 in Rowan County, N.C. She married Wilson Smith.

More About Wilson Smith:
Fact 1: Business partner of Ralph Ketner.

Children of Margaret Wyatt and Wilson Smith are:
739   i.   Ronald Lee[23] Smith, born June 05, 1946.
+ 740   ii.   Timothy Ray Smith, born January 30, 1949 in Rowan, N.C.

592. David Eli[22] Wyatt (James "Jim" Noah[21], William Wesley "Brantly"[20], Noah Calvin[19], Thomas "Tommy"[18] Wiatt, Sr. (Wyatt, Wiett), John[17], Henry[16], Richard[15], George[14], Rev. Haute "Haut" "Hawte"[13], Sir George "Georgius" Thomas[12], Sir Thomas "The Younger"[11], Sir Thomas "The Elder"[10], Sir Henry[9], Richard Wiat or[8] Wyatt, Geoffrey "Jeoffrey" Wiot or[7] Wiat, Robert or Richard[6] Wiot, William Wiot or[5] Wyot, Adam Wiot or Wyote or[4], Guyott[3], Guyott[2], Captain or Admiral Adam Guyott or[1] Wiot) was born November 21, 1887 in Rowan County N.C., and died March 01, 1966 in Rowan County N.C. He married Amanda Fannie L. Esther Frick April 16, 1913 in Rowan County N.C., daughter of Frick and Unknown Wife.

More About David Eli Wyatt:
Remains are buried at the Flat Creek Primitive Baptist Church Cemetery, Rowan County, N.C.; Row #4.

More About Amanda Fannie L. Esther Frick:
Died at age 95 years -- old age.
Remains are buried at the Flat Creek Primitive Baptist Church Cemetery, Rowan; age 95; North Carolina Dept of Health, N.C. Deaths 1983-87. was widowed at the time of demise.

Children of David Wyatt and Amanda Frick are:
+ 741   i.   Lula Marie[23] Wyatt, born January 19, 1914 in Rowan County N.C.; died March 07, 2002 in Rowan County N.C.

+ 742   ii.   Paul Woodrow Wyatt, born December 11, 1918 in Richfield, N.C.; died June 08, 2014 in Stanly County, N.C.

743   iii.   Mary Elizabeth Wyatt, born August 21, 1926 in Rowan County, N.C. She married Carter. More About Mary Elizabeth Wyatt: Fact 1: of Conover, N.C.

744   iv.   Roy Eli Wyatt, born September 08, 1929 in Rowan County, N.C.; died June 28, 2005 in Rowan County N.C.

More About Roy Eli Wyatt:
Fact 1: Never married.
Fact 2: Was a farmer.
Fact 3: Served in the U.S. Army; stationed in Louisiana.
Fact 4: Wrote to his cousin Jim Hinson, M.D. when he was in Indiana in army.
Fact 5: Was a childhood playmate with my father Jim Hinson, M.D.
Fact 6: Lived on Orchard Road when he was growing up.
Remains are buried at the Flat Creek Primitive Baptist Church Cemetery, Rowan County, N.C.; Row #4.

595. Freda Maybelle[22] Kirk (Rhoda Isabelle[21] Morgan, Lila Delilah "Delila"[20] Wyatt, Noah Calvin[19], Thomas "Tommy"[18] Wiatt, Sr. (Wyatt, Wiett), John[17], Henry[16], Richard[15], George[14], Rev. Haute "Haut" "Hawte"[13], Sir George "Georgius" Thomas[12], Sir Thomas "The Younger"[11], Sir Thomas "The Elder"[10], Sir Henry[9], Richard Wiat or[8] Wyatt, Geoffrey "Jeoffrey" Wiot or[7] Wiat, Robert or Richard[6] Wiot, William Wiot or[5] Wyot, Adam Wiot or Wyote or[4], Guyott[3], Guyott[2], Captain or Admiral Adam Guyott or[1] Wiot) was born December 12, 1886 in Stanly County, N.C., and died January 24, 1955 in Rowan County N.C. She married Joe Tom Morgan May 11, 1909 in Rowan County N.C., son of Jacob Morgan and Ann Kirk.

More About Freda Maybelle Kirk:
Flat Creek Primitive Baptist Church Cemetery, Rowan County, N.C.

More About Joe Tom Morgan:
Fact 1: 1930, listed on N.C. Census with wife and family for Morgan Township, Rowan County, N.C.
Fact 2: September 1882, birth also given.
Fact 3: Also known as *"Jacob Thomas Morgan."*

Children of Freda Kirk and Joe Morgan are:
745   i.   Chester[23] Morgan, born July 03, 1910 in North Carolina; died October 06, 1931.

More About Chester Morgan: Luther's Lurther Church Cemetery, Rowan County, N.C.

+ 746   ii.   Paulie Morgan, born August 08, 1912 in Rowan County N.C.; died October 14, 1970 in Rowan County N.C.

747   iii.   Haywood or Hayward Morgan, born Abt. 1914 in North Carolina.

748   iv.   Atlas Morgan, born Abt. 1916 in North Carolina.

749   v.   J. Thomas Morgan, Jr., born Abt. 1918 in North Carolina.

+ 750   vi.   J.T. Morgan, born October 19, 1919 in North Carolina; died June 25, 1994 in Rowan County N.C.

751   vii.   Annie "Anna" Belle Morgan, born December 06, 1921 in Rowan County N.C.; died October 21, 2008 in Salisbury, Rowan County, N.C. She married Harry Lawrence Hall November 09, 1946 in Rowan County N.C.

> More About Annie "Anna" Belle Morgan: Saint Matthew's Lutheran Church Cemetery, Salisbury, N.C.

752   viii.   Jack Boyd Morgan, born Abt. 1924 in North Carolina.

596. Noah Jenkins[22] Eagle (Mary Jane[21] Morgan, Rachel Evelyn "Eveline"[20] Wyatt, Noah Calvin[19], Thomas "Tommy"[18] Wiatt, Sr. (Wyatt, Wiett), John[17], Henry[16], Richard[15], George[14], Rev. Haute "Haut" "Hawte"[13], Sir George "Georgius" Thomas[12], Sir Thomas "The Younger"[11], Sir Thomas "The Elder"[10], Sir Henry[9], Richard Wiat or[8] Wyatt, Geoffrey "Jeoffrey" Wiot or[7] Wiat, Robert or Richard[6] Wiot, William Wiot or[5] Wyot, Adam Wiot or Wyote or[4], Guyott[3], Guyott[2], Captain or Admiral Adam Guyott or[1] Wiot) was born January 28, 1878 in Morgan Township, Rowan County, N.C., and died August 18, 1976 in Richfield, Rowan County, N.C. He married Laura Lou Eller August 12, 1900 in Liberty Methodist Church, Liberty section of Salisbury, N.C. ?, daughter of Reuben Eller and Martha Stoner.

> More About Noah Jenkins Eagle:
> Fact 1: Farmer.
> Fact 2: 1/32 Cherokee Indian, according to William Ashley Hinson (1987).
> Fact 3: Resided in Morgan Township, Rowan County, N.C.
> Fact 4: 1900, built his home in Morgan Township, Rowan County, N.C.
> Fact 5: June 22, 1880, appears on N.C. Federal Census for Morgan Township, Rowan County, N.C.
> Fact 6: 1880, appears on census with his parents and grandmother.
> Fact 7: 1880, His name is misspelled as "Joel J." or "Jill J."
> Fact 8: 1910, listed with his family on the Morgan Township, Rowan County, N.C. Census.
> Was 98 years old at demise. Buried at Wyatt Grove Baptist Church Cemetery, Richfield, N.C.

The April 19th, 1910 United States Federal Census for Morgan Township, Rowan County, N.C. lists on the *"Delaware Yadkin River"* and a indiscernible word followed by

"Larry Publer Road to Richfield." The 13th Census lists Noah J., head, age 32, married for 10 years; his wife: Laura L., 26; Virgie I., daughter, 7; Edwin L., son,5; Helen M., daughter, 3; Gladys M., daughter, 10 months -- written as 10/12. Birthplaces for all: North Carolina.

Other households that appear on this April 19th, 1910 census page include: a few of Morgan, Shaver, Miller, Briggs, Carroll, Surratt. Noah's father's household is directly next door. It may be interesting to some researchers that Noah Jenkins Eagle is in 1910 living in the same general area and is listed on the same page of the census as James W. Wyatt, his first cousin once removed and third cousin once removed. He is also listed on the same page as Jacob -- written on the census as *"J."* Love Surratt, his first cousin once removed and third cousin once removed. Also, listed on the same page is Rhoda Isabelle Morgan Surratt -- wife of Alfred Surratt. She is a second cousin twice removed to Noah. Rhoda Isabelle Morgan Surratt is also Noah's great aunt. Rhoda is a sister to John Calvin Morgan – the husband of Rachel Wyatt – parents of Mary Jane Morgan Eagle – Noah's mother.

Noah Jenkins Eagle is listed on the February 1920 Census, the Fourteenth Census of the United States, Department of Commerce, Bureau of the Census for the Morgan Township of Rowan County. Noah is listed as the head of household, then at age 43; Laura, wife, then age 36; daughter Virgie, then age 17; son Edwin, then age 15; daughter Helen, then age 14; daughter Gladys, then age 10; son Paul, then age, 6; daughter Agnes. The age for Agnes is illegible. She would have been around a year old. All are listed as being born in North Carolina.

♀ | | ♂

Story on Noah Jenkins Eagle [1878-1976]

Memories do not always fade. They are inscribed
in these stories passed to descendants.

THE RED clay and gravel roads are not too much different today as they were in 1894. They are fewer in number – but nevertheless, call to us from other times. Oxen, mules and horses no longer pull the wagons and buggies that traveled here. If we close our eyes we might imagine the gentle wind at night fall bending corn stalks or the morning sun kissing the fuzzy skins of peaches or the sweet softness of figs.

In 1894 in Rowan County, N.C. the teenage Noah feels this need to impress his lady friends. He is trusted to oversee his father Solomon Eagle's freshly cleaned buggy. Noah loves to socialize and is said to have had 13 girlfriends prior to marrying his wife Laura in 1900. Laura is not yet in his limelight. He is distracted with his Saturday night date plans.

A brand new suit he finds in his parents' bedroom. The pants are too big for Noah's small stature. The sixteen-year-old takes the suit coat and puts it on. It looks good, he says to himself.

That evening during the return trip to River Road, where he lived at the time with his parents, he places the suit coat on the dashboard. The lull of the hooves and moving wheels against the road are like the parent who holds an exhausted infant.

While his eyes are closing -- the horse's chocolate eyes are wide alert. It has made this trip so many times, it does not require the navigations of a whip, reins or voice. The cool sweat under the mane, the smell of leather and the sound of the horse's breathing wake Noah. He sits up and looks around a bit disoriented. The horse has stopped.

Noah's sleepy eyes grow wider. His focus is on the dashboard. He must put the suit coat where he first found it. The dashboard is empty. Noah turns the buggy and horse around and heads out to search for it.

In the dark he is unsuccessful. No matter where he searches, it is not discernible.

On Sunday morning, Solomon begins to get ready for church.

"Mary Jane," he says to his wife, *"Have you seen my new suit - the jacket that goes with these pants?"*

She replies:

"I did not know you bought a new suit."

Solomon adores his wife. Her response is viewed as if she plays a secret game. He believes she is jealous. Solomon bought something new for himself and not her. Mary Jane hid the suit coat is what he presumes. He bought the suit because of repeated comments from his mother-in-law Rachel Wyatt Morgan. Rachel said he always wore the same old suit to church. Solomon wants to wear his new suit to please her.

Days pass into weeks. Solomon is out walking. He stops in front of a mud hole, which has begun to dry up. He stares into the mud. He asks:

"Did a man fall into this hole? Is this a body or what?"

Solomon leans over the mud hole. Digging at the gooey mess of red clay with a stick, he fishes out a suit coat. As he stares at the coat, he reasons his wife's jealousy over a coat would never go to the extent of destroying it.

Noah is out again at night socializing. Somehow, word finds itself to Noah that his father has found the suit coat. Noah stays out late to avoid a conversation about it. When Noah returns, it is dark. He moves around the windows looking inside. Not seeing his father who is standing and waiting with a buggy whip, he enters. It does not take much imagination to figure out what happened next.

A lot of growing can happen in six years. Despite Noah's teenage rebellion, in 1900 he finds himself on Orchard Road pounding nails into wood. He is designing and building a house for the woman he wishes to marry – Laura Lou Eller.

He built it on 10 acres of family land he used later for orchards. His father Solomon Eagle, Jr. owned a house on River Road in Richfield. That house was moved to Orchard Road later. It was called the Old Rock House, built in 1806 – and had been the former home of John Calvin Morgan – husband of Rachel Wyatt and father of Mary Jane Morgan Eagle. It was used to store apples.

Both Noah and Solomon's houses still stand today and are owned outside the family.

Nearly seventy-six years of living in the home brought with it the aches and pains of a spirit preparing itself to exit the body. Noah – although of good demeanor, is moved to Hinson Road, where is he lived with his daughter Virgie.

His grandson Jim was his physician and required Noah have with his meals a glass of water and a glass of milk. Before dinner, my brother retrieves a hand mirror, brush and comb. Noah's hair is soft like baby chick feathers. Hans combs Grandpa's hair straight up. Noah looks into the mirror.

"How do you like your hair?" Häns asks.

"It's fine. That's nice." he replies.

When I was a little girl, we visited him at his home. I run about his yard chasing cats with my brother. We run indoors and eat vanilla wafers. When I greet Noah, I ask:

"Do you know who I am?"

He answers:

"You're Jim's daughter."

He asks:

"Where's the little red head?" referring to my sister.

On Thanksgiving Day, 2001, my father James Noah Hinson, M.D. recounts:

"When I was a little boy, Grandpa Eagle told me about Barbara Shaver -- Noah's great grandmother. Barbara was one-quarter Cherokee Indian. Barbara Shaver was married to Moses Green Morgan.

Noah's mother was Mary Jane Morgan who married Solomon Eagle, Junior. Mary Jane Morgan Eagle's mother was Rachel Evelyn Wyatt, and her father was John Noah Calvin Morgan -- the son of Barbara Shaver and Moses Green Morgan. Noah told me when he was growing up his great grandmother Barbara smoked a pipe. She liked to smoke in bed. A small screen was fashioned over the opening of the pipe to keep the embers from falling out onto her mattress in case Barbara fell asleep smoking. Sometimes, Barbara did not want to get out of bed to light her pipe. She asked Noah to light her pipe. He got her pipe. He added tobacco to it. He walked to the fireplace to light it. He said that was his earliest memories of smoking.

"*Noah caught fish with a fish trap he placed at the Yadkin River. He placed his trap under water between rocks that held it in place. Eels swam into the trap along with the fish. Buzzards saw this and landed on top of the fish trap to sample what had been caught. Noah, as a boy, checked his trap each day. He freed buzzards that landed on top. He knew if their feathers got wet, they would not be able to fly away.*

"*Noah experimented with moonshine one evening. When he returned home he slept late the following day. His mother attempted to wake him. She found Noah unresponsive. She pulled him out of bed and down the stairs bumping his head against the stairs in an attempt to wake him for work.*"

More About Laura Lou Eller:
Buried at Wyatt Grove Baptist Church Cemetery, Richfield, N.C.

Children of Noah Eagle and Laura Eller are:

+   753   i.   Virgie Irene[23] Eagle, born November 15, 1902 in Richfield, Rowan County, N.C.; died July 12, 1984 in Salisbury, Rowan County, N.C.

+   754   ii.   Edwin "Ed" Lee Eagle, born July 25, 1904 in Morgan Township, Rowan County, N.C.; died January 09, 1984 in North Carolina.

+   755   iii.   Helen Madelene Eagle, born September 30, 1906 in Morgan Township, Rowan County, N.C.; died May 23, 1978.

+   756   iv.   Gladys Marie Eagle, born June 03, 1909 in Morgan Township, Rowan County, N.C.; died September 03, 1977.

       757   v.   Paul Murray Eagle, born December 01, 1913 in Rowan County, N.C.; died May 31, 1995 in Rowan County N.C. He married (1) Lonie Bame (Ketchie). He married (2) Thelma Lucille Moore November 29, 1941. More About Paul Murray Eagle: Fact 1: Served in the US Army for 17 years -- including during WWII. Remains are buried at Wyatts Grove Missionary Baptist Church Cemetery, Richfield, Rowan County, N.C. More About Thelma Lucille Moore: Fact 1: Buried at Pennisula Memorial Park Cemetery, Va.

+   758   vi.   Agnes Evelyn Eagle, born May 31, 1919 in Richfield, N.C.; died June 1999 in Carrboro, N.C.

+   759   vii.   Robert "Bob" Noah Eagle, born January 09, 1923 in Rowan County, N.C.

♀ | | ♂

Story on Paul Murray Eagle [1913-1995]

ON MAY 31st, 1995, the angels of Heaven greeted the spirit of Paul Eagle. When his funeral and burial had taken place, his wife remarked to Paul's niece Margaret Gordon, *"This is not the first time Paul has been buried."* It was then Margaret remembered – as later this was recounted by other relatives too.

During World War II, Paul was in Germany. *"He was on duty with two other boys in the field,"* Margaret recollected. They were in their fox holes when a bomb came down and scattered the dirt – burying each. Two soldiers who knew Paul began immediately digging themselves out. They remembered where Paul was and ran to him. Unknown to either soldier, though, Paul was praying. He said to God, as he recounted later, *"Lord, is this what you want for me?"*

He was running out of oxygen. He had no sooner said this prayer when his two comrades uncovered him and pulled him into the air.

597. Rachel Minnie Dora[22] Eagle (Mary Jane[21] Morgan, Rachel Evelyn "Eveline"[20] Wyatt, Noah Calvin[19], Thomas "Tommy"[18] Wiatt, Sr. (Wyatt, Wiett), John[17], Henry[16], Richard[15], George[14], Rev. Haute "Haut" "Hawte"[13], Sir George "Georgius" Thomas[12], Sir Thomas "The Younger"[11], Sir Thomas "The Elder"[10], Sir Henry[9], Richard Wiat or[8] Wyatt, Geoffrey "Jeoffrey" Wiot or[7] Wiat, Robert or Richard[6] Wiot, William Wiot or[5] Wyot, Adam Wiot or Wyote or[4], Guyott[3], Guyott[2], Captain or Admiral Adam Guyott or[1] Wiot) was born February 1885 in Rowan County, N.C. She married Cain Morgan.

More About Cain Morgan:
Fact 1: Also known as Camy Morgan.

     Child of Rachel Eagle and Cain Morgan is:
     760   i.   Zeda[23] Morgan.

598. Mary Lillie[22] Eagle (Mary Jane[21] Morgan, Rachel Evelyn "Eveline"[20] Wyatt, Noah Calvin[19], Thomas "Tommy"[18] Wiatt, Sr. (Wyatt, Wiett), John[17], Henry[16], Richard[15], George[14], Rev. Haute "Haut" "Hawte"[13], Sir George "Georgius" Thomas[12], Sir Thomas "The Younger"[11], Sir Thomas "The Elder"[10], Sir Henry[9], Richard Wiat or[8] Wyatt, Geoffrey "Jeoffrey" Wiot or[7] Wiat, Robert or Richard[6] Wiot, William Wiot or[5] Wyot, Adam Wiot or Wyote or[4], Guyott[3], Guyott[2], Captain or Admiral Adam Guyott or[1] Wiot) was born May 18, 1898 in Providence Township, Rowan County, N.C., and died July 12, 1979 in North Carolina. She married Love Troutman, son of Daniel Troutman and Amanda Frick.

Children of Mary Eagle and Love Troutman are:

+ 761   i.   Ray Clayton[23] Troutman, born October 14, 1920.

+ 762   ii.   Lonie Mae Troutman, born March 18, 1923 in Rowan County, N.C.

599. Mary Frances[22] Eagle (Noah Calvin[21], Mary Ann[20] Wyatt, Noah Calvin[19], Thomas "Tommy"[18] Wiatt, Sr. (Wyatt, Wiett), John[17], Henry[16], Richard[15], George[14], Rev. Haute "Haut" "Hawte"[13], Sir George "Georgius" Thomas[12], Sir Thomas "The Younger"[11], Sir Thomas "The Elder"[10], Sir Henry[9], Richard Wiat or[8] Wyatt, Geoffrey "Jeoffrey" Wiot or[7] Wiat, Robert or Richard[6] Wiot, William Wiot or[5] Wyot, Adam Wiot or Wyote or[4], Guyott[3], Guyott[2], Captain or Admiral Adam Guyott or[1] Wiot) was born November 25, 1884 in Jan. 30, 1979, and died January 30, 1979. She married Charles Franklin Morgan March 29, 1908, son of Ivey Morgan and Reney Rimer.

More About Mary Frances Eagle:
Buried Chestnut Hill Cemetery, Rowna County, N.C.

More About Charles Franklin Morgan:
Buried at Chestnut Hill Cemetery, Rowan County, N.C.

Children of Mary Eagle and Charles Morgan are:

763   i.   Lester Everett[23] Morgan, born January 20, 1909 in Rowan County, N.C.; died March 04, 1987. He married Mary Boyd October 31, 1936.

       More About Lester Everett Morgan:
       Buried at Chestnut Hill Cemetery, N.C.

       More About Mary Boyd:
       Buried at Chestnut Hill Cemetery, N.C.

+ 764   ii.   Nellie Manola Morgan, born February 12, 1912 in Rowan County, N.C.

600. Albert Thadeus[22] Eagle (Noah Calvin[21], Mary Ann[20] Wyatt, Noah Calvin[19], Thomas "Tommy"[18] Wiatt, Sr. (Wyatt, Wiett), John[17], Henry[16], Richard[15], George[14], Rev. Haute "Haut" "Hawte"[13], Sir George "Georgius" Thomas[12], Sir Thomas "The Younger"[11], Sir Thomas "The Elder"[10], Sir Henry[9], Richard Wiat or[8] Wyatt, Geoffrey "Jeoffrey" Wiot or[7] Wiat, Robert or Richard[6] Wiot, William Wiot or[5] Wyot, Adam Wiot or Wyote or[4], Guyott[3], Guyott[2], Captain or Admiral Adam Guyott or[1] Wiot) was born December 24, 1885, and died May 19, 1986. He married Mary Anna Canup June 20, 1919, daughter of William Canup and Josie Frick.

More About Albert Thadeus Eagle:
Remains are buried at Liberty Methodist Church Cemetery, N.C.

More About Mary Anna Canup:
Buried at Liberty Methodist Church Cemetery, N.C.

    Children of Albert Eagle and Mary Canup are:

+   765   i.   Ruby Mae[23] Eagle, born June 11, 1916 in Rowan County, N.C.
+   766   ii.   Moody Van Calvin Eagle, born September 08, 1917 in Rowan County, N.C.
+   767   iii.   James Albert Eagle, born June 20, 1920 in Rowan County, N.C.
+   768   iv.   Marjorie Lucille Eagle, born July 07, 1923 in Rowan County, N.C.

601. Roxie Dora[22] Eagle (Noah Calvin[21], Mary Ann[20] Wyatt, Noah Calvin[19], Thomas "Tommy"[18] Wiatt, Sr. (Wyatt, Wiett), John[17], Henry[16], Richard[15], George[14], Rev. Haute "Haut" "Hawte"[13], Sir George "Georgius" Thomas[12], Sir Thomas "The Younger"[11], Sir Thomas "The Elder"[10], Sir Henry[9], Richard Wiat or[8] Wyatt, Geoffrey "Jeoffrey" Wiot or[7] Wiat, Robert or Richard[6] Wiot, William Wiot or[5] Wyot, Adam Wiot or Wyote or[4], Guyott[3], Guyott[2], Captain or Admiral Adam Guyott or[1] Wiot) was born August 14, 1887, and died September 24, 1955. She married James William Whitley July 01, 1906, son of Pleasant Whitley and Nancy Arey.

    Children of Roxie Eagle and James Whitley are:

+   769   i.   Ervin Oscar[23] Whitley, born April 16, 1907 in Stanly County, N.C.
+   770   ii.   Vertie May Whitley, born August 16, 1908 in Stanly County, N.C.
   771   iii.   Pearle Esther Whitley, born April 25, 1910; died January 21, 1912.

    More About Pearle Esther Whitley:
    Cause of death: Dress caught fire while playing around a wash pot.

+   772   iv.   Marybelle Lucille Whitley, born October 30, 1911 in Stanly County, N.C.
+   773   v.   Agnes Marie Whitley, born March 08, 1915 in Stanly County, N.C.
+   774   vi.   Marvin L. Whitley, born September 13, 1916 in Stanly County, N.C.; died July 21, 1989.
+   775   vii.   Georgia (Georgie) Kathleen Whitley, born February 22, 1919.
+   776   viii.   Robert Clifford Whitley, born March 21, 1921 in Rowan County, N.C.; died November 16, 1983 in Az.
   777   ix.   Jasper Leroy Whitley, born March 09, 1924. He married (1) Ruth Secrest June 06, 1950. He married (2) Pauline Locke Owens October 25, 1968.

More About Ruth Secrest:
Died as the result of injuries sustained in car accident.

+   778   x.   John Calvin Whitley, born May 07, 1926.

     779   xi.   James Everett Whitley, born November 19, 1927 in Rowan County, N.C.

     780   xii.   Martha Louise Whitley, born July 30, 1929; died March 25, 1985 in Az. She married Jack Farrington April 07, 1949.

602. Annie Luada[22] Eagle (Noah Calvin[21], Mary Ann[20] Wyatt, Noah Calvin[19], Thomas "Tommy"[18] Wiatt, Sr. (Wyatt, Wiett), John[17], Henry[16], Richard[15], George[14], Rev. Haute "Haut" "Hawte"[13], Sir George "Georgius" Thomas[12], Sir Thomas "The Younger"[11], Sir Thomas "The Elder"[10], Sir Henry[9], Richard Wiat or[8] Wyatt, Geoffrey "Jeoffrey" Wiot or[7] Wiat, Robert or Richard[6] Wiot, William Wiot or[5] Wyot, Adam Wiot or Wyote or[4], Guyott[3], Guyott[2], Captain or Admiral Adam Guyott or[1] Wiot) was born November 03, 1890, and died August 21, 1929. She married George Freeland Jones, Sr. May 10, 1912, son of R.B. Jones and Maggie Hillard.

     Children of Annie Eagle and George Jones are:

+   781   i.   Helen Marie[23] Jones, born June 06, 1915 in Rowan County, N.C.

+   782   ii.   George Freeland Jones, Jr., born April 30, 1920 in Rowan County, N.C.; died May 14, 1968.

+   783   iii   Ruby May Jones, born September 16, 1923 in Rowan County, N.C.; died March 30, 1926.

603. Nannie Manola[22] Eagle (Noah Calvin[21], Mary Ann[20] Wyatt, Noah Calvin[19], Thomas "Tommy"[18] Wiatt, Sr. (Wyatt, Wiett), John[17], Henry[16], Richard[15], George[14], Rev. Haute "Haut" "Hawte"[13], Sir George "Georgius" Thomas[12], Sir Thomas "The Younger"[11], Sir Thomas "The Elder"[10], Sir Henry[9], Richard Wiat or[8] Wyatt, Geoffrey "Jeoffrey" Wiot or[7] Wiat, Robert or Richard[6] Wiot, William Wiot or[5] Wyot, Adam Wiot or Wyote or[4], Guyott[3], Guyott[2], Captain or Admiral Adam Guyott or[1] Wiot) was born January 03, 1894, and died June 03, 1965. She married Albert Alexander Safrit February 21, 1929, son of Daniel Safrit and Laura Cress.

     Child of Nannie Eagle and Albert Safrit is:

+   784   i.   Fred Calvin[23] Safrit, born March 24, 1930.

605. Martin Junius[22] Eagle (Noah Calvin[21], Mary Ann[20] Wyatt, Noah Calvin[19], Thomas "Tommy"[18] Wiatt, Sr. (Wyatt, Wiett), John[17], Henry[16], Richard[15], George[14], Rev. Haute "Haut" "Hawte"[13], Sir George "Georgius" Thomas[12], Sir Thomas "The Younger"[11], Sir Thomas "The Elder"[10], Sir Henry[9], Richard Wiat or[8] Wyatt, Geoffrey "Jeoffrey" Wiot or[7] Wiat, Robert or Richard[6] Wiot, William Wiot or[5] Wyot, Adam Wiot or Wyote or[4], Guyott[3], Guyott[2], Captain or Admiral Adam Guyott or[1] Wiot) was born June 08, 1897 in Morgan Township, Rowan County, N.C., and died September 21, 1970. He married Vera Roberts, daughter of Hugh Roberts and Lula Walker.

Children of Martin Eagle and Vera Roberts are:

+ 785   i.   Frances Mildred[23] Eagle, born October 28, 1918 in Rowan County, N.C.

+ 786   ii.   Mabel Eloise Eagle, born August 24, 1920 in Lincoln County, N.C.

   787   iii.   Hugh Calvin Eagle, born November 23, 1922 in Rowan County, N.C.

607. Mattie E.[22] Eagle (Noah Calvin[21], Mary Ann[20] Wyatt, Noah Calvin[19], Thomas "Tommy"[18] Wiatt, Sr. (Wyatt, Wiett), John[17], Henry[16], Richard[15], George[14], Rev. Haute "Haut" "Hawte"[13], Sir George "Georgius" Thomas[12], Sir Thomas "The Younger"[11], Sir Thomas "The Elder"[10], Sir Henry[9], Richard Wiat or[8] Wyatt, Geoffrey "Jeoffrey" Wiot or[7] Wiat, Robert or Richard[6] Wiot, William Wiot or[5] Wyot, Adam Wiot or Wyote or[4], Guyott[3], Guyott[2], Captain or Admiral Adam Guyott or[1] Wiot) was born July 22, 1902. She married Eubert Hugh Graham, Sr. August 20, 1921, son of Hugh Graham and Frances Goodman.

Children of Mattie Eagle and Eubert Graham are:

+ 788   i.   Ronald Alexander[23] Graham, born December 14, 1925 in Rowan County, N.C.; died September 01, 1976.

+ 789   ii.   Theron Eagle Graham, born October 30, 1933 in Rowan County, N.C.

+ 790   iii.   Bobby Eagle Graham, born April 19, 1935 in Rowan County, N.C.

   791   iv.   Eubert Hugh Graham, Jr., born February 02, 1937 in Rowan County, N.C. He married Carol Goodwin Summers July 11, 1975.

608. Carpenter L.[22] Eagle (Noah Calvin[21], Mary Ann[20] Wyatt, Noah Calvin[19], Thomas "Tommy"[18] Wiatt, Sr. (Wyatt, Wiett), John[17], Henry[16], Richard[15], George[14], Rev. Haute "Haut" "Hawte"[13], Sir George "Georgius" Thomas[12], Sir Thomas "The Younger"[11], Sir Thomas "The Elder"[10], Sir Henry[9], Richard Wiat or[8] Wyatt, Geoffrey "Jeoffrey" Wiot or[7] Wiat, Robert or Richard[6] Wiot, William Wiot or[5] Wyot, Adam Wiot or Wyote or[4], Guyott[3], Guyott[2], Captain or Admiral Adam Guyott or[1] Wiot) was born March 29, 1904. He married Joycie Luetitia Snider July 25, 1925, daughter of Samuel Snider and Tronie Walker.

Children of Carpenter Eagle and Joycie Snider are:

+ 792   i.   Thelma Louise[23] Eagle, born June 10, 1926 in Rowan County, N.C.

+ 793   ii.   Billy West Eagle, born June 04, 1928 in Rowan County, N.C.

+ 794   iii.   Carpenter L. Eagle, Jr., born August 25, 1931 in Rowan County, N.C.

+ 795   iv.   Nancy Mae Eagle, born July 20, 1935 in Rowan County, N.C.

+ 796   v.   Glenn Floyd Eagle, born June 10, 1938 in Rowan County, N.C.

611. William Armstrong[22] Eagle (Eli Esau[21], Mary Ann[20] Wyatt, Noah Calvin[19], Thomas "Tommy"[18] Wiatt, Sr. (Wyatt, Wiett), John[17], Henry[16], Richard[15], George[14], Rev. Haute "Haut" "Hawte"[13], Sir George "Georgius" Thomas[12], Sir Thomas "The Younger"[11], Sir Thomas "The Elder"[10], Sir Henry[9], Richard Wiat or[8] Wyatt, Geoffrey "Jeoffrey" Wiot or[7] Wiat, Robert or Richard[6] Wiot, William Wiot or[5] Wyot, Adam Wiot or Wyote or[4], Guyott[3], Guyott[2], Captain or Admiral Adam Guyott or[1] Wiot) was born April 08, 1900, and died February 25, 1978. He married Mary Freda Lyerly, daughter of W. Lyerly and Minnie Morgan.

More About William Armstrong Eagle:
Remains are buried in the Rowan Memorial Park Cemetery, Salisbury, N.C.

Children of William Eagle and Mary Lyerly are:

+ 797   i.   Evelyn[23] Eagle, born November 22, 1919 in Rowan County N.C.

+ 798   ii.   Everett Wayne Eagle, born October 10, 1921 in Rowan County N.C.

612. Carrie Etta[22] Eagle (Eli Esau[21], Mary Ann[20] Wyatt, Noah Calvin[19], Thomas "Tommy"[18] Wiatt, Sr. (Wyatt, Wiett), John[17], Henry[16], Richard[15], George[14], Rev. Haute "Haut" "Hawte"[13], Sir George "Georgius" Thomas[12], Sir Thomas "The Younger"[11], Sir Thomas "The Elder"[10], Sir Henry[9], Richard Wiat or[8] Wyatt, Geoffrey "Jeoffrey" Wiot or[7] Wiat, Robert or Richard[6] Wiot, William Wiot or[5] Wyot, Adam Wiot or Wyote or[4], Guyott[3], Guyott[2], Captain or Admiral Adam Guyott or[1] Wiot) was born March 30, 1884, and died February 19, 1974. She married Adolphus D. Morgan January 21, 1906, son of Otha Morgan and Clarcy Eller.

Children of Carrie Eagle and Adolphus Morgan are:

799   i.   Ruth Etta[23] Morgan. She married Jesse Dickson May 29, 1930.

800   ii.   Oren Adophus Morgan, born November 10, 1906; died June 11, 1957. He married Evelyn Hall Smith.

801   iii.   Nettie Remelle Morgan, born July 25, 1910; died October 18, 1953. She married Enoch Benjamin Goodman.

802   iv.   Ruby Ann Morgan, born July 16, 1915. She married Sam C. Smith November 02, 1950.

+ 803   v.   Rena Elizabeth Morgan, born February 20, 1917.

+ 804   vi.   Billie Mae Morgan, born February 13, 1929; died November 13, 1991.

613. Emma Dora[22] Eagle (Eli Esau[21], Mary Ann[20] Wyatt, Noah Calvin[19], Thomas "Tommy"[18] Wiatt, Sr. (Wyatt, Wiett), John[17], Henry[16], Richard[15], George[14], Rev. Haute "Haut" "Hawte"[13], Sir George "Georgius" Thomas[12], Sir Thomas "The Younger"[11], Sir Thomas "The Elder"[10], Sir Henry[9], Richard Wiat or[8] Wyatt, Geoffrey "Jeoffrey" Wiot or[7] Wiat, Robert or Richard[6] Wiot, William Wiot or[5] Wyot, Adam Wiot or Wyote or[4], Guyott[3], Guyott[2], Captain or Admiral Adam Guyott or[1] Wiot) was born April 24, 1885, and died March 06, 1967. She married (1) Jones Joseph Frick. She married (2) James Monroe Morgan. She married (3) Chalmers Gideon.

Children of Emma Eagle and Jones Frick are:

+ 805   i.   Roy David[23] Frick, born May 26, 1911.

   806   ii.   Dora A. Frick, born July 10, 1905; died December 09, 1905.

+ 807   iii.   Fannie Lillian Frick, born October 25, 1906.

+ 808   iv.   Ernest Jones Frick, born July 08, 1908.

+ 809   v.   Ida Nora Frick, born September 09, 1909; died June 14, 1987 in S.C.

Children of Emma Eagle and James Morgan are:

+ 810   i.   Geneva Voncelle[23] Morgan, born January 17, 1920.

+ 811   ii.   Baxter Monroe Morgan, born September 05, 1924.

+ 812   iii.   Curtis Eli Morgan, born February 19, 1925.

+ 813   iv.   Raymond Emerson Morgan, born February 06, 1926.

+ 814   v.   Pearl Hazelene Morgan, born August 09, 1927.

614. Mary Christine[22] Eagle (Eli Esau[21], Mary Ann[20] Wyatt, Noah Calvin[19], Thomas "Tommy"[18] Wiatt, Sr. (Wyatt, Wiett), John[17], Henry[16], Richard[15], George[14], Rev. Haute "Haut" "Hawte"[13], Sir George "Georgius" Thomas[12], Sir Thomas "The Younger"[11], Sir Thomas "The Elder"[10], Sir Henry[9], Richard Wiat or[8] Wyatt, Geoffrey "Jeoffrey" Wiot or[7] Wiat, Robert or Richard[6] Wiot, William Wiot or[5] Wyot, Adam Wiot or Wyote or[4], Guyott[3], Guyott[2], Captain or Admiral Adam Guyott or[1] Wiot) was born August 07, 1886. She married Chalmers Gideon Frick February 11, 1906, son of Levi Frick and Julia Stoner.

Children of Mary Eagle and Chalmers Frick are:

+ 815   i.   Harvey Lee[23] Frick, born November 15, 1906 in Rowan County, N.C.

+ 816   ii.   Frederick Gideon Frick, born December 20, 1907 in Rowan County, N.C.; died July 01, 1962.

+ 817   iii.   Nellie Mae Frick, born November 07, 1909 in Rowan County, N.C.

+ 818   iv.   Elizabeth Euver Frick, born April 30, 1909 in Rowan County, N.C.

+ 819   v.   Mamie Frances Frick, born September 15, 1913 in Rowan County, N.C.; died December 09, 1983.

+ 820   vi.   Gertrude Esther Frick, born October 17, 1917 in Rowan County, N.C.

   821   vii.   Pearl Ruth Frick, born April 13, 1920 in Rowan County, N.C.; died March 03, 1940.

     More About Pearl Ruth Frick:
     Remains are buried at Liberty Methodist Church Cemetery, Rowan County, N.C.

+ 822   viii.   Norman Grey Frick, born May 06, 1926.

616. Grover Victor[22] Eagle (Eli Esau[21], Mary Ann[20] Wyatt, Noah Calvin[19], Thomas "Tommy"[18] Wiatt, Sr. (Wyatt, Wiett), John[17], Henry[16], Richard[15], George[14], Rev. Haute "Haut" "Hawte"[13], Sir George "Georgius" Thomas[12], Sir Thomas "The Younger"[11], Sir Thomas "The Elder"[10], Sir Henry[9], Richard Wiat or[8] Wyatt, Geoffrey "Jeoffrey" Wiot or[7] Wiat, Robert or Richard[6] Wiot, William Wiot or[5] Wyot, Adam Wiot or Wyote or[4], Guyott[3], Guyott[2], Captain or Admiral Adam Guyott or[1] Wiot) was born February 22, 1891, and died May 28, 1966. He married Mary Lee Poole December 25, 1911, daughter of Joseph Poole and Barbara Kesler.

More About Grover Victor Eagle:
Remains are buried at Rowan Memorial Park Cemetery, Rowan County, N.C.

More About Mary Lee Poole:
Remains are buried at Rowan Memorial Park Cemetery, Rowan County, N.C.

Children of Grover Eagle and Mary Poole are:
+   823   i.   Lucille[23] Eagle, born August 14, 1912 in Rowan County N.C.
+   824   ii.   Joseph Eagle, born July 23, 1914; died November 20, 1969.
+   825   iii.   Pearl Eagle, born August 23, 1916.
+   826   iv.   Irene Eagle, born January 11, 1920.
+   827   v.   Frances Eagle, born November 07, 1925.

617. Joseph Calvin[22] Eagle (Eli Esau[21], Mary Ann[20] Wyatt, Noah Calvin[19], Thomas "Tommy"[18] Wiatt, Sr. (Wyatt, Wiett), John[17], Henry[16], Richard[15], George[14], Rev. Haute "Haut" "Hawte"[13], Sir George "Georgius" Thomas[12], Sir Thomas "The Younger"[11], Sir Thomas "The Elder"[10], Sir Henry[9], Richard Wiat or[8] Wyatt, Geoffrey "Jeoffrey" Wiot or[7] Wiat, Robert or Richard[6] Wiot, William Wiot or[5] Wyot, Adam Wiot or Wyote or[4], Guyott[3], Guyott[2], Captain or Admiral Adam Guyott or[1] Wiot) was born November 14, 1892, and died November 18, 1973. He married Elizabeth Jefferson Dixon August 12, 1914, daughter of Thomas Dixon and Betty Stuart.

More About Joseph Calvin Eagle:
Remains are buried at the Rowan Memorial Park Cemetery, Rowan County, N.C.

More About Elizabeth Jefferson Dixon:
Remains are buried at the Rowan Memorial Park Cemetery, Rowan County, N.C.

Children of Joseph Eagle and Elizabeth Dixon are:
+   828   i.   Joseph Charles[23] Eagle, born December 03, 1916 in Mecklenburg County, N.C.
+   829   ii.   Mabel Inez Eagle, born May 29, 1919.
+   830   iii.   Maurice Edison Eagle, Sr., born September 12, 1921 in USA; died December 23, 1986.

618. Walter Eli[22] Eagle (Eli Esau[21], Mary Ann[20] Wyatt, Noah Calvin[19], Thomas "Tommy"[18] Wiatt, Sr. (Wyatt, Wiett), John[17], Henry[16], Richard[15], George[14], Rev. Haute "Haut" "Hawte"[13], Sir George "Georgius" Thomas[12], Sir Thomas "The Younger"[11], Sir Thomas "The Elder"[10], Sir Henry[9], Richard Wiat or[8] Wyatt, Geoffrey "Jeoffrey" Wiot or[7] Wiat, Robert or Richard[6] Wiot, William Wiot or[5] Wyot, Adam Wiot or Wyote or[4], Guyott[3], Guyott[2], Captain or Admiral Adam Guyott or[1] Wiot) was born September 11, 1894. He married Minnie Mary Catharine Morgan August 30, 1914, daughter of John Morgan and Margaret Troutman.

More About Walter Eli Eagle:
Died Augst 10, 19__; remains buried at Rowan Memorial Park Cemetery, Rowan County, N.C.

Children of Walter Eagle and Minnie Morgan are:

+ 831   i.   Edna Elizabeth[23] Eagle, born June 19, 1915 in Rowan County N.C.

+ 832   ii.   Reba Odessa Eagle, born September 10, 1916 in Rowan County N.C.

+ 833   iii.   Wade Preston Eagle, born February 04, 1920 in Rowan County N.C.

   834   iv.   Nancy L. Eagle, born June 13, 1926 in Rowan County N.C. She married Charles B. Duncan, Jr. October 01, 1977.

             More About Charles B. Duncan, Jr.:
             Fact 1: Served in the U.S. Air Force.

+ 835   v.   James Donald Eagle, born March 07, 1934 in Rowan County N.C.

619. Annie Zenobia[22] Eagle (Eli Esau[21], Mary Ann[20] Wyatt, Noah Calvin[19], Thomas "Tommy"[18] Wiatt, Sr. (Wyatt, Wiett), John[17], Henry[16], Richard[15], George[14], Rev. Haute "Haut" "Hawte"[13], Sir George "Georgius" Thomas[12], Sir Thomas "The Younger"[11], Sir Thomas "The Elder"[10], Sir Henry[9], Richard Wiat or[8] Wyatt, Geoffrey "Jeoffrey" Wiot or[7] Wiat, Robert or Richard[6] Wiot, William Wiot or[5] Wyot, Adam Wiot or Wyote or[4], Guyott[3], Guyott[2], Captain or Admiral Adam Guyott or[1] Wiot) was born September 20, 1896, and died May 12, 1962. She married William Henry Morgan May 03, 1914.

Children of Annie Eagle and William Morgan are:

+ 836   i.   Esther Viola[23] Morgan, born in Rowan County N.C.; died March 25, 1983.

+ 837   ii.   Reather Armstrong Morgan, born in Rowan County N.C.; died April 15, 1974.

+ 838   iii.   William Henry Morgan, born in Rowan County N.C.

+ 839   iv.   Dorothy Ann Morgan, born August 14, 1928 in Bilozi, Missouri.

+ 840   v.   Rachel Lee Morgan, born in Rowan County N.C.

620. Ida Lou[22] Eagle (Eli Esau[21], Mary Ann[20] Wyatt, Noah Calvin[19], Thomas "Tommy"[18] Wiatt, Sr. (Wyatt, Wiett), John[17], Henry[16], Richard[15], George[14], Rev. Haute "Haut" "Hawte"[13], Sir George "Georgius" Thomas[12], Sir Thomas "The Younger"[11], Sir Thomas "The Elder"[10], Sir Henry[9], Richard Wiat or[8] Wyatt, Geoffrey "Jeoffrey" Wiot or[7] Wiat, Robert or Richard[6] Wiot, William Wiot or[5] Wyot, Adam Wiot or Wyote or[4], Guyott[3], Guyott[2], Captain or Admiral Adam Guyott or[1] Wiot) was born July 10, 1899, and died April 27, 1952. She married John Wilson Jackson December 17, 1911, son of William Jackson and Eva Croter.

More About John Wilson Jackson:
Remains are buried next to his wife's remains at Liberty Methodist Church Cemetery, Rowan County, N.C.

Children of Ida Eagle and John Jackson are:

+ 841   i.   William Eli[23] Jackson, born November 07, 1912 in Rowan County, N.C.

842   ii.   Thelma Ruth Jackson, born May 04, 1914 in Rowan County, N.C. She married Kendrick Whitson Thompson February 29, 1936.

More About Kendrick Whitson Thompson:
Fact 1: No children born.
Remains are buried at Mount View Memorial Gardens, N.C.

+ 843   iii.   Manteo Monroe Jackson, born January 12, 1916 in Rowan County, N.C.

+ 844   iv.   John David Jackson, born October 10, 1917 in Rowan County, N.C.

845   v.   Glenn Wesley Jackson, born August 14, 1920 in Rowan County, N.C.; died August 17, 1920.

More About Glenn Wesley Jackson:
Remains are buried at the Corinth Baptist Church, Rowan County, N.C.

+ 846   vi.   Ralph Adolphus Jackson, born July 16, 1922 in Rowan County, N.C.

+ 847   vii.   Louie Phenix Jackson, born August 08, 1924 in Rowan County, N.C.

+ 848   viii.   Ruby Ann Jackson, born June 29, 1926 in Rowan County, N.C.

621. Elizabeth "Elisbeth" Nora[22] Eagle (Eli Esau[21], Mary Ann[20] Wyatt, Noah Calvin[19], Thomas "Tommy"[18] Wiatt, Sr. (Wyatt, Wiett), John[17], Henry[16], Richard[15], George[14], Rev. Haute "Haut" "Hawte"[13], Sir George "Georgius" Thomas[12], Sir Thomas "The Younger"[11], Sir Thomas "The Elder"[10], Sir Henry[9], Richard Wiat or[8] Wyatt, Geoffrey "Jeoffrey" Wiot or[7] Wiat, Robert or Richard[6] Wiot, William Wiot or[5] Wyot, Adam Wiot or Wyote or[4], Guyott[3], Guyott[2], Captain or Admiral Adam Guyott or[1] Wiot) was born January 14, 1902 in Gold Hill, N.C., and died January 30, 1983. She married Victor Elvin Edwards, son of William Edwards and Hattie Jones.

> Children of Elizabeth Eagle and Victor Edwards are:

+ 849   i.   James Alois[23] Edwards, born April 13, 1924 in Stark County, Massilon, Ohio.

+ 850   ii.   Stanley Edwards, born March 26, 1926 in Stark County, Massilon, Ohio.

   851   iii.   Elizabeth Jane Edwards, born July 21, 1930 in Stark County, Massilon, Ohio.

+ 852   iv.   Dwight Jerette Edwards, born October 05, 1938 in Stark County, Massilon, Ohio.

622. James Harvey[22] Eagle (Eli Esau[21], Mary Ann[20] Wyatt, Noah Calvin[19], Thomas "Tommy"[18] Wiatt, Sr. (Wyatt, Wiett), John[17], Henry[16], Richard[15], George[14], Rev. Haute "Haut" "Hawte"[13], Sir George "Georgius" Thomas[12], Sir Thomas "The Younger"[11], Sir Thomas "The Elder"[10], Sir Henry[9], Richard Wiat or[8] Wyatt, Geoffrey "Jeoffrey" Wiot or[7] Wiat, Robert or Richard[6] Wiot, William Wiot or[5] Wyot, Adam Wiot or Wyote or[4], Guyott[3], Guyott[2], Captain or Admiral Adam Guyott or[1] Wiot) was born April 30, 1905 in Gold Hill, N.C. He married (1) Eunice Thelma Newsom, daughter of Albert Newsom and Talora Arie. He married (2) Frances Loften Peace.

> More About Eunice Thelma Newsom: Remains are buried at Oakwood Memorial Mausoleum, High Point, N.C.

> Children of James Eagle and Eunice Newsom are:

   853   i.   Bonnie Lou[23] Eagle, born November 11, 1931; died November 11, 1931.

+ 854   ii.   Tolora Anita Eagle, born June 16, 1937.

+ 855   iii.   Mary Lynda Eagle, born March 27, 1942 in High Point, N.C.

624. Enoch Arthur[22] Goodman (Nancy Jane[21] Eagle, Mary Ann[20] Wyatt, Noah Calvin[19], Thomas "Tommy"[18] Wiatt, Sr. (Wyatt, Wiett), John[17], Henry[16], Richard[15], George[14], Rev. Haute "Haut" "Hawte"[13], Sir George "Georgius" Thomas[12], Sir Thomas "The Younger"[11], Sir Thomas "The Elder"[10], Sir Henry[9], Richard Wiat or[8] Wyatt, Geoffrey "Jeoffrey" Wiot or[7] Wiat, Robert or Richard[6] Wiot, William Wiot or[5] Wyot, Adam Wiot or Wyote or[4], Guyott[3], Guyott[2], Captain or Admiral Adam Guyott or[1] Wiot) was born February 07, 1881, and died

April 17, 1974. He married Frances Josephine Park, daughter of Noah Trexler and Sarah Parker.

More About Enoch Arthur Goodman:
Fact 1: 1974, Buried Chestnut Hill Cemetery, N.C.

More About Frances Josephine Park:
Buried at Chestnut Hill Cemetery, N.C.

Children of Enoch Goodman and Frances Park are:

	856	i.	Francis Roy[23] Goodman.
+	857	ii.	Ree Velt Goodman, born August 10, 1907.
+	858	iii.	Myron A.O. Goodman, born April 12, 1909; died May 01, 1982.
+	859	iv.	Loyd Calvin Goodman, born April 24, 1911.
+	860	v.	Harold Moses Goodman, born April 02, 1913; died January 12, 1963.
+	861	vi.	Enoch Alvin Goodman, born July 30, 1915.
+	862	vii.	Sara Jane Goodman, born September 11, 1923; died August 30, 1979.

625. Linus Giles[22] Goodman (Nancy Jane[21] Eagle, Mary Ann[20] Wyatt, Noah Calvin[19], Thomas "Tommy"[18] Wiatt, Sr. (Wyatt, Wiett), John[17], Henry[16], Richard[15], George[14], Rev. Haute "Haut" "Hawte"[13], Sir George "Georgius" Thomas[12], Sir Thomas "The Younger"[11], Sir Thomas "The Elder"[10], Sir Henry[9], Richard Wiat or[8] Wyatt, Geoffrey "Jeoffrey" Wiot or[7] Wiat, Robert or Richard[6] Wiot, William Wiot or[5] Wyot, Adam Wiot or Wyote or[4], Guyott[3], Guyott[2], Captain or Admiral Adam Guyott or[1] Wiot) was born September 05, 1884, and died October 03, 1971. He married Carrie Lingle June 08, 1913, daughter of Littleton Lingle and Margaret Bost.

Children of Linus Goodman and Carrie Lingle are:

+	863	i.	Mildred Louise[23] Goodman, born September 26, 1916.
+	864	ii.	Linus Giles Goodman, Jr., born June 25, 1920.
+	865	iii.	Nancy Elizabeth Goodman, born September 08, 1932.

626. Amanda Louise[22] Goodman (Nancy Jane[21] Eagle, Mary Ann[20] Wyatt, Noah Calvin[19], Thomas "Tommy"[18] Wiatt, Sr. (Wyatt, Wiett), John[17], Henry[16], Richard[15], George[14], Rev. Haute "Haut" "Hawte"[13], Sir George "Georgius" Thomas[12], Sir Thomas "The Younger"[11], Sir Thomas "The Elder"[10], Sir Henry[9], Richard Wiat or[8] Wyatt, Geoffrey "Jeoffrey" Wiot or[7] Wiat, Robert or Richard[6] Wiot, William Wiot or[5] Wyot, Adam Wiot or Wyote or[4], Guyott[3], Guyott[2], Captain or Admiral Adam Guyott or[1] Wiot) was born September 12, 1886, and died September 29, 1905. She married John A. Arey October 30, 1904.

Child of Amanda Goodman and John Arey is:

| | 866 | i. | Louie Goodman[23] Arey. |

627. Paul Talmadge[22] Goodman (Nancy Jane[21] Eagle, Mary Ann[20] Wyatt, Noah Calvin[19], Thomas "Tommy"[18] Wiatt, Sr. (Wyatt, Wiett), John[17], Henry[16], Richard[15], George[14], Rev. Haute "Haut" "Hawte"[13], Sir George "Georgius" Thomas[12], Sir Thomas "The Younger"[11], Sir Thomas "The Elder"[10], Sir Henry[9], Richard Wiat or[8] Wyatt, Geoffrey "Jeoffrey" Wiot or[7] Wiat, Robert or Richard[6] Wiot, William Wiot or[5] Wyot, Adam Wiot or Wyote or[4], Guyott[3], Guyott[2], Captain or Admiral Adam Guyott or[1] Wiot) was born April 26, 1889, and died July 23, 1965. He married Emma Elizabeth Arey September 13, 1911, daughter of Gabriel Arey and Nancy Casper.

    Children of Paul Goodman and Emma Arey are:

+   867   i.   Gertrude Eliza[23] Goodman, born January 21, 1913.
+   868   ii.   Ruth Estelle Goodman, born October 29, 1914.
+   869   iii.   Emerson Clayton Goodman, born August 15, 1916; died February 20, 1978.
+   870   iv.   Paul Talmadge Goodman, Jr., born August 26, 1918.
+   871   v.   Geneva Lee Goodman, born September 23, 1920.
+   872   vi.   Mabel Arey Goodman, born January 04, 1922.
+   873   vii.   Dwight Wilburn Francis Goodman, born January 25, 1924.
+   874   viii.   Glenna Rachel Goodman, born February 19, 1927.
+   875   ix.   Harry Kale Goodman, born February 10, 1931.

629. Leland Quincy[22] Goodman (Nancy Jane[21] Eagle, Mary Ann[20] Wyatt, Noah Calvin[19], Thomas "Tommy"[18] Wiatt, Sr. (Wyatt, Wiett), John[17], Henry[16], Richard[15], George[14], Rev. Haute "Haut" "Hawte"[13], Sir George "Georgius" Thomas[12], Sir Thomas "The Younger"[11], Sir Thomas "The Elder"[10], Sir Henry[9], Richard Wiat or[8] Wyatt, Geoffrey "Jeoffrey" Wiot or[7] Wiat, Robert or Richard[6] Wiot, William Wiot or[5] Wyot, Adam Wiot or Wyote or[4], Guyott[3], Guyott[2], Captain or Admiral Adam Guyott or[1] Wiot) was born March 20, 1893, and died July 21, 1982. He married Nora Brown January 07, 1917, daughter of John Brown and Martha Bolton.

    Children of Leland Goodman and Nora Brown are:

+   876   i.   Spencer Brown[23] Goodman, born October 22, 1917 in Stanly County, N.C.; died August 26, 1974.
+   877   ii.   Carrie Mae Goodman, born January 12, 1922 in Stanly County, N.C.
+   878   iii.   Annie Katherine Goodman, born April 17, 1926 in Stanly County, N.C.
+   879   iv.   Clyde "Bud" Weir Goodman, born October 01, 1927 in Richfield, N.C.
+   880   v.   Melvine Eagle Goodman, born October 01, 1932 in Stanly County, N.C.
+   881   vi.   Alva Lee Goodman, born February 28, 1937 in Stanly County, N.C.

630. Nannie Jane[22] Goodman (Nancy Jane[21] Eagle, Mary Ann[20] Wyatt, Noah Calvin[19], Thomas "Tommy"[18] Wiatt, Sr. (Wyatt, Wiett), John[17], Henry[16], Richard[15], George[14], Rev. Haute "Haut" "Hawte"[13], Sir George "Georgius" Thomas[12], Sir Thomas "The Younger"[11], Sir Thomas "The Elder"[10], Sir Henry[9], Richard Wiat or[8] Wyatt, Geoffrey "Jeoffrey" Wiot or[7] Wiat, Robert or Richard[6] Wiot, William Wiot or[5] Wyot, Adam Wiot or Wyote or[4], Guyott[3], Guyott[2], Captain or Admiral Adam Guyott or[1] Wiot) was born December 26, 1894. She married Sidney Holmes Morgan April 09, 1916, son of John Morgan and Amanda Trexler.

Children of Nannie Goodman and Sidney Morgan are:

+ 882   i.   Stella Mae[23] Morgan, born January 19, 1917 in Stanly County, N.C.
+ 883   ii.   Rena Margaret Morgan, born April 03, 1918.
+ 884   iii.   Leo Goodman Morgan, born December 06, 1919.
+ 885   iv.   Kathleen Louise Morgan, born November 14, 1926.
+ 886   v.   Lois Helen Morgan, born August 11, 1929.
+ 887   vi.   Jane Virginia Morgan, born February 17, 1932 in Woodleaf, Rowan County, N.C.
+ 888   vii.   Joe Frank Morgan, born March 09, 1938.

631. Bennett Francis[22] Goodman (Nancy Jane[21] Eagle, Mary Ann[20] Wyatt, Noah Calvin[19], Thomas "Tommy"[18] Wiatt, Sr. (Wyatt, Wiett), John[17], Henry[16], Richard[15], George[14], Rev. Haute "Haut" "Hawte"[13], Sir George "Georgius" Thomas[12], Sir Thomas "The Younger"[11], Sir Thomas "The Elder"[10], Sir Henry[9], Richard Wiat or[8] Wyatt, Geoffrey "Jeoffrey" Wiot or[7] Wiat, Robert or Richard[6] Wiot, William Wiot or[5] Wyot, Adam Wiot or Wyote or[4], Guyott[3], Guyott[2], Captain or Admiral Adam Guyott or[1] Wiot) was born July 12, 1883 in Rowan County, N.C., and died December 09, 1964. He married Mary Luticia Morgan December 25, 1905, daughter of Wilson Morgan and Mary Trexler.

Children of Bennett Goodman and Mary Morgan are:

889   i.   Delmer Moses[23] Goodman, born October 26, 1907 in Rowan County N.C.; died November 25, 1995 in Rowan County N.C. He married Viola Polly Morgan.

        More About Delmer Moses Goodman:
        Liberty United Methodist Church Cemetery, Gold Hill, Rowan County, N.C.

        More About Viola Polly Morgan: Remains are buried at Liberty United Methodist Church Cemetery, Gold Hill, Rowan County, N.C.

+ 890   ii.   Enos Roy Goodman, born June 26, 1912 in Rowan County N.C.; died November 09, 2005 in Rowan County N.C.

891   iii.   Leo Francis Goodman, born 1919.

	892	iv.	Eunice Roxana Goodman.
	893	v.	Enos Roy Goodman.
	894	vi.	Myra Eleanor Goodman.
	895	vii.	George Otha Goodman, born October 10, 1906; died February 20, 1954. He married Callie Morgan.
+	896	viii.	Delmar Moses Goodman, born October 26, 1907.
+	897	ix.	Leo Francis Goodman, born August 09, 1919.

632. Josephine Erma[22] Shaver (Mary Malinda[21] Eagle, Mary Ann[20] Wyatt, Noah Calvin[19], Thomas "Tommy"[18] Wiatt, Sr. (Wyatt, Wiett), John[17], Henry[16], Richard[15], George[14], Rev. Haute "Haut" "Hawte"[13], Sir George "Georgius" Thomas[12], Sir Thomas "The Younger"[11], Sir Thomas "The Elder"[10], Sir Henry[9], Richard Wiat or[8] Wyatt, Geoffrey "Jeoffrey" Wiot or[7] Wiat, Robert or Richard[6] Wiot, William Wiot or[5] Wyot, Adam Wiot or Wyote or[4], Guyott[3], Guyott[2], Captain or Admiral Adam Guyott or[1] Wiot) was born August 12, 1890. She married Solomon Clarence Morgan November 10, 1912.

More About Josephine Erma Shaver:
Remains are buried at Liberty Methodist Church Cemetery, Rowan County, N.C.

Children of Josephine Shaver and Solomon Morgan are:

+	898	i.	Onnie Leven[23] Morgan, born November 24, 1913.
+	899	ii.	Stella Marie Morgan, born March 20, 1914.
+	900	iii.	Lena Irene Morgan, born August 21, 1918.
	901	iv.	Hubert Grady Morgan.
	902	v.	Wilma Helen Morgan.
	903	vi.	Robert Oscar Morgan.
	904	vii.	Clifford Ralph Morgan.
	905	viii.	Flossie Gertrude Morgan.

637. Curtis Bewey[22] Shaver (Mary Malinda[21] Eagle, Mary Ann[20] Wyatt, Noah Calvin[19], Thomas "Tommy"[18] Wiatt, Sr. (Wyatt, Wiett), John[17], Henry[16], Richard[15], George[14], Rev. Haute "Haut" "Hawte"[13], Sir George "Georgius" Thomas[12], Sir Thomas "The Younger"[11], Sir Thomas "The Elder"[10], Sir Henry[9], Richard Wiat or[8] Wyatt, Geoffrey "Jeoffrey" Wiot or[7] Wiat, Robert or Richard[6] Wiot, William Wiot or[5] Wyot, Adam Wiot or Wyote or[4], Guyott[3], Guyott[2], Captain or Admiral Adam Guyott or[1] Wiot). He married Minnie Burrage.

Child of Curtis Shaver and Minnie Burrage is:

	906	i.	Bewey Melvin[23] Shaver, born February 16, 1928; died 2013 in Lee County, N.C. He married Vivian Harrington.

638. William Grant[22] Eagle, Jr. (William Grant[21], Mary Ann[20] Wyatt, Noah Calvin[19], Thomas "Tommy"[18] Wiatt, Sr. (Wyatt, Wiett), John[17], Henry[16], Richard[15], George[14], Rev. Haute "Haut" "Hawte"[13], Sir George "Georgius" Thomas[12], Sir Thomas "The Younger"[11], Sir Thomas "The Elder"[10], Sir Henry[9], Richard Wiat or[8] Wyatt, Geoffrey "Jeoffrey" Wiot or[7] Wiat, Robert or

Richard[6] Wiot, William Wiot or[5] Wyot, Adam Wiot or Wyote or[4], Guyott[3], Guyott[2], Captain or Admiral Adam Guyott or[1] Wiot) was born 1894 in Rowan County, N.C., and died 1918. He married Martha Caroline Trexler.

> Child of William Eagle and Martha Trexler is:
> 907   i.   Grant Napolian[23] Eagle.

639. Beulah Ann[22] Eagle (William Grant[21], Mary Ann[20] Wyatt, Noah Calvin[19], Thomas "Tommy"[18] Wiatt, Sr. (Wyatt, Wiett), John[17], Henry[16], Richard[15], George[14], Rev. Haute "Haut" "Hawte"[13], Sir George "Georgius" Thomas[12], Sir Thomas "The Younger"[11], Sir Thomas "The Elder"[10], Sir Henry[9], Richard Wiat or[8] Wyatt, Geoffrey "Jeoffrey" Wiot or[7] Wiat, Robert or Richard[6] Wiot, William Wiot or[5] Wyot, Adam Wiot or Wyote or[4], Guyott[3], Guyott[2], Captain or Admiral Adam Guyott or[1] Wiot) was born 1895 in Rowan County, N.C., and died 1947. She married Glenn Van Trexler, Sr., son of George Trexler and Louisa Brady.

> More About Beulah Ann Eagle:
> Remains are buried in the Saint Matthew's Lutheran Church Cemetery, Salisbury, Rowan County, N.C. Plot #397.

> More About Glenn Van Trexler, Sr.:
> Remains are buried in the Saint Matthew's Lutheran Church Cemetery, Salisbury, Rowan County, N.C. Plot #397.

> Children of Beulah Eagle and Glenn Van Trexler are:
> 908   i.   Odelia[23] Trexler.
> 909   ii.   Glenn Van Trexler, Jr. He married Hazel Boggs March 20, 1947.

> > More About Glenn Van Trexler, Jr.:
> > Remains are buried in the Saint Matthew's Lutheran Church Cemetery, Salisbury, Rowan County, N.C. Plot #397.

> 910   iii.   Thomas S. Trexler.
> 911   iv.   Lucille Trexler.
> 912   v.   Paul Hubert Trexler.
> + 913   vi.   Mary Elizabeth Trexler, born January 01, 1925.
> + 914   vii.   George William Trexler, born March 13, 1927; died July 24, 1949.

640. Addie Louise[22] Eagle (William Grant[21], Mary Ann[20] Wyatt, Noah Calvin[19], Thomas "Tommy"[18] Wiatt, Sr. (Wyatt, Wiett), John[17], Henry[16], Richard[15], George[14], Rev. Haute "Haut" "Hawte"[13], Sir George "Georgius" Thomas[12], Sir Thomas "The Younger"[11], Sir Thomas "The Elder"[10], Sir Henry[9], Richard Wiat or[8] Wyatt, Geoffrey "Jeoffrey" Wiot or[7] Wiat, Robert or

Richard[6] Wiot, William Wiot or[5] Wyot, Adam Wiot or Wyote or[4], Guyott[3], Guyott[2], Captain or Admiral Adam Guyott or[1] Wiot) was born 1897 in Rowan County, N.C., and died 1977. She married Elbert Welker Kluttz.

Children of Addie Eagle and Elbert Kluttz are:
915   i.   Paul Lee[23] Kluttz.
916   ii.   Ray Banks Kluttz.

641. Esther Ethel[22] Eagle (William Grant[21], Mary Ann[20] Wyatt, Noah Calvin[19], Thomas "Tommy"[18] Wiatt, Sr. (Wyatt, Wiett), John[17], Henry[16], Richard[15], George[14], Rev. Haute "Haut" "Hawte"[13], Sir George "Georgius" Thomas[12], Sir Thomas "The Younger"[11], Sir Thomas "The Elder"[10], Sir Henry[9], Richard Wiat or[8] Wyatt, Geoffrey "Jeoffrey" Wiot or[7] Wiat, Robert or Richard[6] Wiot, William Wiot or[5] Wyot, Adam Wiot or Wyote or[4], Guyott[3], Guyott[2], Captain or Admiral Adam Guyott or[1] Wiot) was born 1898 in Rowan County, N.C. She married Lomie Raymond Eller.

Children of Esther Eagle and Lomie Eller are:
917   i.   Lawrence Raymond[23] Eller.
918   ii.   Wade Rudolph Eller, born 1921; died 1944.

642. Octa Mae[22] Eagle (William Grant[21], Mary Ann[20] Wyatt, Noah Calvin[19], Thomas "Tommy"[18] Wiatt, Sr. (Wyatt, Wiett), John[17], Henry[16], Richard[15], George[14], Rev. Haute "Haut" "Hawte"[13], Sir George "Georgius" Thomas[12], Sir Thomas "The Younger"[11], Sir Thomas "The Elder"[10], Sir Henry[9], Richard Wiat or[8] Wyatt, Geoffrey "Jeoffrey" Wiot or[7] Wiat, Robert or Richard[6] Wiot, William Wiot or[5] Wyot, Adam Wiot or Wyote or[4], Guyott[3], Guyott[2], Captain or Admiral Adam Guyott or[1] Wiot) was born July 26, 1903 in Rowan County, N.C., and died 1995. She married Charles Sylvester McHargue December 18, 1920, son of Charles McHargue and Nellie Loflin.

More About Octa Mae Eagle:
Buried at Rowan Memorial Park, Rowan County, N.C.

More About Charles Sylvester McHargue:
Buried at Fairview Cemetery, Stanly County, N.C.

Children of Octa Eagle and Charles McHargue are:
919   i.   Mae Levene[23] McHargue.
+ 920   ii.   Janet Inez McHargue, born March 06, 1922 in Rowan County, N.C.
+ 921   iii.   Marjorie Ellen McHargue, born July 23, 1923 in Rowan County, N.C; died September 26, 1962 in Greensboro, N.C.
     922   iv.   Evelyn Genair McHargue, born June 19, 1925; died October 23, 1929 in Rowan County, N.C.

+ 923   v.   Charles William McHargue, born December 01, 1926 in Rowan County, N.C.

+ 924   vi.   Lucius Baxter McHargue, born May 11, 1928 in Rowan County, N.C; died June 06, 1990.

925   vii.   Mary Kate McHargue, born January 05, 1930; died June 11, 1930 in Stanly County, N.C.

+ 926   viii.   Floyd Richard McHargue, born December 07, 1933 in Stanly County, N.C.

644. Norvie Lundy[22] Eagle (William Grant[21], Mary Ann[20] Wyatt, Noah Calvin[19], Thomas "Tommy"[18] Wiatt, Sr. (Wyatt, Wiett), John[17], Henry[16], Richard[15], George[14], Rev. Haute "Haut" "Hawte"[13], Sir George "Georgius" Thomas[12], Sir Thomas "The Younger"[11], Sir Thomas "The Elder"[10], Sir Henry[9], Richard Wiat or[8] Wyatt, Geoffrey "Jeoffrey" Wiot or[7] Wiat, Robert or Richard[6] Wiot, William Wiot or[5] Wyot, Adam Wiot or Wyote or[4], Guyott[3], Guyott[2], Captain or Admiral Adam Guyott or[1] Wiot) was born March 02, 1907 in Rowan County, N.C. She married Marshall Theodore Myers April 24, 1926, son of Daniel Myers and Dora Meismore.

More About Norvie Lundy Eagle:
Buried at Liberty Methodist Church Cemtery, Rowan County, N.C.

More About Marshall Theodore Myers:
Buried at Liberty Methodist Church Cemtery, Rowan County, N.C.

Children of Norvie Eagle and Marshall Myers are:

+ 927   i.   Margaret Lee[23] Myers, born December 25, 1926 in Rowan County, N.C.

+ 928   ii.   Harold William Myers, born August 12, 1928 in Greenville County, S.C.

645. Paul Thomas[22] Eagle (William Grant[21], Mary Ann[20] Wyatt, Noah Calvin[19], Thomas "Tommy"[18] Wiatt, Sr. (Wyatt, Wiett), John[17], Henry[16], Richard[15], George[14], Rev. Haute "Haut" "Hawte"[13], Sir George "Georgius" Thomas[12], Sir Thomas "The Younger"[11], Sir Thomas "The Elder"[10], Sir Henry[9], Richard Wiat or[8] Wyatt, Geoffrey "Jeoffrey" Wiot or[7] Wiat, Robert or Richard[6] Wiot, William Wiot or[5] Wyot, Adam Wiot or Wyote or[4], Guyott[3], Guyott[2], Captain or Admiral Adam Guyott or[1] Wiot) was born March 13, 1908 in of Misenheimer, Rowan County, N.C. He married Ruth Lucille Reynolds December 01, 1929, daughter of Riley Reynolds and Agnes Peeler.

Child of Paul Eagle and Ruth Reynolds is:

+ 929   i.   Peggy Pauline[23] Eagle, born September 17, 1938 in Stanly County, N.C.

646. Mary (Phene) Josephine[22] Eagle (William Grant[21], Mary Ann[20] Wyatt, Noah Calvin[19], Thomas "Tommy"[18] Wiatt, Sr. (Wyatt, Wiett), John[17], Henry[16], Richard[15], George[14], Rev.

Haute "Haut" "Hawte"[13], Sir George "Georgius" Thomas[12], Sir Thomas "The Younger"[11], Sir Thomas "The Elder"[10], Sir Henry[9], Richard Wiat or[8] Wyatt, Geoffrey "Jeoffrey" Wiot or[7] Wiat, Robert or Richard[6] Wiot, William Wiot or[5] Wyot, Adam Wiot or Wyote or[4], Guyott[3], Guyott[2], Captain or Admiral Adam Guyott or[1] Wiot) was born February 10, 1910 in Rowan County, N.C., and died March 13, 1994. She married Arkles Gray Grubb May 26, 1930, son of John Grubb and Cora Doby.

Children of Mary Eagle and Arkles Grubb are:

+ 930   i.   Jimmy Farrell[23] Grubb, born February 17, 1931 in Rowan County, N.C.
+ 931   ii.   Larry Douglas Grubb, born July 07, 1936 in Rowan County, N.C.
+ 932   iii.   Don Wayne Grubb, born October 16, 1944 in Rowan County, N.C.

647. Kate Eursel "Ercle"[22] Eagle (William Grant[21], Mary Ann[20] Wyatt, Noah Calvin[19], Thomas "Tommy"[18] Wiatt, Sr. (Wyatt, Wiett), John[17], Henry[16], Richard[15], George[14], Rev. Haute "Haut" "Hawte"[13], Sir George "Georgius" Thomas[12], Sir Thomas "The Younger"[11], Sir Thomas "The Elder"[10], Sir Henry[9], Richard Wiat or[8] Wyatt, Geoffrey "Jeoffrey" Wiot or[7] Wiat, Robert or Richard[6] Wiot, William Wiot or[5] Wyot, Adam Wiot or Wyote or[4], Guyott[3], Guyott[2], Captain or Admiral Adam Guyott or[1] Wiot) was born November 09, 1912 in Morgan Township, Rowan County, N.C. She married Paul Buren Smith June 04, 1933, son of Charles Smith and Jessie Ryan.

More About Paul Buren Smith:
Buried at Rowan Memorial Park, Rowan County, N.C.

Children of Kate Eagle and Paul Smith are:

+ 933   i.   Edward Lee[23] Smith, born February 06, 1934.
+ 934   ii.   Patsy Eagle Smith, born November 11, 1943.

648. Doy Hollis[22] Eagle (William Grant[21], Mary Ann[20] Wyatt, Noah Calvin[19], Thomas "Tommy"[18] Wiatt, Sr. (Wyatt, Wiett), John[17], Henry[16], Richard[15], George[14], Rev. Haute "Haut" "Hawte"[13], Sir George "Georgius" Thomas[12], Sir Thomas "The Younger"[11], Sir Thomas "The Elder"[10], Sir Henry[9], Richard Wiat or[8] Wyatt, Geoffrey "Jeoffrey" Wiot or[7] Wiat, Robert or Richard[6] Wiot, William Wiot or[5] Wyot, Adam Wiot or Wyote or[4], Guyott[3], Guyott[2], Captain or Admiral Adam Guyott or[1] Wiot) was born January 10, 1915 in of Gold Hill, Rowan County, N.C., and died 2007 in Rowan County, N.C. He married (1) Daisey League or Daisy Clarine Teague?. He married (2) Gladys Troutman April 09, 1961, daughter of Clyde Troutman and Addie Wagner.

More About Doy Hollis Eagle:
Fact 1: August 2007, attends the Eagle reunion in Liberty, Salisbury, N.C.
Remains buried at Liberty United Methodist Church Cemetery, Gold Hill, N.C.

Children of Doy Eagle and Daisey Teague? are:

+ 935   i.   Linda Clarine[23] Eagle, born April 22, 1942.

+ 936   ii.   Janice Eagle, born February 02, 1947.

Children of Doy Eagle and Gladys Troutman are:

+ 937   i.   Heidi Virginia[23] Eagle, born January 20, 1962 in Rowan County or Cabarrus County, N.C.

938   ii.   Hollis William Eagle, born March 11, 1962 in Rowan County, N.C.

939   iii.   Lisa Laura Eagle, born August 21, 1967 in Rowan County, N.C.

940   iv.   David Clyde Eagle, born March 08, 1971 in Rowan County, N.C.

941   v.   Clara Addie Eagle, born July 19, 1974 in Rowan County, N.C.

649. Jessie Bernice[22] Eagle (William Grant[21], Mary Ann[20] Wyatt, Noah Calvin[19], Thomas "Tommy"[18] Wiatt, Sr. (Wyatt, Wiett), John[17], Henry[16], Richard[15], George[14], Rev. Haute "Haut" "Hawte"[13], Sir George "Georgius" Thomas[12], Sir Thomas "The Younger"[11], Sir Thomas "The Elder"[10], Sir Henry[9], Richard Wiat or[8] Wyatt, Geoffrey "Jeoffrey" Wiot or[7] Wiat, Robert or Richard[6] Wiot, William Wiot or[5] Wyot, Adam Wiot or Wyote or[4], Guyott[3], Guyott[2], Captain or Admiral Adam Guyott or[1] Wiot) was born September 10, 1916 in Rowan County, N.C. She married (1) Raymond Franklin Misenheimer December 22, 1940, son of Napolean Misenheimer and Ollie Cruse. She married (2) Macauley C. Byrum May 21, 1994.

Children of Jessie Eagle and Raymond Misenheimer are:

+ 942   i.   Laura Ann[23] Misenheimer, born June 03, 1951.

+ 943   ii.   Franklin Eugene Misenheimer, born April 26, 1948.

651. Emma Dora[22] Eagle (William Grant[21], Mary Ann[20] Wyatt, Noah Calvin[19], Thomas "Tommy"[18] Wiatt, Sr. (Wyatt, Wiett), John[17], Henry[16], Richard[15], George[14], Rev. Haute "Haut" "Hawte"[13], Sir George "Georgius" Thomas[12], Sir Thomas "The Younger"[11], Sir Thomas "The Elder"[10], Sir Henry[9], Richard Wiat or[8] Wyatt, Geoffrey "Jeoffrey" Wiot or[7] Wiat, Robert or Richard[6] Wiot, William Wiot or[5] Wyot, Adam Wiot or Wyote or[4], Guyott[3], Guyott[2], Captain or Admiral Adam Guyott or[1] Wiot) was born June 26, 1901 in Morgan Township, Rowan County, N.C., and died September 21, 1993. She married Joseph Calvin Arey, Sr. December 03, 1921 in Rowan County N.C., son of James Arey and Amanda Miller.

More About Joseph Calvin Arey, Sr.:
Buried at Liberty United Methodist Church Cemetery, Gold Hill, Rowan County, N.C.

Children of Emma Eagle and Joseph Arey are:

944   i.   Lorraine Eagle[23] Arey. She married Boger.

945   ii.   Robert Stanton Arey.

946   iii.   Joseph Calvin Arey, Jr., born 1922-2011.

947   iv.   Melvin Lee Arey, born 1929-1987.

652. McCoy Lee[22] Cranford (Josephine[21] Eagle, Mary Ann[20] Wyatt, Noah Calvin[19], Thomas "Tommy"[18] Wiatt, Sr. (Wyatt, Wiett), John[17], Henry[16], Richard[15], George[14], Rev. Haute "Haut" "Hawte"[13], Sir George "Georgius" Thomas[12], Sir Thomas "The Younger"[11], Sir Thomas "The Elder"[10], Sir Henry[9], Richard Wiat or[8] Wyatt, Geoffrey "Jeoffrey" Wiot or[7] Wiat, Robert or Richard[6] Wiot, William Wiot or[5] Wyot, Adam Wiot or Wyote or[4], Guyott[3], Guyott[2], Captain or Admiral Adam Guyott or[1] Wiot) was born September 30, 1899 in Rowan County, N.C, and died June 18, 1984. He married Lettie L. Agner December 19, 1920, daughter of David Agner and Mary Wyatt.

More About McCoy Lee Cranford:
Buried at Providence Methodist Church Cemetery, Rowan County, N.C.

More About Lettie L. Agner:
Buried at Providence Methodist Church Cemetery, Rowan County, N.C.

Children of McCoy Cranford and Lettie Agner are:

	948	i.	Cathern Earline[23] Cranford, born in Rowan County, N.C.
	949	ii.	Jimmie David Cranford, born in Rowan County, N.C.
	950	iii.	Mary Lou Cranford, born in Rowan County, N.C.
+	951	iv.	Marie Cranford, born January 03, 1922.
	952	v.	Madoline May Cranford, born January 26, 1924 in Rowan County, N.C; died June 09, 1924.

More About Madoline May Cranford:
Buried at Provience Methodist Church Cemetery, Rowan County, N.C.

659. MacDonald[22] Wyatt (William Mock[21], Eli[20], Noah Calvin[19], Thomas "Tommy"[18] Wiatt, Sr. (Wyatt, Wiett), John[17], Henry[16], Richard[15], George[14], Rev. Haute "Haut" "Hawte"[13], Sir George "Georgius" Thomas[12], Sir Thomas "The Younger"[11], Sir Thomas "The Elder"[10], Sir Henry[9], Richard Wiat or[8] Wyatt, Geoffrey "Jeoffrey" Wiot or[7] Wiat, Robert or Richard[6] Wiot, William Wiot or[5] Wyot, Adam Wiot or Wyote or[4], Guyott[3], Guyott[2], Captain or Admiral Adam Guyott or[1] Wiot). He married X.

Child of MacDonald Wyatt and X is:
953   i.   Amy[23] Wyatt.

661. J. Columbus[22] Parker (Ollie Lou Ada[21] Shaver, Rhoda E.[20] Wyatt, Noah Calvin[19], Thomas "Tommy"[18] Wiatt, Sr. (Wyatt, Wiett), John[17], Henry[16], Richard[15], George[14], Rev. Haute "Haut" "Hawte"[13], Sir George "Georgius" Thomas[12], Sir Thomas "The Younger"[11], Sir Thomas "The Elder"[10], Sir Henry[9], Richard Wiat or[8] Wyatt, Geoffrey "Jeoffrey" Wiot or[7] Wiat, Robert or Richard[6] Wiot, William Wiot or[5] Wyot, Adam Wiot or Wyote or[4], Guyott[3], Guyott[2], Captain or Admiral Adam Guyott or[1] Wiot) was born March 17, 1849, and died June 18, 1926. He married Catherine L. Miller.

Child of J. Parker and Catherine Miller is:

+   954   i.   Harvey Adophus[23] Parker, born July 04, 1881; died April 12, 1961.

664. Bertha Lillie Ann[22] Parker (Ollie Lou Ada[21] Shaver, Rhoda E.[20] Wyatt, Noah Calvin[19], Thomas "Tommy"[18] Wiatt, Sr. (Wyatt, Wiett), John[17], Henry[16], Richard[15], George[14], Rev. Haute "Haut" "Hawte"[13], Sir George "Georgius" Thomas[12], Sir Thomas "The Younger"[11], Sir Thomas "The Elder"[10], Sir Henry[9], Richard Wiat or[8] Wyatt, Geoffrey "Jeoffrey" Wiot or[7] Wiat, Robert or Richard[6] Wiot, William Wiot or[5] Wyot, Adam Wiot or Wyote or[4], Guyott[3], Guyott[2], Captain or Admiral Adam Guyott or[1] Wiot) was born 1894-1981. She married Kesler.

Child of Bertha Parker and Kesler is:

955   i.   Bobby[23] Kesler, born Abt. 1933.

671. Jacob Frank[22] Shaver (Emanuel Calvin[21], Rhoda E.[20] Wyatt, Noah Calvin[19], Thomas "Tommy"[18] Wiatt, Sr. (Wyatt, Wiett), John[17], Henry[16], Richard[15], George[14], Rev. Haute "Haut" "Hawte"[13], Sir George "Georgius" Thomas[12], Sir Thomas "The Younger"[11], Sir Thomas "The Elder"[10], Sir Henry[9], Richard Wiat or[8] Wyatt, Geoffrey "Jeoffrey" Wiot or[7] Wiat, Robert or Richard[6] Wiot, William Wiot or[5] Wyot, Adam Wiot or Wyote or[4], Guyott[3], Guyott[2], Captain or Admiral Adam Guyott or[1] Wiot) was born 1900. He married Unknown Wife.

Child of Jacob Shaver and Unknown Wife is:

956   i.   Frank B.[23] Shaver.

More About Frank B. Shaver:
Fact 1: Principal of Knox Junior School, Salisbury, N.C.

678. Calvin DeBerry[22] Eagle (William Lawson[21], Amanda Jane[20] Wyatt, Noah Calvin[19], Thomas "Tommy"[18] Wiatt, Sr. (Wyatt, Wiett), John[17], Henry[16], Richard[15], George[14], Rev. Haute "Haut" "Hawte"[13], Sir George "Georgius" Thomas[12], Sir Thomas "The Younger"[11], Sir Thomas "The Elder"[10], Sir Henry[9], Richard Wiat or[8] Wyatt, Geoffrey "Jeoffrey" Wiot or[7] Wiat, Robert or Richard[6] Wiot, William Wiot or[5] Wyot, Adam Wiot or Wyote or[4], Guyott[3], Guyott[2], Captain or Admiral Adam Guyott or[1] Wiot) was born March 09, 1898 in Rowan County N.C., and died June 18, 1973 in Salisbury, Rowan County, N.C. He married Martha Carolina "Callie" Trexler, daughter of Napolean Trexler and Mary Eller.

More About Calvin DeBerry Eagle:
Fact 1: October 09, 1898, another date of birth given.
Fact 2: June 17, 1973, another date of demise given.
Buried at Rowan Memorial Park Cemetery, Salisbury, N.C.

More About Martha Carolina "Callie" Trexler:
Buried in Rowan Memorial Park, Salisbury, N.C.

Children of Calvin Eagle and Martha Trexler are:

+ 957   i.   Murray or Murry Lee "Red"[23] Eagle, born February 14, 1921 in Rowan County N.C.; died March 23, 1992 in Rowan County N.C.

+ 958   ii.   Frances Virginia Eagle, born January 03, 1923.

+ 959   iii.   Betty Lorene Eagle, born August 10, 1927.

+ 960   iv.   Alice Maretta Eagle, born October 30, 1930.

+ 961   v.   Donald Ray Eagle, born June 19, 1934.

+ 962   vi.   Nancy Jean Eagle, born June 15, 1936.

679. Anna "Anner" Lillian Pauline[22] Eagle (William Lawson[21], Amanda Jane[20] Wyatt, Noah Calvin[19], Thomas "Tommy"[18] Wiatt, Sr. (Wyatt, Wiett), John[17], Henry[16], Richard[15], George[14], Rev. Haute "Haut" "Hawte"[13], Sir George "Georgius" Thomas[12], Sir Thomas "The Younger"[11], Sir Thomas "The Elder"[10], Sir Henry[9], Richard Wiat or[8] Wyatt, Geoffrey "Jeoffrey" Wiot or[7] Wiat, Robert or Richard[6] Wiot, William Wiot or[5] Wyot, Adam Wiot or Wyote or[4], Guyott[3], Guyott[2], Captain or Admiral Adam Guyott or[1] Wiot) was born June 21, 1911 in Rowan County N.C., and died August 14, 1993 in Salisbury, Rowan County, N.C. She married James Ross Arey December 16, 1933 in Rowan County N.C., son of James Arey and Mary Honeycutt.

More About Anna "Anner" Lillian Pauline Eagle:
Buried at Luther's Lutheran Church Cemetery, Richfield, N.C.; Row #15.

Children of Anna Eagle and James Arey are:

+ 963   i.   Sherley "Shirley" Ann[23] Arey, born November 09, 1935.

+ 964   ii.   Roberta Gayle Arey, born March 24, 1943.

680. Virgie Lou Vera[22] Eagle (William Lawson[21], Amanda Jane[20] Wyatt, Noah Calvin[19], Thomas "Tommy"[18] Wiatt, Sr. (Wyatt, Wiett), John[17], Henry[16], Richard[15], George[14], Rev. Haute "Haut" "Hawte"[13], Sir George "Georgius" Thomas[12], Sir Thomas "The Younger"[11], Sir Thomas "The Elder"[10], Sir Henry[9], Richard Wiat or[8] Wyatt, Geoffrey "Jeoffrey" Wiot or[7] Wiat, Robert or Richard[6] Wiot, William Wiot or[5] Wyot, Adam Wiot or Wyote or[4], Guyott[3], Guyott[2], Captain or Admiral Adam Guyott or[1] Wiot) was born September 25, 1900, and died 1980. She married Guy Earl Wise December 1920, son of Wiley Wise and Anner Smith.

Child of Virgie Eagle and Guy Wise is:

+ 965   i.   Raymond Monroe[23] Wise, born October 25, 1925.

681. Sarah Jane[22] Eagle (William Lawson[21], Amanda Jane[20] Wyatt, Noah Calvin[19], Thomas "Tommy"[18] Wiatt, Sr. (Wyatt, Wiett), John[17], Henry[16], Richard[15], George[14], Rev. Haute "Haut" "Hawte"[13], Sir George "Georgius" Thomas[12], Sir Thomas "The Younger"[11], Sir Thomas "The Elder"[10], Sir Henry[9], Richard Wiat or[8] Wyatt, Geoffrey "Jeoffrey" Wiot or[7] Wiat, Robert or Richard[6] Wiot, William Wiot or[5] Wyot, Adam Wiot or Wyote or[4], Guyott[3], Guyott[2], Captain

or Admiral Adam Guyott or[1] Wiot) was born July 11, 1904. She married David Thomas Frye November 23, 1923, son of Jesse Frye and Eva Parker.

Child of Sarah Eagle and David Frye is:
+   966   i.   Clara Sue[23] Frye, born August 08, 1930.

682. Esther Mae[22] Eagle (William Lawson[21], Amanda Jane[20] Wyatt, Noah Calvin[19], Thomas "Tommy"[18] Wiatt, Sr. (Wyatt, Wiett), John[17], Henry[16], Richard[15], George[14], Rev. Haute "Haut" "Hawte"[13], Sir George "Georgius" Thomas[12], Sir Thomas "The Younger"[11], Sir Thomas "The Elder"[10], Sir Henry[9], Richard Wiat or[8] Wyatt, Geoffrey "Jeoffrey" Wiot or[7] Wiat, Robert or Richard[6] Wiot, William Wiot or[5] Wyot, Adam Wiot or Wyote or[4], Guyott[3], Guyott[2], Captain or Admiral Adam Guyott or[1] Wiot) was born November 20, 1906. She married Arthur Glenn Stoker March 23, 1930, son of John Stoker and Lavine.

More About Arthur Glenn Stoker:
Fact 1: Served in U.S. Navy.
Remains are buried at Luther's Lutheran Church Cemetery, Richfield, N.C.

Children of Esther Eagle and Arthur Stoker are:
967   i.   Dorthy Lavine "Louise"[23] Stoker, born December 02, 1929 in Rowan County N.C. She married Elwood Carter June 30, 1956.
+   968   ii.   Hazeline Marell Stoker, born July 21, 1931 in Rowan County N.C.
+   969   iii.   Glenn Edward Stoker, born March 13, 1948 in Rowan County N.C.

683. Bertha Louise[22] Eagle (Adolphus Grant[21], Amanda Jane[20] Wyatt, Noah Calvin[19], Thomas "Tommy"[18] Wiatt, Sr. (Wyatt, Wiett), John[17], Henry[16], Richard[15], George[14], Rev. Haute "Haut" "Hawte"[13], Sir George "Georgius" Thomas[12], Sir Thomas "The Younger"[11], Sir Thomas "The Elder"[10], Sir Henry[9], Richard Wiat or[8] Wyatt, Geoffrey "Jeoffrey" Wiot or[7] Wiat, Robert or Richard[6] Wiot, William Wiot or[5] Wyot, Adam Wiot or Wyote or[4], Guyott[3], Guyott[2], Captain or Admiral Adam Guyott or[1] Wiot) was born February 1900 in North Carolina, and died December 24, 1932. She married Jasper A. Hoover, son of James Hoover and Rena Sheffield.

More About Bertha Louise Eagle:
Fact 1: 1910, Census spells her name: "Birtha."
Fact 2: January 31, 1899, Birthdate, according to Rachel Hill published research.
Remains are buried in the Tabernacle M.E. Cemetery, Trinity, N.C.

Children of Bertha Eagle and Jasper Hoover are:
+   970   i.   Margaret Pauline[23] Hoover, born June 26, 1921 in Stanly County, N.C.

+	971	ii.	Ernst Edwin Hoover, born October 16, 1923.
+	972	iii.	Gladys Mae Hoover, born January 15, 1926.

684. Beulah Jane[22] Eagle (Adolphus Grant[21], Amanda Jane[20] Wyatt, Noah Calvin[19], Thomas "Tommy"[18] Wiatt, Sr. (Wyatt, Wiett), John[17], Henry[16], Richard[15], George[14], Rev. Haute "Haut" "Hawte"[13], Sir George "Georgius" Thomas[12], Sir Thomas "The Younger"[11], Sir Thomas "The Elder"[10], Sir Henry[9], Richard Wiat or[8] Wyatt, Geoffrey "Jeoffrey" Wiot or[7] Wiat, Robert or Richard[6] Wiot, William Wiot or[5] Wyot, Adam Wiot or Wyote or[4], Guyott[3], Guyott[2], Captain or Admiral Adam Guyott or[1] Wiot) was born March 06, 1900 in Morgan Township, Rowan County, N.C. She married Jonah Bascom Swanner, son of Joseph Swanner and Nancy Peiffer.

> More About Beulah Jane Eagle:
> Remains are buried at Westlawn Mausoleum [Memorial Park], China Grove, Rowan County, N.C.

> Child of Beulah Eagle and Jonah Swanner is:

+	973	i.	Leslie Francis[23] Swanner, born January 30, 1934.

687. Jennie Elizabeth[22] Eagle (Adolphus Grant[21], Amanda Jane[20] Wyatt, Noah Calvin[19], Thomas "Tommy"[18] Wiatt, Sr. (Wyatt, Wiett), John[17], Henry[16], Richard[15], George[14], Rev. Haute "Haut" "Hawte"[13], Sir George "Georgius" Thomas[12], Sir Thomas "The Younger"[11], Sir Thomas "The Elder"[10], Sir Henry[9], Richard Wiat or[8] Wyatt, Geoffrey "Jeoffrey" Wiot or[7] Wiat, Robert or Richard[6] Wiot, William Wiot or[5] Wyot, Adam Wiot or Wyote or[4], Guyott[3], Guyott[2], Captain or Admiral Adam Guyott or[1] Wiot) was born September 01, 1906 in Rowan County, N.C. She married Grady Henry Turner June 13, 1925, son of Joseph Turner and Lottie Wheless.

> Children of Jennie Eagle and Grady Turner are:

+	974	i.	Mae Elizabeth[23] Turner, born July 19, 1926.
	975	ii.	Clara Jean Turner, born July 16, 1928 in Rowan County N.C. She married Clarence Troy Mayhew, Jr.
+	976	iii.	Lois Evelyn Turner, born October 06, 1931.
	977	iv.	Elbert Grady Turner, born July 28, 1933.

689. Viola Martha[22] Eagle (Adolphus Grant[21], Amanda Jane[20] Wyatt, Noah Calvin[19], Thomas "Tommy"[18] Wiatt, Sr. (Wyatt, Wiett), John[17], Henry[16], Richard[15], George[14], Rev. Haute "Haut" "Hawte"[13], Sir George "Georgius" Thomas[12], Sir Thomas "The Younger"[11], Sir Thomas "The Elder"[10], Sir Henry[9], Richard Wiat or[8] Wyatt, Geoffrey "Jeoffrey" Wiot or[7] Wiat, Robert or Richard[6] Wiot, William Wiot or[5] Wyot, Adam Wiot or Wyote or[4], Guyott[3], Guyott[2], Captain or Admiral Adam Guyott or[1] Wiot) was born November 10, 1910 in North Carolina. She married Jennings D. Ramseur September 05, 1936, son of George Ramseur and Callie Lenora.

Children of Viola Eagle and Jennings Ramseur are:

+ 978   i.   Nancy Lenora[23] Ramseur, born July 30, 1940 in Cabarrus County, N.C.

   979   ii.   Jennings Dodson Ramseur, Jr., born October 09, 1942 in Cabarrus County, N.C. He married Hilda Mae McIntosh June 21, 1975.

690. Bessie Carolina "Caroline"[22] Eagle (Adolphus Grant[21], Amanda Jane[20] Wyatt, Noah Calvin[19], Thomas "Tommy"[18] Wiatt, Sr. (Wyatt, Wiett), John[17], Henry[16], Richard[15], George[14], Rev. Haute "Haut" "Hawte"[13], Sir George "Georgius" Thomas[12], Sir Thomas "The Younger"[11], Sir Thomas "The Elder"[10], Sir Henry[9], Richard Wiat or[8] Wyatt, Geoffrey "Jeoffrey" Wiot or[7] Wiat, Robert or Richard[6] Wiot, William Wiot or[5] Wyot, Adam Wiot or Wyote or[4], Guyott[3], Guyott[2], Captain or Admiral Adam Guyott or[1] Wiot) was born June 20, 1913 in Rowan County, N.C. She married John Hubert Eller.

     Children of Bessie Eagle and John Eller are:

   980   i.   Margaret Jane[23] Eller, born May 10, 1931. She married Arthur V. Bocchino July 21, 1957.

+ 981   ii.   Joan Eller, born January 06, 1933.

+ 982   iii.   Nancy Loraine Eller, born March 21, 1939 in Iredell County, N.C.

692. Marnie Della "Delle"[22] Eagle (Adolphus Grant[21], Amanda Jane[20] Wyatt, Noah Calvin[19], Thomas "Tommy"[18] Wiatt, Sr. (Wyatt, Wiett), John[17], Henry[16], Richard[15], George[14], Rev. Haute "Haut" "Hawte"[13], Sir George "Georgius" Thomas[12], Sir Thomas "The Younger"[11], Sir Thomas "The Elder"[10], Sir Henry[9], Richard Wiat or[8] Wyatt, Geoffrey "Jeoffrey" Wiot or[7] Wiat, Robert or Richard[6] Wiot, William Wiot or[5] Wyot, Adam Wiot or Wyote or[4], Guyott[3], Guyott[2], Captain or Admiral Adam Guyott or[1] Wiot) was born May 10, 1916 in Rowan County, N.C. She married Melvin Layfaette Ramseur December 24, 1935, son of Charlie Ramseur and Eliza Elliott.

     More About Marnie Della "Delle" Eagle:
Fact 1: May 09, 1917, date of birth, according to Rachel Hill's published research.

     Children of Marnie Eagle and Melvin Ramseur are:

+ 983   i.   Brenda Sue[23] Ramseur, born November 22, 1944 in Iredell County, N.C.

+ 984   ii.   Melvin Layaette Rameur, Jr., born July 23, 1938.

693. Weathler Lee[22] Eagle (John Murphy[21], Amanda Jane[20] Wyatt, Noah Calvin[19], Thomas "Tommy"[18] Wiatt, Sr. (Wyatt, Wiett), John[17], Henry[16], Richard[15], George[14], Rev. Haute "Haut" "Hawte"[13], Sir George "Georgius" Thomas[12], Sir Thomas "The Younger"[11], Sir Thomas "The Elder"[10], Sir Henry[9], Richard Wiat or[8] Wyatt, Geoffrey "Jeoffrey" Wiot or[7] Wiat, Robert or

Richard[6] Wiot, William Wiot or[5] Wyot, Adam Wiot or Wyote or[4], Guyott[3], Guyott[2], Captain or Admiral Adam Guyott or[1] Wiot) was born October 06, 1900 in Rowan County N.C., and died February 11, 1947. He married Daisy Pierce July 04, 1919, daughter of George Pierce and Amanda Morris.

More About Weathler Lee Eagle:
Remains are buried with those of his wife at Chestnut Hill Cemetery, Salisbury, N.C.

Children of Weathler Eagle and Daisy Pierce are:

+ 985   i.   Kenneth Lee[23] Eagle, born May 09, 1921 in Rowan County N.C.
+ 986   ii.   Margaret Eagle, born March 17, 1925.
+ 987   iii.   Charles Eagle, born October 11, 1929 in Rowan County N.C.; died August 11, 1977.

694. Mary Kate[22] Eagle (John Murphy[21], Amanda Jane[20] Wyatt, Noah Calvin[19], Thomas "Tommy"[18] Wiatt, Sr. (Wyatt, Wiett), John[17], Henry[16], Richard[15], George[14], Rev. Haute "Haut" "Hawte"[13], Sir George "Georgius" Thomas[12], Sir Thomas "The Younger"[11], Sir Thomas "The Elder"[10], Sir Henry[9], Richard Wiat or[8] Wyatt, Geoffrey "Jeoffrey" Wiot or[7] Wiat, Robert or Richard[6] Wiot, William Wiot or[5] Wyot, Adam Wiot or Wyote or[4], Guyott[3], Guyott[2], Captain or Admiral Adam Guyott or[1] Wiot) was born January 30, 1903, and died November 08, 1968. She married Wiley Lee Kluttz February 15, 1920, son of Albert Kluttz and Mary Ribelin.

More About Mary Kate Eagle:
Remains are buried at Organ Luther Church Cemetery, Rowan County, N.C. with spouse.

Children of Mary Eagle and Wiley Kluttz are:

+ 988   i.   Warren Keith[23] Kluttz, born March 15, 1921 in Rowan County N.C.
+ 989   ii.   Novice Bernita Kluttz, born August 20, 1922 in Rowan County N.C.
+ 990   iii.   Roberta Myraline Kluttz, born October 15, 1924 in Rowan County N.C.
+ 991   iv.   Zelma Jestine Kluttz, born June 23, 1927 in Rowan County N.C.

695. Ethel Viola[22] Eagle (John Murphy[21], Amanda Jane[20] Wyatt, Noah Calvin[19], Thomas "Tommy"[18] Wiatt, Sr. (Wyatt, Wiett), John[17], Henry[16], Richard[15], George[14], Rev. Haute "Haut" "Hawte"[13], Sir George "Georgius" Thomas[12], Sir Thomas "The Younger"[11], Sir Thomas "The Elder"[10], Sir Henry[9], Richard Wiat or[8] Wyatt, Geoffrey "Jeoffrey" Wiot or[7] Wiat, Robert or Richard[6] Wiot, William Wiot or[5] Wyot, Adam Wiot or Wyote or[4], Guyott[3], Guyott[2], Captain

or Admiral Adam Guyott or[1] Wiot) was born November 05, 1908, and died March 13, 1977. She married Charlie Wagoner, son of John Wagoner and Ida Honeycutt.

More About Ethel Viola Eagle:
Remains are buried Saint Stevens Church Cemetery, Cabarrus County, N.C.

More About Charlie Wagoner:
Remains are buried at Rowan Memorial Park Cemetery, Salisbury, N.C.

    Children of Ethel Eagle and Charlie Wagoner are:
+   992   i.   Charles Robert[23] Wagoner, born April 10, 1938 in Rowan County N.C.
+   993   ii.   Larry Dean Wagoner, born January 15, 1944 in Rowan County N.C.

696. Lizzie Remelle[22] Eagle (John Murphy[21], Amanda Jane[20] Wyatt, Noah Calvin[19], Thomas "Tommy"[18] Wiatt, Sr. (Wyatt, Wiett), John[17], Henry[16], Richard[15], George[14], Rev. Haute "Haut" "Hawte"[13], Sir George "Georgius" Thomas[12], Sir Thomas "The Younger"[11], Sir Thomas "The Elder"[10], Sir Henry[9], Richard Wiat or[8] Wyatt, Geoffrey "Jeoffrey" Wiot or[7] Wiat, Robert or Richard[6] Wiot, William Wiot or[5] Wyot, Adam Wiot or Wyote or[4], Guyott[3], Guyott[2], Captain or Admiral Adam Guyott or[1] Wiot) was born September 23, 1912. She married W. Max Brannock.

    Children of Lizzie Eagle and W. Brannock are:
+   994   i.   Eugene A.[23] Brannock, born January 01, 1933.
+   995   ii.   Patricia Ann Brannock, born January 19, 1935 in Rome, Ga.

697. Margaret Marie[22] Eagle (John Murphy[21], Amanda Jane[20] Wyatt, Noah Calvin[19], Thomas "Tommy"[18] Wiatt, Sr. (Wyatt, Wiett), John[17], Henry[16], Richard[15], George[14], Rev. Haute "Haut" "Hawte"[13], Sir George "Georgius" Thomas[12], Sir Thomas "The Younger"[11], Sir Thomas "The Elder"[10], Sir Henry[9], Richard Wiat or[8] Wyatt, Geoffrey "Jeoffrey" Wiot or[7] Wiat, Robert or Richard[6] Wiot, William Wiot or[5] Wyot, Adam Wiot or Wyote or[4], Guyott[3], Guyott[2], Captain or Admiral Adam Guyott or[1] Wiot) was born July 22, 1916, and died July 03, 1971. She married Eearnest William Cook April 11, 1934.

More About Margaret Marie Eagle:
Remains are buried in the Memorial Park Cemetery, Salisbury, N.C.

    Children of Margaret Eagle and Eearnest Cook are:
+   996   i.   Barbara[23] Cook, born December 07, 1935.
+   997   ii.   Genelda Cook, born January 09, 1937.
+   998   iii.   Jerry William Cook, born March 29, 1940 in Rowan County N.C.

698. Martin L.[22] Harkey (Mary Lillie[21] Eagle, Amanda Jane[20] Wyatt, Noah Calvin[19], Thomas "Tommy"[18] Wiatt, Sr. (Wyatt, Wiett), John[17], Henry[16], Richard[15], George[14], Rev. Haute "Haut" "Hawte"[13], Sir George "Georgius" Thomas[12], Sir Thomas "The Younger"[11], Sir Thomas "The Elder"[10], Sir Henry[9], Richard Wiat or[8] Wyatt, Geoffrey "Jeoffrey" Wiot or[7] Wiat, Robert or Richard[6] Wiot, William Wiot or[5] Wyot, Adam Wiot or Wyote or[4], Guyott[3], Guyott[2], Captain or Admiral Adam Guyott or[1] Wiot). He married Gladys Terry.

Children of Martin Harkey and Gladys Terry are:
999   i.   William Richard[23] Harkey, born July 30, 1931; died 1977.

More About William Richard Harkey:
Remains are buried at Fairview Memorial Park Cemetery, Stanly County, N.C.

1000   ii.   Clifford Harold Harkey.

699. Annie[22] Harkey (Mary Lillie[21] Eagle, Amanda Jane[20] Wyatt, Noah Calvin[19], Thomas "Tommy"[18] Wiatt, Sr. (Wyatt, Wiett), John[17], Henry[16], Richard[15], George[14], Rev. Haute "Haut" "Hawte"[13], Sir George "Georgius" Thomas[12], Sir Thomas "The Younger"[11], Sir Thomas "The Elder"[10], Sir Henry[9], Richard Wiat or[8] Wyatt, Geoffrey "Jeoffrey" Wiot or[7] Wiat, Robert or Richard[6] Wiot, William Wiot or[5] Wyot, Adam Wiot or Wyote or[4], Guyott[3], Guyott[2], Captain or Admiral Adam Guyott or[1] Wiot). She married Charles Murry.

Children of Annie Harkey and Charles Murry are:
1001   i.   Son[23] Murry.
1002   ii.   Daughter Murry.

700. Onnie[22] Harkey (Mary Lillie[21] Eagle, Amanda Jane[20] Wyatt, Noah Calvin[19], Thomas "Tommy"[18] Wiatt, Sr. (Wyatt, Wiett), John[17], Henry[16], Richard[15], George[14], Rev. Haute "Haut" "Hawte"[13], Sir George "Georgius" Thomas[12], Sir Thomas "The Younger"[11], Sir Thomas "The Elder"[10], Sir Henry[9], Richard Wiat or[8] Wyatt, Geoffrey "Jeoffrey" Wiot or[7] Wiat, Robert or Richard[6] Wiot, William Wiot or[5] Wyot, Adam Wiot or Wyote or[4], Guyott[3], Guyott[2], Captain or Admiral Adam Guyott or[1] Wiot). She married Coy Fine.

Children of Onnie Harkey and Coy Fine are:
1003   i.   Son #1[23] Fine.
1004   ii.   Son #2 Fine.
1005   iii.   Son #3 Fine.
1006   iv.   Daughter Fine.

703. Mary Frances[22] Eagle (David Leo[21], Amanda Jane[20] Wyatt, Noah Calvin[19], Thomas "Tommy"[18] Wiatt, Sr. (Wyatt, Wiett), John[17], Henry[16], Richard[15], George[14], Rev. Haute "Haut" "Hawte"[13], Sir George "Georgius" Thomas[12], Sir Thomas "The Younger"[11], Sir Thomas "The

Elder"[10], Sir Henry[9], Richard Wiat or[8] Wyatt, Geoffrey "Jeoffrey" Wiot or[7] Wiat, Robert or Richard[6] Wiot, William Wiot or[5] Wyot, Adam Wiot or Wyote or[4], Guyott[3], Guyott[2], Captain or Admiral Adam Guyott or[1] Wiot) was born January 25, 1932 in Rowan County N.C. She married Harold Jack Hand December 25, 1948, son of James Hand and Bessie Thompson.

Children of Mary Eagle and Harold Hand are:

+ 1007   i.   James David[23] Hand, born October 07, 1956 in Rowan County N.C.

+ 1008   ii.   Timothy Irvin Hand, born March 29, 1959 in Rowan County N.C.

+ 1009   iii.   Harold Wayne Hand, born August 01, 1950 in Rowan County N.C.

705. Janie Catherine[22] Eagle (David Leo[21], Amanda Jane[20] Wyatt, Noah Calvin[19], Thomas "Tommy"[18] Wiatt, Sr. (Wyatt, Wiett), John[17], Henry[16], Richard[15], George[14], Rev. Haute "Haut" "Hawte"[13], Sir George "Georgius" Thomas[12], Sir Thomas "The Younger"[11], Sir Thomas "The Elder"[10], Sir Henry[9], Richard Wiat or[8] Wyatt, Geoffrey "Jeoffrey" Wiot or[7] Wiat, Robert or Richard[6] Wiot, William Wiot or[5] Wyot, Adam Wiot or Wyote or[4], Guyott[3], Guyott[2], Captain or Admiral Adam Guyott or[1] Wiot) was born August 01, 1935 in Rowan County N.C. She married Japard Lee Harrington, Jr. November 25, 1954, son of Japard Harrington and Mary Link.

Children of Janie Eagle and Japard Harrington are:

1010   i.   Beverly Dawn[23] Harrington, born July 24, 1961.

1011   ii.   Robin Gay Harrington, born July 24, 1964 in Iredell County, N.C.

706. Barbara Jean[22] Eagle (David Leo[21], Amanda Jane[20] Wyatt, Noah Calvin[19], Thomas "Tommy"[18] Wiatt, Sr. (Wyatt, Wiett), John[17], Henry[16], Richard[15], George[14], Rev. Haute "Haut" "Hawte"[13], Sir George "Georgius" Thomas[12], Sir Thomas "The Younger"[11], Sir Thomas "The Elder"[10], Sir Henry[9], Richard Wiat or[8] Wyatt, Geoffrey "Jeoffrey" Wiot or[7] Wiat, Robert or Richard[6] Wiot, William Wiot or[5] Wyot, Adam Wiot or Wyote or[4], Guyott[3], Guyott[2], Captain or Admiral Adam Guyott or[1] Wiot) was born April 17, 1942 in Rowan County N.C. She married Henry Varner Ludwick, Jr. December 25, 1960, son of Henry Ludwick and Bertha Shulenberger.

Children of Barbara Eagle and Henry Ludwick are:

+ 1012   i.   Kimberly Cheryl[23] Ludwick, born July 01, 1964.

1013   ii.   Karen Machelle Ludwick, born December 19, 1968.

707. Martin Luther[22] Eagle (David Leo[21], Amanda Jane[20] Wyatt, Noah Calvin[19], Thomas "Tommy"[18] Wiatt, Sr. (Wyatt, Wiett), John[17], Henry[16], Richard[15], George[14], Rev. Haute "Haut" "Hawte"[13], Sir George "Georgius" Thomas[12], Sir Thomas "The Younger"[11], Sir Thomas "The Elder"[10], Sir Henry[9], Richard Wiat or[8] Wyatt, Geoffrey "Jeoffrey" Wiot or[7] Wiat, Robert or Richard[6] Wiot, William Wiot or[5] Wyot, Adam Wiot or Wyote or[4], Guyott[3], Guyott[2], Captain

or Admiral Adam Guyott or[1] Wiot) was born October 04, 1944 in Rowan County N.C. He married Jo Annelle Clark August 08, 1965, daughter of James Clark and Nina Peele.

    Children of Martin Eagle and Jo Clark are:

+   1014   i.   Christopher Martin[23] Eagle, born January 13, 1970 in Rowan County N.C.

    1015   ii.   Bradley Scott Eagle, born February 10, 1979 in Rowan County N.C.

710. Helen Lois[22] Eagle (Noah Walter[21], Amanda Jane[20] Wyatt, Noah Calvin[19], Thomas "Tommy"[18] Wiatt, Sr. (Wyatt, Wiett), John[17], Henry[16], Richard[15], George[14], Rev. Haute "Haut" "Hawte"[13], Sir George "Georgius" Thomas[12], Sir Thomas "The Younger"[11], Sir Thomas "The Elder"[10], Sir Henry[9], Richard Wiat or[8] Wyatt, Geoffrey "Jeoffrey" Wiot or[7] Wiat, Robert or Richard[6] Wiot, William Wiot or[5] Wyot, Adam Wiot or Wyote or[4], Guyott[3], Guyott[2], Captain or Admiral Adam Guyott or[1] Wiot) was born December 16, 1912 in Wilmington, Del. She married Richard Alexander Shaw, Jr. July 05, 1937, son of Richard Shaw and Mary Craft.

    Children of Helen Eagle and Richard Shaw are:

+   1016   i.   Richard Eagle[23] Shaw, born August 20, 1938.
+   1017   ii.   Willie Kay Shaw, born May 05, 1949 in McDowell County, N.C.

711. Ruth Anne[22] Eagle (Albert Lee[21], Amanda Jane[20] Wyatt, Noah Calvin[19], Thomas "Tommy"[18] Wiatt, Sr. (Wyatt, Wiett), John[17], Henry[16], Richard[15], George[14], Rev. Haute "Haut" "Hawte"[13], Sir George "Georgius" Thomas[12], Sir Thomas "The Younger"[11], Sir Thomas "The Elder"[10], Sir Henry[9], Richard Wiat or[8] Wyatt, Geoffrey "Jeoffrey" Wiot or[7] Wiat, Robert or Richard[6] Wiot, William Wiot or[5] Wyot, Adam Wiot or Wyote or[4], Guyott[3], Guyott[2], Captain or Admiral Adam Guyott or[1] Wiot) was born May 18, 1901 in Rowan County, N.C. She married Joseph Ray Kepley June 21, 1930.

    Children of Ruth Eagle and Joseph Kepley are:

+   1018   i.   Hilda Joyce[23] Kepley.
+   1019   ii.   Albert Ray Kepley, born October 31, 1931.
+   1020   iii.   Joseph Lewis Kepley, born November 27, 1936.
    1021   iv.   Gene Alton Kepley, born April 26, 1941. He married Judy Hudson 1961.
+   1022   v.   Jerry Lee Kepley, born April 18, 1943.

712. Carrie Etta[22] Eagle (Albert Lee[21], Amanda Jane[20] Wyatt, Noah Calvin[19], Thomas "Tommy"[18] Wiatt, Sr. (Wyatt, Wiett), John[17], Henry[16], Richard[15], George[14], Rev. Haute "Haut" "Hawte"[13], Sir George "Georgius" Thomas[12], Sir Thomas "The Younger"[11], Sir Thomas "The Elder"[10], Sir Henry[9], Richard Wiat or[8] Wyatt, Geoffrey "Jeoffrey" Wiot or[7] Wiat, Robert or Richard[6] Wiot, William Wiot or[5] Wyot, Adam Wiot or Wyote or[4], Guyott[3], Guyott[2], Captain or Admiral Adam Guyott or[1] Wiot) was born December 13, 1917 in Rowan County, N.C. She married (1) William Glenn Wilcox, son of James Wilcox and Sarah Jones. She married (2) Howard Bailey Hollar April 20, 1974.

Children of Carrie Eagle and William Wilcox are:

+ 1023   i.   Larry Eugene[23] Wilcox, born November 12, 1940.
+ 1024   ii.   Linda Lee Wilcox, born December 23, 1942.
+ 1025   iii.   Donnie Lynn Wilcox, born March 12, 1951.

713. Rosa Belle[22] Morgan (Amanda Dora[21] Eagle, Amanda Jane[20] Wyatt, Noah Calvin[19], Thomas "Tommy"[18] Wiatt, Sr. (Wyatt, Wiett), John[17], Henry[16], Richard[15], George[14], Rev. Haute "Haut" "Hawte"[13], Sir George "Georgius" Thomas[12], Sir Thomas "The Younger"[11], Sir Thomas "The Elder"[10], Sir Henry[9], Richard Wiat or[8] Wyatt, Geoffrey "Jeoffrey" Wiot or[7] Wiat, Robert or Richard[6] Wiot, William Wiot or[5] Wyot, Adam Wiot or Wyote or[4], Guyott[3], Guyott[2], Captain or Admiral Adam Guyott or[1] Wiot) was born February 07, 1909. She married Stephen Jasper Terry April 05, 1931.

More About Stephen Jasper Terry:
Buried at the Rourl Presbyterian Cemetery in Elerbee, N.C.

Children of Rosa Morgan and Stephen Terry are:

+ 1026   i.   Arthur Lewis[23] Terry, born in Richmond County, N.C.
+ 1027   ii.   Stephen Jasper Terry, Jr., born October 20, 1930 in Richmond County, N.C.
+ 1028   iii.   Ralph Gilbert Terry, born January 28, 1932 in Richmond County, N.C.
+ 1029   iv.   Sam Coy Terry, born July 03, 1933 in Richmond County, N.C.
+ 1030   v.   Charles Ray Terry, born December 02, 1937 in Richmond County, N.C.
+ 1031   vi.   Leonard Leon Terry, born August 21, 1939 in Richmond County, N.C.
+ 1032   vii.   Jo Ann Terry, born November 19, 1941 in Richmond County, N.C.
+ 1033   viii.   Rachael Maxine Terry, born June 23, 1943 in Richmond County, N.C.

718. Amanda Catherine[22] Morgan (Amanda Dora[21] Eagle, Amanda Jane[20] Wyatt, Noah Calvin[19], Thomas "Tommy"[18] Wiatt, Sr. (Wyatt, Wiett), John[17], Henry[16], Richard[15], George[14], Rev. Haute "Haut" "Hawte"[13], Sir George "Georgius" Thomas[12], Sir Thomas "The Younger"[11], Sir Thomas "The Elder"[10], Sir Henry[9], Richard Wiat or[8] Wyatt, Geoffrey "Jeoffrey" Wiot or[7] Wiat, Robert or Richard[6] Wiot, William Wiot or[5] Wyot, Adam Wiot or Wyote or[4], Guyott[3], Guyott[2], Captain or Admiral Adam Guyott or[1] Wiot) was born March 08, 1921. She married Raymond Bruce Williams November 24, 1949.

Children of Amanda Morgan and Raymond Williams are:

+ 1034   i.   Kenneth Ray[23] Williams, born July 24, 1952.

1035　ii.　Ricky Dean Williams, born May 18, 1957. He married Connie Fesperman June 07, 1979.

719. John Calvin[22] Morgan, Jr. (Amanda Dora[21] Eagle, Amanda Jane[20] Wyatt, Noah Calvin[19], Thomas "Tommy"[18] Wiatt, Sr. (Wyatt, Wiett), John[17], Henry[16], Richard[15], George[14], Rev. Haute "Haut" "Hawte"[13], Sir George "Georgius" Thomas[12], Sir Thomas "The Younger"[11], Sir Thomas "The Elder"[10], Sir Henry[9], Richard Wiat or[8] Wyatt, Geoffrey "Jeoffrey" Wiot or[7] Wiat, Robert or Richard[6] Wiot, William Wiot or[5] Wyot, Adam Wiot or Wyote or[4], Guyott[3], Guyott[2], Captain or Admiral Adam Guyott or[1] Wiot) was born August 20, 1923, and died 1995. He married Susie Dorthy McRea December 18, 1954.

More About Susie Dorthy McRea:
Fact 1: Born Oct. 16th.

Children of John Morgan and Susie McRea are:

1036　i.　Donald Lee[23] Morgan, born October 21, 1955 in Richmond County, N.C.

1037　ii.　Albert Dale Morgan, born December 02, 1956 in Richmond County, N.C.

1038　iii.　Patricia Gale Morgan, born December 02, 1956 in Richmond County, N.C.

1039　iv.　Larry Wayne Morgan, born June 15, 1961.

720. William Howard[22] Morgan (Amanda Dora[21] Eagle, Amanda Jane[20] Wyatt, Noah Calvin[19], Thomas "Tommy"[18] Wiatt, Sr. (Wyatt, Wiett), John[17], Henry[16], Richard[15], George[14], Rev. Haute "Haut" "Hawte"[13], Sir George "Georgius" Thomas[12], Sir Thomas "The Younger"[11], Sir Thomas "The Elder"[10], Sir Henry[9], Richard Wiat or[8] Wyatt, Geoffrey "Jeoffrey" Wiot or[7] Wiat, Robert or Richard[6] Wiot, William Wiot or[5] Wyot, Adam Wiot or Wyote or[4], Guyott[3], Guyott[2], Captain or Admiral Adam Guyott or[1] Wiot) was born September 24, 1925. He married Audrey Catherine Smith January 01, 1951, daughter of Joseph Smith and Carrie Cauble.

Children of William Morgan and Audrey Smith are:

+　1040　i.　Linda Catherine[23] Morgan, born April 09, 1952 in Moore County, N.C.

1041　ii.　John Williams Morgan, born March 24, 1953 in Moore County, N.C.

+　1042　iii.　Lee Howard Morgan, born May 14, 1954.

+　1043　iv.　Nancy Faye Morgan, born June 03, 1955 in Moore County, N.C.

1044　v.　Jerry Lewis Morgan, born January 21, 1957 in Moore County, N.C.

1045　vi.　Sam Smith Morgan, born March 15, 1958.

1046　vii.　Ralph Morris Morgan, born June 12, 1959.

+　1047　viii.　Mary Jane Morgan, born October 24, 1961.

1048　ix.　Calvin Ray Morgan, born July 24, 1967.

721. Mildred Bernice[22] Morgan (Amanda Dora[21] Eagle, Amanda Jane[20] Wyatt, Noah Calvin[19], Thomas "Tommy"[18] Wiatt, Sr. (Wyatt, Wiett), John[17], Henry[16], Richard[15], George[14], Rev. Haute "Haut" "Hawte"[13], Sir George "Georgius" Thomas[12], Sir Thomas "The Younger"[11], Sir Thomas "The Elder"[10], Sir Henry[9], Richard Wiat or[8] Wyatt, Geoffrey "Jeoffrey" Wiot or[7] Wiat, Robert or Richard[6] Wiot, William Wiot or[5] Wyot, Adam Wiot or Wyote or[4], Guyott[3], Guyott[2], Captain or Admiral Adam Guyott or[1] Wiot) was born August 16, 1927. She married Robert M. Ward June 17, 1951.

> Children of Mildred Morgan and Robert Ward are:
>
> | 1049 | i. | David Morgan[23] Ward, born September 25, 1953 in Chattahochee County, Ga. |
> | 1050 | ii. | Deborah Denise Ward, born May 30, 1955 in Davidson County, Tenn. |
> | 1051 | iii. | Donald William Ward, born July 19, 1957 in Hamilton County, Tenn. |
> | 1052 | iv. | Deeanne Ward, born August 31, 1960 in Rowan County, N.C. |
> | 1053 | v. | Douglas Wesley Ward, born February 16, 1965 in Rowan County, N.C; died February 16, 1965 in Rowan County, N.C. |

Generation No. 23

729. Joseph Marshall[23] (James Frankin[22], Martha C.[21] Sykes, James B.[20], frances[19] Cates, Thomas[18], Rebecca[17] Sykes, Frances[16] Wiatt, Richard[15], George[14], Rev. Haute "Haut" "Hawte"[13], Sir George "Georgius" Thomas[12], Sir Thomas "The Younger"[11], Sir Thomas "The Elder"[10], Sir Henry[9], Richard Wiat or[8] Wyatt, Geoffrey "Jeoffrey" Wiot or[7] Wiat, Robert or Richard[6] Wiot, William Wiot or[5] Wyot, Adam Wiot or Wyote or[4], Guyott[3], Guyott[2], Captain or Admiral Adam Guyott or[1] Wiot) was born March 10, 1900 in mebane, alabance co, n.c., and died August 26, 1980 in Graham, Alamance County, N.C. He married Dula "Sweet" Darling Montgomery.

> Children of Joseph Qualls and Dula Montgomery are:
>
> | + | 1054 | i. | Lucy[24] Qualls. |
> | | 1055 | ii. | Alise Qualls. |
> | | 1056 | iii. | Rae Qualls. |
> | | 1057 | iv. | Marsa Qualls. |

738. Effie Jeanette "Genetta" Eagle[23] Wyatt (Harvey Addison[22], Columbus Ciscero[21], Wilson Riley[20], Jesse "Jessey"[19], John "Johney"[18], John[17] Wiatt, Henry[16], Richard[15], George[14], Rev. Haute "Haut" "Hawte"[13], Sir George "Georgius" Thomas[12], Sir Thomas "The Younger"[11], Sir Thomas "The Elder"[10], Sir Henry[9], Richard Wiat or[8] Wyatt, Geoffrey "Jeoffrey" Wiot or[7] Wiat, Robert or Richard[6] Wiot, William Wiot or[5] Wyot, Adam Wiot or Wyote or[4], Guyott[3], Guyott[2], Captain or Admiral Adam Guyott or[1] Wiot) was born March 21, 1900, and died July 08, 1986. She married Calvin L. Basinger January 07, 1917.

More About Effie Jeanette "Genetta" Eagle Wyatt:
Fact 1: March 02, 1900, possible birthday.
Fact 2: Effie's mother Charity Eagle Wyatt was a daughter of Moses Eagle, brother of Solomon Eagle, Jr. --both sons of Solomon Eagle, Sr.

Children of Effie Wyatt and Calvin Basinger are:

+	1058	i.	Edith Hope[24] Basinger, born January 07, 1918.
+	1059	ii.	Eltha Pauline Basinger, born October 07, 1919.
+	1060	iii.	Elma Eunice Basinger, born May 31, 1922.
+	1061	iv.	Claude V. Basinger, born December 15, 1924; died October 20, 1980.
+	1062	v.	Clinton E. Basinger, born January 12, 1928; died November 24, 1968.
+	1063	vi.	Chester Clyde Basinger, born May 06, 1932.
+	1064	vii.	Evelyn Ruth Basinger, born September 02, 1937.
+	1065	viii.	Elva Kay Basinger, born May 04, 1944.

740. Timothy Ray[23] Smith (Margaret Evelyeen[22] Wyatt, Pleasant Loveless[21], Ciscero "Cicero" L.[20], Lazerus Pleasant[19], Thomas "Tommy"[18] Wiatt, Sr. (Wyatt, Wiett), John[17], Henry[16], Richard[15], George[14], Rev. Haute "Haut" "Hawte"[13], Sir George "Georgius" Thomas[12], Sir Thomas "The Younger"[11], Sir Thomas "The Elder"[10], Sir Henry[9], Richard Wiat or[8] Wyatt, Geoffrey "Jeoffrey" Wiot or[7] Wiat, Robert or Richard[6] Wiot, William Wiot or[5] Wyot, Adam Wiot or Wyote or[4], Guyott[3], Guyott[2], Captain or Admiral Adam Guyott or[1] Wiot) was born January 30, 1949 in Rowan, N.C. He married Rosemary Penley, daughter of Ross Penley and Mary Gales.

Children of Timothy Smith and Rosemary Penley are:

+	1066	i.	Ashley Elizabeth[24] Smith, born March 12, 1977 in Wake County, N.C.
	1067	ii.	Timothy Stuwart Smith, born June 26, 1979 in Wake County, N.C.

741. Lula Marie[23] Wyatt (David Eli[22], James "Jim" Noah[21], William Wesley "Brantly"[20], Noah Calvin[19], Thomas "Tommy"[18] Wiatt, Sr. (Wyatt, Wiett), John[17], Henry[16], Richard[15], George[14], Rev. Haute "Haut" "Hawte"[13], Sir George "Georgius" Thomas[12], Sir Thomas "The Younger"[11], Sir Thomas "The Elder"[10], Sir Henry[9], Richard Wiat or[8] Wyatt, Geoffrey "Jeoffrey" Wiot or[7] Wiat, Robert or Richard[6] Wiot, William Wiot or[5] Wyot, Adam Wiot or Wyote or[4], Guyott[3], Guyott[2], Captain or Admiral Adam Guyott or[1] Wiot) was born January 19, 1914 in Rowan County N.C., and died March 07, 2002 in Rowan County N.C. She married Enos Roy Goodman August 22, 1940, son of Bennett Goodman and Mary Morgan.

More About Lula Marie Wyatt:
Remains are buried at Liberty United Methodist Church Cemetery, Gold Hill, Rowan County, N.C.

Child of Lula Wyatt and Enos Goodman is:

1068 i. Larry Wyatt[24] Goodman, born 1944; died February 15, 2000.

742. Paul Woodrow[23] Wyatt (David Eli[22], James "Jim" Noah[21], William Wesley "Brantly"[20], Noah Calvin[19], Thomas "Tommy"[18] Wiatt, Sr. (Wyatt, Wiett), John[17], Henry[16], Richard[15], George[14], Rev. Haute "Haut" "Hawte"[13], Sir George "Georgius" Thomas[12], Sir Thomas "The Younger"[11], Sir Thomas "The Elder"[10], Sir Henry[9], Richard Wiat or[8] Wyatt, Geoffrey "Jeoffrey" Wiot or[7] Wiat, Robert or Richard[6] Wiot, William Wiot or[5] Wyot, Adam Wiot or Wyote or[4], Guyott[3], Guyott[2], Captain or Admiral Adam Guyott or[1] Wiot) was born December 11, 1918 in Richfield, N.C., and died June 08, 2014 in Stanly County, N.C. He married Ethrillian Thompson.

More About Paul Woodrow Wyatt:
Providence Baptist Church, Rowan County, N.C.

Child of Paul Wyatt and Ethrillian Thompson is:

+ 1069 i. Dr. Roger D.[24] Wyatt, born Abt. 1946 in Rowan County, N.C.

746. Paulie[23] Morgan (Freda Maybelle[22] Kirk, Rhoda Isabelle[21] Morgan, Lila Delilah "Delila"[20] Wyatt, Noah Calvin[19], Thomas "Tommy"[18] Wiatt, Sr. (Wyatt, Wiett), John[17], Henry[16], Richard[15], George[14], Rev. Haute "Haut" "Hawte"[13], Sir George "Georgius" Thomas[12], Sir Thomas "The Younger"[11], Sir Thomas "The Elder"[10], Sir Henry[9], Richard Wiat or[8] Wyatt, Geoffrey "Jeoffrey" Wiot or[7] Wiat, Robert or Richard[6] Wiot, William Wiot or[5] Wyot, Adam Wiot or Wyote or[4], Guyott[3], Guyott[2], Captain or Admiral Adam Guyott or[1] Wiot) was born August 08, 1912 in Rowan County N.C., and died October 14, 1970 in Rowan County N.C. He married Zadie Weary, daughter of A.L. Weary and Saphronia Currin.

More About Paulie Morgan:
Wyatt's Grove Baptist Church Cemetery, Rowan County, N.C.

More About Zadie Weary:
Wyatt's Grove Baptist Church Cemetery, Rowan County, N.C.

Children of Paulie Morgan and Zadie Weary are:

1070 i. William Thomas[24] Morgan, born January 27, 1943; died November 25, 2013.

1071 ii. Gene Edward Morgan, born March 18, 1945 in Rowan County N.C.; died June 17, 2004 in Rowan County N.C.

     More About Gene Edward Morgan:
     Wyatt's Grove Baptist Church Cemetery, Rowan County, N.C.

1072 iii. Harry Leon Morgan.

750. J.T.[23] Morgan (Freda Maybelle[22] Kirk, Rhoda Isabelle[21] Morgan, Lila Delilah "Delila"[20] Wyatt, Noah Calvin[19], Thomas "Tommy"[18] Wiatt, Sr. (Wyatt, Wiett), John[17], Henry[16], Richard[15], George[14], Rev. Haute "Haut" "Hawte"[13], Sir George "Georgius" Thomas[12], Sir Thomas "The Younger"[11], Sir Thomas "The Elder"[10], Sir Henry[9], Richard Wiat or[8] Wyatt, Geoffrey "Jeoffrey" Wiot or[7] Wiat, Robert or Richard[6] Wiot, William Wiot or[5] Wyot, Adam Wiot or Wyote or[4], Guyott[3], Guyott[2], Captain or Admiral Adam Guyott or[1] Wiot) was born October 19, 1919 in North Carolina, and died June 25, 1994 in Rowan County N.C. He married Arlene Hoffner January 30, 1942 in Rowan County N.C., daughter of Challie Hoffner and Lena Owens.

More About J.T. Morgan:
Fact 1: Oct. 12, 1919 another date of birth found.
Saint Matthew's Lutheran Church Cemetery, Rowan County, N.C.

More About Arlene Hoffner:
Saint Matthew's Lutheran Church Cemetery, Salisbury, Rowan County, N.C. Row #13; Plot #135.

 Child of J.T. Morgan and Arlene Hoffner is:
+ 1073 i. Mike Michael Lynn[24] Morgan, born Abt. 1959 in North Carolina.

753. Virgie Irene[23] Eagle (Noah Jenkins[22], Mary Jane[21] Morgan, Rachel Evelyn "Eveline"[20] Wyatt, Noah Calvin[19], Thomas "Tommy"[18] Wiatt, Sr. (Wyatt, Wiett), John[17], Henry[16], Richard[15], George[14], Rev. Haute "Haut" "Hawte"[13], Sir George "Georgius" Thomas[12], Sir Thomas "The Younger"[11], Sir Thomas "The Elder"[10], Sir Henry[9], Richard Wiat or[8] Wyatt, Geoffrey "Jeoffrey" Wiot or[7] Wiat, Robert or Richard[6] Wiot, William Wiot or[5] Wyot, Adam Wiot or Wyote or[4], Guyott[3], Guyott[2], Captain or Admiral Adam Guyott or[1] Wiot) was born November 15, 1902 in Richfield, Rowan County, N.C., and died July 12, 1984 in Salisbury, Rowan County, N.C. She married William Crowell Hinson, Sr. May 31, 1925 in Richfield, Rowan County, N.C., son of James Hinson and Lucy Floyd.

More About Virgie Irene Eagle:
Fact 1: 1902, born in the home her father Noah built in Morgan Township, Rowan County, N.C.
Fact 2: 1910, poses in group school photo for Poole School, Morgan Township, Rowan County, N.C.
Fact 3: 1910, listed on Rowan County Census with parents and siblings.
Fact 4: 1911, poses in group school photo for Poole School, Morgan Township, Rowan County, N.C
Fact 5: October 02, 1913, poses in Morgan, Wyatt, Shaver birthday dinner for Rachel Evelyn Wyatt Morgan.
Fact 6: 1919, poses with sister Agnes (baby) in photo.
Fact 7: 1920-1925, taught school at Pond's School House, Richfield area of N.C.
Remains are buried in the Wyatt Grove Baptist Church, Richfield, N.C.

More About William Crowell Hinson, Sr.:
Fact 1: Was a farmer in Richfield, N.C.
Fact 2: 1899-1997, resided: Rocky River Springs, N.C.; Texas; Morgan Township and Rowan County, N.C.
Remains are buried at Wyatt Grove Baptist Church Cemetery, Richfield, N.C.

    Children of Virgie Eagle and William Hinson are:

+   1074   i.   William "Bill" Crowell[24] Hinson, Jr., born March 05, 1926 in Rowan County, N.C.; died December 24, 2014 in Myrtle Beach, S.C.

+   1075   ii.   Richard "Chubby" "Chub" Clyde Hinson, born April 11, 1927 in Richfield, Rowan County, N.C.; died October 23, 2006 in Salisbury, Rowan County, N.C.

+   1076   iii.   James "Jim" Noah Hinson, M.D., born January 12, 1929 in Mabery Place, Porter Station, Stanly County, N.C.; died March 30, 2015 in Salisbury, Rowan County, N.C.

+   1077   iv.   Betty Lou Hinson, born October 24, 1930 in Rowan County, N.C.

+   1078   v.   Rachel Evelyn Hinson, born September 03, 1932 in Stanly County, N.C.; died March 12, 1994 in Rowan County, N.C.

+   1079   vi.   Margaret Ann Hinson, born June 07, 1934 in Palmerville, Stanly County, N.C.

754. Edwin "Ed" Lee[23] Eagle (Noah Jenkins[22], Mary Jane[21] Morgan, Rachel Evelyn "Eveline"[20] Wyatt, Noah Calvin[19], Thomas "Tommy"[18] Wiatt, Sr. (Wyatt, Wiett), John[17], Henry[16], Richard[15], George[14], Rev. Haute "Haut" "Hawte"[13], Sir George "Georgius" Thomas[12], Sir Thomas "The Younger"[11], Sir Thomas "The Elder"[10], Sir Henry[9], Richard Wiat or[8] Wyatt, Geoffrey "Jeoffrey" Wiot or[7] Wiat, Robert or Richard[6] Wiot, William Wiot or[5] Wyot, Adam Wiot or Wyote or[4], Guyott[3], Guyott[2], Captain or Admiral Adam Guyott or[1] Wiot) was born July 25, 1904 in Morgan Township, Rowan County, N.C., and died January 09, 1984 in North Carolina. He married Jesse Viola Reid May 14, 1927, daughter of Earl Reid and Sarah Copley.

More About Edwin "Ed" Lee Eagle:
Buried in Luthers Lutheran Church Cemetery in Richfield, N.C. next to his wife.

More About Jesse Viola Reid:
Fact 1: *"Aunt Vi."*
Buried in Luthers Lutheran Church Cemetery in Richfield, N.C. next to her husband.

    Children of Edwin Eagle and Jesse Reid are:

+   1080   i.   Olga Bruce[24] Eagle, born August 09, 1928 in Cabarrus County, N.C.

1081   ii.   Gene Lee Eagle, born October 21, 1933 in Davidson County, N.C. He married Hazel Loretta Troutman May 04, 1958.

More About Gene Lee Eagle:
Fact 1: 1954-1958, Served in the US Airforce.

755. Helen Madelene[23] Eagle (Noah Jenkins[22], Mary Jane[21] Morgan, Rachel Evelyn "Eveline"[20] Wyatt, Noah Calvin[19], Thomas "Tommy"[18] Wiatt, Sr. (Wyatt, Wiett), John[17], Henry[16], Richard[15], George[14], Rev. Haute "Haut" "Hawte"[13], Sir George "Georgius" Thomas[12], Sir Thomas "The Younger"[11], Sir Thomas "The Elder"[10], Sir Henry[9], Richard Wiat or[8] Wyatt, Geoffrey "Jeoffrey" Wiot or[7] Wiat, Robert or Richard[6] Wiot, William Wiot or[5] Wyot, Adam Wiot or Wyote or[4], Guyott[3], Guyott[2], Captain or Admiral Adam Guyott or[1] Wiot) was born September 30, 1906 in Morgan Township, Rowan County, N.C., and died May 23, 1978. She married Alton Parker Basinger February 04, 1928, son of Walter Basinger and Hattie Williams.

More About Helen Madelene Eagle:
Fact 1: Nicknamed: "Nell."

More About Alton Parker Basinger:
Fact 1: Buried at the Luthers Lutheran Church Cemetery.

Children of Helen Eagle and Alton Basinger are:

+   1082   i.   Hattie Laura[24] Basinger, born June 01, 1928 in Rowan County, N.C.; died March 22, 2007 in Statesville, N.C.
+   1083   ii.   Jerry Zane Grey Basinger, born December 18, 1931 in Rowan County, N.C.
+   1084   iii.   Hayden Murray Basinger, born September 19, 1934 in Rowan County, N.C.
+   1085   iv.   Alton Parker Basinger, Jr., born June 23, 1938.
+   1086   v.   Robert Noah Basinger, born January 19, 1942.
+   1087   vi.   Dorothy Jean Basinger, born February 27, 1944.

756. Gladys Marie[23] Eagle (Noah Jenkins[22], Mary Jane[21] Morgan, Rachel Evelyn "Eveline"[20] Wyatt, Noah Calvin[19], Thomas "Tommy"[18] Wiatt, Sr. (Wyatt, Wiett), John[17], Henry[16], Richard[15], George[14], Rev. Haute "Haut" "Hawte"[13], Sir George "Georgius" Thomas[12], Sir Thomas "The Younger"[11], Sir Thomas "The Elder"[10], Sir Henry[9], Richard Wiat or[8] Wyatt, Geoffrey "Jeoffrey" Wiot or[7] Wiat, Robert or Richard[6] Wiot, William Wiot or[5] Wyot, Adam Wiot or Wyote or[4], Guyott[3], Guyott[2], Captain or Admiral Adam Guyott or[1] Wiot) was born June 03, 1909 in Morgan Township, Rowan County, N.C., and died September 03, 1977. She married Glenn George Barringer December 24, 1927.

More About Gladys Marie Eagle:
Fact 1: Remains are buried at Wesley Chapel Methodist Church Cemetery, Rowan County, N.C.

More About Glenn George Barringer:
Fact 1: Buried at Wesley Chapel Methodist Church Cemetery.

Children of Gladys Eagle and Glenn Barringer are:

+ 1088 i. Norman Paige[24] Barringer, born December 10, 1928 in Stanly County, N.C.; died 2013 in North Carolina.
+ 1089 ii. George Wilson Barringer, born February 22, 1931 in Stanly County, N.C.
+ 1090 iii. Sylvia Ann Barringer, born May 01, 1938.
+ 1091 iv. Edward Zane Barringer, born December 07, 1939.

758. Agnes Evelyn[23] Eagle (Noah Jenkins[22], Mary Jane[21] Morgan, Rachel Evelyn "Eveline"[20] Wyatt, Noah Calvin[19], Thomas "Tommy"[18] Wiatt, Sr. (Wyatt, Wiett), John[17], Henry[16], Richard[15], George[14], Rev. Haute "Haut" "Hawte"[13], Sir George "Georgius" Thomas[12], Sir Thomas "The Younger"[11], Sir Thomas "The Elder"[10], Sir Henry[9], Richard Wiat or[8] Wyatt, Geoffrey "Jeoffrey" Wiot or[7] Wiat, Robert or Richard[6] Wiot, William Wiot or[5] Wyot, Adam Wiot or Wyote or[4], Guyott[3], Guyott[2], Captain or Admiral Adam Guyott or[1] Wiot) was born May 31, 1919 in Richfield, N.C., and died June 1999 in Carrboro, N.C. She married (1) Mark Calton Whitaker, Jr., son of Mark Whitaker and Tommie Johnson. She married (2) William B. Palmer. She married (3) Reese Cranford, son of Samuel Cranford and Dellie Cannup.

More About Reese Cranford:
Fact 1: Lived in Richfield, N.C.

Died young at Baden in factory accident. Just before he passed away, he told his rescuers: "Tell Agnes that I will see her in Heaven."

Children of Agnes Eagle and Mark Whitaker are:

+ 1092 i. Nina Marcella[24] Whitaker, born September 20, 1950 in Durham County, N.C.
  1093 ii. Martha Evelyn Whitaker, born November 21, 1954 in Durham County, N.C. She married Jack Lamar Whitehead, Jr. July 02, 1977.

Child of Agnes Eagle and Reese Cranford is:
  1094 i. Daughter[24] Cranford.

More About Daughter Cranford:
Died at soon after birth. Delivered by Dr. Allen. Born alive.

759. Robert "Bob" Noah[23] Eagle (Noah Jenkins[22], Mary Jane[21] Morgan, Rachel Evelyn "Eveline"[20] Wyatt, Noah Calvin[19], Thomas "Tommy"[18] Wiatt, Sr. (Wyatt, Wiett), John[17], Henry[16], Richard[15], George[14], Rev. Haute "Haut" "Hawte"[13], Sir George "Georgius" Thomas[12],

Sir Thomas "The Younger"[11], Sir Thomas "The Elder"[10], Sir Henry[9], Richard Wiat or[8] Wyatt, Geoffrey "Jeoffrey" Wiot or[7] Wiat, Robert or Richard[6] Wiot, William Wiot or[5] Wyot, Adam Wiot or Wyote or[4], Guyott[3], Guyott[2], Captain or Admiral Adam Guyott or[1] Wiot) was born January 09, 1923 in Rowan County, N.C. He married Zylpha Almetta Wright November 22, 1945, daughter of Samuel Wright and Lutee Bass.

Children of Robert Eagle and Zylpha Wright are:

+   1095   i.   Elizabeth Anne[24] Eagle, M.D., born February 23, 1953 in High Point, Guilford County, N.C.

+   1096   ii.   Robert Nathan Eagle, born October 16, 1955 in High Point, Guilford County, N.C.

    1097   iii.   John David Wright Eagle, born March 25, 1961 in Nome, Alaska; Adopted child.

Robert Noah Eagle

♀ | | ♂

LETTER FROM ROBERT NOAH EAGLE [BORN: 1923]

ON AUGUST 10th, 2007, Robert Noah Eagle sends due to my request a written account of an accident he had at age 18. My father, James -- a nephew to Robert -- recollected this accident as well, and clarified that drunken men had wandered out onto the road when this accident occurred.

Robert Noah Eagle writes in August, 2007:

My near fatal accident on March 13th or
April 13th, 1941. Anyway, it was Friday before Easter.
My Brother-in-law, Bill Palmer and I were on
our way home from Salisbury, N.C. via China Grove, N.C.
(Home being Rockwell, N.C.) while passing by the
"Blue Moon Roadhouse," a tavern well known in
those days. This is where a lot of beer + whiskey
was being served. Three or four drunks tried to
run us off the road. We were able to dodge
all of them but one, which one hit + killed him
outright. We were riding a Harley Davidson motorcycle.
We were both on the motorcycle, with me behind
Bill on the same motor. I was thrown from the
motorcycle and landed 7 feet from where the
motorcycle had stopped. I was injured with (2) two
compound skull fractures, 2 broken ribs, left shoulder,
collar bone, left leg and arm and nose. I was
in a coma for four (4) days and five (5) units
of blood. I was hospitalized for about 10 days.
At that time we had not thought about
Hospital Insurance, so my sister-Agnes,
"Bill's wife," paid my expenses. I have no idea
how much!
It is my belief that a *"Guardian Angel"*
was looking after me and *"Thanks be to God"*
I'm still here."

761. Ray Clayton[23] Troutman (Mary Lillie[22] Eagle, Mary Jane[21] Morgan, Rachel Evelyn "Eveline"[20] Wyatt, Noah Calvin[19], Thomas "Tommy"[18] Wiatt, Sr. (Wyatt, Wiett), John[17], Henry[16], Richard[15], George[14], Rev. Haute "Haut" "Hawte"[13], Sir George "Georgius" Thomas[12], Sir Thomas "The Younger"[11], Sir Thomas "The Elder"[10], Sir Henry[9], Richard Wiat or[8] Wyatt, Geoffrey "Jeoffrey" Wiot or[7] Wiat, Robert or Richard[6] Wiot, William Wiot or[5] Wyot, Adam

Wiot or Wyote or[4], Guyott[3], Guyott[2], Captain or Admiral Adam Guyott or[1] Wiot) was born October 14, 1920. He married Martha Jeraldine Mackie March 07, 1959, daughter of Martin Mackie and Verna.

Child of Ray Troutman and Martha Mackie is:
1098 i. Elizabeth Ann[24] Troutman, born September 23, 1959 in Forsythe County, N.C.; died September 28, 1959.

762. Lonie Mae[23] Troutman (Mary Lillie[22] Eagle, Mary Jane[21] Morgan, Rachel Evelyn "Eveline"[20] Wyatt, Noah Calvin[19], Thomas "Tommy"[18] Wiatt, Sr. (Wyatt, Wiett), John[17], Henry[16], Richard[15], George[14], Rev. Haute "Haut" "Hawte"[13], Sir George "Georgius" Thomas[12], Sir Thomas "The Younger"[11], Sir Thomas "The Elder"[10], Sir Henry[9], Richard Wiat or[8] Wyatt, Geoffrey "Jeoffrey" Wiot or[7] Wiat, Robert or Richard[6] Wiot, William Wiot or[5] Wyot, Adam Wiot or Wyote or[4], Guyott[3], Guyott[2], Captain or Admiral Adam Guyott or[1] Wiot) was born March 18, 1923 in Rowan County, N.C. She married Berry Edward Jones, son of Sanford Jones and Ida Basinger.

Children of Lonie Troutman and Berry Jones are:
+ 1099 i. Patricia Ann[24] Jones, born October 16, 1941 in Rowan County, N.C.
+ 1100 ii. Pamela Jane Jones, born October 16, 1950 in Gaston County, N.C.

764. Nellie Manola[23] Morgan (Mary Frances[22] Eagle, Noah Calvin[21], Mary Ann[20] Wyatt, Noah Calvin[19], Thomas "Tommy"[18] Wiatt, Sr. (Wyatt, Wiett), John[17], Henry[16], Richard[15], George[14], Rev. Haute "Haut" "Hawte"[13], Sir George "Georgius" Thomas[12], Sir Thomas "The Younger"[11], Sir Thomas "The Elder"[10], Sir Henry[9], Richard Wiat or[8] Wyatt, Geoffrey "Jeoffrey" Wiot or[7] Wiat, Robert or Richard[6] Wiot, William Wiot or[5] Wyot, Adam Wiot or Wyote or[4], Guyott[3], Guyott[2], Captain or Admiral Adam Guyott or[1] Wiot) was born February 12, 1912 in Rowan County, N.C. She married Glenn Caldwell White, Sr. June 19, 1932, son of Walter White and Ida Peeler.

More About Glenn Caldwell White, Sr.:
Buried at Chestnut Hill Cemetery, N.C.

Children of Nellie Morgan and Glenn White are:
+ 1101 i. Glenn Caldwell[24] White, Jr., born June 27, 1936 in Rowan County, N.C.
+ 1102 ii. John W. White, born August 10, 1937 in Rowan County, N.C.
+ 1103 iii. Fred S. White, born January 04, 1943 in Rowan County, N.C.

765. Ruby Mae[23] Eagle (Albert Thadeus[22], Noah Calvin[21], Mary Ann[20] Wyatt, Noah Calvin[19], Thomas "Tommy"[18] Wiatt, Sr. (Wyatt, Wiett), John[17], Henry[16], Richard[15], George[14], Rev.

Haute "Haut" "Hawte"[13], Sir George "Georgius" Thomas[12], Sir Thomas "The Younger"[11], Sir Thomas "The Elder"[10], Sir Henry[9], Richard Wiat or[8] Wyatt, Geoffrey "Jeoffrey" Wiot or[7] Wiat, Robert or Richard[6] Wiot, William Wiot or[5] Wyot, Adam Wiot or Wyote or[4], Guyott[3], Guyott[2], Captain or Admiral Adam Guyott or[1] Wiot) was born June 11, 1916 in Rowan County, N.C. She married Oilis Clark London January 04, 1948, son of Robert London and Carrie Ownesby.

More About Oilis Clark London:
Fact 1: Served in U.S. military during WWII.

Children of Ruby Eagle and Oilis London are:

1104	i.	Marilyn Jo[24] London, born October 29, 1948.
1105	ii.	Gerald Eugene London, born March 20, 1950.
1106	iii.	Kerry Dean London, born April 24, 1960 in McDowell County, N.C.

766. Moody Van Calvin[23] Eagle (Albert Thadeus[22], Noah Calvin[21], Mary Ann[20] Wyatt, Noah Calvin[19], Thomas "Tommy"[18] Wiatt, Sr. (Wyatt, Wiett), John[17], Henry[16], Richard[15], George[14], Rev. Haute "Haut" "Hawte"[13], Sir George "Georgius" Thomas[12], Sir Thomas "The Younger"[11], Sir Thomas "The Elder"[10], Sir Henry[9], Richard Wiat or[8] Wyatt, Geoffrey "Jeoffrey" Wiot or[7] Wiat, Robert or Richard[6] Wiot, William Wiot or[5] Wyot, Adam Wiot or Wyote or[4], Guyott[3], Guyott[2], Captain or Admiral Adam Guyott or[1] Wiot) was born September 08, 1917 in Rowan County, N.C. He married Mary Louise Alexander April 04, 1942, daughter of James Alexander and Annie Garris.

More About Moody Van Calvin Eagle:
Fact 1: Served in U.S. military during WWII.

Children of Moody Eagle and Mary Alexander are:

+	1107	i.	Jerry Richard[24] Eagle, born November 25, 1943; died April 28, 1984.
+	1108	ii.	Glenn Torrence Eagle, born December 07, 1946.
+	1109	iii.	David Marshall Eagle, born August 08, 1949.
+	1110	iv.	Sue Anne Eagle, born December 16, 1954.

767. James Albert[23] Eagle (Albert Thadeus[22], Noah Calvin[21], Mary Ann[20] Wyatt, Noah Calvin[19], Thomas "Tommy"[18] Wiatt, Sr. (Wyatt, Wiett), John[17], Henry[16], Richard[15], George[14], Rev. Haute "Haut" "Hawte"[13], Sir George "Georgius" Thomas[12], Sir Thomas "The Younger"[11], Sir Thomas "The Elder"[10], Sir Henry[9], Richard Wiat or[8] Wyatt, Geoffrey "Jeoffrey" Wiot or[7] Wiat, Robert or Richard[6] Wiot, William Wiot or[5] Wyot, Adam Wiot or Wyote or[4], Guyott[3], Guyott[2], Captain or Admiral Adam Guyott or[1] Wiot) was born June 20, 1920 in Rowan County, N.C. He married Maxine Cartin September 08, 1945, daughter of Nebraska Cartlin and Maggie Garrick.

Children of James Eagle and Maxine Cartin are:

1111 i. Donald Wayne[24] Eagle, born July 15, 1951 in Sumter, S.C. He married Carol Lee Gulow November 1974.

1112 ii. Terrance Lee Eagle, born July 07, 1954 in Sulfolk, England.

1113 iii. Bruce Edwin Eagle, born April 10, 1956 in Sumter, S.C.

768. Marjorie Lucille[23] Eagle (Albert Thadeus[22], Noah Calvin[21], Mary Ann[20] Wyatt, Noah Calvin[19], Thomas "Tommy"[18] Wiatt, Sr. (Wyatt, Wiett), John[17], Henry[16], Richard[15], George[14], Rev. Haute "Haut" "Hawte"[13], Sir George "Georgius" Thomas[12], Sir Thomas "The Younger"[11], Sir Thomas "The Elder"[10], Sir Henry[9], Richard Wiat or[8] Wyatt, Geoffrey "Jeoffrey" Wiot or[7] Wiat, Robert or Richard[6] Wiot, William Wiot or[5] Wyot, Adam Wiot or Wyote or[4], Guyott[3], Guyott[2], Captain or Admiral Adam Guyott or[1] Wiot) was born July 07, 1923 in Rowan County, N.C. She married George Boger Miller, son of John Miller and Imogene Rudisill.

Children of Marjorie Eagle and George Miller are:

+ 1114 i. Carol Ann[24] Miller, born December 14, 1943 in Rowan County, N.C.

1115 ii. Teresa Gail Miller, born November 07, 1949 in Rowan County, N.C. She married Grady Pickler, Jr. August 29, 1971.

+ 1116 iii. George Albert Miller, born January 30, 1953 in Rowan County, N.C.

769. Ervin Oscar[23] Whitley (Roxie Dora[22] Eagle, Noah Calvin[21], Mary Ann[20] Wyatt, Noah Calvin[19], Thomas "Tommy"[18] Wiatt, Sr. (Wyatt, Wiett), John[17], Henry[16], Richard[15], George[14], Rev. Haute "Haut" "Hawte"[13], Sir George "Georgius" Thomas[12], Sir Thomas "The Younger"[11], Sir Thomas "The Elder"[10], Sir Henry[9], Richard Wiat or[8] Wyatt, Geoffrey "Jeoffrey" Wiot or[7] Wiat, Robert or Richard[6] Wiot, William Wiot or[5] Wyot, Adam Wiot or Wyote or[4], Guyott[3], Guyott[2], Captain or Admiral Adam Guyott or[1] Wiot) was born April 16, 1907 in Stanly County, N.C. He married Sadie Louise Shuping June 06, 1926, daughter of William Shuping and Della Swicegood.

Children of Ervin Whitley and Sadie Shuping are:

1117 i. Margueritte Louise[24] Whitley, born June 10, 1927; died June 10, 1927.

+ 1118 ii. Mary Jo Whitley, born July 18, 1935 in Burke County, N.C.

770. Vertie May[23] Whitley (Roxie Dora[22] Eagle, Noah Calvin[21], Mary Ann[20] Wyatt, Noah Calvin[19], Thomas "Tommy"[18] Wiatt, Sr. (Wyatt, Wiett), John[17], Henry[16], Richard[15], George[14], Rev. Haute "Haut" "Hawte"[13], Sir George "Georgius" Thomas[12], Sir Thomas "The Younger"[11], Sir Thomas "The Elder"[10], Sir Henry[9], Richard Wiat or[8] Wyatt, Geoffrey "Jeoffrey" Wiot or[7] Wiat, Robert or Richard[6] Wiot, William Wiot or[5] Wyot, Adam Wiot or Wyote or[4], Guyott[3], Guyott[2], Captain or Admiral Adam Guyott or[1] Wiot) was born August 16, 1908 in Stanly County, N.C. She married Ralph Howard Johnson, Sr. November 16, 1940, son of Clarence Johnson and Barbara Lake.

Children of Vertie Whitley and Ralph Johnson are:

1119	i.	Ralph Howard[24] Johnson, born June 25, 1942 in Rowan County, N.C.
+ 1120	ii.	Elizabeth May Johnson, born September 23, 1945 in Rowan County, N.C.

772. Marybelle Lucille[23] Whitley (Roxie Dora[22] Eagle, Noah Calvin[21], Mary Ann[20] Wyatt, Noah Calvin[19], Thomas "Tommy"[18] Wiatt, Sr. (Wyatt, Wiett), John[17], Henry[16], Richard[15], George[14], Rev. Haute "Haut" "Hawte"[13], Sir George "Georgius" Thomas[12], Sir Thomas "The Younger"[11], Sir Thomas "The Elder"[10], Sir Henry[9], Richard Wiat or[8] Wyatt, Geoffrey "Jeoffrey" Wiot or[7] Wiat, Robert or Richard[6] Wiot, William Wiot or[5] Wyot, Adam Wiot or Wyote or[4], Guyott[3], Guyott[2], Captain or Admiral Adam Guyott or[1] Wiot) was born October 30, 1911 in Stanly County, N.C. She married Clifford Roderick Penley, Sr. May 23, 1931, son of John Penley and Robertia Ward.

Children of Marybelle Whitley and Clifford Penley are:

+ 1121	i.	Doris Louise[24] Penley, born November 14, 1933 in Rowan County, N.C.
+ 1122	ii.	Clifford Roderick Penley, Jr., born November 02, 1935 in Rowan County, N.C.
+ 1123	iii.	James William Penley, born February 23, 1938 in Alamance County, N.C.

773. Agnes Marie[23] Whitley (Roxie Dora[22] Eagle, Noah Calvin[21], Mary Ann[20] Wyatt, Noah Calvin[19], Thomas "Tommy"[18] Wiatt, Sr. (Wyatt, Wiett), John[17], Henry[16], Richard[15], George[14], Rev. Haute "Haut" "Hawte"[13], Sir George "Georgius" Thomas[12], Sir Thomas "The Younger"[11], Sir Thomas "The Elder"[10], Sir Henry[9], Richard Wiat or[8] Wyatt, Geoffrey "Jeoffrey" Wiot or[7] Wiat, Robert or Richard[6] Wiot, William Wiot or[5] Wyot, Adam Wiot or Wyote or[4], Guyott[3], Guyott[2], Captain or Admiral Adam Guyott or[1] Wiot) was born March 08, 1915 in Stanly County, N.C. She married (1) Robert Lee Hall. She married (2) Rudyard Kipling Fries October 08, 1933, son of Cahnnis Fries and Mittie Poole.

Children of Agnes Whitley and Rudyard Fries are:

+ 1124	i.	Dorothy Jean[24] Fries, born September 26, 1934.
+ 1125	ii.	Terry Gorman Fries, born July 31, 1936.

774. Marvin L.[23] Whitley (Roxie Dora[22] Eagle, Noah Calvin[21], Mary Ann[20] Wyatt, Noah Calvin[19], Thomas "Tommy"[18] Wiatt, Sr. (Wyatt, Wiett), John[17], Henry[16], Richard[15], George[14], Rev. Haute "Haut" "Hawte"[13], Sir George "Georgius" Thomas[12], Sir Thomas "The Younger"[11], Sir Thomas "The Elder"[10], Sir Henry[9], Richard Wiat or[8] Wyatt, Geoffrey "Jeoffrey" Wiot or[7] Wiat, Robert or Richard[6] Wiot, William Wiot or[5] Wyot, Adam Wiot or Wyote or[4], Guyott[3], Guyott[2], Captain or Admiral Adam Guyott or[1] Wiot) was born September 13, 1916 in Stanly County, N.C., and died July 21, 1989. He married Dorothy Jane Setzer July 26, 1952, daughter of Simon Setzer and Lottie Weaver.

Children of Marvin Whitley and Dorothy Setzer are:

1126	i.	Jane Ellen[24] Whitley, born July 13, 1956 in Rowan County, N.C.
1127	ii.	Jeffrey Whitley, born October 10, 1957 in Rowan County, N.C.
+ 1128	iii.	Jody Wayne Whitley, born May 04, 1963 in Rowan County, N.C.

775. Georgia (Georgie) Kathleen[23] Whitley (Roxie Dora[22] Eagle, Noah Calvin[21], Mary Ann[20] Wyatt, Noah Calvin[19], Thomas "Tommy"[18] Wiatt, Sr. (Wyatt, Wiett), John[17], Henry[16], Richard[15], George[14], Rev. Haute "Haut" "Hawte"[13], Sir George "Georgius" Thomas[12], Sir Thomas "The Younger"[11], Sir Thomas "The Elder"[10], Sir Henry[9], Richard Wiat or[8] Wyatt, Geoffrey "Jeoffrey" Wiot or[7] Wiat, Robert or Richard[6] Wiot, William Wiot or[5] Wyot, Adam Wiot or Wyote or[4], Guyott[3], Guyott[2], Captain or Admiral Adam Guyott or[1] Wiot) was born February 22, 1919. She married James Archie Hutchinson April 09, 1939, son of James Hutchinson and Pearl Lentz.

Children of Georgia Whitley and James Hutchinson are:

+ 1129	i.	Cecil Ray[24] Hutchinson, born February 27, 1940 in Rowan County, N.C.
1130	ii.	James Franklin Hutchinson, born June 08, 1961 in Rowan County, N.C.; died March 16, 1977. He married Patsy Caudill June 26, 1971.

776. Robert Clifford[23] Whitley (Roxie Dora[22] Eagle, Noah Calvin[21], Mary Ann[20] Wyatt, Noah Calvin[19], Thomas "Tommy"[18] Wiatt, Sr. (Wyatt, Wiett), John[17], Henry[16], Richard[15], George[14], Rev. Haute "Haut" "Hawte"[13], Sir George "Georgius" Thomas[12], Sir Thomas "The Younger"[11], Sir Thomas "The Elder"[10], Sir Henry[9], Richard Wiat or[8] Wyatt, Geoffrey "Jeoffrey" Wiot or[7] Wiat, Robert or Richard[6] Wiot, William Wiot or[5] Wyot, Adam Wiot or Wyote or[4], Guyott[3], Guyott[2], Captain or Admiral Adam Guyott or[1] Wiot) was born March 21, 1921 in Rowan County, N.C., and died November 16, 1983 in Az. He married Florence Mae Allen, daughter of William Allen and Tina Williams.

Children of Robert Whitley and Florence Allen are:

+ 1131	i.	Victoria Ellen[24] Whitley, born July 30, 1946.
1132	ii.	Robert Allen Whitley, born July 27, 1949.
1133	iii.	Scott Wayne Whitley, born September 27, 1953.
+ 1134	iv.	Kay Gwynn Whitley, born March 19, 1955.

778. John Calvin[23] Whitley (Roxie Dora[22] Eagle, Noah Calvin[21], Mary Ann[20] Wyatt, Noah Calvin[19], Thomas "Tommy"[18] Wiatt, Sr. (Wyatt, Wiett), John[17], Henry[16], Richard[15], George[14], Rev. Haute "Haut" "Hawte"[13], Sir George "Georgius" Thomas[12], Sir Thomas "The Younger"[11], Sir Thomas "The Elder"[10], Sir Henry[9], Richard Wiat or[8] Wyatt, Geoffrey "Jeoffrey" Wiot or[7] Wiat, Robert or Richard[6] Wiot, William Wiot or[5] Wyot, Adam Wiot or Wyote or[4], Guyott[3], Guyott[2], Captain or Admiral Adam Guyott or[1] Wiot) was born May 07, 1926. He married Patsy Jean Wilson October 29, 1948, daughter of Raymon Wilson and Bessie McSwain.

Children of John Whitley and Patsy Wilson are:

+ 1135   i.   John Calvin[24] Whitley, Jr., born February 02, 1951 in Iredell County, N.C.

+ 1136   ii.   Suzanne Amanda Whitley, born June 30, 1953 in Mecklenburg County, N.C.

   1137   iii.   Luann Amelia Whitley, born December 20, 1956.

+ 1138   iv.   Gene Nelson Whitley, born December 27, 1960 in Mecklenburg County, N.C.

781. Helen Marie[23] Jones (Annie Luada[22] Eagle, Noah Calvin[21], Mary Ann[20] Wyatt, Noah Calvin[19], Thomas "Tommy"[18] Wiatt, Sr. (Wyatt, Wiett), John[17], Henry[16], Richard[15], George[14], Rev. Haute "Haut" "Hawte"[13], Sir George "Georgius" Thomas[12], Sir Thomas "The Younger"[11], Sir Thomas "The Elder"[10], Sir Henry[9], Richard Wiat or[8] Wyatt, Geoffrey "Jeoffrey" Wiot or[7] Wiat, Robert or Richard[6] Wiot, William Wiot or[5] Wyot, Adam Wiot or Wyote or[4], Guyott[3], Guyott[2], Captain or Admiral Adam Guyott or[1] Wiot) was born June 06, 1915 in Rowan County, N.C. She married (1) Roland Poindexter Craven, son of Frank Craven and Bertha Kimmons. She married (2) Benton Glover June 09, 1935.

     Children of Helen Jones and Roland Craven are:

   1139   i.   Margaret Elizabeth (Elisbeth)[24] Craven, born December 05, 1949 in Cabarrus County, N.C. She married (1) John Gantt June 27, 1971. She married (2) Richard Lynn Ervin June 15, 1979.

+ 1140   ii.   Sara Jeanette Craven, born March 07, 1951 in Cabarrus County, N.C.

   1141   iii.   Debbie Kay Craven, born November 25, 1953 in Cabarrus County, N.C.

   1142   iv.   Frank McKnight Craven, born May 31, 1956 in Cabarrus County, N.C. He married Debbie Beeker September 11, 1976.

     Child of Helen Jones and Benton Glover is:

+ 1143   i.   Nancy Marie[24] Glover, born May 22, 1938.

782. George Freeland[23] Jones, Jr. (Annie Luada[22] Eagle, Noah Calvin[21], Mary Ann[20] Wyatt, Noah Calvin[19], Thomas "Tommy"[18] Wiatt, Sr. (Wyatt, Wiett), John[17], Henry[16], Richard[15], George[14], Rev. Haute "Haut" "Hawte"[13], Sir George "Georgius" Thomas[12], Sir Thomas "The Younger"[11], Sir Thomas "The Elder"[10], Sir Henry[9], Richard Wiat or[8] Wyatt, Geoffrey "Jeoffrey" Wiot or[7] Wiat, Robert or Richard[6] Wiot, William Wiot or[5] Wyot, Adam Wiot or Wyote or[4], Guyott[3], Guyott[2], Captain or Admiral Adam Guyott or[1] Wiot) was born April 30, 1920 in Rowan County, N.C., and died May 14, 1968. He married Margaret Elizabeth Fortune May 08, 1943, daughter of Thomas Fortune and Bessie Troutman.

     Children of George Jones and Margaret Fortune are:

+ 1144   i.   Ada Elisabeth[24] Jones, born February 25, 1944.

+	1145	ii.	Ruby Mae Jones, born August 07, 1946; died January 09, 1967.
	1146	iii.	Donna Sue Jones, born September 09, 1947. She married (1) Terry Holloway November 30, 1977. She married (2) Larry Thomas Swinson September 06, 1980.
	1147	iv.	George Freeland Jones III, born November 30, 1951; died November 04, 1964.
+	1148	v.	Leonard DeWitt Jones, born March 15, 1953.

783. Ruby May[23] Jones (Annie Luada[22] Eagle, Noah Calvin[21], Mary Ann[20] Wyatt, Noah Calvin[19], Thomas "Tommy"[18] Wiatt, Sr. (Wyatt, Wiett), John[17], Henry[16], Richard[15], George[14], Rev. Haute "Haut" "Hawte"[13], Sir George "Georgius" Thomas[12], Sir Thomas "The Younger"[11], Sir Thomas "The Elder"[10], Sir Henry[9], Richard Wiat or[8] Wyatt, Geoffrey "Jeoffrey" Wiot or[7] Wiat, Robert or Richard[6] Wiot, William Wiot or[5] Wyot, Adam Wiot or Wyote or[4], Guyott[3], Guyott[2], Captain or Admiral Adam Guyott or[1] Wiot) was born September 16, 1923 in Rowan County, N.C., and died March 30, 1926. She married John Thomas Rinehardt.

Child of Ruby Jones and John Rinehardt is:
1149   i.   Craig Harlan[24] Rinehardt.

784. Fred Calvin[23] Safrit (Nannie Manola[22] Eagle, Noah Calvin[21], Mary Ann[20] Wyatt, Noah Calvin[19], Thomas "Tommy"[18] Wiatt, Sr. (Wyatt, Wiett), John[17], Henry[16], Richard[15], George[14], Rev. Haute "Haut" "Hawte"[13], Sir George "Georgius" Thomas[12], Sir Thomas "The Younger"[11], Sir Thomas "The Elder"[10], Sir Henry[9], Richard Wiat or[8] Wyatt, Geoffrey "Jeoffrey" Wiot or[7] Wiat, Robert or Richard[6] Wiot, William Wiot or[5] Wyot, Adam Wiot or Wyote or[4], Guyott[3], Guyott[2], Captain or Admiral Adam Guyott or[1] Wiot) was born March 24, 1930. He married Doris Juanita Watson July 04, 1952, daughter of Robert Watson and Ethel Boyd.

Child of Fred Safrit and Doris Watson is:
1150   i.   Sandra Leigh[24] Safrit, born November 27, 1960.

785. Frances Mildred[23] Eagle (Martin Junius[22], Noah Calvin[21], Mary Ann[20] Wyatt, Noah Calvin[19], Thomas "Tommy"[18] Wiatt, Sr. (Wyatt, Wiett), John[17], Henry[16], Richard[15], George[14], Rev. Haute "Haut" "Hawte"[13], Sir George "Georgius" Thomas[12], Sir Thomas "The Younger"[11], Sir Thomas "The Elder"[10], Sir Henry[9], Richard Wiat or[8] Wyatt, Geoffrey "Jeoffrey" Wiot or[7] Wiat, Robert or Richard[6] Wiot, William Wiot or[5] Wyot, Adam Wiot or Wyote or[4], Guyott[3], Guyott[2], Captain or Admiral Adam Guyott or[1] Wiot) was born October 28, 1918 in Rowan County, N.C. She married Albert Grey Wiliard September 06, 1940, son of Roboh Williard and Bessie Bennett.

Children of Frances Eagle and Albert Wiliard are:
1151   i.   Hugh Grey[24] Wiliard, born April 27, 1944; died December 23, 1967.

More About Hugh Grey Wiliard:
Killed during the Vietnam War.

1152   ii.   Robert Bennett Wiliard, born February 12, 1955. He married Kathryn Joyce Tyler May 30, 1981.

786. Mabel Eloise[23] Eagle (Martin Junius[22], Noah Calvin[21], Mary Ann[20] Wyatt, Noah Calvin[19], Thomas "Tommy"[18] Wiatt, Sr. (Wyatt, Wiett), John[17], Henry[16], Richard[15], George[14], Rev. Haute "Haut" "Hawte"[13], Sir George "Georgius" Thomas[12], Sir Thomas "The Younger"[11], Sir Thomas "The Elder"[10], Sir Henry[9], Richard Wiat or[8] Wyatt, Geoffrey "Jeoffrey" Wiot or[7] Wiat, Robert or Richard[6] Wiot, William Wiot or[5] Wyot, Adam Wiot or Wyote or[4], Guyott[3], Guyott[2], Captain or Admiral Adam Guyott or[1] Wiot) was born August 24, 1920 in Lincoln County, N.C. She married Howard Burwell Abernethy June 08, 1945, son of Hoy Abernathy and Mary Hahn.

Children of Mabel Eagle and Howard Abernethy are:
+   1153   i.   Pamela Jean[24] Abernethy, born May 16, 1947.
+   1154   ii.   Donna Eloise Abernethy, born February 23, 1950.

788. Ronald Alexander[23] Graham (Mattie E.[22] Eagle, Noah Calvin[21], Mary Ann[20] Wyatt, Noah Calvin[19], Thomas "Tommy"[18] Wiatt, Sr. (Wyatt, Wiett), John[17], Henry[16], Richard[15], George[14], Rev. Haute "Haut" "Hawte"[13], Sir George "Georgius" Thomas[12], Sir Thomas "The Younger"[11], Sir Thomas "The Elder"[10], Sir Henry[9], Richard Wiat or[8] Wyatt, Geoffrey "Jeoffrey" Wiot or[7] Wiat, Robert or Richard[6] Wiot, William Wiot or[5] Wyot, Adam Wiot or Wyote or[4], Guyott[3], Guyott[2], Captain or Admiral Adam Guyott or[1] Wiot) was born December 14, 1925 in Rowan County, N.C., and died September 01, 1976. He married Doris Coleen Hillard December 21, 1946, daughter of Ray Hillard and Pauline Cartner.

Child of Ronald Graham and Doris Hillard is:
+   1155   i.   Ronald Dean[24] Graham, born August 30, 1954.

789. Theron Eagle[23] Graham (Mattie E.[22] Eagle, Noah Calvin[21], Mary Ann[20] Wyatt, Noah Calvin[19], Thomas "Tommy"[18] Wiatt, Sr. (Wyatt, Wiett), John[17], Henry[16], Richard[15], George[14], Rev. Haute "Haut" "Hawte"[13], Sir George "Georgius" Thomas[12], Sir Thomas "The Younger"[11], Sir Thomas "The Elder"[10], Sir Henry[9], Richard Wiat or[8] Wyatt, Geoffrey "Jeoffrey" Wiot or[7] Wiat, Robert or Richard[6] Wiot, William Wiot or[5] Wyot, Adam Wiot or Wyote or[4], Guyott[3], Guyott[2], Captain or Admiral Adam Guyott or[1] Wiot) was born October 30, 1933 in Rowan County, N.C. He married Mary E. Dellinger March 28, 1959, daughter of William Dellinger and Zulia F.

Child of Theron Graham and Mary Dellinger is:
1156   i.   John Michael[24] Graham, born March 10, 1963 in Mecklenburg County, N.C.

790. Bobby Eagle[23] Graham (Mattie E.[22] Eagle, Noah Calvin[21], Mary Ann[20] Wyatt, Noah Calvin[19], Thomas "Tommy"[18] Wiatt, Sr. (Wyatt, Wiett), John[17], Henry[16], Richard[15], George[14], Rev. Haute "Haut" "Hawte"[13], Sir George "Georgius" Thomas[12], Sir Thomas "The Younger"[11], Sir Thomas "The Elder"[10], Sir Henry[9], Richard Wiat or[8] Wyatt, Geoffrey "Jeoffrey" Wiot or[7] Wiat, Robert or Richard[6] Wiot, William Wiot or[5] Wyot, Adam Wiot or Wyote or[4], Guyott[3], Guyott[2], Captain or Admiral Adam Guyott or[1] Wiot) was born April 19, 1935 in Rowan County, N.C. He married Etha Christine Bame June 05, 1960, daughter of Adam Bame and Amanda Bean.

> Children of Bobby Graham and Etha Bame are:
>
> 1157 i. Janet Christine[24] Graham, born May 02, 1961 in Gaston County, N.C. She married Nick Reagan McAlister March 23, 1985.
>
> 1158 ii. Karen Leigh Graham, born October 07, 1962 in Forsyth County, N.C. She married John Galloway Harrill June 23, 1984.

792. Thelma Louise[23] Eagle (Carpenter L.[22], Noah Calvin[21], Mary Ann[20] Wyatt, Noah Calvin[19], Thomas "Tommy"[18] Wiatt, Sr. (Wyatt, Wiett), John[17], Henry[16], Richard[15], George[14], Rev. Haute "Haut" "Hawte"[13], Sir George "Georgius" Thomas[12], Sir Thomas "The Younger"[11], Sir Thomas "The Elder"[10], Sir Henry[9], Richard Wiat or[8] Wyatt, Geoffrey "Jeoffrey" Wiot or[7] Wiat, Robert or Richard[6] Wiot, William Wiot or[5] Wyot, Adam Wiot or Wyote or[4], Guyott[3], Guyott[2], Captain or Admiral Adam Guyott or[1] Wiot) was born June 10, 1926 in Rowan County, N.C. She married Edmond Ray Silliman, Jr. February 07, 1947, son of Edmond Silliman and Mary Earnhardt.

> Children of Thelma Eagle and Edmond Silliman are:
>
> + 1159 i. Joyce Marie[24] Silliman, born November 14, 1949 in Rowan County, N.C.
>
> + 1160 ii. Janice Louise Silliman, born January 19, 1953 in Rowan County, N.C.

793. Billy West[23] Eagle (Carpenter L.[22], Noah Calvin[21], Mary Ann[20] Wyatt, Noah Calvin[19], Thomas "Tommy"[18] Wiatt, Sr. (Wyatt, Wiett), John[17], Henry[16], Richard[15], George[14], Rev. Haute "Haut" "Hawte"[13], Sir George "Georgius" Thomas[12], Sir Thomas "The Younger"[11], Sir Thomas "The Elder"[10], Sir Henry[9], Richard Wiat or[8] Wyatt, Geoffrey "Jeoffrey" Wiot or[7] Wiat, Robert or Richard[6] Wiot, William Wiot or[5] Wyot, Adam Wiot or Wyote or[4], Guyott[3], Guyott[2], Captain or Admiral Adam Guyott or[1] Wiot) was born June 04, 1928 in Rowan County, N.C. He married Ethel Marie Martin January 26, 1952, daughter of Floyd Martin and Ethel Wooten.

> Children of Billy Eagle and Ethel Martin are:
>
> + 1161 i. Melba Sue[24] Eagle, born January 21, 1954 in Rowan County, N.C.

+ 1162   ii.   David Kent Eagle, born September 25, 1956 in Rowan County, N.C.

   1163   iii.   Mark William Eagle, born February 14, 1958 in Rowan County, N.C.

794. Carpenter L.[23] Eagle, Jr. (Carpenter L.[22], Noah Calvin[21], Mary Ann[20] Wyatt, Noah Calvin[19], Thomas "Tommy"[18] Wiatt, Sr. (Wyatt, Wiett), John[17], Henry[16], Richard[15], George[14], Rev. Haute "Haut" "Hawte"[13], Sir George "Georgius" Thomas[12], Sir Thomas "The Younger"[11], Sir Thomas "The Elder"[10], Sir Henry[9], Richard Wiat or[8] Wyatt, Geoffrey "Jeoffrey" Wiot or[7] Wiat, Robert or Richard[6] Wiot, William Wiot or[5] Wyot, Adam Wiot or Wyote or[4], Guyott[3], Guyott[2], Captain or Admiral Adam Guyott or[1] Wiot) was born August 25, 1931 in Rowan County, N.C. He married Mona Yvonne Marlowe November 08, 1956, daughter of Dallie Marlowe and Amber Knight.

More About Carpenter L. Eagle, Jr.:
Fact 1: 1951-1955, Served in the U.S. Navy.

More About Mona Yvonne Marlowe:
Fact 1: Worked as a school busdriver for Rowan County Schools, Salisbury, N.C.

   Children of Carpenter Eagle and Mona Marlowe are:
+ 1164   i.   Lisa Lynn[24] Eagle, born August 14, 1960.
   1165   ii.   Laura Lee Eagle, born February 20, 1963. She married Stephen Ralphg Stoner December 17, 1983.

795. Nancy Mae[23] Eagle (Carpenter L.[22], Noah Calvin[21], Mary Ann[20] Wyatt, Noah Calvin[19], Thomas "Tommy"[18] Wiatt, Sr. (Wyatt, Wiett), John[17], Henry[16], Richard[15], George[14], Rev. Haute "Haut" "Hawte"[13], Sir George "Georgius" Thomas[12], Sir Thomas "The Younger"[11], Sir Thomas "The Elder"[10], Sir Henry[9], Richard Wiat or[8] Wyatt, Geoffrey "Jeoffrey" Wiot or[7] Wiat, Robert or Richard[6] Wiot, William Wiot or[5] Wyot, Adam Wiot or Wyote or[4], Guyott[3], Guyott[2], Captain or Admiral Adam Guyott or[1] Wiot) was born July 20, 1935 in Rowan County, N.C. She married Joseph William Watson December 26, 1955, son of Robert Watson and Ethel Boyd.

More About Joseph William Watson:
Fact 1: Served U.S. military during WWII.
Buried Burke Memorial Cemetery, N.C.

   Children of Nancy Eagle and Joseph Watson are:
   1166   i.   Wendy Lynne[24] Watson, born October 20, 1958 in Deridder, La. She married Frankie Phillip Luther.
   1167   ii.   Wanda Kaye Watson, born January 26, 1963 in Bluefield, W.Va. She married Rick Ned May 21, 1983.

796. Glenn Floyd[23] Eagle (Carpenter L.[22], Noah Calvin[21], Mary Ann[20] Wyatt, Noah Calvin[19], Thomas "Tommy"[18] Wiatt, Sr. (Wyatt, Wiett), John[17], Henry[16], Richard[15], George[14], Rev.

Haute "Haut" "Hawte"[13], Sir George "Georgius" Thomas[12], Sir Thomas "The Younger"[11], Sir Thomas "The Elder"[10], Sir Henry[9], Richard Wiat or[8] Wyatt, Geoffrey "Jeoffrey" Wiot or[7] Wiat, Robert or Richard[6] Wiot, William Wiot or[5] Wyot, Adam Wiot or Wyote or[4], Guyott[3], Guyott[2], Captain or Admiral Adam Guyott or[1] Wiot) was born June 10, 1938 in Rowan County, N.C. He married Mary Sue Taylor May 21, 1961, daughter of Adam Taylor and Alice Goodman.

More About Glenn Floyd Eagle:
Fact 1: Served in the U.S. Navy.

Children of Glenn Eagle and Mary Taylor are:

1168	i.	Jeffrey Glenn[24] Eagle, born April 27, 1962 in Rowan County, N.C. He married Lisa Michelle Veach June 04, 1983.
1169	ii.	Kevin Duane Eagle, born February 08, 1965 in Rowan County, N.C.
1170	iii.	Timothy O'Neal Eagle, born July 21, 1971 in Richland County, S.C.

797. Evelyn[23] Eagle (William Armstrong[22], Eli Esau[21], Mary Ann[20] Wyatt, Noah Calvin[19], Thomas "Tommy"[18] Wiatt, Sr. (Wyatt, Wiett), John[17], Henry[16], Richard[15], George[14], Rev. Haute "Haut" "Hawte"[13], Sir George "Georgius" Thomas[12], Sir Thomas "The Younger"[11], Sir Thomas "The Elder"[10], Sir Henry[9], Richard Wiat or[8] Wyatt, Geoffrey "Jeoffrey" Wiot or[7] Wiat, Robert or Richard[6] Wiot, William Wiot or[5] Wyot, Adam Wiot or Wyote or[4], Guyott[3], Guyott[2], Captain or Admiral Adam Guyott or[1] Wiot) was born November 22, 1919 in Rowan County N.C. She married L. Richard Hicks, son of Lee Hicks and Virginia Bruce.

More About L. Richard Hicks:
Buried at Peninsula Memorial Park Cemetery, Newport News, Va.

Children of Evelyn Eagle and L. Hicks are:

+	1171	i.	Carole Jean[24] Hicks, born January 03, 1939.
+	1172	ii.	Sandra Gail Hicks, born May 08, 1943.
+	1173	iii.	Ronald Richard Hicks, born May 29, 1952 in Newport News, Virginia.

798. Everett Wayne[23] Eagle (William Armstrong[22], Eli Esau[21], Mary Ann[20] Wyatt, Noah Calvin[19], Thomas "Tommy"[18] Wiatt, Sr. (Wyatt, Wiett), John[17], Henry[16], Richard[15], George[14], Rev. Haute "Haut" "Hawte"[13], Sir George "Georgius" Thomas[12], Sir Thomas "The Younger"[11], Sir Thomas "The Elder"[10], Sir Henry[9], Richard Wiat or[8] Wyatt, Geoffrey "Jeoffrey" Wiot or[7] Wiat, Robert or Richard[6] Wiot, William Wiot or[5] Wyot, Adam Wiot or Wyote or[4], Guyott[3], Guyott[2], Captain or Admiral Adam Guyott or[1] Wiot) was born October 10, 1921 in Rowan County N.C. He married (1) Jacqueline Deloris Suttle October 31, 1939, daughter of William Suttle and Elizabeth McCowan. He married (2) Judith Smith Hodge September 11, 1976.

More About Everett Wayne Eagle:
Fact 1: 1944-1946, served in U.S. Navy during World War II.

More About Jacqueline Deloris Suttle:
Buried at Providence Church Cemetery, Dare, Va.

Children of Everett Eagle and Jacqueline Suttle are:
+ 1174 i. Everett Wayne[24] Eagle, born January 11, 1943.
+ 1175 ii. Sharon Ann Eagle, born March 14, 1945.
+ 1176 iii. Ronald William Eagle, born November 06, 1949 in Newport News, Virginia.

803. Rena Elizabeth[23] Morgan (Carrie Etta[22] Eagle, Eli Esau[21], Mary Ann[20] Wyatt, Noah Calvin[19], Thomas "Tommy"[18] Wiatt, Sr. (Wyatt, Wiett), John[17], Henry[16], Richard[15], George[14], Rev. Haute "Haut" "Hawte"[13], Sir George "Georgius" Thomas[12], Sir Thomas "The Younger"[11], Sir Thomas "The Elder"[10], Sir Henry[9], Richard Wiat or[8] Wyatt, Geoffrey "Jeoffrey" Wiot or[7] Wiat, Robert or Richard[6] Wiot, William Wiot or[5] Wyot, Adam Wiot or Wyote or[4], Guyott[3], Guyott[2], Captain or Admiral Adam Guyott or[1] Wiot) was born February 20, 1917. She married Frank Ripley Brown, son of Herbert Brown and Annie Nickerson.

Children of Rena Morgan and Frank Brown are:
1177 i. Frank Ripley[24] Brown, Jr., Ph.D., born November 17, 1952 in Mecklenburg County, N.C. He married Ada Gloria MilenKovic November 29, 1980.
1178 ii. Anne Carol Brown, born June 26, 1954.
1179 iii. Rena Elizabeth Brown, born July 13, 1955 in Mecklenburg County, N.C. She married Randy Leigh Richards October 06, 1979.

804. Billie Mae[23] Morgan (Carrie Etta[22] Eagle, Eli Esau[21], Mary Ann[20] Wyatt, Noah Calvin[19], Thomas "Tommy"[18] Wiatt, Sr. (Wyatt, Wiett), John[17], Henry[16], Richard[15], George[14], Rev. Haute "Haut" "Hawte"[13], Sir George "Georgius" Thomas[12], Sir Thomas "The Younger"[11], Sir Thomas "The Elder"[10], Sir Henry[9], Richard Wiat or[8] Wyatt, Geoffrey "Jeoffrey" Wiot or[7] Wiat, Robert or Richard[6] Wiot, William Wiot or[5] Wyot, Adam Wiot or Wyote or[4], Guyott[3], Guyott[2], Captain or Admiral Adam Guyott or[1] Wiot) was born February 13, 1929, and died November 13, 1991. She married Herman Alexander Ribelin July 10, 1949, son of Nathaniel Ribelin and Mary Heilig.

Children of Billie Morgan and Herman Ribelin are:
+ 1180 i. Norman Grey[24] Ribelin, born October 02, 1950.
+ 1181 ii. Kyle Morgan Ribelin, born November 08, 1952.
1182 iii. Connie Ann Ribelin, born July 13, 1954. She married Christopher Turner Jenkins May 28, 1978.

805. Roy David[23] Frick (Emma Dora[22] Eagle, Eli Esau[21], Mary Ann[20] Wyatt, Noah Calvin[19], Thomas "Tommy"[18] Wiatt, Sr. (Wyatt, Wiett), John[17], Henry[16], Richard[15], George[14], Rev. Haute "Haut" "Hawte"[13], Sir George "Georgius" Thomas[12], Sir Thomas "The Younger"[11], Sir Thomas "The Elder"[10], Sir Henry[9], Richard Wiat or[8] Wyatt, Geoffrey "Jeoffrey" Wiot or[7] Wiat, Robert or Richard[6] Wiot, William Wiot or[5] Wyot, Adam Wiot or Wyote or[4], Guyott[3], Guyott[2], Captain or Admiral Adam Guyott or[1] Wiot) was born May 26, 1911. He married Annie Lou Hodge April 25, 1935, daughter of Luther Hodge and Eliza Morgan.

Children of Roy Frick and Annie Hodge are:

	1183	i.	Roy Eugene[24] Frick, born November 07, 1936 in Rowan County, N.C.
+	1184	ii.	Betty Elaine Frick, born July 11, 1938 in Davidson County, N.C.
+	1185	iii.	David Lee Frick, born June 17, 1943 in Stanly County, N.C.
	1186	iv.	Terry Milton Frick, born November 23, 1949 in Stanly County, N.C.

More About Terry Milton Frick:
Fact 1: Served in the U.S. NG.

807. Fannie Lillian[23] Frick (Emma Dora[22] Eagle, Eli Esau[21], Mary Ann[20] Wyatt, Noah Calvin[19], Thomas "Tommy"[18] Wiatt, Sr. (Wyatt, Wiett), John[17], Henry[16], Richard[15], George[14], Rev. Haute "Haut" "Hawte"[13], Sir George "Georgius" Thomas[12], Sir Thomas "The Younger"[11], Sir Thomas "The Elder"[10], Sir Henry[9], Richard Wiat or[8] Wyatt, Geoffrey "Jeoffrey" Wiot or[7] Wiat, Robert or Richard[6] Wiot, William Wiot or[5] Wyot, Adam Wiot or Wyote or[4], Guyott[3], Guyott[2], Captain or Admiral Adam Guyott or[1] Wiot) was born October 25, 1906. She married Jehu Gaither April 01, 1928, son of William Gaither and Sophia Carter.

Children of Fannie Frick and Jehu Gaither are:

+	1187	i.	Lawrence J.[24] Gaither, born July 07, 1929 in Guilford County, N.C.
+	1188	ii.	Wallace Claude Gaither, Sr., born April 25, 1931 in Rowan County, N.C.
+	1189	iii.	Lillian S. Gaither, born March 16, 1936 in Rowan County, N.C.
+	1190	iv.	Emma Deane (Diane?) Gaither, born March 09, 1943 in Davidson County, N.C.

808. Ernest Jones[23] Frick (Emma Dora[22] Eagle, Eli Esau[21], Mary Ann[20] Wyatt, Noah Calvin[19], Thomas "Tommy"[18] Wiatt, Sr. (Wyatt, Wiett), John[17], Henry[16], Richard[15], George[14], Rev. Haute "Haut" "Hawte"[13], Sir George "Georgius" Thomas[12], Sir Thomas "The Younger"[11], Sir Thomas "The Elder"[10], Sir Henry[9], Richard Wiat or[8] Wyatt, Geoffrey "Jeoffrey" Wiot or[7] Wiat, Robert or Richard[6] Wiot, William Wiot or[5] Wyot, Adam Wiot or Wyote or[4], Guyott[3],

Guyott[2], Captain or Admiral Adam Guyott or[1] Wiot) was born July 08, 1908. He married Pauline Vesta Lentz May 18, 1933, daughter of Joseph Lentz and Nancy Morgan.

Children of Ernest Frick and Pauline Lentz are:

+ 1191   i.   Gertrude Frances[24] Frick, born February 24, 1934 in Rowan County, N.C.
+ 1192   ii.   Dora Jeanne Frick, born July 14, 1936 in Rowan County, N.C.
+ 1193   iii.   Gaye Erlene Frick, born October 31, 1940 in Rowan County, N.C.
   1194   iv.   Everette Jones Frick, born May 28, 1943 in Rowan County, N.C. He married Phyllis Jan Blume October 12, 1969.

809.   Ida Nora[23] Frick (Emma Dora[22] Eagle, Eli Esau[21], Mary Ann[20] Wyatt, Noah Calvin[19], Thomas "Tommy"[18] Wiatt, Sr. (Wyatt, Wiett), John[17], Henry[16], Richard[15], George[14], Rev. Haute "Haut" "Hawte"[13], Sir George "Georgius" Thomas[12], Sir Thomas "The Younger"[11], Sir Thomas "The Elder"[10], Sir Henry[9], Richard Wiat or[8] Wyatt, Geoffrey "Jeoffrey" Wiot or[7] Wiat, Robert or Richard[6] Wiot, William Wiot or[5] Wyot, Adam Wiot or Wyote or[4], Guyott[3], Guyott[2], Captain or Admiral Adam Guyott or[1] Wiot) was born September 09, 1909, and died June 14, 1987 in S.C. She married Jesse Stonewall Smith May 08, 1927, son of Garland Smith and Sara Bridges.

Children of Ida Frick and Jesse Smith are:

+ 1195   i.   Mason Gilbert[24] Smith, born May 12, 1936 in York County, S.C.
+ 1196   ii.   Margaret Melba Smith, born March 21, 1928 in Cherokee County, S.C.
+ 1197   iii.   Marshall Thomas Smith, born May 28, 1930 in Cherokee County, S.C.
+ 1198   iv.   Marion (Marian) Louise Smith, born April 07, 1932 in Union County, S.C.
+ 1199   v.   Joseph Milton Smith, born June 12, 1934 in Cherokee County, S.C.
+ 1200   vi.   Mitchell Adron Smith, born April 01, 1938 in York County, S.C.

810.   Geneva Voncelle[23] Morgan (Emma Dora[22] Eagle, Eli Esau[21], Mary Ann[20] Wyatt, Noah Calvin[19], Thomas "Tommy"[18] Wiatt, Sr. (Wyatt, Wiett), John[17], Henry[16], Richard[15], George[14], Rev. Haute "Haut" "Hawte"[13], Sir George "Georgius" Thomas[12], Sir Thomas "The Younger"[11], Sir Thomas "The Elder"[10], Sir Henry[9], Richard Wiat or[8] Wyatt, Geoffrey "Jeoffrey" Wiot or[7] Wiat, Robert or Richard[6] Wiot, William Wiot or[5] Wyot, Adam Wiot or Wyote or[4], Guyott[3], Guyott[2], Captain or Admiral Adam Guyott or[1] Wiot) was born January 17, 1920. She married Charles William Long December 21, 1940, son of Benjamin Long and Mary Smith.

Children of Geneva Morgan and Charles Long are:

+ 1201   i.   Barbara Ann[24] Long, born August 27, 1948.

+ 1202 ii. Betty Sue Long, born October 13, 1951 in Davidson County, N.C.

  1203 iii. Charles William Long, Jr., born October 21, 1959 in Davidson County, N.C.

811. Baxter Monroe[23] Morgan (Emma Dora[22] Eagle, Eli Esau[21], Mary Ann[20] Wyatt, Noah Calvin[19], Thomas "Tommy"[18] Wiatt, Sr. (Wyatt, Wiett), John[17], Henry[16], Richard[15], George[14], Rev. Haute "Haut" "Hawte"[13], Sir George "Georgius" Thomas[12], Sir Thomas "The Younger"[11], Sir Thomas "The Elder"[10], Sir Henry[9], Richard Wiat or[8] Wyatt, Geoffrey "Jeoffrey" Wiot or[7] Wiat, Robert or Richard[6] Wiot, William Wiot or[5] Wyot, Adam Wiot or Wyote or[4], Guyott[3], Guyott[2], Captain or Admiral Adam Guyott or[1] Wiot) was born September 05, 1924. He married Doris R. Russell April 29, 1947, daughter of William Russell and Martha Leazer.

    Children of Baxter Morgan and Doris Russell are:
+   1204 i. George Russell[24] Morgan, born October 08, 1951.

    1205 ii. Jennifer Kay Morgan, born February 15, 1955. She married Barry Bell May 27, 1978.

    1206 iii. Pamela Sue Morgan, born January 21, 1958.

812. Curtis Eli[23] Morgan (Emma Dora[22] Eagle, Eli Esau[21], Mary Ann[20] Wyatt, Noah Calvin[19], Thomas "Tommy"[18] Wiatt, Sr. (Wyatt, Wiett), John[17], Henry[16], Richard[15], George[14], Rev. Haute "Haut" "Hawte"[13], Sir George "Georgius" Thomas[12], Sir Thomas "The Younger"[11], Sir Thomas "The Elder"[10], Sir Henry[9], Richard Wiat or[8] Wyatt, Geoffrey "Jeoffrey" Wiot or[7] Wiat, Robert or Richard[6] Wiot, William Wiot or[5] Wyot, Adam Wiot or Wyote or[4], Guyott[3], Guyott[2], Captain or Admiral Adam Guyott or[1] Wiot) was born February 19, 1925. He married (1) Helen Canup. He married (2) Allie Bane October 25, 1964, daughter of David Bane and Gertha Huffman.

    Children of Curtis Morgan and Helen Canup are:
    1207 i. Betty Sue[24] Morgan, born May 10, 1952 in Rowan County, N.C.; died May 12, 1952 in Rowan County, N.C.

    1208 ii. Peggy Lee Morgan, born April 13, 1955 in Rowan County, N.C.

813. Raymond Emerson[23] Morgan (Emma Dora[22] Eagle, Eli Esau[21], Mary Ann[20] Wyatt, Noah Calvin[19], Thomas "Tommy"[18] Wiatt, Sr. (Wyatt, Wiett), John[17], Henry[16], Richard[15], George[14], Rev. Haute "Haut" "Hawte"[13], Sir George "Georgius" Thomas[12], Sir Thomas "The Younger"[11], Sir Thomas "The Elder"[10], Sir Henry[9], Richard Wiat or[8] Wyatt, Geoffrey "Jeoffrey" Wiot or[7] Wiat, Robert or Richard[6] Wiot, William Wiot or[5] Wyot, Adam Wiot or Wyote or[4], Guyott[3], Guyott[2], Captain or Admiral Adam Guyott or[1] Wiot) was born February 06, 1926. He married Jean Elmeta Hartman October 05, 1947, daughter of Oscar Hartman and Berdie Bame.

    Children of Raymond Morgan and Jean Hartman are:
+   1209 i. Linda Jean[24] Morgan, born October 11, 1948.

+ 1210   ii.   Raymond Emerson Morgan, Jr., born March 07, 1952 in Rowan County, N.C.

814. Pearl Hazelene[23] Morgan (Emma Dora[22] Eagle, Eli Esau[21], Mary Ann[20] Wyatt, Noah Calvin[19], Thomas "Tommy"[18] Wiatt, Sr. (Wyatt, Wiett), John[17], Henry[16], Richard[15], George[14], Rev. Haute "Haut" "Hawte"[13], Sir George "Georgius" Thomas[12], Sir Thomas "The Younger"[11], Sir Thomas "The Elder"[10], Sir Henry[9], Richard Wiat or[8] Wyatt, Geoffrey "Jeoffrey" Wiot or[7] Wiat, Robert or Richard[6] Wiot, William Wiot or[5] Wyot, Adam Wiot or Wyote or[4], Guyott[3], Guyott[2], Captain or Admiral Adam Guyott or[1] Wiot) was born August 09, 1927. She married Louie Alexander Swicegood, Jr., son of Louie Swicegood and Mary Kluttz.

Child of Pearl Morgan and Louie Swicegood is:
1211   i.   Julie Ann[24] Swicegood, born March 04, 1959 in Rowan County, N.C.

815. Harvey Lee[23] Frick (Mary Christine[22] Eagle, Eli Esau[21], Mary Ann[20] Wyatt, Noah Calvin[19], Thomas "Tommy"[18] Wiatt, Sr. (Wyatt, Wiett), John[17], Henry[16], Richard[15], George[14], Rev. Haute "Haut" "Hawte"[13], Sir George "Georgius" Thomas[12], Sir Thomas "The Younger"[11], Sir Thomas "The Elder"[10], Sir Henry[9], Richard Wiat or[8] Wyatt, Geoffrey "Jeoffrey" Wiot or[7] Wiat, Robert or Richard[6] Wiot, William Wiot or[5] Wyot, Adam Wiot or Wyote or[4], Guyott[3], Guyott[2], Captain or Admiral Adam Guyott or[1] Wiot) was born November 15, 1906 in Rowan County, N.C. He married Ruthanna Jaquish December 24, 1933, daughter of Charles Jaquish and Lenora Culver.

More About Harvey Lee Frick:
Fact 1: Served from the U.S. in WWII.

Children of Harvey Frick and Ruthanna Jaquish are:
1212   i.   Thomas Lee Rhyne[24] Frick, born April 24, 1936 in Detroit, Mich.
+ 1213   ii.   Lenora Frick, born April 22, 1943 in Detroit, Mich.

816. Frederick Gideon[23] Frick (Mary Christine[22] Eagle, Eli Esau[21], Mary Ann[20] Wyatt, Noah Calvin[19], Thomas "Tommy"[18] Wiatt, Sr. (Wyatt, Wiett), John[17], Henry[16], Richard[15], George[14], Rev. Haute "Haut" "Hawte"[13], Sir George "Georgius" Thomas[12], Sir Thomas "The Younger"[11], Sir Thomas "The Elder"[10], Sir Henry[9], Richard Wiat or[8] Wyatt, Geoffrey "Jeoffrey" Wiot or[7] Wiat, Robert or Richard[6] Wiot, William Wiot or[5] Wyot, Adam Wiot or Wyote or[4], Guyott[3], Guyott[2], Captain or Admiral Adam Guyott or[1] Wiot) was born December 20, 1907 in Rowan County, N.C., and died July 01, 1962. He married Ada Bell Fink February 25, 1930, daughter of Fitzhugh Fink and Maggie Stirewalt.

More About Frederick Gideon Frick:
Remains are buried at Liberty Methodist Church Cemetery, Rowan County, N.C.

More About Ada Bell Fink:
Remains are buried at Liberty Methodist Church Cemetery, Rowan County, N.C.

Children of Frederick Frick and Ada Fink are:
+   1214   i.   Terrence Frederick[24] Frick, born Abt. December 24, 1935 in Rowan County, N.C.
     1215   ii.   Eric Frick, born October 31, 1947.

817. Nellie Mae[23] Frick (Mary Christine[22] Eagle, Eli Esau[21], Mary Ann[20] Wyatt, Noah Calvin[19], Thomas "Tommy"[18] Wiatt, Sr. (Wyatt, Wiett), John[17], Henry[16], Richard[15], George[14], Rev. Haute "Haut" "Hawte"[13], Sir George "Georgius" Thomas[12], Sir Thomas "The Younger"[11], Sir Thomas "The Elder"[10], Sir Henry[9], Richard Wiat or[8] Wyatt, Geoffrey "Jeoffrey" Wiot or[7] Wiat, Robert or Richard[6] Wiot, William Wiot or[5] Wyot, Adam Wiot or Wyote or[4], Guyott[3], Guyott[2], Captain or Admiral Adam Guyott or[1] Wiot) was born November 07, 1909 in Rowan County, N.C. She married Durant A. Thompson August 06, 1933, son of Edmond Thompson and Ida Poplin.

Child of Nellie Frick and Durant Thompson is:
+   1216   i.   Carolyn Kay[24] Thompson, born February 03, 1939 in Rowan County, N.C.

818. Elizabeth Euver[23] Frick (Mary Christine[22] Eagle, Eli Esau[21], Mary Ann[20] Wyatt, Noah Calvin[19], Thomas "Tommy"[18] Wiatt, Sr. (Wyatt, Wiett), John[17], Henry[16], Richard[15], George[14], Rev. Haute "Haut" "Hawte"[13], Sir George "Georgius" Thomas[12], Sir Thomas "The Younger"[11], Sir Thomas "The Elder"[10], Sir Henry[9], Richard Wiat or[8] Wyatt, Geoffrey "Jeoffrey" Wiot or[7] Wiat, Robert or Richard[6] Wiot, William Wiot or[5] Wyot, Adam Wiot or Wyote or[4], Guyott[3], Guyott[2], Captain or Admiral Adam Guyott or[1] Wiot) was born April 30, 1909 in Rowan County, N.C. She married Luther Adam Fry April 20, 1930, son of Jesse Fry and Eva Parker.

More About Luther Adam Fry:
Remains are buried at the Liberty Methodist Church Cemetery, Rowan County, N.C.

Children of Elizabeth Frick and Luther Fry are:
+   1217   i.   Mary Oma[24] Fry, born November 28, 1930 in Rowan County, N.C.
+   1218   ii.   Jerry Luther Fry, born August 24, 1936 in Rowan County, N.C.

819. Mamie Frances[23] Frick (Mary Christine[22] Eagle, Eli Esau[21], Mary Ann[20] Wyatt, Noah Calvin[19], Thomas "Tommy"[18] Wiatt, Sr. (Wyatt, Wiett), John[17], Henry[16], Richard[15], George[14], Rev. Haute "Haut" "Hawte"[13], Sir George "Georgius" Thomas[12], Sir Thomas "The Younger"[11], Sir Thomas "The Elder"[10], Sir Henry[9], Richard Wiat or[8] Wyatt, Geoffrey "Jeoffrey" Wiot or[7] Wiat, Robert or Richard[6] Wiot, William Wiot or[5] Wyot, Adam Wiot or Wyote or[4], Guyott[3],

Guyott[2], Captain or Admiral Adam Guyott or[1] Wiot) was born September 15, 1913 in Rowan County, N.C., and died December 09, 1983. She married Franklin Monroe Page December 23, 1934, son of Daniel Page and Elizabeth Dunn.

More About Franklin Monroe Page:
Remains are buried next to his wife's remains at Liberty Methodist Church Cemetery, Rowan County, N.C.

Children of Mamie Frick and Franklin Page are:

+ 1219   i.   Nelson Franklin[24] Page, born November 17, 1938 in Rowan County, N.C.
+ 1220   ii.   Lavon Barry Page, born May 28, 1943.

820. Gertrude Esther[23] Frick (Mary Christine[22] Eagle, Eli Esau[21], Mary Ann[20] Wyatt, Noah Calvin[19], Thomas "Tommy"[18] Wiatt, Sr. (Wyatt, Wiett), John[17], Henry[16], Richard[15], George[14], Rev. Haute "Haut" "Hawte"[13], Sir George "Georgius" Thomas[12], Sir Thomas "The Younger"[11], Sir Thomas "The Elder"[10], Sir Henry[9], Richard Wiat or[8] Wyatt, Geoffrey "Jeoffrey" Wiot or[7] Wiat, Robert or Richard[6] Wiot, William Wiot or[5] Wyot, Adam Wiot or Wyote or[4], Guyott[3], Guyott[2], Captain or Admiral Adam Guyott or[1] Wiot) was born October 17, 1917 in Rowan County, N.C. She married Leo J. Misenheimer April 18, 1942, son of Delmar Misenheimer and Carrie Trexler.

More About Leo J. Misenheimer:
Fact 1: Served in the U.S. Air Force.

Children of Gertrude Frick and Leo Misenheimer are:

+ 1221   i.   Leo Gary[24] Misenheimer, born October 26, 1944 in Mecklenburg County, N.C.
   1222   ii.   Stephen Misenheimer, born November 29, 1949 in Fairfax County, Va,. He married Carolyn Ayers.
   1223   iii.   Mary Christina Misenheimer, born December 26, 1956 in Md.

822. Norman Grey[23] Frick (Mary Christine[22] Eagle, Eli Esau[21], Mary Ann[20] Wyatt, Noah Calvin[19], Thomas "Tommy"[18] Wiatt, Sr. (Wyatt, Wiett), John[17], Henry[16], Richard[15], George[14], Rev. Haute "Haut" "Hawte"[13], Sir George "Georgius" Thomas[12], Sir Thomas "The Younger"[11], Sir Thomas "The Elder"[10], Sir Henry[9], Richard Wiat or[8] Wyatt, Geoffrey "Jeoffrey" Wiot or[7] Wiat, Robert or Richard[6] Wiot, William Wiot or[5] Wyot, Adam Wiot or Wyote or[4], Guyott[3], Guyott[2], Captain or Admiral Adam Guyott or[1] Wiot) was born May 06, 1926. He married Annie Geraldine Maness January 17, 1952, daughter of Quincy Maness and Georgia Brown.

More About Norman Grey Frick:
Fact 1: 1944-1953, Served in the U.S. Marine Corps. in WWII.

Children of Norman Frick and Annie Maness are:

+ 1224   i.   Christina Jeanette[24] Frick, born August 05, 1952 in Rowan County, N.C.

  1225   ii.   Jeffry Frick, born December 10, 1954 in Rowan County, N.C.; died March 28, 1955.

  1226   iii.   Tad Grey Frick, born February 22, 1956 in Rowan County, N.C. He married Janice Kathryn Brady July 20, 1975.

+ 1227   iv.   Roger Frick, born March 28, 1958 in Rowan County, N.C.

  1228   v.   Andrew Frick, born in Rowan County, N.C.

823.   Lucille[23] Eagle (Grover Victor[22], Eli Esau[21], Mary Ann[20] Wyatt, Noah Calvin[19], Thomas "Tommy"[18] Wiatt, Sr. (Wyatt, Wiett), John[17], Henry[16], Richard[15], George[14], Rev. Haute "Haut" "Hawte"[13], Sir George "Georgius" Thomas[12], Sir Thomas "The Younger"[11], Sir Thomas "The Elder"[10], Sir Henry[9], Richard Wiat or[8] Wyatt, Geoffrey "Jeoffrey" Wiot or[7] Wiat, Robert or Richard[6] Wiot, William Wiot or[5] Wyot, Adam Wiot or Wyote or[4], Guyott[3], Guyott[2], Captain or Admiral Adam Guyott or[1] Wiot) was born August 14, 1912 in Rowan County N.C. She married Charles M. Baker, Jr. August 11, 1931, son of Charles Baker and Senora Todd.

More About Lucille Eagle:
Remains are buried at Rowan Memorial Park Cemetery, Rowan County, N.C.

More About Charles M. Baker, Jr.:
Remains are buried at Rowan Memorial Park Cemetery, Rowan County, N.C.

Children of Lucille Eagle and Charles Baker are:

  1229   i.   Richard[24] Baker, born September 10, 1935 in Rowan County N.C.; died May 05, 1938.

  1230   ii.   Mary Ruth Baker, born February 24, 1938 in Rowan County N.C. She married Harry Brown January 01, 1960.

+ 1231   iii.   Alice Faye Baker, born May 11, 1940 in Rowan County N.C.

824.   Joseph[23] Eagle (Grover Victor[22], Eli Esau[21], Mary Ann[20] Wyatt, Noah Calvin[19], Thomas "Tommy"[18] Wiatt, Sr. (Wyatt, Wiett), John[17], Henry[16], Richard[15], George[14], Rev. Haute "Haut" "Hawte"[13], Sir George "Georgius" Thomas[12], Sir Thomas "The Younger"[11], Sir Thomas "The Elder"[10], Sir Henry[9], Richard Wiat or[8] Wyatt, Geoffrey "Jeoffrey" Wiot or[7] Wiat, Robert or Richard[6] Wiot, William Wiot or[5] Wyot, Adam Wiot or Wyote or[4], Guyott[3], Guyott[2], Captain or Admiral Adam Guyott or[1] Wiot) was born July 23, 1914, and died November 20, 1969. He married Weldon Whirlow, daughter of Joseph Whirlow and Virginia Brown.

More About Joseph Eagle:
Remains are buried at the Rowan National Cemetery, Rowan County, N.C.

Child of Joseph Eagle and Weldon Whirlow is:

+   1232   i.   Joseph Victor[24] Eagle, born March 26, 1935.

825.   Pearl[23] Eagle (Grover Victor[22], Eli Esau[21], Mary Ann[20] Wyatt, Noah Calvin[19], Thomas "Tommy"[18] Wiatt, Sr. (Wyatt, Wiett), John[17], Henry[16], Richard[15], George[14], Rev. Haute "Haut" "Hawte"[13], Sir George "Georgius" Thomas[12], Sir Thomas "The Younger"[11], Sir Thomas "The Elder"[10], Sir Henry[9], Richard Wiat or[8] Wyatt, Geoffrey "Jeoffrey" Wiot or[7] Wiat, Robert or Richard[6] Wiot, William Wiot or[5] Wyot, Adam Wiot or Wyote or[4], Guyott[3], Guyott[2], Captain or Admiral Adam Guyott or[1] Wiot) was born August 23, 1916. She married Roy Howard Campbell August 27, 1932.

Children of Pearl Eagle and Roy Campbell are:

+   1233   i.   Roy Howard[24] Campbell, Jr, born March 11, 1935.
+   1234   ii.   Barbara Annette Campbell, born April 19, 1937.

826.   Irene[23] Eagle (Grover Victor[22], Eli Esau[21], Mary Ann[20] Wyatt, Noah Calvin[19], Thomas "Tommy"[18] Wiatt, Sr. (Wyatt, Wiett), John[17], Henry[16], Richard[15], George[14], Rev. Haute "Haut" "Hawte"[13], Sir George "Georgius" Thomas[12], Sir Thomas "The Younger"[11], Sir Thomas "The Elder"[10], Sir Henry[9], Richard Wiat or[8] Wyatt, Geoffrey "Jeoffrey" Wiot or[7] Wiat, Robert or Richard[6] Wiot, William Wiot or[5] Wyot, Adam Wiot or Wyote or[4], Guyott[3], Guyott[2], Captain or Admiral Adam Guyott or[1] Wiot) was born January 11, 1920. She married Thomas H. Webb October 24, 1937, son of David Webb and Laura Innis.

Child of Irene Eagle and Thomas Webb is:

1235   i.   Thomas Michael[24] Webb, born January 25, 1950. He married Trudy Eakins August 11, 1978.

827.   Frances[23] Eagle (Grover Victor[22], Eli Esau[21], Mary Ann[20] Wyatt, Noah Calvin[19], Thomas "Tommy"[18] Wiatt, Sr. (Wyatt, Wiett), John[17], Henry[16], Richard[15], George[14], Rev. Haute "Haut" "Hawte"[13], Sir George "Georgius" Thomas[12], Sir Thomas "The Younger"[11], Sir Thomas "The Elder"[10], Sir Henry[9], Richard Wiat or[8] Wyatt, Geoffrey "Jeoffrey" Wiot or[7] Wiat, Robert or Richard[6] Wiot, William Wiot or[5] Wyot, Adam Wiot or Wyote or[4], Guyott[3], Guyott[2], Captain or Admiral Adam Guyott or[1] Wiot) was born November 07, 1925. She married William Woodford February 03, 1946, son of William Woodford and Irma Meder.

Children of Frances Eagle and William Woodford are:

1236   i.   Stephen W.[24] Woodford, born July 24, 1950 in Georgia. He married Carol F. Roberts April 07, 1973.
1237   ii.   Daniel Lynn Woodford, born May 31, 1955 in Atlanta, Ga.

828.   Joseph Charles[23] Eagle (Joseph Calvin[22], Eli Esau[21], Mary Ann[20] Wyatt, Noah Calvin[19], Thomas "Tommy"[18] Wiatt, Sr. (Wyatt, Wiett), John[17], Henry[16], Richard[15], George[14], Rev. Haute "Haut" "Hawte"[13], Sir George "Georgius" Thomas[12], Sir Thomas "The Younger"[11], Sir

Thomas "The Elder"[10], Sir Henry[9], Richard Wiat or[8] Wyatt, Geoffrey "Jeoffrey" Wiot or[7] Wiat, Robert or Richard[6] Wiot, William Wiot or[5] Wyot, Adam Wiot or Wyote or[4], Guyott[3], Guyott[2], Captain or Admiral Adam Guyott or[1] Wiot) was born December 03, 1916 in Mecklenburg County, N.C. He married Etta Maguerite Holshouser, daughter of Lewis Holshouser and Margie Lylery.

Children of Joseph Eagle and Etta Holshouser are:

| | 1238 | i. | Joseph Charles[24] Eagle, Jr., born June 24, 1936; died June 15, 1938. |

More About Joseph Charles Eagle, Jr.:
Remains are buried at Saint Peters Lutheran Church Cemetery, Rowan County, N.C.

+	1239	ii.	Harold Gene Eagle, born June 27, 1937.
+	1240	iii.	Carl Ray Eagle, born May 09, 1939.
+	1241	iv.	Jerry Lee Eagle, born December 08, 1940.
+	1242	v.	Rebecca Jane Eagle, born November 15, 1943.
	1243	vi.	Barbara Ann Eagle, born January 16, 1956.

829. Mabel Inez[23] Eagle (Joseph Calvin[22], Eli Esau[21], Mary Ann[20] Wyatt, Noah Calvin[19], Thomas "Tommy"[18] Wiatt, Sr. (Wyatt, Wiett), John[17], Henry[16], Richard[15], George[14], Rev. Haute "Haut" "Hawte"[13], Sir George "Georgius" Thomas[12], Sir Thomas "The Younger"[11], Sir Thomas "The Elder"[10], Sir Henry[9], Richard Wiat or[8] Wyatt, Geoffrey "Jeoffrey" Wiot or[7] Wiat, Robert or Richard[6] Wiot, William Wiot or[5] Wyot, Adam Wiot or Wyote or[4], Guyott[3], Guyott[2], Captain or Admiral Adam Guyott or[1] Wiot) was born May 29, 1919. She married Bunch Harding Fraley June 29, 1946, son of John Fraley and Ann Lanier.

More About Bunch Harding Fraley:
Fact 1: ROC in WWII.

Children of Mabel Eagle and Bunch Fraley are:

| + | 1244 | i. | Sandra Kay[24] Fraley, born December 18, 1947. |
| | 1245 | ii. | David Wendell Fraley, born November 27, 1951. He married Patricia Vutter Booths January 16, 1976. |

830. Maurice Edison[23] Eagle, Sr. (Joseph Calvin[22], Eli Esau[21], Mary Ann[20] Wyatt, Noah Calvin[19], Thomas "Tommy"[18] Wiatt, Sr. (Wyatt, Wiett), John[17], Henry[16], Richard[15], George[14], Rev. Haute "Haut" "Hawte"[13], Sir George "Georgius" Thomas[12], Sir Thomas "The Younger"[11], Sir Thomas "The Elder"[10], Sir Henry[9], Richard Wiat or[8] Wyatt, Geoffrey "Jeoffrey" Wiot or[7] Wiat, Robert or Richard[6] Wiot, William Wiot or[5] Wyot, Adam Wiot or Wyote or[4], Guyott[3], Guyott[2], Captain or Admiral Adam Guyott or[1] Wiot) was born September 12, 1921 in USA, and died December 23, 1986. He married Margaret Mozelle Price August 27, 1945, daughter of Millard Price and Hettie Witherspoon.

More About Maurice Edison Eagle, Sr.:
Remains are buried in the Matthews Church Cemetery, Salisbury, Liberty section of Rowan County, N.C.

    Children of Maurice Eagle and Margaret Price are:
+   1246   i.   Maurice Edison[24] Eagle, Jr., born July 22, 1946.
+   1247   ii.   Kenneth Michael Eagle, born August 20, 1948.

831. Edna Elizabeth[23] Eagle (Walter Eli[22], Eli Esau[21], Mary Ann[20] Wyatt, Noah Calvin[19], Thomas "Tommy"[18] Wiatt, Sr. (Wyatt, Wiett), John[17], Henry[16], Richard[15], George[14], Rev. Haute "Haut" "Hawte"[13], Sir George "Georgius" Thomas[12], Sir Thomas "The Younger"[11], Sir Thomas "The Elder"[10], Sir Henry[9], Richard Wiat or[8] Wyatt, Geoffrey "Jeoffrey" Wiot or[7] Wiat, Robert or Richard[6] Wiot, William Wiot or[5] Wyot, Adam Wiot or Wyote or[4], Guyott[3], Guyott[2], Captain or Admiral Adam Guyott or[1] Wiot) was born June 19, 1915 in Rowan County N.C. She married William J. Edwards June 12, 1937, son of Walter Edwards and Lena.

    More About William J. Edwards:
Remains are buried at the Oakdale Cemetery in Statesville, Iredell County, N.C.

    Children of Edna Eagle and William Edwards are:
     1248   i.   Patrica Ann[24] Edwards, born June 15, 1939. She married Darley Sean Montgomery July 18, 1955.
     1249   ii.   William Joseph Edwards, born January 11, 1941. He married Linda Solomon August 02, 1963.
     1250   iii.   Larry Glenn Edwards, born March 02, 1944. He married Sally Dobson March 16, 1973.

832. Reba Odessa[23] Eagle (Walter Eli[22], Eli Esau[21], Mary Ann[20] Wyatt, Noah Calvin[19], Thomas "Tommy"[18] Wiatt, Sr. (Wyatt, Wiett), John[17], Henry[16], Richard[15], George[14], Rev. Haute "Haut" "Hawte"[13], Sir George "Georgius" Thomas[12], Sir Thomas "The Younger"[11], Sir Thomas "The Elder"[10], Sir Henry[9], Richard Wiat or[8] Wyatt, Geoffrey "Jeoffrey" Wiot or[7] Wiat, Robert or Richard[6] Wiot, William Wiot or[5] Wyot, Adam Wiot or Wyote or[4], Guyott[3], Guyott[2], Captain or Admiral Adam Guyott or[1] Wiot) was born September 10, 1916 in Rowan County N.C. She married Myron Luther Cauble June 14, 1941, son of Luther Cauble and Pearl Safrit.

    Children of Reba Eagle and Myron Cauble are:
     1251   i.   Myron Luther[24] Cauble, Jr., born December 25, 1945. He married Diana Seitz August 25, 1973.
     1252   ii.   Ronald Dean Cauble, born January 30, 1947 in Rowan County N.C.

833. Wade Preston[23] Eagle (Walter Eli[22], Eli Esau[21], Mary Ann[20] Wyatt, Noah Calvin[19], Thomas "Tommy"[18] Wiatt, Sr. (Wyatt, Wiett), John[17], Henry[16], Richard[15], George[14], Rev.

Haute "Haut" "Hawte"[13], Sir George "Georgius" Thomas[12], Sir Thomas "The Younger"[11], Sir Thomas "The Elder"[10], Sir Henry[9], Richard Wiat or[8] Wyatt, Geoffrey "Jeoffrey" Wiot or[7] Wiat, Robert or Richard[6] Wiot, William Wiot or[5] Wyot, Adam Wiot or Wyote or[4], Guyott[3], Guyott[2], Captain or Admiral Adam Guyott or[1] Wiot) was born February 04, 1920 in Rowan County N.C. He married Ruth Elizabeth Cummings September 26, 1946, daughter of Cyrus Cummings and Arnie Morgan.

More About Wade Preston Eagle:
Fact 1: 1941, United States Army Captain during World War II.

Child of Wade Eagle and Ruth Cummings is:
1253   i.   Wade Hampton[24] Eagle, born January 22, 1943 in Headland, A/A; died June 02, 1945 in buried in Edgewood, Maryland.

835. James Donald[23] Eagle (Walter Eli[22], Eli Esau[21], Mary Ann[20] Wyatt, Noah Calvin[19], Thomas "Tommy"[18] Wiatt, Sr. (Wyatt, Wiett), John[17], Henry[16], Richard[15], George[14], Rev. Haute "Haut" "Hawte"[13], Sir George "Georgius" Thomas[12], Sir Thomas "The Younger"[11], Sir Thomas "The Elder"[10], Sir Henry[9], Richard Wiat or[8] Wyatt, Geoffrey "Jeoffrey" Wiot or[7] Wiat, Robert or Richard[6] Wiot, William Wiot or[5] Wyot, Adam Wiot or Wyote or[4], Guyott[3], Guyott[2], Captain or Admiral Adam Guyott or[1] Wiot) was born March 07, 1934 in Rowan County N.C. He married Doris Jean Stiller June 30, 1957, daughter of John Stiller and Beatrice Baity.

More About James Donald Eagle:
Fact 1: 1955-1975, served in the U.S. Air Force.

Children of James Eagle and Doris Stiller are:
1254   i.   James David[24] Eagle, born August 20, 1958 in Marietta, Georgia.
1255   ii.   Jean Elizabeth Eagle, born April 15, 1960 in Marietta, Georgia.
1256   iii. John Christopher Eagle, born July 09, 1963 in Okinawa, Ryuku Islands, Japan.

836. Esther Viola[23] Morgan (Annie Zenobia[22] Eagle, Eli Esau[21], Mary Ann[20] Wyatt, Noah Calvin[19], Thomas "Tommy"[18] Wiatt, Sr. (Wyatt, Wiett), John[17], Henry[16], Richard[15], George[14], Rev. Haute "Haut" "Hawte"[13], Sir George "Georgius" Thomas[12], Sir Thomas "The Younger"[11], Sir Thomas "The Elder"[10], Sir Henry[9], Richard Wiat or[8] Wyatt, Geoffrey "Jeoffrey" Wiot or[7] Wiat, Robert or Richard[6] Wiot, William Wiot or[5] Wyot, Adam Wiot or Wyote or[4], Guyott[3], Guyott[2], Captain or Admiral Adam Guyott or[1] Wiot) was born in Rowan County N.C., and died March 25, 1983. She married Martin Franklin Iddings.

More About Esther Viola Morgan:
Remains are buried in the Rowan Memorial Park Cemetery, Salisbury, N.C.

Children of Esther Morgan and Martin Iddings are:

     1257   i.   Jerry Martin[24] Iddings.

+ 1258   ii.   Kenneth Paul Iddings.

+ 1259   iii.   Trudy Francis Iddings.

837. Reather Armstrong[23] Morgan (Annie Zenobia[22] Eagle, Eli Esau[21], Mary Ann[20] Wyatt, Noah Calvin[19], Thomas "Tommy"[18] Wiatt, Sr. (Wyatt, Wiett), John[17], Henry[16], Richard[15], George[14], Rev. Haute "Haut" "Hawte"[13], Sir George "Georgius" Thomas[12], Sir Thomas "The Younger"[11], Sir Thomas "The Elder"[10], Sir Henry[9], Richard Wiat or[8] Wyatt, Geoffrey "Jeoffrey" Wiot or[7] Wiat, Robert or Richard[6] Wiot, William Wiot or[5] Wyot, Adam Wiot or Wyote or[4], Guyott[3], Guyott[2], Captain or Admiral Adam Guyott or[1] Wiot) was born in Rowan County N.C., and died April 15, 1974. He married Rozelle Pickard.

More About Reather Armstrong Morgan:
Remains are buried in the Rowan Memorial Park Cemetery, Salisbury, N.C.

More About Rozelle Pickard:
Remains are buried in the Rowan Memorial Park Cemetery, Salisbury, N.C.

Children of Reather Morgan and Rozelle Pickard are:

     1260   i.   Timothy Paul[24] Morgan.

+ 1261   ii.   Phillip Armstrong Morgan.

838. William Henry[23] Morgan (Annie Zenobia[22] Eagle, Eli Esau[21], Mary Ann[20] Wyatt, Noah Calvin[19], Thomas "Tommy"[18] Wiatt, Sr. (Wyatt, Wiett), John[17], Henry[16], Richard[15], George[14], Rev. Haute "Haut" "Hawte"[13], Sir George "Georgius" Thomas[12], Sir Thomas "The Younger"[11], Sir Thomas "The Elder"[10], Sir Henry[9], Richard Wiat or[8] Wyatt, Geoffrey "Jeoffrey" Wiot or[7] Wiat, Robert or Richard[6] Wiot, William Wiot or[5] Wyot, Adam Wiot or Wyote or[4], Guyott[3], Guyott[2], Captain or Admiral Adam Guyott or[1] Wiot) was born in Rowan County N.C. He married Faye Hartmen.

Children of William Morgan and Faye Hartmen are:

1262   i.   Debra[24] Morgan.

1263   ii.   William Henry Morgan, Jr.

1264   iii.   Sherry Morgan.

839. Dorothy Ann[23] Morgan (Annie Zenobia[22] Eagle, Eli Esau[21], Mary Ann[20] Wyatt, Noah Calvin[19], Thomas "Tommy"[18] Wiatt, Sr. (Wyatt, Wiett), John[17], Henry[16], Richard[15], George[14], Rev. Haute "Haut" "Hawte"[13], Sir George "Georgius" Thomas[12], Sir Thomas "The Younger"[11], Sir Thomas "The Elder"[10], Sir Henry[9], Richard Wiat or[8] Wyatt, Geoffrey "Jeoffrey" Wiot or[7] Wiat, Robert or Richard[6] Wiot, William Wiot or[5] Wyot, Adam Wiot or Wyote or[4], Guyott[3], Guyott[2], Captain or Admiral Adam Guyott or[1] Wiot) was born August 14, 1928 in Bilozi, Missouri. She married Harold Ray Hutchins, son of William Hutchins and Bertha Taylor.

More About Harold Ray Hutchins:

Fact 1: Served in the U.S. Navy during World War II.

Children of Dorothy Morgan and Harold Hutchins are:

+   1265   i.   Bonnie Carol[24] Hutchins, born December 25, 1948 in Rowan County N.C.

    1266   ii.   Robert Harold Hutchins, born April 18, 1950 in Rowan County N.C. He married Seldon Deborah Pigford.

    1267   iii.   Patricia Ann Hutchins, born December 31, 1951 in Rowan County N.C. She married Robert Thomas Wirtel.

    1268   iv.   David Ray Hutchins, born August 26, 1953 in Rowan County N.C. He married Deborah Jean Huneycutt.

    1269   v.   Randall Morgan Hutchins, born November 13, 1955 in Rowan County N.C. He married Tracy Jo Cope August 14, 1978.

840.   Rachel Lee[23] Morgan (Annie Zenobia[22] Eagle, Eli Esau[21], Mary Ann[20] Wyatt, Noah Calvin[19], Thomas "Tommy"[18] Wiatt, Sr. (Wyatt, Wiett), John[17], Henry[16], Richard[15], George[14], Rev. Haute "Haut" "Hawte"[13], Sir George "Georgius" Thomas[12], Sir Thomas "The Younger"[11], Sir Thomas "The Elder"[10], Sir Henry[9], Richard Wiat or[8] Wyatt, Geoffrey "Jeoffrey" Wiot or[7] Wiat, Robert or Richard[6] Wiot, William Wiot or[5] Wyot, Adam Wiot or Wyote or[4], Guyott[3], Guyott[2], Captain or Admiral Adam Guyott or[1] Wiot) was born in Rowan County N.C. She married (1) Roy Trexler Smith. She married (2) Unknown.

Child of Rachel Morgan and Roy Smith is:

    1270   i.   Gerald Wayne[24] Smith.

Children of Rachel Morgan and Unknown are:

    1271   i.   Phillip Wayne[24] Unknown.

    1272   ii.   Richard Unknown.

    1273   iii.   Gary Lee Unknown, born August 26, 1954.

    1274   iv.   Teresa Ann Unknown.

841.   William Eli[23] Jackson (Ida Lou[22] Eagle, Eli Esau[21], Mary Ann[20] Wyatt, Noah Calvin[19], Thomas "Tommy"[18] Wiatt, Sr. (Wyatt, Wiett), John[17], Henry[16], Richard[15], George[14], Rev. Haute "Haut" "Hawte"[13], Sir George "Georgius" Thomas[12], Sir Thomas "The Younger"[11], Sir Thomas "The Elder"[10], Sir Henry[9], Richard Wiat or[8] Wyatt, Geoffrey "Jeoffrey" Wiot or[7] Wiat, Robert or Richard[6] Wiot, William Wiot or[5] Wyot, Adam Wiot or Wyote or[4], Guyott[3], Guyott[2], Captain or Admiral Adam Guyott or[1] Wiot) was born November 07, 1912 in Rowan County, N.C. He married Thelma Louise Monroe December 14, 1935, daughter of Henry Monroe and Wife.

Children of William Jackson and Thelma Monroe are:

+   1275   i.   Nancy Ann[24] Jackson, born December 05, 1936 in Rowan County, N.C.

+ 1276 ii. Jimmy Monroe Jackson, born October 13, 1939 in Rowan County, N.C.

+ 1277 iii. Phyllis Jean Jackson, born July 01, 1943 in Rowan County, N.C.

843. Manteo Monroe[23] Jackson (Ida Lou[22] Eagle, Eli Esau[21], Mary Ann[20] Wyatt, Noah Calvin[19], Thomas "Tommy"[18] Wiatt, Sr. (Wyatt, Wiett), John[17], Henry[16], Richard[15], George[14], Rev. Haute "Haut" "Hawte"[13], Sir George "Georgius" Thomas[12], Sir Thomas "The Younger"[11], Sir Thomas "The Elder"[10], Sir Henry[9], Richard Wiat or[8] Wyatt, Geoffrey "Jeoffrey" Wiot or[7] Wiat, Robert or Richard[6] Wiot, William Wiot or[5] Wyot, Adam Wiot or Wyote or[4], Guyott[3], Guyott[2], Captain or Admiral Adam Guyott or[1] Wiot) was born January 12, 1916 in Rowan County, N.C. He married Odessa Estelle Waller June 04, 1938.

Children of Manteo Jackson and Odessa Waller are:
+ 1278 i. Rodney Frederick[24] Jackson, born April 04, 1939 in Rowan County, N.C.

1279 ii. Ginger Dare Jackson, born March 09, 1948 in Rowan County, N.C. She married (1) Dennis K. Vicent August 25, 1970. She married (2) James Wesley Ingold III September 03, 1977.

+ 1280 iii. Melody Jane Jackson, born June 08, 1948 in Rowan County, N.C.

844. John David[23] Jackson (Ida Lou[22] Eagle, Eli Esau[21], Mary Ann[20] Wyatt, Noah Calvin[19], Thomas "Tommy"[18] Wiatt, Sr. (Wyatt, Wiett), John[17], Henry[16], Richard[15], George[14], Rev. Haute "Haut" "Hawte"[13], Sir George "Georgius" Thomas[12], Sir Thomas "The Younger"[11], Sir Thomas "The Elder"[10], Sir Henry[9], Richard Wiat or[8] Wyatt, Geoffrey "Jeoffrey" Wiot or[7] Wiat, Robert or Richard[6] Wiot, William Wiot or[5] Wyot, Adam Wiot or Wyote or[4], Guyott[3], Guyott[2], Captain or Admiral Adam Guyott or[1] Wiot) was born October 10, 1917 in Rowan County, N.C. He married Virgie Juanita Gallimore February 25, 1942, daughter of Edmond Gallimore and Lillie Dunning.

More About John David Jackson:
Fact 1: Served four years in the U.S. military.

Children of John Jackson and Virgie Gallimore are:
+ 1281 i. Linda Carolyn[24] Jackson, born March 23, 1942 in Randolph County, N.C.

1282 ii. Eddie Lawrence Jackson, born June 14, 1948. He married Cathy Diana Hunt.

1283 iii. Tony Eugene Jackson, born March 14, 1953 in Davidson County, N.C.

846. Ralph Adolphus[23] Jackson (Ida Lou[22] Eagle, Eli Esau[21], Mary Ann[20] Wyatt, Noah Calvin[19], Thomas "Tommy"[18] Wiatt, Sr. (Wyatt, Wiett), John[17], Henry[16], Richard[15], George[14], Rev. Haute "Haut" "Hawte"[13], Sir George "Georgius" Thomas[12], Sir Thomas "The Younger"[11],

Sir Thomas "The Elder"[10], Sir Henry[9], Richard Wiat or[8] Wyatt, Geoffrey "Jeoffrey" Wiot or[7] Wiat, Robert or Richard[6] Wiot, William Wiot or[5] Wyot, Adam Wiot or Wyote or[4], Guyott[3], Guyott[2], Captain or Admiral Adam Guyott or[1] Wiot) was born July 16, 1922 in Rowan County, N.C. He married Mary Elizabeth Beaver August 09, 1942, daughter of Ernest Beaver and Carrie Webb.

More About Ralph Adolphus Jackson:
Fact 1: 1942-1947, served in the U.S. military.

Children of Ralph Jackson and Mary Beaver are:

+ 1284   i.   Ronald Ralph[24] Jackson, born February 19, 1944 in Abilene, Tx.
+ 1285   ii.   Joyce Elizabeth Jackson, born June 28, 1945.
+ 1286   iii.   Thomas Lee Jackson, born 1947.
+ 1287   iv.   Robert Ray Jackson, born July 31, 1949.
+ 1288   v.   Randy Steven Jackson, born December 16, 1950 in Rowan County N.C.
+ 1289   vi.   Ernest John Jackson, born December 18, 1952 in Rowan County, N.C.

847. Louie Phenix[23] Jackson (Ida Lou[22] Eagle, Eli Esau[21], Mary Ann[20] Wyatt, Noah Calvin[19], Thomas "Tommy"[18] Wiatt, Sr. (Wyatt, Wiett), John[17], Henry[16], Richard[15], George[14], Rev. Haute "Haut" "Hawte"[13], Sir George "Georgius" Thomas[12], Sir Thomas "The Younger"[11], Sir Thomas "The Elder"[10], Sir Henry[9], Richard Wiat or[8] Wyatt, Geoffrey "Jeoffrey" Wiot or[7] Wiat, Robert or Richard[6] Wiot, William Wiot or[5] Wyot, Adam Wiot or Wyote or[4], Guyott[3], Guyott[2], Captain or Admiral Adam Guyott or[1] Wiot) was born August 08, 1924 in Rowan County, N.C. He married Edith Kathleen Waller February 19, 1949, daughter of Nathaniel Waller and Ethel Cordelia.

Children of Louie Jackson and Edith Waller are:

+ 1290   i.   Judy Ann[24] Jackson, born December 20, 1949.
   1291   ii.   Donna Jean Jackson, born June 29, 1951. She married Ricky Dale Graham May 24, 1971.
   1292   iii.   Ricky Lane Jackson, born April 12, 1956. He married Jane Deaver September 03, 1978.

848. Ruby Ann[23] Jackson (Ida Lou[22] Eagle, Eli Esau[21], Mary Ann[20] Wyatt, Noah Calvin[19], Thomas "Tommy"[18] Wiatt, Sr. (Wyatt, Wiett), John[17], Henry[16], Richard[15], George[14], Rev. Haute "Haut" "Hawte"[13], Sir George "Georgius" Thomas[12], Sir Thomas "The Younger"[11], Sir Thomas "The Elder"[10], Sir Henry[9], Richard Wiat or[8] Wyatt, Geoffrey "Jeoffrey" Wiot or[7] Wiat, Robert or Richard[6] Wiot, William Wiot or[5] Wyot, Adam Wiot or Wyote or[4], Guyott[3], Guyott[2], Captain or Admiral Adam Guyott or[1] Wiot) was born June 29, 1926 in Rowan County, N.C. She married David Gwin Page November 30, 1944, son of Daniel Page and Mary Fisher.

More About David Gwin Page:

Fact 1: Served U.S. Army during World War II.

Children of Ruby Jackson and David Page are:

+ 1293   i.   David Wesley[24] Page, born May 10, 1945 in Rowan County N.C.
+ 1294   ii.   Charles Lee Page, born March 14, 1947 in Rowan County N.C.
+ 1295   iii.   Shirley Jean Page, born May 29, 1949 in Rowan County N.C.
+ 1296   iv.   Joseph Andrew Page, born October 13, 1950 in Rowan County N.C.

849.   James Alois[23] Edwards (Elizabeth "Elisbeth" Nora[22] Eagle, Eli Esau[21], Mary Ann[20] Wyatt, Noah Calvin[19], Thomas "Tommy"[18] Wiatt, Sr. (Wyatt, Wiett), John[17], Henry[16], Richard[15], George[14], Rev. Haute "Haut" "Hawte"[13], Sir George "Georgius" Thomas[12], Sir Thomas "The Younger"[11], Sir Thomas "The Elder"[10], Sir Henry[9], Richard Wiat or[8] Wyatt, Geoffrey "Jeoffrey" Wiot or[7] Wiat, Robert or Richard[6] Wiot, William Wiot or[5] Wyot, Adam Wiot or Wyote or[4], Guyott[3], Guyott[2], Captain or Admiral Adam Guyott or[1] Wiot) was born April 13, 1924 in Stark County, Massilon, Ohio. He married Bernadine Miller August 05, 1948, daughter of Clarence Miller and Lilla B.

More About James Alois Edwards:

Fact 1: Served in the U.S. Army.

Children of James Edwards and Bernadine Miller are:

+ 1297   i.   Lucinda Kay[24] Edwards, born April 10, 1950 in Lamar, Colorado.
   1298   ii.   Marilyn Anne Edwards, born September 01, 1952 in Lamar, Colorado.
   1299   iii.   James Keith Edwards, born in Lamar, Colorado.

850.   Stanley[23] Edwards (Elizabeth "Elisbeth" Nora[22] Eagle, Eli Esau[21], Mary Ann[20] Wyatt, Noah Calvin[19], Thomas "Tommy"[18] Wiatt, Sr. (Wyatt, Wiett), John[17], Henry[16], Richard[15], George[14], Rev. Haute "Haut" "Hawte"[13], Sir George "Georgius" Thomas[12], Sir Thomas "The Younger"[11], Sir Thomas "The Elder"[10], Sir Henry[9], Richard Wiat or[8] Wyatt, Geoffrey "Jeoffrey" Wiot or[7] Wiat, Robert or Richard[6] Wiot, William Wiot or[5] Wyot, Adam Wiot or Wyote or[4], Guyott[3], Guyott[2], Captain or Admiral Adam Guyott or[1] Wiot) was born March 26, 1926 in Stark County, Massilon, Ohio. He married Harriet Huprick September 18, 1948, daughter of John Huprick and Olvie Mathey.

Children of Stanley Edwards and Harriet Huprick are:

+ 1300   i.   Jeffrey Lynn[24] Edwards, born September 07, 1949.
+ 1301   ii.   Rebecca Ann Edwards, born October 06, 1950 in Massillon, Ohio.

852. Dwight Jerette[23] Edwards (Elizabeth "Elisbeth" Nora[22] Eagle, Eli Esau[21], Mary Ann[20] Wyatt, Noah Calvin[19], Thomas "Tommy"[18] Wiatt, Sr. (Wyatt, Wiett), John[17], Henry[16], Richard[15], George[14], Rev. Haute "Haut" "Hawte"[13], Sir George "Georgius" Thomas[12], Sir Thomas "The Younger"[11], Sir Thomas "The Elder"[10], Sir Henry[9], Richard Wiat or[8] Wyatt, Geoffrey "Jeoffrey" Wiot or[7] Wiat, Robert or Richard[6] Wiot, William Wiot or[5] Wyot, Adam Wiot or Wyote or[4], Guyott[3], Guyott[2], Captain or Admiral Adam Guyott or[1] Wiot) was born October 05, 1938 in Stark County, Massilon, Ohio. He married Shirley Jones May 26, 1967, daughter of Edward Jones and Proctor.

> Child of Dwight Edwards and Shirley Jones is:
> 1302   i.   Michael J.[24] Edwards, born September 18, 1970 in Santa Barbara, California.

854. Tolora Anita[23] Eagle (James Harvey[22], Eli Esau[21], Mary Ann[20] Wyatt, Noah Calvin[19], Thomas "Tommy"[18] Wiatt, Sr. (Wyatt, Wiett), John[17], Henry[16], Richard[15], George[14], Rev. Haute "Haut" "Hawte"[13], Sir George "Georgius" Thomas[12], Sir Thomas "The Younger"[11], Sir Thomas "The Elder"[10], Sir Henry[9], Richard Wiat or[8] Wyatt, Geoffrey "Jeoffrey" Wiot or[7] Wiat, Robert or Richard[6] Wiot, William Wiot or[5] Wyot, Adam Wiot or Wyote or[4], Guyott[3], Guyott[2], Captain or Admiral Adam Guyott or[1] Wiot) was born June 16, 1937. She married Michael Victor Levine June 06, 1958.

> Children of Tolora Eagle and Michael Levine are:
> 1303   i.   Gabriella[24] Levine, born July 08, 1959 in Palo Alto, California.
> 1304   ii.   Joseph David Levine, born September 05, 1962 in Phildelphia, Pennsylvania.
> 1305   iii. Rebecca Suzanne Margaret Levine, born February 08, 1965 in Phildelphia, Pennsylvania.

855. Mary Lynda[23] Eagle (James Harvey[22], Eli Esau[21], Mary Ann[20] Wyatt, Noah Calvin[19], Thomas "Tommy"[18] Wiatt, Sr. (Wyatt, Wiett), John[17], Henry[16], Richard[15], George[14], Rev. Haute "Haut" "Hawte"[13], Sir George "Georgius" Thomas[12], Sir Thomas "The Younger"[11], Sir Thomas "The Elder"[10], Sir Henry[9], Richard Wiat or[8] Wyatt, Geoffrey "Jeoffrey" Wiot or[7] Wiat, Robert or Richard[6] Wiot, William Wiot or[5] Wyot, Adam Wiot or Wyote or[4], Guyott[3], Guyott[2], Captain or Admiral Adam Guyott or[1] Wiot) was born March 27, 1942 in High Point, N.C. She married Donald Wilson Livingston September 05, 1962, son of Claude Livingston and Lorene.

> Children of Mary Eagle and Donald Livingston are:
> 1306   i.   Virginia Christine[24] Livingston, born February 04, 1967 in Saint Louis, Missouri.
> 1307   ii.   Mary Margaret Livingston, born January 20, 1971 in De Kalb, Illiniois.

857. Ree Velt[23] Goodman (Enoch Arthur[22], Nancy Jane[21] Eagle, Mary Ann[20] Wyatt, Noah Calvin[19], Thomas "Tommy"[18] Wiatt, Sr. (Wyatt, Wiett), John[17], Henry[16], Richard[15], George[14],

Rev. Haute "Haut" "Hawte"[13], Sir George "Georgius" Thomas[12], Sir Thomas "The Younger"[11], Sir Thomas "The Elder"[10], Sir Henry[9], Richard Wiat or[8] Wyatt, Geoffrey "Jeoffrey" Wiot or[7] Wiat, Robert or Richard[6] Wiot, William Wiot or[5] Wyot, Adam Wiot or Wyote or[4], Guyott[3], Guyott[2], Captain or Admiral Adam Guyott or[1] Wiot) was born August 10, 1907. He married Willie Mets Brown September 14, 1930.

> Children of Ree Goodman and Willie Brown are:
>
> +   1308   i.   John Cameron[24] Goodman, born October 05, 1936.
> +   1309   ii.   Dorothy Kay Goodman, born July 12, 1940.
>   1310   iii.   Thomas Rie Goodman, born 1944.

858.   Myron A.O.[23] Goodman (Enoch Arthur[22], Nancy Jane[21] Eagle, Mary Ann[20] Wyatt, Noah Calvin[19], Thomas "Tommy"[18] Wiatt, Sr. (Wyatt, Wiett), John[17], Henry[16], Richard[15], George[14], Rev. Haute "Haut" "Hawte"[13], Sir George "Georgius" Thomas[12], Sir Thomas "The Younger"[11], Sir Thomas "The Elder"[10], Sir Henry[9], Richard Wiat or[8] Wyatt, Geoffrey "Jeoffrey" Wiot or[7] Wiat, Robert or Richard[6] Wiot, William Wiot or[5] Wyot, Adam Wiot or Wyote or[4], Guyott[3], Guyott[2], Captain or Admiral Adam Guyott or[1] Wiot) was born April 12, 1909, and died May 01, 1982. He married Madelerie Dameron September 02, 1931, daughter of Eugene Dameron and Catherine Kent.

> Children of Myron Goodman and Madelerie Dameron are:
>
> +   1311   i.   Myron Arthur[24] Goodman, M.D., born October 17, 1939.
>   1312   ii.   Charles Dameron Goodman, born August 04, 1943.
>   1313   iii.   William Gordon Goodman, born November 09, 1946.
>   1314   iv.   Francis Edward Goodman, born August 11, 1949. He married Brenda Masters.
> +   1315   v.   Prudence Penelope Goodman, born October 24, 1950.

859.   Loyd Calvin[23] Goodman (Enoch Arthur[22], Nancy Jane[21] Eagle, Mary Ann[20] Wyatt, Noah Calvin[19], Thomas "Tommy"[18] Wiatt, Sr. (Wyatt, Wiett), John[17], Henry[16], Richard[15], George[14], Rev. Haute "Haut" "Hawte"[13], Sir George "Georgius" Thomas[12], Sir Thomas "The Younger"[11], Sir Thomas "The Elder"[10], Sir Henry[9], Richard Wiat or[8] Wyatt, Geoffrey "Jeoffrey" Wiot or[7] Wiat, Robert or Richard[6] Wiot, William Wiot or[5] Wyot, Adam Wiot or Wyote or[4], Guyott[3], Guyott[2], Captain or Admiral Adam Guyott or[1] Wiot) was born April 24, 1911. He married Hazel Virginia Connell August 31, 1937, daughter of John Connell and Dorie Macall.

> Children of Loyd Goodman and Hazel Connell are:
>
> +   1316   i.   Melinda Connell[24] Goodman, born November 07, 1940 in Guilford County, N.C.
> +   1317   ii.   James Arthur Goodman, born January 31, 1944.
> +   1318   iii.   Susan Frances Goodman, born February 19, 1946.
> +   1319   iv.   Jennie Elizabeth Goodman, born February 28, 1948.
> +   1320   v.   Jane Catherine Goodman, born November 16, 1951.

860. Harold Moses[23] Goodman (Enoch Arthur[22], Nancy Jane[21] Eagle, Mary Ann[20] Wyatt, Noah Calvin[19], Thomas "Tommy"[18] Wiatt, Sr. (Wyatt, Wiett), John[17], Henry[16], Richard[15], George[14], Rev. Haute "Haut" "Hawte"[13], Sir George "Georgius" Thomas[12], Sir Thomas "The Younger"[11], Sir Thomas "The Elder"[10], Sir Henry[9], Richard Wiat or[8] Wyatt, Geoffrey "Jeoffrey" Wiot or[7] Wiat, Robert or Richard[6] Wiot, William Wiot or[5] Wyot, Adam Wiot or Wyote or[4], Guyott[3], Guyott[2], Captain or Admiral Adam Guyott or[1] Wiot) was born April 02, 1913, and died January 12, 1963. He married Marion Emerson April 20, 1940, daughter of Lewis Emerson and Marion Sanders.

Children of Harold Goodman and Marion Emerson are:
+ 1321 i.   Harold Kent[24] Goodman, born January 24, 1942.
+ 1322 ii.   Sanders Emerson Goodman, born September 10, 1944.
+ 1323 iii. Richard Park Goodman, born May 02, 1946.

861. Enoch Alvin[23] Goodman (Enoch Arthur[22], Nancy Jane[21] Eagle, Mary Ann[20] Wyatt, Noah Calvin[19], Thomas "Tommy"[18] Wiatt, Sr. (Wyatt, Wiett), John[17], Henry[16], Richard[15], George[14], Rev. Haute "Haut" "Hawte"[13], Sir George "Georgius" Thomas[12], Sir Thomas "The Younger"[11], Sir Thomas "The Elder"[10], Sir Henry[9], Richard Wiat or[8] Wyatt, Geoffrey "Jeoffrey" Wiot or[7] Wiat, Robert or Richard[6] Wiot, William Wiot or[5] Wyot, Adam Wiot or Wyote or[4], Guyott[3], Guyott[2], Captain or Admiral Adam Guyott or[1] Wiot) was born July 30, 1915. He married Dorthy Gail Hedrick April 22, 1939, daughter of Burl Hedrick and Alma Harris.

Children of Enoch Goodman and Dorthy Hedrick are:
+ 1324 i.   Michael Alvin[24] Goodman, born April 07, 1941.
+ 1325 ii.   Jeffrey Vance Goodman, born May 06, 1943.
+ 1326 iii. Dorthy Gail Goodman, born July 28, 1947.

862. Sara Jane[23] Goodman (Enoch Arthur[22], Nancy Jane[21] Eagle, Mary Ann[20] Wyatt, Noah Calvin[19], Thomas "Tommy"[18] Wiatt, Sr. (Wyatt, Wiett), John[17], Henry[16], Richard[15], George[14], Rev. Haute "Haut" "Hawte"[13], Sir George "Georgius" Thomas[12], Sir Thomas "The Younger"[11], Sir Thomas "The Elder"[10], Sir Henry[9], Richard Wiat or[8] Wyatt, Geoffrey "Jeoffrey" Wiot or[7] Wiat, Robert or Richard[6] Wiot, William Wiot or[5] Wyot, Adam Wiot or Wyote or[4], Guyott[3], Guyott[2], Captain or Admiral Adam Guyott or[1] Wiot) was born September 11, 1923, and died August 30, 1979. She married Donald Elsworth Nussman January 17, 1942, son of Ira Nussman and Martha McLaughlin.

Children of Sara Goodman and Donald Nussman are:
+ 1327 i.   Donald O'Brien[24] Nussman, born July 15, 1946.
  1328 ii.   Timothy Park Nussman, born July 06, 1947.
+ 1329 iii. Enoch Anthony Nussman, born October 26, 1950.

863. Mildred Louise[23] Goodman (Linus Giles[22], Nancy Jane[21] Eagle, Mary Ann[20] Wyatt, Noah Calvin[19], Thomas "Tommy"[18] Wiatt, Sr. (Wyatt, Wiett), John[17], Henry[16], Richard[15],

George[14], Rev. Haute "Haut" "Hawte"[13], Sir George "Georgius" Thomas[12], Sir Thomas "The Younger"[11], Sir Thomas "The Elder"[10], Sir Henry[9], Richard Wiat or[8] Wyatt, Geoffrey "Jeoffrey" Wiot or[7] Wiat, Robert or Richard[6] Wiot, William Wiot or[5] Wyot, Adam Wiot or Wyote or[4], Guyott[3], Guyott[2], Captain or Admiral Adam Guyott or[1] Wiot) was born September 26, 1916. She married (1) L. Harvey Robertson, Sr. She married (2) Ray David Beaver September 29, 1940, son of Ray Beaver and Mary Nussman.

Child of Mildred Goodman and Ray Beaver is:
+   1330   i.   David Allen[24] Beaver, born March 24, 1951.

864. Linus Giles[23] Goodman, Jr. (Linus Giles[22], Nancy Jane[21] Eagle, Mary Ann[20] Wyatt, Noah Calvin[19], Thomas "Tommy"[18] Wiatt, Sr. (Wyatt, Wiett), John[17], Henry[16], Richard[15], George[14], Rev. Haute "Haut" "Hawte"[13], Sir George "Georgius" Thomas[12], Sir Thomas "The Younger"[11], Sir Thomas "The Elder"[10], Sir Henry[9], Richard Wiat or[8] Wyatt, Geoffrey "Jeoffrey" Wiot or[7] Wiat, Robert or Richard[6] Wiot, William Wiot or[5] Wyot, Adam Wiot or Wyote or[4], Guyott[3], Guyott[2], Captain or Admiral Adam Guyott or[1] Wiot) was born June 25, 1920. He married Katherine Cress February 10, 1943, daughter of Kirby Cress and Thetis White.

Children of Linus Goodman and Katherine Cress are:
+   1331   i.   Linus[24] Giles III, born July 16, 1950 in Moore County, N.C.
       1332   ii.   Gregory Giles, born November 21, 1955. He married Elizabeth Baskerville April 21, 1984.

865. Nancy Elizabeth[23] Goodman (Linus Giles[22], Nancy Jane[21] Eagle, Mary Ann[20] Wyatt, Noah Calvin[19], Thomas "Tommy"[18] Wiatt, Sr. (Wyatt, Wiett), John[17], Henry[16], Richard[15], George[14], Rev. Haute "Haut" "Hawte"[13], Sir George "Georgius" Thomas[12], Sir Thomas "The Younger"[11], Sir Thomas "The Elder"[10], Sir Henry[9], Richard Wiat or[8] Wyatt, Geoffrey "Jeoffrey" Wiot or[7] Wiat, Robert or Richard[6] Wiot, William Wiot or[5] Wyot, Adam Wiot or Wyote or[4], Guyott[3], Guyott[2], Captain or Admiral Adam Guyott or[1] Wiot) was born September 08, 1932. She married Larry Donald Bowden, Sr. February 27, 1954, son of James Bowen and Mazie Williams.

Children of Nancy Goodman and Larry Bowden are:
       1333   i.   Donald[24] Bowden, Jr., born July 01, 1961.
       1334   ii.   Jeffy Lingle Bowden, born March 24, 1965.
       1335   iii.   Mark Goodman Bowden, born March 04, 1969.

867. Gertrude Eliza[23] Goodman (Paul Talmadge[22], Nancy Jane[21] Eagle, Mary Ann[20] Wyatt, Noah Calvin[19], Thomas "Tommy"[18] Wiatt, Sr. (Wyatt, Wiett), John[17], Henry[16], Richard[15], George[14], Rev. Haute "Haut" "Hawte"[13], Sir George "Georgius" Thomas[12], Sir Thomas "The Younger"[11], Sir Thomas "The Elder"[10], Sir Henry[9], Richard Wiat or[8] Wyatt, Geoffrey "Jeoffrey" Wiot or[7] Wiat, Robert or Richard[6] Wiot, William Wiot or[5] Wyot, Adam Wiot or Wyote or[4], Guyott[3], Guyott[2], Captain or Admiral Adam Guyott or[1] Wiot) was born January

21, 1913. She married John Allen Hemrick August 31, 1940, son of George Hemrick and Mary Sale.

Children of Gertrude Goodman and John Hemrick are:

	1336	i.	Stephen Allen[24] Hemrick.
+	1337	ii.	Sharyn Lynn Hemrick, born October 11, 1949.
	1338	iii.	Robbin Dawn Hemrick, born April 20, 1955.

868. Ruth Estelle[23] Goodman (Paul Talmadge[22], Nancy Jane[21] Eagle, Mary Ann[20] Wyatt, Noah Calvin[19], Thomas "Tommy"[18] Wiatt, Sr. (Wyatt, Wiett), John[17], Henry[16], Richard[15], George[14], Rev. Haute "Haut" "Hawte"[13], Sir George "Georgius" Thomas[12], Sir Thomas "The Younger"[11], Sir Thomas "The Elder"[10], Sir Henry[9], Richard Wiat or[8] Wyatt, Geoffrey "Jeoffrey" Wiot or[7] Wiat, Robert or Richard[6] Wiot, William Wiot or[5] Wyot, Adam Wiot or Wyote or[4], Guyott[3], Guyott[2], Captain or Admiral Adam Guyott or[1] Wiot) was born October 29, 1914. She married John Allen Hammill April 20, 1936, son of John Hammill and Hannah Lentz.

Children of Ruth Goodman and John Hammill are:

| | 1339 | i. | Bobby Gene[24] Hammill, born March 17, 1940. |
| + | 1340 | ii. | John Allen Hammill, Jr., born March 26, 1945. |

869. Emerson Clayton[23] Goodman (Paul Talmadge[22], Nancy Jane[21] Eagle, Mary Ann[20] Wyatt, Noah Calvin[19], Thomas "Tommy"[18] Wiatt, Sr. (Wyatt, Wiett), John[17], Henry[16], Richard[15], George[14], Rev. Haute "Haut" "Hawte"[13], Sir George "Georgius" Thomas[12], Sir Thomas "The Younger"[11], Sir Thomas "The Elder"[10], Sir Henry[9], Richard Wiat or[8] Wyatt, Geoffrey "Jeoffrey" Wiot or[7] Wiat, Robert or Richard[6] Wiot, William Wiot or[5] Wyot, Adam Wiot or Wyote or[4], Guyott[3], Guyott[2], Captain or Admiral Adam Guyott or[1] Wiot) was born August 15, 1916, and died February 20, 1978. He married Lena Mae Winecoff July 09, 1945, daughter of David Winecoff and Bertha File.

Children of Emerson Goodman and Lena Winecoff are:

	1341	i.	Brenda Kay[24] Goodman, born June 27, 1947; died July 04, 1947.
	1342	ii.	Linda Faye Goodman, born June 27, 1947; died July 05, 1947.
+	1343	iii.	Robert Clayton Goodman, born August 20, 1952.

870. Paul Talmadge[23] Goodman, Jr. (Paul Talmadge[22], Nancy Jane[21] Eagle, Mary Ann[20] Wyatt, Noah Calvin[19], Thomas "Tommy"[18] Wiatt, Sr. (Wyatt, Wiett), John[17], Henry[16], Richard[15], George[14], Rev. Haute "Haut" "Hawte"[13], Sir George "Georgius" Thomas[12], Sir Thomas "The Younger"[11], Sir Thomas "The Elder"[10], Sir Henry[9], Richard Wiat or[8] Wyatt, Geoffrey "Jeoffrey" Wiot or[7] Wiat, Robert or Richard[6] Wiot, William Wiot or[5] Wyot, Adam Wiot or Wyote or[4], Guyott[3], Guyott[2], Captain or Admiral Adam Guyott or[1] Wiot) was born August 26, 1918. He married Nellie Margaret Woodberry March 22, 1947, daughter of Charles Woodberry and Addie Barnam.

Children of Paul Goodman and Nellie Woodberry are:

+ 1344   i.   Michael Douglas[24] Goodman, born December 23, 1948.
+ 1345   ii.   Paulette Elisbeth Goodman, born January 25, 1950.

871. Geneva Lee[23] Goodman (Paul Talmadge[22], Nancy Jane[21] Eagle, Mary Ann[20] Wyatt, Noah Calvin[19], Thomas "Tommy"[18] Wiatt, Sr. (Wyatt, Wiett), John[17], Henry[16], Richard[15], George[14], Rev. Haute "Haut" "Hawte"[13], Sir George "Georgius" Thomas[12], Sir Thomas "The Younger"[11], Sir Thomas "The Elder"[10], Sir Henry[9], Richard Wiat or[8] Wyatt, Geoffrey "Jeoffrey" Wiot or[7] Wiat, Robert or Richard[6] Wiot, William Wiot or[5] Wyot, Adam Wiot or Wyote or[4], Guyott[3], Guyott[2], Captain or Admiral Adam Guyott or[1] Wiot) was born September 23, 1920. She married Robert Lee Phillips June 14, 1947, son of Clarence Phillips and Bessie James.

       Children of Geneva Goodman and Robert Phillips are:

      1346   i.   Reva Arlette[24] Phillips.
      1347   ii.   Karon Lynn Phillips, born April 14, 1952. She married Danny Wayne Worshan June 22, 1974.
+ 1348   iii.   Kinsey Lea Phillips, born March 22, 1954.
      1349   iv.   Kirby Dale Phillips, born February 27, 1959. He married Melissa Kay Sloan July 29, 1979.
      1350   v.   Kevin Brian Phillips, born July 29, 1960.

872. Mabel Arey[23] Goodman (Paul Talmadge[22], Nancy Jane[21] Eagle, Mary Ann[20] Wyatt, Noah Calvin[19], Thomas "Tommy"[18] Wiatt, Sr. (Wyatt, Wiett), John[17], Henry[16], Richard[15], George[14], Rev. Haute "Haut" "Hawte"[13], Sir George "Georgius" Thomas[12], Sir Thomas "The Younger"[11], Sir Thomas "The Elder"[10], Sir Henry[9], Richard Wiat or[8] Wyatt, Geoffrey "Jeoffrey" Wiot or[7] Wiat, Robert or Richard[6] Wiot, William Wiot or[5] Wyot, Adam Wiot or Wyote or[4], Guyott[3], Guyott[2], Captain or Admiral Adam Guyott or[1] Wiot) was born January 04, 1922. She married Hill Alexander Carpenter August 17, 1947, son of David Carpenter and Della Hallman.

       Children of Mabel Goodman and Hill Carpenter are:

+ 1351   i.   Ronald Alan[24] Carpenter, born February 25, 1954.
      1352   ii.   Kenneth Brian Carpenter, born February 25, 1956. He married Robyn Denise Fulk September 10, 1978.
+ 1353   iii.   Larry Charles Carpenter, born April 04, 1958.

873. Dwight Wilburn Francis[23] Goodman (Paul Talmadge[22], Nancy Jane[21] Eagle, Mary Ann[20] Wyatt, Noah Calvin[19], Thomas "Tommy"[18] Wiatt, Sr. (Wyatt, Wiett), John[17], Henry[16], Richard[15], George[14], Rev. Haute "Haut" "Hawte"[13], Sir George "Georgius" Thomas[12], Sir Thomas "The Younger"[11], Sir Thomas "The Elder"[10], Sir Henry[9], Richard Wiat or[8] Wyatt, Geoffrey "Jeoffrey" Wiot or[7] Wiat, Robert or Richard[6] Wiot, William Wiot or[5] Wyot, Adam Wiot or Wyote or[4], Guyott[3], Guyott[2], Captain or Admiral Adam Guyott or[1] Wiot) was born

January 25, 1924. He married Lois Ethel Lomax June 04, 1965, daughter of George Lomax and Ethel Rogers.

Child of Dwight Goodman and Lois Lomax is:
1354   i.   Lynn[24] Goodman, born December 04, 1967.

874.   Glenna Rachel[23] Goodman (Paul Talmadge[22], Nancy Jane[21] Eagle, Mary Ann[20] Wyatt, Noah Calvin[19], Thomas "Tommy"[18] Wiatt, Sr. (Wyatt, Wiett), John[17], Henry[16], Richard[15], George[14], Rev. Haute "Haut" "Hawte"[13], Sir George "Georgius" Thomas[12], Sir Thomas "The Younger"[11], Sir Thomas "The Elder"[10], Sir Henry[9], Richard Wiat or[8] Wyatt, Geoffrey "Jeoffrey" Wiot or[7] Wiat, Robert or Richard[6] Wiot, William Wiot or[5] Wyot, Adam Wiot or Wyote or[4], Guyott[3], Guyott[2], Captain or Admiral Adam Guyott or[1] Wiot) was born February 19, 1927. She married George Richter Hahn, Sr. March 24, 1946, son of Willis Hahn and Annie Fisher.

Children of Glenna Goodman and George Hahn are:
1355   i.   John Timothy[24] Hahn.
1356   ii.   George Richter Hahn, Jr., born October 17, 1947. He married Dr. Ruth Wilks May 07, 1977.
+   1357   iii.   Leah Jane Hahn, born February 21, 1949.
+   1358   iv.   Rodger Burk Hahn, born May 11, 1953.

875.   Harry Kale[23] Goodman (Paul Talmadge[22], Nancy Jane[21] Eagle, Mary Ann[20] Wyatt, Noah Calvin[19], Thomas "Tommy"[18] Wiatt, Sr. (Wyatt, Wiett), John[17], Henry[16], Richard[15], George[14], Rev. Haute "Haut" "Hawte"[13], Sir George "Georgius" Thomas[12], Sir Thomas "The Younger"[11], Sir Thomas "The Elder"[10], Sir Henry[9], Richard Wiat or[8] Wyatt, Geoffrey "Jeoffrey" Wiot or[7] Wiat, Robert or Richard[6] Wiot, William Wiot or[5] Wyot, Adam Wiot or Wyote or[4], Guyott[3], Guyott[2], Captain or Admiral Adam Guyott or[1] Wiot) was born February 10, 1931. He married Betty Jane Hill November 15, 1969, daughter of John Hill and Neva Hoover.

Child of Harry Goodman and Betty Hill is:
1359   i.   Dennis Allan[24] Goodman, born November 03, 1970.

876.   Spencer Brown[23] Goodman (Leland Quincy[22], Nancy Jane[21] Eagle, Mary Ann[20] Wyatt, Noah Calvin[19], Thomas "Tommy"[18] Wiatt, Sr. (Wyatt, Wiett), John[17], Henry[16], Richard[15], George[14], Rev. Haute "Haut" "Hawte"[13], Sir George "Georgius" Thomas[12], Sir Thomas "The Younger"[11], Sir Thomas "The Elder"[10], Sir Henry[9], Richard Wiat or[8] Wyatt, Geoffrey "Jeoffrey" Wiot or[7] Wiat, Robert or Richard[6] Wiot, William Wiot or[5] Wyot, Adam Wiot or Wyote or[4], Guyott[3], Guyott[2], Captain or Admiral Adam Guyott or[1] Wiot) was born October 22, 1917 in Stanly County, N.C., and died August 26, 1974. He married Sara Jane Moses November 30, 1940, daughter of Grover Moses and Pearl Harris.

Child of Spencer Goodman and Sara Moses is:
1360   i.   Vickie Brown[24] Goodman, born January 13, 1943 in Pa.

877. Carrie Mae[23] Goodman (Leland Quincy[22], Nancy Jane[21] Eagle, Mary Ann[20] Wyatt, Noah Calvin[19], Thomas "Tommy"[18] Wiatt, Sr. (Wyatt, Wiett), John[17], Henry[16], Richard[15], George[14], Rev. Haute "Haut" "Hawte"[13], Sir George "Georgius" Thomas[12], Sir Thomas "The Younger"[11], Sir Thomas "The Elder"[10], Sir Henry[9], Richard Wiat or[8] Wyatt, Geoffrey "Jeoffrey" Wiot or[7] Wiat, Robert or Richard[6] Wiot, William Wiot or[5] Wyot, Adam Wiot or[4], Guyott[3], Guyott[2], Captain or Admiral Adam Guyott or[1] Wiot) was born January 12, 1922 in Stanly County, N.C. She married Mack Hubert Wood June 14, 1942, son of Thompson Wood and Esther Miller.

> Children of Carrie Goodman and Mack Wood are:
> + 1361   i.   Tommie Leland[24] Wood, born August 07, 1945.
>   1362   ii.   Gary Lee Wood, born June 09, 1950.
> + 1363   iii.   Yonnie Kay Wood, born September 26, 1954.

878. Annie Katherine[23] Goodman (Leland Quincy[22], Nancy Jane[21] Eagle, Mary Ann[20] Wyatt, Noah Calvin[19], Thomas "Tommy"[18] Wiatt, Sr. (Wyatt, Wiett), John[17], Henry[16], Richard[15], George[14], Rev. Haute "Haut" "Hawte"[13], Sir George "Georgius" Thomas[12], Sir Thomas "The Younger"[11], Sir Thomas "The Elder"[10], Sir Henry[9], Richard Wiat or[8] Wyatt, Geoffrey "Jeoffrey" Wiot or[7] Wiat, Robert or Richard[6] Wiot, William Wiot or[5] Wyot, Adam Wiot or Wyote or[4], Guyott[3], Guyott[2], Captain or Admiral Adam Guyott or[1] Wiot) was born April 17, 1926 in Stanly County, N.C. She married Richard Elliot Robinson July 12, 1947, son of Eilliam Robinson and Viola Richard.

> Children of Annie Goodman and Richard Robinson are:
>   1364   i.   Richard William[24] Robinson, born February 04, 1951 in Forsyth County, N.C.
> + 1365   ii.   Sherry Ann Robinson, born December 19, 1952.
> + 1366   iii.   Kristi Lee Robinson, born December 10, 1954.

879. Clyde "Bud" Weir[23] Goodman (Leland Quincy[22], Nancy Jane[21] Eagle, Mary Ann[20] Wyatt, Noah Calvin[19], Thomas "Tommy"[18] Wiatt, Sr. (Wyatt, Wiett), John[17], Henry[16], Richard[15], George[14], Rev. Haute "Haut" "Hawte"[13], Sir George "Georgius" Thomas[12], Sir Thomas "The Younger"[11], Sir Thomas "The Elder"[10], Sir Henry[9], Richard Wiat or[8] Wyatt, Geoffrey "Jeoffrey" Wiot or[7] Wiat, Robert or Richard[6] Wiot, William Wiot or[5] Wyot, Adam Wiot or Wyote or[4], Guyott[3], Guyott[2], Captain or Admiral Adam Guyott or[1] Wiot) was born October 01, 1927 in Richfield, N.C. He married Jeanette Williams January 22, 1950 in Chesterfield, S.C., daughter of Coleman Williams and Hazel Earnhardt.

More About Clyde "Bud" Weir Goodman:
Fact 1: Served in the U.S. Army.

> Children of Clyde Goodman and Jeanette Williams are:
> + 1367   i.   Tony Stephen[24] Goodman, born February 22, 1951 in Stanly County, N.C.

1368	ii.	Jackie Weir Goodman, born February 15, 1954 in Stanly County, N.C. He married Carol Suzette Honeycutt.
+ 1369	iii.	Timothy Noel Goodman, born September 15, 1959 in Stanly County, N.C.

880. Melvine Eagle[23] Goodman (Leland Quincy[22], Nancy Jane[21] Eagle, Mary Ann[20] Wyatt, Noah Calvin[19], Thomas "Tommy"[18] Wiatt, Sr. (Wyatt, Wiett), John[17], Henry[16], Richard[15], George[14], Rev. Haute "Haut" "Hawte"[13], Sir George "Georgius" Thomas[12], Sir Thomas "The Younger"[11], Sir Thomas "The Elder"[10], Sir Henry[9], Richard Wiat or[8] Wyatt, Geoffrey "Jeoffrey" Wiot or[7] Wiat, Robert or Richard[6] Wiot, William Wiot or[5] Wyot, Adam Wiot or Wyote or[4], Guyott[3], Guyott[2], Captain or Admiral Adam Guyott or[1] Wiot) was born October 01, 1932 in Stanly County, N.C. She married Edwin Earle Koontz July 14, 1968, son of Allen Koontz and Emma Poole.

Child of Melvine Goodman and Edwin Koontz is:
1370	i.	Earle Allen[24] Koontz, born February 06, 1971.

881. Alva Lee[23] Goodman (Leland Quincy[22], Nancy Jane[21] Eagle, Mary Ann[20] Wyatt, Noah Calvin[19], Thomas "Tommy"[18] Wiatt, Sr. (Wyatt, Wiett), John[17], Henry[16], Richard[15], George[14], Rev. Haute "Haut" "Hawte"[13], Sir George "Georgius" Thomas[12], Sir Thomas "The Younger"[11], Sir Thomas "The Elder"[10], Sir Henry[9], Richard Wiat or[8] Wyatt, Geoffrey "Jeoffrey" Wiot or[7] Wiat, Robert or Richard[6] Wiot, William Wiot or[5] Wyot, Adam Wiot or Wyote or[4], Guyott[3], Guyott[2], Captain or Admiral Adam Guyott or[1] Wiot) was born February 28, 1937 in Stanly County, N.C. She married Robert Lewis Sells August 30, 1968, son of Henry Sells and Hallie Barringer.

Children of Alva Goodman and Robert Sells are:
1371	i.	Kelley Renée[24] Sells, born June 24, 1959 in Stanly County, N.C. She married Mark Stephen McCullah June 24, 1978.
1372	ii.	Robin Anita Sells, born January 14, 1961 in Stanly County, N.C. She married Thomas Moody Rogers August 29, 1981.
1373	iii.	Wesley Robert Sells, born November 29, 1965 in Stanly County, N.C.

882. Stella Mae[23] Morgan (Nannie Jane[22] Goodman, Nancy Jane[21] Eagle, Mary Ann[20] Wyatt, Noah Calvin[19], Thomas "Tommy"[18] Wiatt, Sr. (Wyatt, Wiett), John[17], Henry[16], Richard[15], George[14], Rev. Haute "Haut" "Hawte"[13], Sir George "Georgius" Thomas[12], Sir Thomas "The Younger"[11], Sir Thomas "The Elder"[10], Sir Henry[9], Richard Wiat or[8] Wyatt, Geoffrey "Jeoffrey" Wiot or[7] Wiat, Robert or Richard[6] Wiot, William Wiot or[5] Wyot, Adam Wiot or Wyote or[4], Guyott[3], Guyott[2], Captain or Admiral Adam Guyott or[1] Wiot) was born January 19, 1917 in Stanly County, N.C. She married Harold David Isenburg May 23, 1941, son of John Isenburg and Lura Schultz.

Children of Stella Morgan and Harold Isenburg are:
+ 1374	i.	John David[24] Isenburg, born August 29, 1944.

1375	ii.	Stephen Morgan Isenburg, born December 20, 1945. He married Patsy Woody June 14, 1972.
+ 1376	iii.	Timothy Douglas Isenburg, born February 14, 1947.
+ 1377	iv.	Paul Galen Isenburg, born November 18, 1952.

883. Rena Margaret[23] Morgan (Nannie Jane[22] Goodman, Nancy Jane[21] Eagle, Mary Ann[20] Wyatt, Noah Calvin[19], Thomas "Tommy"[18] Wiatt, Sr. (Wyatt, Wiett), John[17], Henry[16], Richard[15], George[14], Rev. Haute "Haut" "Hawte"[13], Sir George "Georgius" Thomas[12], Sir Thomas "The Younger"[11], Sir Thomas "The Elder"[10], Sir Henry[9], Richard Wiat or[8] Wyatt, Geoffrey "Jeoffrey" Wiot or[7] Wiat, Robert or Richard[6] Wiot, William Wiot or[5] Wyot, Adam Wiot or Wyote or[4], Guyott[3], Guyott[2], Captain or Admiral Adam Guyott or[1] Wiot) was born April 03, 1918. She married John Ludwig April 19, 1941, son of John Ludwig and Annie.

Children of Rena Morgan and John Ludwig are:
+ 1378	i.	Judy Ann[24] Ludwig, born January 06, 1942.
+ 1379	ii.	James Stanley Ludwig, born August 16, 1944.
+ 1380	iii.	John Franklin Ludwig, born September 11, 1946 in Va.

884. Leo Goodman[23] Morgan (Nannie Jane[22] Goodman, Nancy Jane[21] Eagle, Mary Ann[20] Wyatt, Noah Calvin[19], Thomas "Tommy"[18] Wiatt, Sr. (Wyatt, Wiett), John[17], Henry[16], Richard[15], George[14], Rev. Haute "Haut" "Hawte"[13], Sir George "Georgius" Thomas[12], Sir Thomas "The Younger"[11], Sir Thomas "The Elder"[10], Sir Henry[9], Richard Wiat or[8] Wyatt, Geoffrey "Jeoffrey" Wiot or[7] Wiat, Robert or Richard[6] Wiot, William Wiot or[5] Wyot, Adam Wiot or Wyote or[4], Guyott[3], Guyott[2], Captain or Admiral Adam Guyott or[1] Wiot) was born December 06, 1919. He married Marion Christine Finger August 08, 1941, daughter of Sidney Finger and Ann Carpenter.

Children of Leo Morgan and Marion Finger are:
| + 1381 | i. | Susan Jeanette[24] Morgan, born August 30, 1952. |
| + 1382 | ii. | Mark Sidney Morgan, born March 29, 1957. |

885. Kathleen Louise[23] Morgan (Nannie Jane[22] Goodman, Nancy Jane[21] Eagle, Mary Ann[20] Wyatt, Noah Calvin[19], Thomas "Tommy"[18] Wiatt, Sr. (Wyatt, Wiett), John[17], Henry[16], Richard[15], George[14], Rev. Haute "Haut" "Hawte"[13], Sir George "Georgius" Thomas[12], Sir Thomas "The Younger"[11], Sir Thomas "The Elder"[10], Sir Henry[9], Richard Wiat or[8] Wyatt, Geoffrey "Jeoffrey" Wiot or[7] Wiat, Robert or Richard[6] Wiot, William Wiot or[5] Wyot, Adam Wiot or Wyote or[4], Guyott[3], Guyott[2], Captain or Admiral Adam Guyott or[1] Wiot) was born November 14, 1926. She married Benjamin Hudson Bridges, Jr. November 27, 1946, son of Benjamin Bridges and Lillie White.

Children of Kathleen Morgan and Benjamin Bridges are:
+ 1383	i.	Benjamin Hudson[24] Bridges III, born December 10, 1947.
+ 1384	ii.	William Douglas Bridges, born 1949.
1385	iii.	Jacob Morgan Bridges, born November 03, 1954.

886. Lois Helen[23] Morgan (Nannie Jane[22] Goodman, Nancy Jane[21] Eagle, Mary Ann[20] Wyatt, Noah Calvin[19], Thomas "Tommy"[18] Wiatt, Sr. (Wyatt, Wiett), John[17], Henry[16], Richard[15], George[14], Rev. Haute "Haut" "Hawte"[13], Sir George "Georgius" Thomas[12], Sir Thomas "The Younger"[11], Sir Thomas "The Elder"[10], Sir Henry[9], Richard Wiat or[8] Wyatt, Geoffrey "Jeoffrey" Wiot or[7] Wiat, Robert or Richard[6] Wiot, William Wiot or[5] Wyot, Adam Wiot or Wyote or[4], Guyott[3], Guyott[2], Captain or Admiral Adam Guyott or[1] Wiot) was born August 11, 1929. She married Graham Hoyt Sowers December 23, 1951, son of Paul Sowers and Zella Everhardt.

      Children of Lois Morgan and Graham Sowers are:

	1386	i.	Jonathan Paul[24] Sowers, born August 20, 1958 in Davidson County, N.C.
+	1387	ii.	Janie Elisbeth Sowers, born October 21, 1961 in Davidson County, N.C.

887. Jane Virginia[23] Morgan (Nannie Jane[22] Goodman, Nancy Jane[21] Eagle, Mary Ann[20] Wyatt, Noah Calvin[19], Thomas "Tommy"[18] Wiatt, Sr. (Wyatt, Wiett), John[17], Henry[16], Richard[15], George[14], Rev. Haute "Haut" "Hawte"[13], Sir George "Georgius" Thomas[12], Sir Thomas "The Younger"[11], Sir Thomas "The Elder"[10], Sir Henry[9], Richard Wiat or[8] Wyatt, Geoffrey "Jeoffrey" Wiot or[7] Wiat, Robert or Richard[6] Wiot, William Wiot or[5] Wyot, Adam Wiot or Wyote or[4], Guyott[3], Guyott[2], Captain or Admiral Adam Guyott or[1] Wiot) was born February 17, 1932 in Woodleaf, Rowan County, N.C. She married Donald Kluttz Watson July 23, 1960 in Woodleaf, Rowan County, N.C., son of Arthur Watson and Mary Kluttz.

      Children of Jane Morgan and Donald Watson are:

+	1388	i.	Joseph Arthur[24] Watson, born June 24, 1961 in Salisbury, N.C.
+	1389	ii.	Janice Rebecca Watson, born April 25, 1963 in Salisbury, N.C.
+	1390	iii.	Miriam Estelle Watson, born June 24, 1965 in Salisbury, N.C.

888. Joe Frank[23] Morgan (Nannie Jane[22] Goodman, Nancy Jane[21] Eagle, Mary Ann[20] Wyatt, Noah Calvin[19], Thomas "Tommy"[18] Wiatt, Sr. (Wyatt, Wiett), John[17], Henry[16], Richard[15], George[14], Rev. Haute "Haut" "Hawte"[13], Sir George "Georgius" Thomas[12], Sir Thomas "The Younger"[11], Sir Thomas "The Elder"[10], Sir Henry[9], Richard Wiat or[8] Wyatt, Geoffrey "Jeoffrey" Wiot or[7] Wiat, Robert or Richard[6] Wiot, William Wiot or[5] Wyot, Adam Wiot or Wyote or[4], Guyott[3], Guyott[2], Captain or Admiral Adam Guyott or[1] Wiot) was born March 09, 1938. He married Barbara Sue Kluttz September 03, 1960, daughter of Walter Kluttz and Margaret Wetmore.

      Children of Joe Morgan and Barbara Kluttz are:

1391	i.	Matthew Keith[24] Morgan, born February 08, 1965.
1392	ii.	Molly Elisbeth Morgan, born March 22, 1968.

890. Enos Roy[23] Goodman (Bennett Francis[22], Nancy Jane[21] Eagle, Mary Ann[20] Wyatt, Noah Calvin[19], Thomas "Tommy"[18] Wiatt, Sr. (Wyatt, Wiett), John[17], Henry[16], Richard[15], George[14],

Rev. Haute "Haut" "Hawte"[13], Sir George "Georgius" Thomas[12], Sir Thomas "The Younger"[11], Sir Thomas "The Elder"[10], Sir Henry[9], Richard Wiat or[8] Wyatt, Geoffrey "Jeoffrey" Wiot or[7] Wiat, Robert or Richard[6] Wiot, William Wiot or[5] Wyot, Adam Wiot or Wyote or[4], Guyott[3], Guyott[2], Captain or Admiral Adam Guyott or[1] Wiot) was born June 26, 1912 in Rowan County N.C., and died November 09, 2005 in Rowan County N.C. He married Lula Marie Wyatt August 22, 1940, daughter of David Wyatt and Amanda Frick.

More About Lula Marie Wyatt:
Remains are buried at Liberty United Methodist Church Cemetery, Gold Hill, Rowan County, N.C.

Child of Enos Goodman and Lula Wyatt is:
1393   i.   Larry Wyatt[24] Goodman, born 1944; died February 15, 2000.

896. Delmar Moses[23] Goodman (Bennett Francis[22], Nancy Jane[21] Eagle, Mary Ann[20] Wyatt, Noah Calvin[19], Thomas "Tommy"[18] Wiatt, Sr. (Wyatt, Wiett), John[17], Henry[16], Richard[15], George[14], Rev. Haute "Haut" "Hawte"[13], Sir George "Georgius" Thomas[12], Sir Thomas "The Younger"[11], Sir Thomas "The Elder"[10], Sir Henry[9], Richard Wiat or[8] Wyatt, Geoffrey "Jeoffrey" Wiot or[7] Wiat, Robert or Richard[6] Wiot, William Wiot or[5] Wyot, Adam Wiot or Wyote or[4], Guyott[3], Guyott[2], Captain or Admiral Adam Guyott or[1] Wiot) was born October 26, 1907. He married Trula Viola Morgan August 03, 1929, daughter of James Morgan and Jacey Morgan.

Children of Delmar Goodman and Trula Morgan are:
1394   i.   Rosena Jeanette[24] Goodman.
1395   ii.   Naomi Louise Goodman.
1396   iii.   Eunice Yvonne Goodman.
1397   iv.   Mavis Pauline Goodman.

897. Leo Francis[23] Goodman (Bennett Francis[22], Nancy Jane[21] Eagle, Mary Ann[20] Wyatt, Noah Calvin[19], Thomas "Tommy"[18] Wiatt, Sr. (Wyatt, Wiett), John[17], Henry[16], Richard[15], George[14], Rev. Haute "Haut" "Hawte"[13], Sir George "Georgius" Thomas[12], Sir Thomas "The Younger"[11], Sir Thomas "The Elder"[10], Sir Henry[9], Richard Wiat or[8] Wyatt, Geoffrey "Jeoffrey" Wiot or[7] Wiat, Robert or Richard[6] Wiot, William Wiot or[5] Wyot, Adam Wiot or Wyote or[4], Guyott[3], Guyott[2], Captain or Admiral Adam Guyott or[1] Wiot) was born August 09, 1919. He married Martha Edith Shepherd.

Children of Leo Goodman and Martha Shepherd are:
+ 1398   i.   Robert Lee[24] Goodman, born March 12, 1941 in Rowan County, N.C.
+ 1399   ii.   Jane Eleanor Goodman, born January 19, 1943 in Rowan County, N.C.
+ 1400   iii.   Martha (Mary) Jo Goodman, born May 03, 1948.
+ 1401   iv.   Randall Gwen Goodman, born September 22, 1954.

898.   Onnie Leven[23] Morgan (Josephine Erma[22] Shaver, Mary Malinda[21] Eagle, Mary Ann[20] Wyatt, Noah Calvin[19], Thomas "Tommy"[18] Wiatt, Sr. (Wyatt, Wiett), John[17], Henry[16], Richard[15], George[14], Rev. Haute "Haut" "Hawte"[13], Sir George "Georgius" Thomas[12], Sir Thomas "The Younger"[11], Sir Thomas "The Elder"[10], Sir Henry[9], Richard Wiat or[8] Wyatt, Geoffrey "Jeoffrey" Wiot or[7] Wiat, Robert or Richard[6] Wiot, William Wiot or[5] Wyot, Adam Wiot or Wyote or[4], Guyott[3], Guyott[2], Captain or Admiral Adam Guyott or[1] Wiot) was born November 24, 1913. She married William Elpherd Phillips.

Child of Onnie Morgan and William Phillips is:
+   1402   i.   Dorothy Mae[24] Phillips.

899.   Stella Marie[23] Morgan (Josephine Erma[22] Shaver, Mary Malinda[21] Eagle, Mary Ann[20] Wyatt, Noah Calvin[19], Thomas "Tommy"[18] Wiatt, Sr. (Wyatt, Wiett), John[17], Henry[16], Richard[15], George[14], Rev. Haute "Haut" "Hawte"[13], Sir George "Georgius" Thomas[12], Sir Thomas "The Younger"[11], Sir Thomas "The Elder"[10], Sir Henry[9], Richard Wiat or[8] Wyatt, Geoffrey "Jeoffrey" Wiot or[7] Wiat, Robert or Richard[6] Wiot, William Wiot or[5] Wyot, Adam Wiot or Wyote or[4], Guyott[3], Guyott[2], Captain or Admiral Adam Guyott or[1] Wiot) was born March 20, 1914. She married Felix Wesley Morgan, son of Charlie Morgan and Fannie Morgan.

More About Stella Marie Morgan:
Corinth Baptist Church Cemetery, Rowan County, N.C.

Children of Stella Morgan and Felix Morgan are:
+   1403   i.   Felix Eugene[24] Morgan, born August 08, 1940.
     1404   ii.   Norman Ray Morgan, born February 26, 1946.
     1405   iii.   Robert Wayen Morgan, born March 13, 1948.

900.   Lena Irene[23] Morgan (Josephine Erma[22] Shaver, Mary Malinda[21] Eagle, Mary Ann[20] Wyatt, Noah Calvin[19], Thomas "Tommy"[18] Wiatt, Sr. (Wyatt, Wiett), John[17], Henry[16], Richard[15], George[14], Rev. Haute "Haut" "Hawte"[13], Sir George "Georgius" Thomas[12], Sir Thomas "The Younger"[11], Sir Thomas "The Elder"[10], Sir Henry[9], Richard Wiat or[8] Wyatt, Geoffrey "Jeoffrey" Wiot or[7] Wiat, Robert or Richard[6] Wiot, William Wiot or[5] Wyot, Adam Wiot or Wyote or[4], Guyott[3], Guyott[2], Captain or Admiral Adam Guyott or[1] Wiot) was born August 21, 1918. She married Navel Newmen Mesimer, son of Walter Mesimer and Nancy Flossie.

Children of Lena Morgan and Navel Mesimer are:
+   1406   i.   Harold Craig[24] Mesimer, born April 13, 1944.
+   1407   ii.   Billie Wayne Mesimer, born August 07, 1951.

913.   Mary Elizabeth[23] Trexler (Beulah Ann[22] Eagle, William Grant[21], Mary Ann[20] Wyatt, Noah Calvin[19], Thomas "Tommy"[18] Wiatt, Sr. (Wyatt, Wiett), John[17], Henry[16], Richard[15], George[14], Rev. Haute "Haut" "Hawte"[13], Sir George "Georgius" Thomas[12], Sir Thomas "The Younger"[11], Sir Thomas "The Elder"[10], Sir Henry[9], Richard Wiat or[8] Wyatt, Geoffrey

"Jeoffrey" Wiot or[7] Wiat, Robert or Richard[6] Wiot, William Wiot or[5] Wyot, Adam Wiot or Wyote or[4], Guyott[3], Guyott[2], Captain or Admiral Adam Guyott or[1] Wiot) was born January 01, 1925. She married Delmar Louvern Misenheimer August 02, 1946, son of Francis Misenheimer and Carrie Trexler.

Children of Mary Trexler and Delmar Misenheimer are:
+   1408   i.   Dennis Wayne[24] Misenheimer, born August 02, 1946.
+   1409   ii.   Randy Allen Misenheimer, born May 02, 1951.
+   1410   iii.   Judith Elizabeth Misenheimer, born November 25, 1953.

914.   George William[23] Trexler (Beulah Ann[22] Eagle, William Grant[21], Mary Ann[20] Wyatt, Noah Calvin[19], Thomas "Tommy"[18] Wiatt, Sr. (Wyatt, Wiett), John[17], Henry[16], Richard[15], George[14], Rev. Haute "Haut" "Hawte"[13], Sir George "Georgius" Thomas[12], Sir Thomas "The Younger"[11], Sir Thomas "The Elder"[10], Sir Henry[9], Richard Wiat or[8] Wyatt, Geoffrey "Jeoffrey" Wiot or[7] Wiat, Robert or Richard[6] Wiot, William Wiot or[5] Wyot, Adam Wiot or Wyote or[4], Guyott[3], Guyott[2], Captain or Admiral Adam Guyott or[1] Wiot) was born March 13, 1927, and died July 24, 1949. He married Doris Phillips April 04, 1947, daughter of William Phillips and Roxie Fields.

More About George William Trexler:
Buried at St. Matthews Luthern Cemetery, N.C.

Children of George Trexler and Doris Phillips are:
  1411   i.   William Allen[24] Trexler, born in Rowan County, N.C.
  1412   ii.   Gene Scott Trexler, born in Rowan County, N.C.
+   1413   iii.   Cheryl Darlene Trexler, born July 11, 1949 in Rowan County, N.C.

920. Janet Inez[23] McHargue (Octa Mae[22] Eagle, William Grant[21], Mary Ann[20] Wyatt, Noah Calvin[19], Thomas "Tommy"[18] Wiatt, Sr. (Wyatt, Wiett), John[17], Henry[16], Richard[15], George[14], Rev. Haute "Haut" "Hawte"[13], Sir George "Georgius" Thomas[12], Sir Thomas "The Younger"[11], Sir Thomas "The Elder"[10], Sir Henry[9], Richard Wiat or[8] Wyatt, Geoffrey "Jeoffrey" Wiot or[7] Wiat, Robert or Richard[6] Wiot, William Wiot or[5] Wyot, Adam Wiot or Wyote or[4], Guyott[3], Guyott[2], Captain or Admiral Adam Guyott or[1] Wiot) was born March 06, 1922 in Rowan County, N.C. She married Elwood Keith Hill, son of John Hill and Martha Basinger.

More About Elwood Keith Hill:
Fact 1: Serves in the U.S. military during WWII.

Children of Janet McHargue and Elwood Hill are:
+   1414   i.   Betty Carol[24] Hill, born February 26, 1942 in Rowan County, N.C.
+   1415   ii.   Ronald Keith Hill, born November 17, 1943 in Stanly County, N.C.

921. Marjorie Ellen[23] McHargue (Octa Mae[22] Eagle, William Grant[21], Mary Ann[20] Wyatt, Noah Calvin[19], Thomas "Tommy"[18] Wiatt, Sr. (Wyatt, Wiett), John[17], Henry[16], Richard[15], George[14], Rev. Haute "Haut" "Hawte"[13], Sir George "Georgius" Thomas[12], Sir Thomas "The Younger"[11], Sir Thomas "The Elder"[10], Sir Henry[9], Richard Wiat or[8] Wyatt, Geoffrey "Jeoffrey" Wiot or[7] Wiat, Robert or Richard[6] Wiot, William Wiot or[5] Wyot, Adam Wiot or Wyote or[4], Guyott[3], Guyott[2], Captain or Admiral Adam Guyott or[1] Wiot) was born July 23, 1923 in Rowan County, N.C, and died September 26, 1962 in Greensboro, N.C. She married James Harris Brown February 17, 1953, son of Fidey Brown and Alice Howard.

More About James Harris Brown:
Fact 1: Serves in U.S. Army during the Korean War.

Children of Marjorie McHargue and James Brown are:

+ 1416   i.   James Stephen[24] Brown, born October 25, 1953 in Guilford County, N.C.
  1417   ii.   David Harris Brown, born November 20, 1956 in Guilford County, N.C.
  1418   iii. Michael Joe Brown, born June 18, 1960 in Alamance County, N.C. He married Karen Elizabeth Isley.

923. Charles William[23] McHargue (Octa Mae[22] Eagle, William Grant[21], Mary Ann[20] Wyatt, Noah Calvin[19], Thomas "Tommy"[18] Wiatt, Sr. (Wyatt, Wiett), John[17], Henry[16], Richard[15], George[14], Rev. Haute "Haut" "Hawte"[13], Sir George "Georgius" Thomas[12], Sir Thomas "The Younger"[11], Sir Thomas "The Elder"[10], Sir Henry[9], Richard Wiat or[8] Wyatt, Geoffrey "Jeoffrey" Wiot or[7] Wiat, Robert or Richard[6] Wiot, William Wiot or[5] Wyot, Adam Wiot or Wyote or[4], Guyott[3], Guyott[2], Captain or Admiral Adam Guyott or[1] Wiot) was born December 01, 1926 in Rowan County, N.C. He married Rebecca Ruth Jester June 14, 1949, daughter of Charles Jester and Grace Farmer.

Children of Charles McHargue and Rebecca Jester are:

  1419   i.   Bradford Lee[24] McHargue, born March 01, 1951 in Frankford, Ind. He married Laura Jo Hicks December 19, 1971.
  1420   ii.   Timothy Charles McHargue, born August 18, 1955 in Fayetteville, N.C.
  1421   iii. Kristin Lynette McHargue, born December 27, 1958 in Siler City, Chatham County, N.C. She married Thaddeus Dana Brown June 29, 1985.
  1422   iv.   Evangeline Gaye McHargue, born February 20, 1962 in Chatham County, N.C. She married Christopher Delane Gardner May 04, 1985.

924. Lucius Baxter[23] McHargue (Octa Mae[22] Eagle, William Grant[21], Mary Ann[20] Wyatt, Noah Calvin[19], Thomas "Tommy"[18] Wiatt, Sr. (Wyatt, Wiett), John[17], Henry[16], Richard[15], George[14], Rev. Haute "Haut" "Hawte"[13], Sir George "Georgius" Thomas[12], Sir Thomas

"The Younger"[11], Sir Thomas "The Elder"[10], Sir Henry[9], Richard Wiat or[8] Wyatt, Geoffrey "Jeoffrey" Wiot or[7] Wiat, Robert or Richard[6] Wiot, William Wiot or[5] Wyot, Adam Wiot or Wyote or[4], Guyott[3], Guyott[2], Captain or Admiral Adam Guyott or[1] Wiot) was born May 11, 1928 in Rowan County, N.C, and died June 06, 1990. He married Lyllus Jessie Whited June 27, 1947, daughter of Charles Whited and Maggie Turner.

More About Lucius Baxter McHargue:
Buried in Michigan.

Children of Lucius McHargue and Lyllus Whited are:

+ 1423   i.   Lynda Jo[24] McHargue, born October 10, 1952 in Washtenau County, Ann Arbor, Mich.
1424   ii.   Lori Jean McHargue, born January 29, 1958. She married David Jimmie Walker July 19, 1984.
1425   iii.   Larry Bryan McHargue, born January 06, 1961 in Monroe County, Mich.

926. Floyd Richard[23] McHargue (Octa Mae[22] Eagle, William Grant[21], Mary Ann[20] Wyatt, Noah Calvin[19], Thomas "Tommy"[18] Wiatt, Sr. (Wyatt, Wiett), John[17], Henry[16], Richard[15], George[14], Rev. Haute "Haut" "Hawte"[13], Sir George "Georgius" Thomas[12], Sir Thomas "The Younger"[11], Sir Thomas "The Elder"[10], Sir Henry[9], Richard Wiat or[8] Wyatt, Geoffrey "Jeoffrey" Wiot or[7] Wiat, Robert or Richard[6] Wiot, William Wiot or[5] Wyot, Adam Wiot or Wyote or[4], Guyott[3], Guyott[2], Captain or Admiral Adam Guyott or[1] Wiot) was born December 07, 1933 in Stanly County, N.C. He married Clara Dee Schoonover August 18, 1955, daughter of Henry Schoonover and Susan Funkhouser.

Children of Floyd McHargue and Clara Schoonover are:

+ 1426   i.   Victoria Mae[24] McHargue, born March 17, 1956 in Oceanside, Ca.
1427   ii.   Marlene Gail McHargue, born September 07, 1957 in Los Angeles County, Ca. She married Randal Ray Nelson.
1428   iii.   Terri Lynn McHargue, born October 03, 1958 in Los Angeles County, Ca.
1429   iv.   Sandra Dee McHargue, born August 04, 1961 in Los Angeles County, Ca. She married Randall Gene Nelson August 18, 1984.

927. Margaret Lee[23] Myers (Norvie Lundy[22] Eagle, William Grant[21], Mary Ann[20] Wyatt, Noah Calvin[19], Thomas "Tommy"[18] Wiatt, Sr. (Wyatt, Wiett), John[17], Henry[16], Richard[15], George[14], Rev. Haute "Haut" "Hawte"[13], Sir George "Georgius" Thomas[12], Sir Thomas "The Younger"[11], Sir Thomas "The Elder"[10], Sir Henry[9], Richard Wiat or[8] Wyatt, Geoffrey "Jeoffrey" Wiot or[7] Wiat, Robert or Richard[6] Wiot, William Wiot or[5] Wyot, Adam Wiot or Wyote or[4], Guyott[3], Guyott[2], Captain or Admiral Adam Guyott or[1] Wiot) was born December 25, 1926 in Rowan County, N.C. She married Hilton Ketchie October 06, 1945, son of Walter Ketchie and Sally Jackson.

Children of Margaret Myers and Hilton Ketchie are:

	1430	i.	Chad Kyle[24] Ketchie, born in Rowan County, N.C.
+	1431	ii.	Hilton Michael Ketchie, born May 24, 1946 in Rowan County, N.C.
	1432	iii.	Sherry Lyn Ketchie, born January 18, 1952 in Rowan County, N.C.
+	1433	iv.	Tonya Kay Ketchie, born March 07, 1958 in Rowan County, N.C.

928. Harold William[23] Myers (Norvie Lundy[22] Eagle, William Grant[21], Mary Ann[20] Wyatt, Noah Calvin[19], Thomas "Tommy"[18] Wiatt, Sr. (Wyatt, Wiett), John[17], Henry[16], Richard[15], George[14], Rev. Haute "Haut" "Hawte"[13], Sir George "Georgius" Thomas[12], Sir Thomas "The Younger"[11], Sir Thomas "The Elder"[10], Sir Henry[9], Richard Wiat or[8] Wyatt, Geoffrey "Jeoffrey" Wiot or[7] Wiat, Robert or Richard[6] Wiot, William Wiot or[5] Wyot, Adam Wiot or Wyote or[4], Guyott[3], Guyott[2], Captain or Admiral Adam Guyott or[1] Wiot) was born August 12, 1928 in Greenville County, S.C. He married Alice Elaine Corl March 03, 1951, daughter of David Corl and Agnes Cress.

Children of Harold Myers and Alice Corl are:

+	1434	i.	Sarita Joy[24] Myers, born June 22, 1952 in Rowan County, N.C.
+	1435	ii.	Melody Kim Myers, born February 15, 1957 in Rowan County, N.C.
	1436	iii.	Marsha Leigh Myers, born in Rowan County, N.C.

929. Peggy Pauline[23] Eagle (Paul Thomas[22], William Grant[21], Mary Ann[20] Wyatt, Noah Calvin[19], Thomas "Tommy"[18] Wiatt, Sr. (Wyatt, Wiett), John[17], Henry[16], Richard[15], George[14], Rev. Haute "Haut" "Hawte"[13], Sir George "Georgius" Thomas[12], Sir Thomas "The Younger"[11], Sir Thomas "The Elder"[10], Sir Henry[9], Richard Wiat or[8] Wyatt, Geoffrey "Jeoffrey" Wiot or[7] Wiat, Robert or Richard[6] Wiot, William Wiot or[5] Wyot, Adam Wiot or Wyote or[4], Guyott[3], Guyott[2], Captain or Admiral Adam Guyott or[1] Wiot) was born September 17, 1938 in Stanly County, N.C. She married Norman E. Rogers August 18, 1957, son of Hall Rogers and Zola Brown.

Children of Peggy Eagle and Norman Rogers are:

1437	i.	Kelly Ruth[24] Rogers, born January 28, 1959; died April 13, 1986. She married Edward Lee Pennington April 10, 1982.

More About Kelly Ruth Rogers:
Buried at Stanly Gardens of Memory in Albemarle, N.C.

1438	ii.	Rex Allen Rogers, born December 15, 1962.

930. Jimmy Farrell[23] Grubb (Mary (Phene) Josephine[22] Eagle, William Grant[21], Mary Ann[20] Wyatt, Noah Calvin[19], Thomas "Tommy"[18] Wiatt, Sr. (Wyatt, Wiett), John[17], Henry[16], Richard[15], George[14], Rev. Haute "Haut" "Hawte"[13], Sir George "Georgius" Thomas[12], Sir

Thomas "The Younger"[11], Sir Thomas "The Elder"[10], Sir Henry[9], Richard Wiat or[8] Wyatt, Geoffrey "Jeoffrey" Wiot or[7] Wiat, Robert or Richard[6] Wiot, William Wiot or[5] Wyot, Adam Wiot or Wyote or[4], Guyott[3], Guyott[2], Captain or Admiral Adam Guyott or[1] Wiot) was born February 17, 1931 in Rowan County, N.C. He married Phyllis Ann Freeland May 27, 1956, daughter of James Freeland and Bertie Spry.

> Children of Jimmy Grubb and Phyllis Freeland are:
> 1439   i.   Mitchell Farrell[24] Grubb, born April 06, 1957 in Rowan County, N.C.
> 1440   ii.   Jimmy Dana Grubb, born July 01, 1962 in Rowan County, N.C.
> 1441   iii. Alesia Ann Grubb, born February 02, 1965 in Rowan County, N.C.

931.   Larry Douglas[23] Grubb (Mary (Phene) Josephine[22] Eagle, William Grant[21], Mary Ann[20] Wyatt, Noah Calvin[19], Thomas "Tommy"[18] Wiatt, Sr. (Wyatt, Wiett), John[17], Henry[16], Richard[15], George[14], Rev. Haute "Haut" "Hawte"[13], Sir George "Georgius" Thomas[12], Sir Thomas "The Younger"[11], Sir Thomas "The Elder"[10], Sir Henry[9], Richard Wiat or[8] Wyatt, Geoffrey "Jeoffrey" Wiot or[7] Wiat, Robert or Richard[6] Wiot, William Wiot or[5] Wyot, Adam Wiot or Wyote or[4], Guyott[3], Guyott[2], Captain or Admiral Adam Guyott or[1] Wiot) was born July 07, 1936 in Rowan County, N.C. He married Sally Pierce December 02, 1960, daughter of Robert Pierce and Geneva Morton.

> Child of Larry Grubb and Sally Pierce is:
> 1442   i.   Jennifer Dawn[24] Grubb, born December 26, 1961 in Rowan County, N.C.

932.   Don Wayne[23] Grubb (Mary (Phene) Josephine[22] Eagle, William Grant[21], Mary Ann[20] Wyatt, Noah Calvin[19], Thomas "Tommy"[18] Wiatt, Sr. (Wyatt, Wiett), John[17], Henry[16], Richard[15], George[14], Rev. Haute "Haut" "Hawte"[13], Sir George "Georgius" Thomas[12], Sir Thomas "The Younger"[11], Sir Thomas "The Elder"[10], Sir Henry[9], Richard Wiat or[8] Wyatt, Geoffrey "Jeoffrey" Wiot or[7] Wiat, Robert or Richard[6] Wiot, William Wiot or[5] Wyot, Adam Wiot or Wyote or[4], Guyott[3], Guyott[2], Captain or Admiral Adam Guyott or[1] Wiot) was born October 16, 1944 in Rowan County, N.C. He married Sue Elaine Byrd July 19, 1970, daughter of Marvin Byrd and Sue Effard.

> Children of Don Grubb and Sue Byrd are:
> 1443   i.   Penelope Trisha[24] Grubb, born February 19, 1971 in Rowan County, N.C.
> 1444   ii.   Darren Wayne Grubb, born July 27, 1975 in Rowan County, N.C.

933.   Edward Lee[23] Smith (Kate Eursel "Ercle"[22] Eagle, William Grant[21], Mary Ann[20] Wyatt, Noah Calvin[19], Thomas "Tommy"[18] Wiatt, Sr. (Wyatt, Wiett), John[17], Henry[16], Richard[15], George[14], Rev. Haute "Haut" "Hawte"[13], Sir George "Georgius" Thomas[12], Sir Thomas

"The Younger"[11], Sir Thomas "The Elder"[10], Sir Henry[9], Richard Wiat or[8] Wyatt, Geoffrey "Jeoffrey" Wiot or[7] Wiat, Robert or Richard[6] Wiot, William Wiot or[5] Wyot, Adam Wiot or Wyote or[4], Guyott[3], Guyott[2], Captain or Admiral Adam Guyott or[1] Wiot) was born February 06, 1934. He married Polly Patton Wood September 06, 1958, daughter of Henry Wood and Pauline Patton.

Children of Edward Smith and Polly Wood are:

1445	i.	Edward Lee[24] Smith, Jr., born May 17, 1959.
1446	ii.	Wade Louis Smith, born May 05, 1961.
1447	iii.	Alice Wood Smith, born September 05, 1966. She married Linwood Cleveland Harp, Jr.? June 20, 1987.

934. Patsy Eagle[23] Smith (Kate Eursel "Ercle"[22] Eagle, William Grant[21], Mary Ann[20] Wyatt, Noah Calvin[19], Thomas "Tommy"[18] Wiatt, Sr. (Wyatt, Wiett), John[17], Henry[16], Richard[15], George[14], Rev. Haute "Haut" "Hawte"[13], Sir George "Georgius" Thomas[12], Sir Thomas "The Younger"[11], Sir Thomas "The Elder"[10], Sir Henry[9], Richard Wiat or[8] Wyatt, Geoffrey "Jeoffrey" Wiot or[7] Wiat, Robert or Richard[6] Wiot, William Wiot or[5] Wyot, Adam Wiot or Wyote or[4], Guyott[3], Guyott[2], Captain or Admiral Adam Guyott or[1] Wiot) was born November 11, 1943. She married Richard Lee Davis July 14, 1967, son of John Davis and Willie Wright.

Children of Patsy Smith and Richard Davis are:

1448	i.	Craig Buren[24] Davis, born February 20, 1968.
1449	ii.	Bradley Wright Davis, born December 18, 1970.

935. Linda Clarine[23] Eagle (Doy Hollis[22], William Grant[21], Mary Ann[20] Wyatt, Noah Calvin[19], Thomas "Tommy"[18] Wiatt, Sr. (Wyatt, Wiett), John[17], Henry[16], Richard[15], George[14], Rev. Haute "Haut" "Hawte"[13], Sir George "Georgius" Thomas[12], Sir Thomas "The Younger"[11], Sir Thomas "The Elder"[10], Sir Henry[9], Richard Wiat or[8] Wyatt, Geoffrey "Jeoffrey" Wiot or[7] Wiat, Robert or Richard[6] Wiot, William Wiot or[5] Wyot, Adam Wiot or Wyote or[4], Guyott[3], Guyott[2], Captain or Admiral Adam Guyott or[1] Wiot) was born April 22, 1942. She married Stephen Frank Moorefield July 03, 1960, son of Leo Moorefield and Gladys Setzer.

Children of Linda Eagle and Stephen Moorefield are:

1450	i.	Dana Linn[24] Moorefield, born April 22, 1961 in Rowan County, N.C.
1451	ii.	Stephen Mark Moorefield, born July 25, 1963 in Rowan County, N.C.

936. Janice[23] Eagle (Doy Hollis[22], William Grant[21], Mary Ann[20] Wyatt, Noah Calvin[19], Thomas "Tommy"[18] Wiatt, Sr. (Wyatt, Wiett), John[17], Henry[16], Richard[15], George[14], Rev. Haute "Haut" "Hawte"[13], Sir George "Georgius" Thomas[12], Sir Thomas "The Younger"[11], Sir Thomas "The Elder"[10], Sir Henry[9], Richard Wiat or[8] Wyatt, Geoffrey "Jeoffrey" Wiot or[7] Wiat, Robert or Richard[6] Wiot, William Wiot or[5] Wyot, Adam Wiot or Wyote or[4], Guyott[3], Guyott[2], Captain

or Admiral Adam Guyott or[1] Wiot) was born February 02, 1947. She married Gary Edward Mull September 25, 1966, son of Edward Mull and Mary Ridenhour.

> Children of Janice Eagle and Gary Mull are:
> 1452 i. Stacey Leigh[24] Mull, born April 04, 1974.
> 1453 ii. Beth Marie Mull, born December 09, 1975.

937. Heidi Virginia[23] Eagle (Doy Hollis[22], William Grant[21], Mary Ann[20] Wyatt, Noah Calvin[19], Thomas "Tommy"[18] Wiatt, Sr. (Wyatt, Wiett), John[17], Henry[16], Richard[15], George[14], Rev. Haute "Haut" "Hawte"[13], Sir George "Georgius" Thomas[12], Sir Thomas "The Younger"[11], Sir Thomas "The Elder"[10], Sir Henry[9], Richard Wiat or[8] Wyatt, Geoffrey "Jeoffrey" Wiot or[7] Wiat, Robert or Richard[6] Wiot, William Wiot or[5] Wyot, Adam Wiot or Wyote or[4], Guyott[3], Guyott[2], Captain or Admiral Adam Guyott or[1] Wiot) was born January 20, 1962 in Rowan County or Cabarrus County, N.C. She married Dennis Christopher "Chris" Hatley April 17, 1983, son of Eddie Hatley and Abby Hahn.

> Children of Heidi Eagle and Dennis Hatley are:
> 1454 i. Holly Virginia[24] Hatley, born September 25, 1984 in Rowan County, N.C.
> 1455 ii. Heather Emma Hatley, born March 1989.

942. Laura Ann[23] Misenheimer (Jessie Bernice[22] Eagle, William Grant[21], Mary Ann[20] Wyatt, Noah Calvin[19], Thomas "Tommy"[18] Wiatt, Sr. (Wyatt, Wiett), John[17], Henry[16], Richard[15], George[14], Rev. Haute "Haut" "Hawte"[13], Sir George "Georgius" Thomas[12], Sir Thomas "The Younger"[11], Sir Thomas "The Elder"[10], Sir Henry[9], Richard Wiat or[8] Wyatt, Geoffrey "Jeoffrey" Wiot or[7] Wiat, Robert or Richard[6] Wiot, William Wiot or[5] Wyot, Adam Wiot or Wyote or[4], Guyott[3], Guyott[2], Captain or Admiral Adam Guyott or[1] Wiot) was born June 03, 1951. She married (1) John Patrick Morris III. She married (2) Todd Alan Robinson December 17, 1972, son of Thomas Robinson and Betty Grier.

> Children of Laura Misenheimer and Todd Robinson are:
> 1456 i. Andrew Todd[24] Robinson, born September 01, 1977.
> 1457 ii. William Alan Robinson, born March 21, 1979.
> 1458 iii. Laura Kathryn Robinson, born February 14, 1987 in Gastonia, N.C.

943. Franklin Eugene[23] Misenheimer (Jessie Bernice[22] Eagle, William Grant[21], Mary Ann[20] Wyatt, Noah Calvin[19], Thomas "Tommy"[18] Wiatt, Sr. (Wyatt, Wiett), John[17], Henry[16], Richard[15], George[14], Rev. Haute "Haut" "Hawte"[13], Sir George "Georgius" Thomas[12], Sir Thomas "The Younger"[11], Sir Thomas "The Elder"[10], Sir Henry[9], Richard Wiat or[8] Wyatt, Geoffrey "Jeoffrey" Wiot or[7] Wiat, Robert or Richard[6] Wiot, William Wiot or[5] Wyot, Adam Wiot or Wyote or[4], Guyott[3], Guyott[2], Captain or Admiral Adam Guyott or[1] Wiot) was born April 26, 1948. He married Carlin Faye Earnhardt July 07, 1968, daughter of Carl Earnhardt and Susie Drye.

Children of Franklin Misenheimer and Carlin Earnhardt are:

1459	i.	Kreth Matthew[24] Misenheimer, born January 21, 1971 in Carobou, ME.
1460	ii.	Wesley Adam Misenheimer, born May 21, 1974 in Orlando, Fla.

951. Marie[23] Cranford (McCoy Lee[22], Josephine[21] Eagle, Mary Ann[20] Wyatt, Noah Calvin[19], Thomas "Tommy"[18] Wiatt, Sr. (Wyatt, Wiett), John[17], Henry[16], Richard[15], George[14], Rev. Haute "Haut" "Hawte"[13], Sir George "Georgius" Thomas[12], Sir Thomas "The Younger"[11], Sir Thomas "The Elder"[10], Sir Henry[9], Richard Wiat or[8] Wyatt, Geoffrey "Jeoffrey" Wiot or[7] Wiat, Robert or Richard[6] Wiot, William Wiot or[5] Wyot, Adam Wiot or Wyote or[4], Guyott[3], Guyott[2], Captain or Admiral Adam Guyott or[1] Wiot) was born January 03, 1922. She married Keith Lewis Poole January 11, 1947, son of Lewis Poole and Ada Smith.

More About Keith Lewis Poole:
Fact 1: was in USA in WWII.

Children of Marie Cranford and Keith Poole are:

1461	i.	Barbara Ann[24] Poole, born in Rowan County, N.C.
1462	ii.	Judy Diane Poole, born August 18, 1947 in Rowan County, N.C. She married Frank Vestal April 06, 1985.
1463	iii.	Larry Wayne Poole, born in Rowan County, N.C.
1464	iv.	Richard Keith Poole, born July 09, 1957 in Rowan County, N.C; died July 08, 1984.

More About Richard Keith Poole:
Buried at Providence Methodist Church Cemetery, Rowan County, N.C.

954. Harvey Adophus[23] Parker (J. Columbus[22], Ollie Lou Ada[21] Shaver, Rhoda E.[20] Wyatt, Noah Calvin[19], Thomas "Tommy"[18] Wiatt, Sr. (Wyatt, Wiett), John[17], Henry[16], Richard[15], George[14], Rev. Haute "Haut" "Hawte"[13], Sir George "Georgius" Thomas[12], Sir Thomas "The Younger"[11], Sir Thomas "The Elder"[10], Sir Henry[9], Richard Wiat or[8] Wyatt, Geoffrey "Jeoffrey" Wiot or[7] Wiat, Robert or Richard[6] Wiot, William Wiot or[5] Wyot, Adam Wiot or Wyote or[4], Guyott[3], Guyott[2], Captain or Admiral Adam Guyott or[1] Wiot) was born July 04, 1881, and died April 12, 1961. He married Carrie Isabelle "Belle" Ribelin August 24, 1909, daughter of Isaac Ribelin and Julia Parks.

Children of Harvey Parker and Carrie Ribelin are:

+	1465	i.	Annie Marie[24] Parker.
+	1466	ii.	Rena Catherine Parker, born December 14, 1912.
+	1467	iii.	Guy Ray Parker, born July 05, 1915; died July 17, 1988.
	1468	iv.	J.B. Parker, born May 28, 1921; died June 07, 1945.
	1469	v.	L.C. Parker, born June 15, 1923; died March 04, 1925.
+	1470	vi.	Harvey Adophus Parker, Jr., born August 06, 1926.

957. Murray or Murry Lee "Red"[23] Eagle (Calvin DeBerry[22], William Lawson[21], Amanda Jane[20] Wyatt, Noah Calvin[19], Thomas "Tommy"[18] Wiatt, Sr. (Wyatt, Wiett), John[17], Henry[16], Richard[15], George[14], Rev. Haute "Haut" "Hawte"[13], Sir George "Georgius" Thomas[12], Sir Thomas "The Younger"[11], Sir Thomas "The Elder"[10], Sir Henry[9], Richard Wiat or[8] Wyatt, Geoffrey "Jeoffrey" Wiot or[7] Wiat, Robert or Richard[6] Wiot, William Wiot or[5] Wyot, Adam Wiot or Wyote or[4], Guyott[3], Guyott[2], Captain or Admiral Adam Guyott or[1] Wiot) was born February 14, 1921 in Rowan County N.C., and died March 23, 1992 in Rowan County N.C. He married Gladys Irene Bolden August 20, 1938, daughter of William Bolden and Elisabeth Sarah.

       Children of Murray Eagle and Gladys Bolden are:

+	1471	i.	Harry Wayne[24] Eagle, born August 08, 1939.
+	1472	ii.	Martha Elisabeth Eagle, born August 02, 1940 in Guilford County, N.C.
+	1473	iii.	Willard Lee Eagle, born June 26, 1942; died January 22, 1975 in buried in Stokesdale, N.C.
+	1474	iv.	Calvin Henderson Eagle, born March 26, 1943.
+	1475	v.	Larry Curtis Eagle, born April 16, 1945.
+	1476	vi.	Alice Jane Eagle, born December 28, 1947.
+	1477	vii.	Harold Timothy Eagle, born August 27, 1952.
+	1478	viii.	Barbara Irene Eagle, born February 12, 1952 in Guilford County, N.C.

958. Frances Virginia[23] Eagle (Calvin DeBerry[22], William Lawson[21], Amanda Jane[20] Wyatt, Noah Calvin[19], Thomas "Tommy"[18] Wiatt, Sr. (Wyatt, Wiett), John[17], Henry[16], Richard[15], George[14], Rev. Haute "Haut" "Hawte"[13], Sir George "Georgius" Thomas[12], Sir Thomas "The Younger"[11], Sir Thomas "The Elder"[10], Sir Henry[9], Richard Wiat or[8] Wyatt, Geoffrey "Jeoffrey" Wiot or[7] Wiat, Robert or Richard[6] Wiot, William Wiot or[5] Wyot, Adam Wiot or Wyote or[4], Guyott[3], Guyott[2], Captain or Admiral Adam Guyott or[1] Wiot) was born January 03, 1923. She married (1) Paul Adren Osborne, son of Zeb Osborne and Minnie Snipe. She married (2) William Carl Keller July 31, 1947, son of Clarence Keller and X.

       Children of Frances Eagle and William Keller are:

1479	i.	Carl Michael[24] Keller, born November 26, 1949; died July 01, 1966.
1480	ii.	Larry Eugene Keller, born January 01, 1954. He married Sandy October 03, 1980.

959. Betty Lorene[23] Eagle (Calvin DeBerry[22], William Lawson[21], Amanda Jane[20] Wyatt, Noah Calvin[19], Thomas "Tommy"[18] Wiatt, Sr. (Wyatt, Wiett), John[17], Henry[16], Richard[15], George[14], Rev. Haute "Haut" "Hawte"[13], Sir George "Georgius" Thomas[12], Sir Thomas "The Younger"[11], Sir Thomas "The Elder"[10], Sir Henry[9], Richard Wiat or[8] Wyatt, Geoffrey "Jeoffrey" Wiot or[7] Wiat, Robert or Richard[6] Wiot, William Wiot or[5] Wyot, Adam Wiot or Wyote or[4], Guyott[3], Guyott[2], Captain or Admiral Adam Guyott or[1] Wiot) was born August 10, 1927. She married James Franklin Beattie September 15, 1947 in Lincoln County, N.C., son of Steve Beattie and Josie Armstrong.

Children of Betty Eagle and James Beattie are:

+   1481   i.   James Richard[24] Beattie, born March 1949 in Rowan County N.C.

      1482   ii.   Terry Lee Beattie, born March 31, 1954 in Rowan County N.C.

960. Alice Maretta[23] Eagle (Calvin DeBerry[22], William Lawson[21], Amanda Jane[20] Wyatt, Noah Calvin[19], Thomas "Tommy"[18] Wiatt, Sr. (Wyatt, Wiett), John[17], Henry[16], Richard[15], George[14], Rev. Haute "Haut" "Hawte"[13], Sir George "Georgius" Thomas[12], Sir Thomas "The Younger"[11], Sir Thomas "The Elder"[10], Sir Henry[9], Richard Wiat or[8] Wyatt, Geoffrey "Jeoffrey" Wiot or[7] Wiat, Robert or Richard[6] Wiot, William Wiot or[5] Wyot, Adam Wiot or Wyote or[4], Guyott[3], Guyott[2], Captain or Admiral Adam Guyott or[1] Wiot) was born October 30, 1930. She married Alex Franklin McClamrock July 19, 1960, son of Lloyd McClamrock and Gennie Myers.

Child of Alice Eagle and Alex McClamrock is:

      1483   i.   Kim Renee[24] McClamrock, born December 10, 1963.

961. Donald Ray[23] Eagle (Calvin DeBerry[22], William Lawson[21], Amanda Jane[20] Wyatt, Noah Calvin[19], Thomas "Tommy"[18] Wiatt, Sr. (Wyatt, Wiett), John[17], Henry[16], Richard[15], George[14], Rev. Haute "Haut" "Hawte"[13], Sir George "Georgius" Thomas[12], Sir Thomas "The Younger"[11], Sir Thomas "The Elder"[10], Sir Henry[9], Richard Wiat or[8] Wyatt, Geoffrey "Jeoffrey" Wiot or[7] Wiat, Robert or Richard[6] Wiot, William Wiot or[5] Wyot, Adam Wiot or Wyote or[4], Guyott[3], Guyott[2], Captain or Admiral Adam Guyott or[1] Wiot) was born June 19, 1934. He married Barbara Anne Eubanks September 04, 1953, daughter of Edward Eubanks and Edna Cullpepper.

Children of Donald Eagle and Barbara Eubanks are:

      1484   i.   Donna Jean[24] Eagle, born April 23, 1956.

      1485   ii.   Virginia Anne Eagle, born February 05, 1958 in Duval, Fla.

962. Nancy Jean[23] Eagle (Calvin DeBerry[22], William Lawson[21], Amanda Jane[20] Wyatt, Noah Calvin[19], Thomas "Tommy"[18] Wiatt, Sr. (Wyatt, Wiett), John[17], Henry[16], Richard[15], George[14], Rev. Haute "Haut" "Hawte"[13], Sir George "Georgius" Thomas[12], Sir Thomas "The Younger"[11], Sir Thomas "The Elder"[10], Sir Henry[9], Richard Wiat or[8] Wyatt, Geoffrey "Jeoffrey" Wiot or[7] Wiat, Robert or Richard[6] Wiot, William Wiot or[5] Wyot, Adam Wiot or Wyote or[4], Guyott[3], Guyott[2], Captain or Admiral Adam Guyott or[1] Wiot) was born June 15, 1936. She married Tommy Wayne Coggins September 28, 1957, son of Fred Coggins and Maude Morris.

Children of Nancy Eagle and Tommy Coggins are:

      1486   i.   Gary Wayne[24] Coggins, born July 14, 1959.

      1487   ii.   Mark Eugene Coggins, born November 03, 1960.

      1488   iii.   Pamela Lynn Coggins, born March 31, 1964.

963. Sherley "Shirley" Ann[23] Arey (Anna "Anner" Lillian Pauline[22] Eagle, William Lawson[21], Amanda Jane[20] Wyatt, Noah Calvin[19], Thomas "Tommy"[18] Wiatt, Sr. (Wyatt, Wiett), John[17],

Henry[16], Richard[15], George[14], Rev. Haute "Haut" "Hawte"[13], Sir George "Georgius" Thomas[12], Sir Thomas "The Younger"[11], Sir Thomas "The Elder"[10], Sir Henry[9], Richard Wiat or[8] Wyatt, Geoffrey "Jeoffrey" Wiot or[7] Wiat, Robert or Richard[6] Wiot, William Wiot or[5] Wyot, Adam Wiot or Wyote or[4], Guyott[3], Guyott[2], Captain or Admiral Adam Guyott or[1] Wiot) was born November 09, 1935. She married Albert Shepherd November 14, 1953, son of Charlie Shepherd and Minnie Smith.

Children of Sherley Arey and Albert Shepherd are:

+   1489   i.   Avis Jenice "Geneice"[24] Shepherd, born March 23, 1961.
+   1490   ii.   Sandra Elaine Shepherd, born July 03, 1957.

964.   Roberta Gayle[23] Arey (Anna "Anner" Lillian Pauline[22] Eagle, William Lawson[21], Amanda Jane[20] Wyatt, Noah Calvin[19], Thomas "Tommy"[18] Wiatt, Sr. (Wyatt, Wiett), John[17], Henry[16], Richard[15], George[14], Rev. Haute "Haut" "Hawte"[13], Sir George "Georgius" Thomas[12], Sir Thomas "The Younger"[11], Sir Thomas "The Elder"[10], Sir Henry[9], Richard Wiat or[8] Wyatt, Geoffrey "Jeoffrey" Wiot or[7] Wiat, Robert or Richard[6] Wiot, William Wiot or[5] Wyot, Adam Wiot or Wyote or[4], Guyott[3], Guyott[2], Captain or Admiral Adam Guyott or[1] Wiot) was born March 24, 1943. She married Richard Wayne Furr October 20, 1968, son of Charlie Furr and Alice Davis.

Children of Roberta Arey and Richard Furr are:

     1491   i.   Shane Ross[24] Furr, born August 31, 1971.
     1492   ii.   Travis Brent Furr, born June 20, 1974.

965.   Raymond Monroe[23] Wise (Virgie Lou Vera[22] Eagle, William Lawson[21], Amanda Jane[20] Wyatt, Noah Calvin[19], Thomas "Tommy"[18] Wiatt, Sr. (Wyatt, Wiett), John[17], Henry[16], Richard[15], George[14], Rev. Haute "Haut" "Hawte"[13], Sir George "Georgius" Thomas[12], Sir Thomas "The Younger"[11], Sir Thomas "The Elder"[10], Sir Henry[9], Richard Wiat or[8] Wyatt, Geoffrey "Jeoffrey" Wiot or[7] Wiat, Robert or Richard[6] Wiot, William Wiot or[5] Wyot, Adam Wiot or Wyote or[4], Guyott[3], Guyott[2], Captain or Admiral Adam Guyott or[1] Wiot) was born October 25, 1925. He married Bette Sabastian December 12, 1946, daughter of Charles Sebastian and Etta Holbrook.

Children of Raymond Wise and Bette Sabastian are:

+   1493   i.   Romona Lynn[24] Wise, born October 06, 1951.
     1494   ii.   Kevin Bruce Wise.

966.   Clara Sue[23] Frye (Sarah Jane[22] Eagle, William Lawson[21], Amanda Jane[20] Wyatt, Noah Calvin[19], Thomas "Tommy"[18] Wiatt, Sr. (Wyatt, Wiett), John[17], Henry[16], Richard[15], George[14], Rev. Haute "Haut" "Hawte"[13], Sir George "Georgius" Thomas[12], Sir Thomas "The Younger"[11], Sir Thomas "The Elder"[10], Sir Henry[9], Richard Wiat or[8] Wyatt, Geoffrey "Jeoffrey" Wiot or[7] Wiat, Robert or Richard[6] Wiot, William Wiot or[5] Wyot, Adam Wiot or Wyote or[4], Guyott[3], Guyott[2], Captain or Admiral Adam Guyott or[1] Wiot) was born August 08, 1930. She married Billy Joe Fraley November 08, 1952, son of Adam Fraley and Mary.

Children of Clara Frye and Billy Fraley are:

1495	i.	Carol Annette[24] Fraley, born July 27, 1961.
+ 1496	ii.	Thomas Lloyd Fraley, born July 25, 1953.

968. Hazeline Marell[23] Stoker (Esther Mae[22] Eagle, William Lawson[21], Amanda Jane[20] Wyatt, Noah Calvin[19], Thomas "Tommy"[18] Wiatt, Sr. (Wyatt, Wiett), John[17], Henry[16], Richard[15], George[14], Rev. Haute "Haut" "Hawte"[13], Sir George "Georgius" Thomas[12], Sir Thomas "The Younger"[11], Sir Thomas "The Elder"[10], Sir Henry[9], Richard Wiat or[8] Wyatt, Geoffrey "Jeoffrey" Wiot or[7] Wiat, Robert or Richard[6] Wiot, William Wiot or[5] Wyot, Adam Wiot or Wyote or[4], Guyott[3], Guyott[2], Captain or Admiral Adam Guyott or[1] Wiot) was born July 21, 1931 in Rowan County N.C. She married William Luck August 28, 1951, son of Thomas Luck and Myrtle.

Children of Hazeline Stoker and William Luck are:

+ 1497	i.	Terry Michael[24] Luck, born August 15, 1956 in Chicago, Ill.
+ 1498	ii.	Thomas Arthur Luck, born October 15, 1957 in West Bend, Ind.
1499	iii.	Dale Allen Luck, born March 03, 1961 in Stanly County, N.C.
1500	iv.	Debra Dawn Luck, born December 19, 1964 in Stanly County, N.C.

969. Glenn Edward[23] Stoker (Esther Mae[22] Eagle, William Lawson[21], Amanda Jane[20] Wyatt, Noah Calvin[19], Thomas "Tommy"[18] Wiatt, Sr. (Wyatt, Wiett), John[17], Henry[16], Richard[15], George[14], Rev. Haute "Haut" "Hawte"[13], Sir George "Georgius" Thomas[12], Sir Thomas "The Younger"[11], Sir Thomas "The Elder"[10], Sir Henry[9], Richard Wiat or[8] Wyatt, Geoffrey "Jeoffrey" Wiot or[7] Wiat, Robert or Richard[6] Wiot, William Wiot or[5] Wyot, Adam Wiot or Wyote or[4], Guyott[3], Guyott[2], Captain or Admiral Adam Guyott or[1] Wiot) was born March 13, 1948 in Rowan County N.C. He married Sandra Speight August 26, 1968, daughter of William Speight and Wanda Council.

Child of Glenn Stoker and Sandra Speight is:

1501	i.	Camden Lane[24] Stoker, born December 27, 1968 in Stanly County, N.C.

970. Margaret Pauline[23] Hoover (Bertha Louise[22] Eagle, Adolphus Grant[21], Amanda Jane[20] Wyatt, Noah Calvin[19], Thomas "Tommy"[18] Wiatt, Sr. (Wyatt, Wiett), John[17], Henry[16], Richard[15], George[14], Rev. Haute "Haut" "Hawte"[13], Sir George "Georgius" Thomas[12], Sir Thomas "The Younger"[11], Sir Thomas "The Elder"[10], Sir Henry[9], Richard Wiat or[8] Wyatt, Geoffrey "Jeoffrey" Wiot or[7] Wiat, Robert or Richard[6] Wiot, William Wiot or[5] Wyot, Adam Wiot or Wyote or[4], Guyott[3], Guyott[2], Captain or Admiral Adam Guyott or[1] Wiot) was born June 26, 1921 in Stanly County, N.C. She married James Wilson Clodfelter April 08, 1950, son of Alexander Clodfelter and Mattie Moore.

Children of Margaret Hoover and James Clodfelter are:

+   1502   i.   Michael Alan[24] Clodfelter, born March 19, 1951.

      1503   ii.   Stephen Douglas Clodfelter, born April 01, 1951 in Asheville, N.C.

971. Ernst Edwin[23] Hoover (Bertha Louise[22] Eagle, Adolphus Grant[21], Amanda Jane[20] Wyatt, Noah Calvin[19], Thomas "Tommy"[18] Wiatt, Sr. (Wyatt, Wiett), John[17], Henry[16], Richard[15], George[14], Rev. Haute "Haut" "Hawte"[13], Sir George "Georgius" Thomas[12], Sir Thomas "The Younger"[11], Sir Thomas "The Elder"[10], Sir Henry[9], Richard Wiat or[8] Wyatt, Geoffrey "Jeoffrey" Wiot or[7] Wiat, Robert or Richard[6] Wiot, William Wiot or[5] Wyot, Adam Wiot or Wyote or[4], Guyott[3], Guyott[2], Captain or Admiral Adam Guyott or[1] Wiot) was born October 16, 1923. He married Helen Darr, daughter of Jacob Darr and Hallie Conrad.

      Children of Ernst Hoover and Helen Darr are:

      1504   i.   Annette Marie[24] Hoover, born November 12, 1958 in Guilford County, N.C.

      1505   ii.   Marcia Elaine Hoover, born April 06, 1962 in Guilford County, N.C.

      1506   iii.   Ernie Andrew Hoover, born August 31, 1965 in Guilford County, N.C.

972. Gladys Mae[23] Hoover (Bertha Louise[22] Eagle, Adolphus Grant[21], Amanda Jane[20] Wyatt, Noah Calvin[19], Thomas "Tommy"[18] Wiatt, Sr. (Wyatt, Wiett), John[17], Henry[16], Richard[15], George[14], Rev. Haute "Haut" "Hawte"[13], Sir George "Georgius" Thomas[12], Sir Thomas "The Younger"[11], Sir Thomas "The Elder"[10], Sir Henry[9], Richard Wiat or[8] Wyatt, Geoffrey "Jeoffrey" Wiot or[7] Wiat, Robert or Richard[6] Wiot, William Wiot or[5] Wyot, Adam Wiot or Wyote or[4], Guyott[3], Guyott[2], Captain or Admiral Adam Guyott or[1] Wiot) was born January 15, 1926. She married John Russell Coman December 03, 1955, son of Franklin Coman and Vonnie Fouts.

      Children of Gladys Hoover and John Coman are:

      1507   i.   Mark Russell[24] Coman, born July 23, 1957.

      1508   ii.   Beverly Lynn Coman, born June 13, 1959.

973. Leslie Francis[23] Swanner (Beulah Jane[22] Eagle, Adolphus Grant[21], Amanda Jane[20] Wyatt, Noah Calvin[19], Thomas "Tommy"[18] Wiatt, Sr. (Wyatt, Wiett), John[17], Henry[16], Richard[15], George[14], Rev. Haute "Haut" "Hawte"[13], Sir George "Georgius" Thomas[12], Sir Thomas "The Younger"[11], Sir Thomas "The Elder"[10], Sir Henry[9], Richard Wiat or[8] Wyatt, Geoffrey "Jeoffrey" Wiot or[7] Wiat, Robert or Richard[6] Wiot, William Wiot or[5] Wyot, Adam Wiot or Wyote or[4], Guyott[3], Guyott[2], Captain or Admiral Adam Guyott or[1] Wiot) was born January 30, 1934. He married Barbara Ann Jones July 08, 1955, daughter of Johnny Jones and Hazel Rogers.

Children of Leslie Swanner and Barbara Jones are:

1509   i.   Leslie Douglas[24] Swanner, born November 08, 1956 in Forsyth County, N.C.

1510   ii.   Joy Ellen Swanner, born December 18, 1962 in Forsyth County, N.C.

1511   iii.   Ann Marie Swanner, born October 05, 1966 in Forsyth County, N.C.

974. Mae Elizabeth[23] Turner (Jennie Elizabeth[22] Eagle, Adolphus Grant[21], Amanda Jane[20] Wyatt, Noah Calvin[19], Thomas "Tommy"[18] Wiatt, Sr. (Wyatt, Wiett), John[17], Henry[16], Richard[15], George[14], Rev. Haute "Haut" "Hawte"[13], Sir George "Georgius" Thomas[12], Sir Thomas "The Younger"[11], Sir Thomas "The Elder"[10], Sir Henry[9], Richard Wiat or[8] Wyatt, Geoffrey "Jeoffrey" Wiot or[7] Wiat, Robert or Richard[6] Wiot, William Wiot or[5] Wyot, Adam Wiot or Wyote or[4], Guyott[3], Guyott[2], Captain or Admiral Adam Guyott or[1] Wiot) was born July 19, 1926. She married Robert J. Sweatt, son of Raleigh Sweatt and Ruby Smart.

Children of Mae Turner and Robert Sweatt are:

+ 1512   i.   Ronald Wayne[24] Sweatt, born December 29, 1947.

+ 1513   ii.   Robert Allen Sweatt, born November 07, 1949.

+ 1514   iii.   Dwight Turner Sweatt, born April 13, 1955 in Cabarrus County, N.C.

976. Lois Evelyn[23] Turner (Jennie Elizabeth[22] Eagle, Adolphus Grant[21], Amanda Jane[20] Wyatt, Noah Calvin[19], Thomas "Tommy"[18] Wiatt, Sr. (Wyatt, Wiett), John[17], Henry[16], Richard[15], George[14], Rev. Haute "Haut" "Hawte"[13], Sir George "Georgius" Thomas[12], Sir Thomas "The Younger"[11], Sir Thomas "The Elder"[10], Sir Henry[9], Richard Wiat or[8] Wyatt, Geoffrey "Jeoffrey" Wiot or[7] Wiat, Robert or Richard[6] Wiot, William Wiot or[5] Wyot, Adam Wiot or Wyote or[4], Guyott[3], Guyott[2], Captain or Admiral Adam Guyott or[1] Wiot) was born October 06, 1931. She married John S. Chamberlain January 01, 1965, son of James Chamberlain and Mildred Briggs.

Children of Lois Turner and John Chamberlain are:

1515   i.   Gina Elizabeth[24] Chamberlain, born September 22, 1956 in Caldwell County, N.C.

1516   ii.   Robert Kent Chamberlain, born June 25, 1958 in Caldwell County, N.C.

978. Nancy Lenora[23] Ramseur (Viola Martha[22] Eagle, Adolphus Grant[21], Amanda Jane[20] Wyatt, Noah Calvin[19], Thomas "Tommy"[18] Wiatt, Sr. (Wyatt, Wiett), John[17], Henry[16], Richard[15], George[14], Rev. Haute "Haut" "Hawte"[13], Sir George "Georgius" Thomas[12], Sir Thomas "The Younger"[11], Sir Thomas "The Elder"[10], Sir Henry[9], Richard Wiat or[8] Wyatt, Geoffrey "Jeoffrey" Wiot or[7] Wiat, Robert or Richard[6] Wiot, William Wiot or[5] Wyot, Adam

Wiot or Wyote or[4], Guyott[3], Guyott[2], Captain or Admiral Adam Guyott or[1] Wiot) was born July 30, 1940 in Cabarrus County, N.C. She married Kenneth Larry Marlow October 28, 1961, son of Matthew Marlow and Lula Patterson.

More About Kenneth Larry Marlow:
Fact 1: June 26, 1965, date of birth given in Eagle book.

Children of Nancy Ramseur and Kenneth Marlow are:
1517	i.	Lisa Ann[24] Marlow, born May 28, 1963.
1518	ii.	Kenneth Larry Marlow, born June 26, 1965.
1519	iii.	Philip Scott Marlow, born May 12, 1970.

981. Joan[23] Eller (Bessie Carolina "Caroline"[22] Eagle, Adolphus Grant[21], Amanda Jane[20] Wyatt, Noah Calvin[19], Thomas "Tommy"[18] Wiatt, Sr. (Wyatt, Wiett), John[17], Henry[16], Richard[15], George[14], Rev. Haute "Haut" "Hawte"[13], Sir George "Georgius" Thomas[12], Sir Thomas "The Younger"[11], Sir Thomas "The Elder"[10], Sir Henry[9], Richard Wiat or[8] Wyatt, Geoffrey "Jeoffrey" Wiot or[7] Wiat, Robert or Richard[6] Wiot, William Wiot or[5] Wyot, Adam Wiot or Wyote or[4], Guyott[3], Guyott[2], Captain or Admiral Adam Guyott or[1] Wiot) was born January 06, 1933. She married Donald Eugene Frye, son of Jay Frye and Violet Davis.

Children of Joan Eller and Donald Frye are:
1520	i.	John Darrell[24] Frye, born March 22, 1957.
1521	ii.	Stan Eugene Frye, born August 28, 1960 in Cabarrus County, N.C.
1522	iii.	Donna Kay Frye, born July 29, 1963 in Cabarrus County, N.C.

982. Nancy Loraine[23] Eller (Bessie Carolina "Caroline"[22] Eagle, Adolphus Grant[21], Amanda Jane[20] Wyatt, Noah Calvin[19], Thomas "Tommy"[18] Wiatt, Sr. (Wyatt, Wiett), John[17], Henry[16], Richard[15], George[14], Rev. Haute "Haut" "Hawte"[13], Sir George "Georgius" Thomas[12], Sir Thomas "The Younger"[11], Sir Thomas "The Elder"[10], Sir Henry[9], Richard Wiat or[8] Wyatt, Geoffrey "Jeoffrey" Wiot or[7] Wiat, Robert or Richard[6] Wiot, William Wiot or[5] Wyot, Adam Wiot or Wyote or[4], Guyott[3], Guyott[2], Captain or Admiral Adam Guyott or[1] Wiot) was born March 21, 1939 in Iredell County, N.C. She married Burley Thomas Day, Jr., son of Burley Day and Louise Long.

Children of Nancy Eller and Burley Day are:
1523	i.	Burley Thomas[24] Day III, born June 07, 1961 in Cabarrus County, N.C.
1524	ii.	John Bradley Day, born November 21, 1962 in Cabarrus County, N.C.
1525	iii.	Kemerlyn Caroline Day, born December 22, 1966 in Davidson County, N.C.

983. Brenda Sue[23] Ramseur (Marnie Della "Delle"[22] Eagle, Adolphus Grant[21], Amanda Jane[20] Wyatt, Noah Calvin[19], Thomas "Tommy"[18] Wiatt, Sr. (Wyatt, Wiett), John[17], Henry[16], Richard[15], George[14], Rev. Haute "Haut" "Hawte"[13], Sir George "Georgius" Thomas[12], Sir Thomas "The Younger"[11], Sir Thomas "The Elder"[10], Sir Henry[9], Richard Wiat or[8] Wyatt, Geoffrey "Jeoffrey" Wiot or[7] Wiat, Robert or Richard[6] Wiot, William Wiot or[5] Wyot, Adam Wiot or Wyote or[4], Guyott[3], Guyott[2], Captain or Admiral Adam Guyott or[1] Wiot) was born November 22, 1944 in Iredell County, N.C. She married James Russell Adams, Jr. 1966, son of James Adams and Virginia Cauthen.

Child of Brenda Ramseur and James Adams is:

1526   i.   Marnie Virginia[24] Adams, born February 04, 1967 in Cabarrus County, N.C.

984. Melvin Layaette[23] Rameur, Jr. (Marnie Della "Delle"[22] Eagle, Adolphus Grant[21], Amanda Jane[20] Wyatt, Noah Calvin[19], Thomas "Tommy"[18] Wiatt, Sr. (Wyatt, Wiett), John[17], Henry[16], Richard[15], George[14], Rev. Haute "Haut" "Hawte"[13], Sir George "Georgius" Thomas[12], Sir Thomas "The Younger"[11], Sir Thomas "The Elder"[10], Sir Henry[9], Richard Wiat or[8] Wyatt, Geoffrey "Jeoffrey" Wiot or[7] Wiat, Robert or Richard[6] Wiot, William Wiot or[5] Wyot, Adam Wiot or Wyote or[4], Guyott[3], Guyott[2], Captain or Admiral Adam Guyott or[1] Wiot) was born July 23, 1938. He married Rebecca Joyce Hinson July 04, 1957, daughter of Bennie Hinson and Margaret Gragg.

Children of Melvin Rameur and Rebecca Hinson are:

1527   i.   Milton Todd[24] Rameur, born January 18, 1958 in Watauga County, N.C.
1528   ii.   Timothy Scott Rameur, born December 29, 1958 in Mecklenburg County, N.C.
1529   iii. Margaret Remel Rameur, born January 26, 1966 in Cabarrus County, N.C.
1530   iv.   Susan Rebecca Rameur, born April 27, 1971 in Cabarrus County, N.C.

985. Kenneth Lee[23] Eagle (Weathler Lee[22], John Murphy[21], Amanda Jane[20] Wyatt, Noah Calvin[19], Thomas "Tommy"[18] Wiatt, Sr. (Wyatt, Wiett), John[17], Henry[16], Richard[15], George[14], Rev. Haute "Haut" "Hawte"[13], Sir George "Georgius" Thomas[12], Sir Thomas "The Younger"[11], Sir Thomas "The Elder"[10], Sir Henry[9], Richard Wiat or[8] Wyatt, Geoffrey "Jeoffrey" Wiot or[7] Wiat, Robert or Richard[6] Wiot, William Wiot or[5] Wyot, Adam Wiot or Wyote or[4], Guyott[3], Guyott[2], Captain or Admiral Adam Guyott or[1] Wiot) was born May 09, 1921 in Rowan County N.C. He married Elisabeth Weisner February 16, 1963, daughter of Emory Weisner and Julia Reynolds.

Children of Kenneth Eagle and Elisabeth Weisner are:

1531   i.   Kenneth[24] Lee, Eagle, Jr., born June 18, 1949.

More About Kenneth Lee, Eagle, Jr.:
Fact 1: Lawyer, Rowan County, N.C.

1532   ii.   Elizabeth Gayle, born December 03, 1951. She married Thomas Hill Crabtree.

986.   Margaret[23] Eagle (Weathler Lee[22], John Murphy[21], Amanda Jane[20] Wyatt, Noah Calvin[19], Thomas "Tommy"[18] Wiatt, Sr. (Wyatt, Wiett), John[17], Henry[16], Richard[15], George[14], Rev. Haute "Haut" "Hawte"[13], Sir George "Georgius" Thomas[12], Sir Thomas "The Younger"[11], Sir Thomas "The Elder"[10], Sir Henry[9], Richard Wiat or[8] Wyatt, Geoffrey "Jeoffrey" Wiot or[7] Wiat, Robert or Richard[6] Wiot, William Wiot or[5] Wyot, Adam Wiot or Wyote or[4], Guyott[3], Guyott[2], Captain or Admiral Adam Guyott or[1] Wiot) was born March 17, 1925. She married David Thomas Haynes, son of James Haynes and Grace Cook.

Children of Margaret Eagle and David Haynes are:

1533   i.   David Lee[24] Haynes, born June 11, 1954 in Rowan County N.C.
1534   ii.   Tammy Sue Haynes, born March 16, 1959 in Rowan County N.C.

987.   Charles[23] Eagle (Weathler Lee[22], John Murphy[21], Amanda Jane[20] Wyatt, Noah Calvin[19], Thomas "Tommy"[18] Wiatt, Sr. (Wyatt, Wiett), John[17], Henry[16], Richard[15], George[14], Rev. Haute "Haut" "Hawte"[13], Sir George "Georgius" Thomas[12], Sir Thomas "The Younger"[11], Sir Thomas "The Elder"[10], Sir Henry[9], Richard Wiat or[8] Wyatt, Geoffrey "Jeoffrey" Wiot or[7] Wiat, Robert or Richard[6] Wiot, William Wiot or[5] Wyot, Adam Wiot or Wyote or[4], Guyott[3], Guyott[2], Captain or Admiral Adam Guyott or[1] Wiot) was born October 11, 1929 in Rowan County N.C., and died August 11, 1977. He married Sue Frayer December 26, 1954, daughter of Fred Frayer and Nan McDaniel.

Children of Charles Eagle and Sue Frayer are:

1535   i.   Bonnie Sue[24] Eagle, born March 16, 1959 in Rowan County N.C.
1536   ii.   Charles Steven Eagle, born September 11, 1958 in Rowan County N.C.

988.   Warren Keith[23] Kluttz (Mary Kate[22] Eagle, John Murphy[21], Amanda Jane[20] Wyatt, Noah Calvin[19], Thomas "Tommy"[18] Wiatt, Sr. (Wyatt, Wiett), John[17], Henry[16], Richard[15], George[14], Rev. Haute "Haut" "Hawte"[13], Sir George "Georgius" Thomas[12], Sir Thomas "The Younger"[11], Sir Thomas "The Elder"[10], Sir Henry[9], Richard Wiat or[8] Wyatt, Geoffrey "Jeoffrey" Wiot or[7] Wiat, Robert or Richard[6] Wiot, William Wiot or[5] Wyot, Adam Wiot or Wyote or[4], Guyott[3], Guyott[2], Captain or Admiral Adam Guyott or[1] Wiot) was born March 15, 1921 in Rowan County N.C. He married Verna Beatrice Bost, daughter of Roy Bost and Lola Kluttz.

Child of Warren Kluttz and Verna Bost is:

+ 1537   i.   Pamela Nesta[24] Kluttz, born April 15, 1948 in Stanly County, N.C.

989. Novice Bernita[23] Kluttz (Mary Kate[22] Eagle, John Murphy[21], Amanda Jane[20] Wyatt, Noah Calvin[19], Thomas "Tommy"[18] Wiatt, Sr. (Wyatt, Wiett), John[17], Henry[16], Richard[15], George[14], Rev. Haute "Haut" "Hawte"[13], Sir George "Georgius" Thomas[12], Sir Thomas "The Younger"[11], Sir Thomas "The Elder"[10], Sir Henry[9], Richard Wiat or[8] Wyatt, Geoffrey "Jeoffrey" Wiot or[7] Wiat, Robert or Richard[6] Wiot, William Wiot or[5] Wyot, Adam Wiot or Wyote or[4], Guyott[3], Guyott[2], Captain or Admiral Adam Guyott or[1] Wiot) was born August 20, 1922 in Rowan County N.C. She married (1) Greer S. Abernathy. She married (2) Walter Reid Sifford May 02, 1942, son of Lewis Sifford and Lula Castor.

More About Novice Bernita Kluttz:
Remains are buried in Organ Lutheran Church, Rowan County, N.C. with spouse.

Children of Novice Kluttz and Walter Sifford are:

+ 1538   i.   Walter Roy[24] Sifford, born January 19, 1947 in Rowan County N.C.
+ 1539   ii.   Dennis Andrew Sifford, born October 11, 1951 in Rowan County N.C.

990. Roberta Myraline[23] Kluttz (Mary Kate[22] Eagle, John Murphy[21], Amanda Jane[20] Wyatt, Noah Calvin[19], Thomas "Tommy"[18] Wiatt, Sr. (Wyatt, Wiett), John[17], Henry[16], Richard[15], George[14], Rev. Haute "Haut" "Hawte"[13], Sir George "Georgius" Thomas[12], Sir Thomas "The Younger"[11], Sir Thomas "The Elder"[10], Sir Henry[9], Richard Wiat or[8] Wyatt, Geoffrey "Jeoffrey" Wiot or[7] Wiat, Robert or Richard[6] Wiot, William Wiot or[5] Wyot, Adam Wiot or Wyote or[4], Guyott[3], Guyott[2], Captain or Admiral Adam Guyott or[1] Wiot) was born October 15, 1924 in Rowan County N.C. She married Osco Clay Basinger, son of Basinger and Ada Johnson.

Children of Roberta Kluttz and Osco Basinger are:

+ 1540   i.   Osco Clay[24] Basinger, Jr., born March 16, 1943.
+ 1541   ii.   Olin Lane Basinger, born September 26, 1944.
+ 1542   iii.   Myraline Kluttz Basinger, born March 03, 1958.

991. Zelma Jestine[23] Kluttz (Mary Kate[22] Eagle, John Murphy[21], Amanda Jane[20] Wyatt, Noah Calvin[19], Thomas "Tommy"[18] Wiatt, Sr. (Wyatt, Wiett), John[17], Henry[16], Richard[15], George[14], Rev. Haute "Haut" "Hawte"[13], Sir George "Georgius" Thomas[12], Sir Thomas "The Younger"[11], Sir Thomas "The Elder"[10], Sir Henry[9], Richard Wiat or[8] Wyatt, Geoffrey "Jeoffrey" Wiot or[7] Wiat, Robert or Richard[6] Wiot, William Wiot or[5] Wyot, Adam Wiot or Wyote or[4], Guyott[3], Guyott[2], Captain or Admiral Adam Guyott or[1] Wiot) was born June 23, 1927 in Rowan County N.C. She married Leith C. Foster, Jr., son of Leith Foster and Troy Michael.

Children of Zelma Kluttz and Leith Foster are:

1543   i.   Gerald[24] Foster, born 1946; died 1946.

        More About Gerald Foster:
        Remains are buried at Chestnut Hill Cemetery, Salisbury, Rowan County, N.C.

+   1544   ii.   Melda Jestene Foster, born July 15, 1948.
+   1545   iii.   Sandra Ilene Foster, born December 30, 1949.
+   1546   iv.   Michael Leith Foster, born August 14, 1951.

992. Charles Robert[23] Wagoner (Ethel Viola[22] Eagle, John Murphy[21], Amanda Jane[20] Wyatt, Noah Calvin[19], Thomas "Tommy"[18] Wiatt, Sr. (Wyatt, Wiett), John[17], Henry[16], Richard[15], George[14], Rev. Haute "Haut" "Hawte"[13], Sir George "Georgius" Thomas[12], Sir Thomas "The Younger"[11], Sir Thomas "The Elder"[10], Sir Henry[9], Richard Wiat or[8] Wyatt, Geoffrey "Jeoffrey" Wiot or[7] Wiat, Robert or Richard[6] Wiot, William Wiot or[5] Wyot, Adam Wiot or Wyote or[4], Guyott[3], Guyott[2], Captain or Admiral Adam Guyott or[1] Wiot) was born April 10, 1938 in Rowan County N.C. He married Helen Rachel Agner, daughter of Joseph Agner and Abbie Cauble.

        Child of Charles Wagoner and Helen Agner is:
        1547   i.   Charlie Robert[24] Wagoner, Jr., born January 30, 1977 in Rowan County N.C.

993. Larry Dean[23] Wagoner (Ethel Viola[22] Eagle, John Murphy[21], Amanda Jane[20] Wyatt, Noah Calvin[19], Thomas "Tommy"[18] Wiatt, Sr. (Wyatt, Wiett), John[17], Henry[16], Richard[15], George[14], Rev. Haute "Haut" "Hawte"[13], Sir George "Georgius" Thomas[12], Sir Thomas "The Younger"[11], Sir Thomas "The Elder"[10], Sir Henry[9], Richard Wiat or[8] Wyatt, Geoffrey "Jeoffrey" Wiot or[7] Wiat, Robert or Richard[6] Wiot, William Wiot or[5] Wyot, Adam Wiot or Wyote or[4], Guyott[3], Guyott[2], Captain or Admiral Adam Guyott or[1] Wiot) was born January 15, 1944 in Rowan County N.C. He married Carolina Lois Kirkpatrick June 30, 1965, daughter of C.H. Kirkpatrick and Edith Holland.

        Children of Larry Wagoner and Carolina Kirkpatrick are:
        1548   i.   Donna Marie[24] Wagoner, born June 13, 1970.
        1549   ii.   Lori Dawn Wagoner, born November 28, 1972 in Rowan County N.C.

994. Eugene A.[23] Brannock (Lizzie Remelle[22] Eagle, John Murphy[21], Amanda Jane[20] Wyatt, Noah Calvin[19], Thomas "Tommy"[18] Wiatt, Sr. (Wyatt, Wiett), John[17], Henry[16], Richard[15], George[14], Rev. Haute "Haut" "Hawte"[13], Sir George "Georgius" Thomas[12], Sir Thomas "The Younger"[11], Sir Thomas "The Elder"[10], Sir Henry[9], Richard Wiat or[8] Wyatt, Geoffrey "Jeoffrey" Wiot or[7] Wiat, Robert or Richard[6] Wiot, William Wiot or[5] Wyot, Adam Wiot or Wyote or[4], Guyott[3], Guyott[2], Captain or Admiral Adam Guyott or[1] Wiot) was born January 01, 1933. He married Roberta Helen Busch.

Children of Eugene Brannock and Roberta Busch are:

1550   i.   John Wesley[24] Brannock, born June 15, 1958.

1551   ii.   Cynthia Helen Brannock, born August 18, 1959.

995. Patricia Ann[23] Brannock (Lizzie Remelle[22] Eagle, John Murphy[21], Amanda Jane[20] Wyatt, Noah Calvin[19], Thomas "Tommy"[18] Wiatt, Sr. (Wyatt, Wiett), John[17], Henry[16], Richard[15], George[14], Rev. Haute "Haut" "Hawte"[13], Sir George "Georgius" Thomas[12], Sir Thomas "The Younger"[11], Sir Thomas "The Elder"[10], Sir Henry[9], Richard Wiat or[8] Wyatt, Geoffrey "Jeoffrey" Wiot or[7] Wiat, Robert or Richard[6] Wiot, William Wiot or[5] Wyot, Adam Wiot or Wyote or[4], Guyott[3], Guyott[2], Captain or Admiral Adam Guyott or[1] Wiot) was born January 19, 1935 in Rome, Ga. She married W.T. Lipscomb 1959.

Child of Patricia Brannock and W.T. Lipscomb is:

1552   i.   Scott Sterline[24] Lipscomb, born January 13, 1960 in Gladsden, Ala.

996. Barbara[23] Cook (Margaret Marie[22] Eagle, John Murphy[21], Amanda Jane[20] Wyatt, Noah Calvin[19], Thomas "Tommy"[18] Wiatt, Sr. (Wyatt, Wiett), John[17], Henry[16], Richard[15], George[14], Rev. Haute "Haut" "Hawte"[13], Sir George "Georgius" Thomas[12], Sir Thomas "The Younger"[11], Sir Thomas "The Elder"[10], Sir Henry[9], Richard Wiat or[8] Wyatt, Geoffrey "Jeoffrey" Wiot or[7] Wiat, Robert or Richard[6] Wiot, William Wiot or[5] Wyot, Adam Wiot or Wyote or[4], Guyott[3], Guyott[2], Captain or Admiral Adam Guyott or[1] Wiot) was born December 07, 1935. She married James Russell Lambert April 14, 1956, son of Floyd Lambert and Annie Riddle.

Children of Barbara Cook and James Lambert are:

+   1553   i.   Deborah[24] Lambert, born October 06, 1957.

+   1554   ii.   Amanda Lambert, born November 19, 1957.

+   1555   iii.   James Michael Lambert, born April 06, 1961.

997. Genelda[23] Cook (Margaret Marie[22] Eagle, John Murphy[21], Amanda Jane[20] Wyatt, Noah Calvin[19], Thomas "Tommy"[18] Wiatt, Sr. (Wyatt, Wiett), John[17], Henry[16], Richard[15], George[14], Rev. Haute "Haut" "Hawte"[13], Sir George "Georgius" Thomas[12], Sir Thomas "The Younger"[11], Sir Thomas "The Elder"[10], Sir Henry[9], Richard Wiat or[8] Wyatt, Geoffrey "Jeoffrey" Wiot or[7] Wiat, Robert or Richard[6] Wiot, William Wiot or[5] Wyot, Adam Wiot or Wyote or[4], Guyott[3], Guyott[2], Captain or Admiral Adam Guyott or[1] Wiot) was born January 09, 1937. She married (1) Donald Carl Pickler, son of Pickler and Helen. She married (2) William Ray Hunt, son of Willie Hunt and Crissie Tratham.

Child of Genelda Cook and Donald Pickler is:

+   1556   i.   Sheila Marie[24] Pickler, born April 13, 1957.

Children of Genelda Cook and William Hunt are:

1557   i.   William Ray[24] Hunt, Jr., born July 20, 1963.

| 1558 | ii. | Steven Wayne Hunt, born May 20, 1966. |
| 1559 | iii. | Lynn Michelle Hunt, born August 02, 1969. |

998. Jerry William[23] Cook (Margaret Marie[22] Eagle, John Murphy[21], Amanda Jane[20] Wyatt, Noah Calvin[19], Thomas "Tommy"[18] Wiatt, Sr. (Wyatt, Wiett), John[17], Henry[16], Richard[15], George[14], Rev. Haute "Haut" "Hawte"[13], Sir George "Georgius" Thomas[12], Sir Thomas "The Younger"[11], Sir Thomas "The Elder"[10], Sir Henry[9], Richard Wiat or[8] Wyatt, Geoffrey "Jeoffrey" Wiot or[7] Wiat, Robert or Richard[6] Wiot, William Wiot or[5] Wyot, Adam Wiot or Wyote or[4], Guyott[3], Guyott[2], Captain or Admiral Adam Guyott or[1] Wiot) was born March 29, 1940 in Rowan County N.C. He married Peggy Ann Livengood, daughter of Cecil Livengood and Katherine Goodman.

Children of Jerry Cook and Peggy Livengood are:

| 1560 | i. | Michael William[24] Cook, born June 23, 1962. |
| 1561 | ii. | Angela Kathleen Cook, born February 04, 1965. |

1007. James David[23] Hand (Mary Frances[22] Eagle, David Leo[21], Amanda Jane[20] Wyatt, Noah Calvin[19], Thomas "Tommy"[18] Wiatt, Sr. (Wyatt, Wiett), John[17], Henry[16], Richard[15], George[14], Rev. Haute "Haut" "Hawte"[13], Sir George "Georgius" Thomas[12], Sir Thomas "The Younger"[11], Sir Thomas "The Elder"[10], Sir Henry[9], Richard Wiat or[8] Wyatt, Geoffrey "Jeoffrey" Wiot or[7] Wiat, Robert or Richard[6] Wiot, William Wiot or[5] Wyot, Adam Wiot or Wyote or[4], Guyott[3], Guyott[2], Captain or Admiral Adam Guyott or[1] Wiot) was born October 07, 1956 in Rowan County N.C. He married (1) Cynthia "Cindy" Sprinkle. He married (2) Cynthia "Cindy" Rose Mahaley December 01, 1974, daughter of Alfred Mahaley and Eda Hoffner.

Child of James Hand and Cynthia Sprinkle is:

| + | 1562 | i. | Cassie Camille[24] Hand, born October 10, 1986. |

Child of James Hand and Cynthia Mahaley is:

| 1563 | i. | James Athan[24] Hand, born January 01, 1979 in Rowan County, N.C. |

1008. Timothy Irvin[23] Hand (Mary Frances[22] Eagle, David Leo[21], Amanda Jane[20] Wyatt, Noah Calvin[19], Thomas "Tommy"[18] Wiatt, Sr. (Wyatt, Wiett), John[17], Henry[16], Richard[15], George[14], Rev. Haute "Haut" "Hawte"[13], Sir George "Georgius" Thomas[12], Sir Thomas "The Younger"[11], Sir Thomas "The Elder"[10], Sir Henry[9], Richard Wiat or[8] Wyatt, Geoffrey "Jeoffrey" Wiot or[7] Wiat, Robert or Richard[6] Wiot, William Wiot or[5] Wyot, Adam Wiot or Wyote or[4], Guyott[3], Guyott[2], Captain or Admiral Adam Guyott or[1] Wiot) was born March 29, 1959 in Rowan County N.C. He married Texie Gayle Clontz June 05, 1977, daughter of Elmer Clontz and Texie Money.

Child of Timothy Hand and Texie Clontz is:

| 1564 | i. | Tabitha Dawn24 Hand, born June 08, 1980 in Rowan County N.C. |

1009. Harold Wayne[23] Hand (Mary Frances[22] Eagle, David Leo[21], Amanda Jane[20] Wyatt, Noah Calvin[19], Thomas "Tommy"[18] Wiatt, Sr. (Wyatt, Wiett), John[17], Henry[16], Richard[15], George[14], Rev. Haute "Haut" "Hawte"[13], Sir George "Georgius" Thomas[12], Sir Thomas "The Younger"[11], Sir Thomas "The Elder"[10], Sir Henry[9], Richard Wiat or[8] Wyatt, Geoffrey "Jeoffrey" Wiot or[7] Wiat, Robert or Richard[6] Wiot, William Wiot or[5] Wyot, Adam Wiot or Wyote or[4], Guyott[3], Guyott[2], Captain or Admiral Adam Guyott or[1] Wiot) was born August 01, 1950 in Rowan County N.C. He married (1) Patrica Lynn Teasly, daughter of Grandville Teasly and Lyda Nelson. He married (2) Tammy Pennington.

> Child of Harold Hand and Patrica Teasly is:
> 1565   i.   Amanda Suzanne[24] Hand, born November 19, 1974 in England.

> Child of Harold Hand and Tammy Pennington is:
> 1566   i.   Mary Cole[24] Hand.

1012. Kimberly Cheryl[23] Ludwick (Barbara Jean[22] Eagle, David Leo[21], Amanda Jane[20] Wyatt, Noah Calvin[19], Thomas "Tommy"[18] Wiatt, Sr. (Wyatt, Wiett), John[17], Henry[16], Richard[15], George[14], Rev. Haute "Haut" "Hawte"[13], Sir George "Georgius" Thomas[12], Sir Thomas "The Younger"[11], Sir Thomas "The Elder"[10], Sir Henry[9], Richard Wiat or[8] Wyatt, Geoffrey "Jeoffrey" Wiot or[7] Wiat, Robert or Richard[6] Wiot, William Wiot or[5] Wyot, Adam Wiot or Wyote or[4], Guyott[3], Guyott[2], Captain or Admiral Adam Guyott or[1] Wiot) was born July 01, 1964. She married Bruce Climan Rogers, Jr. May 27, 1989.

> Child of Kimberly Ludwick and Bruce Rogers is:
> 1567   i.   Preston Bruce24 Rogers, born March 28, 1993.

1014. Christopher Martin[23] Eagle (Martin Luther[22], David Leo[21], Amanda Jane[20] Wyatt, Noah Calvin[19], Thomas "Tommy"[18] Wiatt, Sr. (Wyatt, Wiett), John[17], Henry[16], Richard[15], George[14], Rev. Haute "Haut" "Hawte"[13], Sir George "Georgius" Thomas[12], Sir Thomas "The Younger"[11], Sir Thomas "The Elder"[10], Sir Henry[9], Richard Wiat or[8] Wyatt, Geoffrey "Jeoffrey" Wiot or[7] Wiat, Robert or Richard[6] Wiot, William Wiot or[5] Wyot, Adam Wiot or Wyote or[4], Guyott[3], Guyott[2], Captain or Admiral Adam Guyott or[1] Wiot) was born January 13, 1970 in Rowan County N.C. He married Leslie DeAnn Jones, daughter of Paul Jones and Carolyn Fisher.

> Children of Christopher Eagle and Leslie Jones are:
> 1568   i.   Christopher Brian[24] Eagle, born June 07, 1988.
> 1569   ii.   Hunter Lynn Eagle, born June 30, 1989.
> 1570   iii.   Sadie Verline Eagle, born November 16, 1990.
> 1571   iv.   Lindsay Elizabeth Eagle, born July 30, 1992.

1016. Richard Eagle[23] Shaw (Helen Lois[22] Eagle, Noah Walter[21], Amanda Jane[20] Wyatt, Noah Calvin[19], Thomas "Tommy"[18] Wiatt, Sr. (Wyatt, Wiett), John[17], Henry[16], Richard[15], George[14], Rev. Haute "Haut" "Hawte"[13], Sir George "Georgius" Thomas[12], Sir Thomas "The Younger"[11],

Sir Thomas "The Elder"[10], Sir Henry[9], Richard Wiat or[8] Wyatt, Geoffrey "Jeoffrey" Wiot or[7] Wiat, Robert or Richard[6] Wiot, William Wiot or[5] Wyot, Adam Wiot or Wyote or[4], Guyott[3], Guyott[2], Captain or Admiral Adam Guyott or[1] Wiot) was born August 20, 1938. He married Rebecca Anne Faggart, daughter of Alonzo Faggart and Mary Edleman.

Children of Richard Shaw and Rebecca Faggart are:

| 1572 | i. | Phillip Lee[24] Shaw, born March 09, 1966. |
| 1573 | ii. | Anne Elizabeth Shaw, born March 06, 1970 in Cabarrus County, N.C. |

1017. Willie Kay[23] Shaw (Helen Lois[22] Eagle, Noah Walter[21], Amanda Jane[20] Wyatt, Noah Calvin[19], Thomas "Tommy"[18] Wiatt, Sr. (Wyatt, Wiett), John[17], Henry[16], Richard[15], George[14], Rev. Haute "Haut" "Hawte"[13], Sir George "Georgius" Thomas[12], Sir Thomas "The Younger"[11], Sir Thomas "The Elder"[10], Sir Henry[9], Richard Wiat or[8] Wyatt, Geoffrey "Jeoffrey" Wiot or[7] Wiat, Robert or Richard[6] Wiot, William Wiot or[5] Wyot, Adam Wiot or Wyote or[4], Guyott[3], Guyott[2], Captain or Admiral Adam Guyott or[1] Wiot) was born May 05, 1949 in McDowell County, N.C. She married Howard Claude Jenkins June 06, 1971, son of Thaddus Jenkins and Evon Leatherman.

Child of Willie Shaw and Howard Jenkins is:

| 1574 | i. | David Wayne[24] Jenkins, born February 03, 1973 in Pinebluff, Ark. |

1018. Hilda Joyce[23] Kepley (Ruth Anne[22] Eagle, Albert Lee[21], Amanda Jane[20] Wyatt, Noah Calvin[19], Thomas "Tommy"[18] Wiatt, Sr. (Wyatt, Wiett), John[17], Henry[16], Richard[15], George[14], Rev. Haute "Haut" "Hawte"[13], Sir George "Georgius" Thomas[12], Sir Thomas "The Younger"[11], Sir Thomas "The Elder"[10], Sir Henry[9], Richard Wiat or[8] Wyatt, Geoffrey "Jeoffrey" Wiot or[7] Wiat, Robert or Richard[6] Wiot, William Wiot or[5] Wyot, Adam Wiot or Wyote or[4], Guyott[3], Guyott[2], Captain or Admiral Adam Guyott or[1] Wiot). She married Emery Linwood Butler, Jr. April 16, 1968.

Children of Hilda Kepley and Emery Butler are:

1575	i.	Darren Scott[24] Butler, born March 23, 1969 in Cabarrus County, N.C.
1576	ii.	Kimberly Charlene Butler, born September 02, 1972 in Cabarrus County, N.C.
1577	iii.	Crystal Anne Butler, born December 23, 1974 in Cabarrus County, N.C.

1019. Albert Ray[23] Kepley (Ruth Anne[22] Eagle, Albert Lee[21], Amanda Jane[20] Wyatt, Noah Calvin[19], Thomas "Tommy"[18] Wiatt, Sr. (Wyatt, Wiett), John[17], Henry[16], Richard[15], George[14], Rev. Haute "Haut" "Hawte"[13], Sir George "Georgius" Thomas[12], Sir Thomas "The Younger"[11], Sir Thomas "The Elder"[10], Sir Henry[9], Richard Wiat or[8] Wyatt, Geoffrey "Jeoffrey" Wiot or[7] Wiat, Robert or Richard[6] Wiot, William Wiot or[5] Wyot, Adam Wiot or Wyote or[4], Guyott[3],

Guyott^2, Captain or Admiral Adam Guyott or^1 Wiot) was born October 31, 1931. He married Carol Jean Black June 26, 1964.

Child of Albert Kepley and Carol Black is:

1578   i.   Kelley Jo^{24} Kepley, born December 06, 1961.

1020. Joseph Lewis^{23} Kepley (Ruth Anne^{22} Eagle, Albert Lee^{21}, Amanda Jane^{20} Wyatt, Noah Calvin^{19}, Thomas "Tommy"^{18} Wiatt, Sr. (Wyatt, Wiett), John^{17}, Henry^{16}, Richard^{15}, George^{14}, Rev. Haute "Haut" "Hawte"^{13}, Sir George "Georgius" Thomas^{12}, Sir Thomas "The Younger"^{11}, Sir Thomas "The Elder"^{10}, Sir Henry^9, Richard Wiat or^8 Wyatt, Geoffrey "Jeoffrey" Wiot or^7 Wiat, Robert or Richard^6 Wiot, William Wiot or^5 Wyot, Adam Wiot or Wyote or^4, Guyott^3, Guyott^2, Captain or Admiral Adam Guyott or^1 Wiot) was born November 27, 1936. He married Salita Jean Sasser March 25, 1955.

Children of Joseph Kepley and Salita Sasser are:

1579   i.   Patricia Jolene^{24} Kepley, born in Rowan County, N.C.

1580   ii.   Melinda Anne Kepley, born in Rowan County, N.C.

1022. Jerry Lee^{23} Kepley (Ruth Anne^{22} Eagle, Albert Lee^{21}, Amanda Jane^{20} Wyatt, Noah Calvin^{19}, Thomas "Tommy"^{18} Wiatt, Sr. (Wyatt, Wiett), John^{17}, Henry^{16}, Richard^{15}, George^{14}, Rev. Haute "Haut" "Hawte"^{13}, Sir George "Georgius" Thomas^{12}, Sir Thomas "The Younger"^{11}, Sir Thomas "The Elder"^{10}, Sir Henry^9, Richard Wiat or^8 Wyatt, Geoffrey "Jeoffrey" Wiot or^7 Wiat, Robert or Richard^6 Wiot, William Wiot or^5 Wyot, Adam Wiot or Wyote or^4, Guyott^3, Guyott^2, Captain or Admiral Adam Guyott or^1 Wiot) was born April 18, 1943. He married Patricia Faye Evain June 29, 1963.

Child of Jerry Kepley and Patricia Evain is:

1581   i.   Chad Lee^{24} Kepley, born December 30, 1969.

1023. Larry Eugene^{23} Wilcox (Carrie Etta^{22} Eagle, Albert Lee^{21}, Amanda Jane^{20} Wyatt, Noah Calvin^{19}, Thomas "Tommy"^{18} Wiatt, Sr. (Wyatt, Wiett), John^{17}, Henry^{16}, Richard^{15}, George^{14}, Rev. Haute "Haut" "Hawte"^{13}, Sir George "Georgius" Thomas^{12}, Sir Thomas "The Younger"^{11}, Sir Thomas "The Elder"^{10}, Sir Henry^9, Richard Wiat or^8 Wyatt, Geoffrey "Jeoffrey" Wiot or^7 Wiat, Robert or Richard^6 Wiot, William Wiot or^5 Wyot, Adam Wiot or Wyote or^4, Guyott^3, Guyott^2, Captain or Admiral Adam Guyott or^1 Wiot) was born November 12, 1940. He married Tammie Ann Freeze July 10, 1960, daughter of Thomas Freeze and Nevada Benson.

Children of Larry Wilcox and Tammie Freeze are:

1582   i.   Randall Eugene^{24} Wilcox, born November 02, 1963.

1583   ii.   Susan Annett Wilcox, born July 20, 1966.

1024. Linda Lee^{23} Wilcox (Carrie Etta^{22} Eagle, Albert Lee^{21}, Amanda Jane^{20} Wyatt, Noah Calvin^{19}, Thomas "Tommy"^{18} Wiatt, Sr. (Wyatt, Wiett), John^{17}, Henry^{16}, Richard^{15}, George^{14}, Rev. Haute "Haut" "Hawte"^{13}, Sir George "Georgius" Thomas^{12}, Sir Thomas "The Younger"^{11},

Sir Thomas "The Elder"[10], Sir Henry[9], Richard Wiat or[8] Wyatt, Geoffrey "Jeoffrey" Wiot or[7] Wiat, Robert or Richard[6] Wiot, William Wiot or[5] Wyot, Adam Wiot or Wyote or[4], Guyott[3], Guyott[2], Captain or Admiral Adam Guyott or[1] Wiot) was born December 23, 1942. She married James Melvin Freeman November 28, 1965, son of William Freeman and Thelma B.

Children of Linda Wilcox and James Freeman are:
1584   i.   James Scott[24] Freeman, born October 16, 1967.
1585   ii.   Bryan Lynn Freeman, born November 07, 1971.

1025. Donnie Lynn[23] Wilcox (Carrie Etta[22] Eagle, Albert Lee[21], Amanda Jane[20] Wyatt, Noah Calvin[19], Thomas "Tommy"[18] Wiatt, Sr. (Wyatt, Wiett), John[17], Henry[16], Richard[15], George[14], Rev. Haute "Haut" "Hawte"[13], Sir George "Georgius" Thomas[12], Sir Thomas "The Younger"[11], Sir Thomas "The Elder"[10], Sir Henry[9], Richard Wiat or[8] Wyatt, Geoffrey "Jeoffrey" Wiot or[7] Wiat, Robert or Richard[6] Wiot, William Wiot or[5] Wyot, Adam Wiot or Wyote or[4], Guyott[3], Guyott[2], Captain or Admiral Adam Guyott or[1] Wiot) was born March 12, 1951. He married Sharon Lynn Stafford, daughter of James Stafford and Mary Rodgers.

Children of Donnie Wilcox and Sharon Stafford are:
1586   i.   Gregory Lynn[24] Wilcox, born November 25, 1975.
1587   ii.   Cynthia Dawn Wilcox, born March 25, 1978.

1026. Arthur Lewis[23] Terry (Rosa Belle[22] Morgan, Amanda Dora[21] Eagle, Amanda Jane[20] Wyatt, Noah Calvin[19], Thomas "Tommy"[18] Wiatt, Sr. (Wyatt, Wiett), John[17], Henry[16], Richard[15], George[14], Rev. Haute "Haut" "Hawte"[13], Sir George "Georgius" Thomas[12], Sir Thomas "The Younger"[11], Sir Thomas "The Elder"[10], Sir Henry[9], Richard Wiat or[8] Wyatt, Geoffrey "Jeoffrey" Wiot or[7] Wiat, Robert or Richard[6] Wiot, William Wiot or[5] Wyot, Adam Wiot or Wyote or[4], Guyott[3], Guyott[2], Captain or Admiral Adam Guyott or[1] Wiot) was born in Richmond County, N.C. He married Brenda Olean English June 16, 1961.

More About Arthur Lewis Terry:
Fact 1: December 15, 1950, birthday in Eagle Book by Hill and Heath.

Children of Arthur Terry and Brenda English are:
1588   i.   Vickie Jean[24] Terry, born February 05, 1963 in Richmond County, N.C.
1589   ii.   Lynnie Rose Terry, born 1964 in Richmond County, N.C.
1590   iii.   Lewis Alexander Terry, born April 06, 1967.
1591   iv.   Brenda Jeanette Terry, born November 24, 1971 in Guilford County, N.C.

1027. Stephen Jasper[23] Terry, Jr. (Rosa Belle[22] Morgan, Amanda Dora[21] Eagle, Amanda Jane[20] Wyatt, Noah Calvin[19], Thomas "Tommy"[18] Wiatt, Sr. (Wyatt, Wiett), John[17], Henry[16], Richard[15], George[14], Rev. Haute "Haut" "Hawte"[13], Sir George "Georgius" Thomas[12], Sir Thomas "The Younger"[11], Sir Thomas "The Elder"[10], Sir Henry[9], Richard Wiat or[8] Wyatt,

Geoffrey "Jeoffrey" Wiot or[7] Wiat, Robert or Richard[6] Wiot, William Wiot or[5] Wyot, Adam Wiot or Wyote or[4], Guyott[3], Guyott[2], Captain or Admiral Adam Guyott or[1] Wiot) was born October 20, 1930 in Richmond County, N.C. He married (1) Mary Louise Lovin February 29, 1956. He married (2) Carolyn Matthew August 24, 1968.

Children of Stephen Terry and Mary Lovin are:

1592	i.	Pamuela Ann[24] Terry, born April 03, 1959.
1593	ii.	Cathy Lynne Terry, born April 03, 1961.
1594	iii.	Jack Gregg Terry, born February 07, 1966.

Child of Stephen Terry and Carolyn Matthew is:

| 1595 | i. | David Matthew[24] Terry, born September 28, 1970. |

1028. Ralph Gilbert[23] Terry (Rosa Belle[22] Morgan, Amanda Dora[21] Eagle, Amanda Jane[20] Wyatt, Noah Calvin[19], Thomas "Tommy"[18] Wiatt, Sr. (Wyatt, Wiett), John[17], Henry[16], Richard[15], George[14], Rev. Haute "Haut" "Hawte"[13], Sir George "Georgius" Thomas[12], Sir Thomas "The Younger"[11], Sir Thomas "The Elder"[10], Sir Henry[9], Richard Wiat or[8] Wyatt, Geoffrey "Jeoffrey" Wiot or[7] Wiat, Robert or Richard[6] Wiot, William Wiot or[5] Wyot, Adam Wiot or Wyote or[4], Guyott[3], Guyott[2], Captain or Admiral Adam Guyott or[1] Wiot) was born January 28, 1932 in Richmond County, N.C. He married Linda Gail Cockman May 25, 1951.

Children of Ralph Terry and Linda Cockman are:

| 1596 | i. | Ralph Allen[24] Terry, born August 21, 1963 in Rockingham, N.C. |
| 1597 | ii. | Mark Allen Terry, born April 14, 1968. |

1029. Sam Coy[23] Terry (Rosa Belle[22] Morgan, Amanda Dora[21] Eagle, Amanda Jane[20] Wyatt, Noah Calvin[19], Thomas "Tommy"[18] Wiatt, Sr. (Wyatt, Wiett), John[17], Henry[16], Richard[15], George[14], Rev. Haute "Haut" "Hawte"[13], Sir George "Georgius" Thomas[12], Sir Thomas "The Younger"[11], Sir Thomas "The Elder"[10], Sir Henry[9], Richard Wiat or[8] Wyatt, Geoffrey "Jeoffrey" Wiot or[7] Wiat, Robert or Richard[6] Wiot, William Wiot or[5] Wyot, Adam Wiot or Wyote or[4], Guyott[3], Guyott[2], Captain or Admiral Adam Guyott or[1] Wiot) was born July 03, 1933 in Richmond County, N.C. He married Joan Mary Curie October 13, 1956.

Children of Sam Terry and Joan Curie are:

| 1598 | i. | Michael Eugene[24] Terry, born August 21, 1957. |
| 1599 | ii. | Judy Kay Terry, born July 16, 1960 in Rockingham, N.C. |

1030. Charles Ray[23] Terry (Rosa Belle[22] Morgan, Amanda Dora[21] Eagle, Amanda Jane[20] Wyatt, Noah Calvin[19], Thomas "Tommy"[18] Wiatt, Sr. (Wyatt, Wiett), John[17], Henry[16], Richard[15], George[14], Rev. Haute "Haut" "Hawte"[13], Sir George "Georgius" Thomas[12], Sir Thomas "The Younger"[11], Sir Thomas "The Elder"[10], Sir Henry[9], Richard Wiat or[8] Wyatt, Geoffrey "Jeoffrey" Wiot or[7] Wiat, Robert or Richard[6] Wiot, William Wiot or[5] Wyot, Adam

Wiot or Wyote or[4], Guyott[3], Guyott[2], Captain or Admiral Adam Guyott or[1] Wiot) was born December 02, 1937 in Richmond County, N.C. He married Shirley Ann Levin July 05, 1959.

Children of Charles Terry and Shirley Levin are:

1600	i.	Lori Ann[24] Terry, born August 13, 1963.
1601	ii.	Patsy Ray Terry, born May 13, 1965.
1602	iii.	Brian Clark Terry, born August 16, 1968 in Richmond County, N.C.

1031. Leonard Leon[23] Terry (Rosa Belle[22] Morgan, Amanda Dora[21] Eagle, Amanda Jane[20] Wyatt, Noah Calvin[19], Thomas "Tommy"[18] Wiatt, Sr. (Wyatt, Wiett), John[17], Henry[16], Richard[15], George[14], Rev. Haute "Haut" "Hawte"[13], Sir George "Georgius" Thomas[12], Sir Thomas "The Younger"[11], Sir Thomas "The Elder"[10], Sir Henry[9], Richard Wiat or[8] Wyatt, Geoffrey "Jeoffrey" Wiot or[7] Wiat, Robert or Richard[6] Wiot, William Wiot or[5] Wyot, Adam Wiot or Wyote or[4], Guyott[3], Guyott[2], Captain or Admiral Adam Guyott or[1] Wiot) was born August 21, 1939 in Richmond County, N.C. He married Patricia Fay Curie December 03, 1960.

Children of Leonard Terry and Patricia Curie are:

1603	i.	Danny Ray[24] Terry, born June 16, 1961.
1604	ii.	Randy Dean Terry, born June 28, 1963 in Rockingham, N.C.

1032. Jo Ann[23] Terry (Rosa Belle[22] Morgan, Amanda Dora[21] Eagle, Amanda Jane[20] Wyatt, Noah Calvin[19], Thomas "Tommy"[18] Wiatt, Sr. (Wyatt, Wiett), John[17], Henry[16], Richard[15], George[14], Rev. Haute "Haut" "Hawte"[13], Sir George "Georgius" Thomas[12], Sir Thomas "The Younger"[11], Sir Thomas "The Elder"[10], Sir Henry[9], Richard Wiat or[8] Wyatt, Geoffrey "Jeoffrey" Wiot or[7] Wiat, Robert or Richard[6] Wiot, William Wiot or[5] Wyot, Adam Wiot or Wyote or[4], Guyott[3], Guyott[2], Captain or Admiral Adam Guyott or[1] Wiot) was born November 19, 1941 in Richmond County, N.C. She married Wayne Alexander English.

Children of Jo Terry and Wayne English are:

1605	i.	Stephen Wayne[24] English, born June 17, 1961.
1606	ii.	Terry Joe English, born June 28, 1964 in Richmond County, N.C.

1033. Rachael Maxine[23] Terry (Rosa Belle[22] Morgan, Amanda Dora[21] Eagle, Amanda Jane[20] Wyatt, Noah Calvin[19], Thomas "Tommy"[18] Wiatt, Sr. (Wyatt, Wiett), John[17], Henry[16], Richard[15], George[14], Rev. Haute "Haut" "Hawte"[13], Sir George "Georgius" Thomas[12], Sir Thomas "The Younger"[11], Sir Thomas "The Elder"[10], Sir Henry[9], Richard Wiat or[8] Wyatt, Geoffrey "Jeoffrey" Wiot or[7] Wiat, Robert or Richard[6] Wiot, William Wiot or[5] Wyot, Adam Wiot or Wyote or[4], Guyott[3], Guyott[2], Captain or Admiral Adam Guyott or[1] Wiot) was born June 23, 1943 in Richmond County, N.C. She married James Dwight Russell May 12, 1962.

Children of Rachael Terry and James Russell are:

1607 i. Cynthia Jo[24] Russell, born April 09, 1963.

1608 ii. James Dwight Russell, Jr., born October 10, 1966.

1609 iii. Anthony Andrew Russell, born August 21, 1970 in Richmond County, N.C.

1034. Kenneth Ray[23] Williams (Amanda Catherine[22] Morgan, Amanda Dora[21] Eagle, Amanda Jane[20] Wyatt, Noah Calvin[19], Thomas "Tommy"[18] Wiatt, Sr. (Wyatt, Wiett), John[17], Henry[16], Richard[15], George[14], Rev. Haute "Haut" "Hawte"[13], Sir George "Georgius" Thomas[12], Sir Thomas "The Younger"[11], Sir Thomas "The Elder"[10], Sir Henry[9], Richard Wiat or[8] Wyatt, Geoffrey "Jeoffrey" Wiot or[7] Wiat, Robert or Richard[6] Wiot, William Wiot or[5] Wyot, Adam Wiot or Wyote or[4], Guyott[3], Guyott[2], Captain or Admiral Adam Guyott or[1] Wiot) was born July 24, 1952. He married Teresa Ferrell January 24, 1974.

Children of Kenneth Williams and Teresa Ferrell are:

1610 i. Laura Price[24] Williams, born April 29, 1972.

1611 ii. Kevin Ray Williams, born March 04, 1974.

1612 iii. Kimberly Nicole Williams, born March 07, 1976.

1040. Linda Catherine[23] Morgan (William Howard[22], Amanda Dora[21] Eagle, Amanda Jane[20] Wyatt, Noah Calvin[19], Thomas "Tommy"[18] Wiatt, Sr. (Wyatt, Wiett), John[17], Henry[16], Richard[15], George[14], Rev. Haute "Haut" "Hawte"[13], Sir George "Georgius" Thomas[12], Sir Thomas "The Younger"[11], Sir Thomas "The Elder"[10], Sir Henry[9], Richard Wiat or[8] Wyatt, Geoffrey "Jeoffrey" Wiot or[7] Wiat, Robert or Richard[6] Wiot, William Wiot or[5] Wyot, Adam Wiot or Wyote or[4], Guyott[3], Guyott[2], Captain or Admiral Adam Guyott or[1] Wiot) was born April 09, 1952 in Moore County, N.C. She married Daniel Keith Gardner June 01, 1974, son of Baxter Gardner and Marjorie Moore.

Child of Linda Morgan and Daniel Gardner is:

1613 i. Keith Baxter[24] Gardner, born July 21, 1978 in Columbia, S.C.

1042. Lee Howard[23] Morgan (William Howard[22], Amanda Dora[21] Eagle, Amanda Jane[20] Wyatt, Noah Calvin[19], Thomas "Tommy"[18] Wiatt, Sr. (Wyatt, Wiett), John[17], Henry[16], Richard[15], George[14], Rev. Haute "Haut" "Hawte"[13], Sir George "Georgius" Thomas[12], Sir Thomas "The Younger"[11], Sir Thomas "The Elder"[10], Sir Henry[9], Richard Wiat or[8] Wyatt, Geoffrey "Jeoffrey" Wiot or[7] Wiat, Robert or Richard[6] Wiot, William Wiot or[5] Wyot, Adam Wiot or Wyote or[4], Guyott[3], Guyott[2], Captain or Admiral Adam Guyott or[1] Wiot) was born May 14, 1954. He married Phoebe Joy Dawkins February 09, 1974, daughter of Ned Dawkins and Ernestine Nightingale.

Child of Lee Morgan and Phoebe Dawkins is:

1614 i. Cicki Leigh[24] Morgan, born January 09, 1978.

1043. Nancy Faye[23] Morgan (William Howard[22], Amanda Dora[21] Eagle, Amanda Jane[20] Wyatt, Noah Calvin[19], Thomas "Tommy"[18] Wiatt, Sr. (Wyatt, Wiett), John[17], Henry[16], Richard[15], George[14], Rev. Haute "Haut" "Hawte"[13], Sir George "Georgius" Thomas[12], Sir Thomas "The Younger"[11], Sir Thomas "The Elder"[10], Sir Henry[9], Richard Wiat or[8] Wyatt, Geoffrey "Jeoffrey" Wiot or[7] Wiat, Robert or Richard[6] Wiot, William Wiot or[5] Wyot, Adam Wiot or Wyote or[4], Guyott[3], Guyott[2], Captain or Admiral Adam Guyott or[1] Wiot) was born June 03, 1955 in Moore County, N.C. She married Kenneth Warren Lathan May 17, 1974.

> Child of Nancy Morgan and Kenneth Lathan is:
> 1615   i.   Donald Eugene[24] Lathan, born May 18, 1978 in Moore County, N.C.

1047. Mary Jane[23] Morgan (William Howard[22], Amanda Dora[21] Eagle, Amanda Jane[20] Wyatt, Noah Calvin[19], Thomas "Tommy"[18] Wiatt, Sr. (Wyatt, Wiett), John[17], Henry[16], Richard[15], George[14], Rev. Haute "Haut" "Hawte"[13], Sir George "Georgius" Thomas[12], Sir Thomas "The Younger"[11], Sir Thomas "The Elder"[10], Sir Henry[9], Richard Wiat or[8] Wyatt, Geoffrey "Jeoffrey" Wiot or[7] Wiat, Robert or Richard[6] Wiot, William Wiot or[5] Wyot, Adam Wiot or Wyote or[4], Guyott[3], Guyott[2], Captain or Admiral Adam Guyott or[1] Wiot) was born October 24, 1961. She married Phillip McArgue Sharpe July 23, 1978.

> Child of Mary Morgan and Phillip Sharpe is:
> 1616   i.   David Christopher[24] Sharpe.

Generation No. 24

1054. Lucy[24] Qualls (Joseph Marshall[23], James Frankin[22], Martha C.[21] Sykes, James B.[20], Frances[19] Cates, Thomas[18], Rebecca[17] Sykes, Frances[16] Wiatt, Richard[15], George[14], Rev. Haute "Haut" "Hawte"[13], Sir George "Georgius" Thomas[12], Sir Thomas "The Younger"[11], Sir Thomas "The Elder"[10], Sir Henry[9], Richard Wiat or[8] Wyatt, Geoffrey "Jeoffrey" Wiot or[7] Wiat, Robert or Richard[6] Wiot, William Wiot or[5] Wyot, Adam Wiot or Wyote or[4], Guyott[3], Guyott[2], Captain or Admiral Adam Guyott or[1] Wiot). She married Crews.

> Child of Lucy Qualls and Crews is:
> 1617   i.   Joseph Mcneal[25] Crews, born June 15, 1961.

1058. Edith Hope[24] Basinger (Effie Jeanette "Genetta" Eagle[23] Wyatt, Harvey Addison[22], Columbus Ciscero[21], Wilson Riley[20], Jesse "Jessey"[19], John "Johney"[18], John[17] Wiatt, Henry[16], Richard[15], George[14], Rev. Haute "Haut" "Hawte"[13], Sir George "Georgius" Thomas[12], Sir Thomas "The Younger"[11], Sir Thomas "The Elder"[10], Sir Henry[9], Richard Wiat or[8] Wyatt, Geoffrey "Jeoffrey" Wiot or[7] Wiat, Robert or Richard[6] Wiot, William Wiot or[5] Wyot, Adam Wiot or Wyote or[4], Guyott[3], Guyott[2], Captain or Admiral Adam Guyott or[1] Wiot) was born January 07, 1918. She married Clifford Alexander Brown December 24, 1936.

Children of Edith Basinger and Clifford Brown are:

+   1618   i.   Patsy Carolyn[25] Brown, born May 12, 1937.

    1619   ii.   Franklin Max Brown, born August 27, 1938.

+   1620   iii.   James Ray Brown, born June 24, 1940.

+   1621   iv.   Alice "Faye" Brown, born February 16, 1942.

+   1622   v.   Bobby Curtis Brown, born June 02, 1943.

    1623   vi.   Stephen Joe Brown, born April 10, 1948. He married Carole Kesler Davis March 23, 1974.

1059.   Eltha Pauline[24] Basinger (Effie Jeanette "Genetta" Eagle[23] Wyatt, Harvey Addison[22], Columbus Ciscero[21], Wilson Riley[20], Jesse "Jessey"[19], John "Johney"[18], John[17] Wiatt, Henry[16], Richard[15], George[14], Rev. Haute "Haut" "Hawte"[13], Sir George "Georgius" Thomas[12], Sir Thomas "The Younger"[11], Sir Thomas "The Elder"[10], Sir Henry[9], Richard Wiat or[8] Wyatt, Geoffrey "Jeoffrey" Wiot or[7] Wiat, Robert or Richard[6] Wiot, William Wiot or[5] Wyot, Adam Wiot or Wyote or[4], Guyott[3], Guyott[2], Captain or Admiral Adam Guyott or[1] Wiot) was born October 07, 1919. She married Lee B. Castor.

Children of Eltha Basinger and Lee Castor are:

+   1624   i.   Ronald Paul[25] Castor, born December 05, 1936.

+   1625   ii.   Patricia Lee Castor, born March 21, 1945.

1060.   Elma Eunice[24] Basinger (Effie Jeanette "Genetta" Eagle[23] Wyatt, Harvey Addison[22], Columbus Ciscero[21], Wilson Riley[20], Jesse "Jessey"[19], John "Johney"[18], John[17] Wiatt, Henry[16], Richard[15], George[14], Rev. Haute "Haut" "Hawte"[13], Sir George "Georgius" Thomas[12], Sir Thomas "The Younger"[11], Sir Thomas "The Elder"[10], Sir Henry[9], Richard Wiat or[8] Wyatt, Geoffrey "Jeoffrey" Wiot or[7] Wiat, Robert or Richard[6] Wiot, William Wiot or[5] Wyot, Adam Wiot or Wyote or[4], Guyott[3], Guyott[2], Captain or Admiral Adam Guyott or[1] Wiot) was born May 31, 1922. She married Clyde Mitchell Robinson March 30, 1940.

Children of Elma Basinger and Clyde Robinson are:

+   1626   i.   Nellie Jean[25] Robinson, born February 03, 1940.

+   1627   ii.   Ginger Dale Robinson, born August 08, 1950.

1061.   Claude V.[24] Basinger (Effie Jeanette "Genetta" Eagle[23] Wyatt, Harvey Addison[22], Columbus Ciscero[21], Wilson Riley[20], Jesse "Jessey"[19], John "Johney"[18], John[17] Wiatt, Henry[16], Richard[15], George[14], Rev. Haute "Haut" "Hawte"[13], Sir George "Georgius" Thomas[12], Sir Thomas "The Younger"[11], Sir Thomas "The Elder"[10], Sir Henry[9], Richard Wiat or[8] Wyatt, Geoffrey "Jeoffrey" Wiot or[7] Wiat, Robert or Richard[6] Wiot, William Wiot or[5] Wyot, Adam Wiot or Wyote or[4], Guyott[3], Guyott[2], Captain or Admiral Adam Guyott or[1] Wiot) was born December 15, 1924, and died October 20, 1980. He married Ruby Kluttz.

Children of Claude Basinger and Ruby Kluttz are:

+   1628   i.   Vernon[25] Basinger, born June 24, 1946.

+ 1629 ii. Sylvia Basinger, born November 24, 1948.

1630 iii. Sidney Basinger.

1062. Clinton E.[24] Basinger (Effie Jeanette "Genetta" Eagle[23] Wyatt, Harvey Addison[22], Columbus Ciscero[21], Wilson Riley[20], Jesse "Jessey"[19], John "Johney"[18], John[17] Wiatt, Henry[16], Richard[15], George[14], Rev. Haute "Haut" "Hawte"[13], Sir George "Georgius" Thomas[12], Sir Thomas "The Younger"[11], Sir Thomas "The Elder"[10], Sir Henry[9], Richard Wiat or[8] Wyatt, Geoffrey "Jeoffrey" Wiot or[7] Wiat, Robert or Richard[6] Wiot, William Wiot or[5] Wyot, Adam Wiot or Wyote or[4], Guyott[3], Guyott[2], Captain or Admiral Adam Guyott or[1] Wiot) was born January 12, 1928, and died November 24, 1968. He married Ghelia Ridenhour.

Children of Clinton Basinger and Ghelia Ridenhour are:
+ 1631 i. Susan[25] Basinger, born January 21, 1947.
+ 1632 ii. Janie Roseanne Basinger, born December 11, 1954.

1063. Chester Clyde[24] Basinger (Effie Jeanette "Genetta" Eagle[23] Wyatt, Harvey Addison[22], Columbus Ciscero[21], Wilson Riley[20], Jesse "Jessey"[19], John "Johney"[18], John[17] Wiatt, Henry[16], Richard[15], George[14], Rev. Haute "Haut" "Hawte"[13], Sir George "Georgius" Thomas[12], Sir Thomas "The Younger"[11], Sir Thomas "The Elder"[10], Sir Henry[9], Richard Wiat or[8] Wyatt, Geoffrey "Jeoffrey" Wiot or[7] Wiat, Robert or Richard[6] Wiot, William Wiot or[5] Wyot, Adam Wiot or Wyote or[4], Guyott[3], Guyott[2], Captain or Admiral Adam Guyott or[1] Wiot) was born May 06, 1932. He married Doris Miller.

Children of Chester Basinger and Doris Miller are:
+ 1633 i. Vickie Cheryl[25] Basinger, born September 06, 1948.
1634 ii. Rocky Lynn Basinger, born September 28, 1953.
1635 iii. Mickey Dee Basinger, born October 12, 1961.

1064. Evelyn Ruth[24] Basinger (Effie Jeanette "Genetta" Eagle[23] Wyatt, Harvey Addison[22], Columbus Ciscero[21], Wilson Riley[20], Jesse "Jessey"[19], John "Johney"[18], John[17] Wiatt, Henry[16], Richard[15], George[14], Rev. Haute "Haut" "Hawte"[13], Sir George "Georgius" Thomas[12], Sir Thomas "The Younger"[11], Sir Thomas "The Elder"[10], Sir Henry[9], Richard Wiat or[8] Wyatt, Geoffrey "Jeoffrey" Wiot or[7] Wiat, Robert or Richard[6] Wiot, William Wiot or[5] Wyot, Adam Wiot or Wyote or[4], Guyott[3], Guyott[2], Captain or Admiral Adam Guyott or[1] Wiot) was born September 02, 1937. She married Edward Franklin Holt September 06, 1958.

Children of Evelyn Basinger and Edward Holt are:
1636 i. Timothy Edward[25] Holt, born November 26, 1960.
1637 ii. Stanley Wayne Holt, born December 12, 1964.

1065. Elva Kay[24] Basinger (Effie Jeanette "Genetta" Eagle[23] Wyatt, Harvey Addison[22], Columbus Ciscero[21], Wilson Riley[20], Jesse "Jessey"[19], John "Johney"[18], John[17] Wiatt, Henry[16], Richard[15], George[14], Rev. Haute "Haut" "Hawte"[13], Sir George "Georgius" Thomas[12], Sir Thomas "The Younger"[11], Sir Thomas "The Elder"[10], Sir Henry[9], Richard Wiat or[8] Wyatt,

Geoffrey "Jeoffrey" Wiot or[7] Wiat, Robert or Richard[6] Wiot, William Wiot or[5] Wyot, Adam Wiot or Wyote or[4], Guyott[3], Guyott[2], Captain or Admiral Adam Guyott or[1] Wiot) was born May 04, 1944. She married (1) Henry Turner September 08, 1961, son of John Turner and Mattie Craddock. She married (2) Clarence Alexander Basinger June 10, 1966, son of James Basinger and Esther Shuping.

        Child of Elva Basinger and Henry Turner is:

+   1638   i.   Teresa Gail[25] Turner, born March 21, 1963.

        Children of Elva Basinger and Clarence Basinger are:

  1639   i.   Martin Robin[25] Basinger, born April 06, 1968.

  1640   ii.   Amy Reneé Basinger, born January 28, 1974.

1066.   Ashley Elizabeth[24] Smith (Timothy Ray[23], Margaret Evelyeen[22] Wyatt, Pleasant Loveless[21], Ciscero "Cicero" L.[20], Lazerus Pleasant[19], Thomas "Tommy"[18] Wiatt, Sr. (Wyatt, Wiett), John[17], Henry[16], Richard[15], George[14], Rev. Haute "Haut" "Hawte"[13], Sir George "Georgius" Thomas[12], Sir Thomas "The Younger"[11], Sir Thomas "The Elder"[10], Sir Henry[9], Richard Wiat or[8] Wyatt, Geoffrey "Jeoffrey" Wiot or[7] Wiat, Robert or Richard[6] Wiot, William Wiot or[5] Wyot, Adam Wiot or Wyote or[4], Guyott[3], Guyott[2], Captain or Admiral Adam Guyott or[1] Wiot) was born March 12, 1977 in Wake County, N.C. She married James Thomas McMillan November 20, 2005 in Wake County, N.C.

        Child of Ashley Smith and James McMillan is:

  1641   i.   Emerson Rose[25] McMillan, born June 23, 2010 in Wake County, N.C.

1069.   Dr. Roger D.[24] Wyatt (Paul Woodrow[23], David Eli[22], James "Jim" Noah[21], William Wesley "Brantly"[20], Noah Calvin[19], Thomas "Tommy"[18] Wiatt, Sr. (Wyatt, Wiett), John[17], Henry[16], Richard[15], George[14], Rev. Haute "Haut" "Hawte"[13], Sir George "Georgius" Thomas[12], Sir Thomas "The Younger"[11], Sir Thomas "The Elder"[10], Sir Henry[9], Richard Wiat or[8] Wyatt, Geoffrey "Jeoffrey" Wiot or[7] Wiat, Robert or Richard[6] Wiot, William Wiot or[5] Wyot, Adam Wiot or Wyote or[4], Guyott[3], Guyott[2], Captain or Admiral Adam Guyott or[1] Wiot) was born Abt. 1946 in Rowan County, N.C. He married Freida Bryson.

More About Dr. Roger D. Wyatt:

Fact 1: Born on Orchard Road, Rowan County, N.C.

        Children of Dr. Wyatt and Freida Bryson are:

  1642   i.   Derek[25] Wyatt, born in of Nashville, Tenn. He married Heather.

+   1643   ii.   Tamara Wyatt.

1073. Mike Michael Lynn[24] Morgan (J.T.[23], Freda Maybelle[22] Kirk, Rhoda Isabelle[21] Morgan, Lila Delilah "Delila"[20] Wyatt, Noah Calvin[19], Thomas "Tommy"[18] Wiatt, Sr. (Wyatt, Wiett),

John[17], Henry[16], Richard[15], George[14], Rev. Haute "Haut" "Hawte"[13], Sir George "Georgius" Thomas[12], Sir Thomas "The Younger"[11], Sir Thomas "The Elder"[10], Sir Henry[9], Richard Wiat or[8] Wyatt, Geoffrey "Jeoffrey" Wiot or[7] Wiat, Robert or Richard[6] Wiot, William Wiot or[5] Wyot, Adam Wiot or Wyote or[4], Guyott[3], Guyott[2], Captain or Admiral Adam Guyott or[1] Wiot) was born Abt. 1959 in North Carolina. He married Crystal Kluttz, daughter of Donald Kluttz and X.

Child of Mike Morgan and Crystal Kluttz is:
1644   i.   Cam[25] Morgan, born Abt. 1993 in Rowan County, N.C.

1074.   William "Bill" Crowell[24] Hinson, Jr. (Virgie Irene[23] Eagle, Noah Jenkins[22], Mary Jane[21] Morgan, Rachel Evelyn "Eveline"[20] Wyatt, Noah Calvin[19], Thomas "Tommy"[18] Wiatt, Sr. (Wyatt, Wiett), John[17], Henry[16], Richard[15], George[14], Rev. Haute "Haut" "Hawte"[13], Sir George "Georgius" Thomas[12], Sir Thomas "The Younger"[11], Sir Thomas "The Elder"[10], Sir Henry[9], Richard Wiat or[8] Wyatt, Geoffrey "Jeoffrey" Wiot or[7] Wiat, Robert or Richard[6] Wiot, William Wiot or[5] Wyot, Adam Wiot or Wyote or[4], Guyott[3], Guyott[2], Captain or Admiral Adam Guyott or[1] Wiot) was born March 05, 1926 in Rowan County, N.C., and died December 24, 2014 in Myrtle Beach, S.C. He married Delah Mae Brady March 23, 1951 in Eloped., daughter of William Brady and Mary Eudy.

Remains are buried at the Gold Hill Wesleyan Church Cemetery in Gold Hill, N.C. His funeral was held December 29, 2014.

Children of William Hinson and Delah Brady are:
+   1645   i.   Rebecca "Becky" Ann[25] Hinson, born January 22, 1952 in Salisbury, Rowan County, N.C.
+   1646   ii.   Mary Lynn Hinson, born August 02, 1954 in Salisbury, Rowan County, N.C.
+   1647   iii.   Melanie Joan Hinson, born September 21, 1956 in Salisbury, Rowan County, N.C.
+   1648   iv.   William "Billy" Ashley Hinson, born September 09, 1958 in Washington County, Phymouth, N.C.

1075.   Richard "Chubby" "Chub" Clyde[24] Hinson (Virgie Irene[23] Eagle, Noah Jenkins[22], Mary Jane[21] Morgan, Rachel Evelyn "Eveline"[20] Wyatt, Noah Calvin[19], Thomas "Tommy"[18] Wiatt, Sr. (Wyatt, Wiett), John[17], Henry[16], Richard[15], George[14], Rev. Haute "Haut" "Hawte"[13], Sir George "Georgius" Thomas[12], Sir Thomas "The Younger"[11], Sir Thomas "The Elder"[10], Sir Henry[9], Richard Wiat or[8] Wyatt, Geoffrey "Jeoffrey" Wiot or[7] Wiot, Robert or Richard[6] Wiot, William Wiot or[5] Wyot, Adam Wiot or Wyote or[4], Guyott[3], Guyott[2], Captain or Admiral Adam Guyott or[1] Wiot) was born April 11, 1927 in Richfield, Rowan County, N.C., and died October 23, 2006 in Salisbury, Rowan County, N.C. He married (1) Merrell Lenora Goodman April 30, 1950, daughter of Brown Goodman and Minnie Barger. He married (2) Pansy Ruth Hampton October 22, 1988 in Rowan County, N.C., daughter of David Hampton and Ila Furr.

More About Merrell Lenora Goodman:
Buried at the Brookhill Cemetery, Rockwell, Rowan County, N.C.

    Children of Richard Hinson and Merrell Goodman are:

+   1649   i.   Richard Merrell[25] Hinson, born September 28, 1950 in Salisbury, Rowan County, N.C.

     1650   ii.   Steven Clyde Hinson, born October 08, 1952 in Salisbury, Rowan County, N.C. He married Ardith Lee Grubb February 19, 1972 in July 15, 1972 -- date from his sister Patty.

+   1651   iii.   Pamela "Pam" Irene Hinson, born October 15, 1953 in Salisbury, Rowan County, N.C.

+   1652   iv.   Lesa Ann Hinson, born December 04, 1961 in Salisbury, Rowan County, N.C.

     1653   v.   Patricia "Patty" Margaret Hinson, born April 29, 1966 in Salisbury, Rowan County, N.C. She married (1) Johnny Ivester 1993 in N.C. She married (2) Mark Fisher 2004.

1076. James "Jim" Noah[24] Hinson, M.D. (Virgie Irene[23] Eagle, Noah Jenkins[22], Mary Jane[21] Morgan, Rachel Evelyn "Eveline"[20] Wyatt, Noah Calvin[19], Thomas "Tommy"[18] Wiatt, Sr. (Wyatt, Wiett), John[17], Henry[16], Richard[15], George[14], Rev. Haute "Haut" "Hawte"[13], Sir George "Georgius" Thomas[12], Sir Thomas "The Younger"[11], Sir Thomas "The Elder"[10], Sir Henry[9], Richard Wiat or[8] Wyatt, Geoffrey "Jeoffrey" Wiot or[7] Wiat, Robert or Richard[6] Wiot, William Wiot or[5] Wyot, Adam Wiot or Wyote or[4], Guyott[3], Guyott[2], Captain or Admiral Adam Guyott or[1] Wiot) was born January 12, 1929 in Mabery Place, Porter Station, Stanly County, N.C., and died March 30, 2015 in Salisbury, Rowan County, N.C. He married Patricia Ann Leighton, B.S.N., M.Ed., C.I.C. March 03, 1962 in Saint Mark's Lutheran Church, Oakland, Garrett County, Md., daughter of Clarence Leighton and Mary McTall.

Remains are buried in the Luther's Church Cemetery, Richfield, N.C. He passed into Heaven at 4:25 p.m., Monday, March 30, 2015.

    Children of James Hinson and Patricia Leighton are:

+   1654   i.   Hélène "Lynnie" Andorre[25] Hinson, born February 04, 1963 in New Orleans, New Orleans Parish, La.

+   1655   ii.   Häns Leighton Hinson, M.D., born June 02, 1964 in New Orleans, New Orleans Parish, La.

     1656   iii.   Nicole "Nicky" Suzanne Hinson, M.D., born August 31, 1967 in Salisbury, Rowan County, N.C.

1077. Betty Lou[24] Hinson (Virgie Irene[23] Eagle, Noah Jenkins[22], Mary Jane[21] Morgan, Rachel Evelyn "Eveline"[20] Wyatt, Noah Calvin[19], Thomas "Tommy"[18] Wiatt, Sr. (Wyatt, Wiett), John[17], Henry[16], Richard[15], George[14], Rev. Haute "Haut" "Hawte"[13], Sir George "Georgius" Thomas[12], Sir Thomas "The Younger"[11], Sir Thomas "The Elder"[10], Sir Henry[9], Richard Wiat or[8] Wyatt, Geoffrey "Jeoffrey" Wiot or[7] Wiat, Robert or Richard[6] Wiot, William Wiot or[5] Wyot, Adam Wiot or Wyote or[4], Guyott[3], Guyott[2], Captain or Admiral Adam Guyott or[1] Wiot) was born October 24, 1930 in Rowan County, N.C. She married James Edwin "Ed" Heath November 16, 1957, son of Thomas Heath and Minnie Lewallen.

Children of Betty Hinson and James Heath are:

+ 1657   i.   William Eugene[25] Heath, born October 08, 1965 in High Point, Guilford County, N.C.
+ 1658   ii.   Frances "LuAnne" LuAnne Heath, born February 18, 1967 in High Point, N.C.

1078. Rachel Evelyn[24] Hinson (Virgie Irene[23] Eagle, Noah Jenkins[22], Mary Jane[21] Morgan, Rachel Evelyn "Eveline"[20] Wyatt, Noah Calvin[19], Thomas "Tommy"[18] Wiatt, Sr. (Wyatt, Wiett), John[17], Henry[16], Richard[15], George[14], Rev. Haute "Haut" "Hawte"[13], Sir George "Georgius" Thomas[12], Sir Thomas "The Younger"[11], Sir Thomas "The Elder"[10], Sir Henry[9], Richard Wiat or[8] Wyatt, Geoffrey "Jeoffrey" Wiot or[7] Wiat, Robert or Richard[6] Wiot, William Wiot or[5] Wyot, Adam Wiot or Wyote or[4], Guyott[3], Guyott[2], Captain or Admiral Adam Guyott or[1] Wiot) was born September 03, 1932 in Stanly County, N.C., and died March 12, 1994 in Rowan County, N.C. She married Paul Junior "Bud" Hill October 15, 1950 in Rowan County, N.C., son of Joseph Hill and Josephine Isenhour.

Children of Rachel Hinson and Paul Hill are:

1659   i.   Glenda Ruth[25] Hill, born November 05, 1954 in Stanly County, N.C. She married (1) Unknown. She married (2) Unknown. She married (3) Thomas Bruce Stoner October 30, 1977 in Rowan County, N.C. She married (4) Wallace Daniel Wagoner, Jr. October 31, 1992.

1660   ii.   Norman Ray Hill, born September 26, 1957 in Stanly County, N.C. He married (1) Margaret Louise Butler April 17, 1988 in N.C. He married (2) Nancy Marie Smith April 17, 1989.

More About Nancy Marie Smith:
Buried at Liberty St. Matthews Methodist Church Cemetery, Salisbury, N.C.

1661   iii.   Paula Evelyn Hill, born May 07, 1962 in Rowan County, N.C.; died September 25, 1981 in Rowan County, N.C.
Died in vehicle-horse accident on Highway #52. Remains are buried at Liberty St. Matthews Methodist Church Cemetery, Salisbury, N.C.

1079. Margaret Ann[24] Hinson (Virgie Irene[23] Eagle, Noah Jenkins[22], Mary Jane[21] Morgan, Rachel Evelyn "Eveline"[20] Wyatt, Noah Calvin[19], Thomas "Tommy"[18] Wiatt, Sr. (Wyatt, Wiett), John[17], Henry[16], Richard[15], George[14], Rev. Haute "Haut" "Hawte"[13], Sir George "Georgius" Thomas[12], Sir Thomas "The Younger"[11], Sir Thomas "The Elder"[10], Sir Henry[9], Richard

Wiat or[8] Wyatt, Geoffrey "Jeoffrey" Wiot or[7] Wiat, Robert or Richard[6] Wiot, William Wiot or[5] Wyot, Adam Wiot or Wyote or[4], Guyott[3], Guyott[2], Captain or Admiral Adam Guyott or[1] Wiot) was born June 07, 1934 in Palmerville, Stanly County, N.C. She married John Arthur Gordon August 30, 1959 in N.C., son of William Gordon and Vera Jordon.

Child of Margaret Hinson and John Gordon is:

+ 1662   i.   Phillip V.[25] Gordon, Ph.D, M.D., born April 28, 1964 in High Point, Guilford County, N.C.

1080. Olga Bruce[24] Eagle (Edwin "Ed" Lee[23], Noah Jenkins[22], Mary Jane[21] Morgan, Rachel Evelyn "Eveline"[20] Wyatt, Noah Calvin[19], Thomas "Tommy"[18] Wiatt, Sr. (Wyatt, Wiett), John[17], Henry[16], Richard[15], George[14], Rev. Haute "Haut" "Hawte"[13], Sir George "Georgius" Thomas[12], Sir Thomas "The Younger"[11], Sir Thomas "The Elder"[10], Sir Henry[9], Richard Wiat or[8] Wyatt, Geoffrey "Jeoffrey" Wiot or[7] Wiat, Robert or Richard[6] Wiot, William Wiot or[5] Wyot, Adam Wiot or Wyote or[4], Guyott[3], Guyott[2], Captain or Admiral Adam Guyott or[1] Wiot) was born August 09, 1928 in Cabarrus County, N.C. She married James Mitchell Hinson August 09, 1948, son of Albert Hinson and Hattie Russell.

More About James Mitchell Hinson:
Buried at Greenlawn, Asheboro, N.C.

Children of Olga Eagle and James Hinson are:

+ 1663   i.   James Edward[25] Hinson, born August 09, 1949 in Stanly County, N.C.
+ 1664   ii.   Lynda Darlene Hinson, born June 10, 1951 in Stanly County, N.C.
+ 1665   iii.   Shirley Rebecca Hinson, born February 14, 1953 in Stanly County, N.C.

1082. Hattie Laura[24] Basinger (Helen Madelene[23] Eagle, Noah Jenkins[22], Mary Jane[21] Morgan, Rachel Evelyn "Eveline"[20] Wyatt, Noah Calvin[19], Thomas "Tommy"[18] Wiatt, Sr. (Wyatt, Wiett), John[17], Henry[16], Richard[15], George[14], Rev. Haute "Haut" "Hawte"[13], Sir George "Georgius" Thomas[12], Sir Thomas "The Younger"[11], Sir Thomas "The Elder"[10], Sir Henry[9], Richard Wiat or[8] Wyatt, Geoffrey "Jeoffrey" Wiot or[7] Wiat, Robert or Richard[6] Wiot, William Wiot or[5] Wyot, Adam Wiot or Wyote or[4], Guyott[3], Guyott[2], Captain or Admiral Adam Guyott or[1] Wiot) was born June 01, 1928 in Rowan County, N.C., and died March 22, 2007 in Statesville, N.C. She married Hubert Doylas Davis April 19, 1948, son of William Davis and Mary Taylor.

More About Hattie Laura Basinger:
Fact 1: Hattie's middle name was chosen in honor of her grandmother Laura Lou Eller.

The funeral was held at Old Mountain Road Baptist Church, Statesville, N.C.; buried in a cemetery located about five miles away on highway 21 just after Boiling Springs, N.C.

More About Hubert Doylas Davis:
Fact 1: 1943-1945, served in the US Marines.

    Child of Hattie Basinger and Hubert Davis is:

+   1666   i.   Sheri Elaine[25] Davis, born April 09, 1956 in Iredell County, N.C.

1083. Jerry Zane Grey[24] Basinger (Helen Madelene[23] Eagle, Noah Jenkins[22], Mary Jane[21] Morgan, Rachel Evelyn "Eveline"[20] Wyatt, Noah Calvin[19], Thomas "Tommy"[18] Wiatt, Sr. (Wyatt, Wiett), John[17], Henry[16], Richard[15], George[14], Rev. Haute "Haut" "Hawte"[13], Sir George "Georgius" Thomas[12], Sir Thomas "The Younger"[11], Sir Thomas "The Elder"[10], Sir Henry[9], Richard Wiat or[8] Wyatt, Geoffrey "Jeoffrey" Wiot or[7] Wiat, Robert or Richard[6] Wiot, William Wiot or[5] Wyot, Adam Wiot or Wyote or[4], Guyott[3], Guyott[2], Captain or Admiral Adam Guyott or[1] Wiot) was born December 18, 1931 in Rowan County, N.C. He married Barbara June Culp June 09, 1956, daughter of Claude Culp and Letha Canup.

    Child of Jerry Basinger and Barbara Culp is:

   1667   i.   Laura Lorraine[25] Basinger, born March 04, 1959 in Rowan County, N.C. She married Russell Earl Shuping September 20, 1980.

1084. Hayden Murray[24] Basinger (Helen Madelene[23] Eagle, Noah Jenkins[22], Mary Jane[21] Morgan, Rachel Evelyn "Eveline"[20] Wyatt, Noah Calvin[19], Thomas "Tommy"[18] Wiatt, Sr. (Wyatt, Wiett), John[17], Henry[16], Richard[15], George[14], Rev. Haute "Haut" "Hawte"[13], Sir George "Georgius" Thomas[12], Sir Thomas "The Younger"[11], Sir Thomas "The Elder"[10], Sir Henry[9], Richard Wiat or[8] Wyatt, Geoffrey "Jeoffrey" Wiot or[7] Wiat, Robert or Richard[6] Wiot, William Wiot or[5] Wyot, Adam Wiot or Wyote or[4], Guyott[3], Guyott[2], Captain or Admiral Adam Guyott or[1] Wiot) was born September 19, 1934 in Rowan County, N.C. He married (1) Clara Belle Barnes Walker June 04, 1964, daughter of Barnes and Irene Russell. He married (2) Pauline Barr July 18, 1976, daughter of Fred Bare and Laura Church.

Hayden Murray Basinger:
Fact 1: Served in the U.S. Army.

    Children of Hayden Basinger and Clara Walker are:

   1668   i.   Stephen Hayden[25] Basinger. He married Katheryn Victoria McKee June 21, 1984.

   1669   ii.   Debra Jean Basinger, born December 26, 1953.

| 1670 | iii. | Bobbie Davie Basinger, born June 26, 1958. He married Margaret McLoud. |
| 1671 | iv. | Beth Renei Basinger, born July 25, 1970 in Stanly County, N.C. |

1085. Alton Parker[24] Basinger, Jr. (Helen Madelene[23] Eagle, Noah Jenkins[22], Mary Jane[21] Morgan, Rachel Evelyn "Eveline"[20] Wyatt, Noah Calvin[19], Thomas "Tommy"[18] Wiatt, Sr. (Wyatt, Wiett), John[17], Henry[16], Richard[15], George[14], Rev. Haute "Haut" "Hawte"[13], Sir George "Georgius" Thomas[12], Sir Thomas "The Younger"[11], Sir Thomas "The Elder"[10], Sir Henry[9], Richard Wiat or[8] Wyatt, Geoffrey "Jeoffrey" Wiot or[7] Wiat, Robert or Richard[6] Wiot, William Wiot or[5] Wyot, Adam Wiot or Wyote or[4], Guyott[3], Guyott[2], Captain or Admiral Adam Guyott or[1] Wiot) was born June 23, 1938. He married Mary Maxine Campbell July 25, 1959, daughter of Floyd Campbell and Sara Johnson.

More About Alton Parker Basinger, Jr.:

Children of Alton Basinger and Mary Campbell are:

1672	i.	Helen Victoria[25] Parker, born July 22, 1960.
1673	ii.	Gregory Todd Parker, born August 03, 1961. He married Rachel Teresa Alexander.
1674	iii.	Michael Scott Parker, born October 20, 1962.
1675	iv.	Cynthia Lynn Parker, born October 31, 1964.
1676	v.	Janet Marie Parker, born May 04, 1969 in Stanly County, N.C.; died May 04, 1969 in Stanly County, N.C.

1086. Robert Noah[24] Basinger (Helen Madelene[23] Eagle, Noah Jenkins[22], Mary Jane[21] Morgan, Rachel Evelyn "Eveline"[20] Wyatt, Noah Calvin[19], Thomas "Tommy"[18] Wiatt, Sr. (Wyatt, Wiett), John[17], Henry[16], Richard[15], George[14], Rev. Haute "Haut" "Hawte"[13], Sir George "Georgius" Thomas[12], Sir Thomas "The Younger"[11], Sir Thomas "The Elder"[10], Sir Henry[9], Richard Wiat or[8] Wyatt, Geoffrey "Jeoffrey" Wiot or[7] Wiat, Robert or Richard[6] Wiot, William Wiot or[5] Wyot, Adam Wiot or Wyote or[4], Guyott[3], Guyott[2], Captain or Admiral Adam Guyott or[1] Wiot) was born January 19, 1942. He married Dolly Linda Boger July 02, 1963, daughter of Carl Boger and X.

Child of Robert Basinger and Dolly Boger is:

| 1677 | i. | Mark Allen[25] Basinger, born November 01, 1967. |

1087. Dorothy Jean[24] Basinger (Helen Madelene[23] Eagle, Noah Jenkins[22], Mary Jane[21] Morgan, Rachel Evelyn "Eveline"[20] Wyatt, Noah Calvin[19], Thomas "Tommy"[18] Wiatt, Sr. (Wyatt, Wiett), John[17], Henry[16], Richard[15], George[14], Rev. Haute "Haut" "Hawte"[13], Sir George "Georgius" Thomas[12], Sir Thomas "The Younger"[11], Sir Thomas "The Elder"[10], Sir Henry[9], Richard Wiat or[8] Wyatt, Geoffrey "Jeoffrey" Wiot or[7] Wiat, Robert or Richard[6] Wiot, William Wiot or[5] Wyot, Adam Wiot or Wyote or[4], Guyott[3], Guyott[2], Captain or Admiral Adam Guyott or[1] Wiot) was born February 27, 1944. She married Thomas Lester Lowder November 30, 1967, son of James Lowder and Annie Goodman.

Children of Dorothy Basinger and Thomas Lowder are:

1678	i.	Tommy Gene[25] Lowder, born December 01, 1970 in Cabarrus County, N.C.
1679	ii.	Tony Allen Lowder, born February 02, 1974 in Cabarrus County, N.C.
1680	iii.	Johnny Ray Lowder, born November 23, 1977 in Cabarrus County, N.C.
1681	iv.	Jimmy Alton Lowder, born January 31, 1979 in Cabarrus County, N.C.

1088.   Norman Paige[24] Barringer (Gladys Marie[23] Eagle, Noah Jenkins[22], Mary Jane[21] Morgan, Rachel Evelyn "Eveline"[20] Wyatt, Noah Calvin[19], Thomas "Tommy"[18] Wiatt, Sr. (Wyatt, Wiett), John[17], Henry[16], Richard[15], George[14], Rev. Haute "Haut" "Hawte"[13], Sir George "Georgius" Thomas[12], Sir Thomas "The Younger"[11], Sir Thomas "The Elder"[10], Sir Henry[9], Richard Wiat or[8] Wyatt, Geoffrey "Jeoffrey" Wiot or[7] Wiat, Robert or Richard[6] Wiot, William Wiot or[5] Wyot, Adam Wiot or Wyote or[4], Guyott[3], Guyott[2], Captain or Admiral Adam Guyott or[1] Wiot) was born December 10, 1928 in Stanly County, N.C., and died 2013 in North Carolina. He married Mary Ruth Pinion August 28, 1954, daughter of Dossie Pinion and Martha Hurt.

More About Norman Paige Barringer:
Fact 1: 1951-1952, served in the US Army during the Korean War.

Children of Norman Barringer and Mary Pinion are:

+	1682	i.	David Monroe[25] Barringer, born September 18, 1957 in Forsyth County, Winston-Salem, N.C.
	1683	ii.	Kevin Stuart Barringer, born January 11, 1961 in Forsyth County, N.C.
	1684	iii.	Todd Andrew Barringer, born April 29, 1971 in Forsyth County, N.C.

♀ | | ♂

Story on Norman Paige Barringer [1928-2013]

THE DUSTY GRAVEL of a country road leads to a house that once contained a framed photograph of Norman Barringer and his first cousin James Hinson. It rested on a desk. For James' mother Virgie, it was a special keepsake. Photos are like that. They capture time on paper. Glass and frame preserve the moment. Norman was in a military uniform. He was posing with James or Jim, as he was called by family and friends. Jim was dressed in uniform as well. It was in 1950 when the Korean War occupied the worries and prayers of the American way of life.

In his older years, Jim professed to have not spoken until he was nearly four years old. Possibly, he was three. No doubt, he remembered it. It was some profound thing that cemented his childhood to his adult years. It kept the bond he forged with Norman close to his heart. The day was like any other day in the world of play. Jim ran along behind Norman who entertained him with adventures. One day Norman who was a year older, ran through a door as his cousin James [Jim] waited for him outside. Suddenly, he yelled: *"Oakie door! Oakie door!"* Certainly, this was babytalk for *"Open the door."* When others in the house heard this, they thought it was Norman yelling.

How could that be? They had just seen Norman run past them. Jim waited for his cousin to return. *"Oakie door!"* he yelled again. The adults of the household opened the door and discovered it was indeed not Norman. More precisely they discovered Jim had found his voice.

Forty-four years later the calendar pages turned to a sad day in March 1994. Jim's sister Rachel had passed to the angels on the 12th. A soft glow of warmth filled the chill of hearts gathered throughout the rooms. Norman approached with a friendly demeanor and said: *"Just in case you don't know who I am ...I am Norman Barringer. I am your first cousin once removed."* He paused between the words *"cousin"* and *"once"* and smiled.

"I recognize you from Grandma's photo of you and Daddy," I professed.

"I know who you are," I told him. Within moments of this, my Uncle June, a brother to Jim, Rachel, Chub, Margaret and Betty, strides over and extends his hand.

Howard, who was standing next to me, said: *"I know you must be Chub."* June smiled:

"No, I'm June. That's okay, though. It's not important that you know who we all are, but more importantly, we know who you are. Of course, we all know who you are."

The pages of the calendar turned as if the wind had fingers of its own. Years are like this. It was 2001. The muffled sounds of conversation floated like a cloud through the rooms. Every relative there wishing me well with hugs and kisses. The breakfast room – as tiny as it is, brought with it privacy to sit next to Norman's wife Mary.

In our little reprieve, I told her a story of a peanutbutter sandwich. I don't particularly enjoy peanutbutter. For children who are not allergic – it is often the first food they learn to spread onto crackers or bread, or watch their mothers or grandmothers make into cookies.

"When Nicholas presented his sandwich to Howard he was maybe five or six," I told Mary, *"I noticed a dirty, frayed and stringy bandage resting against the sandwich. The bandage was attached to one of Nicholas's fingers."* His father asked: *"What is that hair all over the sandwich?"* He soon determined it was not hair at all; only torn gauze and adhesive tape dangling like fringe on an afghan.

Sometimes, it's not too unappetizing, and if one is lucky, a dog might decide to walk by. *"One time, my oldest son Zachary presented me with one pancake to go with a plate of maple syrup. On another occasion Nicholas prepared a plate of ketch-up to go with two fishsticks."*

Mary then began telling me about Norman going on a fishing trip with some buddies. *"Norman had nearly half finished a sandwich someone had added crickets to." "If it wasn't crickets, it was something like crickets,"* she said. Naturally, when I relayed this story to my father, he was not amused.

I replied that the fishing buddies were his friends and possibly they did not believe Norman would actually eat the sandwich, but he had not noticed, so their prank back fired.

1089. George Wilson[24] Barringer (Gladys Marie[23] Eagle, Noah Jenkins[22], Mary Jane[21] Morgan, Rachel Evelyn "Eveline"[20] Wyatt, Noah Calvin[19], Thomas "Tommy"[18] Wiatt, Sr. (Wyatt, Wiett), John[17], Henry[16], Richard[15], George[14], Rev. Haute "Haut" "Hawte"[13], Sir George "Georgius" Thomas[12], Sir Thomas "The Younger"[11], Sir Thomas "The Elder"[10], Sir Henry[9], Richard Wiat or[8] Wyatt, Geoffrey "Jeoffrey" Wiot or[7] Wiat, Robert or Richard[6] Wiot, William Wiot or[5] Wyot, Adam Wiot or Wyote or[4], Guyott[3], Guyott[2], Captain or Admiral Adam Guyott or[1] Wiot) was born February 22, 1931 in Stanly County, N.C. He married Eunice Marie Simpson January 26, 1958, daughter of Adam Simpson and Pattie Goodman.

More About George Wilson Barringer:
Fact 1: Served in the U.S. Navy.

Children of George Barringer and Eunice Simpson are:

1685　　i.　　Stephan Vance[25] Barringer, born December 25, 1960 in Mecklanburg County, N.C. He married (1) X. He married (2) Kathryn Tucker January 19, 1980.

1686　　ii.　　Alan Leslie Barringer, born March 27, 1962 in Mecklanburg County, N.C.

1090.　Sylvia Ann[24] Barringer (Gladys Marie[23] Eagle, Noah Jenkins[22], Mary Jane[21] Morgan, Rachel Evelyn "Eveline"[20] Wyatt, Noah Calvin[19], Thomas "Tommy"[18] Wiatt, Sr. (Wyatt, Wiett), John[17], Henry[16], Richard[15], George[14], Rev. Haute "Haut" "Hawte"[13], Sir George "Georgius" Thomas[12], Sir Thomas "The Younger"[11], Sir Thomas "The Elder"[10], Sir Henry[9], Richard Wiat or[8] Wyatt, Geoffrey "Jeoffrey" Wiot or[7] Wiat, Robert or Richard[6] Wiot, William Wiot or[5] Wyot, Adam Wiot or Wyote or[4], Guyott[3], Guyott[2], Captain or Admiral Adam Guyott or[1] Wiot) was born May 01, 1938. She married Robert Livingston Faulk April 20, 1958, son of Joseph Faulk and Annie Sexton.

Children of Sylvia Barringer and Robert Faulk are:

+　1687　　i.　　Beverly Suzanne[25] Faulk, born January 18, 1959 in Stanly County, N.C.

+　1688　　ii.　　Daniel Robert Faulk, born April 15, 1962 in Stanly County, N.C.

1091.　Edward Zane[24] Barringer (Gladys Marie[23] Eagle, Noah Jenkins[22], Mary Jane[21] Morgan, Rachel Evelyn "Eveline"[20] Wyatt, Noah Calvin[19], Thomas "Tommy"[18] Wiatt, Sr. (Wyatt, Wiett), John[17], Henry[16], Richard[15], George[14], Rev. Haute "Haut" "Hawte"[13], Sir George "Georgius" Thomas[12], Sir Thomas "The Younger"[11], Sir Thomas "The Elder"[10], Sir Henry[9], Richard Wiat or[8] Wyatt, Geoffrey "Jeoffrey" Wiot or[7] Wiat, Robert or Richard[6] Wiot, William Wiot or[5] Wyot, Adam Wiot or Wyote or[4], Guyott[3], Guyott[2], Captain or Admiral Adam Guyott or[1] Wiot) was born December 07, 1939. He married Margaret Kay Williams July 02, 1961, daughter of Grey Williams and Margaret Kennedy.

Children of Edward Barringer and Margaret Williams are:

1689　　i.　　Edward Zane[25] Barringer, Jr., born July 09, 1962 in Fort Benning, Ga.

1690　　ii.　　Anne Caroline Barringer, born July 09, 1964 in Stanly County, N.C. She married Jeff London.

1092.　Nina Marcella[24] Whitaker (Agnes Evelyn[23] Eagle, Noah Jenkins[22], Mary Jane[21] Morgan, Rachel Evelyn "Eveline"[20] Wyatt, Noah Calvin[19], Thomas "Tommy"[18] Wiatt, Sr. (Wyatt, Wiett), John[17], Henry[16], Richard[15], George[14], Rev. Haute "Haut" "Hawte"[13], Sir George "Georgius" Thomas[12], Sir Thomas "The Younger"[11], Sir Thomas "The Elder"[10], Sir Henry[9], Richard

Wiat or[8] Wyatt, Geoffrey "Jeoffrey" Wiot or[7] Wiat, Robert or Richard[6] Wiot, William Wiot or[5] Wyot, Adam Wiot or Wyote or[4], Guyott[3], Guyott[2], Captain or Admiral Adam Guyott or[1] Wiot) was born September 20, 1950 in Durham County, N.C. She married William Bryant Hackney June 12, 1971, son of Henry Hackney and Beulah Hobby.

Child of Nina Whitaker and William Hackney is:

1691   i.   William Bryant[25] Hackney, born July 30, 1976 in Chapel Hill, Orange County, N.C.

1095. Elizabeth Anne[24] Eagle, M.D. (Robert "Bob" Noah[23], Noah Jenkins[22], Mary Jane[21] Morgan, Rachel Evelyn "Eveline"[20] Wyatt, Noah Calvin[19], Thomas "Tommy"[18] Wiatt, Sr. (Wyatt, Wiett), John[17], Henry[16], Richard[15], George[14], Rev. Haute "Haut" "Hawte"[13], Sir George "Georgius" Thomas[12], Sir Thomas "The Younger"[11], Sir Thomas "The Elder"[10], Sir Henry[9], Richard Wiat or[8] Wyatt, Geoffrey "Jeoffrey" Wiot or[7] Wiat, Robert or Richard[6] Wiot, William Wiot or[5] Wyot, Adam Wiot or Wyote or[4], Guyott[3], Guyott[2], Captain or Admiral Adam Guyott or[1] Wiot) was born February 23, 1953 in High Point, Guilford County, N.C. She married David Allen Crews December 27, 1975, son of James Crews and Vivian Kreiger.

Children of Elizabeth Eagle and David Crews are:

1692   i.   Meredith Logan[25] Crews, born July 07, 1985 in Guilford County, N.C.
1693   ii.   Connor Harris Crews, born April 17, 1989.
1694   iii.   Dixon Crews, born April 19, 1992.

1096. Robert Nathan[24] Eagle (Robert "Bob" Noah[23], Noah Jenkins[22], Mary Jane[21] Morgan, Rachel Evelyn "Eveline"[20] Wyatt, Noah Calvin[19], Thomas "Tommy"[18] Wiatt, Sr. (Wyatt, Wiett), John[17], Henry[16], Richard[15], George[14], Rev. Haute "Haut" "Hawte"[13], Sir George "Georgius" Thomas[12], Sir Thomas "The Younger"[11], Sir Thomas "The Elder"[10], Sir Henry[9], Richard Wiat or[8] Wyatt, Geoffrey "Jeoffrey" Wiot or[7] Wiat, Robert or Richard[6] Wiot, William Wiot or[5] Wyot, Adam Wiot or Wyote or[4], Guyott[3], Guyott[2], Captain or Admiral Adam Guyott or[1] Wiot) was born October 16, 1955 in High Point, Guilford County, N.C. He married Mary Lyndon McNair June 26, 1982, daughter of Grover McNair and Jane Castenena.

Children of Robert Eagle and Mary McNair are:

1695   i.   Robert Christopher[25] Eagle, born January 29, 1984 in Guilford County, N.C.
1696   ii.   Jane Catherine Eagle, born June 27, 1986 in Guilford County, N.C.

         More About Jane Catherine Eagle:
         Fact 1: Nicknamed: "Katy."

1697   iii.   Taylor McNair Eagle, born April 19, 1994.

1099. Patricia Ann[24] Jones (Lonie Mae[23] Troutman, Mary Lillie[22] Eagle, Mary Jane[21] Morgan, Rachel Evelyn "Eveline"[20] Wyatt, Noah Calvin[19], Thomas "Tommy"[18] Wiatt, Sr. (Wyatt, Wiett), John[17], Henry[16], Richard[15], George[14], Rev. Haute "Haut" "Hawte"[13], Sir George "Georgius" Thomas[12], Sir Thomas "The Younger"[11], Sir Thomas "The Elder"[10], Sir Henry[9], Richard Wiat or[8] Wyatt, Geoffrey "Jeoffrey" Wiot or[7] Wiat, Robert or Richard[6] Wiot, William Wiot or[5] Wyot, Adam Wiot or Wyote or[4], Guyott[3], Guyott[2], Captain or Admiral Adam Guyott or[1] Wiot) was born October 16, 1941 in Rowan County, N.C. She married Cecil Stanly Little August 13, 1960, son of C. Little and Laura Stanley.

Children of Patricia Jones and Cecil Little are:

| 1698 | i. | Angela Lynn[25] Little, born October 21, 1961 in Forsythe County, N.C. She married Gary Fulp September 09, 1984. |
| 1699 | ii. | Amy Carol Little, born May 08, 1964 in Forsythe County, N.C. She married Kenneth Allen Rush August 02, 1986. |

1100. Pamela Jane[24] Jones (Lonie Mae[23] Troutman, Mary Lillie[22] Eagle, Mary Jane[21] Morgan, Rachel Evelyn "Eveline"[20] Wyatt, Noah Calvin[19], Thomas "Tommy"[18] Wiatt, Sr. (Wyatt, Wiett), John[17], Henry[16], Richard[15], George[14], Rev. Haute "Haut" "Hawte"[13], Sir George "Georgius" Thomas[12], Sir Thomas "The Younger"[11], Sir Thomas "The Elder"[10], Sir Henry[9], Richard Wiat or[8] Wyatt, Geoffrey "Jeoffrey" Wiot or[7] Wiat, Robert or Richard[6] Wiot, William Wiot or[5] Wyot, Adam Wiot or Wyote or[4], Guyott[3], Guyott[2], Captain or Admiral Adam Guyott or[1] Wiot) was born October 16, 1950 in Gaston County, N.C. She married Roy Wayne Dudley February 06, 1972, son of William Dudley and Carrie.

Children of Pamela Jones and Roy Dudley are:

| 1700 | i. | Brian Wayne[25] Dudley, born February 14, 1973. |
| 1701 | ii. | April Renée Dudley, born June 12, 1976 in Mecklenburg County, N.C. |

1101. Glenn Caldwell[24] White, Jr. (Nellie Manola[23] Morgan, Mary Frances[22] Eagle, Noah Calvin[21], Mary Ann[20] Wyatt, Noah Calvin[19], Thomas "Tommy"[18] Wiatt, Sr. (Wyatt, Wiett), John[17], Henry[16], Richard[15], George[14], Rev. Haute "Haut" "Hawte"[13], Sir George "Georgius" Thomas[12], Sir Thomas "The Younger"[11], Sir Thomas "The Elder"[10], Sir Henry[9], Richard Wiat or[8] Wyatt, Geoffrey "Jeoffrey" Wiot or[7] Wiat, Robert or Richard[6] Wiot, William Wiot or[5] Wyot, Adam Wiot or Wyote or[4], Guyott[3], Guyott[2], Captain or Admiral Adam Guyott or[1] Wiot) was born June 27, 1936 in Rowan County, N.C. He married Nancy Patterson August 20, 1960, daughter of James Patterson and Katherine Cauble.

Children of Glenn White and Nancy Patterson are:

| 1702 | i. | Dean B.[25] White, born February 23, 1967. |
| 1703 | ii. | Darin S. White, born September 03, 1970 in Mecklenburg County, N.C. |

1102. John W.[24] White (Nellie Manola[23] Morgan, Mary Frances[22] Eagle, Noah Calvin[21], Mary Ann[20] Wyatt, Noah Calvin[19], Thomas "Tommy"[18] Wiatt, Sr. (Wyatt, Wiett), John[17], Henry[16], Richard[15], George[14], Rev. Haute "Haut" "Hawte"[13], Sir George "Georgius" Thomas[12], Sir Thomas "The Younger"[11], Sir Thomas "The Elder"[10], Sir Henry[9], Richard Wiat or[8] Wyatt, Geoffrey "Jeoffrey" Wiot or[7] Wiat, Robert or Richard[6] Wiot, William Wiot or[5] Wyot, Adam Wiot or Wyote or[4], Guyott[3], Guyott[2], Captain or Admiral Adam Guyott or[1] Wiot) was born August 10, 1937 in Rowan County, N.C. He married Dora Elaine McSherry August 27, 1959, daughter of George McSherry and Georgia Manious.

Children of John White and Dora McSherry are:
1704   i.   James Blair[25] White, born September 29, 1960.
1705   ii. Michael Frederick White, born October 02, 1962.

1103. Fred S.[24] White (Nellie Manola[23] Morgan, Mary Frances[22] Eagle, Noah Calvin[21], Mary Ann[20] Wyatt, Noah Calvin[19], Thomas "Tommy"[18] Wiatt, Sr. (Wyatt, Wiett), John[17], Henry[16], Richard[15], George[14], Rev. Haute "Haut" "Hawte"[13], Sir George "Georgius" Thomas[12], Sir Thomas "The Younger"[11], Sir Thomas "The Elder"[10], Sir Henry[9], Richard Wiat or[8] Wyatt, Geoffrey "Jeoffrey" Wiot or[7] Wiat, Robert or Richard[6] Wiot, William Wiot or[5] Wyot, Adam Wiot or Wyote or[4], Guyott[3], Guyott[2], Captain or Admiral Adam Guyott or[1] Wiot) was born January 04, 1943 in Rowan County, N.C. He married Rosemary Grubb August 22, 1959, daughter of William Grubb and Martha Clayton.

Child of Fred White and Rosemary Grubb is:
1706   i.   Julie[25] White, born March 04, 1970 in Petersburg, Va.

1107. Jerry Richard[24] Eagle (Moody Van Calvin[23], Albert Thadeus[22], Noah Calvin[21], Mary Ann[20] Wyatt, Noah Calvin[19], Thomas "Tommy"[18] Wiatt, Sr. (Wyatt, Wiett), John[17], Henry[16], Richard[15], George[14], Rev. Haute "Haut" "Hawte"[13], Sir George "Georgius" Thomas[12], Sir Thomas "The Younger"[11], Sir Thomas "The Elder"[10], Sir Henry[9], Richard Wiat or[8] Wyatt, Geoffrey "Jeoffrey" Wiot or[7] Wiat, Robert or Richard[6] Wiot, William Wiot or[5] Wyot, Adam Wiot or Wyote or[4], Guyott[3], Guyott[2], Captain or Admiral Adam Guyott or[1] Wiot) was born November 25, 1943, and died April 28, 1984. He married (1) Brenda Brooks August 25, 1961, daughter of Guy Brooks and Christine Laws. He married (2) Gunda Schuchert March 01, 1967.

Child of Jerry Eagle and Brenda Brooks is:
1707   i.   Karen Elaine[25] Eagle, born August 25, 1964 in Seattle, Wash. She married Yount.

Children of Jerry Eagle and Gunda Schuchert are:
1708   i.   Linda Suzanne[25] Eagle, born January 08, 1968 in Germany.
1709   ii. Jerry Richard Eagle, born March 28, 1982 in Rowan County, N.C.

1108.   Glenn Torrence[24] Eagle (Moody Van Calvin[23], Albert Thadeus[22], Noah Calvin[21], Mary Ann[20] Wyatt, Noah Calvin[19], Thomas "Tommy"[18] Wiatt, Sr. (Wyatt, Wiett), John[17], Henry[16], Richard[15], George[14], Rev. Haute "Haut" "Hawte"[13], Sir George "Georgius" Thomas[12], Sir Thomas "The Younger"[11], Sir Thomas "The Elder"[10], Sir Henry[9], Richard Wiat or[8] Wyatt, Geoffrey "Jeoffrey" Wiot or[7] Wiat, Robert or Richard[6] Wiot, William Wiot or[5] Wyot, Adam Wiot or Wyote or[4], Guyott[3], Guyott[2], Captain or Admiral Adam Guyott or[1] Wiot) was born December 07, 1946. He married Nancy Elaine Walter June 17, 1973, daughter of George Walter and Ruth Sloop.

   Children of Glenn Eagle and Nancy Walter are:
  1710 i. Angela Joy[25] Eagle, born February 13, 1977 in Rowan County, N.C.
  1711 ii. Mark Glenn Eagle, born January 01, 1980 in Rowan County, N.C.

1109. David Marshall[24] Eagle (Moody Van Calvin[23], Albert Thadeus[22], Noah Calvin[21], Mary Ann[20] Wyatt, Noah Calvin[19], Thomas "Tommy"[18] Wiatt, Sr. (Wyatt, Wiett), John[17], Henry[16], Richard[15], George[14], Rev. Haute "Haut" "Hawte"[13], Sir George "Georgius" Thomas[12], Sir Thomas "The Younger"[11], Sir Thomas "The Elder"[10], Sir Henry[9], Richard Wiat or[8] Wyatt, Geoffrey "Jeoffrey" Wiot or[7] Wiat, Robert or Richard[6] Wiot, William Wiot or[5] Wyot, Adam Wiot or Wyote or[4], Guyott[3], Guyott[2], Captain or Admiral Adam Guyott or[1] Wiot) was born August 08, 1949. He married Jackie Estes July 18, 1977, daughter of Gene Estes and Betty Scardina.

   Child of David Eagle and Jackie Estes is:
  1712 i. Matthew David[25] Eagle, born June 13, 1978 in Rowan County, N.C.

1110.   Sue Anne[24] Eagle (Moody Van Calvin[23], Albert Thadeus[22], Noah Calvin[21], Mary Ann[20] Wyatt, Noah Calvin[19], Thomas "Tommy"[18] Wiatt, Sr. (Wyatt, Wiett), John[17], Henry[16], Richard[15], George[14], Rev. Haute "Haut" "Hawte"[13], Sir George "Georgius" Thomas[12], Sir Thomas "The Younger"[11], Sir Thomas "The Elder"[10], Sir Henry[9], Richard Wiat or[8] Wyatt, Geoffrey "Jeoffrey" Wiot or[7] Wiat, Robert or Richard[6] Wiot, William Wiot or[5] Wyot, Adam Wiot or Wyote or[4], Guyott[3], Guyott[2], Captain or Admiral Adam Guyott or[1] Wiot) was born December 16, 1954. She married Christopher Adam Troutman June 23, 1973, son of Fred Troutman and Dolly Safrit.

   Child of Sue Eagle and Christopher Troutman is:
  1713 i. Lisa Suzanne[25] Troutman, born October 12, 1975 in Rowan County, N.C.

1114.   Carol Ann[24] Miller (Marjorie Lucille[23] Eagle, Albert Thadeus[22], Noah Calvin[21], Mary Ann[20] Wyatt, Noah Calvin[19], Thomas "Tommy"[18] Wiatt, Sr. (Wyatt, Wiett), John[17], Henry[16], Richard[15], George[14], Rev. Haute "Haut" "Hawte"[13], Sir George "Georgius" Thomas[12], Sir

Thomas "The Younger"[11], Sir Thomas "The Elder"[10], Sir Henry[9], Richard Wiat or[8] Wyatt, Geoffrey "Jeoffrey" Wiot or[7] Wiat, Robert or Richard[6] Wiot, William Wiot or[5] Wyot, Adam Wiot or Wyote or[4], Guyott[3], Guyott[2], Captain or Admiral Adam Guyott or[1] Wiot) was born December 14, 1943 in Rowan County, N.C. She married (1) Larry Wagoner. She married (2) Terry Edwards.

Child of Carol Miller and Larry Wagoner is:
1714   i.   Kathy[25] Wagoner, born April 10, 1964.

Child of Carol Miller and Terry Edwards is:
1715   i.   Angela[25] Edwards, born December 1974.

1116. George Albert[24] Miller (Marjorie Lucille[23] Eagle, Albert Thadeus[22], Noah Calvin[21], Mary Ann[20] Wyatt, Noah Calvin[19], Thomas "Tommy"[18] Wiatt, Sr. (Wyatt, Wiett), John[17], Henry[16], Richard[15], George[14], Rev. Haute "Haut" "Hawte"[13], Sir George "Georgius" Thomas[12], Sir Thomas "The Younger"[11], Sir Thomas "The Elder"[10], Sir Henry[9], Richard Wiat or[8] Wyatt, Geoffrey "Jeoffrey" Wiot or[7] Wiat, Robert or Richard[6] Wiot, William Wiot or[5] Wyot, Adam Wiot or Wyote or[4], Guyott[3], Guyott[2], Captain or Admiral Adam Guyott or[1] Wiot) was born January 30, 1953 in Rowan County, N.C. He married Donna Jean Tesh July 04, 1971, daughter of Donald Tesh and Betty House.

Child of George Miller and Donna Tesh is:
1716   i.   Jason Kelly[25] Miller, born June 21, 1974 in Rowan County, N.C.

1118. Mary Jo[24] Whitley (Ervin Oscar[23], Roxie Dora[22] Eagle, Noah Calvin[21], Mary Ann[20] Wyatt, Noah Calvin[19], Thomas "Tommy"[18] Wiatt, Sr. (Wyatt, Wiett), John[17], Henry[16], Richard[15], George[14], Rev. Haute "Haut" "Hawte"[13], Sir George "Georgius" Thomas[12], Sir Thomas "The Younger"[11], Sir Thomas "The Elder"[10], Sir Henry[9], Richard Wiat or[8] Wyatt, Geoffrey "Jeoffrey" Wiot or[7] Wiat, Robert or Richard[6] Wiot, William Wiot or[5] Wyot, Adam Wiot or Wyote or[4], Guyott[3], Guyott[2], Captain or Admiral Adam Guyott or[1] Wiot) was born July 18, 1935 in Burke County, N.C. She married (1) Clarence Harmon Smith, son of Archie Smith and Bessie Lyles. She married (2) Robert Franklin Godfrey June 05, 1955, son of George Godfrey and Una Weaver.

Children of Mary Whitley and Robert Godfrey are:
1717   i.   Virginia Louise[25] Godfrey, born July 16, 1956 in Davidson County, N.C.
1718   ii.   Robert (Ronald?) Ervin Godfrey, born July 11, 1961 in Davidson County, N.C.

1120. Elizabeth May[24] Johnson (Vertie May[23] Whitley, Roxie Dora[22] Eagle, Noah Calvin[21], Mary Ann[20] Wyatt, Noah Calvin[19], Thomas "Tommy"[18] Wiatt, Sr. (Wyatt, Wiett), John[17], Henry[16], Richard[15], George[14], Rev. Haute "Haut" "Hawte"[13], Sir George "Georgius" Thomas[12], Sir Thomas "The Younger"[11], Sir Thomas "The Elder"[10], Sir Henry[9], Richard Wiat or[8] Wyatt,

Geoffrey "Jeoffrey" Wiot or[7] Wiat, Robert or Richard[6] Wiot, William Wiot or[5] Wyot, Adam Wiot or Wyote or[4], Guyott[3], Guyott[2], Captain or Admiral Adam Guyott or[1] Wiot) was born September 23, 1945 in Rowan County, N.C. She married (1) Roger Lee Brown November 20, 1965, son of Grady (?) and Elvira. She married (2) Pink Carpenter May 11, 1974.

Children of Elizabeth Johnson and Pink Carpenter are:

1719	i.	Wendy Elizabeth[25] Carpenter, born March 13, 1975.
1720	ii.	Martin Jill Carpenter, born November 19, 1975; died November 19, 1975.
1721	iii.	Jason Ryan Carpenter, born August 12, 1977.

1121.   Doris Louise[24] Penley (Marybelle Lucille[23] Whitley, Roxie Dora[22] Eagle, Noah Calvin[21], Mary Ann[20] Wyatt, Noah Calvin[19], Thomas "Tommy"[18] Wiatt, Sr. (Wyatt, Wiett), John[17], Henry[16], Richard[15], George[14], Rev. Haute "Haut" "Hawte"[13], Sir George "Georgius" Thomas[12], Sir Thomas "The Younger"[11], Sir Thomas "The Elder"[10], Sir Henry[9], Richard Wiat or[8] Wyatt, Geoffrey "Jeoffrey" Wiot or[7] Wiat, Robert or Richard[6] Wiot, William Wiot or[5] Wyot, Adam Wiot or Wyote or[4], Guyott[3], Guyott[2], Captain or Admiral Adam Guyott or[1] Wiot) was born November 14, 1933 in Rowan County, N.C. She married Rodriques Brittingham Von Müeller June 07, 1952, son of William Von Müeller and Una Adams.

Children of Doris Penley and Rodriques Von Müeller are:

1722	i.	James Roderick[25] Von Mueller, born December 23, 1956 in San Diego, Ca.
1723	ii.	Gilford Penley Von Mueller, born April 10, 1958 in San Diego, Ca.
1724	iii.	Guy Brittingham Von Mueller, born December 13, 1959 in Ca.; died December 13, 1959 in Ca.

1122. Clifford Roderick[24] Penley, Jr. (Marybelle Lucille[23] Whitley, Roxie Dora[22] Eagle, Noah Calvin[21], Mary Ann[20] Wyatt, Noah Calvin[19], Thomas "Tommy"[18] Wiatt, Sr. (Wyatt, Wiett), John[17], Henry[16], Richard[15], George[14], Rev. Haute "Haut" "Hawte"[13], Sir George "Georgius" Thomas[12], Sir Thomas "The Younger"[11], Sir Thomas "The Elder"[10], Sir Henry[9], Richard Wiat or[8] Wyatt, Geoffrey "Jeoffrey" Wiot or[7] Wiat, Robert or Richard[6] Wiot, William Wiot or[5] Wyot, Adam Wiot or Wyote or[4], Guyott[3], Guyott[2], Captain or Admiral Adam Guyott or[1] Wiot) was born November 02, 1935 in Rowan County, N.C. He married Gloria Castro December 06, 1958, daughter of Carlos Castro and Rosario Marquez.

Children of Clifford Penley and Gloria Castro are:

1725	i.	David William[25] Penley, born January 15, 1961 in San Pedro, Ca.
1726	ii.	Edward Dean Penley, born July 30, 1963 in La Mesa, Ca.
1727	iii.	Denise Michelle Penley, born April 23, 1965 in La Mesa, Ca.

1123. James William[24] Penley (Marybelle Lucille[23] Whitley, Roxie Dora[22] Eagle, Noah Calvin[21], Mary Ann[20] Wyatt, Noah Calvin[19], Thomas "Tommy"[18] Wiatt, Sr. (Wyatt, Wiett), John[17], Henry[16], Richard[15], George[14], Rev. Haute "Haut" "Hawte"[13], Sir George "Georgius" Thomas[12], Sir Thomas "The Younger"[11], Sir Thomas "The Elder"[10], Sir Henry[9], Richard Wiat or[8] Wyatt, Geoffrey "Jeoffrey" Wiot or[7] Wiat, Robert or Richard[6] Wiot, William Wiot or[5] Wyot, Adam Wiot or Wyote or[4], Guyott[3], Guyott[2], Captain or Admiral Adam Guyott or[1] Wiot) was born February 23, 1938 in Alamance County, N.C. He married Beatriz Edith San Doval June 18, 1967, daughter of Alezandro San Doval and Delores Villanicencio.

> Children of James Penley and Beatriz San Doval are:
>
> 1728   i.   Roderick William[25] Penley, born March 29, 1968 in San Diego, Ca.
>
> 1729   ii.   Richard Allen Penley, born July 06, 1973 in Gretna, La.

1124. Dorothy Jean[24] Fries (Agnes Marie[23] Whitley, Roxie Dora[22] Eagle, Noah Calvin[21], Mary Ann[20] Wyatt, Noah Calvin[19], Thomas "Tommy"[18] Wiatt, Sr. (Wyatt, Wiett), John[17], Henry[16], Richard[15], George[14], Rev. Haute "Haut" "Hawte"[13], Sir George "Georgius" Thomas[12], Sir Thomas "The Younger"[11], Sir Thomas "The Elder"[10], Sir Henry[9], Richard Wiat or[8] Wyatt, Geoffrey "Jeoffrey" Wiot or[7] Wiat, Robert or Richard[6] Wiot, William Wiot or[5] Wyot, Adam Wiot or Wyote or[4], Guyott[3], Guyott[2], Captain or Admiral Adam Guyott or[1] Wiot) was born September 26, 1934. She married Kenneth Lloyd Honeycutt April 14, 1952, son of Kenneth Honeycutt and Edna Dean.

> Children of Dorothy Fries and Kenneth Honeycutt are:
>
> + 1730   i.   Jeanie Lynn[25] Honeycutt, born August 15, 1952 in Rowan County, N.C.
>
> + 1731   ii.   Kenneth Kipling Honeycutt, born July 13, 1953 in Rowan County, N.C.
>
> + 1732   iii.   Stanley Dean Honeycutt, born August 02, 1957 in Rowan County, N.C.
>
> 1733   iv.   Gregory Wayne Honeycutt, born December 15, 1958 in Rowan County, N.C.

1125. Terry Gorman[24] Fries (Agnes Marie[23] Whitley, Roxie Dora[22] Eagle, Noah Calvin[21], Mary Ann[20] Wyatt, Noah Calvin[19], Thomas "Tommy"[18] Wiatt, Sr. (Wyatt, Wiett), John[17], Henry[16], Richard[15], George[14], Rev. Haute "Haut" "Hawte"[13], Sir George "Georgius" Thomas[12], Sir Thomas "The Younger"[11], Sir Thomas "The Elder"[10], Sir Henry[9], Richard Wiat or[8] Wyatt, Geoffrey "Jeoffrey" Wiot or[7] Wiat, Robert or Richard[6] Wiot, William Wiot or[5] Wyot, Adam Wiot or Wyote or[4], Guyott[3], Guyott[2], Captain or Admiral Adam Guyott or[1] Wiot) was born July 31, 1936. He married Sheila Rochelle Cain April 10, 1955, daughter of Herbert Cain and Addie Dedmon.

Children of Terry Fries and Sheila Cain are:

	1734	i.	Mark Gorman[25] Fries, born August 16, 1956; died August 16, 1956.
+	1735	ii.	Marc Christopher Fries, born June 07, 1957.
+	1736	iii.	Todd Gorman Fries, born April 02, 1959.
+	1737	iv.	Robin Rochelle Fries, born September 13, 1961.

1128. Jody Wayne[24] Whitley (Marvin L.[23], Roxie Dora[22] Eagle, Noah Calvin[21], Mary Ann[20] Wyatt, Noah Calvin[19], Thomas "Tommy"[18] Wiatt, Sr. (Wyatt, Wiett), John[17], Henry[16], Richard[15], George[14], Rev. Haute "Haut" "Hawte"[13], Sir George "Georgius" Thomas[12], Sir Thomas "The Younger"[11], Sir Thomas "The Elder"[10], Sir Henry[9], Richard Wiat or[8] Wyatt, Geoffrey "Jeoffrey" Wiot or[7] Wiat, Robert or Richard[6] Wiot, William Wiot or[5] Wyot, Adam Wiot or Wyote or[4], Guyott[3], Guyott[2], Captain or Admiral Adam Guyott or[1] Wiot) was born May 04, 1963 in Rowan County, N.C. He married Angella Machelle Mungo June 28, 1986, daughter of Ernest Mungo and Jerolyn Courtney.

Child of Jody Whitley and Angella Mungo is:

| 1738 | i. | Ryan Mattew[25] Whitley, born November 26, 1988 in Mecklenburg County, N.C. |

1129. Cecil Ray[24] Hutchinson (Georgia (Georgie) Kathleen[23] Whitley, Roxie Dora[22] Eagle, Noah Calvin[21], Mary Ann[20] Wyatt, Noah Calvin[19], Thomas "Tommy"[18] Wiatt, Sr. (Wyatt, Wiett), John[17], Henry[16], Richard[15], George[14], Rev. Haute "Haut" "Hawte"[13], Sir George "Georgius" Thomas[12], Sir Thomas "The Younger"[11], Sir Thomas "The Elder"[10], Sir Henry[9], Richard Wiat or[8] Wyatt, Geoffrey "Jeoffrey" Wiot or[7] Wiat, Robert or Richard[6] Wiot, William Wiot or[5] Wyot, Adam Wiot or Wyote or[4], Guyott[3], Guyott[2], Captain or Admiral Adam Guyott or[1] Wiot) was born February 27, 1940 in Rowan County, N.C. He married Melvia Louise Hall July 01, 1961, daughter of Melvin Hall and Helen Miller.

Children of Cecil Hutchinson and Melvia Hall are:

| 1739 | i. | Jeffrey Todd[25] Hutchinson, born October 07, 1962 in Rowan County, N.C. |
| 1740 | ii. | Blair Lurae Hutchinson, born January 17, 1966 in Rowan County, N.C. She married Bryan David Green August 11, 1984. |

1131. Victoria Ellen[24] Whitley (Robert Clifford[23], Roxie Dora[22] Eagle, Noah Calvin[21], Mary Ann[20] Wyatt, Noah Calvin[19], Thomas "Tommy"[18] Wiatt, Sr. (Wyatt, Wiett), John[17], Henry[16], Richard[15], George[14], Rev. Haute "Haut" "Hawte"[13], Sir George "Georgius" Thomas[12], Sir Thomas "The Younger"[11], Sir Thomas "The Elder"[10], Sir Henry[9], Richard Wiat or[8] Wyatt, Geoffrey "Jeoffrey" Wiot or[7] Wiat, Robert or Richard[6] Wiot, William Wiot or[5] Wyot, Adam Wiot or Wyote or[4], Guyott[3], Guyott[2], Captain or Admiral Adam Guyott or[1] Wiot) was born July 30, 1946. She married Theodore Parker Jensen, Jr. June 24, 1972, son of Theodore Jensen and Faye Turner.

Child of Victoria Whitley and Theodore Jensen is:

1741   i.   John A. Thomas[25] Jensen, born December 23, 1975 in Stockton, Ca.

1134. Kay Gwynn[24] Whitley (Robert Clifford[23], Roxie Dora[22] Eagle, Noah Calvin[21], Mary Ann[20] Wyatt, Noah Calvin[19], Thomas "Tommy"[18] Wiatt, Sr. (Wyatt, Wiett), John[17], Henry[16], Richard[15], George[14], Rev. Haute "Haut" "Hawte"[13], Sir George "Georgius" Thomas[12], Sir Thomas "The Younger"[11], Sir Thomas "The Elder"[10], Sir Henry[9], Richard Wiat or[8] Wyatt, Geoffrey "Jeoffrey" Wiot or[7] Wiat, Robert or Richard[6] Wiot, William Wiot or[5] Wyot, Adam Wiot or Wyote or[4], Guyott[3], Guyott[2], Captain or Admiral Adam Guyott or[1] Wiot) was born March 19, 1955. She married Mark C. Harris January 19, 1979, son of Durwood Harris and Betty Rankin.

Child of Kay Whitley and Mark Harris is:

1742   i.   Annie Jean[25] Harris, born May 14, 1981.

1135. John Calvin[24] Whitley, Jr. (John Calvin[23], Roxie Dora[22] Eagle, Noah Calvin[21], Mary Ann[20] Wyatt, Noah Calvin[19], Thomas "Tommy"[18] Wiatt, Sr. (Wyatt, Wiett), John[17], Henry[16], Richard[15], George[14], Rev. Haute "Haut" "Hawte"[13], Sir George "Georgius" Thomas[12], Sir Thomas "The Younger"[11], Sir Thomas "The Elder"[10], Sir Henry[9], Richard Wiat or[8] Wyatt, Geoffrey "Jeoffrey" Wiot or[7] Wiat, Robert or Richard[6] Wiot, William Wiot or[5] Wyot, Adam Wiot or Wyote or[4], Guyott[3], Guyott[2], Captain or Admiral Adam Guyott or[1] Wiot) was born February 02, 1951 in Iredell County, N.C. He married Diane Corl.

Child of John Whitley and Diane Corl is:

1743   i.   Angelia Love[25] Whitley, born September 1970 in Cabarrus County, N.C.

1136. Suzanne Amanda[24] Whitley (John Calvin[23], Roxie Dora[22] Eagle, Noah Calvin[21], Mary Ann[20] Wyatt, Noah Calvin[19], Thomas "Tommy"[18] Wiatt, Sr. (Wyatt, Wiett), John[17], Henry[16], Richard[15], George[14], Rev. Haute "Haut" "Hawte"[13], Sir George "Georgius" Thomas[12], Sir Thomas "The Younger"[11], Sir Thomas "The Elder"[10], Sir Henry[9], Richard Wiat or[8] Wyatt, Geoffrey "Jeoffrey" Wiot or[7] Wiat, Robert or Richard[6] Wiot, William Wiot or[5] Wyot, Adam Wiot or Wyote or[4], Guyott[3], Guyott[2], Captain or Admiral Adam Guyott or[1] Wiot) was born June 30, 1953 in Mecklenburg County, N.C. She married Jeffry Everett Hege June 15, 1974, son of Everett Hege and Maxine.

Child of Suzanne Whitley and Jeffry Hege is:

1744   i.   Darrell Lennon[25] Hege, born April 16, 1975 in Cabarrus County, N.C.

1138. Gene Nelson[24] Whitley (John Calvin[23], Roxie Dora[22] Eagle, Noah Calvin[21], Mary Ann[20] Wyatt, Noah Calvin[19], Thomas "Tommy"[18] Wiatt, Sr. (Wyatt, Wiett), John[17], Henry[16],

Richard[15], George[14], Rev. Haute "Haut" "Hawte"[13], Sir George "Georgius" Thomas[12], Sir Thomas "The Younger"[11], Sir Thomas "The Elder"[10], Sir Henry[9], Richard Wiat or[8] Wyatt, Geoffrey "Jeoffrey" Wiot or[7] Wiat, Robert or Richard[6] Wiot, William Wiot or[5] Wyot, Adam Wiot or Wyote or[4], Guyott[3], Guyott[2], Captain or Admiral Adam Guyott or[1] Wiot) was born December 27, 1960 in Mecklenburg County, N.C. He married Karen Nancy Nordhausen, daughter of Eric Nordhausen and Joan Bohn.

Child of Gene Whitley and Karen Nordhausen is:

1745   i.   Kyle Nolan[25] Whitley, born September 15, 1985 in Tucson, Ca.

1140. Sara Jeanette[24] Craven (Helen Marie[23] Jones, Annie Luada[22] Eagle, Noah Calvin[21], Mary Ann[20] Wyatt, Noah Calvin[19], Thomas "Tommy"[18] Wiatt, Sr. (Wyatt, Wiett), John[17], Henry[16], Richard[15], George[14], Rev. Haute "Haut" "Hawte"[13], Sir George "Georgius" Thomas[12], Sir Thomas "The Younger"[11], Sir Thomas "The Elder"[10], Sir Henry[9], Richard Wiat or[8] Wyatt, Geoffrey "Jeoffrey" Wiot or[7] Wiat, Robert or Richard[6] Wiot, William Wiot or[5] Wyot, Adam Wiot or Wyote or[4], Guyott[3], Guyott[2], Captain or Admiral Adam Guyott or[1] Wiot) was born March 07, 1951 in Cabarrus County, N.C. She married (1) John Avery Wood August 26, 1972. She married (2) Guy Angster April 03, 1976, son of Capt. Angster and Grete Cielke.

Child of Sara Craven and Guy Angster is:

1746   i.   Zachary Scott[25] Angster, born June 11, 1977 in Wake County, N.C.

1143. Nancy Marie[24] Glover (Helen Marie[23] Jones, Annie Luada[22] Eagle, Noah Calvin[21], Mary Ann[20] Wyatt, Noah Calvin[19], Thomas "Tommy"[18] Wiatt, Sr. (Wyatt, Wiett), John[17], Henry[16], Richard[15], George[14], Rev. Haute "Haut" "Hawte"[13], Sir George "Georgius" Thomas[12], Sir Thomas "The Younger"[11], Sir Thomas "The Elder"[10], Sir Henry[9], Richard Wiat or[8] Wyatt, Geoffrey "Jeoffrey" Wiot or[7] Wiat, Robert or Richard[6] Wiot, William Wiot or[5] Wyot, Adam Wiot or Wyote or[4], Guyott[3], Guyott[2], Captain or Admiral Adam Guyott or[1] Wiot) was born May 22, 1938. She married James Thurman Allman, Sr. December 27, 1956, son of James Allman and Azilee Eugenia.

Children of Nancy Glover and James Allman are:

1747   i.   Jackie Yvonne[25] Allman, born February 13, 1958 in Cabarrus County, N.C. She married Terry Lyndon Treece June 26, 1973.

1748   ii.   James Thurman Allman, Jr., born July 25, 1959 in Cabarrus County, N.C.

+ 1749   iii.   Boyd Allen Allman, born September 02, 1960 in Cabarrus County, N.C.

1750   iv.   Jerry Lee Allman, born July 07, 1964 in Cabarrus County, N.C.

1144. Ada Elisabeth[24] Jones (George Freeland[23], Annie Luada[22] Eagle, Noah Calvin[21], Mary Ann[20] Wyatt, Noah Calvin[19], Thomas "Tommy"[18] Wiatt, Sr. (Wyatt, Wiett), John[17], Henry[16],

Richard[15], George[14], Rev. Haute "Haut" "Hawte"[13], Sir George "Georgius" Thomas[12], Sir Thomas "The Younger"[11], Sir Thomas "The Elder"[10], Sir Henry[9], Richard Wiat or[8] Wyatt, Geoffrey "Jeoffrey" Wiot or[7] Wiat, Robert or Richard[6] Wiot, William Wiot or[5] Wyot, Adam Wiot or Wyote or[4], Guyott[3], Guyott[2], Captain or Admiral Adam Guyott or[1] Wiot) was born February 25, 1944. She married Jerry Wayne Mills February 22, 1964, son of Robert Mills and Helen Smith.

> Children of Ada Jones and Jerry Mills are:
> 1751   i.   Elizabeth Dawn25 Mills, born May 11, 1964 in Rowan County, N.C.
> 1752   ii. Jason Wayne Mills, born March 22, 1978 in Rowan County, N.C.

1145.   Ruby Mae[24] Jones (George Freeland[23], Annie Luada[22] Eagle, Noah Calvin[21], Mary Ann[20] Wyatt, Noah Calvin[19], Thomas "Tommy"[18] Wiatt, Sr. (Wyatt, Wiett), John[17], Henry[16], Richard[15], George[14], Rev. Haute "Haut" "Hawte"[13], Sir George "Georgius" Thomas[12], Sir Thomas "The Younger"[11], Sir Thomas "The Elder"[10], Sir Henry[9], Richard Wiat or[8] Wyatt, Geoffrey "Jeoffrey" Wiot or[7] Wiat, Robert or Richard[6] Wiot, William Wiot or[5] Wyot, Adam Wiot or Wyote or[4], Guyott[3], Guyott[2], Captain or Admiral Adam Guyott or[1] Wiot) was born August 07, 1946, and died January 09, 1967. She married John Thomas Rinehardt December 20, 1964, son of Adam Rinehardt and Maude Hill.

More About Ruby Mae Jones:
Died of injuries sustained from an auto accident.

> Child of Ruby Jones and John Rinehardt is:
> 1753   i.   Craig Harlan[25] Rinehardt, born July 23, 1966 in Rowan County, N.C.; died December 31, 1983.
>
> > More About Craig Harlan Rinehardt:
> > Died of injuries sustained from auto accident.

1148.   Leonard DeWitt[24] Jones (George Freeland[23], Annie Luada[22] Eagle, Noah Calvin[21], Mary Ann[20] Wyatt, Noah Calvin[19], Thomas "Tommy"[18] Wiatt, Sr. (Wyatt, Wiett), John[17], Henry[16], Richard[15], George[14], Rev. Haute "Haut" "Hawte"[13], Sir George "Georgius" Thomas[12], Sir Thomas "The Younger"[11], Sir Thomas "The Elder"[10], Sir Henry[9], Richard Wiat or[8] Wyatt, Geoffrey "Jeoffrey" Wiot or[7] Wiat, Robert or Richard[6] Wiot, William Wiot or[5] Wyot, Adam Wiot or Wyote or[4], Guyott[3], Guyott[2], Captain or Admiral Adam Guyott or[1] Wiot) was born March 15, 1953. He married Phyllis Inez Albright June 12, 1971, daughter of James Albright and Ruth Morgan.

> Child of Leonard Jones and Phyllis Albright is:
> 1754   i.   Wendy Michelle[25] Jones, born January 05, 1972 in Rowan County, N.C.

1153.   Pamela Jean[24] Abernethy (Mabel Eloise[23] Eagle, Martin Junius[22], Noah Calvin[21], Mary Ann[20] Wyatt, Noah Calvin[19], Thomas "Tommy"[18] Wiatt, Sr. (Wyatt, Wiett), John[17], Henry[16], Richard[15], George[14], Rev. Haute "Haut" "Hawte"[13], Sir George "Georgius" Thomas[12], Sir Thomas "The Younger"[11], Sir Thomas "The Elder"[10], Sir Henry[9], Richard Wiat or[8] Wyatt, Geoffrey "Jeoffrey" Wiot or[7] Wiat, Robert or Richard[6] Wiot, William Wiot or[5] Wyot, Adam Wiot or Wyote or[4], Guyott[3], Guyott[2], Captain or Admiral Adam Guyott or[1] Wiot) was born May 16, 1947. She married Timothy Parlier December 21, 1968.

Children of Pamela Abernethy and Timothy Parlier are:
1755   i.   Angela Jean[25] Parlier, born May 16, 1971.
1756   ii.   David Timothy Parlier, born June 14, 1974.
1757   iii. Howard Benjamin Parlier, born 1977.

1154. Donna Eloise[24] Abernethy (Mabel Eloise[23] Eagle, Martin Junius[22], Noah Calvin[21], Mary Ann[20] Wyatt, Noah Calvin[19], Thomas "Tommy"[18] Wiatt, Sr. (Wyatt, Wiett), John[17], Henry[16], Richard[15], George[14], Rev. Haute "Haut" "Hawte"[13], Sir George "Georgius" Thomas[12], Sir Thomas "The Younger"[11], Sir Thomas "The Elder"[10], Sir Henry[9], Richard Wiat or[8] Wyatt, Geoffrey "Jeoffrey" Wiot or[7] Wiat, Robert or Richard[6] Wiot, William Wiot or[5] Wyot, Adam Wiot or Wyote or[4], Guyott[3], Guyott[2], Captain or Admiral Adam Guyott or[1] Wiot) was born February 23, 1950. She married (1) Williard R. Pittman, Jr., son of Willard Pittman and Bertha Buchanan. She married (2) Gary Arthur Raines, Jr. November 14, 1970, son of Arthur Raines and Pearl Parker.

Children of Donna Abernethy and Gary Raines are:
1758   i.   Gary Arthur[25] Raines III, born June 04, 1971.
1759   ii.   Deirdre Michelle Raines, born July 03, 1973.

1155. Ronald Dean[24] Graham (Ronald Alexander[23], Mattie E.[22] Eagle, Noah Calvin[21], Mary Ann[20] Wyatt, Noah Calvin[19], Thomas "Tommy"[18] Wiatt, Sr. (Wyatt, Wiett), John[17], Henry[16], Richard[15], George[14], Rev. Haute "Haut" "Hawte"[13], Sir George "Georgius" Thomas[12], Sir Thomas "The Younger"[11], Sir Thomas "The Elder"[10], Sir Henry[9], Richard Wiat or[8] Wyatt, Geoffrey "Jeoffrey" Wiot or[7] Wiat, Robert or Richard[6] Wiot, William Wiot or[5] Wyot, Adam Wiot or Wyote or[4], Guyott[3], Guyott[2], Captain or Admiral Adam Guyott or[1] Wiot) was born August 30, 1954. He married Joanne Vacchiano March 27, 1957, daughter of Joseph Vacchiano and Marilou McCory.

Children of Ronald Graham and Joanne Vacchiano are:
1760   i.   Joseph Ronald[25] Graham, born January 14, 1981.
1761   ii.   Jonathan Graham, born June 1984.

1159. Joyce Marie[24] Silliman (Thelma Louise[23] Eagle, Carpenter L.[22], Noah Calvin[21], Mary Ann[20] Wyatt, Noah Calvin[19], Thomas "Tommy"[18] Wiatt, Sr. (Wyatt, Wiett), John[17], Henry[16], Richard[15], George[14], Rev. Haute "Haut" "Hawte"[13], Sir George "Georgius" Thomas[12], Sir

Thomas "The Younger"[11], Sir Thomas "The Elder"[10], Sir Henry[9], Richard Wiat or[8] Wyatt, Geoffrey "Jeoffrey" Wiot or[7] Wiat, Robert or Richard[6] Wiot, William Wiot or[5] Wyot, Adam Wiot or Wyote or[4], Guyott[3], Guyott[2], Captain or Admiral Adam Guyott or[1] Wiot) was born November 14, 1949 in Rowan County, N.C. She married Ronald D. Keistler, Jr. July 12, 1970, son of Ronald Keistler and Jean Howard.

> Children of Joyce Silliman and Ronald Keistler are:
> 1762   i.   Christina Marie[25] Keistler, born November 01, 1977.
> 1763   ii.   Emily Stewart Keistler, born August 04, 1981 in Wake County, N.C.

1160. Janice Louise[24] Silliman (Thelma Louise[23] Eagle, Carpenter L.[22], Noah Calvin[21], Mary Ann[20] Wyatt, Noah Calvin[19], Thomas "Tommy"[18] Wiatt, Sr. (Wyatt, Wiett), John[17], Henry[16], Richard[15], George[14], Rev. Haute "Haut" "Hawte"[13], Sir George "Georgius" Thomas[12], Sir Thomas "The Younger"[11], Sir Thomas "The Elder"[10], Sir Henry[9], Richard Wiat or[8] Wyatt, Geoffrey "Jeoffrey" Wiot or[7] Wiat, Robert or Richard[6] Wiot, William Wiot or[5] Wyot, Adam Wiot or Wyote or[4], Guyott[3], Guyott[2], Captain or Admiral Adam Guyott or[1] Wiot) was born January 19, 1953 in Rowan County, N.C. She married Michael Lee Spears July 10, 1976, son of Craig Spears and Betty.

> Child of Janice Silliman and Michael Spears is:
> 1764   i.   Catherine Balir[25] Spears, born February 02, 1983 in Wake County, N.C.

1161. Melba Sue[24] Eagle (Billy West[23], Carpenter L.[22], Noah Calvin[21], Mary Ann[20] Wyatt, Noah Calvin[19], Thomas "Tommy"[18] Wiatt, Sr. (Wyatt, Wiett), John[17], Henry[16], Richard[15], George[14], Rev. Haute "Haut" "Hawte"[13], Sir George "Georgius" Thomas[12], Sir Thomas "The Younger"[11], Sir Thomas "The Elder"[10], Sir Henry[9], Richard Wiat or[8] Wyatt, Geoffrey "Jeoffrey" Wiot or[7] Wiat, Robert or Richard[6] Wiot, William Wiot or[5] Wyot, Adam Wiot or Wyote or[4], Guyott[3], Guyott[2], Captain or Admiral Adam Guyott or[1] Wiot) was born January 21, 1954 in Rowan County, N.C. She married Larry Melton May 24, 1983.

> Child of Melba Eagle and Larry Melton is:
> 1765   i.   Noah McKenley[25] Melton, born October 19, 1983.

1162. David Kent[24] Eagle (Billy West[23], Carpenter L.[22], Noah Calvin[21], Mary Ann[20] Wyatt, Noah Calvin[19], Thomas "Tommy"[18] Wiatt, Sr. (Wyatt, Wiett), John[17], Henry[16], Richard[15], George[14], Rev. Haute "Haut" "Hawte"[13], Sir George "Georgius" Thomas[12], Sir Thomas "The Younger"[11], Sir Thomas "The Elder"[10], Sir Henry[9], Richard Wiat or[8] Wyatt, Geoffrey "Jeoffrey" Wiot or[7] Wiat, Robert or Richard[6] Wiot, William Wiot or[5] Wyot, Adam Wiot or Wyote or[4], Guyott[3], Guyott[2], Captain or Admiral Adam Guyott or[1] Wiot) was born September 25, 1956 in Rowan County, N.C. He married Ramonda Gaye Houck February 25, 1978, daughter of James Houck and Estella Wyatt.

Children of David Eagle and Ramonda Houck are:

| 1766 | i. | Lori Dawn[25] Eagle, born September 20, 1978 in Cabarrus County, N.C. |
| 1767 | ii. | Brian Scott Eagle, born December 12, 1981 in Cabarrus County, N.C. |

1164. Lisa Lynn[24] Eagle (Carpenter L.[23], Carpenter L.[22], Noah Calvin[21], Mary Ann[20] Wyatt, Noah Calvin[19], Thomas "Tommy"[18] Wiatt, Sr. (Wyatt, Wiett), John[17], Henry[16], Richard[15], George[14], Rev. Haute "Haut" "Hawte"[13], Sir George "Georgius" Thomas[12], Sir Thomas "The Younger"[11], Sir Thomas "The Elder"[10], Sir Henry[9], Richard Wiat or[8] Wyatt, Geoffrey "Jeoffrey" Wiot or[7] Wiat, Robert or Richard[6] Wiot, William Wiot or[5] Wyot, Adam Wiot or Wyote or[4], Guyott[3], Guyott[2], Captain or Admiral Adam Guyott or[1] Wiot) was born August 14, 1960. She married Charles David Shuping, son of Charles Shuping and Carol Hoffman.

Child of Lisa Eagle and Charles Shuping is:

| 1768 | i. | Shawn[25] Shuping, born May 17, 1988. |

1171. Carole Jean[24] Hicks (Evelyn[23] Eagle, William Armstrong[22], Eli Esau[21], Mary Ann[20] Wyatt, Noah Calvin[19], Thomas "Tommy"[18] Wiatt, Sr. (Wyatt, Wiett), John[17], Henry[16], Richard[15], George[14], Rev. Haute "Haut" "Hawte"[13], Sir George "Georgius" Thomas[12], Sir Thomas "The Younger"[11], Sir Thomas "The Elder"[10], Sir Henry[9], Richard Wiat or[8] Wyatt, Geoffrey "Jeoffrey" Wiot or[7] Wiat, Robert or Richard[6] Wiot, William Wiot or[5] Wyot, Adam Wiot or Wyote or[4], Guyott[3], Guyott[2], Captain or Admiral Adam Guyott or[1] Wiot) was born January 03, 1939. She married Eugene Crawford Autry September 04, 1959, son of James Autry and Grace.

Children of Carole Hicks and Eugene Autry are:

| 1769 | i. | Tina Lynn[25] Autry, born January 28, 1966. |
| 1770 | ii. | Keith Eugene Autry, born August 17, 1967 in Newport News, Virginia. |

1172. Sandra Gail[24] Hicks (Evelyn[23] Eagle, William Armstrong[22], Eli Esau[21], Mary Ann[20] Wyatt, Noah Calvin[19], Thomas "Tommy"[18] Wiatt, Sr. (Wyatt, Wiett), John[17], Henry[16], Richard[15], George[14], Rev. Haute "Haut" "Hawte"[13], Sir George "Georgius" Thomas[12], Sir Thomas "The Younger"[11], Sir Thomas "The Elder"[10], Sir Henry[9], Richard Wiat or[8] Wyatt, Geoffrey "Jeoffrey" Wiot or[7] Wiat, Robert or Richard[6] Wiot, William Wiot or[5] Wyot, Adam Wiot or Wyote or[4], Guyott[3], Guyott[2], Captain or Admiral Adam Guyott or[1] Wiot) was born May 08, 1943. She married William H. Jarrett September 02, 1967, son of Edward Jarrett and Lucille.

Children of Sandra Hicks and William Jarrett are:

1771	i.	Jennifer Denise[25] Jarrett, born May 22, 1971 in Leesbury, Florida.
1772	ii.	William Jarrett, born February 02, 1973 in Leesbury, Florida.
1773	iii.	Joseph Edward Jarrett, Jr., born May 28, 1977 in Leesbury, Florida.

1173. Ronald Richard[24] Hicks (Evelyn[23] Eagle, William Armstrong[22], Eli Esau[21], Mary Ann[20] Wyatt, Noah Calvin[19], Thomas "Tommy"[18] Wiatt, Sr. (Wyatt, Wiett), John[17], Henry[16], Richard[15], George[14], Rev. Haute "Haut" "Hawte"[13], Sir George "Georgius" Thomas[12], Sir Thomas "The Younger"[11], Sir Thomas "The Elder"[10], Sir Henry[9], Richard Wiat or[8] Wyatt, Geoffrey "Jeoffrey" Wiot or[7] Wiat, Robert or Richard[6] Wiot, William Wiot or[5] Wyot, Adam Wiot or Wyote or[4], Guyott[3], Guyott[2], Captain or Admiral Adam Guyott or[1] Wiot) was born May 29, 1952 in Newport News, Virginia. He married Betty Jane Hayter December 21, 1973, daughter of Curtis Hayter and Unknown.

> Child of Ronald Hicks and Betty Hayter is:
> 1774   i.   Christopher Ronald[25] Hicks, born April 23, 1978 in Newport News, Virginia.

1174. Everett Wayne[24] Eagle (Everett Wayne[23], William Armstrong[22], Eli Esau[21], Mary Ann[20] Wyatt, Noah Calvin[19], Thomas "Tommy"[18] Wiatt, Sr. (Wyatt, Wiett), John[17], Henry[16], Richard[15], George[14], Rev. Haute "Haut" "Hawte"[13], Sir George "Georgius" Thomas[12], Sir Thomas "The Younger"[11], Sir Thomas "The Elder"[10], Sir Henry[9], Richard Wiat or[8] Wyatt, Geoffrey "Jeoffrey" Wiot or[7] Wiat, Robert or Richard[6] Wiot, William Wiot or[5] Wyot, Adam Wiot or Wyote or[4], Guyott[3], Guyott[2], Captain or Admiral Adam Guyott or[1] Wiot) was born January 11, 1943. He married Ann Elizabeth Bonniwell June 01, 1963, daughter of James Bonniwell and Agnes Camden.

> Children of Everett Eagle and Ann Bonniwell are:
> 1775   i.   Everett Wayne[25] Eagle III, born June 11, 1968 in Richmond, Virginia.
> 1776   ii.   Elizabeth Diane Eagle, born June 06, 1971.

1175. Sharon Ann[24] Eagle (Everett Wayne[23], William Armstrong[22], Eli Esau[21], Mary Ann[20] Wyatt, Noah Calvin[19], Thomas "Tommy"[18] Wiatt, Sr. (Wyatt, Wiett), John[17], Henry[16], Richard[15], George[14], Rev. Haute "Haut" "Hawte"[13], Sir George "Georgius" Thomas[12], Sir Thomas "The Younger"[11], Sir Thomas "The Elder"[10], Sir Henry[9], Richard Wiat or[8] Wyatt, Geoffrey "Jeoffrey" Wiot or[7] Wiat, Robert or Richard[6] Wiot, William Wiot or[5] Wyot, Adam Wiot or Wyote or[4], Guyott[3], Guyott[2], Captain or Admiral Adam Guyott or[1] Wiot) was born March 14, 1945. She married Wendell Bernard Sparrer March 17, 1962, son of Wendell Sparrer and Mary Diggs.

> Children of Sharon Eagle and Wendell Sparrer are:
> 1777   i.   Wendell Bernard[25] Sparrer, Jr., born February 12, 1963.
> 1778   ii.   John David Sparrer, born September 15, 1964.
> 1779   iii.   Deborah Gail Sparrer, born March 20, 1968.

1176. Ronald William[24] Eagle (Everett Wayne[23], William Armstrong[22], Eli Esau[21], Mary Ann[20] Wyatt, Noah Calvin[19], Thomas "Tommy"[18] Wiatt, Sr. (Wyatt, Wiett), John[17], Henry[16], Richard[15], George[14], Rev. Haute "Haut" "Hawte"[13], Sir George "Georgius" Thomas[12], Sir

Thomas "The Younger"[11], Sir Thomas "The Elder"[10], Sir Henry[9], Richard Wiat or[8] Wyatt, Geoffrey "Jeoffrey" Wiot or[7] Wiat, Robert or Richard[6] Wiot, William Wiot or[5] Wyot, Adam Wiot or Wyote or[4], Guyott[3], Guyott[2], Captain or Admiral Adam Guyott or[1] Wiot) was born November 06, 1949 in Newport News, Virginia. He married Deborah Ruth Jamison January 24, 1972, daughter of Fran Jamison and Shirley Bryan.

> Child of Ronald Eagle and Deborah Jamison is:
> 1780   i.   Tracie Ann[25] Eagle, born July 26, 1973.

1180. Norman Grey[24] Ribelin (Billie Mae[23] Morgan, Carrie Etta[22] Eagle, Eli Esau[21], Mary Ann[20] Wyatt, Noah Calvin[19], Thomas "Tommy"[18] Wiatt, Sr. (Wyatt, Wiett), John[17], Henry[16], Richard[15], George[14], Rev. Haute "Haut" "Hawte"[13], Sir George "Georgius" Thomas[12], Sir Thomas "The Younger"[11], Sir Thomas "The Elder"[10], Sir Henry[9], Richard Wiat or[8] Wyatt, Geoffrey "Jeoffrey" Wiot or[7] Wiat, Robert or Richard[6] Wiot, William Wiot or[5] Wyot, Adam Wiot or Wyote or[4], Guyott[3], Guyott[2], Captain or Admiral Adam Guyott or[1] Wiot) was born October 02, 1950. He married Pamela Ray Misenheimer January 07, 1973, daughter of Rayford Misenheimer and Madge Lingle.

> Child of Norman Ribelin and Pamela Misenheimer is:
> 1781   i.   Carrie Grey[25] Ribelin, born August 07, 1978 in Rowan County, N.C.

1181. Kyle Morgan[24] Ribelin (Billie Mae[23] Morgan, Carrie Etta[22] Eagle, Eli Esau[21], Mary Ann[20] Wyatt, Noah Calvin[19], Thomas "Tommy"[18] Wiatt, Sr. (Wyatt, Wiett), John[17], Henry[16], Richard[15], George[14], Rev. Haute "Haut" "Hawte"[13], Sir George "Georgius" Thomas[12], Sir Thomas "The Younger"[11], Sir Thomas "The Elder"[10], Sir Henry[9], Richard Wiat or[8] Wyatt, Geoffrey "Jeoffrey" Wiot or[7] Wiat, Robert or Richard[6] Wiot, William Wiot or[5] Wyot, Adam Wiot or Wyote or[4], Guyott[3], Guyott[2], Captain or Admiral Adam Guyott or[1] Wiot) was born November 08, 1952. He married Frances Claudine Trexler April 24, 1976, daughter of Claude Trexler and Martha Fisher.

> Child of Kyle Ribelin and Frances Trexler is:
> 1782   i.   Dana Marie[25] Ribelin, born August 05, 1980 in Rowan County, N.C.

1184. Betty Elaine[24] Frick (Roy David[23], Emma Dora[22] Eagle, Eli Esau[21], Mary Ann[20] Wyatt, Noah Calvin[19], Thomas "Tommy"[18] Wiatt, Sr. (Wyatt, Wiett), John[17], Henry[16], Richard[15], George[14], Rev. Haute "Haut" "Hawte"[13], Sir George "Georgius" Thomas[12], Sir Thomas "The Younger"[11], Sir Thomas "The Elder"[10], Sir Henry[9], Richard Wiat or[8] Wyatt, Geoffrey "Jeoffrey" Wiot or[7] Wiat, Robert or Richard[6] Wiot, William Wiot or[5] Wyot, Adam Wiot or Wyote or[4], Guyott[3], Guyott[2], Captain or Admiral Adam Guyott or[1] Wiot) was born July 11, 1938 in Davidson County, N.C. She married David Orland Mason August 23, 1964, son of Frank Mason and Helen Trasscasky.

Children of Betty Frick and David Mason are:

1783	i.	Erin David Kenndy[25] Mason, born September 01, 1968 in Chattanooga, Tenn.
1784	ii.	Shaun Alan Frick Mason, born December 17, 1972 in Austell County, Ga.
1785	iii.	Kyle Brett Wesley Mason, born April 23, 1977 in Athens, Ga.

1185. David Lee[24] Frick (Roy David[23], Emma Dora[22] Eagle, Eli Esau[21], Mary Ann[20] Wyatt, Noah Calvin[19], Thomas "Tommy"[18] Wiatt, Sr. (Wyatt, Wiett), John[17], Henry[16], Richard[15], George[14], Rev. Haute "Haut" "Hawte"[13], Sir George "Georgius" Thomas[12], Sir Thomas "The Younger"[11], Sir Thomas "The Elder"[10], Sir Henry[9], Richard Wiat or[8] Wyatt, Geoffrey "Jeoffrey" Wiot or[7] Wiat, Robert or Richard[6] Wiot, William Wiot or[5] Wyot, Adam Wiot or Wyote or[4], Guyott[3], Guyott[2], Captain or Admiral Adam Guyott or[1] Wiot) was born June 17, 1943 in Stanly County, N.C. He married Bennie Sherrill Sides March 21, 1970, daughter of William Sides and Essie Burris.

More About David Lee Frick:
Fact 1: Served in the U.S. ANG.

Children of David Frick and Bennie Sides are:

1786	i.	Brent David[25] Frick, born April 24, 1971.
1787	ii.	Gregory Bennett Frick, born February 27, 1977.

1187. Lawrence J.[24] Gaither (Fannie Lillian[23] Frick, Emma Dora[22] Eagle, Eli Esau[21], Mary Ann[20] Wyatt, Noah Calvin[19], Thomas "Tommy"[18] Wiatt, Sr. (Wyatt, Wiett), John[17], Henry[16], Richard[15], George[14], Rev. Haute "Haut" "Hawte"[13], Sir George "Georgius" Thomas[12], Sir Thomas "The Younger"[11], Sir Thomas "The Elder"[10], Sir Henry[9], Richard Wiat or[8] Wyatt, Geoffrey "Jeoffrey" Wiot or[7] Wiat, Robert or Richard[6] Wiot, William Wiot or[5] Wyot, Adam Wiot or Wyote or[4], Guyott[3], Guyott[2], Captain or Admiral Adam Guyott or[1] Wiot) was born July 07, 1929 in Guilford County, N.C. He married Minnie Reita Durham July 19, 1952, daughter of Ervin Durham and Delores Grubb.

Children of Lawrence Gaither and Minnie Durham are:

1788	i.	Pamela Rae[25] Gaither, born December 22, 1958 in Alamance County, N.C.
1789	ii.	Vicki Marie Gaither, born August 27, 1964 in Alamance County, N.C.
1790	iii.	David Lawrence Gaither, born June 16, 1969 in Alamance County, N.C.

1188. Wallace Claude[24] Gaither, Sr. (Fannie Lillian[23] Frick, Emma Dora[22] Eagle, Eli Esau[21], Mary Ann[20] Wyatt, Noah Calvin[19], Thomas "Tommy"[18] Wiatt, Sr. (Wyatt, Wiett), John[17], Henry[16], Richard[15], George[14], Rev. Haute "Haut" "Hawte"[13], Sir George "Georgius" Thomas[12],

Sir Thomas "The Younger"[11], Sir Thomas "The Elder"[10], Sir Henry[9], Richard Wiat or[8] Wyatt, Geoffrey "Jeoffrey" Wiot or[7] Wiat, Robert or Richard[6] Wiot, William Wiot or[5] Wyot, Adam Wiot or Wyote or[4], Guyott[3], Guyott[2], Captain or Admiral Adam Guyott or[1] Wiot) was born April 25, 1931 in Rowan County, N.C. He married Betty Lou Lingle June 12, 1969, daughter of Claude Lingle and Buna Kesler.

Children of Wallace Gaither and Betty Lingle are:

1791	i.	Melinda Joan[25] Gaither, born December 28, 1956. She married James Michael Phillips December 04, 1976.
1792	ii.	Crystal Dawn Gaither, born May 16, 1960.
1793	iii.	Wallace Claude Gaither, Jr., born July 02, 1964.

1189.   Lillian S.[24] Gaither (Fannie Lillian[23] Frick, Emma Dora[22] Eagle, Eli Esau[21], Mary Ann[20] Wyatt, Noah Calvin[19], Thomas "Tommy"[18] Wiatt, Sr. (Wyatt, Wiett), John[17], Henry[16], Richard[15], George[14], Rev. Haute "Haut" "Hawte"[13], Sir George "Georgius" Thomas[12], Sir Thomas "The Younger"[11], Sir Thomas "The Elder"[10], Sir Henry[9], Richard Wiat or[8] Wyatt, Geoffrey "Jeoffrey" Wiot or[7] Wiat, Robert or Richard[6] Wiot, William Wiot or[5] Wyot, Adam Wiot or Wyote or[4], Guyott[3], Guyott[2], Captain or Admiral Adam Guyott or[1] Wiot) was born March 16, 1936 in Rowan County, N.C. She married Darwin Jacobs Bruce August 26, 1956, son of Armond Bruce and Lillian Jacobs.

Children of Lillian Gaither and Darwin Bruce are:

1794	i.	William Keith[25] Bruce, born April 13, 1960.
1795	ii.	Darrell Andrew Bruce, born December 30, 1963.
1796	iii.	Linda Kay Bruce, born February 25, 1966.

1190.   Emma Deane (Diane?)[24] Gaither (Fannie Lillian[23] Frick, Emma Dora[22] Eagle, Eli Esau[21], Mary Ann[20] Wyatt, Noah Calvin[19], Thomas "Tommy"[18] Wiatt, Sr. (Wyatt, Wiett), John[17], Henry[16], Richard[15], George[14], Rev. Haute "Haut" "Hawte"[13], Sir George "Georgius" Thomas[12], Sir Thomas "The Younger"[11], Sir Thomas "The Elder"[10], Sir Henry[9], Richard Wiat or[8] Wyatt, Geoffrey "Jeoffrey" Wiot or[7] Wiat, Robert or Richard[6] Wiot, William Wiot or[5] Wyot, Adam Wiot or Wyote or[4], Guyott[3], Guyott[2], Captain or Admiral Adam Guyott or[1] Wiot) was born March 09, 1943 in Davidson County, N.C. She married Rolland Ray Basinger January 06, 1962, son of Lewis Basinger and Sarah Earnhardt.

Children of Emma Gaither and Rolland Basinger are:

| 1797 | i. | Rolland Ray[25] Basinger, Jr., born August 18, 1964 in Newport News, Va. |
| 1798 | ii. | Donald Scott Basinger, born August 10, 1965 in Hampton, Va. |

1191.   Gertrude Frances[24] Frick (Ernest Jones[23], Emma Dora[22] Eagle, Eli Esau[21], Mary Ann[20] Wyatt, Noah Calvin[19], Thomas "Tommy"[18] Wiatt, Sr. (Wyatt, Wiett), John[17], Henry[16], Richard[15], George[14], Rev. Haute "Haut" "Hawte"[13], Sir George "Georgius" Thomas[12], Sir Thomas "The Younger"[11], Sir Thomas "The Elder"[10], Sir Henry[9], Richard Wiat or[8] Wyatt,

Geoffrey "Jeoffrey" Wiot or[7] Wiat, Robert or Richard[6] Wiot, William Wiot or[5] Wyot, Adam Wiot or Wyote or[4], Guyott[3], Guyott[2], Captain or Admiral Adam Guyott or[1] Wiot) was born February 24, 1934 in Rowan County, N.C. She married Kent Bunting August 29, 1953, son of Solomon Bunting and Flossie Jones.

Children of Gertrude Frick and Kent Bunting are:

1799   i.   Michael Kent[25] Bunting, born September 19, 1954.

1800   ii.   Patricia Ann Bunting, born April 27, 1957.

1801   iii.   Linda Carol Bunting, born August 19, 1958.

1192.   Dora Jeanne[24] Frick (Ernest Jones[23], Emma Dora[22] Eagle, Eli Esau[21], Mary Ann[20] Wyatt, Noah Calvin[19], Thomas "Tommy"[18] Wiatt, Sr. (Wyatt, Wiett), John[17], Henry[16], Richard[15], George[14], Rev. Haute "Haut" "Hawte"[13], Sir George "Georgius" Thomas[12], Sir Thomas "The Younger"[11], Sir Thomas "The Elder"[10], Sir Henry[9], Richard Wiat or[8] Wyatt, Geoffrey "Jeoffrey" Wiot or[7] Wiat, Robert or Richard[6] Wiot, William Wiot or[5] Wyot, Adam Wiot or Wyote or[4], Guyott[3], Guyott[2], Captain or Admiral Adam Guyott or[1] Wiot) was born July 14, 1936 in Rowan County, N.C. She married Misenheimer, son of Love Misenheimer and Eunice Ritchie.

Children of Dora Frick and Misenheimer are:

1802   i.   Bryan Reid[25] Misenheimer, born September 30, 1960 in Front Royal, Va.

1803   ii.   Eric Rodney Misenheimer, born June 21, 1964 in Richmond, Va.

1193.   Gaye Erlene[24] Frick (Ernest Jones[23], Emma Dora[22] Eagle, Eli Esau[21], Mary Ann[20] Wyatt, Noah Calvin[19], Thomas "Tommy"[18] Wiatt, Sr. (Wyatt, Wiett), John[17], Henry[16], Richard[15], George[14], Rev. Haute "Haut" "Hawte"[13], Sir George "Georgius" Thomas[12], Sir Thomas "The Younger"[11], Sir Thomas "The Elder"[10], Sir Henry[9], Richard Wiat or[8] Wyatt, Geoffrey "Jeoffrey" Wiot or[7] Wiat, Robert or Richard[6] Wiot, William Wiot or[5] Wyot, Adam Wiot or Wyote or[4], Guyott[3], Guyott[2], Captain or Admiral Adam Guyott or[1] Wiot) was born October 31, 1940 in Rowan County, N.C. She married Herman S. Caldwell, Jr. November 19, 1966, son of Herman Caldwell and Doris Bandy.

Children of Gaye Frick and Herman Caldwell are:

1804   i.   Carolyn Jeanne[25] Caldwell, born September 11, 1968.

1805   ii.   Catherine Elaine Caldwell, born June 22, 1970 in Athens, Ga.

1195.   Mason Gilbert[24] Smith (Ida Nora[23] Frick, Emma Dora[22] Eagle, Eli Esau[21], Mary Ann[20] Wyatt, Noah Calvin[19], Thomas "Tommy"[18] Wiatt, Sr. (Wyatt, Wiett), John[17], Henry[16], Richard[15], George[14], Rev. Haute "Haut" "Hawte"[13], Sir George "Georgius" Thomas[12], Sir Thomas "The Younger"[11], Sir Thomas "The Elder"[10], Sir Henry[9], Richard Wiat or[8] Wyatt, Geoffrey "Jeoffrey" Wiot or[7] Wiat, Robert or Richard[6] Wiot, William Wiot or[5] Wyot, Adam Wiot or Wyote or[4], Guyott[3], Guyott[2], Captain or Admiral Adam Guyott or[1] Wiot) was born

May 12, 1936 in York County, S.C. He married Blanche Elizabeth Howell September 16, 1960, daughter of William Howell and Wilma Bratton.

Children of Mason Smith and Blanche Howell are:

1806   i.   James Mason[25] Smith, born July 04, 1961 in York County, S.C.

1807   ii.   Elizabeth Ann Smith, born October 13, 1967 in York County, S.C.

1196. Margaret Melba[24] Smith (Ida Nora[23] Frick, Emma Dora[22] Eagle, Eli Esau[21], Mary Ann[20] Wyatt, Noah Calvin[19], Thomas "Tommy"[18] Wiatt, Sr. (Wyatt, Wiett), John[17], Henry[16], Richard[15], George[14], Rev. Haute "Haut" "Hawte"[13], Sir George "Georgius" Thomas[12], Sir Thomas "The Younger"[11], Sir Thomas "The Elder"[10], Sir Henry[9], Richard Wiat or[8] Wyatt, Geoffrey "Jeoffrey" Wiot or[7] Wiat, Robert or Richard[6] Wiot, William Wiot or[5] Wyot, Adam Wiot or Wyote or[4], Guyott[3], Guyott[2], Captain or Admiral Adam Guyott or[1] Wiot) was born March 21, 1928 in Cherokee County, S.C. She married Thomas Logan Brandon May 15, 1951, son of George Brandon and Ola Daniels.

Child of Margaret Smith and Thomas Brandon is:

1808   i.   Donna Lynn[25] Brandon, born October 23, 1954 in York, S.C.

1197. Marshall Thomas[24] Smith (Ida Nora[23] Frick, Emma Dora[22] Eagle, Eli Esau[21], Mary Ann[20] Wyatt, Noah Calvin[19], Thomas "Tommy"[18] Wiatt, Sr. (Wyatt, Wiett), John[17], Henry[16], Richard[15], George[14], Rev. Haute "Haut" "Hawte"[13], Sir George "Georgius" Thomas[12], Sir Thomas "The Younger"[11], Sir Thomas "The Elder"[10], Sir Henry[9], Richard Wiat or[8] Wyatt, Geoffrey "Jeoffrey" Wiot or[7] Wiat, Robert or Richard[6] Wiot, William Wiot or[5] Wyot, Adam Wiot or Wyote or[4], Guyott[3], Guyott[2], Captain or Admiral Adam Guyott or[1] Wiot) was born May 28, 1930 in Cherokee County, S.C. He married Margaret Melissa Robinson November 23, 1950, daughter of Baxter Robinson and Sudie Stewart.

Children of Marshall Smith and Margaret Robinson are:

1809   i.   Edward Thomas[25] Smith, born July 22, 1951. He married Nellie Jean Bradley July 31, 1976.

1810   ii.   Wayne Barnett Smith, born October 19, 1953 in York, S.C. He married Deborah Jane Adkins.

1811   iii.   David Michael Smith, born April 20, 1961.

1198. Marion (Marian) Louise[24] Smith (Ida Nora[23] Frick, Emma Dora[22] Eagle, Eli Esau[21], Mary Ann[20] Wyatt, Noah Calvin[19], Thomas "Tommy"[18] Wiatt, Sr. (Wyatt, Wiett), John[17], Henry[16], Richard[15], George[14], Rev. Haute "Haut" "Hawte"[13], Sir George "Georgius" Thomas[12], Sir Thomas "The Younger"[11], Sir Thomas "The Elder"[10], Sir Henry[9], Richard Wiat or[8] Wyatt, Geoffrey "Jeoffrey" Wiot or[7] Wiat, Robert or Richard[6] Wiot, William Wiot or[5] Wyot, Adam Wiot or Wyote or[4], Guyott[3], Guyott[2], Captain or Admiral Adam Guyott or[1] Wiot) was born April 07, 1932 in Union County, S.C. She married Barr Walker Huddeston, Jr. January 30, 1956, son of Barr Huddeston and Esma Ashe.

Children of Marion Smith and Barr Huddeston are:

| 1812 | i. | Debra Jane[25] Huddeston, born February 12, 1957 in York, S.C. She married David Lamar Brown December 27, 1975. |
| 1813 | ii. | Deanna Ellen Huddeston, born April 25, 1960 in York, S.C. |

1199. Joseph Milton[24] Smith (Ida Nora[23] Frick, Emma Dora[22] Eagle, Eli Esau[21], Mary Ann[20] Wyatt, Noah Calvin[19], Thomas "Tommy"[18] Wiatt, Sr. (Wyatt, Wiett), John[17], Henry[16], Richard[15], George[14], Rev. Haute "Haut" "Hawte"[13], Sir George "Georgius" Thomas[12], Sir Thomas "The Younger"[11], Sir Thomas "The Elder"[10], Sir Henry[9], Richard Wiat or[8] Wyatt, Geoffrey "Jeoffrey" Wiot or[7] Wiat, Robert or Richard[6] Wiot, William Wiot or[5] Wyot, Adam Wiot or Wyote or[4], Guyott[3], Guyott[2], Captain or Admiral Adam Guyott or[1] Wiot) was born June 12, 1934 in Cherokee County, S.C. He married Catherine Ann Heubener August 25, 1959, daughter of Archie Heubener and Catherine (Wright?).

Children of Joseph Smith and Catherine Heubener are:

1814	i.	Randall Lee[25] Smith, born March 25, 1961 in San Antonio, Tx.
1815	ii.	Ronda Lannette Smith, born September 13, 1963 in Port Lavoca, Tx.
1816	iii.	Regina LaRue Smith, born November 19, 1964 in San Antonio, Tx.

1200. Mitchell Adron[24] Smith (Ida Nora[23] Frick, Emma Dora[22] Eagle, Eli Esau[21], Mary Ann[20] Wyatt, Noah Calvin[19], Thomas "Tommy"[18] Wiatt, Sr. (Wyatt, Wiett), John[17], Henry[16], Richard[15], George[14], Rev. Haute "Haut" "Hawte"[13], Sir George "Georgius" Thomas[12], Sir Thomas "The Younger"[11], Sir Thomas "The Elder"[10], Sir Henry[9], Richard Wiat or[8] Wyatt, Geoffrey "Jeoffrey" Wiot or[7] Wiat, Robert or Richard[6] Wiot, William Wiot or[5] Wyot, Adam Wiot or Wyote or[4], Guyott[3], Guyott[2], Captain or Admiral Adam Guyott or[1] Wiot) was born April 01, 1938 in York County, S.C. He married Mary Alice Sipe February 09, 1957, daughter of Wilburn Sipe and Crystal Hopper.

Children of Mitchell Smith and Mary Sipe are:

| 1817 | i. | Richard Adron[25] Smith, born August 18, 1958 in York County, S.C. He married Pamela Madine Mathis May 07, 1977. |

More About Richard Adron Smith:
Fact 1: Served in the U.S. Air Force.

| 1818 | ii. | Tammy Norine Smith, born October 1961 in York County, S.C. |
| 1819 | iii. | Wilburn Allen Smith, born June 18, 1962 in Gastonia, N.C. |

1201. Barbara Ann[24] Long (Geneva Voncelle[23] Morgan, Emma Dora[22] Eagle, Eli Esau[21], Mary Ann[20] Wyatt, Noah Calvin[19], Thomas "Tommy"[18] Wiatt, Sr. (Wyatt, Wiett), John[17], Henry[16], Richard[15], George[14], Rev. Haute "Haut" "Hawte"[13], Sir George "Georgius" Thomas[12], Sir Thomas "The Younger"[11], Sir Thomas "The Elder"[10], Sir Henry[9], Richard Wiat or[8] Wyatt, Geoffrey

"Jeoffrey" Wiot or[7] Wiat, Robert or Richard[6] Wiot, William Wiot or[5] Wyot, Adam Wiot or Wyote or[4], Guyott[3], Guyott[2], Captain or Admiral Adam Guyott or[1] Wiot) was born August 27, 1948. She married Jeffrey Britt Barnes June 08, 1969, son of Paul Barnes and Betty Phillips.

Children of Barbara Long and Jeffrey Barnes are:

1820   i.   Lori Christine[25] Barnes, born November 15, 1970 in Md.

1821   ii.   Andrew Britt Barnes, born October 23, 1976 in Forsyth County, N.C.

1202. Betty Sue[24] Long (Geneva Voncelle[23] Morgan, Emma Dora[22] Eagle, Eli Esau[21], Mary Ann[20] Wyatt, Noah Calvin[19], Thomas "Tommy"[18] Wiatt, Sr. (Wyatt, Wiett), John[17], Henry[16], Richard[15], George[14], Rev. Haute "Haut" "Hawte"[13], Sir George "Georgius" Thomas[12], Sir Thomas "The Younger"[11], Sir Thomas "The Elder"[10], Sir Henry[9], Richard Wiat or[8] Wyatt, Geoffrey "Jeoffrey" Wiot or[7] Wiat, Robert or Richard[6] Wiot, William Wiot or[5] Wyot, Adam Wiot or Wyote or[4], Guyott[3], Guyott[2], Captain or Admiral Adam Guyott or[1] Wiot) was born October 13, 1951 in Davidson County, N.C. She married Richard Elliot Cain September 12, 1976, son of Thomas Cain and Pauline Cain?.

Child of Betty Long and Richard Cain is:

1822   i.   Dana Marie[25] Cain, born January 13, 1978 in Forsyth County, N.C.

1204. George Russell[24] Morgan (Baxter Monroe[23], Emma Dora[22] Eagle, Eli Esau[21], Mary Ann[20] Wyatt, Noah Calvin[19], Thomas "Tommy"[18] Wiatt, Sr. (Wyatt, Wiett), John[17], Henry[16], Richard[15], George[14], Rev. Haute "Haut" "Hawte"[13], Sir George "Georgius" Thomas[12], Sir Thomas "The Younger"[11], Sir Thomas "The Elder"[10], Sir Henry[9], Richard Wiat or[8] Wyatt, Geoffrey "Jeoffrey" Wiot or[7] Wiat, Robert or Richard[6] Wiot, William Wiot or[5] Wyot, Adam Wiot or Wyote or[4], Guyott[3], Guyott[2], Captain or Admiral Adam Guyott or[1] Wiot) was born October 08, 1951. He married Martha Louise Lay August 29, 1971, daughter of John Lay and Edna McCaskell.

Children of George Morgan and Martha Lay are:

1823   i.   Danielle Elizabeth[25] Morgan, born December 10, 1974 in Rowan County, N.C.

1824   ii.   Michael Shawn Morgan, born March 02, 1979.

1209. Linda Jean[24] Morgan (Raymond Emerson[23], Emma Dora[22] Eagle, Eli Esau[21], Mary Ann[20] Wyatt, Noah Calvin[19], Thomas "Tommy"[18] Wiatt, Sr. (Wyatt, Wiett), John[17], Henry[16], Richard[15], George[14], Rev. Haute "Haut" "Hawte"[13], Sir George "Georgius" Thomas[12], Sir Thomas "The Younger"[11], Sir Thomas "The Elder"[10], Sir Henry[9], Richard Wiat or[8] Wyatt, Geoffrey "Jeoffrey" Wiot or[7] Wiat, Robert or Richard[6] Wiot, William Wiot or[5] Wyot, Adam Wiot or Wyote or[4], Guyott[3], Guyott[2], Captain or Admiral Adam Guyott or[1] Wiot) was born October 11, 1948. She married Floyd Gilmer Rusher, Jr. July 07, 1968, son of Floyd Rusher and Ruby Randall.

Children of Linda Morgan and Floyd Rusher are:

1825   i.   Tonya Michelle[25] Rusher, born April 19, 1971 in Rowan County, N.C.

1826   ii.   Stephanie Alyce Rusher, born July 07, 1973 in Rowan County, N.C.

1210. Raymond Emerson[24] Morgan, Jr. (Raymond Emerson[23], Emma Dora[22] Eagle, Eli Esau[21], Mary Ann[20] Wyatt, Noah Calvin[19], Thomas "Tommy"[18] Wiatt, Sr. (Wyatt, Wiett), John[17], Henry[16], Richard[15], George[14], Rev. Haute "Haut" "Hawte"[13], Sir George "Georgius" Thomas[12], Sir Thomas "The Younger"[11], Sir Thomas "The Elder"[10], Sir Henry[9], Richard Wiat or[8] Wyatt, Geoffrey "Jeoffrey" Wiot or[7] Wiat, Robert or Richard[6] Wiot, William Wiot or[5] Wyot, Adam Wiot or Wyote or[4], Guyott[3], Guyott[2], Captain or Admiral Adam Guyott or[1] Wiot) was born March 07, 1952 in Rowan County, N.C. He married Marilyn Kirkland Gardner September 07, 1974, daughter of Albert Gardner and Margaret Kirkland.

Child of Raymond Morgan and Marilyn Gardner is:

1827   i.   Courtney Taylor[25] Morgan, born November 22, 1977 in Rowan County, N.C.

1213. Lenora[24] Frick (Harvey Lee[23], Mary Christine[22] Eagle, Eli Esau[21], Mary Ann[20] Wyatt, Noah Calvin[19], Thomas "Tommy"[18] Wiatt, Sr. (Wyatt, Wiett), John[17], Henry[16], Richard[15], George[14], Rev. Haute "Haut" "Hawte"[13], Sir George "Georgius" Thomas[12], Sir Thomas "The Younger"[11], Sir Thomas "The Elder"[10], Sir Henry[9], Richard Wiat or[8] Wyatt, Geoffrey "Jeoffrey" Wiot or[7] Wiat, Robert or Richard[6] Wiot, William Wiot or[5] Wyot, Adam Wiot or Wyote or[4], Guyott[3], Guyott[2], Captain or Admiral Adam Guyott or[1] Wiot) was born April 22, 1943 in Detroit, Mich. She married Gerald Brochowski May 30, 1964.

Children of Lenora Frick and Gerald Brochowski are:

1828   i.   Christine Marie[25] Brochowski, born March 15, 1970 in Detroit, Mich.

1829   ii.   Kathy Brochowski, born October 17, 1971 in Ashtabila, Ohio.

1214. Terrence Frederick[24] Frick (Frederick Gideon[23], Mary Christine[22] Eagle, Eli Esau[21], Mary Ann[20] Wyatt, Noah Calvin[19], Thomas "Tommy"[18] Wiatt, Sr. (Wyatt, Wiett), John[17], Henry[16], Richard[15], George[14], Rev. Haute "Haut" "Hawte"[13], Sir George "Georgius" Thomas[12], Sir Thomas "The Younger"[11], Sir Thomas "The Elder"[10], Sir Henry[9], Richard Wiat or[8] Wyatt, Geoffrey "Jeoffrey" Wiot or[7] Wiat, Robert or Richard[6] Wiot, William Wiot or[5] Wyot, Adam Wiot or Wyote or[4], Guyott[3], Guyott[2], Captain or Admiral Adam Guyott or[1] Wiot) was born Abt. December 24, 1935 in Rowan County, N.C. He married Peggy McKaughn.

Children of Terrence Frick and Peggy McKaughn are:

1830   i.   Kathy25 Frick, born February 10, 1958.

1831   ii.   Tracy Frick, born December 26, 1960.

1832　　iii.　　Terrence Frederic Frick, Jr., born June 30, 1964 in Hickory, N.C.

1216. Carolyn Kay[24] Thompson (Nellie Mae[23] Frick, Mary Christine[22] Eagle, Eli Esau[21], Mary Ann[20] Wyatt, Noah Calvin[19], Thomas "Tommy"[18] Wiatt, Sr. (Wyatt, Wiett), John[17], Henry[16], Richard[15], George[14], Rev. Haute "Haut" "Hawte"[13], Sir George "Georgius" Thomas[12], Sir Thomas "The Younger"[11], Sir Thomas "The Elder"[10], Sir Henry[9], Richard Wiat or[8] Wyatt, Geoffrey "Jeoffrey" Wiot or[7] Wiat, Robert or Richard[6] Wiot, William Wiot or[5] Wyot, Adam Wiot or Wyote or[4], Guyott[3], Guyott[2], Captain or Admiral Adam Guyott or[1] Wiot) was born February 03, 1939 in Rowan County, N.C. She married Bill Kirland March 11, 1958.

More About Bill Kirland:
Remains are buried at Lakeland, Fla.

Children of Carolyn Thompson and Bill Kirland are:
1833　　i.　　Carma Kay[25] Kirland, born February 18, 1959 in Lakeland, Fla.
1834　　ii.　　Kolette Kirland, born May 14, 1960 in Lakeland, Fla.

1217. Mary Oma[24] Fry (Elizabeth Euver[23] Frick, Mary Christine[22] Eagle, Eli Esau[21], Mary Ann[20] Wyatt, Noah Calvin[19], Thomas "Tommy"[18] Wiatt, Sr. (Wyatt, Wiett), John[17], Henry[16], Richard[15], George[14], Rev. Haute "Haut" "Hawte"[13], Sir George "Georgius" Thomas[12], Sir Thomas "The Younger"[11], Sir Thomas "The Elder"[10], Sir Henry[9], Richard Wiat or[8] Wyatt, Geoffrey "Jeoffrey" Wiot or[7] Wiat, Robert or Richard[6] Wiot, William Wiot or[5] Wyot, Adam Wiot or Wyote or[4], Guyott[3], Guyott[2], Captain or Admiral Adam Guyott or[1] Wiot) was born November 28, 1930 in Rowan County, N.C. She married Irving Kenneth Shepherd July 12, 1950, son of David Shepherd and Maggie Trexler.

Children of Mary Fry and Irving Shepherd are:
+　1835　　i.　　Kenneth Ray[25] Shepherd, born May 11, 1952.
+　1836　　ii.　　Edward Eugene Shepherd, born September 04, 1953.
　1837　　iii.　　James Patrick Shepherd, born January 19, 1957.

1218. Jerry Luther[24] Fry (Elizabeth Euver[23] Frick, Mary Christine[22] Eagle, Eli Esau[21], Mary Ann[20] Wyatt, Noah Calvin[19], Thomas "Tommy"[18] Wiatt, Sr. (Wyatt, Wiett), John[17], Henry[16], Richard[15], George[14], Rev. Haute "Haut" "Hawte"[13], Sir George "Georgius" Thomas[12], Sir Thomas "The Younger"[11], Sir Thomas "The Elder"[10], Sir Henry[9], Richard Wiat or[8] Wyatt, Geoffrey "Jeoffrey" Wiot or[7] Wiat, Robert or Richard[6] Wiot, William Wiot or[5] Wyot, Adam Wiot or Wyote or[4], Guyott[3], Guyott[2], Captain or Admiral Adam Guyott or[1] Wiot) was born August 24, 1936 in Rowan County, N.C. He married Naomi Louise Goodman June 17, 1956, daughter of Delmar Goodman and Viola Morgan.

Children of Jerry Fry and Naomi Goodman are:

1838   i.   Timothy Luther[25] Fry, born June 27, 1967 in Davidson County, N.C.

1839   ii.   Christopher Jerry Fry, born April 10, 1969 in Davidson County, N.C.

1219.   Nelson Franklin[24] Page (Mamie Frances[23] Frick, Mary Christine[22] Eagle, Eli Esau[21], Mary Ann[20] Wyatt, Noah Calvin[19], Thomas "Tommy"[18] Wiatt, Sr. (Wyatt, Wiett), John[17], Henry[16], Richard[15], George[14], Rev. Haute "Haut" "Hawte"[13], Sir George "Georgius" Thomas[12], Sir Thomas "The Younger"[11], Sir Thomas "The Elder"[10], Sir Henry[9], Richard Wiat or[8] Wyatt, Geoffrey "Jeoffrey" Wiot or[7] Wiat, Robert or Richard[6] Wiot, William Wiot or[5] Wyot, Adam Wiot or Wyote or[4], Guyott[3], Guyott[2], Captain or Admiral Adam Guyott or[1] Wiot) was born November 17, 1938 in Rowan County, N.C. He married Betty Ann Lupberger June 06, 1964, daughter of Adolph Lupberger and Ezma Hines.

Remains are buried at the Liberty Methodist Church Cemetery, Rowan County, N.C.

Children of Nelson Page and Betty Lupberger are:

1840   i.   Eileen Virginia[25] Page, born August 06, 1965 in Chapel Hill, Orange County, N.C.

1841   ii.   Frank Douglas Page, born December 14, 1967 in Greensboro, N.C.

1842   iii.   Daniel Nelson Page, born October 13, 1975 in High Point, N.C.

1220.   Lavon Barry[24] Page (Mamie Frances[23] Frick, Mary Christine[22] Eagle, Eli Esau[21], Mary Ann[20] Wyatt, Noah Calvin[19], Thomas "Tommy"[18] Wiatt, Sr. (Wyatt, Wiett), John[17], Henry[16], Richard[15], George[14], Rev. Haute "Haut" "Hawte"[13], Sir George "Georgius" Thomas[12], Sir Thomas "The Younger"[11], Sir Thomas "The Elder"[10], Sir Henry[9], Richard Wiat or[8] Wyatt, Geoffrey "Jeoffrey" Wiot or[7] Wiat, Robert or Richard[6] Wiot, William Wiot or[5] Wyot, Adam Wiot or Wyote or[4], Guyott[3], Guyott[2], Captain or Admiral Adam Guyott or[1] Wiot) was born May 28, 1943. He married Rebecca Joyce Jones May 31, 1964, daughter of William Jones and Daisy Lyerly.

Child of Lavon Page and Rebecca Jones is:

1843   i.   Kimberly Leigh[25] Page, born September 21, 1969 in Wake County, N.C.

1221.   Leo Gary[24] Misenheimer (Gertrude Esther[23] Frick, Mary Christine[22] Eagle, Eli Esau[21], Mary Ann[20] Wyatt, Noah Calvin[19], Thomas "Tommy"[18] Wiatt, Sr. (Wyatt, Wiett), John[17], Henry[16], Richard[15], George[14], Rev. Haute "Haut" "Hawte"[13], Sir George "Georgius"

Thomas[12], Sir Thomas "The Younger"[11], Sir Thomas "The Elder"[10], Sir Henry[9], Richard Wiat or[8] Wyatt, Geoffrey "Jeoffrey" Wiot or[7] Wiat, Robert or Richard[6] Wiot, William Wiot or[5] Wyot, Adam Wiot or Wyote or[4], Guyott[3], Guyott[2], Captain or Admiral Adam Guyott or[1] Wiot) was born October 26, 1944 in Mecklenburg County, N.C. He married Mary Aletha Myers October 02, 1971, daughter of Leroy Myers and Betty Kriver.

More About Leo Gary Misenheimer:
Fact 1: Served in the U.S. Air Force.

> Child of Leo Misenheimer and Mary Myers is:
> 1844   i.   Jeromie[25] Misenheimer, born February 12, 1976 in Spartenburg, S.C.

1224. Christina Jeanette[24] Frick (Norman Grey[23], Mary Christine[22] Eagle, Eli Esau[21], Mary Ann[20] Wyatt, Noah Calvin[19], Thomas "Tommy"[18] Wiatt, Sr. (Wyatt, Wiett), John[17], Henry[16], Richard[15], George[14], Rev. Haute "Haut" "Hawte"[13], Sir George "Georgius" Thomas[12], Sir Thomas "The Younger"[11], Sir Thomas "The Elder"[10], Sir Henry[9], Richard Wiat or[8] Wyatt, Geoffrey "Jeoffrey" Wiot or[7] Wiat, Robert or Richard[6] Wiot, William Wiot or[5] Wyot, Adam Wiot or Wyote or[4], Guyott[3], Guyott[2], Captain or Admiral Adam Guyott or[1] Wiot) was born August 05, 1952 in Rowan County, N.C. She married Stephen Whitaker May 28, 1972, son of Paul Whitaker and Pauline Joyce.

> Child of Christina Frick and Stephen Whitaker is:
> 1845   i.   Jennifer C.[25] Whitaker, born November 10, 1972 in Guilford County, N.C.

1227. Roger[24] Frick (Norman Grey[23], Mary Christine[22] Eagle, Eli Esau[21], Mary Ann[20] Wyatt, Noah Calvin[19], Thomas "Tommy"[18] Wiatt, Sr. (Wyatt, Wiett), John[17], Henry[16], Richard[15], George[14], Rev. Haute "Haut" "Hawte"[13], Sir George "Georgius" Thomas[12], Sir Thomas "The Younger"[11], Sir Thomas "The Elder"[10], Sir Henry[9], Richard Wiat or[8] Wyatt, Geoffrey "Jeoffrey" Wiot or[7] Wiat, Robert or Richard[6] Wiot, William Wiot or[5] Wyot, Adam Wiot or Wyote or[4], Guyott[3], Guyott[2], Captain or Admiral Adam Guyott or[1] Wiot) was born March 28, 1958 in Rowan County, N.C. He married Avis Jenice "Geneice" Shepherd July 21, 1980, daughter of Albert Shepherd and Sherley Arey.

> Children of Roger Frick and Avis Shepherd are:
> 1846   i.   Tristan Ross[25] Frick, born January 18, 1986.
> 1847   ii.   Atalie Ann Frick, born November 29, 1988.

1231. Alice Faye[24] Baker (Lucille[23] Eagle, Grover Victor[22], Eli Esau[21], Mary Ann[20] Wyatt, Noah Calvin[19], Thomas "Tommy"[18] Wiatt, Sr. (Wyatt, Wiett), John[17], Henry[16], Richard[15], George[14], Rev. Haute "Haut" "Hawte"[13], Sir George "Georgius" Thomas[12], Sir Thomas "The Younger"[11], Sir Thomas "The Elder"[10], Sir Henry[9], Richard Wiat or[8] Wyatt, Geoffrey "Jeoffrey" Wiot or[7] Wiat, Robert or Richard[6] Wiot, William Wiot or[5] Wyot, Adam Wiot or

Wyote or[4], Guyott[3], Guyott[2], Captain or Admiral Adam Guyott or[1] Wiot) was born May 11, 1940 in Rowan County N.C. She married Dale Lippard Cobb October 03, 1959, son of Clarence Cobb and Grace Lippard.

Children of Alice Baker and Dale Cobb are:

1848	i.	Jeffrey Dale[25] Cobb, born Bef. 1966.
1849	ii.	Richard Todd Cobb, born August 21, 1963.
1850	iii.	Kenneth Michael Cobb, born September 13, 1966 in Rowan County N.C.

1232. Joseph Victor[24] Eagle (Joseph[23], Grover Victor[22], Eli Esau[21], Mary Ann[20] Wyatt, Noah Calvin[19], Thomas "Tommy"[18] Wiatt, Sr. (Wyatt, Wiett), John[17], Henry[16], Richard[15], George[14], Rev. Haute "Haut" "Hawte"[13], Sir George "Georgius" Thomas[12], Sir Thomas "The Younger"[11], Sir Thomas "The Elder"[10], Sir Henry[9], Richard Wiat or[8] Wyatt, Geoffrey "Jeoffrey" Wiot or[7] Wiat, Robert or Richard[6] Wiot, William Wiot or[5] Wyot, Adam Wiot or Wyote or[4], Guyott[3], Guyott[2], Captain or Admiral Adam Guyott or[1] Wiot) was born March 26, 1935. He married Sherry Lee Fink, daughter of Cletus Fink and Thelma Whitman.

Children of Joseph Eagle and Sherry Fink are:

| 1851 | i. | Joseph Victor[25] Eagle, Jr., born August 07, 1957. |
| 1852 | ii. | Russell Lee Eagle, born August 30, 1959 in Greenville, S.C. |

1233. Roy Howard[24] Campbell, Jr (Pearl[23] Eagle, Grover Victor[22], Eli Esau[21], Mary Ann[20] Wyatt, Noah Calvin[19], Thomas "Tommy"[18] Wiatt, Sr. (Wyatt, Wiett), John[17], Henry[16], Richard[15], George[14], Rev. Haute "Haut" "Hawte"[13], Sir George "Georgius" Thomas[12], Sir Thomas "The Younger"[11], Sir Thomas "The Elder"[10], Sir Henry[9], Richard Wiat or[8] Wyatt, Geoffrey "Jeoffrey" Wiot or[7] Wiat, Robert or Richard[6] Wiot, William Wiot or[5] Wyot, Adam Wiot or Wyote or[4], Guyott[3], Guyott[2], Captain or Admiral Adam Guyott or[1] Wiot) was born March 11, 1935. He married Sonja Bowers August 16, 1956, daughter of Edgar Bowers and Frances Sparrow.

Children of Roy Campbell and Sonja Bowers are:

1853	i.	Greg Howard[25] Campbell, born December 29, 1958 in Rowan County N.C.
1854	ii.	Jana Lee Campbell, born December 10, 1960 in Atlanta, Ga.
1855	iii.	Jodie Campbell, born July 21, 1962 in High Point, N.C.

1234. Barbara Annette[24] Campbell (Pearl[23] Eagle, Grover Victor[22], Eli Esau[21], Mary Ann[20] Wyatt, Noah Calvin[19], Thomas "Tommy"[18] Wiatt, Sr. (Wyatt, Wiett), John[17], Henry[16], Richard[15], George[14], Rev. Haute "Haut" "Hawte"[13], Sir George "Georgius" Thomas[12], Sir Thomas "The Younger"[11], Sir Thomas "The Elder"[10], Sir Henry[9], Richard Wiat or[8] Wyatt, Geoffrey "Jeoffrey" Wiot or[7] Wiat, Robert or Richard[6] Wiot, William Wiot or[5] Wyot, Adam Wiot or Wyote or[4], Guyott[3], Guyott[2], Captain or Admiral Adam Guyott or[1] Wiot) was born April 19, 1937. She married Jack A. Poole September 08, 1957, son of Ralph Poole and Ruth Miller.

Child of Barbara Campbell and Jack Poole is:

| 1856 | i. | Scott Arron[25] Poole, born April 13, 1961 in Rowan County N.C. |

1239. Harold Gene[24] Eagle (Joseph Charles[23], Joseph Calvin[22], Eli Esau[21], Mary Ann[20] Wyatt, Noah Calvin[19], Thomas "Tommy"[18] Wiatt, Sr. (Wyatt, Wiett), John[17], Henry[16], Richard[15], George[14], Rev. Haute "Haut" "Hawte"[13], Sir George "Georgius" Thomas[12], Sir Thomas "The Younger"[11], Sir Thomas "The Elder"[10], Sir Henry[9], Richard Wiat or[8] Wyatt, Geoffrey "Jeoffrey" Wiot or[7] Wiat, Robert or Richard[6] Wiot, William Wiot or[5] Wyot, Adam Wiot or Wyote or[4], Guyott[3], Guyott[2], Captain or Admiral Adam Guyott or[1] Wiot) was born June 27, 1937. He married Carole Beulah Steele February 01, 1960, daughter of Car Steele and Elizabeth McNeely.

Children of Harold Eagle and Carole Steele are:

| 1857 | i. | Andra Elisbeth[25] Eagle, born June 06, 1963. |
| 1858 | ii. | Amber Fawn Eagle, born August 23, 1965 in Mecklenburg County, N.C. |

1240. Carl Ray[24] Eagle (Joseph Charles[23], Joseph Calvin[22], Eli Esau[21], Mary Ann[20] Wyatt, Noah Calvin[19], Thomas "Tommy"[18] Wiatt, Sr. (Wyatt, Wiett), John[17], Henry[16], Richard[15], George[14], Rev. Haute "Haut" "Hawte"[13], Sir George "Georgius" Thomas[12], Sir Thomas "The Younger"[11], Sir Thomas "The Elder"[10], Sir Henry[9], Richard Wiat or[8] Wyatt, Geoffrey "Jeoffrey" Wiot or[7] Wiat, Robert or Richard[6] Wiot, William Wiot or[5] Wyot, Adam Wiot or Wyote or[4], Guyott[3], Guyott[2], Captain or Admiral Adam Guyott or[1] Wiot) was born May 09, 1939. He married Dottie Lane Bassinger, daughter of Haywood Bassinger and Edith Ellis.

Children of Carl Eagle and Dottie Bassinger are:

1859	i.	Linda Gun[25] Eagle, born November 15, 1960 in Rowan County, N.C.
1860	ii.	Russell Craig Eagle, born November 10, 1961 in Rowan County, N.C.
1861	iii.	Kathy Lynn Eagle, born June 06, 1967 in Rowan County, N.C.

1241. Jerry Lee[24] Eagle (Joseph Charles[23], Joseph Calvin[22], Eli Esau[21], Mary Ann[20] Wyatt, Noah Calvin[19], Thomas "Tommy"[18] Wiatt, Sr. (Wyatt, Wiett), John[17], Henry[16], Richard[15], George[14], Rev. Haute "Haut" "Hawte"[13], Sir George "Georgius" Thomas[12], Sir Thomas "The Younger"[11], Sir Thomas "The Elder"[10], Sir Henry[9], Richard Wiat or[8] Wyatt, Geoffrey "Jeoffrey" Wiot or[7] Wiat, Robert or Richard[6] Wiot, William Wiot or[5] Wyot, Adam Wiot or Wyote or[4], Guyott[3], Guyott[2], Captain or Admiral Adam Guyott or[1] Wiot) was born December 08, 1940. He married Mary Levon Upright June 08, 1967, daughter of Grady Upright and Mary Troutman.

Children of Jerry Eagle and Mary Upright are:

| 1862 | i. | Shana Leigh[25] Eagle, born November 13, 1972 in Guilford County, N.C. |
| 1863 | ii. | Brett Kyle Eagle, born November 22, 1974 in Guilford County, N.C. |

1242. Rebecca Jane[24] Eagle (Joseph Charles[23], Joseph Calvin[22], Eli Esau[21], Mary Ann[20] Wyatt, Noah Calvin[19], Thomas "Tommy"[18] Wiatt, Sr. (Wyatt, Wiett), John[17], Henry[16], Richard[15], George[14], Rev. Haute "Haut" "Hawte"[13], Sir George "Georgius" Thomas[12], Sir Thomas "The Younger"[11], Sir Thomas "The Elder"[10], Sir Henry[9], Richard Wiat or[8] Wyatt, Geoffrey "Jeoffrey" Wiot or[7] Wiat, Robert or Richard[6] Wiot, William Wiot or[5] Wyot, Adam Wiot or Wyote or[4], Guyott[3], Guyott[2], Captain or Admiral Adam Guyott or[1] Wiot) was born November 15, 1943. She married (1) Thomas Jacob Lee. She married (2) James Walker Lunsford March 17, 1973, son of James Lunsford and Edna Goodwin.

> Children of Rebecca Eagle and James Lunsford are:
> 1864   i.   Michael Cameron[25] Lunsford, born December 05, 1967.
> 1865   ii.   Brandon David Lunsford, born August 08, 1978 in Rowan County, N.C.

1244. Sandra Kay[24] Fraley (Mabel Inez[23] Eagle, Joseph Calvin[22], Eli Esau[21], Mary Ann[20] Wyatt, Noah Calvin[19], Thomas "Tommy"[18] Wiatt, Sr. (Wyatt, Wiett), John[17], Henry[16], Richard[15], George[14], Rev. Haute "Haut" "Hawte"[13], Sir George "Georgius" Thomas[12], Sir Thomas "The Younger"[11], Sir Thomas "The Elder"[10], Sir Henry[9], Richard Wiat or[8] Wyatt, Geoffrey "Jeoffrey" Wiot or[7] Wiat, Robert or Richard[6] Wiot, William Wiot or[5] Wyot, Adam Wiot or Wyote or[4], Guyott[3], Guyott[2], Captain or Admiral Adam Guyott or[1] Wiot) was born December 18, 1947. She married Harold Craven McClellan, Jr. December 30, 1972, son of Harold McClellan and Virginia Clifton.

> Child of Sandra Fraley and Harold McClellan is:
> 1866   i.   Kelly Michelle[25] McClellan, born March 13, 1978 in Guilford County, N.C.

1246. Maurice Edison[24] Eagle, Jr. (Maurice Edison[23], Joseph Calvin[22], Eli Esau[21], Mary Ann[20] Wyatt, Noah Calvin[19], Thomas "Tommy"[18] Wiatt, Sr. (Wyatt, Wiett), John[17], Henry[16], Richard[15], George[14], Rev. Haute "Haut" "Hawte"[13], Sir George "Georgius" Thomas[12], Sir Thomas "The Younger"[11], Sir Thomas "The Elder"[10], Sir Henry[9], Richard Wiat or[8] Wyatt, Geoffrey "Jeoffrey" Wiot or[7] Wiat, Robert or Richard[6] Wiot, William Wiot or[5] Wyot, Adam Wiot or Wyote or[4], Guyott[3], Guyott[2], Captain or Admiral Adam Guyott or[1] Wiot) was born July 22, 1946. He married (1) Beverly Kimmer. He married (2) Diane Janette Hodges, daughter of Richard Hodges and Betty Sharp.

> Children of Maurice Eagle and Beverly Kimmer are:
> 1867   i.   Lisa Beverly[25] Eagle, born December 20, 1964 in Rowan County, N.C.
> 1868   ii.   David Bradley Eagle, born July 18, 1967 in Charleston, S.C.
>
> Children of Maurice Eagle and Diane Hodges are:
> 1869   i.   Maurice Edison[25] Eagle III, born October 02, 1972 in Elizabeth, Ky.
> 1870   ii.   Mary Jo Eagle, born November 27, 1976 in Rowan County, N.C.

1247.   Kenneth Michael[24] Eagle (Maurice Edison[23], Joseph Calvin[22], Eli Esau[21], Mary Ann[20] Wyatt, Noah Calvin[19], Thomas "Tommy"[18] Wiatt, Sr. (Wyatt, Wiett), John[17], Henry[16], Richard[15], George[14], Rev. Haute "Haut" "Hawte"[13], Sir George "Georgius" Thomas[12], Sir Thomas "The Younger"[11], Sir Thomas "The Elder"[10], Sir Henry[9], Richard Wiat or[8] Wyatt, Geoffrey "Jeoffrey" Wiot or[7] Wiat, Robert or Richard[6] Wiot, William Wiot or[5] Wyot, Adam Wiot or Wyote or[4], Guyott[3], Guyott[2], Captain or Admiral Adam Guyott or[1] Wiot) was born August 20, 1948. He married (1) Gloria Ann Raby, daughter of Larry Raby and Betty Livengood. He married (2) Wife January 26, 1969.

> Children of Kenneth Eagle and Wife are:
> 1871   i.   Anita Michelle[25] Eagle, born August 30, 1969.
> 1872   ii.   Margaret Jean Eagle, born October 29, 1970.

1258.   Kenneth Paul[24] Iddings (Esther Viola[23] Morgan, Annie Zenobia[22] Eagle, Eli Esau[21], Mary Ann[20] Wyatt, Noah Calvin[19], Thomas "Tommy"[18] Wiatt, Sr. (Wyatt, Wiett), John[17], Henry[16], Richard[15], George[14], Rev. Haute "Haut" "Hawte"[13], Sir George "Georgius" Thomas[12], Sir Thomas "The Younger"[11], Sir Thomas "The Elder"[10], Sir Henry[9], Richard Wiat or[8] Wyatt, Geoffrey "Jeoffrey" Wiot or[7] Wiat, Robert or Richard[6] Wiot, William Wiot or[5] Wyot, Adam Wiot or Wyote or[4], Guyott[3], Guyott[2], Captain or Admiral Adam Guyott or[1] Wiot). He married Unknown.

> Children of Kenneth Iddings and Unknown are:
> 1873   i.   Jeffrey Paul[25] Iddings.
> 1874   ii.   Joseph Martin Iddings.
> 1875   iii. Julie Diane Iddings.

1259.   Trudy Francis[24] Iddings (Esther Viola[23] Morgan, Annie Zenobia[22] Eagle, Eli Esau[21], Mary Ann[20] Wyatt, Noah Calvin[19], Thomas "Tommy"[18] Wiatt, Sr. (Wyatt, Wiett), John[17], Henry[16], Richard[15], George[14], Rev. Haute "Haut" "Hawte"[13], Sir George "Georgius" Thomas[12], Sir Thomas "The Younger"[11], Sir Thomas "The Elder"[10], Sir Henry[9], Richard Wiat or[8] Wyatt, Geoffrey "Jeoffrey" Wiot or[7] Wiat, Robert or Richard[6] Wiot, William Wiot or[5] Wyot, Adam Wiot or Wyote or[4], Guyott[3], Guyott[2], Captain or Admiral Adam Guyott or[1] Wiot). She married Howard Wilde.

> Children of Trudy Iddings and Howard Wilde are:
> 1876   i.   Howard Dowagne[25] Wilde.
> 1877   ii.   Katie Francis Wilde.

1261.   Phillip Armstrong[24] Morgan (Reather Armstrong[23], Annie Zenobia[22] Eagle, Eli Esau[21], Mary Ann[20] Wyatt, Noah Calvin[19], Thomas "Tommy"[18] Wiatt, Sr. (Wyatt, Wiett), John[17], Henry[16], Richard[15], George[14], Rev. Haute "Haut" "Hawte"[13], Sir George "Georgius" Thomas[12], Sir Thomas "The Younger"[11], Sir Thomas "The Elder"[10], Sir Henry[9], Richard Wiat or[8] Wyatt, Geoffrey "Jeoffrey" Wiot or[7] Wiat, Robert or Richard[6] Wiot, William Wiot or[5] Wyot, Adam Wiot or Wyote or[4], Guyott[3], Guyott[2], Captain or Admiral Adam Guyott or[1] Wiot). He married Unknown 1981.

Child of Phillip Morgan and Unknown is:

1878   i.   Phillip Armstrong[25] Morgan, Jr., born in Rowan County N.C.

1265. Bonnie Carol[24] Hutchins (Dorothy Ann[23] Morgan, Annie Zenobia[22] Eagle, Eli Esau[21], Mary Ann[20] Wyatt, Noah Calvin[19], Thomas "Tommy"[18] Wiatt, Sr. (Wyatt, Wiett), John[17], Henry[16], Richard[15], George[14], Rev. Haute "Haut" "Hawte"[13], Sir George "Georgius" Thomas[12], Sir Thomas "The Younger"[11], Sir Thomas "The Elder"[10], Sir Henry[9], Richard Wiat or[8] Wyatt, Geoffrey "Jeoffrey" Wiot or[7] Wiat, Robert or Richard[6] Wiot, William Wiot or[5] Wyot, Adam Wiot or Wyote or[4], Guyott[3], Guyott[2], Captain or Admiral Adam Guyott or[1] Wiot) was born December 25, 1948 in Rowan County N.C. She married James Thomas Hill December 20, 1967, son of James Hill and Helen Ketchie.

More About James Thomas Hill:
Fact 1: Served in the U.S. Army during the Vietnam War.

Child of Bonnie Hutchins and James Hill is:

1879   i.   Christy Carol[25] Hill, born November 09, 1970. She married Mark Stiller December 1995.

1275. Nancy Ann[24] Jackson (William Eli[23], Ida Lou[22] Eagle, Eli Esau[21], Mary Ann[20] Wyatt, Noah Calvin[19], Thomas "Tommy"[18] Wiatt, Sr. (Wyatt, Wiett), John[17], Henry[16], Richard[15], George[14], Rev. Haute "Haut" "Hawte"[13], Sir George "Georgius" Thomas[12], Sir Thomas "The Younger"[11], Sir Thomas "The Elder"[10], Sir Henry[9], Richard Wiat or[8] Wyatt, Geoffrey "Jeoffrey" Wiot or[7] Wiat, Robert or Richard[6] Wiot, William Wiot or[5] Wyot, Adam Wiot or Wyote or[4], Guyott[3], Guyott[2], Captain or Admiral Adam Guyott or[1] Wiot) was born December 05, 1936 in Rowan County, N.C. She married (1) John Clark. She married (2) William Edward Miller December 27, 1953.

Children of Nancy Jackson and William Miller are:

1880   i.   Angie Rae[25] Miller, born January 29, 1955. She married Charles Pickford August 14, 1976.
1881   ii.   William Edward Miller, Jr., born July 02, 1958 in Rowan County, N.C.
1882   iii.   Melanie Jane Miller, born May 13, 1962 in Rowan County, N.C.

1276. Jimmy Monroe[24] Jackson (William Eli[23], Ida Lou[22] Eagle, Eli Esau[21], Mary Ann[20] Wyatt, Noah Calvin[19], Thomas "Tommy"[18] Wiatt, Sr. (Wyatt, Wiett), John[17], Henry[16], Richard[15], George[14], Rev. Haute "Haut" "Hawte"[13], Sir George "Georgius" Thomas[12], Sir Thomas "The Younger"[11], Sir Thomas "The Elder"[10], Sir Henry[9], Richard Wiat or[8] Wyatt, Geoffrey "Jeoffrey" Wiot or[7] Wiat, Robert or Richard[6] Wiot, William Wiot or[5] Wyot, Adam Wiot or

Wyote or[4], Guyott[3], Guyott[2], Captain or Admiral Adam Guyott or[1] Wiot) was born October 13, 1939 in Rowan County, N.C. He married Judy Panter.

Children of Jimmy Jackson and Judy Panter are:
1883 i. Michael[25] Jackson.
1884 ii. Michelle Jackson.

1277. Phyllis Jean[24] Jackson (William Eli[23], Ida Lou[22] Eagle, Eli Esau[21], Mary Ann[20] Wyatt, Noah Calvin[19], Thomas "Tommy"[18] Wiatt, Sr. (Wyatt, Wiett), John[17], Henry[16], Richard[15], George[14], Rev. Haute "Haut" "Hawte"[13], Sir George "Georgius" Thomas[12], Sir Thomas "The Younger"[11], Sir Thomas "The Elder"[10], Sir Henry[9], Richard Wiat or[8] Wyatt, Geoffrey "Jeoffrey" Wiot or[7] Wiat, Robert or Richard[6] Wiot, William Wiot or[5] Wyot, Adam Wiot or Wyote or[4], Guyott[3], Guyott[2], Captain or Admiral Adam Guyott or[1] Wiot) was born July 01, 1943 in Rowan County, N.C. She married Robert Lama Williams III, son of Robert Williams and Wife.

Child of Phyllis Jackson and Robert Williams is:
1885 i. Robert Lama[25] Williams IV, born April 23, 1965.

1278. Rodney Frederick[24] Jackson (Manteo Monroe[23], Ida Lou[22] Eagle, Eli Esau[21], Mary Ann[20] Wyatt, Noah Calvin[19], Thomas "Tommy"[18] Wiatt, Sr. (Wyatt, Wiett), John[17], Henry[16], Richard[15], George[14], Rev. Haute "Haut" "Hawte"[13], Sir George "Georgius" Thomas[12], Sir Thomas "The Younger"[11], Sir Thomas "The Elder"[10], Sir Henry[9], Richard Wiat or[8] Wyatt, Geoffrey "Jeoffrey" Wiot or[7] Wiat, Robert or Richard[6] Wiot, William Wiot or[5] Wyot, Adam Wiot or Wyote or[4], Guyott[3], Guyott[2], Captain or Admiral Adam Guyott or[1] Wiot) was born April 04, 1939 in Rowan County, N.C. He married Harriet Faye Joiner January 28, 1961.

Children of Rodney Jackson and Harriet Joiner are:
1886 i. Rodney Frederick[25] Jackson, Jr., born September 07, 1962 in Tenn.
1887 ii. Kristen L. Jackson, born October 25, 1964 in Fla.
1888 iii. Timothy S. Jackson, born September 13, 1966 in Fla.

1280. Melody Jane[24] Jackson (Manteo Monroe[23], Ida Lou[22] Eagle, Eli Esau[21], Mary Ann[20] Wyatt, Noah Calvin[19], Thomas "Tommy"[18] Wiatt, Sr. (Wyatt, Wiett), John[17], Henry[16], Richard[15], George[14], Rev. Haute "Haut" "Hawte"[13], Sir George "Georgius" Thomas[12], Sir Thomas "The Younger"[11], Sir Thomas "The Elder"[10], Sir Henry[9], Richard Wiat or[8] Wyatt, Geoffrey "Jeoffrey" Wiot or[7] Wiat, Robert or Richard[6] Wiot, William Wiot or[5] Wyot, Adam Wiot or Wyote or[4], Guyott[3], Guyott[2], Captain or Admiral Adam Guyott or[1] Wiot) was born June 08, 1948 in Rowan County, N.C. She married Harold Scott Neely May 11, 1974.

Child of Melody Jackson and Harold Neely is:
1889 i. Matthew Scott[25] Neely, born October 27, 1977.

1281. Linda Carolyn[24] Jackson (John David[23], Ida Lou[22] Eagle, Eli Esau[21], Mary Ann[20] Wyatt, Noah Calvin[19], Thomas "Tommy"[18] Wiatt, Sr. (Wyatt, Wiett), John[17], Henry[16], Richard[15], George[14], Rev. Haute "Haut" "Hawte"[13], Sir George "Georgius" Thomas[12], Sir Thomas "The Younger"[11], Sir Thomas "The Elder"[10], Sir Henry[9], Richard Wiat or[8] Wyatt, Geoffrey "Jeoffrey" Wiot or[7] Wiat, Robert or Richard[6] Wiot, William Wiot or[5] Wyot, Adam Wiot or Wyote or[4], Guyott[3], Guyott[2], Captain or Admiral Adam Guyott or[1] Wiot) was born March 23, 1942 in Randolph County, N.C. She married Kenneth Wayne Markham April 28, 1962, son of Clarence Markham and Irene Wilson.

Child of Linda Jackson and Kenneth Markham is:

1890   i.   Kim[25] Markham, born September 12, 1963 in Davidson County, N.C.

1284. Ronald Ralph[24] Jackson (Ralph Adolphus[23], Ida Lou[22] Eagle, Eli Esau[21], Mary Ann[20] Wyatt, Noah Calvin[19], Thomas "Tommy"[18] Wiatt, Sr. (Wyatt, Wiett), John[17], Henry[16], Richard[15], George[14], Rev. Haute "Haut" "Hawte"[13], Sir George "Georgius" Thomas[12], Sir Thomas "The Younger"[11], Sir Thomas "The Elder"[10], Sir Henry[9], Richard Wiat or[8] Wyatt, Geoffrey "Jeoffrey" Wiot or[7] Wiat, Robert or Richard[6] Wiot, William Wiot or[5] Wyot, Adam Wiot or Wyote or[4], Guyott[3], Guyott[2], Captain or Admiral Adam Guyott or[1] Wiot) was born February 19, 1944 in Abilene, Tx. He married Lena Frances Ward December 23, 1961, daughter of Kirk Ward and Mary Hoffner.

Children of Ronald Jackson and Lena Ward are:

+   1891   i.   Connie Frances[25] Jackson, born December 30, 1962.

1892   ii.   Victor Dale Jackson, born February 08, 1965 in Rowan County, N.C.

1285. Joyce Elizabeth[24] Jackson (Ralph Adolphus[23], Ida Lou[22] Eagle, Eli Esau[21], Mary Ann[20] Wyatt, Noah Calvin[19], Thomas "Tommy"[18] Wiatt, Sr. (Wyatt, Wiett), John[17], Henry[16], Richard[15], George[14], Rev. Haute "Haut" "Hawte"[13], Sir George "Georgius" Thomas[12], Sir Thomas "The Younger"[11], Sir Thomas "The Elder"[10], Sir Henry[9], Richard Wiat or[8] Wyatt, Geoffrey "Jeoffrey" Wiot or[7] Wiat, Robert or Richard[6] Wiot, William Wiot or[5] Wyot, Adam Wiot or Wyote or[4], Guyott[3], Guyott[2], Captain or Admiral Adam Guyott or[1] Wiot) was born June 28, 1945. She married Walter Clyde Koontz November 01, 1965, son of Walter Koontz and Mary Harris.

Children of Joyce Jackson and Walter Koontz are:

1893   i.   Walter Darren[25] Koontz, born March 01, 1967 in Rowan County N.C.

1894   ii.   Webster Brian Koontz, born August 24, 1968 in Rowan County N.C.

1286. Thomas Lee[24] Jackson (Ralph Adolphus[23], Ida Lou[22] Eagle, Eli Esau[21], Mary Ann[20] Wyatt, Noah Calvin[19], Thomas "Tommy"[18] Wiatt, Sr. (Wyatt, Wiett), John[17], Henry[16],

Richard[15], George[14], Rev. Haute "Haut" "Hawte"[13], Sir George "Georgius" Thomas[12], Sir Thomas "The Younger"[11], Sir Thomas "The Elder"[10], Sir Henry[9], Richard Wiat or[8] Wyatt, Geoffrey "Jeoffrey" Wiot or[7] Wiat, Robert or Richard[6] Wiot, William Wiot or[5] Wyot, Adam Wiot or Wyote or[4], Guyott[3], Guyott[2], Captain or Admiral Adam Guyott or[1] Wiot) was born 1947. He married Barbara Jean Miller 1967, daughter of Raymond Miller and Marie Leazer.

> Children of Thomas Jackson and Barbara Miller are:
>
> 1895   i.   Thomas Lee[25] Jackson, Jr., born February 09, 1969 in Rowan County N.C.
>
> 1896   ii.   Gregory Scott Jackson, born August 09, 1971 in Rowan County N.C.

1287. Robert Ray[24] Jackson (Ralph Adolphus[23], Ida Lou[22] Eagle, Eli Esau[21], Mary Ann[20] Wyatt, Noah Calvin[19], Thomas "Tommy"[18] Wiatt, Sr. (Wyatt, Wiett), John[17], Henry[16], Richard[15], George[14], Rev. Haute "Haut" "Hawte"[13], Sir George "Georgius" Thomas[12], Sir Thomas "The Younger"[11], Sir Thomas "The Elder"[10], Sir Henry[9], Richard Wiat or[8] Wyatt, Geoffrey "Jeoffrey" Wiot or[7] Wiat, Robert or Richard[6] Wiot, William Wiot or[5] Wyot, Adam Wiot or Wyote or[4], Guyott[3], Guyott[2], Captain or Admiral Adam Guyott or[1] Wiot) was born July 31, 1949. He married Jo Ann Riley October 14, 1967, daughter of Ervin Riley and Mae Owen.

> Children of Robert Jackson and Jo Riley are:
>
> 1897   i.   Denise Kay[25] Jackson, born July 17, 1968 in Rowan County N.C.
>
> 1898   ii.   Jeffrey Todd Jackson, born March 13, 1972 in Rowan County N.C.
>
> 1899   iii.   Robin Ann Jackson, born October 06, 1973 in Rowan County N.C.

1288. Randy Steven[24] Jackson (Ralph Adolphus[23], Ida Lou[22] Eagle, Eli Esau[21], Mary Ann[20] Wyatt, Noah Calvin[19], Thomas "Tommy"[18] Wiatt, Sr. (Wyatt, Wiett), John[17], Henry[16], Richard[15], George[14], Rev. Haute "Haut" "Hawte"[13], Sir George "Georgius" Thomas[12], Sir Thomas "The Younger"[11], Sir Thomas "The Elder"[10], Sir Henry[9], Richard Wiat or[8] Wyatt, Geoffrey "Jeoffrey" Wiot or[7] Wiat, Robert or Richard[6] Wiot, William Wiot or[5] Wyot, Adam Wiot or Wyote or[4], Guyott[3], Guyott[2], Captain or Admiral Adam Guyott or[1] Wiot) was born December 16, 1950 in Rowan County N.C. He married Cynthia Lee Bonds July 09, 1970, daughter of Kenneth Bonds and Eve Carter.

> Children of Randy Jackson and Cynthia Bonds are:
>
> 1900   i.   Russell Matthew[25] Jackson, born November 09, 1972 in Coral Gables, Florida.
>
> 1901   ii.   Nathan Mark Jackson, born September 04, 1977 in Rowan County N.C.

1289. Ernest John[24] Jackson (Ralph Adolphus[23], Ida Lou[22] Eagle, Eli Esau[21], Mary Ann[20] Wyatt, Noah Calvin[19], Thomas "Tommy"[18] Wiatt, Sr. (Wyatt, Wiett), John[17], Henry[16], Richard[15], George[14], Rev. Haute "Haut" "Hawte"[13], Sir George "Georgius" Thomas[12], Sir Thomas "The Younger"[11], Sir Thomas "The Elder"[10], Sir Henry[9], Richard Wiat or[8] Wyatt, Geoffrey "Jeoffrey" Wiot or[7] Wiat, Robert or Richard[6] Wiot, William Wiot or[5] Wyot, Adam Wiot or Wyote or[4], Guyott[3], Guyott[2], Captain or Admiral Adam Guyott or[1] Wiot) was born December 18, 1952 in Rowan County, N.C. He married Donna Ann Curlee February 18, 1971, daughter of Carson Curlee and Ophelia Williams.

More About Ernest John Jackson:
Fact 1: 1973-1976, served in the U.S. Army.

Children of Ernest Jackson and Donna Curlee are:
1902   i.   Christopher Eric[25] Jackson, born September 11, 1972 in Fayetteville, N.C.
1903   ii.   Melissa Dawn Jackson, born February 14, 1976 in Rowan County N.C.

1290. Judy Ann[24] Jackson (Louie Phenix[23], Ida Lou[22] Eagle, Eli Esau[21], Mary Ann[20] Wyatt, Noah Calvin[19], Thomas "Tommy"[18] Wiatt, Sr. (Wyatt, Wiett), John[17], Henry[16], Richard[15], George[14], Rev. Haute "Haut" "Hawte"[13], Sir George "Georgius" Thomas[12], Sir Thomas "The Younger"[11], Sir Thomas "The Elder"[10], Sir Henry[9], Richard Wiat or[8] Wyatt, Geoffrey "Jeoffrey" Wiot or[7] Wiat, Robert or Richard[6] Wiot, William Wiot or[5] Wyot, Adam Wiot or Wyote or[4], Guyott[3], Guyott[2], Captain or Admiral Adam Guyott or[1] Wiot) was born December 20, 1949. She married Richard Allen Isenhour March 08, 1972, son of Robert Isenhour and Macie Wells.

Child of Judy Jackson and Richard Isenhour is:
1904   i.   Richard Allen[25] Isenhour, Jr., born November 20, 1975 in Rowan County N.C.

1293. David Wesley[24] Page (Ruby Ann[23] Jackson, Ida Lou[22] Eagle, Eli Esau[21], Mary Ann[20] Wyatt, Noah Calvin[19], Thomas "Tommy"[18] Wiatt, Sr. (Wyatt, Wiett), John[17], Henry[16], Richard[15], George[14], Rev. Haute "Haut" "Hawte"[13], Sir George "Georgius" Thomas[12], Sir Thomas "The Younger"[11], Sir Thomas "The Elder"[10], Sir Henry[9], Richard Wiat or[8] Wyatt, Geoffrey "Jeoffrey" Wiot or[7] Wiat, Robert or Richard[6] Wiot, William Wiot or[5] Wyot, Adam Wiot or Wyote or[4], Guyott[3], Guyott[2], Captain or Admiral Adam Guyott or[1] Wiot) was born May 10, 1945 in Rowan County N.C. He married Ellen Ruth Sutton October 13, 1965, daughter of William Sutton and Mary Reasoner.

Children of David Page and Ellen Sutton are:
1905   i.   Rebecca Lyn[25] Page, born July 18, 1966.
1906   ii.   Sandra Denise Page, born November 17, 1969.
1907   iii.   David Wesley, Jr. Page, born April 08, 1975.

1294. Charles Lee[24] Page (Ruby Ann[23] Jackson, Ida Lou[22] Eagle, Eli Esau[21], Mary Ann[20] Wyatt, Noah Calvin[19], Thomas "Tommy"[18] Wiatt, Sr. (Wyatt, Wiett), John[17], Henry[16], Richard[15], George[14], Rev. Haute "Haut" "Hawte"[13], Sir George "Georgius" Thomas[12], Sir Thomas "The Younger"[11], Sir Thomas "The Elder"[10], Sir Henry[9], Richard Wiat or[8] Wyatt, Geoffrey "Jeoffrey" Wiot or[7] Wiat, Robert or Richard[6] Wiot, William Wiot or[5] Wyot, Adam Wiot or Wyote or[4], Guyott[3], Guyott[2], Captain or Admiral Adam Guyott or[1] Wiot) was born March 14, 1947 in Rowan County N.C. He married Joan Miller October 23, 1970, daughter of John Miller and Unknown.

More About Charles Lee Page:
Fact 1: Served in the U.S. Air Force for 9 years.

Children of Charles Page and Joan Miller are:
1908   i.   Charles Lee[25] Page II, born December 17, 1972 in Kansas.
1909   ii.   Christie Dawn Page, born August 09, 1974 in Hawaii.

1295. Shirley Jean[24] Page (Ruby Ann[23] Jackson, Ida Lou[22] Eagle, Eli Esau[21], Mary Ann[20] Wyatt, Noah Calvin[19], Thomas "Tommy"[18] Wiatt, Sr. (Wyatt, Wiett), John[17], Henry[16], Richard[15], George[14], Rev. Haute "Haut" "Hawte"[13], Sir George "Georgius" Thomas[12], Sir Thomas "The Younger"[11], Sir Thomas "The Elder"[10], Sir Henry[9], Richard Wiat or[8] Wyatt, Geoffrey "Jeoffrey" Wiot or[7] Wiat, Robert or Richard[6] Wiot, William Wiot or[5] Wyot, Adam Wiot or Wyote or[4], Guyott[3], Guyott[2], Captain or Admiral Adam Guyott or[1] Wiot) was born May 29, 1949 in Rowan County N.C. She married William A. Sutton, Jr. December 24, 1966, son of William Sutton and Mary Reasoner.

Children of Shirley Page and William Sutton are:
1910   i.   William Arlen[25] Sutton, born February 09, 1968.
1911   ii.   John Arron Sutton, born April 20, 1971 in Rowan County N.C.

1296. Joseph Andrew[24] Page (Ruby Ann[23] Jackson, Ida Lou[22] Eagle, Eli Esau[21], Mary Ann[20] Wyatt, Noah Calvin[19], Thomas "Tommy"[18] Wiatt, Sr. (Wyatt, Wiett), John[17], Henry[16], Richard[15], George[14], Rev. Haute "Haut" "Hawte"[13], Sir George "Georgius" Thomas[12], Sir Thomas "The Younger"[11], Sir Thomas "The Elder"[10], Sir Henry[9], Richard Wiat or[8] Wyatt, Geoffrey "Jeoffrey" Wiot or[7] Wiat, Robert or Richard[6] Wiot, William Wiot or[5] Wyot, Adam Wiot or Wyote or[4], Guyott[3], Guyott[2], Captain or Admiral Adam Guyott or[1] Wiot) was born October 13, 1950 in Rowan County N.C. He married Mary Evelyn Williams July 27, 1969, daughter of E.P. Williams and Evelyn Wyrick.

Children of Joseph Page and Mary Williams are:
1912   i.   Wendy Kaye[25] Page, born November 29, 1971.
1913   ii.   Joseph Andrew Page, Jr., born September 26, 1975.

1297. Lucinda Kay[24] Edwards (James Alois[23], Elizabeth "Elisbeth" Nora[22] Eagle, Eli Esau[21], Mary Ann[20] Wyatt, Noah Calvin[19], Thomas "Tommy"[18] Wiatt, Sr. (Wyatt, Wiett), John[17],

Henry[16], Richard[15], George[14], Rev. Haute "Haut" "Hawte"[13], Sir George "Georgius" Thomas[12], Sir Thomas "The Younger"[11], Sir Thomas "The Elder"[10], Sir Henry[9], Richard Wiat or[8] Wyatt, Geoffrey "Jeoffrey" Wiot or[7] Wiat, Robert or Richard[6] Wiot, William Wiot or[5] Wyot, Adam Wiot or Wyote or[4], Guyott[3], Guyott[2], Captain or Admiral Adam Guyott or[1] Wiot) was born April 10, 1950 in Lamar, Colorado. She married Timothy Callihan June 18, 1969.

Children of Lucinda Edwards and Timothy Callihan are:
1914   i.   Amy Kathlee[25] Callihan, born July 17, 1974 in Colorado.
1915   ii.   Kelly Jean Callihan, born February 24, 1977.

1300. Jeffrey Lynn[24] Edwards (Stanley[23], Elizabeth "Elisbeth" Nora[22] Eagle, Eli Esau[21], Mary Ann[20] Wyatt, Noah Calvin[19], Thomas "Tommy"[18] Wiatt, Sr. (Wyatt, Wiett), John[17], Henry[16], Richard[15], George[14], Rev. Haute "Haut" "Hawte"[13], Sir George "Georgius" Thomas[12], Sir Thomas "The Younger"[11], Sir Thomas "The Elder"[10], Sir Henry[9], Richard Wiat or[8] Wyatt, Geoffrey "Jeoffrey" Wiot or[7] Wiat, Robert or Richard[6] Wiot, William Wiot or[5] Wyot, Adam Wiot or Wyote or[4], Guyott[3], Guyott[2], Captain or Admiral Adam Guyott or[1] Wiot) was born September 07, 1949. He married Vicky Lynn Murray May 05, 1973.

Children of Jeffrey Edwards and Vicky Murray are:
1916   i.   Hilary Suzanne[25] Edwards, born July 03, 1975 in Santa Barbara, Ca.
1917   ii.   Joseph Michael Edwards, born January 26, 1977 in Santa Barbara, Ca.

1301. Rebecca Ann[24] Edwards (Stanley[23], Elizabeth "Elisbeth" Nora[22] Eagle, Eli Esau[21], Mary Ann[20] Wyatt, Noah Calvin[19], Thomas "Tommy"[18] Wiatt, Sr. (Wyatt, Wiett), John[17], Henry[16], Richard[15], George[14], Rev. Haute "Haut" "Hawte"[13], Sir George "Georgius" Thomas[12], Sir Thomas "The Younger"[11], Sir Thomas "The Elder"[10], Sir Henry[9], Richard Wiat or[8] Wyatt, Geoffrey "Jeoffrey" Wiot or[7] Wiat, Robert or Richard[6] Wiot, William Wiot or[5] Wyot, Adam Wiot or Wyote or[4], Guyott[3], Guyott[2], Captain or Admiral Adam Guyott or[1] Wiot) was born October 06, 1950 in Massillon, Oh. She married Charles A. Bischof September 05, 1970.

Child of Rebecca Edwards and Charles Bischof is:
1918   i.   Matthew Jonathan[25] Bischof, born May 01, 1974 in Santa Barbara, Ca.

1308. John Cameron[24] Goodman (Ree Velt[23], Enoch Arthur[22], Nancy Jane[21] Eagle, Mary Ann[20] Wyatt, Noah Calvin[19], Thomas "Tommy"[18] Wiatt, Sr. (Wyatt, Wiett), John[17], Henry[16], Richard[15], George[14], Rev. Haute "Haut" "Hawte"[13], Sir George "Georgius" Thomas[12], Sir Thomas "The Younger"[11], Sir Thomas "The Elder"[10], Sir Henry[9], Richard Wiat or[8] Wyatt, Geoffrey "Jeoffrey" Wiot or[7] Wiat, Robert or Richard[6] Wiot, William Wiot or[5] Wyot, Adam Wiot or Wyote or[4], Guyott[3], Guyott[2], Captain or Admiral Adam Guyott or[1] Wiot) was born October 05, 1936. He married Susan Raker McIntyre January 30, 1960, daughter of Stephen McIntyre and E. Boyer.

Children of John Goodman and Susan McIntyre are:

1919   i.   Cameron Ree[25] Goodman, born 1961 in Wash.

1920   ii.   Lyn Boyer Goodman, born 1965 in Mecklenburg County, N.C.

1309.   Dorothy Kay[24] Goodman (Ree Velt[23], Enoch Arthur[22], Nancy Jane[21] Eagle, Mary Ann[20] Wyatt, Noah Calvin[19], Thomas "Tommy"[18] Wiatt, Sr. (Wyatt, Wiett), John[17], Henry[16], Richard[15], George[14], Rev. Haute "Haut" "Hawte"[13], Sir George "Georgius" Thomas[12], Sir Thomas "The Younger"[11], Sir Thomas "The Elder"[10], Sir Henry[9], Richard Wiat or[8] Wyatt, Geoffrey "Jeoffrey" Wiot or[7] Wiat, Robert or Richard[6] Wiot, William Wiot or[5] Wyot, Adam Wiot or Wyote or[4], Guyott[3], Guyott[2], Captain or Admiral Adam Guyott or[1] Wiot) was born July 12, 1940. She married Norde David Wilson, Sr. August 29, 1965.

Children of Dorothy Goodman and Norde Wilson are:

1921   i.   Dorothy Kay[25] Wilson, born 1965.

1922   ii.   David Wilson, Jr., born 1968.

1923   iii. Gary Wilson, born 1969.

1311.   Myron Arthur[24] Goodman, M.D. (Myron A.O.[23], Enoch Arthur[22], Nancy Jane[21] Eagle, Mary Ann[20] Wyatt, Noah Calvin[19], Thomas "Tommy"[18] Wiatt, Sr. (Wyatt, Wiett), John[17], Henry[16], Richard[15], George[14], Rev. Haute "Haut" "Hawte"[13], Sir George "Georgius" Thomas[12], Sir Thomas "The Younger"[11], Sir Thomas "The Elder"[10], Sir Henry[9], Richard Wiat or[8] Wyatt, Geoffrey "Jeoffrey" Wiot or[7] Wiat, Robert or Richard[6] Wiot, William Wiot or[5] Wyot, Adam Wiot or Wyote or[4], Guyott[3], Guyott[2], Captain or Admiral Adam Guyott or[1] Wiot) was born October 17, 1939. He married Mary Helen Schomer October 16, 1971, daughter of Joseph Schomer and Bernice Buman.

Children of Myron Goodman and Mary Schomer are:

1924   i.   Catherine Schomer[25] Goodman, born September 09, 1972 in Salibury, Rowan County, N.C.

1925   ii.   Mary Elizabeth Goodman, born January 01, 1974 in Salibury, Rowan County, N.C.

1926   iii. Myron Joseph Goodman, born June 07, 1975 in Salibury, Rowan County, N.C.

1927   iv.   Michael Moses Goodman, born January 07, 1977 in Salibury, Rowan County, N.C. He married Julianne Kennedy.

1928   v.   Christopher Goodman, born 1982 in Salibury, Rowan County, N.C.

1315.   Prudence Penelope[24] Goodman (Myron A.O.[23], Enoch Arthur[22], Nancy Jane[21] Eagle, Mary Ann[20] Wyatt, Noah Calvin[19], Thomas "Tommy"[18] Wiatt, Sr. (Wyatt, Wiett), John[17], Henry[16], Richard[15], George[14], Rev. Haute "Haut" "Hawte"[13], Sir George "Georgius" Thomas[12], Sir Thomas "The Younger"[11], Sir Thomas "The Elder"[10], Sir Henry[9], Richard Wiat or[8] Wyatt, Geoffrey "Jeoffrey" Wiot or[7] Wiat, Robert or Richard[6] Wiot, William Wiot or[5] Wyot, Adam

Wiot or Wyote or[4], Guyott[3], Guyott[2], Captain or Admiral Adam Guyott or[1] Wiot) was born October 24, 1950. She married Charles David Taylor, Sr. June 03, 1967, son of Charles Taylor and Charlotte Ruffner.

Children of Prudence Goodman and Charles Taylor are:
1929   i.   Charles David[25] Taylor, Jr., born August 07, 1969.
1930   ii.   Charlotte Dameron Taylor, born January 07, 1971.
1931   iii.   Elizabeth Ruffner Taylor, born June 08, 1981.

1316.   Melinda Connell[24] Goodman (Loyd Calvin[23], Enoch Arthur[22], Nancy Jane[21] Eagle, Mary Ann[20] Wyatt, Noah Calvin[19], Thomas "Tommy"[18] Wiatt, Sr. (Wyatt, Wiett), John[17], Henry[16], Richard[15], George[14], Rev. Haute "Haut" "Hawte"[13], Sir George "Georgius" Thomas[12], Sir Thomas "The Younger"[11], Sir Thomas "The Elder"[10], Sir Henry[9], Richard Wiat or[8] Wyatt, Geoffrey "Jeoffrey" Wiot or[7] Wiat, Robert or Richard[6] Wiot, William Wiot or[5] Wyot, Adam Wiot or Wyote or[4], Guyott[3], Guyott[2], Captain or Admiral Adam Guyott or[1] Wiot) was born November 07, 1940 in Guilford County, N.C. She married David Sherrill Heilig, Sr. June 14, 1964, son of Charles Heilig and Mary Linn.

Children of Melinda Goodman and David Heilig are:
1932   i.   David Sherrill[25] Heilig, Jr., born April 10, 1967.
1933   ii.   Michael Linn Heilig, born June 29, 1969 in Lenoir County, N.C.
1934   iii.   Douglas Arthur Heilig, born June 29, 1969 in Lenoir County, N.C.

1317.   James Arthur[24] Goodman (Loyd Calvin[23], Enoch Arthur[22], Nancy Jane[21] Eagle, Mary Ann[20] Wyatt, Noah Calvin[19], Thomas "Tommy"[18] Wiatt, Sr. (Wyatt, Wiett), John[17], Henry[16], Richard[15], George[14], Rev. Haute "Haut" "Hawte"[13], Sir George "Georgius" Thomas[12], Sir Thomas "The Younger"[11], Sir Thomas "The Elder"[10], Sir Henry[9], Richard Wiat or[8] Wyatt, Geoffrey "Jeoffrey" Wiot or[7] Wiat, Robert or Richard[6] Wiot, William Wiot or[5] Wyot, Adam Wiot or Wyote or[4], Guyott[3], Guyott[2], Captain or Admiral Adam Guyott or[1] Wiot) was born January 31, 1944. He married Sonja Sarah Reese December 28, 1968, daughter of Willard Reese and Betty McPhail.

Children of James Goodman and Sonja Reese are:
1935   i.   James Steven[25] Goodman, born August 10, 1977 in Ga.
1936   ii.   Emily Elizabeth Goodman, born June 30, 1981 in Ill.

1318.   Susan Frances[24] Goodman (Loyd Calvin[23], Enoch Arthur[22], Nancy Jane[21] Eagle, Mary Ann[20] Wyatt, Noah Calvin[19], Thomas "Tommy"[18] Wiatt, Sr. (Wyatt, Wiett), John[17], Henry[16], Richard[15], George[14], Rev. Haute "Haut" "Hawte"[13], Sir George "Georgius" Thomas[12], Sir Thomas "The Younger"[11], Sir Thomas "The Elder"[10], Sir Henry[9], Richard Wiat or[8] Wyatt, Geoffrey "Jeoffrey" Wiot or[7] Wiat, Robert or Richard[6] Wiot, William Wiot or[5] Wyot, Adam

Wiot or Wyote or[4], Guyott[3], Guyott[2], Captain or Admiral Adam Guyott or[1] Wiot) was born February 19, 1946. She married Steven Eugene Jarrell December 06, 1966, son of Charles Jarrell and Ruth David.

    Children of Susan Goodman and Steven Jarrell are:

1937   i.   Charles Gregory[25] Jarrell, born August 21, 1970.
1938   ii.   Matthew Lloyd Jarrell, born January 26, 1973.
1939   iii.   Allison Virginia Jarrell, born September 17, 1974 in Wake County, N.C.

1319. Jennie Elizabeth[24] Goodman (Loyd Calvin[23], Enoch Arthur[22], Nancy Jane[21] Eagle, Mary Ann[20] Wyatt, Noah Calvin[19], Thomas "Tommy"[18] Wiatt, Sr. (Wyatt, Wiett), John[17], Henry[16], Richard[15], George[14], Rev. Haute "Haut" "Hawte"[13], Sir George "Georgius" Thomas[12], Sir Thomas "The Younger"[11], Sir Thomas "The Elder"[10], Sir Henry[9], Richard Wiat or[8] Wyatt, Geoffrey "Jeoffrey" Wiot or[7] Wiat, Robert or Richard[6] Wiot, William Wiot or[5] Wyot, Adam Wiot or Wyote or[4], Guyott[3], Guyott[2], Captain or Admiral Adam Guyott or[1] Wiot) was born February 28, 1948. She married Tony Ray Deal June 09, 1973, son of Floyd Deal and Pauline Moore.

    Children of Jennie Goodman and Tony Deal are:

1940   i.   Adam Goodman[25] Deal, born October 12, 1976.
1941   ii.   Carrie Connell Deal, born August 23, 1978.

1320. Jane Catherine[24] Goodman (Loyd Calvin[23], Enoch Arthur[22], Nancy Jane[21] Eagle, Mary Ann[20] Wyatt, Noah Calvin[19], Thomas "Tommy"[18] Wiatt, Sr. (Wyatt, Wiett), John[17], Henry[16], Richard[15], George[14], Rev. Haute "Haut" "Hawte"[13], Sir George "Georgius" Thomas[12], Sir Thomas "The Younger"[11], Sir Thomas "The Elder"[10], Sir Henry[9], Richard Wiat or[8] Wyatt, Geoffrey "Jeoffrey" Wiot or[7] Wiat, Robert or Richard[6] Wiot, William Wiot or[5] Wyot, Adam Wiot or Wyote or[4], Guyott[3], Guyott[2], Captain or Admiral Adam Guyott or[1] Wiot) was born November 16, 1951. She married Larry Wayne Britt March 29, 1975, son of Andy Britt and Hazel Thompson.

    Child of Jane Goodman and Larry Britt is:

1942   i.   Catherine Goodman[25] Britt, born 1982.

1321. Harold Kent[24] Goodman (Harold Moses[23], Enoch Arthur[22], Nancy Jane[21] Eagle, Mary Ann[20] Wyatt, Noah Calvin[19], Thomas "Tommy"[18] Wiatt, Sr. (Wyatt, Wiett), John[17], Henry[16], Richard[15], George[14], Rev. Haute "Haut" "Hawte"[13], Sir George "Georgius" Thomas[12], Sir Thomas "The Younger"[11], Sir Thomas "The Elder"[10], Sir Henry[9], Richard Wiat or[8] Wyatt, Geoffrey "Jeoffrey" Wiot or[7] Wiat, Robert or Richard[6] Wiot, William Wiot or[5] Wyot, Adam Wiot or Wyote or[4], Guyott[3], Guyott[2], Captain or Admiral Adam Guyott or[1] Wiot) was born January 24, 1942. He married Gloria Florence Misenheimer February 08, 1969, daughter of Guy Misenheimer and Faye Culp.

Children of Harold Goodman and Gloria Misenheimer are:

1943   i.   Catherine Page[25] Goodman, born September 30, 1973 in Tenn.

1944   ii.   Brandley Kent Goodman, born December 1975 in Tenn.

1322.   Sanders Emerson[24] Goodman (Harold Moses[23], Enoch Arthur[22], Nancy Jane[21] Eagle, Mary Ann[20] Wyatt, Noah Calvin[19], Thomas "Tommy"[18] Wiatt, Sr. (Wyatt, Wiett), John[17], Henry[16], Richard[15], George[14], Rev. Haute "Haut" "Hawte"[13], Sir George "Georgius" Thomas[12], Sir Thomas "The Younger"[11], Sir Thomas "The Elder"[10], Sir Henry[9], Richard Wiat or[8] Wyatt, Geoffrey "Jeoffrey" Wiot or[7] Wiat, Robert or Richard[6] Wiot, William Wiot or[5] Wyot, Adam Wiot or Wyote or[4], Guyott[3], Guyott[2], Captain or Admiral Adam Guyott or[1] Wiot) was born September 10, 1944. He married Judith Irene Main May 27, 1970, daughter of George Main and Marjorie Eddins.

Children of Sanders Goodman and Judith Main are:

1945   i.   Harold David[25] Goodman, born March 26, 1976.

1946   ii.   George Andrew Goodman, born June 02, 1977.

1323.   Richard Park[24] Goodman (Harold Moses[23], Enoch Arthur[22], Nancy Jane[21] Eagle, Mary Ann[20] Wyatt, Noah Calvin[19], Thomas "Tommy"[18] Wiatt, Sr. (Wyatt, Wiett), John[17], Henry[16], Richard[15], George[14], Rev. Haute "Haut" "Hawte"[13], Sir George "Georgius" Thomas[12], Sir Thomas "The Younger"[11], Sir Thomas "The Elder"[10], Sir Henry[9], Richard Wiat or[8] Wyatt, Geoffrey "Jeoffrey" Wiot or[7] Wiat, Robert or Richard[6] Wiot, William Wiot or[5] Wyot, Adam Wiot or Wyote or[4], Guyott[3], Guyott[2], Captain or Admiral Adam Guyott or[1] Wiot) was born May 02, 1946. He married Elizabeth Manning Collier December 18, 1971, daughter of Charles Collier and Elizabeth Manning.

Children of Richard Goodman and Elizabeth Collier are:

1947   i.   Marion Elisabeth[25] Goodman, born March 27, 1976.

1948   ii.   Charles Emerson Goodman, born December 31, 1978.

1324.   Michael Alvin[24] Goodman (Enoch Alvin[23], Enoch Arthur[22], Nancy Jane[21] Eagle, Mary Ann[20] Wyatt, Noah Calvin[19], Thomas "Tommy"[18] Wiatt, Sr. (Wyatt, Wiett), John[17], Henry[16], Richard[15], George[14], Rev. Haute "Haut" "Hawte"[13], Sir George "Georgius" Thomas[12], Sir Thomas "The Younger"[11], Sir Thomas "The Elder"[10], Sir Henry[9], Richard Wiat or[8] Wyatt, Geoffrey "Jeoffrey" Wiot or[7] Wiat, Robert or Richard[6] Wiot, William Wiot or[5] Wyot, Adam Wiot or Wyote or[4], Guyott[3], Guyott[2], Captain or Admiral Adam Guyott or[1] Wiot) was born April 07, 1941. He married Kay Nussman July 09, 1966, daughter of Wayne Nussman and Kitty Cadell.

Children of Michael Goodman and Kay Nussman are:

1949   i.   Louisa Harris[25] Goodman, born November 19, 1968 in Buncombe County, N.C.

1950   ii.   Lauren Hadley Goodman, born January 02, 1972 in Buncombe County, N.C.

1325. Jeffrey Vance[24] Goodman (Enoch Alvin[23], Enoch Arthur[22], Nancy Jane[21] Eagle, Mary Ann[20] Wyatt, Noah Calvin[19], Thomas "Tommy"[18] Wiatt, Sr. (Wyatt, Wiett), John[17], Henry[16], Richard[15], George[14], Rev. Haute "Haut" "Hawte"[13], Sir George "Georgius" Thomas[12], Sir Thomas "The Younger"[11], Sir Thomas "The Elder"[10], Sir Henry[9], Richard Wiat or[8] Wyatt, Geoffrey "Jeoffrey" Wiot or[7] Wiat, Robert or Richard[6] Wiot, William Wiot or[5] Wyot, Adam Wiot or Wyote or[4], Guyott[3], Guyott[2], Captain or Admiral Adam Guyott or[1] Wiot) was born May 06, 1943. He married Dianna Mae Blackwell February 06, 1971, daughter of Robert Blackwell and Peggy Watts.

> Children of Jeffrey Goodman and Dianna Blackwell are:
> 1951   i.   Sarah Vance[25] Goodman, born October 10, 1979 in Buncombe County, N.C.
> 1952   ii.   Catherine Park Goodman, born May 10, 1981 in Buncombe County, N.C.
> 1953   iii.   Dorthy Madison Goodman, born 1985 in Buncombe County, N.C.

1326. Dorthy Gail[24] Goodman (Enoch Alvin[23], Enoch Arthur[22], Nancy Jane[21] Eagle, Mary Ann[20] Wyatt, Noah Calvin[19], Thomas "Tommy"[18] Wiatt, Sr. (Wyatt, Wiett), John[17], Henry[16], Richard[15], George[14], Rev. Haute "Haut" "Hawte"[13], Sir George "Georgius" Thomas[12], Sir Thomas "The Younger"[11], Sir Thomas "The Elder"[10], Sir Henry[9], Richard Wiat or[8] Wyatt, Geoffrey "Jeoffrey" Wiot or[7] Wiat, Robert or Richard[6] Wiot, William Wiot or[5] Wyot, Adam Wiot or Wyote or[4], Guyott[3], Guyott[2], Captain or Admiral Adam Guyott or[1] Wiot) was born July 28, 1947. She married Robert Daniel Settle, Jr. November 28, 1970, son of Robert Settle and Gloria.

> Children of Dorthy Goodman and Robert Settle are:
> 1954   i.   Robert Daniel[25] Settle III, born February 13, 1974.
> 1955   ii.   Christopher Arthur Settle, born August 28, 1976.
> 1956   iii.   Michael Harris Settle, born 1980 in Tx.

1327. Donald O'Brien[24] Nussman (Sara Jane[23] Goodman, Enoch Arthur[22], Nancy Jane[21] Eagle, Mary Ann[20] Wyatt, Noah Calvin[19], Thomas "Tommy"[18] Wiatt, Sr. (Wyatt, Wiett), John[17], Henry[16], Richard[15], George[14], Rev. Haute "Haut" "Hawte"[13], Sir George "Georgius" Thomas[12], Sir Thomas "The Younger"[11], Sir Thomas "The Elder"[10], Sir Henry[9], Richard Wiat or[8] Wyatt, Geoffrey "Jeoffrey" Wiot or[7] Wiat, Robert or Richard[6] Wiot, William Wiot or[5] Wyot, Adam Wiot or Wyote or[4], Guyott[3], Guyott[2], Captain or Admiral Adam Guyott or[1] Wiot) was born July 15, 1946. He married Melanie Zumbrunnen, daughter of Thomas Zumbrunnen and Jerry Fisher.

> Child of Donald Nussman and Melanie Zumbrunnen is:
> 1957   i.   Patrick O'Brien[25] Nussman, born February 24, 1970.

1329. Enoch Anthony[24] Nussman (Sara Jane[23] Goodman, Enoch Arthur[22], Nancy Jane[21] Eagle, Mary Ann[20] Wyatt, Noah Calvin[19], Thomas "Tommy"[18] Wiatt, Sr. (Wyatt, Wiett),

John[17], Henry[16], Richard[15], George[14], Rev. Haute "Haut" "Hawte"[13], Sir George "Georgius" Thomas[12], Sir Thomas "The Younger"[11], Sir Thomas "The Elder"[10], Sir Henry[9], Richard Wiat or[8] Wyatt, Geoffrey "Jeoffrey" Wiot or[7] Wiat, Robert or Richard[6] Wiot, William Wiot or[5] Wyot, Adam Wiot or Wyote or[4], Guyott[3], Guyott[2], Captain or Admiral Adam Guyott or[1] Wiot) was born October 26, 1950. He married (1) Jennifer Lynn Hunt. He married (2) Bonnie Coggins October 06, 1974.

> Child of Enoch Nussman and Jennifer Hunt is:
> 1958   i.   Christopher Michael[25] Nussman, born 1984.

> Child of Enoch Nussman and Bonnie Coggins is:
> 1959   i.   Anthony Scott[25] Nussman, born July 11, 1975.

1330. David Allen[24] Beaver (Mildred Louise[23] Goodman, Linus Giles[22], Nancy Jane[21] Eagle, Mary Ann[20] Wyatt, Noah Calvin[19], Thomas "Tommy"[18] Wiatt, Sr. (Wyatt, Wiett), John[17], Henry[16], Richard[15], George[14], Rev. Haute "Haut" "Hawte"[13], Sir George "Georgius" Thomas[12], Sir Thomas "The Younger"[11], Sir Thomas "The Elder"[10], Sir Henry[9], Richard Wiat or[8] Wyatt, Geoffrey "Jeoffrey" Wiot or[7] Wiat, Robert or Richard[6] Wiot, William Wiot or[5] Wyot, Adam Wiot or Wyote or[4], Guyott[3], Guyott[2], Captain or Admiral Adam Guyott or[1] Wiot) was born March 24, 1951. He married Robecca Moser July 21, 1971, daughter of Wilson Moser and Frances Sohmer.

> Children of David Beaver and Robecca Moser are:
> 1960   i.   Adrienne F.[25] Beaver, born 1972 in Forsyth County, N.C.
> 1961   ii.   Wilson Moser Beaver, born 1979 in Stanly County, N.C.
> 1962   iii. Roy David Beaver III, born 1983 in Mecklenburg County, N.C.

1331. Linus[24] Giles III (Linus Giles[23] Goodman, Jr., Linus Giles[22], Nancy Jane[21] Eagle, Mary Ann[20] Wyatt, Noah Calvin[19], Thomas "Tommy"[18] Wiatt, Sr. (Wyatt, Wiett), John[17], Henry[16], Richard[15], George[14], Rev. Haute "Haut" "Hawte"[13], Sir George "Georgius" Thomas[12], Sir Thomas "The Younger"[11], Sir Thomas "The Elder"[10], Sir Henry[9], Richard Wiat or[8] Wyatt, Geoffrey "Jeoffrey" Wiot or[7] Wiat, Robert or Richard[6] Wiot, William Wiot or[5] Wyot, Adam Wiot or Wyote or[4], Guyott[3], Guyott[2], Captain or Admiral Adam Guyott or[1] Wiot) was born July 16, 1950 in Moore County, N.C. He married Betty Anne Bost August 28, 1975, daughter of Robert Bost and Mildred Steele.

> Children of Linus Giles and Betty Bost are:
> 1963   i.   Linus[25] Giles IV, born 1980.
> 1964   ii.   Katherine Anne Giles, born 1982.

1337. Sharyn Lynn[24] Hemrick (Gertrude Eliza[23] Goodman, Paul Talmadge[22], Nancy Jane[21] Eagle, Mary Ann[20] Wyatt, Noah Calvin[19], Thomas "Tommy"[18] Wiatt, Sr. (Wyatt, Wiett), John[17], Henry[16], Richard[15], George[14], Rev. Haute "Haut" "Hawte"[13], Sir George "Georgius" Thomas[12], Sir Thomas "The Younger"[11], Sir Thomas "The Elder"[10], Sir Henry[9], Richard

Wiat or[8] Wyatt, Geoffrey "Jeoffrey" Wiot or[7] Wiat, Robert or Richard[6] Wiot, William Wiot or[5] Wyot, Adam Wiot or Wyote or[4], Guyott[3], Guyott[2], Captain or Admiral Adam Guyott or[1] Wiot) was born October 11, 1949. She married Harold Leonard West, Jr., son of Harold West and Jean Thomas.

Children of Sharyn Hemrick and Harold West are:
1965   i.   Jennifer[25] Lynn, born June 14, 1977.
1966   ii. Kathern Jorden, born March 09, 1980.

1339. Bobby Gene[24] Hammill (Ruth Estelle[23] Goodman, Paul Talmadge[22], Nancy Jane[21] Eagle, Mary Ann[20] Wyatt, Noah Calvin[19], Thomas "Tommy"[18] Wiatt, Sr. (Wyatt, Wiett), John[17], Henry[16], Richard[15], George[14], Rev. Haute "Haut" "Hawte"[13], Sir George "Georgius" Thomas[12], Sir Thomas "The Younger"[11], Sir Thomas "The Elder"[10], Sir Henry[9], Richard Wiat or[8] Wyatt, Geoffrey "Jeoffrey" Wiot or[7] Wiat, Robert or Richard[6] Wiot, William Wiot or[5] Wyot, Adam Wiot or Wyote or[4], Guyott[3], Guyott[2], Captain or Admiral Adam Guyott or[1] Wiot) was born March 17, 1940. He married Glenda Ann Auten November 09, 1958, daughter of Robert Auten and Nannie Shue.

Children of Bobby Hammill and Glenda Auten are:
+ 1967   i.   Cheryl Anita[25] Hammill, born December 01, 1959.
   1968   ii.   Nancy Jane Hammill, born December 22, 1960. She married Jerry Glenn Cain November 06, 1981.
   1969   iii. Bobby Gene Hammill, Jr., born November 22, 1962. He married Annette Barnhardt June 17, 1984.

1340. John Allen[24] Hammill, Jr. (Ruth Estelle[23] Goodman, Paul Talmadge[22], Nancy Jane[21] Eagle, Mary Ann[20] Wyatt, Noah Calvin[19], Thomas "Tommy"[18] Wiatt, Sr. (Wyatt, Wiett), John[17], Henry[16], Richard[15], George[14], Rev. Haute "Haut" "Hawte"[13], Sir George "Georgius" Thomas[12], Sir Thomas "The Younger"[11], Sir Thomas "The Elder"[10], Sir Henry[9], Richard Wiat or[8] Wyatt, Geoffrey "Jeoffrey" Wiot or[7] Wiat, Robert or Richard[6] Wiot, William Wiot or[5] Wyot, Adam Wiot or Wyote or[4], Guyott[3], Guyott[2], Captain or Admiral Adam Guyott or[1] Wiot) was born March 26, 1945. He married Rebecca Jan Barnard April 05, 1969, daughter of Quentine Barnard and Artie Anderson.

Child of John Hammill and Rebecca Barnard is:
1970   i.   John Allen[25] Hammill III, born June 03, 1972.

1343. Robert Clayton[24] Goodman (Emerson Clayton[23], Paul Talmadge[22], Nancy Jane[21] Eagle, Mary Ann[20] Wyatt, Noah Calvin[19], Thomas "Tommy"[18] Wiatt, Sr. (Wyatt, Wiett), John[17], Henry[16], Richard[15], George[14], Rev. Haute "Haut" "Hawte"[13], Sir George "Georgius" Thomas[12], Sir Thomas "The Younger"[11], Sir Thomas "The Elder"[10], Sir Henry[9], Richard Wiat or[8] Wyatt, Geoffrey "Jeoffrey" Wiot or[7] Wiat, Robert or Richard[6] Wiot, William Wiot or[5] Wyot, Adam Wiot or Wyote or[4], Guyott[3], Guyott[2], Captain or Admiral Adam Guyott or[1] Wiot) was born August 20, 1952. He married Vinetta Farmer August 20, 1972, daughter of Hubert Farmer and Bernice Richeson.

Children of Robert Goodman and Vinetta Farmer are:
1971   i.   Robert Christopher[25] Goodman, born April 29, 1973.
1972   ii.   Teresa Ann Goodman, born August 10, 1976.

1344.   Michael Douglas[24] Goodman (Paul Talmadge[23], Paul Talmadge[22], Nancy Jane[21] Eagle, Mary Ann[20] Wyatt, Noah Calvin[19], Thomas "Tommy"[18] Wiatt, Sr. (Wyatt, Wiett), John[17], Henry[16], Richard[15], George[14], Rev. Haute "Haut" "Hawte"[13], Sir George "Georgius" Thomas[12], Sir Thomas "The Younger"[11], Sir Thomas "The Elder"[10], Sir Henry[9], Richard Wiat or[8] Wyatt, Geoffrey "Jeoffrey" Wiot or[7] Wiat, Robert or Richard[6] Wiot, William Wiot or[5] Wyot, Adam Wiot or Wyote or[4], Guyott[3], Guyott[2], Captain or Admiral Adam Guyott or[1] Wiot) was born December 23, 1948. He married Janet Carol Burdashaw October 07, 1971, daughter of Charles Burdashaw and Mary Parker.

Children of Michael Goodman and Janet Burdashaw are:
1973   i.   Allyson Marie[25] Goodman, born July 29, 1973.
1974   ii.   Michael Russ Goodman, born August 11, 1975.
1975   iii.   Parker Douglas Goodman, born 1982.

1345.   Paulette Elisbeth[24] Goodman (Paul Talmadge[23], Paul Talmadge[22], Nancy Jane[21] Eagle, Mary Ann[20] Wyatt, Noah Calvin[19], Thomas "Tommy"[18] Wiatt, Sr. (Wyatt, Wiett), John[17], Henry[16], Richard[15], George[14], Rev. Haute "Haut" "Hawte"[13], Sir George "Georgius" Thomas[12], Sir Thomas "The Younger"[11], Sir Thomas "The Elder"[10], Sir Henry[9], Richard Wiat or[8] Wyatt, Geoffrey "Jeoffrey" Wiot or[7] Wiat, Robert or Richard[6] Wiot, William Wiot or[5] Wyot, Adam Wiot or Wyote or[4], Guyott[3], Guyott[2], Captain or Admiral Adam Guyott or[1] Wiot) was born January 25, 1950. She married Robert P. O'Brien August 21, 1976, son of Edward O'Brien and Ruth Nelson.

Children of Paulette Goodman and Robert O'Brien are:
1976   i.   Travis Jason[25] O'Brien, born June 25, 1978.
1977   ii.   Margaret Ruth O'Brien, born 1980.

1348.   Kinsey Lea[24] Phillips (Geneva Lee[23] Goodman, Paul Talmadge[22], Nancy Jane[21] Eagle, Mary Ann[20] Wyatt, Noah Calvin[19], Thomas "Tommy"[18] Wiatt, Sr. (Wyatt, Wiett), John[17], Henry[16], Richard[15], George[14], Rev. Haute "Haut" "Hawte"[13], Sir George "Georgius" Thomas[12], Sir Thomas "The Younger"[11], Sir Thomas "The Elder"[10], Sir Henry[9], Richard Wiat or[8] Wyatt, Geoffrey "Jeoffrey" Wiot or[7] Wiat, Robert or Richard[6] Wiot, William Wiot or[5] Wyot, Adam Wiot or Wyote or[4], Guyott[3], Guyott[2], Captain or Admiral Adam Guyott or[1] Wiot) was born March 22, 1954. She married Joyce Elaine Myers August 10, 1974, son of Robert Myers and Betty Archild.

Children of Kinsey Phillips and Joyce Myers are:

1978 i. Robert Jason[25] Myers, born February 05, 1978.

1979 ii. Eric Kinsey Myers, born 1979.

1980 iii. Nathan Christopher Myers, born November 06, 1980.

1351. Ronald Alan[24] Carpenter (Mabel Arey[23] Goodman, Paul Talmadge[22], Nancy Jane[21] Eagle, Mary Ann[20] Wyatt, Noah Calvin[19], Thomas "Tommy"[18] Wiatt, Sr. (Wyatt, Wiett), John[17], Henry[16], Richard[15], George[14], Rev. Haute "Haut" "Hawte"[13], Sir George "Georgius" Thomas[12], Sir Thomas "The Younger"[11], Sir Thomas "The Elder"[10], Sir Henry[9], Richard Wiat or[8] Wyatt, Geoffrey "Jeoffrey" Wiot or[7] Wiat, Robert or Richard[6] Wiot, William Wiot or[5] Wyot, Adam Wiot or Wyote or[4], Guyott[3], Guyott[2], Captain or Admiral Adam Guyott or[1] Wiot) was born February 25, 1954. He married Phillis Susanne Grayson June 29, 1980, daughter of Howard Grayson and Betty Gettys.

Child of Ronald Carpenter and Phillis Grayson is:

1981 i. Ronda Ellen[25] Carpenter, born 1984.

1353. Larry Charles[24] Carpenter (Mabel Arey[23] Goodman, Paul Talmadge[22], Nancy Jane[21] Eagle, Mary Ann[20] Wyatt, Noah Calvin[19], Thomas "Tommy"[18] Wiatt, Sr. (Wyatt, Wiett), John[17], Henry[16], Richard[15], George[14], Rev. Haute "Haut" "Hawte"[13], Sir George "Georgius" Thomas[12], Sir Thomas "The Younger"[11], Sir Thomas "The Elder"[10], Sir Henry[9], Richard Wiat or[8] Wyatt, Geoffrey "Jeoffrey" Wiot or[7] Wiat, Robert or Richard[6] Wiot, William Wiot or[5] Wyot, Adam Wiot or Wyote or[4], Guyott[3], Guyott[2], Captain or Admiral Adam Guyott or[1] Wiot) was born April 04, 1958. He married Dena Mitchem Hicks April 08, 1979, daughter of Frank Hicks and Adene Mitchem.

Child of Larry Carpenter and Dena Hicks is:

1982 i. Justin Lee[25] Carpenter, born 1983.

1357. Leah Jane[24] Hahn (Glenna Rachel[23] Goodman, Paul Talmadge[22], Nancy Jane[21] Eagle, Mary Ann[20] Wyatt, Noah Calvin[19], Thomas "Tommy"[18] Wiatt, Sr. (Wyatt, Wiett), John[17], Henry[16], Richard[15], George[14], Rev. Haute "Haut" "Hawte"[13], Sir George "Georgius" Thomas[12], Sir Thomas "The Younger"[11], Sir Thomas "The Elder"[10], Sir Henry[9], Richard Wiat or[8] Wyatt, Geoffrey "Jeoffrey" Wiot or[7] Wiat, Robert or Richard[6] Wiot, William Wiot or[5] Wyot, Adam Wiot or Wyote or[4], Guyott[3], Guyott[2], Captain or Admiral Adam Guyott or[1] Wiot) was born February 21, 1949. She married (1) Steven Ray Propst August 09, 1970, son of Ray Propst and Shirley Reynolds. She married (2) William J. Houch June 1978.

Child of Leah Hahn and Steven Propst is:

1983 i. Matthew Steven[25] Propst, born November 11, 1974.

1358. Rodger Burk[24] Hahn (Glenna Rachel[23] Goodman, Paul Talmadge[22], Nancy Jane[21] Eagle, Mary Ann[20] Wyatt, Noah Calvin[19], Thomas "Tommy"[18] Wiatt, Sr. (Wyatt, Wiett), John[17], Henry[16], Richard[15], George[14], Rev. Haute "Haut" "Hawte"[13], Sir George "Georgius"

Thomas[12], Sir Thomas "The Younger"[11], Sir Thomas "The Elder"[10], Sir Henry[9], Richard Wiat or[8] Wyatt, Geoffrey "Jeoffrey" Wiot or[7] Wiat, Robert or Richard[6] Wiot, William Wiot or[5] Wyot, Adam Wiot or Wyote or[4], Guyott[3], Guyott[2], Captain or Admiral Adam Guyott or[1] Wiot) was born May 11, 1953. He married Tresa Jan Atwood March 08, 1975, daughter of Calvin Atwood and Hegrow.

Children of Rodger Hahn and Tresa Atwood are:

1984	i.	Jason Daniel[25] Hahn, born October 10, 1975.
1985	ii.	Eric Noelle Hahn, born December 22, 1978.

1361. Tommie Leland[24] Wood (Carrie Mae[23] Goodman, Leland Quincy[22], Nancy Jane[21] Eagle, Mary Ann[20] Wyatt, Noah Calvin[19], Thomas "Tommy"[18] Wiatt, Sr. (Wyatt, Wiett), John[17], Henry[16], Richard[15], George[14], Rev. Haute "Haut" "Hawte"[13], Sir George "Georgius" Thomas[12], Sir Thomas "The Younger"[11], Sir Thomas "The Elder"[10], Sir Henry[9], Richard Wiat or[8] Wyatt, Geoffrey "Jeoffrey" Wiot or[7] Wiat, Robert or Richard[6] Wiot, William Wiot or[5] Wyot, Adam Wiot or Wyote or[4], Guyott[3], Guyott[2], Captain or Admiral Adam Guyott or[1] Wiot) was born August 07, 1945. He married Mildred Sue McCanless February 05, 1973, daughter of Ross McCanless and Mildred Lentz.

Children of Tommie Wood and Mildred McCanless are:

1986	i.	Tommie LeLand[25] Wood, Jr., born October 08, 1971 in Mecklenburg County, N.C.
1987	ii.	Todd Lentz Wood, born July 14, 1976 in Mecklenburg County, N.C.

1363. Yonnie Kay[24] Wood (Carrie Mae[23] Goodman, Leland Quincy[22], Nancy Jane[21] Eagle, Mary Ann[20] Wyatt, Noah Calvin[19], Thomas "Tommy"[18] Wiatt, Sr. (Wyatt, Wiett), John[17], Henry[16], Richard[15], George[14], Rev. Haute "Haut" "Hawte"[13], Sir George "Georgius" Thomas[12], Sir Thomas "The Younger"[11], Sir Thomas "The Elder"[10], Sir Henry[9], Richard Wiat or[8] Wyatt, Geoffrey "Jeoffrey" Wiot or[7] Wiat, Robert or Richard[6] Wiot, William Wiot or[5] Wyot, Adam Wiot or Wyote or[4], Guyott[3], Guyott[2], Captain or Admiral Adam Guyott or[1] Wiot) was born September 26, 1954. She married David Collier Holland October 06, 1973, son of Thurston Holland and Emily Presley.

Children of Yonnie Wood and David Holland are:

1988	i.	Jessie Ryan[25] Holland, born 1979.
1989	ii.	Carrie Beth Holland, born June 12, 1979.

1365. Sherry Ann[24] Robinson (Annie Katherine[23] Goodman, Leland Quincy[22], Nancy Jane[21] Eagle, Mary Ann[20] Wyatt, Noah Calvin[19], Thomas "Tommy"[18] Wiatt Sr. (Wyatt, Wiett), John[17], Henry[16], Richard[15], George[14], Rev. Haute "Haut" "Hawte"[13], Sir George "Georgius" Thomas[12], Sir Thomas "The Younger"[11], Sir Thomas "The Elder"[10], Sir Henry[9], Richard Wiat or[8] Wyatt, Geoffrey "Jeoffrey" Wiot or[7] Wiat, Robert or Richard[6] Wiot, William Wiot or[5] Wyot, Adam Wiot or Wyote or[4], Guyott[3], Guyott[2], Captain or Admiral Adam Guyott or[1]

Wiot) was born December 19, 1952. She married Richard Dean White November 10, 1970, son of Robert White and Leslie Greene.

Children of Sherry Robinson and Richard White are:

1990   i.   Shannon Elisbeth[25] White, born February 05, 1971 in Watauga County, N.C.

1991   ii.   Travis Wesley White, born August 02, 1974 in Md.

1366. Kristi Lee[24] Robinson (Annie Katherine[23] Goodman, Leland Quincy[22], Nancy Jane[21] Eagle, Mary Ann[20] Wyatt, Noah Calvin[19], Thomas "Tommy"[18] Wiatt, Sr. (Wyatt, Wiett), John[17], Henry[16], Richard[15], George[14], Rev. Haute "Haut" "Hawte"[13], Sir George "Georgius" Thomas[12], Sir Thomas "The Younger"[11], Sir Thomas "The Elder"[10], Sir Henry[9], Richard Wiat or[8] Wyatt, Geoffrey "Jeoffrey" Wiot or[7] Wiat, Robert or Richard[6] Wiot, William Wiot or[5] Wyot, Adam Wiot or Wyote or[4], Guyott[3], Guyott[2], Captain or Admiral Adam Guyott or[1] Wiot) was born December 10, 1954. She married Robert Harvey Deal February 10, 1973, son of Marvin Deal and Jennie Bingham.

Children of Kristi Robinson and Robert Deal are:

1992   i.   Brady Allan[25] Deal, born September 10, 1973.

1993   ii.   Chad Nolan Deal, born January 18, 1975 in S.C.

1367. Tony Stephen[24] Goodman (Clyde "Bud" Weir[23], Leland Quincy[22], Nancy Jane[21] Eagle, Mary Ann[20] Wyatt, Noah Calvin[19], Thomas "Tommy"[18] Wiatt, Sr. (Wyatt, Wiett), John[17], Henry[16], Richard[15], George[14], Rev. Haute "Haut" "Hawte"[13], Sir George "Georgius" Thomas[12], Sir Thomas "The Younger"[11], Sir Thomas "The Elder"[10], Sir Henry[9], Richard Wiat or[8] Wyatt, Geoffrey "Jeoffrey" Wiot or[7] Wiat, Robert or Richard[6] Wiot, William Wiot or[5] Wyot, Adam Wiot or Wyote or[4], Guyott[3], Guyott[2], Captain or Admiral Adam Guyott or[1] Wiot) was born February 22, 1951 in Stanly County, N.C. He married Joan Coggins November 23, 1968, daughter of James Coggins and Betty Tysinger.

Children of Tony Goodman and Joan Coggins are:

1994   i.   Stephen Scott[25] Goodman, born June 14, 1969.

1995   ii.   Amy Elizabeth Goodman, born February 10, 1972.

1369. Timothy Noel[24] Goodman (Clyde "Bud" Weir[23], Leland Quincy[22], Nancy Jane[21] Eagle, Mary Ann[20] Wyatt, Noah Calvin[19], Thomas "Tommy"[18] Wiatt, Sr. (Wyatt, Wiett), John[17], Henry[16], Richard[15], George[14], Rev. Haute "Haut" "Hawte"[13], Sir George "Georgius" Thomas[12], Sir Thomas "The Younger"[11], Sir Thomas "The Elder"[10], Sir Henry[9], Richard Wiat or[8] Wyatt, Geoffrey "Jeoffrey" Wiot or[7] Wiat, Robert or Richard[6] Wiot, William Wiot or[5] Wyot, Adam Wiot or Wyote or[4], Guyott[3], Guyott[2], Captain or Admiral Adam Guyott or[1] Wiot) was born September 15, 1959 in Stanly County, N.C. He married Cynthia Ellen Edwards May 28, 1978, daughter of Joe Edwards and Rachel Forrest.

Children of Timothy Goodman and Cynthia Edwards are:

1996   i.   Adam Quincy[25] Goodman, born December 08, 1983.

1997   ii.   Jodi Megan Goodman, born May 08, 1986.

1374. John David[24] Isenburg (Stella Mae[23] Morgan, Nannie Jane[22] Goodman, Nancy Jane[21] Eagle, Mary Ann[20] Wyatt, Noah Calvin[19], Thomas "Tommy"[18] Wiatt, Sr. (Wyatt, Wiett), John[17], Henry[16], Richard[15], George[14], Rev. Haute "Haut" "Hawte"[13], Sir George "Georgius" Thomas[12], Sir Thomas "The Younger"[11], Sir Thomas "The Elder"[10], Sir Henry[9], Richard Wiat or[8] Wyatt, Geoffrey "Jeoffrey" Wiot or[7] Wiat, Robert or Richard[6] Wiot, William Wiot or[5] Wyot, Adam Wiot or Wyote or[4], Guyott[3], Guyott[2], Captain or Admiral Adam Guyott or[1] Wiot) was born August 29, 1944. He married Dawn Carpenter February 22, 1970, daughter of Elmo Carpenter and Katie Norwood.

Children of John Isenburg and Dawn Carpenter are:

1998   i.   Amy Virginia[25] Isenburg, born April 19, 1971.

1999   ii.   Jill Elisabeth Isenburg, born August 29, 1973.

2000   iii.   David Alexander Isenburg, born July 15, 1977.

2001   iv.   Erin Rebekah Isenburg, born 1981.

1376. Timothy Douglas[24] Isenburg (Stella Mae[23] Morgan, Nannie Jane[22] Goodman, Nancy Jane[21] Eagle, Mary Ann[20] Wyatt, Noah Calvin[19], Thomas "Tommy"[18] Wiatt, Sr. (Wyatt, Wiett), John[17], Henry[16], Richard[15], George[14], Rev. Haute "Haut" "Hawte"[13], Sir George "Georgius" Thomas[12], Sir Thomas "The Younger"[11], Sir Thomas "The Elder"[10], Sir Henry[9], Richard Wiat or[8] Wyatt, Geoffrey "Jeoffrey" Wiot or[7] Wiat, Robert or Richard[6] Wiot, William Wiot or[5] Wyot, Adam Wiot or Wyote or[4], Guyott[3], Guyott[2], Captain or Admiral Adam Guyott or[1] Wiot) was born February 14, 1947. He married Carol Teal June 14, 1969, daughter of Robert Teal and Marjorie Rice.

Children of Timothy Isenburg and Carol Teal are:

2002   i.   Jennifer Brooke[25] Isenburg, born November 21, 1969.

2003   ii.   Amanda Morgan Isenburg, born August 05, 1975.

2004   iii.   Douglas Rice Isenburg, born September 24, 1981.

1377. Paul Galen[24] Isenburg (Stella Mae[23] Morgan, Nannie Jane[22] Goodman, Nancy Jane[21] Eagle, Mary Ann[20] Wyatt, Noah Calvin[19], Thomas "Tommy"[18] Wiatt, Sr. (Wyatt, Wiett), John[17], Henry[16], Richard[15], George[14], Rev. Haute "Haut" "Hawte"[13], Sir George "Georgius" Thomas[12], Sir Thomas "The Younger"[11], Sir Thomas "The Elder"[10], Sir Henry[9], Richard Wiat or[8] Wyatt, Geoffrey "Jeoffrey" Wiot or[7] Wiat, Robert or Richard[6] Wiot, William Wiot or[5] Wyot, Adam Wiot or Wyote or[4], Guyott[3], Guyott[2], Captain or Admiral Adam Guyott or[1] Wiot) was born November 18, 1952. He married Barbara Haden April 06, 1977, daughter of James Haden and Barbara Hoffman.

Child of Paul Isenburg and Barbara Haden is:

2005   i.   Grayson Paul[25] Isenburg, born May 31, 1981.

1378. Judy Ann[24] Ludwig (Rena Margaret[23] Morgan, Nannie Jane[22] Goodman, Nancy Jane[21] Eagle, Mary Ann[20] Wyatt, Noah Calvin[19], Thomas "Tommy"[18] Wiatt, Sr. (Wyatt, Wiett), John[17], Henry[16], Richard[15], George[14], Rev. Haute "Haut" "Hawte"[13], Sir George "Georgius" Thomas[12], Sir Thomas "The Younger"[11], Sir Thomas "The Elder"[10], Sir Henry[9], Richard Wiat or[8] Wyatt, Geoffrey "Jeoffrey" Wiot or[7] Wiat, Robert or Richard[6] Wiot, William Wiot or[5] Wyot, Adam Wiot or Wyote or[4], Guyott[3], Guyott[2], Captain or Admiral Adam Guyott or[1] Wiot) was born January 06, 1942. She married Weldon J. Hawkins June 24, 1961, son of Charlie Hawkins and Maggie Jan.

Children of Judy Ludwig and Weldon Hawkins are:

+   2006   i.   William Jack[25] Hawkins, born October 02, 1960 in Germany.

      2007   ii.   Deborah Ann Hawkins, born February 02, 1964 in Cumberland County, N.C.

      2008 iii.   Jeffery Hawkins, born December 1965 in Cumberland County, N.C.

1379. James Stanley[24] Ludwig (Rena Margaret[23] Morgan, Nannie Jane[22] Goodman, Nancy Jane[21] Eagle, Mary Ann[20] Wyatt, Noah Calvin[19], Thomas "Tommy"[18] Wiatt, Sr. (Wyatt, Wiett), John[17], Henry[16], Richard[15], George[14], Rev. Haute "Haut" "Hawte"[13], Sir George "Georgius" Thomas[12], Sir Thomas "The Younger"[11], Sir Thomas "The Elder"[10], Sir Henry[9], Richard Wiat or[8] Wyatt, Geoffrey "Jeoffrey" Wiot or[7] Wiat, Robert or Richard[6] Wiot, William Wiot or[5] Wyot, Adam Wiot or Wyote or[4], Guyott[3], Guyott[2], Captain or Admiral Adam Guyott or[1] Wiot) was born August 16, 1944. He married Ann Marie Ratcliff September 24, 1971, daughter of John Ratcliff and Mary Murphy.

Children of James Ludwig and Ann Ratcliff are:

2009   i.   Jeremy John[25] Ludwig, born March 28, 1975 in Wash.

2010   ii.   Eagan James Ludwig, born March 01, 1977 in Wash.

2011 iii.   Heather Anne Ludwig, born December 02, 1978 in Wash.

1380. John Franklin[24] Ludwig (Rena Margaret[23] Morgan, Nannie Jane[22] Goodman, Nancy Jane[21] Eagle, Mary Ann[20] Wyatt, Noah Calvin[19], Thomas "Tommy"[18] Wiatt, Sr. (Wyatt, Wiett), John[17], Henry[16], Richard[15], George[14], Rev. Haute "Haut" "Hawte"[13], Sir George "Georgius" Thomas[12], Sir Thomas "The Younger"[11], Sir Thomas "The Elder"[10], Sir Henry[9], Richard Wiat or[8] Wyatt, Geoffrey "Jeoffrey" Wiot or[7] Wiat, Robert or Richard[6] Wiot, William Wiot or[5] Wyot, Adam Wiot or Wyote or[4], Guyott[3], Guyott[2], Captain or Admiral Adam Guyott or[1] Wiot) was born September 11, 1946 in Va. He married Jean Faye Rickman April 09, 1970, daughter of Noah Rickman and Beulah.

Children of John Ludwig and Jean Rickman are:

2012 i. Lynn William[25] Ludwig, born 1974 in Cumberland County, N.C.

2013 ii. Robert Lee Ludwig, born 1978 in Cumberland County, N.C.

1381. Susan Jeanette[24] Morgan (Leo Goodman[23], Nannie Jane[22] Goodman, Nancy Jane[21] Eagle, Mary Ann[20] Wyatt, Noah Calvin[19], Thomas "Tommy"[18] Wiatt, Sr. (Wyatt, Wiett), John[17], Henry[16], Richard[15], George[14], Rev. Haute "Haut" "Hawte"[13], Sir George "Georgius" Thomas[12], Sir Thomas "The Younger"[11], Sir Thomas "The Elder"[10], Sir Henry[9], Richard Wiat or[8] Wyatt, Geoffrey "Jeoffrey" Wiot or[7] Wiat, Robert or Richard[6] Wiot, William Wiot or[5] Wyot, Adam Wiot or Wyote or[4], Guyott[3], Guyott[2], Captain or Admiral Adam Guyott or[1] Wiot) was born August 30, 1952. She married Richard Eugene Moore August 02, 1975.

Child of Susan Morgan and Richard Moore is:

2014 i. Morgan[25] Moore, born June 12, 1979.

1382. Mark Sidney[24] Morgan (Leo Goodman[23], Nannie Jane[22] Goodman, Nancy Jane[21] Eagle, Mary Ann[20] Wyatt, Noah Calvin[19], Thomas "Tommy"[18] Wiatt, Sr. (Wyatt, Wiett), John[17], Henry[16], Richard[15], George[14], Rev. Haute "Haut" "Hawte"[13], Sir George "Georgius" Thomas[12], Sir Thomas "The Younger"[11], Sir Thomas "The Elder"[10], Sir Henry[9], Richard Wiat or[8] Wyatt, Geoffrey "Jeoffrey" Wiot or[7] Wiat, Robert or Richard[6] Wiot, William Wiot or[5] Wyot, Adam Wiot or Wyote or[4], Guyott[3], Guyott[2], Captain or Admiral Adam Guyott or[1] Wiot) was born March 29, 1957. He married Sandy Rae Sink August 22, 1970, daughter of Raymond Sink and Clodfelter.

Children of Mark Morgan and Sandy Sink are:

2015 i. Jacob[25] Morgan, born May 10, 1979.

2016 ii. Anna Katherine Morgan, born December 30, 1980.

1383. Benjamin Hudson[24] Bridges III (Kathleen Louise[23] Morgan, Nannie Jane[22] Goodman, Nancy Jane[21] Eagle, Mary Ann[20] Wyatt, Noah Calvin[19], Thomas "Tommy"[18] Wiatt, Sr. (Wyatt, Wiett), John[17], Henry[16], Richard[15], George[14], Rev. Haute "Haut" "Hawte"[13], Sir George "Georgius" Thomas[12], Sir Thomas "The Younger"[11], Sir Thomas "The Elder"[10], Sir Henry[9], Richard Wiat or[8] Wyatt, Geoffrey "Jeoffrey" Wiot or[7] Wiat, Robert or Richard[6] Wiot, William Wiot or[5] Wyot, Adam Wiot or Wyote or[4], Guyott[3], Guyott[2], Captain or Admiral Adam Guyott or[1] Wiot) was born December 10, 1947. He married Elinor Brook Reynolds January 18, 1970, daughter of Paul Reynolds and Elinor Beckett.

Children of Benjamin Bridges and Elinor Reynolds are:

2017 i. Brooke Beckette[25] Bridges, born December 13, 1973.

2018 ii. Sarah Chancellor Wroe Bridges, born July 13, 1976.

1384. William Douglas[24] Bridges (Kathleen Louise[23] Morgan, Nannie Jane[22] Goodman, Nancy Jane[21] Eagle, Mary Ann[20] Wyatt, Noah Calvin[19], Thomas "Tommy"[18] Wiatt, Sr. (Wyatt, Wiett), John[17], Henry[16], Richard[15], George[14], Rev. Haute "Haut" "Hawte"[13], Sir George "Georgius" Thomas[12], Sir Thomas "The Younger"[11], Sir Thomas "The Elder"[10], Sir Henry[9], Richard Wiat or[8] Wyatt, Geoffrey "Jeoffrey" Wiot or[7] Wiat, Robert or Richard[6] Wiot, William Wiot or[5] Wyot, Adam Wiot or Wyote or[4], Guyott[3], Guyott[2], Captain or Admiral Adam Guyott or[1] Wiot) was born 1949. He married Barbara Anne Plonk June 11, 1971, daughter of George Plonk and Margaret Cooper.

> Children of William Bridges and Barbara Plonk are:
>
> 2019   i.   William Douglas[25] Bridges, Jr., born January 25, 1975 in Gaston County, N.C.
>
> 2020   ii.   Sidney Sloan Bridges, born February 14, 1977 in Gaston County, N.C.
>
> 2021   iii.   Wesley Hudson Bridges, born 1979 in Gaston County, N.C.

1387. Janie Elisbeth[24] Sowers (Lois Helen[23] Morgan, Nannie Jane[22] Goodman, Nancy Jane[21] Eagle, Mary Ann[20] Wyatt, Noah Calvin[19], Thomas "Tommy"[18] Wiatt, Sr. (Wyatt, Wiett), John[17], Henry[16], Richard[15], George[14], Rev. Haute "Haut" "Hawte"[13], Sir George "Georgius" Thomas[12], Sir Thomas "The Younger"[11], Sir Thomas "The Elder"[10], Sir Henry[9], Richard Wiat or[8] Wyatt, Geoffrey "Jeoffrey" Wiot or[7] Wiat, Robert or Richard[6] Wiot, William Wiot or[5] Wyot, Adam Wiot or Wyote or[4], Guyott[3], Guyott[2], Captain or Admiral Adam Guyott or[1] Wiot) was born October 21, 1961 in Davidson County, N.C. She married Kenny Keiker.

> Child of Janie Sowers and Kenny Keiker is:
>
> 2022   i.   Kelly Elizabeth[25] Keiker, born February 03, 1981.

1388. Joseph Arthur[24] Watson (Jane Virginia[23] Morgan, Nannie Jane[22] Goodman, Nancy Jane[21] Eagle, Mary Ann[20] Wyatt, Noah Calvin[19], Thomas "Tommy"[18] Wiatt, Sr. (Wyatt, Wiett), John[17], Henry[16], Richard[15], George[14], Rev. Haute "Haut" "Hawte"[13], Sir George "Georgius" Thomas[12], Sir Thomas "The Younger"[11], Sir Thomas "The Elder"[10], Sir Henry[9], Richard Wiat or[8] Wyatt, Geoffrey "Jeoffrey" Wiot or[7] Wiat, Robert or Richard[6] Wiot, William Wiot or[5] Wyot, Adam Wiot or Wyote or[4], Guyott[3], Guyott[2], Captain or Admiral Adam Guyott or[1] Wiot) was born June 24, 1961 in Salisbury, N.C. He married Elizabeth Wetmore June 03, 1984 in Woodleaf, Rowan County, N.C.

More About Joseph Arthur Watson:

> Children of Joseph Watson and Elizabeth Wetmore are:
>
> 2023   i.   Laura Elizabeth[25] Watson, born March 16, 1991 in Salisbury, N.C.
>
> 2024   ii.   Jacob Donald Watson, born February 25, 1995 in Salisbury, N.C.

1389. Janice Rebecca[24] Watson (Jane Virginia[23] Morgan, Nannie Jane[22] Goodman, Nancy Jane[21] Eagle, Mary Ann[20] Wyatt, Noah Calvin[19], Thomas "Tommy"[18] Wiatt, Sr. (Wyatt, Wiett), John[17], Henry[16], Richard[15], George[14], Rev. Haute "Haut" "Hawte"[13], Sir George "Georgius" Thomas[12], Sir Thomas "The Younger"[11], Sir Thomas "The Elder"[10], Sir Henry[9], Richard Wiat or[8] Wyatt, Geoffrey "Jeoffrey" Wiot or[7] Wiat, Robert or Richard[6] Wiot, William Wiot or[5] Wyot, Adam Wiot or Wyote or[4], Guyott[3], Guyott[2], Captain or Admiral Adam Guyott or[1] Wiot) was born April 25, 1963 in Salisbury, N.C. She married (1) Max Elbert Menius April 25, 1987 in Woodleaf, Rowan County, N.C., son of Max Menius and Sue Hart. She married (2) Philip Stafford December 1994 in Rowan County, N.C., son of Robert Stafford and Jean.

> Children of Janice Watson and Philip Stafford are:
>
> 2025   i.   Morgan Elizabeth[25] Stafford, born July 08, 1996.
>
> 2026   ii. Robert Watson Stafford, born May 19, 1997.

1390. Miriam Estelle[24] Watson (Jane Virginia[23] Morgan, Nannie Jane[22] Goodman, Nancy Jane[21] Eagle, Mary Ann[20] Wyatt, Noah Calvin[19], Thomas "Tommy"[18] Wiatt, Sr. (Wyatt, Wiett), John[17], Henry[16], Richard[15], George[14], Rev. Haute "Haut" "Hawte"[13], Sir George "Georgius" Thomas[12], Sir Thomas "The Younger"[11], Sir Thomas "The Elder"[10], Sir Henry[9], Richard Wiat or[8] Wyatt, Geoffrey "Jeoffrey" Wiot or[7] Wiat, Robert or Richard[6] Wiot, William Wiot or[5] Wyot, Adam Wiot or Wyote or[4], Guyott[3], Guyott[2], Captain or Admiral Adam Guyott or[1] Wiot) was born June 24, 1965 in Salisbury, N.C. She married Richard Crandall Lindrooth July 05, 1997 in Woodleaf, Rowan County, N.C., son of Richard Lindwooth and Beverly Crandall.

> Children of Miriam Watson and Richard Lindrooth are:
>
> 2027   i.   Estelle "Ellie" Jane[25] Lindrooth, born July 29, 1999 in Chicago, Ill.
>
> 2028   ii. Anna Morgan Lindrooth, born October 17, 2001 in Chicago, Ill.

1398. Robert Lee[24] Goodman (Leo Francis[23], Bennett Francis[22], Nancy Jane[21] Eagle, Mary Ann[20] Wyatt, Noah Calvin[19], Thomas "Tommy"[18] Wiatt, Sr. (Wyatt, Wiett), John[17], Henry[16], Richard[15], George[14], Rev. Haute "Haut" "Hawte"[13], Sir George "Georgius" Thomas[12], Sir Thomas "The Younger"[11], Sir Thomas "The Elder"[10], Sir Henry[9], Richard Wiat or[8] Wyatt, Geoffrey "Jeoffrey" Wiot or[7] Wiat, Robert or Richard[6] Wiot, William Wiot or[5] Wyot, Adam Wiot or Wyote or[4], Guyott[3], Guyott[2], Captain or Admiral Adam Guyott or[1] Wiot) was born March 12, 1941 in Rowan County, N.C. He married Judy Ann Everhart May 30, 1965, daughter of Farris Everhart and HIlda Grubb.

> Children of Robert Goodman and Judy Everhart are:
>
> 2029   i.   Samuel Bennett[25] Goodman, born December 27, 1967.
>
> 2030   ii.   Ginger Dare Goodman, born January 25, 1969.
>
> 2031   iii. Mary Lutricia Goodman, born June 07, 1971.

1399. Jane Eleanor[24] Goodman (Leo Francis[23], Bennett Francis[22], Nancy Jane[21] Eagle, Mary Ann[20] Wyatt, Noah Calvin[19], Thomas "Tommy"[18] Wiatt, Sr. (Wyatt, Wiett), John[17], Henry[16], Richard[15], George[14], Rev. Haute "Haut" "Hawte"[13], Sir George "Georgius" Thomas[12], Sir Thomas "The Younger"[11], Sir Thomas "The Elder"[10], Sir Henry[9], Richard Wiat or[8] Wyatt, Geoffrey "Jeoffrey" Wiot or[7] Wiat, Robert or Richard[6] Wiot, William Wiot or[5] Wyot, Adam Wiot or Wyote or[4], Guyott[3], Guyott[2], Captain or Admiral Adam Guyott or[1] Wiot) was born January 19, 1943 in Rowan County, N.C. She married Jacob Marion Boggs, son of Harvey Boggs and Mary Anna.

Children of Jane Goodman and Jacob Boggs are:
+   2032   i.   Tamara Letitia[25] Boggs, born October 24, 1962.
+   2033   ii.   Derek Anthony Boggs, born December 09, 1964.
     2034   iii.   Amanda Kristina Boggs, born May 10, 1970.

1400. Martha (Mary) Jo[24] Goodman (Leo Francis[23], Bennett Francis[22], Nancy Jane[21] Eagle, Mary Ann[20] Wyatt, Noah Calvin[19], Thomas "Tommy"[18] Wiatt, Sr. (Wyatt, Wiett), John[17], Henry[16], Richard[15], George[14], Rev. Haute "Haut" "Hawte"[13], Sir George "Georgius" Thomas[12], Sir Thomas "The Younger"[11], Sir Thomas "The Elder"[10], Sir Henry[9], Richard Wiat or[8] Wyatt, Geoffrey "Jeoffrey" Wiot or[7] Wiat, Robert or Richard[6] Wiot, William Wiot or[5] Wyot, Adam Wiot or Wyote or[4], Guyott[3], Guyott[2], Captain or Admiral Adam Guyott or[1] Wiot) was born May 03, 1948. She married Ricky Gene Kluttz.

Children of Martha Goodman and Ricky Kluttz are:
     2035   i.   Gary[25] Michael, born 1968.
     2036   ii.   Edward Anthony, born 1972.
     2037   iii.   Emily Suzanne, born May 31, 1981.

1401. Randall Gwen[24] Goodman (Leo Francis[23], Bennett Francis[22], Nancy Jane[21] Eagle, Mary Ann[20] Wyatt, Noah Calvin[19], Thomas "Tommy"[18] Wiatt, Sr. (Wyatt, Wiett), John[17], Henry[16], Richard[15], George[14], Rev. Haute "Haut" "Hawte"[13], Sir George "Georgius" Thomas[12], Sir Thomas "The Younger"[11], Sir Thomas "The Elder"[10], Sir Henry[9], Richard Wiat or[8] Wyatt, Geoffrey "Jeoffrey" Wiot or[7] Wiat, Robert or Richard[6] Wiot, William Wiot or[5] Wyot, Adam Wiot or Wyote or[4], Guyott[3], Guyott[2], Captain or Admiral Adam Guyott or[1] Wiot) was born September 22, 1954. He married Christine Sloop, daughter of Grady Sloop and Margaret Basinger.

Children of Randall Goodman and Christine Sloop are:
     2038   i.   David Michael[25] Goodman.
     2039   ii.   Matthew Goodman.

1402. Dorothy Mae[24] Phillips (Onnie Leven[23] Morgan, Josephine Erma[22] Shaver, Mary Malinda[21] Eagle, Mary Ann[20] Wyatt, Noah Calvin[19], Thomas "Tommy"[18] Wiatt, Sr. (Wyatt, Wiett), John[17], Henry[16], Richard[15], George[14], Rev. Haute "Haut" "Hawte"[13], Sir George "Georgius" Thomas[12], Sir Thomas "The Younger"[11], Sir Thomas "The Elder"[10], Sir Henry[9],

Richard Wiat or[8] Wyatt, Geoffrey "Jeoffrey" Wiot or[7] Wiat, Robert or Richard[6] Wiot, William Wiot or[5] Wyot, Adam Wiot or Wyote or[4], Guyott[3], Guyott[2], Captain or Admiral Adam Guyott or[1] Wiot). She married Jerry Stinson.

> Children of Dorothy Phillips and Jerry Stinson are:
> 2040   i.   Rondy Dawn[25] Stinson, born September 18, 1965.
> 2041   ii.   William Dewane Stinson, born June 05, 1968.
> 2042   iii.   Windy Michelle Stinson, born May 12, 1971.
> 2043   iv.   Brenda Denise Stinson, born August 09, 1977.

1403. Felix Eugene[24] Morgan (Stella Marie[23], Josephine Erma[22] Shaver, Mary Malinda[21] Eagle, Mary Ann[20] Wyatt, Noah Calvin[19], Thomas "Tommy"[18] Wiatt, Sr. (Wyatt, Wiett), John[17], Henry[16], Richard[15], George[14], Rev. Haute "Haut" "Hawte"[13], Sir George "Georgius" Thomas[12], Sir Thomas "The Younger"[11], Sir Thomas "The Elder"[10], Sir Henry[9], Richard Wiat or[8] Wyatt, Geoffrey "Jeoffrey" Wiot or[7] Wiat, Robert or Richard[6] Wiot, William Wiot or[5] Wyot, Adam Wiot or Wyote or[4], Guyott[3], Guyott[2], Captain or Admiral Adam Guyott or[1] Wiot) was born August 08, 1940. He married Hilda Ann Hoffner August 07, 1961, daughter of Johnny Mac Hoffner and Lottie Basinger.

> Children of Felix Morgan and Hilda Hoffner are:
> 2044   i.   Jennifer Ann[25] Morgan, born September 07, 1962.
> 2045   ii.   Crystal Dianne Morgan.
> 2046   iii.   Donnie Michelle Morgan, born September 15, 1964.

1406. Harold Craig[24] Mesimer (Lena Irene[23] Morgan, Josephine Erma[22] Shaver, Mary Malinda[21] Eagle, Mary Ann[20] Wyatt, Noah Calvin[19], Thomas "Tommy"[18] Wiatt, Sr. (Wyatt, Wiett), John[17], Henry[16], Richard[15], George[14], Rev. Haute "Haut" "Hawte"[13], Sir George "Georgius" Thomas[12], Sir Thomas "The Younger"[11], Sir Thomas "The Elder"[10], Sir Henry[9], Richard Wiat or[8] Wyatt, Geoffrey "Jeoffrey" Wiot or[7] Wiat, Robert or Richard[6] Wiot, William Wiot or[5] Wyot, Adam Wiot or Wyote or[4], Guyott[3], Guyott[2], Captain or Admiral Adam Guyott or[1] Wiot) was born April 13, 1944. He married Susan Huffman.

> Children of Harold Mesimer and Susan Huffman are:
> 2047   i.   Jonathan Craig[25] Mesimer, born December 18, 1975.
> 2048   ii.   Ryan Alexander Mesimer, born March 14, 1977.

1407. Billie Wayne[24] Mesimer (Lena Irene[23] Morgan, Josephine Erma[22] Shaver, Mary Malinda[21] Eagle, Mary Ann[20] Wyatt, Noah Calvin[19], Thomas "Tommy"[18] Wiatt, Sr. (Wyatt, Wiett), John[17], Henry[16], Richard[15], George[14], Rev. Haute "Haut" "Hawte"[13], Sir George "Georgius" Thomas[12], Sir Thomas "The Younger"[11], Sir Thomas "The Elder"[10], Sir Henry[9], Richard Wiat or[8] Wyatt, Geoffrey "Jeoffrey" Wiot or[7] Wiat, Robert or Richard[6] Wiot, William Wiot or[5] Wyot, Adam Wiot or Wyote or[4], Guyott[3], Guyott[2], Captain or Admiral Adam Guyott or[1] Wiot) was born August 07, 1951. He married Gloria Gibbins, daughter of Bill Gibbins and Unknown.

Child of Billie Mesimer and Gloria Gibbins is:

2049   i.   Jason Wayne[25] Mesimer, born March 11, 1977.

1408. Dennis Wayne[24] Misenheimer (Mary Elizabeth[23] Trexler, Beulah Ann[22] Eagle, William Grant[21], Mary Ann[20] Wyatt, Noah Calvin[19], Thomas "Tommy"[18] Wiatt, Sr. (Wyatt, Wiett), John[17], Henry[16], Richard[15], George[14], Rev. Haute "Haut" "Hawte"[13], Sir George "Georgius" Thomas[12], Sir Thomas "The Younger"[11], Sir Thomas "The Elder"[10], Sir Henry[9], Richard Wiat or[8] Wyatt, Geoffrey "Jeoffrey" Wiot or[7] Wiat, Robert or Richard[6] Wiot, William Wiot or[5] Wyot, Adam Wiot or Wyote or[4], Guyott[3], Guyott[2], Captain or Admiral Adam Guyott or[1] Wiot) was born August 02, 1946. He married Connie Gail Overby, daughter of Charles Overby and Clonnie Richardson.

Child of Dennis Misenheimer and Connie Overby is:

2050   i.   Roxie Shayne[25] Misenheimer, born February 17, 1987.

1409. Randy Allen[24] Misenheimer (Mary Elizabeth[23] Trexler, Beulah Ann[22] Eagle, William Grant[21], Mary Ann[20] Wyatt, Noah Calvin[19], Thomas "Tommy"[18] Wiatt, Sr. (Wyatt, Wiett), John[17], Henry[16], Richard[15], George[14], Rev. Haute "Haut" "Hawte"[13], Sir George "Georgius" Thomas[12], Sir Thomas "The Younger"[11], Sir Thomas "The Elder"[10], Sir Henry[9], Richard Wiat or[8] Wyatt, Geoffrey "Jeoffrey" Wiot or[7] Wiat, Robert or Richard[6] Wiot, William Wiot or[5] Wyot, Adam Wiot or Wyote or[4], Guyott[3], Guyott[2], Captain or Admiral Adam Guyott or[1] Wiot) was born May 02, 1951. He married Annette Prince July 02, 1972, daughter of Carl Prince and Edna Thomas.

Children of Randy Misenheimer and Annette Prince are:

2051   i.   Samatha Ann[25] Misenheimer, born September 05, 1974 in Rowan County, N.C.
2052   ii.   Sam Allen Misenheimer, born March 26, 1980 in Rowan County, N.C.

1410. Judith Elizabeth[24] Misenheimer (Mary Elizabeth[23] Trexler, Beulah Ann[22] Eagle, William Grant[21], Mary Ann[20] Wyatt, Noah Calvin[19], Thomas "Tommy"[18] Wiatt, Sr. (Wyatt, Wiett), John[17], Henry[16], Richard[15], George[14], Rev. Haute "Haut" "Hawte"[13], Sir George "Georgius" Thomas[12], Sir Thomas "The Younger"[11], Sir Thomas "The Elder"[10], Sir Henry[9], Richard Wiat or[8] Wyatt, Geoffrey "Jeoffrey" Wiot or[7] Wiat, Robert or Richard[6] Wiot, William Wiot or[5] Wyot, Adam Wiot or Wyote or[4], Guyott[3], Guyott[2], Captain or Admiral Adam Guyott or[1] Wiot) was born November 25, 1953. She married Fidel Clyde Goodnight May 20, 1979, son of Fidel Goodnight and Betty Everett.

Children of Judith Misenheimer and Fidel Goodnight are:

2053   i.   Karrie Elizabeth[25] Goodnight, born December 18, 1982.
2054   ii.   Kacie Marie Goodnight, born June 16, 1986.

1413. Cheryl Darlene[24] Trexler (George William[23], Beulah Ann[22] Eagle, William Grant[21], Mary Ann[20] Wyatt, Noah Calvin[19], Thomas "Tommy"[18] Wiatt, Sr. (Wyatt, Wiett), John[17], Henry[16], Richard[15], George[14], Rev. Haute "Haut" "Hawte"[13], Sir George "Georgius" Thomas[12], Sir Thomas "The Younger"[11], Sir Thomas "The Elder"[10], Sir Henry[9], Richard Wiat or[8] Wyatt, Geoffrey "Jeoffrey" Wiot or[7] Wiat, Robert or Richard[6] Wiot, William Wiot or[5] Wyot, Adam Wiot or Wyote or[4], Guyott[3], Guyott[2], Captain or Admiral Adam Guyott or[1] Wiot) was born July 11, 1949 in Rowan County, N.C. She married Randy Bost December 24, 1967, son of Herbert Bost and Pauline Bowls.

> Children of Cheryl Trexler and Randy Bost are:
>
> | 2055 | i. | David[25] Bost, born April 12, 1969. |
> | 2056 | ii. | Christopher Bost, born October 18, 1970. |
> | 2057 | iii. | Bryan Scott Bost, born January 18, 1979. |

1414. Betty Carol[24] Hill (Janet Inez[23] McHargue, Octa Mae[22] Eagle, William Grant[21], Mary Ann[20] Wyatt, Noah Calvin[19], Thomas "Tommy"[18] Wiatt, Sr. (Wyatt, Wiett), John[17], Henry[16], Richard[15], George[14], Rev. Haute "Haut" "Hawte"[13], Sir George "Georgius" Thomas[12], Sir Thomas "The Younger"[11], Sir Thomas "The Elder"[10], Sir Henry[9], Richard Wiat or[8] Wyatt, Geoffrey "Jeoffrey" Wiot or[7] Wiat, Robert or Richard[6] Wiot, William Wiot or[5] Wyot, Adam Wiot or Wyote or[4], Guyott[3], Guyott[2], Captain or Admiral Adam Guyott or[1] Wiot) was born February 26, 1942 in Rowan County, N.C. She married Joseph Wayne Osborne September 30, 1962, son of William Osborne and Opal Parson.

> More About Joseph Wayne Osborne:
> Fact 1: Served in the USAF, Vietnam.

> Children of Betty Hill and Joseph Osborne are:
>
> | + | 2058 | i. | Carla Waynette[25] Osborne, born October 17, 1963 in Md. |
> | | 2059 | ii. | Terry Scott Osborne. |

1415. Ronald Keith[24] Hill (Janet Inez[23] McHargue, Octa Mae[22] Eagle, William Grant[21], Mary Ann[20] Wyatt, Noah Calvin[19], Thomas "Tommy"[18] Wiatt, Sr. (Wyatt, Wiett), John[17], Henry[16], Richard[15], George[14], Rev. Haute "Haut" "Hawte"[13], Sir George "Georgius" Thomas[12], Sir Thomas "The Younger"[11], Sir Thomas "The Elder"[10], Sir Henry[9], Richard Wiat or[8] Wyatt, Geoffrey "Jeoffrey" Wiot or[7] Wiat, Robert or Richard[6] Wiot, William Wiot or[5] Wyot, Adam Wiot or Wyote or[4], Guyott[3], Guyott[2], Captain or Admiral Adam Guyott or[1] Wiot) was born November 17, 1943 in Stanly County, N.C. He married Yvonne Lucille Bost January 10, 1973, daughter of Julian Bost and Ruby Dorris.

> More About Ronald Keith Hill:
> Fact 1: Serves in the USN, Vietman.

Children of Ronald Hill and Yvonne Bost are:

2060   i.   Pamela Denice[25] Hill, born June 10, 1973 in Rowan County, N.C.

2061   ii.   Tricia Gail Hill, born February 16, 1977 in Rowan County, N.C.

1416.   James Stephen[24] Brown (Marjorie Ellen[23] McHargue, Octa Mae[22] Eagle, William Grant[21], Mary Ann[20] Wyatt, Noah Calvin[19], Thomas "Tommy"[18] Wiatt, Sr. (Wyatt, Wiett), John[17], Henry[16], Richard[15], George[14], Rev. Haute "Haut" "Hawte"[13], Sir George "Georgius" Thomas[12], Sir Thomas "The Younger"[11], Sir Thomas "The Elder"[10], Sir Henry[9], Richard Wiat or[8] Wyatt, Geoffrey "Jeoffrey" Wiot or[7] Wiat, Robert or Richard[6] Wiot, William Wiot or[5] Wyot, Adam Wiot or Wyote or[4], Guyott[3], Guyott[2], Captain or Admiral Adam Guyott or[1] Wiot) was born October 25, 1953 in Guilford County, N.C. He married Rachel Yvonne Flowers January 12, 1972, daughter of Harry Flowers and June Woodridge.

Children of James Brown and Rachel Flowers are:

2062   i.   Jason Scott[25] Brown, born June 11, 1974 in Guilford County, N.C.

2063   ii.   Stephanie Lynne Brown, born April 27, 1979 in Guilford County, N.C.

1423.   Lynda Jo[24] McHargue (Lucius Baxter[23], Octa Mae[22] Eagle, William Grant[21], Mary Ann[20] Wyatt, Noah Calvin[19], Thomas "Tommy"[18] Wiatt, Sr. (Wyatt, Wiett), John[17], Henry[16], Richard[15], George[14], Rev. Haute "Haut" "Hawte"[13], Sir George "Georgius" Thomas[12], Sir Thomas "The Younger"[11], Sir Thomas "The Elder"[10], Sir Henry[9], Richard Wiat or[8] Wyatt, Geoffrey "Jeoffrey" Wiot or[7] Wiat, Robert or Richard[6] Wiot, William Wiot or[5] Wyot, Adam Wiot or Wyote or[4], Guyott[3], Guyott[2], Captain or Admiral Adam Guyott or[1] Wiot) was born October 10, 1952 in Washtenau County, Ann Arbor, Mich. She married Michael Charles Bleyaert August 10, 1979, son of Kenneth Bleyaert and Betty Skidmore.

Children of Lynda McHargue and Michael Bleyaert are:

2064   i.   Amy Jo Lynn[25] Bleyaert, born May 23, 1983 in Monroe County, Mich.

2065   ii.   Lisa Michelle Bleyaert, born April 04, 1985 in Monroe County, Mich.

1426.   Victoria Mae[24] McHargue (Floyd Richard[23], Octa Mae[22] Eagle, William Grant[21], Mary Ann[20] Wyatt, Noah Calvin[19], Thomas "Tommy"[18] Wiatt, Sr. (Wyatt, Wiett), John[17], Henry[16], Richard[15], George[14], Rev. Haute "Haut" "Hawte"[13], Sir George "Georgius" Thomas[12], Sir Thomas "The Younger"[11], Sir Thomas "The Elder"[10], Sir Henry[9], Richard Wiat or[8] Wyatt, Geoffrey "Jeoffrey" Wiot or[7] Wiat, Robert or Richard[6] Wiot, William Wiot or[5] Wyot, Adam Wiot or Wyote or[4], Guyott[3], Guyott[2], Captain or Admiral Adam Guyott or[1] Wiot) was born March 17, 1956 in Oceanside, Ca. She married Gerald Edwin Sutherland February 14, 1976, son of John Sutherland and Vera Grove.

Children of Victoria McHargue and Gerald Sutherland are:

2066	i.	Christina Rae[25] Sutherland, born February 15, 1977.
2067	ii.	Susan Marie Sutherland, born June 12, 1978.
2068	iii.	Becky Ann Sutherland, born March 16, 1981.
2069	iv.	Kimberly Michelle Sutherland, born October 20, 1985 in Medford, Ore.

1431.   Hilton Michael[24] Ketchie (Margaret Lee[23] Myers, Norvie Lundy[22] Eagle, William Grant[21], Mary Ann[20] Wyatt, Noah Calvin[19], Thomas "Tommy"[18] Wiatt, Sr. (Wyatt, Wiett), John[17], Henry[16], Richard[15], George[14], Rev. Haute "Haut" "Hawte"[13], Sir George "Georgius" Thomas[12], Sir Thomas "The Younger"[11], Sir Thomas "The Elder"[10], Sir Henry[9], Richard Wiat or[8] Wyatt, Geoffrey "Jeoffrey" Wiot or[7] Wiat, Robert or Richard[6] Wiot, William Wiot or[5] Wyot, Adam Wiot or Wyote or[4], Guyott[3], Guyott[2], Captain or Admiral Adam Guyott or[1] Wiot) was born May 24, 1946 in Rowan County, N.C. He married Laura Janette McDaniel July 17, 1966, daughter of George McDaniel and Jo.

Children of Hilton Ketchie and Laura McDaniel are:

| 2070 | i. | Tom Michael[25] Ketchie, born May 12, 1967 in Rowan County, N.C. |
| 2071 | ii. | Camara Chasy Ketchie, born November 12, 1970 in Rowan County, N.C. |

1433.   Tonya Kay[24] Ketchie (Margaret Lee[23] Myers, Norvie Lundy[22] Eagle, William Grant[21], Mary Ann[20] Wyatt, Noah Calvin[19], Thomas "Tommy"[18] Wiatt, Sr. (Wyatt, Wiett), John[17], Henry[16], Richard[15], George[14], Rev. Haute "Haut" "Hawte"[13], Sir George "Georgius" Thomas[12], Sir Thomas "The Younger"[11], Sir Thomas "The Elder"[10], Sir Henry[9], Richard Wiat or[8] Wyatt, Geoffrey "Jeoffrey" Wiot or[7] Wiat, Robert or Richard[6] Wiot, William Wiot or[5] Wyot, Adam Wiot or Wyote or[4], Guyott[3], Guyott[2], Captain or Admiral Adam Guyott or[1] Wiot) was born March 07, 1958 in Rowan County, N.C. She married Lester Mark Wilhelm June 28, 1981, son of William Wilhelm and Mary White.

Child of Tonya Ketchie and Lester Wilhelm is:

| 2072 | i. | Ashley Jewel[25] Wilhelm, born October 06, 1983 in Rowan County, N.C. |

1434.   Sarita Joy[24] Myers (Harold William[23], Norvie Lundy[22] Eagle, William Grant[21], Mary Ann[20] Wyatt, Noah Calvin[19], Thomas "Tommy"[18] Wiatt, Sr. (Wyatt, Wiett), John[17], Henry[16], Richard[15], George[14], Rev. Haute "Haut" "Hawte"[13], Sir George "Georgius" Thomas[12], Sir Thomas "The Younger"[11], Sir Thomas "The Elder"[10], Sir Henry[9], Richard Wiat or[8] Wyatt, Geoffrey "Jeoffrey" Wiot or[7] Wiat, Robert or Richard[6] Wiot, William Wiot or[5] Wyot, Adam Wiot or Wyote or[4], Guyott[3], Guyott[2], Captain or Admiral Adam Guyott or[1] Wiot) was born June 22, 1952 in Rowan County, N.C. She married William Harold Mull February 05, 1971, son of James Mull and Esther Kimball.

Children of Sarita Myers and William Mull are:

2073   i.   Greyland Blaine[25] Mull, born August 17, 1971 in Rowan County, N.C.

2074   ii.   William Adam Mull, born May 11, 1980 in Rowan County, N.C.

1435. Melody Kim[24] Myers (Harold William[23], Norvie Lundy[22] Eagle, William Grant[21], Mary Ann[20] Wyatt, Noah Calvin[19], Thomas "Tommy"[18] Wiatt, Sr. (Wyatt, Wiett), John[17], Henry[16], Richard[15], George[14], Rev. Haute "Haut" "Hawte"[13], Sir George "Georgius" Thomas[12], Sir Thomas "The Younger"[11], Sir Thomas "The Elder"[10], Sir Henry[9], Richard Wiat or[8] Wyatt, Geoffrey "Jeoffrey" Wiot or[7] Wiat, Robert or Richard[6] Wiot, William Wiot or[5] Wyot, Adam Wiot or Wyote or[4], Guyott[3], Guyott[2], Captain or Admiral Adam Guyott or[1] Wiot) was born February 15, 1957 in Rowan County, N.C. She married Banks Rudolph Cline, Jr. February 03, 1979, son of Banks Cline and Ruby Miller.

Children of Melody Myers and Banks Cline are:

2075   i.   Rebekah Allison[25] Cline, born April 03, 1981 in Rowan County, N.C.

2076   ii.   Rachel Anna Cline, born February 14, 1984 in Rowan County, N.C.

1465. Annie Marie[24] Parker (Harvey Adophus[23], J. Columbus[22], Ollie Lou Ada[21] Shaver, Rhoda E.[20] Wyatt, Noah Calvin[19], Thomas "Tommy"[18] Wiatt, Sr. (Wyatt, Wiett), John[17], Henry[16], Richard[15], George[14], Rev. Haute "Haut" "Hawte"[13], Sir George "Georgius" Thomas[12], Sir Thomas "The Younger"[11], Sir Thomas "The Elder"[10], Sir Henry[9], Richard Wiat or[8] Wyatt, Geoffrey "Jeoffrey" Wiot or[7] Wiat, Robert or Richard[6] Wiot, William Wiot or[5] Wyot, Adam Wiot or Wyote or[4], Guyott[3], Guyott[2], Captain or Admiral Adam Guyott or[1] Wiot). She married Arthur Burns Cannon October 20, 1930.

Children of Annie Parker and Arthur Cannon are:

+   2077   i.   Darleen[25] Cannon.
+   2078   ii.   Leon Cannon.
    2079   iii.   Eugene Cannon. He married Betty Morris.
+   2080   iv.   Irvin Cannon.
    2081   v.   Ruth Cannon. She married Pope.
+   2082   vi.   Edna Cannon.
+   2083   vii.   Richard Cannon.
+   2084   viii. Glenn Cannon, born February 11, 1937; died June 17, 1984.
+   2085   ix.   Jay Cannon, born November 01, 1945; died April 26, 1987.
    2086   x.   Joyce Cannon, born November 19, 1949; died January 16, 1950.

1466. Rena Catherine[24] Parker (Harvey Adophus[23], J. Columbus[22], Ollie Lou Ada[21] Shaver, Rhoda E.[20] Wyatt, Noah Calvin[19], Thomas "Tommy"[18] Wiatt, Sr. (Wyatt, Wiett), John[17],

Henry[16], Richard[15], George[14], Rev. Haute "Haut" "Hawte"[13], Sir George "Georgius" Thomas[12], Sir Thomas "The Younger"[11], Sir Thomas "The Elder"[10], Sir Henry[9], Richard Wiat or[8] Wyatt, Geoffrey "Jeoffrey" Wiot or[7] Wiat, Robert or Richard[6] Wiot, William Wiot or[5] Wyot, Adam Wiot or Wyote or[4], Guyott[3], Guyott[2], Captain or Admiral Adam Guyott or[1] Wiot) was born December 14, 1912. She married Adam R. Walton.

Children of Rena Parker and Adam Walton are:

	2087	i.	Adam R.[25] Walton, born June 14, 1932.
+	2088	ii.	Hugh Brittle Walton, born October 23, 1933.

1467.   Guy Ray[24] Parker (Harvey Adophus[23], J. Columbus[22], Ollie Lou Ada[21] Shaver, Rhoda E.[20] Wyatt, Noah Calvin[19], Thomas "Tommy"[18] Wiatt, Sr. (Wyatt, Wiett), John[17], Henry[16], Richard[15], George[14], Rev. Haute "Haut" "Hawte"[13], Sir George "Georgius" Thomas[12], Sir Thomas "The Younger"[11], Sir Thomas "The Elder"[10], Sir Henry[9], Richard Wiat or[8] Wyatt, Geoffrey "Jeoffrey" Wiot or[7] Wiat, Robert or Richard[6] Wiot, William Wiot or[5] Wyot, Adam Wiot or Wyote or[4], Guyott[3], Guyott[2], Captain or Admiral Adam Guyott or[1] Wiot) was born July 05, 1915, and died July 17, 1988. He married Alice Clementine Canup August 17, 1941, daughter of Edgar Canup and Eva Shepherd.

Children of Guy Parker and Alice Canup are:

+	2089	i.	Ronald Clifton[25] Parker, born June 27, 1946.
+	2090	ii.	Katie Jane Parker, born April 11, 1949.
	2091	iii.	Betty Ruth Parker, born September 13, 1950. She married Sammy Allen December 24, 1967.
+	2092	iv.	Connie Sue Parker, born November 1958.

1470.   Harvey Adophus[24] Parker, Jr. (Harvey Adophus[23], J. Columbus[22], Ollie Lou Ada[21] Shaver, Rhoda E.[20] Wyatt, Noah Calvin[19], Thomas "Tommy"[18] Wiatt, Sr. (Wyatt, Wiett), John[17], Henry[16], Richard[15], George[14], Rev. Haute "Haut" "Hawte"[13], Sir George "Georgius" Thomas[12], Sir Thomas "The Younger"[11], Sir Thomas "The Elder"[10], Sir Henry[9], Richard Wiat or[8] Wyatt, Geoffrey "Jeoffrey" Wiot or[7] Wiat, Robert or Richard[6] Wiot, William Wiot or[5] Wyot, Adam Wiot or Wyote or[4], Guyott[3], Guyott[2], Captain or Admiral Adam Guyott or[1] Wiot) was born August 06, 1926. He married Martha Lovoda Basinger November 1947, daughter of William Basinger and Addie Rinehardt.

Children of Harvey Parker and Martha Basinger are:

	2093	i.	Marilyn Fay[25] Parker, born July 31, 1949. She married Greg Marshall Nelson June 24, 1979.
+	2094	ii.	Jimmy Darrell Parker, born June 02, 1951.
+	2095	iii.	Robert Keith Parker, born October 25, 1953.
+	2096	iv.	Brenda Catherine Parker, born December 28, 1955.

1471.   Harry Wayne[24] Eagle (Murray or Murry Lee "Red"[23], Calvin DeBerry[22], William Lawson[21], Amanda Jane[20] Wyatt, Noah Calvin[19], Thomas "Tommy"[18] Wiatt, Sr. (Wyatt, Wiett),

John[17], Henry[16], Richard[15], George[14], Rev. Haute "Haut" "Hawte"[13], Sir George "Georgius" Thomas[12], Sir Thomas "The Younger"[11], Sir Thomas "The Elder"[10], Sir Henry[9], Richard Wiat or[8] Wyatt, Geoffrey "Jeoffrey" Wiot or[7] Wiat, Robert or Richard[6] Wiot, William Wiot or[5] Wyot, Adam Wiot or Wyote or[4], Guyott[3], Guyott[2], Captain or Admiral Adam Guyott or[1] Wiot) was born August 08, 1939. He married (1) Lexie Hendion. He married (2) Linda Martin.

Children of Harry Eagle and Lexie Hendion are:
2097   i.   Tony Wayne[25] Eagle, born August 03, 1958.
2098   ii.   Sherri Dianne Eagle, born September 09, 1962.

Child of Harry Eagle and Linda Martin is:
2099   i.   Michael Todd[25] Eagle, born June 12, 1971.

1472.   Martha Elisabeth[24] Eagle (Murray or Murry Lee "Red"[23], Calvin DeBerry[22], William Lawson[21], Amanda Jane[20] Wyatt, Noah Calvin[19], Thomas "Tommy"[18] Wiatt, Sr. (Wyatt, Wiett), John[17], Henry[16], Richard[15], George[14], Rev. Haute "Haut" "Hawte"[13], Sir George "Georgius" Thomas[12], Sir Thomas "The Younger"[11], Sir Thomas "The Elder"[10], Sir Henry[9], Richard Wiat or[8] Wyatt, Geoffrey "Jeoffrey" Wiot or[7] Wiat, Robert or Richard[6] Wiot, William Wiot or[5] Wyot, Adam Wiot or Wyote or[4], Guyott[3], Guyott[2], Captain or Admiral Adam Guyott or[1] Wiot) was born August 02, 1940 in Guilford County, N.C. She married Henry Max Patton.

Children of Martha Eagle and Henry Patton are:
2100   i.   Debra Irene[25] Patton, born September 27, 1957. She married Edward Johnson.
2101   ii.   Henry Max Patton, Jr., born November 29, 1958.
2102   iii.   Christopher Lee Patton, born July 01, 1960.
+   2103   iv.   Tammy Jean Patton, born June 19, 1961.
2104   v.   Linda Carol Patton, born August 10, 1962.
2105   vi.   Jerry Ray Patton, born August 12, 1963.

1473.   Willard Lee[24] Eagle (Murray or Murry Lee "Red"[23], Calvin DeBerry[22], William Lawson[21], Amanda Jane[20] Wyatt, Noah Calvin[19], Thomas "Tommy"[18] Wiatt, Sr. (Wyatt, Wiett), John[17], Henry[16], Richard[15], George[14], Rev. Haute "Haut" "Hawte"[13], Sir George "Georgius" Thomas[12], Sir Thomas "The Younger"[11], Sir Thomas "The Elder"[10], Sir Henry[9], Richard Wiat or[8] Wyatt, Geoffrey "Jeoffrey" Wiot or[7] Wiat, Robert or Richard[6] Wiot, William Wiot or[5] Wyot, Adam Wiot or Wyote or[4], Guyott[3], Guyott[2], Captain or Admiral Adam Guyott or[1] Wiot) was born June 26, 1942, and died January 22, 1975 in buried in Stokesdale, N.C. He married Rebecca Ann Warren, daughter of G.W. Warren and X.

Children of Willard Eagle and Rebecca Warren are:
2106   i.   Rhonda Renne[25] Eagle, born August 16, 1962.
2107   ii.   Brenda Lynn Eagle, born March 29, 1967.
2108   iii.   Brian Lee Eagle, born May 26, 1971.

1474. Calvin Henderson[24] Eagle (Murray or Murry Lee "Red"[23], Calvin DeBerry[22], William Lawson[21], Amanda Jane[20] Wyatt, Noah Calvin[19], Thomas "Tommy"[18] Wiatt, Sr. (Wyatt, Wiett), John[17], Henry[16], Richard[15], George[14], Rev. Haute "Haut" "Hawte"[13], Sir George "Georgius" Thomas[12], Sir Thomas "The Younger"[11], Sir Thomas "The Elder"[10], Sir Henry[9], Richard Wiat or[8] Wyatt, Geoffrey "Jeoffrey" Wiot or[7] Wiat, Robert or Richard[6] Wiot, William Wiot or[5] Wyot, Adam Wiot or Wyote or[4], Guyott[3], Guyott[2], Captain or Admiral Adam Guyott or[1] Wiot) was born March 26, 1943. He married Wendy Donna Brett, daughter of George Brett and Lou.

> Children of Calvin Eagle and Wendy Brett are:
> 2109   i.   Jason Christopher[25] Eagle, born October 01, 1971.
> 2110   ii.   Christopher George Eagle, born March 10, 1976.

1475. Larry Curtis[24] Eagle (Murray or Murry Lee "Red"[23], Calvin DeBerry[22], William Lawson[21], Amanda Jane[20] Wyatt, Noah Calvin[19], Thomas "Tommy"[18] Wiatt, Sr. (Wyatt, Wiett), John[17], Henry[16], Richard[15], George[14], Rev. Haute "Haut" "Hawte"[13], Sir George "Georgius" Thomas[12], Sir Thomas "The Younger"[11], Sir Thomas "The Elder"[10], Sir Henry[9], Richard Wiat or[8] Wyatt, Geoffrey "Jeoffrey" Wiot or[7] Wiat, Robert or Richard[6] Wiot, William Wiot or[5] Wyot, Adam Wiot or Wyote or[4], Guyott[3], Guyott[2], Captain or Admiral Adam Guyott or[1] Wiot) was born April 16, 1945. He married Judith Alice Bass, daughter of Jay Bass and Doris Walser.

> Children of Larry Eagle and Judith Bass are:
> 2111   i.   Larry Scott[25] Eagle, born March 12, 1964 in Rowan County N.C.
> 2112   ii.   Pamela Dawn Eagle, born October 22, 1966.

1476. Alice Jane[24] Eagle (Murray or Murry Lee "Red"[23], Calvin DeBerry[22], William Lawson[21], Amanda Jane[20] Wyatt, Noah Calvin[19], Thomas "Tommy"[18] Wiatt, Sr. (Wyatt, Wiett), John[17], Henry[16], Richard[15], George[14], Rev. Haute "Haut" "Hawte"[13], Sir George "Georgius" Thomas[12], Sir Thomas "The Younger"[11], Sir Thomas "The Elder"[10], Sir Henry[9], Richard Wiat or[8] Wyatt, Geoffrey "Jeoffrey" Wiot or[7] Wiat, Robert or Richard[6] Wiot, William Wiot or[5] Wyot, Adam Wiot or Wyote or[4], Guyott[3], Guyott[2], Captain or Admiral Adam Guyott or[1] Wiot) was born December 28, 1947. She married (1) Leonard Mabe. She married (2) Dan Peller.

> Children of Alice Eagle and Leonard Mabe are:
> 2113   i.   Bonnie Kay[25] Mabe, born January 11, 1964 in Rowan County N.C.
> 2114   ii.   Donnie Ray Mabe, born August 16, 1967 in Rowan County N.C.
> 2115   iii.   Connie Gay Mabe, born June 16, 1969 in Rowan County N.C.
> 2116   iv.   Deana Faye Mabe, born November 09, 1973 in Rowan County N.C.

1477. Harold Timothy[24] Eagle (Murray or Murry Lee "Red"[23], Calvin DeBerry[22], William Lawson[21], Amanda Jane[20] Wyatt, Noah Calvin[19], Thomas "Tommy"[18] Wiatt, Sr. (Wyatt, Wiett),

John[17], Henry[16], Richard[15], George[14], Rev. Haute "Haut" "Hawte"[13], Sir George "Georgius" Thomas[12], Sir Thomas "The Younger"[11], Sir Thomas "The Elder"[10], Sir Henry[9], Richard Wiat or[8] Wyatt, Geoffrey "Jeoffrey" Wiot or[7] Wiat, Robert or Richard[6] Wiot, William Wiot or[5] Wyot, Adam Wiot or Wyote or[4], Guyott[3], Guyott[2], Captain or Admiral Adam Guyott or[1] Wiot) was born August 27, 1952. He married (1) Barbara Ann Julian, daughter of Everette Julian and Shirley Kestler. He married (2) Beverly Stevens.

Child of Harold Eagle and Barbara Julian is:
2117　i.　Junior Lee[25] Eagle, born August 06, 1973 in Rowan County N.C.

1478.　Barbara Irene[24] Eagle (Murray or Murry Lee "Red"[23], Calvin DeBerry[22], William Lawson[21], Amanda Jane[20] Wyatt, Noah Calvin[19], Thomas "Tommy"[18] Wiatt, Sr. (Wyatt, Wiett), John[17], Henry[16], Richard[15], George[14], Rev. Haute "Haut" "Hawte"[13], Sir George "Georgius" Thomas[12], Sir Thomas "The Younger"[11], Sir Thomas "The Elder"[10], Sir Henry[9], Richard Wiat or[8] Wyatt, Geoffrey "Jeoffrey" Wiot or[7] Wiat, Robert or Richard[6] Wiot, William Wiot or[5] Wyot, Adam Wiot or Wyote or[4], Guyott[3], Guyott[2], Captain or Admiral Adam Guyott or[1] Wiot) was born February 12, 1952 in Guilford County, N.C. She married Everette Graham Julian, son of Everette Julian and Shirley Kestler.

Child of Barbara Eagle and Everette Julian is:
2118　i.　Shannon Delane[25] Julian, born January 27, 1947.

1481.　James Richard[24] Beattie (Betty Lorene[23] Eagle, Calvin DeBerry[22], William Lawson[21], Amanda Jane[20] Wyatt, Noah Calvin[19], Thomas "Tommy"[18] Wiatt, Sr. (Wyatt, Wiett), John[17], Henry[16], Richard[15], George[14], Rev. Haute "Haut" "Hawte"[13], Sir George "Georgius" Thomas[12], Sir Thomas "The Younger"[11], Sir Thomas "The Elder"[10], Sir Henry[9], Richard Wiat or[8] Wyatt, Geoffrey "Jeoffrey" Wiot or[7] Wiat, Robert or Richard[6] Wiot, William Wiot or[5] Wyot, Adam Wiot or Wyote or[4], Guyott[3], Guyott[2], Captain or Admiral Adam Guyott or[1] Wiot) was born March 1949 in Rowan County N.C. He married Gloria Jean Mitchell June 25, 1967, daughter of Herman Mitchell and Lillian Beard.

Children of James Beattie and Gloria Mitchell are:
2119　i.　Kristina Renae[25] Beattie, born September 15, 1969.
2120　ii.　Richard Brian Beattie, born May 19, 1973.
2121　iii.　Jonathan Blane Beattie, born December 11, 1975.

1489.　Avis Jenice "Geneice"[24] Shepherd (Sherley "Shirley" Ann[23] Arey, Anna "Anner" Lillian Pauline[22] Eagle, William Lawson[21], Amanda Jane[20] Wyatt, Noah Calvin[19], Thomas "Tommy"[18] Wiatt, Sr. (Wyatt, Wiett), John[17], Henry[16], Richard[15], George[14], Rev. Haute "Haut" "Hawte"[13], Sir George "Georgius" Thomas[12], Sir Thomas "The Younger"[11], Sir Thomas "The Elder"[10], Sir Henry[9], Richard Wiat or[8] Wyatt, Geoffrey "Jeoffrey" Wiot or[7] Wiat, Robert or Richard[6] Wiot, William Wiot or[5] Wyot, Adam Wiot or Wyote or[4], Guyott[3], Guyott[2], Captain or Admiral Adam Guyott or[1] Wiot) was born March 23, 1961. She married Roger Frick July 21, 1980, son of Norman Frick and Annie Maness.

Children of Avis Shepherd and Roger Frick are:

2122   i.   Tristan Ross[25] Frick, born January 18, 1986.

2123   ii.   Atalie Ann Frick, born November 29, 1988.

1490.   Sandra Elaine[24] Shepherd (Sherley "Shirley" Ann[23] Arey, Anna "Anner" Lillian Pauline[22] Eagle, William Lawson[21], Amanda Jane[20] Wyatt, Noah Calvin[19], Thomas "Tommy"[18] Wiatt, Sr. (Wyatt, Wiett), John[17], Henry[16], Richard[15], George[14], Rev. Haute "Haut" "Hawte"[13], Sir George "Georgius" Thomas[12], Sir Thomas "The Younger"[11], Sir Thomas "The Elder"[10], Sir Henry[9], Richard Wiat or[8] Wyatt, Geoffrey "Jeoffrey" Wiot or[7] Wiat, Robert or Richard[6] Wiot, William Wiot or[5] Wyot, Adam Wiot or Wyote or[4], Guyott[3], Guyott[2], Captain or Admiral Adam Guyott or[1] Wiot) was born July 03, 1957. She married James Louis Erik December 17, 1977, son of John Erik and Mary Hoflund.

        Child of Sandra Shepherd and James Erik is:

2124   i.   Carl Louis[25] Erik, born January 04, 1981.

1493.   Romona Lynn[24] Wise (Raymond Monroe[23], Virgie Lou Vera[22] Eagle, William Lawson[21], Amanda Jane[20] Wyatt, Noah Calvin[19], Thomas "Tommy"[18] Wiatt, Sr. (Wyatt, Wiett), John[17], Henry[16], Richard[15], George[14], Rev. Haute "Haut" "Hawte"[13], Sir George "Georgius" Thomas[12], Sir Thomas "The Younger"[11], Sir Thomas "The Elder"[10], Sir Henry[9], Richard Wiat or[8] Wyatt, Geoffrey "Jeoffrey" Wiot or[7] Wiat, Robert or Richard[6] Wiot, William Wiot or[5] Wyot, Adam Wiot or Wyote or[4], Guyott[3], Guyott[2], Captain or Admiral Adam Guyott or[1] Wiot) was born October 06, 1951. She married Tom Tilton August 07, 1971.

        Children of Romona Wise and Tom Tilton are:

2125   i.   Cheryl Lynn[25] Tilton.

2126   ii.   Susan Elisbeth Tilton.

1496.   Thomas Lloyd[24] Fraley (Clara Sue[23] Frye, Sarah Jane[22] Eagle, William Lawson[21], Amanda Jane[20] Wyatt, Noah Calvin[19], Thomas "Tommy"[18] Wiatt, Sr. (Wyatt, Wiett), John[17], Henry[16], Richard[15], George[14], Rev. Haute "Haut" "Hawte"[13], Sir George "Georgius" Thomas[12], Sir Thomas "The Younger"[11], Sir Thomas "The Elder"[10], Sir Henry[9], Richard Wiat or[8] Wyatt, Geoffrey "Jeoffrey" Wiot or[7] Wiat, Robert or Richard[6] Wiot, William Wiot or[5] Wyot, Adam Wiot or Wyote or[4], Guyott[3], Guyott[2], Captain or Admiral Adam Guyott or[1] Wiot) was born July 25, 1953. He married Patty Sue Panther August 31, 1973, daughter of Lawrence Panther and Lena Grubb.

        Child of Thomas Fraley and Patty Panther is:

2127   i.   Heath Aaron[25] Fraley, born October 09, 1978.

1497. Terry Michael[24] Luck (Hazeline Marell[23] Stoker, Esther Mae[22] Eagle, William Lawson[21], Amanda Jane[20] Wyatt, Noah Calvin[19], Thomas "Tommy"[18] Wiatt, Sr. (Wyatt, Wiett), John[17], Henry[16], Richard[15], George[14], Rev. Haute "Haut" "Hawte"[13], Sir George "Georgius" Thomas[12], Sir Thomas "The Younger"[11], Sir Thomas "The Elder"[10], Sir Henry[9], Richard Wiat or[8] Wyatt, Geoffrey "Jeoffrey" Wiot or[7] Wiat, Robert or Richard[6] Wiot, William Wiot or[5] Wyot, Adam

Wiot or Wyote or[4], Guyott[3], Guyott[2], Captain or Admiral Adam Guyott or[1] Wiot) was born August 15, 1956 in Chicago, Ill. He married Debbie July 10, 1976.

Child of Terry Luck and Debbie is:

2128   i.   Jason Michael[25] Luck, born August 01, 1978.

1498.   Thomas Arthur[24] Luck (Hazeline Marell[23] Stoker, Esther Mae[22] Eagle, William Lawson[21], Amanda Jane[20] Wyatt, Noah Calvin[19], Thomas "Tommy"[18] Wiatt, Sr. (Wyatt, Wiett), John[17], Henry[16], Richard[15], George[14], Rev. Haute "Haut" "Hawte"[13], Sir George "Georgius" Thomas[12], Sir Thomas "The Younger"[11], Sir Thomas "The Elder"[10], Sir Henry[9], Richard Wiat or[8] Wyatt, Geoffrey "Jeoffrey" Wiot or[7] Wiat, Robert or Richard[6] Wiot, William Wiot or[5] Wyot, Adam Wiot or Wyote or[4], Guyott[3], Guyott[2], Captain or Admiral Adam Guyott or[1] Wiot) was born October 15, 1957 in West Bend, Ind. He married Jasmia May 22, 1977.

Child of Thomas Luck and Jasmia is:

2129   i.   Bamba Shoe[25] Luck, born October 02, 1978.

1502.   Michael Alan[24] Clodfelter (Margaret Pauline[23] Hoover, Bertha Louise[22] Eagle, Adolphus Grant[21], Amanda Jane[20] Wyatt, Noah Calvin[19], Thomas "Tommy"[18] Wiatt, Sr. (Wyatt, Wiett), John[17], Henry[16], Richard[15], George[14], Rev. Haute "Haut" "Hawte"[13], Sir George "Georgius" Thomas[12], Sir Thomas "The Younger"[11], Sir Thomas "The Elder"[10], Sir Henry[9], Richard Wiat or[8] Wyatt, Geoffrey "Jeoffrey" Wiot or[7] Wiat, Robert or Richard[6] Wiot, William Wiot or[5] Wyot, Adam Wiot or Wyote or[4], Guyott[3], Guyott[2], Captain or Admiral Adam Guyott or[1] Wiot) was born March 19, 1951. He married Judy Ann Silvers February 14, 1970, daughter of Hollis Silvers and Ruby Morris.

Child of Michael Clodfelter and Judy Silvers is:

2130   i.   Daisha Lynn[25] Clodfelter, born October 26, 1977 in California.

1512. Ronald Wayne[24] Sweatt (Mae Elizabeth[23] Turner, Jennie Elizabeth[22] Eagle, Adolphus Grant[21], Amanda Jane[20] Wyatt, Noah Calvin[19], Thomas "Tommy"[18] Wiatt, Sr. (Wyatt, Wiett), John[17], Henry[16], Richard[15], George[14], Rev. Haute "Haut" "Hawte"[13], Sir George "Georgius" Thomas[12], Sir Thomas "The Younger"[11], Sir Thomas "The Elder"[10], Sir Henry[9], Richard Wiat or[8] Wyatt, Geoffrey "Jeoffrey" Wiot or[7] Wiat, Robert or Richard[6] Wiot, William Wiot or[5] Wyot, Adam Wiot or Wyote or[4], Guyott[3], Guyott[2], Captain or Admiral Adam Guyott or[1] Wiot) was born December 29, 1947. He married (1) Lea. He married (2) Lupi.

Child of Ronald Sweatt and Lea is:

2131   i.   Ronald Leon[25] Sweatt, born 1974 in New Jersey.

Children of Ronald Sweatt and Lupi are:

2132   i.   Grady Turner[25] Sweatt.
2133   ii.   Michael Sweatt.

1513. Robert Allen[24] Sweatt (Mae Elizabeth[23] Turner, Jennie Elizabeth[22] Eagle, Adolphus Grant[21], Amanda Jane[20] Wyatt, Noah Calvin[19], Thomas "Tommy"[18] Wiatt, Sr. (Wyatt, Wiett), John[17], Henry[16], Richard[15], George[14], Rev. Haute "Haut" "Hawte"[13], Sir George "Georgius" Thomas[12], Sir Thomas "The Younger"[11], Sir Thomas "The Elder"[10], Sir Henry[9], Richard Wiat or[8] Wyatt, Geoffrey "Jeoffrey" Wiot or[7] Wiat, Robert or Richard[6] Wiot, William Wiot or[5] Wyot, Adam Wiot or Wyote or[4], Guyott[3], Guyott[2], Captain or Admiral Adam Guyott or[1] Wiot) was born November 07, 1949. He married Frances Marlene Trexler, daughter of Thomas Trexler and Mary Bostian.

> Children of Robert Sweatt and Frances Trexler are:
> 2134 i. Laura Marlene[25] Sweatt, born May 21, 1971 in Rowan County N.C. She married Raymond Pierce July 15, 1995.
> 2135 ii. Kevin Wayne Sweatt, born August 21, 1978 in Rowan County N.C.

1514. Dwight Turner[24] Sweatt (Mae Elizabeth[23] Turner, Jennie Elizabeth[22] Eagle, Adolphus Grant[21], Amanda Jane[20] Wyatt, Noah Calvin[19], Thomas "Tommy"[18] Wiatt, Sr. (Wyatt, Wiett), John[17], Henry[16], Richard[15], George[14], Rev. Haute "Haut" "Hawte"[13], Sir George "Georgius" Thomas[12], Sir Thomas "The Younger"[11], Sir Thomas "The Elder"[10], Sir Henry[9], Richard Wiat or[8] Wyatt, Geoffrey "Jeoffrey" Wiot or[7] Wiat, Robert or Richard[6] Wiot, William Wiot or[5] Wyot, Adam Wiot or Wyote or[4], Guyott[3], Guyott[2], Captain or Admiral Adam Guyott or[1] Wiot) was born April 13, 1955 in Cabarrus County, N.C. He married (1) Terry. He married (2) Vivian Lilette Gomez March 02, 1973.

> Children of Dwight Sweatt and Vivian Gomez are:
> 2136 i. Vivian Elizabeth[25] Sweatt, born January 10, 1974 in New Jersey.
> 2137 ii. Jeanette Christine Sweatt, born 1980 in Burlington, N.C.

1537. Pamela Nesta[24] Kluttz (Warren Keith[23], Mary Kate[22] Eagle, John Murphy[21], Amanda Jane[20] Wyatt, Noah Calvin[19], Thomas "Tommy"[18] Wiatt, Sr. (Wyatt, Wiett), John[17], Henry[16], Richard[15], George[14], Rev. Haute "Haut" "Hawte"[13], Sir George "Georgius" Thomas[12], Sir Thomas "The Younger"[11], Sir Thomas "The Elder"[10], Sir Henry[9], Richard Wiat or[8] Wyatt, Geoffrey "Jeoffrey" Wiot or[7] Wiat, Robert or Richard[6] Wiot, William Wiot or[5] Wyot, Adam Wiot or Wyote or[4], Guyott[3], Guyott[2], Captain or Admiral Adam Guyott or[1] Wiot) was born April 15, 1948 in Stanly County, N.C. She married Johnny Caswell.

> Child of Pamela Kluttz and Johnny Caswell is:
> 2138 i. Amanda Leigh[25] Caswell, born April 21, 1980 in Wake County, N.C.

1538. Walter Roy[24] Sifford (Novice Bernita[23] Kluttz, Mary Kate[22] Eagle, John Murphy[21], Amanda Jane[20] Wyatt, Noah Calvin[19], Thomas "Tommy"[18] Wiatt, Sr. (Wyatt, Wiett), John[17], Henry[16], Richard[15], George[14], Rev. Haute "Haut" "Hawte"[13], Sir George "Georgius" Thomas[12], Sir Thomas "The Younger"[11], Sir Thomas "The Elder"[10], Sir Henry[9], Richard Wiat or[8] Wyatt,

Geoffrey "Jeoffrey" Wiot or[7] Wiat, Robert or Richard[6] Wiot, William Wiot or[5] Wyot, Adam Wiot or Wyote or[4], Guyott[3], Guyott[2], Captain or Admiral Adam Guyott or[1] Wiot) was born January 19, 1947 in Rowan County N.C. He married Frances Renee Deal February 12, 1966, daughter of Ralph Deal and Jennie Holshouser.

Children of Walter Sifford and Frances Deal are:
+   2139   i.   Lori Lachelle[25] Sifford, born September 16, 1968.
      2140   ii.   Bradley Walter Sifford, born March 19, 1974.

1539. Dennis Andrew[24] Sifford (Novice Bernita[23] Kluttz, Mary Kate[22] Eagle, John Murphy[21], Amanda Jane[20] Wyatt, Noah Calvin[19], Thomas "Tommy"[18] Wiatt, Sr. (Wyatt, Wiett), John[17], Henry[16], Richard[15], George[14], Rev. Haute "Haut" "Hawte"[13], Sir George "Georgius" Thomas[12], Sir Thomas "The Younger"[11], Sir Thomas "The Elder"[10], Sir Henry[9], Richard Wiat or[8] Wyatt, Geoffrey "Jeoffrey" Wiot or[7] Wiat, Robert or Richard[6] Wiot, William Wiot or[5] Wyot, Adam Wiot or Wyote or[4], Guyott[3], Guyott[2], Captain or Admiral Adam Guyott or[1] Wiot) was born October 11, 1951 in Rowan County N.C. He married Karen J. Williams September 29, 1979, daughter of James Williams and Julia Page.

Child of Dennis Sifford and Karen Williams is:
      2141   i.   Aaron Kyle[25] Sifford, born April 23, 1988.

1540. Osco Clay[24] Basinger, Jr. (Roberta Myraline[23] Kluttz, Mary Kate[22] Eagle, John Murphy[21], Amanda Jane[20] Wyatt, Noah Calvin[19], Thomas "Tommy"[18] Wiatt, Sr. (Wyatt, Wiett), John[17], Henry[16], Richard[15], George[14], Rev. Haute "Haut" "Hawte"[13], Sir George "Georgius" Thomas[12], Sir Thomas "The Younger"[11], Sir Thomas "The Elder"[10], Sir Henry[9], Richard Wiat or[8] Wyatt, Geoffrey "Jeoffrey" Wiot or[7] Wiat, Robert or Richard[6] Wiot, William Wiot or[5] Wyot, Adam Wiot or Wyote or[4], Guyott[3], Guyott[2], Captain or Admiral Adam Guyott or[1] Wiot) was born March 16, 1943. He married Barbara Jean Ketchie November 24, 1962, daughter of Harold Ketchie and Myrtle Cauble.

Children of Osco Basinger and Barbara Ketchie are:
      2142   i.   Marnie Leigh[25] Basinger, born May 24, 1974.
      2143   ii.   Daniel Scott Basinger, born February 06, 1980.

1541. Olin Lane[24] Basinger (Roberta Myraline[23] Kluttz, Mary Kate[22] Eagle, John Murphy[21], Amanda Jane[20] Wyatt, Noah Calvin[19], Thomas "Tommy"[18] Wiatt, Sr. (Wyatt, Wiett), John[17], Henry[16], Richard[15], George[14], Rev. Haute "Haut" "Hawte"[13], Sir George "Georgius" Thomas[12], Sir Thomas "The Younger"[11], Sir Thomas "The Elder"[10], Sir Henry[9], Richard Wiat or[8] Wyatt, Geoffrey "Jeoffrey" Wiot or[7] Wiat, Robert or Richard[6] Wiot, William Wiot or[5] Wyot, Adam Wiot or Wyote or[4], Guyott[3], Guyott[2], Captain or Admiral Adam Guyott or[1] Wiot) was born September 26, 1944. He married Audrey Gail Hill April 04, 1971, daughter of Arlie Hill and Eula Brown.

Children of Olin Basinger and Audrey Hill are:

2144   i.   Gina Michelle[25] Basinger, born May 11, 1972.

2145   ii.   Kristie Lea Basinger, born October 12, 1974.

1542. Myraline Kluttz[24] Basinger (Roberta Myraline[23] Kluttz, Mary Kate[22] Eagle, John Murphy[21], Amanda Jane[20] Wyatt, Noah Calvin[19], Thomas "Tommy"[18] Wiatt, Sr. (Wyatt, Wiett), John[17], Henry[16], Richard[15], George[14], Rev. Haute "Haut" "Hawte"[13], Sir George "Georgius" Thomas[12], Sir Thomas "The Younger"[11], Sir Thomas "The Elder"[10], Sir Henry[9], Richard Wiat or[8] Wyatt, Geoffrey "Jeoffrey" Wiot or[7] Wiat, Robert or Richard[6] Wiot, William Wiot or[5] Wyot, Adam Wiot or Wyote or[4], Guyott[3], Guyott[2], Captain or Admiral Adam Guyott or[1] Wiot) was born March 03, 1958. She married Jerry Dean Trexler April 29, 1978, son of Purcell Trexler and Ruth Merritt.

Child of Myraline Basinger and Jerry Trexler is:

2146   i.   David Scott[25] Trexler, born March 23, 1980 in Rowan County N.C.

1544. Melda Jestene[24] Foster (Zelma Jestine[23] Kluttz, Mary Kate[22] Eagle, John Murphy[21], Amanda Jane[20] Wyatt, Noah Calvin[19], Thomas "Tommy"[18] Wiatt, Sr. (Wyatt, Wiett), John[17], Henry[16], Richard[15], George[14], Rev. Haute "Haut" "Hawte"[13], Sir George "Georgius" Thomas[12], Sir Thomas "The Younger"[11], Sir Thomas "The Elder"[10], Sir Henry[9], Richard Wiat or[8] Wyatt, Geoffrey "Jeoffrey" Wiot or[7] Wiat, Robert or Richard[6] Wiot, William Wiot or[5] Wyot, Adam Wiot or Wyote or[4], Guyott[3], Guyott[2], Captain or Admiral Adam Guyott or[1] Wiot) was born July 15, 1948. She married Joseph Robert Walston, son of Myldred Walston and Ruth Skinner.

Children of Melda Foster and Joseph Walston are:

2147   i.   Steven Robert[25] Walston, born November 28, 1968.

2148   ii.   Melda Annette Walston, born October 09, 1972 in Wake County, N.C.

1545. Sandra Ilene[24] Foster (Zelma Jestine[23] Kluttz, Mary Kate[22] Eagle, John Murphy[21], Amanda Jane[20] Wyatt, Noah Calvin[19], Thomas "Tommy"[18] Wiatt, Sr. (Wyatt, Wiett), John[17], Henry[16], Richard[15], George[14], Rev. Haute "Haut" "Hawte"[13], Sir George "Georgius" Thomas[12], Sir Thomas "The Younger"[11], Sir Thomas "The Elder"[10], Sir Henry[9], Richard Wiat or[8] Wyatt, Geoffrey "Jeoffrey" Wiot or[7] Wiat, Robert or Richard[6] Wiot, William Wiot or[5] Wyot, Adam Wiot or Wyote or[4], Guyott[3], Guyott[2], Captain or Admiral Adam Guyott or[1] Wiot) was born December 30, 1949. She married Kenneth Starling Bissette June 01, 1969, son of Starling Bissette and X.

Children of Sandra Foster and Kenneth Bissette are:

2149   i.   Mary Amanda[25] Bissette, born January 28, 1976.

2150   ii.   Kenneth Starling Bissette, born March 20, 1978 in Wilson County, N.C.

1546. Michael Leith[24] Foster (Zelma Jestine[23] Kluttz, Mary Kate[22] Eagle, John Murphy[21], Amanda Jane[20] Wyatt, Noah Calvin[19], Thomas "Tommy"[18] Wiatt, Sr. (Wyatt, Wiett), John[17], Henry[16], Richard[15], George[14], Rev. Haute "Haut" "Hawte"[13], Sir George "Georgius" Thomas[12], Sir Thomas "The Younger"[11], Sir Thomas "The Elder"[10], Sir Henry[9], Richard Wiat or[8] Wyatt, Geoffrey "Jeoffrey" Wiot or[7] Wiat, Robert or Richard[6] Wiot, William Wiot or[5] Wyot, Adam Wiot or Wyote or[4], Guyott[3], Guyott[2], Captain or Admiral Adam Guyott or[1] Wiot) was born August 14, 1951. He married (1) Teresa Taylor Stallings, daughter of Melvin Taylor and Nancy. He married (2) Martha E. Thompson July 23, 1970, daughter of James Thompson and Edna.

> Children of Michael Foster and Martha Thompson are:
> 2151 i. Amy Lynn[25] Foster, born January 08, 1971.
> 2152 ii. Michael Leith Foster, born November 17, 1972.

1553. Deborah[24] Lambert (Barbara[23] Cook, Margaret Marie[22] Eagle, John Murphy[21], Amanda Jane[20] Wyatt, Noah Calvin[19], Thomas "Tommy"[18] Wiatt, Sr. (Wyatt, Wiett), John[17], Henry[16], Richard[15], George[14], Rev. Haute "Haut" "Hawte"[13], Sir George "Georgius" Thomas[12], Sir Thomas "The Younger"[11], Sir Thomas "The Elder"[10], Sir Henry[9], Richard Wiat or[8] Wyatt, Geoffrey "Jeoffrey" Wiot or[7] Wiat, Robert or Richard[6] Wiot, William Wiot or[5] Wyot, Adam Wiot or Wyote or[4], Guyott[3], Guyott[2], Captain or Admiral Adam Guyott or[1] Wiot) was born October 06, 1957. She married Randy Lee Crowell June 22, 1974, son of Bob Crowell and Geraldine Beaver.

> Child of Deborah Lambert and Randy Crowell is:
> 2153 i. Sharon Marie[25] Crowell, born June 12, 1977.

1554. Amanda[24] Lambert (Barbara[23] Cook, Margaret Marie[22] Eagle, John Murphy[21], Amanda Jane[20] Wyatt, Noah Calvin[19], Thomas "Tommy"[18] Wiatt, Sr. (Wyatt, Wiett), John[17], Henry[16], Richard[15], George[14], Rev. Haute "Haut" "Hawte"[13], Sir George "Georgius" Thomas[12], Sir Thomas "The Younger"[11], Sir Thomas "The Elder"[10], Sir Henry[9], Richard Wiat or[8] Wyatt, Geoffrey "Jeoffrey" Wiot or[7] Wiat, Robert or Richard[6] Wiot, William Wiot or[5] Wyot, Adam Wiot or Wyote or[4], Guyott[3], Guyott[2], Captain or Admiral Adam Guyott or[1] Wiot) was born November 19, 1957. She married Johnny Alan Taylor, son of James Taylor and Doris.

> Child of Amanda Lambert and Johnny Taylor is:
> 2154 i. Barbara Ann[25] Taylor, born January 08, 1978.

1555. James Michael[24] Lambert (Barbara[23] Cook, Margaret Marie[22] Eagle, John Murphy[21], Amanda Jane[20] Wyatt, Noah Calvin[19], Thomas "Tommy"[18] Wiatt, Sr. (Wyatt, Wiett), John[17], Henry[16], Richard[15], George[14], Rev. Haute "Haut" "Hawte"[13], Sir George "Georgius" Thomas[12], Sir Thomas "The Younger"[11], Sir Thomas "The Elder"[10], Sir Henry[9], Richard Wiat or[8] Wyatt, Geoffrey "Jeoffrey" Wiot or[7] Wiat, Robert or Richard[6] Wiot, William Wiot or[5] Wyot, Adam Wiot or Wyote or[4], Guyott[3], Guyott[2], Captain or Admiral Adam Guyott or[1] Wiot) was born

April 06, 1961. He married Wendy Broadway February 20, 1978, daughter of Billy Broadway and Carol Tomason.

Child of James Lambert and Wendy Broadway is:
2155   i.   Amy Michelle[25] Lambert, born April 05, 1980.

1556.   Sheila Marie[24] Pickler (Genelda[23] Cook, Margaret Marie[22] Eagle, John Murphy[21], Amanda Jane[20] Wyatt, Noah Calvin[19], Thomas "Tommy"[18] Wiatt, Sr. (Wyatt, Wiett), John[17], Henry[16], Richard[15], George[14], Rev. Haute "Haut" "Hawte"[13], Sir George "Georgius" Thomas[12], Sir Thomas "The Younger"[11], Sir Thomas "The Elder"[10], Sir Henry[9], Richard Wiat or[8] Wyatt, Geoffrey "Jeoffrey" Wiot or[7] Wiat, Robert or Richard[6] Wiot, William Wiot or[5] Wyot, Adam Wiot or Wyote or[4], Guyott[3], Guyott[2], Captain or Admiral Adam Guyott or[1] Wiot) was born April 13, 1957. She married (1) Gary Lee Fesperman, son of David Fesperman and Coleen. She married (2) Tim Goodman August 19, 1979.

Child of Sheila Pickler and Gary Fesperman is:
2156   i.   Jennifer Lee[25] Fesperman, born November 02, 1975.

1562.   Cassie Camille[24] Hand (James David[23], Mary Frances[22] Eagle, David Leo[21], Amanda Jane[20] Wyatt, Noah Calvin[19], Thomas "Tommy"[18] Wiatt, Sr. (Wyatt, Wiett), John[17], Henry[16], Richard[15], George[14], Rev. Haute "Haut" "Hawte"[13], Sir George "Georgius" Thomas[12], Sir Thomas "The Younger"[11], Sir Thomas "The Elder"[10], Sir Henry[9], Richard Wiat or[8] Wyatt, Geoffrey "Jeoffrey" Wiot or[7] Wiat, Robert or Richard[6] Wiot, William Wiot or[5] Wyot, Adam Wiot or Wyote or[4], Guyott[3], Guyott[2], Captain or Admiral Adam Guyott or[1] Wiot) was born October 10, 1986. She married Joshua Clawson December 06, 2004 in Rowan County, N.C.

Children of Cassie Hand and Joshua Clawson are:
2157   i.   Braden[25] Clawson, born November 17, 2005.
2158   ii.   Logan Clawson, born November 17, 2005.
2159   iii. Grayson Clawson, born July 29, 2008.

Generation No. 25

1618.   Patsy Carolyn[25] Brown (Edith Hope[24] Basinger, Effie Jeanette "Genetta" Eagle[23] Wyatt, Harvey Addison[22], Columbus Ciscero[21], Wilson Riley[20], Jesse "Jessey"[19], John "Johney"[18], John[17] Wiatt, Henry[16], Richard[15], George[14], Rev. Haute "Haut" "Hawte"[13], Sir George "Georgius" Thomas[12], Sir Thomas "The Younger"[11], Sir Thomas "The Elder"[10], Sir Henry[9], Richard Wiat or[8] Wyatt, Geoffrey "Jeoffrey" Wiot or[7] Wiat, Robert or Richard[6] Wiot, William Wiot or[5] Wyot, Adam Wiot or Wyote or[4], Guyott[3], Guyott[2], Captain or Admiral Adam Guyott or[1] Wiot) was born May 12, 1937. She married Lloyd Thomas Story September 29, 1956.

Children of Patsy Brown and Lloyd Story are:
+   2160   i.   Kathy Renea[26] Story, born February 17, 1958.
+   2161   ii.   Randal Thomas Story, born June 28, 1959.

+ 2162   iii.   Rhonda LuAnne Story, born July 08, 1961.

   2163   iv.   Gregory Alexander Story, born June 20, 1965.

1620. James Ray[25] Brown (Edith Hope[24] Basinger, Effie Jeanette "Genetta" Eagle[23] Wyatt, Harvey Addison[22], Columbus Ciscero[21], Wilson Riley[20], Jesse "Jessey"[19], John "Johney"[18], John[17] Wiatt, Henry[16], Richard[15], George[14], Rev. Haute "Haut" "Hawte"[13], Sir George "Georgius" Thomas[12], Sir Thomas "The Younger"[11], Sir Thomas "The Elder"[10], Sir Henry[9], Richard Wiat or[8] Wyatt, Geoffrey "Jeoffrey" Wiot or[7] Wiat, Robert or Richard[6] Wiot, William Wiot or[5] Wyot, Adam Wiot or Wyote or[4], Guyott[3], Guyott[2], Captain or Admiral Adam Guyott or[1] Wiot) was born June 24, 1940. He married Judith Carolyn Hawkins May 07, 1961, daughter of James Hawkins and Evelyn Smith.

      Children of James Brown and Judith Hawkins are:

+ 2164   i.   Gary Wayne[26] Brown, born February 24, 1962.

   2165   ii.   Danny Calvin Brown, born December 27, 1964.

1621. Alice "Faye"[25] Brown (Edith Hope[24] Basinger, Effie Jeanette "Genetta" Eagle[23] Wyatt, Harvey Addison[22], Columbus Ciscero[21], Wilson Riley[20], Jesse "Jessey"[19], John "Johney"[18], John[17] Wiatt, Henry[16], Richard[15], George[14], Rev. Haute "Haut" "Hawte"[13], Sir George "Georgius" Thomas[12], Sir Thomas "The Younger"[11], Sir Thomas "The Elder"[10], Sir Henry[9], Richard Wiat or[8] Wyatt, Geoffrey "Jeoffrey" Wiot or[7] Wiat, Robert or Richard[6] Wiot, William Wiot or[5] Wyot, Adam Wiot or Wyote or[4], Guyott[3], Guyott[2], Captain or Admiral Adam Guyott or[1] Wiot) was born February 16, 1942. She married (1) Bennett. She married (2) John Wayne Stirewalt February 28, 1960.

      Children of Alice Brown and John Stirewalt are:

+ 2166   i.   John Michael[26] Stirewalt, born November 21, 1960.

   2167   ii.   Mitchell Braine Stirewalt, born March 17, 1964.

1622. Bobby Curtis[25] Brown (Edith Hope[24] Basinger, Effie Jeanette "Genetta" Eagle[23] Wyatt, Harvey Addison[22], Columbus Ciscero[21], Wilson Riley[20], Jesse "Jessey"[19], John "Johney"[18], John[17] Wiatt, Henry[16], Richard[15], George[14], Rev. Haute "Haut" "Hawte"[13], Sir George "Georgius" Thomas[12], Sir Thomas "The Younger"[11], Sir Thomas "The Elder"[10], Sir Henry[9], Richard Wiat or[8] Wyatt, Geoffrey "Jeoffrey" Wiot or[7] Wiat, Robert or Richard[6] Wiot, William Wiot or[5] Wyot, Adam Wiot or Wyote or[4], Guyott[3], Guyott[2], Captain or Admiral Adam Guyott or[1] Wiot) was born June 02, 1943. He married Margaret Ann Edwards Spry November 20, 1964.

      Children of Bobby Brown and Margaret Spry are:

   2168   i.   Philip Shane[26] Brown, born May 26, 1965 in Rowan County N.C.; died August 27, 1981 in Rowan County N.C.

      More About Philip Shane Brown:
      Remains buried at Rock Grove Methodist Church Cemetery, Rowan County, N.C.

2169   ii.   Christi Dawn Brown, born January 18, 1971.

1624.   Ronald Paul[25] Castor (Eltha Pauline[24] Basinger, Effie Jeanette "Genetta" Eagle[23] Wyatt, Harvey Addison[22], Columbus Ciscero[21], Wilson Riley[20], Jesse "Jessey"[19], John "Johney"[18], John[17] Wiatt, Henry[16], Richard[15], George[14], Rev. Haute "Haut" "Hawte"[13], Sir George "Georgius" Thomas[12], Sir Thomas "The Younger"[11], Sir Thomas "The Elder"[10], Sir Henry[9], Richard Wiat or[8] Wyatt, Geoffrey "Jeoffrey" Wiot or[7] Wiat, Robert or Richard[6] Wiot, William Wiot or[5] Wyot, Adam Wiot or Wyote or[4], Guyott[3], Guyott[2], Captain or Admiral Adam Guyott or[1] Wiot) was born December 05, 1936. He married Lois Jane Sellers.

Children of Ronald Castor and Lois Sellers are:
2170   i.   Rhonda Lee[26] Castor, born December 15, 1964.
2171   ii.   Lisa Susab Castor, born November 12, 1967.

1625.   Patricia Lee[25] Castor (Eltha Pauline[24] Basinger, Effie Jeanette "Genetta" Eagle[23] Wyatt, Harvey Addison[22], Columbus Ciscero[21], Wilson Riley[20], Jesse "Jessey"[19], John "Johney"[18], John[17] Wiatt, Henry[16], Richard[15], George[14], Rev. Haute "Haut" "Hawte"[13], Sir George "Georgius" Thomas[12], Sir Thomas "The Younger"[11], Sir Thomas "The Elder"[10], Sir Henry[9], Richard Wiat or[8] Wyatt, Geoffrey "Jeoffrey" Wiot or[7] Wiat, Robert or Richard[6] Wiot, William Wiot or[5] Wyot, Adam Wiot or Wyote or[4], Guyott[3], Guyott[2], Captain or Admiral Adam Guyott or[1] Wiot) was born March 21, 1945. She married Donald Lee Perry III.

Children of Patricia Castor and Donald Perry are:
2172   i.   Carolyn[26] Perry, born July 01, 1968.
2173   ii.   Cathy Perry, born July 01, 1968.

1626.   Nellie Jean[25] Robinson (Elma Eunice[24] Basinger, Effie Jeanette "Genetta" Eagle[23] Wyatt, Harvey Addison[22], Columbus Ciscero[21], Wilson Riley[20], Jesse "Jessey"[19], John "Johney"[18], John[17] Wiatt, Henry[16], Richard[15], George[14], Rev. Haute "Haut" "Hawte"[13], Sir George "Georgius" Thomas[12], Sir Thomas "The Younger"[11], Sir Thomas "The Elder"[10], Sir Henry[9], Richard Wiat or[8] Wyatt, Geoffrey "Jeoffrey" Wiot or[7] Wiat, Robert or Richard[6] Wiot, William Wiot or[5] Wyot, Adam Wiot or Wyote or[4], Guyott[3], Guyott[2], Captain or Admiral Adam Guyott or[1] Wiot) was born February 03, 1940. She married (1) Vernon R. Overcash June 27, 1959. She married (2) Clonnie David Deese, Jr. October 09, 1983.

Children of Nellie Robinson and Vernon Overcash are:
2174   i.   Tammy Annette[26] Overcash, born September 21, 1960.
2175   ii.   Gregory Todd Overcash, born February 24, 1963.

1627.   Ginger Dale[25] Robinson (Elma Eunice[24] Basinger, Effie Jeanette "Genetta" Eagle[23] Wyatt, Harvey Addison[22], Columbus Ciscero[21], Wilson Riley[20], Jesse "Jessey"[19], John "Johney"[18], John[17] Wiatt, Henry[16], Richard[15], George[14], Rev. Haute "Haut" "Hawte"[13], Sir George "Georgius" Thomas[12], Sir Thomas "The Younger"[11], Sir Thomas "The Elder"[10], Sir Henry[9], Richard Wiat or[8] Wyatt, Geoffrey "Jeoffrey" Wiot or[7] Wiat, Robert or Richard[6] Wiot,

William Wiot or[5] Wyot, Adam Wiot or Wyote or[4], Guyott[3], Guyott[2], Captain or Admiral Adam Guyott or[1] Wiot) was born August 08, 1950. She married James Cornelius III May 10, 1968.

Children of Ginger Robinson and James Cornelius are:

2176   i.   Tracy Shawn[26] Cornelius, born July 18, 1970.

2177   ii.   Jeremy Shane Cornelius, born July 04, 1972.

2178   iii.   Rusty Dale Cornelius, born May 1979; died May 1979.

1628.   Vernon[25] Basinger (Claude V.[24], Effie Jeanette "Genetta" Eagle[23] Wyatt, Harvey Addison[22], Columbus Ciscero[21], Wilson Riley[20], Jesse "Jessey"[19], John "Johney"[18], John[17] Wiatt, Henry[16], Richard[15], George[14], Rev. Haute "Haut" "Hawte"[13], Sir George "Georgius" Thomas[12], Sir Thomas "The Younger"[11], Sir Thomas "The Elder"[10], Sir Henry[9], Richard Wiat or[8] Wyatt, Geoffrey "Jeoffrey" Wiot or[7] Wiat, Robert or Richard[6] Wiot, William Wiot or[5] Wyot, Adam Wiot or Wyote or[4], Guyott[3], Guyott[2], Captain or Admiral Adam Guyott or[1] Wiot) was born June 24, 1946. He married Susan.

Children of Vernon Basinger and Susan are:

2179   i.   Wendy[26] Basinger, born January 18, 1969.

2180   ii.   Donna Basinger, born April 12, 1971.

2181   iii.   Crystal Basinger, born April 12, 1973.

2182   iv.   Marie Basinger, born October 21, 1975.

1629.   Sylvia[25] Basinger (Claude V.[24], Effie Jeanette "Genetta" Eagle[23] Wyatt, Harvey Addison[22], Columbus Ciscero[21], Wilson Riley[20], Jesse "Jessey"[19], John "Johney"[18], John[17] Wiatt, Henry[16], Richard[15], George[14], Rev. Haute "Haut" "Hawte"[13], Sir George "Georgius" Thomas[12], Sir Thomas "The Younger"[11], Sir Thomas "The Elder"[10], Sir Henry[9], Richard Wiat or[8] Wyatt, Geoffrey "Jeoffrey" Wiot or[7] Wiat, Robert or Richard[6] Wiot, William Wiot or[5] Wyot, Adam Wiot or Wyote or[4], Guyott[3], Guyott[2], Captain or Admiral Adam Guyott or[1] Wiot) was born November 24, 1948. She married Robert Leazer.

Child of Sylvia Basinger and Robert Leazer is:

2183   i.   Daren[26] Leazer.

1631.   Susan[25] Basinger (Clinton E.[24], Effie Jeanette "Genetta" Eagle[23] Wyatt, Harvey Addison[22], Columbus Ciscero[21], Wilson Riley[20], Jesse "Jessey"[19], John "Johney"[18], John[17] Wiatt, Henry[16], Richard[15], George[14], Rev. Haute "Haut" "Hawte"[13], Sir George "Georgius" Thomas[12], Sir Thomas "The Younger"[11], Sir Thomas "The Elder"[10], Sir Henry[9], Richard Wiat or[8] Wyatt, Geoffrey "Jeoffrey" Wiot or[7] Wiat, Robert or Richard[6] Wiot, William Wiot or[5] Wyot, Adam Wiot or Wyote or[4], Guyott[3], Guyott[2], Captain or Admiral Adam Guyott or[1] Wiot) was born January 21, 1947. She married Ruddy Edwin Shipton.

Children of Susan Basinger and Ruddy Shipton are:

2184   i.   Jodi Suzanne[26] Shipton, born April 29, 1966.

2185   ii.   Windy Beth Shipton, born January 22, 1968.

2186   iii.   Clinton Ray Shipton, born March 12, 1978; died March 12, 1978.

1632. Janie Roseanne[25] Basinger (Clinton E.[24], Effie Jeanette "Genetta" Eagle[23] Wyatt, Harvey Addison[22], Columbus Ciscero[21], Wilson Riley[20], Jesse "Jessey"[19], John "Johney"[18], John[17] Wiatt, Henry[16], Richard[15], George[14], Rev. Haute "Haut" "Hawte"[13], Sir George "Georgius" Thomas[12], Sir Thomas "The Younger"[11], Sir Thomas "The Elder"[10], Sir Henry[9], Richard Wiat or[8] Wyatt, Geoffrey "Jeoffrey" Wiot or[7] Wiat, Robert or Richard[6] Wiot, William Wiot or[5] Wyot, Adam Wiot or Wyote or[4], Guyott[3], Guyott[2], Captain or Admiral Adam Guyott or[1] Wiot) was born December 11, 1954. She married Stephen Linn Walker.

     Child of Janie Basinger and Stephen Walker is:

2187   i.   Jason Linn[26] Walker, born May 18, 1975.

1633. Vickie Cheryl[25] Basinger (Chester Clyde[24], Effie Jeanette "Genetta" Eagle[23] Wyatt, Harvey Addison[22], Columbus Ciscero[21], Wilson Riley[20], Jesse "Jessey"[19], John "Johney"[18], John[17] Wiatt, Henry[16], Richard[15], George[14], Rev. Haute "Haut" "Hawte"[13], Sir George "Georgius" Thomas[12], Sir Thomas "The Younger"[11], Sir Thomas "The Elder"[10], Sir Henry[9], Richard Wiat or[8] Wyatt, Geoffrey "Jeoffrey" Wiot or[7] Wiat, Robert or Richard[6] Wiot, William Wiot or[5] Wyot, Adam Wiot or Wyote or[4], Guyott[3], Guyott[2], Captain or Admiral Adam Guyott or[1] Wiot) was born September 06, 1948. She married Jimmy Miles.

     Child of Vickie Basinger and Jimmy Miles is:

2188   i.   Son[26] Miles.

1638. Teresa Gail[25] Turner (Elva Kay[24] Basinger, Effie Jeanette "Genetta" Eagle[23] Wyatt, Harvey Addison[22], Columbus Ciscero[21], Wilson Riley[20], Jesse "Jessey"[19], John "Johney"[18], John[17] Wiatt, Henry[16], Richard[15], George[14], Rev. Haute "Haut" "Hawte"[13], Sir George "Georgius" Thomas[12], Sir Thomas "The Younger"[11], Sir Thomas "The Elder"[10], Sir Henry[9], Richard Wiat or[8] Wyatt, Geoffrey "Jeoffrey" Wiot or[7] Wiat, Robert or Richard[6] Wiot, William Wiot or[5] Wyot, Adam Wiot or Wyote or[4], Guyott[3], Guyott[2], Captain or Admiral Adam Guyott or[1] Wiot) was born March 21, 1963. She married (1) Gary Wayne Martin. She married (2) Teddy Joseph Phipps.

     Child of Teresa Turner and Gary Martin is:

2189   i.   Nicklas Christopher[26] Martin, born November 19, 1980.

     Child of Teresa Turner and Teddy Phipps is:

2190   i.   Cynthia Reneé[26] Phipps, born March 20, 1984.

1643. Tamara[25] Wyatt (Dr. Roger D.[24], Paul Woodrow[23], David Eli[22], James "Jim" Noah[21], William Wesley "Brantly"[20], Noah Calvin[19], Thomas "Tommy"[18] Wiatt, Sr. (Wyatt, Wiett), John[17], Henry[16], Richard[15], George[14], Rev. Haute "Haut" "Hawte"[13], Sir George "Georgius"

Thomas[12], Sir Thomas "The Younger"[11], Sir Thomas "The Elder"[10], Sir Henry[9], Richard Wiat or[8] Wyatt, Geoffrey "Jeoffrey" Wiot or[7] Wiat, Robert or Richard[6] Wiot, William Wiot or[5] Wyot, Adam Wiot or Wyote or[4], Guyott[3], Guyott[2], Captain or Admiral Adam Guyott or[1] Wiot). She married Jensen.

Child of Tamara Wyatt and Jensen is:
2191   i.   Jacob Paul[26] Jensen, born in of Murfreesboro, Tenn.

1645. Rebecca "Becky" Ann[25] Hinson (William "Bill" Crowell[24], Virgie Irene[23] Eagle, Noah Jenkins[22], Mary Jane[21] Morgan, Rachel Evelyn "Eveline"[20] Wyatt, Noah Calvin[19], Thomas "Tommy"[18] Wiatt, Sr. (Wyatt, Wiett), John[17], Henry[16], Richard[15], George[14], Rev. Haute "Haut" "Hawte"[13], Sir George "Georgius" Thomas[12], Sir Thomas "The Younger"[11], Sir Thomas "The Elder"[10], Sir Henry[9], Richard Wiat or[8] Wyatt, Geoffrey "Jeoffrey" Wiot or[7] Wiat, Robert or Richard[6] Wiot, William Wiot or[5] Wyot, Adam Wiot or Wyote or[4], Guyott[3], Guyott[2], Captain or Admiral Adam Guyott or[1] Wiot) was born January 22, 1952 in Salisbury, Rowan County, N.C. She married David Leslie Wikle October 24, 1970 in Pulaski, Va. (southwest), son of Evert Wikle and Mary Stoots.

Children of Rebecca Hinson and David Wikle are:
2192   i.   David Ashley[26] Wikle, born February 19, 1974 in Marion, Smyth County, Va.
+   2193   ii.   Chad Edward Wikle, born November 20, 1977 in Radford, Montgomery County, Va.

1646. Mary Lynn[25] Hinson (William "Bill" Crowell[24], Virgie Irene[23] Eagle, Noah Jenkins[22], Mary Jane[21] Morgan, Rachel Evelyn "Eveline"[20] Wyatt, Noah Calvin[19], Thomas "Tommy"[18] Wiatt, Sr. (Wyatt, Wiett), John[17], Henry[16], Richard[15], George[14], Rev. Haute "Haut" "Hawte"[13], Sir George "Georgius" Thomas[12], Sir Thomas "The Younger"[11], Sir Thomas "The Elder"[10], Sir Henry[9], Richard Wiat or[8] Wyatt, Geoffrey "Jeoffrey" Wiot or[7] Wiat, Robert or Richard[6] Wiot, William Wiot or[5] Wyot, Adam Wiot or Wyote or[4], Guyott[3], Guyott[2], Captain or Admiral Adam Guyott or[1] Wiot) was born August 02, 1954 in Salisbury, Rowan County, N.C. She married Richard Ronald Mangieri August 02, 1975 in Winston-Salem, N.C., son of Silvio Mangieri and Josephine Merolese.

Fact 1: Served in the U.S. military.

Child of Mary Hinson and Richard Mangieri is:
+   2194   i.   Maria Adelinea[26] Mangieri, born December 29, 1986 in Italy; Adopted child.

1647. Melanie Joan[25] Hinson (William "Bill" Crowell[24], Virgie Irene[23] Eagle, Noah Jenkins[22], Mary Jane[21] Morgan, Rachel Evelyn "Eveline"[20] Wyatt, Noah Calvin[19], Thomas "Tommy"[18] Wiatt, Sr. (Wyatt, Wiett), John[17], Henry[16], Richard[15], George[14], Rev. Haute "Haut" "Hawte"[13], Sir George "Georgius" Thomas[12], Sir Thomas "The Younger"[11], Sir Thomas "The Elder"[10],

Sir Henry[9], Richard Wiat or[8] Wyatt, Geoffrey "Jeoffrey" Wiot or[7] Wiat, Robert or Richard[6] Wiot, William Wiot or[5] Wyot, Adam Wiot or Wyote or[4], Guyott[3], Guyott[2], Captain or Admiral Adam Guyott or[1] Wiot) was born September 21, 1956 in Salisbury, Rowan County, N.C. She married Jean "John" Ivan "Iwan" Saramaha September 30, 1984 in Winston-Salem, N.C., son of Nikolaus Saramaha and Iwanna Grymajlo.

Remains are buried in Utica, N.Y., Russian Orthodox Monestary.

Children of Melanie Hinson and Jean Saramaha are:

+ 2195 i. Natalie Paige[26] Hinson, born February 03, 1979 in Winston-Salem, Forsyth County, N.C.
+ 2196 ii. Daniel Michael Saramaha, born June 28, 1986 in Winston-Salem, Forsyth County, N.C.

1648. William "Billy" Ashley[25] Hinson (William "Bill" Crowell[24], Virgie Irene[23] Eagle, Noah Jenkins[22], Mary Jane[21] Morgan, Rachel Evelyn "Eveline"[20] Wyatt, Noah Calvin[19], Thomas "Tommy"[18] Wiatt, Sr. (Wyatt, Wiett), John[17], Henry[16], Richard[15], George[14], Rev. Haute "Haut" "Hawte"[13], Sir George "Georgius" Thomas[12], Sir Thomas "The Younger"[11], Sir Thomas "The Elder"[10], Sir Henry[9], Richard Wiat or[8] Wyatt, Geoffrey "Jeoffrey" Wiot or[7] Wiat, Robert or Richard[6] Wiot, William Wiot or[5] Wyot, Adam Wiot or Wyote or[4], Guyott[3], Guyott[2], Captain or Admiral Adam Guyott or[1] Wiot) was born September 09, 1958 in Washington County, Phymouth, N.C. He married (1) First Wife Bef. 1980. He married (2) Jamie Brooke Smith Abt. 1980, daughter of Dewitt Smith and Locke Faulkner. He married (3) Sheila Ann Adams November 25, 1989 in Ashpole Presbyterian Church, Rowland, Robeson County, N.C., daughter of James Adams and Elizabeth Adcock.

Children of William Hinson and Sheila Adams are:

2197 i. William "Ashe" Ashley[26] Hinson II, born November 02, 1990 in North Carolina.
2198 ii. Elizabeth "Liz" Ann Hinson, born June 06, 1992 in North Carolina.
2199 iii. James "Cooper" Cooper Hinson, born February 03, 1995 in North Carolina.

1649. Richard Merrell[25] Hinson (Richard "Chubby" "Chub" Clyde[24], Virgie Irene[23] Eagle, Noah Jenkins[22], Mary Jane[21] Morgan, Rachel Evelyn "Eveline"[20] Wyatt, Noah Calvin[19], Thomas "Tommy"[18] Wiatt, Sr. (Wyatt, Wiett), John[17], Henry[16], Richard[15], George[14], Rev. Haute "Haut" "Hawte"[13], Sir George "Georgius" Thomas[12], Sir Thomas "The Younger"[11], Sir Thomas "The Elder"[10], Sir Henry[9], Richard Wiat or[8] Wyatt, Geoffrey "Jeoffrey" Wiot or[7] Wiat, Robert or Richard[6] Wiot, William Wiot or[5] Wyot, Adam Wiot or Wyote or[4], Guyott[3], Guyott[2], Captain or Admiral Adam Guyott or[1] Wiot) was born September 28, 1950 in Salisbury, Rowan County, N.C. He married Debra "Debbie" Lea Thomas July 16, 1972 in Salisbury, Rowan County, N.C., daughter of Horace Thomas and Dorothy Honeycutt.

Child of Richard Hinson and Debra Thomas is:

+ 2200   i.   Christopher "Chris" Thomas[26] Hinson, born October 15, 1977 in Salisbury, Rowan County, N.C.

1651. Pamela "Pam" Irene[25] Hinson (Richard "Chubby" "Chub" Clyde[24], Virgie Irene[23] Eagle, Noah Jenkins[22], Mary Jane[21] Morgan, Rachel Evelyn "Eveline"[20] Wyatt, Noah Calvin[19], Thomas "Tommy"[18] Wiatt, Sr. (Wyatt, Wiett), John[17], Henry[16], Richard[15], George[14], Rev. Haute "Haut" "Hawte"[13], Sir George "Georgius" Thomas[12], Sir Thomas "The Younger"[11], Sir Thomas "The Elder"[10], Sir Henry[9], Richard Wiat or[8] Wyatt, Geoffrey "Jeoffrey" Wiot or[7] Wiat, Robert or Richard[6] Wiot, William Wiot or[5] Wyot, Adam Wiot or Wyote or[4], Guyott[3], Guyott[2], Captain or Admiral Adam Guyott or[1] Wiot) was born October 15, 1953 in Salisbury, Rowan County, N.C. She married William Marvin Wilson December 05, 1979 in Salisbury, Rowan County, N.C., son of William Wilson and Betty Bowles.

Children of Pamela Hinson and William Wilson are:

+ 2201   i.   Pamela Michelle[26] Wilson, born July 15, 1972 in Salisbury, Rowan County, N.C.
+ 2202   ii.   Candace Chevonne Wilson, born August 04, 1981 in Salisbury, Rowan County, N.C.
  2203   iii.   William Richard Wilson, born May 04, 1983 in Salisbury, Rowan County, N.C.

1652. Lesa Ann[25] Hinson (Richard "Chubby" "Chub" Clyde[24], Virgie Irene[23] Eagle, Noah Jenkins[22], Mary Jane[21] Morgan, Rachel Evelyn "Eveline"[20] Wyatt, Noah Calvin[19], Thomas "Tommy"[18] Wiatt, Sr. (Wyatt, Wiett), John[17], Henry[16], Richard[15], George[14], Rev. Haute "Haut" "Hawte"[13], Sir George "Georgius" Thomas[12], Sir Thomas "The Younger"[11], Sir Thomas "The Elder"[10], Sir Henry[9], Richard Wiat or[8] Wyatt, Geoffrey "Jeoffrey" Wiot or[7] Wiat, Robert or Richard[6] Wiot, William Wiot or[5] Wyot, Adam Wiot or Wyote or[4], Guyott[3], Guyott[2], Captain or Admiral Adam Guyott or[1] Wiot) was born December 04, 1961 in Salisbury, Rowan County, N.C. She married (1) Dewey Brian McAbee April 10, 1982 in Saint Peter's Lutheran Church, Salisbury, N.C., son of Wallace McAbee and Bertha Huntley. She married (2) David Allen Harris October 05, 2001 in Chimney Rock, near Asheville, N.C., son of William Harris and Joyce Cogar.

More About Dewey Brian McAbee:
Died in car accident.

Children of Lesa Hinson and Dewey McAbee are:

  2204   i.   Natalie Anita[26] McAbee, born January 16, 1983 in Mission Memorial Hospital, Asheville, Buncombe County, N.C.; died August 03, 1994 in Fairview, N.C.

2205 ii. Andrew Brian McAbee, born December 28, 1985 in Mission Memorial Hospital, Asheville, Buncombe County, N.C.; died May 10, 1998 in Died in Hickory, N.C. hospital; buried in Fairview, N.C.

Buried at Cane Creek, Fairview, N.C.

1654. Hélène "Lynnie" Andorre[25] Hinson (James "Jim" Noah[24], Virgie Irene[23] Eagle, Noah Jenkins[22], Mary Jane[21] Morgan, Rachel Evelyn "Eveline"[20] Wyatt, Noah Calvin[19], Thomas "Tommy"[18] Wiatt, Sr. (Wyatt, Wiett), John[17], Henry[16], Richard[15], George[14], Rev. Haute "Haut" "Hawte"[13], Sir George "Georgius" Thomas[12], Sir Thomas "The Younger"[11], Sir Thomas "The Elder"[10], Sir Henry[9], Richard Wiat or[8] Wyatt, Geoffrey "Jeoffrey" Wiot or[7] Wiat, Robert or Richard[6] Wiot, William Wiot or[5] Wyot, Adam Wiot or Wyote or[4], Guyott[3], Guyott[2], Captain or Admiral Adam Guyott or[1] Wiot) was born February 04, 1963 in New Orleans, New Orleans Parish, La. She married Howard "Hal" Anthony Staley, D.P.M. December 29, 1990 in St. Thomas Episcopal Church, Steele Street, Sanford, Lee County, N.C., son of Milton Staley and Marie Euker.

Children of Hélène Hinson and Howard Staley are:
2206 i. Zachary "Zach" Christopher[26] Staley, born March 23, 1992 in Sanford, Lee County, N.C.
2207 ii. Nicholas "Nick" Howard Staley, born September 09, 1994 in Raleigh, Wake County, N.C.
2208 iii. Benjamin "Ben" Noah Patrick Staley, born March 16, 2004 in Raleigh, Wake County, N.C.

1655. Häns Leighton[25] Hinson, M.D. (James "Jim" Noah[24], Virgie Irene[23] Eagle, Noah Jenkins[22], Mary Jane[21] Morgan, Rachel Evelyn "Eveline"[20] Wyatt, Noah Calvin[19], Thomas "Tommy"[18] Wiatt, Sr. (Wyatt, Wiett), John[17], Henry[16], Richard[15], George[14], Rev. Haute "Haut" "Hawte"[13], Sir George "Georgius" Thomas[12], Sir Thomas "The Younger"[11], Sir Thomas "The Elder"[10], Sir Henry[9], Richard Wiat or[8] Wyatt, Geoffrey "Jeoffrey" Wiot or[7] Wiat, Robert or Richard[6] Wiot, William Wiot or[5] Wyot, Adam Wiot or Wyote or[4], Guyott[3], Guyott[2], Captain or Admiral Adam Guyott or[1] Wiot) was born June 02, 1964 in New Orleans, New Orleans Parish, La. He married Vanessa Karsch, Ph.D., M.D. May 30, 1997 in Hamburg, Germany, daughter of Guenter Karsch and Birgit Juenger.

Children of Häns Hinson and Vanessa Karsch are:
2209 i. Jonah Karsch[26] Hinson, born June 16, 2001 in Charleston, S.C.
2210 ii. Noah Karsch Hinson, born July 03, 2004 in Charleston, S.C.
2211 iii. Elijah Karsch Hinson, born August 11, 2006 in Charleston, S.C.

2212   iv.   Micah Karsch Hinson, born February 05, 2010 in Mount Pleasant, S.C.

1657. William Eugene[25] Heath (Betty Lou[24] Hinson, Virgie Irene[23] Eagle, Noah Jenkins[22], Mary Jane[21] Morgan, Rachel Evelyn "Eveline"[20] Wyatt, Noah Calvin[19], Thomas "Tommy"[18] Wiatt, Sr. (Wyatt, Wiett), John[17], Henry[16], Richard[15], George[14], Rev. Haute "Haut" "Hawte"[13], Sir George "Georgius" Thomas[12], Sir Thomas "The Younger"[11], Sir Thomas "The Elder"[10], Sir Henry[9], Richard Wiat or[8] Wyatt, Geoffrey "Jeoffrey" Wiot or[7] Wiat, Robert or Richard[6] Wiot, William Wiot or[5] Wyot, Adam Wiot or Wyote or[4], Guyott[3], Guyott[2], Captain or Admiral Adam Guyott or[1] Wiot) was born October 08, 1965 in High Point, Guilford County, N.C. He married Shannon Reneé Adkins June 24, 1990 in Guilford County, N.C., daughter of James Adkins and Sharon Willard.

     Children of William Heath and Shannon Adkins are:
     2213   i.   William James[26] Heath, born June 15, 1993 in High Point, Guilford County, N.C.
     2214   ii.   Jacob Daniel Heath, born January 21, 1996 in High Point, Guilford County, N.C.
     2215   iii.   Caitlyn Elizabeth Heath, born January 06, 1999 in High Point, Guilford County, N.C.

1658. Frances "LuAnne" LuAnne[25] Heath (Betty Lou[24] Hinson, Virgie Irene[23] Eagle, Noah Jenkins[22], Mary Jane[21] Morgan, Rachel Evelyn "Eveline"[20] Wyatt, Noah Calvin[19], Thomas "Tommy"[18] Wiatt, Sr. (Wyatt, Wiett), John[17], Henry[16], Richard[15], George[14], Rev. Haute "Haut" "Hawte"[13], Sir George "Georgius" Thomas[12], Sir Thomas "The Younger"[11], Sir Thomas "The Elder"[10], Sir Henry[9], Richard Wiat or[8] Wyatt, Geoffrey "Jeoffrey" Wiot or[7] Wiat, Robert or Richard[6] Wiot, William Wiot or[5] Wyot, Adam Wiot or Wyote or[4], Guyott[3], Guyott[2], Captain or Admiral Adam Guyott or[1] Wiot) was born February 18, 1967 in High Point, N.C. She married Lawrence "Larry" Walker Tywater November 18, 2000 in Wesley Memorial United Methodist Church, #1225 Chestnut Drive, High Point, N.C., son of Walker Tywater and Elizabeth Guidry.

     Children of Frances Heath and Lawrence Tywater are:
     2216   i.   Zachary[26] Tywater, born August 01, 2006 in High Point, N.C.
     2217   ii.   Chloe Nicole Tywater, born July 15, 2007 in High Point, Guilford County, N.C.

1662. Phillip V.[25] Gordon, Ph.D, M.D. (Margaret Ann[24] Hinson, Virgie Irene[23] Eagle, Noah Jenkins[22], Mary Jane[21] Morgan, Rachel Evelyn "Eveline"[20] Wyatt, Noah Calvin[19], Thomas "Tommy"[18] Wiatt, Sr. (Wyatt, Wiett), John[17], Henry[16], Richard[15], George[14], Rev. Haute "Haut" "Hawte"[13], Sir George "Georgius" Thomas[12], Sir Thomas "The Younger"[11], Sir Thomas "The Elder"[10], Sir Henry[9], Richard Wiat or[8] Wyatt, Geoffrey "Jeoffrey" Wiot or[7] Wiat, Robert or Richard[6] Wiot, William Wiot or[5] Wyot, Adam Wiot or Wyote or[4], Guyott[3], Guyott[2], Captain or Admiral Adam Guyott or[1] Wiot) was born April 28, 1964 in High Point, Guilford County, N.C. He married SaraBeth Lee Thomas June 12, 1993 in Tallahassee, Fla., daughter of Norris Thomas and Jessie Whitten.

Children of Phillip Gordon and SaraBeth Thomas are:

2218   i.   Megan Eleyn[26] Gordon, born December 06, 2001 in Charlottesville, Va.

2219   ii.   Audrey Leigh Gordon, born September 03, 2003 in Charlottesville, Va.

2220   iii. Jack Angus Gordon, born September 29, 2005 in Charlottesville, Va.

1663. James Edward[25] Hinson (Olga Bruce[24] Eagle, Edwin "Ed" Lee[23], Noah Jenkins[22], Mary Jane[21] Morgan, Rachel Evelyn "Eveline"[20] Wyatt, Noah Calvin[19], Thomas "Tommy"[18] Wiatt, Sr. (Wyatt, Wiett), John[17], Henry[16], Richard[15], George[14], Rev. Haute "Haut" "Hawte"[13], Sir George "Georgius" Thomas[12], Sir Thomas "The Younger"[11], Sir Thomas "The Elder"[10], Sir Henry[9], Richard Wiat or[8] Wyatt, Geoffrey "Jeoffrey" Wiot or[7] Wiat, Robert or Richard[6] Wiot, William Wiot or[5] Wyot, Adam Wiot or Wyote or[4], Guyott[3], Guyott[2], Captain or Admiral Adam Guyott or[1] Wiot) was born August 09, 1949 in Stanly County, N.C. He married Dianne McDowell June 10, 1967, daughter of Howard McDowell and Winsie Daniels.

More About James Edward Hinson:
Fact 1: Served in the U.S. Army.

Children of James Hinson and Dianne McDowell are:

2221   i.   Deanna Michele[26] Hinson, born January 26, 1969 in Randolph County, N.C.

2222   ii.   April Lynn Hinson, born March 30, 1972 in Stanly County, N.C.

2223   iii. Temple Dawn Hinson, born March 23, 1973 in Stanly County, N.C.

1664. Lynda Darlene[25] Hinson (Olga Bruce[24] Eagle, Edwin "Ed" Lee[23], Noah Jenkins[22], Mary Jane[21] Morgan, Rachel Evelyn "Eveline"[20] Wyatt, Noah Calvin[19], Thomas "Tommy"[18] Wiatt, Sr. (Wyatt, Wiett), John[17], Henry[16], Richard[15], George[14], Rev. Haute "Haut" "Hawte"[13], Sir George "Georgius" Thomas[12], Sir Thomas "The Younger"[11], Sir Thomas "The Elder"[10], Sir Henry[9], Richard Wiat or[8] Wyatt, Geoffrey "Jeoffrey" Wiot or[7] Wiat, Robert or Richard[6] Wiot, William Wiot or[5] Wyot, Adam Wiot or Wyote or[4], Guyott[3], Guyott[2], Captain or Admiral Adam Guyott or[1] Wiot) was born June 10, 1951 in Stanly County, N.C. She married Richard Lester Frazier August 02, 1968, son of Clarence Mac Frazier and Ester Hayes.

More About Richard Lester Frazier:
Fact 1: 1966-1968, Served in the U.S. Army.

Children of Lynda Hinson and Richard Frazier are:

2224	i.	Ricky Dean[26] Frazier, born March 03, 1969 in Chatham County, N.C.
2225	ii.	Tammy Darlene Frazier, born April 21, 1970 in Chatham County, N.C.
2226	iii.	Keith Anthony Frazier, born June 10, 1972 in Chatham County, N.C.

1665. Shirley Rebecca[25] Hinson (Olga Bruce[24] Eagle, Edwin "Ed" Lee[23], Noah Jenkins[22], Mary Jane[21] Morgan, Rachel Evelyn "Eveline"[20] Wyatt, Noah Calvin[19], Thomas "Tommy"[18] Wiatt, Sr. (Wyatt, Wiett), John[17], Henry[16], Richard[15], George[14], Rev. Haute "Haut" "Hawte"[13], Sir George "Georgius" Thomas[12], Sir Thomas "The Younger"[11], Sir Thomas "The Elder"[10], Sir Henry[9], Richard Wiat or[8] Wyatt, Geoffrey "Jeoffrey" Wiot or[7] Wiat, Robert or Richard[6] Wiot, William Wiot or[5] Wyot, Adam Wiot or Wyote or[4], Guyott[3], Guyott[2], Captain or Admiral Adam Guyott or[1] Wiot) was born February 14, 1953 in Stanly County, N.C. She married Gilbert Hayes Presnell December 20, 1970, son of Robert Presnell and Etta Sanders.

Children of Shirley Hinson and Gilbert Presnell are:

2227	i.	Robert Mitchell[26] Presnell, born October 15, 1971 in Randolph County, N.C.
2228	ii.	Timothy Lee Presnell, born April 30, 1979 in Randolph County, N.C.

1666. Sheri Elaine[25] Davis (Hattie Laura[24] Basinger, Helen Madelene[23] Eagle, Noah Jenkins[22], Mary Jane[21] Morgan, Rachel Evelyn "Eveline"[20] Wyatt, Noah Calvin[19], Thomas "Tommy"[18] Wiatt, Sr. (Wyatt, Wiett), John[17], Henry[16], Richard[15], George[14], Rev. Haute "Haut" "Hawte"[13], Sir George "Georgius" Thomas[12], Sir Thomas "The Younger"[11], Sir Thomas "The Elder"[10], Sir Henry[9], Richard Wiat or[8] Wyatt, Geoffrey "Jeoffrey" Wiot or[7] Wiat, Robert or Richard[6] Wiot, William Wiot or[5] Wyot, Adam Wiot or Wyote or[4], Guyott[3], Guyott[2], Captain or Admiral Adam Guyott or[1] Wiot) was born April 09, 1956 in Iredell County, N.C. She married (1) Thomas Patrick Davis, son of Lawrence Davis and Catherine Olivia. She married (2) Martin Lewis Smith, Sr. November 21, 1976.

Children of Sheri Davis and Thomas Davis are:

2229	i.	Candance Olivia[26] Davis, born March 22, 1983 in Iredell County, N.C.
2230	ii.	Thomas Patrick Davis, Jr., born September 03, 1985.

Children of Sheri Davis and Martin Smith are:

2231	i.	Martin Lewis[26] Smith, Jr., born August 31, 1977.
2232	ii.	Harold Michael Anthony Smith, born March 11, 1978.

1682. David Monroe[25] Barringer (Norman Paige[24], Gladys Marie[23] Eagle, Noah Jenkins[22], Mary Jane[21] Morgan, Rachel Evelyn "Eveline"[20] Wyatt, Noah Calvin[19], Thomas "Tommy"[18]

Wiatt, Sr. (Wyatt, Wiett), John[17], Henry[16], Richard[15], George[14], Rev. Haute "Haut" "Hawte"[13], Sir George "Georgius" Thomas[12], Sir Thomas "The Younger"[11], Sir Thomas "The Elder"[10], Sir Henry[9], Richard Wiat or[8] Wyatt, Geoffrey "Jeoffrey" Wiot or[7] Wiat, Robert or Richard[6] Wiot, William Wiot or[5] Wyot, Adam Wiot or Wyote or[4], Guyott[3], Guyott[2], Captain or Admiral Adam Guyott or[1] Wiot) was born September 18, 1957 in Forsyth County, Winston-Salem, N.C. He married Terri Susan Manuel September 29, 1981, daughter of John Manuel and Dorothy Dodson.

> Child of David Barringer and Terri Manuel is:
> 2233   i.   Emily Paige[26] Barringer, born July 31, 1989 in Winston-Salem, N.C.

1687. Beverly Suzanne[25] Faulk (Sylvia Ann[24] Barringer, Gladys Marie[23] Eagle, Noah Jenkins[22], Mary Jane[21] Morgan, Rachel Evelyn "Eveline"[20] Wyatt, Noah Calvin[19], Thomas "Tommy"[18] Wiatt, Sr. (Wyatt, Wiett), John[17], Henry[16], Richard[15], George[14], Rev. Haute "Haut" "Hawte"[13], Sir George "Georgius" Thomas[12], Sir Thomas "The Younger"[11], Sir Thomas "The Elder"[10], Sir Henry[9], Richard Wiat or[8] Wyatt, Geoffrey "Jeoffrey" Wiot or[7] Wiat, Robert or Richard[6] Wiot, William Wiot or[5] Wyot, Adam Wiot or Wyote or[4], Guyott[3], Guyott[2], Captain or Admiral Adam Guyott or[1] Wiot) was born January 18, 1959 in Stanly County, N.C. She married Terry Allen Price April 12, 1975, son of Clayton Price and Kathleeen Talbert.

> Children of Beverly Faulk and Terry Price are:
> 2234   i.   Michael Blake[26] Price, born December 05, 1975 in Stanly County, N.C.
> 2235   ii.   Brooke Marie Price, born March 18, 1979 in Stanly County, N.C.

1688. Daniel Robert[25] Faulk (Sylvia Ann[24] Barringer, Gladys Marie[23] Eagle, Noah Jenkins[22], Mary Jane[21] Morgan, Rachel Evelyn "Eveline"[20] Wyatt, Noah Calvin[19], Thomas "Tommy"[18] Wiatt, Sr. (Wyatt, Wiett), John[17], Henry[16], Richard[15], George[14], Rev. Haute "Haut" "Hawte"[13], Sir George "Georgius" Thomas[12], Sir Thomas "The Younger"[11], Sir Thomas "The Elder"[10], Sir Henry[9], Richard Wiat or[8] Wyatt, Geoffrey "Jeoffrey" Wiot or[7] Wiat, Robert or Richard[6] Wiot, William Wiot or[5] Wyot, Adam Wiot or Wyote or[4], Guyott[3], Guyott[2], Captain or Admiral Adam Guyott or[1] Wiot) was born April 15, 1962 in Stanly County, N.C. He married Tammy X.

> Children of Daniel Faulk and Tammy X are:
> 2236   i.   X[26] Faulk.
> 2237   ii.   X Faulk.

1730. Jeanie Lynn[25] Honeycutt (Dorothy Jean[24] Fries, Agnes Marie[23] Whitley, Roxie Dora[22] Eagle, Noah Calvin[21], Mary Ann[20] Wyatt, Noah Calvin[19], Thomas "Tommy"[18] Wiatt, Sr. (Wyatt, Wiett), John[17], Henry[16], Richard[15], George[14], Rev. Haute "Haut" "Hawte"[13], Sir George "Georgius" Thomas[12], Sir Thomas "The Younger"[11], Sir Thomas "The Elder"[10], Sir

Henry[9], Richard Wiat or[8] Wyatt, Geoffrey "Jeoffrey" Wiot or[7] Wiat, Robert or Richard[6] Wiot, William Wiot or[5] Wyot, Adam Wiot or Wyote or[4], Guyott[3], Guyott[2], Captain or Admiral Adam Guyott or[1] Wiot) was born August 15, 1952 in Rowan County, N.C. She married Jacky Reeves Moore February 22, 1975, son of Bascom Moore and Treva Vail.

Children of Jeanie Honeycutt and Jacky Moore are:

2238   i.   Sandy Reeves[26] Moore, born November 30, 1976 in Rowan County, N.C.

2239   ii.   Daniel Tyler Moore, born June 24, 1982 in Rowan County, N.C.

1731. Kenneth Kipling[25] Honeycutt (Dorothy Jean[24] Fries, Agnes Marie[23] Whitley, Roxie Dora[22] Eagle, Noah Calvin[21], Mary Ann[20] Wyatt, Noah Calvin[19], Thomas "Tommy"[18] Wiatt, Sr. (Wyatt, Wiett), John[17], Henry[16], Richard[15], George[14], Rev. Haute "Haut" "Hawte"[13], Sir George "Georgius" Thomas[12], Sir Thomas "The Younger"[11], Sir Thomas "The Elder"[10], Sir Henry[9], Richard Wiat or[8] Wyatt, Geoffrey "Jeoffrey" Wiot or[7] Wiat, Robert or Richard[6] Wiot, William Wiot or[5] Wyot, Adam Wiot or Wyote or[4], Guyott[3], Guyott[2], Captain or Admiral Adam Guyott or[1] Wiot) was born July 13, 1953 in Rowan County, N.C. He married Mitzi Lynn Stutts July 01, 1977, daughter of Rufus Stutts and Ruth Simmons.

Child of Kenneth Honeycutt and Mitzi Stutts is:

2240   i.   Ryan Kipling[26] Honeycutt, born March 27, 1980.

1732. Stanley Dean[25] Honeycutt (Dorothy Jean[24] Fries, Agnes Marie[23] Whitley, Roxie Dora[22] Eagle, Noah Calvin[21], Mary Ann[20] Wyatt, Noah Calvin[19], Thomas "Tommy"[18] Wiatt, Sr. (Wyatt, Wiett), John[17], Henry[16], Richard[15], George[14], Rev. Haute "Haut" "Hawte"[13], Sir George "Georgius" Thomas[12], Sir Thomas "The Younger"[11], Sir Thomas "The Elder"[10], Sir Henry[9], Richard Wiat or[8] Wyatt, Geoffrey "Jeoffrey" Wiot or[7] Wiat, Robert or Richard[6] Wiot, William Wiot or[5] Wyot, Adam Wiot or Wyote or[4], Guyott[3], Guyott[2], Captain or Admiral Adam Guyott or[1] Wiot) was born August 02, 1957 in Rowan County, N.C. He married Rita Miller February 18, 1979, daughter of Grover Miller and Vangie Hamm.

Child of Stanley Honeycutt and Rita Miller is:

2241   i.   Megan Lynn[26] Honeycutt, born December 27, 1981 in Rowan County, N.C.

1735. Marc Christopher[25] Fries (Terry Gorman[24], Agnes Marie[23] Whitley, Roxie Dora[22] Eagle, Noah Calvin[21], Mary Ann[20] Wyatt, Noah Calvin[19], Thomas "Tommy"[18] Wiatt, Sr. (Wyatt, Wiett), John[17], Henry[16], Richard[15], George[14], Rev. Haute "Haut" "Hawte"[13], Sir George "Georgius" Thomas[12], Sir Thomas "The Younger"[11], Sir Thomas "The Elder"[10], Sir Henry[9], Richard Wiat or[8] Wyatt, Geoffrey "Jeoffrey" Wiot or[7] Wiat, Robert or Richard[6] Wiot, William Wiot or[5] Wyot, Adam Wiot or Wyote or[4], Guyott[3], Guyott[2], Captain or Admiral Adam Guyott or[1] Wiot) was born June 07, 1957. He married Tammie Veronica Thomas June 04, 1978, daughter of Michael Thomas and Ruth Bell.

Child of Marc Fries and Tammie Thomas is:

2242   i.   Hillerie Elizabeth[26] Fries, born November 28, 1981.

1736. Todd Gorman[25] Fries (Terry Gorman[24], Agnes Marie[23] Whitley, Roxie Dora[22] Eagle, Noah Calvin[21], Mary Ann[20] Wyatt, Noah Calvin[19], Thomas "Tommy"[18] Wiatt, Sr. (Wyatt, Wiett), John[17], Henry[16], Richard[15], George[14], Rev. Haute "Haut" "Hawte"[13], Sir George "Georgius" Thomas[12], Sir Thomas "The Younger"[11], Sir Thomas "The Elder"[10], Sir Henry[9], Richard Wiat or[8] Wyatt, Geoffrey "Jeoffrey" Wiot or[7] Wiat, Robert or Richard[6] Wiot, William Wiot or[5] Wyot, Adam Wiot or Wyote or[4], Guyott[3], Guyott[2], Captain or Admiral Adam Guyott or[1] Wiot) was born April 02, 1959. He married Janet Carol Morgan September 20, 1981, daughter of Charlie Morgan and Susan Huffman.

Child of Todd Fries and Janet Morgan is:

2243   i.   Abram Tyson[26] Fries.

1737. Robin Rochelle[25] Fries (Terry Gorman[24], Agnes Marie[23] Whitley, Roxie Dora[22] Eagle, Noah Calvin[21], Mary Ann[20] Wyatt, Noah Calvin[19], Thomas "Tommy"[18] Wiatt, Sr. (Wyatt, Wiett), John[17], Henry[16], Richard[15], George[14], Rev. Haute "Haut" "Hawte"[13], Sir George "Georgius" Thomas[12], Sir Thomas "The Younger"[11], Sir Thomas "The Elder"[10], Sir Henry[9], Richard Wiat or[8] Wyatt, Geoffrey "Jeoffrey" Wiot or[7] Wiat, Robert or Richard[6] Wiot, William Wiot or[5] Wyot, Adam Wiot or Wyote or[4], Guyott[3], Guyott[2], Captain or Admiral Adam Guyott or[1] Wiot) was born September 13, 1961. She married Keith Bernard Taylor March 02, 1980, son of Brown Taylor and Louise Linker.

Child of Robin Fries and Keith Taylor is:

2244   i.   Seth Matthews[26] Taylor, born September 13, 1980 in Rowan County, N.C.

1749. Boyd Allen[25] Allman (Nancy Marie[24] Glover, Helen Marie[23] Jones, Annie Luada[22] Eagle, Noah Calvin[21], Mary Ann[20] Wyatt, Noah Calvin[19], Thomas "Tommy"[18] Wiatt, Sr. (Wyatt, Wiett), John[17], Henry[16], Richard[15], George[14], Rev. Haute "Haut" "Hawte"[13], Sir George "Georgius" Thomas[12], Sir Thomas "The Younger"[11], Sir Thomas "The Elder"[10], Sir Henry[9], Richard Wiat or[8] Wyatt, Geoffrey "Jeoffrey" Wiot or[7] Wiat, Robert or Richard[6] Wiot, William Wiot or[5] Wyot, Adam Wiot or Wyote or[4], Guyott[3], Guyott[2], Captain or Admiral Adam Guyott or[1] Wiot) was born September 02, 1960 in Cabarrus County, N.C. He married Rosemarie Faith Adams May 07, 1977, daughter of Bobby Adams and Peggy Ghent.

Child of Boyd Allman and Rosemarie Adams is:

2245   i.   Ashley Hope[26] Allman, born September 26, 1977 in Chester County, S.C.

1835. Kenneth Ray[25] Shepherd (Mary Oma[24] Fry, Elizabeth Euver[23] Frick, Mary Christine[22] Eagle, Eli Esau[21], Mary Ann[20] Wyatt, Noah Calvin[19], Thomas "Tommy"[18] Wiatt, Sr. (Wyatt, Wiett), John[17], Henry[16], Richard[15], George[14], Rev. Haute "Haut" "Hawte"[13], Sir George

"Georgius" Thomas[12], Sir Thomas "The Younger"[11], Sir Thomas "The Elder"[10], Sir Henry[9], Richard Wiat or[8] Wyatt, Geoffrey "Jeoffrey" Wiot or[7] Wiat, Robert or Richard[6] Wiot, William Wiot or[5] Wyot, Adam Wiot or Wyote or[4], Guyott[3], Guyott[2], Captain or Admiral Adam Guyott or[1] Wiot) was born May 11, 1952. He married Betty Reid April 04, 1971, daughter of Clifford Reid and Mary Miller.

> Children of Kenneth Shepherd and Betty Reid are:
> 2246   i.   Mary Ann[26] Shepherd, born September 06, 1973.
> 2247   ii.   Adam Clifford Shepherd, born December 20, 1979.

1836.   Edward Eugene[25] Shepherd (Mary Oma[24] Fry, Elizabeth Euver[23] Frick, Mary Christine[22] Eagle, Eli Esau[21], Mary Ann[20] Wyatt, Noah Calvin[19], Thomas "Tommy"[18] Wiatt, Sr. (Wyatt, Wiett), John[17], Henry[16], Richard[15], George[14], Rev. Haute "Haut" "Hawte"[13], Sir George "Georgius" Thomas[12], Sir Thomas "The Younger"[11], Sir Thomas "The Elder"[10], Sir Henry[9], Richard Wiat or[8] Wyatt, Geoffrey "Jeoffrey" Wiot or[7] Wiat, Robert or Richard[6] Wiot, William Wiot or[5] Wyot, Adam Wiot or Wyote or[4], Guyott[3], Guyott[2], Captain or Admiral Adam Guyott or[1] Wiot) was born September 04, 1953. He married Elizabeth Ann Casper April 28, 1978, daughter of William Casper and Wife Maxine.

> Children of Edward Shepherd and Elizabeth Casper are:
> 2248   i.   Amy Nichole[26] Shepherd, born April 16, 1981.
> 2249   ii.   Lisa Mitchell Shepherd, born April 16, 1981.

1891.   Connie Frances[25] Jackson (Ronald Ralph[24], Ralph Adolphus[23], Ida Lou[22] Eagle, Eli Esau[21], Mary Ann[20] Wyatt, Noah Calvin[19], Thomas "Tommy"[18] Wiatt, Sr. (Wyatt, Wiett), John[17], Henry[16], Richard[15], George[14], Rev. Haute "Haut" "Hawte"[13], Sir George "Georgius" Thomas[12], Sir Thomas "The Younger"[11], Sir Thomas "The Elder"[10], Sir Henry[9], Richard Wiat or[8] Wyatt, Geoffrey "Jeoffrey" Wiot or[7] Wiat, Robert or Richard[6] Wiot, William Wiot or[5] Wyot, Adam Wiot or Wyote or[4], Guyott[3], Guyott[2], Captain or Admiral Adam Guyott or[1] Wiot) was born December 30, 1962. She married Thomas Kelly March 30, 1979.

> Children of Connie Jackson and Thomas Kelly are:
> 2250   i.   Michael Trey[26] Kelly, born August 31, 1979.
> 2251   ii.   Alissha Marie Kelly, born July 16, 1982.

1967.   Cheryl Anita[25] Hammill (Bobby Gene[24], Ruth Estelle[23] Goodman, Paul Talmadge[22], Nancy Jane[21] Eagle, Mary Ann[20] Wyatt, Noah Calvin[19], Thomas "Tommy"[18] Wiatt, Sr. (Wyatt, Wiett), John[17], Henry[16], Richard[15], George[14], Rev. Haute "Haut" "Hawte"[13], Sir George "Georgius" Thomas[12], Sir Thomas "The Younger"[11], Sir Thomas "The Elder"[10], Sir Henry[9], Richard Wiat or[8] Wyatt, Geoffrey "Jeoffrey" Wiot or[7] Wiat, Robert or Richard[6] Wiot, William Wiot or[5] Wyot, Adam Wiot or Wyote or[4], Guyott[3], Guyott[2], Captain or Admiral Adam Guyott or[1] Wiot) was born December 01, 1959. She married James Keith White April 05, 1980, son of James White and Betty Shepherd.

Child of Cheryl Hammill and James White is:

2252 i. Brandon Keith[26] White, born 1985.

2006. William Jack[25] Hawkins (Judy Ann[24] Ludwig, Rena Margaret[23] Morgan, Nannie Jane[22] Goodman, Nancy Jane[21] Eagle, Mary Ann[20] Wyatt, Noah Calvin[19], Thomas "Tommy"[18] Wiatt, Sr. (Wyatt, Wiett), John[17], Henry[16], Richard[15], George[14], Rev. Haute "Haut" "Hawte"[13], Sir George "Georgius" Thomas[12], Sir Thomas "The Younger"[11], Sir Thomas "The Elder"[10], Sir Henry[9], Richard Wiat or[8] Wyatt, Geoffrey "Jeoffrey" Wiot or[7] Wiat, Robert or Richard[6] Wiot, William Wiot or[5] Wyot, Adam Wiot or Wyote or[4], Guyott[3], Guyott[2], Captain or Admiral Adam Guyott or[1] Wiot) was born October 02, 1960 in Germany. He married Ginger.

  Child of William Hawkins and Ginger is:

2253 i. Billy[26] Hawkins, born September 22, 1981.

2032. Tamara Letitia[25] Boggs (Jane Eleanor[24] Goodman, Leo Francis[23], Bennett Francis[22], Nancy Jane[21] Eagle, Mary Ann[20] Wyatt, Noah Calvin[19], Thomas "Tommy"[18] Wiatt, Sr. (Wyatt, Wiett), John[17], Henry[16], Richard[15], George[14], Rev. Haute "Haut" "Hawte"[13], Sir George "Georgius" Thomas[12], Sir Thomas "The Younger"[11], Sir Thomas "The Elder"[10], Sir Henry[9], Richard Wiat or[8] Wyatt, Geoffrey "Jeoffrey" Wiot or[7] Wiat, Robert or Richard[6] Wiot, William Wiot or[5] Wyot, Adam Wiot or Wyote or[4], Guyott[3], Guyott[2], Captain or Admiral Adam Guyott or[1] Wiot) was born October 24, 1962. She married Peter Klingsheim, son of Peter Klingsheim and Gloria.

  Children of Tamara Boggs and Peter Klingsheim are:

2254 i. Peter Harold[26] Klingsheim.

2255 ii. Christopher Theodore Klingsheim, born April 03, 1985.

2033. Derek Anthony[25] Boggs (Jane Eleanor[24] Goodman, Leo Francis[23], Bennett Francis[22], Nancy Jane[21] Eagle, Mary Ann[20] Wyatt, Noah Calvin[19], Thomas "Tommy"[18] Wiatt, Sr. (Wyatt, Wiett), John[17], Henry[16], Richard[15], George[14], Rev. Haute "Haut" "Hawte"[13], Sir George "Georgius" Thomas[12], Sir Thomas "The Younger"[11], Sir Thomas "The Elder"[10], Sir Henry[9], Richard Wiat or[8] Wyatt, Geoffrey "Jeoffrey" Wiot or[7] Wiat, Robert or Richard[6] Wiot, William Wiot or[5] Wyot, Adam Wiot or Wyote or[4], Guyott[3], Guyott[2], Captain or Admiral Adam Guyott or[1] Wiot) was born December 09, 1964. He married Merdith Christine Adams.

  Child of Derek Boggs and Merdith Adams is:

2256 i. Seth Adam[26] Boggs, born May 17, 1987.

2058. Carla Waynette[25] Osborne (Betty Carol[24] Hill, Janet Inez[23] McHargue, Octa Mae[22] Eagle, William Grant[21], Mary Ann[20] Wyatt, Noah Calvin[19], Thomas "Tommy"[18] Wiatt, Sr. (Wyatt, Wiett), John[17], Henry[16], Richard[15], George[14], Rev. Haute "Haut" "Hawte"[13], Sir George "Georgius" Thomas[12], Sir Thomas "The Younger"[11], Sir Thomas "The Elder"[10], Sir Henry[9], Richard Wiat or[8] Wyatt, Geoffrey "Jeoffrey" Wiot or[7] Wiat, Robert or Richard[6] Wiot,

William Wiot or[5] Wyot, Adam Wiot or Wyote or[4], Guyott[3], Guyott[2], Captain or Admiral Adam Guyott or[1] Wiot) was born October 17, 1963 in Md. She married Charles Daniel Sexton January 04, 1982, son of Charles Sexton and Mary Shirley.

Child of Carla Osborne and Charles Sexton is:

2257   i.   Janet Danielle[26] Sexton, born September 02, 1986 in Doylas County, Lithea Springs, Ga.

2077. Darleen[25] Cannon (Annie Marie[24] Parker, Harvey Adophus[23], J. Columbus[22], Ollie Lou Ada[21] Shaver, Rhoda E.[20] Wyatt, Noah Calvin[19], Thomas "Tommy"[18] Wiatt, Sr. (Wyatt, Wiett), John[17], Henry[16], Richard[15], George[14], Rev. Haute "Haut" "Hawte"[13], Sir George "Georgius" Thomas[12], Sir Thomas "The Younger"[11], Sir Thomas "The Elder"[10], Sir Henry[9], Richard Wiat or[8] Wyatt, Geoffrey "Jeoffrey" Wiot or[7] Wiat, Robert or Richard[6] Wiot, William Wiot or[5] Wyot, Adam Wiot or Wyote or[4], Guyott[3], Guyott[2], Captain or Admiral Adam Guyott or[1] Wiot). She married (1) Carl Reavis. She married (2) X.

Children of Darleen Cannon and Carl Reavis are:

+   2258   i.   James[26] Reavis.
+   2259   ii.   William Reavis.
     2260   iii. Susan Reavis.

Children of Darleen Cannon and X are:

2261   i.   Jeremy[26] X.
2262   ii.   Amanda X.

2078. Leon[25] Cannon (Annie Marie[24] Parker, Harvey Adophus[23], J. Columbus[22], Ollie Lou Ada[21] Shaver, Rhoda E.[20] Wyatt, Noah Calvin[19], Thomas "Tommy"[18] Wiatt, Sr. (Wyatt, Wiett), John[17], Henry[16], Richard[15], George[14], Rev. Haute "Haut" "Hawte"[13], Sir George "Georgius" Thomas[12], Sir Thomas "The Younger"[11], Sir Thomas "The Elder"[10], Sir Henry[9], Richard Wiat or[8] Wyatt, Geoffrey "Jeoffrey" Wiot or[7] Wiat, Robert or Richard[6] Wiot, William Wiot or[5] Wyot, Adam Wiot or Wyote or[4], Guyott[3], Guyott[2], Captain or Admiral Adam Guyott or[1] Wiot). He married Ruby Smith.

Children of Leon Cannon and Ruby Smith are:

+   2263   i.   Rebecca[26] Cannon.
     2264   ii.   Randy Cannon.
     2265   iii. Terry Cannon.

2080. Irvin[25] Cannon (Annie Marie[24] Parker, Harvey Adophus[23], J. Columbus[22], Ollie Lou Ada[21] Shaver, Rhoda E.[20] Wyatt, Noah Calvin[19], Thomas "Tommy"[18] Wiatt, Sr. (Wyatt, Wiett), John[17], Henry[16], Richard[15], George[14], Rev. Haute "Haut" "Hawte"[13], Sir George "Georgius" Thomas[12], Sir Thomas "The Younger"[11], Sir Thomas "The Elder"[10], Sir Henry[9], Richard Wiat or[8] Wyatt, Geoffrey "Jeoffrey" Wiot or[7] Wiat, Robert or Richard[6] Wiot, William Wiot or[5] Wyot, Adam Wiot or Wyote or[4], Guyott[3], Guyott[2], Captain or Admiral Adam Guyott or[1] Wiot). He married Joyce Wilhelm.

Children of Irvin Cannon and Joyce Wilhelm are:

+ 2266   i.   Vickie[26] Cannon.
+ 2267   ii.   Sheila Cannon.

2082. Edna[25] Cannon (Annie Marie[24] Parker, Harvey Adophus[23], J. Columbus[22], Ollie Lou Ada[21] Shaver, Rhoda E.[20] Wyatt, Noah Calvin[19], Thomas "Tommy"[18] Wiatt, Sr. (Wyatt, Wiett), John[17], Henry[16], Richard[15], George[14], Rev. Haute "Haut" "Hawte"[13], Sir George "Georgius" Thomas[12], Sir Thomas "The Younger"[11], Sir Thomas "The Elder"[10], Sir Henry[9], Richard Wiat or[8] Wyatt, Geoffrey "Jeoffrey" Wiot or[7] Wiat, Robert or Richard[6] Wiot, William Wiot or[5] Wyot, Adam Wiot or Wyote or[4], Guyott[3], Guyott[2], Captain or Admiral Adam Guyott or[1] Wiot). She married Wade English.

Children of Edna Cannon and Wade English are:

+ 2268   i.   Bobby[26] English.
+ 2269   ii.   Ann English.
+ 2270   iii.   Tammy English.
   2271   iv.   Teresa English.
+ 2272   v.   Ronda English.

2083. Richard[25] Cannon (Annie Marie[24] Parker, Harvey Adophus[23], J. Columbus[22], Ollie Lou Ada[21] Shaver, Rhoda E.[20] Wyatt, Noah Calvin[19], Thomas "Tommy"[18] Wiatt, Sr. (Wyatt, Wiett), John[17], Henry[16], Richard[15], George[14], Rev. Haute "Haut" "Hawte"[13], Sir George "Georgius" Thomas[12], Sir Thomas "The Younger"[11], Sir Thomas "The Elder"[10], Sir Henry[9], Richard Wiat or[8] Wyatt, Geoffrey "Jeoffrey" Wiot or[7] Wiat, Robert or Richard[6] Wiot, William Wiot or[5] Wyot, Adam Wiot or Wyote or[4], Guyott[3], Guyott[2], Captain or Admiral Adam Guyott or[1] Wiot). He married X.

Child of Richard Cannon and X is:

   2273   i.   Sherre[26] Cannon.

2084. Glenn[25] Cannon (Annie Marie[24] Parker, Harvey Adophus[23], J. Columbus[22], Ollie Lou Ada[21] Shaver, Rhoda E.[20] Wyatt, Noah Calvin[19], Thomas "Tommy"[18] Wiatt, Sr. (Wyatt, Wiett), John[17], Henry[16], Richard[15], George[14], Rev. Haute "Haut" "Hawte"[13], Sir George "Georgius" Thomas[12], Sir Thomas "The Younger"[11], Sir Thomas "The Elder"[10], Sir Henry[9], Richard Wiat or[8] Wyatt, Geoffrey "Jeoffrey" Wiot or[7] Wiat, Robert or Richard[6] Wiot, William Wiot or[5] Wyot, Adam Wiot or Wyote or[4], Guyott[3], Guyott[2], Captain or Admiral Adam Guyott or[1] Wiot) was born February 11, 1937, and died June 17, 1984. He married Frances Moss.

Children of Glenn Cannon and Frances Moss are:

+ 2274   i.   Bonita[26] Cannon.
+ 2275   ii.   Tracie Cannon.

2085. Jay[25] Cannon (Annie Marie[24] Parker, Harvey Adophus[23], J. Columbus[22], Ollie Lou Ada[21] Shaver, Rhoda E.[20] Wyatt, Noah Calvin[19], Thomas "Tommy"[18] Wiatt, Sr. (Wyatt, Wiett), John[17], Henry[16], Richard[15], George[14], Rev. Haute "Haut" "Hawte"[13], Sir George "Georgius"

Thomas[12], Sir Thomas "The Younger"[11], Sir Thomas "The Elder"[10], Sir Henry[9], Richard Wiat or[8] Wyatt, Geoffrey "Jeoffrey" Wiot or[7] Wiat, Robert or Richard[6] Wiot, William Wiot or[5] Wyot, Adam Wiot or Wyote or[4], Guyott[3], Guyott[2], Captain or Admiral Adam Guyott or[1] Wiot) was born November 01, 1945, and died April 26, 1987. He married Brenda Burris.

    Children of Jay Cannon and Brenda Burris are:

2276	i.	Mark[26] Cannon.
2277	ii.	Scott Cannon.

2088. Hugh Brittle[25] Walton (Rena Catherine[24] Parker, Harvey Adophus[23], J. Columbus[22], Ollie Lou Ada[21] Shaver, Rhoda E.[20] Wyatt, Noah Calvin[19], Thomas "Tommy"[18] Wiatt, Sr. (Wyatt, Wiett), John[17], Henry[16], Richard[15], George[14], Rev. Haute "Haut" "Hawte"[13], Sir George "Georgius" Thomas[12], Sir Thomas "The Younger"[11], Sir Thomas "The Elder"[10], Sir Henry[9], Richard Wiat or[8] Wyatt, Geoffrey "Jeoffrey" Wiot or[7] Wiat, Robert or Richard[6] Wiot, William Wiot or[5] Wyot, Adam Wiot or Wyote or[4], Guyott[3], Guyott[2], Captain or Admiral Adam Guyott or[1] Wiot) was born October 23, 1933. He married Sadie Troutman June 17, 1951, daughter of William Troutman and Annie Reeves.

    Child of Hugh Walton and Sadie Troutman is:

+	2278	i.	Janice Elaine[26] Walton, born August 17, 1952.

2089. Ronald Clifton[25] Parker (Guy Ray[24], Harvey Adophus[23], J. Columbus[22], Ollie Lou Ada[21] Shaver, Rhoda E.[20] Wyatt, Noah Calvin[19], Thomas "Tommy"[18] Wiatt, Sr. (Wyatt, Wiett), John[17], Henry[16], Richard[15], George[14], Rev. Haute "Haut" "Hawte"[13], Sir George "Georgius" Thomas[12], Sir Thomas "The Younger"[11], Sir Thomas "The Elder"[10], Sir Henry[9], Richard Wiat or[8] Wyatt, Geoffrey "Jeoffrey" Wiot or[7] Wiat, Robert or Richard[6] Wiot, William Wiot or[5] Wyot, Adam Wiot or Wyote or[4], Guyott[3], Guyott[2], Captain or Admiral Adam Guyott or[1] Wiot) was born June 27, 1946. He married Pearly Mae Bartley.

    Children of Ronald Parker and Pearly Bartley are:

2279	i.	Jeffry[26] Parker.
2280	ii.	Jennifer Parker.

2090. Katie Jane[25] Parker (Guy Ray[24], Harvey Adophus[23], J. Columbus[22], Ollie Lou Ada[21] Shaver, Rhoda E.[20] Wyatt, Noah Calvin[19], Thomas "Tommy"[18] Wiatt, Sr. (Wyatt, Wiett), John[17], Henry[16], Richard[15], George[14], Rev. Haute "Haut" "Hawte"[13], Sir George "Georgius" Thomas[12], Sir Thomas "The Younger"[11], Sir Thomas "The Elder"[10], Sir Henry[9], Richard Wiat or[8] Wyatt, Geoffrey "Jeoffrey" Wiot or[7] Wiat, Robert or Richard[6] Wiot, William Wiot or[5] Wyot, Adam Wiot or Wyote or[4], Guyott[3], Guyott[2], Captain or Admiral Adam Guyott or[1] Wiot) was born April 11, 1949. She married Thomas Edward Stoner, son of Robert Stoner and Freda Shepherd.

    Children of Katie Parker and Thomas Stoner are:

2281	i.	Janie Lee[26] Stoner, born January 15, 1971.
2282	ii.	Angie Marie Stoner, born May 18, 1974.

2092. Connie Sue[25] Parker (Guy Ray[24], Harvey Adophus[23], J. Columbus[22], Ollie Lou Ada[21] Shaver, Rhoda E.[20] Wyatt, Noah Calvin[19], Thomas "Tommy"[18] Wiatt, Sr. (Wyatt, Wiett), John[17], Henry[16], Richard[15], George[14], Rev. Haute "Haut" "Hawte"[13], Sir George "Georgius" Thomas[12], Sir Thomas "The Younger"[11], Sir Thomas "The Elder"[10], Sir Henry[9], Richard Wiat or[8] Wyatt, Geoffrey "Jeoffrey" Wiot or[7] Wiat, Robert or Richard[6] Wiot, William Wiot or[5] Wyot, Adam Wiot or Wyote or[4], Guyott[3], Guyott[2], Captain or Admiral Adam Guyott or[1] Wiot) was born November 1958. She married Robert Poole, son of Robert Poole and Frances Phillips.

> Child of Connie Parker and Robert Poole is:
> 2283   i.   Kelly Leigh[26] Poole, born January 1985.

2094. Jimmy Darrell[25] Parker (Harvey Adophus[24], Harvey Adophus[23], J. Columbus[22], Ollie Lou Ada[21] Shaver, Rhoda E.[20] Wyatt, Noah Calvin[19], Thomas "Tommy"[18] Wiatt, Sr. (Wyatt, Wiett), John[17], Henry[16], Richard[15], George[14], Rev. Haute "Haut" "Hawte"[13], Sir George "Georgius" Thomas[12], Sir Thomas "The Younger"[11], Sir Thomas "The Elder"[10], Sir Henry[9], Richard Wiat or[8] Wyatt, Geoffrey "Jeoffrey" Wiot or[7] Wiat, Robert or Richard[6] Wiot, William Wiot or[5] Wyot, Adam Wiot or Wyote or[4], Guyott[3], Guyott[2], Captain or Admiral Adam Guyott or[1] Wiot) was born June 02, 1951. He married Sandy Genenne Sifford June 18, 1971, daughter of Lindy Stifford and Virginia Kluttz.

> Children of Jimmy Parker and Sandy Sifford are:
> 2284   i.   Jeffrey Darrell[26] Parker, born December 05, 1974.
> 2285   ii.   Cammie Rebecca Parker, born September 06, 1980.

2095. Robert Keith[25] Parker (Harvey Adophus[24], Harvey Adophus[23], J. Columbus[22], Ollie Lou Ada[21] Shaver, Rhoda E.[20] Wyatt, Noah Calvin[19], Thomas "Tommy"[18] Wiatt, Sr. (Wyatt, Wiett), John[17], Henry[16], Richard[15], George[14], Rev. Haute "Haut" "Hawte"[13], Sir George "Georgius" Thomas[12], Sir Thomas "The Younger"[11], Sir Thomas "The Elder"[10], Sir Henry[9], Richard Wiat or[8] Wyatt, Geoffrey "Jeoffrey" Wiot or[7] Wiat, Robert or Richard[6] Wiot, William Wiot or[5] Wyot, Adam Wiot or Wyote or[4], Guyott[3], Guyott[2], Captain or Admiral Adam Guyott or[1] Wiot) was born October 25, 1953. He married Sandra Christine Strange June 1978.

> Child of Robert Parker and Sandra Strange is:
> 2286   i.   Amanda Christine[26] Parker, born September 01, 1978.

2096. Brenda Catherine[25] Parker (Harvey Adophus[24], Harvey Adophus[23], J. Columbus[22], Ollie Lou Ada[21] Shaver, Rhoda E.[20] Wyatt, Noah Calvin[19], Thomas "Tommy"[18] Wiatt, Sr. (Wyatt, Wiett), John[17], Henry[16], Richard[15], George[14], Rev. Haute "Haut" "Hawte"[13], Sir George "Georgius" Thomas[12], Sir Thomas "The Younger"[11], Sir Thomas "The Elder"[10], Sir Henry[9], Richard Wiat or[8] Wyatt, Geoffrey "Jeoffrey" Wiot or[7] Wiat, Robert or Richard[6] Wiot, William Wiot or[5] Wyot, Adam Wiot or Wyote or[4], Guyott[3], Guyott[2], Captain or Admiral Adam Guyott or[1] Wiot) was born December 28, 1955. She married Randy Franklin Goodman June 12, 1974, son of Eli Goodman and Billie.

Children of Brenda Parker and Randy Goodman are:

2287   i.   Chrissy Anne[26] Goodman, born March 16, 1978.

2288   ii.   Randy Franklin Goodman, Jr., born January 25, 1987.

2103. Tammy Jean[25] Patton (Martha Elisabeth[24] Eagle, Murray or Murry Lee "Red"[23], Calvin DeBerry[22], William Lawson[21], Amanda Jane[20] Wyatt, Noah Calvin[19], Thomas "Tommy"[18] Wiatt, Sr. (Wyatt, Wiett), John[17], Henry[16], Richard[15], George[14], Rev. Haute "Haut" "Hawte"[13], Sir George "Georgius" Thomas[12], Sir Thomas "The Younger"[11], Sir Thomas "The Elder"[10], Sir Henry[9], Richard Wiat or[8] Wyatt, Geoffrey "Jeoffrey" Wiot or[7] Wiat, Robert or Richard[6] Wiot, William Wiot or[5] Wyot, Adam Wiot or Wyote or[4], Guyott[3], Guyott[2], Captain or Admiral Adam Guyott or[1] Wiot) was born June 19, 1961. She married Donald Jerry Phillips II, son of Donald Phillips and X.

Child of Tammy Patton and Donald Phillips is:

2289   i.   Donald Jerry[26] Phillips III, born October 02, 1976 in Guilford County, N.C.

2139. Lori Lachelle[25] Sifford (Walter Roy[24], Novice Bernita[23] Kluttz, Mary Kate[22] Eagle, John Murphy[21], Amanda Jane[20] Wyatt, Noah Calvin[19], Thomas "Tommy"[18] Wiatt, Sr. (Wyatt, Wiett), John[17], Henry[16], Richard[15], George[14], Rev. Haute "Haut" "Hawte"[13], Sir George "Georgius" Thomas[12], Sir Thomas "The Younger"[11], Sir Thomas "The Elder"[10], Sir Henry[9], Richard Wiat or[8] Wyatt, Geoffrey "Jeoffrey" Wiot or[7] Wiat, Robert or Richard[6] Wiot, William Wiot or[5] Wyot, Adam Wiot or Wyote or[4], Guyott[3], Guyott[2], Captain or Admiral Adam Guyott or[1] Wiot) was born September 16, 1968. She married Edward K. DeMunbrun December 22, 1985.

Child of Lori Sifford and Edward DeMunbrun is:

2290   i.   Samantha Caroline[26] DeMunbrun, born February 16, 1990.

Generation No. 26

2160. Kathy Renea[26] Story (Patsy Carolyn[25] Brown, Edith Hope[24] Basinger, Effie Jeanette "Genetta" Eagle[23] Wyatt, Harvey Addison[22], Columbus Ciscero[21], Wilson Riley[20], Jesse "Jessey"[19], John "Johney"[18], John[17] Wiatt, Henry[16], Richard[15], George[14], Rev. Haute "Haut" "Hawte"[13], Sir George "Georgius" Thomas[12], Sir Thomas "The Younger"[11], Sir Thomas "The Elder"[10], Sir Henry[9], Richard Wiat or[8] Wyatt, Geoffrey "Jeoffrey" Wiot or[7] Wiat, Robert or Richard[6] Wiot, William Wiot or[5] Wyot, Adam Wiot or Wyote or[4], Guyott[3], Guyott[2], Captain or Admiral Adam Guyott or[1] Wiot) was born February 17, 1958. She married Robert Ervin Basinger February 27, 1976.

Children of Kathy Story and Robert Basinger are:

2291   i.   Levi Robin[27] Basinger, born March 16, 1977.

2292   ii.   Nicholas Christian Basinger, born November 16, 1979.

2161. Randal Thomas[26] Story (Patsy Carolyn[25] Brown, Edith Hope[24] Basinger, Effie Jeanette "Genetta" Eagle[23] Wyatt, Harvey Addison[22], Columbus Ciscero[21], Wilson Riley[20], Jesse "Jessey"[19], John "Johney"[18], John[17] Wiatt, Henry[16], Richard[15], George[14], Rev. Haute "Haut" "Hawte"[13], Sir George "Georgius" Thomas[12], Sir Thomas "The Younger"[11], Sir Thomas "The Elder"[10], Sir Henry[9], Richard Wiat or[8] Wyatt, Geoffrey "Jeoffrey" Wiot or[7] Wiat, Robert or Richard[6] Wiot, William Wiot or[5] Wyot, Adam Wiot or Wyote or[4], Guyott[3], Guyott[2], Captain or Admiral Adam Guyott or[1] Wiot) was born June 28, 1959. He married Brenda Annette Beaver March 20, 1983.

> Child of Randal Story and Brenda Beaver is:
> 2293   i.   Tiffany Brooke[27] Story, born October 03, 1983.

2162. Rhonda LuAnne[26] Story (Patsy Carolyn[25] Brown, Edith Hope[24] Basinger, Effie Jeanette "Genetta" Eagle[23] Wyatt, Harvey Addison[22], Columbus Ciscero[21], Wilson Riley[20], Jesse "Jessey"[19], John "Johney"[18], John[17] Wiatt, Henry[16], Richard[15], George[14], Rev. Haute "Haut" "Hawte"[13], Sir George "Georgius" Thomas[12], Sir Thomas "The Younger"[11], Sir Thomas "The Elder"[10], Sir Henry[9], Richard Wiat or[8] Wyatt, Geoffrey "Jeoffrey" Wiot or[7] Wiat, Robert or Richard[6] Wiot, William Wiot or[5] Wyot, Adam Wiot or Wyote or[4], Guyott[3], Guyott[2], Captain or Admiral Adam Guyott or[1] Wiot) was born July 08, 1961. She married Charlie Leon Harrington April 05, 1980.

> Child of Rhonda Story and Charlie Harrington is:
> 2294   i.   Nathan Leon[27] Harrington, born October 03, 1983.

2164. Gary Wayne[26] Brown (James Ray[25], Edith Hope[24] Basinger, Effie Jeanette "Genetta" Eagle[23] Wyatt, Harvey Addison[22], Columbus Ciscero[21], Wilson Riley[20], Jesse "Jessey"[19], John "Johney"[18], John[17] Wiatt, Henry[16], Richard[15], George[14], Rev. Haute "Haut" "Hawte"[13], Sir George "Georgius" Thomas[12], Sir Thomas "The Younger"[11], Sir Thomas "The Elder"[10], Sir Henry[9], Richard Wiat or[8] Wyatt, Geoffrey "Jeoffrey" Wiot or[7] Wiat, Robert or Richard[6] Wiot, William Wiot or[5] Wyot, Adam Wiot or Wyote or[4], Guyott[3], Guyott[2], Captain or Admiral Adam Guyott or[1] Wiot) was born February 24, 1962. He married Deborah Lynn Holstein November 19, 1983.

> Child of Gary Brown and Deborah Holstein is:
> 2295   i.   Jonathan Taylor[27] Brown, born January 03, 1985.

2166. John Michael[26] Stirewalt (Alice "Faye"[25] Brown, Edith Hope[24] Basinger, Effie Jeanette "Genetta" Eagle[23] Wyatt, Harvey Addison[22], Columbus Ciscero[21], Wilson Riley[20], Jesse "Jessey"[19], John "Johney"[18], John[17] Wiatt, Henry[16], Richard[15], George[14], Rev. Haute "Haut" "Hawte"[13], Sir George "Georgius" Thomas[12], Sir Thomas "The Younger"[11], Sir Thomas "The Elder"[10], Sir Henry[9], Richard Wiat or[8] Wyatt, Geoffrey "Jeoffrey" Wiot or[7] Wiat, Robert or Richard[6] Wiot, William Wiot or[5] Wyot, Adam Wiot or Wyote or[4], Guyott[3], Guyott[2], Captain or Admiral Adam Guyott or[1] Wiot) was born November 21, 1960. He married Linda Delette Goble July 02, 1983.

Child of John Stirewalt and Linda Goble is:

2296   i.   Justin Michael[27] Stirewalt, born May 05, 1985.

2193. Chad Edward[26] Wikle (Rebecca "Becky" Ann[25] Hinson, William "Bill" Crowell[24], Virgie Irene[23] Eagle, Noah Jenkins[22], Mary Jane[21] Morgan, Rachel Evelyn "Eveline"[20] Wyatt, Noah Calvin[19], Thomas "Tommy"[18] Wiatt, Sr. (Wyatt, Wiett), John[17], Henry[16], Richard[15], George[14], Rev. Haute "Haut" "Hawte"[13], Sir George "Georgius" Thomas[12], Sir Thomas "The Younger"[11], Sir Thomas "The Elder"[10], Sir Henry[9], Richard Wiat or[8] Wyatt, Geoffrey "Jeoffrey" Wiot or[7] Wiat, Robert or Richard[6] Wiot, William Wiot or[5] Wyot, Adam Wiot or Wyote or[4], Guyott[3], Guyott[2], Captain or Admiral Adam Guyott or[1] Wiot) was born November 20, 1977 in Radford, Montgomery County, Va. He married Elesha Burnette, daughter of Burnette and Mary.

Child of Chad Wikle and Elesha Burnette is:

2297   i.   Andrew Evert[27] Wikle, born April 11, 1997 in Montgomery Regional Hospital, Blacksburg, Va.

2194. Maria Adelinea[26] Mangieri (Mary Lynn[25] Hinson, William "Bill" Crowell[24], Virgie Irene[23] Eagle, Noah Jenkins[22], Mary Jane[21] Morgan, Rachel Evelyn "Eveline"[20] Wyatt, Noah Calvin[19], Thomas "Tommy"[18] Wiatt, Sr. (Wyatt, Wiett), John[17], Henry[16], Richard[15], George[14], Rev. Haute "Haut" "Hawte"[13], Sir George "Georgius" Thomas[12], Sir Thomas "The Younger"[11], Sir Thomas "The Elder"[10], Sir Henry[9], Richard Wiat or[8] Wyatt, Geoffrey "Jeoffrey" Wiot or[7] Wiat, Robert or Richard[6] Wiot, William Wiot or[5] Wyot, Adam Wiot or Wyote or[4], Guyott[3], Guyott[2], Captain or Admiral Adam Guyott or[1] Wiot) was born December 29, 1986 in Italy. She married Michael Farrow October 2011 in Virginia.

Children of Maria Mangieri and Michael Farrow are:

2298   i.   Rylan Grace[27] Farrow, born November 2011.
2299   ii.   Emmalyn Taylor Farrow.
2300   iii.   Girl Farrow.

2195. Natalie Paige[26] Hinson (Melanie Joan[25], William "Bill" Crowell[24], Virgie Irene[23] Eagle, Noah Jenkins[22], Mary Jane[21] Morgan, Rachel Evelyn "Eveline"[20] Wyatt, Noah Calvin[19], Thomas "Tommy"[18] Wiatt, Sr. (Wyatt, Wiett), John[17], Henry[16], Richard[15], George[14], Rev. Haute "Haut" "Hawte"[13], Sir George "Georgius" Thomas[12], Sir Thomas "The Younger"[11], Sir Thomas "The Elder"[10], Sir Henry[9], Richard Wiat or[8] Wyatt, Geoffrey "Jeoffrey" Wiot or[7] Wiat, Robert or Richard[6] Wiot, William Wiot or[5] Wyot, Adam Wiot or Wyote or[4], Guyott[3], Guyott[2], Captain or Admiral Adam Guyott or[1] Wiot) was born February 03, 1979 in Winston-Salem, Forsyth County, N.C. She met (1) Jerry Autry 1997 in Winston-Salem, Forsyth County, N.C., son of Jerry Autry and Margaret Rice. She married (2) Brad Boyd February 2001 in Winston-Salem, Forsyth County, N.C. She married (3) Chadd Andrew Wolfanger April 19, 2003 in Courthouse, Winston-Salem, Forsyth County, N.C., son of Larry Wolfanger and Bonnie.

Child of Natalie Hinson and Jerry Autry is:

2301   i.   Joshua "Josh" Lawrence[27] Hinson, born June 15, 1998 in Winston-Salem, Forsyth County, N.C.

Child of Natalie Hinson and Chadd Wolfanger is:

2302   i.   Ava Paige[27] Wolfanger, born December 05, 2002 in Winston-Salem, N.C.

2196. Daniel Michael[26] Saramaha (Melanie Joan[25] Hinson, William "Bill" Crowell[24], Virgie Irene[23] Eagle, Noah Jenkins[22], Mary Jane[21] Morgan, Rachel Evelyn "Eveline"[20] Wyatt, Noah Calvin[19], Thomas "Tommy"[18] Wiatt, Sr. (Wyatt, Wiett), John[17], Henry[16], Richard[15], George[14], Rev. Haute "Haut" "Hawte"[13], Sir George "Georgius" Thomas[12], Sir Thomas "The Younger"[11], Sir Thomas "The Elder"[10], Sir Henry[9], Richard Wiat or[8] Wyatt, Geoffrey "Jeoffrey" Wiot or[7] Wiat, Robert or Richard[6] Wiot, William Wiot or[5] Wyot, Adam Wiot or Wyote or[4], Guyott[3], Guyott[2], Captain or Admiral Adam Guyott or[1] Wiot) was born June 28, 1986 in Winston-Salem, Forsyth County, N.C. He married Miriam March 2012 in Jacksonville, Fla.

Children of Daniel Saramaha and Miriam are:

2303   i.   Daniel Michael[27] Saramaha, Jr., born June 28, 2013 in Sasebo, Japan.

2304   ii.   Child Saramaha, born February 2015.

2200. Christopher "Chris" Thomas[26] Hinson (Richard Merrell[25], Richard "Chubby" "Chub" Clyde[24], Virgie Irene[23] Eagle, Noah Jenkins[22], Mary Jane[21] Morgan, Rachel Evelyn "Eveline"[20] Wyatt, Noah Calvin[19], Thomas "Tommy"[18] Wiatt, Sr. (Wyatt, Wiett), John[17], Henry[16], Richard[15], George[14], Rev. Haute "Haut" "Hawte"[13], Sir George "Georgius" Thomas[12], Sir Thomas "The Younger"[11], Sir Thomas "The Elder"[10], Sir Henry[9], Richard Wiat or[8] Wyatt, Geoffrey "Jeoffrey" Wiot or[7] Wiat, Robert or Richard[6] Wiot, William Wiot or[5] Wyot, Adam Wiot or Wyote or[4], Guyott[3], Guyott[2], Captain or Admiral Adam Guyott or[1] Wiot) was born October 15, 1977 in Salisbury, Rowan County, N.C. He married Julie Marie Purser June 04, 2004 in Charleston, S.C., daughter of Julius Purser and Joyce X?.

Children of Christopher Hinson and Julie Purser are:

2305   i.   Elizabeth Riley[27] Hinson, born June 11, 2007.

2306   ii.   Madeline Reece Hinson?, born January 12, 2009.

2201. Pamela Michelle[26] Wilson (Pamela "Pam" Irene[25] Hinson, Richard "Chubby" "Chub" Clyde[24], Virgie Irene[23] Eagle, Noah Jenkins[22], Mary Jane[21] Morgan, Rachel Evelyn "Eveline"[20] Wyatt, Noah Calvin[19], Thomas "Tommy"[18] Wiatt, Sr. (Wyatt, Wiett), John[17], Henry[16], Richard[15], George[14], Rev. Haute "Haut" "Hawte"[13], Sir George "Georgius" Thomas[12], Sir Thomas "The Younger"[11], Sir Thomas "The Elder"[10], Sir Henry[9], Richard Wiat or[8] Wyatt, Geoffrey "Jeoffrey" Wiot or[7] Wiat, Robert or Richard[6] Wiot, William Wiot or[5] Wyot, Adam Wiot or Wyote or[4], Guyott[3], Guyott[2], Captain or Admiral Adam Guyott or[1] Wiot) was born

July 15, 1972 in Salisbury, Rowan County, N.C. She married (1) Brian Wacaster August 15, 1993 in Salisbury, Rowan County, N.C. She married (2) Burris Abt. 2007 in Salisbury, Rowan County, N.C.

> Child of Pamela Wilson and Brian Wacaster is:
> 2307   i.   Wacaster[27].
>
> Child of Pamela Wilson and Burris is:
> 2308   i.   Karlie Elizabeth[27] Burris, born February 18, 2009 in Salisbury, Rowan County, N.C.

2202.   Candace Chevonne[26] Wilson (Pamela "Pam" Irene[25] Hinson, Richard "Chubby" "Chub" Clyde[24], Virgie Irene[23] Eagle, Noah Jenkins[22], Mary Jane[21] Morgan, Rachel Evelyn "Eveline"[20] Wyatt, Noah Calvin[19], Thomas "Tommy"[18] Wiatt, Sr. (Wyatt, Wiett), John[17], Henry[16], Richard[15], George[14], Rev. Haute "Haut" "Hawte"[13], Sir George "Georgius" Thomas[12], Sir Thomas "The Younger"[11], Sir Thomas "The Elder"[10], Sir Henry[9], Richard Wiat or[8] Wyatt, Geoffrey "Jeoffrey" Wiot or[7] Wiat, Robert or Richard[6] Wiot, William Wiot or[5] Wyot, Adam Wiot or Wyote or[4], Guyott[3], Guyott[2], Captain or Admiral Adam Guyott or[1] Wiot) was born August 04, 1981 in Salisbury, Rowan County, N.C. She married Adam Carmean.

> Children of Candace Wilson and Adam Carmean are:
> 2309   i.   Nevaeh Gabrielle[27] Carmean, born March 16, 2007 in Salisbury, Rowan County, N.C.
> 2310   ii.   Daughter Carmean, born 2012.

2258.   James[26] Reavis (Darleen[25] Cannon, Annie Marie[24] Parker, Harvey Adophus[23], J. Columbus[22], Ollie Lou Ada[21] Shaver, Rhoda E.[20] Wyatt, Noah Calvin[19], Thomas "Tommy"[18] Wiatt, Sr. (Wyatt, Wiett), John[17], Henry[16], Richard[15], George[14], Rev. Haute "Haut" "Hawte"[13], Sir George "Georgius" Thomas[12], Sir Thomas "The Younger"[11], Sir Thomas "The Elder"[10], Sir Henry[9], Richard Wiat or[8] Wyatt, Geoffrey "Jeoffrey" Wiot or[7] Wiat, Robert or Richard[6] Wiot, William Wiot or[5] Wyot, Adam Wiot or Wyote or[4], Guyott[3], Guyott[2], Captain or Admiral Adam Guyott or[1] Wiot). He married Gragia Galls.

> Children of James Reavis and Gragia Galls are:
> 2311   i.   Jennifer[27] Reavis.
> 2312   ii.   Jeff Reavis.

2259.   William[26] Reavis (Darleen[25] Cannon, Annie Marie[24] Parker, Harvey Adophus[23], J. Columbus[22], Ollie Lou Ada[21] Shaver, Rhoda E.[20] Wyatt, Noah Calvin[19], Thomas "Tommy"[18] Wiatt, Sr. (Wyatt, Wiett), John[17], Henry[16], Richard[15], George[14], Rev. Haute "Haut" "Hawte"[13], Sir George "Georgius" Thomas[12], Sir Thomas "The Younger"[11], Sir Thomas "The Elder"[10], Sir Henry[9], Richard Wiat or[8] Wyatt, Geoffrey "Jeoffrey" Wiot or[7] Wiat, Robert or Richard[6] Wiot, William Wiot or[5] Wyot, Adam Wiot or Wyote or[4], Guyott[3], Guyott[2], Captain or Admiral Adam Guyott or[1] Wiot). He married Cindy Chapman.

Children of William Reavis and Cindy Chapman are:

2313	i.	David[27] Reavis.
2314	ii.	Christy Reavis.

2263. Rebecca[26] Cannon (Leon[25], Annie Marie[24] Parker, Harvey Adophus[23], J. Columbus[22], Ollie Lou Ada[21] Shaver, Rhoda E.[20] Wyatt, Noah Calvin[19], Thomas "Tommy"[18] Wiatt, Sr. (Wyatt, Wiett), John[17], Henry[16], Richard[15], George[14], Rev. Haute "Haut" "Hawte"[13], Sir George "Georgius" Thomas[12], Sir Thomas "The Younger"[11], Sir Thomas "The Elder"[10], Sir Henry[9], Richard Wiat or[8] Wyatt, Geoffrey "Jeoffrey" Wiot or[7] Wiat, Robert or Richard[6] Wiot, William Wiot or[5] Wyot, Adam Wiot or Wyote or[4], Guyott[3], Guyott[2], Captain or Admiral Adam Guyott or[1] Wiot). She married Randy Bringle.

Child of Rebecca Cannon and Randy Bringle is:

2315	i.	Eric[27] Bringle.

2266. Vickie[26] Cannon (Irvin[25], Annie Marie[24] Parker, Harvey Adophus[23], J. Columbus[22], Ollie Lou Ada[21] Shaver, Rhoda E.[20] Wyatt, Noah Calvin[19], Thomas "Tommy"[18] Wiatt, Sr. (Wyatt, Wiett), John[17], Henry[16], Richard[15], George[14], Rev. Haute "Haut" "Hawte"[13], Sir George "Georgius" Thomas[12], Sir Thomas "The Younger"[11], Sir Thomas "The Elder"[10], Sir Henry[9], Richard Wiat or[8] Wyatt, Geoffrey "Jeoffrey" Wiot or[7] Wiat, Robert or Richard[6] Wiot, William Wiot or[5] Wyot, Adam Wiot or Wyote or[4], Guyott[3], Guyott[2], Captain or Admiral Adam Guyott or[1] Wiot). She married Jimmy Brooks.

Child of Vickie Cannon and Jimmy Brooks is:

2316	i.	Ashley Jo[27] Brooks.

2267. Sheila[26] Cannon (Irvin[25], Annie Marie[24] Parker, Harvey Adophus[23], J. Columbus[22], Ollie Lou Ada[21] Shaver, Rhoda E.[20] Wyatt, Noah Calvin[19], Thomas "Tommy"[18] Wiatt, Sr. (Wyatt, Wiett), John[17], Henry[16], Richard[15], George[14], Rev. Haute "Haut" "Hawte"[13], Sir George "Georgius" Thomas[12], Sir Thomas "The Younger"[11], Sir Thomas "The Elder"[10], Sir Henry[9], Richard Wiat or[8] Wyatt, Geoffrey "Jeoffrey" Wiot or[7] Wiat, Robert or Richard[6] Wiot, William Wiot or[5] Wyot, Adam Wiot or Wyote or[4], Guyott[3], Guyott[2], Captain or Admiral Adam Guyott or[1] Wiot). She married Wayne Moore.

Child of Sheila Cannon and Wayne Moore is:

2317	i.	Matthew[27] Moore.

2268. Bobby[26] English (Edna[25] Cannon, Annie Marie[24] Parker, Harvey Adophus[23], J. Columbus[22], Ollie Lou Ada[21] Shaver, Rhoda E.[20] Wyatt, Noah Calvin[19], Thomas "Tommy"[18] Wiatt, Sr. (Wyatt, Wiett), John[17], Henry[16], Richard[15], George[14], Rev. Haute "Haut" "Hawte"[13], Sir George "Georgius" Thomas[12], Sir Thomas "The Younger"[11], Sir Thomas "The Elder"[10], Sir Henry[9], Richard Wiat or[8] Wyatt, Geoffrey "Jeoffrey" Wiot or[7] Wiat, Robert or Richard[6] Wiot, William Wiot or[5] Wyot, Adam Wiot or Wyote or[4], Guyott[3], Guyott[2], Captain or Admiral Adam Guyott or[1] Wiot). He married Carla Matley.

Child of Bobby English and Carla Matley is:

2318   i.   Mercedes[27] English.

2269.   Ann[26] English (Edna[25] Cannon, Annie Marie[24] Parker, Harvey Adophus[23], J. Columbus[22], Ollie Lou Ada[21] Shaver, Rhoda E.[20] Wyatt, Noah Calvin[19], Thomas "Tommy"[18] Wiatt, Sr. (Wyatt, Wiett), John[17], Henry[16], Richard[15], George[14], Rev. Haute "Haut" "Hawte"[13], Sir George "Georgius" Thomas[12], Sir Thomas "The Younger"[11], Sir Thomas "The Elder"[10], Sir Henry[9], Richard Wiat or[8] Wyatt, Geoffrey "Jeoffrey" Wiot or[7] Wiat, Robert or Richard[6] Wiot, William Wiot or[5] Wyot, Adam Wiot or Wyote or[4], Guyott[3], Guyott[2], Captain or Admiral Adam Guyott or[1] Wiot). She married Steve Keck.

Children of Ann English and Steve Keck are:

2319   i.   Ricky[27] Keck.
2320   ii.   Clinton Keck.

2270.   Tammy[26] English (Edna[25] Cannon, Annie Marie[24] Parker, Harvey Adophus[23], J. Columbus[22], Ollie Lou Ada[21] Shaver, Rhoda E.[20] Wyatt, Noah Calvin[19], Thomas "Tommy"[18] Wiatt, Sr. (Wyatt, Wiett), John[17], Henry[16], Richard[15], George[14], Rev. Haute "Haut" "Hawte"[13], Sir George "Georgius" Thomas[12], Sir Thomas "The Younger"[11], Sir Thomas "The Elder"[10], Sir Henry[9], Richard Wiat or[8] Wyatt, Geoffrey "Jeoffrey" Wiot or[7] Wiat, Robert or Richard[6] Wiot, William Wiot or[5] Wyot, Adam Wiot or Wyote or[4], Guyott[3], Guyott[2], Captain or Admiral Adam Guyott or[1] Wiot). She married Steve Foster.

Child of Tammy English and Steve Foster is:

2321   i.   Sharon[27] Foster.

2272.   Ronda[26] English (Edna[25] Cannon, Annie Marie[24] Parker, Harvey Adophus[23], J. Columbus[22], Ollie Lou Ada[21] Shaver, Rhoda E.[20] Wyatt, Noah Calvin[19], Thomas "Tommy"[18] Wiatt, Sr. (Wyatt, Wiett), John[17], Henry[16], Richard[15], George[14], Rev. Haute "Haut" "Hawte"[13], Sir George "Georgius" Thomas[12], Sir Thomas "The Younger"[11], Sir Thomas "The Elder"[10], Sir Henry[9], Richard Wiat or[8] Wyatt, Geoffrey "Jeoffrey" Wiot or[7] Wiat, Robert or Richard[6] Wiot, William Wiot or[5] Wyot, Adam Wiot or Wyote or[4], Guyott[3], Guyott[2], Captain or Admiral Adam Guyott or[1] Wiot). She married Randy Heintz.

Children of Ronda English and Randy Heintz are:

2322   i.   Ammie[27] Heintz.
2323   ii.   Randal Heintz.

2274.   Bonita[26] Cannon (Glenn[25], Annie Marie[24] Parker, Harvey Adophus[23], J. Columbus[22], Ollie Lou Ada[21] Shaver, Rhoda E.[20] Wyatt, Noah Calvin[19], Thomas "Tommy"[18] Wiatt, Sr. (Wyatt, Wiett), John[17], Henry[16], Richard[15], George[14], Rev. Haute "Haut" "Hawte"[13], Sir George "Georgius" Thomas[12], Sir Thomas "The Younger"[11], Sir Thomas "The Elder"[10], Sir Henry[9], Richard Wiat or[8] Wyatt, Geoffrey "Jeoffrey" Wiot or[7] Wiat, Robert or Richard[6] Wiot,

William Wiot or[5] Wyot, Adam Wiot or Wyote or[4], Guyott[3], Guyott[2], Captain or Admiral Adam Guyott or[1] Wiot). She married Steve Jackson.

Children of Bonita Cannon and Steve Jackson are:
2324   i.   Matthew Steven[27] Jackson.
2325   ii.   Glenn Jackson.

2275. Tracie[26] Cannon (Glenn[25], Annie Marie[24] Parker, Harvey Adophus[23], J. Columbus[22], Ollie Lou Ada[21] Shaver, Rhoda E.[20] Wyatt, Noah Calvin[19], Thomas "Tommy"[18] Wiatt, Sr. (Wyatt, Wiett), John[17], Henry[16], Richard[15], George[14], Rev. Haute "Haut" "Hawte"[13], Sir George "Georgius" Thomas[12], Sir Thomas "The Younger"[11], Sir Thomas "The Elder"[10], Sir Henry[9], Richard Wiat or[8] Wyatt, Geoffrey "Jeoffrey" Wiot or[7] Wiat, Robert or Richard[6] Wiot, William Wiot or[5] Wyot, Adam Wiot or Wyote or[4], Guyott[3], Guyott[2], Captain or Admiral Adam Guyott or[1] Wiot). She married Thomas.

Children of Tracie Cannon and Thomas are:
2326   i.   Brian[27] Thomas.
2327   ii.   Michael Thomas.

2278. Janice Elaine[26] Walton (Hugh Brittle[25], Rena Catherine[24] Parker, Harvey Adophus[23], J. Columbus[22], Ollie Lou Ada[21] Shaver, Rhoda E.[20] Wyatt, Noah Calvin[19], Thomas "Tommy"[18] Wiatt, Sr. (Wyatt, Wiett), John[17], Henry[16], Richard[15], George[14], Rev. Haute "Haut" "Hawte"[13], Sir George "Georgius" Thomas[12], Sir Thomas "The Younger"[11], Sir Thomas "The Elder"[10], Sir Henry[9], Richard Wiat or[8] Wyatt, Geoffrey "Jeoffrey" Wiot or[7] Wiat, Robert or Richard[6] Wiot, William Wiot or[5] Wyot, Adam Wiot or Wyote or[4], Guyott[3], Guyott[2], Captain or Admiral Adam Guyott or[1] Wiot) was born August 17, 1952. She married Gary Ray Huffman, son of Raymond Huffman and Marie Lookabill.

Children of Janice Walton and Gary Huffman are:
2328   i.   Matthew Blake[27] Huffman, born September 09, 1982.
2329   ii.   Jordan Blair Huffman, born March 28, 1986.

The Tudor Section

♀ | | ♂

*"Life is for living and working at. If you find anything
or anybody a bore, the fault is in yourself."*

-- QUEEN ELIZABETH I [1533-1603].

THIS TUDOR SECTION IS NOT complete. It is a work in progress. It is true of all notes and trees associated with this work. If there exists some oversight or blunder, apologies are extended. Corrections and clarifications should be sent to Metallo House Publishers.

For the Tudurs or Tudors, historical articles and a few historical references, are not all in one hundred percent agreement. Discrepancies, nevertheless, are pointed out whenever appropriate.

The Welsh name *Tudor* – rather *Tewdwr* or *Tewdr* is the Welsh equvalent to *Theodoric* or *Theodore*. It is the Welsh form of the old Celtic name *Teutorigos*, which means *"ruler of the people."*

DESCENDANTS OF MAREDUDD AP TUDUR

Generation No. 1

1. Maredudd ap[1] Tudur. He married Margaret Ferch Dafydd, daughter of Dafydd Fychan and Nest Leuan.

More About Maredudd ap Tudur:
Fact 1: Names was anglocised to "Meredith Tudor."
Fact 2: Was a Welsh soldier and member of the Tudor family in Penmynydd.

Child of Maredudd Tudur and Margaret Dafydd is:

+   2   i.   Sir Owen Meredith[2] Tudor, born 1400; died February 02, 1460/61 in Hereford, U.K.

Generation No. 2

2. Sir Owen Meredith[2] Tudor (Maredudd ap[1] Tudur) was born 1400, and died February 02, 1460/61 in Hereford, U.K. He married Catherine or Katherine of Valois, daughter of Charles France and Isabeau Bavaria.

More About Sir Owen Meredith Tudor:
Fact 1: Was a Welsh soldier and courtier.
Fact 2: Also known as *"Owain Tudur."*

More About Catherine or Katherine of Valois:
Fact 1: 1420-1422, Was Queen consort of England
Fact 2: Youngest daughter of Charles VI.

Children of Sir Tudor and Catherine Valois are:

+   3   i.   Edmund[3] Tudor, born June 11, 1431; died November 01, 1456.
    4   ii.   Brother of Edmund Tudor.

            More About Brother of Edmund Tudor:
            Fact 1: Fled with Henry VIII who was a child at the time to Brittany.
            Fact 2: Fled as York and Lancaster branches of the family battled for throne.
            Fact 3: August 15, 1485, Richard III defeated at Bosworth Field.
            Fact 4: 1485, The Plantagenet Dynasty ended and Tudor Dynasty began.
            Fact 5: The Plantagenet Dynasty had been in power in England since 1154.

+   5   iii.   Henry VI King of England, born December 06, 1421 in Winsor Castle, Windsor, England; died May 21, 1471 in Tower of London, London, England.
    6   iv.   Jasper Tudor.

Generation No. 3

3. Edmund[3] Tudor (Sir Owen Meredith[2], Maredudd ap[1] Tudur) was born June 11, 1431, and died November 01, 1456. He married Margaret Beaufort, daughter of John Beaufort and Margaret Bletso.

More About Edmund Tudor:
Fact 1: Also known as *"1st Earl of Richmond."*
He died as the York and Lancaster branches of the Tudor family battled for the throne.

More About Margaret Beaufort:
Fact 1: Also known as *"Lady Margaret Beaufort."*
Fact 2: Was an illegitimate child.
Fact 3: Had only one child.
Buried Henry VII Chapel, Westminster Abbey, City of Westminster, England.

Child of Edmund Tudor and Margaret Beaufort is:

+ 7   i.   Henry VII[4] Tudor, born January 28, 1456/57 in Pembroke Castle, Pembroke, West Wales - near River Cleddau, England; died April 21, 1509 in Richmond Palace, Thamesside on right bank of Thames, upstream of Westminster.

5. Henry VI King of[3] England (Sir Owen Meredith[2] Tudor, Maredudd ap[1] Tudur) was born December 06, 1421 in Winsor Castle, Windsor, England, and died May 21, 1471 in Tower of London, London, England. He married Margaret of Anjou April 23, 1445 in Titchfield Abbey, Titchfield -- near Hampshire, England, daughter of René Sicily and Unknown.

More About Henry VI King of England:
Remains buried at Windsor.

More About Margaret of Anjou:
Fact 1: Married one month after her 15 birthday.

Child of Henry England and Margaret Anjou is:

8   i.   Edward of[4] Westminster, born October 13, 1453 in Palace of Westminster, London, England; died May 04, 1471 in Battle of Tewkesbury; buried at Tewkesbury Abbey, England. He married Lady Anne Nevill or Neville.

More About Edward of Westminster:
Fact 1: Killed at the Battle of Tewkesbury
Fact 2: Also known as *"Edward of Lancaster."*
Fact 3: Also known as *"Edward of Westminster."*
Fact 4: Was the only son of Henry IV and Margaret Anjou
Fact 5: 1471, Killed at the battle of Tewkeybury, U.K. on May 4th.
Fact 6: The only heir to the English throne to ever die in battle.
Fact 7: Edward, Prince of Wales.

More About Lady Anne Nevill or Neville:
Fact 1: Became Princess of Wales as the wife of Edward.
Fact 2: Became Queen of England as the wife of Richard III
Buried at Westminster Abbey, Westminster, U.K.

Generation No. 4

7. Henry VII[4] Tudor (Edmund[3], Sir Owen Meredith[2], Maredudd ap[1] Tudur) was born January 28, 1456/57 in Pembroke Castle, Pembroke, West Wales - near River Cleddau, England, and died April 21, 1509 in Richmond Palace, Thamesside on right bank of Thames, upstream of Westminster. He married Elizabeth of York [Plantagenet] January 18, 1485/86 in 1486, Westminster Abbey, London, England, daughter of Edward York and Elizabeth Wydville.

More About Henry VII Tudor:
Fact 1: 1457, born
Fact 2: Henry Wiatt, born in 1460 had for a while been guardian of Henry VIII.
Fact 3: Known as *"King of England"* and *"Lord of Ireland."*
Fact 4: Also known as *"King Henry VII."*
Fact 5: Also known as *"Earl of Richmond."*
Fact 6: August 22, 1485, proclaimed on the field of Bosworth; Died at age 52 years.
Buried at Westminster Abbey, England.

More About Elizabeth of York [Plantagenet]:
Fact 1: 1503, died.
Fact 2: Known as *"Princess Elizabeth Plantagenet."*
Fact 3: Also called: *"Elizabeth of York."*
Fact 4: 1466, born Feb. 11th at Westminster Palace, London, England.
Fact 5: 1487, Coronation: November 25, 1487, Westminster Abbey, London, England.
Buried at the Henry VII *"Lady Chapel,"* Westminster Abbey, London, England.

Children of Henry Tudor and Elizabeth [Plantagenet] are:
9   i.   Edward[5] Tudor?
10   ii.   Arthur Tudor, born September 20, 1486 in Saint Swithin's Priory, Winchester, England; died April 02, 1502 in Ludlow Castle, Shropshire, England. He married Katherine of Aragon, former princess of Spain November 14, 1501 in Saint Paul's Cathedral, London, England.

More About Arthur Tudor:
Fact 1: 1486-1502, was known as "Prince of Wales."
Fact 2: 1490, titled as "Prince of Wales" on Feb. 27th at Westminster Palace, London, England.
Cause of Death: Died April 2, 1502 at Ludlow Castle, Shropshire, England.

Buried at Worcester Cathedral, England.

More About Katherine of Aragon, former princess of Spain:
Fact 1: Was the last child of her father King of Spain Ferdinand V.
Fact 2: Katherine, Katharine, Catherine.
Fact 3: January 06, 1535/36, possible date of demise. 1536.
Buried at Peterborough Cathedral, England.

+ 11   iii.   Margaret "Mary Queen of Scots" Tudor, born November 28, 1489 in Westminster Palace, London, England.

+ 12   iv.   King Henry Tudor VIII, born June 28, 1491 in Palace of Placentia, Greenwich, on banks of Thames River, England; died January 28, 1546/47 in Palace of White Hall, London, England.

13   v.   Elizabeth Tudor, born July 02, 1492 in England; died 1495 in England.

More About Elizabeth Tudor:
Died as toddler.

+ 14   vi.   Mary Tudor, born March 18, 1495/96 in Richmond Palace, Surrey, England; died June 25, 1533 in Westhorpe Hall, Suffolk, England.

15   vii.   Edmund Tudor, born February 21, 1498/99 in England; died 1500 in England.

More About Edmund Tudor:
Fact 1: 1499-1500, Titled: "Duke of Somerset."

16   viii.   Katherine Tudor, born February 02, 1502/03 in England; died February 02, 1502/03 in England.

More About Katherine Tudor:
Fact 1: Died at birth.
Born and died on Feb. 2, 1503.

Generation No. 5

11. Margaret "Mary Queen of Scots"[5] Tudor (Henry VII[4], Edmund[3], Sir Owen Meredith[2], Maredudd ap[1] Tudur) was born November 28, 1489 in Westminster Palace, London, England. She married (1) James Stuart IV of Scotland August 08, 1503 in Holyrood Abbey, Edinburgh, Scotland. She married (2) Archibald Douglas August 04, 1514 in Kinnoul Church. She married (3) Henry Stewart, Lord Darnley March 03, 1527/28.

More About Margaret "Mary Queen of Scots" Tudor:
Fact 1: Known also: *"Princess Margaret Tudor."*
Fact 2: 1503, Titled later as: "Queen of Scots" on August 8th.
Fact 3: Titled at Holyrood Abbey, Edinburgh, Scotland.
Fact 4: Also known as *"Mary Queen of Scots."*
Fact 5: Sister of Henry VIII.

More About James Stuart IV of Scotland:
Fact 1: Also later known as: *"King James IV of Scotland."*
Fact 2: King of the Scots

More About Archibald Douglas:
Fact 1: Also known as *"6th Earl of Angus."*

More About Henry Stewart, Lord Darnley:
Fact 1: Also known as *"Lord of Methven I."*

Children of Margaret Tudor and James Scotland are:

17   i.   James[6] Stuart, born February 21, 1506/07.

More About James Stuart:
Fact 1: Also known as "Duke of Rothesay."

18   ii.   Daughter Stuart, born July 15, 1508.
19   iii.   Arthur Stuart, born October 20, 1509.

More About Arthur Stuart:
Fact 1: Also known as "Duke of Rothesay."

+   20   iv.   King James Stuart V of Scotland, born April 15, 1512 in of Scotland; died December 02, 1542.
21   v.   Daughter Stuart, born November 1512.
22   vi.   Alexander Stuart, born April 30, 1514.

More About Alexander Stuart:
Fact 1: Also known as *"Duke of Ross."*

Child of Margaret Tudor and Archibald Douglas is:

+   23   i.   Margaret[6] Douglas, born October 08, 1515; died March 07, 1577/78.

Child of Margaret Tudor and Henry Stewart is:

24   i.   Dorothea[6] Stewart, born Aft. March 03, 1527/28.

12. King Henry[5] Tudor VIII (Henry VII[4], Edmund[3], Sir Owen Meredith[2], Maredudd ap[1] Tudur) was born June 28, 1491 in Palace of Placentia, Greenwich, on banks of Thames River, England, and died January 28, 1546/47 in Palace of White Hall, London, England. He married (1) Elizabeth Stafford. He met (2) Elizabeth "Bessie" Blount. He married (3) Katherine of Aragon, former princess of Spain June 11, 1509 in Grey Friars Church, Greenwich, England, daughter of Ferdinand Aragon and Isabella. He married (4) Queen Consort Anne Boleyn January 25, 1532/33 in Whitehall, Westminster, London, England, daughter of Thomas Ormonde and Lady Howard. He married (5) Jane Seymour May 20, 1536 in London, England, daughter of Sir Seymour and Margery Wentworth. He married (6) Anne of Cleves January 06, 1538/39 in Greenwich Palace, England - divorced July 1539, daughter of John and Maria Julich-Berg. He married (7) Katherine Howard July 28, 1540 in Hampton Court Palace, England, daughter of Lord Edmund Howard. He married (8) Queen Catherine "Katharine" Parr July 12, 1543 in Hampton Court Palace, England, daughter of Sir Parr and Maude Green.

More About King Henry Tudor VIII:
Fact 1: 1521-1542, King of England and France.
Fact 2: 1542, continued as King of England. France and Ireland.
Fact 3: Was the first English sovereign who bore the title of *"Majesty."*
Fact 4: January 28, 1546/47, died.
Fact 5: Was Duke of York and then later King Henry VIII
Fact 6: January 28, 1491 is sited also as his birthday.
Fact 7: June 24, 1509, titled King of England at Westminster Abbey, London, England.
Fact 8: January 28, 1490/91, 1421 cited as his birthday by some historians.
Buried at Windsor, England.

More About Elizabeth Stafford:
Fact 1: Was a mistress to King Henry VIII.
Fact 2: No children.

More About Elizabeth "Bessie" Blount:
Fact 1: Was a mistress to King Henry VIII.

More About Katherine of Aragon, former princess of Spain:
Fact 1: Was the last child of her father King of Spain Ferdinand V.
Fact 2: Katherine, Katharine, Catherine
Fact 3: January 06, 1535/36, possible date of demise. 1536
Buried at Peterborough Cathedral, England.

More About Queen Consort Anne Boleyn:
Fact 1: 2nd wife of King Henry VIII.
Fact 2: 1532, was titled: Marquess of Pembroke on September 1st.

Fact 3: Became Queen of England.

Fact 4: September 01, 1532, Marchioness of Pembroke.

Fact 5: 1507, Possible year of birth.

Cause of Death: Executed by sword Tower Green at the Tower of London

Buried at Chapel of Saint Peter ad Vincula, Tower of London.

More About Jane Seymour:

Fact 1: 3rd wife of King Henry VIII.

Fact 2: October 14, 1537, another date cited by historians as date of demise for Jane Seymour. She died 12 days after the birth of her son Edward, who later became Edward VI, King of England.

More About Anne of Cleves:

Fact 1: 4th wife of King Henry VIII.

More About Katherine Howard:

Fact 1: February 13, 1541/42, beheaded for adultery.

Fact 2: August 08, 1540, date of marriage cited by some historians.

Cause of Death: Beheaded at Tower Hill, London, England.

Was beheaded after being tried and found guilty of adultry. This wife was a teen and likely had a boyfriend before she was coersed into marrying Henry VIII.

More About Queen Catherine *"Katharine"* Parr:

Fact 1: Sixth wife of King Henry VIII.

Fact 2: Was a widow twice when she married King Henry VIII.

Fact 3: Jan. 28, 1547 death date found in articles.

Fact 4: 1543-1547, was Queen of England. and of Ireland.

Cause of Death: Died in 1547 at Whitehall Palace, London, England.

Buried at Saint George Chapel, Windsor Castle.

Child of King Tudor and Elizabeth Blount is:

25   i.   Henry Fitzroy[6] Tudor, born June 15, 1519 in Priory at Saint Lawrence, Blackmore, Essex, England; died July 23, 1536. He married Mary Howard November 28, 1533.

More About Henry Fitzroy Tudor:

Fact 1: Was the only illegitimate son that Henry VIII acknowledged.

Fact 2: FitzRoy means *"son of the King."*

Fact 3: The name *"FitzRoy"* was given to illegimate children of English royalty.

Fact 4: 1519, Titled: Duke of Richmond

Fact 5: July 22, 1536, Date of demise cited as well.
Fact 6: No heirs.

More About Mary Howard:
Fact 1: A cousin to Anne Boleyn's Henry VIII 2nd wife.

Children of King Tudor and Katherine Aragon are:

26   i.   Daughter[6] Tudor, born January 31, 1509/10.

More About Daughter Tudor:
Fact 1: Born January 31, 1510.
Died as infant.

27   ii.   Henry Tudor, born January 01, 1510/11.

More About Henry Tudor:
Fact 1: Born January 1, 1511.
Fact 2: Given the title "Duke of Cornwall."
Died as infant.

28   iii.   Henry Tudor, born November 1513.

More About Henry Tudor:
Fact 1: Born November 1513.
Fact 2: Given the title *"Duke of Cornwall."*
Died as infant.

29   iv.   Son Tudor, born December 1514.

More About Son Tudor:
Died as infant.

30   v.   Queen Mary Tudor, born February 18, 1515/16 in born Feb. 8, 1516; Palace of Placentia, Greenwich, London, England; died November 17, 1558 in Saint James Palace, London, England. She married Philip II King of Spain July 25, 1554.

More About Queen Mary Tudor:
Fact 1: 4th crowned Monarch in the Tudor dynasty.
Fact 2: Was Roman Catholic.
Fact 3: Mother: Catherne of Aragon of Spain.
Fact 4: Was Princess Mary Tudor and later: Queen Mary I

Fact 5: Born Feb. 18, 1516
Buried at Wesminister Abbey, London, England on Dec. 14, 1558. Died of abdominal tumor after suffering nearly two years with this condition.

31   vi.   Daughter Tudor, born November 10, 1518.

More About Daughter Tudor:
Fact 1: Born November 10, 1518.
Died as infant.

Children of King Tudor and Queen Boleyn are:

32   i.   Queen Elizabeth I[6] Tudor, born September 07, 1533; died March 24, 1602/03 in Richmond Palace, Thamesside on right bank of Thames, upstream of Westminster.

More About Queen Elizabeth I Tudor:
Fact 1: Never married.
Fact 2: Died without descendants.
Fact 3: Was Princess Elizabeth and became Queen of England aft. Mary I's demise.
Fact 4: The Tudor Dynasty died with Elizabeth I .
Buried at Westminster Abbey.

33   ii.   Henry Tudor, born 1534.

More About Henry Tudor:
Fact 1: 1534, Titled: "Duke of Cornwall"
Died as infant.

34   iii.   Son Tudor, born January 29, 1535/36.

More About Son Tudor:
Died as infant.

Child of King Tudor and Jane Seymour is:

35   i.   Edward VI[6] Tudor, born October 12, 1537 in Hampton, Court Palace, Middlesex, England; died July 06, 1553 in Greenwich Palace, Kent, England.

More About Edward VI Tudor:
Fact 1: House of Tudor.
Fact 2: Was Duke of Cornwall and Earl of Chester.

Fact 3: 1547, King of England and Ireland.

Cause of Death: Sickly child. Was in generally good health until the last 6 months of his life.

Died at age 15. Remains are at Henry VII Lady Chapel, Westminster Abbey, England.

14. Mary[5] Tudor (Henry VII[4], Edmund[3], Sir Owen Meredith[2], Maredudd ap[1] Tudur) was born March 18, 1495/96 in Richmond Palace, Surrey, England, and died June 25, 1533 in Westhorpe Hall, Suffolk, England. She married (1) King Louis XII of France October 09, 1514 in Abbeville Cathedral, France. She married (2) Charles Brandon March 03, 1514/15 in Paris, France.

More About Mary Tudor:
Remains are buried at St. Mary's Church, Bury St., Edmunds, England

More About Charles Brandon:
Fact 1: 1st Duke of Suffolk.

  Children of Mary Tudor and Charles Brandon are:
+ 36   i.   Frances[6] Brandon, born July 16, 1517; died 1559 in London, England.
  37   ii.   Henry Brandon, born March 11, 1514/15.
  38   iii. Eleanor Brandon, born 1519.

Generation No. 6

20. King James Stuart V of[6] Scotland (Margaret "Mary Queen of Scots"[5] Tudor, Henry VII[4], Edmund[3], Sir Owen Meredith[2], Maredudd ap[1] Tudur) was born April 15, 1512 in of Scotland, and died December 02, 1542. He married Mary of Guise 1538, daughter of Claude Guise and Antoinette de Bourbon.

More About King James Stuart V of Scotland:
Fact 1: Later known as *"King James V of Scotland."*

More About Mary of Guise:
Fact 1: Was French.
Fact 2: House of Guise.
Remains are buried at Saint Pierre de Reims, France.

  Child of King Scotland and Mary Guise is:
+ 39   i.   Mary "Mary Queen of Scots"[7] Stuart, born December 08, 1542 in Linlithgow, Scotland, U.K.; died February 08, 1586/87 in beheaded Fotheringhay Castle, Northamptonshire, England, U.K.

23. Margaret[6] Douglas (Margaret "Mary Queen of Scots"[5] Tudor, Henry VII[4], Edmund[3], Sir Owen Meredith[2], Maredudd ap[1] Tudur) was born October 08, 1515, and died March 07, 1577/78. She married Matthew Stuart 4th Earl of Lennox, son of John Stuart and Elzabeth Stewart.

More About Margaret Douglas:
Fact 1: Also known as *"Lady Margaret Douglas."*
Fact 2: Countess of Lennox

More About Matthew Stuart 4th Earl of Lennox:
Fact 1: 4th Earl of Lennox.

Children of Margaret Douglas and Matthew Lennox are:
+ 40   i.   Henry Stuart or[7] Stewart, Lord Darnley, born December 07, 1545 in Temple Newsam, Yorkshire, England; died February 10, 1566/67 in Kirk O'Field, Edinburgh, Scotland.
+ 41   ii.   Charles Stewart, born 1555; died 1576.

36. Frances[6] Brandon (Mary[5] Tudor, Henry VII[4], Edmund[3], Sir Owen Meredith[2], Maredudd ap[1] Tudur) was born July 16, 1517, and died 1559 in London, England. She married (1) Henry Grey. She married (2) Henry Grey. She married (3) Adrian Stokes. She married (4) Edward Seymour.

More About Frances Brandon:
Buried at Westminster Abbey, England.

More About Henry Grey:
Fact 1: 1st Duke of Suffolk.

More About Edward Seymour:
Fact 1: 1st Earl of Hertford.

Child of Frances Brandon and Henry Grey is:
+ 42   i.   Catherine[7] Grey, born August 25, 1540 in Bradgate Park, Leicester, England; died January 26, 1567/68 in Cockfield Hall, Yoxford, Suffolk, England.

Children of Frances Brandon and Henry Grey are:
43   i.   Jane[7] Grey, born 1536; died 1554 in Tower of London, London, England. She married Lord Guildford Dudley.

More About Jane Grey:
Fact 1: Lady Jane Grey.

Fact 2: 1553, Was Queen of England and Ireland -- disputed by historians.

Fact 3: was queen for nine days. July 10-19

Buried at Saint Peterad Vincula, London, England.

| 44 | ii. | Mary Grey. She married Keyes. |
| 45 | iii. | Elizabeth Grey. She married Stokes. |

Generation No. 7

39. Mary "Mary Queen of Scots"[7] Stuart (King James Stuart V of[6] Scotland, Margaret "Mary Queen of Scots"[5] Tudor, Henry VII[4], Edmund[3], Sir Owen Meredith[2], Maredudd ap[1] Tudur) was born December 08, 1542 in Linilithgow, Scotland, U.K., and died February 08, 1586/87 in beheaded Fotheringhay Castle, Northamptonshire, England, U.K. She married (1) Francis II 1558, son of King France and Catherine de Medicis. She married (2) Henry Stuart or Stewart, Lord Darnley 1565, son of Matthew Lennox and Margaret Douglas. She married (3) James Hepburn 4th Earl of Bothwell 1567.

More About Mary *"Mary Queen of Scots"* Stuart:

Fact 1: Known as *"Mary -- Queen of Scots."*

Fact 2: Was in the House of Stuart

Fact 3: February 07, 1586/87, executed

Fact 4: Imprisoned by her first cousin Elizabeth I for 18 years

Fact 5: Miscarried twins of Bothwell.

Was beheaded at the order of her cousin Elizabeth I -- a first cousin once removed.

Executed at the age of 44 years after her cousin Elizabeth signed her death warrant.

More About Henry Stuart or Stewart, Lord Darnley:

Fact 1: Also knowns as *"Lord Darnley."*

Fact 2: Is a half first cousin to his wife Mary Queen of Scots

Fact 3: Was Roman Catholic.

More About James Hepburn 4th Earl of Bothwell:

Fact 1: Known as *"4th Earl of Bothwell."*

Child of Mary Stuart and Henry Stewart is:

| + | 46 | i. | James Stuart VI[8] and I, born June 19, 1566 in of England; died March 27, 1625 in Theobalds, Herts, England; buried at Westminster Abbey, London, England. |

40. Henry Stuart or[7] Stewart, Lord Darnley (Margaret[6] Douglas, Margaret "Mary Queen of Scots"[5] Tudor, Henry VII[4], Edmund[3], Sir Owen Meredith[2], Maredudd ap[1] Tudur) was born December 07, 1545 in Temple Newsam, Yorkshire, England, and died February 10, 1566/67

in Kirk O'Field, Edinburgh, Scotland. He married Mary "Mary Queen of Scots" Stuart 1565, daughter of King Scotland and Mary Guise.

More About Henry Stuart or Stewart, Lord Darnley:
Fact 1: Also knowns as *"Lord Darnley."*
Fact 2: Is a half first cousin to his wife Mary Queen of Scots
Fact 3: Was Roman Catholic.

More About Mary *"Mary Queen of Scots"* Stuart:
Fact 1: Known as "Mary -- Queen of Scots."
Fact 2: Was in the House of Stuart
Fact 3: February 07, 1586/87, executed
Fact 4: Imprisoned by her first cousin Elizabeth I for 18 years.
Fact 5: Miscarried twins of Bothwell.
Was beheaded at the order of her cousin Elizabeth I -- a first cousin once removed.
Executed at the age of 44 years after her cousin Elizabeth signed her death warrant.

> Child of Henry Stewart and Mary Stuart is:
> + 47   i.   James Stuart VI[8] and I, born June 19, 1566 in of England; died March 27, 1625 in Theobalds, Herts, England; buried at Westminster Abbey, London, England.

41. Charles[7] Stewart (Margaret[6] Douglas, Margaret "Mary Queen of Scots"[5] Tudor, Henry VII[4], Edmund[3], Sir Owen Meredith[2], Maredudd ap[1] Tudur) was born 1555, and died 1576. He married Elizabeth Cavendish, daughter of Elizabeth Talbot.

More About Charles Stewart:
Fact 1: Received title: Earl of Lennox.

> Child of Charles Stewart and Elizabeth Cavendish is:
> 48   i.   Arbella Stuart or[8] Stewart, born in England. She married William Seymour.
>
> More About William Seymour:
> Fact 1: 2nd Duke of Somerset.
> Fact 2: Was a Royalist commander in the English Civil War.

42. Catherine[7] Grey (Frances[6] Brandon, Mary[5] Tudor, Henry VII[4], Edmund[3], Sir Owen Meredith[2], Maredudd ap[1] Tudur) was born August 25, 1540 in Bradgate Park, Leicester, England, and died January 26, 1567/68 in Cockfield Hall, Yoxford, Suffolk, England. She married (1) Henry Herbert. She married (2) Edward Seymour 1560-1568, son of Edward Seymour and Anne Stanhope.

More About Catherine Grey:
Fact 1: Lady Catherine Grey.
Fact 2: Youngest sister of Lady Jane Grey.
Buried at Cockfield Chapel, Yoxford Church, Suffolk, England.

More About Edward Seymour:
Fact 1: 1st Earl of Hertford.

    Children of Catherine Grey and Edward Seymour are:

+	49	i.	Edward[8] Seymour.
	50	ii.	Beauchamp Seymour.
	51	iii.	Thomas Seymour.

Generation No. 8

47. James Stuart VI[8] and I (Henry Stuart or[7] Stewart, Lord Darnley, Margaret[6] Douglas, Margaret "Mary Queen of Scots"[5] Tudor, Henry VII[4], Edmund[3], Sir Owen Meredith[2], Maredudd ap[1] Tudur) was born June 19, 1566 in of England, and died March 27, 1625 in Theobalds, Herts, England; buried at Westminster Abbey, London, England. He married Princess Anne, daughter of King Frederick II.

More About James Stuart VI and I:
Fact 1: 1567, was King of the Scots, King of Scotland.
Fact 2: July 25, 1603, crowned king of England.
Fact 3: House of Stuart.

    Children of James and and Princess Anne are:

+	52	i.	Elizabeth[9] Stuart, born August 19, 1596; died February 13, 1661/62.
	53	ii.	Henry Frederick Stuart, born February 19, 1593/94.
+	54	iii.	Charles I Stuart, born November 19, 1600; died January 30, 1648/49 in beheaded for high treason Whitehall, buried at St. George's Chapel at Windsor.
	55	iv.	Margaret Stuart, born December 24, 1598.
	56	v.	Robert Stuart, born 1602.
	57	vi.	Mary Stuart, born 1605-1607.
	58	vii.	Sophia Stuart, born 1607.

49. Edward[8] Seymour (Catherine[7] Grey, Frances[6] Brandon, Mary[5] Tudor, Henry VII[4], Edmund[3], Sir Owen Meredith[2], Maredudd ap[1] Tudur). He married Honora Rogers.

More About Edward Seymour:
Fact 1: Lord Beauchamp of Hache.

Child of Edward Seymour and Honora Rogers is:

59 i. William[9] Seymour, born 1588; died 1660. He married Arbella Stuart or Stewart.

More About William Seymour:
Fact 1: 2nd Duke of Somerset.
Fact 2: Was a Royalist commander in the English Civil War.

Generation No. 9

52. Elizabeth[9] Stuart (James Stuart VI[8] and I, Henry Stuart or[7] Stewart, Lord Darnley, Margaret[6] Douglas, Margaret "Mary Queen of Scots"[5] Tudor, Henry VII[4], Edmund[3], Sir Owen Meredith[2], Maredudd ap[1] Tudur) was born August 19, 1596, and died February 13, 1661/62. She married Frederick V, Elector Palatine.

More About Elizabeth Stuart:
Fact 1: Queen of Bohemia.
Fact 2: 2nd child and eldest daughter of her father James VI.
Fact 3: Called: *"The Winter Queen."*
Fact 4: 1714, was the demise of the Stuart Dynasty.
Fact 5: Her reign lasted only one winter.

Children of Elizabeth Stuart and Frederick are:

+ 60 i. Sophia[10], born 1630 in of Hanover -- born in the Hague, The Netherlands; died 1714 in Herrenhausen, Hanover.

 61 ii. 12 others.

54. Charles I[9] Stuart (James Stuart VI[8] and I, Henry Stuart or[7] Stewart, Lord Darnley, Margaret[6] Douglas, Margaret "Mary Queen of Scots"[5] Tudor, Henry VII[4], Edmund[3], Sir Owen Meredith[2], Maredudd ap[1] Tudur) was born November 19, 1600, and died January 30, 1648/49 in beheaded for high treason Whitehall, buried at St. George's Chapel at Windsor. He married Princess Hentrietta Maria May 11, 1625, daughter of Henry IV, King of France.

More About Charles I Stuart:
Fact 1: Found guilty of High Treason bythe High Court of Justice.
Fact 2: The High Court of Justice was appointed by Parliament.
Cause of Death: Beheaded at Whitehall
Remains buried at Saint George Chapel, Windsor, England.

Children of Charles Stuart and Princess Maria are:

+ 62 i. Charles II[10] Stuart, born May 29, 1630; died February 06, 1684/85 in 1685, Whitehall, buried at Westminster Abbey, London, England.

+	63	ii.	Mary Stuart.
+	64	iii.	James II and VII Stuart, born October 14, 1633; died September 16, 1701 in Saint Germain and buried here.
	65	iv.	Elizabeth Stuart.
	66	v.	Anne Stuart.
	67	vi.	Henry Stuart.
	68	vii.	Henrietta Stuart.

Generation No. 10

60. Sophia[10] (Elizabeth[9] Stuart, James Stuart VI[8] and I, Henry Stuart or[7] Stewart, Lord Darnley, Margaret[6] Douglas, Margaret "Mary Queen of Scots"[5] Tudor, Henry VII[4], Edmund[3], Sir Owen Meredith[2], Maredudd ap[1] Tudur) was born 1630 in of Hanover -- born in the Hague, The Netherlands, and died 1714 in Herrenhausen, Hanover. She married Ernest Augustus, Elector of Hanover.

Children of Sophia and Ernest Augustus are:

+	69	i.	George[11] I, born May 28, 1660 in Hanover, which is now Germany; died 1727.
	70	ii.	Maximilian William.
	71	iii.	Sophia Charlotte.

More About Sophia Charlotte:
Fact 1: Queen of Prussia.

	72	iv.	Ernest Augustus.

More About Ernest Augustus:
Fact 1: Duke of York

62. Charles II[10] Stuart (Charles I[9], James Stuart VI[8] and I, Henry Stuart or[7] Stewart, Lord Darnley, Margaret[6] Douglas, Margaret "Mary Queen of Scots"[5] Tudor, Henry VII[4], Edmund[3], Sir Owen Meredith[2], Maredudd ap[1] Tudur) was born May 29, 1630, and died February 06, 1684/85 in 1685, Whitehall, buried at Westminster Abbey, London, England. He married (1) Mistress Lucy Walter. He married (2) Mistress Catherine Pegge, daughter of Thomas Pegge and Unknown. He married (3) Mistress Barbara Villiers. He married (4) Mistress Nell Gwynne. He married (5) Louise de Kérouaille. He married (6) Princess Katharine of Braganza May 21, 1662, daughter of John IV King of Portugal.

More About Charles II Stuart:
Fact 1: January 01, 1650/51, King of Scotland, 1651
Fact 2: April 23, 1661, King of England.

More About Mistress Barbara Villiers:
Fact 1: Countess of Castlemaine
Fact 2: Later 1st Duchess of Cleveland.

More About Louise de Kérouaille:
Fact 1: Duchess of Portsmouth.

Child of Charles Stuart and Mistress Walter is:

73   i.   James Scott[11] Stuart, born April 09, 1649 in Rotterdam, Dutch Republic; died July 15, 1685 in beheaded for treason, London, England.

More About James Scott Stuart:
Fact 1: Eldest illegitimate son of Charles II of England, Sctoland, and Ireland.
Fact 2: 1st Duke of Monmouth.
Fact 3: Also known as *"James Crofts"* and *"James Fitzroy."*
Fact 4: Served in the 2nd Anglo-Dutch War.
Fact 5: Commanded English troops taking part in the 3rd Anglo-Dutch War.
Beheaded for treason July 15, 1685 when he attempted to capitalise on his position as the son of Charles II and led an unsuccessful Monmouth Rebellion to depose his uncle King James II and VII.

Children of Charles Stuart and Mistress Pegge are:

74   i.   Charles FitzCharles[11] Stuart, born Abt. 1657 in Westminster, England; died October 17, 1680 in Colony of Tangier. He married Lady Bridget Osborne.

More About Charles FitzCharles Stuart:
Fact 1: Nicknamed: *"Don Carolos."*
Fact 2: Educated in Spain.

75   ii.   Catherine FitsCharles Stuart.

More About Catherine FitsCharles Stuart:
Fact 1: Became a nun,

Children of Charles Stuart and Mistress Villiers are:

76   i.   Charles FitzRoy[11] Stuart, born June 18, 1662; died September 09, 1730.

More About Charles FitzRoy Stuart:
Fact 1: 2nd Duke of Cleveland
Fact 2: 1670-1675, 1st Duke of South Hampton.
Fact 3: Bef. 1670, known as Baron Limerick.

+ 77   ii.   Charlotte Lee Stuart, born September 05, 1664; died February 17, 1717/18.

78   iii.   Henry FitzRoy Stuart, born September 28, 1663; died October 09, 1690. He married Isabella Bennett November 07, 1679.

More About Henry FitzRoy Stuart:
Fact 1: 1675, Duke of Grafton.
Fact 2: Married at age 9 to 5 year old Isabella.
Fact 3: November 07, 1679, The marriage ceremony was repeated.
Fact 4: Known as *"Earl of Euston, Baron Sudbury, Viscount Ipswich."*
Fact 5: 1680, Knight of Garter
Fact 6: 1681, Colonel of the Grenadier Guards.
Fact 7: Princess Diana of Wales is one of his descendants.
Died at age 27 of a wound received at the storming of Cork while leading William of Orange's forces to voer throw the king in the Revolution of 1688.

79   iv.   George FitzRoy Stuart, born December 28, 1665; died June 28, 1716. He married (1) Catherine Wheatley. He married (2) Mary Dutton.

More About George FitzRoy Stuart:
Fact 1: Earl of Northumberland.
Fact 2: Baron of Pontefract, Yorkshire.
Fact 3: Viscount Falmouth [Cornwall].

Child of Charles Stuart and Mistress Gwynne is:
80   i.   Charles Beauclerk[11] Stuart, born May 08, 1670; died May 10, 1726 in Bath, England; buried Westminster Abbey, England. He married Diana de Vere.

More About Charles Beauclerk Stuart:
Fact 1: 1st Duke of St. Albans

Child of Charles Stuart and Louise de Kérouaille is:
+ 81   i.   Charles Lennox[11] Stuart, born July 29, 1672; died May 27, 1723.

Children of Charles Stuart and Princess Braganza are:

82	i.	Charles FitzRoy[11] Stuart.
83	ii.	Charlotte Lee Stuart.
84	iii.	Henry FitzRoy Stuart.
85	iv.	George FitzRoy Stuart.
86	v.	Charles Beauclerk Stuart.
87	vi.	Charles Lennox Stuart.

63. Mary[10] Stuart (Charles I[9], James Stuart VI[8] and I, Henry Stuart or[7] Stewart, Lord Darnley, Margaret[6] Douglas, Margaret "Mary Queen of Scots"[5] Tudor, Henry VII[4], Edmund[3], Sir Owen Meredith[2], Maredudd ap[1] Tudur).

Child of Mary Stuart is:
88   i.   William[11] Stuart.

More About William Stuart:
Fact 1: Prince of Orange.

64. James II and VII[10] Stuart (Charles I[9], James Stuart VI[8] and I, Henry Stuart or[7] Stewart, Lord Darnley, Margaret[6] Douglas, Margaret "Mary Queen of Scots"[5] Tudor, Henry VII[4], Edmund[3], Sir Owen Meredith[2], Maredudd ap[1] Tudur) was born October 14, 1633, and died September 16, 1701 in Saint Germain and buried here. He married (1) Lady Anne Hyde November 24, 1659, daughter of Edward Clarendon and X. He married (2) Princess Mary Beatrice Eleanora D'Estes September 30, 1673, daughter of Alphonzo III Duke of Modena.

Child of James Stuart and Princess D'Estes is:
89   i.   Mary[11] Stuart, died March 08, 1701/02 in buried at Westminster Abbey; England. She married Prince of Orange William November 14, 1677.

More About Mary Stuart:
Fact 1: February 13, 1688/89, crowned together with William.
Fact 2: Crowned with William as King and Queen of England, Scotland, Ireland and France.

Generation No. 11

69. George[11] I (Sophia[10], Elizabeth[9] Stuart, James Stuart VI[8] and I, Henry Stuart or[7] Stewart, Lord Darnley, Margaret[6] Douglas, Margaret "Mary Queen of Scots"[5] Tudor, Henry VII[4], Edmund[3], Sir Owen Meredith[2], Maredudd ap[1] Tudur) was born May 28, 1660 in Hanover, which is now Germany, and died 1727. He married Sophia Dorothea November 21, 1682.

More About George I:
Fact 1: 1714-1727, was King of Great Britain and Ireland.

    Children of George and Sophia Dorothea are:
+   90   i.   George[12] II, born October 30, 1683; died 1760 in Kensington, buried at Westminster Abbey, England.
     91   ii.   Sophia Dorothea.

77. Charlotte Lee[11] Stuart (Charles II[10], Charles I[9], James Stuart VI[8] and I, Henry Stuart or[7] Stewart, Lord Darnley, Margaret[6] Douglas, Margaret "Mary Queen of Scots"[5] Tudor, Henry VII[4], Edmund[3], Sir Owen Meredith[2], Maredudd ap[1] Tudur) was born September 05, 1664, and died February 17, 1717/18. She married Edward Lee.

    More About Charlotte Lee Stuart:
Fact 1: Countess of Lichfield.
Fact 2: Lady Charlotte Fitzroy.

    Child of Charlotte Stuart and Edward Lee is:
     92   i.   Had 18 children[12] Lee.

81. Charles Lennox[11] Stuart (Charles II[10], Charles I[9], James Stuart VI[8] and I, Henry Stuart or[7] Stewart, Lord Darnley, Margaret[6] Douglas, Margaret "Mary Queen of Scots"[5] Tudor, Henry VII[4], Edmund[3], Sir Owen Meredith[2], Maredudd ap[1] Tudur) was born July 29, 1672, and died May 27, 1723. He married Anne Belasyse Brudenell.

    More About Charles Lennox Stuart:
Fact 1: Duke of Richmond.

    Children of Charles Stuart and Anne Brudenell are:
     93   i.   Louisa Lennox[12] Stuart.
     94   ii.   Charles Lennox Stuart.
     95   iii.   Anne Lennox Stuart.

Generation No. 12

90. George[12] II (George[11] I, Sophia[10], Elizabeth[9] Stuart, James Stuart VI[8] and I, Henry Stuart or[7] Stewart, Lord Darnley, Margaret[6] Douglas, Margaret "Mary Queen of Scots"[5] Tudor, Henry VII[4], Edmund[3], Sir Owen Meredith[2], Maredudd ap[1] Tudur) was born October 30, 1683, and died 1760 in Kensington, buried at Westminster Abbey, England. He married Princess Wilhelmina Charlotte Caroline August 22, 1705, daughter of John Frederick and X.

Children of George and Princess Caroline are:
+ 96   i.   George[13] III, born June 04, 1738 in Norfolk House, St. James'
            Square, London, England; died January 29, 1820 in Windsor
            Castle, Berkshire, England.
  97   ii.   Anne.
  98   iii. Amelia.
  99   iv.   Caroline.
  100 v.   George William.
  101 vi.   William.
  102 vii. Mary.
  103 viii. Louisa.

Generation No. 13

96. George[13] III (George[12] II, George[11] I, Sophia[10], Elizabeth[9] Stuart, James Stuart VI[8] and I, Henry Stuart or[7] Stewart, Lord Darnley, Margaret[6] Douglas, Margaret "Mary Queen of Scots"[5] Tudor, Henry VII[4], Edmund[3], Sir Owen Meredith[2], Maredudd ap[1] Tudur) was born June 04, 1738 in Norfolk House, St. James' Square, London, England, and died January 29, 1820 in Windsor Castle, Berkshire, England. He married Princess Sophia Charlotte September 08, 1761, daughter of Duke Frederick and Princess Albertine.

More About George III:
Fact 1: 1760-1820, served the British throne.
Fact 2: House of Hanover.
Suffered from Porphyria. Buried at Saint George's Chapel, Windsor, England.

More About Princess Sophia Charlotte:
Fact 1: House of Mecklenburg-Strelitz.- a North German dynasty of West Slavic origin.
Saint George's Chapel, Windsor, England

Children of George and Princess Charlotte are:
  104 i.   Adolphus[14].
  105 ii.   Alfred.
  106 iii. Amelia.
  107 iv.   Ernest Augustus II.

       More About Ernest Augustus II:
       Fact 1: Duke of Cumberland and Teviotdale.

  108 v.   Charlotte.
  109 vi.   Elizabeth.
  110 vii. Frederick.
  111 viii. Augustus Frederick.

112	ix.	Mary.
113	x.	Octavia.
114	xi.	Augusta Sophia.
115	xii.	George IV, born August 12, 1762; died June 26, 1830 in buried at Windsor. He married Princess Caroline Amelia Elizabeth.

More About George IV:
Fact 1: 1811-1821, was Regent of the U.K.

| 116 | xiii. | William IV, born August 21, 1765; died June 30, 1827 in buried at Windsor. He married Princess Adelside Louisa Theresa Caroline Amelia. |
| + 117 | xiv. | Prince Edward Augustus, born November 02, 1767 in Buckingham Palace, London, England; died January 23, 1820 in Sidmouth, England. |

Generation No. 14

117. Prince Edward[14] Augustus (George[13] III, George[12] II, George[11] I, Sophia[10], Elizabeth[9] Stuart, James Stuart VI[8] and I, Henry Stuart or[7] Stewart, Lord Darnley, Margaret[6] Douglas, Margaret "Mary Queen of Scots"[5] Tudor, Henry VII[4], Edmund[3], Sir Owen Meredith[2], Maredudd ap[1] Tudur) was born November 02, 1767 in Buckingham Palace, London, England, and died January 23, 1820 in Sidmouth, England. He married Victoria of Saxe-Coburg-Gotha, daughter of Francis Saxe-Coburg-Gotha and Augusta Reuss-Ebersdorf.

More About Prince Edward Augustus:
Fact 1: Duke of Kent and Strathearn.
Fact 2: From the House of Hanover, Germany.

More About Victoria of Saxe-Coburg-Gotha:
Fact 1: Also known as Marie Luise Victorie

Child of Prince Augustus and Victoria Saxe-Coburg-Gotha is:
| + 118 | i. | Alexandrina[15] Victoria, born May 24, 1819 in Kensington Palace, London, England; died January 22, 1901 in Osborne House, Isle of Wight off southern coast of England. |

Generation No. 15

118. Alexandrina[15] Victoria (Prince Edward[14] Augustus, George[13] III, George[12] II, George[11] I, Sophia[10], Elizabeth[9] Stuart, James Stuart VI[8] and I, Henry Stuart or[7] Stewart, Lord Darnley, Margaret[6] Douglas, Margaret "Mary Queen of Scots"[5] Tudor, Henry VII[4], Edmund[3], Sir Owen Meredith[2], Maredudd ap[1] Tudur) was born May 24, 1819 in Kensington Palace, London, England, and died January 22, 1901 in Osborne House, Isle of Wight off southern

coast of England. She married Francis Albert Augustus of Saxe-Coburg-Gotha February 10, 1840, son of Ernest Saxe-Coburg-Gotha and Louise.

More About Alexandrina Victoria:
Fact 1: 1837-1901, Was Queen of Great Britain and Ireland.
Fact 2: Queen Victoria.
Fact 3: January 01, 1877, proclaimed Empress of India.
Remains are buried at Frogmore, England.

More About Francis Albert Augustus of Saxe-Coburg-Gotha:
Fact 1: 1819-1961, Prince Consort.

Children of Alexandrina Victoria and Francis Saxe-Coburg-Gotha are:

+	119	i.	Victoria of[16] Saxe-Coburg-Gotha, born 1840; died 1901.
+	120	ii.	Albert Edward VII of Saxe-Coburg-Gotha, born November 09, 1841; died May 06, 1910 in Buckingham Palace; buried at Windsor; England.
	+121	iii.	Alice Maude Mary of Saxe-Coburg-Gotha, born April 25, 1843 in Buckingham Palace, London, England; died 1879 in Germany.
	122	iv.	Alfred of Saxe-Coburg-Gotha, born 1844; died 1900.

More About Alfred of Saxe-Coburg-Gotha:
Fact 1: Duke of Edinburgh

	123	v.	Helena of Saxe-Coburg-Gotha, born 1846; died 1923.

More About Helena of Saxe-Coburg-Gotha:
Fact 1: Christian of Schleswig-Holstein

	124	vi.	Louise of Saxe-Coburg-Gotha, born 1848; died 1939.

More About Louise of Saxe-Coburg-Gotha:
Fact 1: Duchess of Argyll

	125	vii.	Arthur of Saxe-Coburg-Gotha, born 1850; died 1942.

More About Arthur of Saxe-Coburg-Gotha:
Fact 1: Duke of Connaught.

+	126	viii.	Leopold of Saxe-Coburg-Gotha, born 1853; died 1884.
	127	ix.	Beatrice os Saxe-Coburg-Gotha, born 1858; died 1944.

More About Beatrice os Saxe-Coburg-Gotha:
Fact 1: Princess Henry of Battenberg

Generation No. 16

119. Victoria of[16] Saxe-Coburg-Gotha (Alexandrina[15] Victoria, Prince Edward[14] Augustus, George[13] III, George[12] II, George[11] I, Sophia[10], Elizabeth[9] Stuart, James Stuart VI[8] and I, Henry Stuart or[7] Stewart, Lord Darnley, Margaret[6] Douglas, Margaret "Mary Queen of Scots"[5] Tudor, Henry VII[4], Edmund[3], Sir Owen Meredith[2], Maredudd ap[1] Tudur) was born 1840, and died 1901. She married Frederick III.

More About Victoria of Saxe-Coburg-Gotha:
Fact 1: Princess Royal.

More About Frederick III:
Fact 1: Emperor of Germany

 Child of Victoria Saxe-Coburg-Gotha and Frederick is:
 128 i.   William[17] II, born 1859; died 1941.

    More About William II:
    Fact 1: Emperor of Germany.

120. Albert Edward VII of[16] Saxe-Coburg-Gotha (Alexandrina[15] Victoria, Prince Edward[14] Augustus, George[13] III, George[12] II, George[11] I, Sophia[10], Elizabeth[9] Stuart, James Stuart VI[8] and I, Henry Stuart or[7] Stewart, Lord Darnley, Margaret[6] Douglas, Margaret "Mary Queen of Scots"[5] Tudor, Henry VII[4], Edmund[3], Sir Owen Meredith[2], Maredudd ap[1] Tudur) was born November 09, 1841, and died May 06, 1910 in Buckingham Palace; buried at Windsor; England. He married Alexandra Caroline Marie Charlotte Louise Julia March 10, 1863, daughter of Prince IX and Luise von Hessen-Kassel.

More About Albert Edward VII of Saxe-Coburg-Gotha:
Fact 1: 1901-1910, was King of England and British Dominions
Fact 2: Was also Emperor of India.
Fact 3: In the House of Saxe-Coburg and Gotha.

More About Alexandra Caroline Marie Charlotte Louise Julia:
Fact 1: Was Queen Consort of the United Kingdom of Great Britain and Ireland.
Fact 2: Was Empress Consort of India.
Fact 3: Was Lutheran and later Anglican upon marriage.
Fact 4: House of Schleswig-Holstein-Sonderburg-Glucksburg.
Fact 5: Marie=Mary
Remains are at St. George's Chapel, Windsor Castle, England, U.K. Buried November 28, 1925.

 Children of Albert Saxe-Coburg-Gotha and Alexandra Julia are:
 129 i.   Albert Victor of[17] Saxe-Coburg-Gotha, born 1864; died 1892.

More About Albert Victor of Saxe-Coburg-Gotha:
Fact 1: Duke of Clarence and Avondale.

+ 130   ii.   George V of Saxe-Coburg-Gotha changed to Windsor, born June 03, 1865; died January 20, 1936 in Sandringham; buried at Windsor, England.

131   iii.   Princess Royal Louise of Saxe-Coburg-Gotha, born 1867; died 1931. She married Alexander Duff.

More About Alexander Duff:
Fact 1: Duke of Fife.

132   iv.   Princess Victoria of Saxe-Coburg-Gotha, born 1868; died 1935.

133   v.   Princess Maude of Saxe-Coburg-Gotha, born 1869; died 1938. She married Haakon VII.

More About Princess Maude of Saxe-Coburg-Gotha:
Fact 1: Later Queen of Norway.

134   vi.   Prince John Alexander, born in of Wales.

121. Alice Maude Mary of[16] Saxe-Coburg-Gotha (Alexandrina[15] Victoria, Prince Edward[14] Augustus, George[13] III, George[12] II, George[11] I, Sophia[10], Elizabeth[9] Stuart, James Stuart VI[8] and I, Henry Stuart or[7] Stewart, Lord Darnley, Margaret[6] Douglas, Margaret "Mary Queen of Scots"[5] Tudor, Henry VII[4], Edmund[3], Sir Owen Meredith[2], Maredudd ap[1] Tudur) was born April 25, 1843 in Buckingham Palace, London, England, and died 1879 in Germany. She married Louis IV of Hesse.

More About Louis IV of Hesse:
Fact 1: Gand Duke of Hesse.

Children of Alice Saxe-Coburg-Gotha and Louis Hesse are:
135   i.   Elisabeth17.
136   ii.   Friedrich.
137   iii.   Irene.
138   iv.   Ernest Louis.
139   v.   Marie.
+ 140   vi.   Victoria, born 1863 in of Hesse; died 1950.
+ 141   vii.   Alexandra Hesse or Alix of Hesse, born June 06, 1872 in of Hesse Darmstadt, German Empire; died July 17, 1918 in Yekaterinberg, Russian SFSR Soviet Union.

126. Leopold of[16] Saxe-Coburg-Gotha (Alexandrina[15] Victoria, Prince Edward[14] Augustus, George[13] III, George[12] II, George[11] I, Sophia[10], Elizabeth[9] Stuart, James Stuart VI[8] and I,

Henry Stuart or[7] Stewart, Lord Darnley, Margaret[6] Douglas, Margaret "Mary Queen of Scots"[5] Tudor, Henry VII[4], Edmund[3], Sir Owen Meredith[2], Maredudd ap[1] Tudur) was born 1853, and died 1884. He married Helena.

More About Leopold of Saxe-Coburg-Gotha:
Fact 1: Duke of Albany.

Child of Leopold Saxe-Coburg-Gotha and Helena is:
142   i.   Alice[17] Saxe-Coburg-Gotha, born 1883; died 1981.

More About Alice Saxe-Coburg-Gotha:
Fact 1: Countess of Athlone.

Generation No. 17

130. George V of Saxe-Coburg-Gotha changed to[17] Windsor (Albert Edward VII of[16] Saxe-Coburg-Gotha, Alexandrina[15] Victoria, Prince Edward[14] Augustus, George[13] III, George[12] II, George[11] I, Sophia[10], Elizabeth[9] Stuart, James Stuart VI[8] and I, Henry Stuart or[7] Stewart, Lord Darnley, Margaret[6] Douglas, Margaret "Mary Queen of Scots"[5] Tudor, Henry VII[4], Edmund[3], Sir Owen Meredith[2], Maredudd ap[1] Tudur) was born June 03, 1865, and died January 20, 1936 in Sandringham; buried at Windsor, England. He married Victoria Mary Augusta Louise Olga Pauline July 06, 1893, daughter of Prince Alexander and Princess Cambridge.

More About George V of Saxe-Coburg-Gotha changed to Windsor:
Fact 1: 1910-1936, was King of England, British Dominions and Emperor of India.
Fact 2: House of Windsor.
Fact 3: House of Saxe-Coburg and Gotha.
Fact 4: July 17, 1917, George changed his surname: Windsor due to anti-German sentiment in British Empire.

More About Victoria Mary Augusta Louise Olga Pauline:
Fact 1: Victoria Mary Augusta Louise Olga Pauline Claudine Agnes.
Fact 2: Was Queen Consort of the United Kingdom and the British Dominions.
Fact 3: Was Empress Consort of India.
Fact 4: Technically, was Princess of Teck.
Fact 5: Informally known as *"May."*
Fact 6: House of Wurttemberg [Germany]. Remains are in St. George's Chapel, Windsor, England, U.K.

Children of George Windsor and Victoria Pauline are:
143   i.   Edward VIII of[18] Saxe-Coburg-Gotha, born June 23, 1894; died 1972. He married Wallace Warfield Simpson.

More About Edward VIII of Saxe-Coburg-Gotha:
Fact 1: Also known as "David."

Fact 2: Duke of Windsor.

Fact 3: 1936, Reigned.

Fact 4: No heirs.

Fact 5: December 11, 1936, abdicated and renounced the throne to his descendants.

+	144	ii.	King George VI of Saxe-Coburg-Gotha, born December 14, 1895; died February 06, 1952 in buried at Windsor.
+	145	iii.	Princess Royal Mary of Saxe-Coburg-Gotha, born 1897; died 1965.
+	146	iv.	Prince Henry of Saxe-Coburg-Gotha, born 1900; died 1974.
+	147	v.	Prince George of Saxe-Coburg-Gotha, born 1902; died 1942.
	148	vi.	Prince John of Saxe-Coburg-Gotha, born 1905.

140. Victoria[17] (Alice Maude Mary of[16] Saxe-Coburg-Gotha, Alexandrina[15] Victoria, Prince Edward[14] Augustus, George[13] III, George[12] II, George[11] I, Sophia[10], Elizabeth[9] Stuart, James Stuart VI[8] and I, Henry Stuart or[7] Stewart, Lord Darnley, Margaret[6] Douglas, Margaret "Mary Queen of Scots"[5] Tudor, Henry VII[4], Edmund[3], Sir Owen Meredith[2], Maredudd ap[1] Tudur) was born 1863 in of Hesse, and died 1950. She married Louis of Battenberg.

More About Louis of Battenberg:
Fact 1: 1st Marquess of Milford Haven.

Children of Victoria and Louis Battenberg are:

+	149	i.	George[18] Battenberg, born 1892 in of Battenberg; died 1938.
	150	ii.	Gustaf VI Battenberg, born 1882; died 1973. He married Louise.

More About Gustaf VI Battenberg:
Fact 1: Adolf of Sweden.
Fact 2: King Gustaf VI.

	151	iii.	Louis Battenberg, born 1900 in of Battenberg; died 1979. He married Edwina Ashley.

More About Louis Battenberg:
Fact 1: Earl of Mountbatten of Burma.

141. Alexandra Hesse or Alix of[17] Hesse (Alice Maude Mary of[16] Saxe-Coburg-Gotha, Alexandrina[15] Victoria, Prince Edward[14] Augustus, George[13] III, George[12] II, George[11] I, Sophia[10], Elizabeth[9] Stuart, James Stuart VI[8] and I, Henry Stuart or[7] Stewart, Lord Darnley, Margaret[6] Douglas, Margaret "Mary Queen of Scots"[5] Tudor, Henry VII[4], Edmund[3], Sir

Owen Meredith[2], Maredudd ap[1] Tudur) was born June 06, 1872 in of Hesse Darmstadt, German Empire, and died July 17, 1918 in Yekaterinberg, Russian SFSR Soviet Union. She married Nicholas II Tsar of Russia, son of Emperor Russias and Maria Dagmar.

More About Nicholas II Tsar of Russia:

Fact 1: Was in the House of Holstein-Gottorp-Romanov

Fact 2: Also known as *"Nikolai Alexandrovich Romanov."*

Fact 3: May 26, 1896, coronation.

Fact 4: 1894-1917, reigned.

Remains are in the Peter and Paul Cathedral, Saint Petersburg, Russian Federation.

Children of Alexandra Hesse and Nicholas Russia are:

152	i.	Olga[18], born 1895.
153	ii.	Tatiana, born 1897.
154	iii.	Maria, born 1899.
155	iv.	Anastasia, born 1901.
156	v.	Tsesarevich Alexei Nikolevich, born 1904.

More About Tsesarevich Alexei Nikolevich:

Fact 1: Was a hemophiliac.

Generation No. 18

144. King George VI of[18] Saxe-Coburg-Gotha (George V of Saxe-Coburg-Gotha changed to[17] Windsor, Albert Edward VII of[16] Saxe-Coburg-Gotha, Alexandrina[15] Victoria, Prince Edward[14] Augustus, George[13] III, George[12] II, George[11] I, Sophia[10], Elizabeth[9] Stuart, James Stuart VI[8] and I, Henry Stuart or[7] Stewart, Lord Darnley, Margaret[6] Douglas, Margaret "Mary Queen of Scots"[5] Tudor, Henry VII[4], Edmund[3], Sir Owen Meredith[2], Maredudd ap[1] Tudur) was born December 14, 1895, and died February 06, 1952 in buried at Windsor. He married Lady Elizabeth Angela Marguerite Bowes-Lyon April 26, 1923, daughter of 14th Kinghorne and X.

More About King George VI of Saxe-Coburg-Gotha:

Fact 1: 1936-1952, King of the UK and the Dominions of the British Commonwealth

Fact 2: Duke of York.

More About Lady Elizabeth Angela Marguerite Bowes-Lyon:

Fact 1: Duchess of York.

Children of King Saxe-Coburg-Gotha and Lady Bowes-Lyon are:

+	157	i.	Elizabeth II[19] Windsor, born April 21, 1926 in Mayfair, London, England, U.K.
+	158	ii.	Margaret Rose Windsor, born 1930.

145. Princess Royal Mary of[18] Saxe-Coburg-Gotha (George V of Saxe-Coburg-Gotha changed to[17] Windsor, Albert Edward VII of[16] Saxe-Coburg-Gotha, Alexandrina[15] Victoria, Prince Edward[14] Augustus, George[13] III, George[12] II, George[11] I, Sophia[10], Elizabeth[9] Stuart, James Stuart VI[8] and I, Henry Stuart or[7] Stewart, Lord Darnley, Margaret[6] Douglas, Margaret "Mary Queen of Scots"[5] Tudor, Henry VII[4], Edmund[3], Sir Owen Meredith[2], Maredudd ap[1] Tudur) was born 1897, and died 1965. She married Henry Viscount Lascelles.

More About Princess Royal Mary of Saxe-Coburg-Gotha:
Fact 1: Princess Royal.

More About Henry Viscount Lascelles:
Fact 1: 6th Earl of Harewood

   Child of Princess Saxe-Coburg-Gotha and Henry Lascelles is:
+   159   i.   George[19] Lascelles, born 1923 in of Harewood.

146. Prince Henry of[18] Saxe-Coburg-Gotha (George V of Saxe-Coburg-Gotha changed to[17] Windsor, Albert Edward VII of[16] Saxe-Coburg-Gotha, Alexandrina[15] Victoria, Prince Edward[14] Augustus, George[13] III, George[12] II, George[11] I, Sophia[10], Elizabeth[9] Stuart, James Stuart VI[8] and I, Henry Stuart or[7] Stewart, Lord Darnley, Margaret[6] Douglas, Margaret "Mary Queen of Scots"[5] Tudor, Henry VII[4], Edmund[3], Sir Owen Meredith[2], Maredudd ap[1] Tudur) was born 1900, and died 1974. He married Alice Montagu-Douglas-Scott.

More About Prince Henry of Saxe-Coburg-Gotha:
Fact 1: Duke of Gloucester.

   Children of Prince Saxe-Coburg-Gotha and Alice Montagu-Douglas-Scott are:
    160   i.   William[19] Saxe-Coburg-Gotha, born 1941; died 1972.
+   161   ii.   Richard Saxe-Coburg-Gotha, born 1944.

147. Prince George of[18] Saxe-Coburg-Gotha (George V of Saxe-Coburg-Gotha changed to[17] Windsor, Albert Edward VII of[16] Saxe-Coburg-Gotha, Alexandrina[15] Victoria, Prince Edward[14] Augustus, George[13] III, George[12] II, George[11] I, Sophia[10], Elizabeth[9] Stuart, James Stuart VI[8] and I, Henry Stuart or[7] Stewart, Lord Darnley, Margaret[6] Douglas, Margaret "Mary Queen of Scots"[5] Tudor, Henry VII[4], Edmund[3], Sir Owen Meredith[2], Maredudd ap[1] Tudur) was born 1902, and died 1942. He married Marina.

More About Prince George of Saxe-Coburg-Gotha:
Fact 1: Duke of Kent.

More About Marina:
Fact 1: Princess of Greece.

Children of Prince Saxe-Coburg-Gotha and Marina are:

+   162   i.   Edward[19] Saxe-Coburg-Gotha, born 1935.
+   163   ii.   Alexandra Saxe-Coburg-Gotha, born 1936.
+   164   iii.   Michael Saxe-Coburg-Gotha, born 1942.

149. George[18] Battenberg (Victoria[17], Alice Maude Mary of[16] Saxe-Coburg-Gotha, Alexandrina[15] Victoria, Prince Edward[14] Augustus, George[13] III, George[12] II, George[11] I, Sophia[10], Elizabeth[9] Stuart, James Stuart VI[8] and I, Henry Stuart or[7] Stewart, Lord Darnley, Margaret[6] Douglas, Margaret "Mary Queen of Scots"[5] Tudor, Henry VII[4], Edmund[3], Sir Owen Meredith[2], Maredudd ap[1] Tudur) was born 1892 in of Battenberg, and died 1938.

Child of George Battenberg is:
165   i.   David[19] Battenberg, born 1919; died 1970.

Generation No. 19

157. Elizabeth II[19] Windsor (King George VI of[18] Saxe-Coburg-Gotha, George V of Saxe-Coburg-Gotha changed to[17] Windsor, Albert Edward VII of[16] Saxe-Coburg-Gotha, Alexandrina[15] Victoria, Prince Edward[14] Augustus, George[13] III, George[12] II, George[11] I, Sophia[10], Elizabeth[9] Stuart, James Stuart VI[8] and I, Henry Stuart or[7] Stewart, Lord Darnley, Margaret[6] Douglas, Margaret "Mary Queen of Scots"[5] Tudor, Henry VII[4], Edmund[3], Sir Owen Meredith[2], Maredudd ap[1] Tudur) was born April 21, 1926 in Mayfair, London, England, U.K. She married Prince Philip Mountbatten 1947, son of Prince de Laszlo and Princess Battenberg.

More About Elizabeth II Windsor:
Fact 1: Queen of England.
Fact 2: Elizabeth Alexandra Mary Windsor.
Fact 3: Elizabeth II.

More About Prince Philip Mountbatten:
Fact 1: Duke of Edinburgh.
Fact 2: June 10, 1921, Born: Prince William of Greece and Denmark.

Children of Elizabeth Windsor and Prince Mountbatten are:

+   166   i.   Prince Charles Philip Arthur[20] George, born November 14, 1948 in Buckingham Palace, London, England.
+   167   ii.   Princess Royal Anne Elizabeth Alice Louise, born August 15, 1950.
+   168   iii.   Prince Andrew Albert Christian Edward, born February 19, 1960 in Buckingham Palace, London, England.
+   169   iv.   Prince Edward Anthony Richard Louis, born March 10, 1964 in Buckingham Palace, London, England.

158. Margaret Rose[19] Windsor (King George VI of[18] Saxe-Coburg-Gotha, George V of Saxe-Coburg-Gotha changed to[17] Windsor, Albert Edward VII of[16] Saxe-Coburg-Gotha, Alexandrina[15] Victoria, Prince Edward[14] Augustus, George[13] III, George[12] II, George[11] I, Sophia[10], Elizabeth[9] Stuart, James Stuart VI[8] and I, Henry Stuart or[7] Stewart, Lord Darnley, Margaret[6] Douglas, Margaret "Mary Queen of Scots"[5] Tudor, Henry VII[4], Edmund[3], Sir Owen Meredith[2], Maredudd ap[1] Tudur) was born 1930. She married Anthony Armstrong-Jones.

More About Anthony Armstrong-Jones:
Fact 1: 1st Earl of Snowdon

    Children of Margaret Windsor and Anthony Armstrong-Jones are:
    170   i.   David[20] Armstrong-Jones, born 1961. He married Serena Stanhope.

    More About David Armstrong-Jones:
    Fact 1: Viscount Linley.

+   171   ii.   Sarah Armstrong-Jones, born 1964.

159. George[19] Lascelles (Princess Royal Mary of[18] Saxe-Coburg-Gotha, George V of Saxe-Coburg-Gotha changed to[17] Windsor, Albert Edward VII of[16] Saxe-Coburg-Gotha, Alexandrina[15] Victoria, Prince Edward[14] Augustus, George[13] III, George[12] II, George[11] I, Sophia[10], Elizabeth[9] Stuart, James Stuart VI[8] and I, Henry Stuart or[7] Stewart, Lord Darnley, Margaret[6] Douglas, Margaret "Mary Queen of Scots"[5] Tudor, Henry VII[4], Edmund[3], Sir Owen Meredith[2], Maredudd ap[1] Tudur) was born 1923 in of Harewood. He married (1) Marion Stein. He married (2) Patricia Tuckwell.

    Children of George Lascelles and Marion Stein are:
    172   i.   David[20] Lascelles, born 1950.
    173   ii.   James Lascelles, born 1953.
    174   iii.   Jeremy Lascelles, born 1955.

    Child of George Lascelles and Patricia Tuckwell is:
    175   i.   Mark[20] Lascelles, born 1964.

161. Richard[19] Saxe-Coburg-Gotha (Prince Henry of[18], George V of Saxe-Coburg-Gotha changed to[17] Windsor, Albert Edward VII of[16] Saxe-Coburg-Gotha, Alexandrina[15] Victoria, Prince Edward[14] Augustus, George[13] III, George[12] II, George[11] I, Sophia[10], Elizabeth[9] Stuart, James Stuart VI[8] and I, Henry Stuart or[7] Stewart, Lord Darnley, Margaret[6] Douglas, Margaret "Mary Queen of Scots"[5] Tudor, Henry VII[4], Edmund[3], Sir Owen Meredith[2], Maredudd ap[1] Tudur) was born 1944. He married Birgitte van Deura.

More About Richard Saxe-Coburg-Gotha:
Fact 1: Duke of Gloucester.

Children of Richard Saxe-Coburg-Gotha and Birgitte van Deura are:

176   i.   Alexander[20] Saxe-Coburg-Gotha, born 1974.

More About Alexander Saxe-Coburg-Gotha:
Fact 1: Earl of Ulster.

177   ii.   Davina Saxe-Coburg-Gotha, born 1977.
178   iii.   Rose Saxe-Coburg-Gotha, born 1980.

162. Edward[19] Saxe-Coburg-Gotha (Prince George of[18], George V of Saxe-Coburg-Gotha changed to[17] Windsor, Albert Edward VII of[16] Saxe-Coburg-Gotha, Alexandrina[15] Victoria, Prince Edward[14] Augustus, George[13] III, George[12] II, George[11] I, Sophia[10], Elizabeth[9] Stuart, James Stuart VI[8] and I, Henry Stuart or[7] Stewart, Lord Darnley, Margaret[6] Douglas, Margaret "Mary Queen of Scots"[5] Tudor, Henry VII[4], Edmund[3], Sir Owen Meredith[2], Maredudd ap[1] Tudur) was born 1935. He married Katharine Worsley.

More About Edward Saxe-Coburg-Gotha:
Fact 1: Duke of Kent.

Children of Edward Saxe-Coburg-Gotha and Katharine Worsley are:

179   i.   George[20] Saxe-Coburg-Gotha, born 1962. More About George Saxe-Coburg-Gotha: Fact 1: Earl of Saint Andrews.
180   ii.   Helen Saxe-Coburg-Gotha, born 1964.
181   iii.   Nicholas Saxe-Coburg-Gotha, born 1970.

163. Alexandra[19] Saxe-Coburg-Gotha (Prince George of[18], George V of Saxe-Coburg-Gotha changed to[17] Windsor, Albert Edward VII of[16] Saxe-Coburg-Gotha, Alexandrina[15] Victoria, Prince Edward[14] Augustus, George[13] III, George[12] II, George[11] I, Sophia[10], Elizabeth[9] Stuart, James Stuart VI[8] and I, Henry Stuart or[7] Stewart, Lord Darnley, Margaret[6] Douglas, Margaret "Mary Queen of Scots"[5] Tudor, Henry VII[4], Edmund[3], Sir Owen Meredith[2], Maredudd ap[1] Tudur) was born 1936. She married Angus Ogilvy.

Children of Alexandra Saxe-Coburg-Gotha and Angus Ogilvy are:

182   i.   James[20] Ogilvy, born 1964.
183   ii.   Marina Ogilvy, born 1966.

164. Michael[19] Saxe-Coburg-Gotha (Prince George of[18], George V of Saxe-Coburg-Gotha changed to[17] Windsor, Albert Edward VII of[16] Saxe-Coburg-Gotha, Alexandrina[15] Victoria, Prince Edward[14] Augustus, George[13] III, George[12] II, George[11] I, Sophia[10], Elizabeth[9] Stuart, James Stuart VI[8] and I, Henry Stuart or[7] Stewart, Lord Darnley, Margaret[6] Douglas, Margaret "Mary Queen of Scots"[5] Tudor, Henry VII[4], Edmund[3], Sir Owen Meredith[2], Maredudd ap[1] Tudur) was born 1942. He married Marie-Christine von Reibnitz.

Children of Michael Saxe-Coburg-Gotha and Marie-Christine von Reibnitz are:

184   i.   Frederick[20] Saxe-Coburg-Gotha, born 1979.
185   ii.   Gabriella Saxe-Coburg-Gotha, born 1981.

Generation No. 20

166. Prince Charles Philip Arthur[20] George (Elizabeth II[19] Windsor, King George VI of[18] Saxe-Coburg-Gotha, George V of Saxe-Coburg-Gotha changed to[17] Windsor, Albert Edward VII of[16] Saxe-Coburg-Gotha, Alexandrina[15] Victoria, Prince Edward[14] Augustus, George[13] III, George[12] II, George[11] I, Sophia[10], Elizabeth[9] Stuart, James Stuart VI[8] and I, Henry Stuart or[7] Stewart, Lord Darnley, Margaret[6] Douglas, Margaret "Mary Queen of Scots"[5] Tudor, Henry VII[4], Edmund[3], Sir Owen Meredith[2], Maredudd ap[1] Tudur) was born November 14, 1948 in Buckingham Palace, London, England. He married (1) Lady Diana Frances Spencer July 29, 1981 in Saint Paul's Cathedral, London, England, daughter of John Spencer and Frances Kydd. He married (2) Camilla Rosemary Shand April 09, 2005 in Guildhall, Windsor, Berkshire, England, daughter of Bruce Shand and Hon Cubitt.

More About Prince Charles Philip Arthur George:
Fact 1: Prince of Wales.

More About Lady Diana Frances Spencer:
Fact 1: Princess of Wales.
Fact 2: Born July 1, 1961.

More About Camilla Rosemary Shand:
Fact 1: Duchess of Cornwall.

Fact 2: Born July 17, 1947.

Children of Prince Charles and Lady Spencer are:
+ 186   i.   Prince William Arthur Philip[21] Louis, born June 21, 1982 in Saint Mary's Hospital, Paddington, London, England.
   187   ii.   Prince Henry (Harry) Charles Albert David, born September 15, 1984 in Paddington, London, England.

Children of Prince George and Camilla Shand are:
188   i.   Thomas Henry Charles Parker[21] Bowles, born December 18, 1974. He married Sara Buys September 10, 2005 in St. Nicholas' Church, Rotherfield Grey, Oxon.
189   ii.   Laura Rose Parker Bowles, born 1978. She married Harry Marcus George Lopes May 06, 2006 in St. Cyriac's Church, Lacock, Wiltshire, England.

167. Princess Royal Anne Elizabeth Alice[20] Louise (Elizabeth II[19] Windsor, King George VI of[18] Saxe-Coburg-Gotha, George V of Saxe-Coburg-Gotha changed to[17] Windsor, Albert Edward VII of[16] Saxe-Coburg-Gotha, Alexandrina[15] Victoria, Prince Edward[14] Augustus, George[13] III, George[12] II, George[11] I, Sophia[10], Elizabeth[9] Stuart, James Stuart VI[8] and I, Henry Stuart or[7] Stewart, Lord Darnley, Margaret[6] Douglas, Margaret "Mary Queen of Scots"[5] Tudor, Henry VII[4], Edmund[3], Sir Owen Meredith[2], Maredudd ap[1] Tudur) was born August 15, 1950. She married (1) Mark Phillips. She married (2) Timothy Lawrence.

More About Princess Royal Anne Elizabeth Alice Louise:
Fact 1: Princess Royal.

Children of Princess Louise and Mark Phillips are:
190   i.   Peter[21] Phillips, born 1977.
191   ii.   Zara Tindall Phillips, born 1981.

168. Prince Andrew Albert Christian[20] Edward (Elizabeth II[19] Windsor, King George VI of[18] Saxe-Coburg-Gotha, George V of Saxe-Coburg-Gotha changed to[17] Windsor, Albert Edward VII of[16] Saxe-Coburg-Gotha, Alexandrina[15] Victoria, Prince Edward[14] Augustus, George[13] III, George[12] II, George[11] I, Sophia[10], Elizabeth[9] Stuart, James Stuart VI[8] and I, Henry Stuart or[7] Stewart, Lord Darnley, Margaret[6] Douglas, Margaret "Mary Queen of Scots"[5] Tudor, Henry VII[4], Edmund[3], Sir Owen Meredith[2], Maredudd ap[1] Tudur) was born February 19, 1960 in Buckingham Palace, London, England. He married Sarah Ferguson.

More About Prince Andrew Albert Christian Edward:
Fact 1: Duke of York.

Children of Prince Edward and Sarah Ferguson are:
192   i.   Beatrice[21] Andrew, born 1988.
193   ii.   Eugenie Andrew, born 1990.

169. Prince Edward Anthony Richard[20] Louis (Elizabeth II[19] Windsor, King George VI of[18] Saxe-Coburg-Gotha, George V of Saxe-Coburg-Gotha changed to[17] Windsor, Albert Edward VII of[16] Saxe-Coburg-Gotha, Alexandrina[15] Victoria, Prince Edward[14] Augustus, George[13] III, George[12] II, George[11] I, Sophia[10], Elizabeth[9] Stuart, James Stuart VI[8] and I, Henry Stuart or[7] Stewart, Lord Darnley, Margaret[6] Douglas, Margaret "Mary Queen of Scots"[5] Tudor, Henry VII[4], Edmund[3], Sir Owen Meredith[2], Maredudd ap[1] Tudur) was born March 10, 1964 in Buckingham Palace, London, England. He married Sophie Rhys-Jones 1999.

More About Prince Edward Anthony Richard Louis:
Fact 1: Earl of Wessex.

Children of Prince Louis and Sophie Rhys-Jones are:

194	i.	Lady Louise[21] Windsor.
195	ii.	Viscount James Windsor.

171. Sarah[20] Armstrong-Jones (Margaret Rose[19] Windsor, King George VI of[18] Saxe-Coburg-Gotha, George V of Saxe-Coburg-Gotha changed to[17] Windsor, Albert Edward VII of[16] Saxe-Coburg-Gotha, Alexandrina[15] Victoria, Prince Edward[14] Augustus, George[13] III, George[12] II, George[11] I, Sophia[10], Elizabeth[9] Stuart, James Stuart VI[8] and I, Henry Stuart or[7] Stewart, Lord Darnley, Margaret[6] Douglas, Margaret "Mary Queen of Scots"[5] Tudor, Henry VII[4], Edmund[3], Sir Owen Meredith[2], Maredudd ap[1] Tudur) was born 1964. She married Daniel Chatto.

Child of Sarah Armstrong-Jones and Daniel Chatto is:

196	i.	Samuel[21] Chatto, born 1996.

Generation No. 21

186. Prince William Arthur Philip[21] Louis (Prince Charles Philip Arthur[20] George, Elizabeth II[19] Windsor, King George VI of[18] Saxe-Coburg-Gotha, George V of Saxe-Coburg-Gotha changed to[17] Windsor, Albert Edward VII of[16] Saxe-Coburg-Gotha, Alexandrina[15] Victoria, Prince Edward[14] Augustus, George[13] III, George[12] II, George[11] I, Sophia[10], Elizabeth[9] Stuart, James Stuart VI[8] and I, Henry Stuart or[7] Stewart, Lord Darnley, Margaret[6] Douglas, Margaret "Mary Queen of Scots"[5] Tudor, Henry VII[4], Edmund[3], Sir Owen Meredith[2], Maredudd ap[1] Tudur) was born June 21, 1982 in Saint Mary's Hospital, Paddington, London, England. He married Catherine "Kate" Middleton April 29, 2011 in Westminster Abbey, London, England, daughter of Michael Middleton and Carole Goldsmith.

More About Prince William Arthur Philip Louis:
Fact 1: Duke of Cambridge.

More About Catherine "Kate" Middleton:
Fact 1: Duchess of Cambridge.

Children of Prince Louis and Catherine Middleton are:

197	i.	Prince George Alexander[22] Louis, born July 22, 2013 in Saint Mary's Hospital, London, England.

More About Prince George Alexander Louis:
Fact 1: House of Windsor.

198	ii.	Princess Charlotte Elizabeth Diana, born May 02, 2015 in Saint Mary's Hospital, London, England.

More About Princess Charlotte Elizabeth Diana: Fact 1: May 02, 2015, born at 8:34 a.m. Saturday Fact 2: House of Windsor.

The Boleyn Section

♀ | | ♂

"The most happy,"

MOTTO OF QUEEN ANNE BOLEYN.

THE BOLEYN SECTION CONTAINS ONLY the first seven generations in a quest to save space. The name *Boleyn* is sometimes referred to as *Bullen*. It is a habitational name from the French Channel Port of Boulogne. It comes from the Latin word *bonus*, meaning *good*. It is conceivable that it may be derived from the Gaulic word *bona* meaning *foundation*. Boulogne is a major trading port between England and France.

There are many versions of the name Boleyn.

* Bullan
* Bulloyne
* Bullene
* Bulen
* Bullen
* Bulleyn
* Bullion
* Bullon
* Bullin
* Bullene
* Bullent
* Bollen
* Bouleyne
* Boullin
* Boullen
* Bullan
* Bullant

If discrepancies are discerned, please note them in the note section of the back matter of this book and contact Metallo House Publishers [MHP] with your findings.

DESCENDANTS OF SIR THOMAS BOLEYN

Generation No. 1

1. Sir Thomas[1] Boleyn. He married Anne "Jane" Bracton.

More About Sir Thomas Boleyn:
Fact 1: Was a wealthy London mercer -- cloth merchant.

Child of Sir Boleyn and Anne Bracton is:
+   2   i.   Sir Geoffrey[2] Boleyn, born 1406; died 1471.

Generation No. 2

2. Sir Geoffrey[2] Boleyn (Sir Thomas[1]) was born 1406, and died 1471. He married (1) Unknown Wife. He married (2) Anne Mary Hoo, daughter of Sir Hoo and Elizabeth Wychingham.

More About Sir Geoffrey Boleyn:
Fact 1: 1452, served as alderman for City of London, Lord Mayor of London.
Fact 2: Knighted by King Henry VI.
Fact 3: 1462, purchased Hever Castle, Kent, England.
Fact 4: He and his wife were the great grandparents of Anne Boleyn.
Fact 5: Was a wealthy cloth merchant.
Fact 6: 1463, possible death date.
Fact 7: Great grandfather of Queen Anne Boleyn.

Child of Sir Boleyn and Unknown Wife is:
+   3   i.   Elizabeth or Anne[3] Boleyn.

Children of Sir Boleyn and Anne Hoo are:
+   4   i.   Sir William[3] Boleyn, born 1451 in Blicking, Norfolk, England; died October 10, 1505.
     5   ii.   Sir Thomas Boleyn, died 1471.

Generation No. 3

3. Elizabeth or Anne[3] Boleyn (Sir Geoffrey[2], Sir Thomas[1]). She married Sir Henry Heydon "Haydon" "Hayden".

Child of Elizabeth Boleyn and Sir "Hayden" is:

+ 6   i.   Dorothy⁴ Heydon.

4. Sir William³ Boleyn (Sir Geoffrey², Sir Thomas¹) was born 1451 in Blicking, Norfolk, England, and died October 10, 1505. He married Lady Margaret Ormond Butler, daughter of Thomas Ormond and Anne Hankford.

More About Sir William Boleyn:
Fact 1: Was made *Knight of Bath* by Richard III.
Fact 2: 1489, served as High Sheriff of Kent.
Fact 3: With his wife -- they were the paternal grandparents of Anne Boleyn.
Fact 4: 1449 possible birth year.

     Children of Sir Boleyn and Lady Butler are:
     7   i.   Alice⁴ Boleyn. She married Sir Robert Clere.
     8   ii.   Anne Boleyn. She married Sir John Shelton.
     9   iii.   Anthony Boleyn.
     10   iv.   Jane Boleyn. She married Sir Philip Calthorpe.
     11   v.   John Boleyn.
     12   vi.   Margaret Boleyn. She married John Sackville.
     13   vii.   Sir Edward Boleyn.
     14   viii.   Sir James Boleyn.
     15   ix.   William - Archdeacon of Wincester.
+ 16   x.   Thomas Boleyn --1st Earl of Wiltshire and Ormonde, born 1477 in Hever Castle, Kent, England; died March 12, 1538/39 in Hever, Kent, England.

Generation No. 4

6. Dorothy⁴ Heydon (Elizabeth or Anne³ Boleyn, Sir Geoffrey², Sir Thomas¹). She married Thomas Brooke, 8th Baron of Cobham, son of John Brooke and Margaret de Neville.

More About Thomas Brooke, 8th Baron of Cobham:
Fact 1: Freeth says he died July 19, 1529.
Fact 2: Was the 8th Baron and Lord of Cobham

     Children of Dorothy Heydon and Thomas Brooke are:
+ 17   i.   Elizabeth⁵ Brooke, born 1503 in Cobham, England; died 1560.
+ 18   ii.   George Brooke.

16. Thomas Boleyn --1st Earl of Wiltshire and⁴ Ormonde (Sir William³ Boleyn, Sir Geoffrey², Sir Thomas¹) was born 1477 in Hever Castle, Kent, England, and died March 12, 1538/39 in Hever, Kent, England. He married Lady Elizabeth Howard, Countess of Wiltshire Abt. 1500, daughter of Thomas Howard and Elizabeth Tylney.

More About Thomas Boleyn --1st Earl of Wiltshire and Ormonde:
Fact 1: Father of Queen Anne Boleyn.
Fact 2: Title: Viscount Rochford.
Fact 3: December 08, 1529, Earl of Ormond and Earl of Wiltshire.
Died at age 61 buried at Hever, Kent, England.

    Children of Thomas Ormonde and Lady Howard are:

    19   i.   George[5] Boleyn.

        More About George Boleyn:
        Fact 1: Viscount Rochford.

    20   ii.   Viscount Rochford Boleyn, died May 19, 1536 in condemned to death on charges of adultery the 15th; executed 19th.

+ 21   iii.   Mary Boleyn, born 1499 in Blickling Hall, England; died July 19, 1543 in Essex, England.

+ 22   iv.   Queen Consort Anne Boleyn, born 1501 in Hever or Bickering Hall, Norfolk, England; died May 19, 1536 in executed Tower of London, north bank of River Thames, Central London, England.

Generation No. 5

17. Elizabeth[5] Brooke (Dorothy[4] Heydon, Elizabeth or Anne[3] Boleyn, Sir Geoffrey[2], Sir Thomas[1]) was born 1503 in Cobham, England, and died 1560. She married Sir Thomas "The Elder" Wiatt 1520 in 1521 another possible year of marriage., son of Sir Wiatt and Anne Skinner.

More About Elizabeth Brooke:
Fact 1: Considered possible wife for Henry VIII while his 5th wife awaited execution.
Fact 2: Separated from her husband and lived openly in adultery.

More About Sir Thomas "The Elder" Wiatt:
Fact 1: C.S. Lewis called him the *"Father of the Drab Age."*
Fact 2: 1541, date of death cited by Martyn Freeth.
Buried at the great church of Sherbourne, Dorset, England.

    Children of Elizabeth Brooke and Sir Wiatt are:

+ 23   i.   Sir Thomas "The Younger"[6] Wiatt, born 1521 in Allington Castle, Kent County, England; died April 11, 1554 in Tower Hill, London, England.

    24   ii.   Frances Wiatt?, born Abt. 1522; died July 16, 1578. She married (1) Thomas Lighe. She married (2) William Patrtckson.

18. George[5] Brooke (Dorothy[4] Heydon, Elizabeth or Anne[3] Boleyn, Sir Geoffrey[2], Sir Thomas[1]). He married Anne.

More About George Brooke:
Fact 1: 9th Baron of Cobham of Kent, England.

Child of George Brooke and Anne is:
25   i.   Elisabeth[6] Brooke, born June 25, 1526; died April 02, 1565. She married William Parr, 1st Marquess of Northampton in Bigamously married to William Parr.

More About Elisabeth Brooke:
Fact 1: Was the sister-in-law of Catharine Parr, King Henry VIII's 6th wife/queen.
Fact 2: Was a first cousin to Sir Thomas the Younger.

21. Mary[5] Boleyn (Thomas Boleyn --1st Earl of Wiltshire and[4] Ormonde, Sir William[3] Boleyn, Sir Geoffrey[2], Sir Thomas[1]) was born 1499 in Blickling Hall, England, and died July 19, 1543 in Essex, England. She married (1) William Carey February 04, 1519/20. She married (2) Sir William Stafford 1534, son of Sir Stafford and Margaret Fogge.

More About Mary Boleyn:
Fact 1: Also known as Lady Mary Rochford and as Lady Mary Boleyn.
Fact 2: 1500-1504, possible birth years.

More About William Carey:
Fact 1: Made keeper of the manor, garden and tower of Pleasance, East Greenwich.

Children of Mary Boleyn and William Carey are:
+   26   i.   Catherine or Katherine Cary or[6] Carey, born June 1524; died February 1568/69 in Hampton Court Palace.
+   27   ii.   Henry Carey, born March 04, 1525/26; died July 23, 1596 in Somerset House, London, England.

Child of Mary Boleyn and Sir Stafford is:
28   i.   Son[6] Stafford, born 1534; died 1543.

22. Queen Consort Anne[5] Boleyn (Thomas Boleyn --1st Earl of Wiltshire and[4] Ormonde, Sir William[3] Boleyn, Sir Geoffrey[2], Sir Thomas[1]) was born 1501 in Hever or Bickering Hall, Norfolk, England, and died May 19, 1536 in executed Tower of London, north bank of River Thames, Central London, England. She married King Henry Tudor VIII January 25, 1532/33 in Whitehall, Westminster, London, England, son of Henry Tudor and Elizabeth [Plantagenet].

More About Queen Consort Anne Boleyn:
Fact 1: 2nd wife of King Henry VIII.
Fact 2: 1532, was titled: Marquess of Pembroke on September 1st.
Fact 3: Became Queen of England.
Fact 4: September 01, 1532, Marchioness of Pembroke.
Fact 5: 1507, Possible year of birth.
Cause of Death: Executed by sword Tower Green at the Tower of London
Buried at Chapel of Saint Peter ad Vincula, Tower of London.

More About King Henry Tudor VIII:
Fact 1: 1521-1542, King of England and France.
Fact 2: 1542, Continued as King of England. France and Ireland.
Fact 3: Was the first English sovereign who bore the title of *"Majesty."*
Fact 4: January 28, 1546/47, died.
Fact 5: Was Duke of York and then later King Henry VIII
Fact 6: January 28, 1491 is sited also as his birthday.
Fact 7: June 24, 1509, titled King of England at Westminster Abbey, London, England.
Fact 8: January 28, 1490/91, 1421 cited as his birthday by some historians.
Buried at Windsor, England.

Children of Queen Boleyn and King Tudor are:

29   i.   Queen Elizabeth I[6] Tudor, born September 07, 1533; died March 24, 1602/03 in Richmond Palace, Thamesside on right bank of Thames, upstream of Westminster.

More About Queen Elizabeth I Tudor:
Fact 1: Never married.
Fact 2: Died without descendants.
Fact 3: Was Princess Elizabeth and became Queen of England aft. Mary I's demise.
Fact 4: The Tudor Dynasty died with Elizabeth I. Buried at Westminster Abbey.

30   ii.   Henry Tudor, born 1534.

More About Henry Tudor:
Fact 1: 1534, Titled: *"Duke of Cornwall;"* died as infant.

31   iii.   Son Tudor, born January 29, 1535/36.

More About Son Tudor:
Died as infant.

Generation No. 6

23. Sir Thomas "The Younger"[6] Wiatt (Elizabeth[5] Brooke, Dorothy[4] Heydon, Elizabeth or Anne[3] Boleyn, Sir Geoffrey[2], Sir Thomas[1]) was born 1521 in Allington Castle, Kent County, England, and died April 11, 1554 in Tower Hill, London, England. He married Lady Jane Haute "Hawte" "Haut" "Hawt" 1536 in or 1537 Kent County, England, daughter of Sir Haute and Maria Guldeford.

More About Sir Thomas "The Younger" Wiatt:
Fact 1: Was brought up a Roman Catholic.
Fact 2: Changed to Protestant after witnessing Spanish Inquisition in Spain on trip.
Fact 3: Was imprisoned at Tower of London for breaking windows while drunk.
Fact 4: After release, fought for Hapsburg emperor -- then also king of Spain.
Fact 5: Fragment of Allington Castle still inhabited near Maidstone on bank of Medway
Fact 6: Served King Henry VIII as a squire and soldier.
Fact 7: Was an only son of his parents.
Fact 8: Executed near Hyde Park, London, England.
Fact 9: 1522, cites his birth year as -- Alexander Lloyd Wiatt
Fact 10: 1542, he inherited Allington Castle and Boxley Abbey.
Fact 11: 1543, took part in siege of Landrecies and in 1544 the seige of Boulogne.
Fact 12: 1547, was knighted.
Fact 13: Resting place provided: St. Mary the Virgin and All Saints Churchyard, Boxley, Kent County, England.
Executed. Churchyard, Boxley, Kent County, England.

More About Lady Jane Haute "Hawte" "Haut" "Hawt":
Fact 1: 1537, Manor of Boxley passed to him via his wife Jane Haute.
Fact 2: 1554, Property was confiscated after husband's rebellion by Queen Mary I
Fact 3: 1571, Boxley Manor property was restored to her by Elizabeth I.
Fact 4: Abbey property, abbey house and upper grange.

Children of Sir Wiatt and Lady "Hawt" are:
32	i.	Arthur[7] Wiatt.
33	ii.	Charles "Carolus" Wiatt.
34	iii.	Henry "Henricus" Wiatt.

More About Henry "Henricus" Wiatt:
died 1624?

| 35 | iv. | Jocosa "Joyce" Wiatt. |
| 36 | v. | Richardus "Richard" Wiatt. |

	37	vi.	Ursula Wiatt.
	38	vii.	Frances Wiatt?. He married Sir Thomas Leigh?
+	39	viii.	Anne or Ann Anna Wiatt, born September 19, 1542 in Kent, England; died June 04, 1592 in East Peckham, Kent County, England.
+	40	ix.	Jane or Joan Wiatt, born 1553 in England; died 1617.
+	41	x.	Sir George "Georgius" Thomas Wiatt, Knt., born Abt. 1554 in Allington Castle or Boxley Hall, Kent County, England; died September 16, 1624 in Ireland, buried Nov. 10, 1624 in Boxley, Kent, England.

26. Catherine or Katherine Cary or[6] Carey (Mary[5] Boleyn, Thomas Boleyn --1st Earl of Wiltshire and[4] Ormonde, Sir William[3] Boleyn, Sir Geoffrey[2], Sir Thomas[1]) was born June 1524, and died February 1568/69 in Hampton Court Palace. She married Sir Francis Knollys April 1540 in married in April of May 1540, son of Robert Knollys and Lettice Peniston.

More About Catherine or Katherine Cary or Carey:
Fact 1: 1st cousin to Queen Elizabeth I of England
Fact 2: Katherine Carey
Fact 3: November 1539, at age 15 Maid of Honor in wedding of Anne of Cleves to Henry VIII.
Fact 4: January 15, 1568/69, possible date of demise.
Fact 5: born in the midst of her mother's affair with King Henry VIII.
Fact 6: 1568, was given a royal funeral by Elizabeth I who paid 640 pounds for the funeral.
Cause of Death: Buried at St. Edmund's Chapel April 1569, Westminster Abbey is the only so-called non-royal, found amongst those of Henry III, Henry VI, Queen Mary II, King William III, Prince George of Denmark, Queen Anne and Queen Caroline.

More About Sir Francis Knollys:
Fact 1: Was courtier in service to Henry VIII, Edward VI and Elizabeth I.
Fact 2: Was a member of Parliament,
Fact 3: 1540, became known as Gentleman Pensioner, his first royal appointment.

Children of Catherine Carey and Sir Knollys are:

	42	i.	Cecelia[7] Knollys.
	43	ii.	Dudley Knollys.
	44	iii.	Katherine or Catherine Knollys, died 1632 in buried Dec. 20, 1632. She married (1) Sir Phillip Boteler. She married (2) Gerald Fitzgerald October 1578.

More About Gerald Fitzgerald:
Fact 1: Lord Offaly.

45	iv.	Lettice Knollys.
46	v.	Mary Knollys.
47	vi.	Maud Knollys.
48	vii.	Thomas Knollys, died Aft. August 1596.
+ 49	viii.	Lettice Knollys or Knolles, born 1540 in Rotherfield Greys in Oxfordshire, England; died December 25, 1634.
50	ix.	Henry Knollys, born Abt. 1542; died 1582. He married Margaret Cave 1565.

More About Henry Knollys:
Fact 1: 1563, elected M.P. for reading

| 51 | x. | William Knollys, born Abt. 1545; died May 26, 1632. He married (1) Dorothy Bray March 1572/73. He married (2) Elizabeth Howard 1605. |

More About William Knollys:
Fact 1: 1626, 1st Earl of Branbury.
Fact 2: 1603, Baron Knollys.
Fact 3: 1616, Viscount Wallingford.

More About Elizabeth Howard:
Fact 1: Lady Elizabeth Howard.

52	xi.	Edward Knollys, born Abt. 1546; died 1575.
53	xii.	Robert Knollys, born Abt. 1547; died 1619.
54	xiii.	Richard Knollys, born Abt. 1548; died 1596.
+ 55	xiv.	Elizabeth Knollys, born June 15, 1549; died Abt. 1605.
56	xv.	Francis Knollys, born Abt. 1550; died 1648.
+ 57	xvi.	Lady Anne Knollys or Elizabeth Knollys, born Abt. 1553.

27. Henry[6] Carey (Mary[5] Boleyn, Thomas Boleyn --1st Earl of Wiltshire and[4] Ormonde, Sir William[3] Boleyn, Sir Geoffrey[2], Sir Thomas[1]) was born March 04, 1525/26, and died July 23, 1596 in Somerset House, London, England. He married Ann Morgan.

More About Henry Carey:
Fact 1: 1526-1596, Lord Hunsdon, created Baron Hunsdon of Hunsdon
Fact 2: April 15, 1535, living at Syon, Isleworth, Middlesex when referred to as the Henry VIII's son.
Fact 3: May 1545, at age 19 was living in King Henry VIII's household.
Buried August 12, 1596, Saint John the Baptist Chapel, Westminster Abbey, London, England. He was buried at the Queen's expense.

Children of Henry Carey and Ann Morgan are:

58   i.   George[7] Carey, born 1547; died September 08, 1603.

           More About George Carey:
           Fact 1: 2nd Lord Hunsdon.
           Fact 2: Had been suggested as a possible husband for Mary Queen of Scots when her marriage to an English nobleman was under consideration.

59   ii.   John Carey.

           More About John Carey:
           Fact 1: 3rd Lord Hunsdon.

60   iii.   Henry Carey.
61   iv.   Thomas The Elder Carey.
62   v.   Thomas The Younger Carey.
63   vi.   William Carey.
64   vii.   Sir Edmund Carey.
65   viii. Robert Carey.

           More About Robert Carey:
           Fact 1: 1st Earl of Monmouth.

66   ix.   Son Carey.
67   x.   Catherine Carey. She married Charles Howard.

           More About Charles Howard:
           Fact 1: 1st Earl of Nottingham.

68   xi.   Philadelphia Carey. She married Thomas Bef. 1584.

           More About Thomas:
           Fact 1: 10th Lord Scrope.

69   xii.   Margaret Carey. She married Sir Edward Hoby.

Generation No. 7

39. Anne or Ann Anna[7] Wiatt (Sir Thomas "The Younger"[6], Elizabeth[5] Brooke, Dorothy[4] Heydon, Elizabeth or Anne[3] Boleyn, Sir Geoffrey[2], Sir Thomas[1]) was born September 19, 1542 in Kent, England, and died June 04, 1592 in East Peckham, Kent County, England. She married Sir Roger Twisden de Peckham or Twysden.

More About Anne or Ann Anna Wiatt:
Remains buried at Saint Michael's Churchyard. east Peckham, Tonbrdige and Malling Borough, Kent, England.

More About Sir Roger Twisden de Peckham or Twysden:
Fact 1: Of Royal Hall, England.

    Child of Anne Wiatt and Sir Twysden is:
70   i.   William[8] Twysden, born in of Roydon Hall, England; died January 08, 1627/28. He married Anne Finch.

40. Jane or Joan[7] Wiatt (Sir Thomas "The Younger"[6], Elizabeth[5] Brooke, Dorothy[4] Heydon, Elizabeth or Anne[3] Boleyn, Sir Geoffrey[2], Sir Thomas[1]) was born 1553 in England, and died 1617. She married Sir Charles Scott or Scot, son of Sir Scott and Mary Tuke.

More About Sir Charles Scott or Scot:
Fact 1: A younger son of Sir Reynold Scott.
Fact 2: Was Captain of the Castles of Calais and Langette, France.
Fact 3: 1541-1542, Was Sheriff of Kent.

    Children of Jane Wiatt and Sir Scot are:
71   i.   Dorothea "Deborah"[8] Scott. She married William Fleet.

           More About William Fleet:
           Fact 1: Was a member of the Virginia Company of London under the 3rd charter.

72   ii.   Thomas Scott.

41. Sir George "Georgius" Thomas[7] Wiatt, Knt. (Sir Thomas "The Younger"[6], Elizabeth[5] Brooke, Dorothy[4] Heydon, Elizabeth or Anne[3] Boleyn, Sir Geoffrey[2], Sir Thomas[1]) was born Abt. 1554 in Allington Castle or Boxley Hall, Kent County, England, and died September 16, 1624 in Ireland, buried Nov. 10, 1624 in Boxley, Kent, England. He married Lady Jane Finch October 08, 1582 in Caswell, Kent County, England, daughter of Sir Finch and Lady Moyle.

More About Sir George "Georgius" Thomas Wiatt, Knt.:
Fact 1: 1550, possible birth year.
Fact 2: Admitted to Grays' Inn at age 17
Fact 3: Married at age 18.
Fact 4: Wrote *The Life of Anne Boleyn*.
Fact 5: Recorded a history of the Wyatt family.

Fact 6: Both manuscripts mentioned above are in the British Museum.

Fact 7: Was a soldier.

Fact 8: Wrote Extracts from *The Life of Queen Anne Boleigne*

Fact 9: September 01, 1624, a date cited as a possible as by date of death.

Died at age 73 years.

Buried at Boxley Manor (Abbey), Kent County, England. Possible dead years 1624 and 1625. Sait Mary the Virgin and All Saints Churchyard, Boxley, Maidstone Borough, Kent, England.

More About Lady Jane Finch:

Fact 1: April 29, 1639, takes administration of her son Hawte's estate upon his demise.

Fact 2: With Jane's efforts, she identifies Hawte's children in documents.

Outlived her husband by 20 years. Died at age 84.

Children of Sir Wiatt and Lady Finch are:

73	i.	George Thomas[8] Wiatt?
74	ii.	Thomas Wiatt?
75	iii.	Sir Francis Wyatt, born 1588 in Boxley Abbey, Kent County, England; died August 1644 in Jamestown, Va. buried in Boxley, Kent County, England. He married Lady Margaret Sandys 1618.

More About Sir Francis Wyatt:

Fact 1: 1621-1626, Served as English Royal Colonial Governor of Virginia in November.

Fact 2: 1639-1642, English Royal Colonial Governor of Virginia.

Fact 3: 1618, was knighted.

Fact 4: 1623, inherited "Boxley Abbey," the Wyatt family seat.

Fact 5: March 1621/22, Indians went to war with white settlers.

Fact 6: 1624, Colony at Jameston, Va. came under *"Royal"* control.

Fact 7: Was Crown-appointed Royal Governor of Virginia.

Fact 8: 1626, temporarily leaves Va. to attend to his family's estate matters in England.

Fact 9: 1639, returns in November to resume his position as Governor of Virginia.

Fact 10: August 24, 1644, buried at Boxley Abbey Church, Kent County, England.

Fact 11: 1621, was the first English Royal Governor of Virginia.

Fact 12: 1624, Virginia became a royal colony in this year.

Fact 13: 1621-1639, listed Nov. 18, 1621 and Nov. 1639 in Va. register as Governor of Virginia

Wyatt monument erected in the Boxley Church in 1702 by Francis' son Edwin Wiat states: *"George Wiat left also Hawte Wiat who died vicar of this parish, and hath issue living in Virginia."*

More About Lady Margaret Sandys:
Fact 1: Also known as *"Lady Wyatt."*
Fact 2: 1621, settled in Virginia for a while after her husband became Royal Governor.

76   iv.   Eleanora "Eleanor" Wiatt, born 1591 in Allington Castle, Boxley, Kent County, England. She married Lord John Finch February 06, 1617/18 in Boxley, Kent County, England.

More About Lord John Finch:
Fact 1: 1627, Was Speaker of the House of Commons.
Fact 2: Baron of Fordetch.

77   v.   Rev. Haute "Haut" "Hawte" Wiatt, born June 04, 1594 in Allington Castle, Maidstone, Kent County, England; died July 31, 1638 in Allington Castle, Kent County, England. He married (1) Barbara Elizabeth "Eliza" Mitford February 06, 1618/19 in London, England. He married (2) Anna "Ann" Lee Cox (Cocke) 1629 in England.

More About Rev. Haute "Haut" "Hawte" Wiatt:
Fact 1: November 18, 1621, travels from England to Jamestown on a vessel called the Georgia or George.
Fact 2: 1621-1625, serves as minister at Jamestown, Va.
Fact 3: 1625-1638, Minister or Vicar of Boxley Parish, Kent County, England.
Fact 4: July 31, 1638, possible date of demise at Boxley Abbey, Kent County, England.
Fact 5: 1619, traveled from Kent, England to Virginia.
Fact 6: Was the second son of Sir George Wiat of Allington Castle and Boxley Manor, Kent County.
Fact 7: October 1621, arrived on vessel called: the George at Jamestown, Va.
Fact 8: July 16, 1621, London court Rev. Wiat was *"entertayned as minister"* to accompany his brother.
Fact 9: 1632, was vicar in charge of Boxley Parish, became vicar there.
Fact 10: Attended Queen's College at Oxford and was a student at Gray's Inn.

Cause of Death: Tuberculosis
Buried Aug. 1st, 1638, Boxley Parish, Kent County, England.
Interred in center aisle at Boxley Church.

More About Barbara Elizabeth "Eliza" Mitford:
Fact 1: Barbara Elizabeth Mitford is also name combination listed.
Cause of Death: Had given birth to a third son on Oct. 16, 1626.
In the book titled: *The History of Boxley Parish*, on page 168 of the parish register Barbara is recorded as *"Elizabeth"* with the burial recorded as October 31, 1626.

More About Anna "Ann" Lee Cox (Cocke):
Fact 1: 1607, another possible birth year.
Cause of Death: Died in February 1631
Gave birth to two children before her passing.

78   vi.   Isabel Wiatt, born Abt. 1595 in Allington Castle, Kent, England; died Abt. 1655. She married Francis Page Abt. 1622 in Virginia.

More About Isabel Wiatt:
Fact 1: Lived at Middle Plantation fortified in 1634; Williamsburg by 1700.
Fact 2: Lived also Bedfont in Harrow
Died at age 73.

More About Francis Page:
Remains buried in Bedford, England.

79   vii.   Henry Wiatt, born November 07, 1596 in Kerstening, Berks, Kent County, England; died November 10, 1624 in buried January 1, 1624 Boxley, Kent County, England. He married Catherine Finch December 08, 1618 in Saint Andrews Church,.

More About Henry Wiatt:
Fact 1: Christened November 7, 1596, Otham, Kent County, England

49. Lettice Knollys or[7] Knolles (Catherine or Katherine Cary or[6] Carey, Mary[5] Boleyn, Thomas Boleyn --1st Earl of Wiltshire and[4] Ormonde, Sir William[3] Boleyn, Sir Geoffrey[2], Sir Thomas[1]) was born 1540 in Rotherfield Greys in Oxfordshire, England, and died

December 25, 1634. She married (1) Sir Christopher Blount. She married (2) Walter Devereux 1560 in moved after to Chartley Hall in Staffordshire, England. She married (3) Robert Dudley, Earl of Leicester September 21, 1578 in 1st at Kenilworth and again at Wanstead.

More About Lettice Knollys or Knolles:
Fact 1: Was Countess of Essex, England.
Fact 2: 1st child of her parents.
Buried with her second husband -- Earl of Leicester.

More About Walter Devereux:
Fact 1: Viscount Hereford, later 1st Earl of Essex

More About Robert Dudley, Earl of Leicester:
Fact 1: Was retired early by Elizabeth I for his secret marriage
Fact 2: The Queen did not know of it for one year before she was informed.

Children of Lettice Knolles and Walter Devereux are:
80   i.   Five children[8] Devereux, born in Each born at Chartley Hall, Staffordshire, England.
81   ii.   Penelope Devereux.
82   iii. Dorothy Devereux.

More About Dorothy Devereux:
Fact 1: Lady Percy.

Child of Lettice Knolles and Robert Dudley is:
83   i.   Robert[8] Dudley, born January 1578/79; died 1584.

55. Elizabeth[7] Knollys (Catherine or Katherine Cary or[6] Carey, Mary[5] Boleyn, Thomas Boleyn --1st Earl of Wiltshire and[4] Ormonde, Sir William[3] Boleyn, Sir Geoffrey[2], Sir Thomas[1]) was born June 15, 1549, and died Abt. 1605. She married Sir Thomas Leighton 1578, son of John Leighton and Joyce Sutton.

More About Elizabeth Knollys:
Fact 1: Was a Gentlewoman of the Privy Chamber.
Fact 2: Was a grandniece to Queen consort Anne Boleyn -- Henry VIII 2nd wife.
Fact 3: Admired by Sir Walter Raleigh who wrote her poetry.

More About Sir Thomas Leighton:
Fact 1: Sometimes called *"Layton."*
Fact 2: 1535, possible birth year.
Fact 3: 1611, possible date of demise.

Children of Elizabeth Knollys and Sir Leighton are:

84   i.   Thomas Leighton[8] Jr., born 1584; died September 25, 1617 in buried at Saint Peter Port Church, Guersney. He married Mary Zouche.

More About Thomas Leighton Jr.:
Fact 1: September 10, 1604, served as Lieutenant of Guersney.
Fact 2: No issue.

85   ii.   Elizabeth Leighton, died January 12, 1632/33. She married Sherington Talbot.

86   iii.   Anne Leighton, died 1628. She married Sir John St. John.

More About Anne Leighton:
Died during child birth.

More About Sir John St. John:
Fact 1: was 1st baronet.

57. Lady Anne Knollys or Elizabeth[7] Knollys (Catherine or Katherine Cary or[6] Carey, Mary[5] Boleyn, Thomas Boleyn --1st Earl of Wiltshire and[4] Ormonde, Sir William[3] Boleyn, Sir Geoffrey[2], Sir Thomas[1]) was born Abt. 1553. She married Sir Thomas West de la Warr November 19, 1571, son of Sir de la Warr and Unknown Wife.

More About Lady Anne Knollys or Elizabeth Knollys:
Fact 1: August 30, 1608, living then.

More About Sir Thomas West de la Warr:
Fact 1: Was Baron De La Warr
Fact 2: 2nd Lord de la Warr

Children of Lady Knollys and Sir de la Warr are:

87   i.   Penelope[8] West. She married Herbert Pelham.

88   ii.   Sir Thomas West, born 1577; died 1618.

More About Sir Thomas West:
Fact 1: Was third Lord de la Warr.
Fact 2: February 28, 1609/10, 1st Lord Governor and Capt. General of Virginia
Fact 3: June 1610, his arrival saved the Va. colony from abandonment by disheartened settlers.

89   iii.   Francis West, born 1586; died 1634 in Va.

More About Francis West:
Fact 1: Was a memeber of the Va. Company
Fact 2: 1608, came to Va. with Capt. Christopher Newport.
Fact 3: November 14, 1627, elected to the council and appointed Governor of Virginia.

90 iv. Governor John West, born 1590 in of Virginia; born in Hampshire, England; died 1659 in West Point Plantation, Va. He married Ann.

More About Governor John West:
Fact 1: was 12th child of his parents.
Fact 2: Aft. 1622, After the massacre with indians he commanded a copany of men against the indians.
Fact 3: 1618, moved to the Virginia; served as Governor.

91 v. Nathaniel West, born November 30, 1592; died February 16, 1622/23. He married Virginia Frances Greville.

The Dandridge Section

♀ | | ♂

"In good faith,"

-- Dandridge motto.

"I am determined to be cheerful and happy in whatever situation I may find myself. For I have learned that the greater part of our misery or unhappiness is determined not by our circumstance, but by our disposition."

-- Martha Dandridge Custis Washington
[1731-1802]

THE DANDRIDGE SECTION IN A quest to save space, includes only the first six generations beginning with Bartholomew Dandridge [Abt. 1580-1638]. There are several spellings variations of this name in general: Dandridge, Tandridge and some include: Danbridge and Tanbridge.

The motto of the Dandridge heraldry is *"In adversis etiam fide."* This is Latin and means: *"In adversity, still consistent,"* or *"In adversity, still loyal."* Also: *"With faith, even in adversity."* In English, it translates: *"genuine."*

The surname *"Dandridge"* draws its origin from a locality or place. It literally means *"of Tandridge,"* which is a parish in the diocese of Winchester, England.

A Colonel William Dandridge [1689-1743] has been cited as being the first Dandridge known in America. Bartholomew Dandridge [Abt. 1580-1638] -- father of William Dandridge [b. abt. 1612], father of John Dandridge I [1655-1731] are all evidence of those using the Dandridge name in England -- as John Dandridge I is the father of the brothers William [1689-1743] and John Dandridge II [1700-1756].

According to a book in the Special Collections of the North Carolina Collections at Wilson Library, page 15, this Colonel William Dandridge [1689-1743] – husband of Euphan

Wallace and Unity West, was the founder of those connected to Dandridge descendants in America. He was an officer in the British Navy and commander of the Ludlow Castle. He was a member of the Royal Governor's Council and a successful merchant.

Just before the year 1717, this William Dandridge settled in Virginia. He became a resident of Elsing Green, King William County, Va., and there he served as a burgess in the House of Burgess. His brother was Colonel John Dandridge II -- the father of Martha Dandridge Custis Washington -- first lady of the United States. In a nutshell, this Bartholomew Dandridge is the great-grandfather of the two Dandridge boys and their sister Elizabeth who came to America.

John Dandridge II is thought to have first lived in Hampton, Va. -- possibly in his brother William's home. After William moved to Elsing Green in King William County, Va., John moved close by. John settled on the opposite bank of the Pamunkey River in New Kent County, Va. In 1732, John served as clerk of New Kent County, Va.

The Virginia House of Burgess was the first elected lower house in the Legislative Assembly established July 1619 in the Colony of Virginia. The Virginia colony itself was founded in 1607. It was founded as the first permanent English colony. The Virginia House of Burgess evolved into representing the entire legislative body of the Colony of Virginia.

The word *"Burgess"* originally meant a free man of the burough or burgh. Later, the meaning evolved to mean an elected or un-elected official of a governing municipality. In the English House of Commons, it means *"representative of a borough."*

John Dandridge II [1700-1756] is interred at the burial grounds of St. George's Episcopal Church, Fredericksburg, Va.

On his tombstone:

HERE LIES INFERR'D THE BODY
OF COLONEL JOHN DANDRIDGE
OF NEW KENT COUNTY WHO
DEPARTED THIS LIFE THE 31ST DAY
OF AUGUST 1756 AGED 56 YEARS
TO PRESERVE THE INSCRIPTION NOW
LEGIBLE NEVILLE MITCHELL SMITH,
A LENEAL DESCENDANT OF COLONEL
JOHN DANDRIDGE HAS PLACED THIS
PLAQUE HERE
1956

Elizabeth Dandridge Wyatt [1703-1750], wife of Henry Wyatt [Abt. 1685-1743 or in 1762 is claimed by CLP researchers. This Elizabeth is a sister to the brothers William and John Dandridge mentioned above and an aunt to Martha Dandridge Custis Washington – wife of

U.S. 1st President George Washington, son of Mary Ball [1708-1789] and Captain Augustine Washington [1694-1743].

The husband of this Elizabeth Dandridge as stated earlier was Henry Wyatt, son of Sallie Peyton and Richard Wyatt.

DESCENDANTS OF BARTHOLOMEW DANDRIDGE

Generation No. 1

1. Bartholomew[1] Dandridge was born Abt. 1580 in Oxfordshire, England, and died 1638 in England. He married **Agnes Wilder** 1604 in Drayton or Dreyton St. Leonard, near London, England.

Children of Bartholomew Dandridge and Agnes Wilder are:

+	2	i.	William[2] Dandridge, born 1612.
+	3	ii.	Francis Dandridge, born 1619 in lived in Dorchester, England; died 1708 in buried under the floor of Dorchester Abbey, Dorchester, England.
	4	iii.	Child #3 Dandridge.
	5	iv.	Child #4 Dandridge.
	6	v.	Child #5 Dandridge.
	7	vi.	Child #6 Dandridge.
	8	vii.	Child #7 Dandridge.
	9	viii.	Child #8 Dandridge.

Generation No. 2

2. William[2] Dandridge (Bartholomew[1]) was born 1612. He married **Wife**.

Children of William Dandridge and Wife are:

+	10	i.	John[3] Dandridge I, born 1655 in Great Malvern, Westchestershire, England; died 1731 in England.
	11	ii.	Francis Dandridge, born 1649-1655.
	12	iii.	William Dandridge, born 1649-1655.

3. Francis[2] Dandridge (Bartholomew[1]) was born 1619 in lived in Dorchester, England, and died 1708 in buried under the floor of Dorchester Abbey, Dorchester, England. He married **Ann**.

Children of Francis Dandridge and Ann are:

	13	i.	Francis[3] Dandridge.
+	14	ii.	John Dandridge.

Generation No. 3

10. John³ Dandridge I (William², Bartholomew¹) was born 1655 in Great Malvern, Westchestershire, England, and died 1731 in England. He married **(1) Bridget Dugale** 1676 in St. Mary Magelene Chruch, Fish Street, England. He married **(2) Ann Dugale** 1687 in 1687/88.

Child of John Dandridge and Bridget Dugale is:

15	i.	John⁴ Dandridge, born 1695; died 1695.

Children of John Dandridge and Ann Dugale are:

+	16	i.	Bartholomew⁴ Dandridge.
	17	ii.	Child #7 Dandridge.
	18	iii.	Child #8 Dandridge.
	19	iv.	Child #9 Dandridge.
	20	v.	Child #10 Dandridge.
	21	vi.	Child #11 Dandridge.
	22	vii.	Child #12 Dandridge.
	23	viii.	Child #13 Dandridge.
	24	ix.	Francis Dandridge, died 1765.
+	25	x.	Mary Dandridge.
+	26	xi.	Captain Colonel William Dandridge, born December 29, 1689 in London, England; lived in Elsing Green, King Willliam County, Va.; died 1743.
+	27	xii.	Colonel John Dandridge II, born July 14, 1700 in London, England; lived in Chestnut Grove, New Kent County, Va.; died August 31, 1756 in Fredericksburg, Va.
+	28	xiii.	Elizabeth Dandridge, born 1703 in Oxfordshire, England; died 1750 in Virginia.

14. John³ Dandridge (Francis², Bartholomew¹). He married **Wife**.

Child of John Dandridge and Wife is:

29	i.	Francis⁴ Dandridge, died Abt. 1725 in Dorchester Abbey, Dorchester, England.

Generation No. 4

16. Bartholomew⁴ Dandridge (John³, William², Bartholomew¹). He married **(1) Rachel**. He married **(2) Hannah Asworth** 1725.

Children of Bartholomew Dandridge and Rachel are:

30	i.	Ralph⁵ Dandridge.
31	ii.	William Dandridge.

25. Mary⁴ Dandridge (John³, William², Bartholomew¹). She married **Robert Langborne** Abt. 1711.

>Child of Mary Dandridge and Robert Langborne is:
>32   i.   William⁵ Langborne.

26. Captain Colonel William⁴ Dandridge (John³, William², Bartholomew¹) was born December 29, 1689 in London, England; lived in Elsing Green, King Willliam County, Va., and died 1743. He married **(1) Euphan Wallace**. He married **(2) Unity West** March 18, 1718/19 in March 18, 1719 married West Point, King William County, Va., daughter of Captain West and Martha Woodward.

>Children of Captain Dandridge and Unity West are:
>33   i.   Martha⁵ Dandridge, born 1721; died April 25, 1747 in Fairfield Plantation, King William County, Va. She married Philip Aylett 1739.
>34   ii.   Mary Dandridge, born 1725 in Elsing Green, King William County, Va.; died 1798 in Newport, Giles County, Va. She married (1) John Spotswood. She married (2) John Campbell.
>+ 35   iii.   Nathaniel West Dandridge I, born September 07, 1729; died January 16, 1786.

27. Colonel John⁴ Dandridge II (John³, William², Bartholomew¹) was born July 14, 1700 in London, England; lived in Chestnut Grove, New Kent County, Va., and died August 31, 1756 in Fredericksburg, Va. He married **(1) Slave woman Half African/Half Cherokee**. He married **(2) X**. He married **(3) Frances Orlando Jones** July 22, 1730, daughter of Orlando Jones and Martha Macon.

>Child of Colonel Dandridge and Slave Cherokee is:
>36   i.   Ann Dandridge⁵ Costin.

>Child of Colonel Dandridge and X is:
>37   i.   Ralph⁵ Dandridge.

>Children of Colonel Dandridge and Frances Jones are:
>+ 38   i.   Martha⁵ Dandridge, born June 02, 1731 in Chestnut Grove or New Kent County, Va.; died May 22, 1802 in Mount Vernon, Fairfax County, Va.
>39   ii.   John Dandridge, born 1732; died July 1749.
>40   iii.   William Dandridge, born 1734; died 1776.
>+ 41   iv.   Bartholomew Dandridge, born 1737 in Chestnut Grove, New Kent County, Va.; died 1785.
>+ 42   v.   Anna Maria "Fanny" Dandridge, born 1739; died December 17, 1777 in Eltham, Va.

	43	vi.	Frances Dandridge, born 1744; died 1758.
+	44	vii.	Elizabeth Dandridge, born 1749; died 1800.
	45	viii.	Mary Dandridge, born Abt. 1754; died 1763.

28. Elizabeth[4] Dandridge (John[3], William[2], Bartholomew[1]) was born 1703 in Oxfordshire, England, and died 1750 in Virginia. She married **Henry Wiatt** 1725 in Prince George County, Va., son of Richard Wiatt and Sarah Peyton.

Children of Elizabeth Dandridge and Henry Wiatt are:

	46	i.	Mary[5] Wiatt?, born September 20, 1726 in Saint Peter's Parish, New Kent County, Virginia; died May 10, 1784 in Warren County or Beute County, N.C. She married John Daniel Hawkins 1743 in Grandville, N.C.
+	47	ii.	Colonel Joseph Wyatt, born Abt. 1728 in associated with Saint Peter's Parish, New Kent County, Virginia; died Abt. 1767 in New Kent County, Va.
	48	iii.	Elizabeth Wiatt, born September 15, 1730 in Churchill, Gloucester County, Va.; died February 23, 1803.
	49	iv.	Francis Wiatt, born March 29, 1731 in Churchill, Gloucester County, died 1804 in Gloucester County, Va. Saint Peter's Parish, New Kent County, Va.
	50	v.	Abby Wiatt*?, born 1732; died in Morgan District, Wilkes County, N.C.
	51	vi.	Sarah "Sally" Wiatt, born 1735 in Churchill, Gloucester County, Va.
+	52	vii.	William Wiatt, born April 09, 1738 in Churchill, Gloucester County, Va.; died Abt. 1802 in Lick Creek, Rowan County [1822-Davidson County], N.C.
	53	viii.	Nathan Wiatt, born 1740 in Churchill, Gloucester County, Va.; died in Lick Creek, Rowan County [1822-Davidson County], N.C.
+	54	ix.	John Wiatt, born May 06, 1743 in Virginia or Maryland?; died November 11, 1815 in Lick Creek Baptist Church, Denton, Davidson County, N.C.

Generation No. 5

35. Nathaniel West[5] Dandridge I (Captain Colonel William[4], John[3], William[2], Bartholomew[1]) was born September 07, 1729, and died January 16, 1786. He married **Dorothea Spotswood**.

Children of Nathaniel Dandridge and Dorothea Spotswood are:

	55	i.	Martha[6] Dandridge, born 1748-1791. She married Archibald Archer Payne.
	56	ii.	William Alexander Dandridge, born 1750-1801. He married Anne Bolling.

57	iii.	Alexander Spotswood Dandridge, born 1753-1785. He married Anne Steven.
58	iv.	Dorothea Dandridge, born 1757-1831. She married Patrick Henry I.
59	v.	Nathaniel West Dandridge II, born 1762-1810. He married Sarah Sally Watson.

38. Martha[5] Dandridge (Colonel John[4], John[3], William[2], Bartholomew[1]) was born June 02, 1731 in Chestnut Grove or New Kent County, Va., and died May 22, 1802 in Mount Vernon, Fairfax County, Va. She married **(1) Daniel Parke Custis, Sr.** May 15, 1750 in Chestnut Grove Plantation, Va., son of John Custis and Frances Parke. She married **(2) U.S. President George Washington** January 06, 1759 in The White House Plantation, Pamunkey River, northwest of Williamsburg, Va., son of Captain Washington and Mary Ball.

Children of Martha Dandridge and Daniel Custis are:

60	i.	Daniel Parke[6] Custis, Jr., born November 19, 1751 in White House Plantation, Pamunkey River, northwest of Williamsburg, Va.; died February 19, 1754 in White House Plantation, Pamunkey River, northwest of Williamsburg, Va.
61	ii.	Frances Parke Custis, born April 12, 1753 in White House Plantation, Pamunkey River, northwest of Williamsburg, Va.; died April 01, 1757 in White House Plantation, Pamunkey River, northwest of Williamsburg, Va.
62	iii.	John "Jacky" "Jack" Parke Custis, born November 27, 1754 in White House, New Kent County, Va. or Yorktown, Pa.; died November 05, 1781 in Yorktown, Pa. He married Eleanor "Nelly" Calvert 1774 in Mount Airy, Md.
63	iv.	Martha "Patsy" Parke Custis, born 1756 in White House Plantation, Pamunkey River, northwest of Williamsburg, Va.; died June 19, 1773 in Mount Vernon, Fairfax County, Va.

41. Bartholomew[5] Dandridge (Colonel John[4], John[3], William[2], Bartholomew[1]) was born 1737 in Chestnut Grove, New Kent County, Va., and died 1785. He married **Elizabeth Macon**.

Children of Bartholomew Dandridge and Elizabeth Macon are:

64	i.	7 Children[6] Dandridge.
65	ii.	Anne Dandridge, born 1760-1785. She married William Claiborne.

42. Anna Maria "Fanny"[5] Dandridge (Colonel John[4], John[3], William[2], Bartholomew[1]) was born 1739, and died December 17, 1777 in Eltham, Va. She married **Burwell Bassett**.

Children of Anna Dandridge and Burwell Bassett are:

66   i.   Burwell[6] Bassett, born Abt. 1764.

67   ii.   John Bassett, born Abt. 1766.

68   iii.   Frances "Fanny" Bassett, born Aft. 1766; died Abt. 1796. She married Tobias Lear 1795.

69   iv.   Child Bassett.

70   v.   Child Bassett.

71   vi.   Child Bassett.

72   vii.   Child Bassett.

44. Elizabeth[5] Dandridge (Colonel John[4], John[3], William[2], Bartholomew[1]) was born 1749, and died 1800. She married **(1) Aylet**. She married **(2) Henley**.

Child of Elizabeth Dandridge and Aylet is:

73   i.   Children[6] Aylet.

Child of Elizabeth Dandridge and Henley is:

74   i.   Frances "Fanny" Dandridge[6] Henley. She married Tobias Lear.

47. Colonel Joseph[5] Wyatt (Elizabeth[4] Dandridge, John[3], William[2], Bartholomew[1]) was born Abt. 1728 in associated with Saint Peter's Parish, New Kent County, Virginia, and died Abt. 1767 in New Kent County, Va. He married **Dorothy "Virginia" Peyton Smith**.

Children of Colonel Wyatt and Dorothy Smith are:

75   i.   William Hodges?[6] Wyatt. He married Susannah E. Jones?.

76   ii.   Dorothy Wyatt?, born in Colonial Georgia; died in Harmons Creek, Benton, Tennessee.

77   iii.   James Wyatt, born 1751. He married Lethia Brown.

78   iv.   Peyton Wyatt, born 1755 in Saint Peter's Parish, New Kent County, Virginia; died 1805 in Lincoln, Georgia. He married Hannah Bibb.

79   v.   Sarah Sallie "Sally" Smith Wyatt, born 1759 in New Kent County, Va.; died August 15, 1826 in Robinson Springs, Elmore County, Ala. She married (1) Capt. William Crawford Bibb. She married (2) William Barrett March 21, 1807 in Elbert County, Ga.

80   vi.   Ann Wyatt, born Abt. 1760 in New Kent County, Va.; died Abt. 1836 in Lawrence, Ala.

81   vii.   Nancy Ann "Nannie" Wyatt, born November 17, 1760 in New Kent County, Va.; died 1836 in Lawrence, Ala. She married Capt. Francis Scott.

82   viii.   Ballard S. Wyatt, born 1765 in Va.

83   ix.   Zachariah Sacker Wyatt, born 1765 in Durants Neck, Perquimans, N.C.; died 1807 in Henry, Tennessee.

84   x.   Colonal Joseph Hawte Wyatt, born August 24, 1767 in New Kent County, Virginia; died April 28, 1843 in Charlotte House, Charlotte, Virginia. He married Dorothy.

52. William⁵ Wiatt (Elizabeth⁴ Dandridge, John³, William², Bartholomew¹) was born April 09, 1738 in Churchill, Gloucester County, Va., and died Abt. 1802 in Lick Creek, Rowan County [1822-Davidson County], N.C. He married **Margaret Bostick** 1822 in Davidson County, N.C.

Children of William Wiatt and Margaret Bostick are:

85   i.   Henry⁶ Wyatt, born 1763 in Lick Creek, Rowan County [1822-Davidson County], N.C.

86   ii.   Aaron Wyatt, born Abt. 1765 in Lick Creek, Rowan County [1822-Davidson County], N.C.; died 1831 in Wilkes County, N.C.

54. John⁵ Wiatt (Elizabeth⁴ Dandridge, John³, William², Bartholomew¹) was born May 06, 1743 in Virginia or Maryland?, and died November 11, 1815 in Lick Creek Baptist Church, Denton, Davidson County, N.C. He married **Rachel "Hannah"**.

Children of John Wiatt and Rachel "Hannah" are:

87   i.   Allen⁶ Wiatt?.

88   ii.   Sarah "Sally" Wiatt.

89   iii.   Dempsey "Dempsy" Wyatt.

90   iv.   James Wyatt, born Abt. 1805. He married Unknown.

91   v.   John "Johney" Wyatt, Jr., born in Davidson County, N.C.; died 1819. He married Hannah Park 1789 in Lick Creek, Davidson County, N.C.

92   vi.   Rachel Wyatt?.

93   vii.   Sylvester "Silvester" Wiatt, born 1762 in Church Hill, Va.; died Aft. August 1850 in Marshall County, Ky.

94   viii.   Cecelia "Celia" Wyatt, born 1761 in Churchill, Gloucester, Va. She married William Bean 1778 in Lick Creek Baptist Church, Davidson County, N.C.

95   ix.   Thomas "Tommy" Wiatt, Sr. (Wyatt, Wiett), born 1774 in Rowan County N.C.; died 1845 in buried in Wyatt, Park Bean Graveyard, Rowan County, N.C. He married Rachel "Parks" "Park" Parke January 12, 1793 in Piney Woods District, Rowan County, N.C.

96   x.   Elizabeth Wiatt, born 1778; died Bef. 1820. She married Park.

97   xi.   Eli "Ely" Wyatt, born Abt. 1789. He married Sarah.

THE WILL OF MARTHA WASHINGTON
OF MOUNT VERNON

In the name of God amen

I Martha Washington of Mount Vernon in the
county of Fairfax being of sound mind and capable of
disposing of my worldly estate do make and ordain and
declare this to be my last will and testament hereby
revoling all other wills and testaments by me heretofore
made.

Imprimis it is my desire that all my just debts may be
punctually paid and that as speedily as the same can be
done.

Item I give and devise to my nephew Bartholomew
Dandridge and his heirs my lot in the town of Alexandria situate on Pitt and Cameron streets devided to me
by my late husband George Washington deceased.

Item I give and bequeath to my four nieces Martha
W. Dandridge Mary Dandridge Frances Lucy Dandridge
and Frances Henley, the debt of two thousand pounds
due from Lawrence Lewis and secured by his bond to be
equally divided between them or such of them as shall be
alive at my death and to be paid to them respectively on
the days of their respective marriage or arrival at the age
of twnety one years whichsoever shall first happen
together with all the interest on said debt remaining
unpaid at the time of my death: and in case the whole or

Page 1: [signed Martha Washington]

any part of the said principal sum of two thousand
pounds shall be paid to me during my life then it is my
will that so much money be raised out of my estate as
shall be equal to what I shall have received of the said
principal debt and distributed among my four neices
aforesaid as herein has been bequeathed, and it is my
meaning that the interest accruing after my death on the
said sum of two thousand pounds shall belong to my said
neices and be equally divided between them or such of
them as shall be alive at the time of my death, and be aud
annually for their respective uses until theiur receive their
share of the principal.

Item I give and bequeath to my grandson George
Washington Parke Custis all the silver plate of every
kind of which I shall die possessed, together with the two
large plated coolers, the four small plated coolers with
the bottle castors, and a pipe of wine if there be one in
the house at the time of my death -- also the set of
Cincinnati tea and Table china, the bowl that has a ship in it, the
fine old china jars which usually stand on the chimney
piece in the new room: also all the family pictures of
every sort and the pictures painted by his sister, and two
small skreen worked one by his sister and the other a
present from miss Kitty Brown --- also his choice
of prints -- also the two girandoles and lustres that

Page 2: [signed Martha Washington]

stand on them -- also the new bedstead which I caused to
be made in Philadelphia together with the bed, mattress
bolster & pillows and the white dimity curtains belonging thereto: also two other bed with bolsters and pillows
and the white dimity window curtains in the new
room-- also the iron chest and the desk in the closet
which belonged to my first husband; also all my books of
every kind except the large bible and prayer book, also
the set of tea china that was given to me by Mr.
VanBraam every piece having M W on it.

Item I give and bequeath to my grand daughter
Elizabeth Parke Law, the dressing table and glass that
stands in the chamber called the yellow room, and
Genl. Washington's picture painted by Trumbull.

Item I give and bequeath to my grand daughter
Elizabeth Peter my writing table and the seat to it
standing in my chamber, also the print of Genl. Wash-
inton that hands in the passage.

Item I give and bequeath to my grand daughter
Eleanor Parke Lewis the large looking glass in the front
Parlour and any other looking glass which she
may choose --- Also one of the new side board tables in
the new room -- also twelve chairs with green bottoms
to be selected by herself also the marble table in the
garrett, also the two prints of the dead soldier, a print

Page 3: [signed Martha Washington]

of the Washington family in a box in the Garrett and the
great chair standing in my chamber, also all the plated
ware not hereinafter otherwise bequeathed -- also all the
sheets table linen, napkins towels, pillow cases remaining
in the house at my death, also three beds & bedsteads
curtains bolsters and pillows for each bed such as she
shall choose and not herein particularly otherwise
beqeathed, together with counterpens and a pair of
blankets for each bed, als all the wine glasses &
decanters, of every kind and all the blew and white
china in common use.

Item it is my will and desire that Anna Maria
Washington the daughter of my niece to be put in
homesome mourning at my death at the expense of my
estate and I bequeath to her ten guineas to buy a ring.

Item I give and bequeath to my neighbor Mrs.
Elizabeth Washington five guineas to get something in
remembrance of me.

Item I give and bequeath to Mrs. David Stuart five
guineas to buy her a ring.

Item I give and bequeath to Benjamin Lincoln

Page 4: [signed Martha Washington]

Lear one hundred pounds specie to be vested in the funded
stock of the United States immiedately after my decease
and to stand in his name as his property, which invest-
ment my executors are to cause to be made.

Item When the vestry of Truro parish shall buy a
glebe I devise will and bequeath that my executors shall
pay one hundred pounds to them to aid of the purchase,
provided the said purchase be made in my lifetime or
within three years after my decease.

Item It is my will and desire that all the rest &
residue of my estate of whatever kind and description not
herein specifically devised or bequeathed shall be sold by
the executors of this my last will for ready money as soon
after my decease as the same can be done and that the
proceeds thereof together with all the money in the
house and the debts due me, (the debts due from me and
the legacies herein bequeathed being first satisfied) shall
be invested by my executors in eight percent stock of the

funds of the United States and shall stand on the books
in the name of my executors in their character of
executors of my will; and it is my desire that the interest
there of shall be applied to the proper education of
Bartholomew Henley & Samuel Henley the two youngest
sons of my sister Henley, and also to the education of
John Dandridge son of my deceased nephew John
Dandridge so that they may be severally fitted and

Page 5: [signed Martha Washington]

accomplished in some useful trade and to each of them
who shall have lived to finish his education or to reach
the age of twenty one years I give and bequeath one
hundred pounds to set him up in his trade.

Item m y debts and legacies being paid and the
education of Bartholomew Henley Samuel Henley and
John Dandridge aforesaid being completed, or they
being all dead before the completion thereof it is my will
and desire that all my estates and interests in whatever
form existing whether in money funded stock or any
other species of property shall be equally divided among
all the person hereinafter mentioned who shall be living
at the time that the interest of the funded stock shall
cease to be applicable in pursuance of my will herein
before expressed to the education of my nephews
Bartholomew Henley Samuel Henley and John Dandridge, namely among Anna Maria Washington, daughter of my niece and John Dandridge son of my nephew
and all my great grand children living at the time that the
interest of the said funded stock shall cease to be
applicable to the education of the said B. Henley S.
Henley, and John Dandridge, and the same shall cease
to be applied when all of them shall die before they
arrive at the age of twenty one years, or those living shall
have finished their education or have arrived at the age
of twenty one years, and so long as any one of the three

Page 6: [signed Martha Washington]

lives, who has not finished his education or arrives at the
age of twenty one years, the division of the said residuum
is be deferred and no longer.

Lastly I nominate and appoint my grandson, George Washington Parke Custis, my nephews Julius B. Dandridge & Bartholomew Dandridge and my son in law Thomas Peter executors of this my last will and testament. In Witness whereof I have hereunto set my hand and seal this twenty second day of Sept in the year eighteen hundred.

[signed Martha Washington]

Sealed signed acknowledged and delivered as her last will and testament in the presence of the subscribing witnesses who have been requested to subscribe the same as such in her presence.
ROGER FARRELL
WILLIAM SPENCE
LAW. LEWIS ---
MARTHA PETER,

March 4th 1802
I give to my grandson George Washington Parke Custis my mulatto man Elish -- that I bought of mr Butler Washington to him and his heir forever

[signed Martha Washington]

♀ | | ♂

Martha Dandridge Custis Washington [1731-1802] with her husband
George Washington [1732-1799] & grandchildren.

About the Writer and Compiler…

Hélène Andorre Hinson Staley is a graduate of the School of Journalism at the University of North Carolina at Chapel Hill, known today as the School of Media and Journalism. Staley was born in New Orleans, La. and moved to North Carolina shortly after turning four years old. She was raised in Salisbury, N.C. and is the daughter of Patricia Ann Leighton Hinson and the late James Noah Hinson, M.D.

Hélène is a third great grand daughter of Rachel Wyatt [1835-1915] and John Morgan [1834-1864] formerly of Rowan County, N.C. Hélène's Wyatt connections come through her paternal side via her father's mother's side. The John Wiatt [1743-1815] is a 6th great grand-father to Hélène. This John Wiatt's son Thomas Wiatt [1774-1845] and his wife Rachel Park [1774-1850] and their son Noah Calvin Wiatt [1805-1871] and his wife Mary Polly Hendly Wiatt [1806-Abt. 1861] have their remains in the Park-Wyatt-Bean Graveyard, which is pro-tected on family property.

The Park-Wyatt-Bean Graveyard is located off River Road on Cedar Creek. River Road runs next to the Yadkin River between Bringle Ferry and Stokes Ferry roads, in the eastern section of Rowan County. The cemetery is located on a section of land formerly owned by the Noah Park Sr. family.

When the owner, George A. Park [1808-1882] died, his estate was insufficient to pay his debts. [This George is the son of Joanna Peeler and Noah Park, Jr., both of whom have their remains in the Park-Wyatt-Bean Graveyard. Noah Park, Jr., 1779-1829, is a brother to Rachel Park, 1774-1850, wife of Thomas Wiatt, 1774-1845.]

A petition dated December 18, 1886, was to sell 100 acres of land to the highest bidder on February 24, 1887, 1/3 in cash, balance in 12 months with interest from date of sale. James E. Wyatt bought the land for $585.00. Dr. James Noah Hinson, who descends from Noah Park, Sr., owned it for many years and passed this property to his family in 2015.

Elizabeth *"Betty"* Park Morgan [b. 1781, Rowan County, N.C.], daughter of Noah Park Sr., 1742-1815-or 1820, married Nathan Morgan, Jr., [1785-1844] who served in the 1st Rowan N.C. during the War of 1812. This Nathan Morgan, Jr. is a son of Nathan Morgan, Sr. [1756-1842] and Naomi or Naomie Poole [1760-1851]. Nathan Morgan, Jr. was a father to Moses Green Morgan [1810-1879] – husband of Barbara Shaver Morgan [1813-1896] – this Moses being the father of John Calvin Morgan whose wife was Rachel Wyatt Morgan.

The gravesite of Noah Park Sr., born: 1742; died: 1820, is the oldest plot in the Park-Wyatt-Bean Graveyard. Patricia B. Beck and Mary Jane Fowler documented this cemetery on April 4, 1983 as having 134 gravesites, many without stones, many with stones but no markings. This Noah Park, Sr. is a 6th great grandfather to Hélène.

Source: James Noah Hinson, M.D. & *Rowan County Cemeteries, Volume V* by The Genealogical Society of Rowan County, N.C.

John Wiatt [1743-1815] – the John Wiatt who gave some land for the Lick Creek Church – the John whose remains are buried in that church cemetery, is a 6th great grandfather to the author.

If this John Wiatt indeed connects with Elizabeth Dandridge and Henry Wiatt, this couple are her 7th great grandparents – making Rev. Haute *"Haut" "Hawte" "Hawt"* Wiatt and his wife Barbara Elizabeth *"Eliza"* Mitford her 10th great grandparents and Sir Thomas *"The Younger"* Wiatt [1521-1554] and his wife Lady Jane Haute *"Hawte" "Haut"* [Abt. 1522-1600] her 12th great grandparents.

Hélène's writings and research include:

* *The Rungs of Ladders, A Wyatt History in England & the United States from 1066 to Modern Times,* dedicated to James Noah Hinson, M.D. [2016];
* *Paper & Stone, A Leighton History in England & the United States* – co-researched with Robert Allen DeVries, Ph.D, [2011];
* *The Fairyselves,* [fiction] illustrated by Kaspars Gail tis [fiction] [2012];
* *The Dish Keepers of Honest House;* [fiction] [2010];
* *Dishonest Housekeepers* [fiction] illustrated by Noah Campbell Smith [fiction] [2007];
* *To Escape Into Dreams* volume 1; family stories [2003, 2004]; revised edition: [2005];
* *Appendices of: To Escape Into Dreams,* volumes 2-3; genealogical trees [2004, 2005];
* *Shielding Our Innocents, A Prevention Plan On Child Sexual Abuse* with a foreword by Roland C. Summit, M.D. [1997]

Hélène Andorre Hinson Staley

Suggested Reading & References

♀ | | ♂

AMERICAN CIVIL WAR [1861-1865] SOURCES

* Not all references are listed. Some references are cited within the text of this compilation.

American Civil War – or War Between the States [1861-1865] The American Heritage, Picture History of The Civil War. The Epic Struggle of the Blue and the Gray by Bruce Catton.

Andersonville, Giving Up the Ghost, A Collection of Prisoner's Diaries, Letters & Memoirs (1996) editors: William B. Styple, Nancy Styple, Jack Fitzpatrick, Bill Dekker, et. al.

The Appomattox Paroles, April 9-15, 1865, The Virginia Civil War Battles and Leaders Series, 3rd Edition, editors William G. Nine and Ronald G. Wilson, 1989, H.E. Howard, Inc., Lynchburg, Va.

The Civil War Gettysburg, The Confederate High Tide by Champ Clark and the editors of Time-Life Books. Copyright 1985; Alexandria, Va.

Confederate Chaplain William Edward Wiatt, Annotated Diary by Alex L. Wiatt; First Edition; Copyright 1994 by H.E. Howard, Inc., manufactured in the United States by H.E. Howard, Inc., Lynchburg, Virginia.

Descendants of Point Lookout POW Organization [PLPOW]; Names of Interred Pt. Lookout Cemetery; March 22, 2014

Gettysburg, The Confederate High Tide by Champ Clark and the editors of Time-Life Books, Alexandria, Va.

Iverson's Pits & 60 Confederates who bagged 500 Yankees, kindle edition (2015) by William A. Hinson.

The Little Bugler, The True Story of A Twelve-Year-Old Boy in the Civil War by William B. Styple, Belle Grove Publishing Company, Kearny, New Jersey, 1998.

McClellan's Other Story, The Political Intrigue of Colonel Thomas M. Key, Confidential Aide to General George B. McClellan, edited by William B. Styple, layout designer Kim Styple & photography by Brad Styple; Belle Grove Publishing Company, Kearny, New Jersey; 2012.

North Carolina History Project, Rowan County, 1753; March 22, 2014.

Our Noble Blood, The Civil War Letters of Major-general Régis de Trobriand, translated by Nathalie Chartrain; edited by William B. Styple, Belle Grove Publishing Company, Kearny, New Jersey, 1997.

Picture History of The Civil War, The Epic Struggle of the Blue and the Gray by Bruce Catten; 1960, 1982; American Heritage Publishing Company.

StoppingPoints.com; Stoneman's Raid; Confederate Prison, Catawba College; John W. Ellis, March 22, 2014.

Writing & Fighting the Confederate War, The Letters of Peter Wellington Alexander Confederate War Correspondent edited by William B. Styple; foreword by Edwin C. Bearss, Belle Grove Publishing Company, Kearny, New Jersey, 2002.

Writing and Fighting the Civil War, Soldier Correspondence to The New York Sunday Mercury, edited by William B. Styple, with chapter introductions by Brian C. Pohanka, Edwin C. Bearss, Dr. James M. McPherson, Dr. Richard J. Sommers and William B. Styple; epilogue by Robert Lee Hodge, Belle Grove Publishing Company, Kearny, New Jersey; 2000.

Writing & Fighting from the Army of Northern Virginia, A Collection of Confederate Soldier Correspondence, edited by William B. Styple, Belle Grove Publishing Company, 2003.

North Carolina Troops Records [1861-1865]: Refer to North Carolina Sources & . American Civil War [1861-1865] Sources

Oakwood Cemetery, #701 Oakwood Avenue, Raleigh, N.C. 27601.

♀ | | ♂

BRITISH GENEALOGICAL SOURCES

Abbeys, Castles and Ancient Balls of England and Wales, their Legendary Lore by John Timbs.

Burke's Peerage compiled by John Burke, 1826; London, England.

Burke's Presidential Families of the U.S.

The General Armory of England, Scotland, Ireland, and Wales, Comprising A Registry of Armorial Bearings from the Earliest to the Present Time, Volume 3, Sir Bernard Burke, C.B., L.L.D., Ulster King of Arms.

The History of Boxley by J. Cave-Brown, Maidstone, 1892, pps. 117 & 171.

Modern Language Notes, Vol. 49, No. 7 (Nov. 1934), pp. 446-449. Wyatt's Letters to his son; Albert McHarg Hayes; John Hopkins University Press.

Freeth, Martyn, genealogist contact

Genealogymagazine.com/boleyn.html

The official website of The British Monarchy: www.royal.gov.uk/HistoryoftheMonarchy/KingsandQueensofEngland

The Records of The Virginia Company of London, THE COURT BOOK, FROM THE MANUSCRIPT IN THE LIBRARY OF CONGRESS, volumes 1-2; edited with an introduction & bibliography by Susan Myra Kingsbury, A.M., Ph.D, instructor in history and economics, Simmons College, preface by Herbert Levi Osgood, A.M., Ph.D.; Washington Government Printing Office, Library of Congress, United States Government Printing Office, Washington, D.C. 1906. [quotes from 516-17].

The Records of The Virginia Company of London, Volume 3, Documents I. [quotes from pages 484-485].

The Records of The Virginia Company of London, Volume 4; edited by Susan Myra Kingsbury, A.M., Ph.D, Carola Woerishoffer Professor of Social Economy, Bryn Mawr College, Washington Government Printing Office, Library of Congress, United States Government Printing Office, Washington, D.C. 1935. [quotes from 228-229].

Video Documentaries:

Inside the Court of Henry VIII

Secrets of King Henry VIII

♀ | | ♂

THE VIRGINIA COLONY

Adventurers of Purse and Person, Virginia 1607-1625 and Their Families, compiled and edited by Annie Lash Jester in Collaboration with Martha Woodroof Hiden, F.A.S.G. (1883-1959), sponsored by the Order of First Families of Virginia, 1607-1624, second edition 1964; copyright 1954, 1964, Order of First Families of Virginia; Printed in the United States of America.

The Records of The Virginia Company of London, THE COURT BOOK, FROM THE MANUSCRIPT IN THE LIBRARY OF CONGRESS, volumes 1-2; edited with an introduction & bibliography by Susan Myra Kingsbury, A.M., Ph.D, instructor in history and economics, Simmons College, preface by Herbert Levi Osgood, A.M., Ph.D.; Washington Government Printing Office, Library of Congress, United States Government Printing Office, Washington, D.C. 1906. [quotes from 516-17].

The Records of The Virginia Company of London, Volume 3, Documents I. [quotes from pages 484-485].

The Records of The Virginia Company of London, Volume 4; edited by Susan Myra Kingsbury, A.M., Ph.D, Carola Woerishoffer Professor of Social Economy, Bryn Mawr College, Washington Government Printing Office, Library of Congress, United States Government Printing Office, Washington, D.C. 1935. [quotes from 228-229].

A Tale of Two Colonies, What Really Happened in Virginia and Bermuda by Virginia Bernhard, published by the University of Missouri Press, Columbia and London; copyright 2011 by the Curators of the University of Missouri, University of Missouri Press, Columbia, Missouri 65201; printed and bounded in the United States.

♀ | | ♂

ARKANSAS
Partial Genealogy of the Wyatts (of Arkansas) 1600-1900 by CLP Research, genealogical tree connecting genealogically U.S. Senator of Arkansas Harriet *"Hattie"* Ophelia Wyatt [1878-1950], wife 3of Thaddeus Horatius Caraway [1871-1931] to Rev. Haute Wyatt [1594-1638].

♀ | | ♂

KENTUCKY
Lexington Public Library, #140 E. Main Street, Lexington, Ky. 1840 & 1850 U.S. Federal Census Records for Kentucky counties of Calloway, McCracken & Marshall.

♀ | | ♂

NORTH CAROLINA

Abstracts of Deed Books 11-14 of Rowan County, North Carolina, 1786-1797, Jo White Linn Collection, Rowan Public Library. Deed Book 12, Rowan County, #1277, pg. 206.

Abstracts of Deed Books 11-14 of Rowan County North Carolina 1786-1797; Rowan Public Library; Jo White Linn Collection #1277 p. 206. 18 May 1789; State Grant #1786 @ 50 sh per 100 acres to John Wyatt, 300 A on Lick Crk and Yadkin R adj Moses Park and William Cole.

Abstracts of Deed Books 20-24 of Rowan County North Carolina 1807-1818, donated by James W.Kluttz. Deed Book #20, 493, 494.

Abstracts of Deed Books 25-29 of Rowan County North Carolina 1818-1828, Genealogical Society of Rowan County, Salisbury, North Carolina; year 2002.

Cemetery Records of Davidson County, N.C., Volume 2, Southern Section, compiled by The Genealogical Society of Davidson County, Post Office Box 1665, Lexington, N.C. 27292, Davidson County Public Library, #602 South Main Street, Lexington, N.C. 27292.

Cemetery Records of Davidson County, N.C., Volume 2, Southern Section; compiled by The Genealogical Society of Davidson County, P.O. Box 1665, Lexington, N.C. 27292.

Civil War Courts-Martial of North Carolina Troops by Aldo S. Perry; McFarland & Company, Inc., Publishers, Box 611, Jefferson, N.C. 28640; 2012 ; pages 69-70; 129-131.

Descendants of Roger Parke, Immigrant, 1648-1739, compiled by Cecelia B. Parke, #7162 Cambridge Street, Spring Hill, Fla. 34606;
May 2000.

The Dandridge Family of Virginia [family motto: "In Adversis Etiam Fide" Ten Generations of Descendants from William Dandridge (1689-1747) of Elsing Green, King William County, Va.; John Dandridge (1700-1756) of Chestnut Grove, New Kent County, Va., and their nephew William Langbourne (1723-1766) of the Island, King William County, Va., compiled by Charles J. Ragland, Winston-Salem, N.C. 1999.

To Escape Into Dreams, volumes 1 & 3, written and compiled by Hélène Andorre Hinson Staley, Metallo House Publishers [MHP] 2005.

The Eagle Family of America: Egley, Egle, Egli, Eagle, 1690-1998 by Rachel Hinson Hill, edited by Rachel Hinson Hill, Co-Editor: Betty Hinson Heath, Publisher: Glenda Wagoner, Salisbury, N.C. 1998; printed by Diversified Graphics, Inc., Salisbury, N.C.

Find A Grave on the Internet at findagrave.com, 2014.

Hinson & Related Families compiled by William *"Billy"* Ashley Hinson in 1986, page 304, *"Stories Handed Down."* Current contact: Myrtle Beach, S.C.

History of Lick Creek Baptist Church, Davidson County, N.C., Rowan Public Library, History & Genealogy Department, Salisbury, N.C.

John T. Wyatt Collection MSS #9816; presented January 1999, pgs. 1-6. Rowan Public Library, Edith M. Clark History Room.

Venus Of Faith Is Remembered, SAGE OF FAITH; J.T. Wyatt "VENUS OF DEAD FOLLOWING LONG SEIGE OF ILLNESS, Far Famed Writer Of "Items" Was 82 Years Old, The Salisbury Post, November 3, 1933; Salisbury, N.C.

The Raleigh News & Observer, Tuesday, November 23, 1999, *"Entrepreneur Edgar Wyatt, 82; Seed Seller, local historian"* by Martha Quillin, staff writer. & Edgar Marshall Wyatt, Jr.; Raleigh, N.C.

The Raleigh News & Observer, Monday, November 22, 1999, *"Wyatt, Edgar Marshall (1917-1999),"* Raleigh, N.C.

The Salisbury Evening Post, Friday, November 3, 1933 *"Venus is Dead Following Long Seige of Illness; Far Famed Writer Of 'Items' Was 82 Years Old."* Salisbury, N.C.

The Salisbury Post Bicentennial Edition, Tuesday, April 29, 1975, page 1P. *"Venus of Faith, Country Correspondent's Motto's 'If You Can Beat That, Trot It Out.' "*

State of North Carolina No. 1786; Handwritten Land Grant for John Wiatt [Wyatt] Transcribed and interpreted April-August 2014 by Hélène Andorre Hinson Staley & James Noah Hinson, M.D., Metallo House Publishers, Moncure, N.C.

Last Will & Testment of John Wiatt [1743-1815] recorded in the November Session 1816, page 453-454. This is a photocopy of the original, which is handwritten. This is transcribed in *The Rungs of Ladders, A Wyatt History in England & the United States, from 1066 to Modern Times.*

List of Taxable Property in the County of Rowan Anno 1778 by Ad Osborne, Clerk of Court.

List of Names Appearing in the Rowan County Tax Lists Anno 1778.

1784 Taxable Return of Cap: Runnions Co. A Lis [sic: List] of the Taxable Property of the Inhabitants of Capt Runyons District, Rowan County, North Carolina, Taken by William Cole for the year 1784; pps. 140; year 1794 pps. 326; 346.

NORTH CAROLINA CENSUS RECORDS

INDEX TO THE 1800 CENSUS OF NORTH CAROLINA, Compiled by Elizabeth Petty Bentley, Baltimore, Genealogical Publishing Co., Inc. 1982.

INDEX OF NORTH CAROLINA ANCESTORS VOLUME II, contributed 656 of their descendants, North Carolina Genealogical Society, Raleigh, N.C. 1984.

NORTH CAROLINA 1810 CENSUS INDEX, 1976; 1979; editor: Ronald Vern Jackson, Accelerated Indexing Systems, Inc., 3346 South Orchard Drive, Bountiful, Utah 84010.

The July 23, *1870 United States Federal Census* for Morgan Township, Rowan County, North Carolina at the Gold Hill Post Office shows Solomon Eagle at age 13, a white, male living with his parents and siblings. It states he *"works on farm"* and was born in North Carolina.

The *1880 United States Federal Census* for the Morgan Township, Rowan County, N.C. shows Solomon at the age of 23, as the head of household with his wife Mary Jane, then age, 23; "keeping house," his mother Agnes N. Eagle, then age 63, "at home," and his son, then age 2. Discrepancy transcription reads: *"Joel J."* as his son. The original appears as *"Jill J."* Obviously, this has to be *"Noah J."* because he was born in 1878. Although a discrepancy – it is a matched record. Solomon is listed as a farmer.

On the same page their *"neighbors"* are the families of Roy C. Morgan, Isaac Goodman, J.C. Canup, Alfred Goodman, Charles Morgan.

The June 2nd, *1900 12th United States Federal Census* for Morgan Township, Rowan County, North Carolina shows Solomon Eagle, then age 43, head of household, farmer, living with his wife, Mary S., then 43; his mother-in-law: Rachel C., then 64 and children: Noah J., 22; Rachel M., 15, Mary L., 2. The birhplaces for all listed and all that appear on the same page are *"North Carolina."* This is the birthplace for all parents as well.

* Note: The *"C"* in Rachel's name is a discrepancy. It should be an *"E."* This record is nevertheless, the correct family.

This census page of information was originally collected by a William L. Eagle. I wonder if this census taker is William Lawson Eagle -- son of Daniel Calvin (1848-1925) and Amanda Jane Wyatt Eagle (1848-1907)? This William Lawson Eagle had a brother named Solomon Luther Eagle, among other siblings. Notice as well most of the families listed on the same page are connected or affiliated with the Eagle family either by marriage or blood. Some of the other households are mentioned in other areas of this genealogical report, and those families on the same page of Solomon's family include households for William N. Morgan, David Reid, Adam Parker, Nathan Morgan, Jacob Morgan, Sallie Hodge, John Wyatt and others. To understand this, you will need to look at other entries herein.

The April 19th, *1910 United States Federal Census* for the Morgan Township, Rowan County, N.C. shows Solomon at age 53, his wife, Mary J., then age 53; Lillie, daughter, 11; and mother-in-law: Rachel E. Morgan, 74. Directly above this family is the family of Noah Jenkins Eagle -- Solomon's son. See entry for Noah J. Eagle. See entries for the households of Jacob Love Surratt, James Noah Wyatt and Alfred Surratt, as they appear on the same page of this census and living in the area of the *"Delaware Yadkin River and* [some indiscernible word] *Larry Publer Road to Richfield."*

The *1920 United States Federal Census* for the Morgan Township, Rowan County, N.C. shows Solomon at the age of 63, head of household and living on a private road. He is listed as owning his property and married to Mary J. and having a daughter named: *"Lillie,"* then age 21. His occupation is listed as farmer on a *"General Farm."*

The *1930 United States Federal Census* for the Morgan Township, Rowan County, N.C. shows Solomon at age 73, then living with his second wife Hattie, 46.

According to the *North Carolina State Archives, North Carolina Deaths, 1908-1967,* Solomon died December 27th, 1939 in Rowan County, N.C. at the age of 82, having been born in 1857.

1820 United States Federal Census for Rowan County, N.C. shows individuals who connect genealogically with one another in this county – Thomas Wiatt on the same page as John and Amos Park [Parks] brothers, John and Joseph Hodge, James Reed, Samuel Miller – all of whom are related to one another.

COURTS
North Carolina Higher-Court Records, 1670-1696, editor Mattie Erma Edwards Parker; State Department of Archives and History, Raleigh, N.C., 1968 – specficially *Records of the County Court of Albemarle,* pps. 352-353.

TROOP RECORDS
North Carolina Troop Records 1861-1865, A Roster, Volume 1 Artillery, compiled by Louis H. Manarin;

North Carolina Troop Records 1861-1865, A Roster, Volume II Cavalry, compiled by Louis H. Manarin, 1st printing 1968, 1989, 2004.

North Carolina Troop Records 1861-1865, A Roster Volume III, Infantry, compiled by Louis H. Manarin, Raleigh, N.C., State Department of Archives & History; 1971.

North Carolina Troops 1861-1865, A Roster, Volume IV, Infantry; compiled by Weymouth T. Jordan, Jr.; 1973.

North Carolina Troops 1861-1865, A Roster, Volume VI, Infantry; edited & compiled by Weymouth T. Jordan, Jr.; 1977.

North Carolina Troops 1861-1865, A Roster, Volume VII, Infantry 22nd-26th Regiments; edited & compiled by Weymouth T. Jordan, Jr.

North Carolina Troops 1861-1865, A Roster, Volume VIII, Infantry 22nd-26th Regiments; edited & compiled by Weymouth T. Jordan, Jr.

North Carolina Troops 1861-1865, A Roster, Volume IX, Infantry 32nd-35th & 37^{h} Regiments; edited & compiled by Weymouth T. Jordan, Jr.; Division of Archives & History, Raleigh, N.C.; 1983.

North Carolina Troops 1861-1865, A Roster, Volume X, 38th, 39^{h}, 42nd, 44th Regiments.

North Carolina Troops 1861-1865, A Roster, Volume XI, Infantry, Company B, 46th Regiment, N.C.; compiled by Weymouth T. Jordan, Jr.

North Carolina Troops 1861-1865, Roster, Volume XIII.

North Carolina Troops 1861-1865, A Roster, Volume XIV, 2008.

North Carolina Troops 1861-1865, A Roster, Volume XV, Infantry, 62nd, 64th, 66th, 67^{h} & 68th Regiments; Raleigh, N.C. 2009; Office of Archives & History; 2003.

North Carolina Troops 1861-1865, A Roster, Volume XVI, Raleigh, N.C. 2008; Matthew M. Brown & Michael W. Coffey.

North Carolina Troops 1861-1865, A Roster, Volume XVII, Junior Reserves, Raleigh, N.C. 2009; Matthew M. Brown & Michael W. Coffey.

North Carolina Troops 1861-1865, A Roster, Volume XVIII, Junior Reserves, Raleigh, N.C. 2009; Matthew M. Brown & Michael W. Coffey.

ROSTER OF SOLDIERS FROM NORTH CAROLINA IN THE AMERICAN REVOLUTION WITH AN APPENDIX CONTAINING A COLLECTION OF MISCELLANEOUS RECORDS, ROWAN PUBLIC LIBRARY, Jo White Linn Collection, 1972; GENEALOGICAL PUBLISHING CO., INC. BALTIMORE 1972.

Rowan County Marriage Bonds page #61111

Rowan County, North Carolina Will Abstracts Volume II, 1805-1850; Abstracts of Books G-K-1850, abstracted and compiled by Jo White Linn, indexed by Edith Montcalm Clark; 1971 pps. 137, 199.

Rowan County, North Carolina Tax Lists, 1757-1800, Annotated Transcriptions, Jo White Linn Collection, Davidson County Public Library, #602 South Main Street, Lexington, N.C. 27292.

Rowan County North Carolina Will Abstracts Vol. II 1805-1850 Abstracts of Books G-K 1850; abstracted and compiled by Jo White Linn; indexed by Edith Montcalm Clark, copyright Jo White Linn 1971, published by Mrs. Stable Linn, Jr., Box 978, Salisbury, N.C. 28144.

Will Book G, Rowan County, North Carolina, Stahle Linn, Jr., Regent, Elizabeth Maxwell Steele Chapter, Salisbury, N.C. Mrs. Noble Shumate, State Chairman, Will of Noah Parke, Rowan County, N.C. page 217; pps. 381-384.

MUSEUMS

North Carolina Museum of Natural Sciences, #11 West Jones Street, Raleigh, N.C.

♀ | | ♂

VIRGINIA

Genealogical Gleanings in England, pps. 84-87; pps. 151-152.

The Descendants of Stephen Field of King and Queen County, Virginia 1721 with notes on the Armistead, Booth, Catesby-Cocke, Catlett, Jones, Lightfoot, Smith, Tabb, Todd and Wiatt Families by Alex L. Wiatt; copyright 1992 by Alexander Lloyd Wiatt; printed and bound in the United States by BookCrafters, 3591 Lee Hill Drive, Fredericksburg, Virginia 22408.

The Wyatt Family of Virginia: with special interest in the descendants of Maude Roberta Sinclair and Alexander Taliaferro Wiatt and their collateral; Second Edition by Alexander Lloyd Wiatt available from Earl Gregg Swem Library, College of William and Mary, 400 Landrum Drive, Post Office Box 8794, Williamsburg, Virginia 23187-8794.; copyright 2010 by Alexander Lloyd Wiatt; printed and bound in the United States by Bookmasters, Inc.

The Wiatt Family of Virginia, The Descendants of John Wiatt, Jr. [1732-1805] of Gloucester County, Virginia with notes on the Field, Carter, Todd, Ball, Montague and Jones Families. Compiled by Alexander Lloyd Wiatt; copyrighted 1980 by Alexander Lloyd Wiatt; printed and bound in the United States of America by the McClure Printing Company, Inc., Vernon, Virginia.

OTHER SOURCES

Ancestry.com

DAR PATRIOT INDEX CENTENNIAL EDITION PART III,

National Society of the Daughters of the American Revolution Centennial Administration, Mrs. Eldred Martin Yochim, President General, Washington: 1900.

Good New Bible, Today's English Version, Thomas Nelson Publishers, Inc. under license of the American Bible Society, Nashville, Tenn.; New York, N.Y.

High on History by Daniel Wyatt, author, sports fanatic and history buff; Ancestry.com, March 26, 2014.

TO LAY DOWN ONE'S LIFE FOR YOU, BROTHER, a novel by Dr. Sean M.J. McCarthy, 1994.

Other works and records are mentioned within the body of *The Rungs of Ladders* and do not appear in this list.

Some North Carolina cemeteries containing Wyatts and Wyatt descendants in Rowan County, N.C. [unless otherwise indicated] located:

- Calvary Baptist Church, Old Mocksville Highway, Salisbury, Rowan County, N.C.
- East Corinth Baptist Church, Stokesferry Road, Rowan County, N.C.
- Flat Creek Primitive Baptist Church Cemetery, Flat Creek Church Road, Richfield, Rowan County, N.C.
- Forsyth Memorial Park, Winston-Salem, N.C.
- Gold Hill Wesleyan Church Cemetery, #830 Liberty Road, Gold Hill, Rowan County, N.C.
- Guilford Memorial Park, Greensboro, N.C.
- Liberty United Methodist Church Cemetery, #3640 Liberty Road, Gold Hill, Rowan County, N.C.
- Lick Creek Baptist Church, Denton, Davidson County, N.C.
- Luther's Lutheran Church Cemetery, #4955 Richfield Road, Richfield, Rowan County, N.C.
- M.E. Methodist Church, Mt. Pleasant, N.C.
- Memorial Park Cemetery, intersection of West Innes and Grove streets, Salisbury, N.C. [known as City Memorial Park.]
- Morgan Cemetery – served as muster ground for Confederate soldiers, 1842-1964, Stokes Ferry Road, Salisbury, N.C.
- Old English Cemetery, Salisbury, N.C. [Cornwallis' men are buried in this cemetery. It was granted to the city of Salisbury in 1770 by the British Government. The grave of John. W. Ellis is in this cemetery.
- Park-Wyatt-Bean Graveyard, off River Road on Cedar Creek, Rowan County, N.C.
- Rockwell Cemetery or Rockwell City Cemetery, Rockwell, Rowan County, N.C. – now known as Ursinus Cemetery and Saint James Lutheran Church Cemetery.
- Rowan Memorial Park, Salisbury, N.C.
- Saint Matthews Lutheran Church Cemetery, #9275 Bringle Ferry Road, Salisbury, N.C.

- Saint Peter's Lutheran Church, #2570 Saint Peter's Church Road, Rockwell, Rowan County, N.C., three miles east of Rockwell.
- Saint Stephen's Lutheran Church, Cabarrus County, N.C.
- Stanly Gardens of Memory, Albemarle, N.C.
- Tabernacle M.E. Church, Trinity, N.C.
- Union Lutheran Church, Bringle Ferry Road, Rowan County, N.C.
- United Presbyterian Church, Stanly County, N.C.
- Westlawn Memorial Park, China Grove, Rowan County, N.C.
- Wesley Chapel United Methodist Church, #579 Weathers Creek Road, Troutman, N.C. 28166.
- Wyatt Grove Missionary Baptist Chruch Cemetery, #2995 Wyatt Grove Church Road, Richfield, N.C.
- Zion United Methodist Church Cemetery, #15055 Stokes Ferry Road, Richfield community, Rowan County, N.C.

Searching for Wyatts takes a researcher to all sorts of cemeteries. Not all are currently connected into sections of this book. This does not mean, however, they do not connect some where or another. It simply means the research is ongoing.

If you find one not mentioned in the tree sections of this book, note them in the note section. Send your thoughts and notations to the publisher of *The Rungs of Ladders*. The remains of several Wyatts are buried in the Old English Cemetery, including: Susan Wyatt Moit [1856-1934]; Arthur Lee Wyatt [1875-1877]; N.C. Wyatt [1842-1912]; Nancy E. Wyatt [1837-1903]; Sarah Jane McKenzie Wyatt [1828-1908].

Some Wyatt stones are found Salisbury National Cemetery, #202 Government Road, Salisbury, N.C. Wyatts are scattered in many North Carolina counties and Wyatt remains found in cemeteries such as Rowan Memorial Park, #4125 Franklin Community Center, Salisbury, N.C.

There are additionally Wyatts in McDowell County, N.C. – specifically in the McDowell Memorial Park, Memorial Park Road, Marion, N.C. Iredell County, N.C. contains several Wyatts specifically in the Iredell Memorial Gardens, #2304 Shelton Avenue, Statesville, N.C.

There is even one Wyatt – a William Franklin *"Frank"* Wyatt [1901-1964] in the Buffalo Presbyterian Church, #1333 Carthage Street, Sanford, Lee County, N.C.

Some Wyatts who lost track of their closest ancestors have some curiosity about Wyatt families and may not be mentioned in this book. Pencil in their names, birthdates, birth places, names of spouses, marriage dates, the names of their parents, grandparents, etc. in the note sections and contact the compiler.

Libraries are mentioned within the body of this work.

Footnote:

On Thursday, April 2nd, 2015, *The Salisbury Post* ran the obituary for my father James Noah Hinson, M.D. on page 4A. On page 3A of this same issue there is an article titled: *"On a mission, Online Daily 'Gazette' tracks people, stories behind Stoneman's Raid"* by Mark Wineka. The story is continued to page 6A. It seems ironic that such a story regarding ACW Union Maj. Gen. George Stoneman – whose raid in Salisbury, N.C. my father loved discussing, should run on the same day my father's passing was announced.

THE GLOBE ILLUSTRATED SHAKESPEARE, THE COMPLETE WORKS ANNOTATED, DELUXE EDITION, EDITED BY HOWARD STAUNTON; *King Richard the Third;* © Copyright 1983 Edition, The Globe Illustrated Shakespeare, Greenwich House Crown Publishers, Inc. New York. This Shakespearian play mentioned in the Introduction of *The Rungs of Ladders* is dominated by the character Richard the hunchback, Duke of Gloucester. He becomes King Richard III via a sequence of actions. He kills his enemies, kinsmen, wife and many of his supporters before arriving at the Battle of Bosworth. He cries out: *"My kingdom for a horse!"* His evil essence leads him to defeat by the Duke of Richmond [the one who becomes Henry VII] by the last act.

MOTHER TONGUE, English & How It Got That Way by Bill Bryson, 1990; William Morrow & Company, New York, N.Y.

A Poem to Honor Our Heavenly Father

♀ | | ♂

By Hélène Hinson Staley

Friday, New Year's Day, 2016

God, I beckon to my heart
I've had You from the very start
But in this world of fit and rage,
The evils pretend to be a Sage
That whispers things to confuse our goals
Until we call to You to save our souls!

The love from You is this light that shines
It keeps us in a world sublime
Without You, we would all be dead
Nothing would exist to even be said.
We could not strive with or against the forces
That give us both good and bad resources.

You are essential to win this battle
Good over bad, we are in the saddle.
The horse's energy comes from You.
It gallops on a path narrow and true.
It aligns itself with good so pure
You are the only cure

New, it is, as it does not age
When we listen we hear the real Sage
Who sounds the trumpet in the sky

And claims the truth, we do not die!
We merely step out of the body we used
And continue the lives we did choose

To love those things worthy and good
To reject evil the way we should.

Notes

♀ | | ♂

"God doesn't require us to succeed; He only requires that you try."

– MOTHER TERESA [ANJEZË GONXHE BOJAXHIU], BORN AUGUST 26, 1910, SKOPJE, NOW CAPITAL OF THE REPUBLIC OF MACEDONIA- DIED SEPTEMBER 5, 1997, ROMAN CATHOLIC NUN WHO LIVED MOST OF HER LIFE IN INDIA.

Notes

"We are all pencils in the hand of God."

-- MOTHER TERESA [ANJEZË GONXHE BOJAXHIU] [BORN
AUGUST 26, 1910, SKOPJE, NOW CAPITAL OF THE REPUBLIC
OF MACEDONIA- DIED SEPTEMBER 5, 1997, ROMAN CATHOLIC
NUN WHO LIVED MOST OF HER LIFE IN INDIA.

Notes

"What we think, we become."

-- BUDDHA [GAUTAMA SHAKYAMUNI, BORN 563 BCE, LUMBINI, SAKYA REPUBLIC; DIED 483 BCE, KUSHINAGAR, MALLA REPUBLIC]
A SAGE WHO LIVED AND TAUGHT IN EASTERN INDIA.

Notes

"Whatever you do may seem insignificant, but it is most important that you do it."

– Mahatma Gandhi [a.k.a: Mohandas Karamchand Gandhi, born October 2, 1869, Porbandar, Kathiawar Agency, British India; died January 30, 1948, New Delhi, Delhi, India], led India to independence and inspired civil rights and freedom movements worldwide.

Notes

"I disapprove of what you say, but I will defend to the death your right to say it."

— Voltaire

Notes

"Steps one's ancestors have made were steps taken toward our existence…
Without them, we would not experience the life we have today…."

--Hélène Staley

Notes

"We should strive to understand where we have come from so we can make responsible decisions on where we are going."

-- HÉLÈNE STALEY

Notes

"My imperfections and failures are as much a blessing from God as my successes and my talents, and I lay them both at his feet."

– MAHATMA GANDHI

Notes

"Every stick has two ends,"

-- ANONYMOUS LATVIAN SAYING.

Notes

*"Birthdays are good for you. Statistics show that people
who have the most live the longest!"*

– LARRY LORENZONI, SALESIAN OF DON BOSCO, PRIEST AND EDUCATOR.

Notes

"When the past no longer illuminates the future, the spirit walks in darkness."

-- ALEXIS DE TOCQUEVILLE.

Notes

"There is history in all men's lives,"

-- WILLIAM SHAKESPEARE, BRITISH PLAYWRIGHT.

Notes

"The healthy soul is a miniature heaven, the sick soul a miniature hell."

– GREGORY R. JOHNSON IN THE INTRODUCTION OF
DIVINE PROVIDENCE BY EMANUEL SWEDENBORG.

Notes

"A clear and innocent conscience fears nothing."

-- QUEEN ELIZABETH I